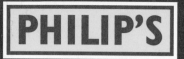

STREET ATLAS
Dorset
Bournemouth and Poole

First published 2002 by

Philip's, a division of
Octopus Publishing Group Ltd
2–4 Heron Quays, London E14 4JP

First colour edition 2002
First impression 2002

ISBN 0-540-08119-1 (hardback)
ISBN 0-540-08120-5 (spiral)

Printed and bound in Spain
by Cayfosa-Quebecor

Contents

III **Key to map symbols**

IV **Key to map pages**

VI **Route planning**

VIII **Administrative and Postcode boundaries**

1 **Street maps** at 3½ inches to 1 mile

188 **Street maps** at 1¾ inches to 1 mile

212 **Street map** at 3½ inches to 1 mile

213 **Town map of** Salisbury

214 **Index** of towns and villages

217 **Index** of streets, hospitals, industrial estates, railway
stations, schools, shopping centres, universities
and places of interest

Digital Data

The exceptionally high-quality mapping found in this atlas is available as digital data in TIFF format,
which is easily convertible to other bit mapped (raster) image formats.

The index is also available in digital form as a standard database table. It contains all the details
found in the printed index together with the National Grid reference for the map square in which
each entry is named.

For further information and to discuss your requirements, please contact Philip's on
020 7531 8439 or george.philip@philips-maps.co.uk

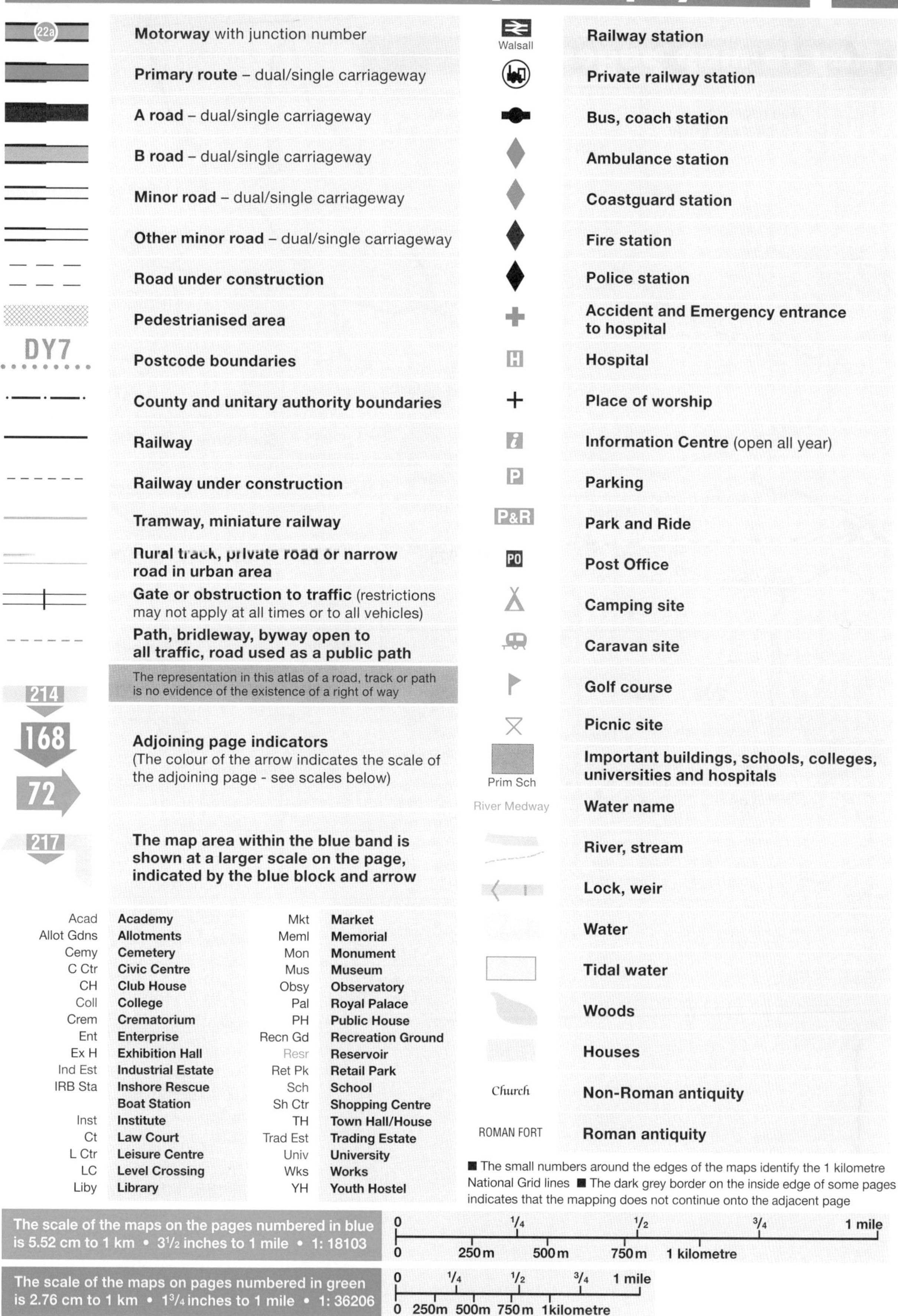 22a	Motorway with junction number	Railway station Walsall	Railway station
	Primary route – dual/single carriageway		Private railway station
	A road – dual/single carriageway		Bus, coach station
	B road – dual/single carriageway		Ambulance station
	Minor road – dual/single carriageway		Coastguard station
	Other minor road – dual/single carriageway		Fire station
	Road under construction		Police station
	Pedestrianised area		Accident and Emergency entrance to hospital
DY7	Postcode boundaries	H	Hospital
	County and unitary authority boundaries	+	Place of worship
	Railway	i	Information Centre (open all year)
	Railway under construction	P	Parking
	Tramway, miniature railway	P&R	Park and Ride
	Rural track, private road or narrow road in urban area	PO	Post Office
	Gate or obstruction to traffic (restrictions may not apply at all times or to all vehicles)		Camping site
	Path, bridleway, byway open to all traffic, road used as a public path		Caravan site
	The representation in this atlas of a road, track or path is no evidence of the existence of a right of way		Golf course
			Picnic site
214 168 72	Adjoining page indicators (The colour of the arrow indicates the scale of the adjoining page - see scales below)	Prim Sch	Important buildings, schools, colleges, universities and hospitals
		River Medway	Water name
217	The map area within the blue band is shown at a larger scale on the page, indicated by the blue block and arrow		River, stream
			Lock, weir
			Water
			Tidal water
			Woods
			Houses
		Church	Non-Roman antiquity
		ROMAN FORT	Roman antiquity

Acad	Academy	Mkt	Market
Allot Gdns	Allotments	Meml	Memorial
Cemy	Cemetery	Mon	Monument
C Ctr	Civic Centre	Mus	Museum
CH	Club House	Obsy	Observatory
Coll	College	Pal	Royal Palace
Crem	Crematorium	PH	Public House
Ent	Enterprise	Recn Gd	Recreation Ground
Ex H	Exhibition Hall	Resr	Reservoir
Ind Est	Industrial Estate	Ret Pk	Retail Park
IRB Sta	Inshore Rescue Boat Station	Sch	School
		Sh Ctr	Shopping Centre
Inst	Institute	TH	Town Hall/House
Ct	Law Court	Trad Est	Trading Estate
L Ctr	Leisure Centre	Univ	University
LC	Level Crossing	Wks	Works
Liby	Library	YH	Youth Hostel

■ The small numbers around the edges of the maps identify the 1 kilometre National Grid lines ■ The dark grey border on the inside edge of some pages indicates that the mapping does not continue onto the adjacent page

The scale of the maps on the pages numbered in blue is 5.52 cm to 1 km • 3½ inches to 1 mile • 1: 18103

0	¼	½	¾	1 mile

| 0 | 250m | 500m | 750m | 1 kilometre |

The scale of the maps on pages numbered in green is 2.76 cm to 1 km • 1¾ inches to 1 mile • 1: 36206

0	¼	½	¾	1 mile

| 0 | 250m | 500m | 750m | 1kilometre |

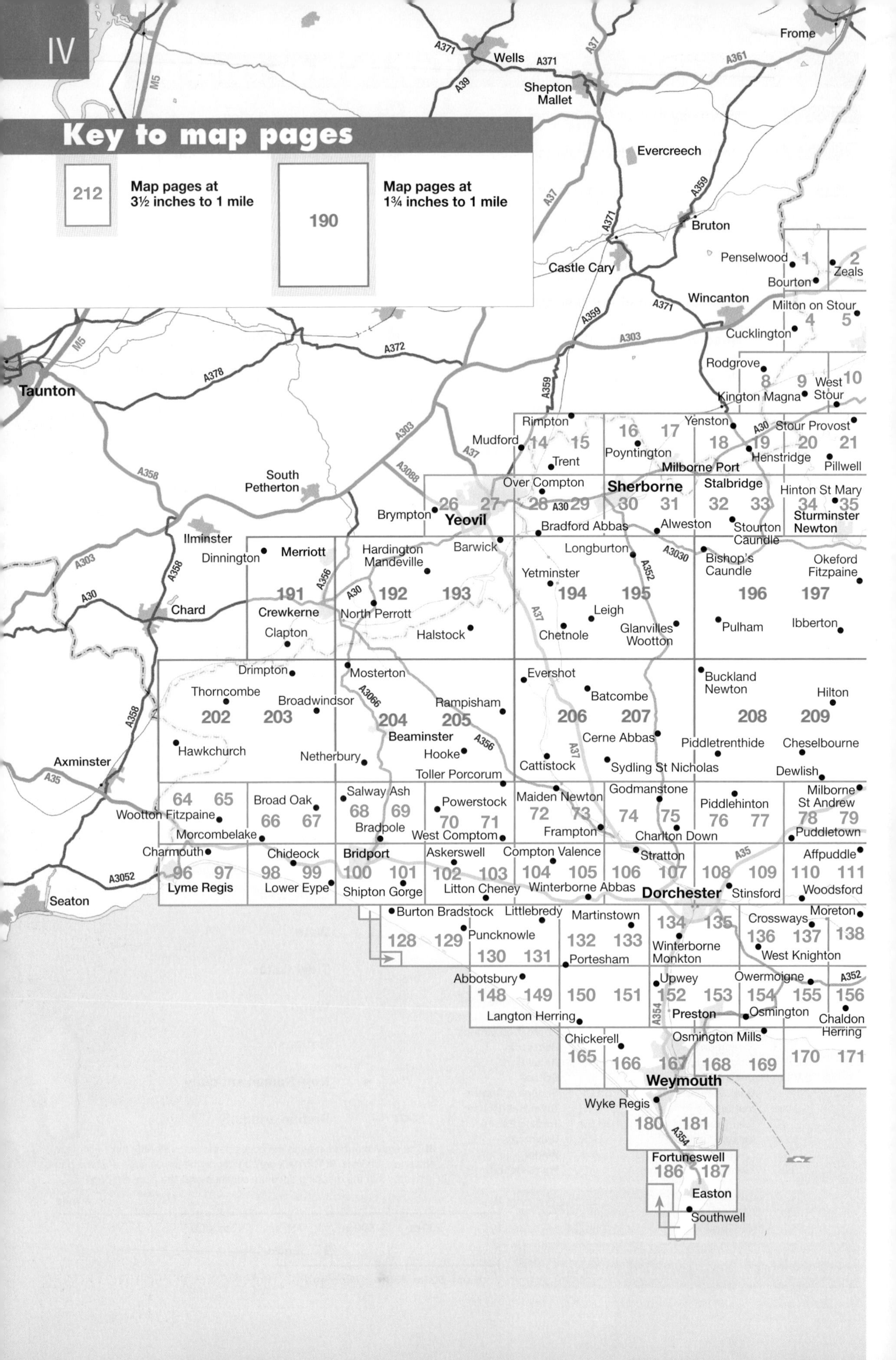

IV

Key to map pages

| 212 | Map pages at 3½ inches to 1 mile |
| 190 | Map pages at 1¾ inches to 1 mile |

Frome

Wells

Shepton Mallet

Evercreech

Bruton

Penselwood 1 2 Zeals

Bourton

Milton on Stour 4 5

Cucklington

Castle Cary

Rodgrove

8 9 West 10 Stour

Kington Magna

Wincanton

Taunton

Rimpton 14 15 16 17 Yenston 18 19 Stour Provost 20 21

Mudford

Trent

Poyntington

Milborne Port Henstridge Pillwell

Over Compton

Sherborne Stalbridge Hinton St Mary

South Petherton

Brympton 26 27 28 A30 29 30 31 32 33 34 35 Sturminster Newton

Yeovil

Bradford Abbas Alweston Stourton Caundle

Ilminster

Merriott

Hardington Mandeville

Barwick

Longburton A3030 Bishop's Caundle Okeford Fitzpaine

Dinnington

Crewkerne 191 192 193 194 195 196 197

North Perrott

Yetminster

Leigh

Pulham Ibberton

Chard

Clapton

Halstock

Chetnole

Glanvilles Wootton

Drimpton

Mosterton

Evershot

Buckland Newton

Hilton

Thorncombe

Broadwindsor

Rampisham

Batcombe

202 203 204 205 206 207 208 209

Beaminster

Hooke

Cerne Abbas Piddletrenthide Cheselbourne

Hawkchurch

Netherbury

Toller Porcorum

Cattistock

Sydling St Nicholas

Dewlish

Axminster

Maiden Newton Godmanstone Milborne St Andrew

64 65 68 69 70 71 72 73 74 75 76 77 78 79

Wootton Fitzpaine 66 67 Bradpole West Comptom Frampton Charlton Down Piddlehinton Puddletown

Morcombelake

Charmouth Chideock Bridport Askerswell Compton Valence Stratton Affpuddle

96 97 98 99 100 101 102 103 104 105 106 107 108 109 110 111

Lyme Regis Lower Eype Shipton Gorge Litton Cheney Winterborne Abbas Dorchester Stinsford Woodsford

Seaton

Burton Bradstock Littlebredy Martinstown Moreton

128 129 Punknowle 132 133 134 135 Crossways 136 137 138

130 131 Portesham Winterborne Monkton West Knighton

Abbotsbury Upwey Owermoigne

148 149 150 151 152 153 154 155 156

Langton Herring Preston Osmington Chaldon Herring

Chickerell Osmington Mills 170 171

165 166 167 168 169

Weymouth

Wyke Regis

180 181

Fortuneswell

186 187

Easton

Southwell

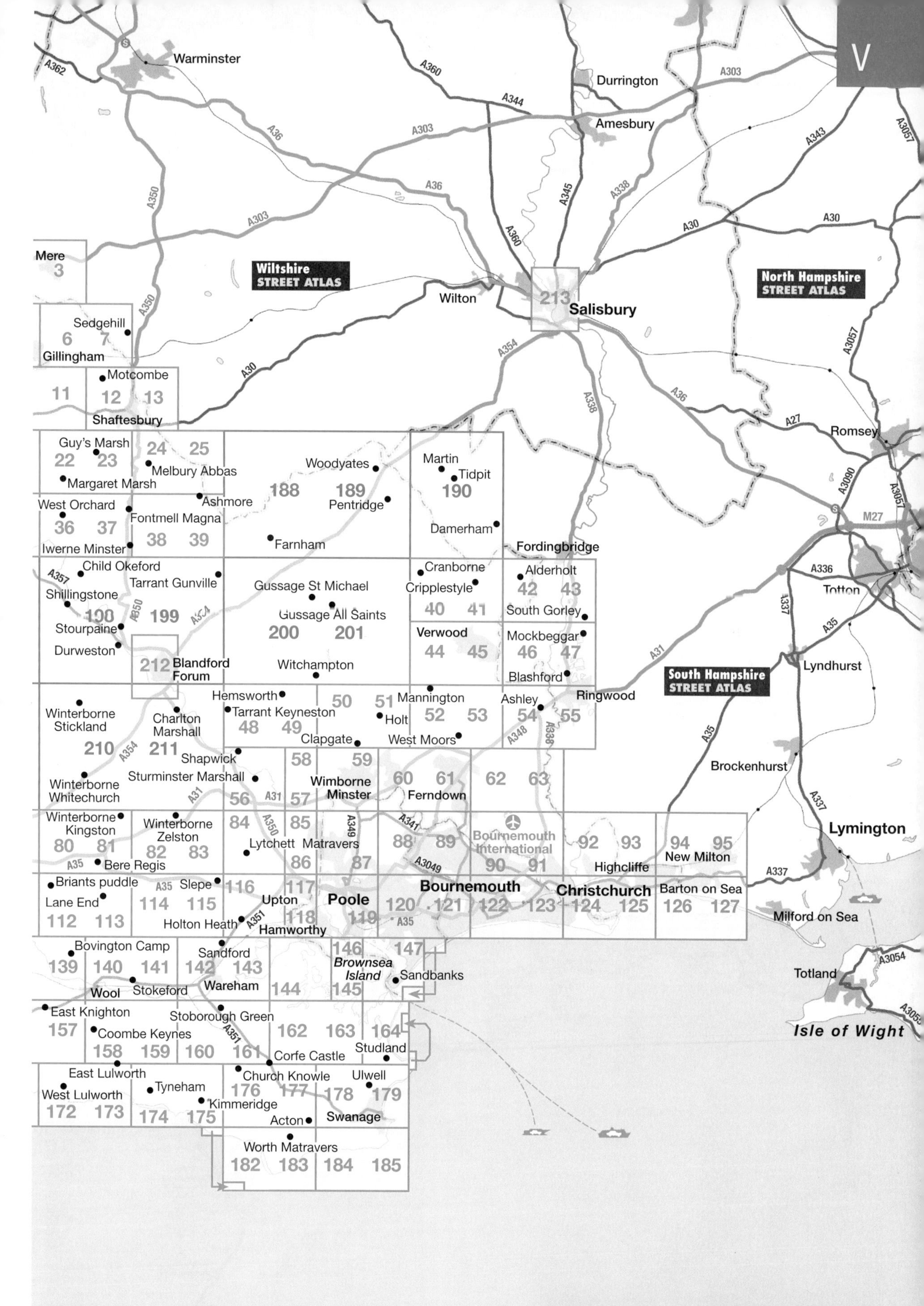

Warminster

Durrington

Amesbury

Wiltshire STREET ATLAS

North Hampshire STREET ATLAS

Mere
3

Wilton

213 Salisbury

Romsey

Sedgehill
6 **7**

Gillingham

Motcombe

11 **12** **13**

Shaftesbury

M27

Guy's Marsh
22 **23** **24** **25**

Melbury Abbas

Margaret Marsh

Woodyates

Martin
Tidpit

188 **189** **190**

A3090

West Orchard
36 **37**

Ashmore

Pentridge

Damerham

Fordingbridge

Totton

Iwerne Minster
Fontmell Magna
38 **39**

Farnham

Child Okeford

Cranborne
Cripplestyle

Alderholt
42 **43**

Shillingstone
Tarrant Gunville

Gussage St Michael

40 **41**

South Gorley

198 **199**

Gussage All Saints

Verwood

Mockbeggar
46 **47**

Lyndhurst

Stourpaine
Durweston

200 **201**

44 **45**

Blashford

212 Blandford
Forum

Witchampton

Ringwood

South Hampshire STREET ATLAS

Hemsworth
Tarrant Keyneston

50 **51** Mannington

Ashley

Brockenhurst

Winterborne
Stickland

Charlton
Marshall

48 **49**

Holt
52 **53**

54 **55**

Lymington

210 **211**

Clapgate

West Moors

Shapwick

Sturminster Marshall

58 **59**

Winterborne
Whitechurch

56 **57**

Wimborne
Minster

Ferndown

60 **61** **62** **63**

Winterborne
Kingston
80 **81**

Winterborne
Zelston
82 **83**

84 **85**

Lytchett Matravers

88 **89**

Bournemouth
International

92 **93** **94** **95**

New Milton

Bere Regis

86 **87**

90 **91**

Highcliffe

Barton on Sea
126 **127**

Briants puddle
Lane End

Slepe
116 **117**

Poole

120 **121** **122** **123** **124** **125**

112 **113** **114** **115**

Upton

Christchurch

Milford on Sea

Holton Heath

118 **119**

Hamworthy

Totland

Bovington Camp

139 **140** **141**

Sandford

142 **143**

146 **147**

Brownsea
Island

Sandbanks

Isle of Wight

Wool Stokeford

Wareham

144 **145**

East Knighton
157

Coombe Keynes

Stoborough Green

162 **163** **164**

158 **159** **160** **161**

Corfe Castle

Studland

East Lulworth

West Lulworth
172 **173**

Tyneham

Church Knowle

Ulwell

176 **177** **178** **179**

174 **175**

Kimmeridge

Acton

Swanage

Worth Matravers

182 **183** **184** **185**

Scale

0   5   10   15   20 km

0   5   10 miles

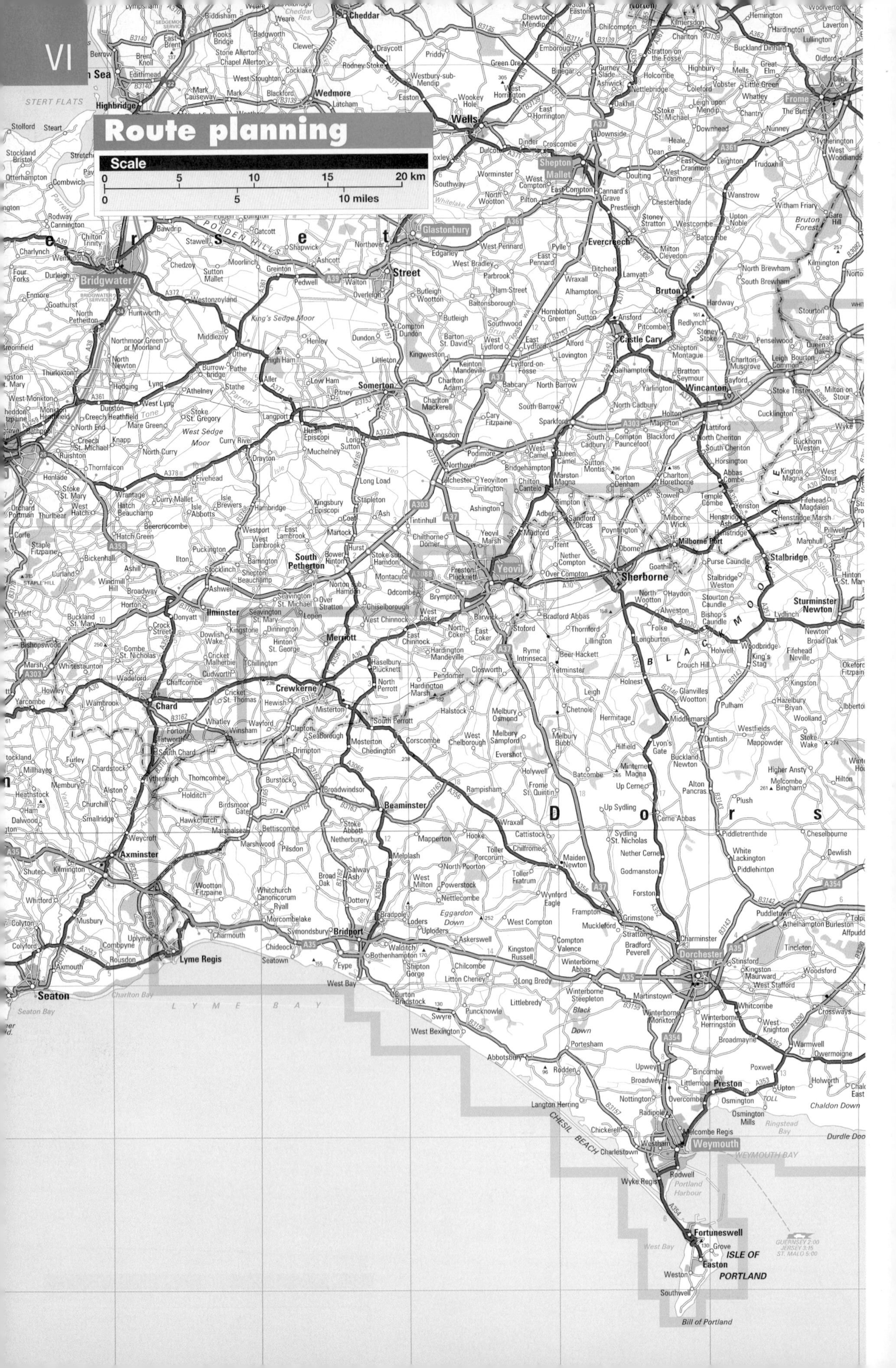
Route planning
Scale
0
5
10
15
20 km
0
5
10 miles
Cheddar
Wedmore
Highbridge
Wells
Shepton Mallet
Frome
Glastonbury
Street
Bridgwater
Evercreech
Bruton
Castle Cary
Somerton
Wincanton
Langport
South Petherton
Yeovil
Sherborne
Milborne Port
Stalbridge
Sturminster Newton
Ilminster
Merriott
Crewkerne
Chard
Beaminster
Axminster
Lyme Regis
Seaton
Bridport
Dorchester
Weymouth
Fortuneswell
Easton
ISLE OF PORTLAND
Bill of Portland
LYME BAY
CHESIL BEACH
WEYMOUTH BAY
POLDEN HILLS
BLACKMOOR VALE
Dorset
Somerset

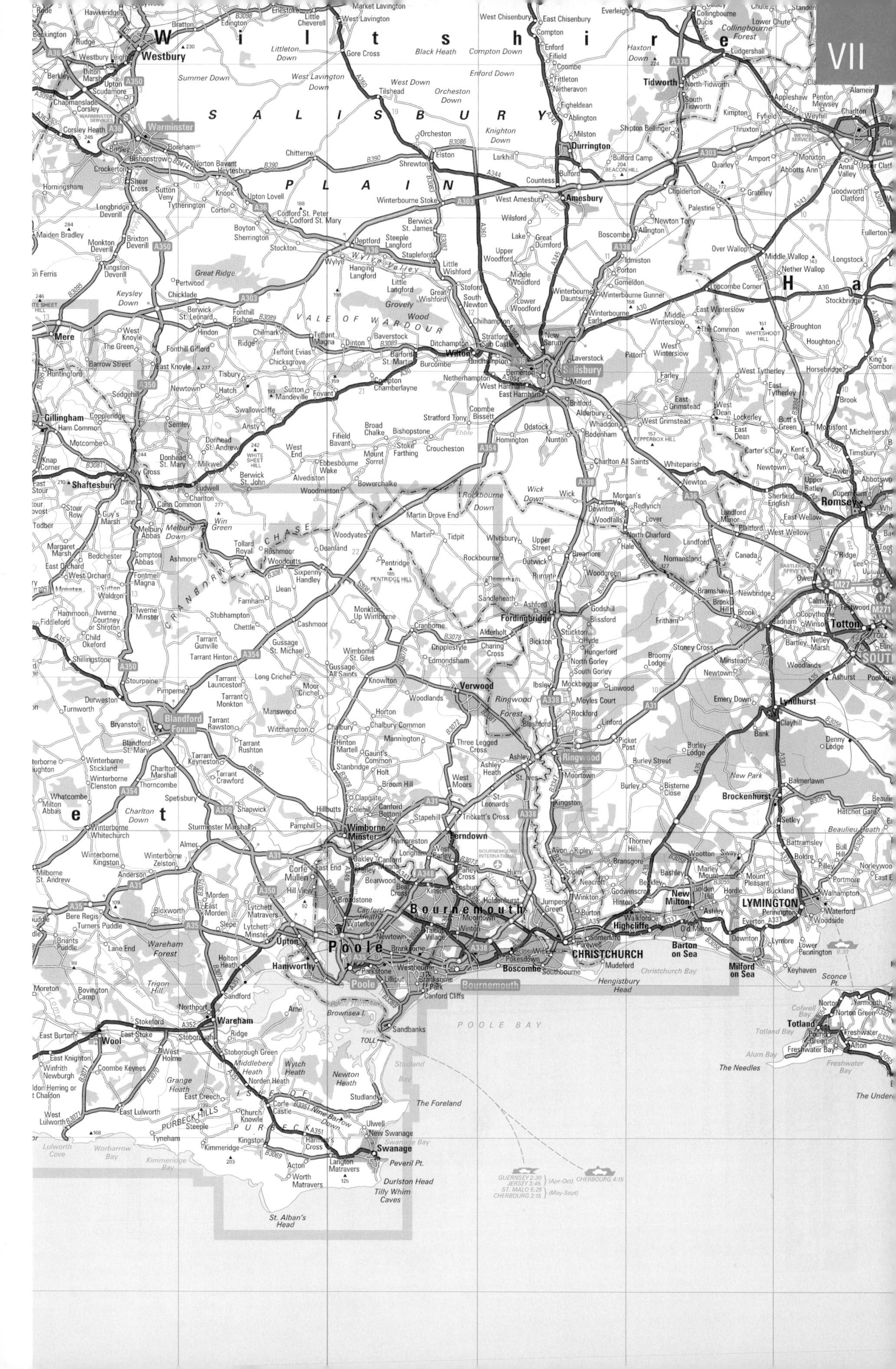

VII
Wiltshire
SALISBURY PLAIN
Westbury
Warminster
Tidworth
Durrington
Amesbury
Ludgershall
Collingbourne Forest
Market Lavington
West Lavington
Tilshead
Shrewton
Orcheston
Larkhill
Bulford
Chitterne
Heytesbury
Codford St. Peter
Codford St. Mary
Winterbourne Stoke
Wylye
Wylye Valley
Great Ridge
Grovely Wood
VALE OF WARDOUR
Mere
Gillingham
Shaftesbury
Tisbury
Hindon
Wilton
Salisbury
Old Sarum
Stockbridge
Romsey
Totton
Downton
Fordingbridge
Ringwood
Verwood
Cranborne
CRANBORNE CHASE
Blandford Forum
Wimborne Minster
Ferndown
Bournemouth
Poole
Boscombe
Christchurch
Highcliffe
New Milton
Barton on Sea
Milford on Sea
Lymington
Brockenhurst
Lyndhurst
New Park
Ringwood Forest
Wareham
Wareham Forest
Wool
Swanage
Corfe Castle
Studland
Sandbanks
Brownsea I.
POOLE BAY
Christchurch Bay
Hengistbury Head
Durlston Head
St. Alban's Head
Peveril Pt.
The Foreland
PURBECK HILLS
Kimmeridge
Worbarrow Bay
Lulworth Cove
East Lulworth
Totland
Yarmouth
Freshwater Bay
The Needles
Hurst Castle
GUERNSEY 2:30
JERSEY 3:45
ST. MALO 5:25
CHERBOURG 2:15
CHERBOURG 4:15
BOURNEMOUTH INTERNATIONAL

Administrative and Postcode boundaries

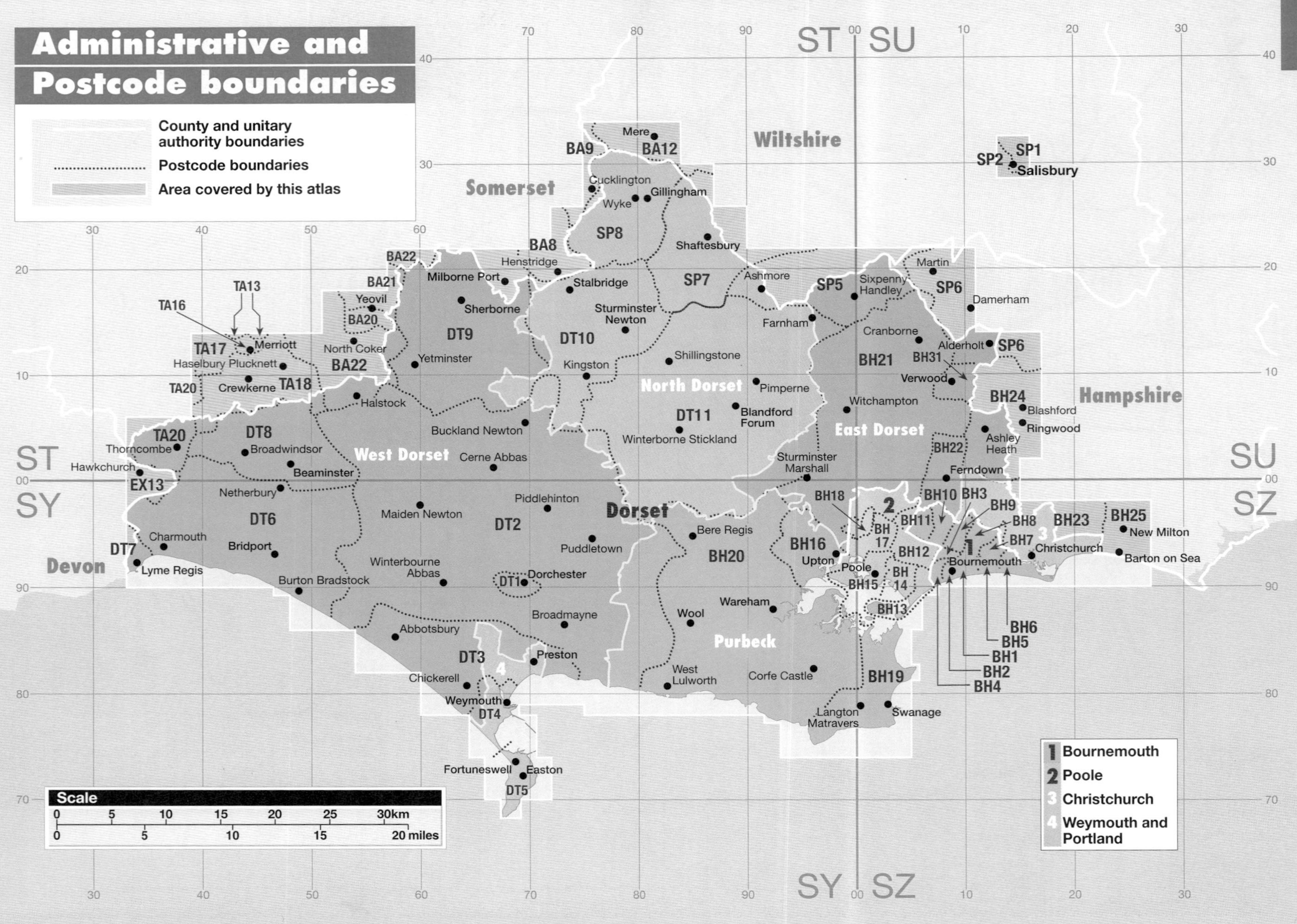

County and unitary authority boundaries

Postcode boundaries

Area covered by this atlas

Legend:

1 Bournemouth
2 Poole
3 Christchurch
4 Weymouth and Portland

Scale

0 5 10 15 20 25 30km
0 5 10 15 20 miles

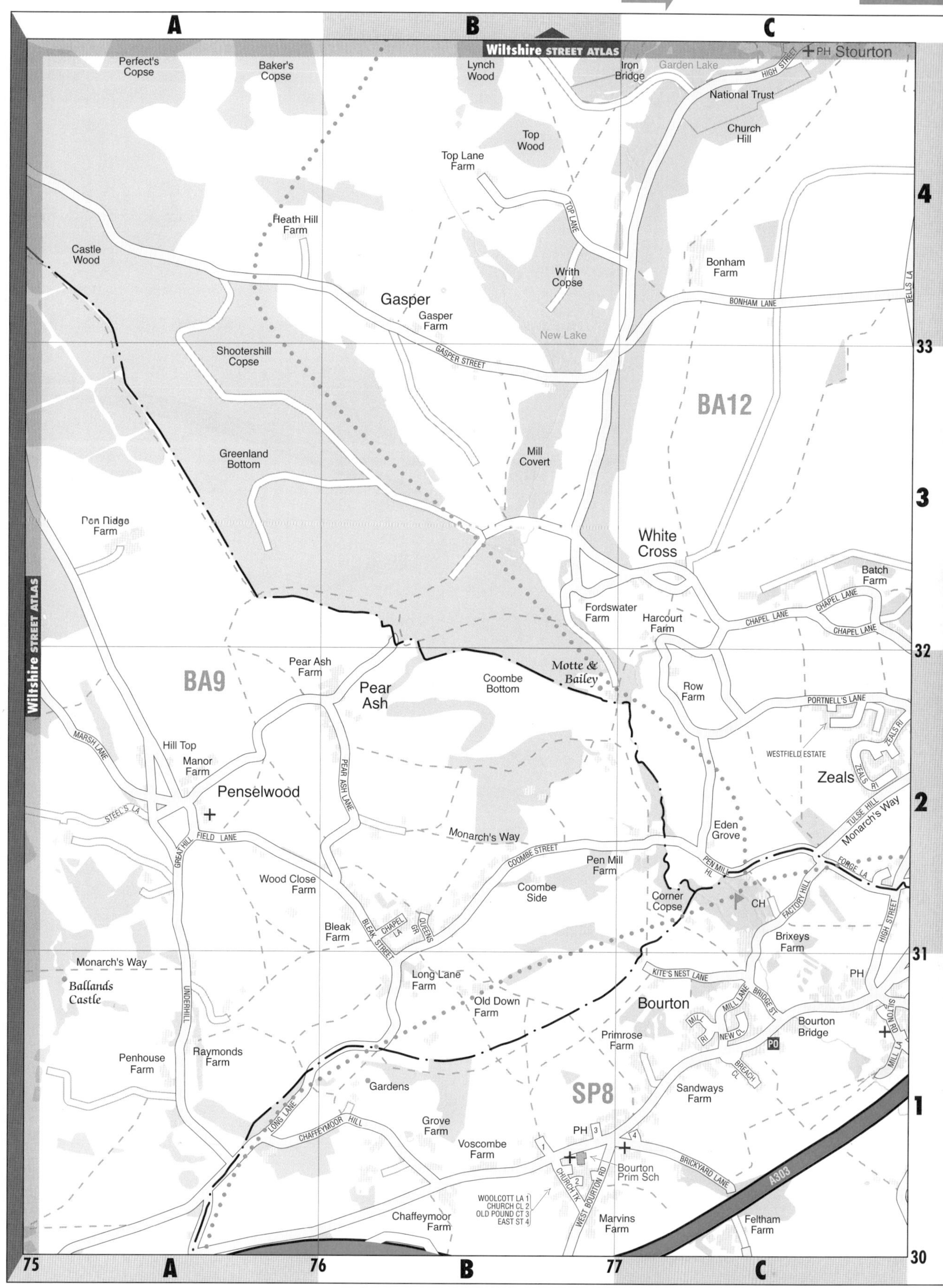

A   B   C

PH Stourton

Perfect's Copse

Baker's Copse

Lynch Wood

Iron Bridge

Garden Lake

National Trust

Church Hill

4

Top Lane Farm

Top Wood

Heath Hill Farm

Castle Wood

Bonham Farm

Writh Copse

Gasper

BONHAM LANE

BELLS LA

Gasper Farm

New Lake

33

Shootershill Copse

GASPER STREET

BA12

Greenland Bottom

Mill Covert

Don Ridge Farm

3

White Cross

Batch Farm

Fordswater Farm

Harcourt Farm

CHAPEL LANE

CHAPEL LANE

CHAPEL LANE

Pear Ash Farm

Coombe Bottom

Motte & Bailey

Row Farm

32

BA9

Pear Ash

PORTNELL'S LANE

MARSH LANE

Hill Top Manor Farm

PEAR ASH LANE

WESTFIELD ESTATE

ZEALS RI

Zeals

ZEALS RI

Penselwood

Monarch's Way

Eden Grove

Monarch's Way

STEEL'S LA

COOMBE STREET

Pen Mill Farm

PEN MILL HL

TULSE HILL

2

FIELD LANE

Wood Close Farm

Coombe Side

Corner Copse

CH

FACTORY HILL

HIGH STREET

Brixeys Farm

GREAT HILL

Bleak Farm

BLEAK STREET

CHAPEL LA

QUEENS GRT

FORGE LA

31

Monarch's Way

Long Lane Farm

KITE'S NEST LANE

PH

Ballands Castle

UNDERHILL

Old Down Farm

Bourton

MILL LANE

BRIDGE ST

Bourton Bridge

OLD MILLS

Penhouse Farm

Raymonds Farm

Primrose Farm

NEW CL

BREACH CL

PO

Gardens

SP8

Sandways Farm

MILL LA

1

LONG LANE

CHAFFEYMOOR HILL

Grove Farm

Voscombe Farm

PH 3

4

Bourton Prim Sch

BRICKYARD LANE

A303

Feltham Farm

WEST BOURTON RD

CHURCH TK

Marvins Farm

Chaffeymoor Farm

WOOLCOTT LA 1
CHURCH CL 2
OLD POUND CT 3
EAST ST 4

30

75   A   76   B   77   C   30

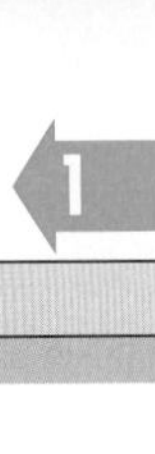
1

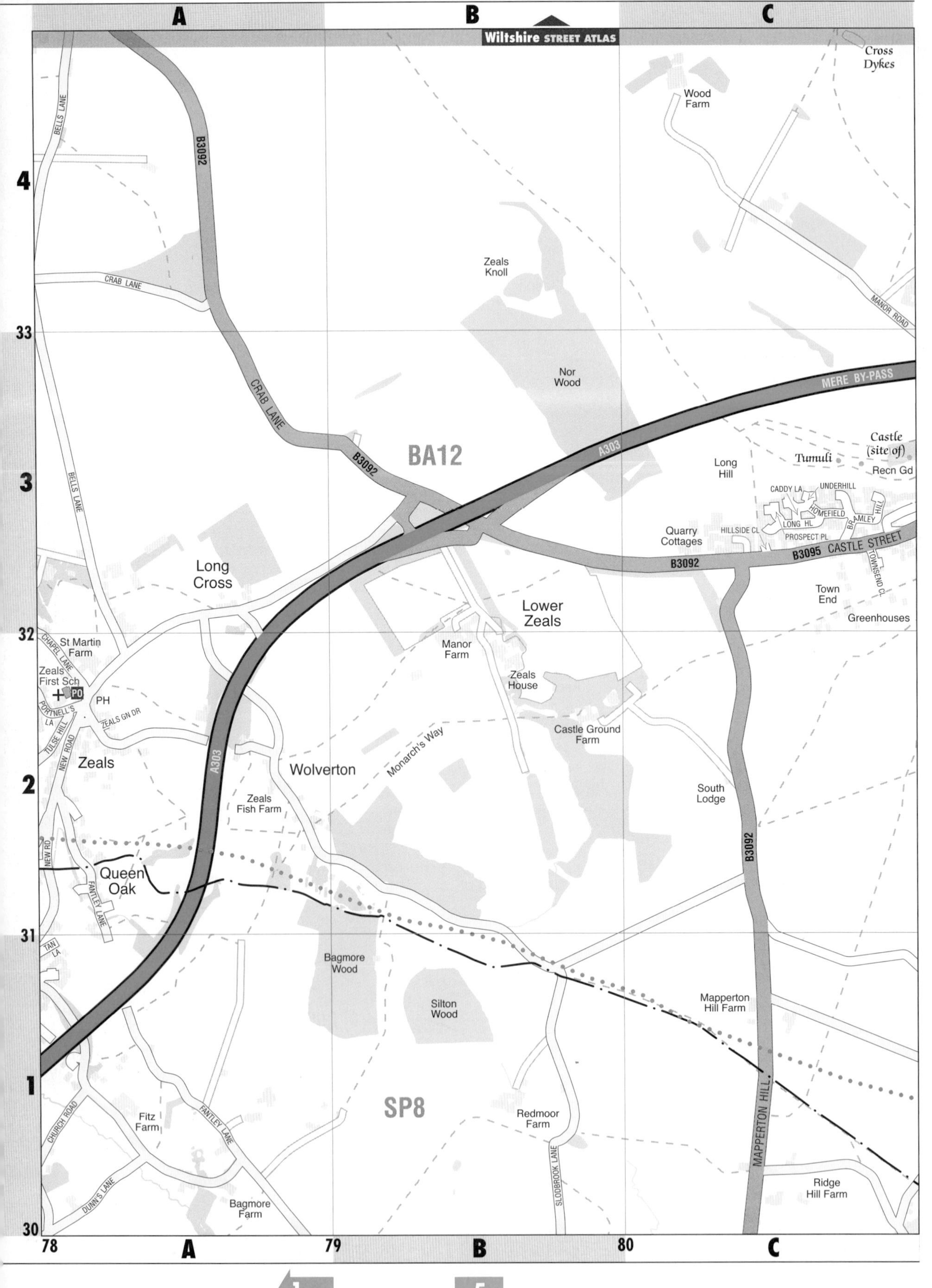
A
B
C
Wiltshire STREET ATLAS
Cross
Dykes
Wood
Farm
BELLS LANE
B3092
4
CRAB LANE
Zeals
Knoll
MANOR ROAD
33
Nor
Wood
MERE BY-PASS
CRAB LANE
Castle
(site of)
BA12
B3092
A303
Tumuli
Long
Hill
Recn Gd
3
BELLS LANE
CADDY LA
UNDERHILL
HOMEFIELD
BRAMLEY HILL
Quarry
Cottages
HILLSIDE CL
LONG HL
PROSPECT PL
CASTLE STREET
B3092
B3095
Long
Cross
TOWNSEND CL
Lower
Zeals
Town
End
Greenhouses
32
St Martin
Farm
CHAPEL LANE
Manor
Farm
Zeals
First Sch
PO
PH
Zeals
House
PORTNELL'S LA
ZEALS GN DR
Castle Ground
Farm
Monarch's Way
TULSE HILL
NEW ROAD
Zeals
A303
Wolverton
2
South
Lodge
Zeals
Fish Farm
NEW RD
B3092
Queen
Oak
FANTLEY LANE
31
TAN LA
Bagmore
Wood
Mapperton
Hill Farm
Silton
Wood
1
MAPPERTON HILL
CHURCH ROAD
SP8
Fitz
Farm
FANTLEY LANE
Redmoor
Farm
SLODBROOK LANE
Ridge
Hill Farm
DUNN'S LANE
Bagmore
Farm
30
78
A
79
B
80
C

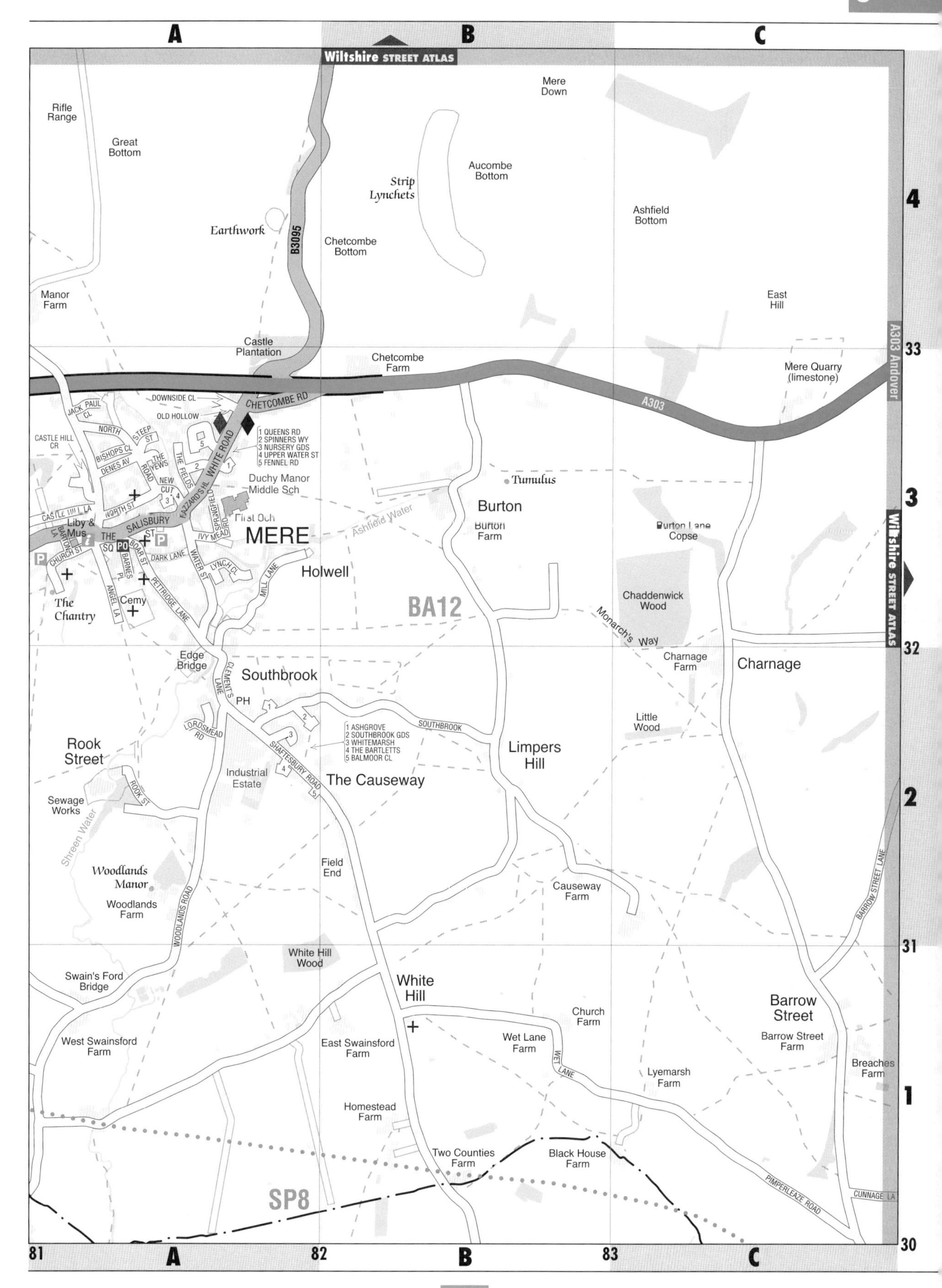

A **B** **C**

4

Rifle Range

Great Bottom

Mere Down

Strip Lynchets

Aucombe Bottom

Earthwork

Chetcombe Bottom

Ashfield Bottom

Manor Farm

East Hill

33

Castle Plantation

Chetcombe Farm

Mere Quarry (limestone)

DOWNSIDE CL

CHETCOMBE RD

A303

A303 Andover

JACK PAUL CL

OLD HOLLOW

1 QUEENS RD
2 SPINNERS WY
3 NURSERY GDS
4 UPPER WATER ST
5 FENNEL RD

NORTH ST

STEEP ST

CASTLE HILL CR

BISHOPS CL

DENES AV

WHITE ROAD

THE VIEWS

Duchy Manor Middle Sch

Tumulus

Burton

3

Wiltshire STREET ATLAS

NEW CUT

CASTLE HILL LA

First Sch

Ashfield Water

Burton Farm

Burton Lane Copse

Liby & Mus

SALISBURY

IVY MEAD

MERE

BARTONS

THE SQ

PO

BARNES PL

Dark Lane

WATER ST

LYNCH CL

MILL LANE

Holwell

BA12

Chaddenwick Wood

The Chantry

Cemy

ANGEL LA

Edge Bridge

Southbrook

Monarch's Way

Charnage Farm

Charnage

32

CLEMENT'S LANE

PH

SOUTHBROOK

1 ASHGROVE
2 SOUTHBROOK GDS
3 WHITEMARSH
4 THE BARTLETTS
5 BALMOOR CL

Limpers Hill

Little Wood

Rook Street

LORDSMEAD RD

ROOK ST

Industrial Estate

SHAFTESBURY ROAD

The Causeway

2

Sewage Works

Shreen Water

Woodlands Manor

Causeway Farm

Woodlands Farm

WOODLANDS ROAD

Field End

31

Swain's Ford Bridge

White Hill Wood

White Hill

Church Farm

Barrow Street

West Swainsford Farm

East Swainsford Farm

Wet Lane Farm

WET LANE

Barrow Street Farm

Breaches Farm

1

Homestead Farm

Lyemarsh Farm

SP8

Two Counties Farm

Black House Farm

PIMPERLEAZE ROAD

CUNNAGE LA

30

81 **A** 82 **B** 83 **C**

1

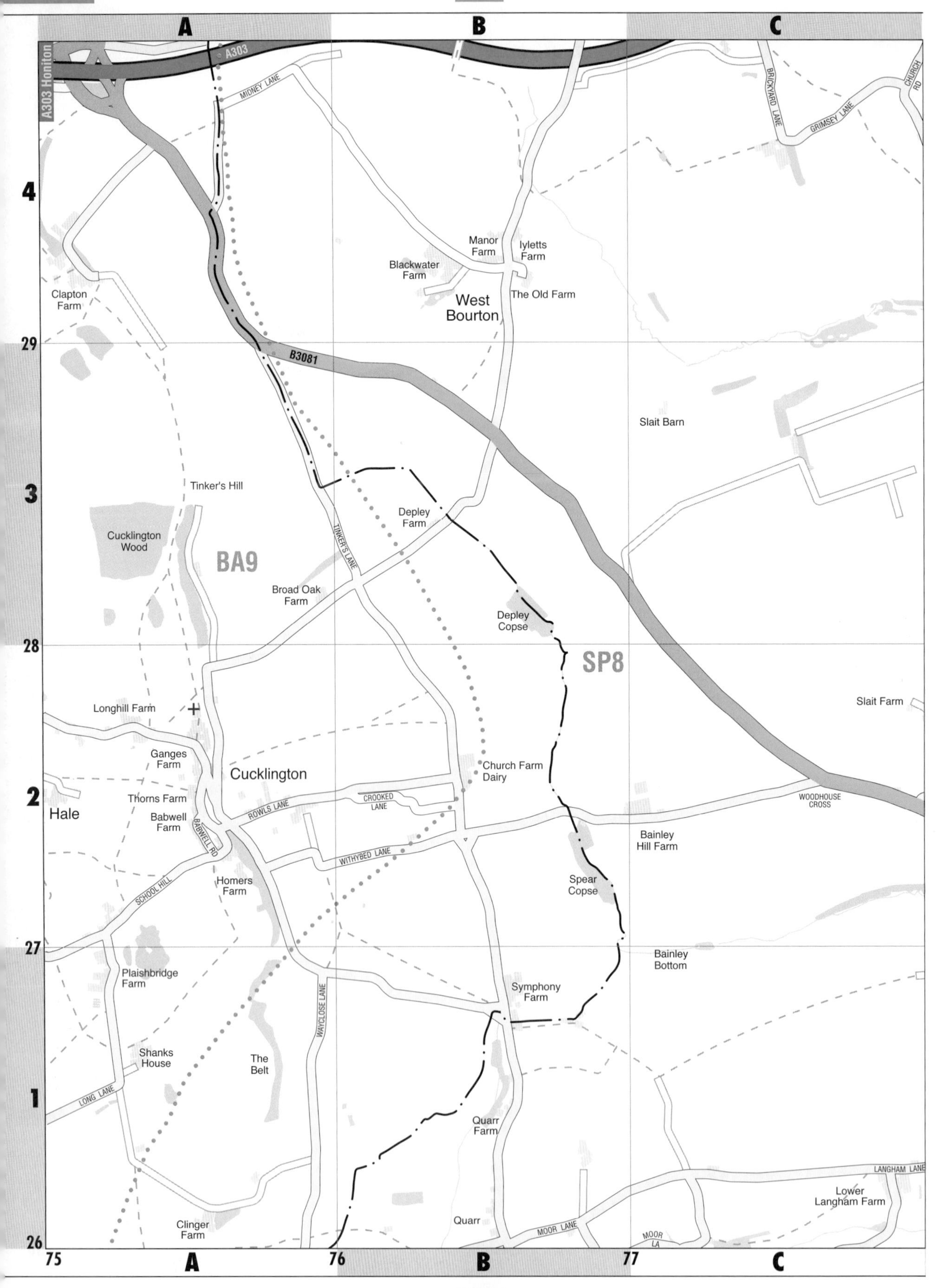

A
B
C
A303 Honiton
A303
MIDNEY LANE
BRICKYARD LANE
GRIMSEY LANE
CHURCH RD
4
Manor Farm
Iyletts Farm
Blackwater Farm
The Old Farm
West Bourton
Clapton Farm
29
B3081
Slait Barn
Tinker's Hill
3
Depley Farm
Cucklington Wood
BA9
TINKER'S LANE
Broad Oak Farm
Depley Copse
28
SP8
Slait Farm
Longhill Farm
Ganges Farm
Cucklington
Church Farm Dairy
2
Hale
Thorns Farm
CROOKED LANE
WOODHOUSE CROSS
Babwell Farm
ROWLS LANE
BABWELL RD
WITHYBED LANE
Bainley Hill Farm
SCHOOL HILL
Homers Farm
Spear Copse
27
Bainley Bottom
Plaishbridge Farm
WAYCLOSE LANE
Symphony Farm
Shanks House
The Belt
1
LONG LANE
Quarr Farm
LANGHAM LANE
Lower Langham Farm
Quarr
Clinger Farm
MOOR LANE
MOOR LA
26
75
76
77

9

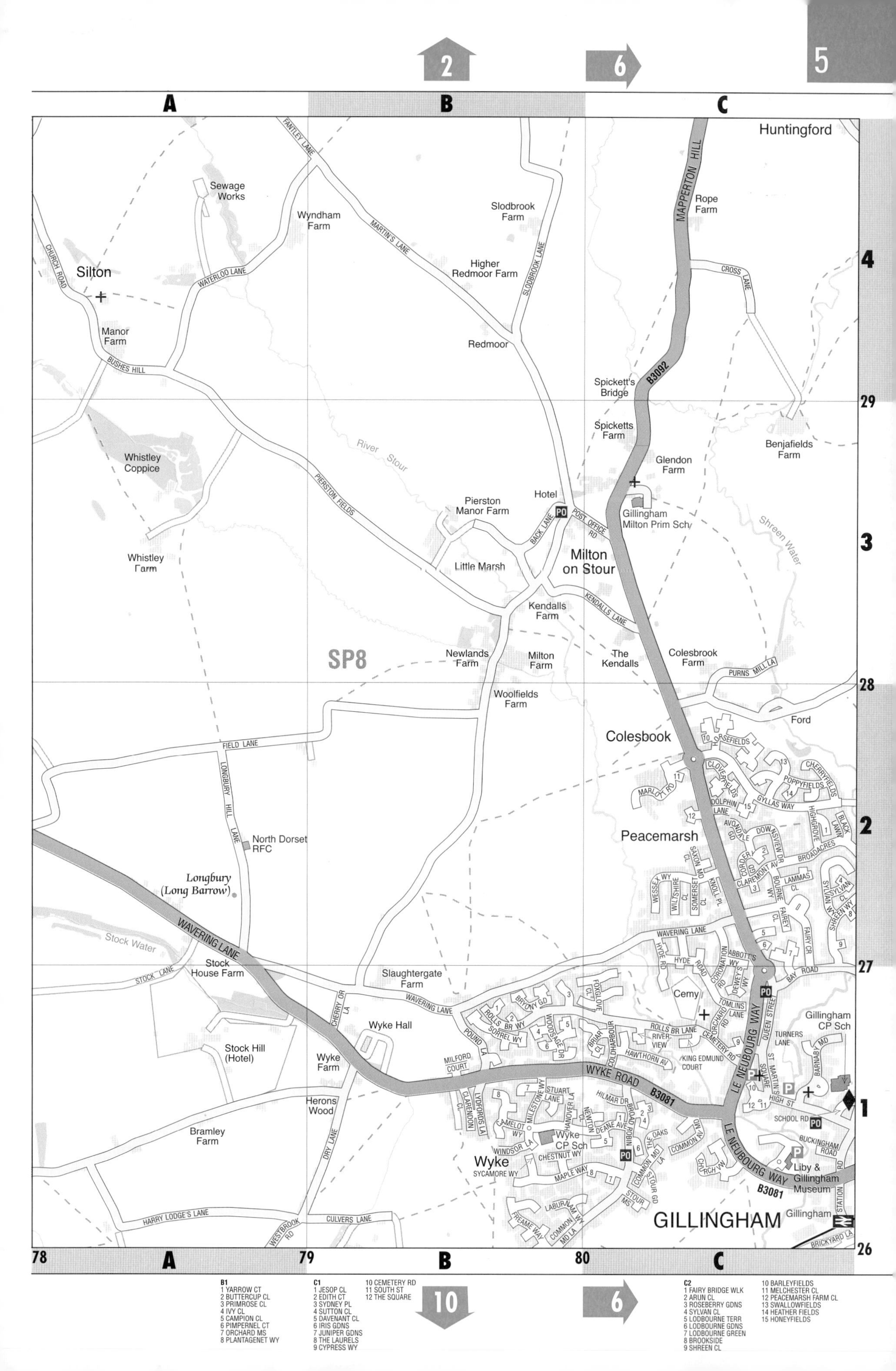

5
2
6
A
B
C
Huntingford
Sewage Works
Wyndham Farm
Slodbrook Farm
Rope Farm
MAPPERTON HILL
FANTLEY LANE
MARTIN'S LANE
SLODBROOK LANE
CROSS LANE
CHURCH ROAD
Silton
WATERLOO LANE
Higher Redmoor Farm
Manor Farm
Redmoor
BUSHES HILL
B3092
Spickett's Bridge
Spicketts Farm
Benjafields Farm
Glendon Farm
Whistley Coppice
River Stour
PIERSTON FIELDS
Hotel
Pierston Manor Farm
BACK LANE
POST OFFICE RD
Gillingham Milton Prim Sch
Shreen Water
Whistley Farm
Little Marsh
Milton on Stour
KENDALLS LANE
Kendalls Farm
SP8
Newlands Farm
Milton Farm
The Kendalls
Colesbrook Farm
PURNS MILL LA
Woolfields Farm
Ford
Colesbook
FIELD LANE
HORSEFIELDS
CHERRYFIELDS
POPPYFIELDS
CLOVERFIELDS
MARLOTT RD
GYLLAS WAY
DOLPHIN LANE
AVONDALE
Peacemarsh
LONGBURY HILL LANE
North Dorset RFC
Longbury (Long Barrow)
BROADACRES
CLAREMONT AV
LAMMAS
WESSEX WY
WILTSHIRE CL
SOMERSET CL
KNOLL PL
SAXON MD
BOURNE WY
FAIREY CL
Stock Water
WAVERING LANE
HYDE RD
HYDE ROAD
CORONATION RD
ABBOTT'S WY
DEWEY'S WY
FAIRY CR
SHREEN WY
BAY ROAD
Stock House Farm
STOCK LANE
Slaughtergate Farm
CHERRY ORCHARD LA
Cemy
FOXGLOVE CL
TOMLINS LANE
BRYONY GD
ROLLS BR WY
SORREL WY
WOODSAGE DR
COLDHARBOUR
ROLLS BR LANE
RIVER VIEW
HAWTHORN AV
CEMETERY RD
Gillingham CP Sch
Wyke Hall
Stock Hill (Hotel)
POUND LA
MILFORD COURT
KING EDMUND COURT
TURNERS LANE
QUEEN STREET
LE NEUBOURG WAY
ST MARTIN'S SQUARE
BARNABY MD
Wyke Farm
WYKE ROAD
B3081
HIGH ST
Herons Wood
LYDFORDS LA
CLARENDON CL
MILESTONE WY
STUART LANE
HILMAR DR
BROAD ROBIN
SCHOOL RD
Bramley Farm
CAMELOT WY
HANOVER LA
NEWTON RD
DEANE AVE
THE OAKS
COMMON MD LA
COMMON AV MD
BUCKINGHAM ROAD
WINDSOR LA
Wyke CP Sch
CHESTNUT WY
CHURCH WK
Liby & Gillingham Museum
DRY LANE
Wyke
SYCAMORE WY
MAPLE WAY
STOUR GD
STOUR MS
LABURNAM WY
STATION RD
Gillingham
HARRY LODGE'S LANE
WESTBROOK RD
CULVERS LANE
FREAME WAY
COMMON MD LA
GILLINGHAM
BRICKYARD LA
PO
P
4
29
3
28
2
27
1
26
78
79
80
B1
1 YARROW CT
2 BUTTERCUP CL
3 PRIMROSE CL
4 IVY CL
5 CAMPION CL
6 PIMPERNEL CT
7 ORCHARD MS
8 PLANTAGENET WY
C1
1 JESOP CL
2 EDITH CT
3 SYDNEY PL
4 SUTTON CL
5 DAVENANT CL
6 IRIS GDNS
7 JUNIPER GDNS
8 THE LAURELS
9 CYPRESS WY
10 CEMETERY RD
11 SOUTH ST
12 THE SQUARE
10
6
C2
1 FAIRY BRIDGE WLK
2 ARUN CL
3 ROSEBERRY GDNS
4 SYLVAN CL
5 LODBOURNE TERR
6 LODBOURNE GDNS
7 LODBOURNE GREEN
8 BROOKSIDE
9 SHREEN CL
10 BARLEYFIELDS
11 MELCHESTER CL
12 PEACEMARSH FARM CL
13 SWALLOWFIELDS
14 HEATHER FIELDS
15 HONEYFIELDS

A

B

C

Huntingford

Forest
Farm

Forest Deer

BA12

Bushhayes
Farm

PIMPERLEAZE ROAD

Shreen Water

4

Forest Side
Farm

Longmoor
Farm

SP8

East
Lawn Farm

29

North Lawn
Farm

3

Bloomer's
Farm

Lawn
Farm

Gutchpool
Farm

Lower Bowridge
Hill Farm

Savage
Cat Farm

28

Easterley
Copse

River Lodden

Larkinglass
Farm

Bowridge
Hill Farm

Bowridge
Hill

2

Paddock
Farm

Wolfridge
Farm

Shreen Way

Woodwater
Farm

SP8

SP7

BAY ROAD

Windyridge
Farm

27

BAY LANE

Bay

King's Court
Wood

GILLINGHAM

Gillingham
Sch

SCHOOL
LANE

HARDING'S LANE

Leisure
Centre

1

Hotel

Gillingham Town
Football Club

NEWBURY

VICTORIA

King's
Court Palace

Donedge Lodge
Farm

LE
NEUBOURG
WY

NEWBURY

Lodden
Farm

Lodden
Bridge

KINGSCOURT RD

KINGSCOURT

NEW ROAD

2

SHAFTESBURY RD

BRIDGE
CL

6

26

B3092

ADDISON CL

B3081

5

7

Ham Common

81

A

82

B

83

C

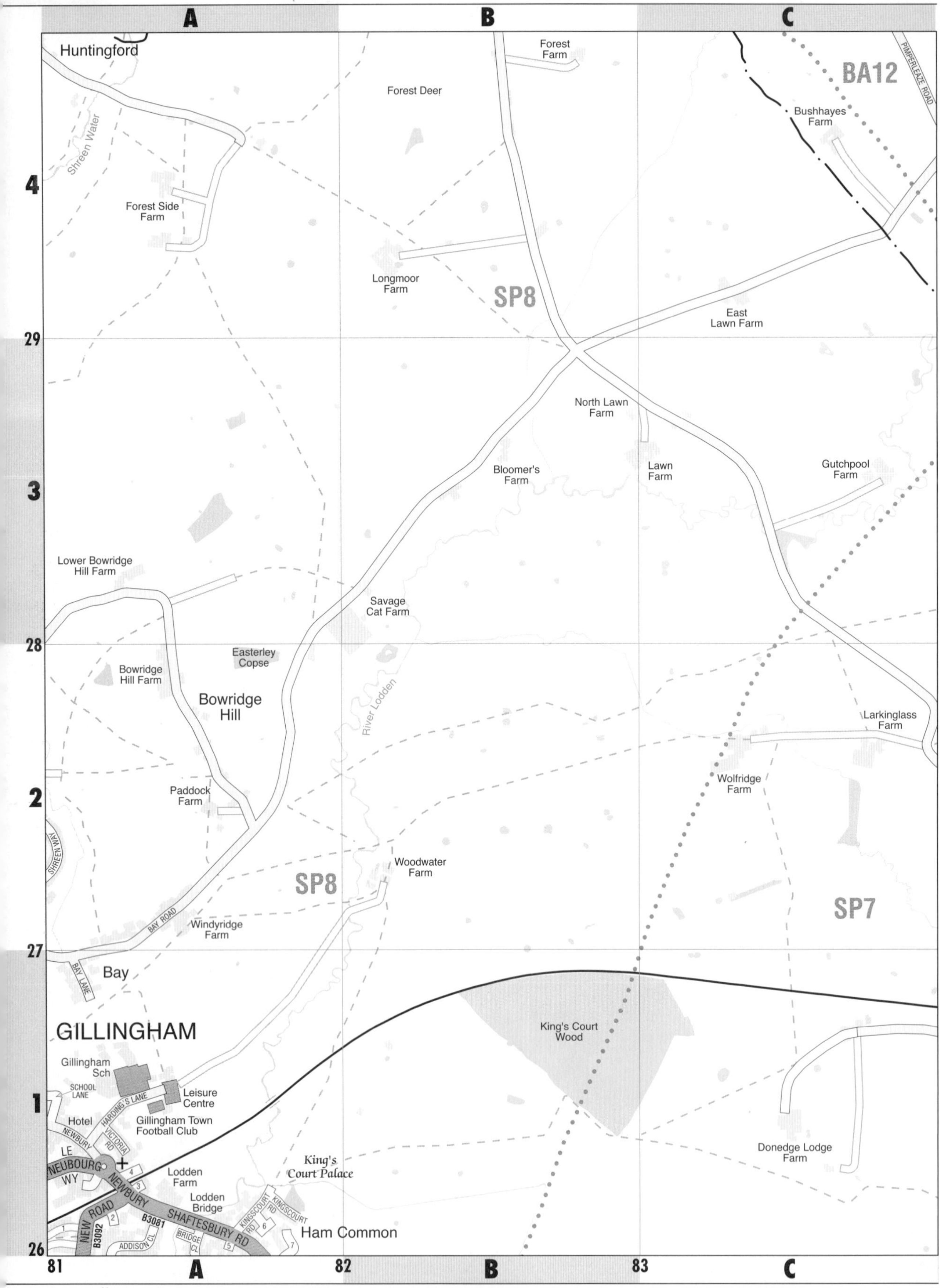

A1
1 BRICKYARD LA
2 PROSPECT CL
3 ROSE CT
4 RAILWAY TR
5 HAM LA
6 KINGSCOURT CL
7 ROOKERY CL

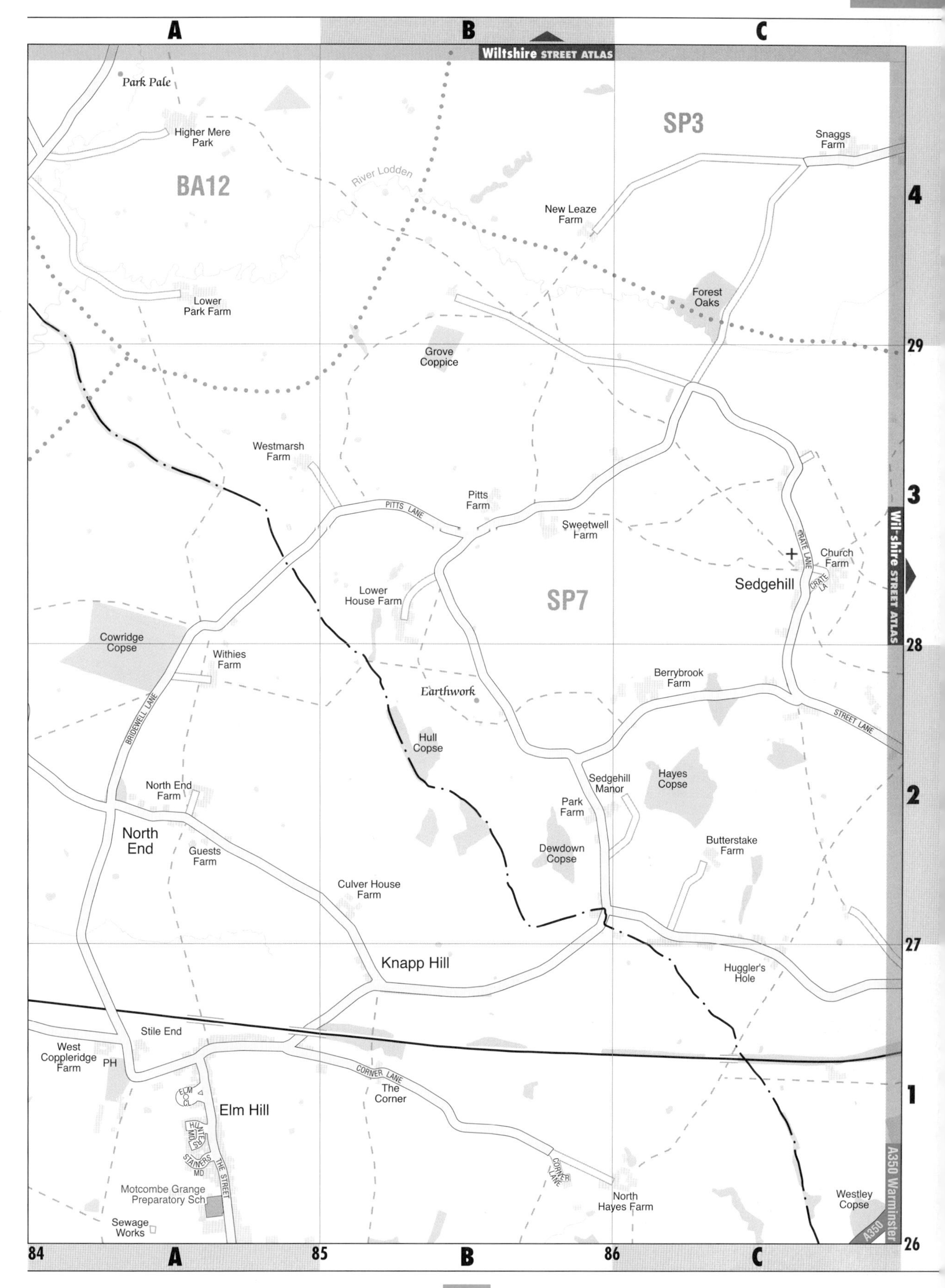

Park Pale

Higher Mere Park

BA12

River Lodden

SP3

Snaggs Farm

New Leaze Farm

4

Lower Park Farm

Forest Oaks

29

Grove Coppice

Westmarsh Farm

PITTS LANE

Pitts Farm

Sweetwell Farm

3

Wiltshire STREET ATLAS

CRATE LANE

CRATE LA

Church Farm

Sedgehill

SP7

Lower House Farm

Cowridge Copse

Withies Farm

BRIDEWELL LANE

Earthwork

Berrybrook Farm

STREET LANE

28

Hull Copse

Hayes Copse

North End Farm

Sedgehill Manor

2

North End

Guests Farm

Park Farm

Butterstake Farm

Culver House Farm

Dewdown Copse

27

Knapp Hill

Huggler's Hole

Stile End

West Coppleridge Farm

PH

CORNER LANE

The Corner

1

ELM CS

Elm Hill

HUNTS MD CS

STAINERS

THE STREET

MD

CORNER LANE

North Hayes Farm

A350 Warminster

A350

Westley Copse

Motcombe Grange Preparatory Sch

Sewage Works

26

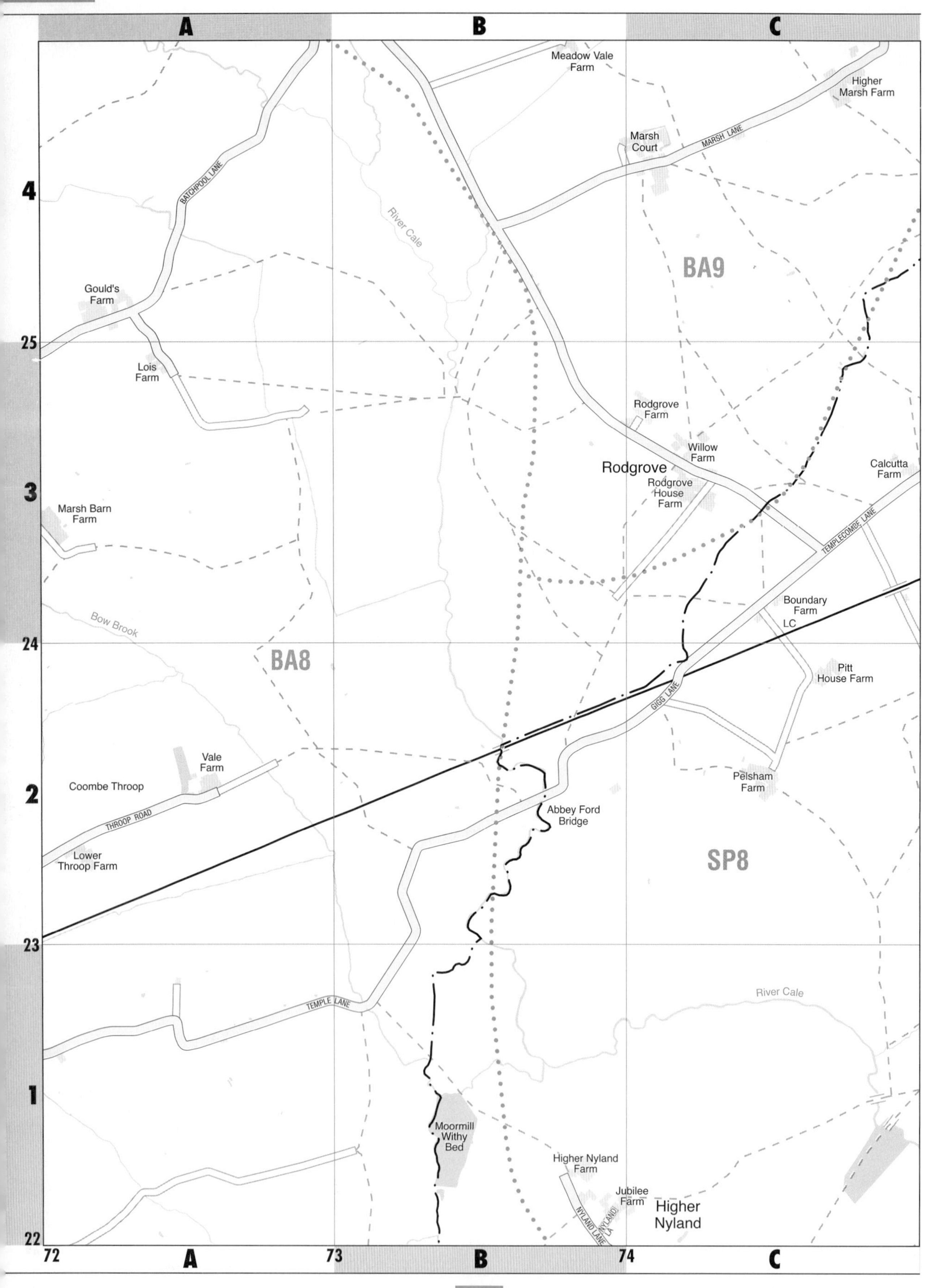
A
B
C
Meadow Vale Farm
Higher Marsh Farm
Marsh Court
MARSH LANE
BATCHPOOL LANE
River Cale
BA9
Gould's Farm
Lois Farm
Rodgrove Farm
Willow Farm
Rodgrove
Rodgrove House Farm
Calcutta Farm
Marsh Barn Farm
TEMPLECOMBE LANE
Boundary Farm
LC
Bow Brook
BA8
Pitt House Farm
GIGG LANE
Vale Farm
Coombe Throop
THROOP ROAD
Pelsham Farm
Abbey Ford Bridge
Lower Throop Farm
SP8
TEMPLE LANE
River Cale
Moormill Withy Bed
Higher Nyland Farm
Jubilee Farm
Higher Nyland
NYLAND LANE
NYLAND LA
4
25
3
24
2
23
1
22
72
73
74

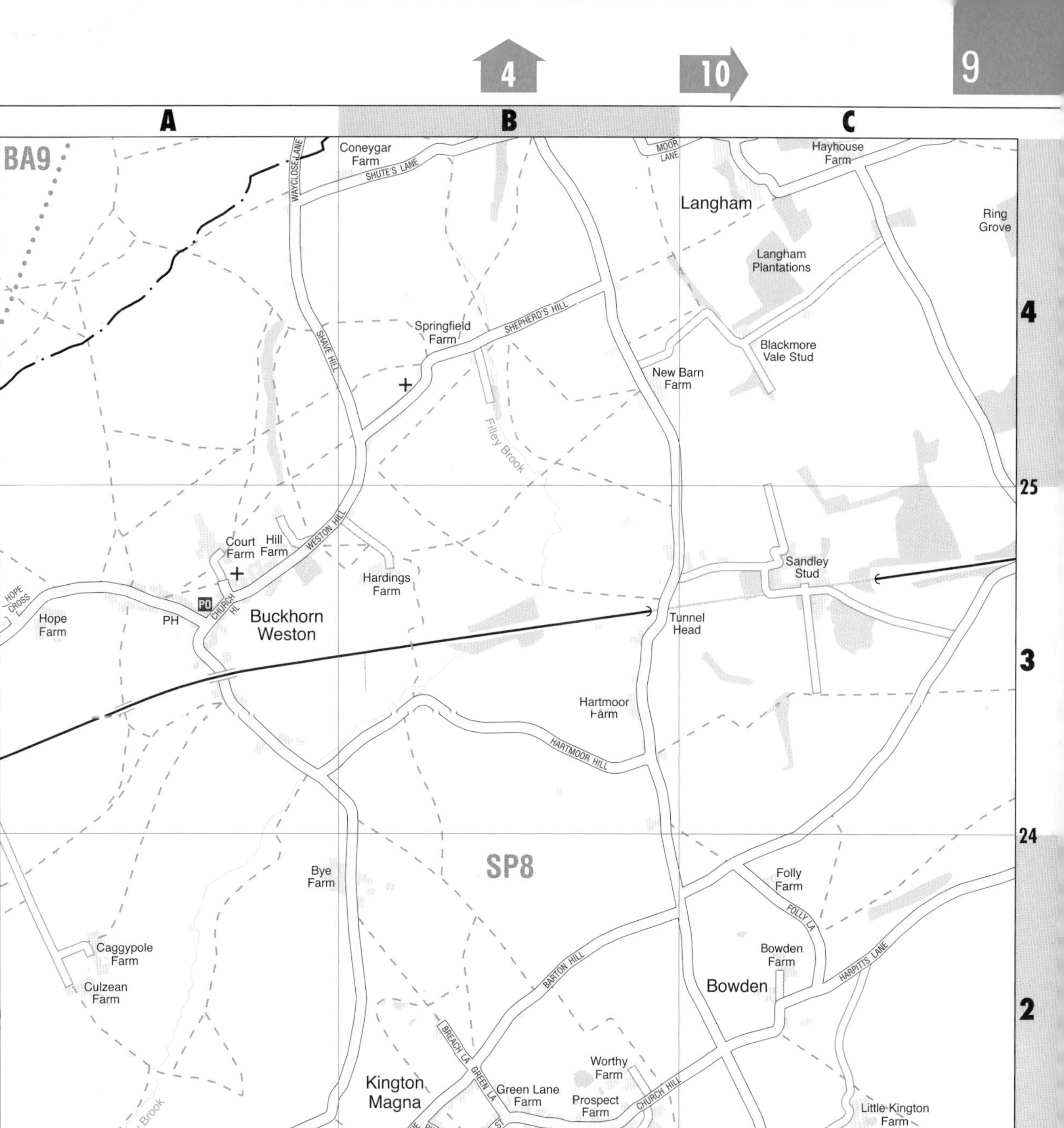

BA9

A   B   C

Coneygar Farm
WAYCLOSE LANE
SHUTE'S LANE
MOOR LANE
Hayhouse Farm
Langham
Ring Grove
Langham Plantations
Springfield Farm
SHEPHERD'S HILL
SHAVE HILL
New Barn Farm
Blackmore Vale Stud
Filley Brook

25

Court Farm
Hill Farm
WESTON HILL
Hardings Farm
Sandley Stud
HOPE CROSS
Hope Farm
PO
PH
CHURCH HILL
Buckhorn Weston
Tunnel Head

3

Hartmoor Farm
HARTMOOR HILL

24

Bye Farm
SP8
Folly Farm
FOLLY LA
Bowden Farm
HARPITTS LANE
Bowden
Caggypole Farm
BARTON HILL
Culzean Farm
Worthy Farm
Little Kington Farm

2

Kington Magna
BREACH LA
GREEN LA
Green Lane Farm
Prospect Farm
CHURCH HILL
BACK LANE
PILL MDW
CHURCH ST
Dairy House Farm
Kington Manor Farm
Filley Brook
JUAN'S LA
JUAN'S LA

23

Old Rectory Farm
WEST ST
CHAPEL HILL
Tanners Farm
SOUTH STREET
CHAPEL HL
FIELD LANE
Lower Farm
New Town
Gaines Farm
Stour Cross Farm

1

Orchard Farm
COMMON LANE
Stour Hill
A30
STOUR HILL
Stour Hill Farm
STOUR PK
STOUR HL

75   A   76   B   77   C   22

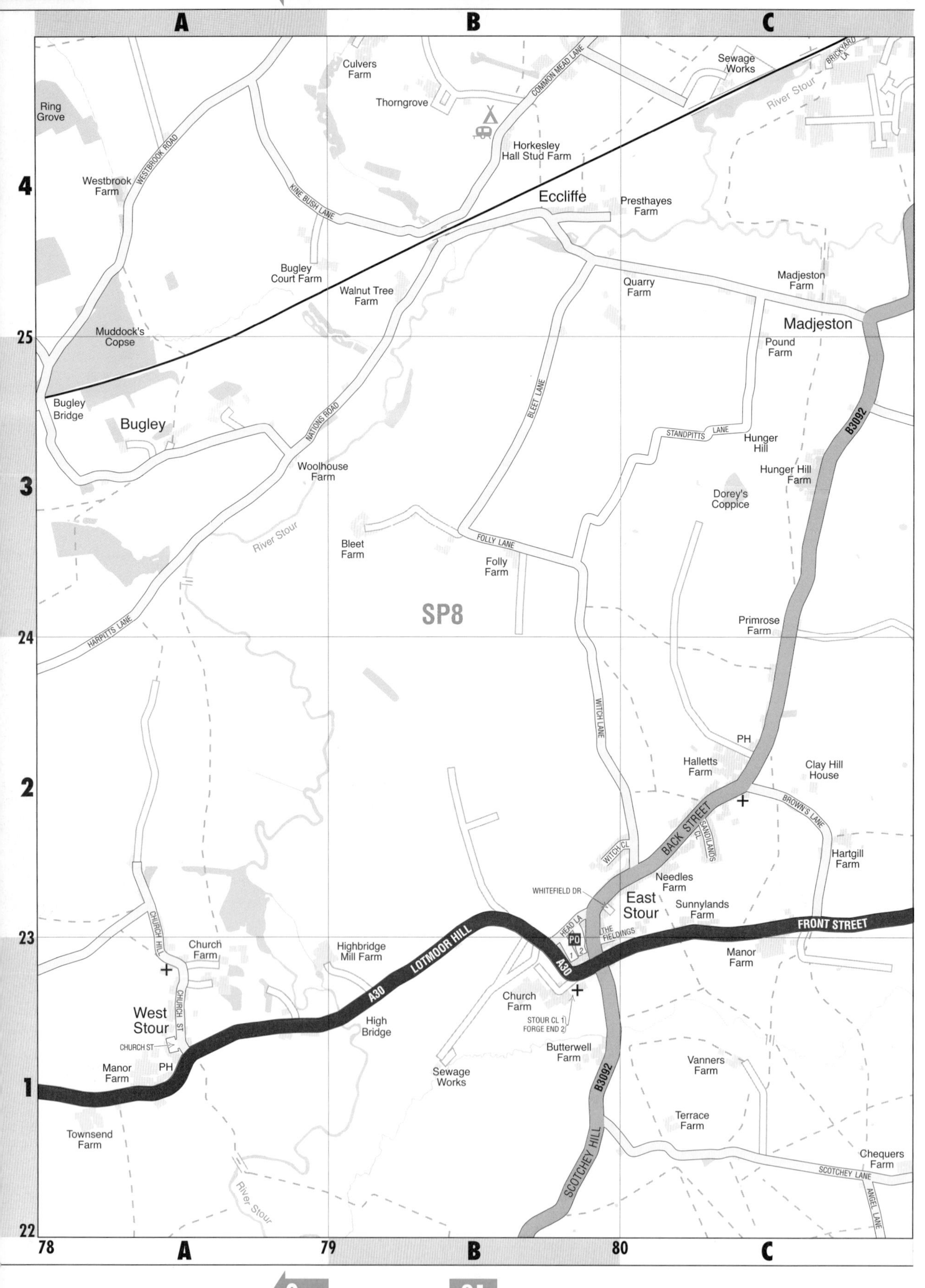

A   B   C

Ring Grove

Westbrook Farm

WESTBROOK ROAD

Culvers Farm

Thorngrove

Common Mead Lane

Sewage Works

BRICKYARD LA

River Stour

Horkesley Hall Stud Farm

Eccliffe

Presthayes Farm

KINE BUSH LANE

Bugley Court Farm

Walnut Tree Farm

Quarry Farm

Madjeston Farm

Madjeston

Muddock's Copse

Pound Farm

B3092

Bugley Bridge

NATIONS ROAD

Bugley

Woolhouse Farm

River Stour

BLEET LANE

STANDPITTS LANE

Hunger Hill

Hunger Hill Farm

Dorey's Coppice

Bleet Farm

FOLLY LANE

Folly Farm

SP8

HARPITTS LANE

Primrose Farm

WITCH LANE

PH

Halletts Farm

Clay Hill House

BACK STREET

SANDLANDS CL

BROWN'S LANE

Hartgill Farm

WITCH CL

Needles Farm

Sunnylands Farm

WHITEFIELD DR

East Stour

FRONT STREET

HEAD LA

PO

THE FIELDINGS

Manor Farm

CHURCH HILL

Church Farm

Highbridge Mill Farm

LOTMOOR HILL

A30

A30

West Stour

CHURCH ST

High Bridge

Church Farm

STOUR CL 1
FORGE END 2

Butterwell Farm

B3092

Vanners Farm

CHURCH ST

Manor Farm

PH

Sewage Works

Terrace Farm

Townsend Farm

SCOTCHEY HILL

River Stour

Chequers Farm

SCOTCHEY LANE

ANGEL LANE

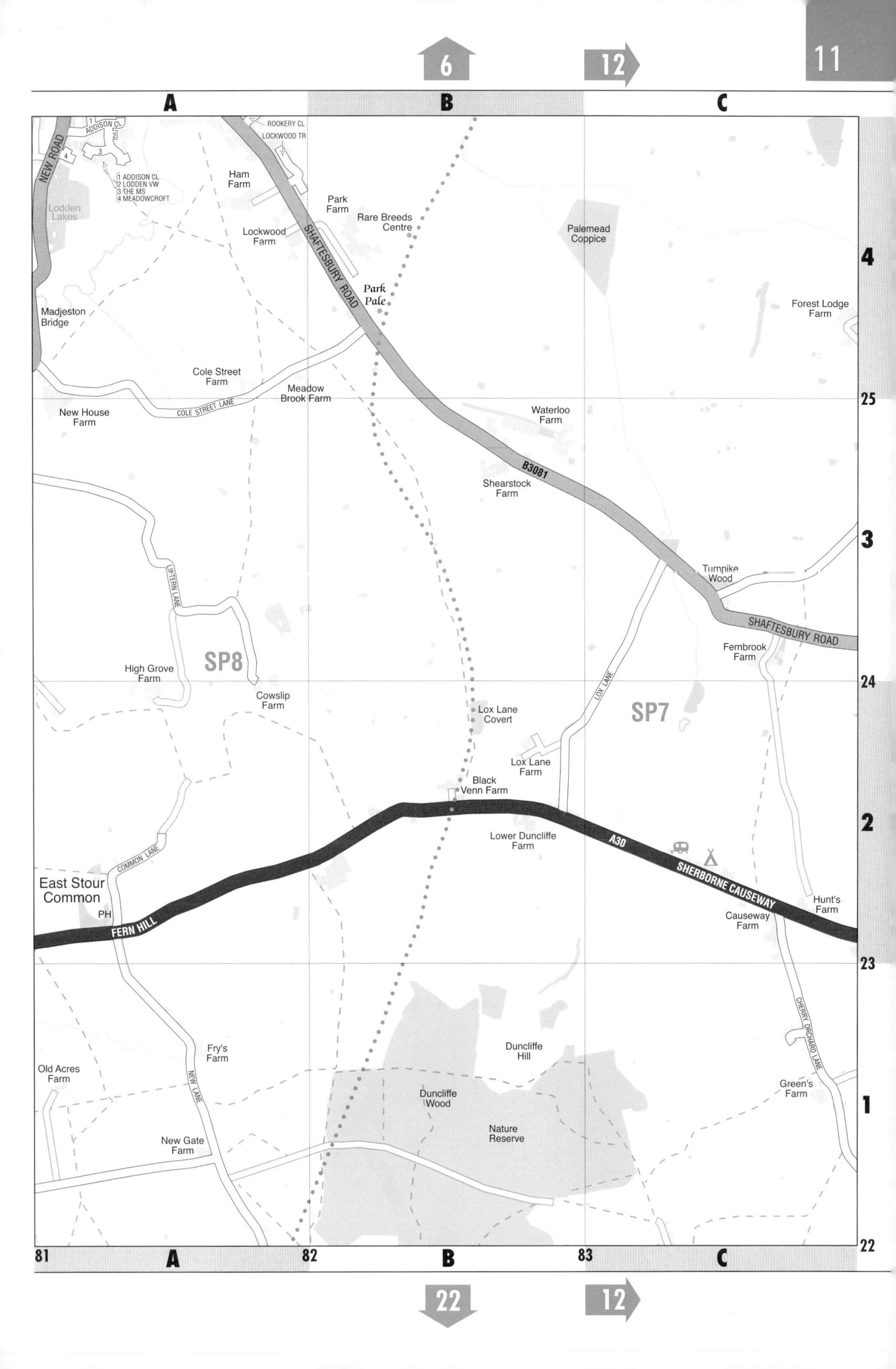

A

B

C

NEW ROAD

ADDISON CL

ROOKERY CL
LOCKWOOD TR

1 ADDISON CL
2 LODDEN VW
3 THE MS
4 MEADOWCROFT

Ham
Farm

Park
Farm

Rare Breeds
Centre

Palemead
Coppice

Lodden
Lakes

Lockwood
Farm

SHAFTESBURY ROAD

Park
Pale

Forest Lodge
Farm

Madjeston
Bridge

Cole Street
Farm

Meadow
Brook Farm

COLE STREET LANE

Waterloo
Farm

25

New House
Farm

B3081

Shearstock
Farm

LANTERN LANE

3

Turnpike
Wood

SHAFTESBURY ROAD

SP8

High Grove
Farm

Fernbrook
Farm

Cowslip
Farm

24

LOX LANE

SP7

Lox Lane
Covert

Lox Lane
Farm

Black
Venn Farm

Lower Duncliffe
Farm

A30

2

COMMON LANE

SHERBORNE CAUSEWAY

Hunt's
Farm

East Stour
Common

PH

FERN HILL

Causeway
Farm

23

Fry's
Farm

Duncliffe
Hill

CHERRY ORCHARD LANE

Old Acres
Farm

NEW LANE

Green's
Farm

Duncliffe
Wood

1

New Gate
Farm

Nature
Reserve

22

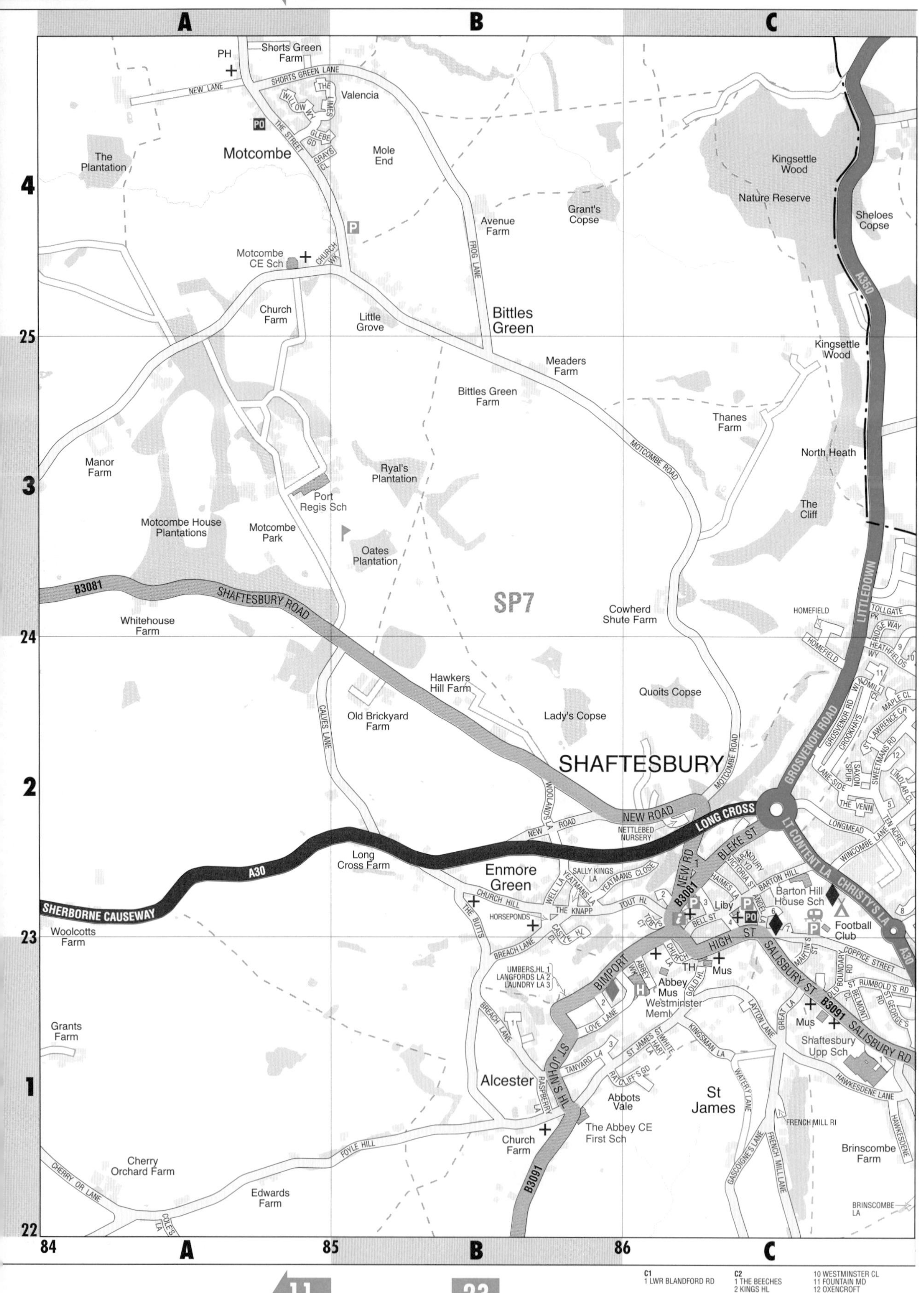

4

25

3

24

2

23

1

22

84   A   85   B   86   C

C1
1 LWR BLANDFORD RD

C2
1 THE BEECHES
2 KINGS HL
3 PARSONS POOL
4 MUSTONS LA
5 ST EDWARDS
6 GRANVILLE GD
7 CHARLES GARRETT CL
8 JEANNEAU CL
9 CRANBORNE DR

10 WESTMINSTER CL
11 FOUNTAIN MD
12 OXENCROFT

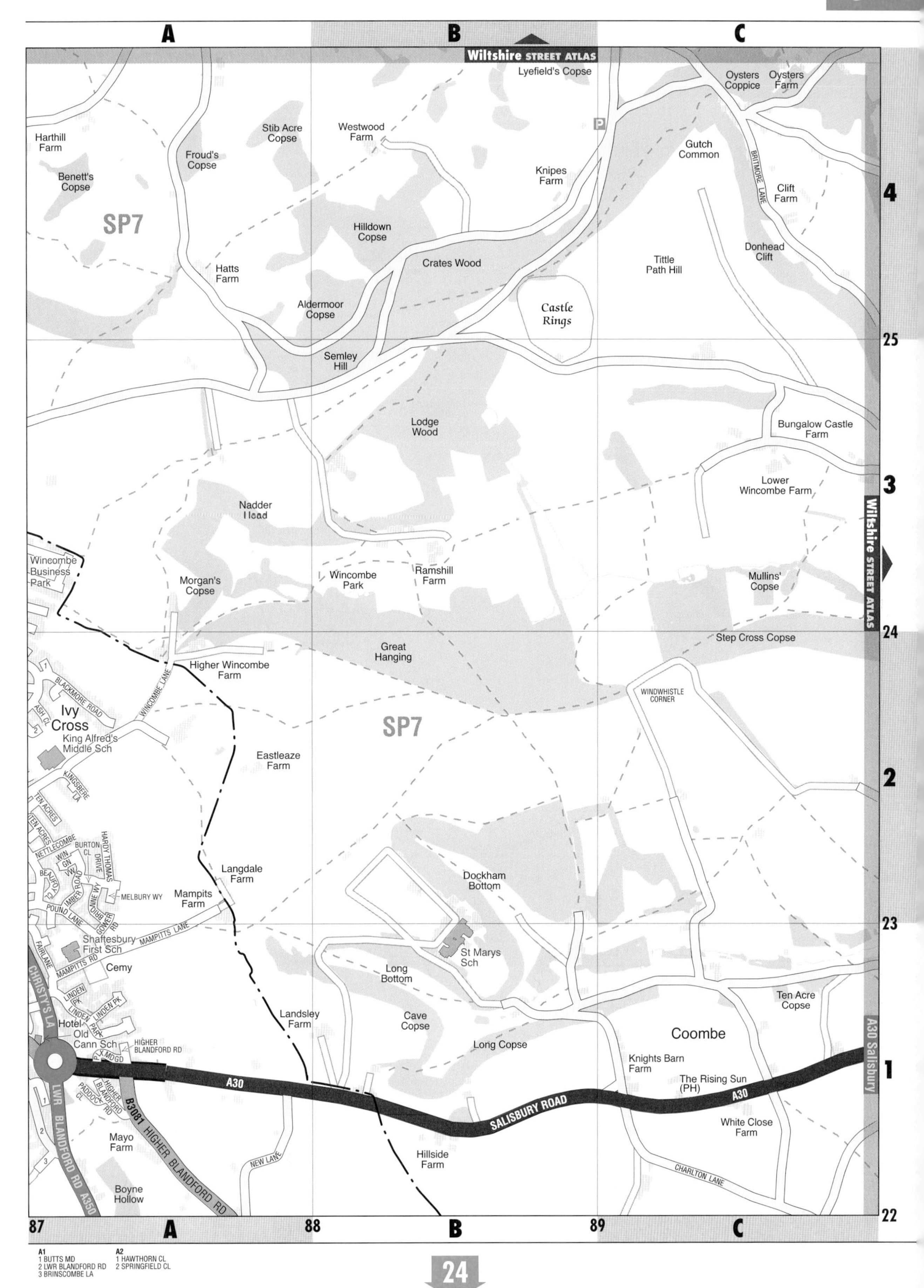

Lyefield's Copse

Oysters Coppice

Oysters Farm

Harthill Farm

Stib Acre Copse

Westwood Farm

Gutch Common

Benett's Copse

Froud's Copse

Knipes Farm

BRITMORE LANE

Clift Farm

SP7

Hilldown Copse

Crates Wood

Tittle Path Hill

Donhead Clift

Hatts Farm

Aldermoor Copse

Castle Rings

25

Semley Hill

Lodge Wood

Bungalow Castle Farm

Nadder Road

Lower Wincombe Farm

3

Wincombe Business Park

Morgan's Copse

Wincombe Park

Ramshill Farm

Mullins' Copse

Wiltshire STREET ATLAS

24

Higher Wincombe Farm

Great Hanging

Step Cross Copse

WINDWHISTLE CORNER

BLACKMORE ROAD

ASH CL

Ivy Cross

King Alfred's Middle Sch

KINGSMEAD LA

Eastleaze Farm

SP7

2

TEN ACRES

NETTLECOMBE

WIN GN

HARDY THOMAS DRIVE

BURTON CL

Langdale Farm

Dockham Bottom

BEAUFORD

IMBER ROAD

JUBILEE WY

MELBURY WY

Mampits Farm

23

POUND LANE

MAMPITTS LANE

St Marys Sch

Ten Acre Copse

LINDEN PK

Shaftesbury First Sch

MAMPITTS LANE

Cemy

Long Bottom

Coombe

LINDEN PK

Landsley Farm

Cave Copse

Knights Barn Farm

A30 Salisbury

HOTEL

Old Cann Sch

HIGHER BLANDFORD RD

EX MO GD

Long Copse

The Rising Sun (PH)

A30

1

CHRISTY'S LA

LWR BLANDFORD RD A350

PADDOCK RD

HIGHER BLANDFORD RD

A30

SALISBURY ROAD

A30

White Close Farm

B3081 HIGHER BLANDFORD RD

NEW LANE

Mayo Farm

Hillside Farm

CHARLTON LANE

Boyne Hollow

22

87

88

89

A1
1 BUTTS MD
2 LWR BLANDFORD RD
3 BRINSCOMBE LA

A2
1 HAWTHORN CL
2 SPRINGFIELD CL.

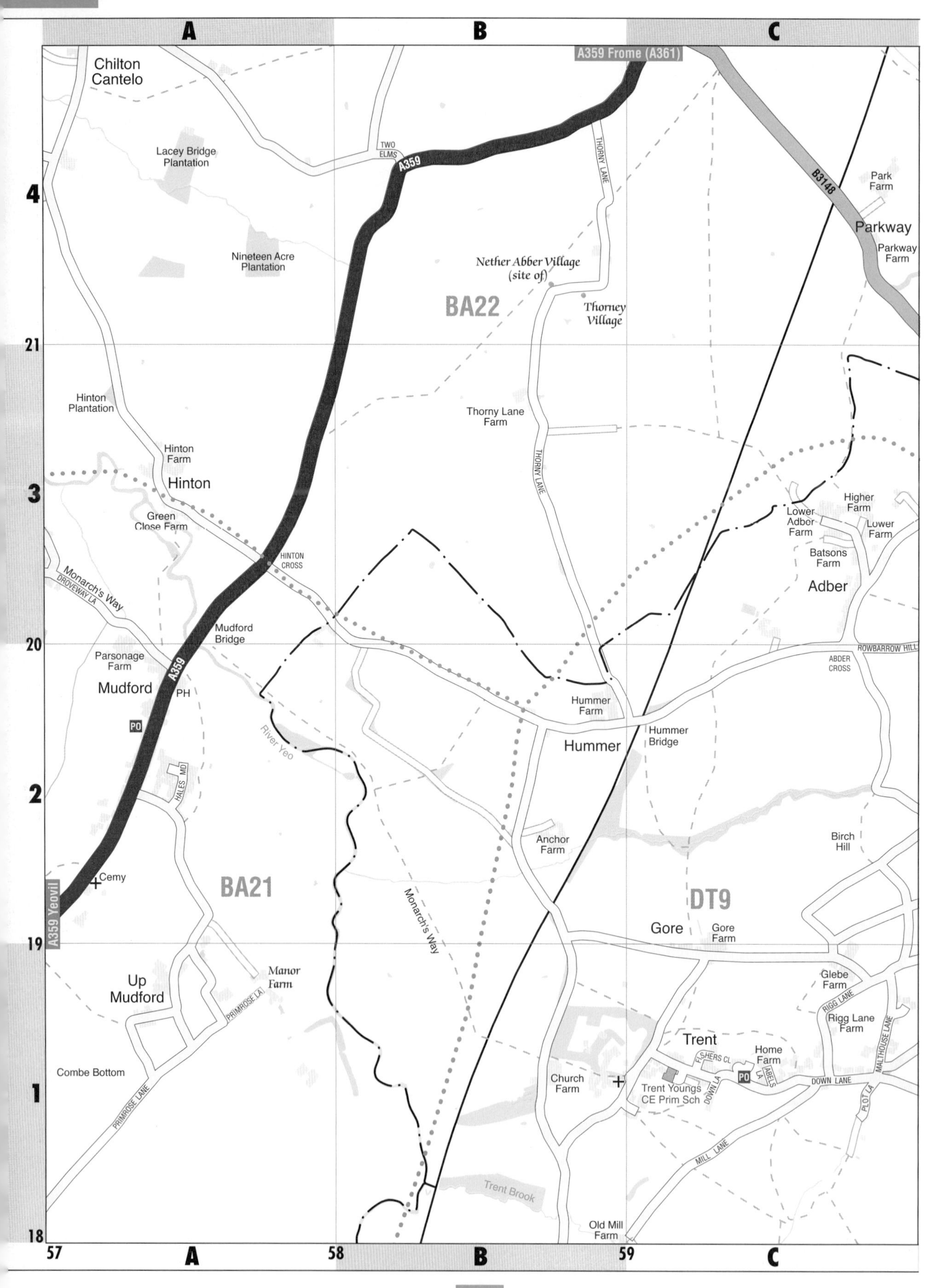

A
B
C
A359 Frome (A361)
Chilton Cantelo
Lacey Bridge Plantation
TWO ELMS
A359
THORNY LANE
B3148
Park Farm
Parkway
Parkway Farm
4
Nineteen Acre Plantation
Nether Abber Village (site of)
Thorney Village
BA22
21
Hinton Plantation
Thorny Lane Farm
Hinton Farm
Hinton
3
Green Close Farm
HINTON CROSS
Higher Farm
Lower Adber Farm
Lower Farm
Batsons Farm
Adber
Monarch's Way
DROVEWAY LA
Mudford Bridge
20
Parsonage Farm
Mudford
PH
PO
ROWBARROW HILL
ABDER CROSS
Hummer Farm
Hummer
Hummer Bridge
River Yeo
HALES MD
2
Anchor Farm
Birch Hill
Cemy
BA21
Monarch's Way
DT9
A359 Yeovil
Gore
Gore Farm
19
Up Mudford
Manor Farm
PRIMROSE LA
Glebe Farm
RIGG LANE
Rigg Lane Farm
MALTHOUSE LANE
Trent
FISHERS CL
Home Farm
Combe Bottom
Church Farm
Trent Youngs CE Prim Sch
DOWN LA
ABELS LA
DOWN LANE
PLOT LA
1
PRIMROSE LANE
MILL LANE
Trent Brook
Old Mill Farm
18
57
58
59

28

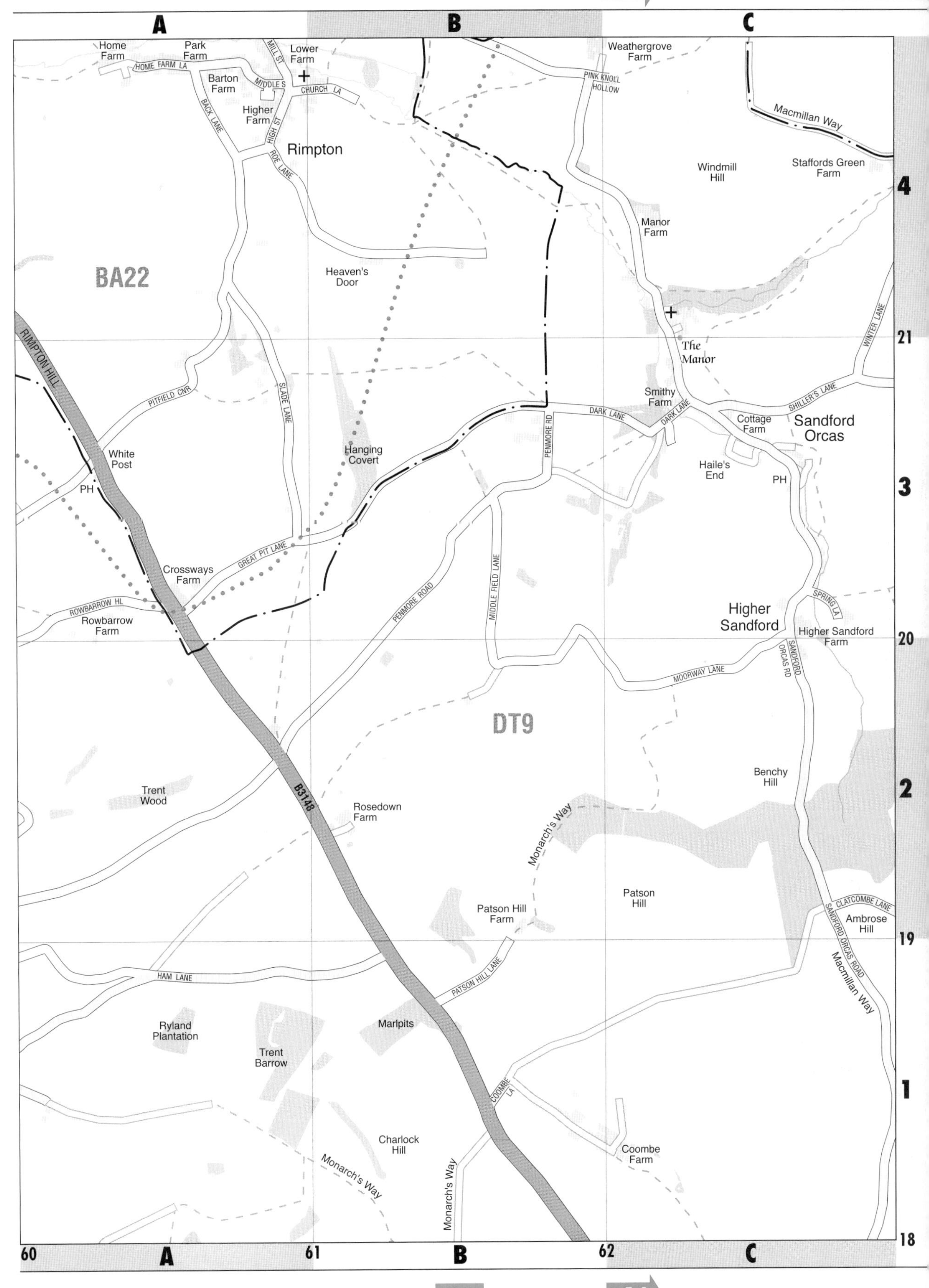

A   **B**   **C**

Home Farm
Park Farm
Barton Farm
HOME FARM LA
MILL ST
MIDDLE S
Lower Farm
Weathergrove Farm
CHURCH LA
PINK KNOLL HOLLOW
Higher Farm
BACK LANE
HIGH ST
Macmillan Way

Rimpton
RGE LANE
Windmill Hill
Staffords Green Farm

4

Manor Farm

BA22
Heaven's Door
SLADE LANE

The Manor

21

PITFIELD CNR
Smithy Farm
SHILLER'S LANE
WINTER LANE

Hanging Covert
DARK LANE
DARK LANE
Cottage Farm
Sandford Orcas

White Post
PENMORE RD
Haile's End
PH

PH
GREAT PIT LANE
3

Crossways Farm

ROWBARROW HL
Rowbarrow Farm
PENMORE ROAD
MIDDLE FIELD LANE
Higher Sandford
SPRING LA
Higher Sandford Farm
SANDFORD ORCAS RD
20

MOORWAY LANE

DT9

Benchy Hill

2

Trent Wood
Rosedown Farm
Monarch's Way
Patson Hill
CLATCOMBE LANE

Patson Hill Farm
Ambrose Hill
SANDFORD ORCAS ROAD
Macmillan Way
19

HAM LANE
PATSON HILL LANE

Ryland Plantation
Marlpits

Trent Barrow
COOMBE LA
1

Charlock Hill
Monarch's Way
Monarch's Way
Monarch's Way
Coombe Farm

18

60   **A**   61   **B**   62   **C**

B3148
RIMPTON HILL

15

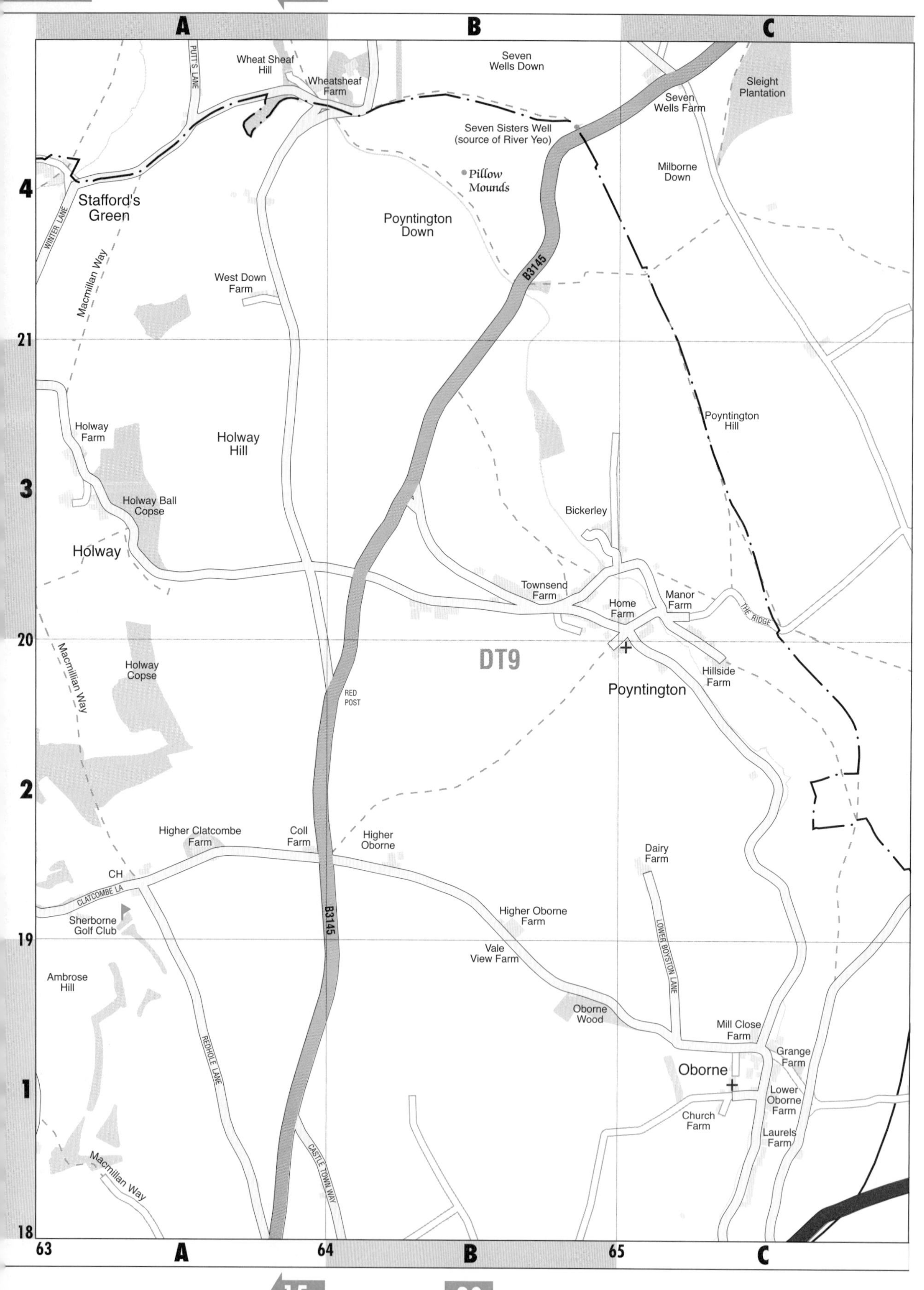

A
B
C
Wheat Sheaf Hill
Wheatsheaf Farm
Seven Wells Down
Seven Wells Farm
Sleight Plantation
PUTT'S LANE
Seven Sisters Well (source of River Yeo)
Pillow Mounds
Milborne Down
Stafford's Green
WINTER LANE
Poyntington Down
Macmillan Way
West Down Farm
B3145
Holway Farm
Holway Hill
Poyntington Hill
Holway Ball Copse
Bickerley
Holway
Townsend Farm
Home Farm
Manor Farm
THE RIDGE
Macmillan Way
Holway Copse
DT9
Hillside Farm
Poyntington
RED POST
Higher Clatcombe Farm
Coll Farm
Higher Oborne
Dairy Farm
CH
CLATCOMBE LA
Sherborne Golf Club
Higher Oborne Farm
B3145
LOWER BOYSTON LANE
Vale View Farm
Ambrose Hill
Oborne Wood
Mill Close Farm
REDHOLE LANE
Grange Farm
Oborne
Lower Oborne Farm
Church Farm
Laurels Farm
CASTLE TOWN WAY
Macmillan Way
4
21
3
20
2
19
1
18
63
64
65

15
30

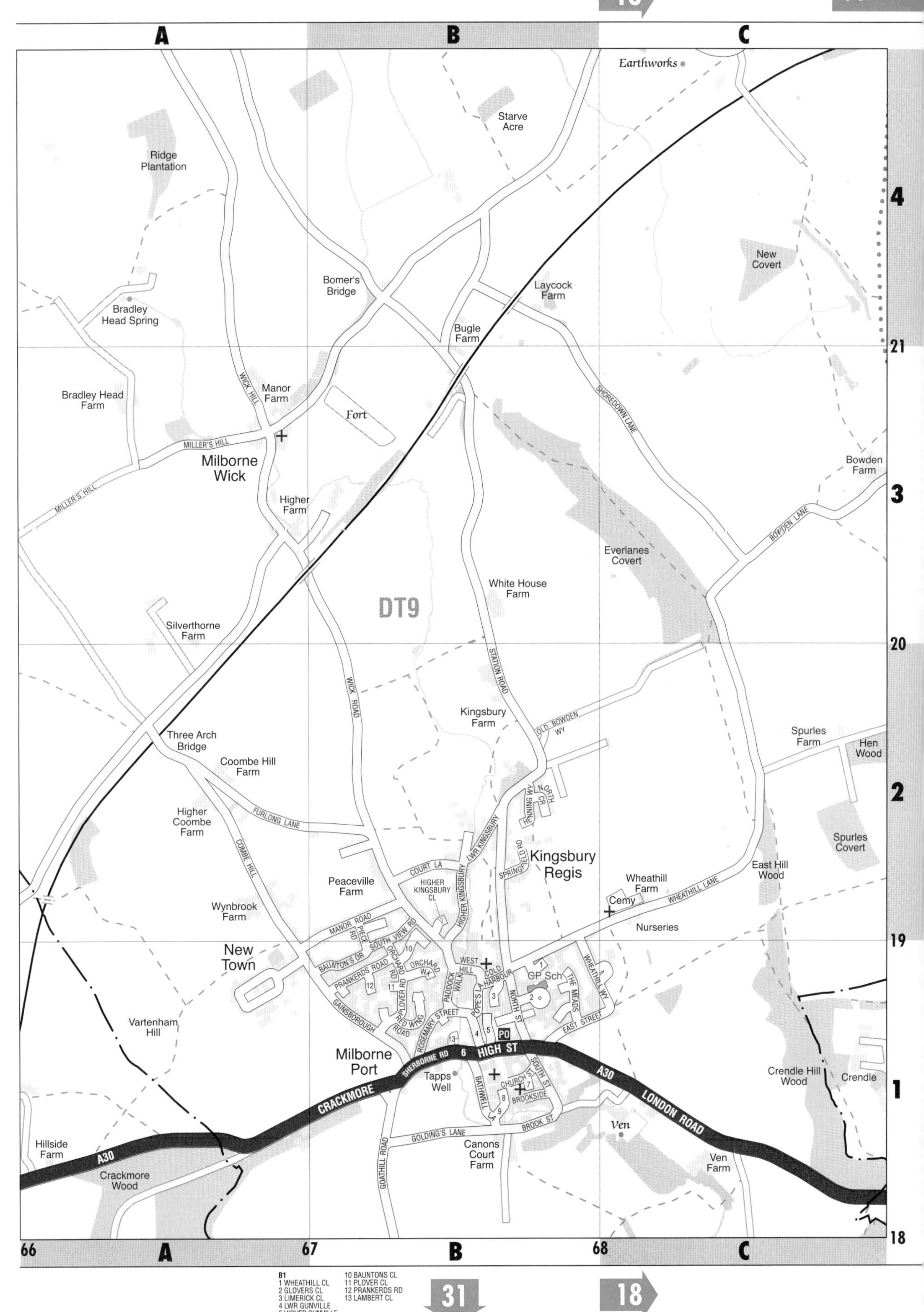

A   B   C

Earthworks

Starve
Acre

Ridge
Plantation

New
Covert

4

Bomer's
Bridge

Laycock
Farm

Bugle
Farm

21

Bradley
Head Spring

WICK HILL

Manor
Farm

SHOREDOWN LANE

Bradley Head
Farm

Fort

Bowden
Farm

MILLER'S HILL

Milborne
Wick

+

Higher
Farm

BLYDEN LANE

3

MILLER'S HILL

Everlanes
Covert

White House
Farm

DT9

Silverthorne
Farm

STATION ROAD

20

Kingsbury
Farm

OLD BOWDEN WY

Spurles
Farm

Hen
Wood

Three Arch
Bridge

WICK ROAD

Coombe Hill
Farm

Higher
Coombe
Farm

FURLONG LANE

COMBE HILL RD

Spurles
Covert

2

Peaceville
Farm

HIGHER KINGSBURY CL

LWR KINGSBURY

HIGHER KINGSBURY

NORTH RD

GUNNING RD

SPRINGFIELD RD

Kingsbury
Regis

Wheathill
Farm

WHEATHILL LANE

East Hill
Wood

Wynbrook
Farm

MANOR ROAD

PADDOCK PIECE

COURT LA

Cemy

+

Nurseries

New
Town

BAUNTON'S OR

SOUTH VIEW RD

PRANKERDS ROAD

ORCHARD WK

PADDOCK WALK

WEST HILL

COLD HARBOUR

GP Sch

WHEATHILL WY

THE MEADS

19

10

9

PED WING

ROPE'S LA

NORTH ST

EAST STREET

Vartenham
Hill

GAINSBOROUGH

ROSEMARY STREET

12

11

5

3

2

PO

Milborne
Port

SHERBORNE RD

6

HIGH ST

SOUTH ST

A30

LONDON ROAD

Crendle Hill
Wood

Crendle

1

CRACKMORE

Tapps
Well

BATHWELL

CHURCH ST

7

BROOKSIDE

9

BROOK ST

Ven

Hillside
Farm

A30

GOATHILL ROAD

GOLDING'S LANE

Canons
Court
Farm

Ven
Farm

Crackmore
Wood

18

66   A   67   B   68   C   18

B1
1 WHEATHILL CL
2 GLOVERS CL
3 LIMERICK CL
4 LWR GUNVILLE
5 HIGHER GUNVILLE
6 SANSOME'S HL
7 CHAPEL LA
8 CANNON CT MS
9 PUD BROOK

10 BAUNTONS CL
11 PLOVER CL
12 PRANKERDS RD
13 LAMBERT CL

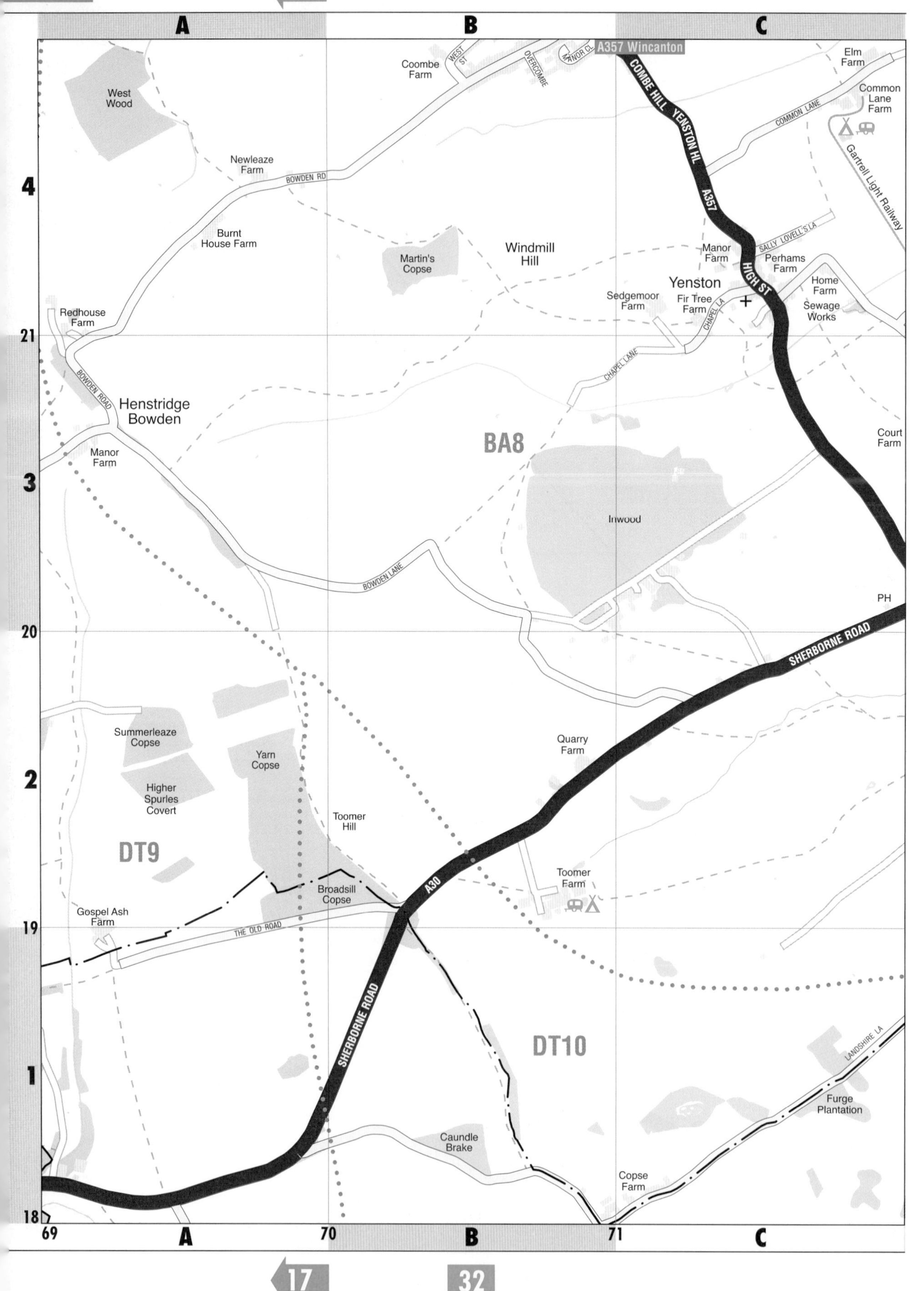

A   B   C

4

West
Wood

Coombe
Farm

WEST ST

OVERCOMBE

MANOR CL

A357 Wincanton

COMBE HILL

YENSTON HL

Elm
Farm

Common
Lane
Farm

COMMON LANE

Gartrell Light Railway

Newleaze
Farm

BOWDEN RD

A357

Martin's
Copse

Windmill
Hill

Manor
Farm

SALLY LOVELL'S LA

Perhams
Farm

Home
Farm

Burnt
House Farm

Yenston

Sedgemoor
Farm

Fir Tree
Farm

HIGH ST

21

Redhouse
Farm

CHAPEL LA

Sewage
Works

BOWDEN ROAD

Henstridge
Bowden

CHAPEL LANE

BA8

Court
Farm

3

Manor
Farm

Inwood

BOWDEN LANE

PH

20

SHERBORNE ROAD

Summerleaze
Copse

Yarn
Copse

Quarry
Farm

2

Higher
Spurles
Covert

Toomer
Hill

Toomer
Farm

DT9

Broadsill
Copse

A30

Gospel Ash
Farm

THE OLD ROAD

19

SHERBORNE ROAD

LANDSHIRE LA

DT10

1

Furge
Plantation

Caundle
Brake

Copse
Farm

18

69   70   71

A   B   C

8
20

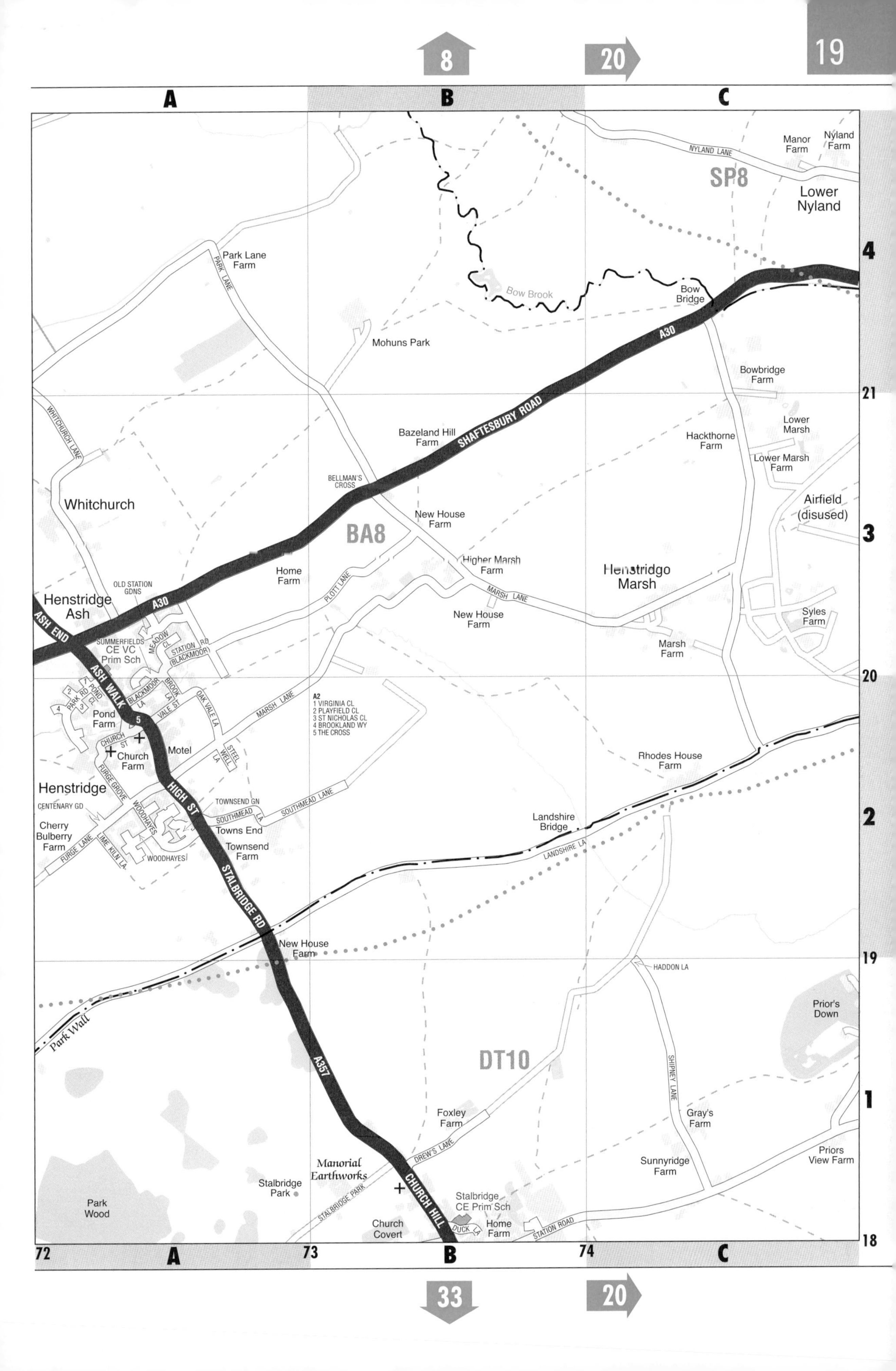
A
B
C
Manor Farm
Nyland Farm
NYLAND LANE
SP8
Lower Nyland
Park Lane Farm
PARK LANE
Bow Brook
Bow Bridge
Mohuns Park
A30
Bowbridge Farm
WHITCHURCH LANE
SHAFTESBURY ROAD
Bazeland Hill Farm
Hackthorne Farm
Lower Marsh
Lower Marsh Farm
BELLMAN'S CROSS
Whitchurch
New House Farm
Airfield (disused)
BA8
Higher Marsh Farm
Henstridge Marsh
Home Farm
OLD STATION GDNS
PLOTT LANE
MARSH LANE
Henstridge Ash
New House Farm
Syles Farm
ASH END
SUMMERFIELDS CE VC Prim Sch
MEADOW CL
STATION RD
BLACKMOOR
Marsh Farm
ASH WALK
BLACKMOOR LA
BROOK LA
VALE ST
OAK VALE LA
PARK RD
POND CL
Pond Farm
A2
1 VIRGINIA CL
2 PLAYFIELD CL
3 ST NICHOLAS CL
4 BROOKLAND WY
5 THE CROSS
CHURCH ST
Church Farm
Motel
STEEL WELL LA
Rhodes House Farm
Henstridge
FURGE GROVE
HIGH ST
TOWNSEND GN
SOUTHMEAD LA
SOUTHMEAD LANE
CENTENARY GD
Cherry Bulberry Farm
WOODHAYES
Towns End
Landshire Bridge
FURGE LANE
LIME KILN LA
Townsend Farm
LANDSHIRE LA
STALBRIDGE RD
New House Farm
HADDON LA
Park Wall
Prior's Down
A357
DT10
SHIPNEY LANE
Foxley Farm
Gray's Farm
DREW'S LANE
Manorial Earthworks
Sunnyridge Farm
Priors View Farm
Stalbridge Park
CHURCH HILL
Stalbridge CE Prim Sch
Park Wood
STALBRIDGE PARK
Church Covert
DUCK LA
Home Farm
STATION ROAD
4
21
3
20
2
19
1
18
72
73
74

33
20

19
9

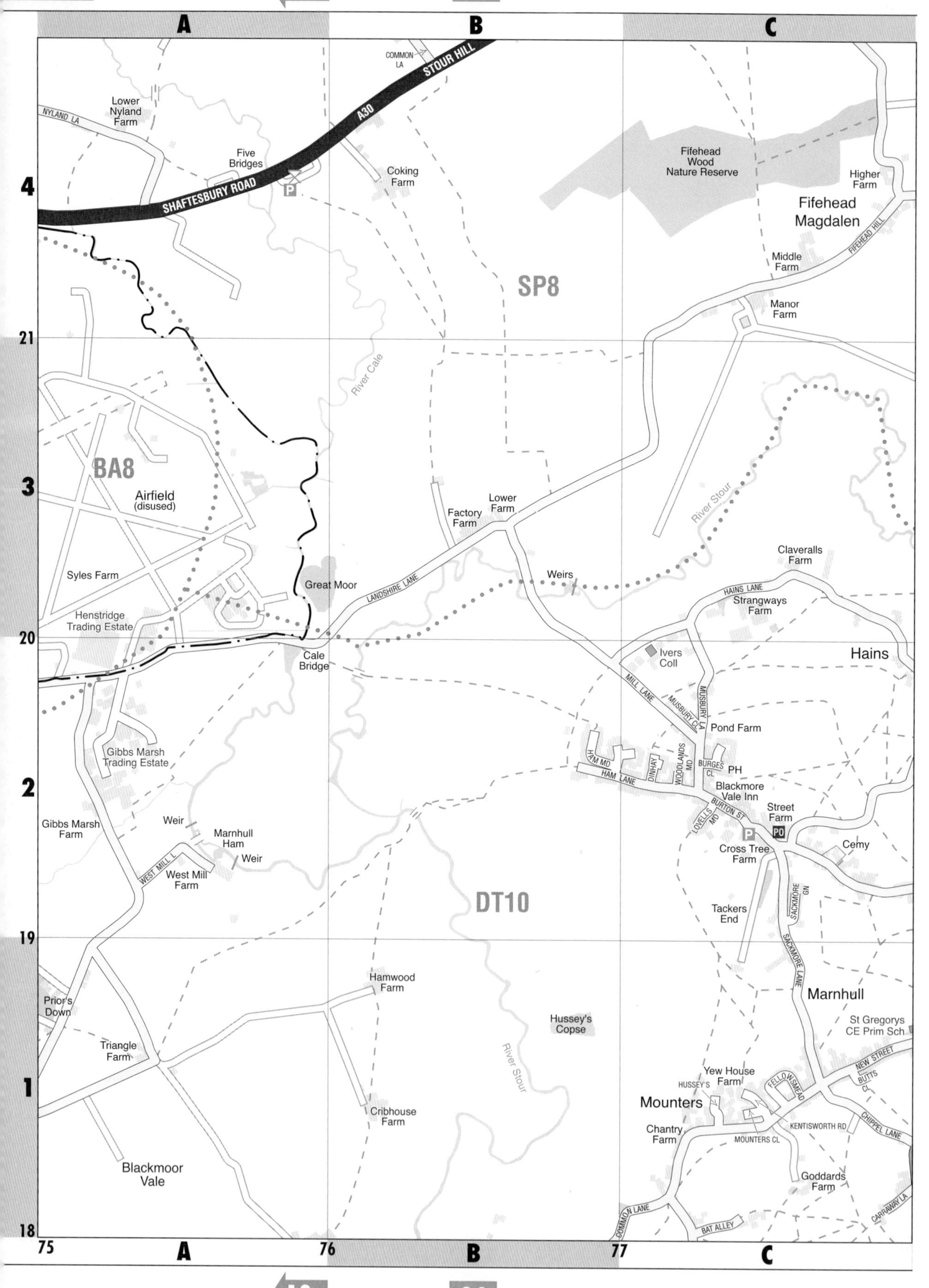
A
B
C
4
3
2
1
21
20
19
18
75
76
77
COMMON LA
STOUR HILL
A30
NYLAND LA
Lower Nyland Farm
Five Bridges
SHAFTESBURY ROAD
Coking Farm
Fifehead Wood Nature Reserve
Higher Farm
Fifehead Magdalen
FIFEHEAD HILL
Middle Farm
Manor Farm
SP8
River Cale
BA8
Airfield (disused)
Syles Farm
Henstridge Trading Estate
Great Moor
Factory Farm
Lower Farm
LANDSHIRE LANE
Weirs
River Stour
Claveralls Farm
HAINS LANE
Strangways Farm
Hains
Ivers Coll
Cale Bridge
MILL LANE
MUSBURY CL
MUSBURY LA
Pond Farm
Gibbs Marsh Trading Estate
HAM MD
HAM LANE
DINHAY
WOODLANDS MD
BURGES CL
PH
Blackmore Vale Inn
BURTON ST
LOVELLS MD
Street Farm
PO
Gibbs Marsh Farm
Weir
Marnhull Ham
Weir
WEST MILL L
West Mill Farm
Cross Tree Farm
Cemy
DT10
Tackers End
SACKMORE GN
SACKMORE LANE
Hamwood Farm
Marnhull
Prior's Down
Hussey's Copse
St Gregorys CE Prim Sch
Triangle Farm
River Stour
Yew House Farm
HUSSEY'S
FELLOWSMEAD
NEW STREET
BUTTS CL
Mounters
Cribhouse Farm
KENTISWORTH RD
CHIPPEL LANE
Chantry Farm
MOUNTERS CL
Blackmoor Vale
Goddards Farm
COMMON LANE
BAT ALLEY
CARRAWAY LA

19
34

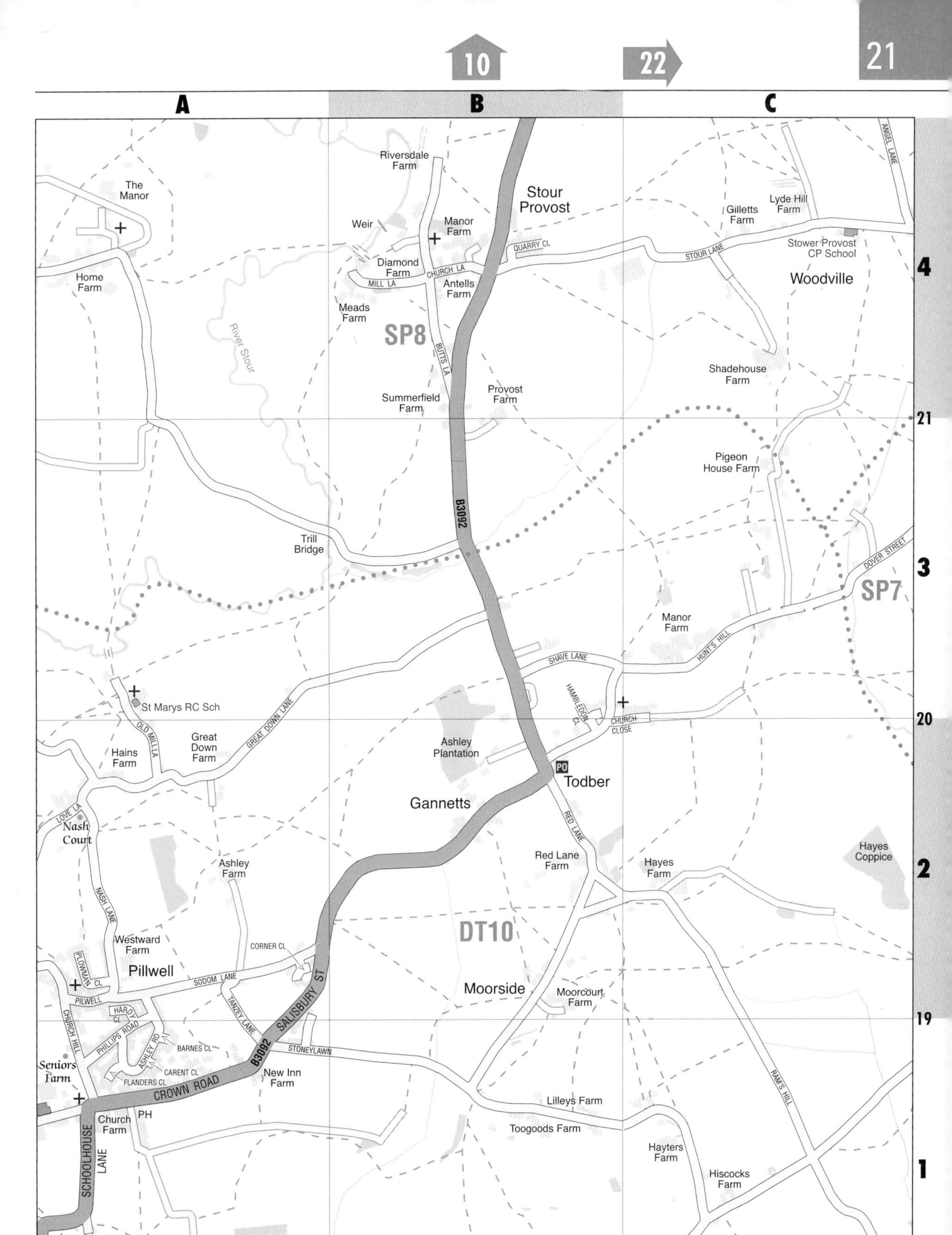

A B C

The Manor

Home Farm

River Stour

Riversdale Farm

Weir

Manor Farm

Diamond Farm

CHURCH LA

MILL LA

Antells Farm

Meads Farm

SP8

Summerfield Farm

BUTTS LA

Provost Farm

Stour Provost

QUARRY CL

STOUR LANE

Gilletts Farm

Lyde Hill Farm

Stower Provost CP School

Woodville

Shadehouse Farm

B3092

Pigeon House Farm

Trill Bridge

ANGEL LANE

21

DOVER STREET

SP7

3

St Marys RC Sch

OLD MILL LA

GREAT DOWN LANE

Great Down Farm

Hains Farm

Ashley Plantation

SHAVE LANE

HAMBLEDON CL

Manor Farm

HUNT'S HILL

CHURCH CLOSE

20

LOVE LA

Nash Court

Ashley Farm

Gannetts

PO

Todber

RED LANE

Red Lane Farm

Hayes Farm

Hayes Coppice

2

NASH LANE

Westward Farm

PLOWMAN CL

Pillwell

CORNER CL

SODOM LANE

DT10

Moorside

Moorcourt Farm

19

PILWELL

HAR CL

TANSEY LANE

SALISBURY ST

Church Hill

PHILLIPS ROAD

ASHLEY RD

BARNES CL

CARENT CL

FLANDERS CL

B3092

STONEYLAWN

New Inn Farm

RAM'S HILL

Seniors Farm

CROWN ROAD

Church Farm

PH

Lilleys Farm

Toogoods Farm

SCHOOLHOUSE LANE

Hayters Farm

Hiscocks Farm

1

WHITE WAY LANE

BOOSMARSH LANE

Thornton Farm

Moat

78 A 79 B 80 C 18

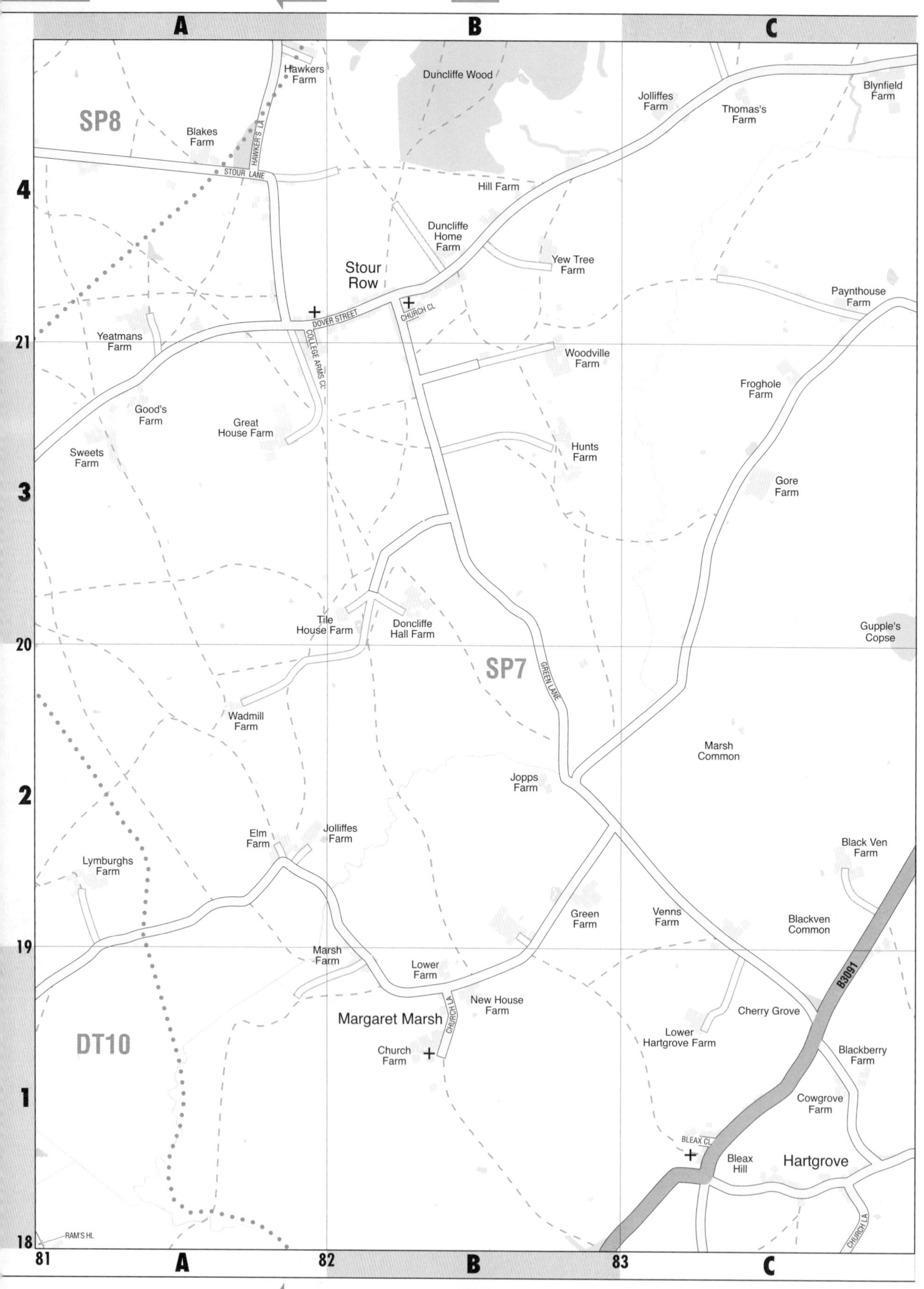

A   B   C

SP8

Hawkers Farm

Duncliffe Wood

Jolliffes Farm

Thomas's Farm

Blynfield Farm

Blakes Farm

STOUR LANE

HAWKER'S LA

4

Hill Farm

Duncliffe Home Farm

Yew Tree Farm

Paynthouse Farm

Stour Row

DOVER STREET

CHURCH CL

COLLEGE ARMS CL

21

Yeatmans Farm

Woodville Farm

Froghole Farm

Good's Farm

Great House Farm

Hunts Farm

Gore Farm

Sweets Farm

3

Tile House Farm

Doncliffe Hall Farm

20

SP7

GREEN LANE

Gupple's Copse

Wadmill Farm

Marsh Common

Jopps Farm

2

Elm Farm

Jolliffes Farm

Black Ven Farm

Lymburghs Farm

Green Farm

Venns Farm

Blackven Common

19

Marsh Farm

Lower Farm

B3031

DT10

CHURCH LA

New House Farm

Cherry Grove

Margaret Marsh

Lower Hartgrove Farm

Blackberry Farm

Church Farm

1

Cowgrove Farm

BLEAX CL

Bleax Hill

Hartgrove

18

RAM'S HL

CHURCH LA

81   A   82   B   83   C

12

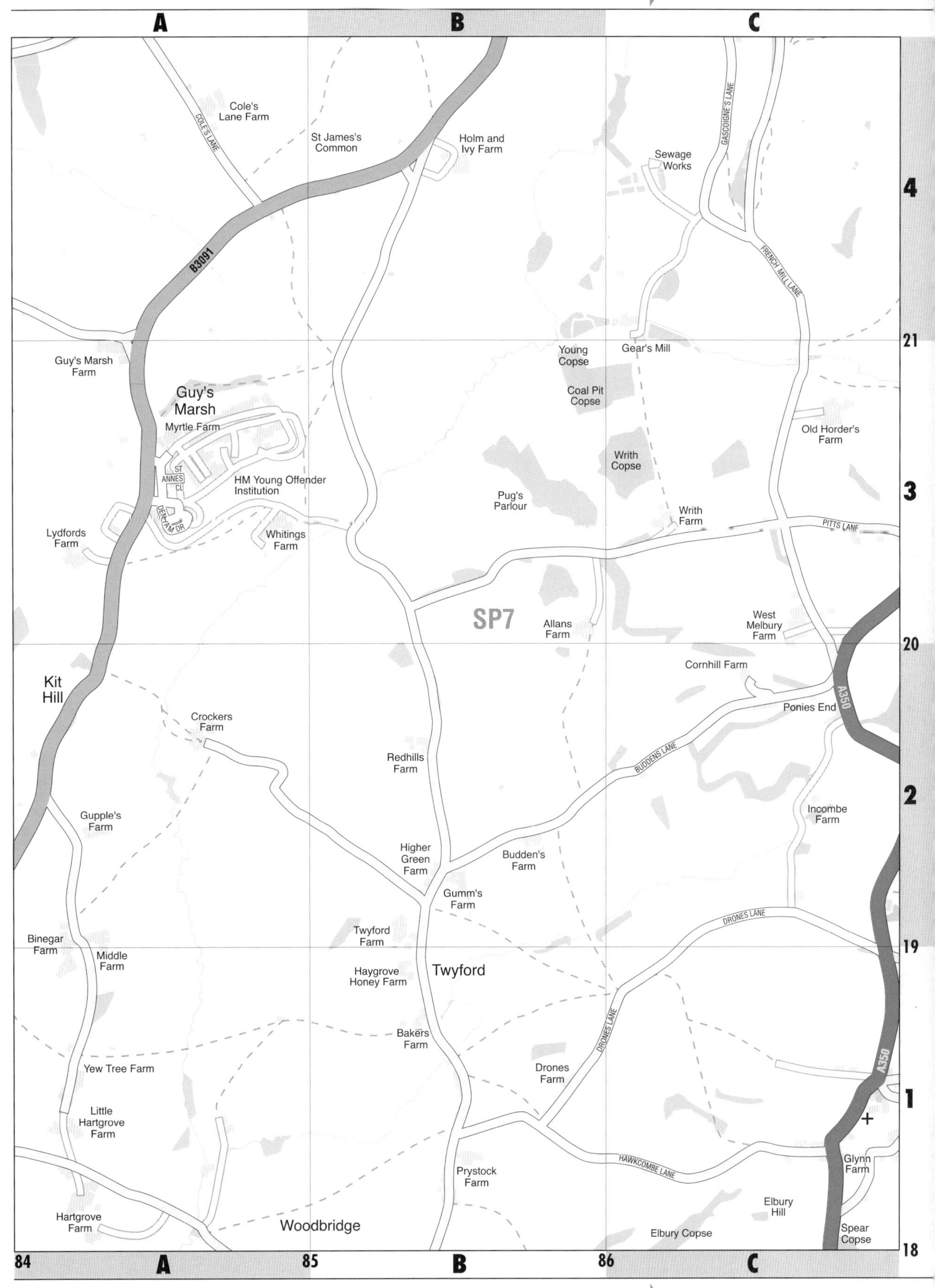

24
A
B
C
Cole's Lane Farm
COLE'S LANE
St James's Common
Holm and Ivy Farm
Sewage Works
GASCOIGNE'S LANE
B3091
FRENCH MILL LANE
Young Copse
Gear's Mill
Guy's Marsh Farm
Guy's Marsh
Coal Pit Copse
Myrtle Farm
Old Horder's Farm
ST ANNES CL
HM Young Offender Institution
Writh Copse
DENHAM DR
Pug's Parlour
Writh Farm
Lydfords Farm
Whitings Farm
PITTS LANE
SP7
Allans Farm
West Melbury Farm
Cornhill Farm
Kit Hill
Crockers Farm
Ponies End
A350
BUDDENS LANE
Redhills Farm
Gupple's Farm
Incombe Farm
Higher Green Farm
Budden's Farm
Gumm's Farm
DRONES LANE
Binegar Farm
Twyford Farm
Middle Farm
Haygrove Honey Farm
Twyford
DRONES LANE
Bakers Farm
Yew Tree Farm
Drones Farm
Little Hartgrove Farm
HAWKCOMBE LANE
Glynn Farm
Prystock Farm
Elbury Hill
Hartgrove Farm
Woodbridge
Elbury Copse
Spear Copse
4
21
3
20
2
19
1
18
84
85
86
37
24

23
13

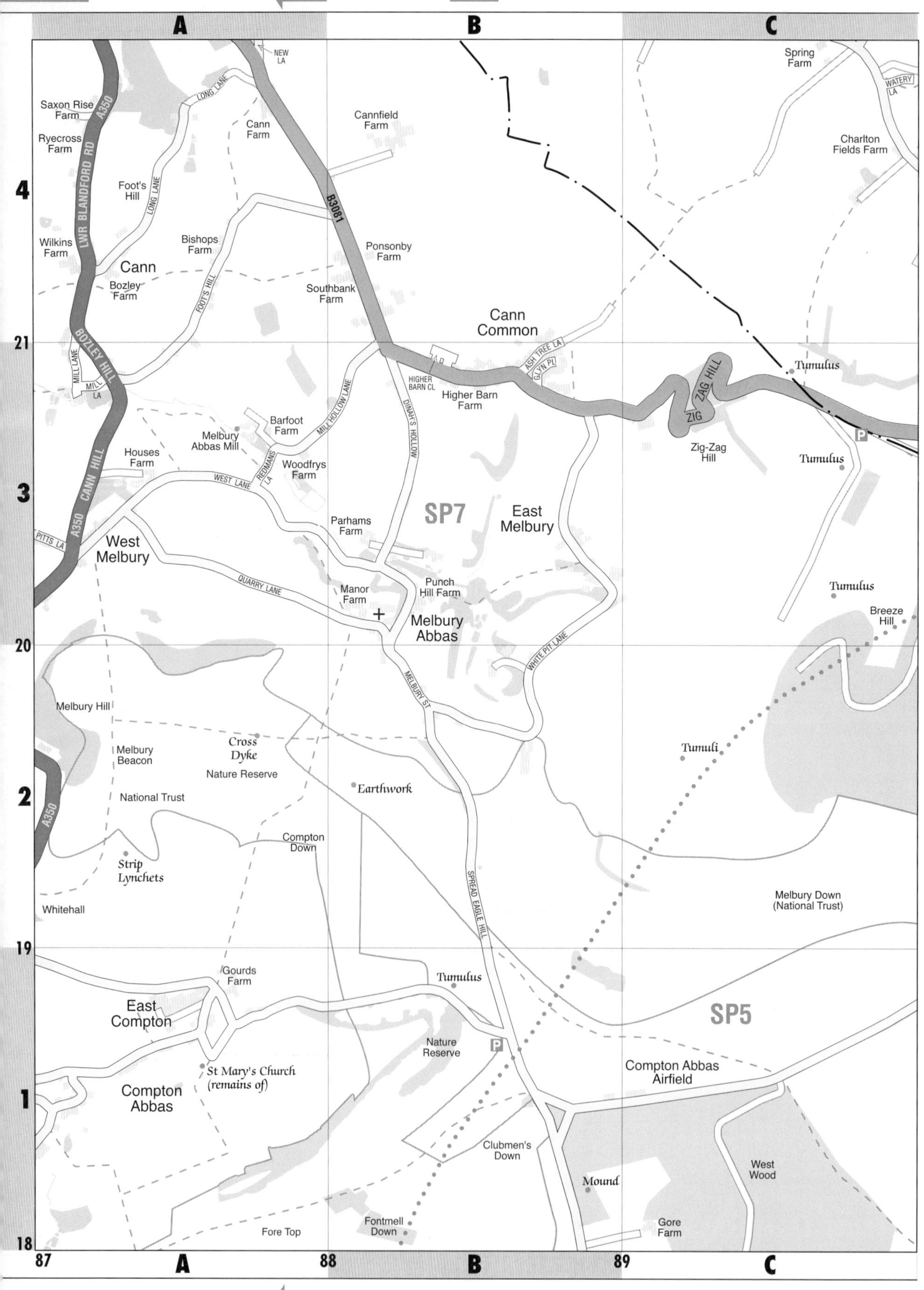
A
B
C
4
21
3
20
2
19
1
18
87
88
89
NEW LA
Saxon Rise Farm
Ryecross Farm
Cann Farm
Cannfield Farm
Spring Farm
WATERY LA
Charlton Fields Farm
LONG LANE
A350
LWR BLANDFORD RD
Foot's Hill
B3081
Wilkins Farm
Bishops Farm
Ponsonby Farm
Cann
Bozley Farm
FOOT'S HILL
Southbank Farm
Cann Common
BOZLEY HILL
MILL LANE
MILL LA
ASH TREE LA
GLYN PL
HIGHER BARN CL
Higher Barn Farm
ZIG ZAG HILL
Tumulus
Barfoot Farm
Melbury Abbas Mill
MILL HOLLOW LANE
DINAH'S HOLLOW
Zig-Zag Hill
Houses Farm
REDMANS LA
Woodfrys Farm
CANN HILL
WEST LANE
SP7
East Melbury
Parhams Farm
PITTS LA
West Melbury
QUARRY LANE
Manor Farm
Punch Hill Farm
Melbury Abbas
WHITE PIT LANE
Breeze Hill
MELBURY ST
Melbury Hill
Cross Dyke
Melbury Beacon
Nature Reserve
Tumuli
Earthwork
National Trust
Compton Down
Strip Lynchets
SPREAD EAGLE HILL
Melbury Down (National Trust)
Whitehall
Gourds Farm
East Compton
SP5
Nature Reserve
Compton Abbas Airfield
St Mary's Church (remains of)
Compton Abbas
Clubmen's Down
West Wood
Mound
Gore Farm
Fontmell Down
Fore Top

23
38

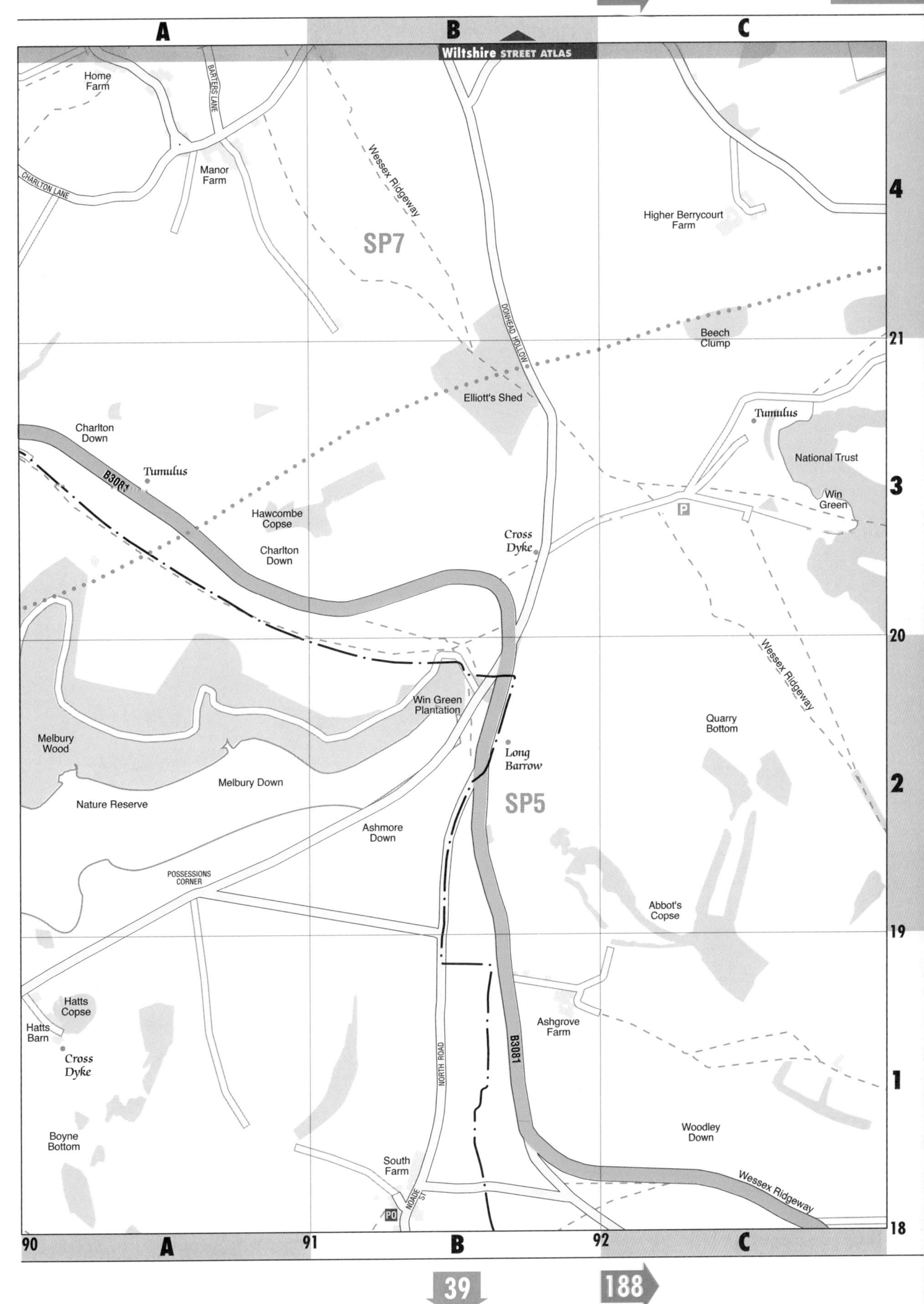

Wiltshire STREET ATLAS

A

Home Farm

Manor Farm

BARTERS LANE

CHARLTON LANE

Wessex Ridgeway

SP7

Charlton Down

Tumulus

B3081

Hawcombe Copse

Charlton Down

DONHEAD HOLLOW

Elliott's Shed

Cross Dyke

Melbury Wood

Win Green Plantation

Melbury Down

Nature Reserve

Ashmore Down

POSSESSIONS CORNER

Long Barrow

SP5

Hatts Copse

Hatts Barn

Cross Dyke

Boyne Bottom

NORTH ROAD

South Farm

MOORE ST

PO

B

Higher Berrycourt Farm

Beech Clump

Tumulus

National Trust

Win Green

P

Wessex Ridgeway

Quarry Bottom

Abbot's Copse

Ashgrove Farm

Woodley Down

Wessex Ridgeway

B3081

C

4

21

3

20

2

19

1

18

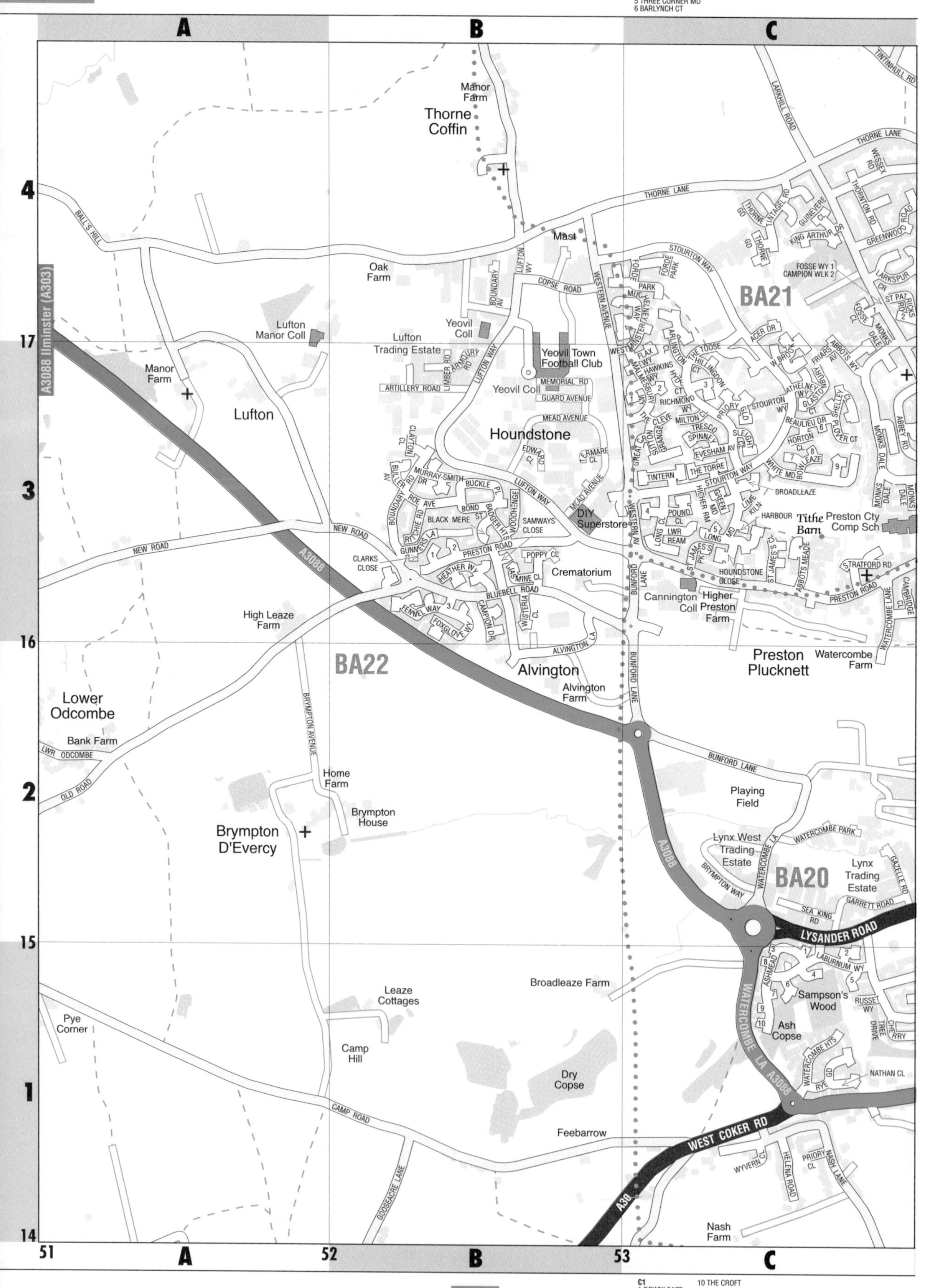

B3
1 BRIGADIER CL
2 HOUNDSTONE CT
3 CELANDINE RD

C3
1 TRELLECH CT
2 THE REGENTS
3 DERWENT WY
4 HILLBORNE GDNS
5 THREE CORNER MD
6 BARLYNCH CT
7 MALVERN CT
8 NETLEY
9 TEWKESBURY

C1
1 DOWNLEAZE
2 WOODCOTE
3 THE BRIARS
4 OAKLEIGH
5 RIDGEMEAD
6 BIRCHDALE
7 THE SPINNEY
8 FOXCOTE
9 THE FURZE
10 THE CROFT

28

C3
1 ST THOMAS CROSS
2 DAMPIER PL
3 DAMPIER ST
4 HILLSIDE TERRACE
5 WYNDHAM ST

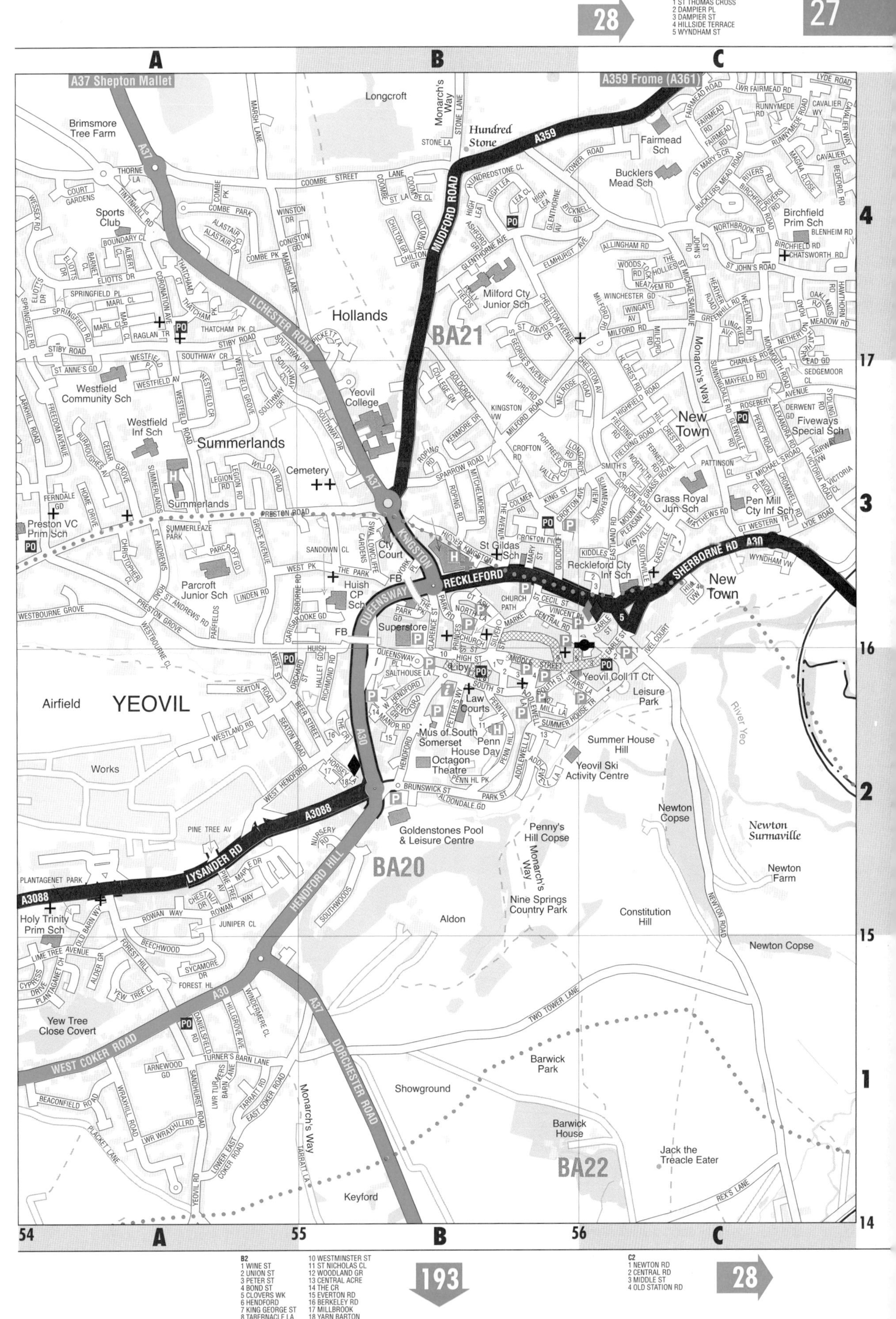

B2
1 WINE ST
2 UNION ST
3 PETER ST
4 BOND ST
5 CLOVERS WK
6 HENDFORD
7 KING GEORGE ST
8 TABERNACLE LA
9 VICARAGE ST
10 WESTMINSTER ST
11 ST NICHOLAS CL
12 WOODLAND GR
13 CENTRAL ACRE
14 THE CR
15 EVERTON RD
16 BERKELEY RD
17 MILLBROOK
18 YARN BARTON

193

C2
1 NEWTON RD
2 CENTRAL RD
3 MIDDLE ST
4 OLD STATION RD

28

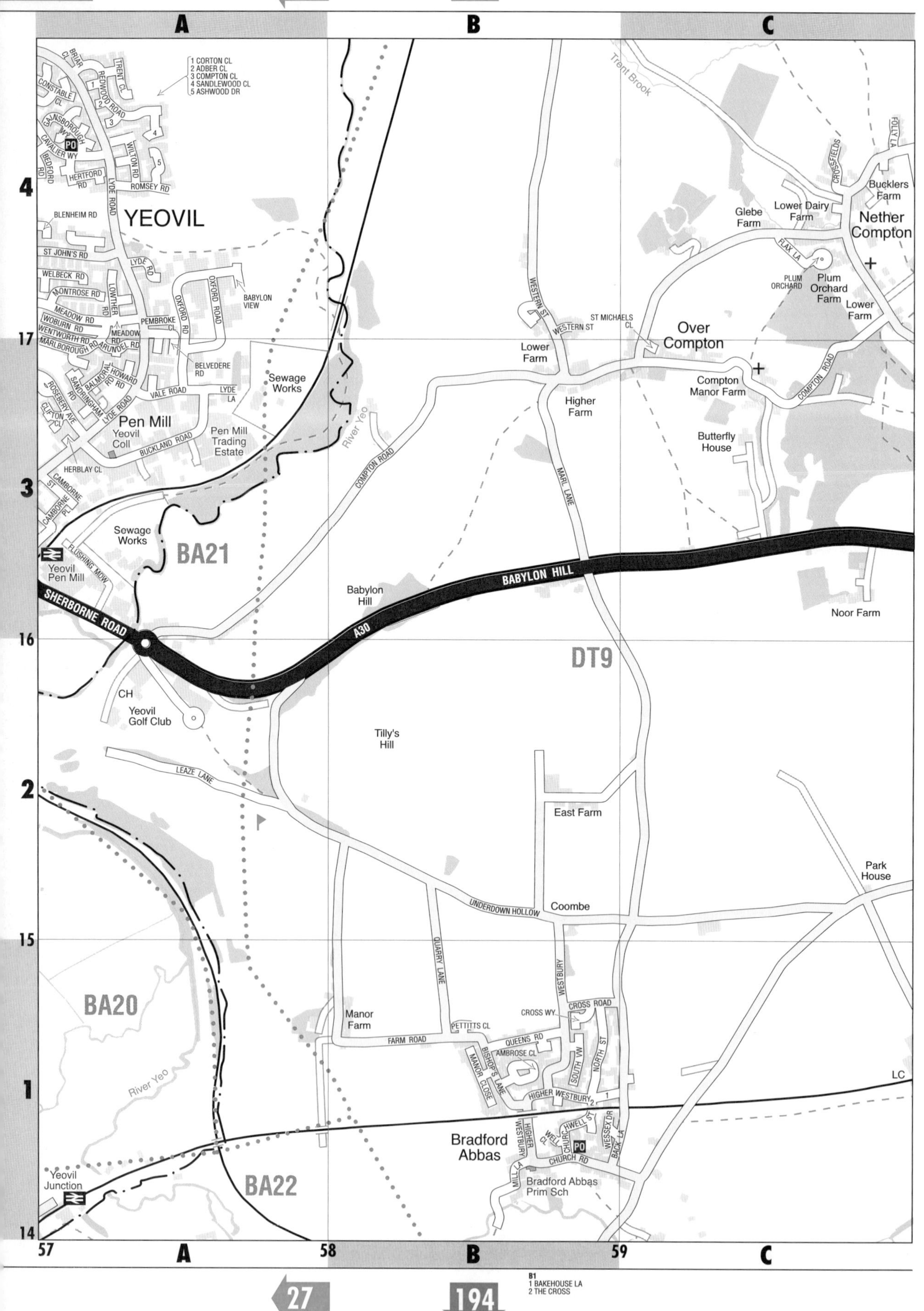

1 CORTON CL
2 ADBER CL
3 COMPTON CL
4 SANDLEWOOD CL
5 ASHWOOD DR

YEOVIL

BABYLON VIEW

Sewage Works

Pen Mill
Yeovil Coll

Pen Mill
Trading
Estate

BA21

Sewage Works

Yeovil Pen Mill

SHERBORNE ROAD

Yeovil Golf Club

CH

River Yeo

Compton Road

Trent Brook

Glebe Farm

Lower Dairy Farm

Nether Compton

Bucklers Farm

FOLLY LA

CROSS-FIELDS

FLAX LA

Plum Orchard
Plum Orchard Farm

Lower Farm

Over Compton

Compton Manor Farm

Butterfly House

Compton Road

Lower Farm

Higher Farm

Western St

Western St

St Michaels Cl

MARL LANE

BABYLON HILL

Babylon Hill

Noor Farm

A30

DT9

Tilly's Hill

LEAZE LANE

East Farm

Park House

Underdown Hollow

Coombe

Quarry Lane

Westbury

Cross Road

Cross Wy

BA20

River Yeo

Manor Farm

FARM ROAD

PETTITTS CL

Queens Rd

Ambrose Cl

Cross Road

Manor Close

Bishop's Lane

South Wv

North St

Higher Westbury

Higher Westbury

LC

Bradford Abbas

Bradford Abbas Prim Sch

Wessex Dr

Back La

PO

Church Rd

Church St

Well

MILL

BA22

Yeovil Junction

57

58

59

B1
1 BAKEHOUSE LA
2 THE CROSS

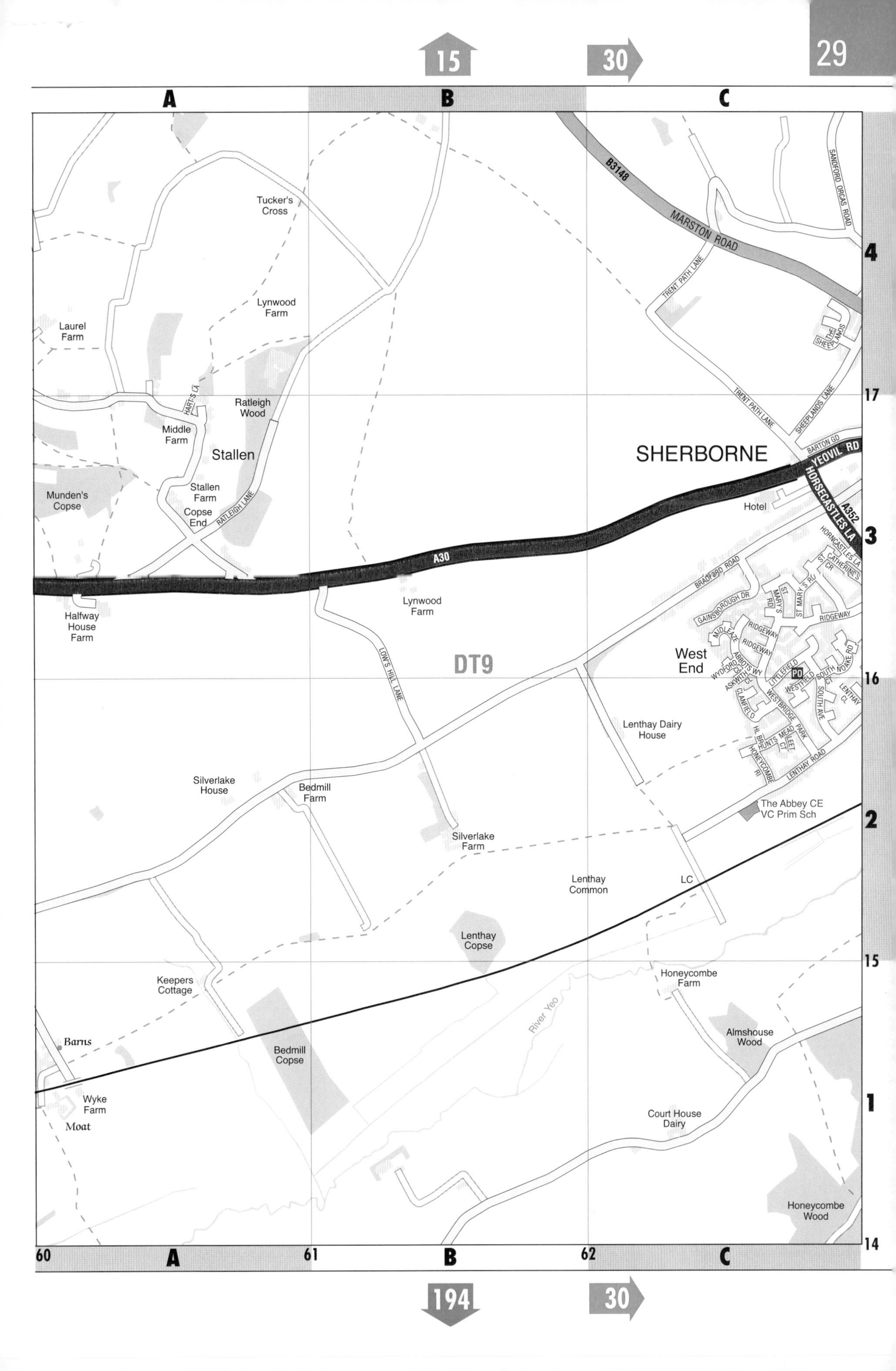

A
B
C

Tucker's Cross

B3148

MARSTON ROAD

4

SANDFORD ORCAS ROAD

TRENT PATH LANE

Lynwood Farm

Laurel Farm

HART'S LA

17

SHEEPLANDS LANE

TRENT PATH LANE

Middle Farm

Ratleigh Wood

Stallen

SHERBORNE

BARTON GD

YEOVIL RD

Munden's Copse

Stallen Farm

Copse End

RATLEIGH LANE

Hotel

HORSECASTLES LA

A352

3

Halfway House Farm

A30

Lynwood Farm

BRADFORD ROAD

GAINSBOROUGH DR

ST MARY'S RD

HORNCASTLES LA

ST CATHERINE'S

ST CR

RIDGEWAY

RIDGEWAY

MID CAZE

RIDGEWAY

ABBOT'S CL

LITTLEFIELD

West End

WYDFORD CL

ASKWITH'S

CLANFIELD

WESTBRIDGE PARK

WESTFIELD

PO

ST CT

LENTHAY CL

SOUTH AVE

NORKE RD

16

DT9

Lenthay Dairy House

HL BRUNTS MEAD

LEET CT

HONEYCOMBE RI

LENTHAY ROAD

Silverlake House

Bedmill Farm

Silverlake Farm

The Abbey CE VC Prim Sch

2

Lenthay Common

LC

15

Keepers Cottage

Lenthay Copse

Honeycombe Farm

River Yeo

Barns

Almshouse Wood

Bedmill Copse

Wyke Farm

Moat

Court House Dairy

1

Honeycombe Wood

14

30

A3
1 HORNCASTLES LA
2 ST CATHERINE'S CR
3 RIDGEWAY
4 WYNNES CL
5 SPRINGFIELD CR
6 WESTRIDGE

← **29**   ↑ **16**

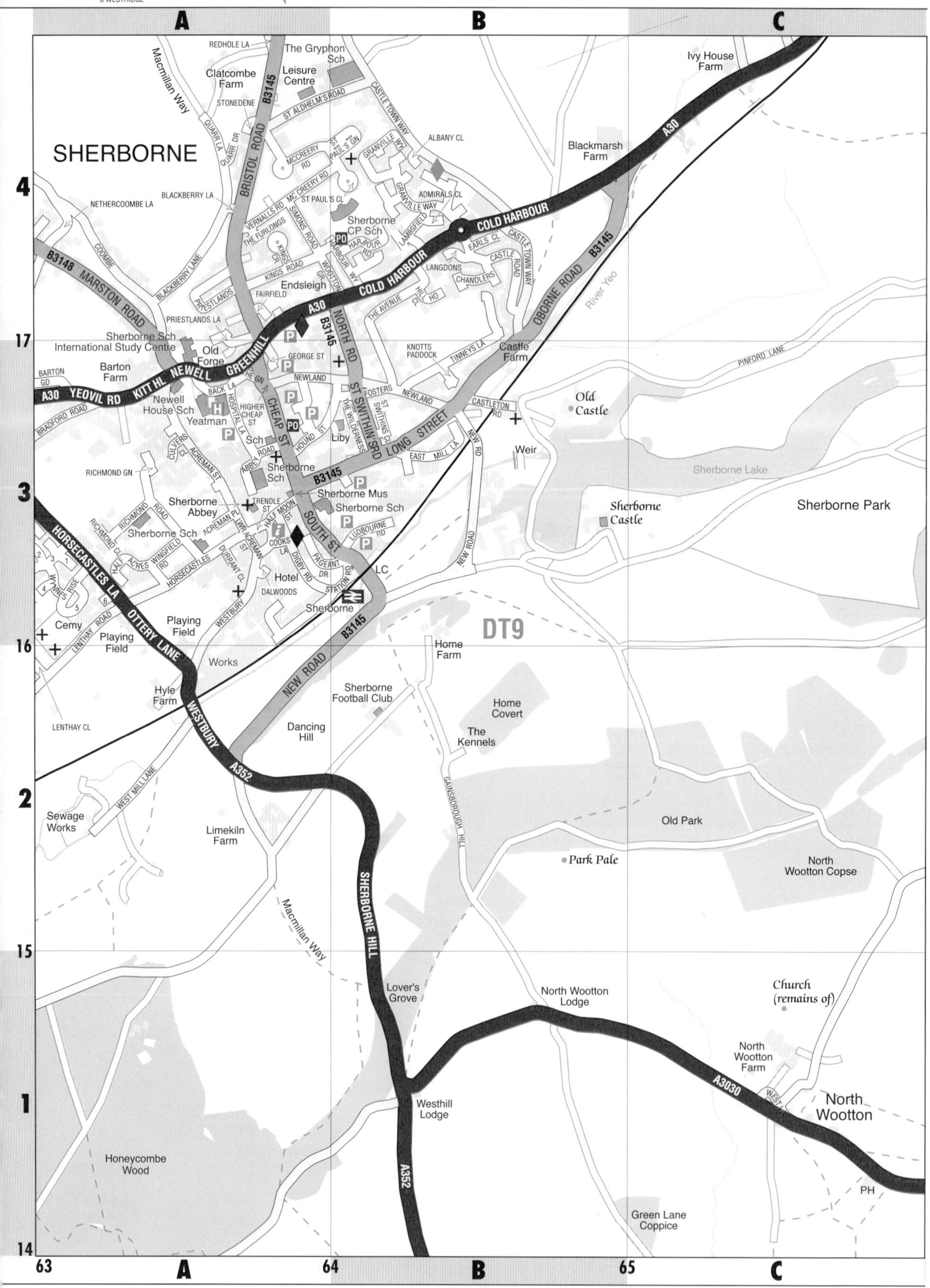

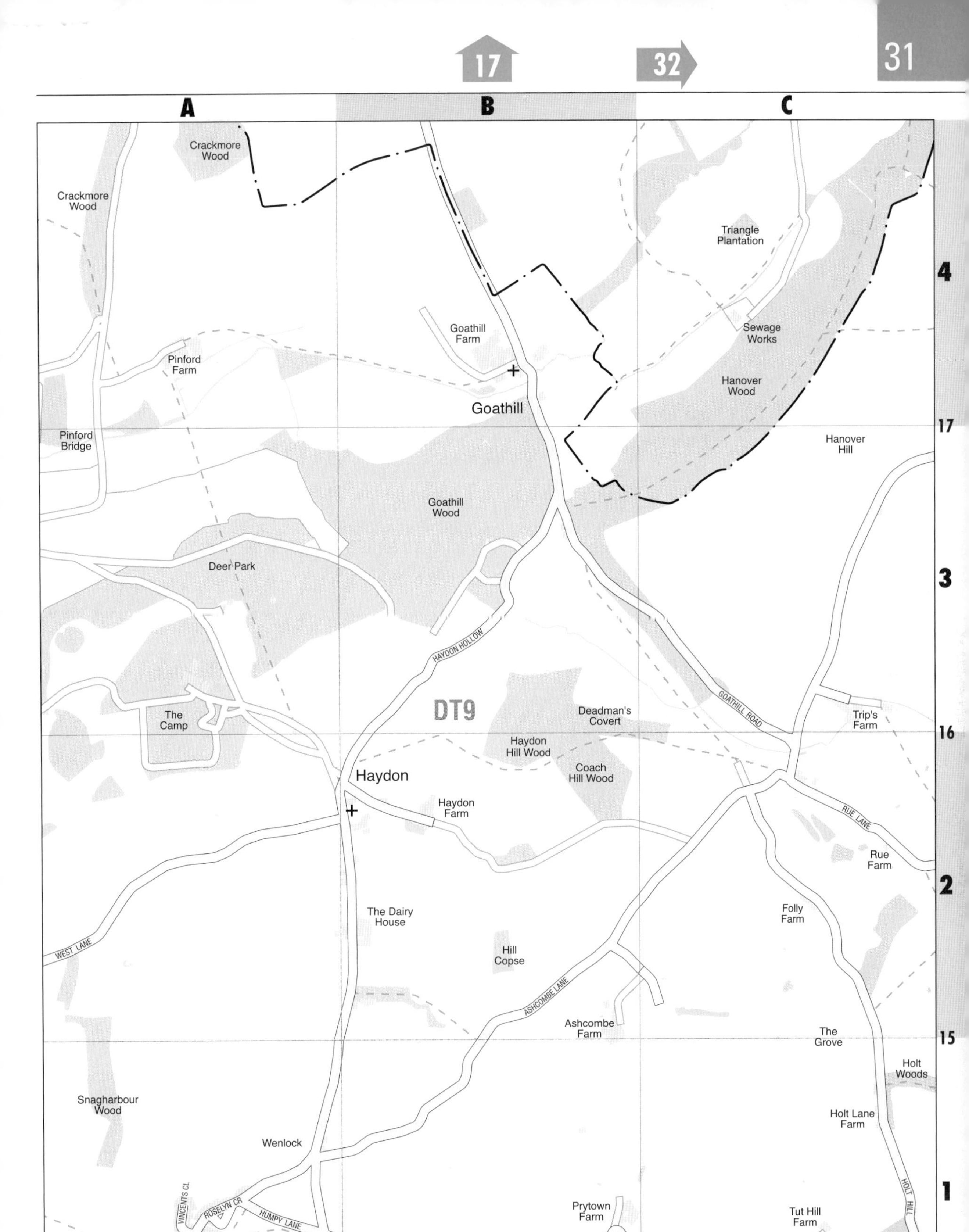

A
B
C

Crackmore
Wood

Crackmore
Wood

Triangle
Plantation

Pinford
Farm

Goathill
Farm

Sewage
Works

4

Hanover
Wood

Goathill

Pinford
Bridge

Hanover
Hill

17

Goathill
Wood

Deer Park

3

HAYDON HOLLOW

GOATHILL ROAD

Trip's
Farm

The
Camp

DT9

Deadman's
Covert

Haydon
Hill Wood

16

Haydon

Coach
Hill Wood

RUE LANE

Haydon
Farm

Rue
Farm

2

The Dairy
House

Folly
Farm

WEST LANE

Hill
Copse

ASHCOMBE LANE

Ashcombe
Farm

The
Grove

15

Holt
Woods

Snagharbour
Wood

Holt Lane
Farm

Wenlock

HOLT HILL

1

VINCENTS CL

ROSELYN CR

HUMPY LANE

Prytown
Farm

Tut Hill
Farm

Tut Hill
Copse

Alweston
Farm

OLD
SCHOOL
CL

Alweston

WRITH ROAD

Birch
Copse

Lower
Farm

Sewage
Works

TUT HILL

HOLT HILL

PO

MUNDEN'S LANE

FOLKE LANE

Mundens
Farm

Yew Tree
Farm

Rowditch
Wood

14

66
67
A
B
68
C

A   B   C

4

Home
Farm
Manor House •
Purse
Caundle
+ Church
Farm
Court
Farm
Manor
Farm
Cemy

Frith
Wood
Frith
House
Dales
Covert
Frith
Farm

Park Wall •

17

Clayhanger

West Coppice

Middle
Farm
Manor
Farm

3

Wood House
Covert

DT9

Cockhill
Farm
Haddon
Lodge
Cockhill Coppice

West
Wood

Rum
Coppice

PILE LA

Herridge
Coppice

16

Plumley Wood

DT10

New Leaze
Wood

Rockhill
Farm

Newlands
Farm

STALBRIDGE ROAD

2

Woodrow
Farm
Bilcombe
Copse
Woodclose
Farm
Woodclose
Poultry Farm

STOKES LANE

Brunsell Knap
+ Farm
Brunsell
Farm
Stourton Caundle

DROVE ROAD

15

Knoll Copse

Manor
Farm
Chapel •
PH
BARROW HILL

1

Holt Woods

HOLT LANE

HOLT LANE

GOLDEN HILL
BOWDEN MILL LANE

Holtwood

CAUNDLE LANE
Caundle
Farm

14

Bishop's
Caundle Wood

69   A   70   B   71   C

19
34

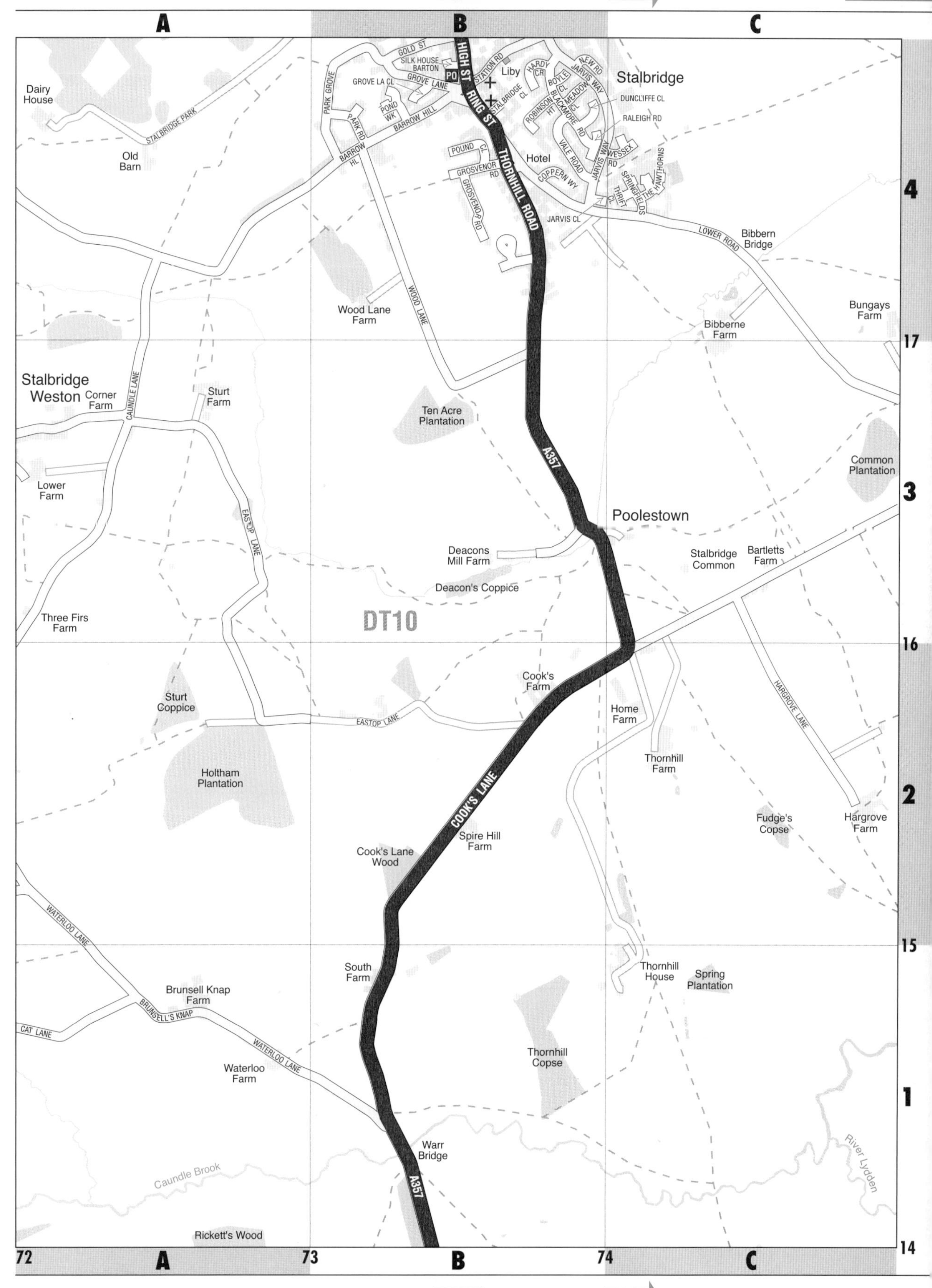
A
B
C
Dairy House
Old Barn
STALBRIDGE PARK
GOLD ST
SILK HOUSE BARTON
HIGH ST
PO
GROVE LA CL
GROVE LANE
PARK GROVE
PARK RD
POND WK
BARROW HILL
BARROW HL
RING ST
STATION RD
Liby
STALBRIDGE CL
HARDY CR
BOYLE CL
NEW RD
JARVIS WAY
Stalbridge
DUNCLIFFE CL
RALEIGH RD
ROBINSON HT
BLACKMORE RD
MEADOW CL
VALE ROAD
POUND CL
GROSVENOR RD
THORNHILL ROAD
Hotel
COPPERN WY
JARVIS WAY
WESSEX RD
SPRINGFIELDS
THE HAWTHORNS
THRIFT CL
JARVIS CL
LOWER ROAD
Bibbern Bridge
4
Wood Lane Farm
WOOD LANE
A357
Bibberne Farm
Bungays Farm
17
Stalbridge Weston
Corner Farm
CAUNDLE LANE
Sturt Farm
Ten Acre Plantation
Common Plantation
Lower Farm
3
EASTOP LANE
Poolestown
Deacons Mill Farm
Stalbridge Common
Bartletts Farm
Deacon's Coppice
Three Firs Farm
DT10
16
Cook's Farm
Sturt Coppice
EASTOP LANE
Home Farm
HARGROVE LANE
Holtham Plantation
Thornhill Farm
COOK'S LANE
2
Fudge's Copse
Hargrove Farm
Spire Hill Farm
Cook's Lane Wood
WATERLOO LANE
15
South Farm
Thornhill House
Spring Plantation
Brunsell Knap Farm
BRUNSELL'S KNAP
CAT LANE
WATERLOO LANE
Thornhill Copse
Waterloo Farm
1
Warr Bridge
River Lydden
Caundle Brook
Rickett's Wood
14
72
73
74

196
34

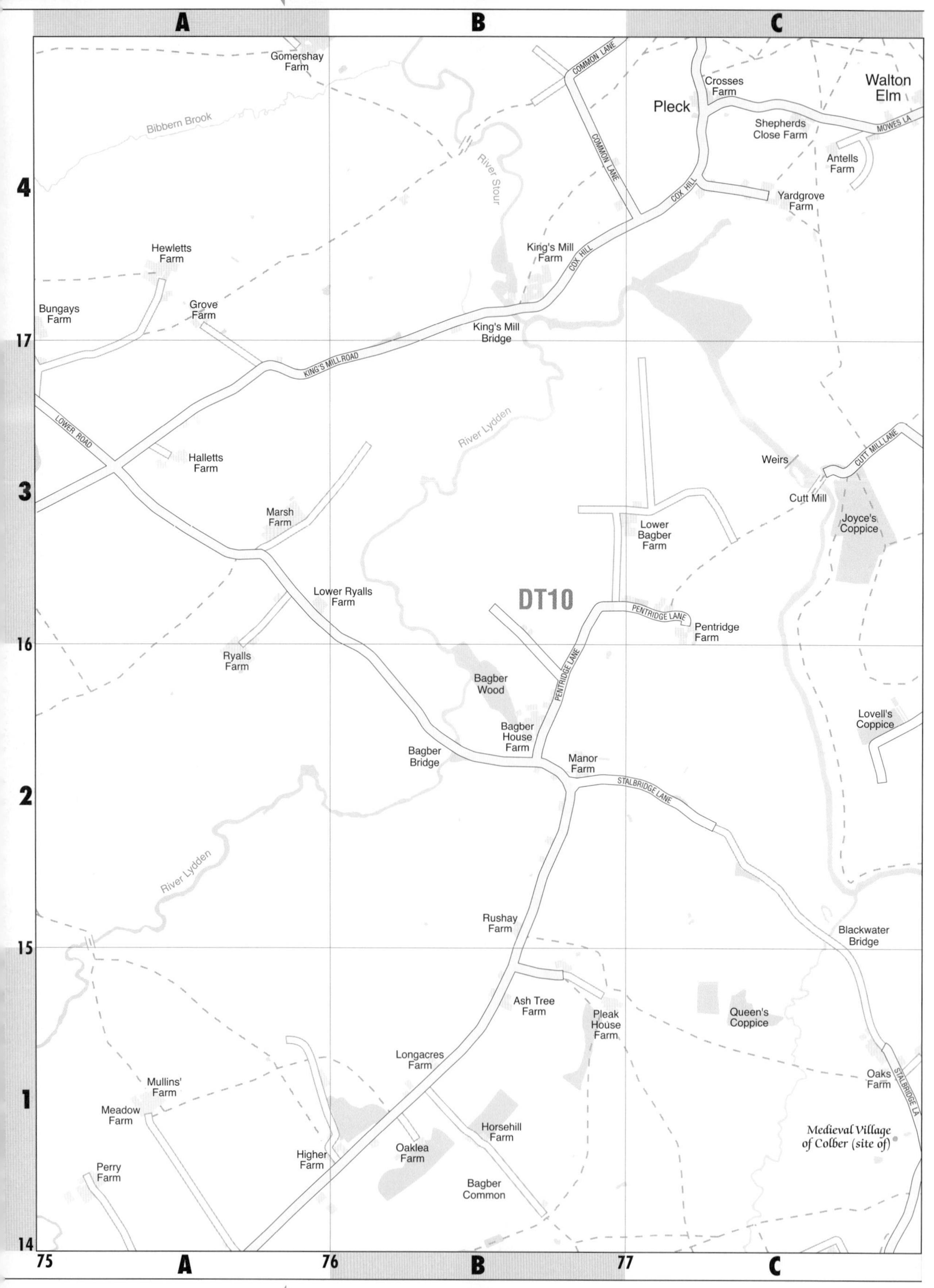
A
B
C
Gomershay Farm
COMMON LANE
Crosses Farm
Walton Elm
Pleck
Shepherds Close Farm
MOWES LA
Bibbern Brook
River Stour
Antells Farm
COX HILL
Yardgrove Farm
4
Hewletts Farm
King's Mill Farm
COX HILL
Bungays Farm
Grove Farm
King's Mill Bridge
17
KING'S MILL ROAD
LOWER ROAD
River Lydden
Halletts Farm
Weirs
CUTT MILL LANE
3
Cutt Mill
Marsh Farm
Lower Bagber Farm
Joyce's Coppice
Lower Ryalls Farm
DT10
PENTRIDGE LANE
Pentridge Farm
16
Ryalls Farm
Bagber Wood
PENTRIDGE LANE
Lovell's Coppice
Bagber House Farm
Bagber Bridge
Manor Farm
2
STALBRIDGE LANE
River Lydden
Rushay Farm
Blackwater Bridge
15
Ash Tree Farm
Pleak House Farm
Queen's Coppice
Longacres Farm
Mullins' Farm
Oaks Farm
STALBRIDGE LA
1
Meadow Farm
Horsehill Farm
Medieval Village of Colber (site of)
Higher Farm
Oaklea Farm
Perry Farm
Bagber Common
14
75
76
77

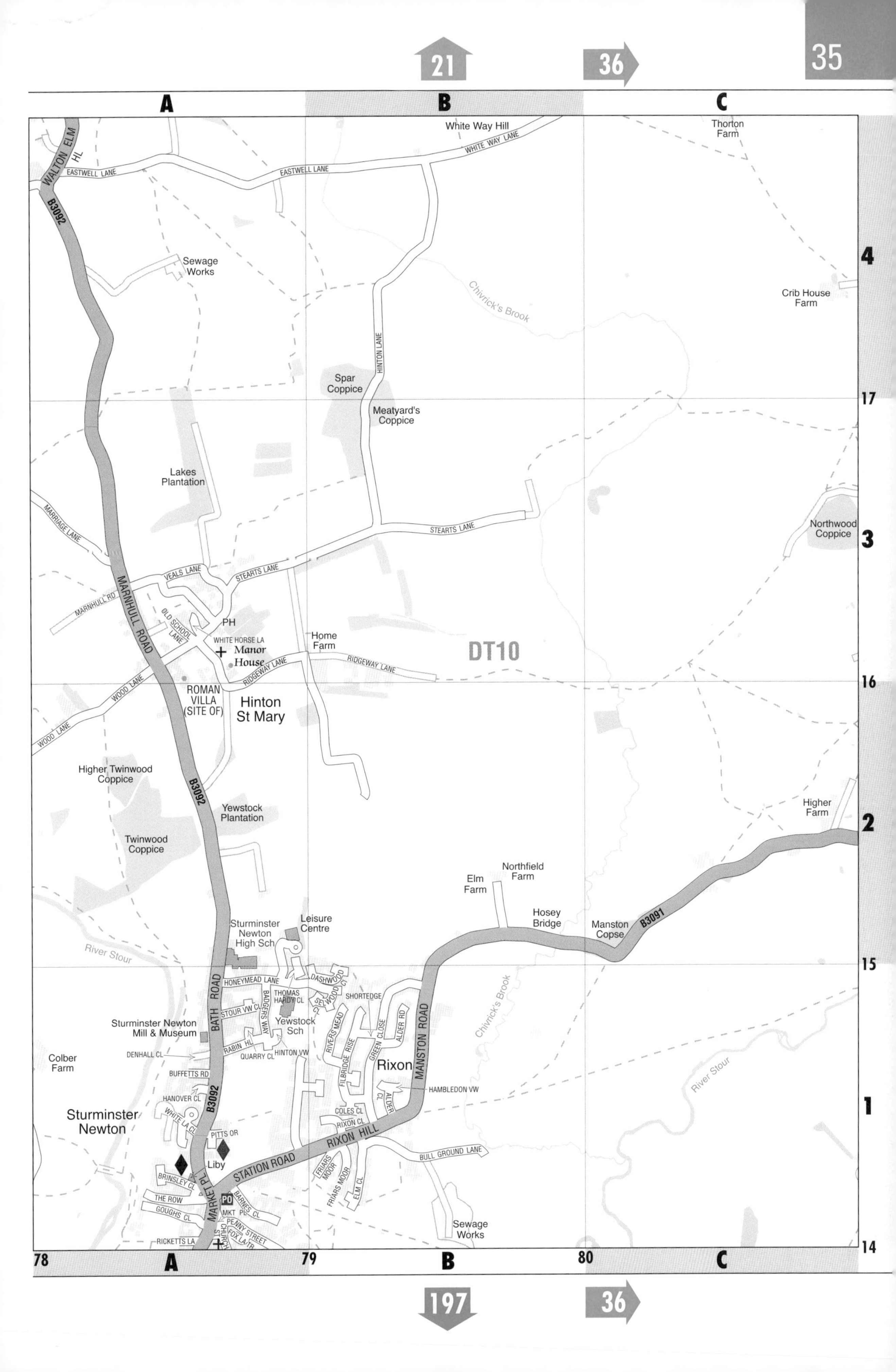

A B C

WALTON ELM HL

White Way Hill

WHITE WAY LANE

Thorton Farm

EASTWELL LANE

EASTWELL LANE

B3092

Sewage Works

Chivrick's Brook

4

Crib House Farm

HINTON LANE

Spar Coppice

17

Meatyard's Coppice

MARRIAGE LANE

Lakes Plantation

Northwood Coppice

3

STEARTS LANE

VEALS LANE

STEARTS LANE

MARNHULL ROAD

MARNHULL RD

OLD SCHOOL LANE

PH

DT10

WHITE HORSE LA

Home Farm

WOOD LANE

ROMAN VILLA (SITE OF)

Manor House

RIDGEWAY LANE

RIDGEWAY LANE

16

Hinton St Mary

WOOD LANE

Higher Twinwood Coppice

Higher Farm

B3092

Yewstock Plantation

2

Twinwood Coppice

Elm Farm

Northfield Farm

Hosey Bridge

Manston Copse

B3091

River Stour

Leisure Centre

Sturminster Newton High Sch

HONEYMEAD LANE

DASHWOOD

15

BATH ROAD

THOMAS HARDY CL

SHORTEDGE

Sturminster Newton Mill & Museum

STOUR VW CL

BADGERS WAY

Yewstock Sch

RIVERS MEAD

GREEN CLOSE

ALDER RD

Chivrick's Brook

River Stour

Colber Farm

DENHALL CL

RABIN HL

QUARRY CL

HINTON VW

FLEBRIDGE RISE

Rixon

MANSTON ROAD

HAMBLEDON VW

BUFFETTS RD

HANOVER CL

COLES CL

ATHOL

1

Sturminster Newton

WHITE LA CL

PITTS OR

RIXON CL

Liby

RIXON HILL

BULL GROUND LANE

BRINSLEY CL

STATION ROAD

FRIARS MOOR

FRIARS MOOR

ELM CL

MARKET PL

THE ROW

GOUGHS CL

MKT PL

PO

PENNY STREET

BARNS CL

Sewage Works

RICKETTS LA

CHURCH ST

FOX LA TR

78 A 79 B 80 C 14

35
22

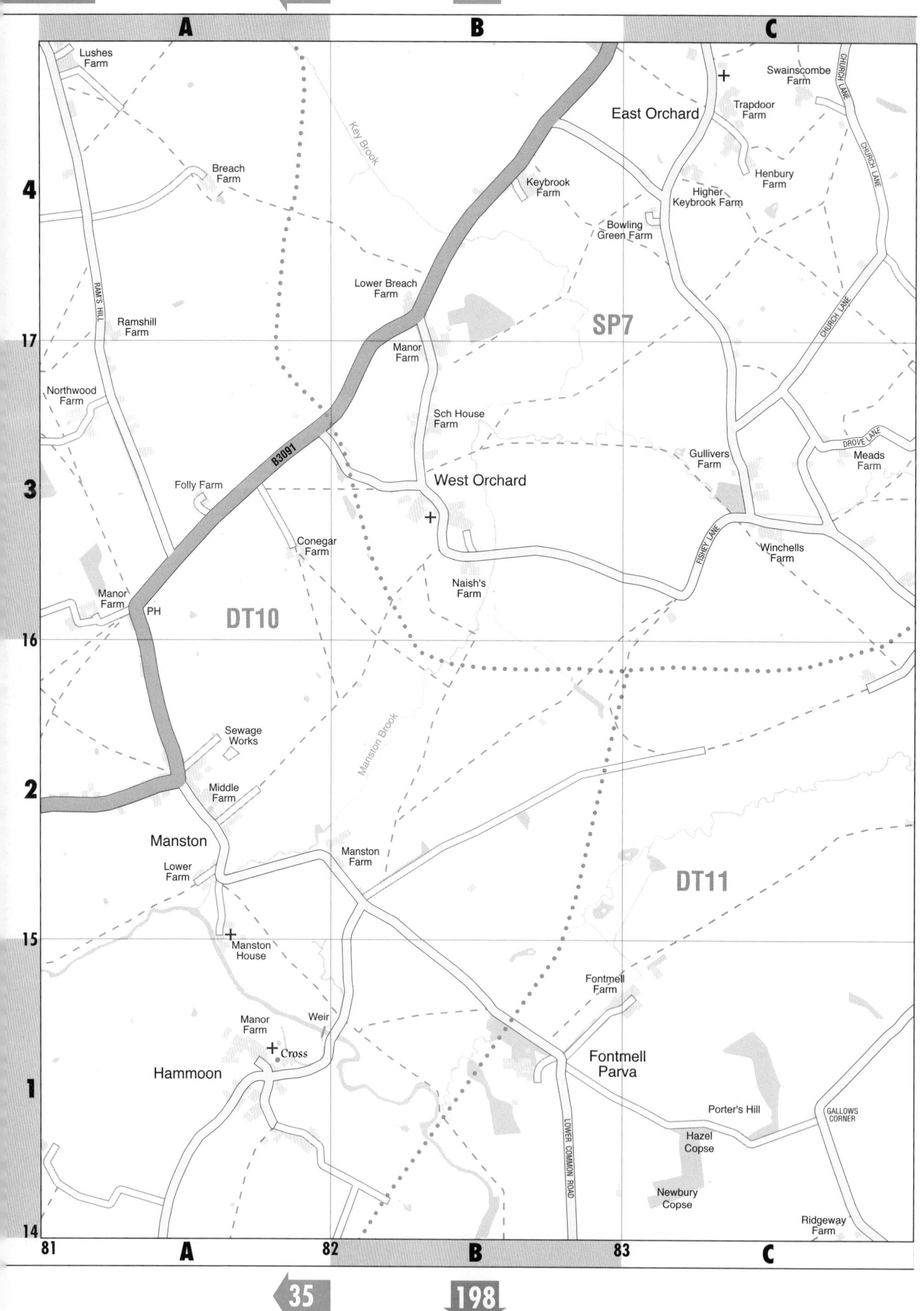
A
B
C
Lushes Farm
Swainscombe Farm
CHURCH LANE
Trapdoor Farm
East Orchard
Key Brook
Breach Farm
Keybrook Farm
Henbury Farm
Higher Keybrook Farm
Bowling Green Farm
Lower Breach Farm
RAM'S HILL
Ramshill Farm
SP7
CHURCH LANE
Manor Farm
Northwood Farm
Sch House Farm
Gullivers Farm
DROVE LANE
Meads Farm
B3091
Folly Farm
West Orchard
Conegar Farm
Winchells Farm
FISHEY LANE
Naish's Farm
Manor Farm
PH
DT10
Sewage Works
Manston Brook
Middle Farm
Manston
Manston Farm
Lower Farm
DT11
Manston House
Fontmell Farm
Weir
Manor Farm
Cross
Fontmell Parva
Hammoon
Porter's Hill
GALLOWS CORNER
Hazel Copse
LOWER COMMON ROAD
Newbury Copse
Ridgeway Farm
4
17
3
16
2
15
1
14
81
82
83

35
198

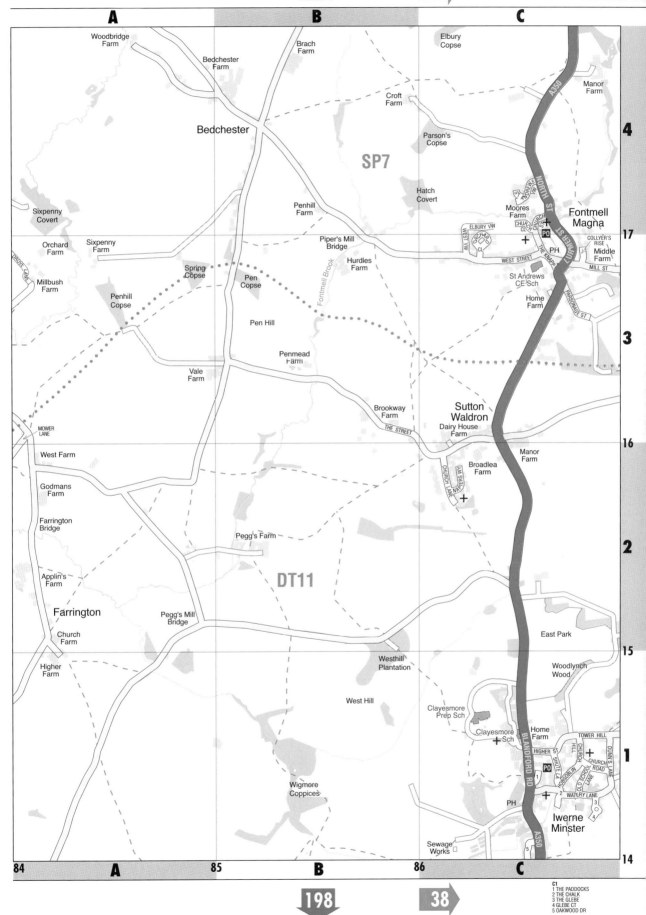

A B C

84 85 86

14 15 16 17

1 2 3 4

Woodbridge Farm
Bedchester Farm
Brach Farm
Elbury Copse
Manor Farm
A350
Croft Farm
Bedchester
SP7
Parson's Copse
Hatch Covert
Moores Farm
NORTH ST
Fontmell Magna
MOORES VW
ELBURY VW
CHUA CL
PO
CL
PH
COLLYER'S RISE
Middle Farm
Penhill Farm
WEST VW
ORCHARD
THE KNAPP
West Street
MILL ST
St Andrews CE Sch
PARSONAGE ST
Sixpenny Covert
Orchard Farm
Sixpenny Farm
Piper's Mill Bridge
Hurdles Farm
Home Farm
Spring Copse
Pen Copse
Fontmell Brook
DROVE LANE
Millbush Farm
Penhill Copse
Pen Hill
Penmead Farm
Vale Farm
Brookway Farm
Sutton Waldron
Dairy House Farm
Manor Farm
THE STREET
MOWER LANE
West Farm
Broadlea Farm
CHURCH LANE
VW SHEPS M
Godmans Farm
Farrington Bridge
Pegg's Farm
DT11
Manor Farm
Applin's Farm
Pegg's Mill Bridge
Farrington
Church Farm
East Park
Westhill Plantation
Woodlynch Wood
Higher Farm
West Hill
Clayesmore Prep Sch
Clayesmore Sch
Home Farm
BLANDFORD RD
TOWER HILL
HIGHER ST
SHUTE LA
CHURCH HILL
DUNN'S LANE
PO
CHURCH ROAD
HOBGOBLIN
OLD SCHOOL LANE
Wigmore Coppices
WATERY LANE
PH
Iwerne Minster
A350
Sewage Works

C1
1 THE PADDOCKS
2 THE CHALK
3 THE GLEBE
4 GLEBE CT
5 OAKWOOD DR

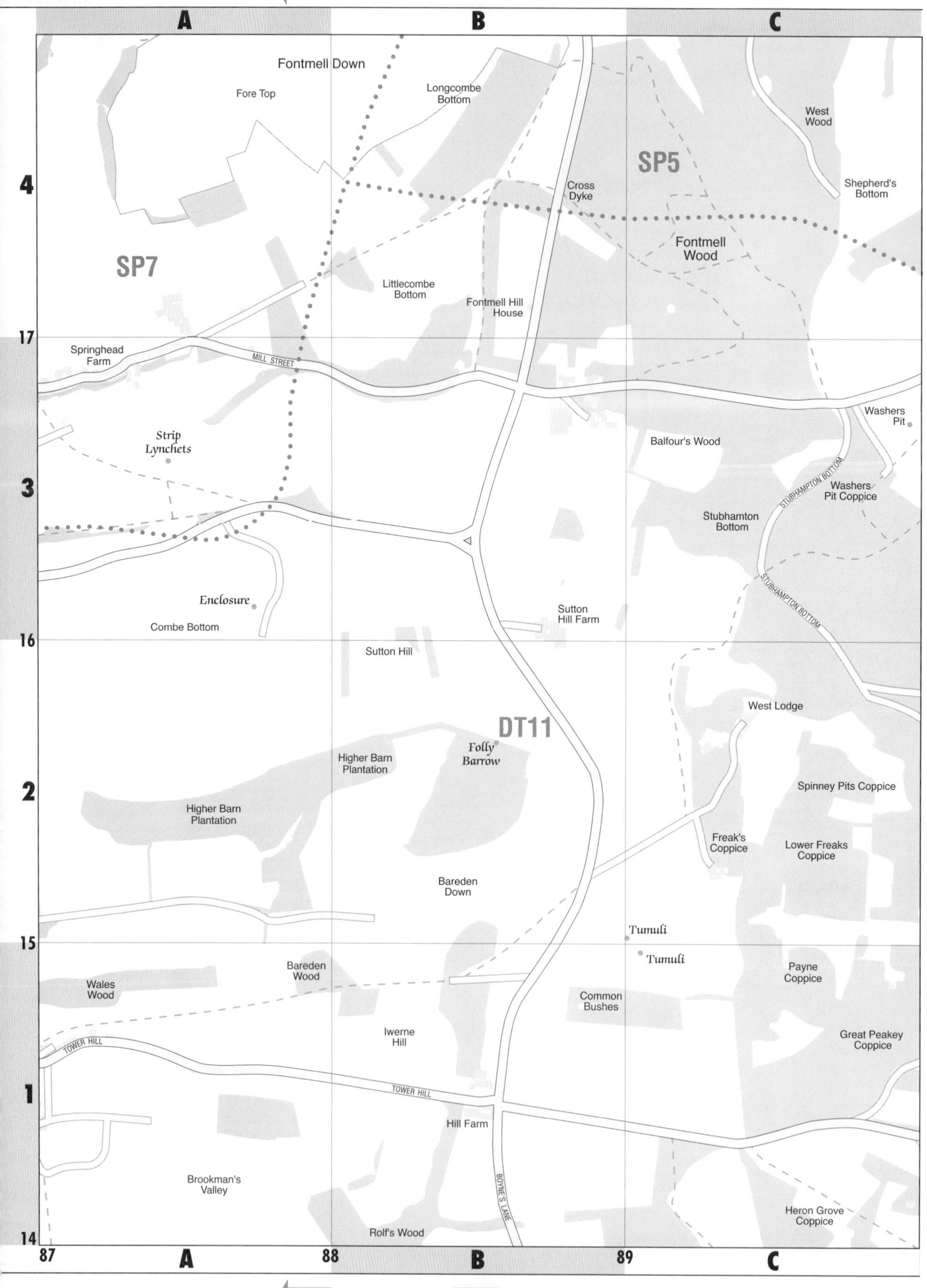

A
B
C

Fontmell Down

Fore Top

Longcombe
Bottom

West
Wood

SP5

4

Cross
Dyke

Shepherd's
Bottom

Fontmell
Wood

SP7

Littlecombe
Bottom

Fontmell Hill
House

17

Springhead
Farm

MILL STREET

Washers
Pit

Balfour's Wood

Washers
Pit Coppice

Strip
Lynchets

STUBHAMPTON BOTTOM

3

Stubhamton
Bottom

Enclosure

STUBHAMPTON BOTTOM

Combe Bottom

Sutton
Hill Farm

16

Sutton Hill

West Lodge

DT11

Higher Barn
Plantation

Folly
Barrow

Spinney Pits Coppice

2

Higher Barn
Plantation

Freak's
Coppice

Lower Freaks
Coppice

Bareden
Down

Tumuli

15

Tumuli

Bareden
Wood

Payne
Coppice

Wales
Wood

Common
Bushes

Great Peakey
Coppice

TOWER HILL

Iwerne
Hill

1

TOWER HILL

Hill Farm

BOYNE'S LANE

Brookman's
Valley

Heron Grove
Coppice

14

Rolf's Wood

87
A
88
B
89
C

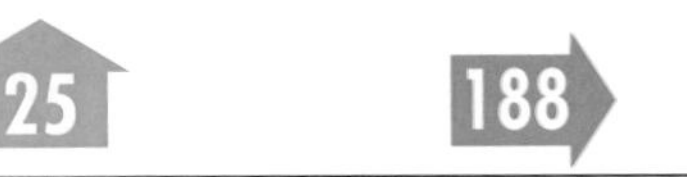

B3081

Shepherd's Bottom

Wessex Ridgeway   *Tumulus*

Ashmore

HIGH ST
NOADE ST
HALFPENNY LANE
GREEN LANE

Wiltshire
Coppice

Hookley
Copse

Ashmore
Farm

SP5

Turkey
Plantation

Earthwork
Mudoak Wood

Gallops

Tollard
Green

Little Alderwood
Coppice

Spring
Farm

Well
Bottom

Great Alderwood
Coppice

Wessex Ridgeway

Earthwork

Tumuli

Great Bench
Coppice

Ashmore Wood

Elderen
Coppice

Tollard
Green Bottom

Deadman's
Coppice

Alner's
Coppice

Little Bench
Coppice

Stony
Bottom

Little Sedge
Oak Coppice

Bussey's
Down

Stone Down Coppice

Upper Broadridge
Coppice

Ashmore
Bottom

CAESAR'S CAMP
(Fort)

Wagbush
Coppice

Ashmore Wood

Ashmore
Plantation

Hill Flower
Coppice

Crabtree
Coppice

Manor
Hill

Higher Downend
Coppice

DT11

Ball
Coppice

Churchill's
Coppice

Little Peakey
Coppice

Stubhampton
Bottom

Tumulus

Ashmore
Barn Farm

Bussey
Stool Farm

Hanging Coppice

Wessex Ridgeway

Stubhampton Bottom

Ashmore
Bottom

ASHMORE BOTTOM

Bossleton Belt

Earl's Hill

Ashmore
Bottom

Tumuli

Dungrove
Hill

Bishop's Coppice

Stubhampton Down

17

4

3

16

2

15

1

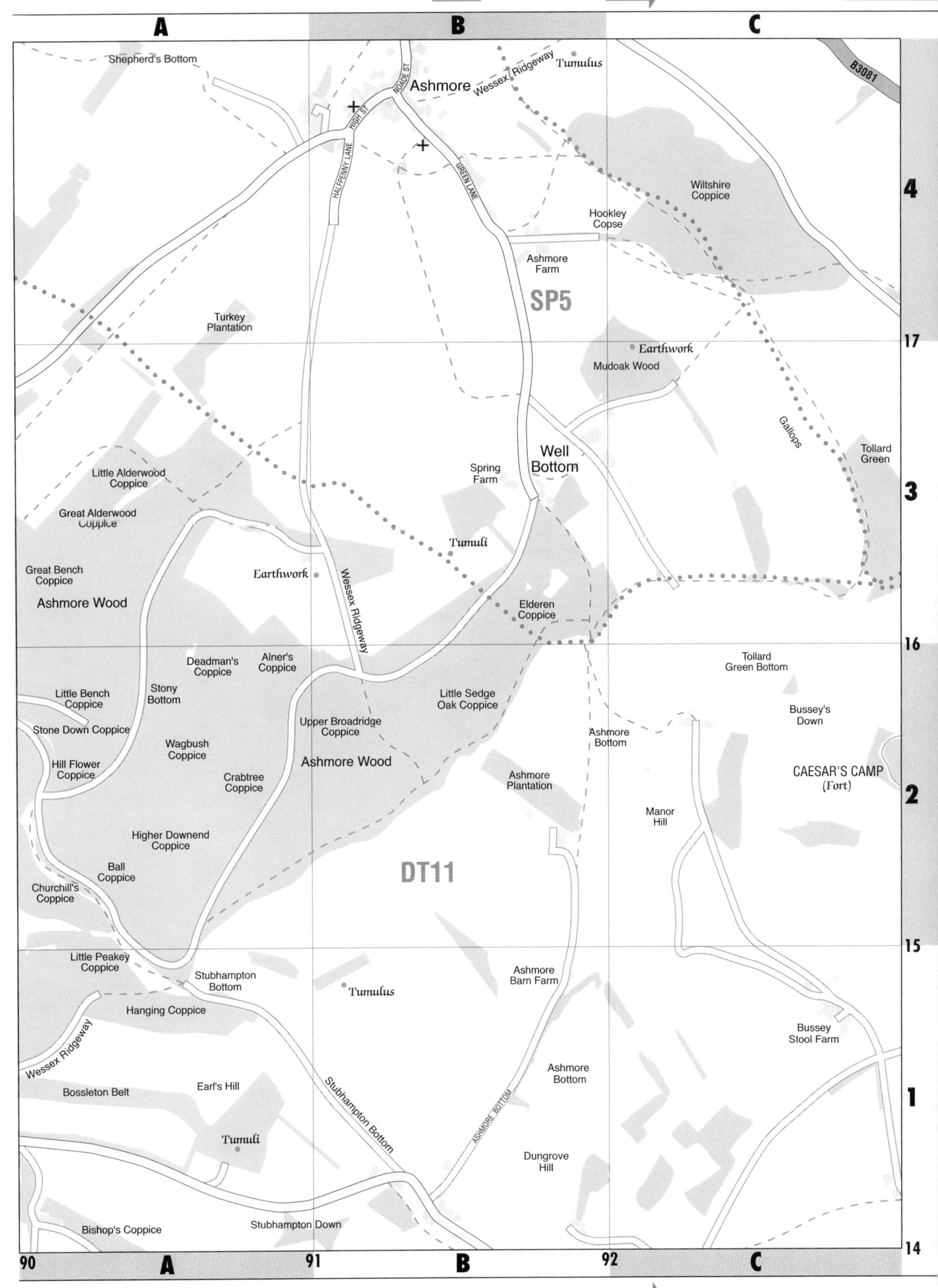

A
B
C

Burwood

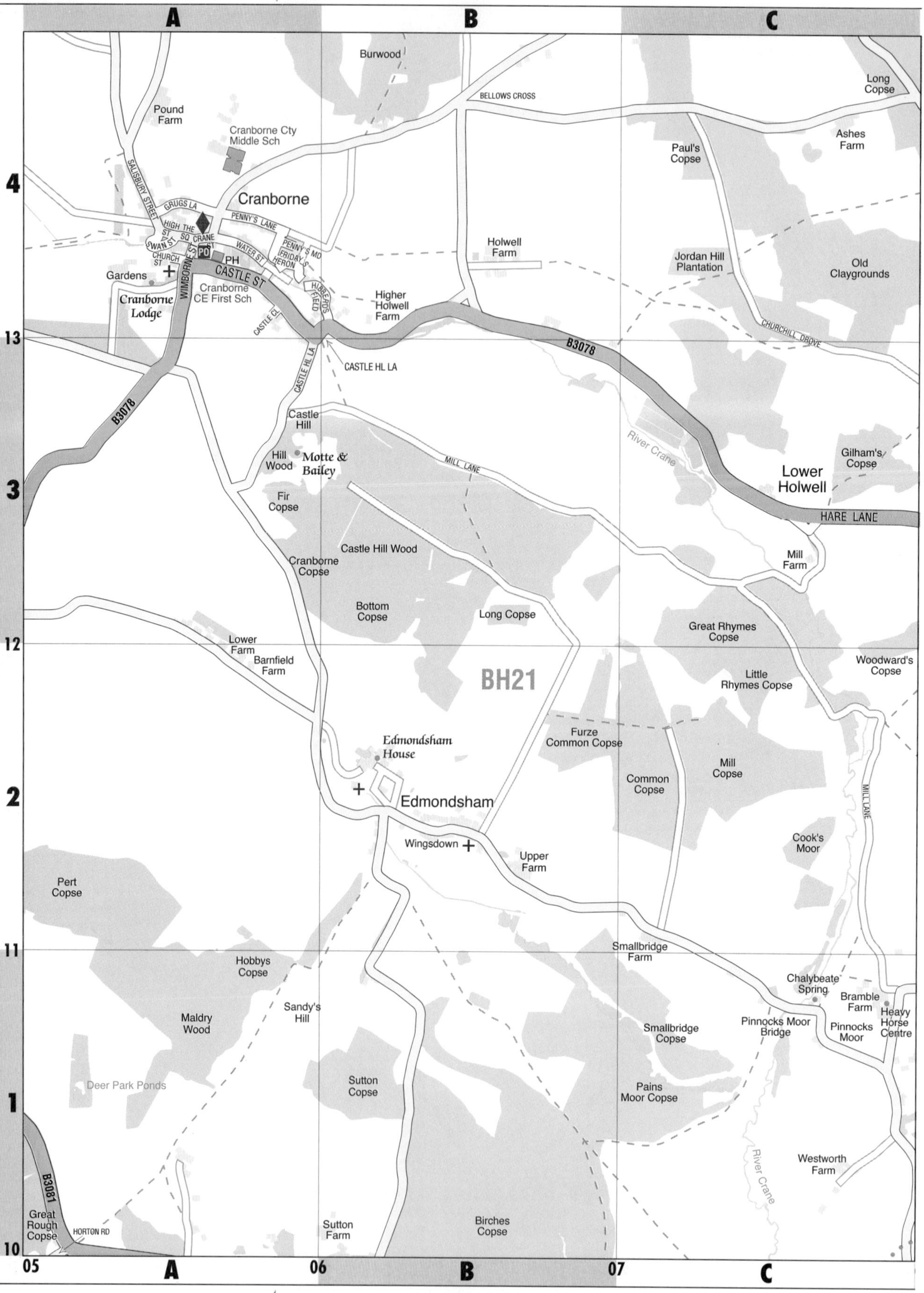

BELLOWS CROSS

Long Copse

Pound Farm

Cranborne Cty Middle Sch

Ashes Farm

Paul's Copse

4

Cranborne

GRUGS LA

PENNY'S LANE

Holwell Farm

Jordan Hill Plantation

Old Claygrounds

HIGH ST
THE SQ
CRANE

SALISBURY STREET

PENNY'S MD
FRIDAY
HERON

SWAN ST
CHURCH ST
PO
PH

WATER ST

PENNY'S

CASTLE ST

Gardens

CHURCHILL DROVE

B3078

Cranborne CE First Sch

Higher Holwell Farm

WIMBORNE ST

Cranborne Lodge

CASTLE CL

HIGHFIELD

HIGHFIELD

13

B3078

CASTLE HL LA

CASTLE HL LA

River Crane

Lower Holwell

Gilham's Copse

Castle Hill

Hill Wood

Motte & Bailey

MILL LANE

HARE LANE

Fir Copse

3

Cranborne Copse

Castle Hill Wood

Mill Farm

Bottom Copse

Long Copse

Great Rhymes Copse

12

Lower Farm

Barnfield Farm

Woodward's Copse

Little Rhymes Copse

BH21

Edmondsham House

Furze Common Copse

Mill Copse

2

Edmondsham

Common Copse

Wingsdown

Upper Farm

Cook's Moor

Pert Copse

MILL LANE

11

Hobbys Copse

Smallbridge Farm

Chalybeate Spring

Bramble Farm

Heavy Horse Centre

Sandy's Hill

Maldry Wood

Smallbridge Copse

Pinnocks Moor Bridge

Pinnocks Moor

Deer Park Ponds

Sutton Copse

Pains Moor Copse

1

B3081

River Crane

Westworth Farm

Great Rough Copse

HORTON RD

Sutton Farm

Birches Copse

10

05
A
06
B
07
C

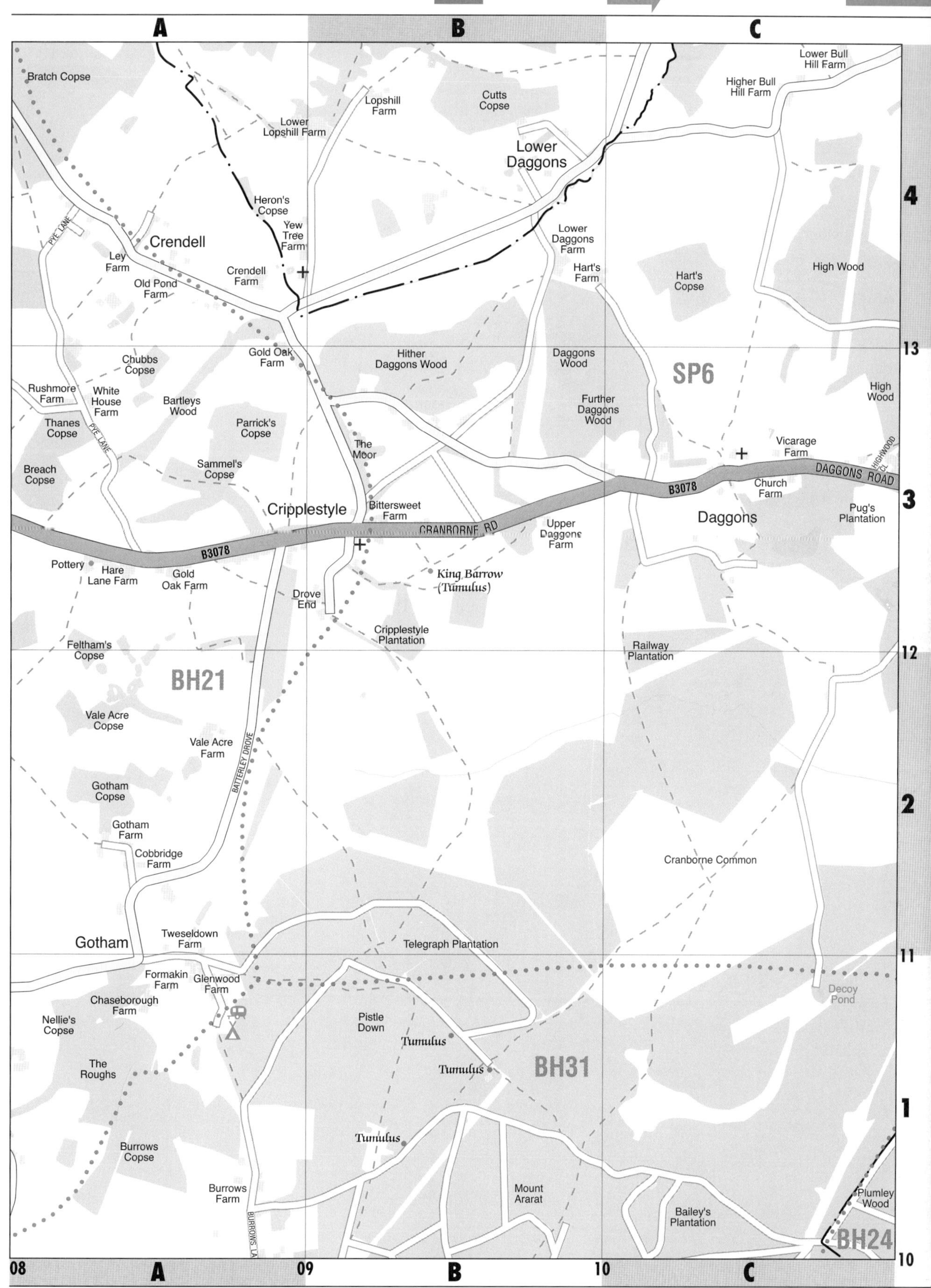

A **B** **C**

Brach Copse

Lower Bull
Hill Farm

Higher Bull
Hill Farm

Lopshill
Farm

Cutts
Copse

Lower
Lopshill Farm

Lower
Daggons

4

Heron's
Copse

Crendell

Ley
Farm

Yew
Tree
Farm

Lower
Daggons
Farm

Hart's
Farm

Hart's
Copse

High Wood

Old Pond
Farm

Crendell
Farm

PYE LANE

13

Chubbs
Copse

Gold Oak
Farm

Hither
Daggons Wood

Daggons
Wood

SP6

High
Wood

Rushmore
Farm

White
House
Farm

Bartleys
Wood

Further
Daggons
Wood

Thanes
Copse

Parrick's
Copse

PYE LANE

The
Moor

Vicarage
Farm

HIGHWOOD

Breach
Copse

Sammel's
Copse

Cripplestyle

Bittersweet
Farm

CRANBORNE RD

Upper
Daggons
Farm

B3078

Church
Farm

DAGGONS ROAD

3

Daggons

Pug's
Plantation

Pottery

Hare
Lane Farm

Gold
Oak Farm

B3078

Drove
End

King Barrow
(Tumulus)

Feltham's
Copse

Cripplestyle
Plantation

Railway
Plantation

12

BH21

Vale Acre
Copse

BATTERLEY DROVE

Vale Acre
Farm

Gotham
Copse

Cranborne Common

2

Gotham
Farm

Cobbridge
Farm

Gotham

Tweseldown
Farm

Telegraph Plantation

11

Formakin
Farm

Glenwood
Farm

Decoy
Pond

Chaseborough
Farm

Pistle
Down

Nellie's
Copse

Tumulus

Tumulus

BH31

The
Roughs

Tumulus

1

Burrows
Copse

Tumulus

BURROWS LA.

Plumley
Wood

Burrows
Farm

Mount
Ararat

Bailey's
Plantation

BH24

08 **A** 09 **B** 10 **C** **10**

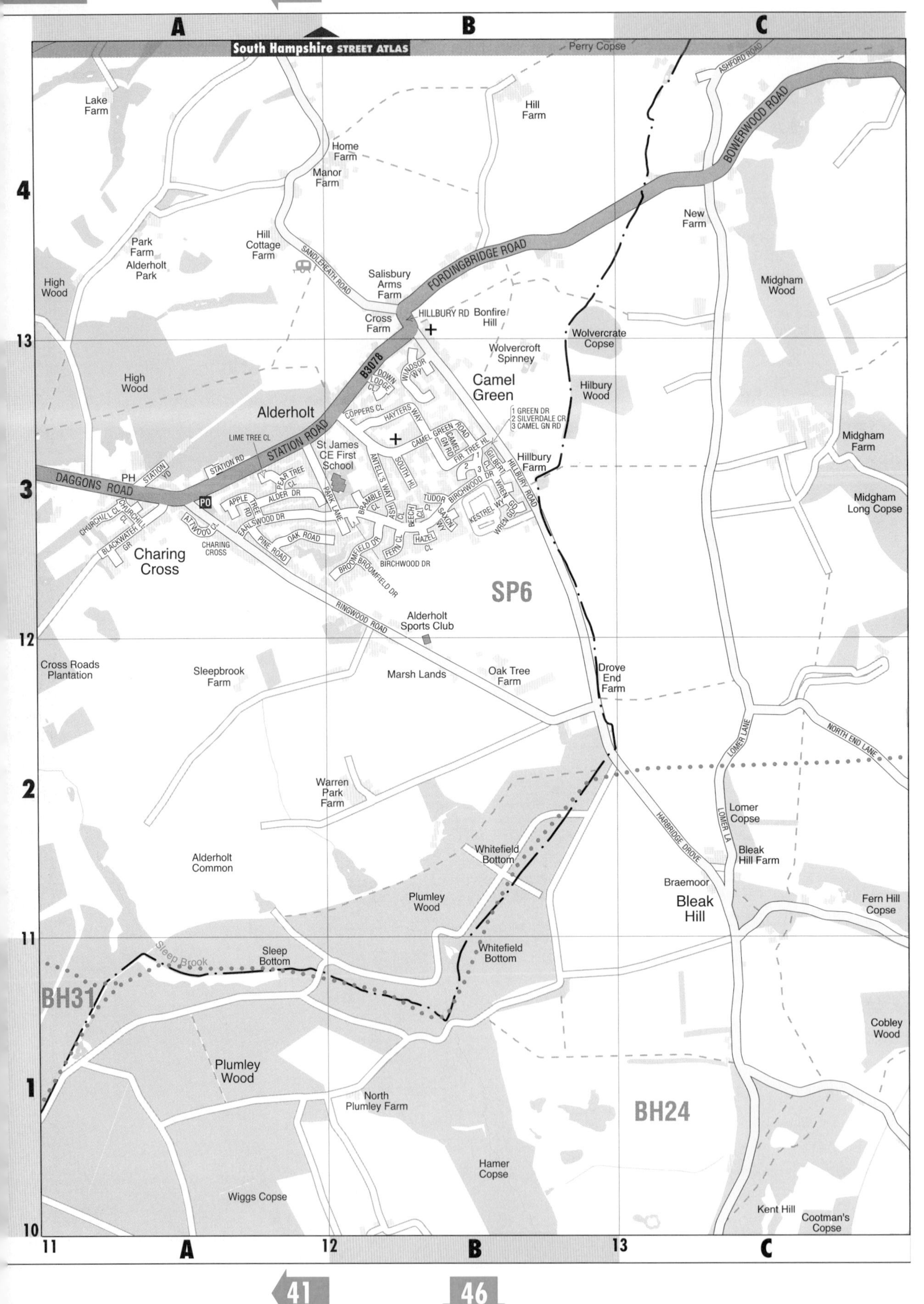

A · B · C

Perry Copse

Lake Farm

Hill Farm

BOWERWOOD ROAD

ASHFORD ROAD

Home Farm

Manor Farm

New Farm

Midgham Wood

4

Park Farm
Alderholt Park

Hill Cottage Farm

SANDLEHEATH ROAD

Salisbury Arms Farm

High Wood

FORDINGBRIDGE ROAD

Wolvercrate Copse

Cross Farm

HILLBURY RD

Bonfire Hill

Wolvercroft Spinney

Hilbury Wood

Midgham Farm

13

High Wood

B3078

DOWN LODGE CL

WINDSOR WY

Camel Green

1 GREEN DR
2 SILVERDALE CR
3 CAMEL GN RD

Midgham Long Copse

Alderholt

COPPERS CL

HAYTERS WAY

CAMEL GREEN ROAD

GILBERT CT

FIR TREE HL

Hillbury Farm

LIME TREE CL

STATION ROAD

St James CE First School

SOUTH HL

BIRCHWOOD DR

HILLBURY ROAD

PH

STATION RD

STATION YD

ANTELL'S WAY

BRAMBLE CL

TUDOR CT

KESTREL WY

WREN CT

3

DAGGONS ROAD

PO

APPLE TREE

ALDER DR

PARK LANE

BEECH CT

HAZEL

WREN CT

CHURCH CL

CHURCH RD

BLACKWATER GR

ATWOOD CL

PINE ROAD

OAK ROAD

BROOMFIELD DR

BIRCHWOOD DR

SP6

Charing Cross

CHARING CROSS

EARLSWOOD DR

BROOMFIELD DR

Alderholt Sports Club

12

Cross Roads Plantation

Sleepbrook Farm

RINGWOOD ROAD

Marsh Lands

Oak Tree Farm

Drove End Farm

LOWER LANE

NORTH END LANE

2

Warren Park Farm

Lomer Copse

LOWER LA

HARBRIDGE DROVE

Bleak Hill Farm

Alderholt Common

Whitefield Bottom

Braemoor

Fern Hill Copse

Plumley Wood

Bleak Hill

11

BH31

Sleep Brook

Sleep Bottom

Whitefield Bottom

Cobley Wood

Plumley Wood

North Plumley Farm

BH24

1

Hamer Copse

Kent Hill

Cootman's Copse

Wiggs Copse

10

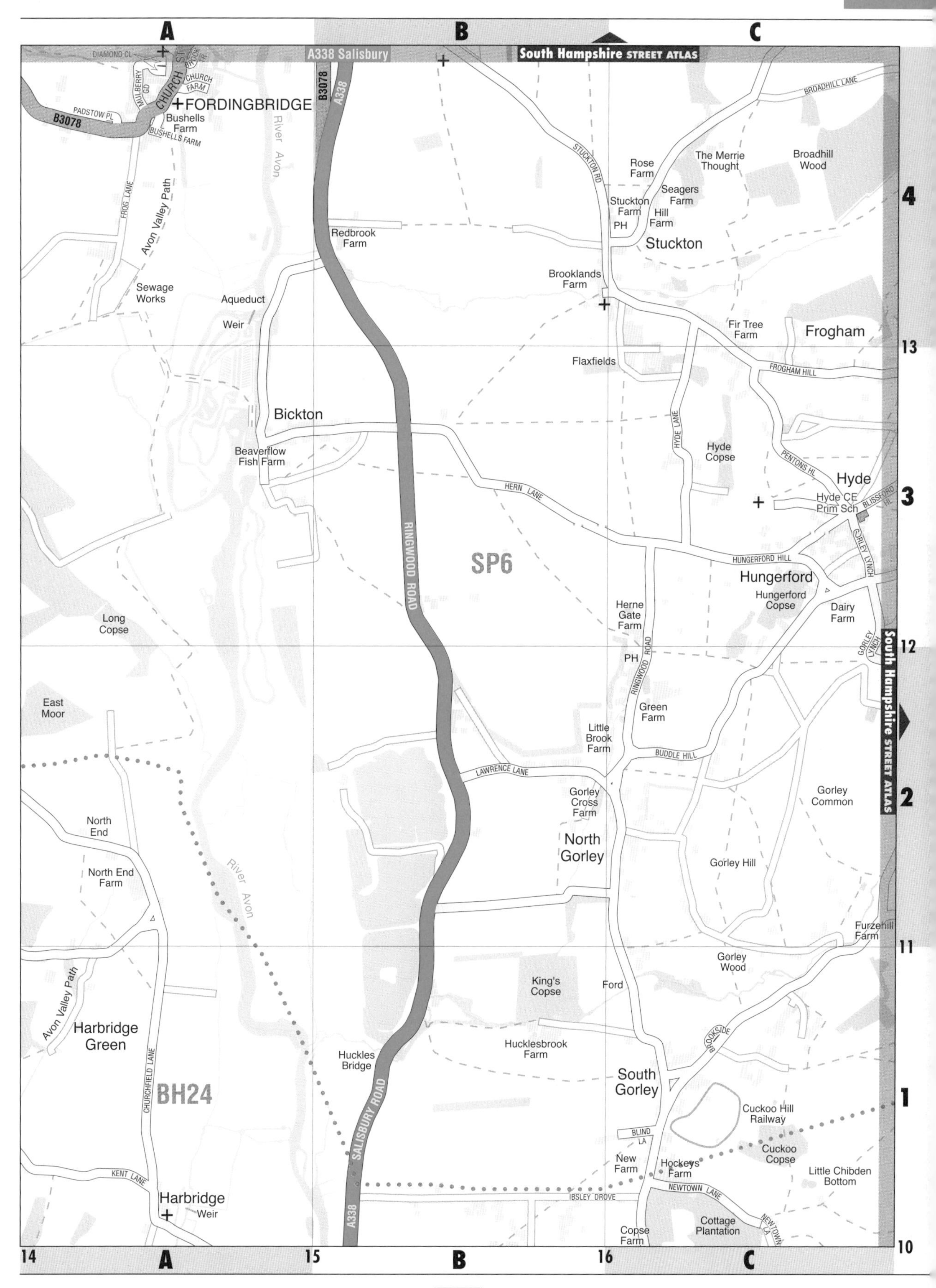

A338 Salisbury

FORDINGBRIDGE

B3078

B3078

DIAMOND CL
MILLBERRY GD
CHURCH ST
PADSTOW PL
CHURCH FARM
Bushells Farm
BUSHELLS FARM

River Avon

Avon Valley Path
FROG LANE

Sewage Works

Aqueduct

Weir

Redbrook Farm

Bickton

Beaverflow Fish Farm

Hern Lane

SP6

Long Copse

East Moor

River Avon

North End

North End Farm

Avon Valley Path

Harbridge Green

BH24

CHURCHFIELD LANE

KENT LANE

Harbridge

Weir

RINGWOOD ROAD

SALISBURY ROAD

A338

Huckles Bridge

Lawrence Lane

Little Brook Farm

Herne Gate Farm

PH

RINGWOOD ROAD

Green Farm

BUDDLE HILL

Gorley Cross Farm

North Gorley

King's Copse

Ford

Hucklesbrook Farm

South Gorley

BROOKSIDE

New Farm

BLIND LA

Hockeys Farm

NEWTOWN LANE

IBSLEY DROVE

Copse Farm

Cottage Plantation

NEWTOWN LA

Cuckoo Hill Railway

Cuckoo Copse

Little Chibden Bottom

Gorley Wood

Furzehill Farm

Gorley Hill

Gorley Common

Stuckton Rd

Rose Farm

The Merrie Thought

Broadhill Wood

BROADHILL LANE

Stuckton Farm PH

Seagers Farm

Hill Farm

Stuckton

Brooklands Farm

Fir Tree Farm

Flaxfields

Frogham

FROGHAM HILL

HYDE LANE

Hyde Copse

PENTONS HL

Hyde

Hyde CE Prim Sch

BLISSFORD HL

Hungerford Hill

Hungerford

Hungerford Copse

Dairy Farm

GORLEY LYNCH

CURLEY LYNCH

4

13

3

12

11

2

1

10

A   B   C

14   15   16

201
40

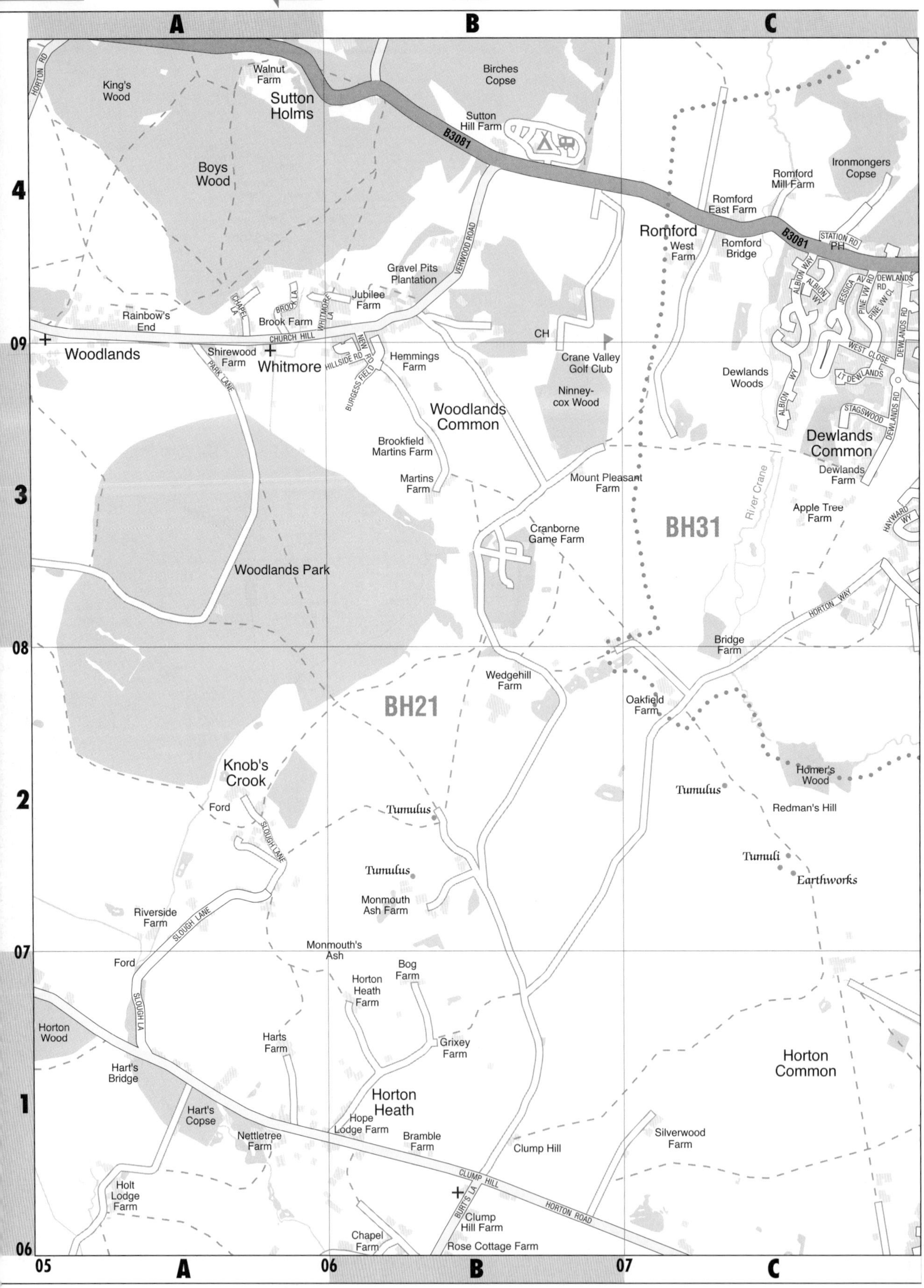
A
B
C
King's Wood
Walnut Farm
Sutton Holms
Birches Copse
Sutton Hill Farm
B3081
Boys Wood
Ironmongers Copse
Romford Mill Farm
Romford East Farm
Romford
West Farm
Romford Bridge
STATION RD
PH
Gravel Pits Plantation
VERWOOD ROAD
Jubilee Farm
Rainbow's End
Brook Farm
CHURCH HILL
CH
Woodlands
Shirewood Farm
Whitmore
Hemmings Farm
Crane Valley Golf Club
Dewlands Woods
Ninney-cox Wood
Woodlands Common
Dewlands Common
Brookfield Martins Farm
Dewlands Farm
Martins Farm
Mount Pleasant Farm
River Crane
Apple Tree Farm
BH31
Cranborne Game Farm
Woodlands Park
HORTON WAY
Bridge Farm
Wedgehill Farm
BH21
Oakfield Farm
Homer's Wood
Knob's Crook
Tumulus
Ford
Tumulus
Redman's Hill
Tumuli
Earthworks
Tumulus
Monmouth Ash Farm
Riverside Farm
SLOUGH LANE
Monmouth's Ash
Ford
Bog Farm
Horton Heath Farm
Horton Wood
Harts Farm
Grixey Farm
Horton Common
Hart's Bridge
Horton Heath
Hart's Copse
Hope Lodge Farm
Nettletree Farm
Bramble Farm
Clump Hill
Silverwood Farm
CLUMP HILL
Holt Lodge Farm
HORTON ROAD
Clump Hill Farm
Chapel Farm
Rose Cottage Farm
4
3
2
1
09
08
07
06
05
06
07

201
52

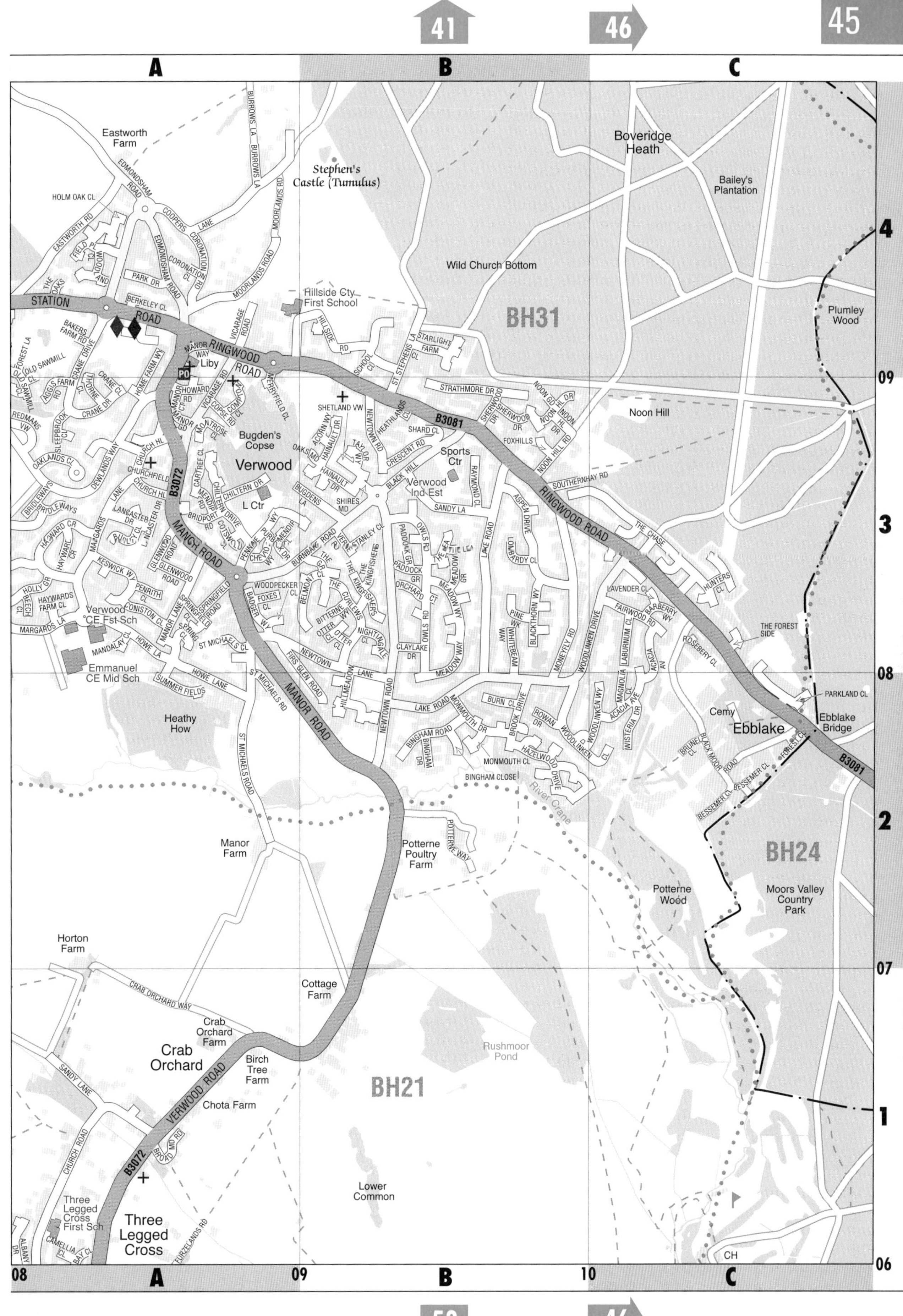

A   B   C

4

3

2

1

09

08

07

06

Eastworth Farm

HOLM OAK CL

Stephen's Castle (Tumulus)

Boveridge Heath

Bailey's Plantation

Plumley Wood

Wild Church Bottom

BH31

Hillside Cty First School

STATION

RINGWOOD ROAD

Verwood

Bugden's Copse

SHETLAND VW

B3081

Noon Hill

Sports Ctr

Verwood Ind Est

Southernhay Rd

RINGWOOD ROAD

THE CHASE

THE FOREST SIDE

PARKLAND CL

Ebblake Bridge

Ebblake

B3081

Cemy

BH24

Moors Valley Country Park

Potterne Wood

Verwood °CE Fst Sch

Emmanuel CE Mid Sch

Heathy How

MANOR ROAD

Potterne Poultry Farm

POTTERNE WAY

River Crane

Manor Farm

Horton Farm

Crab Orchard Farm

Cottage Farm

Crab Orchard

Birch Tree Farm

Chota Farm

VERWOOD ROAD

B3072

Rushmoor Pond

BH21

Lower Common

Three Legged Cross First Sch

Three Legged Cross

CH

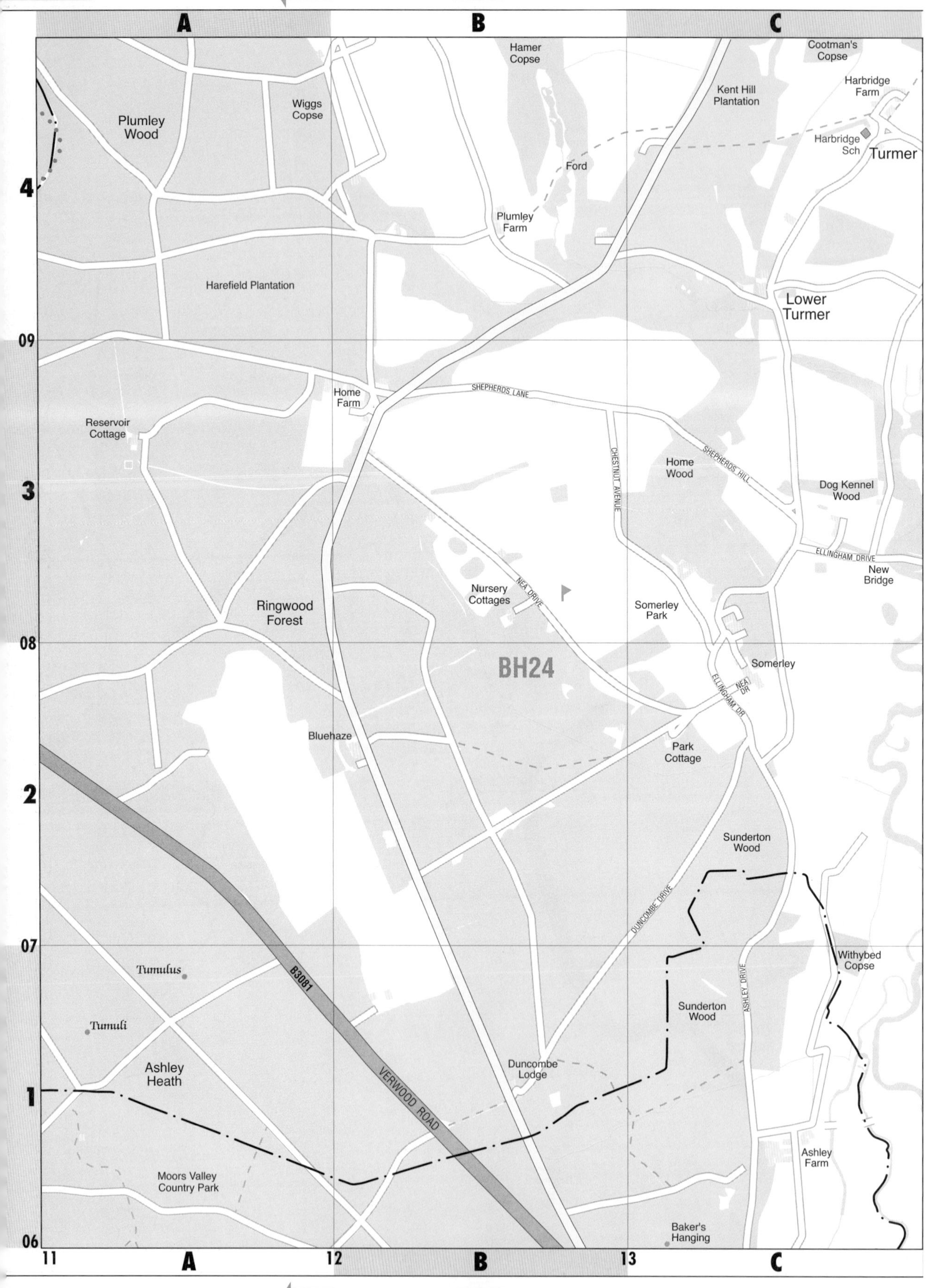

A   B   C

Cootman's Copse

Hamer Copse

Kent Hill Plantation

Harbridge Farm

Plumley Wood

Wiggs Copse

Ford

Harbridge Sch

Turmer

Plumley Farm

Harefield Plantation

Lower Turmer

09

Home Farm

SHEPHERDS LANE

Reservoir Cottage

CHESTNUT AVENUE

Home Wood

SHEPHERDS HILL

Dog Kennel Wood

3

ELLINGHAM DRIVE

New Bridge

Nursery Cottages

NEA DRIVE

Ringwood Forest

Somerley Park

BH24

08

Somerley

ELLINGHAM DR

Bluehaze

NEA DR

Park Cottage

2

Sunderton Wood

DUNCOMBE DRIVE

07

Tumulus

B3081

ASHLEY DRIVE

Withybed Copse

Tumuli

Sunderton Wood

Ashley Heath

Duncombe Lodge

1

VERWOOD ROAD

Ashley Farm

Moors Valley Country Park

Baker's Hanging

06

11   A   12   B   13   C

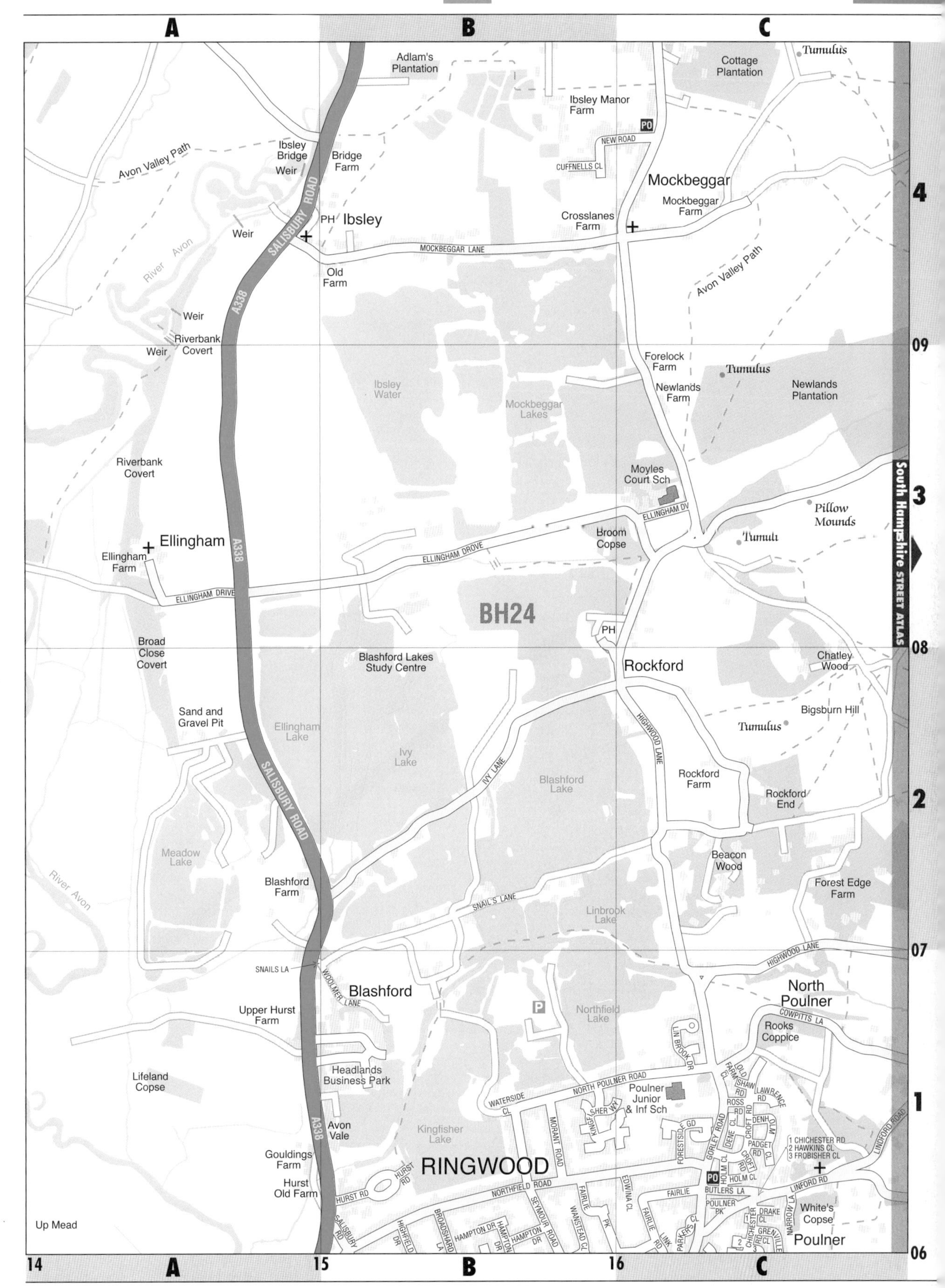

Adlam's Plantation

Cottage Plantation

Tumulus

Ibsley Manor Farm

PO

NEW ROAD

Mockbeggar

CUFFNELLS CL

Mockbeggar Farm

Avon Valley Path

Ibsley Bridge Weir

Bridge Farm

PH Ibsley

Crosslanes Farm

Weir

Old Farm

MOCKBEGGAR LANE

River Avon

Weir

Weir

Riverbank Covert

Ibsley Water

Mockbeggar Lakes

Forelock Farm

Newlands Farm

Tumulus

Newlands Plantation

Riverbank Covert

Moyles Court Sch

Ellingham

Ellingham Farm

A338

ELLINGHAM DRIVE

Broom Copse

Ellingham Dv

Pillow Mounds

Tumuli

ELLINGHAM DROVE

BH24

PH

Broad Close Covert

Blashford Lakes Study Centre

Rockford

Chatley Wood

Sand and Gravel Pit

Ellingham Lake

Ivy Lake

Blashford Lake

HIGHWOOD LANE

Rockford Farm

Bigsburn Hill

Tumulus

Rockford End

SALISBURY ROAD

IVY LANE

2

Meadow Lake

Blashford Farm

River Avon

SNAIL'S LANE

Linbrook Lake

Beacon Wood

Forest Edge Farm

HIGHWOOD LANE

SNAILS LA

WOODMELL LANE

Blashford

Upper Hurst Farm

Lifeland Copse

Headlands Business Park

P

Northfield Lake

North Poulner

COWPITTS LA

Rooks Coppice

LIN BROOK DR

A338

Avon Vale

Gouldings Farm

Hurst Old Farm

Kingfisher Lake

WATERSIDE CL

MORANT ROAD

NORTH POULNER ROAD

SHER W

SPINK...

Poulner Junior & Inf Sch

OLD FARM SHAW RD

ROSS RD

CREDI... RD

DENH...

LAWN...

LAWRENCE RD

GORLEY ROAD

FORESTSIDE GD

HOLM CL

PO

BUTLERS LA

POULNER PK

1 CHICHESTER RD
2 HAWKINS CL
3 FROBISHER CL

White's Copse

LINFORD ROAD

HARROW RD

LINFORD RD

Poulner

RINGWOOD

HURST RD

SALISBURY RD

HIGHFIELD DR

BROADSHARD LA

HAMPTON DR

HAMPTON DR

NORTHFIELD RD

SEYMOUR ROAD

WANSTEAD CL

FAIRLIE CL

EDWINA CL

FAIRLIE PK

FAIRLIE

POULNER LA

PARK RD

LINK

DRAKE CL

GRENVILLE...

CHICHESTER...

PADGET RD

HOLM CL

Up Mead

211
200

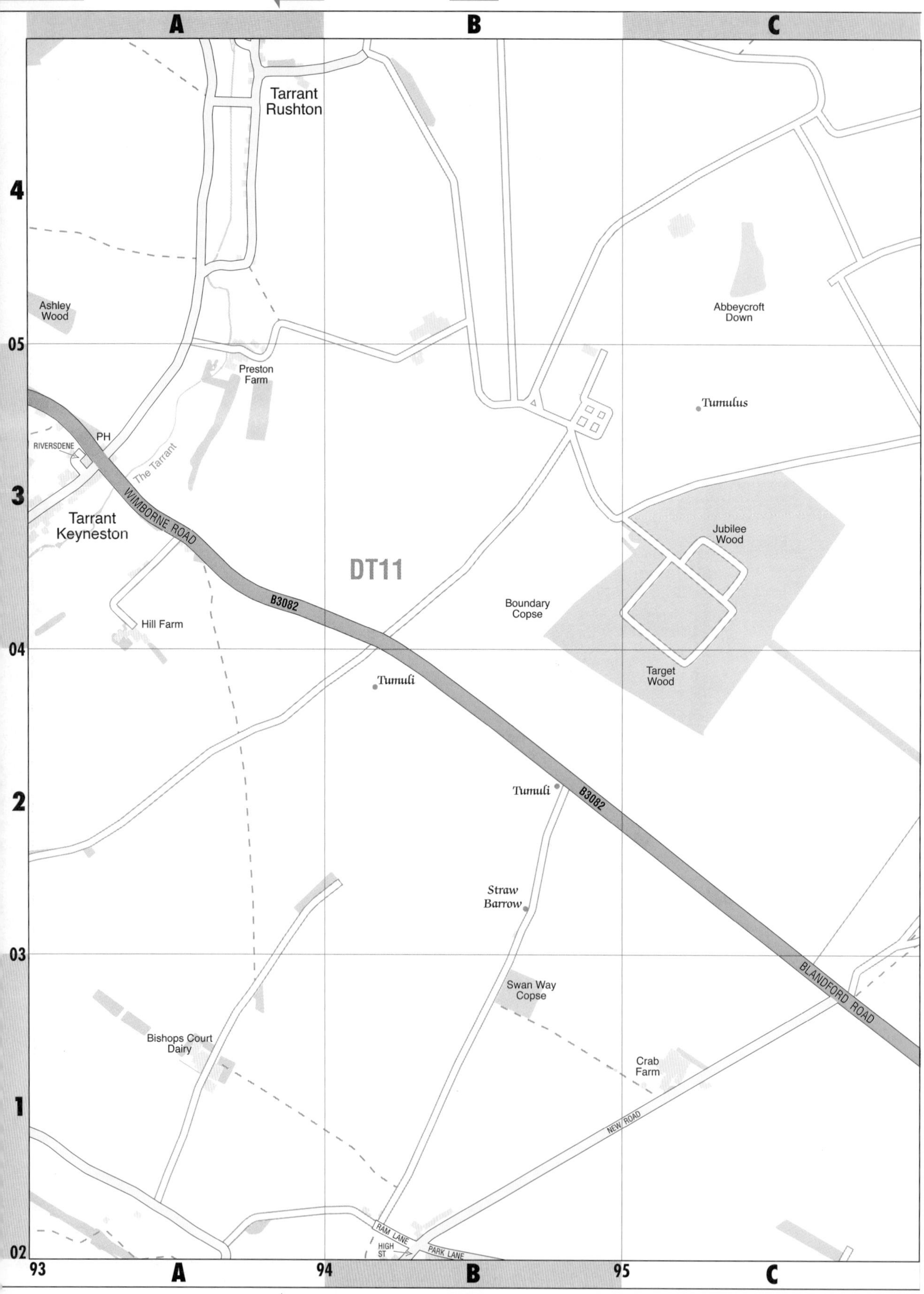
A
B
C
Tarrant
Rushton
4
Ashley
Wood
Abbeycroft
Down
05
Preston
Farm
Tumulus
PH
RIVERSDENE
The Tarrant
3
WIMBORNE ROAD
Tarrant
Keyneston
Jubilee
Wood
DT11
B3082
Boundary
Copse
Hill Farm
04
Target
Wood
Tumuli
2
Tumuli
B3082
Straw
Barrow
03
Swan Way
Copse
BLANDFORD ROAD
Bishops Court
Dairy
Crab
Farm
1
NEW ROAD
RAM LANE
HIGH
ST
PARK LANE
02
93
94
95

211
56

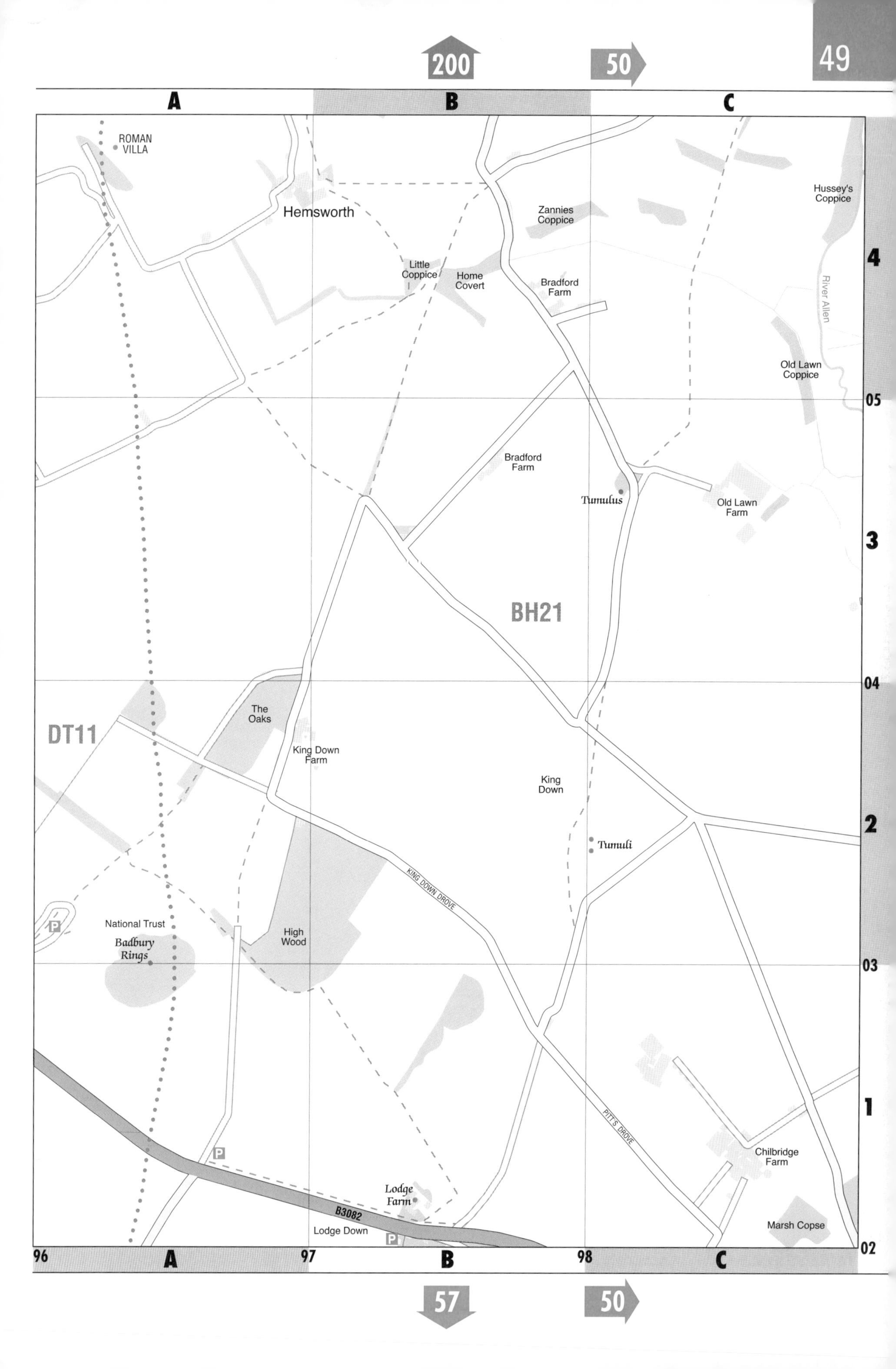

A
B
C

ROMAN VILLA

Hemsworth

Hussey's Coppice

Zannies Coppice

Little Coppice

Home Covert

Bradford Farm

River Allen

Old Lawn Coppice

4

05

Bradford Farm

Tumulus

Old Lawn Farm

3

BH21

04

The Oaks

King Down Farm

King Down

Tumuli

2

DT11

KING DOWN DROVE

National Trust

Badbury Rings

High Wood

PITT'S DROVE

03

1

Chilbridge Farm

Lodge Farm

B3082

Lodge Down

Marsh Copse

02

96
A
97
B
98
C
02

A **B** **C**

WITCHAMPTON LANE

High Lea Farm

High Lea Sch

EMLEY LANE

Clay Hill

4

WOODCUTTS LANE

B3078

Underwood Farm

05

Woodcutts Farm

Gardens

Close Copse

3

Hinton Mill Farm

Hinton Parva

Ashton Wood

Sweet Apple Copse

Gaunt's House

River Allen

CRANBORNE ROAD

Ashton Farm

BH21

04

Stanbridge
+

Barnsley Farm

Brach Copse

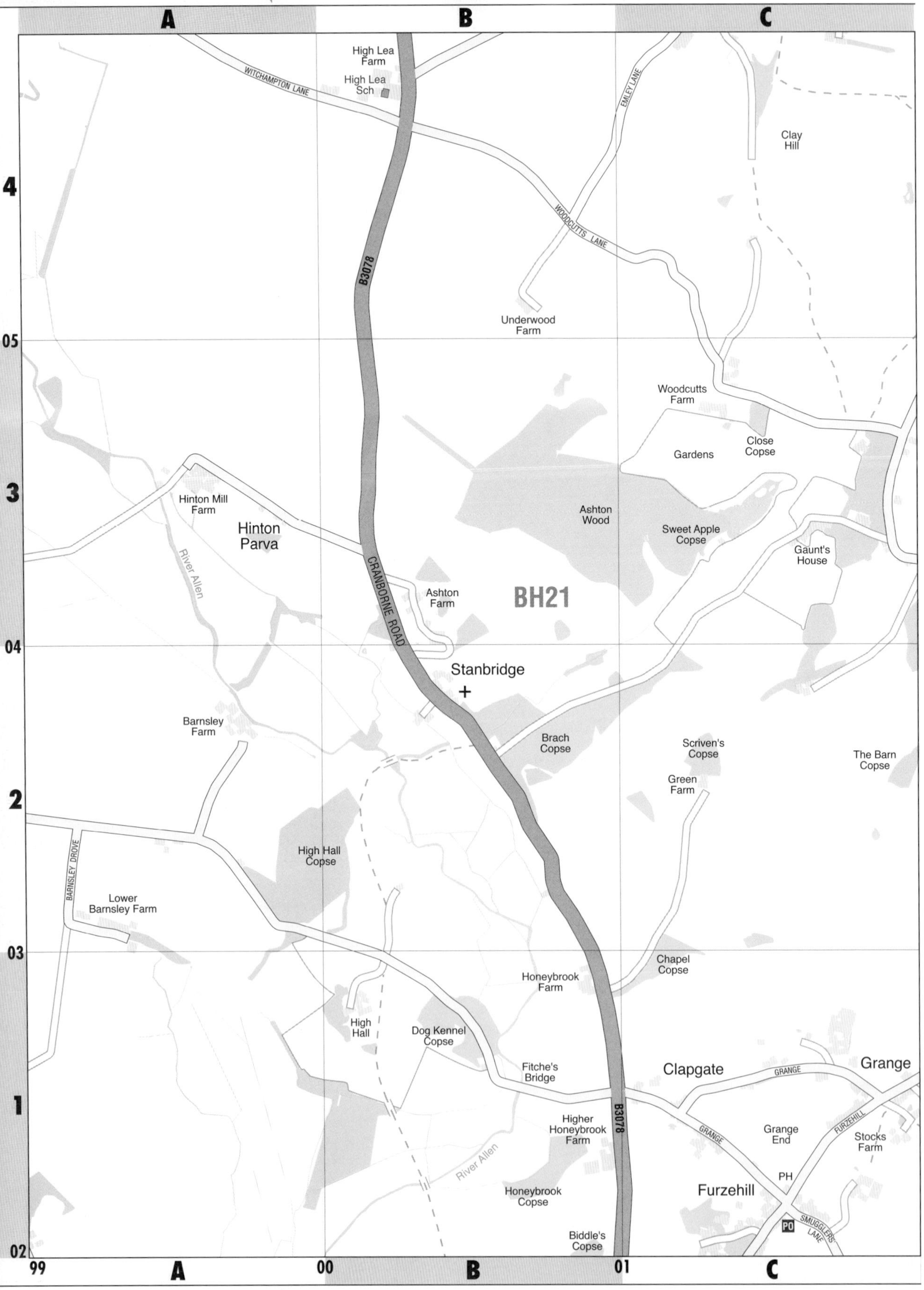

Scriven's Copse

The Barn Copse

2

Green Farm

BARNSLEY DROVE

High Hall Copse

Lower Barnsley Farm

03

Honeybrook Farm

Chapel Copse

High Hall

Dog Kennel Copse

1

Fitche's Bridge

Clapgate

GRANGE

Grange

B3078

Higher Honeybrook Farm

Grange End

GRANGE

FURZEHILL

Stocks Farm

PH

Honeybrook Copse

Furzehill

PO

SMUGGLERS LANE

02

Biddle's Copse

River Allen

99 **A** **00** **B** **01** **C**

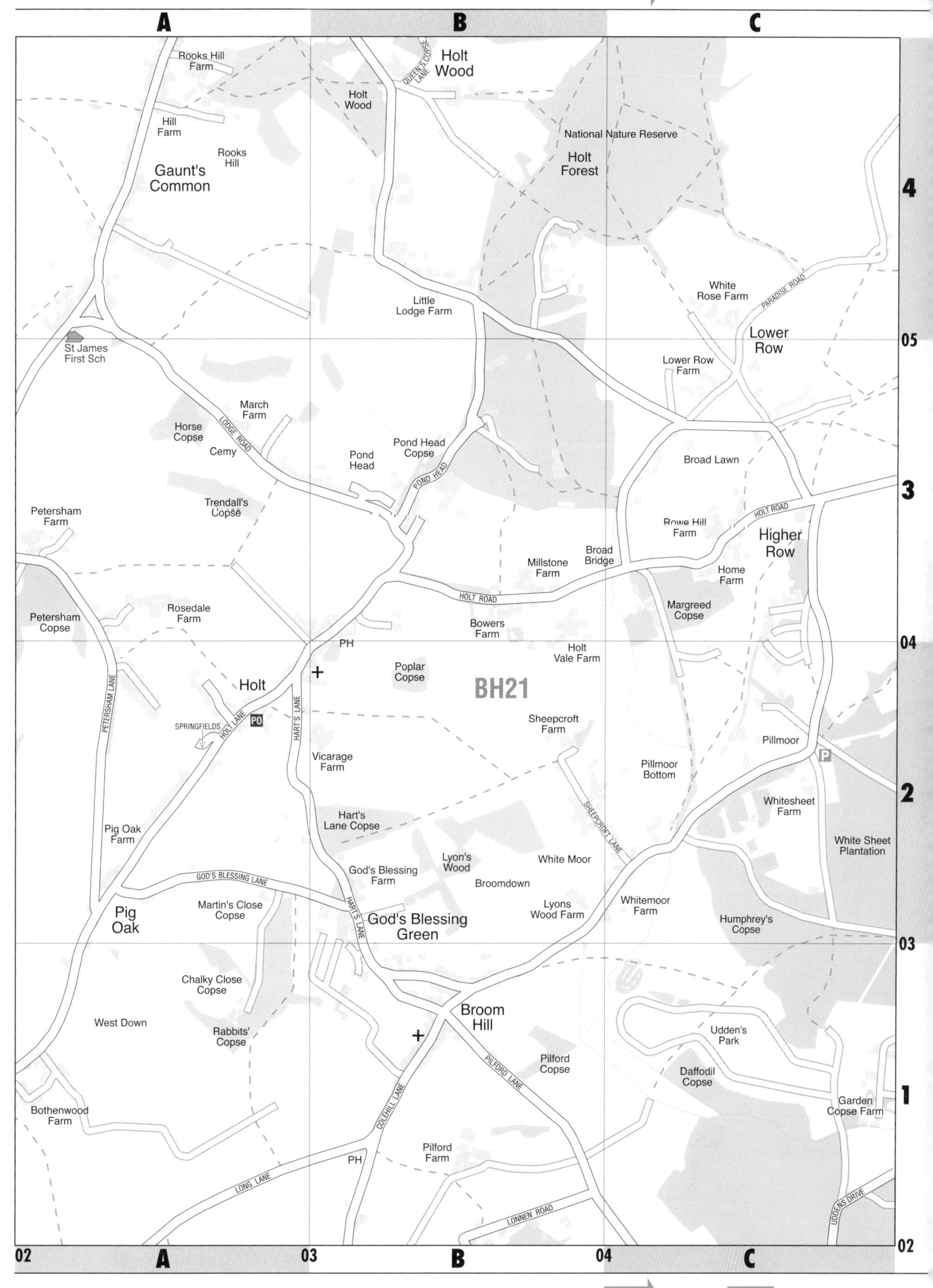

A
B
C

Rooks Hill Farm

Holt Wood

Holt Wood

QUEEN'S COPSE LANE

Hill Farm

National Nature Reserve

Rooks Hill

Holt Forest

Gaunt's Common

4

White Rose Farm

PARADISE ROAD

Little Lodge Farm

Lower Row

05

St James First Sch

Lower Row Farm

March Farm

Pond Head Copse

Broad Lawn

Horse Copse

Cemy

Pond Head

POND HEAD

Rowe Hill Farm

HOLT ROAD

Higher Row

3

Trendall's Copse

Petersham Farm

Broad Bridge

Millstone Farm

Home Farm

Petersham Copse

Rosedale Farm

PH

Bowers Farm

Margreed Copse

Holt Vale Farm

04

PETERSHAM LANE

Holt

+

Poplar Copse

BH21

SPRINGFIELDS

PO

HOLT LANE

HART'S LANE

Sheepcroft Farm

Pillmoor

P

Vicarage Farm

Pillmoor Bottom

Whitesheet Farm

2

Pig Oak Farm

Hart's Lane Copse

White Sheet Plantation

GOD'S BLESSING LANE

God's Blessing Farm

Lyon's Wood

White Moor

SHEEPCROFT LANE

Pig Oak

Martin's Close Copse

HART'S LANE

Broomdown

Lyons Wood Farm

Whitemoor Farm

Humphrey's Copse

God's Blessing Green

03

Chalky Close Copse

Udden's Park

West Down

Rabbits' Copse

+

Broom Hill

Pilford Copse

Daffodil Copse

Garden Copse Farm

1

Bothenwood Farm

COLEHILL LANE

PILFORD LANE

Pilford Farm

UDDENS DRIVE

PH

LONG LANE

LONNEN ROAD

02
A
03
B
04
C
02

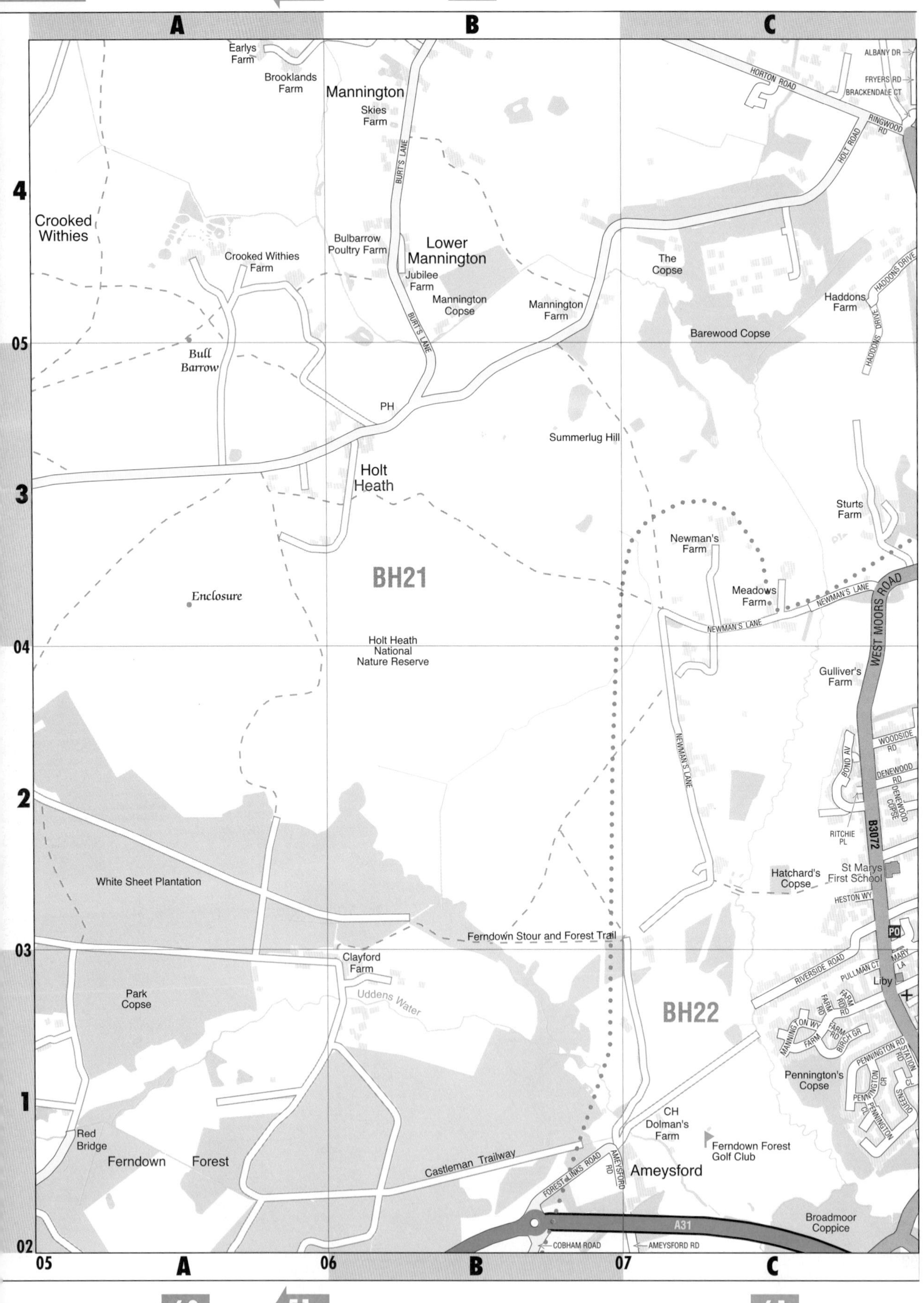

A **B** **C**

4

Crooked
Withies

Earlys
Farm

Brooklands
Farm

Mannington

Skies
Farm

HORTON ROAD

ALBANY DR

FRYERS RD
BRACKENDALE CT

RINGWOOD
RD

BURT'S LANE

Crooked Withies
Farm

Bulbarrow
Poultry Farm

Lower
Mannington

Jubilee
Farm

Mannington
Copse

Mannington
Farm

The
Copse

HADDONS DRIVE

HOLT ROAD

Haddons
Farm

05

Bull
Barrow

BURT'S LANE

Barewood Copse

PH

Holt
Heath

Summerlug Hill

Newman's
Farm

Sturts
Farm

3

BH21

Enclosure

Meadows
Farm

Newman's Lane

WEST MOORS ROAD

NEWMAN'S LANE

04

Holt Heath
National
Nature Reserve

Gulliver's
Farm

NEWMAN'S LANE

WOODSIDE
RD

POND AV

DENEWOOD
RD

DENEWOOD
COPSE

2

RITCHIE
PL

B3072

White Sheet Plantation

Hatchard's
Copse

St Marys
First School

HESTON WY

PO

03

Clayford
Farm

Ferndown Stour and Forest Trail

RIVERSIDE ROAD

PULLMAN CT

Liby

Uddens Water

BH22

MARY
LA

Park
Copse

MANNINGTON WY

FARM

BIRCH GR

FARM RD

FARMFORD

PENNINGTON RD

STATION RD

1

Red
Bridge

Ferndown   Forest

Castleman Trailway

CH
Dolman's
Farm

Ferndown Forest
Golf Club

Ameysford

Pennington's
Copse

PENNINGTON CT

PENNINGTON
CL

GR

FOREST LINKS ROAD

AMEYSFORD
RD

A31

Broadmoor
Coppice

02

COBHAM ROAD

AMEYSFORD RD

05 **A** **06** **B** **07** **C**

45
54

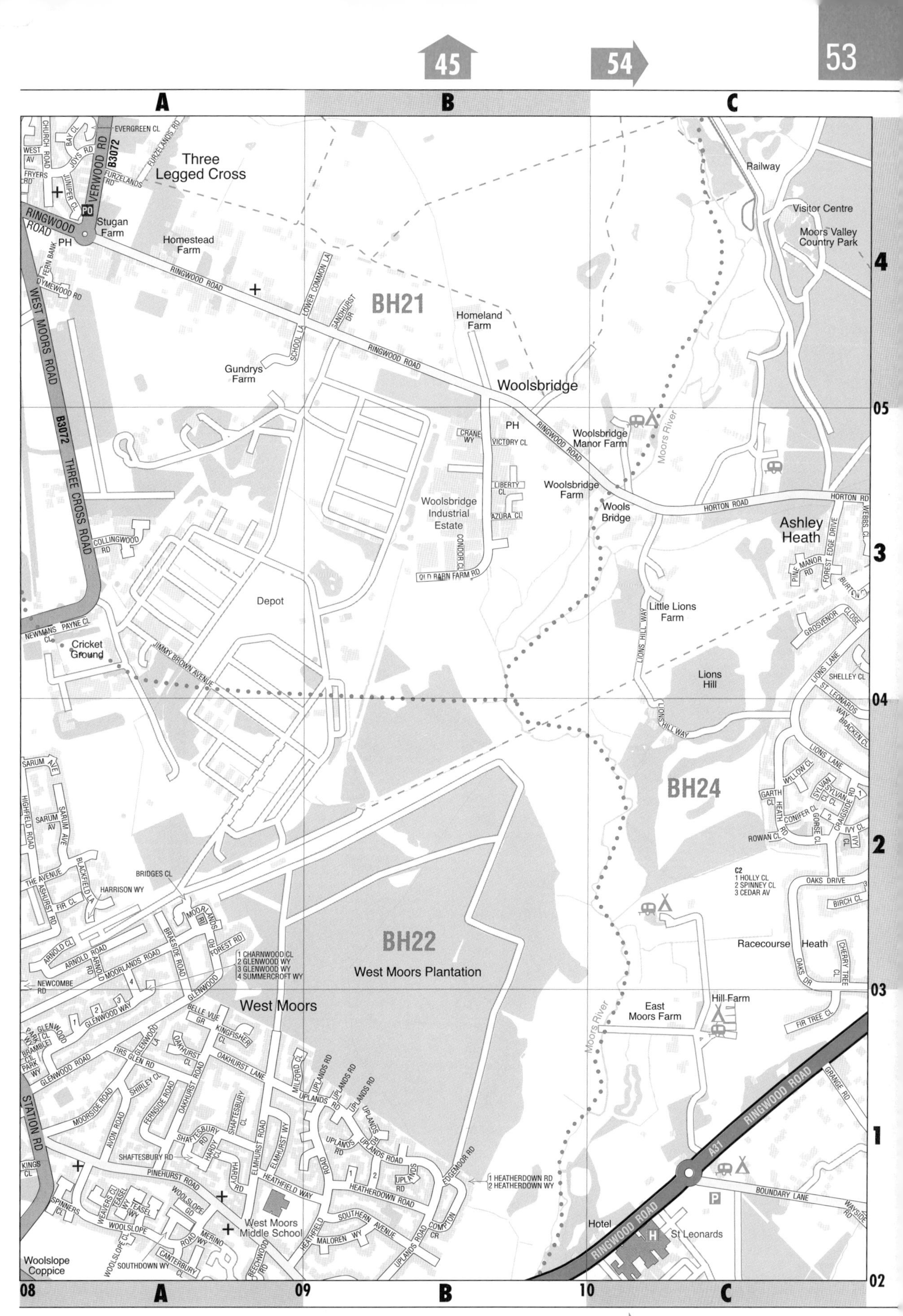
A
B
C
Three Legged Cross
Stugan Farm
Homestead Farm
Railway
Visitor Centre
Moors Valley Country Park
BH21
Homeland Farm
Gundrys Farm
Woolsbridge
Woolsbridge Manor Farm
Woolsbridge Farm
Wools Bridge
Woolsbridge Industrial Estate
Ashley Heath
Depot
Cricket Ground
Little Lions Farm
Lions Hill
BH24
Moors River
RINGWOOD ROAD
VERWOOD RD
B3072
WEST MOORS ROAD
THREE CROSS ROAD
HORTON ROAD
JIMMY BROWN AVENUE
BH22
West Moors Plantation
West Moors
Racecourse
Heath
East Moors Farm
Hill Farm
West Moors Middle School
Hotel
St Leonards
Woolslope Coppice
STATION RD
A31
BOUNDARY LANE
1 CHARNWOOD CL
2 GLENWOOD WY
3 GLENWOOD WY
4 SUMMERCROFT WY
C2
1 HOLLY CL
2 SPINNEY CL
3 CEDAR AV
1 HEATHERDOWN RD
2 HEATHERDOWN WY
08
09
10
02
03
04
05
1
2
3
4

61
54
62

A   B   C

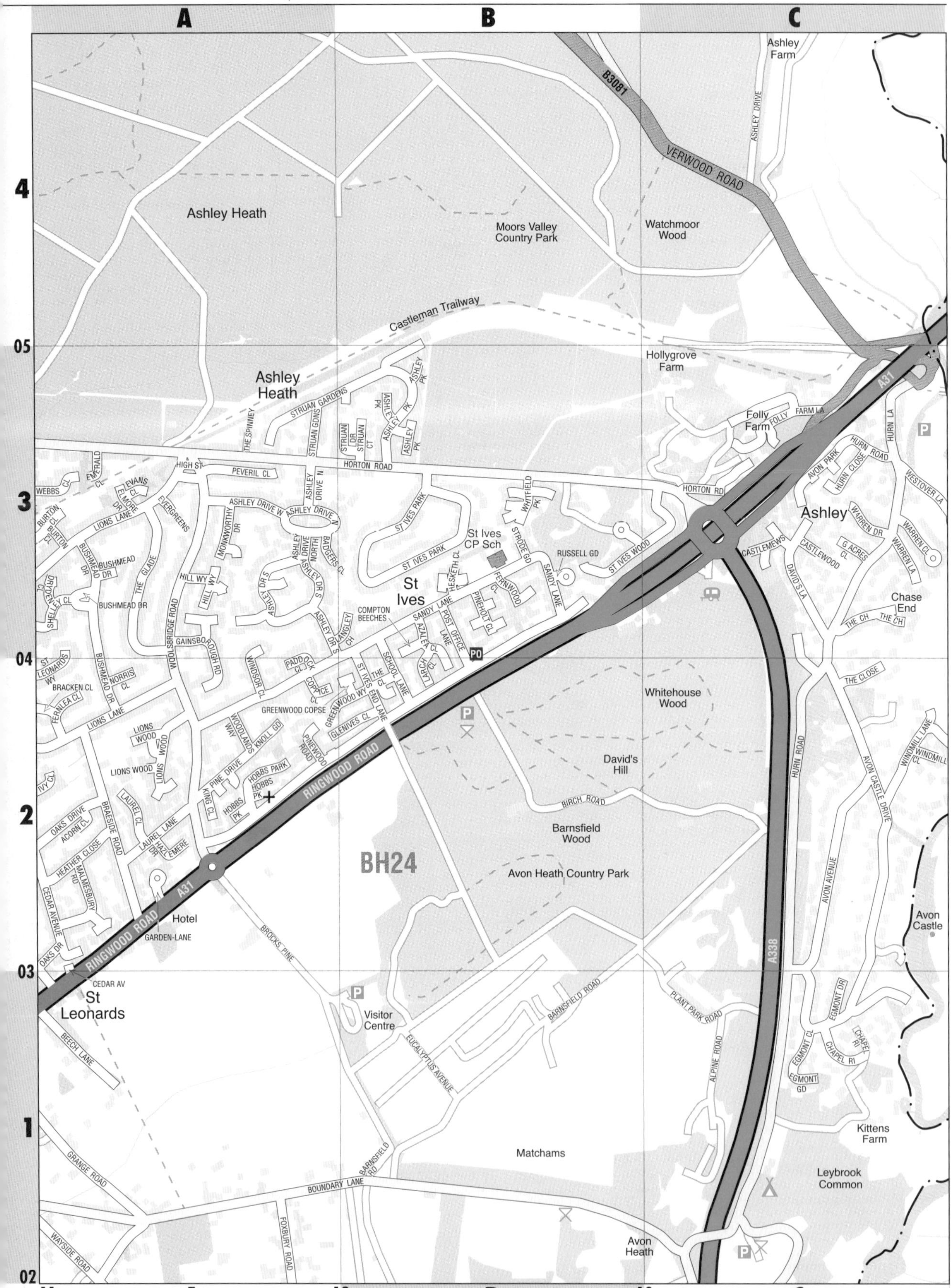

4

Ashley Heath

Moors Valley
Country Park

Watchmoor
Wood

Ashley
Farm

Castleman Trailway

Hollygrove
Farm

05

Ashley
Heath

Folly
Farm

3

High St
PEVERIL CL
HORTON ROAD

St Ives Park

St Ives
CP Sch

RUSSELL GD

HORTON RD

Ashley

Chase
End

St
Ives

RINGWOOD ROAD

PO

04

Whitehouse
Wood

David's
Hill

BIRCH ROAD

Barnsfield
Wood

2

BH24

Avon Heath Country Park

Avon
Castle

RINGWOOD ROAD

A31

Hotel
GARDEN-LANE

03

St
Leonards

CEDAR AV

Visitor
Centre

BARNSFIELD ROAD

A338

Kittens
Farm

Leybrook
Common

1

Matchams

Avon
Heath

BOUNDARY LANE

02

A4
1 LINDEN GD
2 MANOR GD

B3
1 HARRY BARROW CL
2 CHARING CL
3 WATERLOO WY
4 SOUTHFIELD MS
5 CROW ARCH LA
6 JOYCE DICKSON CL

B4
1 BEECHCROFT LA
2 BEECHCROFT MS
3 WANSTEAD CL

C3
1 OLD STACKS GD
2 THE CLOISTERS
3 SANDERLINGS
4 HOLMWOOD GARTH
5 ASHBURN GARTH
6 FOREST CT HILLS

C4
1 WHITEHART FIELDS
2 PIPERS ASH
3 RALEIGH CL
4 CUNNINGHAM CL

47

55

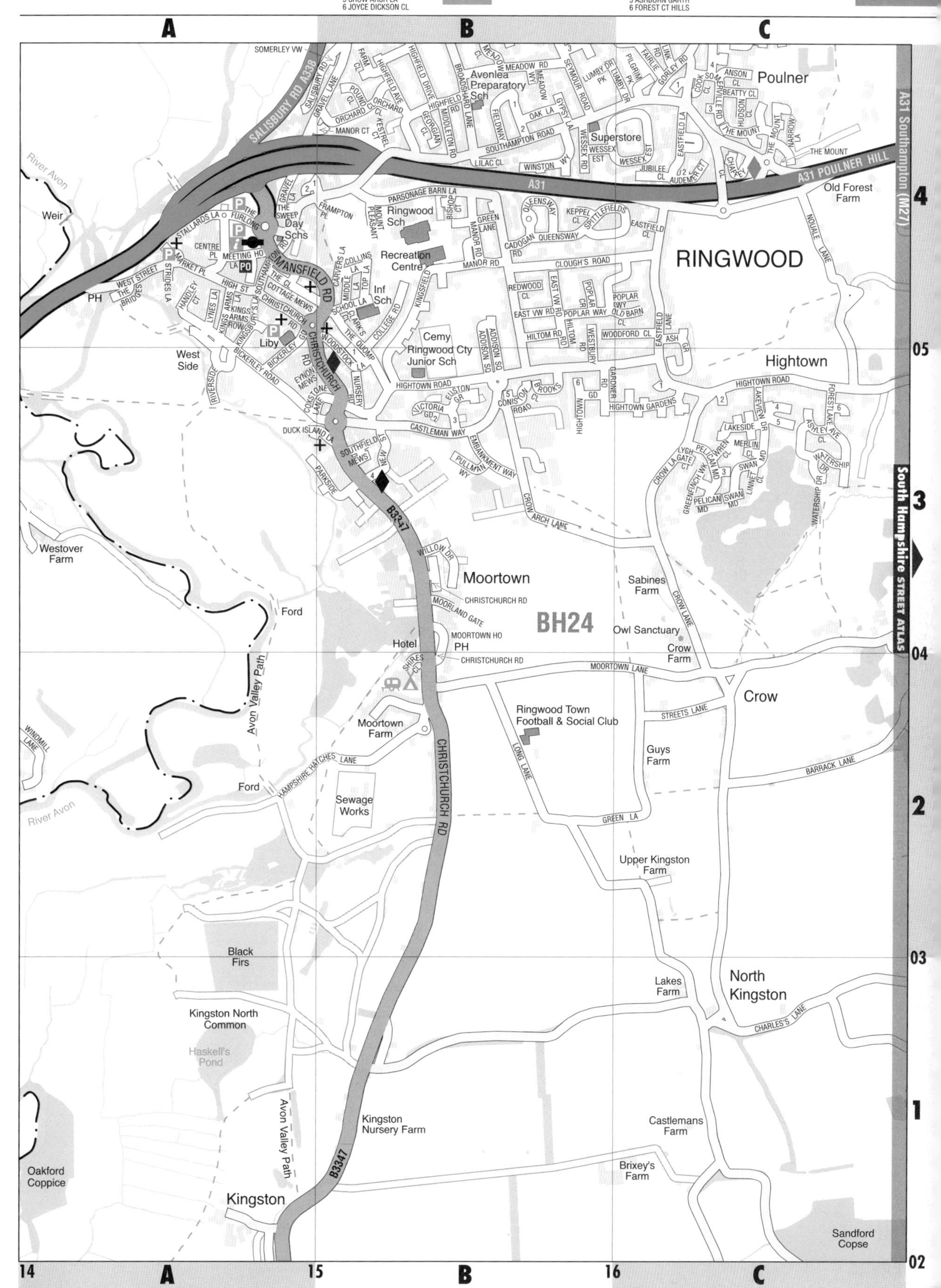

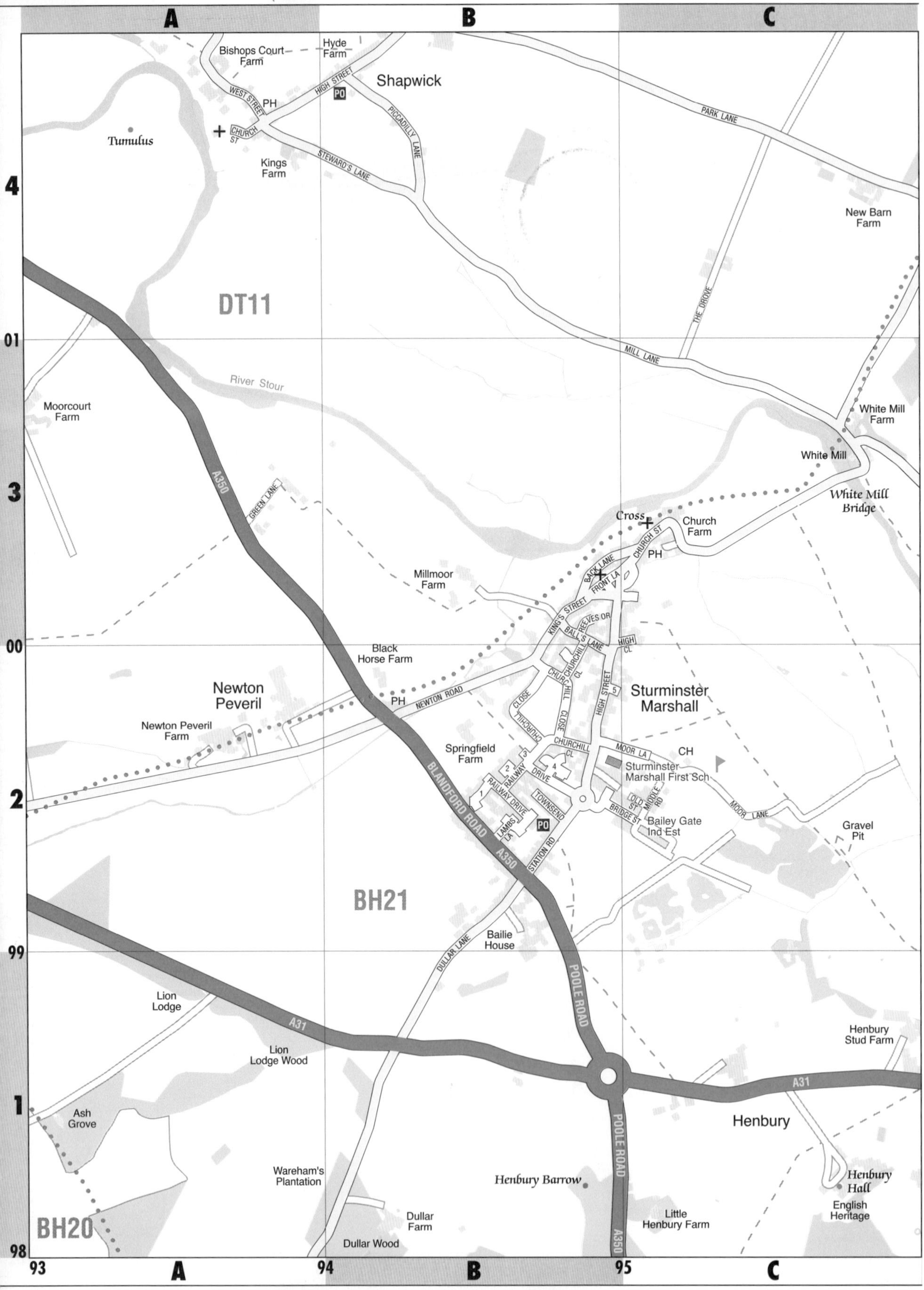

A　　　　B　　　　C

Bishops Court Farm
Hyde Farm
Shapwick
WEST STREET
PH
HIGH STREET
PO
PICCADILLY LANE
CHURCH ST
Kings Farm
STEWARD'S LANE
PARK LANE

4

Tumulus

New Barn Farm

DT11

THE DROVE

01

River Stour

MILL LANE

White Mill Farm

Moorcourt Farm

White Mill

3

GREEN LANE

Cross +
Church Farm
PH

White Mill Bridge

Millmoor Farm

BACK LANE
FRONT LA

KING'S STREET
REEVES DR
BALL'S LANE
HIGH CL

00

Black Horse Farm

CHURCHILL LANE
CHURCHILL CL
HIGH STREET

Sturminster Marshall

Newton Peveril

PH
NEWTON ROAD

THICKTHORN
CL

Newton Peveril Farm

Springfield Farm

CHURCHILL CLOSE
2
RAILWAY
1
RAILWAY DRIVE
4
MOOR LA
CH
Sturminster Marshall First Sch
MOOR LANE

2

BLANDFORD ROAD
A350

LAMBS LA
PO
TOWNSEND
OLD ST
MIDDLE ST
BRIDGE ST
Bailey Gate Ind Est
Gravel Pit

BH21

STATION RD

99

DULLAR LANE

Bailie House

POOLE ROAD

Lion Lodge

A31

Henbury Stud Farm

Lion Lodge Wood

A31

1

Ash Grove

Henbury

POOLE ROAD

BH20

Wareham's Plantation

Dullar Farm

Henbury Barrow

A350

Little Henbury Farm

Henbury Hall
English Heritage

Dullar Wood

93　　　A　　　94　　　B　　　95　　　C

B2
1 CHARBOROUGH WY
2 HAYCOCK WY
3 PARKELEA
4 TATTERSHALL GD
5 SHERIDEN WY

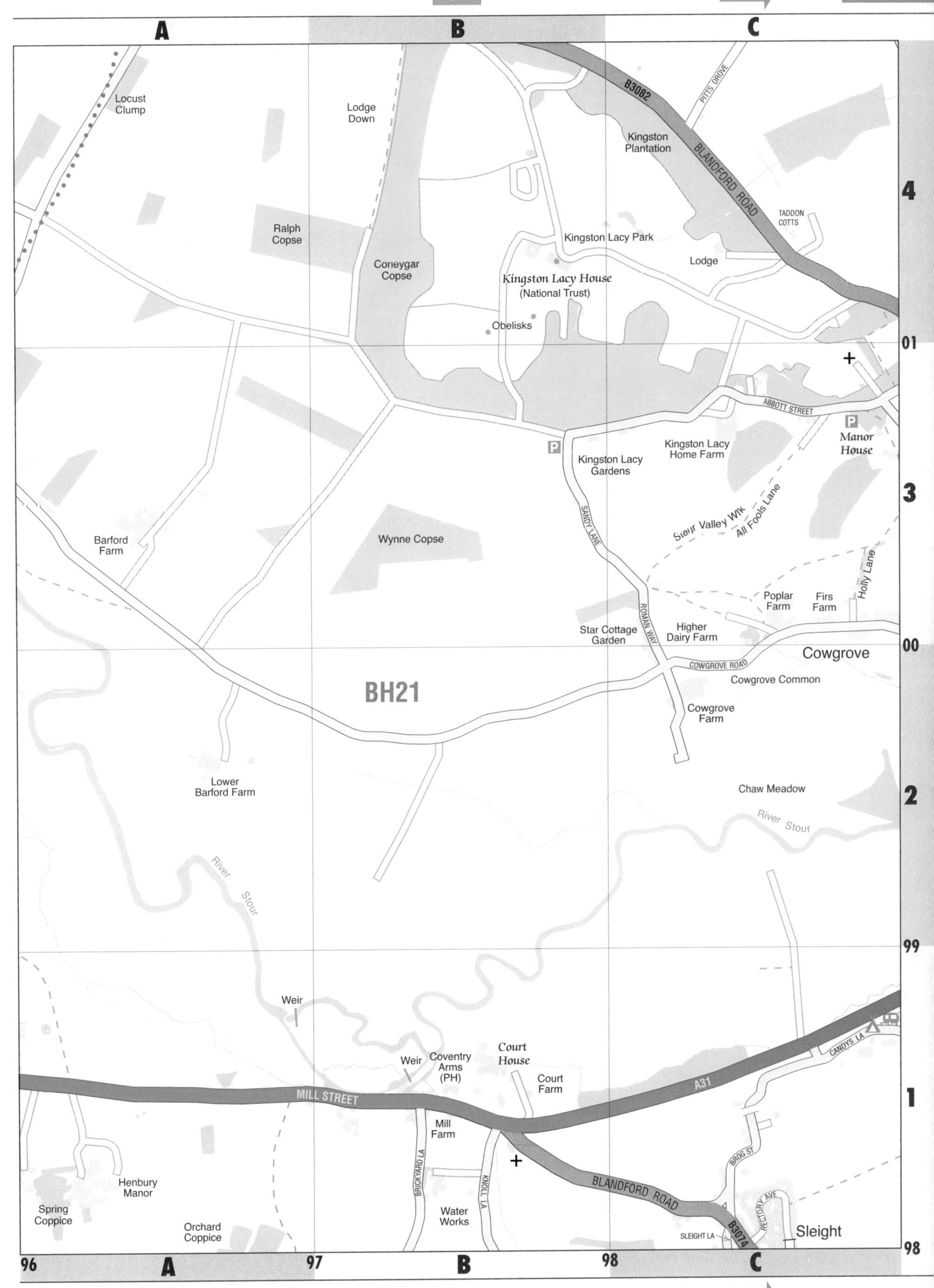
A
B
C
Locust Clump
Lodge Down
B3082
PITTS DROVE
Kingston Plantation
BLANDFORD ROAD
TADDON COTTS
Ralph Copse
Kingston Lacy Park
Lodge
Coneygar Copse
Kingston Lacy House
(National Trust)
Obelisks
01
ABBOTT STREET
Manor House
Kingston Lacy Home Farm
Kingston Lacy Gardens
SANDY LANE
4
3
Stour Valley Wlk
All Fools Lane
Barford Farm
Wynne Copse
Holly Lane
Poplar Farm
Firs Farm
ROMAN WAY
Star Cottage Garden
Higher Dairy Farm
00
Cowgrove
COWGROVE ROAD
Cowgrove Common
BH21
Cowgrove Farm
Lower Barford Farm
Chaw Meadow
2
River Stour
River Stour
99
Weir
Weir
Coventry Arms (PH)
Court House
Court Farm
CANDYS LA
A31
MILL STREET
1
Mill Farm
BRICKYARD LA
KNOLL LA
BLANDFORD ROAD
BROG ST
RECTORY AVE
Henbury Manor
Spring Coppice
Orchard Coppice
Water Works
SLEIGHT LA
B3074
Sleight
98
96
A
97
B
98
C

57
50

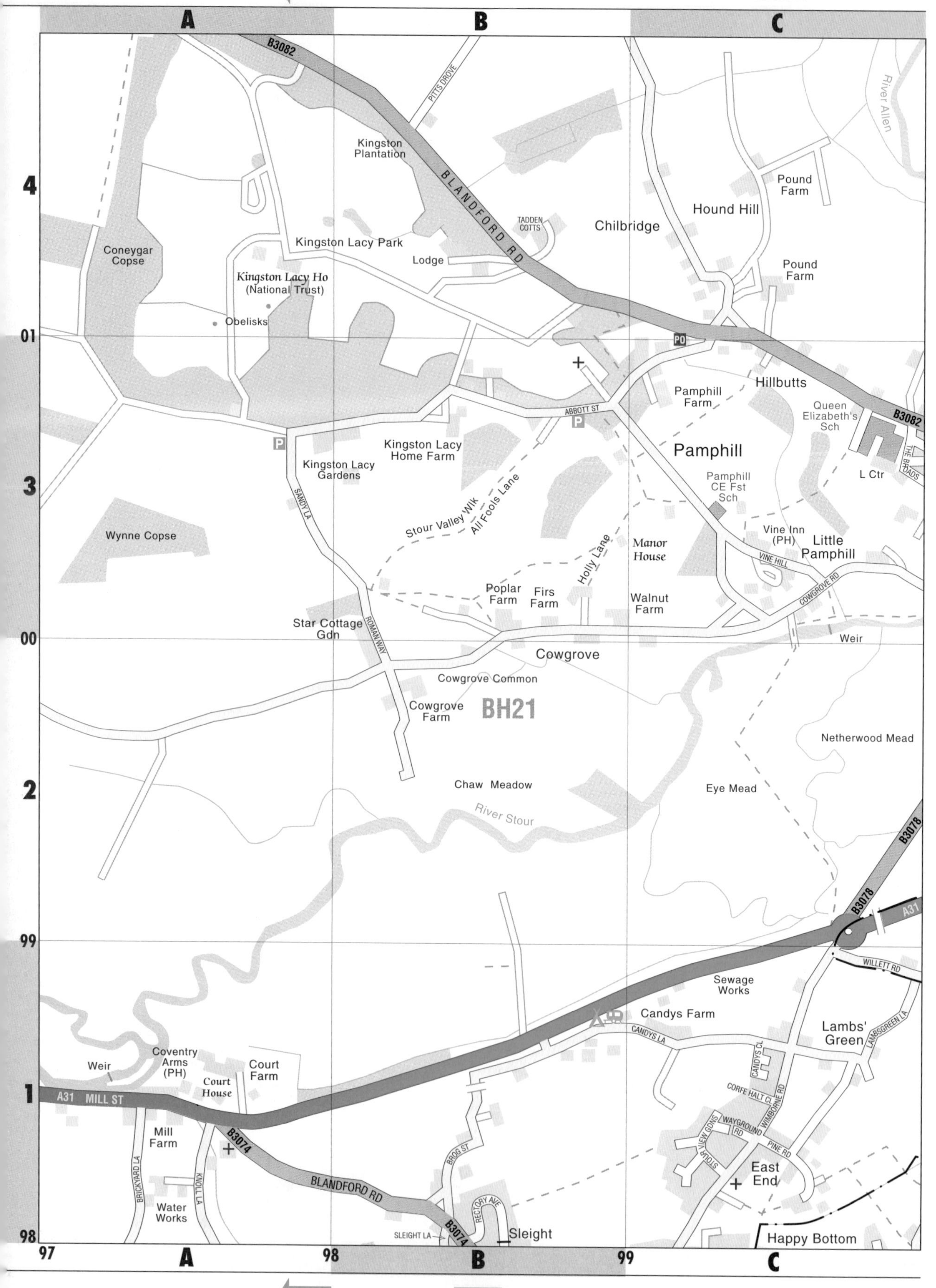
A
B
C
4
3
2
1
01
00
99
98
97
98
99
B3082
BLANDFORD RD
PITTS DROVE
Kingston Plantation
TADDEN COTTS
Chilbridge
Hound Hill
Pound Farm
Pound Farm
River Allen
Coneygar Copse
Kingston Lacy Park
Lodge
Kingston Lacy Ho
(National Trust)
Obelisks
PO
Hillbutts
Pamphill Farm
Queen Elizabeth's Sch
B3082
THE BROADS
ABBOTT ST
Kingston Lacy Home Farm
Kingston Lacy Gardens
SANDY LA
Pamphill
Pamphill CE Fst Sch
L Ctr
Wynne Copse
Stour Valley Wlk
All Fools Lane
Holly Lane
Manor House
Vine Inn (PH)
Little Pamphill
VINE HILL
COWGROVE RD
Poplar Farm
Firs Farm
Walnut Farm
Star Cottage Gdn
ROMAN WAY
Weir
Cowgrove
Cowgrove Common
Cowgrove Farm
BH21
Netherwood Mead
Chaw Meadow
Eye Mead
River Stour
B3078
B3078
A31
WILLETT RD
Sewage Works
Candys Farm
CANDYS LA
Lambs' Green
LAMBSGREEN LA
CANDYS CL
Weir
Coventry Arms (PH)
Court House
Court Farm
A31 MILL ST
CORFE HALT CL
WIMBORNE RD
WAYGROUND RD
STOUR VIEW GDNS
PINE RD
Mill Farm
B3074
BLANDFORD RD
BROG ST
East End
BRICKYARD LA
KNOLL LA
Water Works
RECTORY AVE
B3074
SLEIGHT LA
Sleight
Happy Bottom

57
86

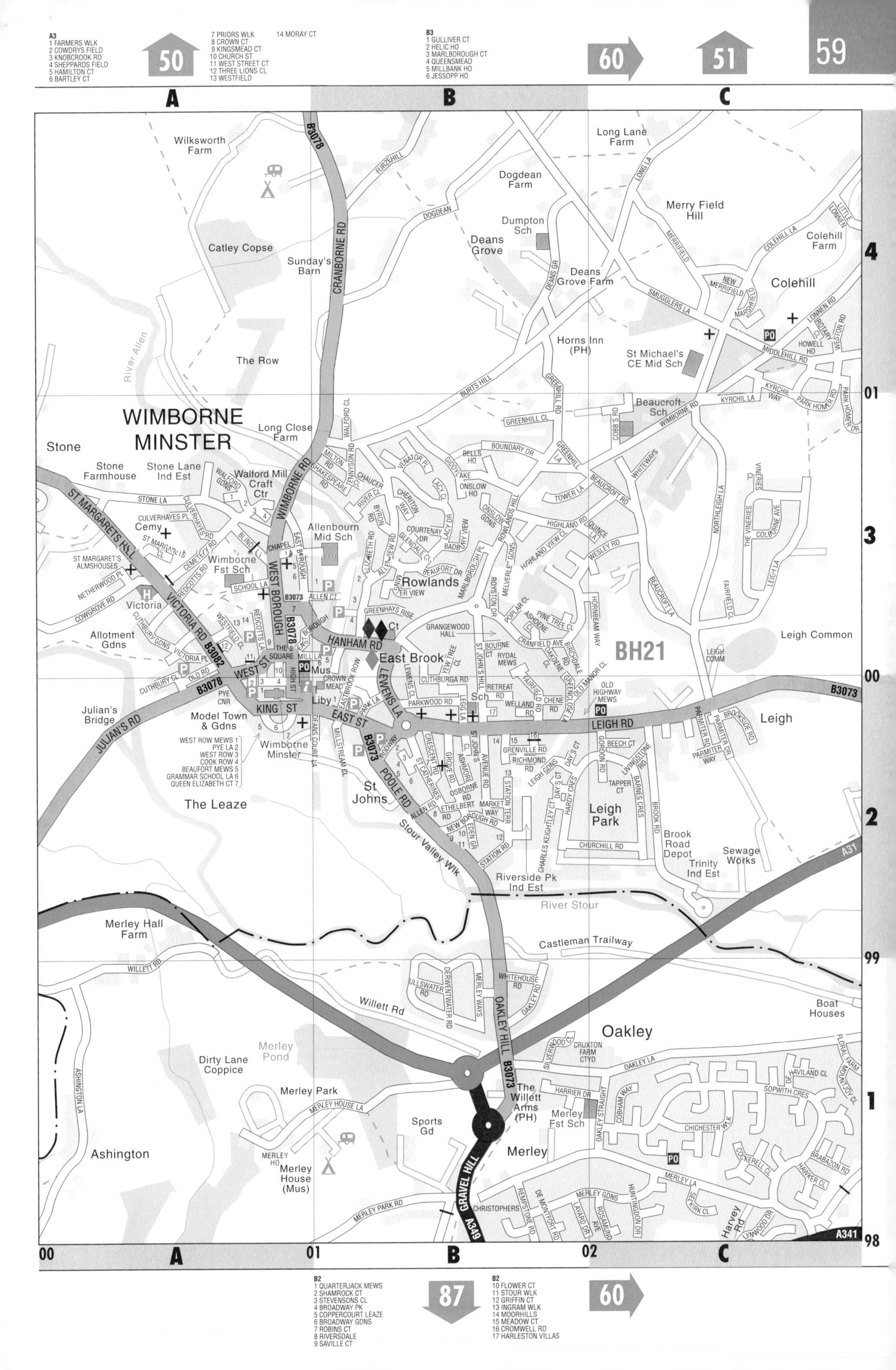
59
50
60
51
87
60
A3
1 FARMERS WLK
2 COWDRYS FIELD
3 KNOBCROOK RD
4 SHEPPARDS FIELD
5 HAMILTON CT
6 BARTLEY CT
7 PRIORS WLK
8 CROWN CT
9 KINGSMEAD CT
10 CHURCH ST
11 WEST STREET CT
12 THREE LIONS CL
13 WESTFIELD
14 MORAY CT
B3
1 GULLIVER CT
2 HELIC HO
3 MARLBOROUGH CT
4 QUEENSMEAD
5 MILLBANK HO
6 JESSOPP HO
A
B
C
4
01
3
00
2
99
1
98
00
01
02
WIMBORNE MINSTER
BH21
Wilksworth Farm
Catley Copse
Sunday's Barn
The Row
River Allen
Long Close Farm
Stone
Stone Farmhouse
Stone Lane Ind Est
Walford Mill Craft Ctr
Allenbourn Mid Sch
Cemy
Wimborne Fst Sch
Victoria
Allotment Gdns
Julian's Bridge
Model Town & Gdns
Wimborne Minster
The Leaze
Mus
Liby
Ct
East Brook
Rowlands
St Johns
Stour Valley Wlk
Riverside Pk Ind Est
River Stour
Castleman Trailway
Merley Hall Farm
Willett Rd
Merley Pond
Dirty Lane Coppice
Merley Park
Sports Gd
Merley House (Mus)
Ashington
The Willett Arms (PH)
Merley Fst Sch
Merley
Oakley
Boat Houses
Long Lane Farm
Dogdean Farm
Dumpton Sch
Deans Grove
Deans Grove Farm
Horns Inn (PH)
Merry Field Hill
Colehill Farm
Colehill
St Michael's CE Mid Sch
Beaucroft Sch
Leigh Common
Leigh
Leigh Park
Brook Road Depot
Trinity Ind Est
Sewage Works
B3078
B3073
B3082
A31
A341
A349
CRANBORNE RD
WIMBORNE RD
WEST BOROUGH
ST MARGARETS HILL
VICTORIA RD
JULIAN'S RD
WEST ST
KING ST
EAST ST
HANHAM RD
LEVENS LA
POOLE RD
LEIGH RD
OAKLEY HILL
GRAVEL HILL
WIMBORNE RD
BURTS HILL
SMUGGLERS LA
OAKLEY LA
MERLEY LA
MERLEY HOUSE LA
MERLEY PARK RD
WILLETT RD
ASHINGTON LA
B2
1 QUARTERJACK MEWS
2 SHAMROCK CT
3 STEVENSONS CL
4 BROADWAY PK
5 COPPERCOURT LEAZE
6 BROADWAY GDNS
7 ROBINS CT
8 RIVERSDALE
9 SAVILLE CT
B2
10 FLOWER CT
11 STOUR WLK
12 GRIFFIN CT
13 INGRAM WLK
14 MOORHILLS
15 MEADOW CT
16 CROMWELL RD
17 HARLESTON VILLAS
WEST ROW MEWS 1
PYE LA 2
WEST ROW 3
COOK ROW 4
BEAUFORT MEWS 5
GRAMMAR SCHOOL LA 6
QUEEN ELIZABETH CT 7

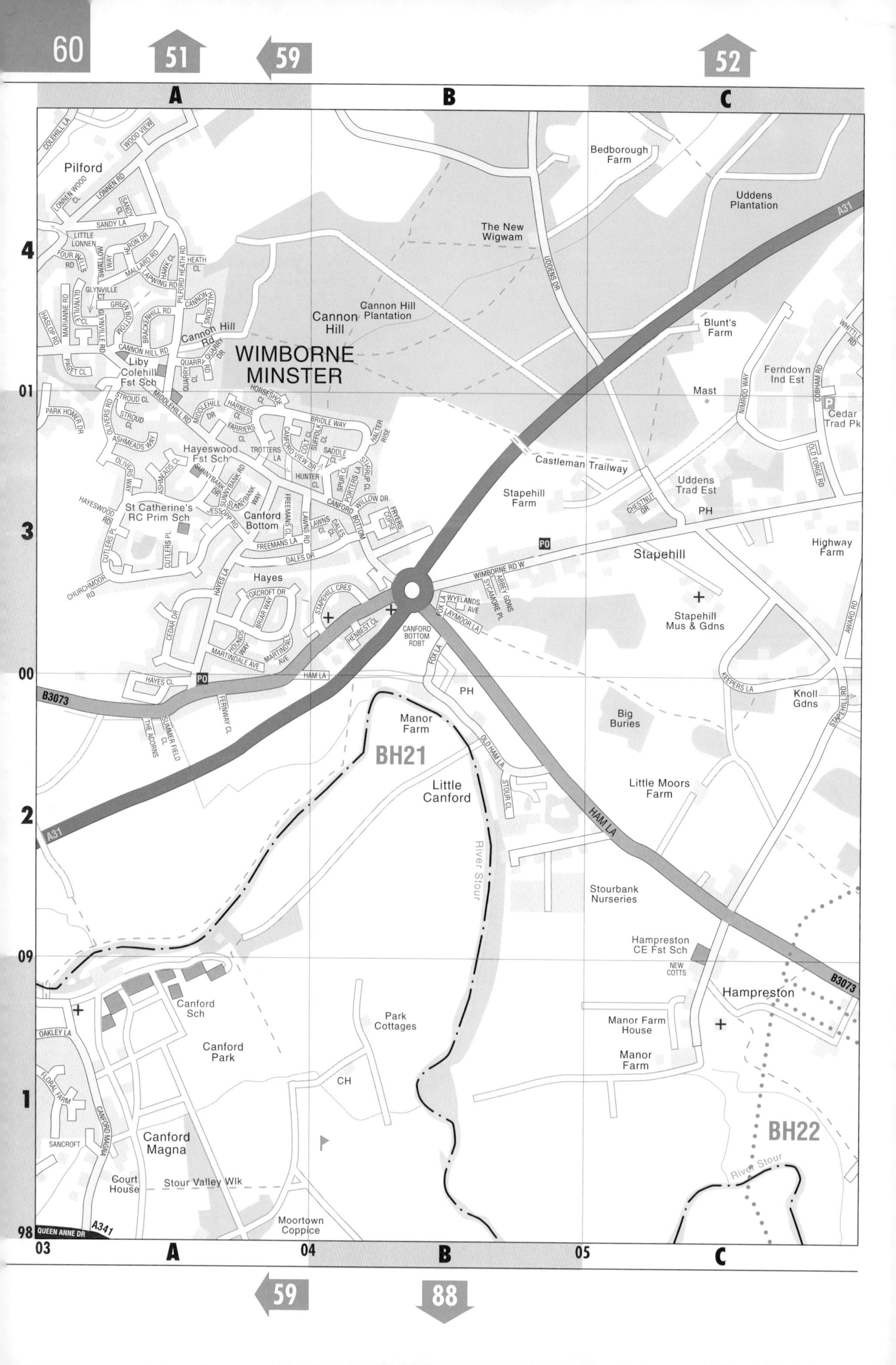

A
B
C

Pilford

COLEHILL LA
WOOD VIEW
LONNEN WOOD CL
LONNEN RD
SANDY RD
SANDY LA

LITTLE LONNEN
FOUR WELLS RD
HERON DR
MOTLINS WAY
MALLARD RD
LAPWING RD
PILFORD HEATH RD
HEATH CL

MARIANNE RD
GLYNVILLE CT
GLYNVILLE RD
GREEN BOTTOM
BRACKENHILL RD
SNOW TRK
CANNON CL

HASLOP RD
PAGET CL
GLYNVILLE CL
CANNON HILL RD
QUARRY CL
QUARRY LA

Liby Colehill Fst Sch

Cannon Hill Rd

Bedborough Farm

The New Wigwam

Cannon Hill Plantation

Cannon Hill

WIMBORNE MINSTER

Uddens Plantation

A31

4

PARK HOMER DR
OLIVERS RD
STROUD CL
STROUD LA
MIDDLEHILL RD
MIDDLEHILL DR
ASHMEADS WAY
OLIVERS WAY
ASHMEADS CL

HORSESHOE
HARNESS CL
FARRIERS
BRIDLE WAY
COLT CL
SUFFOLK CL
SADDLE CL
HALTER RISE

Hayeswood Fst Sch

HAYESWOOD RD
CUTLERS PL
CUTLERS CL

St Catherine's RC Prim Sch

SHINYBANK DR
SUNNYBANK WAY
JESSOPP RD
SUNNYBANK
TROTTERS LA
CANFORD VIEW DR
HUNTER CL
SPUR CL
PORTLES CL
STIRRUP CL
CANFORD BOTTOM
WILLOW DR
LAWNS RD
DALES RD
FRYERS COPSE

Canford Bottom

CHURCHMOOR RD
HAYES CL
HOLLANDS WAY
BRIAR WAY
FOXCROFT DR
CEDAR DR
STAPEHILL CRES
HENBEST CL

Hayes

Blunt's Farm

Mast

Ferndown Ind Est

NIMROD WAY
COBHAM RD
WHITE RD

P Cedar Trad Pk

Castleman Trailway

Stapehill Farm

Uddens Trad Est

PH

CHESTNUT GR

01

3

MARTINDALE AVE
MARTINDALE AVE
HAYES CL
HAM LA
PO
FENWAY CL
THE ACORNS
SUMMER FIELD

P0

WIMBORNE RD W
WYELANDS AVE
LAYMOOR LA
ABBEY GDNS
SYCAMORE PL

CANFORD BOTTOM RDBT

FOX LA

Stapehill

Stapehill Mus & Gdns

Highway Farm

AWARD RD
STAPEHILL RD

00

B3073

PO

PH

Manor Farm

OLD HAM LA
STOUR CL

Big Buries

Little Moors Farm

KEEPERS LA

Knoll Gdns

2

A31

BH21

Little Canford

River Stour

HAM LA

Stourbank Nurseries

Hampreston CE Fst Sch

NEW COTTS

Hampreston

B3073

09

OAKLEY LA

Canford Sch

Park Cottages

Manor Farm House

Manor Farm House

1

FLORAL FARM
SANCROFT
CANFORD MAGNA

Canford Park

Canford Magna

CH

BH22

River Stour

Court House

Stour Valley Wlk

98

QUEEN ANNE DR
A341

Moortown Coppice

A
04
B
05
C

03

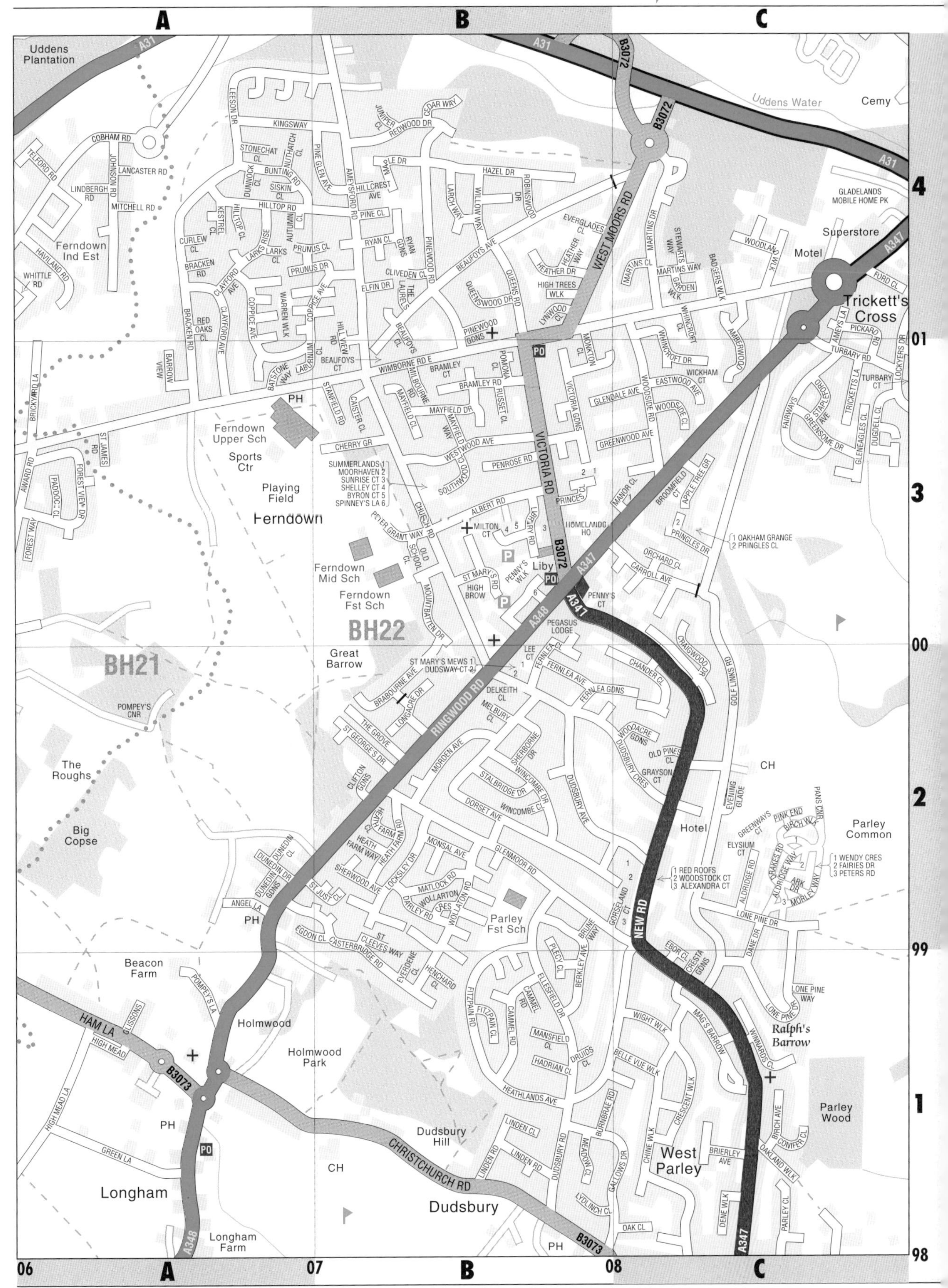

52
62
53
A
B
C
Uddens Plantation
Uddens Water
Cemy
Ferndown Ind Est
Gladelands Mobile Home Pk
Superstore
Motel
Trickett's Cross
Ferndown Upper Sch
Sports Ctr
Playing Field
Ferndown
Ferndown Mid Sch
Ferndown Fst Sch
BH22
BH21
Great Barrow
Pompey's Cnr
The Roughs
Big Copse
Hotel
Parley Common
Parley Fst Sch
Beacon Farm
Holmwood
Holmwood Park
Dudsbury Hill
Dudsbury
Longham
Longham Farm
West Parley
Ralph's Barrow
Parley Wood
Ringwood Rd
Victoria Rd
West Moors Rd
Wimborne Rd E
New Rd
Christchurch Rd
Ham La
Golf Links Rd
A31
A347
A348
B3072
B3073
06
07
08
98
99
00
01
1
2
3
4
89
62

A
B
C

St Leonard's Bridge
H
St Leonards
White Ranch
Grange Estate
PINEHURST RD
UPLANDS RD
ABBEY RD
MONKS CL
ABBOTS
ASHLEY
PRIORY RD
RINGWOOD RD
A31
WAYSIDE RD
FOXBURY RD
St Leonard's Farm
PRIORY GDNS
POL
A347
Palmers Ford Farm
BH24
Trickett's Cross

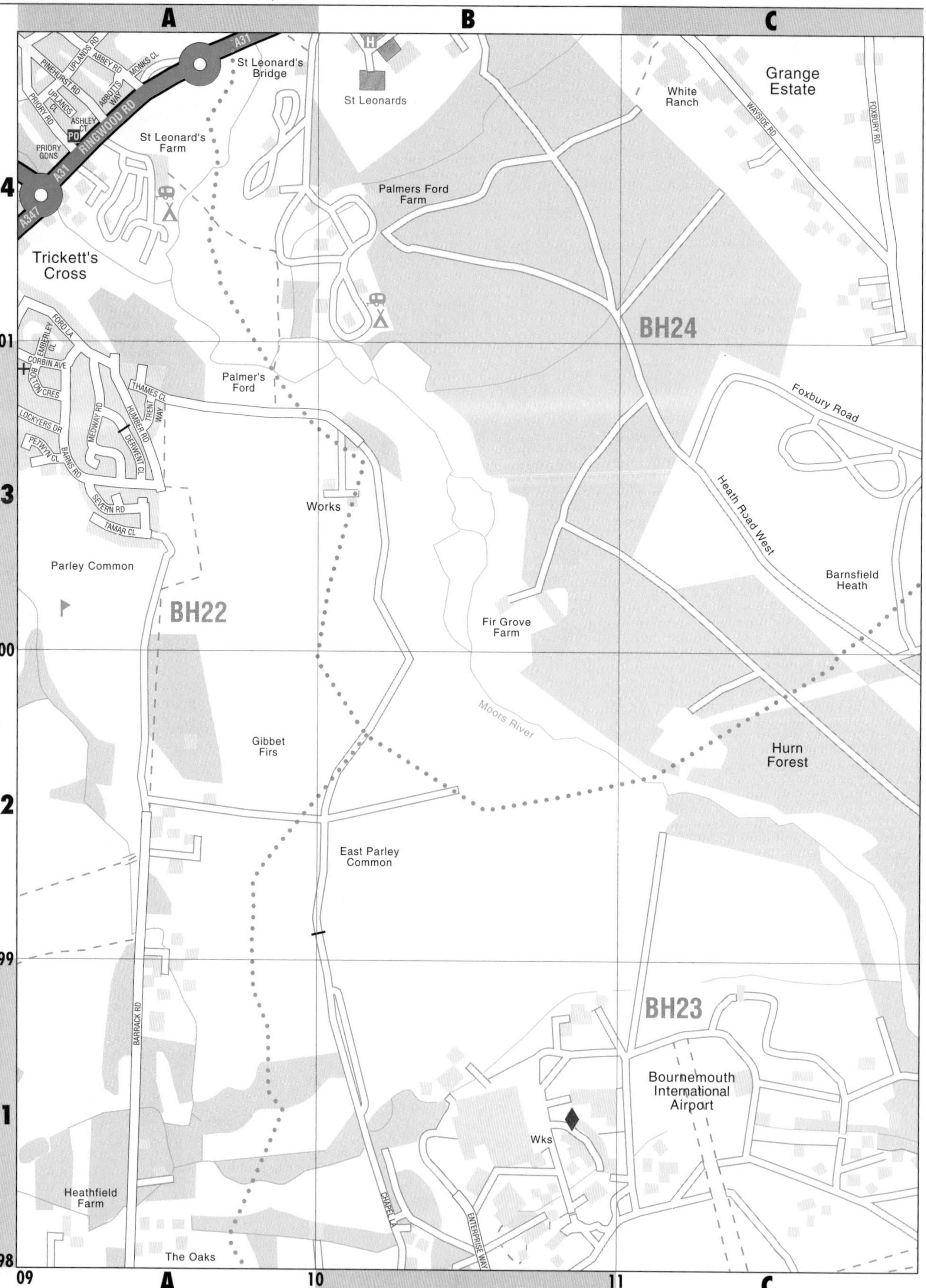

4

FORD LA
EMBERLEY CL
CORBIN AVE
BOLTON CRES
LOCKYERS DR
PETWYN CL
BARNS RD
MEDWAY RD
THAMES CL
TRENT WAY
HUMBER RD
DERWENT CL
SEVERN RD
TAMAR CL
Palmer's Ford
Foxbury Road

01

Works
Heath Road West
Barnsfield Heath

3

Parley Common
BH22
Fir Grove Farm

00

Moors River
Hurn Forest

Gibbet Firs

2

East Parley Common

BARRACK RD

99

BH23

1

Bournemouth International Airport
Wks

Heathfield Farm
CHAPEL LA
ENTERPRISE WAY

98

The Oaks

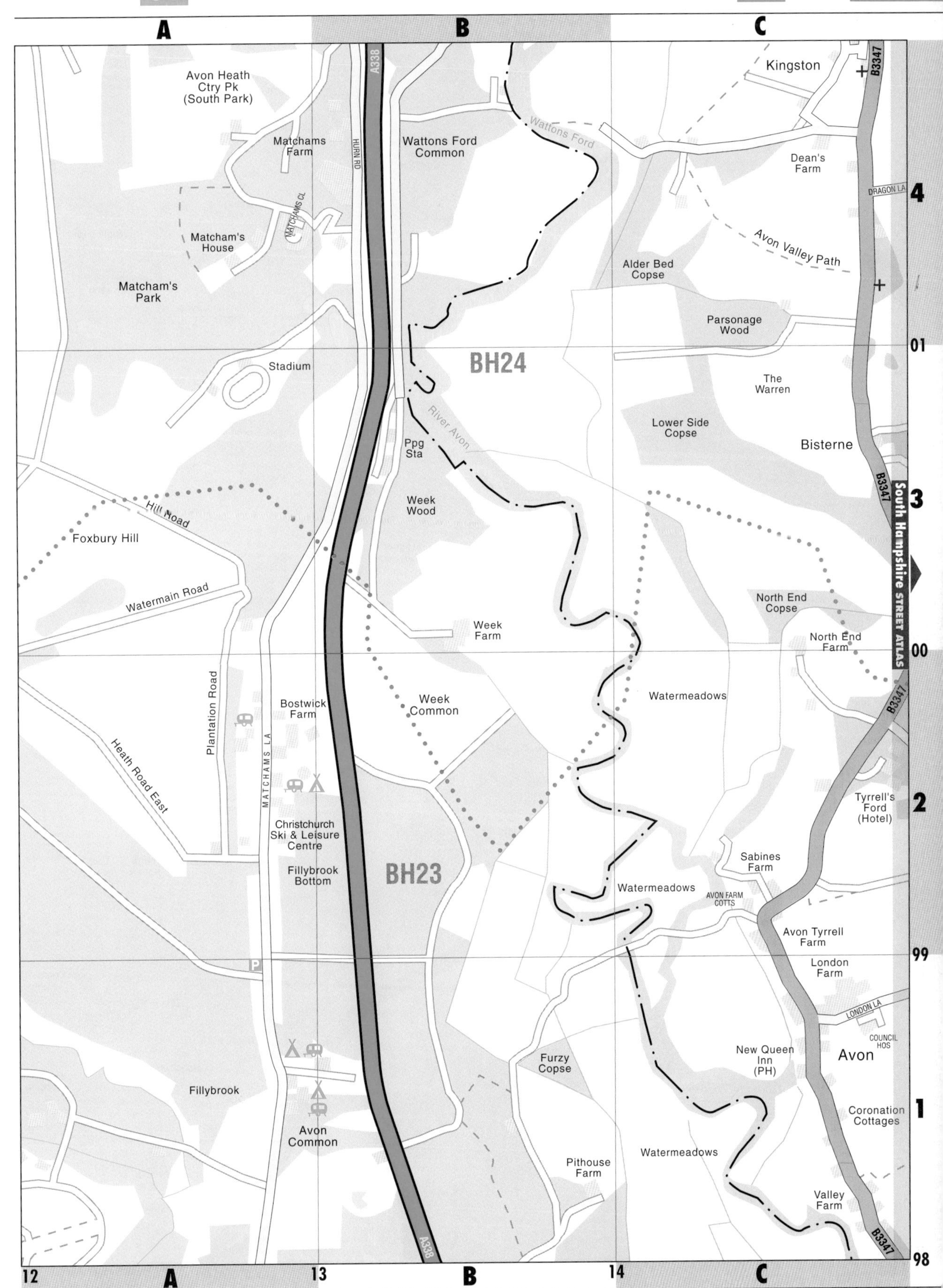

A B C

Avon Heath Ctry Pk (South Park)

Matchams Farm

MATCHAMS CL

Matcham's House

Matcham's Park

Wattons Ford Common

Wattons Ford

Kingston

Dean's Farm

DRAGON LA

4

Avon Valley Path

Alder Bed Copse

Parsonage Wood

01

BH24

The Warren

Bisterne

Lower Side Copse

B3347

South Hampshire STREET ATLAS

Stadium

River Avon

HURN RD

Ppg Sta

Week Wood

3

Hill Road

Foxbury Hill

Watermain Road

Week Farm

North End Copse

North End Farm

00

Plantation Road

MATCHAMS LA

Bostwick Farm

Week Common

Watermeadows

B3347

Heath Road East

Christchurch Ski & Leisure Centre

Tyrrell's Ford (Hotel)

2

BH23

Sabines Farm

Fillybrook Bottom

Watermeadows

AVON FARM COTTS

Avon Tyrrell Farm

London Farm

99

P

LONDON LA

COUNCIL HOS

Furzy Copse

New Queen Inn (PH)

Avon

Fillybrook

Coronation Cottages

1

Avon Common

Pithouse Farm

Watermeadows

Valley Farm

B3347

98

12 A 13 B 14 C

202

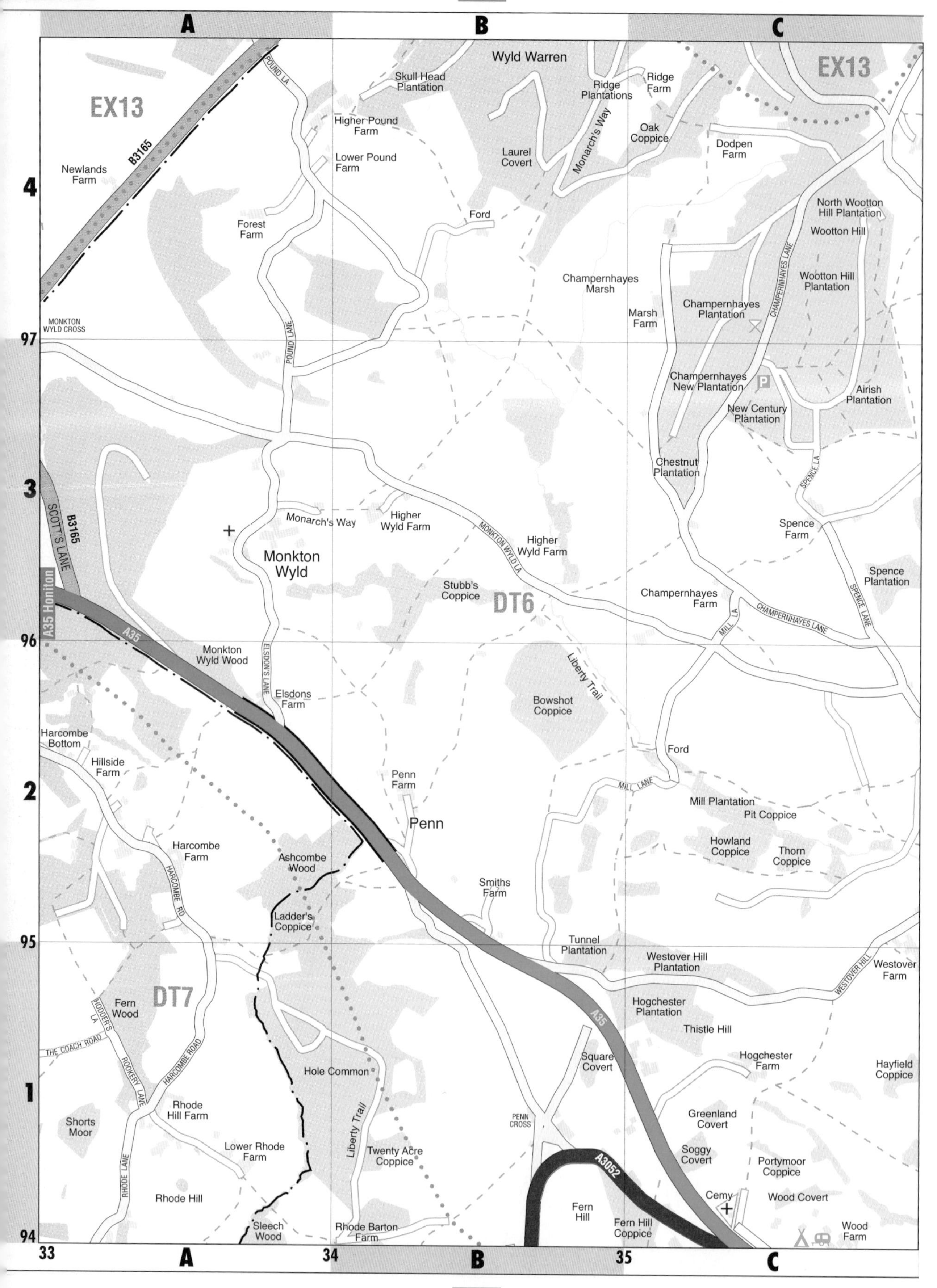
A
B
C
Wyld Warren
EX13
Skull Head Plantation
Ridge Plantations
Ridge Farm
EX13
POUND LA
Higher Pound Farm
Monarch's Way
Oak Coppice
Dodpen Farm
B3165
Newlands Farm
Lower Pound Farm
Laurel Covert
4
Forest Farm
Ford
North Wootton Hill Plantation
Wootton Hill
Wootton Hill Plantation
Champernhayes Marsh
CHAMPERNHAYES LANE
Marsh Farm
Champernhayes Plantation
MONKTON WYLD CROSS
POUND LANE
97
Champernhayes New Plantation
P
Airish Plantation
New Century Plantation
Chestnut Plantation
SPENCE LA
3
SCOTT'S LANE
B3165
Monarch's Way
Higher Wyld Farm
Spence Farm
MONKTON WYLD LA
Higher Wyld Farm
Monkton Wyld
Spence Plantation
Stubb's Coppice
DT6
Champernhayes Farm
A35 Honiton
MILL LA
CHAMPERNHAYES LANE
SPENCE LANE
A35
96
Monkton Wyld Wood
ELSDON'S LANE
Liberty Trail
Elsdons Farm
Bowshot Coppice
Harcombe Bottom
Ford
Hillside Farm
Penn Farm
MILL LANE
2
Mill Plantation
Pit Coppice
Penn
Harcombe Farm
Ashcombe Wood
Howland Coppice
Thorn Coppice
HARCOMBE RD
Smiths Farm
Ladder's Coppice
95
Tunnel Plantation
Westover Hill Plantation
Westover Farm
WESTOVER HILL
DT7
Fern Wood
HODDER'S LA
Hogchester Plantation
A35
Thistle Hill
THE COACH ROAD
HARCOMBE ROAD
Square Covert
Hogchester Farm
Hole Common
Hayfield Coppice
1
ROOKERY LANE
Rhode Hill Farm
Greenland Covert
Shorts Moor
PENN CROSS
Liberty Trail
Lower Rhode Farm
Twenty Acre Coppice
Soggy Covert
Portymoor Coppice
A3052
RHODE LANE
Cemy
Rhode Hill
Fern Hill
Wood Covert
Sleech Wood
Rhode Barton Farm
Fern Hill Coppice
Wood Farm
94
33
A
34
B
35
C

96

A **B** **C**

Sheepwash
Farm

Nettlemore
Farm

Little
Coombe
Farm

Handcock
Coppice

P

Gummershaye
Farm

Harper's
Coppice

Spearpit
Coppice

Hangings
Coppice

National Trust

Coney's Castle
(Fort)

Longhayes
Coppice

4

Prime
Farm

PRIME LA

Coombe

Great
Coombe
Farm

LONG LANE

Northay
Farm

ABBOTT'S WOOTTON LANE

Pottle Oysters
Coppice

Prime
Coppices

GLEBELAND
LANE

Guppy
Plantation

97

Lane
Coppice

Higher Abbots
Wootton Farm

Spiller's
Coppice

3

Wessex Ridgeway

Lower Abbots
Wootton Farm

DT6

Stony
Down

Liberty Trail

STONY DOWN LANE

WOOTTON CROSS

WOOTTON LANE

BAKER'S CROSS

96

**Wootton
Fitzpaine**

Cemy

Knapp
Farm

Dairy
Farm

WOOTTON LA

Manor
Farm

BECKLANDS LANE

Becklands
Farm

MEERHAY LANE

2

Meer Hay
Farm

+

Wootton
House

Conegar Hill
Plantation

Conegar
Hill

Little Pitt
Coppice

PITT LANE

Tun
Coppice

Weir

Pitt
Farm

95

GREEN PITT KNAPP

River Char

Monarch's Way

Nutcombe
Coppice

1

ROUGH DOWN LANE

Manor
House

Berne
Farm

Little
Catherston
Farm

+

LWR CATHERSTON ROAD

**Catherston
Leweston**

Catherston
Coppice

Befferlands
Farm

A35

94

36 **A** **37** **B** **38** **C**

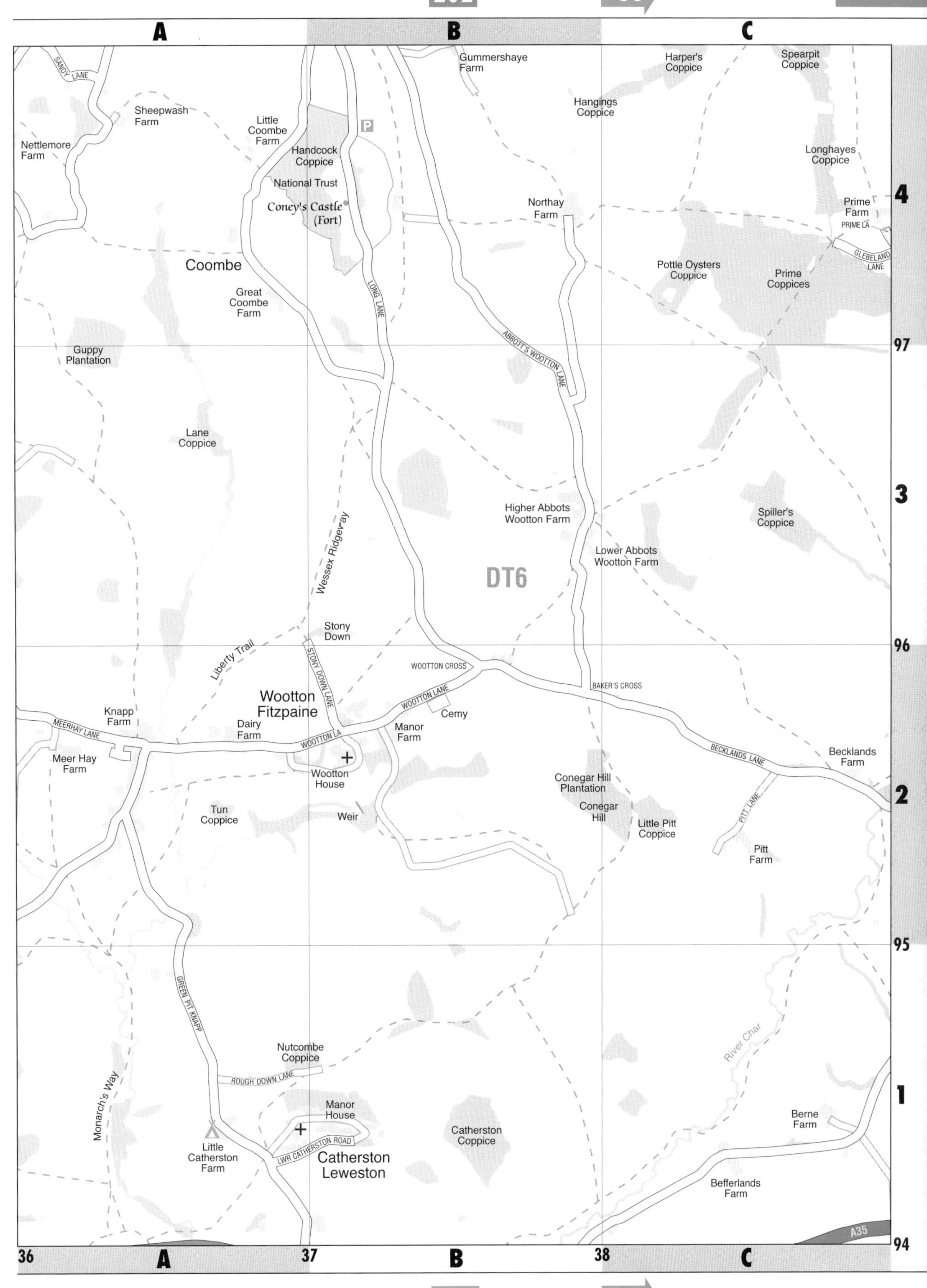

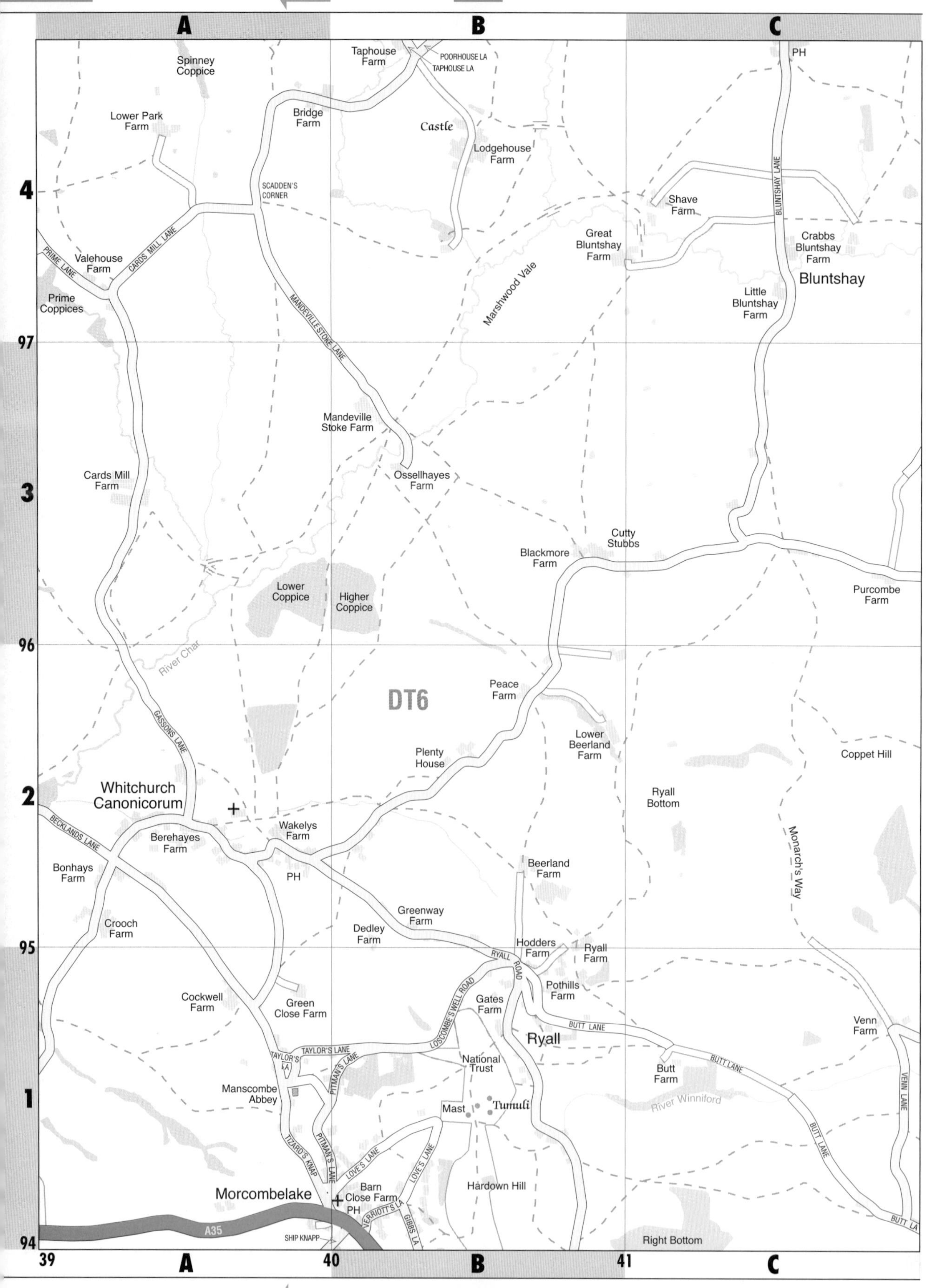

A   B   C

Spinney Coppice

Taphouse Farm

PH

POORHOUSE LA
TAPHOUSE LA

Lower Park Farm

Bridge Farm

Castle

Lodgehouse Farm

Bluntshay

PRIME LANE

SCADDEN'S CORNER

Shave Farm

Crabbs Bluntshay Farm

BLUNTSHAY LANE

4

Valehouse Farm

CARDS MILL LANE

Marshwood Vale

Great Bluntshay Farm

Bluntshay

Prime Coppices

Little Bluntshay Farm

97

MANDEVILLE STOKE LANE

Cards Mill Farm

Mandeville Stoke Farm

Ossellhayes Farm

Cutty Stubbs

3

Blackmore Farm

Purcombe Farm

Lower Coppice

Higher Coppice

96

River Char

Peace Farm

DT6

Coppet Hill

GASSONS LANE

Plenty House

Lower Beerland Farm

Ryall Bottom

2

Whitchurch Canonicorum

Wakelys Farm

Monarch's Way

BECKLANDS LANE

Berehayes Farm

PH

Beerland Farm

Bonhays Farm

Greenway Farm

Venn Farm

Crooch Farm

Dedley Farm

Hodders Farm

Ryall Farm

95

RYALL ROAD

Pothills Farm

Cockwell Farm

Green Close Farm

LOSCOMBE'S WELL ROAD

Gates Farm

Ryall

Butt Farm

BUTT LANE

VENN LANE

TAYLOR'S LANE

National Trust

BUTT LANE

1

TAYLOR'S LA

PITMAN'S LANE

Manscombe Abbey

Mast

Tumuli

River Winniford

BUTT LA

TIZARD'S KNAP

PITMAN'S LANE

LOVE'S LANE

LOVE'S LANE

Hardown Hill

Morcombelake

Barn Close Farm PH

VERRIOTT'S LA

GIBBS LA

94

A35

SHIP KNAPP

Right Bottom

39   A   40   B   41   C

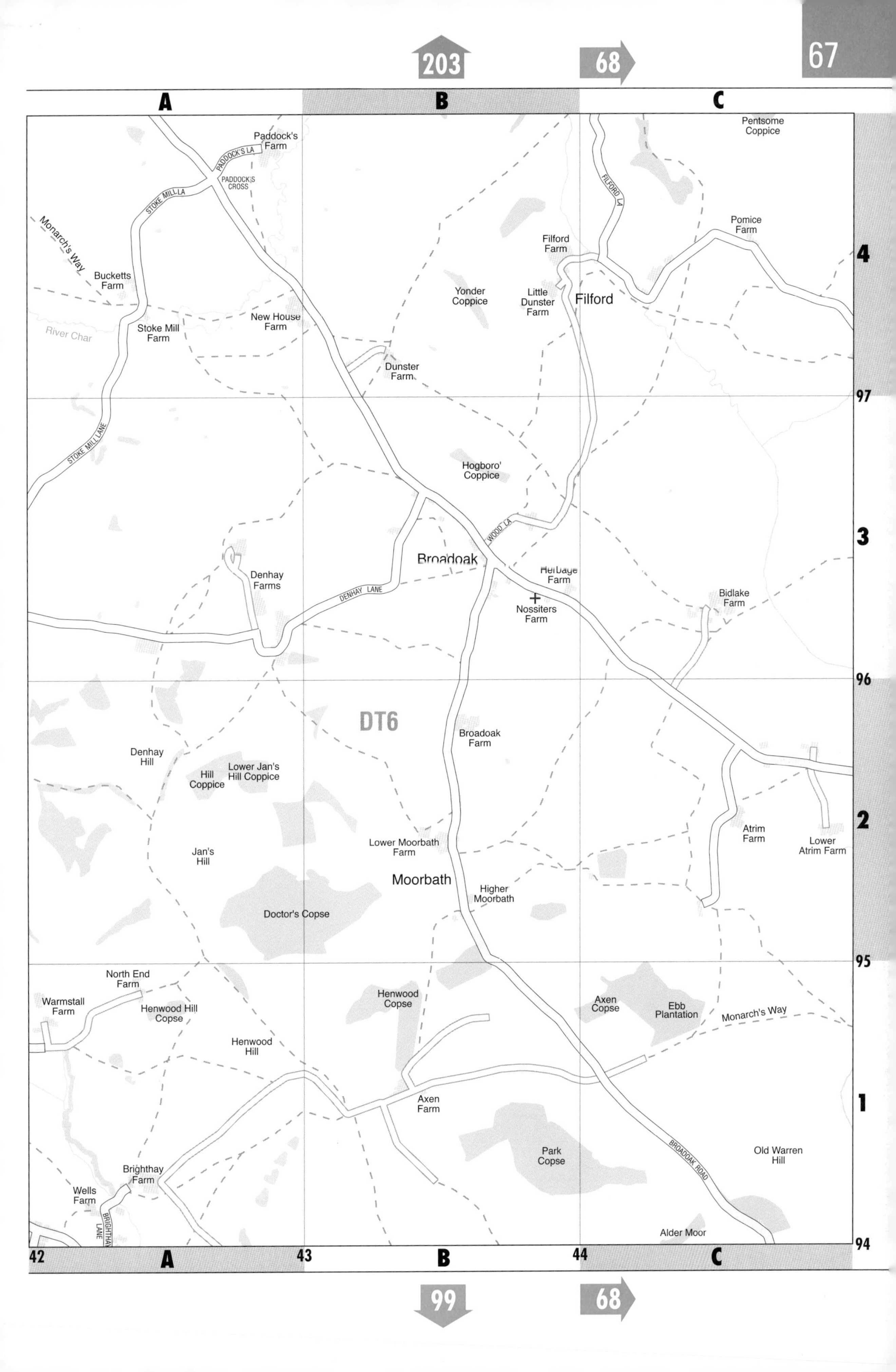

A

B

C

Pentsome
Coppice

Paddock's
Farm

PADDOCK'S LA

FILFORD LA

Pomice
Farm

STOKE MILL LA

4

PADDOCK'S
CROSS

Filford
Farm

Monarch's Way

Bucketts
Farm

Yonder
Coppice

Little
Dunster
Farm

Filford

New House
Farm

Stoke Mill
Farm

River Char

Dunster
Farm

97

STOKE MILL LANE

Hogboro'
Coppice

WOOD LA

3

Broadoak

Herbage
Farm

Denhay
Farms

DENHAY LANE

Bidlake
Farm

✝
Nossiters
Farm

96

DT6

Broadoak
Farm

Denhay
Hill

Lower Jan's
Hill Coppice

Hill
Coppice

2

Atrim
Farm

Lower
Atrim Farm

Jan's
Hill

Lower Moorbath
Farm

Moorbath

Higher
Moorbath

Doctor's Copse

95

North End
Farm

Henwood
Copse

Axen
Copse

Ebb
Plantation

Monarch's Way

Warmstall
Farm

Henwood Hill
Copse

Henwood
Hill

1

BROADOAK ROAD

Axen
Farm

Old Warren
Hill

Brighthay
Farm

Park
Copse

Wells
Farm

BRIGHTHAY LANE

Alder Moor

42

A

43

B

44

C

94

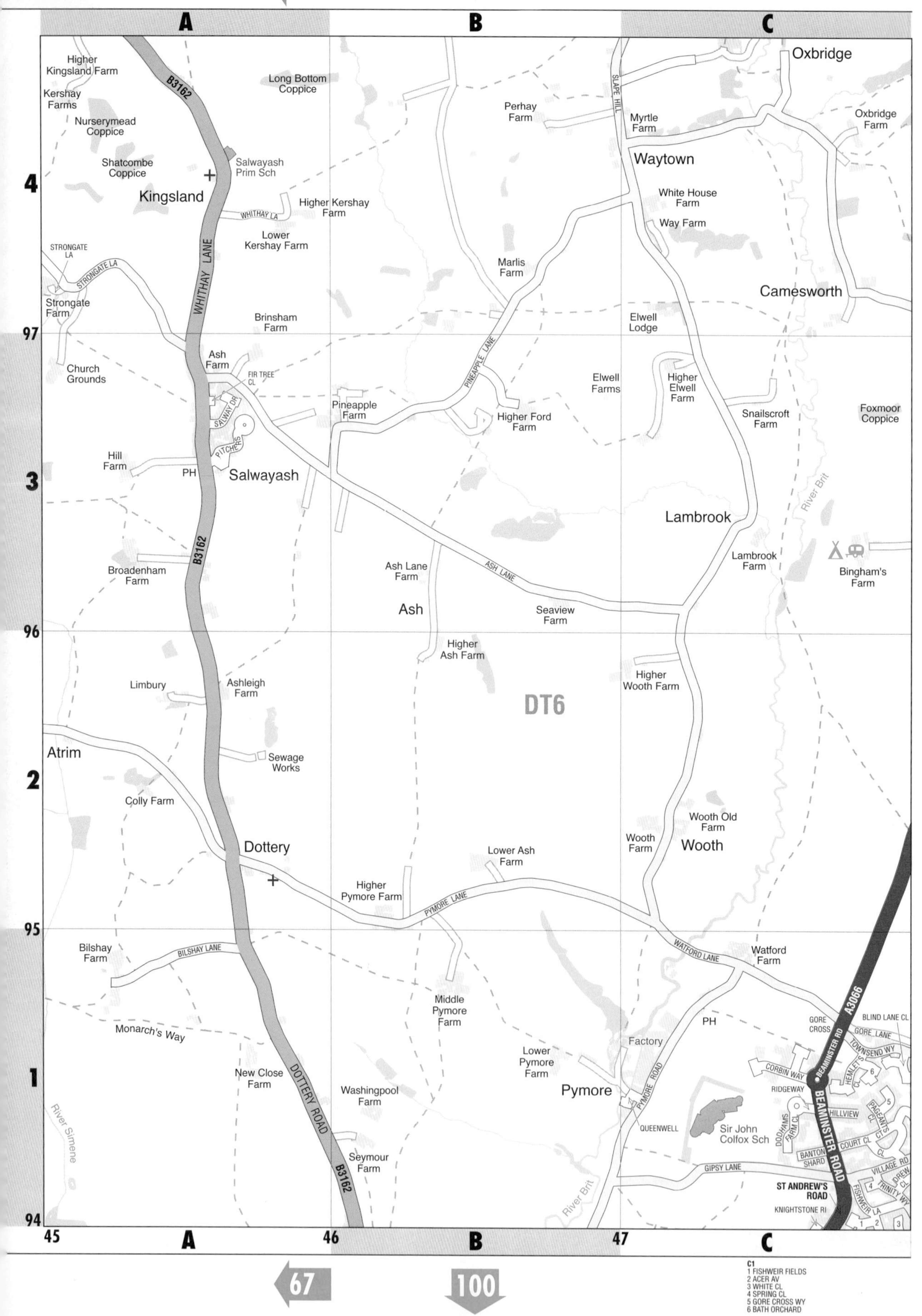

A · B · C

Higher Kingsland Farm
Kershay Farms
Nurserymead Coppice
Long Bottom Coppice
Perhay Farm
Myrtle Farm
Oxbridge
Oxbridge Farm
B3162
Shatcombe Coppice
Salwayash Prim Sch
Waytown
White House Farm
Way Farm

4

Kingsland
WHITHAY LA
Higher Kershay Farm
Lower Kershay Farm
Marlis Farm
SLAPE HILL
Camesworth

STRONGATE LA
STRONGATE LA
Strongate Farm
WHITHAY LANE
Brinsham Farm
Elwell Lodge

97

Church Grounds
Ash Farm
FIR TREE CL
Pineapple Farm
PINEAPPLE LANE
Higher Ford Farm
Elwell Farms
Higher Elwell Farm
Snailscroft Farm
Foxmoor Coppice

Hill Farm
PH
SALWAY DR
PITCHERS
Salwayash
River Brit

3

B3162
Lambrook
Lambrook Farm
Bingham's Farm

Broadenham Farm
Ash Lane Farm
ASH LANE
Ash
Seaview Farm

96

Limbury
Ashleigh Farm
Higher Ash Farm
Higher Wooth Farm
DT6

Atrim
Sewage Works
Wooth Farm
Wooth Old Farm
Wooth

2

Colly Farm
Dottery
Lower Ash Farm
Higher Pymore Farm
PYMORE LANE
Watford Lane
Watford Farm
A3066

95

Bilshay Farm
BILSHAY LANE
Middle Pymore Farm
PH
GORE CROSS
BEAMINSTER RD
GORE LANE
BLIND LANE CL
TOWNSEND WY

Monarch's Way
Factory
CORBIN WAY
HEALEY'S
PAGEANTS CL
RIDGEWAY
HILLVIEW

1

New Close Farm
DOTTERY ROAD
Washingpool Farm
Lower Pymore Farm
Pymore
QUEENWELL
Sir John Colfox Sch
DODHAMS
BANTON SHARD
COURT CL
BEAMINSTER ROAD
VILLAGE RD
TRINITY WY
OPEN
FISHER LA

River Simene
Seymour Farm
B3162
River Brit
GIPSY LANE
ST ANDREW'S ROAD
KNIGHTSTONE RI

94

45 · A · 46 · B · 47 · C

C1
1 FISHWEIR FIELDS
2 ACER AV
3 WHITE CL
4 SPRING CL
5 GORE CROSS WY
6 BATH ORCHARD

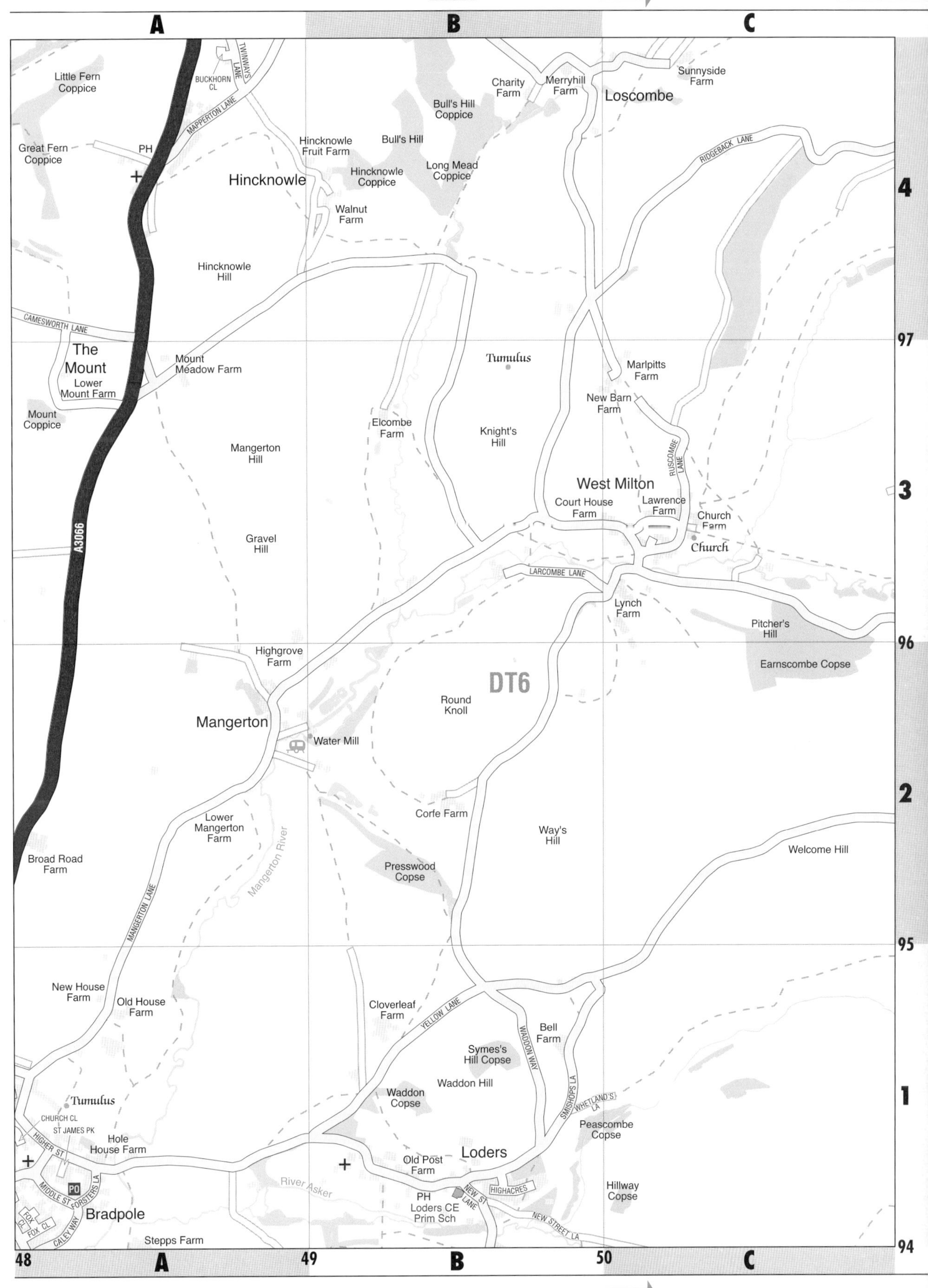

A B C

Little Fern
Coppice

TWINWAYS LA
BUCKHORN CL
MAPPERTON LANE

Great Fern
Coppice

PH

Hincknowle
Fruit Farm

Hincknowle

Bull's Hill
Coppice

Bull's Hill

Hincknowle
Coppice

Long Mead
Coppice

Walnut
Farm

Charity
Farm

Merryhill
Farm

Loscombe

Sunnyside
Farm

RIDGEBACK LANE

4

Hincknowle
Hill

CAMESWORTH LANE

The
Mount

Lower
Mount Farm

Mount
Meadow Farm

Mount
Coppice

Mangerton
Hill

Elcombe
Farm

Tumulus

Knight's
Hill

Marlpitts
Farm

New Barn
Farm

West Milton

Court House
Farm

Lawrence
Farm

Church
Farm

Church

RUSCOMBE LANE

97

3

A3066

Gravel
Hill

LARCOMBE LANE

Lynch
Farm

Pitcher's
Hill

Earnscombe Copse

96

Highgrove
Farm

Mangerton

Water Mill

DT6

Round
Knoll

Lower
Mangerton
Farm

MANGERTON LANE

Mangerton River

Corfe Farm

Way's
Hill

Welcome Hill

Broad Road
Farm

Presswood
Copse

2

95

New House
Farm

Old House
Farm

Cloverleaf
Farm

YELLOW LANE

WADDON WAY

Bell
Farm

SIXBShops LA

WHETLAND'S LA

Tumulus

CHURCH CL
ST JAMES PK

Hole
House Farm

Symes's
Hill Copse

Waddon Hill

Peascombe
Copse

1

Waddon
Copse

Hillway
Copse

HIGHER ST
PO

Old Post
Farm

Loders

HIGHACRES

FOX CL
MIDDLE ST
FORSTERS LA

FOX CL
CALEY WAY

Bradpole

Stepps Farm

River Asker

PH
Loders CE
Prim Sch

NEW ST LANE

NEW STREET LA

94

48 A 49 B 50 C

69
205

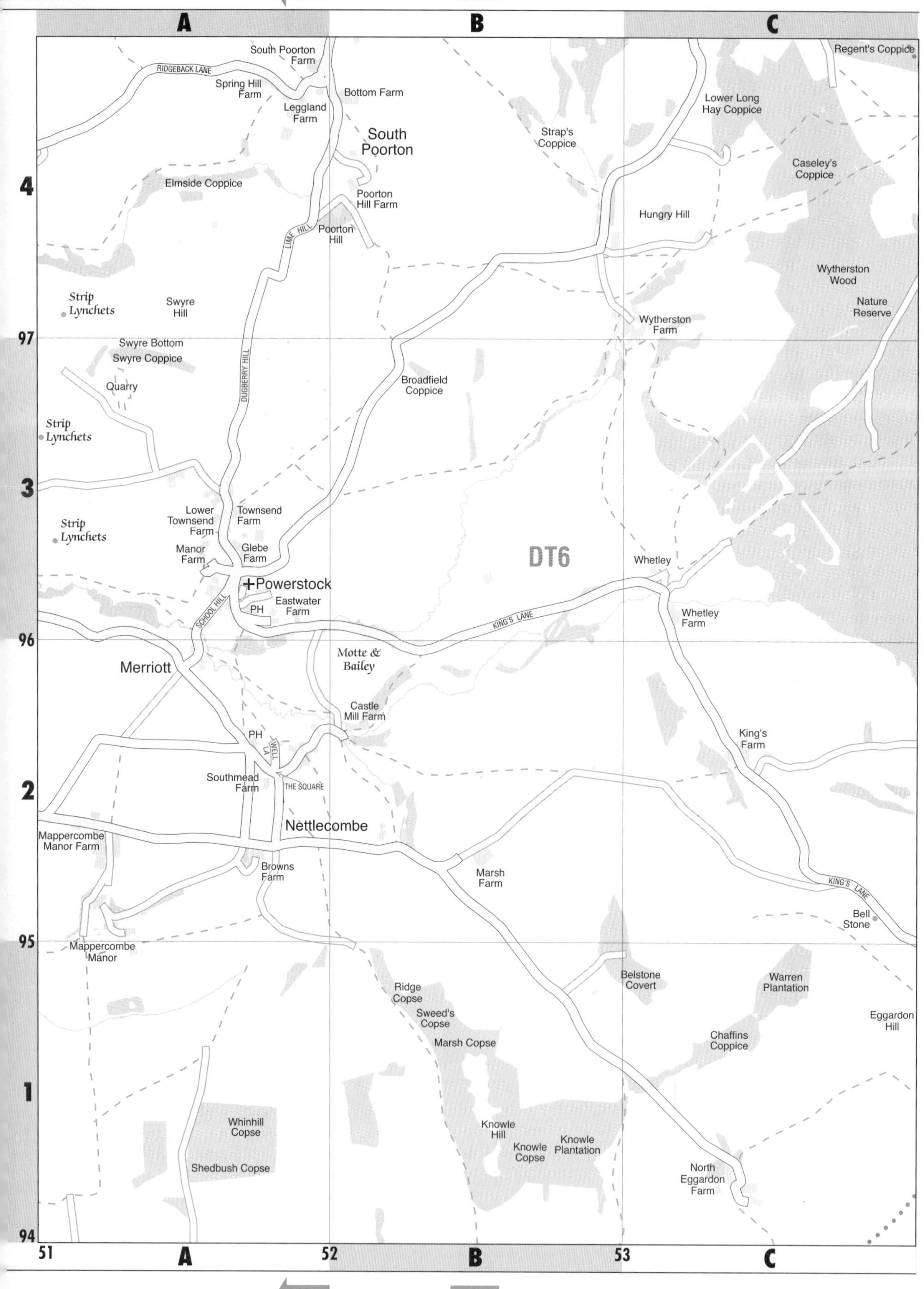
A
B
C
South Poorton Farm
Ridgeback Lane
Spring Hill Farm
Leggland Farm
Bottom Farm
South Poorton
Regent's Coppice
Lower Long Hay Coppice
Strap's Coppice
Caseley's Coppice
Elmside Coppice
Poorton Hill Farm
Poorton Hill
Lime Hill
Hungry Hill
Wytherston Wood
Nature Reserve
Strip Lynchets
Swyre Hill
Wytherston Farm
Swyre Bottom
Swyre Coppice
Quarry
Dugberry Hill
Broadfield Coppice
Strip Lynchets
Strip Lynchets
Lower Townsend Farm
Townsend Farm
Manor Farm
Glebe Farm
DT6
Whetley
Powerstock
School Hill
PH
Eastwater Farm
King's Lane
Whetley Farm
Merriott
Motte & Bailey
Castle Mill Farm
PH
Well La
King's Farm
Southmead Farm
The Square
Nettlecombe
Mappercombe Manor Farm
Browns Farm
Marsh Farm
King's Lane
Bell Stone
Mappercombe Manor
Belstone Covert
Warren Plantation
Ridge Copse
Sweed's Copse
Eggardon Hill
Marsh Copse
Chaffins Coppice
Whinhill Copse
Knowle Hill
Knowle Copse
Knowle Plantation
Shedbush Copse
North Eggardon Farm
4
97
3
96
2
95
1
94
51
52
53

69
102

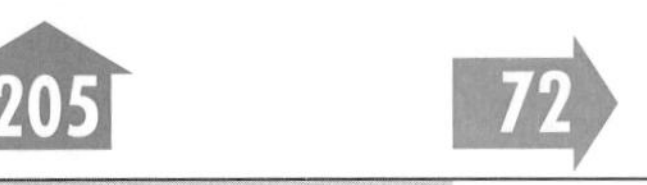
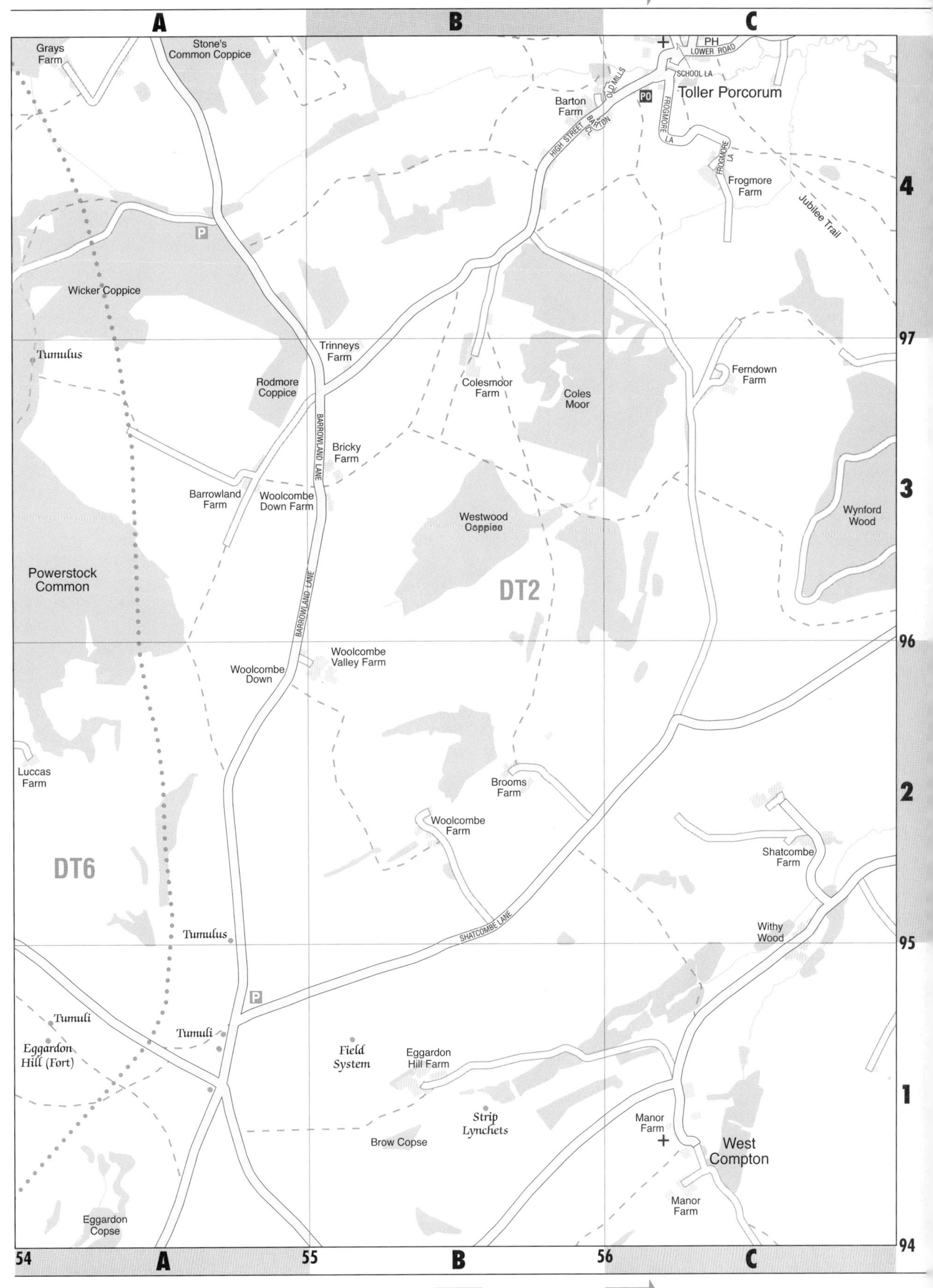

A   B   C

Grays Farm

Stone's Common Coppice

Toller Porcorum

PH
LOWER ROAD
SCHOOL LA

Barton Farm

PO

HIGH STREET

OLD MILLS

BARTON

FROGMORE LA

4

Frogmore Farm

Frogmore LA

Jubilee Trail

P

Wicker Coppice

97

Trinneys Farm

Tumulus

Rodmore Coppice

Colesmoor Farm

Coles Moor

Ferndown Farm

BARROWLAND LANE

Bricky Farm

3

Barrowland Farm

Woolcombe Down Farm

Westwood Coppice

Wynford Wood

Powerstock Common

DT2

BARROWLAND LANE

96

Woolcombe Valley Farm

Woolcombe Down

Luccas Farm

2

Brooms Farm

DT6

Woolcombe Farm

Shatcombe Farm

Tumulus

Withy Wood

SHATCOMBE LANE

95

P

Tumuli

Field System

Eggardon Hill Farm

Tumuli

Eggardon Hill (Fort)

1

Strip Lynchets

Manor Farm

Brow Copse

West Compton

94

Eggardon Copse

Manor Farm

54   A   55   B   56   C

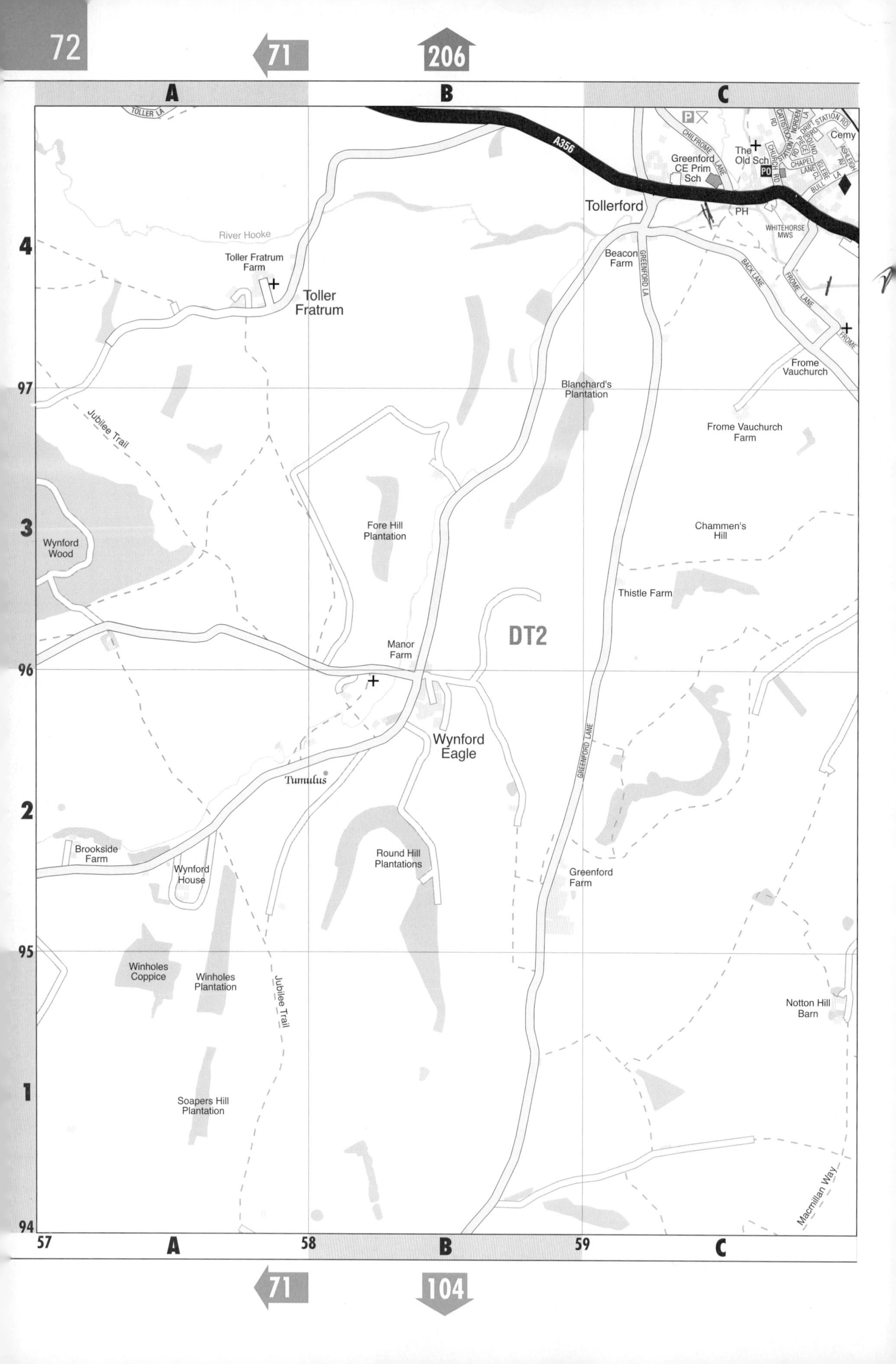

A B C

4

97

3

96

2

95

1

94

TOLLER LA

River Hooke

Toller Fratrum
Farm

Toller
Fratrum

Jubilee Trail

Wynford
Wood

Fore Hill
Plantation

Manor
Farm

Wynford
Eagle

DT2

Tumulus

Brookside
Farm

Wynford
House

Round Hill
Plantations

Winholes
Coppice

Winholes
Plantation

Jubilee Trail

Soapers Hill
Plantation

A356

Greenford
CE Prim
Sch

The
Old Sch

PO

Cemy

CHILFROME LANE

CATISTOCK RD

BROWN PL

PRINCE PL

DRIFT STATION RD

ASH PL

CHAPEL
LANE

BERE LA

BULL LA

Tollerford

PH

WHITEHORSE
MWS

Beacon
Farm

GREENFORD LA

BACK LANE

FROME LANE

FROME

Frome
Vauchurch

Blanchard's
Plantation

Frome Vauchurch
Farm

Chammen's
Hill

Thistle Farm

GREENFORD LANE

Greenford
Farm

Notton Hill
Barn

Macmillan Way

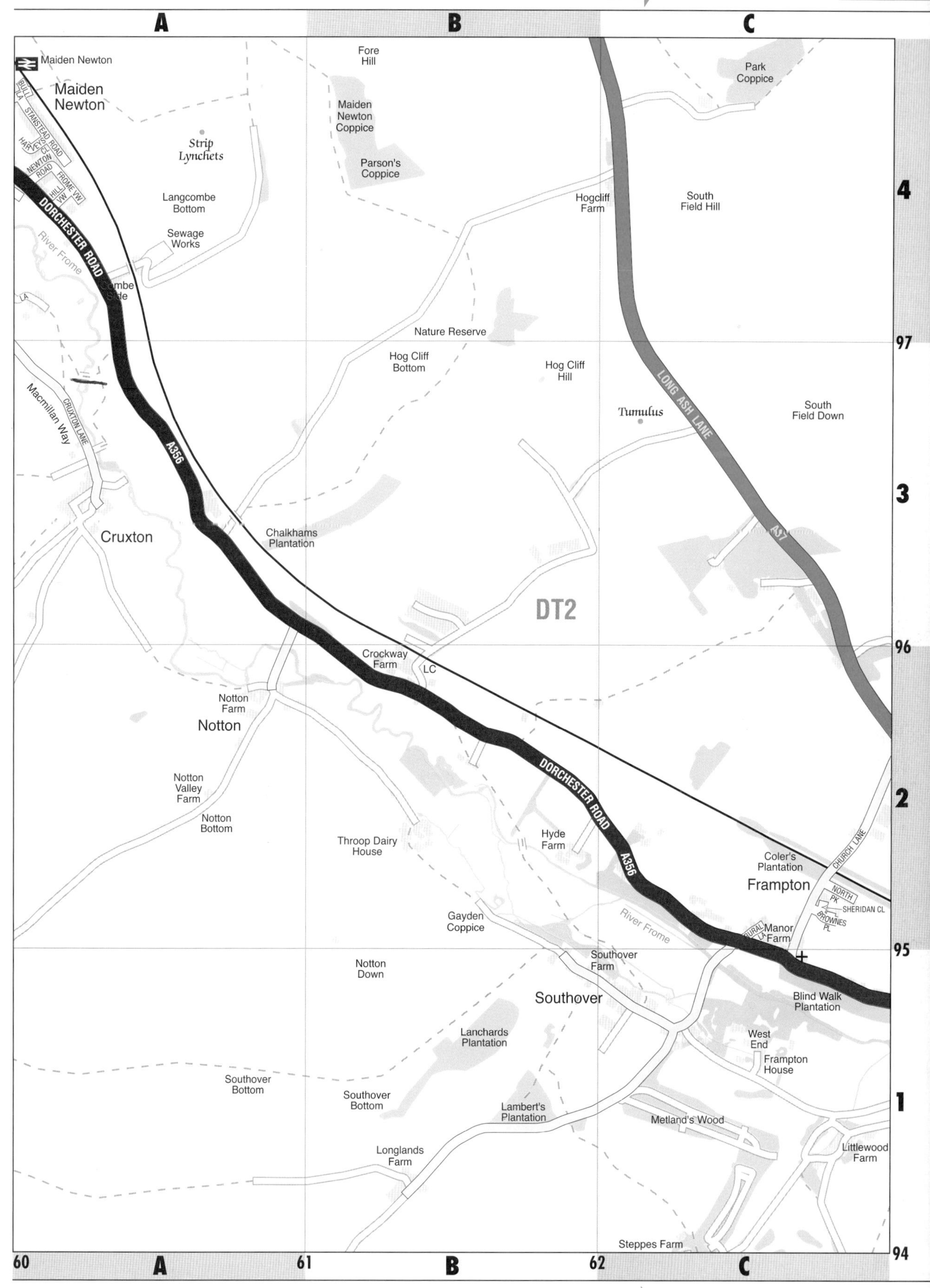

Maiden Newton

Maiden Newton

Fore Hill

Park Coppice

Maiden Newton Coppice

Parson's Coppice

Strip Lynchets

Langcombe Bottom

Sewage Works

Hogcliff Farm

South Field Hill

4

Combe Side

River Frome

Macmillan Way

Nature Reserve

Hog Cliff Bottom

Hog Cliff Hill

South Field Down

Tumulus

97

LONG ASH LANE

A356

Cruxton

Chalkhams Plantation

3

DT2

Crockway Farm

LC

96

Notton Farm

Notton

Notton Valley Farm

Notton Bottom

Throop Dairy House

Hyde Farm

DORCHESTER ROAD

A356

Coler's Plantation

Frampton

CHURCH LANE

NORTH PK

SHERIDAN CL

BROWNIES PL

2

River Frome

RURAL

Manor Farm

Gayden Coppice

Southover Farm

Blind Walk Plantation

95

Notton Down

Southover

West End

Frampton House

Southover Bottom

Lanchards Plantation

Southover Bottom

Lambert's Plantation

Metland's Wood

1

Longlands Farm

Littlewood Farm

Steppes Farm

94

A
B
C

Huish
Plantation

4

Tumulus

Bushes
Barn

Crete
Bottom

Crete
Hill

Magiston
Hill

97

Tumulus

Crete
Bottom

South
Field Down

Magiston
Farm

3

Coronation
Plantation

Lower
Magiston

Cross Dyke

Jackman's
Plantation

Stratton
Down

96

Langford
Farm

DT2

Jackman's
Coppice

Kidney
Plantation

Watcombe
Bottom

Settlement

Lawyer's
Plantation

Howdes Barrow
Plantation

Galhampton
Farm

Tumulus

PICKETTS CROSS

Tumuli

Grimstone
Down

Stratton
Down

Half Moon
Plantation

CHURCH LA

2

Stratton
Down
Plantation

Great War
Plantation

Long
Plantation

Prisoner's of War
Plantation

95

Hog
Hill

Tumulus

Stratton
Down

Stratton
Bottom

Sydling Water

A356

Blind Walk
Plantation

DORCHESTER RD

A37

DORCHESTER ROAD

Peacock
Plantation

Strip
Lynchets

1

River Frome

Manor
Farm

Grimstone

94

63
A
64
B
65
C

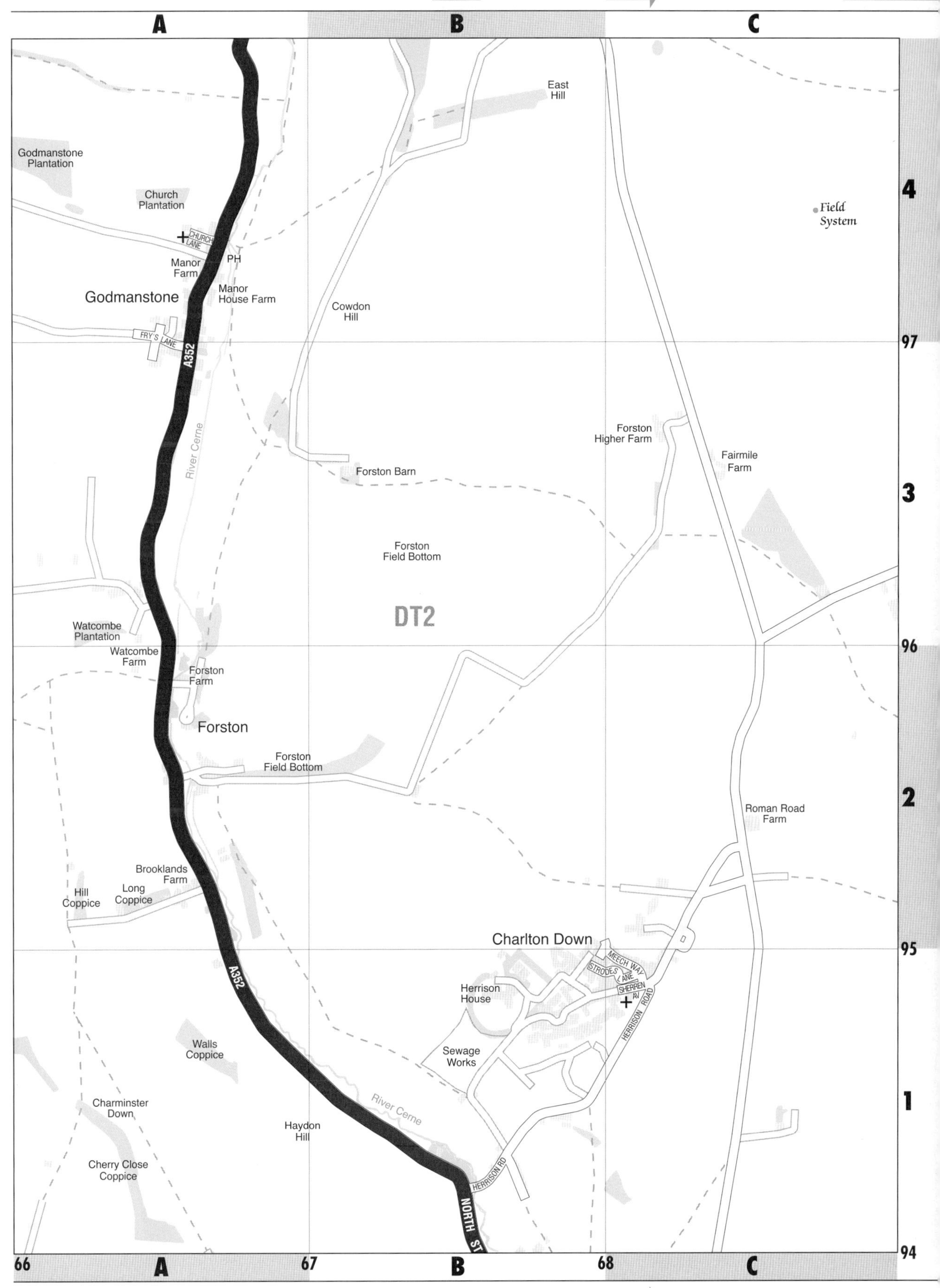

East
Hill

Godmanstone
Plantation

Church
Plantation

CHURCH LANE

PH

Manor
Farm

Cowdon
Hill

Godmanstone

Manor
House Farm

FRY'S LANE

A352

River Cerne

4

Forston
Higher Farm

Fairmile
Farm

97

Field
System

Forston Barn

Forston
Field Bottom

3

DT2

Watcombe
Plantation

96

Watcombe
Farm

Forston
Farm

Forston

Forston
Field Bottom

Roman Road
Farm

2

Brooklands
Farm

Long
Coppice

Hill
Coppice

Charlton Down

95

A352

MEECH WAY
STRODES LANE
SHERREN AV

Herrison
House

Walls
Coppice

Sewage
Works

HERRISON ROAD

River Cerne

1

Charminster
Down

Haydon
Hill

HERRISON RD

Cherry Close
Coppice

NORTH ST

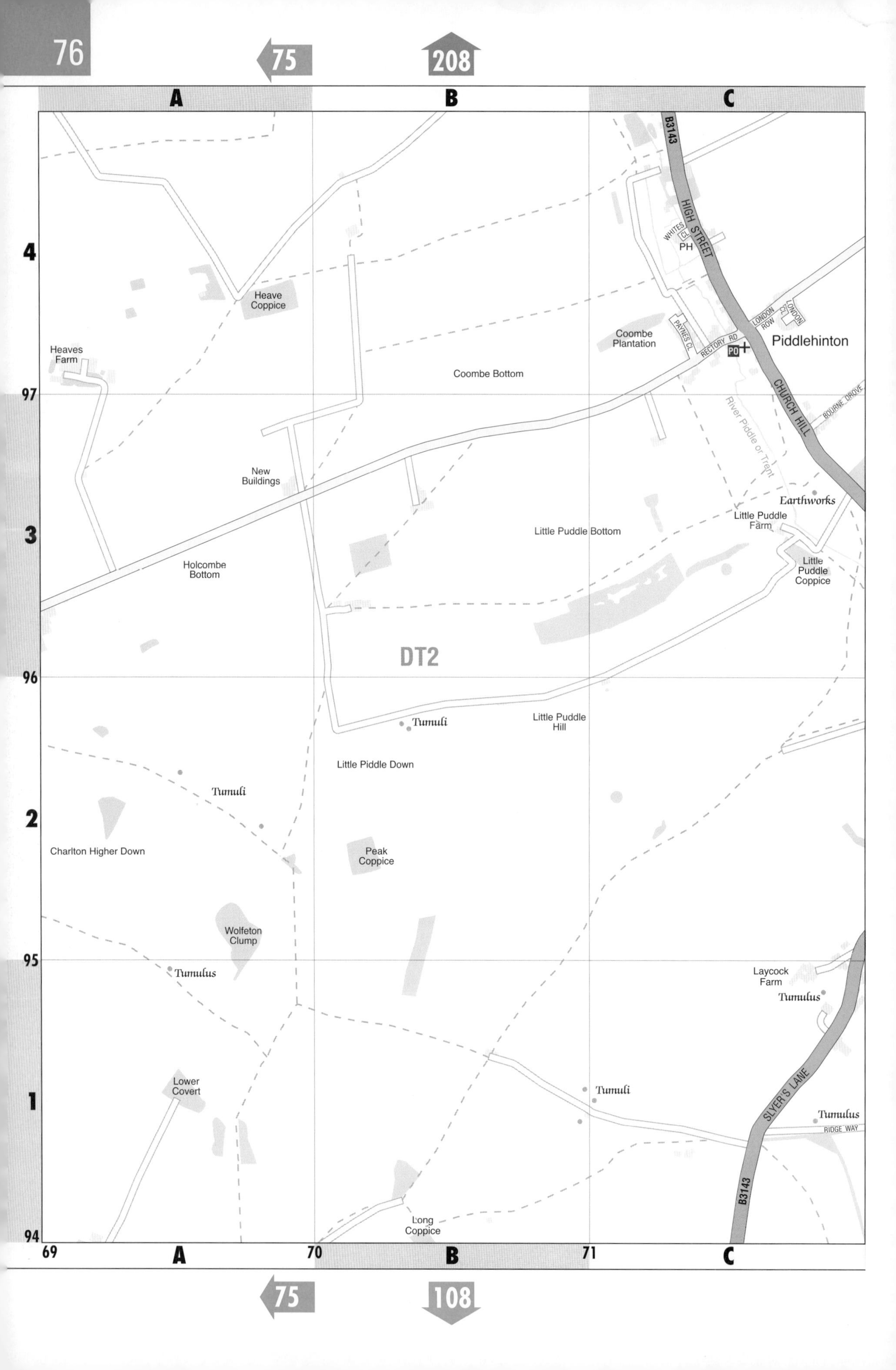

A   B   C

B3143

HIGH STREET

WHITES CL

PH

Heave
Coppice

LONDON ROW

LONDON CL

Coombe
Plantation

PAYNES CL

Heaves
Farm

RECTORY RD

PO ✚

Piddlehinton

Coombe Bottom

CHURCH HILL

BOURNE DROVE

River Piddle or Trent

New
Buildings

Earthworks

Little Puddle
Farm

Little Puddle Bottom

Holcombe
Bottom

Little
Puddle
Coppice

DT2

Tumuli

Little Puddle
Hill

Little Piddle Down

Tumuli

Charlton Higher Down

Peak
Coppice

Wolfeton
Clump

Laycock
Farm

Tumulus

Tumulus

SILVER'S LANE

Lower
Covert

Tumuli

Tumulus

RIDGE WAY

B3143

Long
Coppice

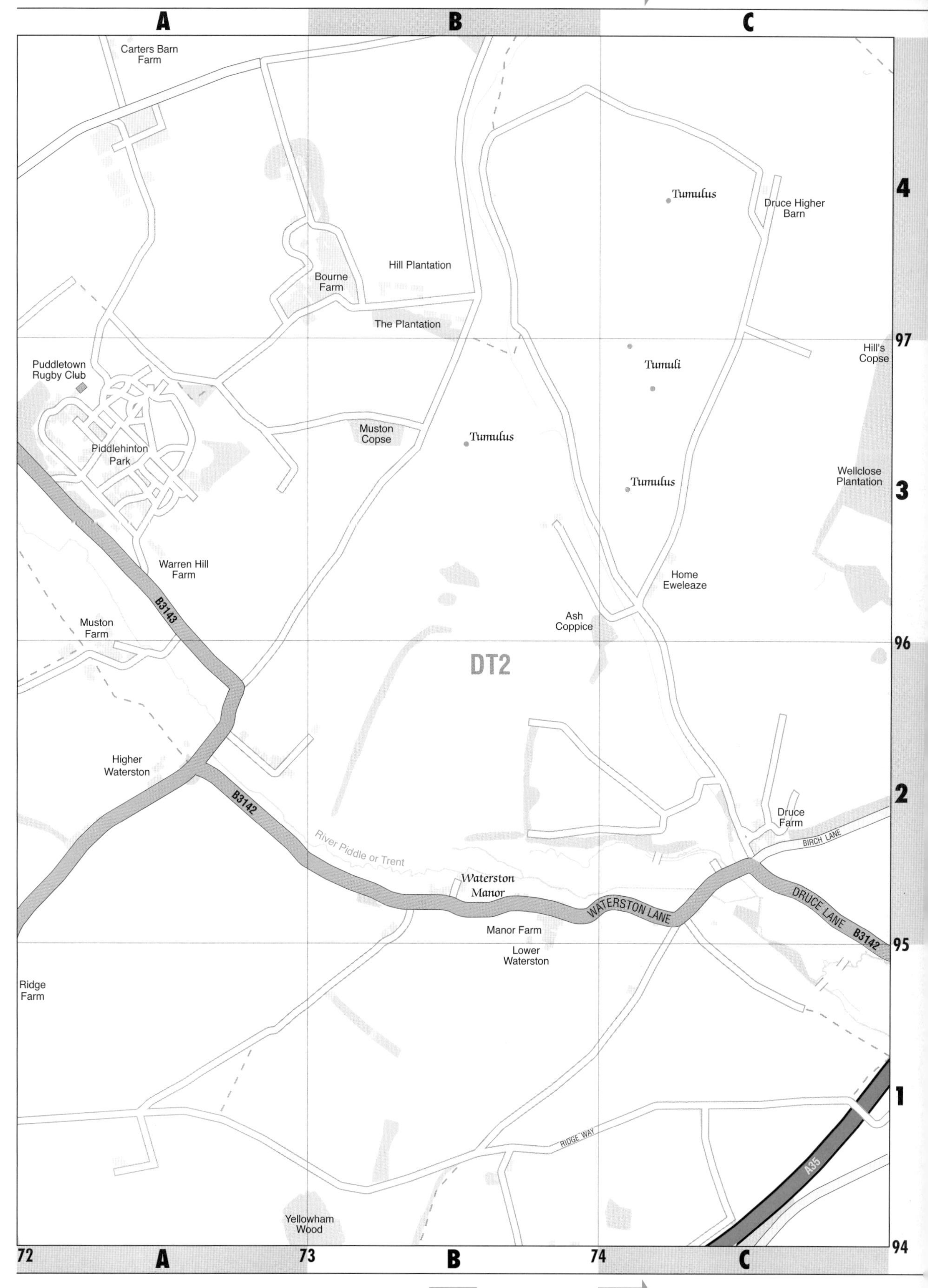

A B C

Carters Barn Farm

4

Tumulus

Druce Higher Barn

Hill Plantation

Bourne Farm

The Plantation

97

Hill's Copse

Puddletown Rugby Club

Tumuli

Muston Copse

Tumulus

Wellclose Plantation

Piddlehinton Park

Tumulus

3

Warren Hill Farm

Home Eweleaze

Muston Farm

Ash Coppice

B3143

96

DT2

Higher Waterston

B3142

Druce Farm

2

BIRCH LANE

River Piddle or Trent

Waterston Manor

WATERSTON LANE

DRUCE LANE B3142

Manor Farm

Lower Waterston

95

Ridge Farm

RIDGE WAY

A35

1

Yellowham Wood

72 A 73 B 74 C 94

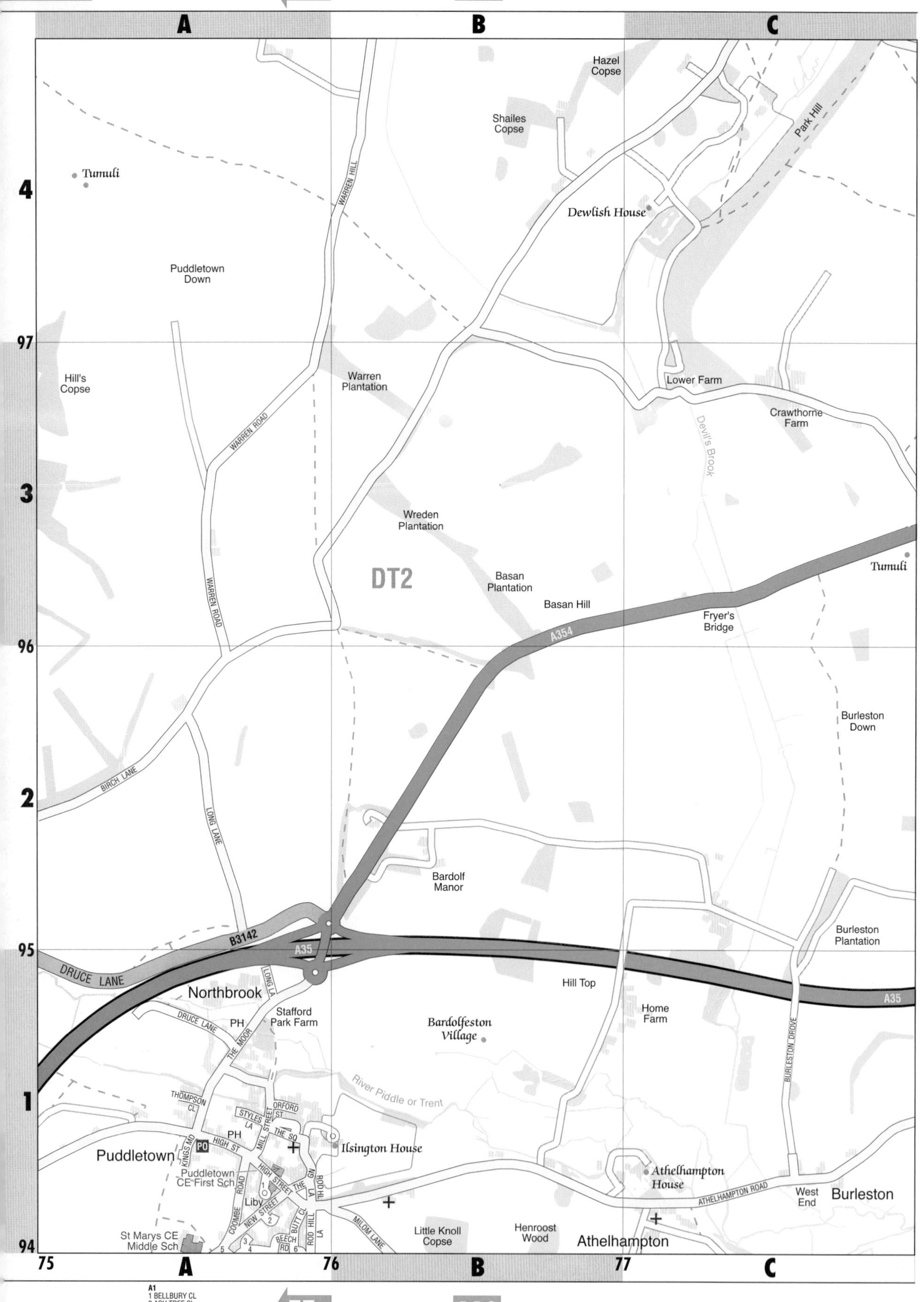

A B C

4

Tumuli

Puddletown Down

Hazel Copse

Shailes Copse

Park Hill

Dewlish House

97

Hill's Copse

Warren Plantation

Lower Farm

Crawthorne Farm

WARREN HILL

WARREN ROAD

Devil's Brook

3

Wreden Plantation

DT2

Basan Plantation

Basan Hill

Tumuli

96

A354

Fryer's Bridge

Burleston Down

BIRCH LANE

LONG LANE

2

Bardolf Manor

Burleston Plantation

95

B3142 A35

DRUCE LANE

Northbrook

Stafford Park Farm

Bardolfeston Village

Hill Top

Home Farm

A35

DRUCE LANE

PH

THE MOOR

LONG LA

River Piddle or Trent

BURLESTON DROVE

West End

Burleston

1

Puddletown

THOMPSON CL

STYLES LA

HIGH ST

PH

KINGS RD

PO

MILL STREET

ORFORD ST

THE SQ

BUTT CL

Ilsington House

Athelhampton House

ATHELHAMPTON ROAD

Puddletown CE First Sch

Liby

HIGH STREET

COOMBE ROAD

NEW STREET

ROD HIL

BUTT LA

GN LA

MILOM LANE

Little Knoll Copse

Henroost Wood

Athelhampton

94

St Marys CE Middle Sch

BEECH RD

75 A 76 B 77 C

A1
1 BELLBURY CL
2 ASH TREE CL
3 WILLOUGHBY CL
4 BRYMER RD
5 WHITE HILL
6 CHAPEL VIEW

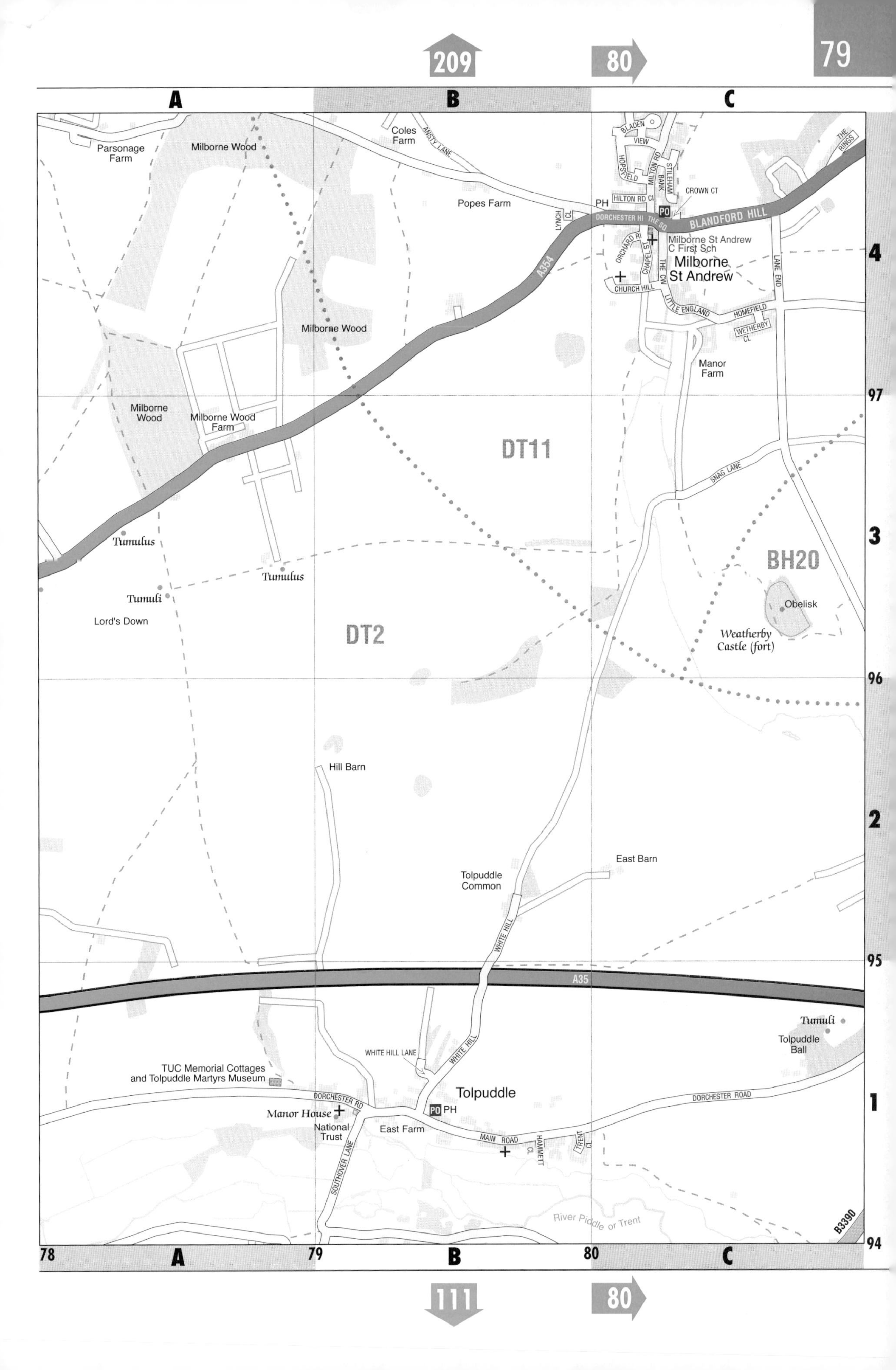
209
80
A
B
C
Parsonage Farm
Milborne Wood
Coles Farm
ANSTY LANE
BLADEN VIEW
HOPSFIELD
MILTON RD
STILEHAM BANK
CROWN CT
HILTON RD CL
PH
PO
Popes Farm
LYNCH CL
DORCHESTER HILL
THE SQ
BLANDFORD HILL
THE RINGS
A354
ORCHARD RI
CHAPEL ST
THE CW
Milborne St Andrew C First Sch
Milborne St Andrew
CHURCH HILL
LITTLE ENGLAND
LANE END
HOMEFIELD
WETHERBY CL
Milborne Wood
Manor Farm
Milborne Wood
Milborne Wood Farm
DT11
SNAG LANE
Tumulus
Tumulus
Tumuli
Lord's Down
BH20
Obelisk
DT2
Weatherby Castle (fort)
Hill Barn
East Barn
Tolpuddle Common
WHITE HILL
A35
Tumuli
Tolpuddle Ball
WHITE HILL LANE
WHITE HILL
TUC Memorial Cottages and Tolpuddle Martyrs Museum
Tolpuddle
DORCHESTER RD
DORCHESTER ROAD
Manor House
PO PH
National Trust
East Farm
MAIN ROAD
HAMMETT CL
TRENT CL
SOUTHOVER LANE
River Piddle or Trent
B3390
4
97
3
96
2
95
1
94
78
A
79
B
80
C
111
80

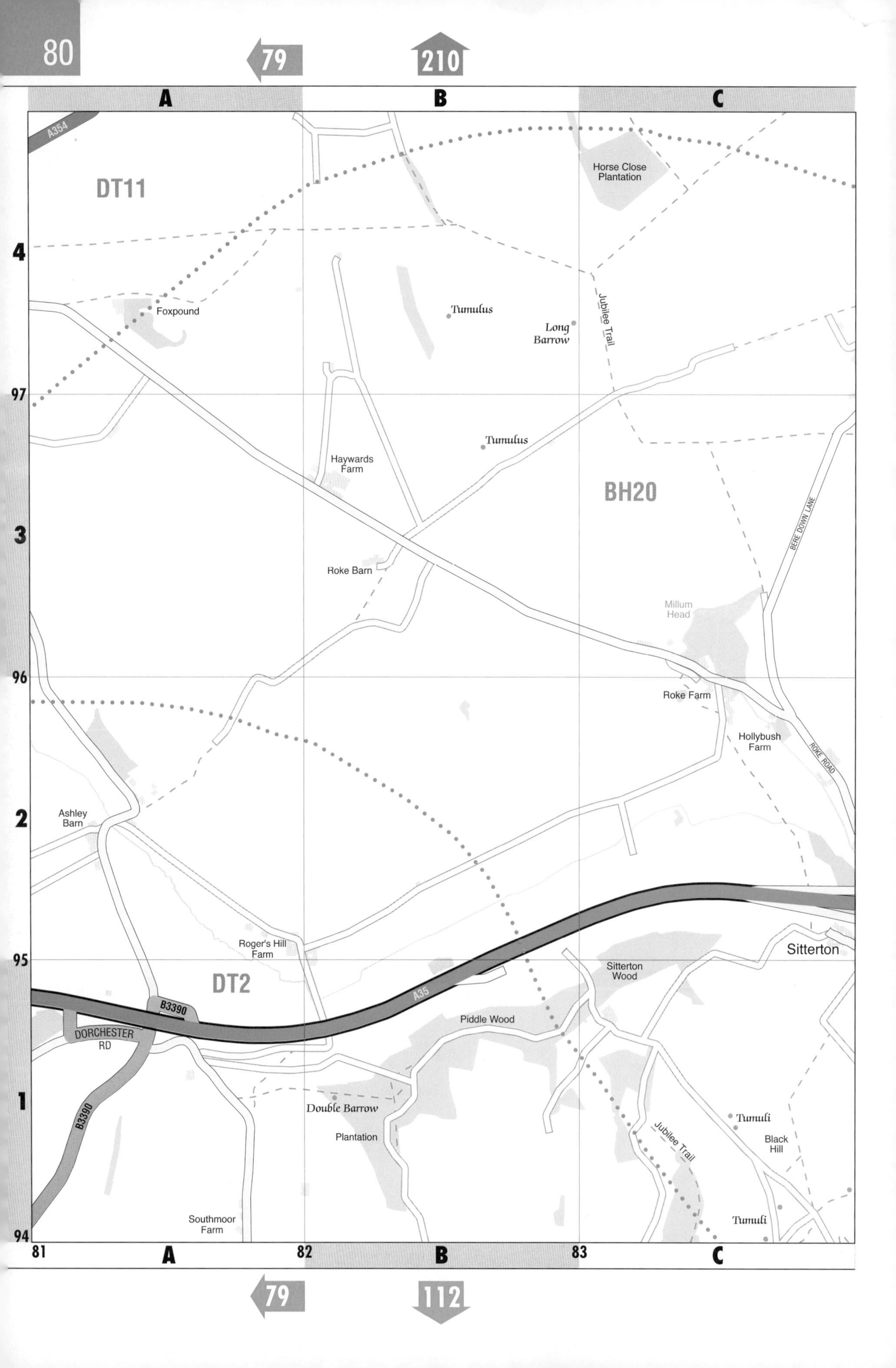

A B C

A354

DT11

Horse Close
Plantation

4

Foxpound

Tumulus

Long
Barrow

Jubilee Trail

97

Tumulus

Haywards
Farm

BH20

BERE DOWN LANE

3

Roke Barn

Millum
Head

96

Roke Farm

Hollybush
Farm

ROKE ROAD

Ashley
Barn

2

Roger's Hill
Farm

95

DT2

Sitterton
Wood

Sitterton

B3390

A35

Piddle Wood

DORCHESTER
RD

1

B3390

Double Barrow

Jubilee Trail

Tumuli

Black
Hill

Plantation

94

Southmoor
Farm

Tumuli

81 A 82 B 83 C

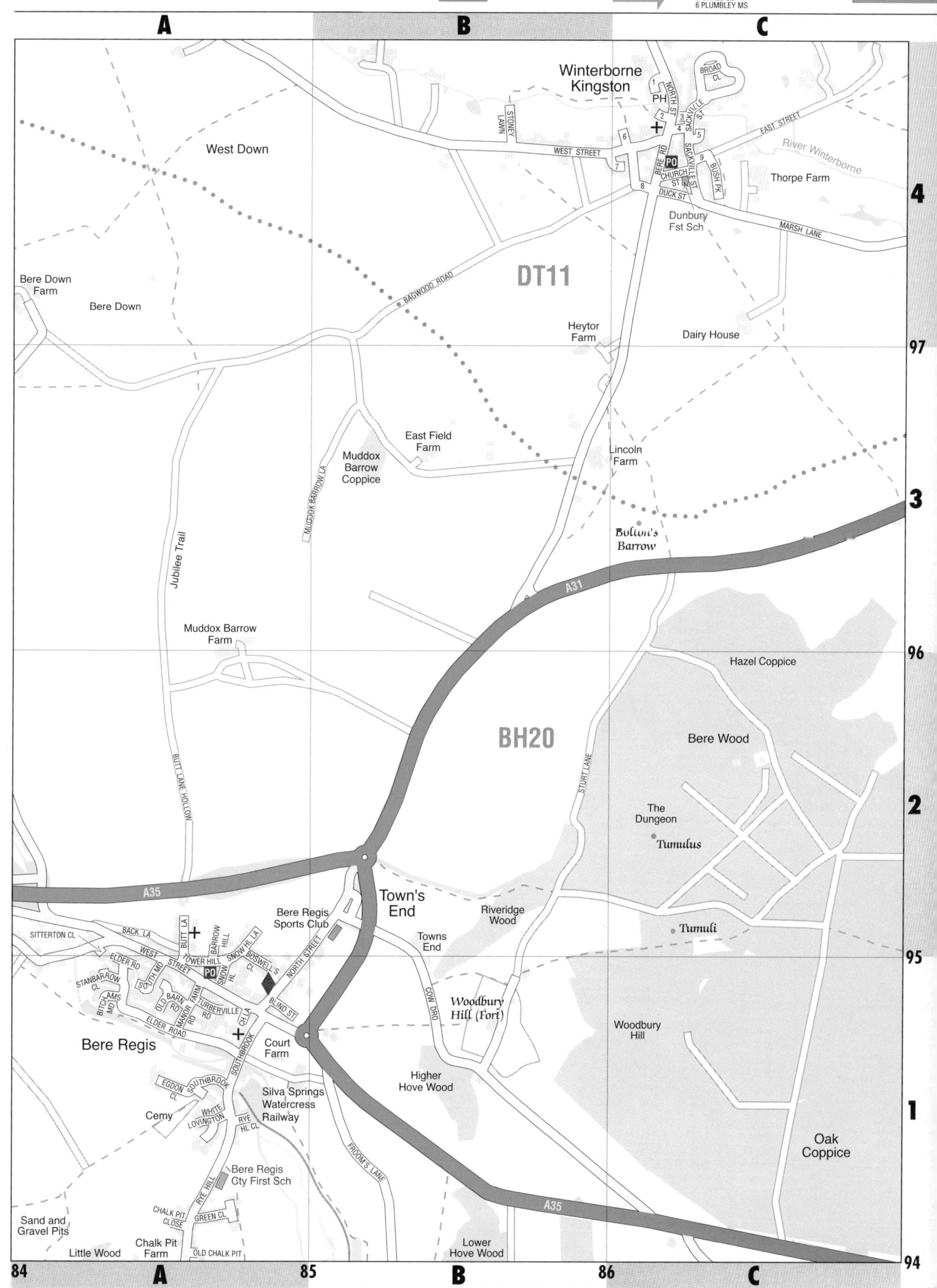

210

82

81

C4
1 WIND WHISTLE FM
2 CLYPETTS
3 PITCHER CL
4 NOAH HENVILLE CNR
5 WARES CL
6 PLUMBLEY MS
7 ORCHARD LA
8 BAGWOOD RD
9 EAST ST

A

B

C

Winterborne Kingston

BROAD CL

PH

STONEY LAWN

NORTH ST

SACKVILLE ST

East Street

River Winterborne

West Down

WEST STREET

PO

CHURCH ST

SACKVILLE ST

BUSH PK

Thorpe Farm

DUCK ST

Dunbury Fst Sch

MARSH LANE

4

Bere Down Farm

Bere Down

DT11

Heytor Farm

Dairy House

97

East Field Farm

Lincoln Farm

Muddox Barrow Coppice

MUDDOX BARROW LA

Bolton's Barrow

3

A31

Jubilee Trail

Muddox Barrow Farm

96

Hazel Coppice

BH20

Bere Wood

BUTT LANE HOLLOW

STURT LANE

The Dungeon

Tumulus

2

A35

Town's End

Riveridge Wood

Tumuli

95

Bere Regis Sports Club

BACK LA

BUTT LA

BARROW HILL

SNOW HL LA

NORTH STREET

Towns End

SITTERTON CL

WEST STREET

TOWER HILL

BOSWELL'S CL

SNOW HL

PO

BLIND ST

COW DRO

Woodbury Hill (Fort)

STANBARROW CL

ELDER RD

STH MD

OLD BARN

MANOR FARM

TURBERVILLE RD

CHL LA

Woodbury Hill

BITCH AMS MD

ELDER ROAD

SOUTHBROOK

Bere Regis

Court Farm

Higher Hove Wood

EGDON CL

SOUTHBROOK

WHITE LOVINGTON

RYE HL CL

Silva Springs Watercress Railway

1

Cemy

FROOM'S LANE

Oak Coppice

RYE HILL

Bere Regis Cty First Sch

Sand and Gravel Pits

CHALK PIT CLOSE

GREEN CL

A35

Little Wood

Chalk Pit Farm

OLD CHALK PIT

Lower Hove Wood

94

84

A

85

B

86

C

94

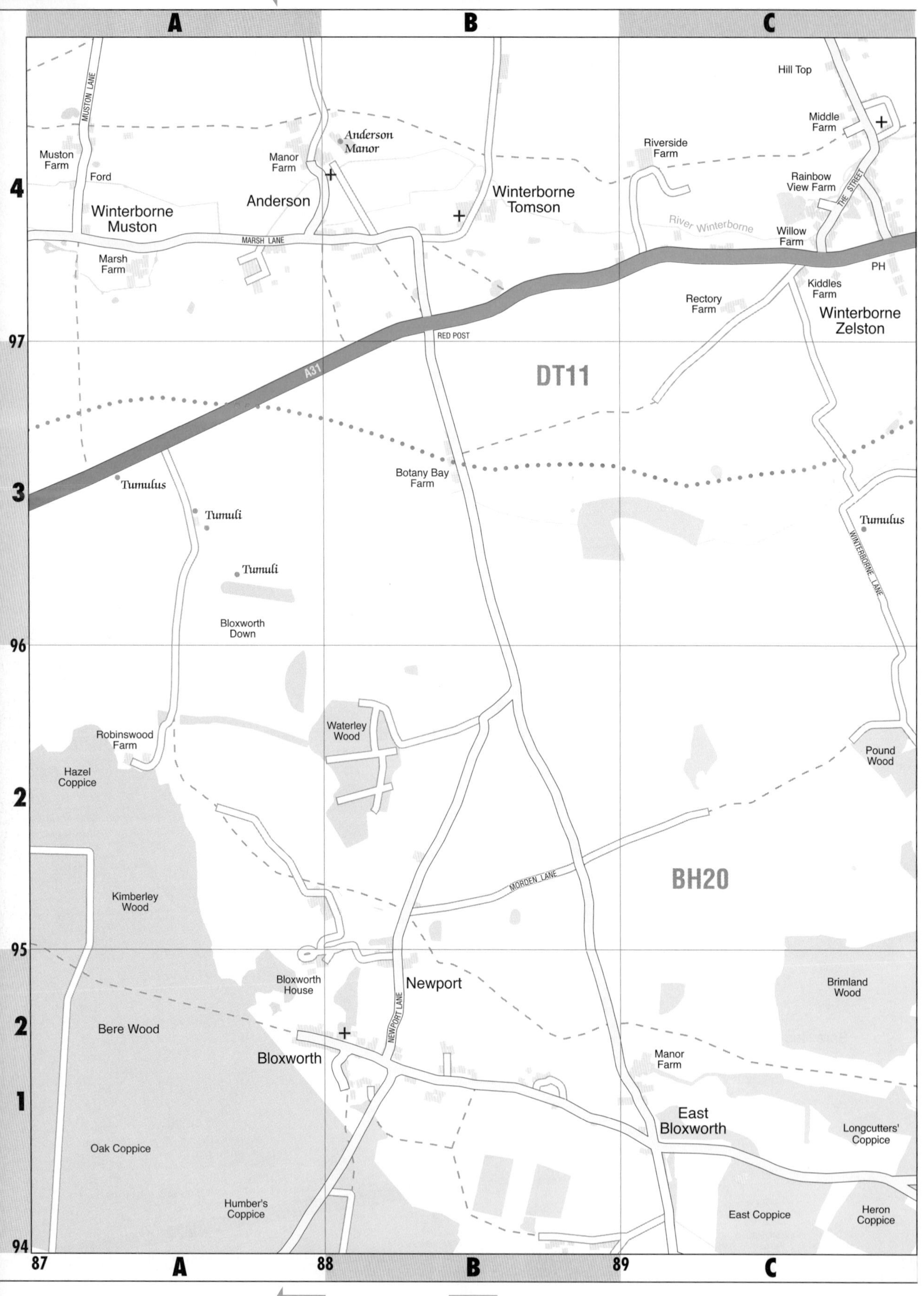

A   **B**   **C**

Hill Top

Middle
Farm

Muston
Farm

Ford

MUSTON LANE

*Anderson
Manor*

Manor
Farm

Riverside
Farm

Rainbow
View Farm

THE STREET

4

Winterborne
Muston

Anderson

Winterborne
Tomson

River Winterborne

Willow
Farm

PH

Marsh
Farm

MARSH LANE

Rectory
Farm

Kiddles
Farm

Winterborne
Zelston

97

RED POST

A31

DT11

Tumulus

Botany Bay
Farm

Tumulus

3

Tumuli

WINTERBORNE LANE

Tumuli

Bloxworth
Down

96

Robinswood
Farm

Waterley
Wood

Pound
Wood

Hazel
Coppice

2

Kimberley
Wood

MORDEN LANE

BH20

95

Bloxworth
House

Newport

Brimland
Wood

2

Bere Wood

NEWPORT LANE

Bloxworth

Manor
Farm

1

East
Bloxworth

Longcutters'
Coppice

Oak Coppice

Humber's
Coppice

East Coppice

Heron
Coppice

94

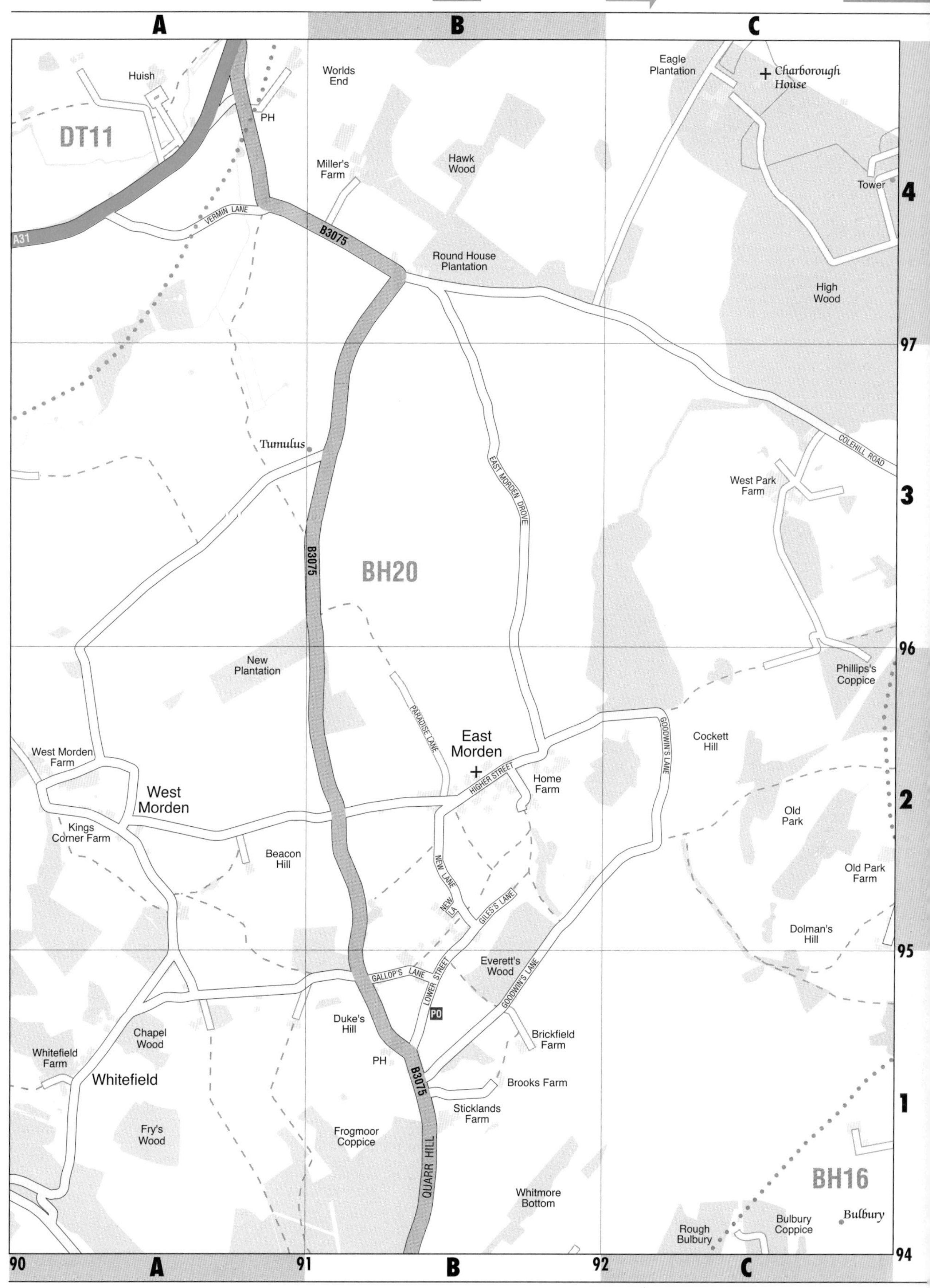

Huish

DT11

Worlds End

Eagle Plantation

Charborough House

Miller's Farm

Hawk Wood

Tower

4

VERMIN LANE

PH

A31

B3075

Round House Plantation

High Wood

97

Tumulus

EAST MORDEN DRIVE

West Park Farm

COLEHILL ROAD

3

B3075

BH20

New Plantation

96

PARADISE LANE

East Morden

Phillips's Coppice

GOODWIN'S LANE

Cockett Hill

West Morden Farm

West Morden

Home Farm

HIGHER STREET

Old Park

2

Kings Corner Farm

Beacon Hill

NEW LANE

NEW ST

GILES'S LANE

Old Park Farm

Dolman's Hill

95

GALLOP'S LANE

LOWER STREET

Everett's Wood

GOODWIN'S LANE

Whitefield Farm

Chapel Wood

Duke's Hill

PO

Brickfield Farm

Whitefield

PH

B3075

Brooks Farm

1

Fry's Wood

Frogmoor Coppice

QUARR HILL

Sticklands Farm

Whitmore Bottom

BH16

Bulbury

Rough Bulbury

Bulbury Coppice

94

83
56

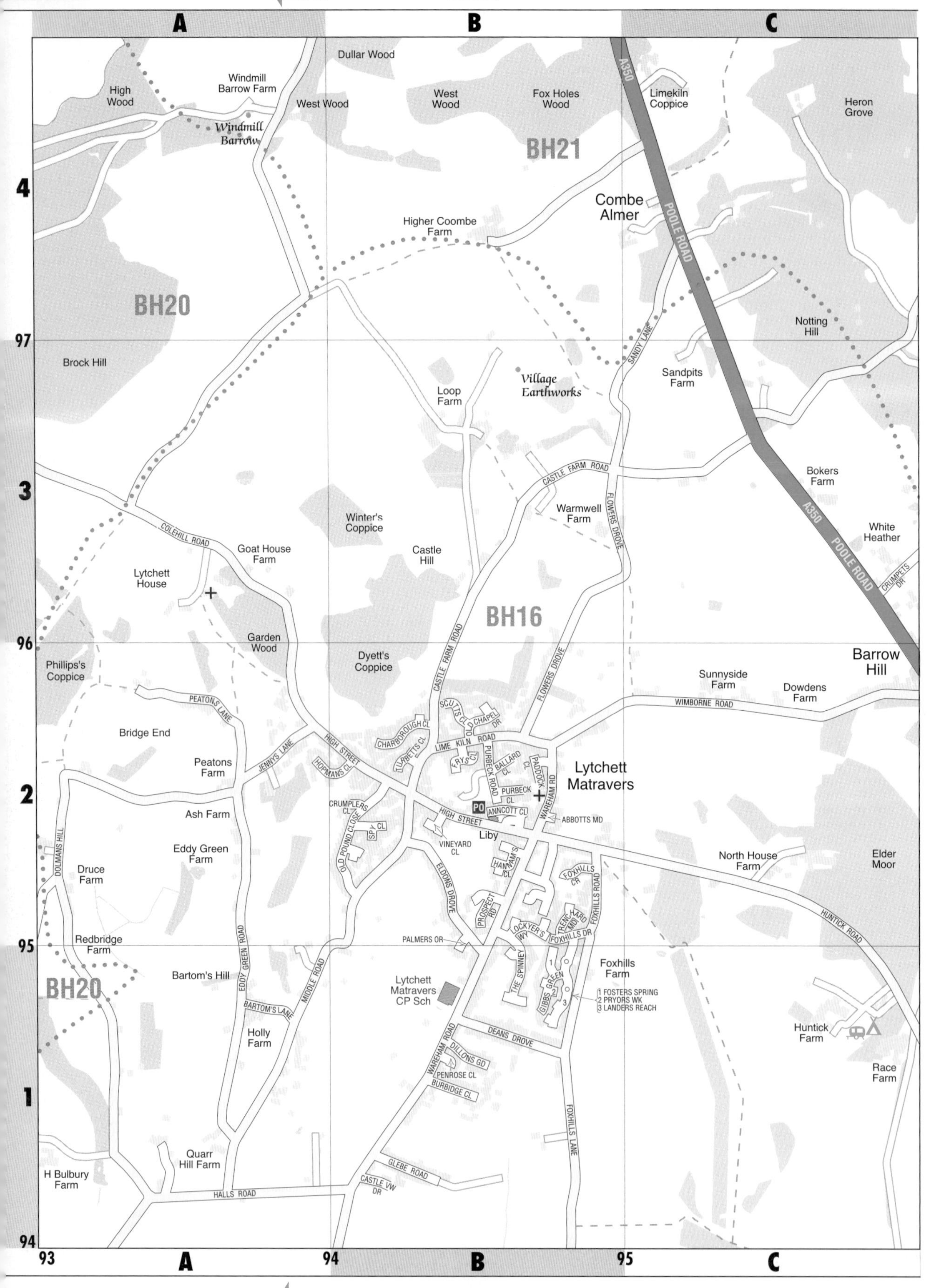
A
B
C
High Wood
Windmill Barrow Farm
Windmill Barrow
Dullar Wood
West Wood
West Wood
Fox Holes Wood
Limekiln Coppice
Heron Grove
BH21
A350
POOLE ROAD
Combe Almer
Higher Coombe Farm
BH20
Notting Hill
Brock Hill
Sandpits Farm
SANDY LANE
Loop Farm
Village Earthworks
Bokers Farm
CASTLE FARM ROAD
Warmwell Farm
FLOWERS DROVE
White Heather
COLEHILL ROAD
Goat House Farm
Winter's Coppice
Castle Hill
Lytchett House
CRUMPETS DR
BH16
Garden Wood
Phillips's Coppice
Dyett's Coppice
CASTLE FARM ROAD
FLOWERS DROVE
Barrow Hill
Sunnyside Farm
Dowdens Farm
WIMBORNE ROAD
PEATONS LANE
Bridge End
SCUTTS CL
OLD CHAPEL DR
CHARBOROUGH CL
TURBETTS CL
LIME KILN ROAD
HIGH STREET
JENNYS LANE
HOPMANS CL
FRYS CL
PURBECK ROAD
BALLARD CL
PADDOCK CL
Peatons Farm
Lytchett Matravers
WAREHAM RD
PURBECK CL
CRUMPLERS CL
PO
ANNCOTT CL
Ash Farm
HIGH STREET
ABBOTTS MD
SPY CL
OLD POUND CLOSE
VINEYARD CL
Liby
Eddy Green Farm
HAM CL
HAYWARDS CL
North House Farm
Elder Moor
DOLMANS HILL
Druce Farm
FOXHILLS CR
ELDONS DROVE
PROSPECT RD
TRENCHARD MD
FOXHILLS ROAD
LOCKYER'S WY
FOXHILLS DR
HUNTICK ROAD
EDDY GREEN ROAD
Redbridge Farm
PALMERS OR
BH20
Bartom's Hill
MIDDLE ROAD
Lytchett Matravers CP Sch
THE SPINNEY
GIBBS GREEN
Foxhills Farm
1 FOSTERS SPRING
2 PRYORS WK
3 LANDERS REACH
BARTOM'S LANE
Holly Farm
WAREHAM ROAD
DEANS DROVE
Huntick Farm
DILLONS GD
PENROSE CL
BURBIDGE CL
Race Farm
FOXHILLS LANE
Quarr Hill Farm
GLEBE ROAD
H Bulbury Farm
HALLS ROAD
CASTLE VW DR
4
97
3
96
2
95
1
94
93
94
95

83
116

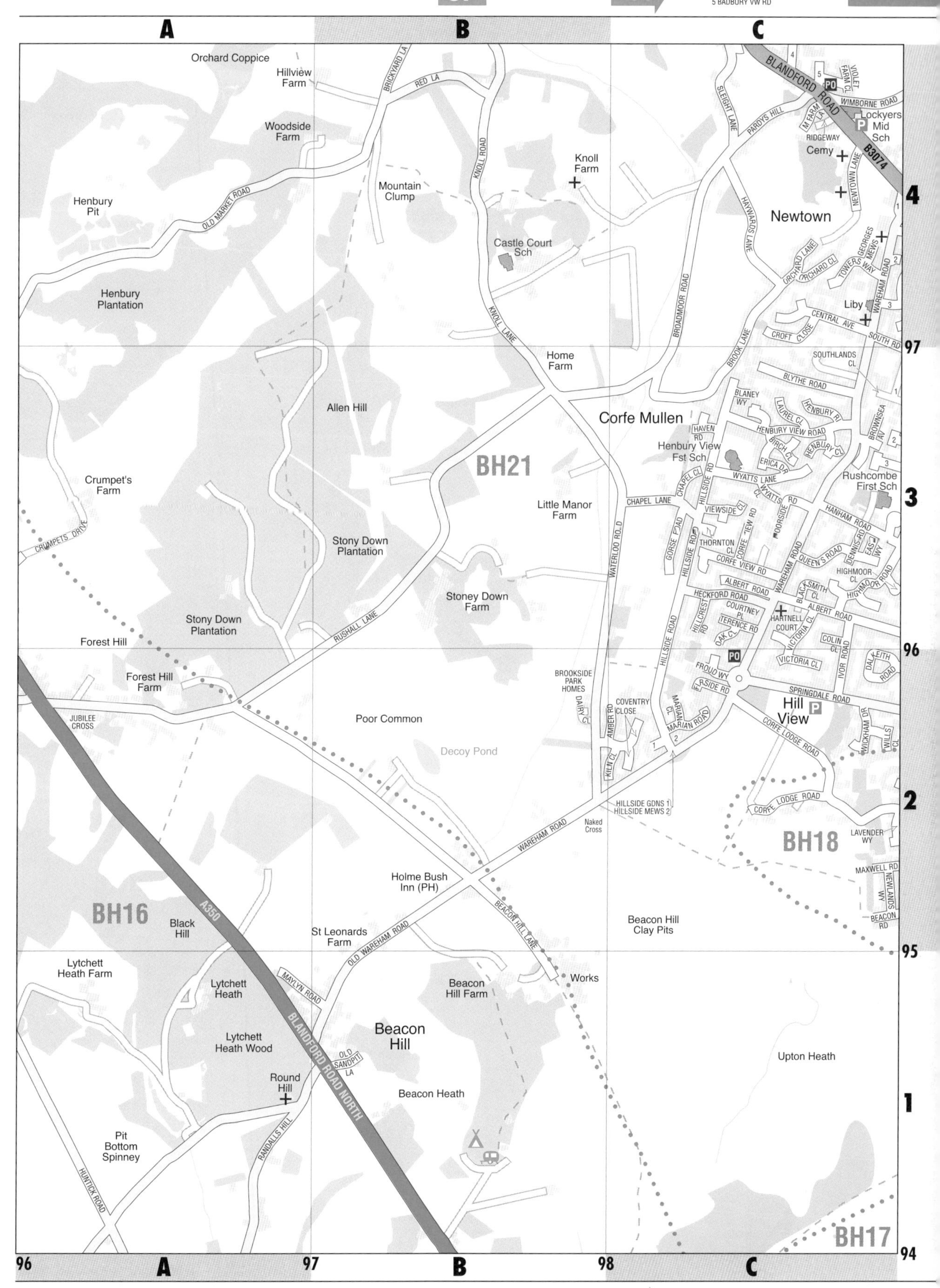

57

C3
1 SOUTHLANDS AV
2 PHELIPPS RD
3 RUSHCOMBE WY

86

C4
1 WAREHAM RD
2 TS FARM
3 PHELIPPS RD
4 OLD RECTORY CL
5 BADBURY VW RD

85

A   **B**   **C**

Orchard Coppice

Hillview Farm

BRICKYARD LA

RED LA

BLANDFORD ROAD

VIOLET FARM LA

Woodside Farm

KNOLL ROAD

Mountain Clump

Knoll Farm

SLEIGHT LANE

PARDYS HILL

PO

WIMBORNE ROAD

Lockyers Mid Sch

P

Henbury Pit

OLD MARKET ROAD

RIDGEWAY

Cemy

B3074

NEWTOWN LANE

Newtown

4

Henbury Plantation

Castle Court Sch

BROADMOOR ROAD

HAYWARDS LANE

ORCHARD LANE

ORCHARD CL

TOWERS WAY

GEORGES MEWS

WAREHAM ROAD

BROWNSEA AV

Liby

Home Farm

KNOLL LANE

BROOK LANE

CENTRAL AVE

SOUTH RD

97

Allen Hill

CROFT CLOSE

SOUTHLANDS CL

BH21

Corfe Mullen

BLANEY WY

BLYTHE ROAD

HENBURY VIEW ROAD

HENBURY CL

Crumpet's Farm

Little Manor Farm

CHAPEL CL

HAVEN RD

Henbury View Fst Sch

BIRCH DR

ERICA DR

WYATTS LANE

WYATTS RD

Rushcombe First Sch

3

CRUMPETS DRIVE

Stony Down Plantation

Stoney Down Farm

CHAPEL LANE

WATERLOO RD

GORSE PAD

HILLSIDE RD

CORFE VIEW RD

VIEWSIDE

THORNTON CL

WOODSIDE RD

HANHAM ROAD

BLACK HILL

BENNION RD

HIGHMOOR CL

HIGHMOOR RD

RUSHALL LANE

ALBERT ROAD

WAREHAM ROAD

QUEEN'S ROAD

ALBERT ROAD

Forest Hill

Stony Down Plantation

HILLSIDE ROAD

HECKFORD ROAD

HILLCREST

COURTNEY PL

TERENCE RD

OAK CL

HARTNELL

Court

VICTORIA CL

IVOR ROAD

COLIN RD

DALE RD

LEITH ROAD

96

Forest Hill Farm

FROUD WY

PO

VICTORIA CL

WICKHAM DR

TWILLS

JUBILEE CROSS

BROOKSIDE PARK HOMES

DAIRY CL

RSIDE RD

Hill View

P

SPRINGDALE ROAD

Poor Common

Decoy Pond

AMBER RD

COVENTRY CLOSE

MANNINGS

CL

MARIAN RD

CORFE LODGE ROAD

BH18

HIGH CL

HILLSIDE GDNS 1

HILLSIDE MEWS 2

CORFE LODGE ROAD

LAVENDER WY

2

WAREHAM ROAD

Naked Cross

MAXWELL RD

BH16

Black Hill

Holme Bush Inn (PH)

BEACON HILL LANE

Beacon Hill Clay Pits

BEACON HILL RD

95

Lytchett Heath Farm

St Leonards Farm

OLD WAREHAM ROAD

Works

Lytchett Heath

MAYLYN ROAD

Beacon Hill Farm

Upton Heath

Lytchett Heath Wood

BLANDFORD ROAD NORTH

A350

Beacon Hill

OLD SANDPIT LA

Round Hill

RANDALLS HILL

Beacon Heath

1

Pit Bottom Spinney

HUNTICK ROAD

BH17

94

96   **A**   **97**   **B**   **98**   **C**

85
58

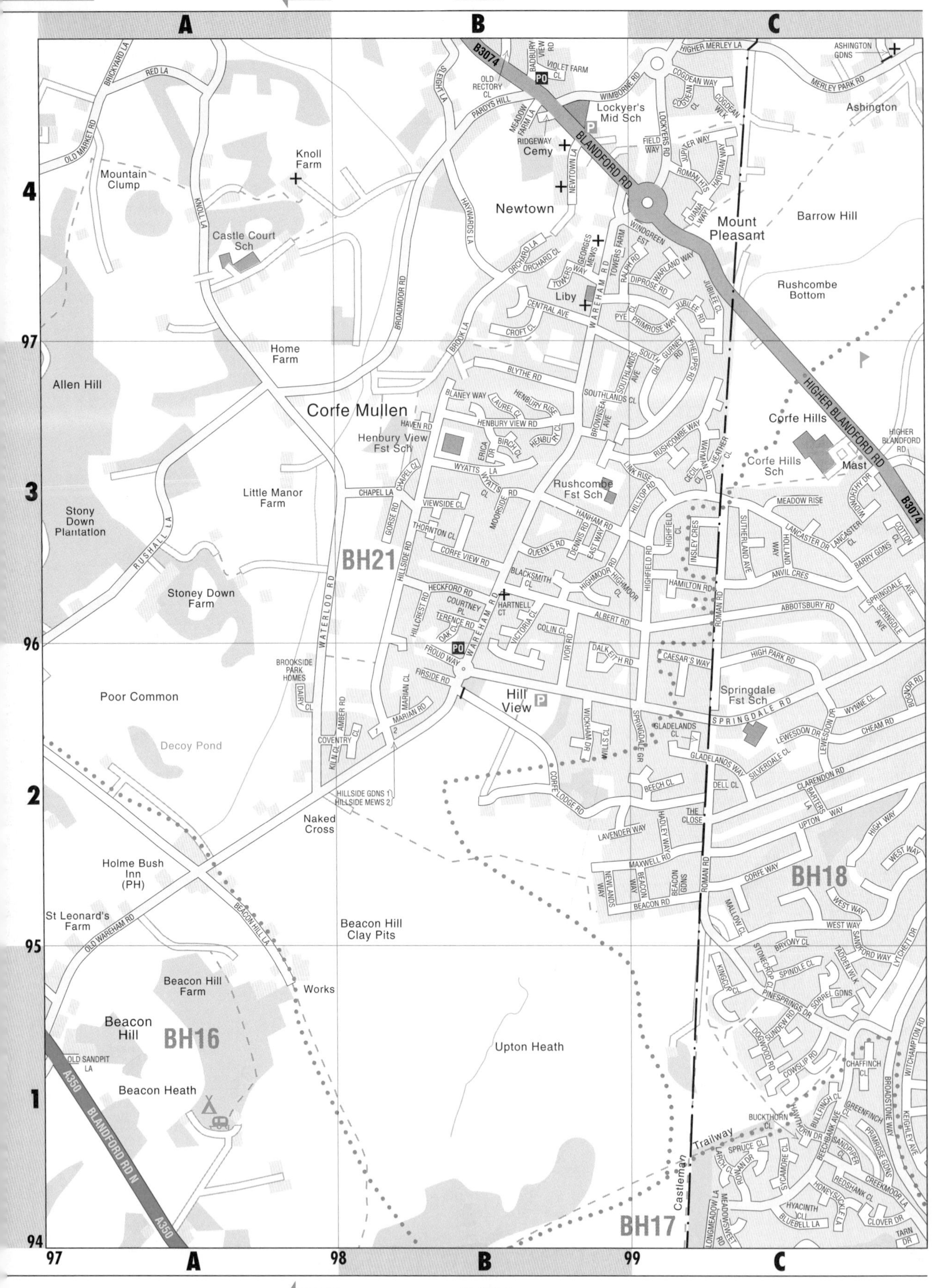
A
B
C
4
3
2
1
97
96
95
94
98
99
Corfe Mullen
Newtown
Mount Pleasant
Barrow Hill
Ashington
Rushcombe Bottom
Corfe Hills
Corfe Hills Sch
Mast
Mountain Clump
Knoll Farm
Castle Court Sch
Home Farm
Allen Hill
Henbury View Fst Sch
Little Manor Farm
Stony Down Plantation
Stoney Down Farm
Rushcombe Fst Sch
Lockyer's Mid Sch
Ridgeway Cemy
Liby
BH21
BH18
BH16
BH17
Poor Common
Decoy Pond
Hill View
Springdale Fst Sch
Naked Cross
Holme Bush Inn (PH)
St Leonard's Farm
Beacon Hill Clay Pits
Beacon Hill Farm
Beacon Hill
Beacon Heath
Works
Upton Heath
Castleman Trailway
B3074
BLANDFORD RD
HIGHER BLANDFORD RD
A350
BLANDFORD RD N
OLD WAREHAM RD
BEACON HILL LA
WAREHAM RD
WATERLOO RD
BROADMOOR RD
RUSHALL LA
KNOLL LA
RED LA
BRICKYARD LA
OLD MARKET RD
HAYWARDS LA
SLEIGHT LA
PARDYS HILL
WIMBORNE RD
HIGHER MERLEY LA
MERLEY PARK RD
ASHINGTON GDNS
ROMAN RD
SPRINGDALE RD
CORFE LODGE RD
UPTON WAY
CLARENDON RD
LEWESDON DR
ABBOTSBURY RD
HIGH PARK RD
WEST WAY
HIGH WAY
CORFE WAY
BROADSTONE WAY
WITCHAMPTON RD
KEIGHLEY AVE
LONGMEADOW LA
OLD SANDPIT LA

85
118

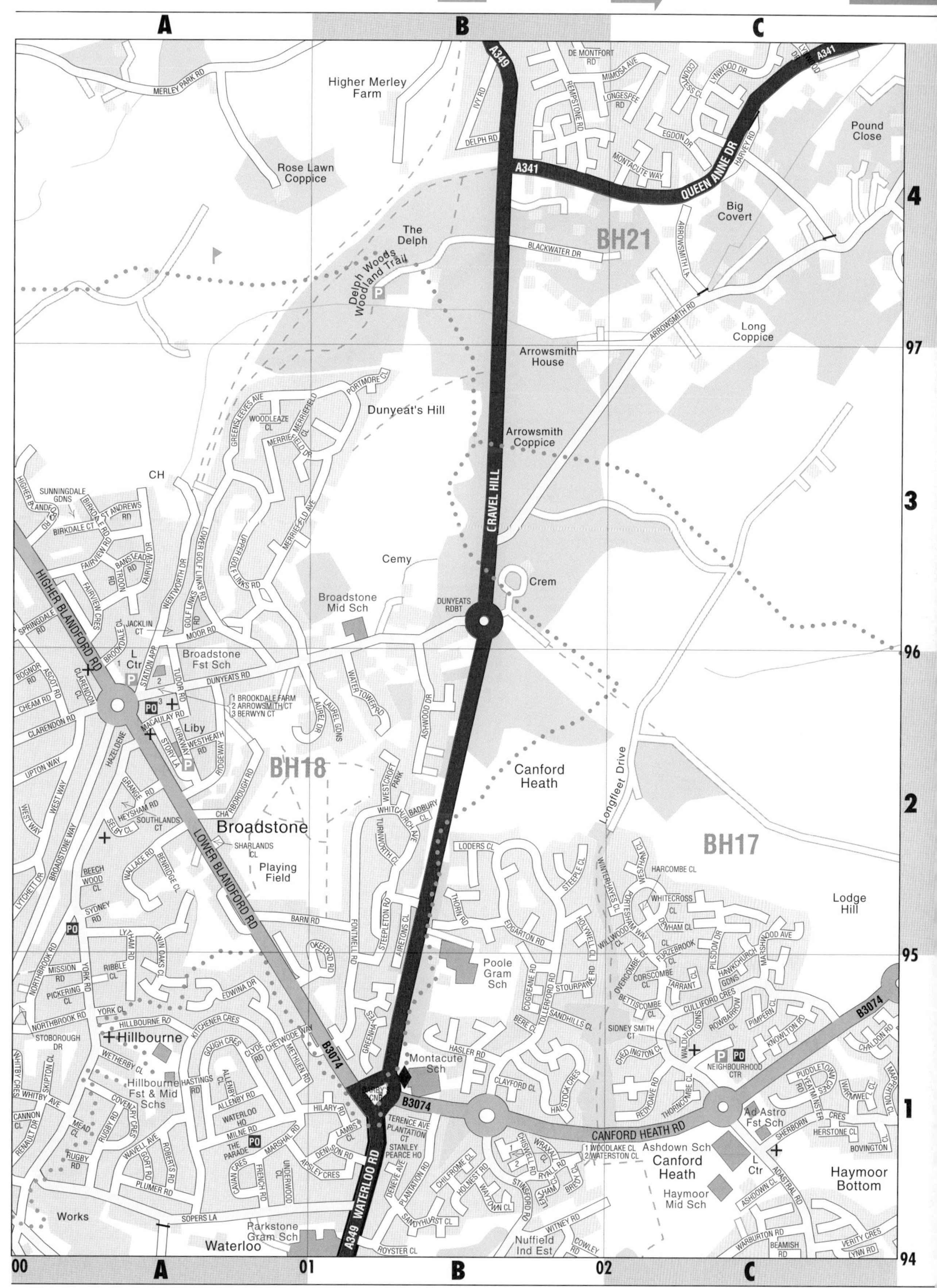
A
B
C
Higher Merley Farm
Rose Lawn Coppice
The Delph
Delph Woods Woodland Trail
BH21
Big Covert
Pound Close
Long Coppice
Arrowsmith House
Dunyeat's Hill
Arrowsmith Coppice
CRAVEL HILL
QUEEN ANNE DR
A341
A349
Cemy
Crem
Broadstone Mid Sch
Broadstone Fst Sch
BH18
Canford Heath
Longfleet Drive
BH17
Broadstone
Playing Field
HIGHER BLANDFORD RD
LOWER BLANDFORD RD
Lodge Hill
Poole Gram Sch
Montacute Sch
Hillbourne
Hillbourne Fst & Mid Schs
B3074
CANFORD HEATH RD
Ad Astra Fst Sch
Ashdown Sch
Haymoor Mid Sch
Haymoor Bottom
Works
Parkstone Gram Sch
Waterloo
WATERLOO RD
Nuffield Ind Est
4
97
3
96
2
95
1
94
00
01
02

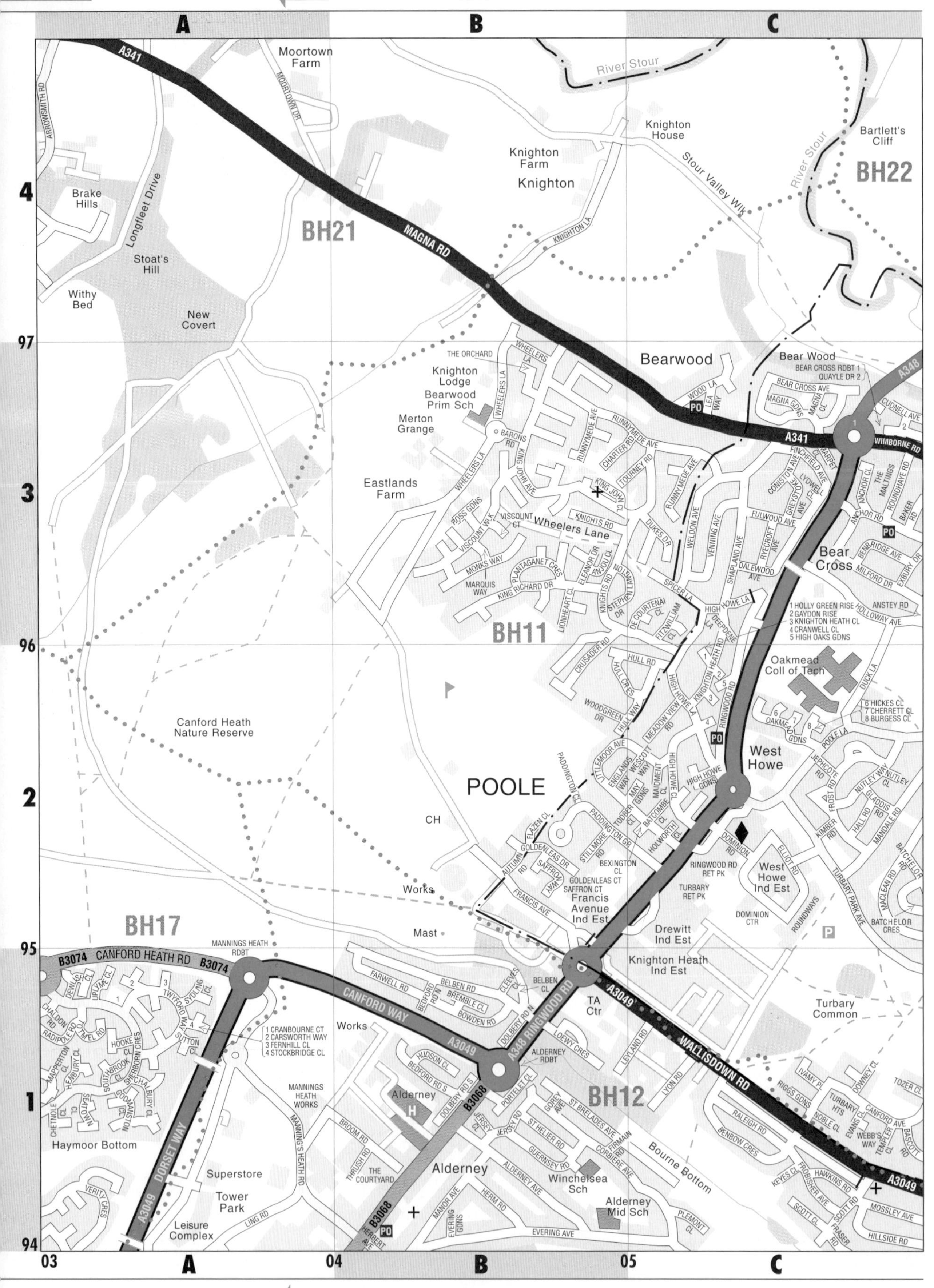

A

B

C

A341

Moortown
Farm

River Stour

Knighton
House

Bartlett's
Cliff

River Stour

4

Brake
Hills

Knighton
Farm

Knighton

BH22

Longfleet Drive

Stour Valley Wlk

BH21

MAGNA RD

Stoat's
Hill

Withy
Bed

New
Covert

97

THE ORCHARD

WHEELERS
LA

Bearwood

Bear Wood

BEAR CROSS RDBT 1
QUAYLE DR 2

A348

Knighton
Lodge

Bearwood
Prim Sch

A341

WIMBORNE RD

Merton
Grange

Eastlands
Farm

Wheelers Lane

Bear
Cross

3

1 HOLLY GREEN RISE
2 GAYDON RISE
3 KNIGHTON HEATH CL
4 CRANWELL CL
5 HIGH OAKS GDNS

Oakmead
Coll of Tech

BH11

6 HICKES CL
7 CHERRETT CL
8 BURGESS CL

96

West
Howe

Canford Heath
Nature Reserve

POOLE

CH

West
Howe
Ind Est

Works

Francis
Avenue
Ind Est

2

Mast

Drewitt
Ind Est

DOMINION
CTR

BH17

MANNINGS HEATH
RDBT

Knighton
Heath
Ind Est

95

B3074 CANFORD HEATH RD B3074

CANFORD WAY

A3049

WALLISDOWN RD

TA
Ctr

Turbary
Common

1 CRANBOURNE CT
2 CARSWORTH WAY
3 FERNHILL CL
4 STOCKBRIDGE CL

Works

A3049

ALDERNEY
RDBT

BH12

1

Mannings
Heath
Works

Alderney

H

Haymoor Bottom

THE
COURTYARD

Alderney

Winchelsea
Sch

Bourne Bottom

A3049

Superstore

Tower
Park

Alderney
Mid Sch

Leisure
Complex

94

03

A

04

B

05

C

61
90

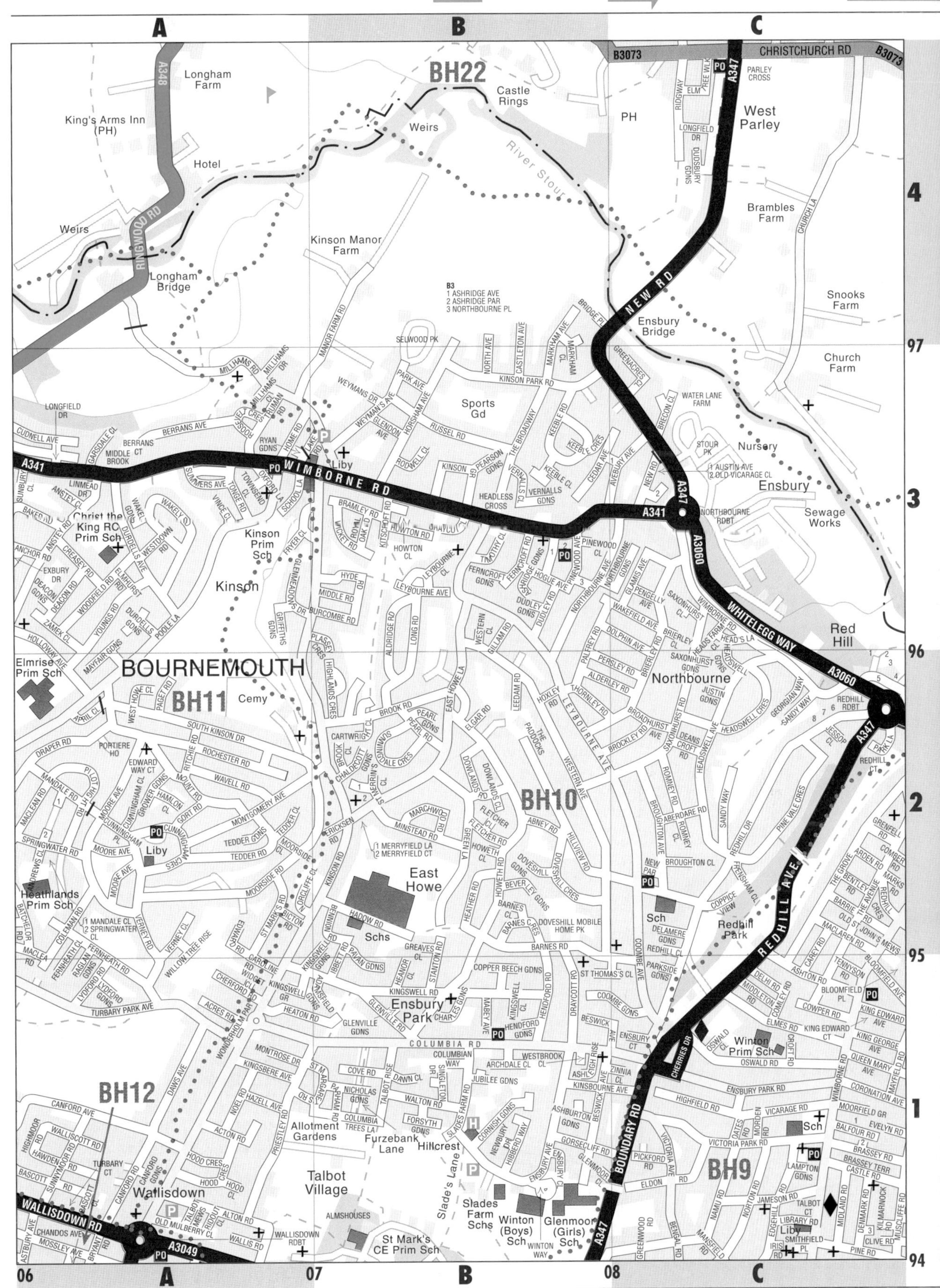
A
B
C
BH22
BH11
BH10
BH12
BH9
BOURNEMOUTH
Longham Farm
King's Arms Inn (PH)
Hotel
Weirs
Longham Bridge
Castle Rings
River Stour
Kinson Manor Farm
West Parley
Parley Cross
Brambles Farm
Snooks Farm
Church Farm
Ensbury Bridge
Water Lane Farm
Nursery
Ensbury
Sewage Works
Red Hill
Northbourne
Kinson
Kinson Prim Sch
Christ the King RC Prim Sch
Elmrise Prim Sch
Heathlands Prim Sch
Cemy
Sports Gd
East Howe
Schs
Ensbury Park
Redhill Park
Winton Prim Sch
Allotment Gardens
Furzebank Lane
Hillcrest
Talbot Village
Wallisdown
Slades Farm Schs
Winton (Boys) Sch
Glenmoor (Girls) Sch
St Mark's CE Prim Sch
Almshouses
A341 WIMBORNE RD
NEW RD
WHITELEGG WAY
REDHILL AVE
BOUNDARY RD
RINGWOOD RD
CHRISTCHURCH RD
WALLISDOWN RD
A347
A348
A3060
A3049
B3073
B3
1 ASHRIDGE AVE
2 ASHRIDGE PAR
3 NORTHBOURNE PL
1 MERRYFIELD LA
2 MERRYFIELD CT
1 MANDALE CL
2 SPRINGWATER CL
1 AUSTIN AVE
2 OLD VICARAGE CL
4
97
3
96
2
95
1
94
06
07
08

121
90

A **B** **C**

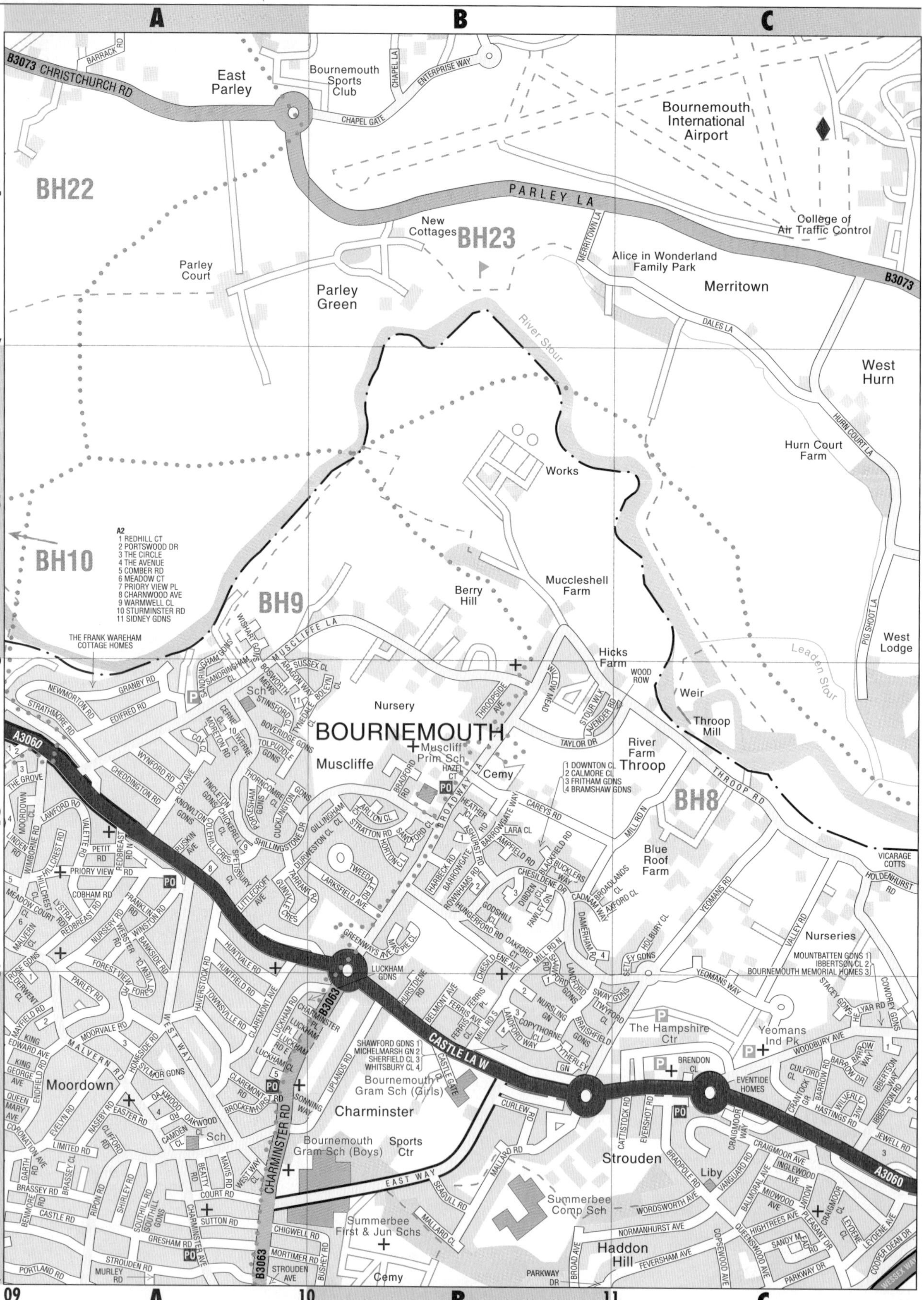

B3073 CHRISTCHURCH RD

BARRACK RD

East Parley

Bournemouth Sports Club

CHAPEL LA
ENTERPRISE WAY

CHAPEL GATE

4

BH22

PARLEY LA

Bournemouth International Airport

New Cottages

BH23

MERRITOWN LA

College of Air Traffic Control

Parley Court

Alice in Wonderland Family Park

Merritown

B3073

Parley Green

DALES LA

River Stour

97

West Hurn

HURN COURT LA

Works

Hurn Court Farm

3

BH10

A2
1 REDHILL CT
2 PORTSWOOD DR
3 THE CIRCLE
4 THE AVENUE
5 COMBER RD
6 MEADOW CT
7 PRIORY VIEW PL
8 CHARNWOOD AVE
9 WARMWELL CL
10 STURMINSTER RD
11 SIDNEY GDNS

Muccleshell Farm

Berry Hill

Leaden Stour

West Lodge

THE FRANK WAREHAM COTTAGE HOMES

BH9

Hicks Farm

WOOD ROW

Weir

PIG SHOOT LA

96

MUSCLIFFE LA

Nursery

BOURNEMOUTH

Throop Mill

NEWMORTON RD
STRATHMORE RD
GRANBY RD
EDIFRED RD

Muscliffe Prim Sch

River Farm

Throop

THROOP RD

Muscliffe

Cemy

1 DOWNTON CL
2 CALMORE CL
3 FRITHAM GDNS
4 BRAMSHAW GDNS

BH8

2

A3060

THE GROVE
MOORDOWN

WYNFORD RD
OAK RD
CHEDDINGTON RD

Blue Roof Farm

VICARAGE COTTS
HOLDENHURST

Nurseries

MOUNTBATTEN GDNS 1
IBBERTSON CL 2
BOURNEMOUTH MEMORIAL HOMES 3

YEOMANS WAY

95

Luckham Gdns

The Hampshire Ctr

Yeomans Ind Pk

WEST WAY
PARLEY RD
FOREST VIEW RD

HUNTVALE RD
HUNTFIELD RD

B3063

CHARMINSTER RD

CASTLE LA W

BRENDON CL

Eventide Homes

Moordown

Shawford Gdns 1
Michelmarsh Gn 2
Sherfield Cl 3
Whitsbury Cl 4

Bournemouth Gram Sch (Girls)

1

Charminster

Bournemouth Gram Sch (Boys)

Sports Ctr

Strouden

Liby

A3060

EAST WAY

MALLARD RD

Summerbee Comp Sch

Haddon Hill

Summerbee First & Jun Schs

B3063

Cemy

PARKWAY DR

94

09 **A** 10 **B** 11 **C**

63
92

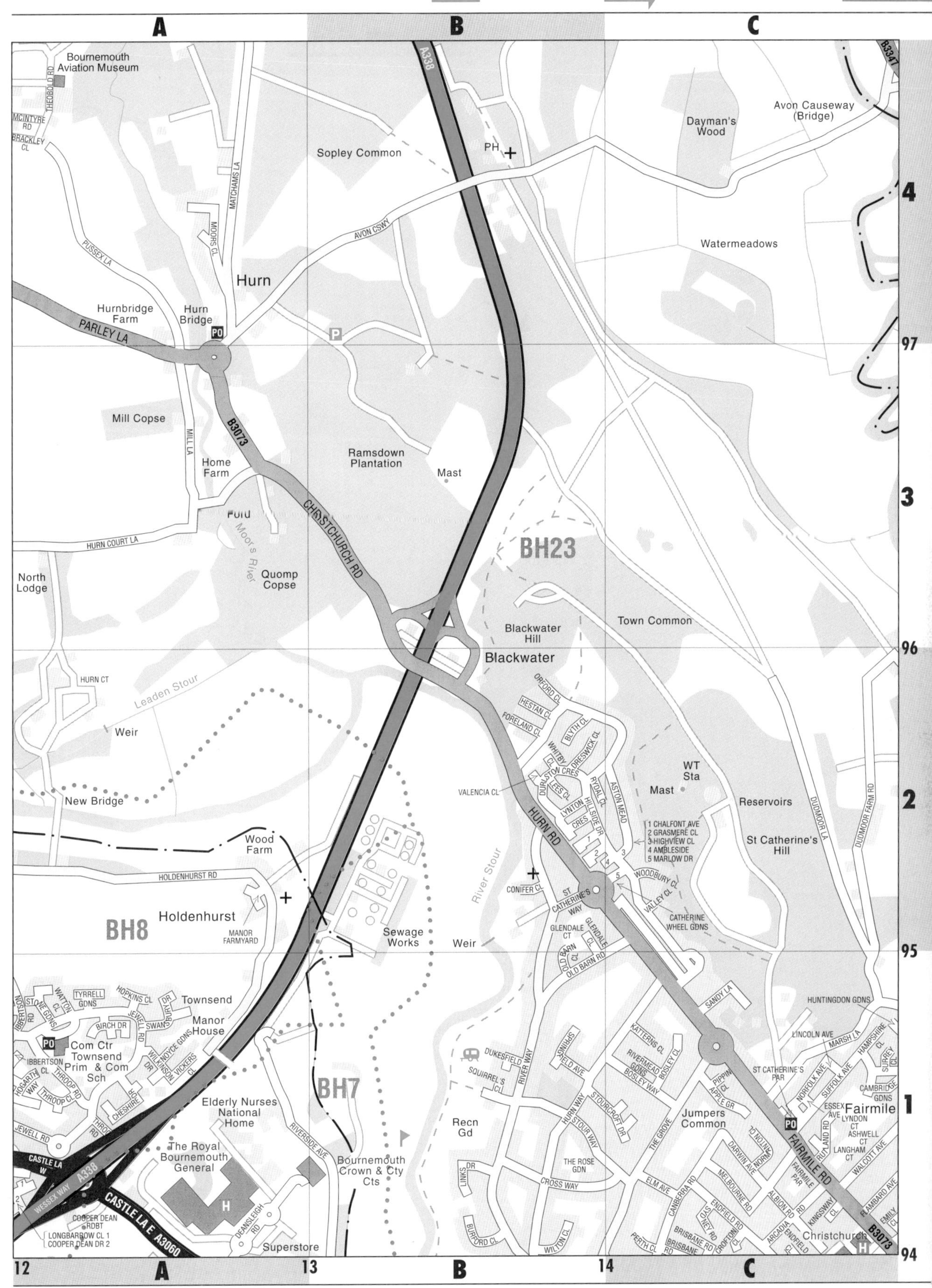
A
B
C
Bournemouth
Aviation Museum
Sopley Common
PH
Dayman's
Wood
Avon Causeway
(Bridge)
Watermeadows
Hurn
Hurnbridge
Farm
Hurn
Bridge
PARLEY LA
AVON CSWY
MATCHAMS LA
MOORS CL
PUSSEX LA
A338
B3347
Mill Copse
MILL LA
B3073
Home
Farm
Ramsdown
Plantation
Mast
CHRISTCHURCH RD
Ford
Moors River
HURN COURT LA
BH23
North
Lodge
Quomp
Copse
Town Common
Blackwater
Hill
Blackwater
HURN CT
Leaden Stour
Weir
New Bridge
WT
Sta
Mast
Reservoirs
St Catherine's
Hill
DUDMOOR LA
DUDMOOR FARM RD
HURN RD
VALENCIA CL
1 CHALFONT AVE
2 GRASMERE CL
3 HIGHVIEW CL
4 AMBLESIDE
5 MARLOW DR
Wood
Farm
HOLDENHURST RD
BH8
Holdenhurst
MANOR
FARMYARD
Sewage
Works
River Stour
Weir
CONIFER CL
ST CATHERINE'S WAY
CATHERINE
WHEEL GDNS
GLENDALE
CT
OLD BARN RD
SANDY LA
HUNTINGDON GDNS
LINCOLN AVE
Townsend
Manor
House
Com Ctr
Townsend
Prim & Com
Sch
BH7
Elderly Nurses
National
Home
The Royal
Bournemouth
General
RIVERSIDE AVE
Bournemouth
Crown & Cty
Cts
Recn
Gd
DUKESFIELD
SQUIRREL'S CL
RIVER WAY
Jumpers
Common
Fairmile
FAIRMILE RD
THE ROSE
GDN
CROSS WAY
ELM AVE
CASTLE LA W
CASTLE LA E A3060
WESSEX WAY
COOPER DEAN
RDBT
LONGBARROW CL 1
COOPER DEAN DR 2
DEANSLEIGH RD
Superstore
Christchurch
BURFORD CL
WILTON CL
PERTH CL
4
97
3
96
2
95
1
94
12
13
14

123
92

91

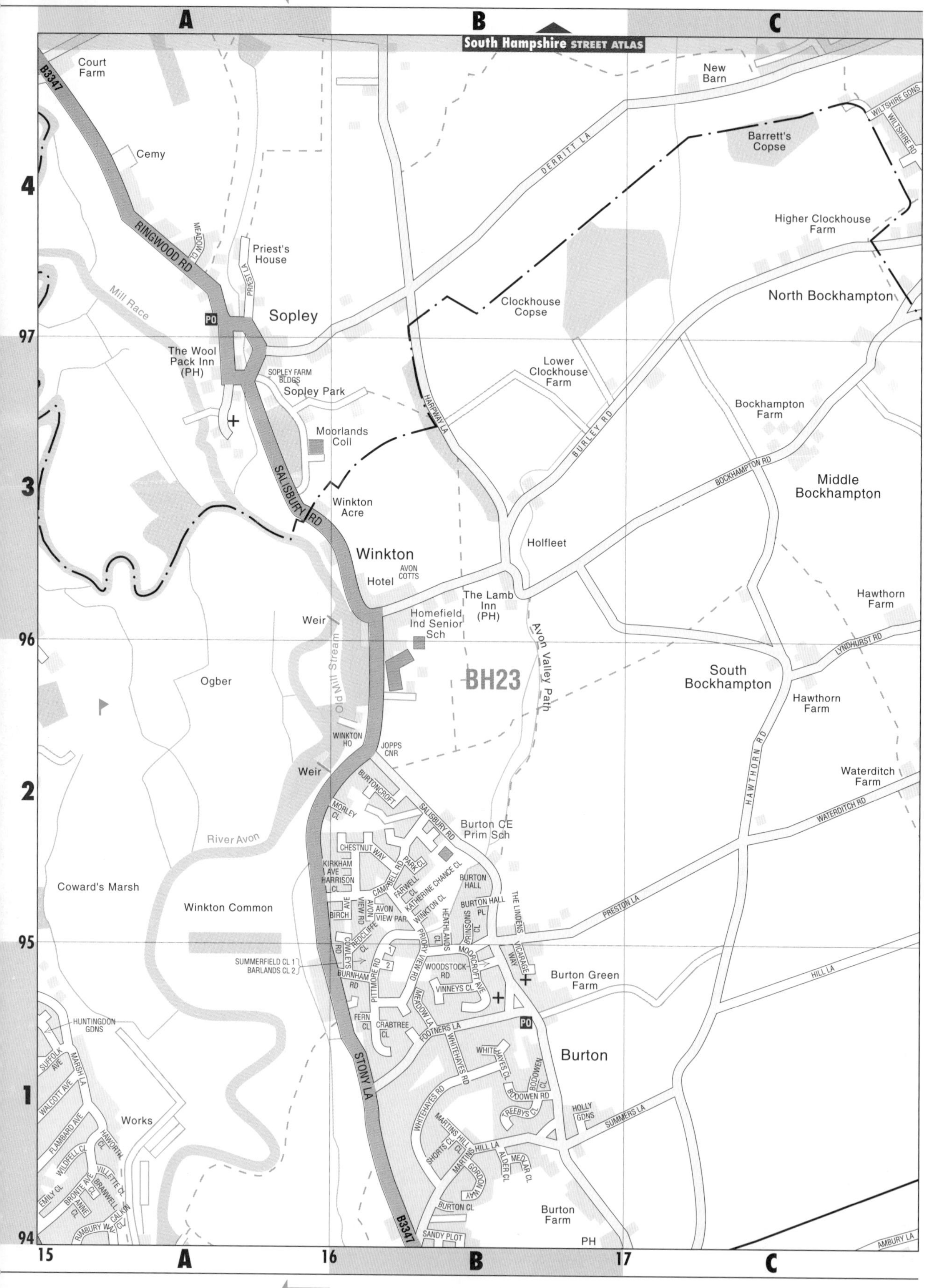
South Hampshire STREET ATLAS
A
B
C
Court Farm
New Barn
Barrett's Copse
Cemy
DERRITT LA
Higher Clockhouse Farm
Priest's House
RINGWOOD RD
Mill Race
Sopley
Clockhouse Copse
North Bockhampton
The Wool Pack Inn (PH)
SOPLEY FARM BLDGS
Sopley Park
Lower Clockhouse Farm
Moorlands Coll
HARPWAY LA
BURLEY RD
Bockhampton Farm
SALISBURY RD
BOCKHAMPTON RD
Middle Bockhampton
Winkton Acre
Winkton
Holfleet
Hotel
AVON COTTS
The Lamb Inn (PH)
Hawthorn Farm
Weir
Homefield Ind Senior Sch
Avon Valley Path
LYNDHURST RD
Ogber
Old Mill Stream
BH23
South Bockhampton
Hawthorn Farm
WINKTON HO
JOPPS CNR
Weir
HAWTHORN RD
Waterditch Farm
BURTONCROFT
MORLEY CL
SALISBURY RD
Burton CE Prim Sch
WATERDITCH RD
River Avon
CHESTNUT WAY
Coward's Marsh
Winkton Common
BURTON HALL
PRESTON LA
THE LINDENS
SUMMERFIELD CL 1
BARLANDS CL 2
WOODSTOCK RD
VICARAGE WAY
Burton Green Farm
HILL LA
VINNEYS CL
HUNTINGDON GDNS
FOOTNERS LA
CRABTREE CL
FERN CL
Burton
STONY LA
Works
HOLLY GDNS
SUMMERS LA
MARTINS HILL LA
Burton Farm
BURTON CL
SANDY PLOT
PH
AMBURY LA
B3347
4
97
3
96
2
95
1
94
15
16
17

91
124

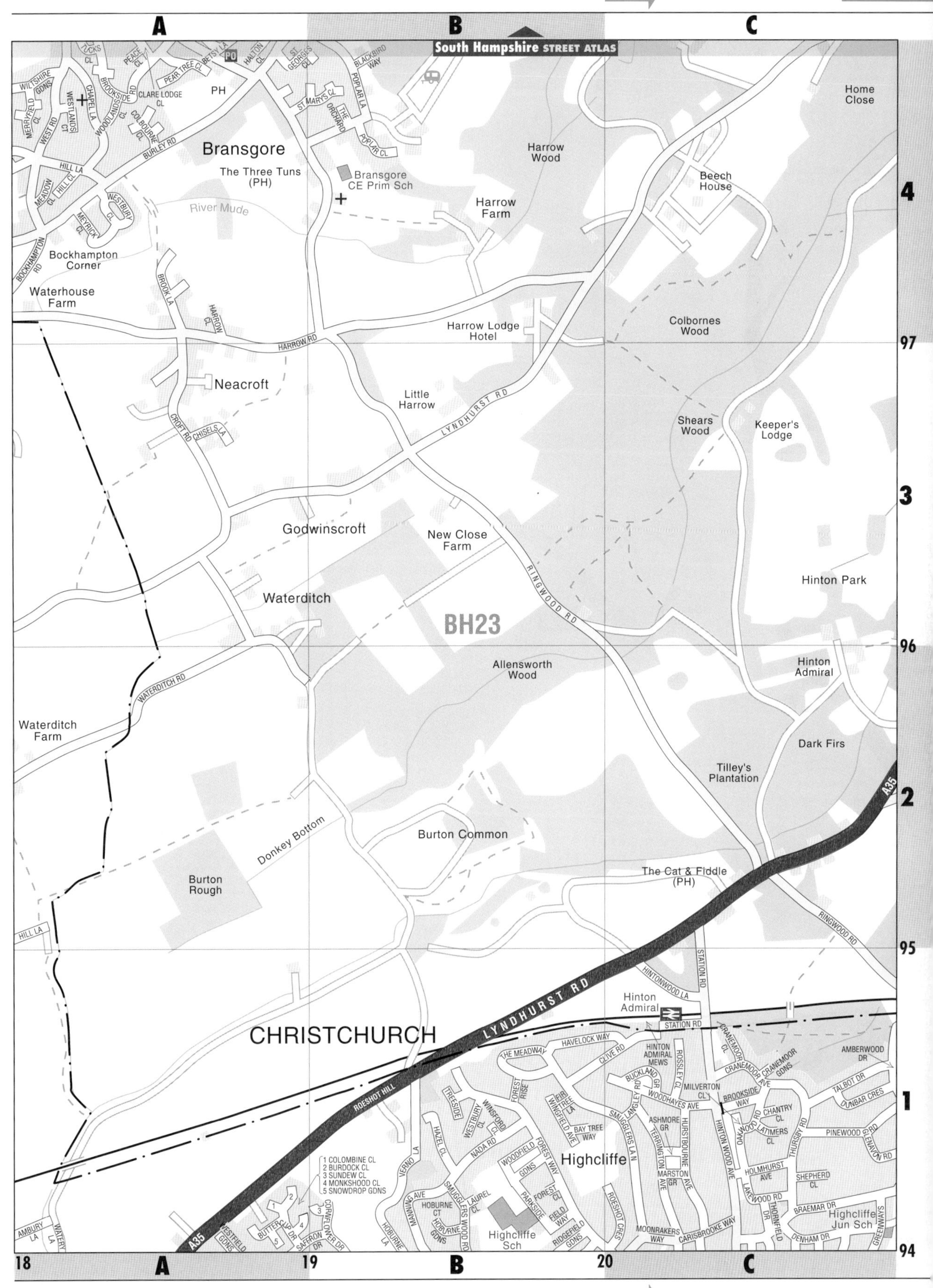

A   B   C

South Hampshire STREET ATLAS

Home Close

Bransgore

The Three Tuns (PH)

Bransgore CE Prim Sch

Harrow Wood

Beech House

Harrow Farm

River Mude

Bockhampton Corner

Waterhouse Farm

Harrow Lodge Hotel

Colbornes Wood

97

Neacroft

Little Harrow

LYNDHURST RD

Shears Wood

Keeper's Lodge

3

Godwinscroft

New Close Farm

RINGWOOD RD

Hinton Park

Waterditch

BH23

96

Allensworth Wood

Hinton Admiral

Waterditch Farm

Dark Firs

Tilley's Plantation

Donkey Bottom

Burton Common

A35

2

Burton Rough

The Cat & Fiddle (PH)

RINGWOOD RD

HILL LA

95

HINTONWOOD LA

STATION RD

CHRISTCHURCH

LYNDHURST RD

Hinton Admiral

STATION RD

Hinton Admiral Mews

AMBERWOOD DR

ROESHOT HILL

Highcliffe

Highcliffe Sch

1 COLOMBINE CL
2 BURDOCK CL
3 SUNDEW CL
4 MONKSHOOD CL
5 SNOWDROP GDNS

Highcliffe Jun Sch

A35

18   A   19   B   20   C   94

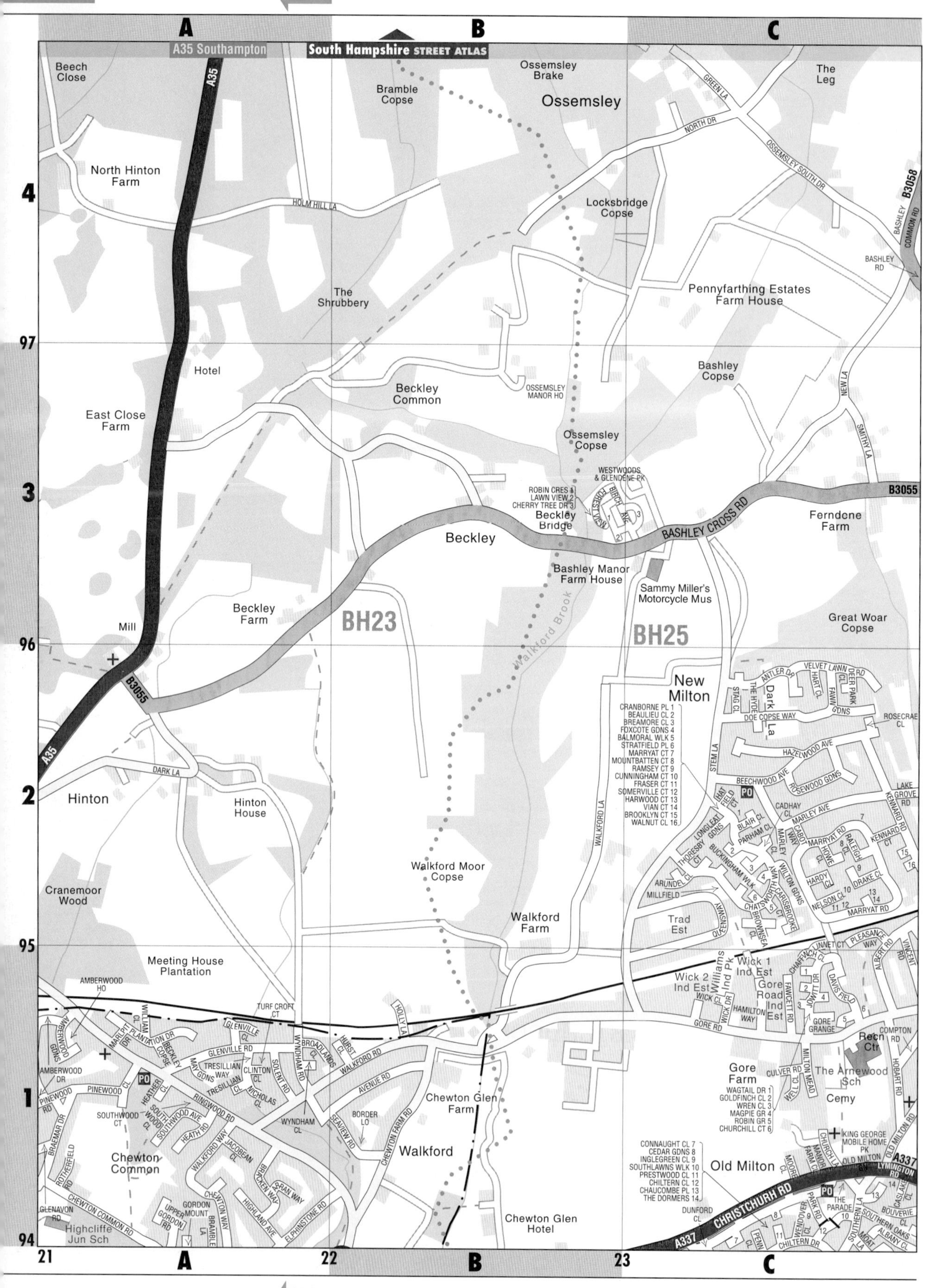

A35 Southampton
A35

Beech Close

North Hinton Farm

HOLM HILL LA

The Shrubbery

Hotel

East Close Farm

Mill

Beckley Farm

BH23

B3055

Hinton

Dark La

Hinton House

Cranemoor Wood

Meeting House Plantation

AMBERWOOD HO

AMBERWOOD DR

Amberwood DR

PO

Pinewood RD

Southwood CT

Chewton Common

Highcliffe Jun Sch

Glenavon RD

Braemar RD

Rotherfield

Heather Cl

Southwood Ave

Southwood Cl

Gordon Mount RD

Upper Gordon RD

Chewton Common RD

Bracken Way

Highland Ave

Elphinstone RD

Bramble La

Jacobean Cl

Walkford Way

Span Way

Gordon RD

Bramble Copse

Beckley Common

OSSEMSLEY MANOR HO

Ossemsley Copse

Beckley

Beckley Bridge

ROBIN CRES 1
LAWN VIEW 2
CHERRY TREE DR 3

Bashley Manor Farm House

Walkford Brook

Walkford Moor Copse

WALKFORD LA

Walkford Farm

HOLLY LA

TURF CROFT CT

GLENVILLE

Glenville RD

Tresillian Way

Tresillian Cl

Clinton Cl

Nicholas Cl

MAZ GDNS

Ringwood RD

Wyndham RD

Broad Lawns

HURST RD

Walkford RD

Solent RD

Avenue RD

Wyndham Cl

Fearview RD

Border Lo

Chewton Glen Farm

Walkford

Chewton Glen Hotel

Ossemsley

Ossemsley Brake

GREEN LA

NORTH DR

Locksbridge Copse

Pennyfarthing Estates Farm House

Bashley Copse

WESTWOODS & GLENDENE PK

BASHLEY CROSS RD

Sammy Miller's Motorcycle Mus

BH25

New Milton

CRANBORNE PL 1
BEAULIEU CL 2
BREAMORE CL 3
FOXCOTE GDNS 4
BALMORAL WLK 5
STRATFIELD PL 6
MARRYAT CT 7
MOUNTBATTEN CT 8
RAMSEY CT 9
CUNNINGHAM CT 10
FRASER CT 11
SOMERVILLE CT 12
HARWOOD CT 13
VIAN CT 14
BROOKLYN CT 15
WALNUT CL 16.

OSSEMSLEY SOUTH DR

The Leg

B3058

BASHLEY COMMON RD

BASHLEY RD

SMITH LA

MILL LN

Bashley Copse

B3055

Ferndene Farm

Great Woar Copse

VELVET LAWN RD

ANTLER CL

HART CL

DEER PARK CL

FAWN CL

Dark La

THE HYDE

STAG CL

DOE COPSE WAY

ROSEWOOD GDNS

ROSECRAE CL

HAZELWOOD AVE

STEM LA

BEECHWOOD AVE

LAKE GROVE RD

KENNARD RD

PO

CADHAY CL

MARLEY AVE

MARRYAT RD

KENNARD RD

THORNLEAT GDNS

LONGLEAT GDNS

BLAIR PL

PARHAM CL

BUCKINGHAM WLK

WILTON GDNS

HARDY CT

DRAKE CL

MARRYAT RD

ARUNDEL

MILLFIELD

CHATSW

BROWNSEA

NELSON CT

Trad Est

Williams Ind Pk

Wick 1 Ind Est

Wick 2 Ind Est

Gore Road Ind Est

HAMILTON WAY

GORE RD

Gore Farm

CULVER RD

WAGTAIL DR 1
GOLDFINCH CL 2
WREN CL 3
MAGPIE GR 4
ROBIN GR 5
CHURCHILL CT 6

CONNAUGHT CL 7
CEDAR GDNS 8
INGLEGREEN CL 9
SOUTHLAWNS WLK 10
PRESTWOOD CL 11
CHILTERN CL 12
CHAUCOMBE PL 13
THE DORMERS 14.

Old Milton

DUNFORD CL

The Arnewood Sch

Cemy

Recn Ctr

Gore Grange

COMPTON RD

HOBART RD

MILTON MEAD

KING GEORGE MOBILE HOME PK

OLD MILTON RD

A337 LYMINGTON

CHRISTCHURH RD

A337

The Parade

PO

CHILTERN DR

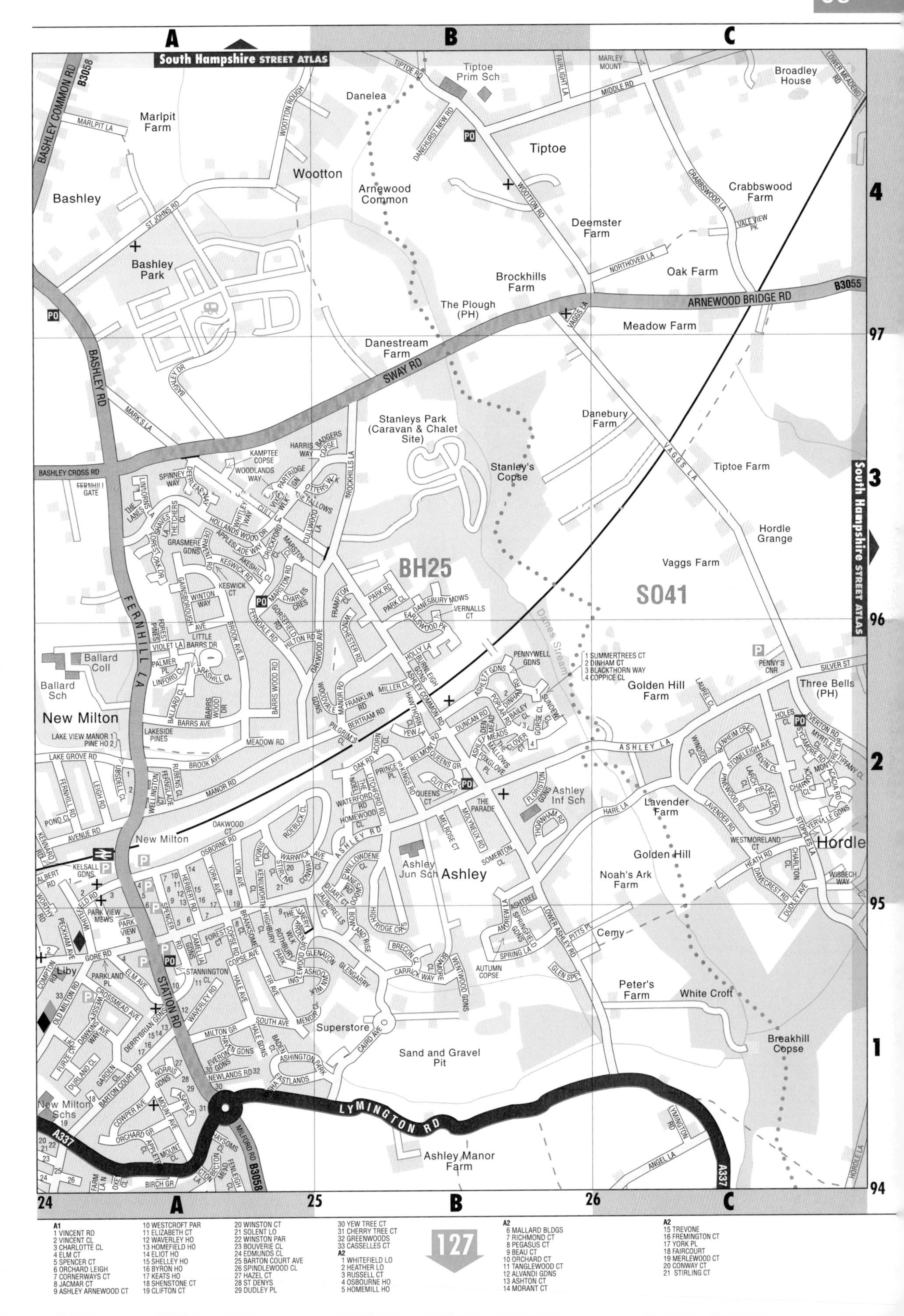

South Hampshire STREET ATLAS

64

B3
1 ELIZABETH CL
2 DOLPHIN CL
3 SHERBOURNE LA
4 POOLE'S CT
5 MONMOUTH ST
6 BRIDGE ST

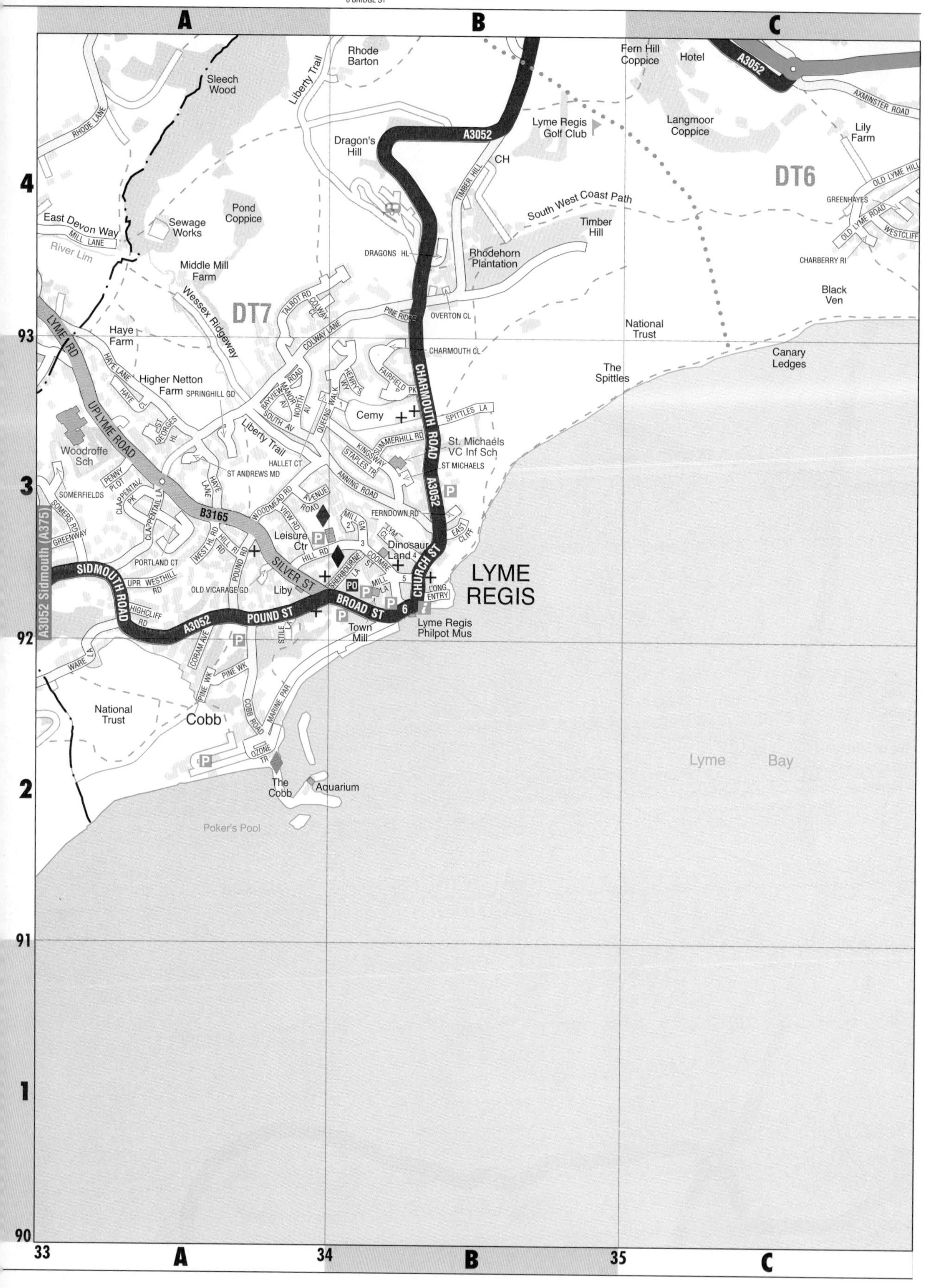

A B C

4

Sleech Wood
Rhode Barton
Fern Hill Coppice
Hotel
A3052

Liberty Trail
Dragon's Hill
A3052
Lyme Regis Golf Club
CH
Langmoor Coppice
DT6
Lily Farm
AXMINSTER ROAD
GREENHAYES
OLD LYME ROAD
WESTCLIFF

RHODE LANE
TIMBER HILL
South West Coast Path
Timber Hill
CHARBERRY RI

East Devon Way
MILL LANE
River Lim
Sewage Works
Pond Coppice
Middle Mill Farm
DRAGONS HL
Rhodehorn Plantation
Black Ven

93

Wessex Ridgeway
DT7
TALBOT RD
GOLWAY
PINE RIDGE
OVERTON CL
CHARMOUTH CL
National Trust
Canary Ledges

Haye Farm
HAYE LANE
Higher Netton Farm
SPRINGHILL GD
GOLWAY LANE
FAIRFIELD
HENRYS
The Spittles
CHARMOUTH ROAD
The Spittles

LYME RD
UPLYME ROAD
Liberty Trail
BAYVIEW ROAD
MANOR AV
SOUTH AV
QUEENS WALK
Cemy
SPITTLES LA
A3052

3

Woodroffe Sch
PENNY PLOT
ST GEORGES HL
HALLET CT
ST ANDREWS MD
KINGSWAY
SUMMERHILL RD
STAPLES TR
ST MICHAELS
St. Michaéls VC Inf Sch

Somerfields
CLAPPENTAIL PK
CLAPPENTAIL LA
HAYE LANE
ANNING ROAD
FERNDOWN RD

B3165
WOODMEAD RD
VIEW RD
AVENUE
MILL GN
COOMBE
LYME CL
EAST CLIFF

GREENWAY
PORTLAND CT
WEST HL RD
HILL RD
Leisure Ctr
SHERBOURNE LA
MILL LA
LONG ENTRY
LYME REGIS

UPR WESTHILL RD
POUND RD
SILVER ST
3
PO
Dinosaur Land

HIGHCLIFF RD
OLD VICARAGE GD
Liby
5
6

92

A3052 Sidmouth (A375)
SIDMOUTH ROAD
A3052
POUND ST
BROAD ST
STILE CL
Town Mill
Lyme Regis Philpot Mus

WARE
CORAM LANE
PINE WK
Cobb
COBB ROAD
MARINE PRR

National Trust
Cobb
OZONE TR

2

The Cobb
Aquarium
Lyme Bay

Poker's Pool

91

1

90

33 A 34 B 35 C

A4
1 GARDENSIDE
2 KIDMORE CL
3 ORCHARD CL
4 OLD RECTORY CL

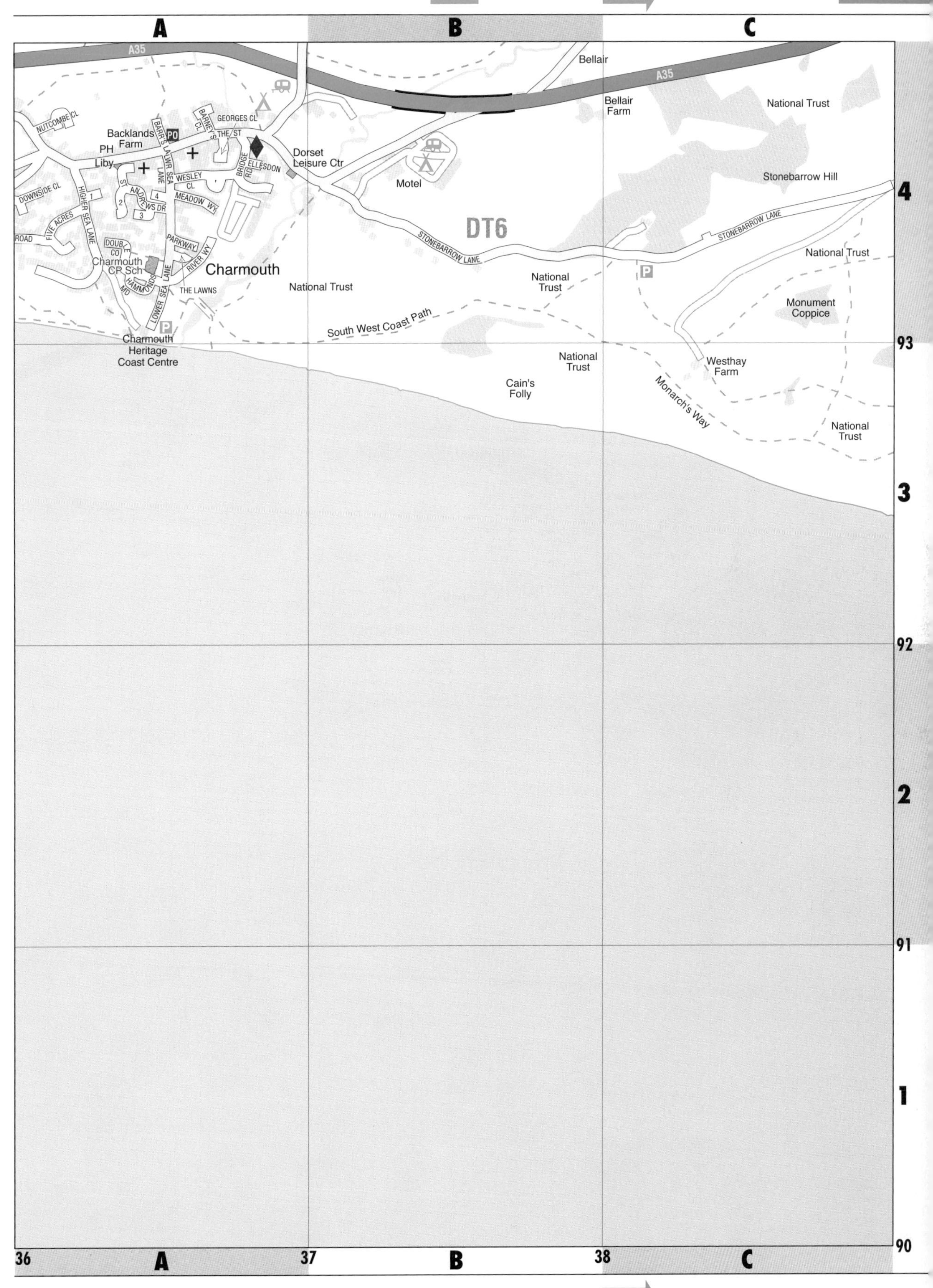

A35

Bellair

A35

National Trust

Bellair
Farm

NUTCOMBE CL

Backlands
Farm

GEORGES CL

Stonebarrow Hill

PH
Liby

THE ST

Dorset
Leisure Ctr

STONEBARROW LANE

National Trust

DOWNSIDE CL

Motel

DT6

Monument
Coppice

ROAD

MEADOW WY

STONEBARROW LANE

National
Trust

National Trust

FIVE ACRES

HIGHER SEA LANE

WESLEY
CL

PARKWAY

Charmouth
C.P. Sch

RIVER WY

Charmouth

National Trust

P

Westhay
Farm

DOUB
CO

LOWER SEA LANE

National
Trust

National
Trust

THE LAWNS

P

Charmouth
Heritage
Coast Centre

South West Coast Path

Cain's
Folly

Monarch's Way

4

93

3

92

2

91

1

90

36   37   38

A   B   C

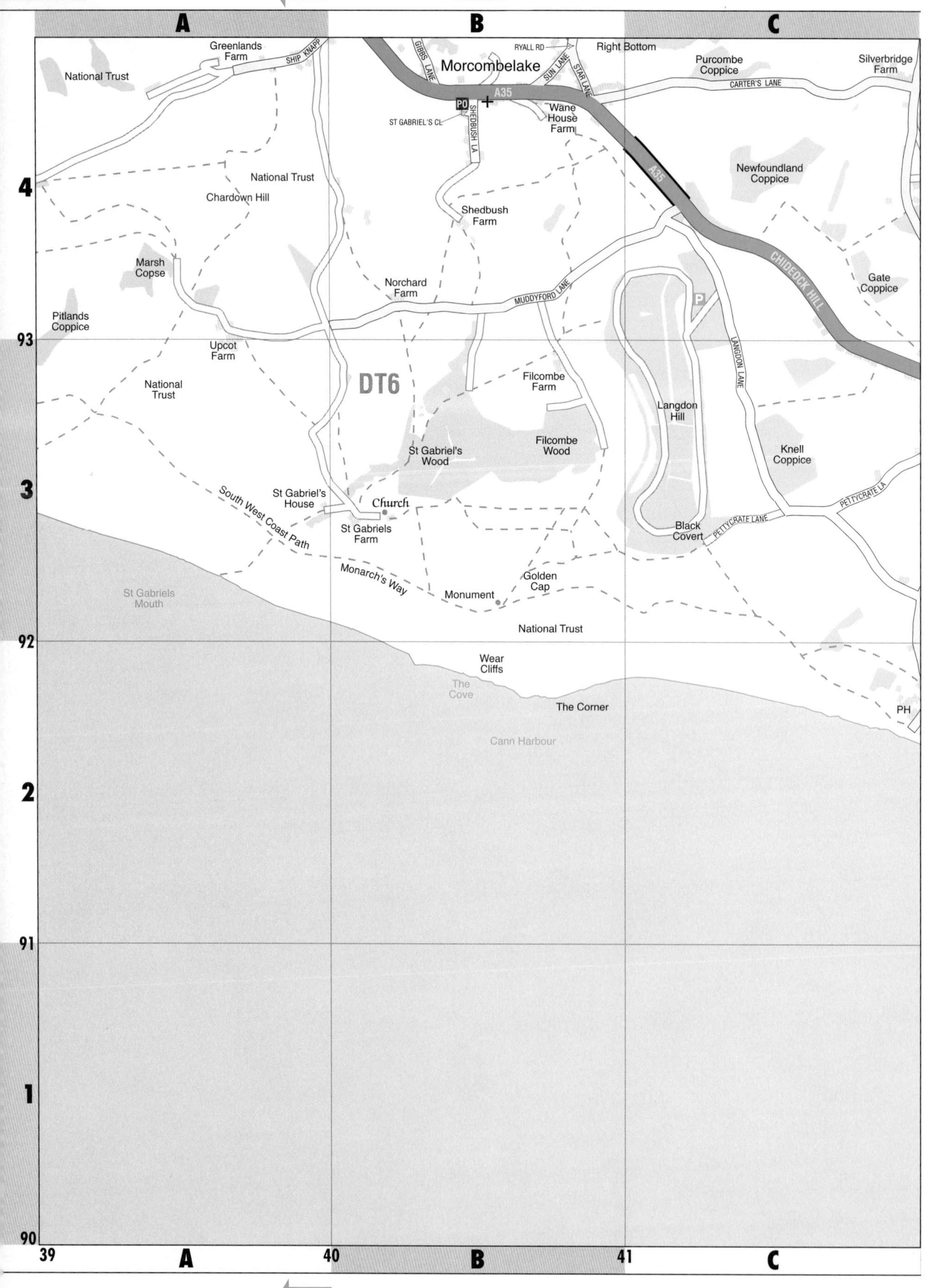

National Trust

Greenlands Farm

SHIP KNAPP

GIBBS LANE

RYALL RD

Morcombelake

Right Bottom

Purcombe Coppice

Silverbridge Farm

CARTER'S LANE

A35

PO

St GABRIEL'S CL

SHEDBUSH LA

SUN LANE

STAR LANE

Wane House Farm

A35

Newfoundland Coppice

CHIDEOCK HILL

National Trust

Chardown Hill

Shedbush Farm

Gate Coppice

Marsh Copse

Norchard Farm

MUDDYFORD LANE

P

Pitlands Coppice

93

Upcot Farm

DT6

Filcombe Farm

Langdon Hill

Knell Coppice

National Trust

St Gabriel's Wood

Filcombe Wood

LANGDON LANE

3

South West Coast Path

St Gabriel's House

Church

St Gabriels Farm

Black Covert

PETTYCRATE LANE

PETTYCRATE LA

St Gabriels Mouth

Monarch's Way

Monument

Golden Cap

92

National Trust

Wear Cliffs

The Cove

The Corner

PH

Cann Harbour

2

91

1

90

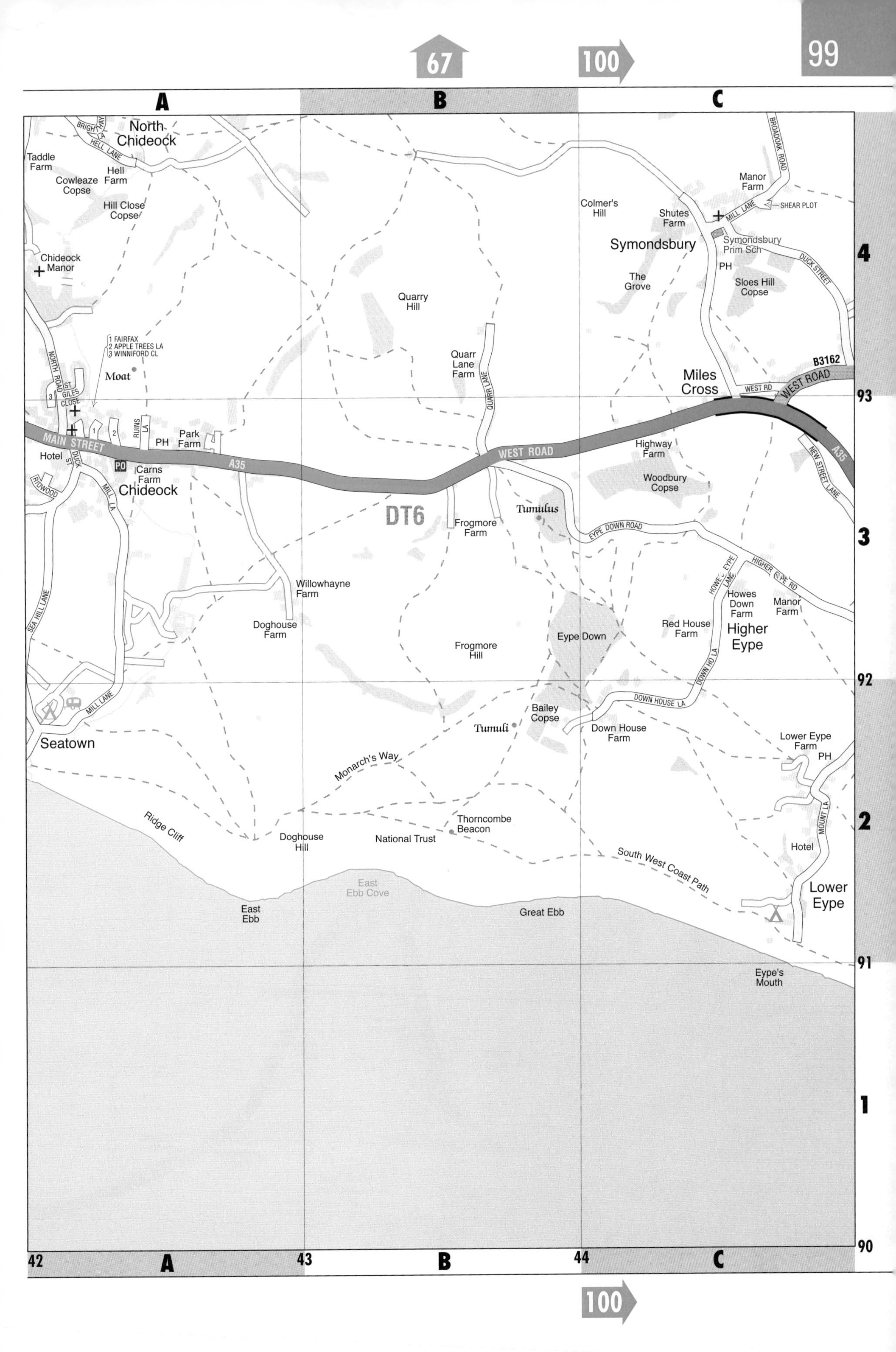

A B C

North
Chideock

Taddle
Farm

Cowleaze
Copse

Hell
Farm

Hill Close
Copse

Chideock
Manor

Moat

1 FAIRFAX
2 APPLE TREES LA
3 WINNIFORD CL

Quarry
Hill

Quarr
Lane
Farm

QUARR LANE

Colmer's
Hill

Manor
Farm

SHEAR PLOT

Symondsbury

Shutes
Farm

MILL LANE

Symondsbury
Prim Sch

PH

BROADOAK ROAD

DUCK STREET

4

The
Grove

Sloes Hill
Copse

ST GILES CLOSE

Main Street

3

Hotel

PO

Carns
Farm

Chideock

RIDWOOD

MILL LA

SEA HILL LANE

NORTH ROAD

Park
Farm

PH

RUINS LA

DUCK ST

Miles
Cross

B3162

WEST RD

WEST ROAD

A35

93

DT6

Frogmore
Farm

Tumulus

WEST ROAD

Highway
Farm

Woodbury
Copse

EYPE DOWN ROAD

NEW STREET LANE

A35

3

Willowhayne
Farm

Doghouse
Farm

Frogmore
Hill

Eype Down

Red House
Farm

HOWE EYPE LANE

Howes
Down
Farm

HIGHER EYPE RD

Manor
Farm

Higher
Eype

DOWN HO LA

92

Seatown

MILL LANE

Tumuli

Bailey
Copse

DOWN HOUSE LA

Down House
Farm

Lower Eype
Farm

PH

MOUNT LA

Monarch's Way

Thorncombe
Beacon

National Trust

South West Coast Path

Hotel

Lower
Eype

2

Ridge Cliff

Doghouse
Hill

East
Ebb

East
Ebb Cove

Great Ebb

Eype's
Mouth

91

1

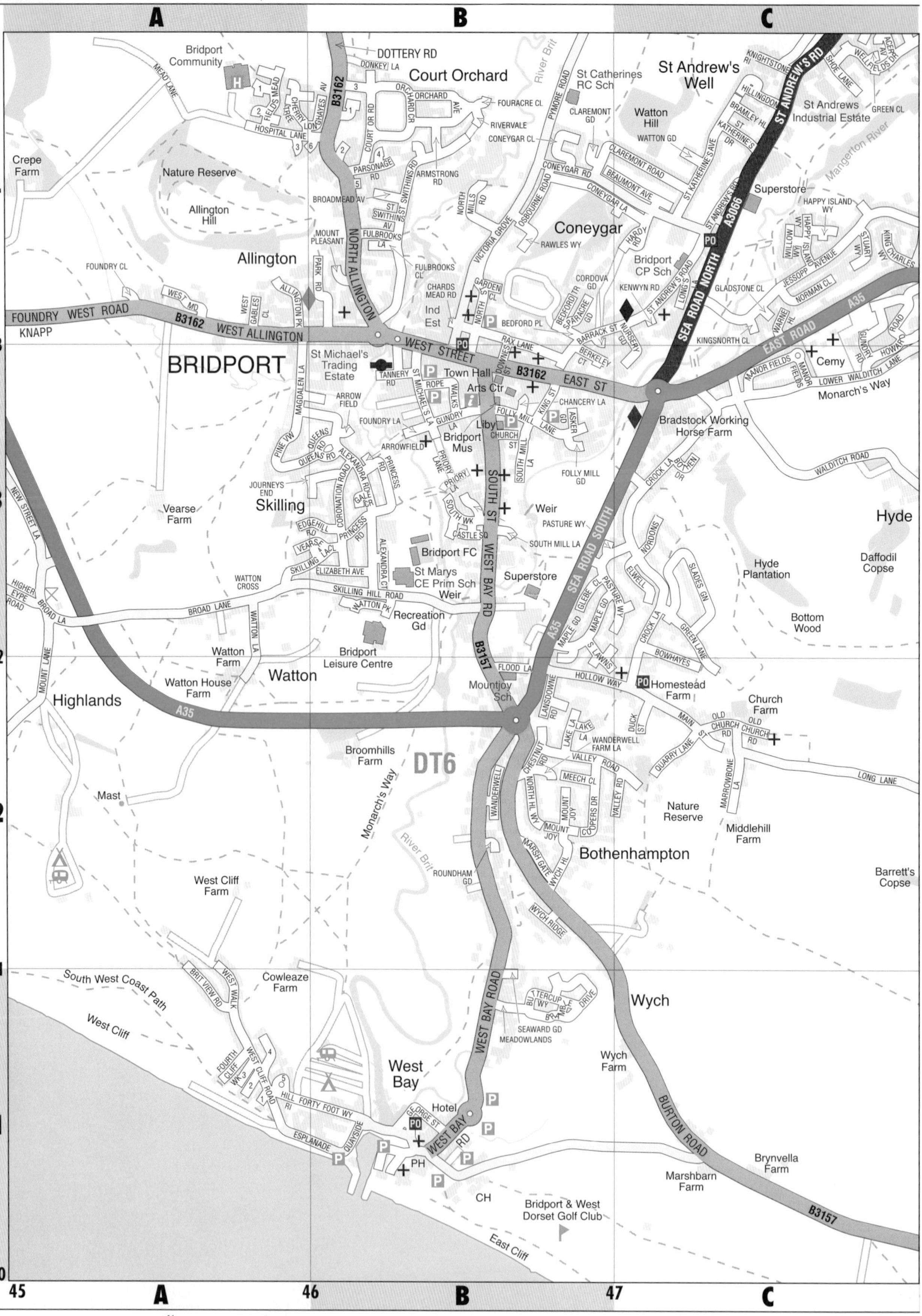

A4
1 LAUREL C
2 ST LUKE'S CT
3 ALLINGTON GD

99

B4
1 HILLVIEW EST
2 DIMENTS GD
3 ALLINGTON MD
4 VICARAGE CT
5 BIDDLECOME OR
6 TRUSTIN CL

68

A **B** **C**

Bridport Community

DOTTERY RD
DONKEY LA
Court Orchard
ORCHARD DR
ORCHARD AVE
FOURACRE CL
RIVERVALE
CONEYGAR CL

River Brit
St Catherines RC Sch
St Andrew's Well
KNIGHTSTONE RI
ST ANDREW'S RD
HILLINGDON
St Andrews Industrial Estate
GREEN CL
SHOE LANE
WELLFIELDS
ACRE
Watton Hill
WATTON GD
BRAMLEY HL
ST KATHERINE S AVE
ST KATHERINE'S DR

Crepe Farm

Nature Reserve

Allington Hill

Allington

PARSONAGE RD
BROADMEAD AV
ST SWITHINS
MOUNT PLEASANT
FULBROOKS LA
ARMSTRONG RD
NORTH MILLS RD
VICTORIA GROVE
OSBOURNE ROAD
Claremont GD
CLAREMONT ROAD
BEAUMONT AVE
CONEYGAR RD
Coneygar
RAWLES WY
HARDY RD
Bridport CP Sch
CORDOVA GD
BEDFORD TR
KENWYN RD
ST ANDREW'S RD
NURSERY
Superstore
HAPPY ISLAND WY
STUART WY
KING CHARLES WY
JESSOPP
NORMAN CL

FOUNDRY CL

FOUNDRY WEST ROAD
B3162
WEST ALLINGTON
KNAPP
WES MD
WEST GABLES
ALLINGTON PK
PARK RD
NORTH ALLINGTON
FULBROOKS CL
CHARDS MEAD RD
Ind Est
GABDEN CL
NORTH ST
BEDFORD PL
RAX LANE
BARRACK ST
BERKELEY CT
A3066
GLADSTONE CL
KINGSNORTH CL
A35
EAST ROAD
MANOR FIELDS
LOWER WALDITCH LANE
Cemy

93

BRIDPORT
St Michael's Trading Estate
TANNERY RD
St MICHAEL S LA
P Town Hall
ROPE WALKS
Arts Ctr
WEST STREET
WEST ST
PO
B3162
EAST ST
CHANCERY LA
KING S LA
ASKER
Bradstock Working Horse Farm
CROCK LA
WALDITCH ROAD
Monarch's Way

FOUNDRY LA
Bridport Mus
ARROWFIELD
ARROW FIELD
PINE FW
MAGDALEN LA
QUEENS RD
GUNDRY LA
PRIORY LANE
Liby
CHURCH
FOLLY MILL LANE
SOUTH ST
SOUTH MILL
Weir
FOLLY MILL GD
NORDONS
Hyde Plantation
Daffodil Copse
Hyde

3

JOURNEYS END
Skilling
EDGEHILL
VEARSE LA
Vearse Farm
PRINCESS RD
ALEXANDRA RD
CORONATION ROAD
CASTLE SQ
SOUTH WK
PASTURE WY
SOUTH MILL LA
ELWELL
MAPLE GD
CROCK LA
Hyde Plantation
Bottom Wood

WATTON CROSS
SKILLING LA
ELIZABETH AVE
Bridport FC
St Marys CE Prim Sch
Weir
SKILLING HILL ROAD
WATTON LA
Recreation Gd
Superstore
GLEBE RD
PASTURE WY
LAWNS
GREEN LANE
BOWHAYES

92

Watton Farm
Watton House Farm
WATTON PK
WEST BAY RD
Bridport Leisure Centre
Watton
B3157
Mountjoy Sch
FLOOD LA
HOLLOW WAY
PO
Homestead Farm
Church Farm
OLD CHURCH RD
LONG LANE

Highlands
MOUNT LANE
A35
Broomhills Farm
Monarch's Way
DT6
WANDERWELL
LAKE LA
WANDERWELL FARM LA
MAIN RD
DUCK ST
QUARRY LANE
MARROWBONE LA
Nature Reserve
Middlehill Farm
Barrett's Copse

2

Mast
NEW STREET LA
HIGHER EYPE ROAD
BROAD LA
West Cliff Farm
River Brit
ROUNDHAM GD
LANSDOWNE RD
CHESTNUT WY
NORTH HL WY
MOUNT JOY
MEECH CL
COPERS DR
VALLEY RD
Bothenhampton
MARSH GATE LA

91

South West Coast Path
BRITT VIEW RD
WEST WALK
Cowleaze Farm
WYCH RIDGE
BURTON ROAD
Wych
Brynvella Farm

West Cliff
FOURTH CLIFF WK
WEST CLIFF ROAD
HILL
FORTY FOOT WY
West Bay
BUTTERCUP WY
SEAWARD GD
MEADOWLANDS
DRIVE
WEST BAY ROAD
Wych Farm

1
Hotel
ESPLANADE
GEORGE ST
QUAYSIDE
WEST BAY RD
PO
PH
CH
Bridport & West Dorset Golf Club
East Cliff
Marshbarn Farm
B3157

90

45 **A** **46** **B** **47** **C**

A1
1 FIRST CLIFF WK
2 SECOND CLIFF WK
3 THIRD CLIFF WK
4 MEADWAY
5 HILL CL

99

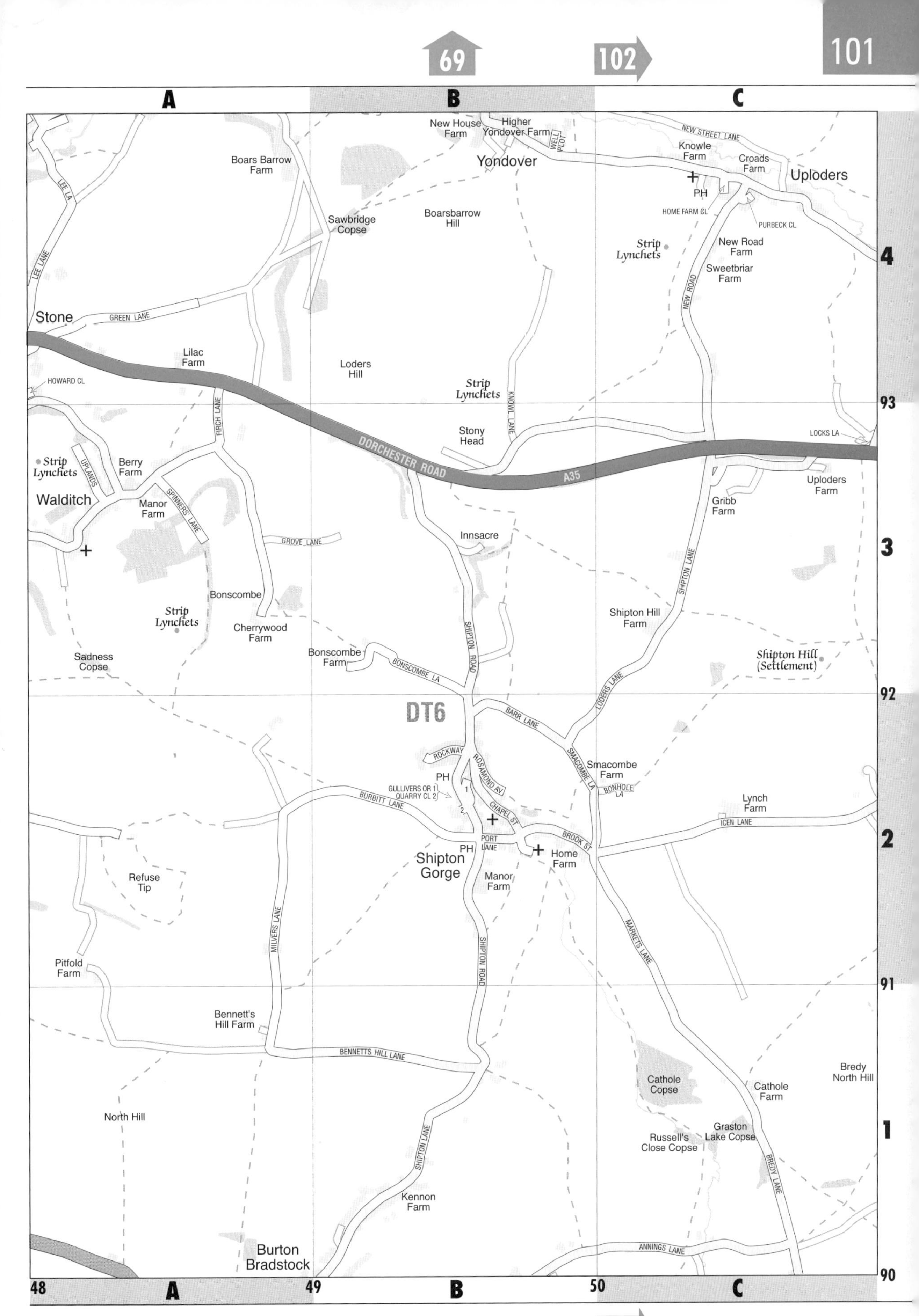

A   B   C

New House Farm
Higher Yondover Farm
WELL PLOT
Knowle Farm
Croads Farm
NEW STREET LANE
Uploders

Boars Barrow Farm
Yondover
✚
PH
HOME FARM CL
PURBECK CL

Sawbridge Copse
Boarsbarrow Hill
Strip Lynchets
New Road Farm
Sweetbriar Farm
4

Stone
GREEN LANE
Loders Hill
Strip Lynchets
NEW ROAD

Lilac Farm
93
LOCKS LA

HOWARD CL
DORCHESTER ROAD
A35
Stony Head

FIRCH LANE
KNOWL LANE
Uploders Farm

• *Strip Lynchets*
Berry Farm
UPLANDS
Innsacre
Gribb Farm
3

Waldditch
SPINNERS LANE
GROVE LANE

✚
Manor Farm
SHIPTON ROAD
Shipton Hill Farm
LODERS LANE

Bonscombe
Shipton Hill (Settlement) •

Sadness Copse
Cherrywood Farm
Strip Lynchets
Bonscombe Farm
BONSCOMBE LA
92

DT6
BARR LANE
Smacombe Farm
SMACOMBE LA
BONHOLE LA
Lynch Farm

ROCKWAY
ROSAMOND AV
ICEN LANE

PH
GULLIVERS OR 1
QUARRY CL 2
BURBITT LANE
CHAPEL ST
BROOK ST
2

Refuse Tip
PORT LANE
PH
✚
Home Farm

Shipton Gorge
Manor Farm

MILVERS LANE
MARKETS LANE

Pitfold Farm
SHIPTON ROAD
91

Bennett's Hill Farm
BENNETTS HILL LANE

Catnole Copse
Bredy North Hill

North Hill
Catnole Farm

SHIPTON LANE
Russell's Close Copse
Graston Lake Copse
BREDY LANE
1

Kennon Farm

Burton Bradstock
ANNINGS LANE

48   A   49   B   50   C   **90**

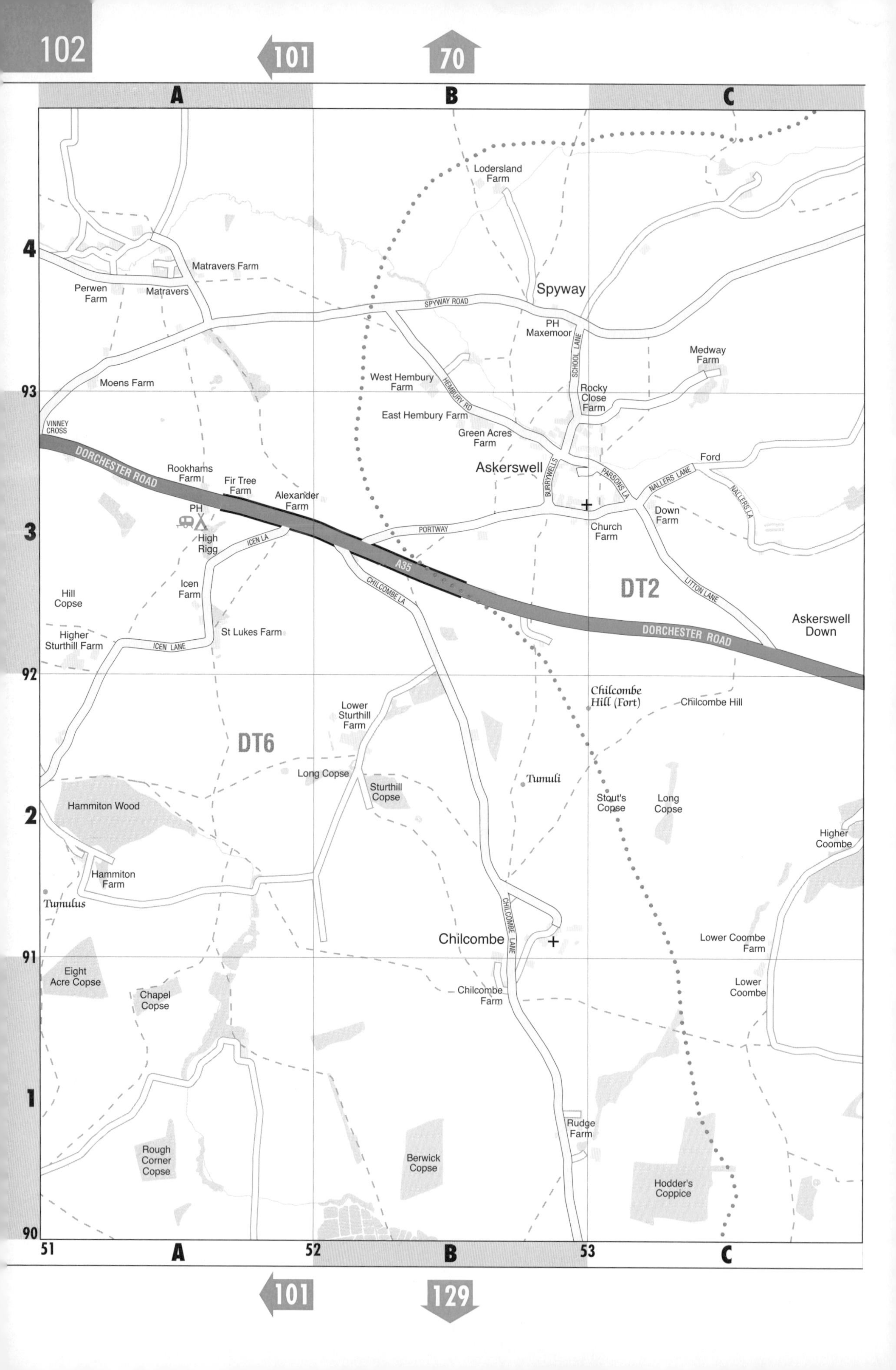

A · B · C

Lodersland Farm

Matravers Farm

Perwen Farm

Matravers

Spyway

SPYWAY ROAD

PH Maxemoor

SCHOOL LANE

Medway Farm

Moens Farm

West Hembury Farm

East Hembury Farm

Green Acres Farm

Rocky Close Farm

93

VINNEY CROSS

DORCHESTER ROAD

Rookhams Farm

Fir Tree Farm

Alexander Farm

Askerswell

HEMBURY RD

BURRYWELLS

PARSONS LA

NALLERS LANE

Ford

NALLERS LA

PH
High Rigg

ICEN LA

PORTWAY

Church Farm

Down Farm

3

Hill Copse

Icen Farm

A35

CHILCOMBE LA

DT2

LITTON LANE

Askerswell Down

Higher Sturthill Farm

ICEN LANE

St Lukes Farm

DORCHESTER ROAD

92

Chilcombe Hill (Fort)

Chilcombe Hill

DT6

Lower Sturthill Farm

Long Copse

Sturthill Copse

Tumuli

Stout's Copse

Long Copse

Higher Coombe

2

Hammiton Wood

Hammiton Farm

CHILCOMBE LANE

Lower Coombe Farm

Tumulus

91

Chilcombe

Lower Coombe

Eight Acre Copse

Chapel Copse

Chilcombe Farm

1

Rudge Farm

Rough Corner Copse

Berwick Copse

Hodder's Coppice

90

51 · A · 52 · B · 53 · C

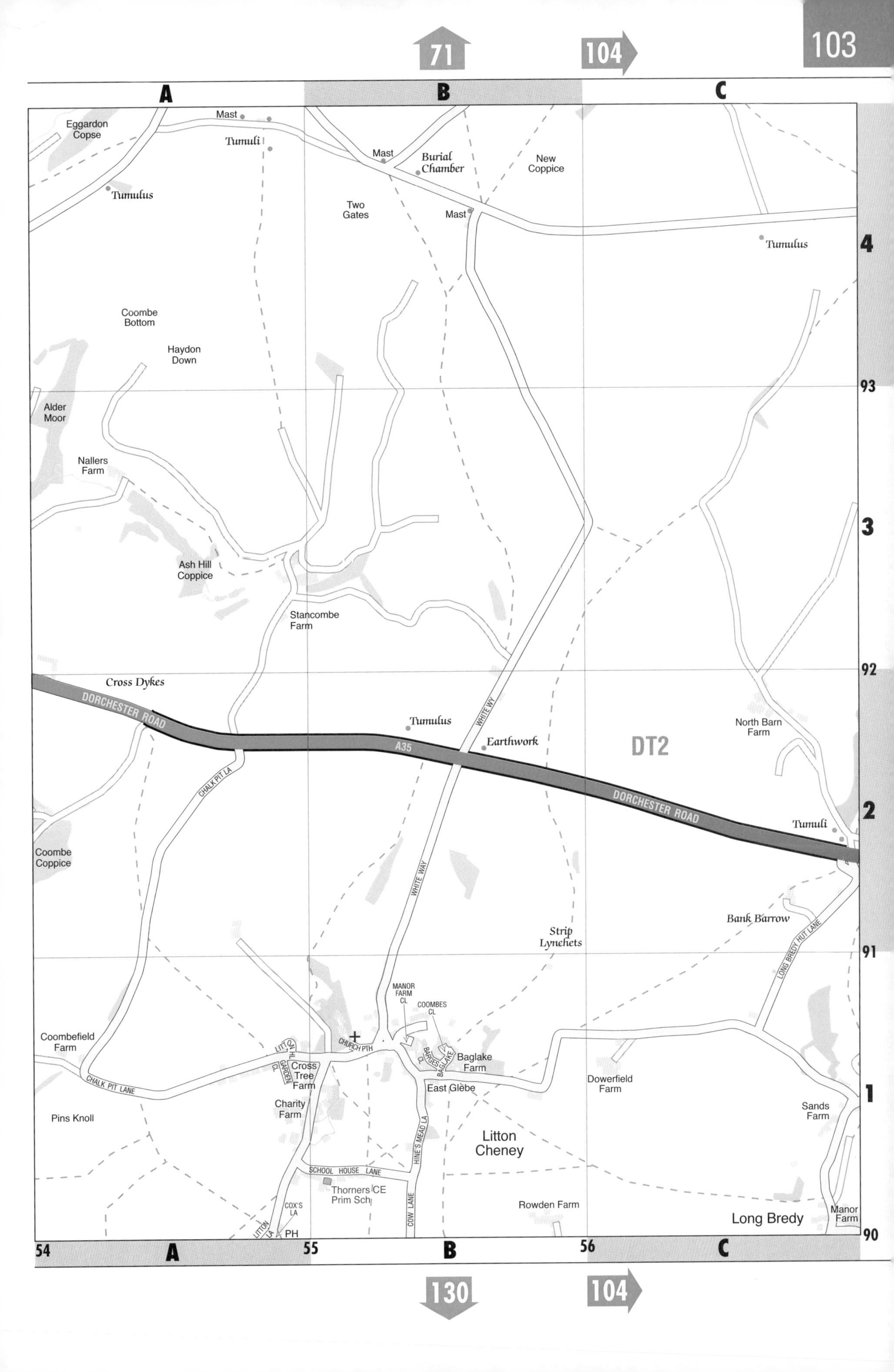

A   **B**   **C**

Eggardon Copse

Mast

Tumuli

Tumulus

Mast

Burial Chamber

New Coppice

Two Gates

Mast

Tumulus

4

Coombe Bottom

Haydon Down

Alder Moor

93

Nallers Farm

Ash Hill Coppice

3

Stancombe Farm

Cross Dykes

92

DORCHESTER ROAD

Tumulus

Earthwork

WHITE WY

DT2

North Barn Farm

A35

DORCHESTER ROAD

Tumuli

2

CHALK PIT LA

Coombe Coppice

WHITE WAY

Strip Lynchets

Bank Barrow

LONG BREDY HUT LANE

91

Coombefield Farm

MANOR FARM CL

COOMBES CL

CHALK PIT LANE

Cross Tree Farm

CHURCH PTH

BAGLAKE CL

Baglake Farm

Dowerfield Farm

Pins Knoll

Charity Farm

HINE'S MEAD LA

East Glebe

Litton Cheney

Sands Farm

1

SCHOOL HOUSE LANE

COX'S LA

Thorners CE Prim Sch

COW LANE

Rowden Farm

Long Bredy

Manor Farm

LITTON LA PH

90

54   **A**   55   **B**   56   **C**

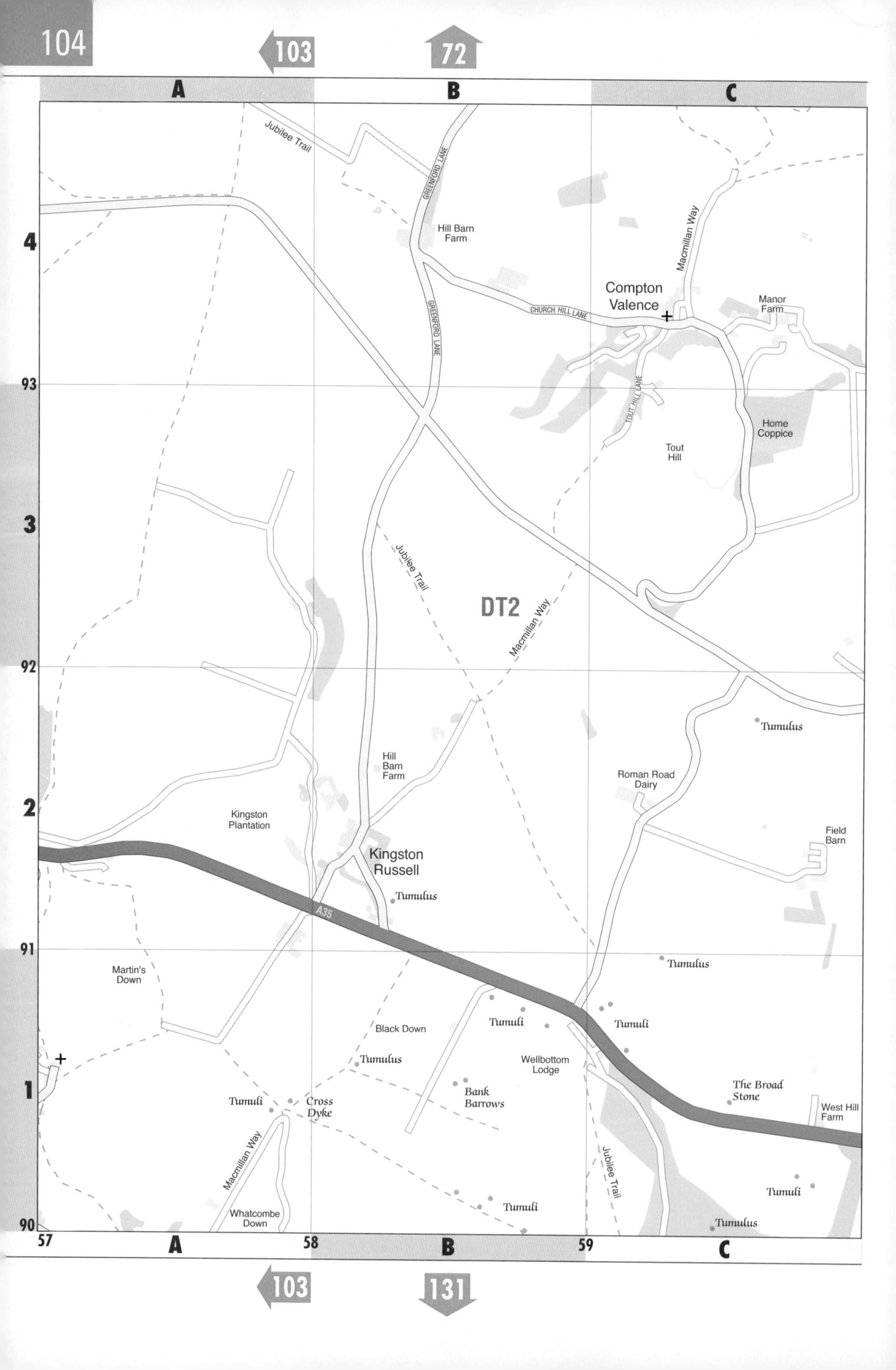

103
72

A   **B**   **C**

4

Jubilee Trail

GREENFORD LANE

Hill Barn Farm

Macmillan Way

Compton Valence

CHURCH HILL LANE

Manor Farm

GREENFORD LANE

93

TOUT HILL LANE

Home Coppice

Tout Hill

3

Jubilee Trail

DT2

Macmillan Way

92

Tumulus

Roman Road Dairy

Hill Barn Farm

2

Kingston Plantation

Field Barn

Kingston Russell

Tumulus

A35

91

Martin's Down

Tumulus

Tumulus

Tumuli

Black Down

Tumuli

Tumulus

Wellbottom Lodge

The Broad Stone

West Hill Farm

1

Tumuli

Cross Dyke

Bank Barrows

Macmillan Way

Jubilee Trail

Tumuli

Tumulus

Whatcombe Down

90

57   **A**   **58**   **B**   **59**   **C**

103
131

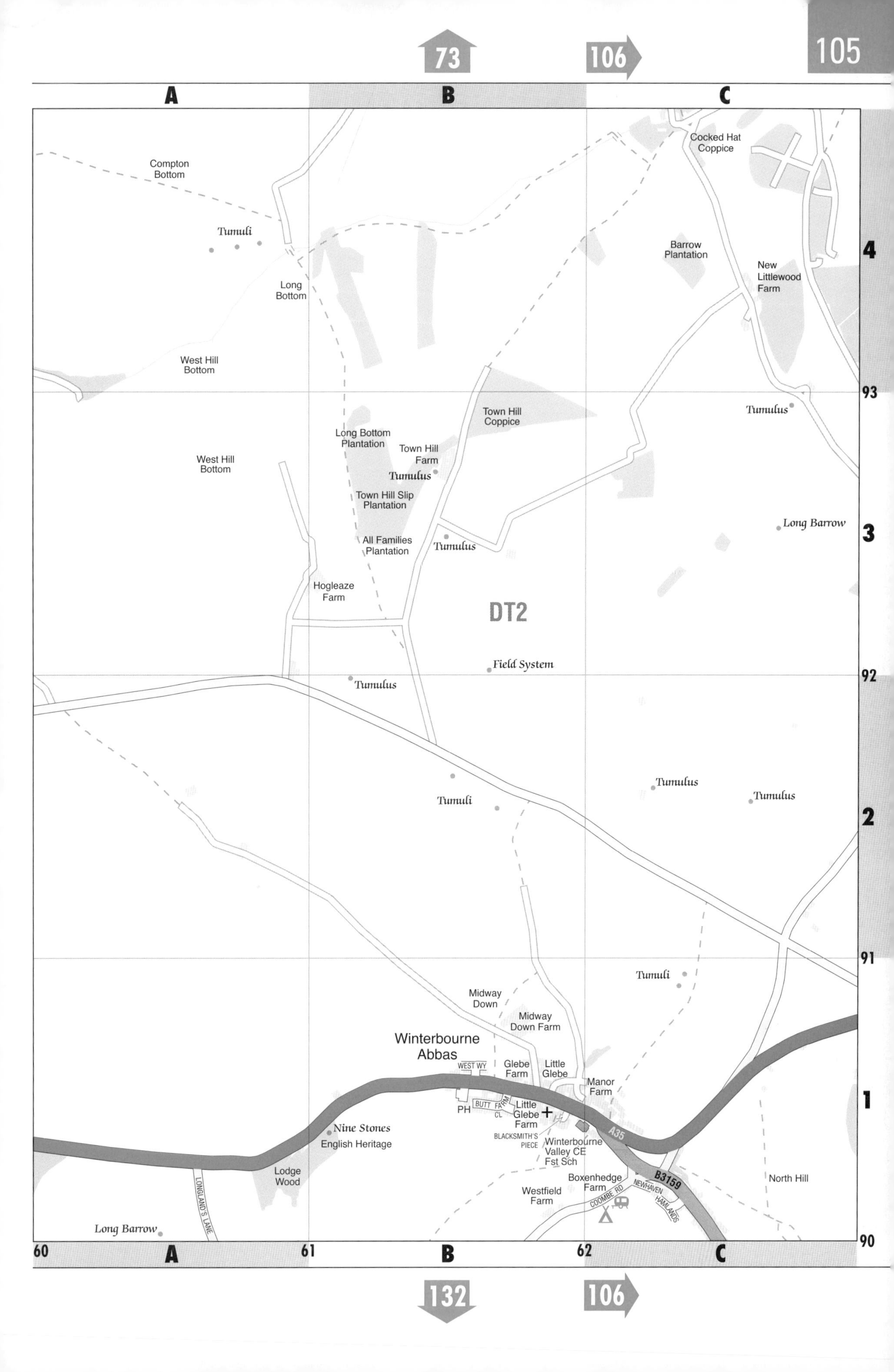

A   **B**   **C**

Compton
Bottom

Tumuli

Long
Bottom

West Hill
Bottom

West Hill
Bottom

Long Bottom
Plantation

Town Hill
Farm

Tumulus

Town Hill Slip
Plantation

All Families
Plantation

Tumulus

Hogleaze
Farm

Cocked Hat
Coppice

Barrow
Plantation

New
Littlewood
Farm

4

Tumulus

93

Town Hill
Coppice

Long Barrow

3

DT2

Field System

92

Tumulus

Tumulus

Tumulus

Tumuli

Tumulus

2

91

Tumuli

Midway
Down

Midway
Down Farm

Winterbourne
Abbas

WEST WY

Glebe
Farm

Little
Glebe

Manor
Farm

1

BUTT FARM
CL

Little
Glebe
Farm

PH

Nine Stones
English Heritage

BLACKSMITH'S
PIECE

Winterbourne
Valley CE
Fst Sch

A35

B3159

North Hill

Lodge
Wood

Boxenhedge
Farm

Westfield
Farm

COOMBE RD

NEWHAVEN

HAMLANDS

LONGLAND'S LANE

Long Barrow

90

60   **A**   **61**   **B**   **62**   **C**

A **B** **C**

A37 DORCHESTER RD

Long Hampton
Plantation

LC

SAWYERS LA 1
BULL CL 2
CARPENTERS CL 3

DORCHESTER RD

LOCKS

A37

Ash
Hill

Lower
Muckleford
Farm

Higher
Muckleford
Farm

Stratton

Church
Farm

WRACKLE CL

MILL LANE

MANOR CL

4

Muckleford

Quatre
Bras

Penns Plantation

River Frome

ROMAN
AQUEDUCT

GLEBEFIELDS

Hampton Hill
Plantation

93

Bradford
Peverell

Home Barn
Farm

YEW TREE
LA

MANOR LA

Strap Bottom

Penn Hill

Coux Plantation

Long
Barrow

Tumuli

New
Barn

3

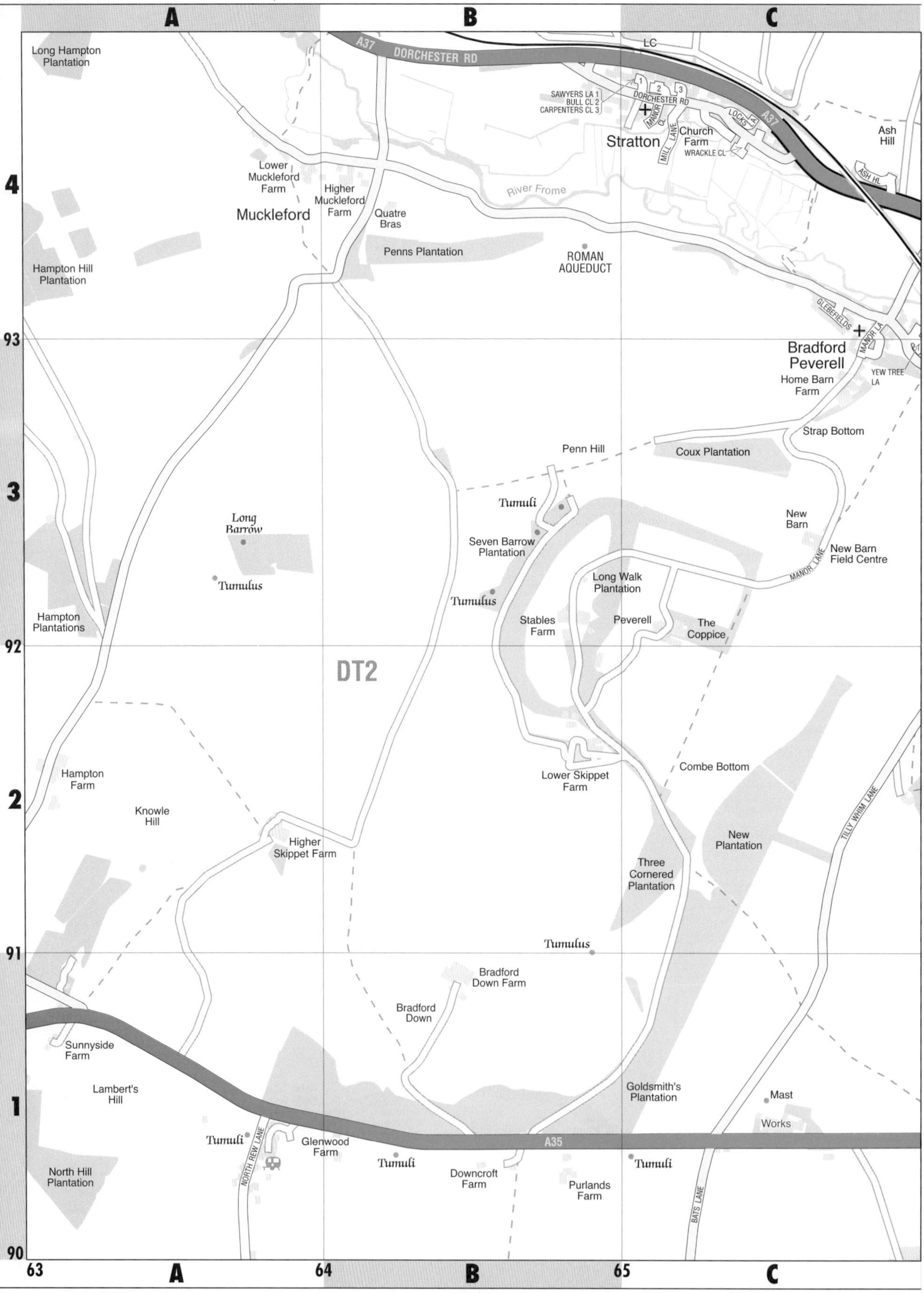

Seven Barrow
Plantation

New Barn
Field Centre

Tumulus

Tumulus

Long Walk
Plantation

MANOR LANE

Hampton
Plantations

Stables
Farm

Peverell

The
Coppice

92

DT2

Combe Bottom

Lower Skippet
Farm

Hampton
Farm

New
Plantation

TILLY WHIM LANE

2

Knowle
Hill

Higher
Skippet Farm

Three
Cornered
Plantation

91

Tumulus

Bradford
Down Farm

Bradford
Down

Sunnyside
Farm

Goldsmith's
Plantation

Mast

Lambert's
Hill

Works

1

Tumuli

NORTH NEW LANE

Glenwood
Farm

A35

Tumuli

Tumuli

North Hill
Plantation

Downcroft
Farm

Purlands
Farm

BATS LANE

90

63 **A** **64** **B** **65** **C**

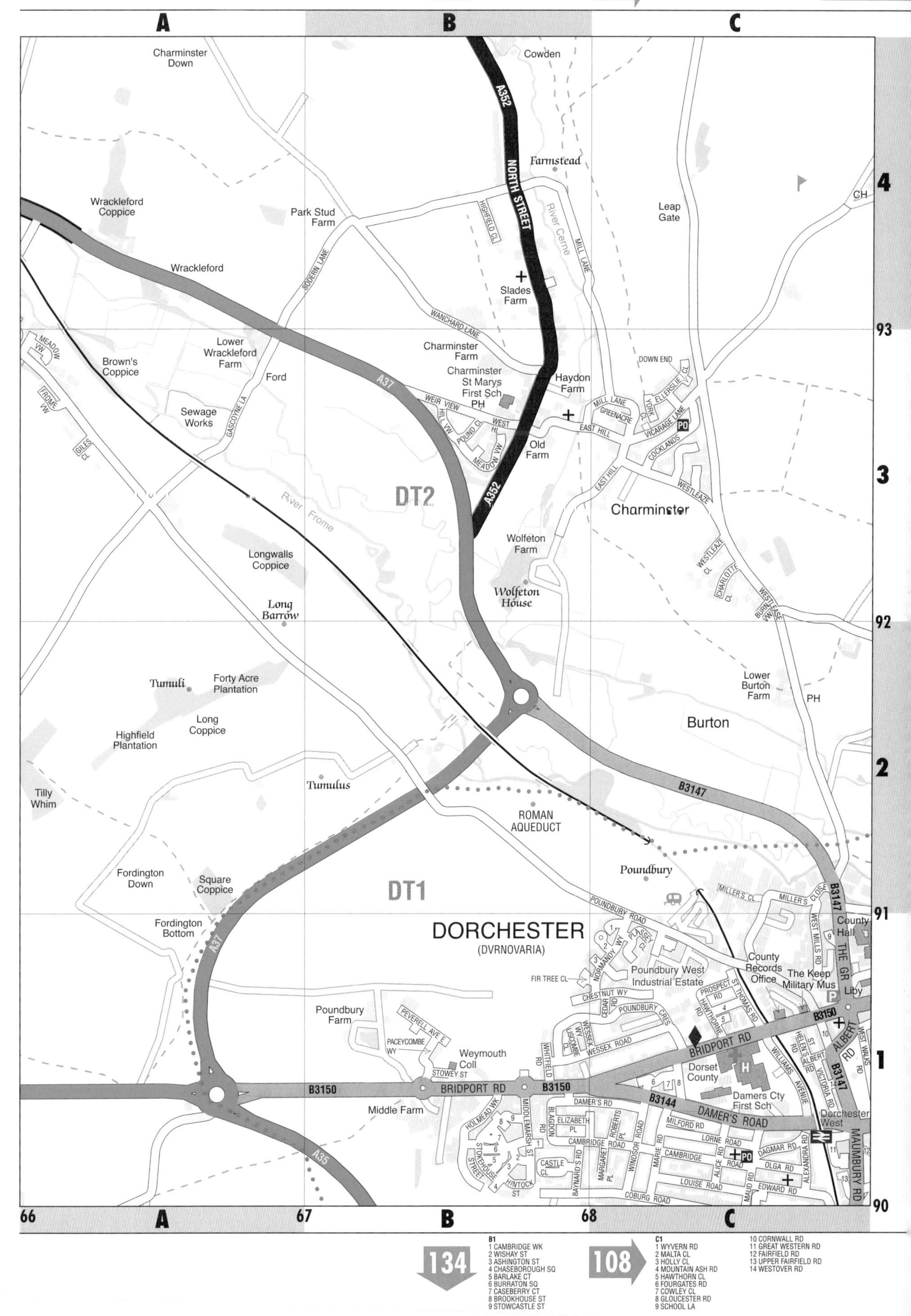

134 108

B1
1 CAMBRIDGE WK
2 WISHAY ST
3 ASHINGTON ST
4 CHASEBOROUGH SQ
5 BARLAKE CT
6 BURRATON SQ
7 CASEBERRY CT
8 BROOKHOUSE ST
9 STOWCASTLE ST

C1
1 WYVERN RD
2 MALTA CL
3 HOLLY CL
4 MOUNTAIN ASH RD
5 HAWTHORN CL
6 FOURGATES RD
7 COWLEY CL
8 GLOUCESTER RD
9 SCHOOL LA
10 CORNWALL RD
11 GREAT WESTERN RD
12 FAIRFIELD RD
13 UPPER FAIRFIELD RD
14 WESTOVER RD

A   B   C

4

Hill Barn

Home Farm

Square Coppice

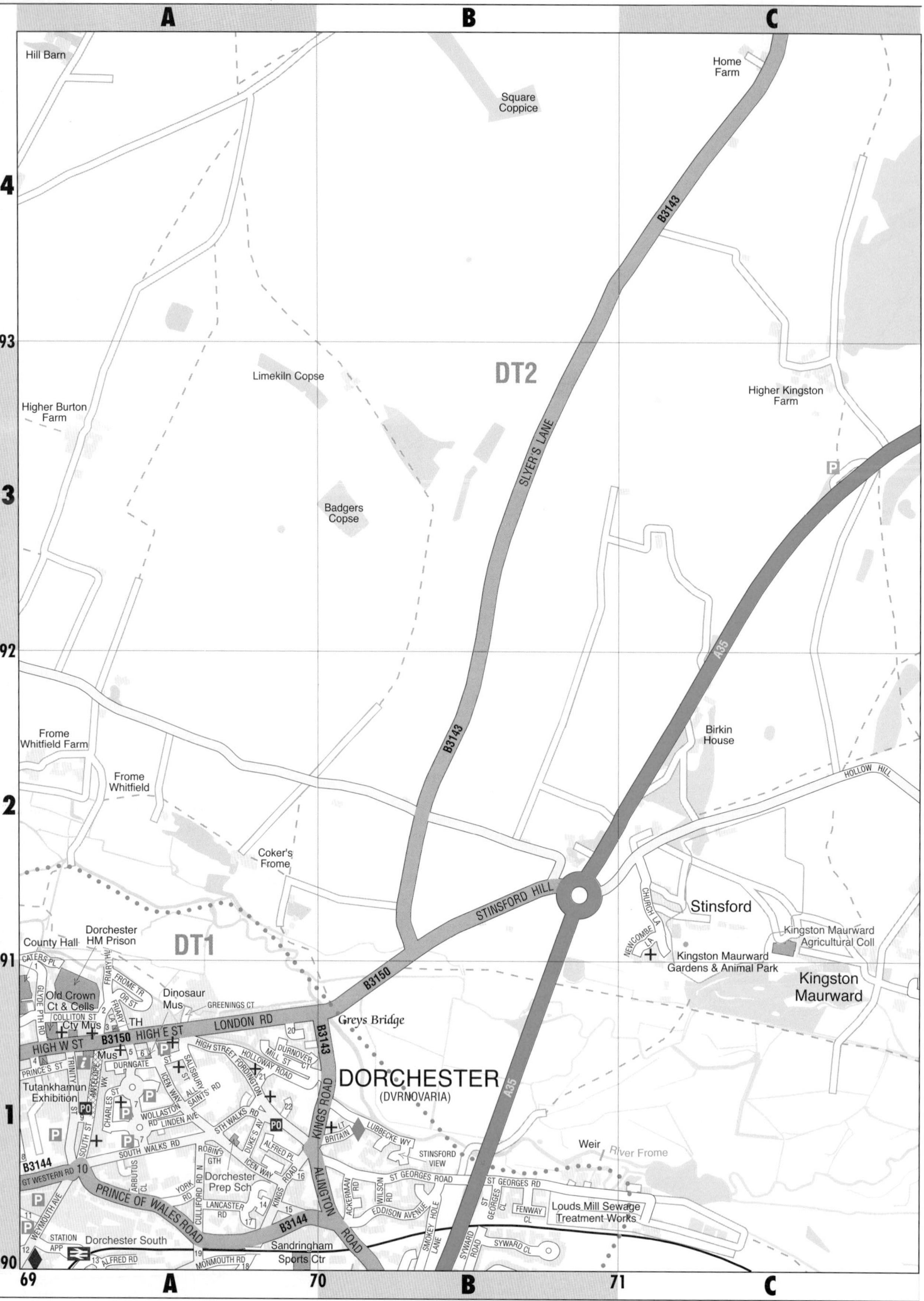

B3143

93

DT2

Limekiln Copse

Higher Burton Farm

Higher Kingston Farm

P

3

Badgers Copse

SLYER'S LANE

A35

92

Frome Whitfield Farm

B3143

Birkin House

Frome Whitfield

HOLLOW HILL

2

Coker's Frome

STINSFORD HILL

Stinsford

CHURCH LA

Kingston Maurward Agricultural Coll

County Hall   Dorchester HM Prison

DT1

NEWCOMBE LA

Kingston Maurward Gardens & Animal Park

Kingston Maurward

91

CATERS' PL

Old Crown Ct & Cells   Cty Mus

Dinosaur Mus   GREENINGS CT

B3150

LONDON RD

Greys Bridge

A35

COLLITON ST   TH

HIGH E ST

GLYDE PTH   FROME TER

FRIARY LA   FRIARY HILL

DURNOVER CT

B3143

HIGH W ST   Mus

High Street Fordington   DURNGATE

MILL ST

PRINCE'S ST   TRINITY ST   i

SALISBURY ST

HOLLOWAY ROAD

DORCHESTER (DVRNOVARIA)

Tutankhamun Exhibition

ICEN WAY   ALL SAINTS' RD

P

CHARLES ST   ACLAND RD

P

STH WALKS RD

P

WOLLASTON RD   LINDEN AVE

KINGS ROAD

Weir   River Frome

1

P

SOUTH ST   DURNGATE ST

SOUTH WALKS RD

DUKE'S AVE

ALFRED PL

BRITAIN

Lubbecke Wy

STINSFORD VIEW

ROBIN'S GTH

ALINGTON ROAD

ST GEORGES ROAD

B3144

GT WESTERN RD 10

PRINCE OF WALES ROAD

CULLIFORD RD N

Dorchester Prep Sch

YORK RD

ICEN WAY

KINGS RD

ACKERMAN RD   WILSON RD

EDDISON AVENUE

ST GEORGES RD

ST GEORGE'S RD

FENWAY CL

Louds Mill Sewage Treatment Works

P

11

WEYMOUTH AVE

P

12

STATION APP

Dorchester South

13   ALFRED RD

LANCASTER RD

14

15

B3144

SMOKEY HOLE LANE

SYWARD ROAD

SYWARD CL

90

19   MONMOUTH RD   18

Sandringham Sports Ctr

69   A   70   B   71   C

A1
1 NORTHERNWAY
2 NORTH SQ
3 THE BOW
4 ALINGTON ST
5 CHURCH ST
6 CHURCH CL
7 ACLAND RD
8 WEST WALKS RD
9 NEW ST
10 WEYMOUTH AVE
11 FAIRFIELD RD
12 UPR FAIRFIELD RD
13 CROMWELL RD
14 EARL CL
15 ATHELSTAN RD
16 FORDINGTON GD
17 SYDENHAM WAY
18 BARNES WAY
19 CULLIFORD RD NTH
20 LONDON CL
21 POUND LANE
22 CHURCH ACRE

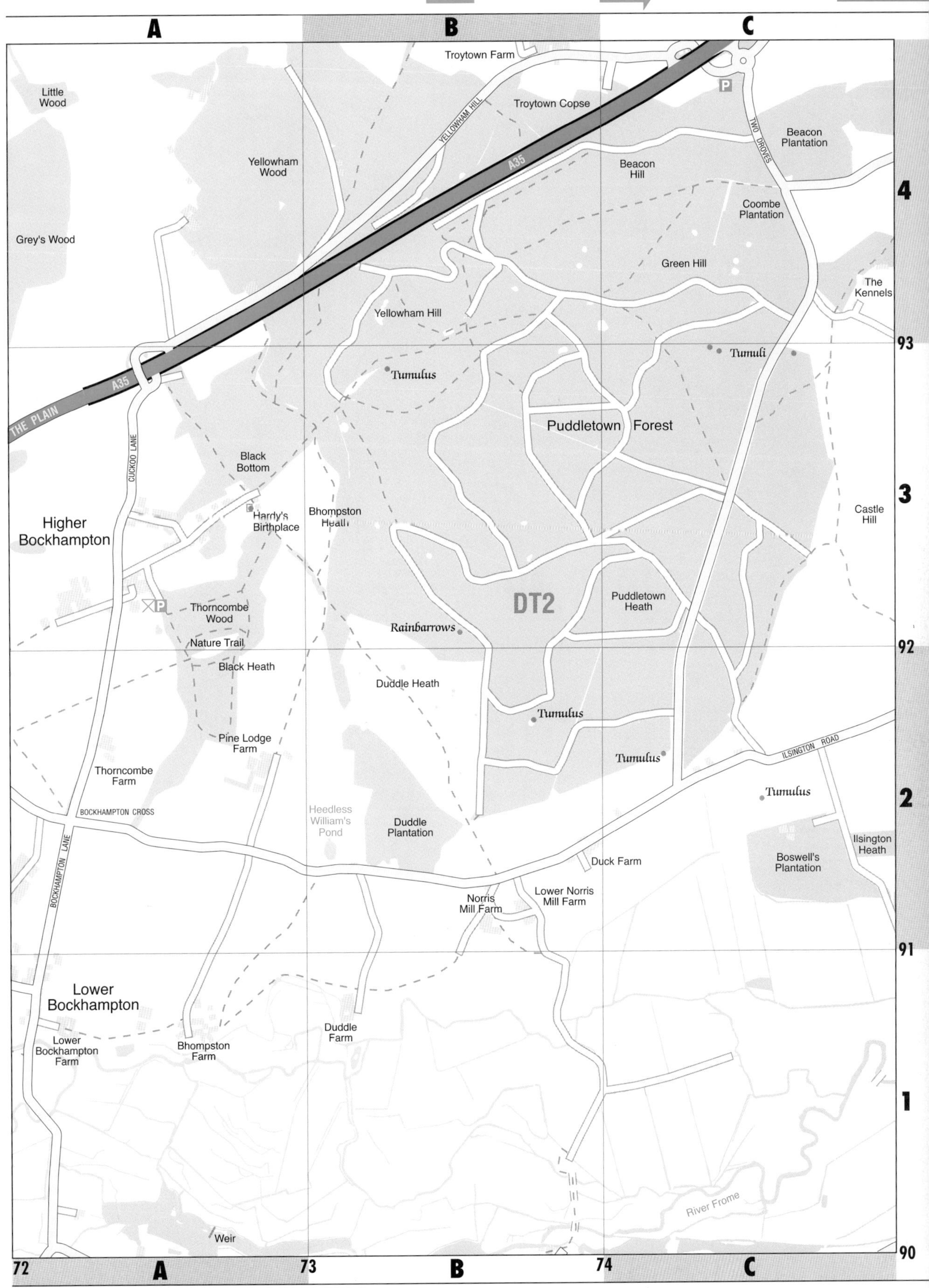
A
B
C
Troytown Farm
Little Wood
Yellowham Hill
Troytown Copse
Two Droves
Beacon Plantation
A35
Yellowham Wood
Beacon Hill
Coombe Plantation
Grey's Wood
Green Hill
The Kennels
Yellowham Hill
Tumuli
Tumulus
The Plain
A35
Cuckoo Lane
Puddletown Forest
Black Bottom
Higher Bockhampton
Hardy's Birthplace
Bhompston Heath
Castle Hill
Thorncombe Wood
DT2
Puddletown Heath
Rainbarrows
Nature Trail
Black Heath
Duddle Heath
Tumulus
Pine Lodge Farm
Tumulus
Ilsington Road
Thorncombe Farm
Tumulus
Bockhampton Cross
Heedless William's Pond
Duddle Plantation
Ilsington Heath
Bockhampton Lane
Duck Farm
Boswell's Plantation
Norris Mill Farm
Lower Norris Mill Farm
Lower Bockhampton
Lower Bockhampton Farm
Bhompston Farm
Duddle Farm
River Frome
Weir
4
93
3
92
2
91
1
90
72
73
74

109
78

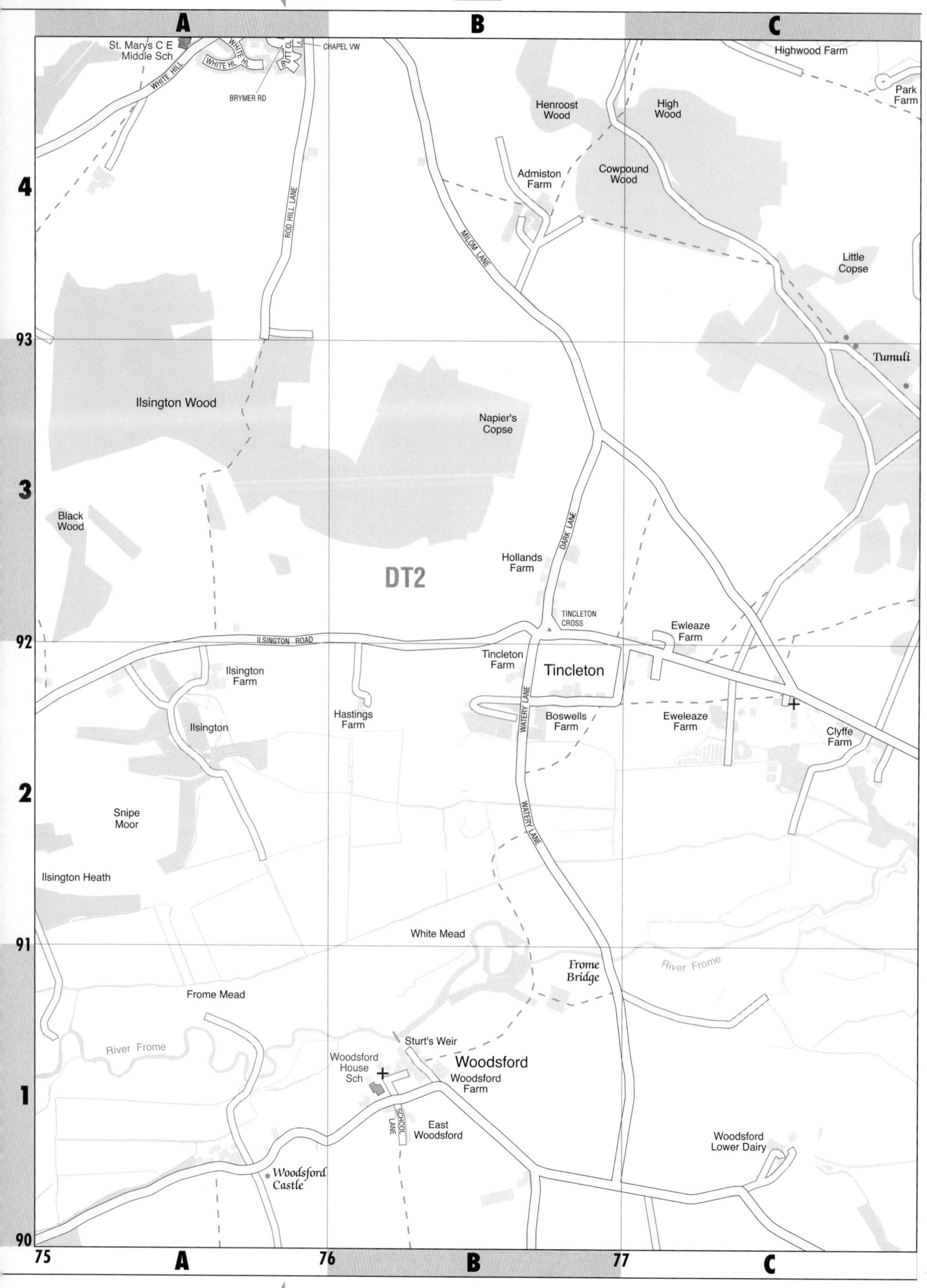

109
137

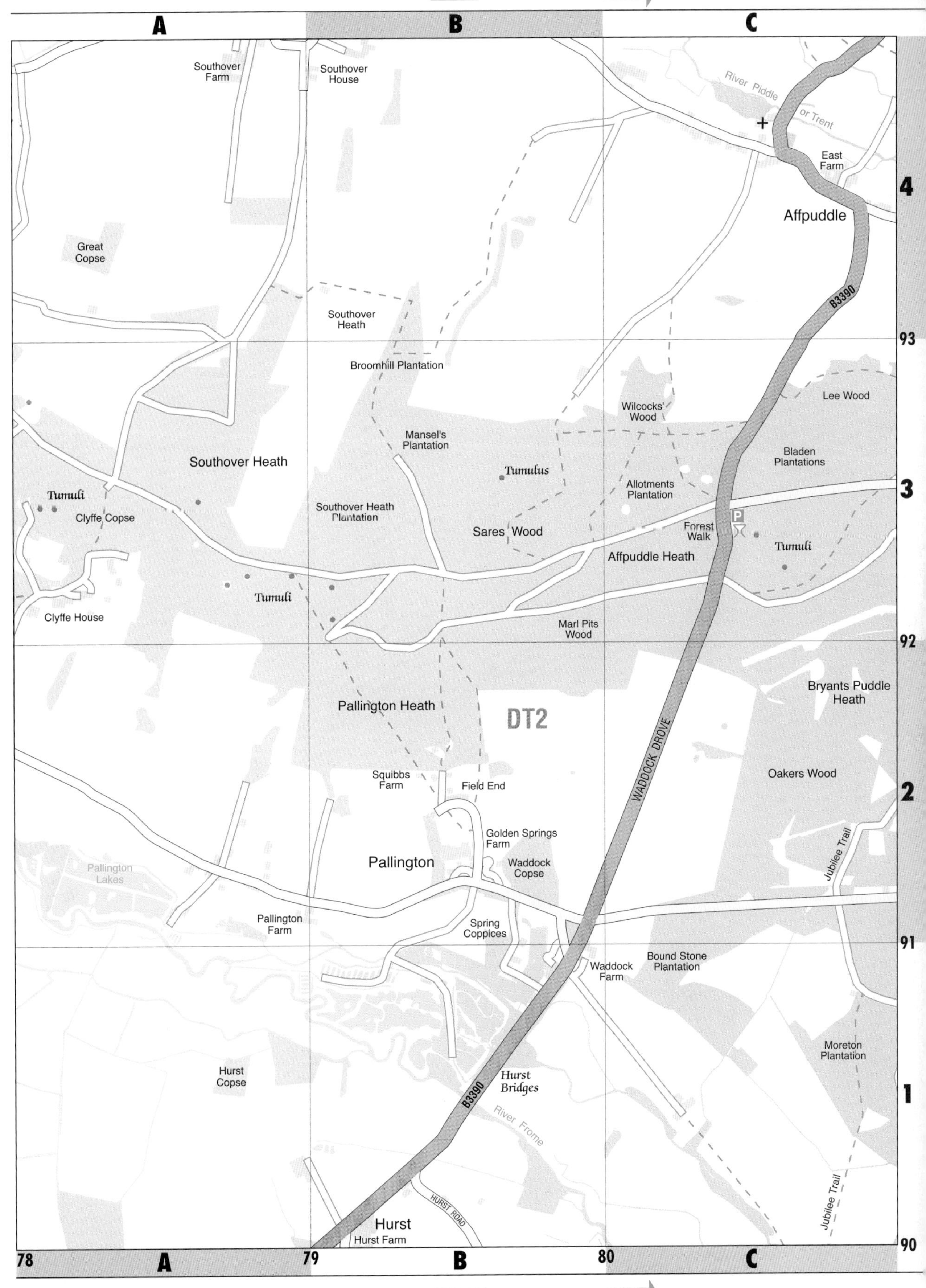

79
112
A
B
C
Southover Farm
Southover House
River Piddle or Trent
East Farm
Affpuddle
4
Great Copse
B3390
Southover Heath
Broomhill Plantation
93
Lee Wood
Wilcocks' Wood
Mansel's Plantation
Bladen Plantations
Southover Heath
Tumulus
Allotments Plantation
3
Tumuli
Clyffe Copse
Southover Heath Plantation
Sares Wood
Forest Walk
Tumuli
Affpuddle Heath
Tumuli
Clyffe House
Marl Pits Wood
92
Bryants Puddle Heath
Pallington Heath
DT2
WADDOCK DROVE
Oakers Wood
Squibbs Farm
Field End
2
Golden Springs Farm
Pallington Lakes
Pallington
Waddock Copse
Jubilee Trail
Pallington Farm
Spring Coppices
91
Waddock Farm
Bound Stone Plantation
Moreton Plantation
Hurst Copse
Hurst Bridges
B3390
1
River Frome
Jubilee Trail
HURST ROAD
Hurst
Hurst Farm
90
78
A
79
B
80
C
138
112

A **B** **C**

4

Spring Garden Coppice

Tumulus

Sand and Gravel Pits

River Puddle or Trent

Damerhill Coppice

Jubilee Trail

Turners Puddle

+

Turnerspuddle Farm

VALLEY BLADEN

Jubilee Trail

Briantspuddle

Throop

93

Bladen Plantations

Landshare Coppice

Throop Farm

Brockhill Coppice

Brockhill Fish Farm

Cecily Bridge

Bryants Puddle Allotments Plantation

Battle Farm

THROOP HOLLOW

Eweleaze Coppice

THE HOLLOW

DT2

Smokeham Bottom

Cull Peppers Dish

3

Tumuli

Tumulus

Longcroft Coppice

Tumulus

Bryants Puddle Heath

Rimsmoor Pond

Jubilee Trail

92

Oakers Wood

Throop Heath

Tumulus

Millicent's Plantation

Tumulus

DANGER AREA

BH20

2

Okers Wood House

Tonerspuddle Heath

Chamberlayne's Heath

Moreton Plantation

East Plantation

Round Barrow

91

Clouds Hill

Lawrence of Arabia's Cottage NT

MORETON DRIVE

1

Moreton Plantation

P

Tank Training Area

90

81 **A** 82 **B** 83 **C**

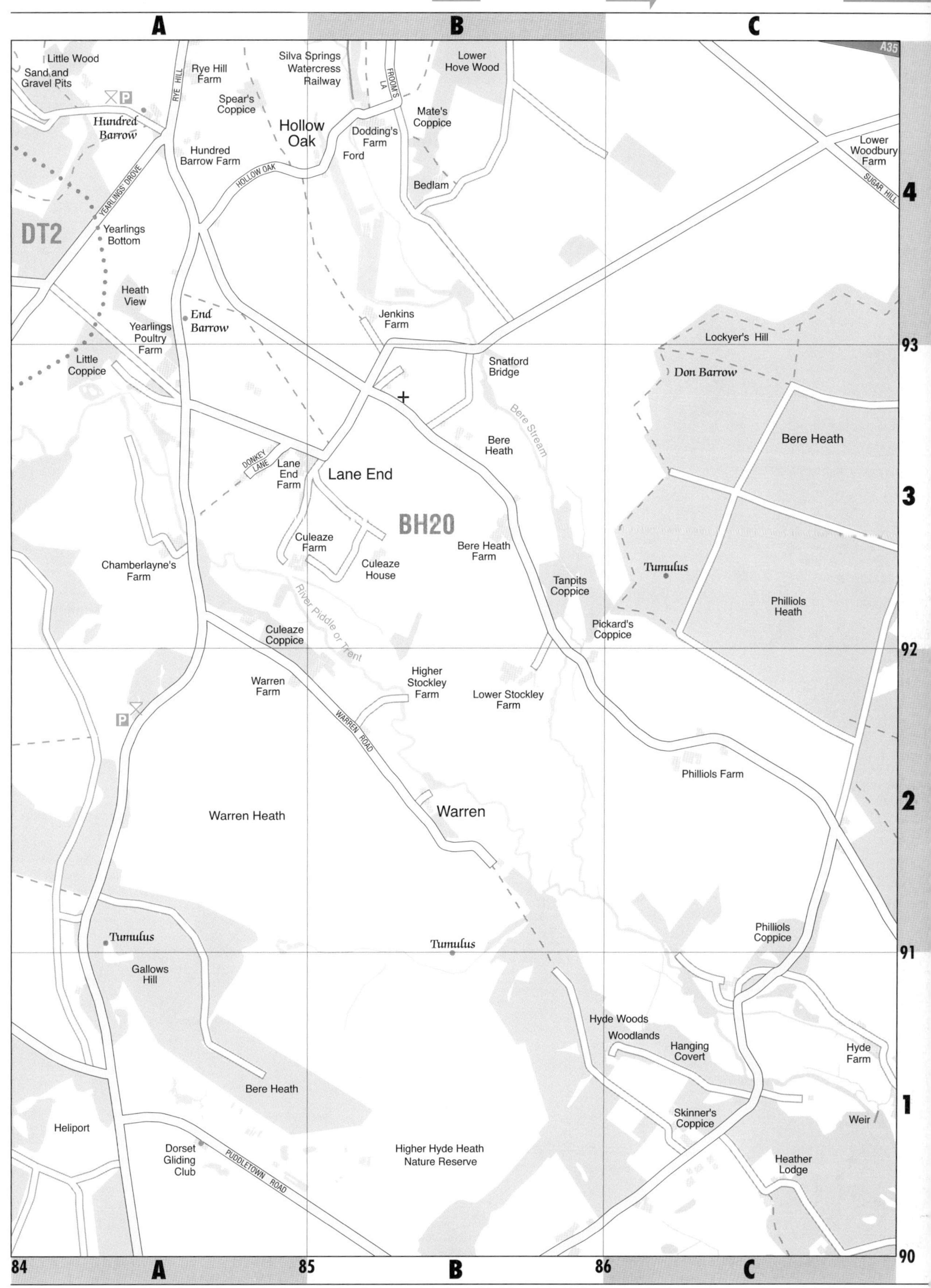

Little Wood
Sand and Gravel Pits
Hundred Barrow
P
Rye Hill Farm
Spear's Coppice
Silva Springs Watercress Railway
Lower Hove Wood
Mate's Coppice
Lower Woodbury Farm

RYE HILL

Hollow Oak
Hundred Barrow Farm
Dodding's Farm
Ford
Bedlam

HOLLOW OAK

DT2
Yearlings Bottom
Heath View
Yearlings Poultry Farm
End Barrow

YEARLINGS DROVE

Jenkins Farm

Little Coppice

Snatford Bridge

Lockyer's Hill
Don Barrow

Bere Stream

Bere Heath

Bere Heath

+

DONKEY LANE
Lane End Farm
Lane End

BH20
Culeaze Farm
Culeaze House
Bere Heath Farm
Tumulus
Philliols Heath

Chamberlayne's Farm

River Piddle or Trent
Culeaze Coppice
Tanpits Coppice
Pickard's Coppice

Warren Farm
Higher Stockley Farm
Lower Stockley Farm

P
WARREN ROAD

Philliols Farm

Warren Heath
Warren

Tumulus
Tumulus

Philliols Coppice

Gallows Hill

Hyde Woods
Woodlands
Hanging Covert
Hyde Farm

Bere Heath

Heliport

Skinner's Coppice
Weir

PUDDLETOWN ROAD
Dorset Gliding Club
Higher Hyde Heath Nature Reserve
Heather Lodge

4

93

3

92

2

91

1

90

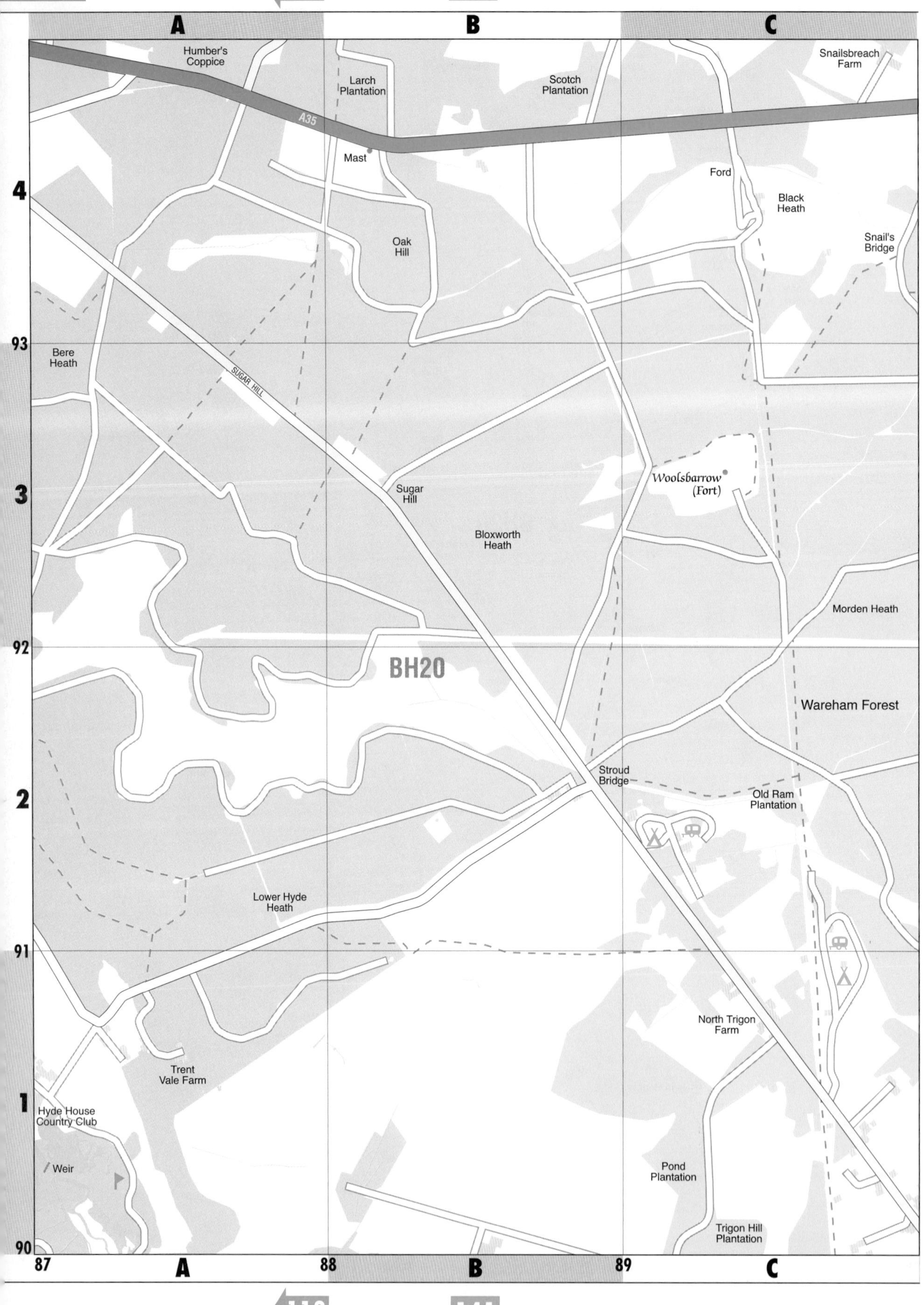

A B C

Humber's
Coppice

Larch
Plantation

Scotch
Plantation

Snailsbreach
Farm

A35

Mast

Ford

Black
Heath

Snail's
Bridge

4

Oak
Hill

93

Bere
Heath

SUGAR HILL

Woolsbarrow
(Fort)

3

Sugar
Hill

Bloxworth
Heath

Morden Heath

92

BH20

Wareham Forest

Stroud
Bridge

Old Ram
Plantation

2

Lower Hyde
Heath

91

North Trigon
Farm

Trent
Vale Farm

1

Hyde House
Country Club

Weir

Pond
Plantation

Trigon Hill
Plantation

90

87   A   88   B   89   C

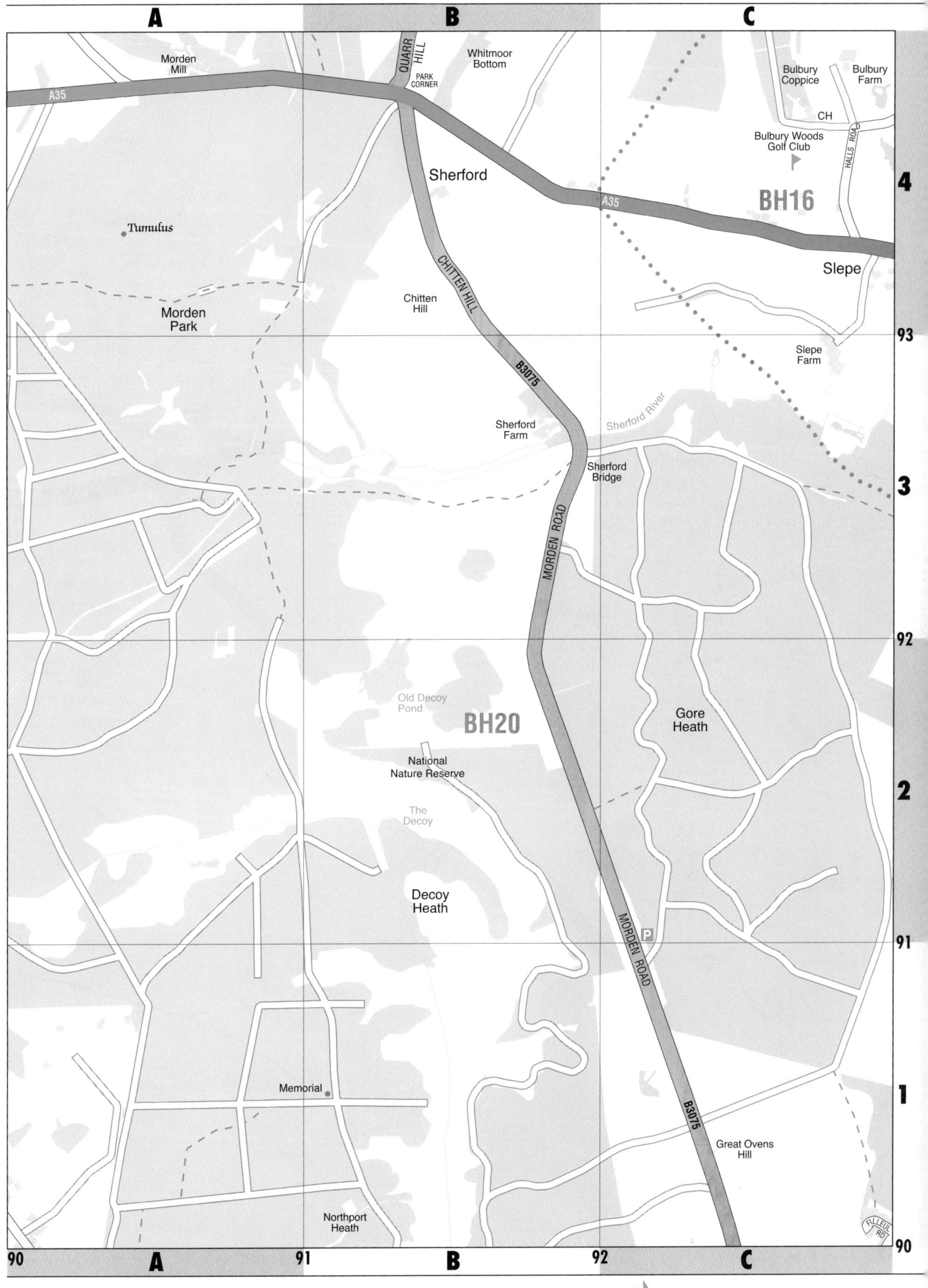
A
B
C
Morden Mill
A35
QUARR HILL
PARK CORNER
Whitmoor Bottom
Bulbury Coppice
Bulbury Farm
CH
HALLS ROAD
Bulbury Woods Golf Club
Sherford
BH16
Slepe
Tumulus
CHITTEN HILL
Chitten Hill
Morden Park
Slepe Farm
B3075
Sherford River
Sherford Farm
Sherford Bridge
MORDEN ROAD
Old Decoy Pond
BH20
Gore Heath
National Nature Reserve
The Decoy
Decoy Heath
P
Memorial
Great Ovens Hill
Northport Heath
FILLEUL RD
4
93
3
92
2
91
1
90
91
92

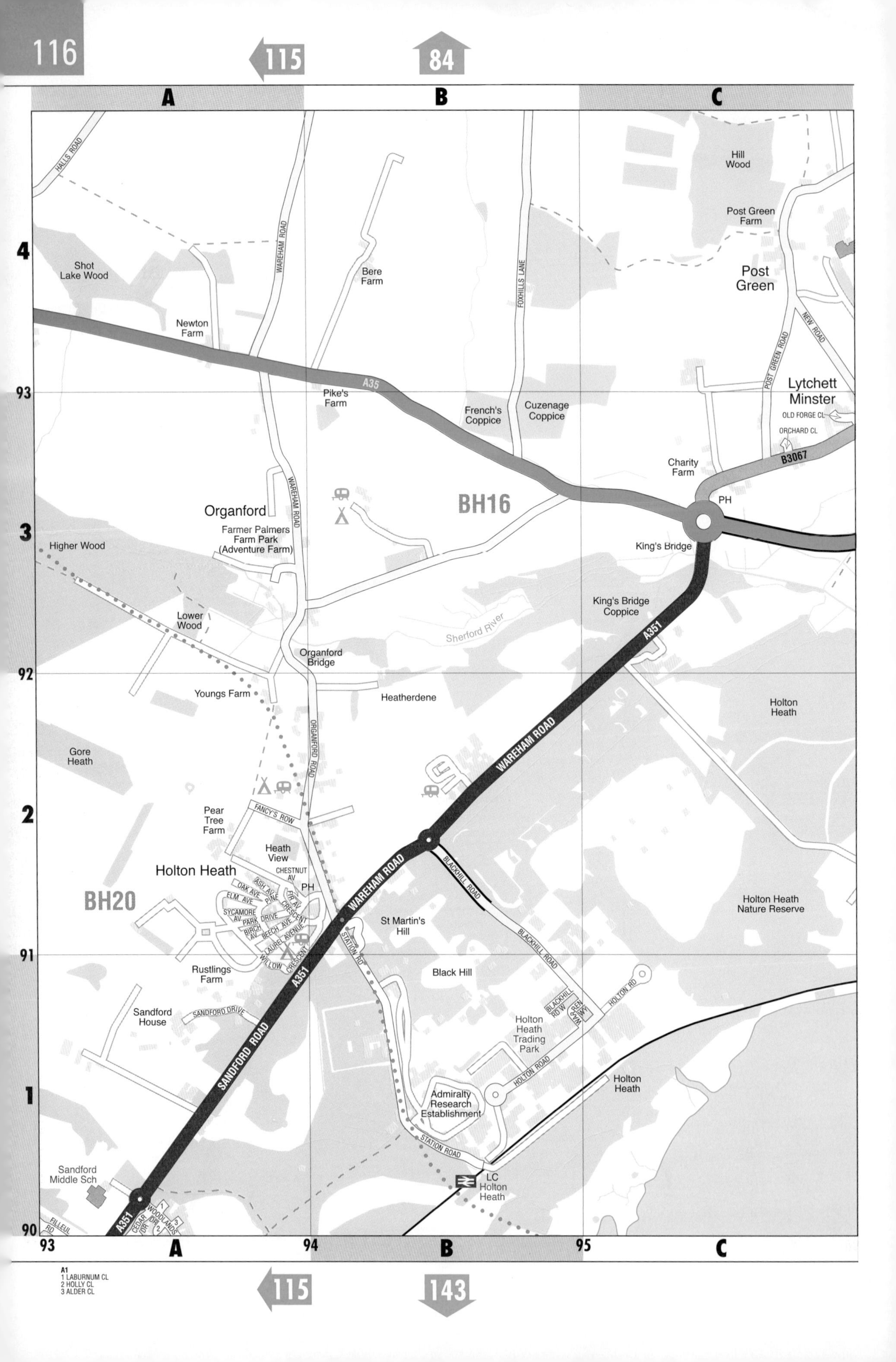
115
84
A
B
C
HALLS ROAD
Hill
Wood
Post Green
Farm
Shot
Lake Wood
WAREHAM ROAD
Bere
Farm
FOXHILLS LANE
Post
Green
NEW ROAD
Newton
Farm
POST GREEN ROAD
A35
Pike's
Farm
French's
Coppice
Cuzenage
Coppice
Lytchett
Minster
OLD FORGE CL
ORCHARD CL
B3067
Charity
Farm
WAREHAM ROAD
BH16
PH
Organford
Farmer Palmers
Farm Park
(Adventure Farm)
Higher Wood
King's Bridge
King's Bridge
Coppice
Lower
Wood
Sherford River
A351
Organford
Bridge
Youngs Farm
Heatherdene
Holton
Heath
ORGANFORD ROAD
WAREHAM ROAD
Gore
Heath
Pear
Tree
Farm
FANCY'S ROW
Heath
View
WAREHAM ROAD
BLACKHILL ROAD
Holton Heath
CHESTNUT AV
ASH AV
OAK AVE
PINE
FIR AV
ELM AVE
CRESCENT
PH
BH20
SYCAMORE AV
PARK DRIVE
BEECH AVE
BIRCH AV
LAUREL AVENUE
WILLOW
CRESCENT
St Martin's
Hill
Holton Heath
Nature Reserve
STATION RD
BLACKHILL ROAD
Rustlings
Farm
Black Hill
A351
HOLTON RD
BLACKHILL RD W
WARREN WY
Sandford
House
SANDFORD DRIVE
Holton
Heath
Trading
Park
SANDFORD ROAD
HOLTON ROAD
Holton
Heath
Admiralty
Research
Establishment
STATION ROAD
Sandford
Middle Sch
LC
Holton
Heath
A351
FILLEUL RD
CEDAR DR
WOODLANDS
1
2
3
4
93
92
91
1
90
93
94
95
A
B
C
115
143

A1
1 LABURNUM CL
2 HOLLY CL
3 ALDER CL

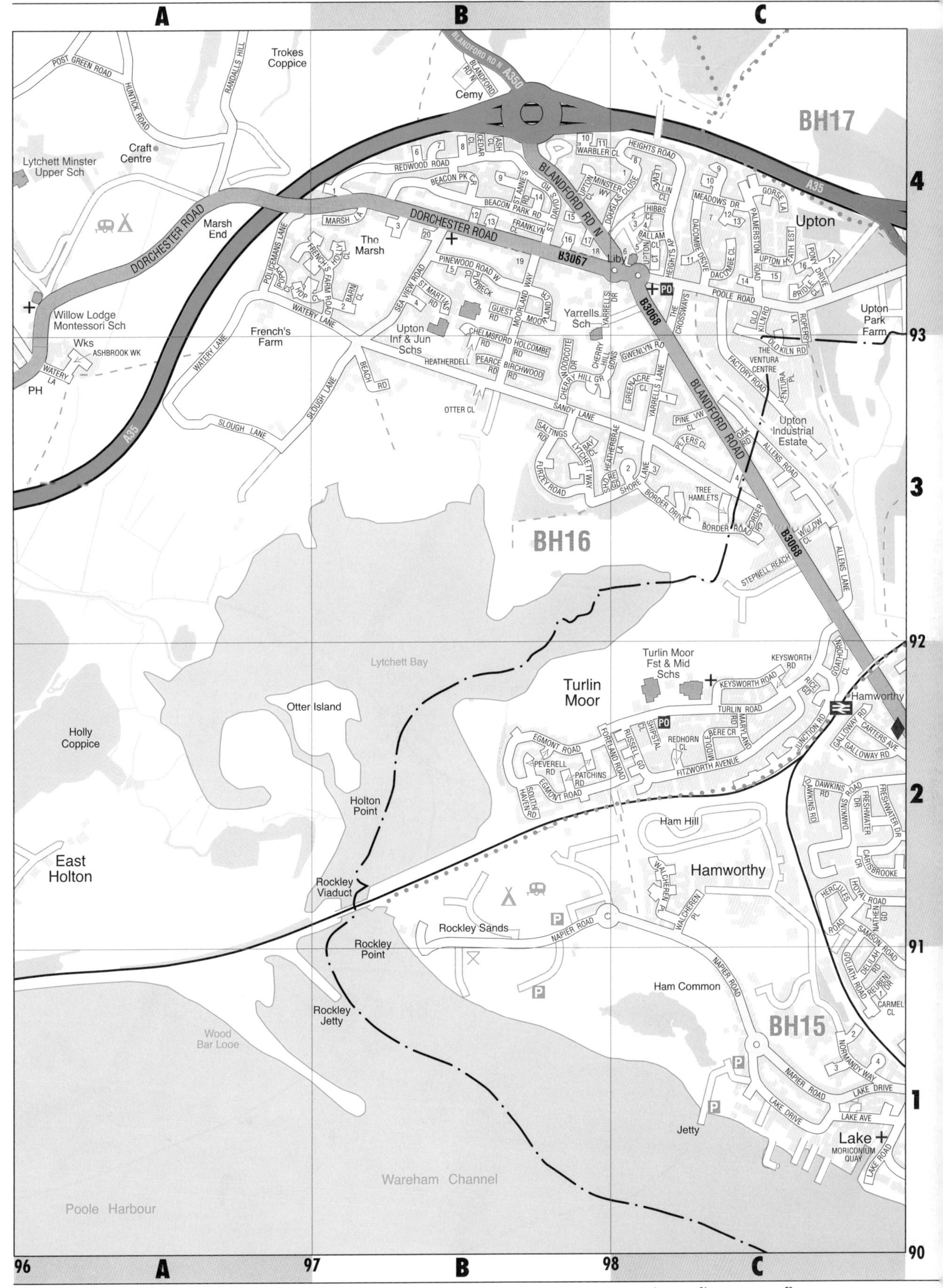

B4
1 DORCHESTER RD
2 GREENWAY CR
3 OAKLEY GD
4 SEABANK CL
5 PINEWOOD CL
6 HICKORY CL
7 GURJUN CL
8 DOUSSIE CL
9 RICHARD CL
10 KESTREL CL
11 BELL HEATHER CL
12 BEACON RD
13 FOXGLOVES
14 STUART CL
15 CORONATION AV
16 EGDON CT
17 THE TRIANGLE
18 DARIAN COURT
19 MOOR LAND PARK
20 OASIS MEWS

85

C4
1 DOUGLAS CL
2 SHIRLEY RD
3 UPTON PARK MOBILE HOME PK
4 ELIZABETH RD
5 CHRIS CR
6 MAPLE LO

118

7 LLEWELLIN CT
8 TURBARY CT
9 MEADOW BANK
10 MEADOWS CL
11 BRIARSWOOD RD
12 MEADOWS DR
13 DAVENPORT CL
14 PRESTON CL
15 PALMERSTON CL
16 STIRRUP CL
17 MARTINGALE CL

117

144 **118**

C1
1 SOLOMON WY
2 FORT CUMBERLAND CL
3 KANGAW PL
4 SALERNO PL

C3
1 YARRELLS CL
2 SHORE AV
3 SHORE CL
4 OLD BOUND RD

117 86

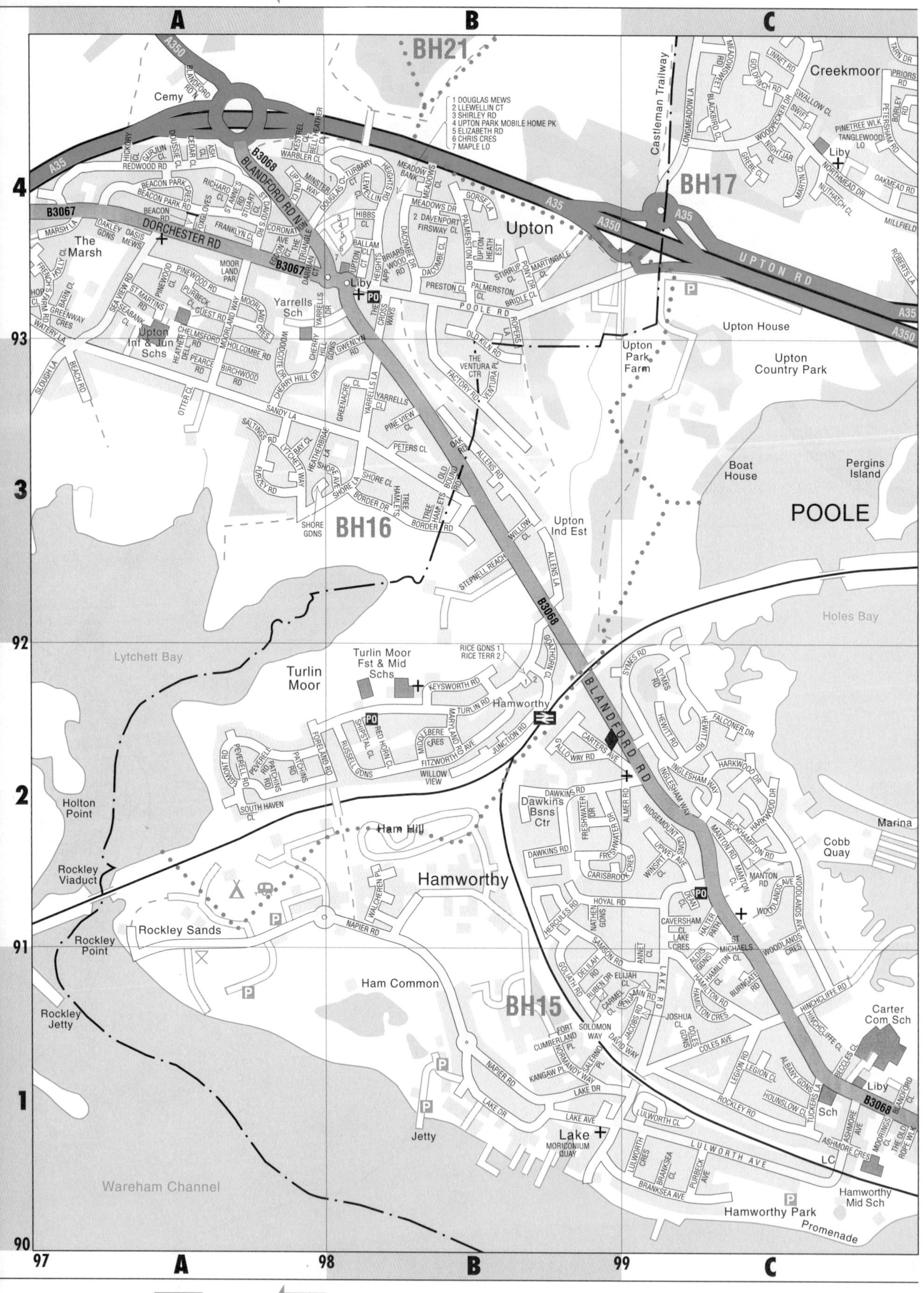
Creekmoor
BH21
BH17
Upton
Cemy
The Marsh
Yarrells Sch
Upton Inf & Jun Schs
Upton House
Upton Country Park
Upton Park Farm
Castleman Trailway
Boat House
Pergins Island
POOLE
BH16
Upton Ind Est
Holes Bay
Lytchett Bay
Turlin Moor
Turlin Moor Fst & Mid Schs
Hamworthy
Holton Point
Rockley Viaduct
Ham Hill
Dawkins Bsns Ctr
Marina
Cobb Quay
Rockley Sands
Rockley Point
Ham Common
BH15
Rockley Jetty
Carter Com Sch
Jetty
Lake
Wareham Channel
Hamworthy Park
Promenade
Hamworthy Mid Sch
1 DOUGLAS MEWS
2 LLEWELLIN CT
3 SHIRLEY RD
4 UPTON PARK MOBILE HOME PK
5 ELIZABETH RD
6 CHRIS CRES
7 MAPLE LO
A35
A350
B3067
B3068
DORCHESTER RD
BLANDFORD RD N
BLANDFORD RD
UPTON RD
POOLE RD
LULWORTH AVE
A B C
97 98 99
90 91 92 93

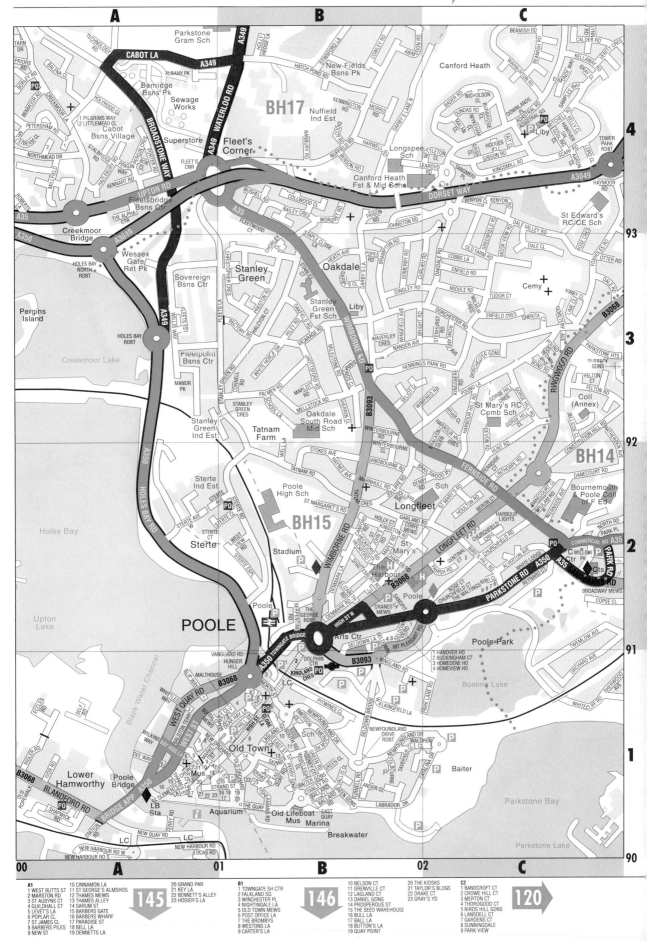

A1
1 WEST BUTTS ST
2 MARSTON RD
3 ST AUBYNS CT
4 GUILDHALL CT
5 LEVET'S LA
6 POPLAR CL
7 ST JAMES CL
8 BARBERS PILES
9 NEW ST
10 CINNAMON LA
11 ST GEORGE'S ALMSHOS
12 THAMES MEWS
13 THAMES ALLEY
14 SARUM ST
15 BARBERS GATE
16 BARBERS WHARF
17 PARADISE ST
18 BELL LA
19 DENNETTS LA
20 GRAND PAR
21 KEY LA
22 BENNETT'S ALLEY
23 HOSIER'S LA

B1
1 TOWNGATE SH CTR
2 FALKLAND SQ
3 WINCHESTER PL
4 NIGHTINGALE LA
5 OLD TOWN MEWS
6 POST OFFICE LA
7 THE BROMBYS
8 WESTONS LA
9 CARTER'S LA
10 NELSON CT
11 GRENVILLE CT
12 LAGLAND CT
13 DANIEL GDNS
14 PROSPEROUS ST
15 THE SEED WAREHOUSE
16 BULL LA
17 BALL LA
18 BUTTON'S LA
19 QUAY POINT
20 THE KIOSKS
21 TAYLOR'S BLDGS
22 DRAKE CT
23 GRAY'S YD

C2
1 BANOCROFT CT
2 CROWE HILL CT
3 MERTON CT
4 THOROGOOD CT
5 BIRDS HILL GDNS
6 LANSDELL CT
7 GARDENS CT
8 SUNNINGDALE
9 PARK VIEW

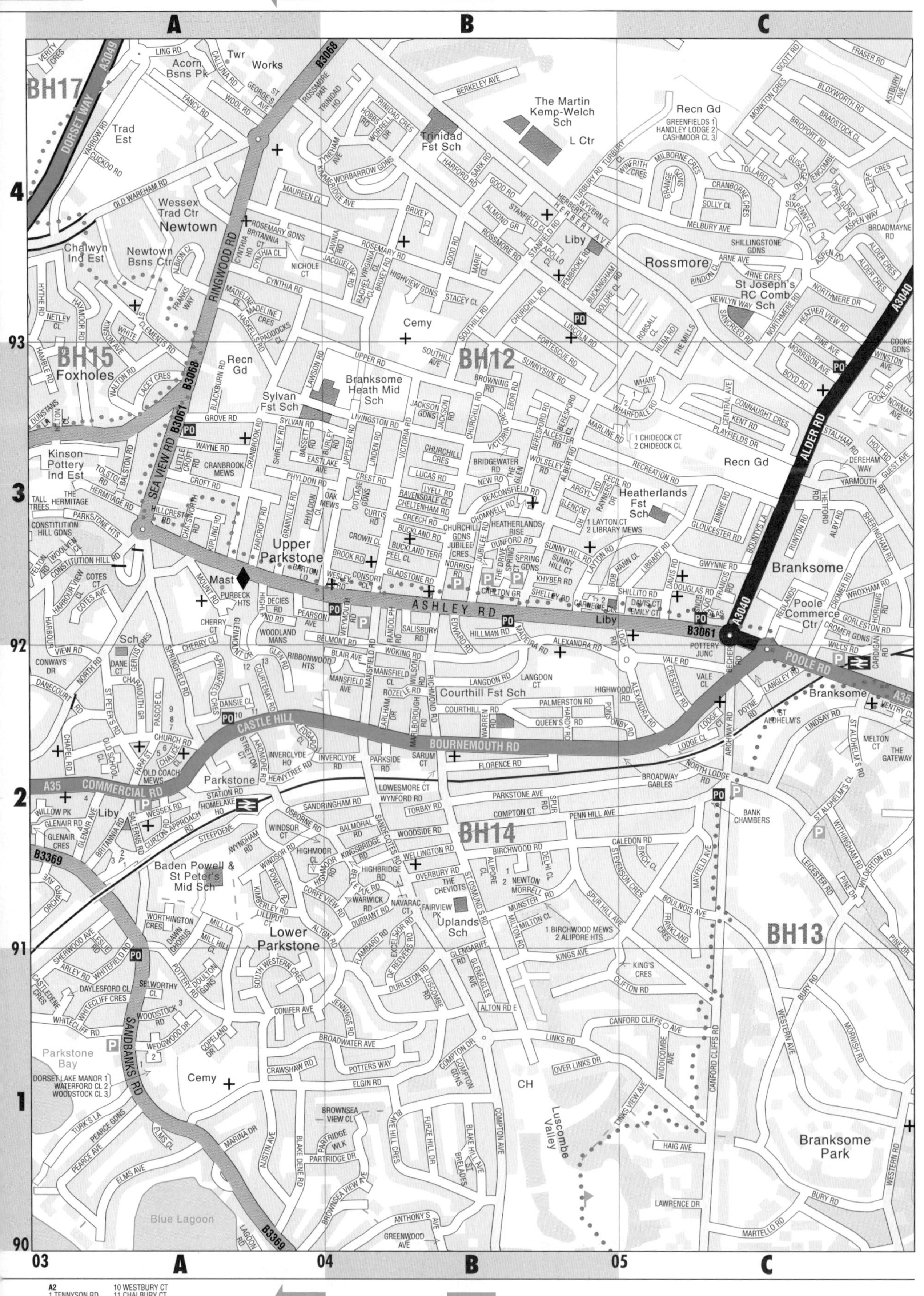

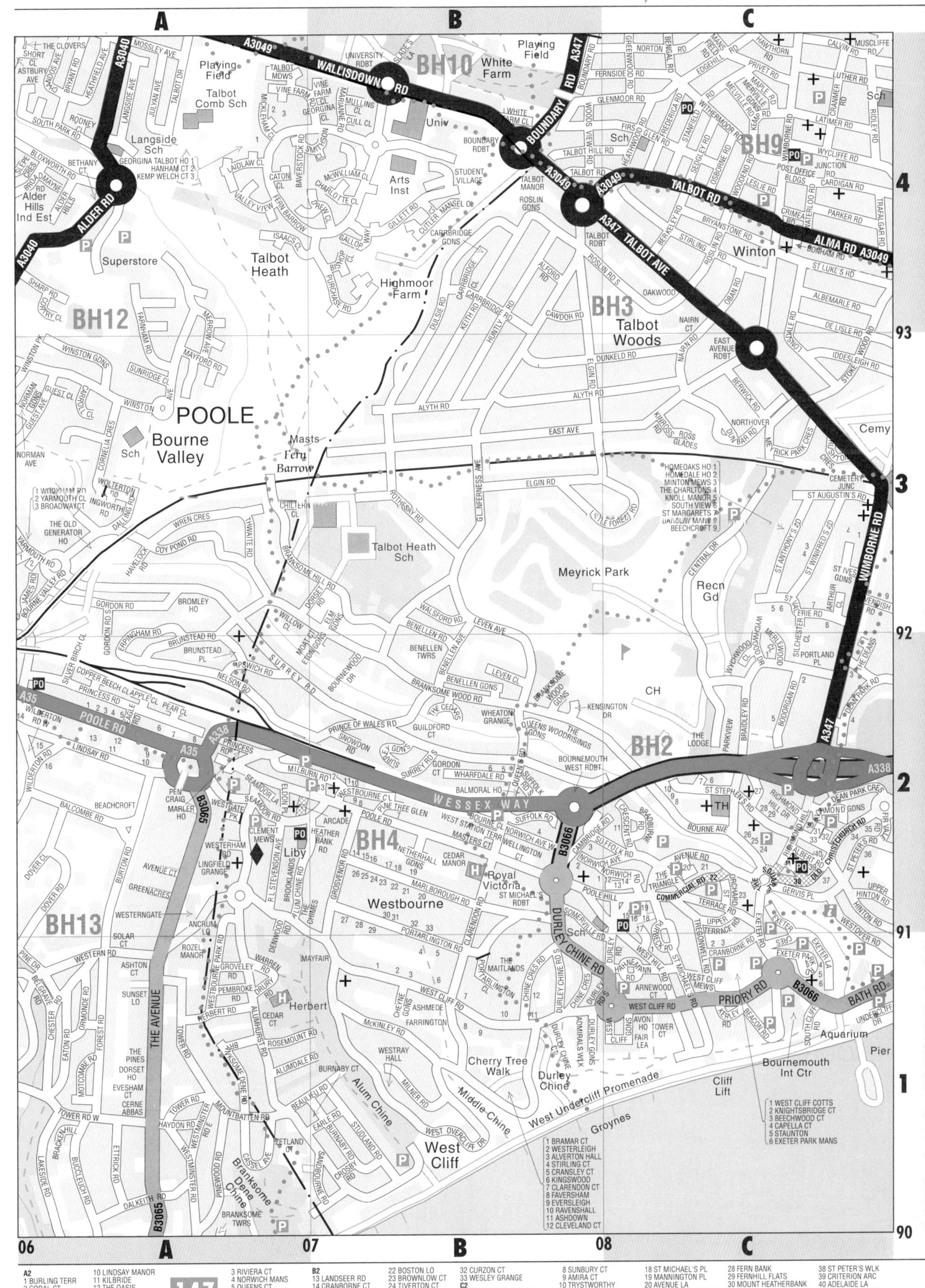

A3
1 CULFORD CT
2 APSLEY CT
3 TRELOEN CT
4 RAVANA CT
5 HOMELEIGH HO
6 BEECHY CT
7 WELLINGTON CT
8 MORINGTON CT
9 PARSONAGE CT
10 HAMILTON CT
11 MOORLEA
12 PORCHESTER CT

B3
1 OPHIR GDNS
2 METHUEN CL
3 LOWTHER GDNS
4 THE LANE
5 STEWART CL
6 HENVILLE CT
7 MALMESBURY PARK PL
8 WESLEY CL

← **121**   ↑ **90**

BOURNEMOUTH

BH9
BH8
BH7
BH1
BH5

Queen's Park
King's Park
Dean Park
Cricket Ground
Springbourne
Boscombe
Russell Cotes Art Gall & Mus
Pier
Promenade

RICHMOND PARK ROAD
CHRISTCHURCH RD
WESSEX WAY
ALMA RD
LANSDOWNE RD
ASHLEY RD
ST PAUL'S RD
BATH RD

1 SHELBOURNE CL
2 CAPSTONE PL
3 AVON CL
4 RICHMOND PARK CL
5 EGERTON GDNS
6 ST LEDGER'S PL

← **121**

A2
1 ASHBOURNE CT
2 TRINITY
3 ST PETERS CT
4 PINE GRANGE
5 BUCKINGHAM MANS
6 ALEXANDRA LO
7 QUEENSBURY MANS
8 AMBERLEY CT
9 BATH HILL CT
10 LITTLE FOREST MANS
11 BERNE CT
12 ELIZABETH CT
13 LANSDOWNE HO
14 CODOGAN CT
15 BURFORD CT
16 GRANGE CT
17 GARDEN HO
18 ATHELNEY CT
19 GROSVENER CT
20 EDEN CT
21 GROVE MANS
22 RIVIERA

B2
1 WILLOW LO
2 GROSVENOR CT
3 PINE MANS
4 VALE MONS
5 KNOLE CT
6 COURTLEIGH MANOR
7 GORSECLIFF CT

C2
1 DONOUGHMORE RD
2 RANDOLPH RD
3 THE CRESCENT
4 CARNARVON RD
5 ROYAL ARC
6 PENNY LA
7 FLORIN MALL
8 SOVEREIGN SQ
9 CROWN WLK
10 HORACE RD
11 ARGYLL MANS
12 FAIRHAVON CT
13 CLIFTON CT
14 WARWICK CT
15 RICHMOND CT
16 GRANTLEY CT
17 THESSALY CT
18 ST GEORGES MANS
19 WATKIN RD
20 ST JAMES'S
21 MARINA CT
22 MERMAID CT
23 SAN REMO TWRS
24 MARINA TWRS
25 WOLLSTONECRAFT RD
26 CLEASBY GRANGE
27 LAVERSTOCK
28 OCEAN HTS
29 CARLINFORD

C3
1 ST ANN'S CT
2 ST GEORGE'S CT
3 ST DAVID'S CT
4 ST JOHN'S CT
5 HAVILAND RD W

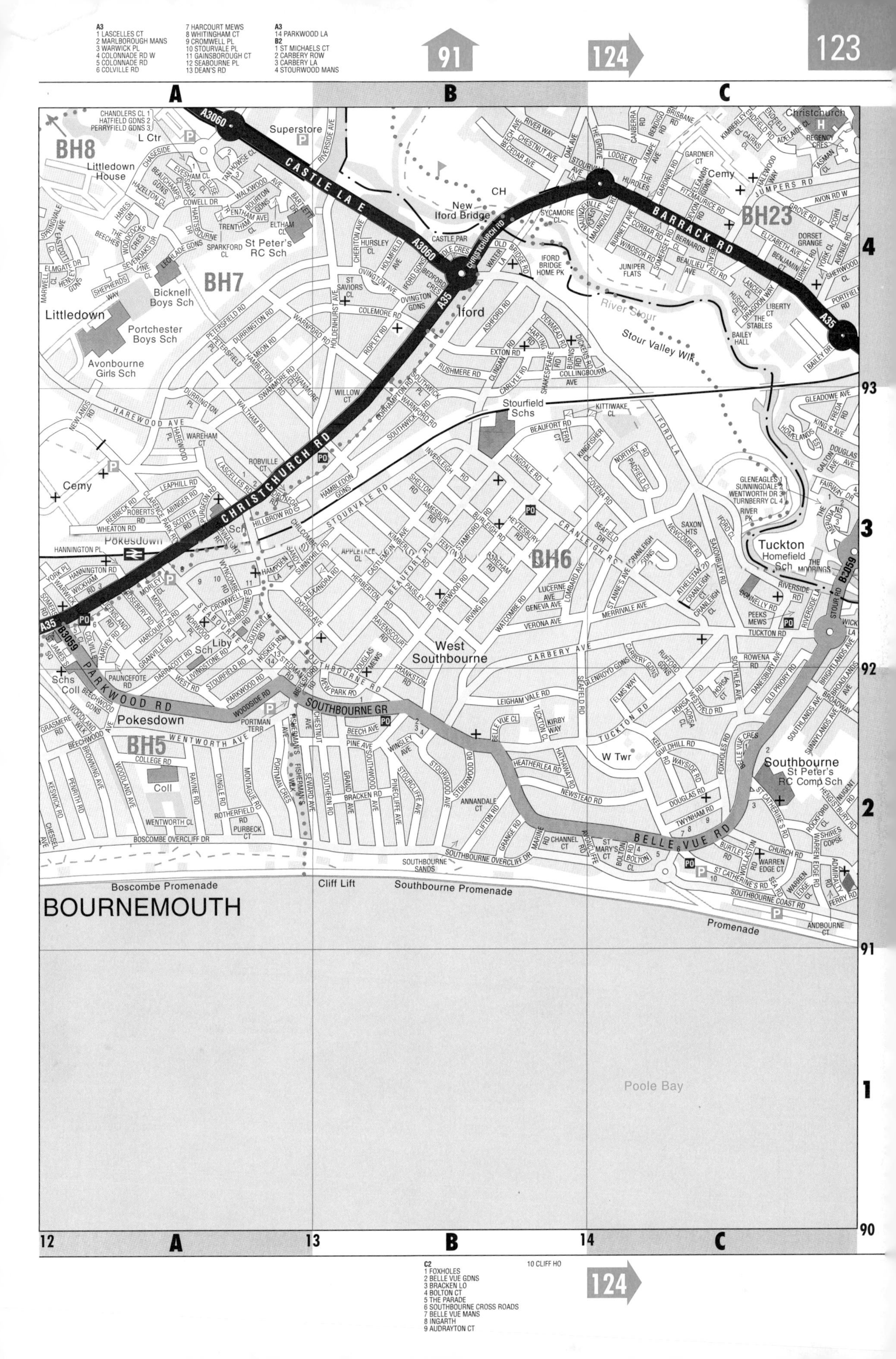

91
124

BOURNEMOUTH

BH8
BH7
BH5
BH6
BH23

Poole Bay

124

124

A3
1 HOMESTOUR HO
2 ORCHARD MEWS
3 POUND LA
4 SAXON SQ SH CTR
5 PRIORY VIEW CT
6 MARINA VIEW
7 THE MOORINGS
8 SWAN GN
9 KINGFISHERS

123

92

A4
1 WINSTON CT
2 KENILWORTH CT
3 ARTHUR LA
4 MULBERRY CT
5 GILBERT CT
6 CENTENARY HO

C3
1 FRANCESCA LO
2 GILLION CT
3 ROSEDALE CL
4 STROUD GDNS
5 GREEN LOANING
6 ALDERBURY CT
7 CHALBURY CT
8 BADBURY CT
9 DUDSBURY CT
C4
1 SOUTHDOWN CT
2 MALVERN CT

C4
3 PURBECK CT
4 MENDIP CT
5 CHILTERN CT
6 COTSWOLD CT
7 QUANTOCK CT
8 PENNINE CT
9 WENLOCK CT
10 STRETE MOUNT
11 PUREWELL CT
12 COURT CL
13 FRANCESCA GRANGE

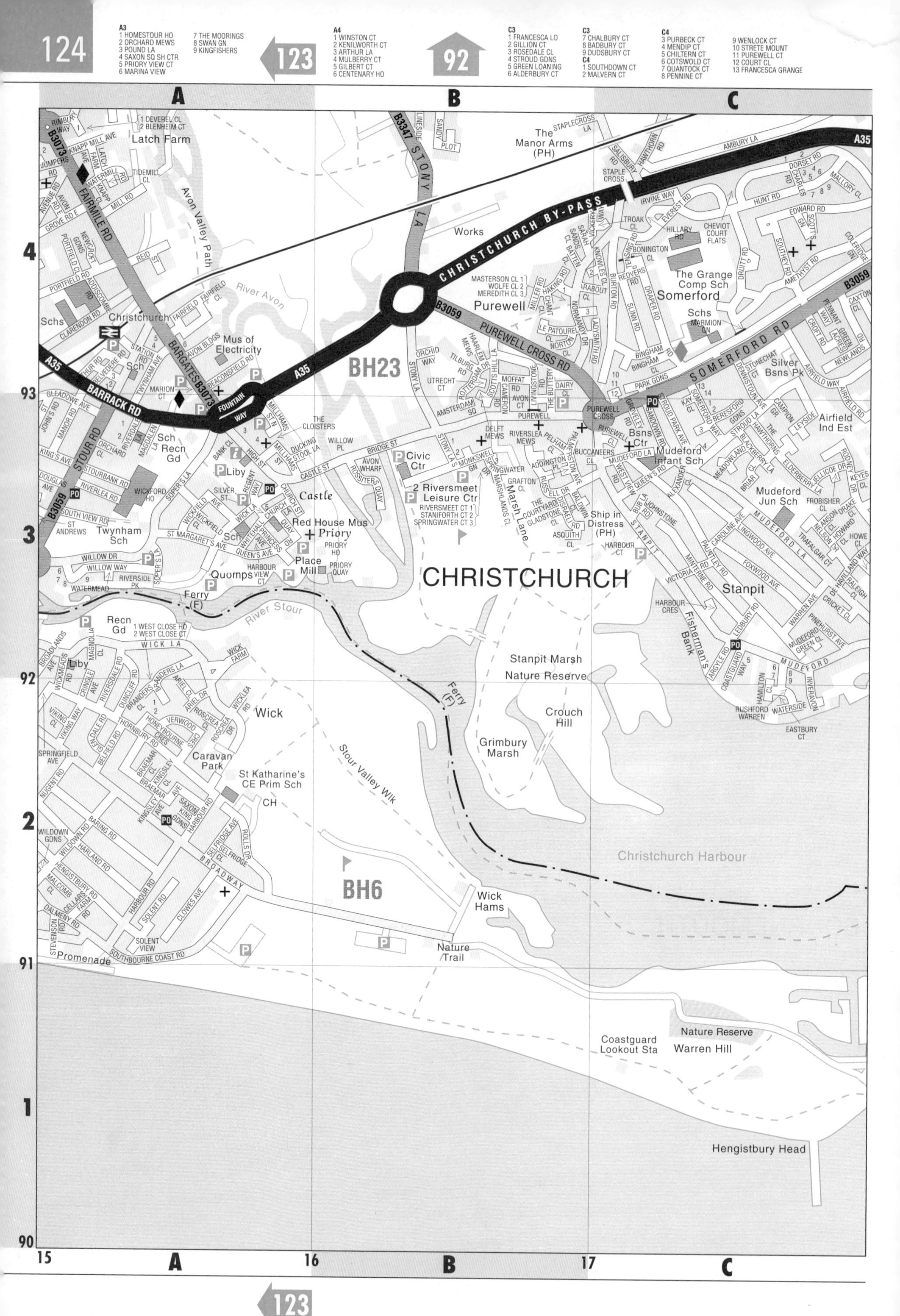

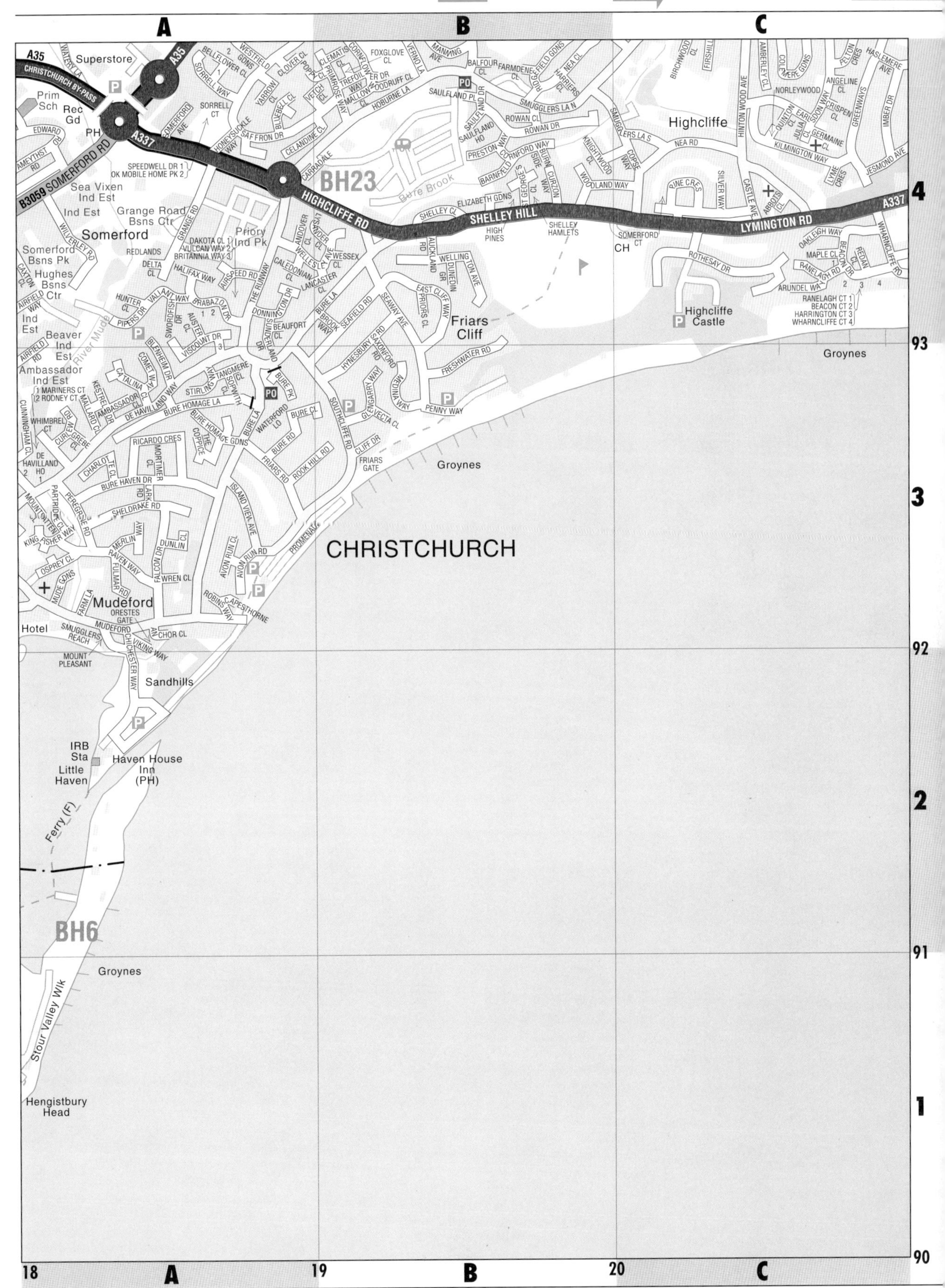

A B C

A35 Superstore
A35
CHRISTCHURCH BY-PASS
Prim Sch
Rec Gd
PH
SOMERFORD RD A337
B3059 SOMERFORD RD
Speedwell Dr 1
OK Mobile Home Pk 2
Sea Vixen Ind Est
Ind Est
Somerford
Grange Road Bsns Ctr
Somerford Bsns Pk
Hughes Bsns Ctr
Ind Est
Beaver Ind Est
Ambassador Ind Est
1 Mariners Ct
2 Rodney Ct
De Havilland Way

BH23
HIGHCLIFFE RD
Priory Ind Pk
Dakota Cl 1
Aullcan Way 2
Britannia Way 3
Redlands
Delta Cl
Halifax Way

SHELLEY HILL
SHELLEY HILL
High Pines
Shelley Hamlets
Somerford CH CT
Friars Cliff

Highcliffe
Nea Rd
LYMINGTON RD A337
Rothesay Dr
Highcliffe Castle
Oakleigh Way
Maple Cl
Ranelagh Rd
Arundel Wa
Ranelagh Ct 1
Beacon Ct 2
Harrington Ct 3
Wharncliffe Ct 4

93
Groynes

4

3
CHRISTCHURCH
Groynes

Mudeford
Hotel
Smugglers Reach
Mudeford

92
MOUNT PLEASANT
Sandhills

IRB Sta
Little Haven
Haven House Inn (PH)

Ferry (F)

2

BH6

91
Groynes

Stour Valley Wlk

Hengistbury Head

1

18 A 19 B 20 C

90

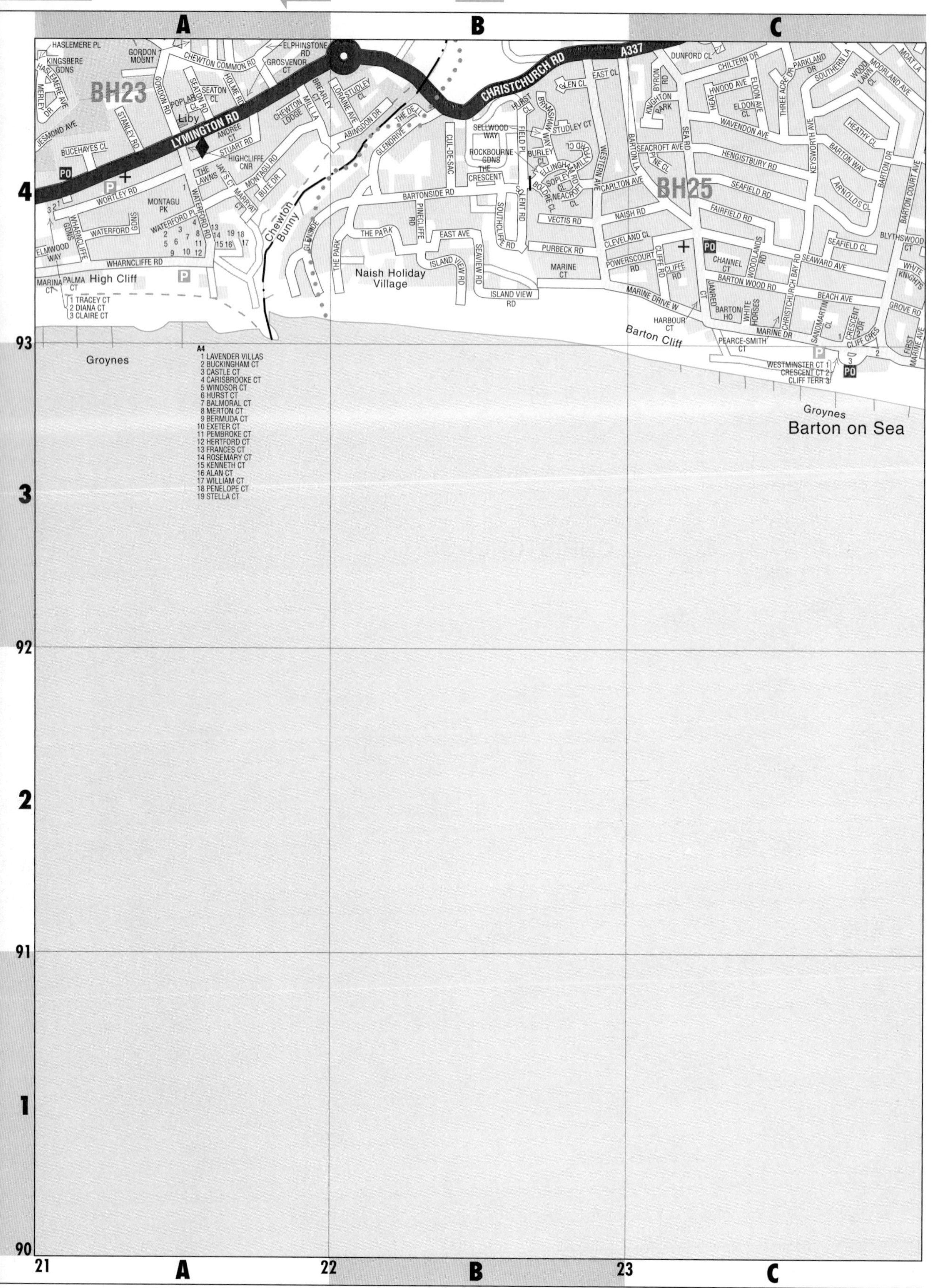
A
B
C
BH23
BH25
LYMINGTON RD
CHRISTCHURCH RD
A337
Liby
High Cliff
Chewton Bunny
Naish Holiday Village
Barton Cliff
Groynes
Barton on Sea
A4
1 LAVENDER VILLAS
2 BUCKINGHAM CT
3 CASTLE CT
4 CARISBROOKE CT
5 WINDSOR CT
6 HURST CT
7 BALMORAL CT
8 MERTON CT
9 BERMUDA CT
10 EXETER CT
11 PEMBROKE CT
12 HERTFORD CT
13 FRANCES CT
14 ROSEMARY CT
15 KENNETH CT
16 ALAN CT
17 WILLIAM CT
18 PENELOPE CT
19 STELLA CT
1 TRACEY CT
2 DIANA CT
3 CLAIRE CT
WESTMINSTER CT 1
CRESCENT CT 2
CLIFF TERR 3
21
22
23
90
91
92
93

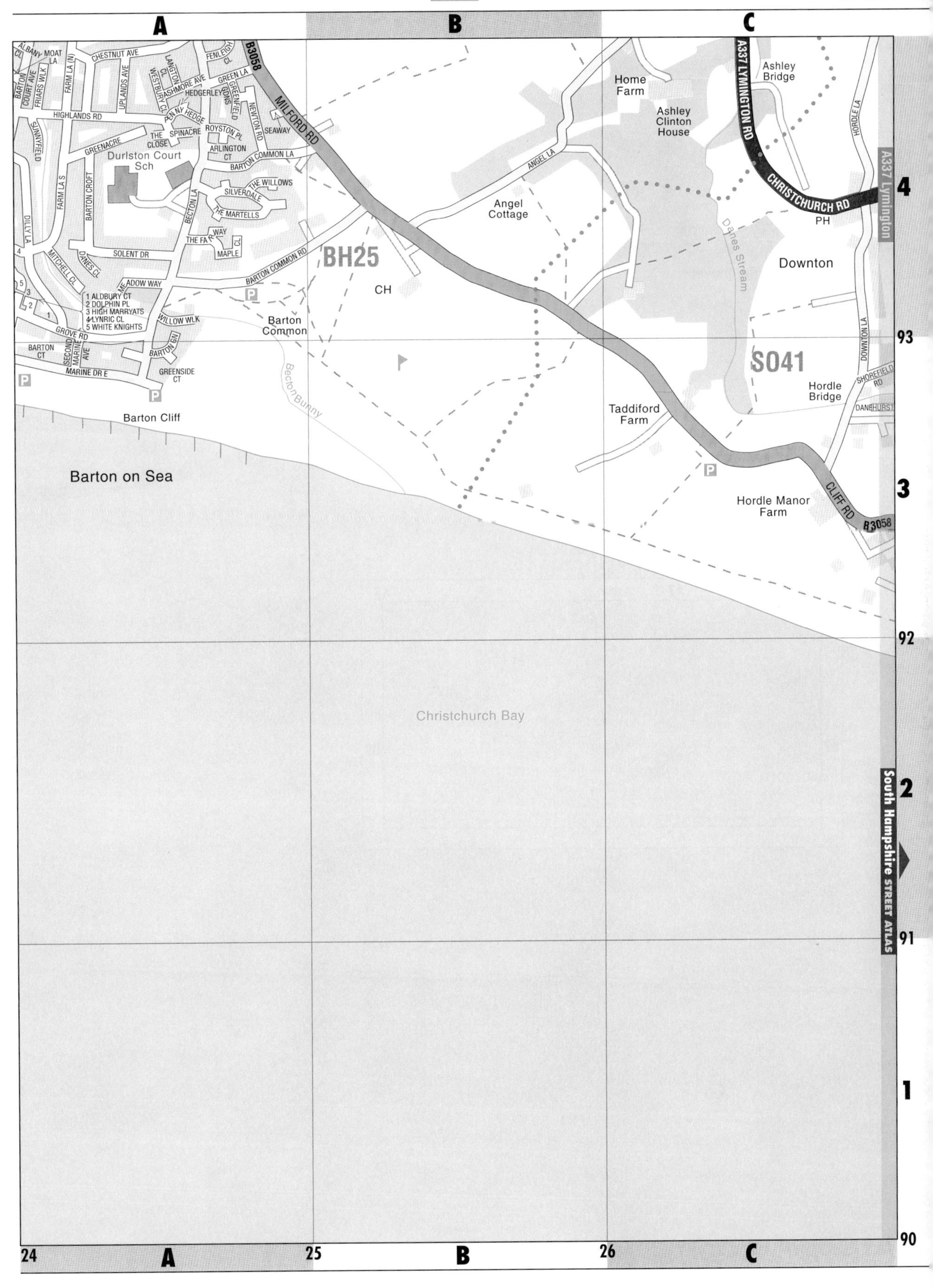

A **B** **C**

B3058

MILFORD RD

ALBANY MOAT CL
CHESTNUT AVE
FARM LA IN
LANGTON CL
FENLEIGH
GREEN LA
NEWTON RD
BARTON CL
COURT AVE
FRIARS WLK
HIGHLANDS RD
CASHMORE AVE
HEDGERLEYS
ROYSTON PL
UPLANDS AVE
ASH HEDGE
WESTERY CL
SPINACRE
ARLINGTON CT
SEAWAY
GREENACRE
THE CLOSE
BARTON COMMON LA
SILVERDALE
THE WILLOWS
BARTON CROFT
THE MARTELLS
SUNNYFIELD
BECTON LA
MAPLE
SOLENT DR
DILLY LA
FARM LA S
MITCHELL CL
MEADOW WAY
THE FAIRWAY
MAPLE CL
DANES CL

Durlston Court Sch

Home Farm

Ashley Bridge

A337 LYMINGTON RD

Ashley Clinton House

CHRISTCHURCH RD
PH

HORDLE LA

Angel La

BH25

Angel Cottage

CH

Downton

SO41

A337 Lymington

Danes Stream

DOWNTON LA

1 ALDBURY CT
2 DOLPHIN PL
3 HIGH MARRYATS
4 LYNRIC CL
5 WHITE KNIGHTS

Barton Common

Hordle Bridge

SHOREFIELD RD

DANEHURST

GROVE RD
BARTON CT
BARTON IN
GREENSIDE CT
MARINE DR E
SECOND MARINE AVE
WILLOW WLK

Becton Bunny

Taddiford Farm

Hordle Manor Farm

CLIFF RD
B3058

Barton Cliff

Barton on Sea

Christchurch Bay

4
93
3
92
2
91
1
90

24   **A**   25   **B**   26   **C**

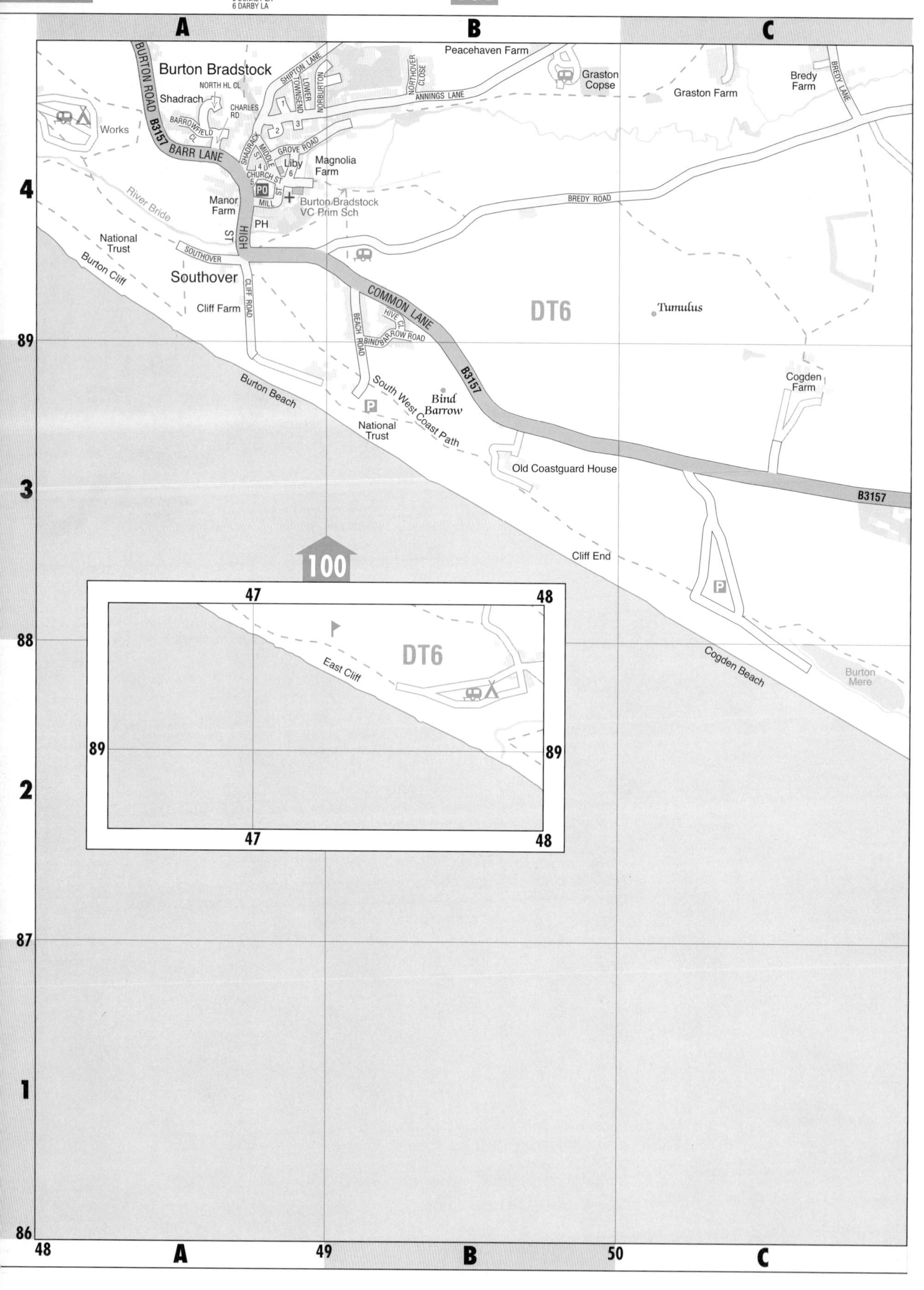

A4
1 HOWARTH CL
2 S ANNINGS
3 GROVE OR
4 ST LAWRENCE
5 DONKEY LA
6 DARBY LA

A

B

C

Burton Bradstock
NORTH HL CL
Shadrach
CHARLES RD
BARROWFIELD CL
BURTON ROAD
B3157
BARR LANE
Works

SHIPTON LANE
LOWER TOWNSEND
NORTHOVER
MILBURN
Peacehaven Farm

Graston Copse
Graston Farm
Bredy Farm

ANNINGS LANE

BREDY LANE

GROVE ROAD
SHADRACK
MIDDLE ST
CHURCH ST
Liby
Magnolia Farm
MILL

4

Manor Farm
PO
Burton Bradstock VC Prim Sch
PH
HIGH ST
SOUTHOVER

Bredy Road

National Trust
River Bride
Burton Cliff
Southover
CLIFF ROAD
Cliff Farm

COMMON LANE
B3157

DT6

Tumulus

89

BEACH ROAD
HIVE CL
ROW ROAD
BIND B'R

South West Coast Path
Burton Beach
P
National Trust

Bind Barrow

Cogden Farm

Old Coastguard House

3

Cliff End

B3157

100

47

48

DT6

East Cliff

88

89

89

Cogden Beach

Burton Mere

2

87

1

86

48

A

49

B

50

C

102
130

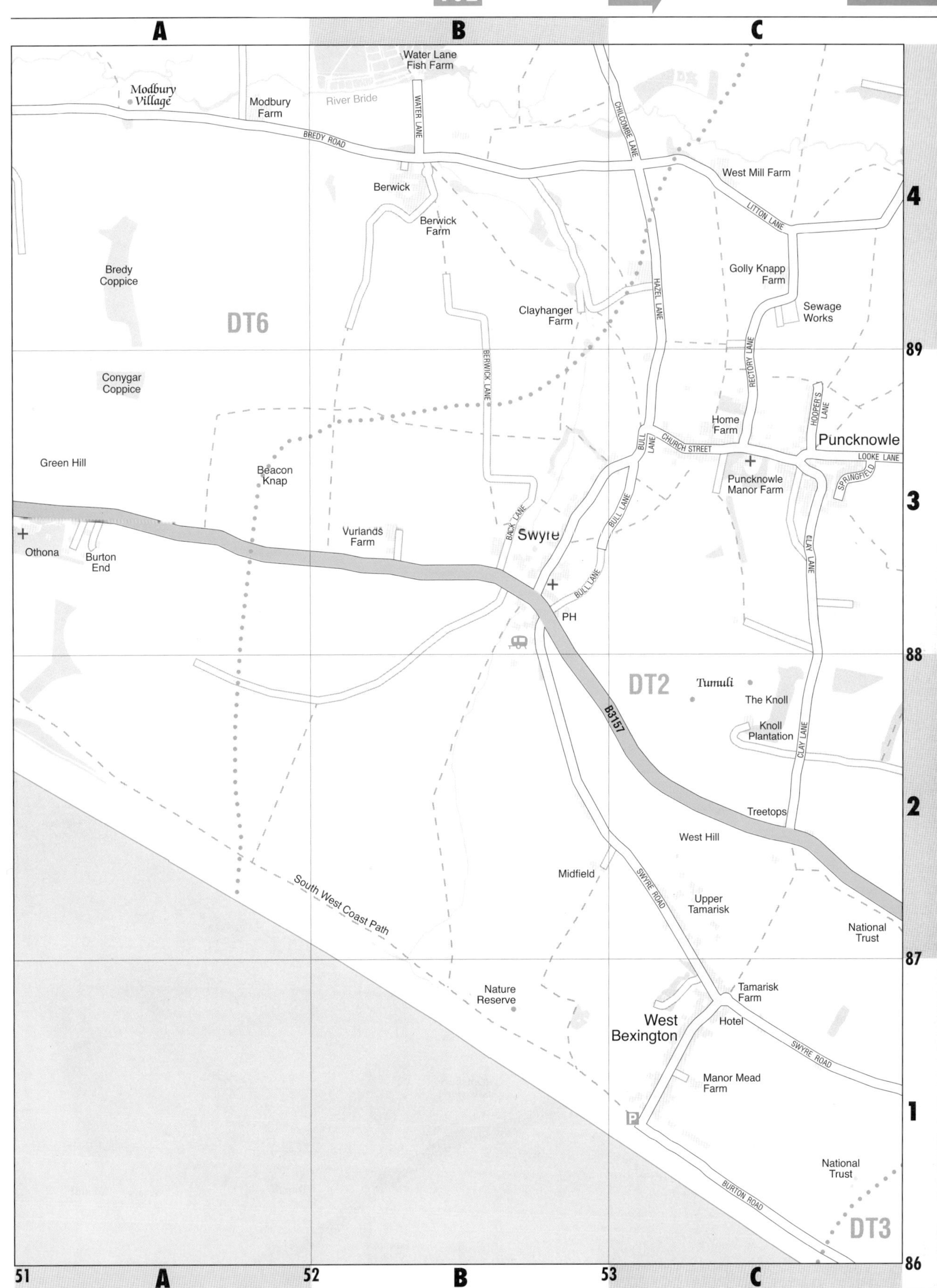
A
B
C
Water Lane
Fish Farm
Modbury
Village
Modbury
Farm
River Bride
WATER LANE
BREDY ROAD
CHILCOMBE LANE
West Mill Farm
Berwick
Berwick
Farm
LITTON LANE
4
Bredy
Coppice
Golly Knapp
Farm
HAZEL LANE
Clayhanger
Farm
Sewage
Works
DT6
89
RECTORY LANE
Conygar
Coppice
BERWICK LANE
HOOPER'S
LANE
Home
Farm
Puncknowle
BULL
LANE
CHURCH STREET
LOOKE LANE
Green Hill
Puncknowle
Manor Farm
SPRINGFIELD
Beacon
Knap
BACK LANE
3
BULL LANE
Swyre
Vurlands
Farm
Othona
Burton
End
CLAY LANE
BULL LANE
PH
88
DT2
Tumuli
The Knoll
B3157
Knoll
Plantation
CLAY LANE
2
Treetops
West Hill
Midfield
South West Coast Path
SWYRE ROAD
Upper
Tamarisk
National
Trust
87
Tamarisk
Farm
Nature
Reserve
Hotel
West
Bexington
SWYRE ROAD
Manor Mead
Farm
1
P
National
Trust
BURTON ROAD
DT3
86
51
52
53

130

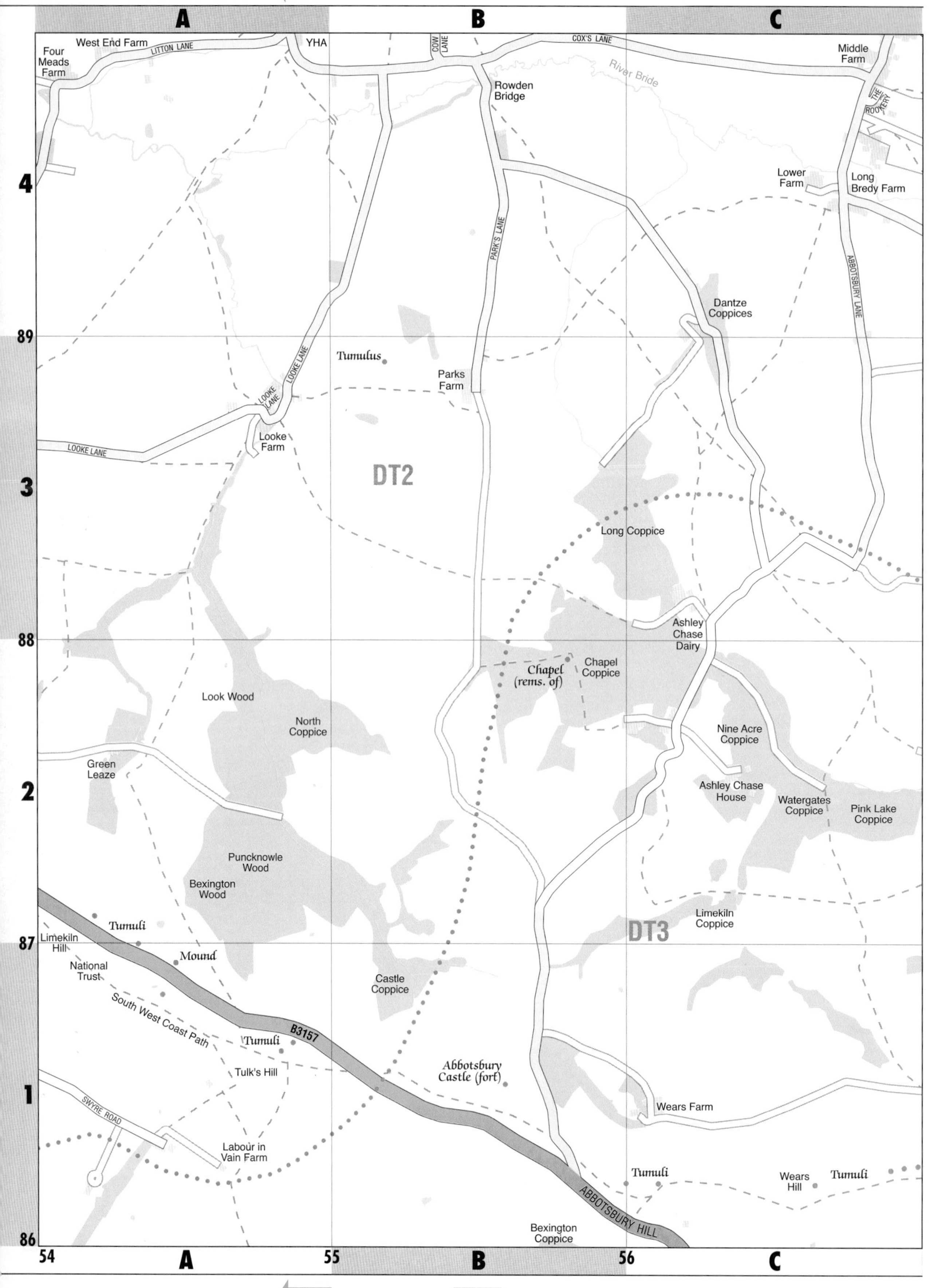

A
B
C

Four Meads Farm

West End Farm

LITTON LANE

YHA

COW LANE

COX'S LANE

Middle Farm

River Bride

Rowden Bridge

THE ROOKERY

4

PARK'S LANE

Lower Farm

Long Bredy Farm

ABBOTSBURY LANE

Dantze Coppices

89

LOOKE LANE

Tumulus

Parks Farm

DT2

Looke Farm

LOOKE LANE

Long Coppice

3

Ashley Chase Dairy

88

Chapel (rems. of)

Chapel Coppice

Look Wood

North Coppice

Nine Acre Coppice

Green Leaze

Ashley Chase House

Watergates Coppice

Pink Lake Coppice

2

Puncknowle Wood

Bexington Wood

Limekiln Coppice

DT3

87

Limekiln Hill

Tumuli

Mound

National Trust

Castle Coppice

South West Coast Path

B3157

Tumuli

Abbotsbury Castle (fort)

Tulk's Hill

Wears Farm

1

SWYRE ROAD

Labour in Vain Farm

Tumuli

Wears Hill

Tumuli

ABBOTSBURY HILL

86

Bexington Coppice

54
A
55
B
56
C

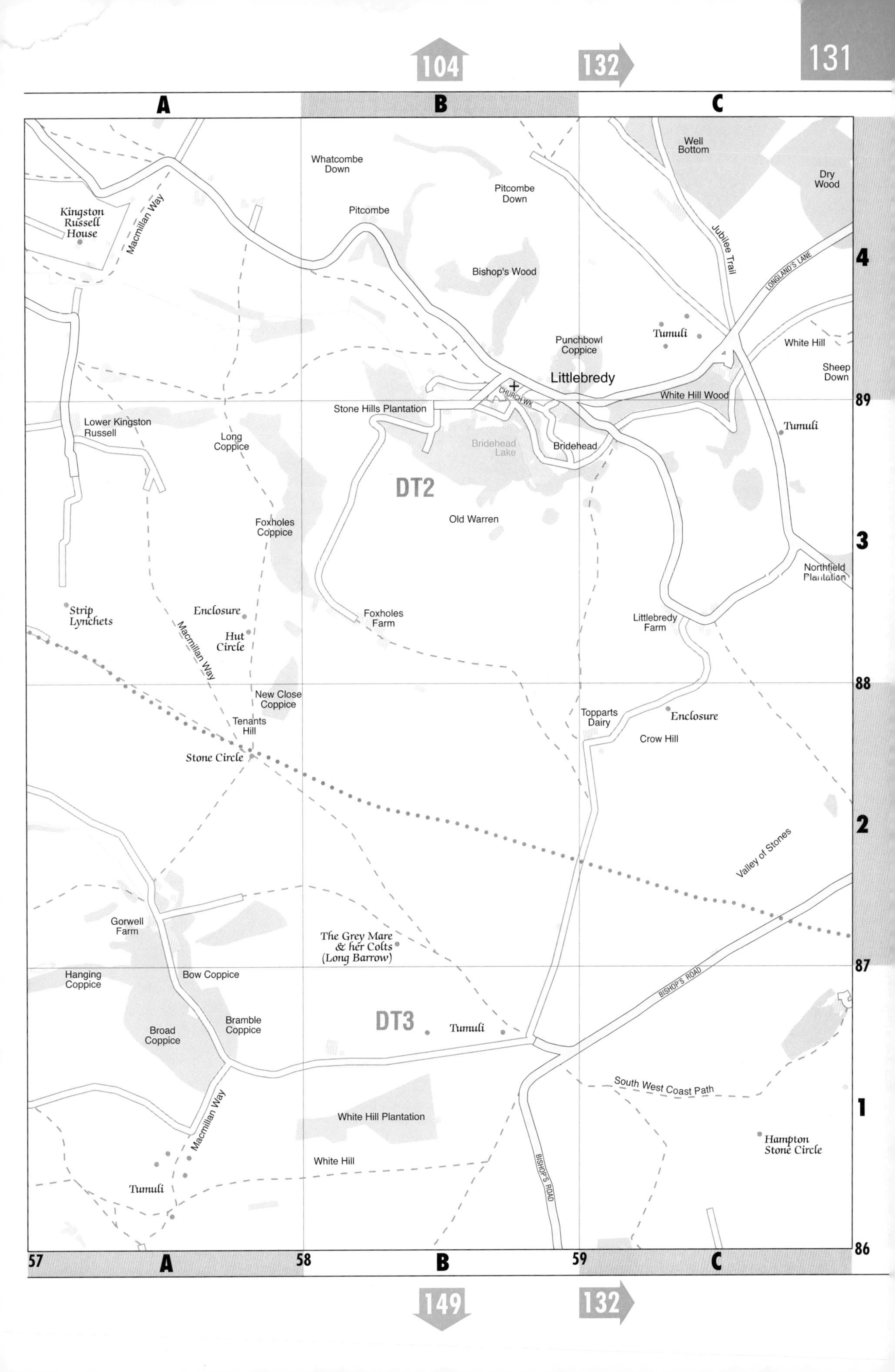

A
B
C

4
89
3
88
2
87
1
86

Well
Bottom

Dry
Wood

Kingston
Russell
House

Macmillan Way

Whatcombe
Down

Pitcombe

Pitcombe
Down

Bishop's Wood

Jubilee Trail

LONGLAND'S LANE

Tumuli

White Hill

Punchbowl
Coppice

Sheep
Down

Littlebredy

CHURCH WK

White Hill Wood

Stone Hills Plantation

Tumuli

Lower Kingston
Russell

Long
Coppice

Bridehead
Lake

Bridehead

DT2

Old Warren

Foxholes
Coppice

Northfield
Plantation

Strip
Lynchets

Enclosure

Macmillan Way

Hut
Circle

Foxholes
Farm

Littlebredy
Farm

New Close
Coppice

Topparts
Dairy

Enclosure

Crow Hill

Tenants
Hill

Stone Circle

Valley of Stones

Gorwell
Farm

The Grey Mare
& her Colts
(Long Barrow)

BISHOP'S ROAD

Hanging
Coppice

Bow Coppice

Bramble
Coppice

DT3

Tumuli

Broad
Coppice

South West Coast Path

Macmillan Way

White Hill Plantation

Hampton
Stone Circle

BISHOP'S ROAD

White Hill

Tumuli

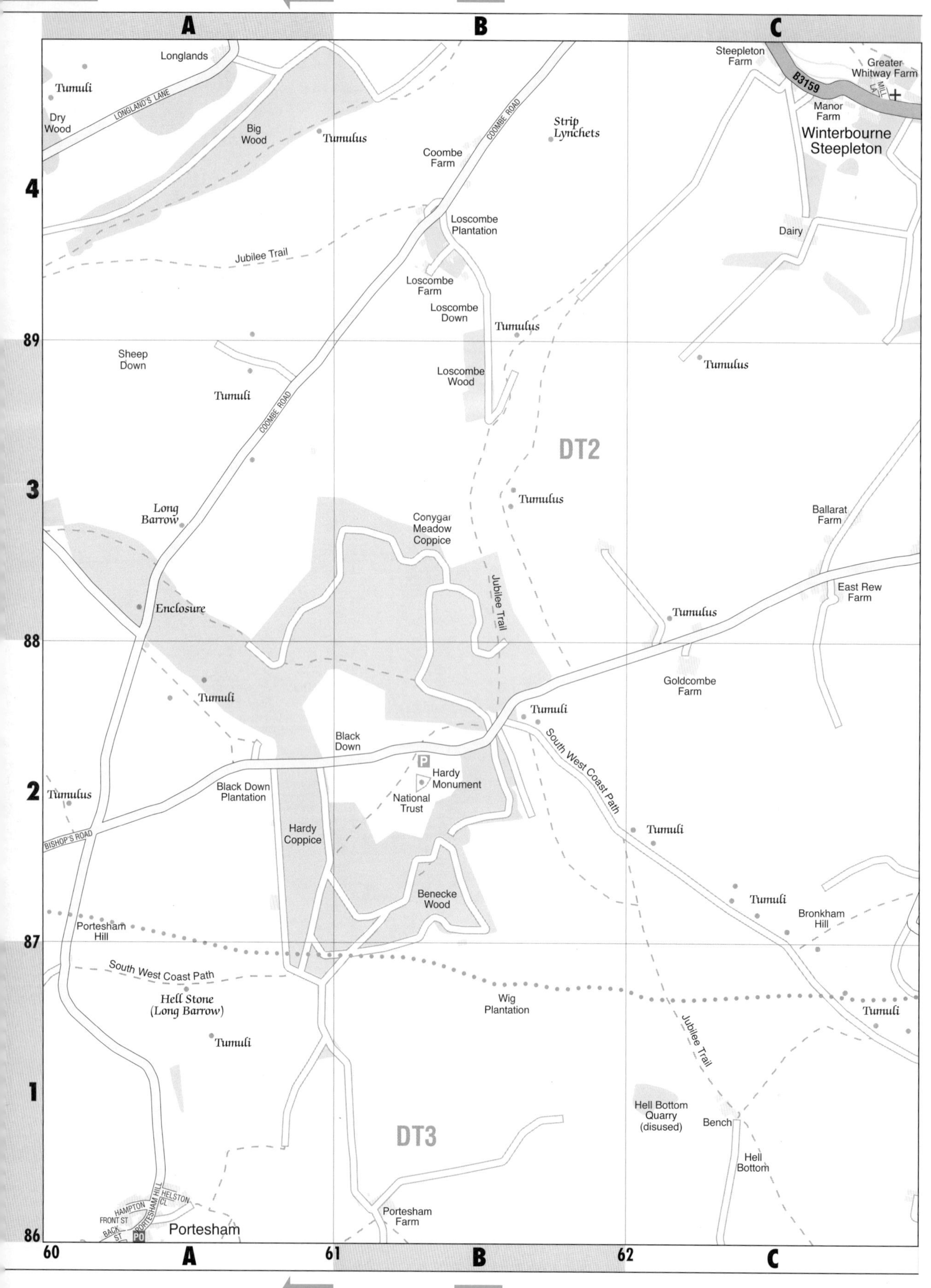

A B C

4

Longlands

Tumuli

Dry
Wood

LONGLAND'S LANE

Big
Wood

Tumulus

Coombe
Farm

COOMBE ROAD

Strip
Lynchets

Loscombe
Plantation

Jubilee Trail

Loscombe
Farm

Loscombe
Down

Steepleton
Farm

B3159

Greater
Whitway Farm

Manor
Farm

Winterbourne
Steepleton

Dairy

89

Sheep
Down

COOMBE ROAD

Tumuli

Loscombe
Wood

Tumulus

Tumulus

DT2

Tumulus

3

Long
Barrow

Conygar
Meadow
Coppice

Jubilee Trail

Tumulus

Ballarat
Farm

Enclosure

Tumulus

East Rew
Farm

88

Goldcombe
Farm

Tumuli

Tumuli

2

Tumulus

Black Down
Plantation

BISHOP'S ROAD

Black
Down

P

Hardy
Monument

National
Trust

Hardy
Coppice

Benecke
Wood

South West Coast Path

Tumuli

Tumuli

Bronkham
Hill

Portesham
Hill

87

South West Coast Path

Hell Stone
(Long Barrow)

Tumuli

Wig
Plantation

Jubilee Trail

Tumuli

1

DT3

Hell Bottom
Quarry
(disused)

Bench

Hell
Bottom

HAMPTON HILL
HELSTON
CL
FRONT ST
PORTESHAM HILL
BACK
ST
PO

Portesham

Portesham
Farm

86

60 A 61 B 62 C

106
134

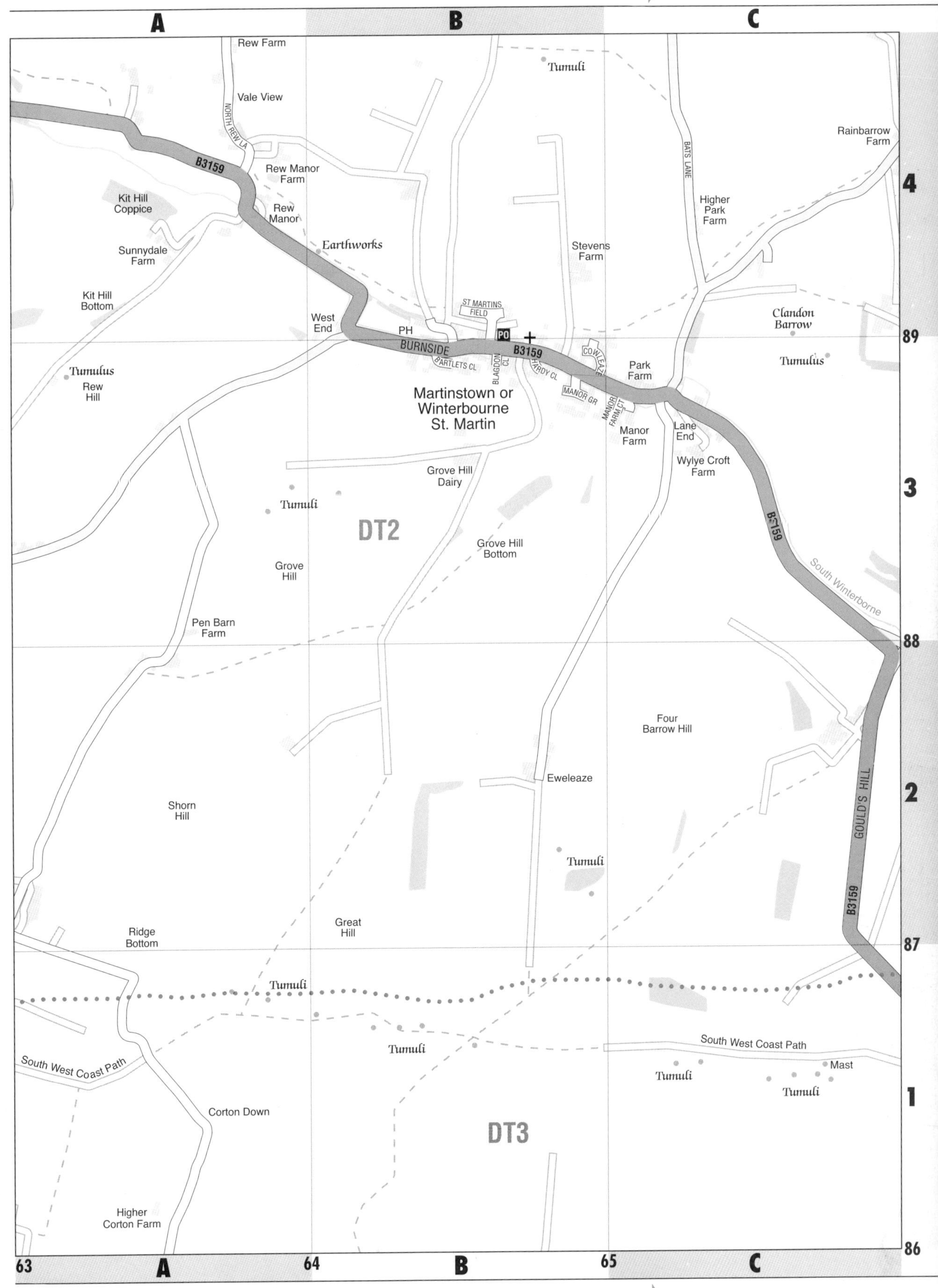
A
B
C
Rew Farm
Vale View
NORTH REW LA
B3159
Rew Manor Farm
Rew Manor
Kit Hill Coppice
Sunnydale Farm
Earthworks
Kit Hill Bottom
West End
PH
BURNSIDE
BARTLETTS CL
BLAGDON CL
PO
B3159
HARDY CL
ST MARTINS FIELD
Tumuli
Stevens Farm
BATS LANE
Higher Park Farm
Rainbarrow Farm
Clandon Barrow
Tumulus
COWLEAZE
MANOR GR
MANOR FARM CT
Park Farm
Manor Farm
Lane End
Wylye Croft Farm
Tumulus
Rew Hill
Martinstown or Winterbourne St. Martin
Grove Hill Dairy
Tumuli
DT2
Grove Hill
Grove Hill Bottom
B3159
South Winterborne
Pen Barn Farm
Four Barrow Hill
Eweleaze
GOULD'S HILL
B3159
Shorn Hill
Tumuli
Ridge Bottom
Great Hill
Tumuli
Tumuli
South West Coast Path
South West Coast Path
Mast
Tumuli
Tumuli
Corton Down
DT3
Higher Corton Farm
4
89
3
88
2
87
1
86
63
64
65

151
134

C4
1 AUGUSTAN CL
2 FARRINGDON CL
3 ELDRIDGE CL
4 D'URBERVILLE CL

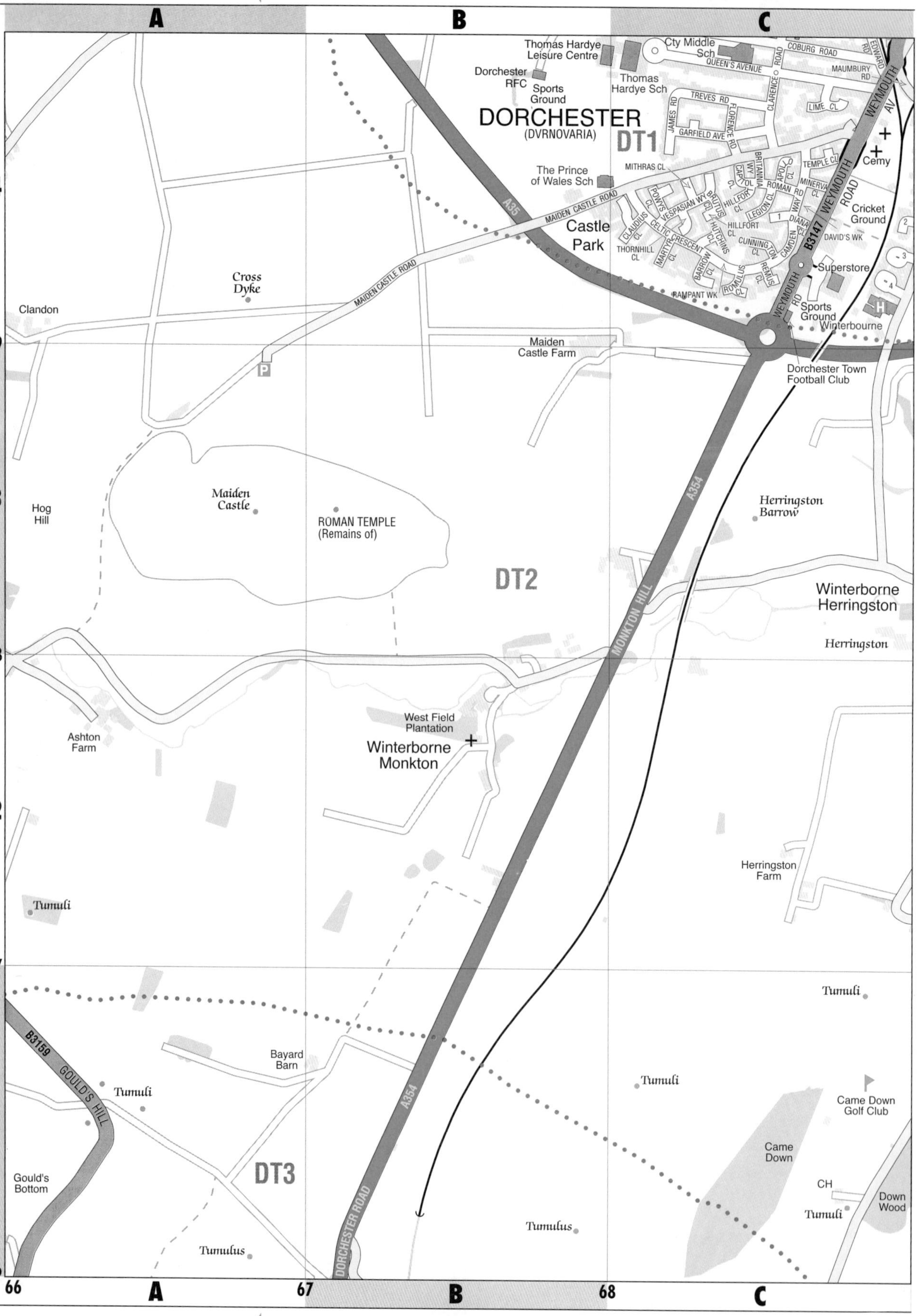

A **B** **C**

4

Thomas Hardye
Leisure Centre

Cty Middle
Sch

COBURG ROAD

QUEEN'S AVENUE

MAUMBURY
RD

Dorchester
RFC

Sports
Ground

Thomas
Hardye Sch

TREVES RD

CLARENCE RD

LIME CL

DORCHESTER
(DVRNOVARIA)

JAMES RD

FLORENCE RD

DT1

Cemy

The Prince
of Wales Sch

MITHRAS CL

GARFIELD AVE

BRITANNIA WY

TEMPLE CL

MINERVA CL

Castle
Park

THORNHILL
CL

CLAUDIUS
CL

PONYS

CELTIC CRESCENT

MARTYRS
CL

BRISTUS
CL

HUTCHINS

HILLFORT

LEGION CL

ROMAN RD

CUNNING
CL

DIANA
WY

CAMDEN
WAY

Cricket
Ground

DAVID'S WK

Superstore

WEYMOUTH AV

B3147 WEYMOUTH ROAD

89

Clandon

Cross
Dyke

BARROW

IRONIUS CL

REBUS

RAMPANT WK

Sports
Ground

Winterbourne

H

Maiden
Castle Farm

Dorchester Town
Football Club

3

Hog
Hill

Maiden
Castle

ROMAN TEMPLE
(Remains of)

DT2

Herringston
Barrow

MONKTON HILL

A354

**Winterborne
Herringston**

Herringston

88

Ashton
Farm

West Field
Plantation

**Winterborne
Monkton**

2

Herringston
Farm

Tumuli

87

B3159

GOULD'S HILL

Tumuli

Bayard
Barn

A354

Tumuli

Tumuli

Came Down
Golf Club

1

Gould's
Bottom

DT3

Came
Down

CH

Down
Wood

Tumuli

86

Tumulus

DORCHESTER ROAD

Tumulus

66 **A** 67 **B** 68 **C**

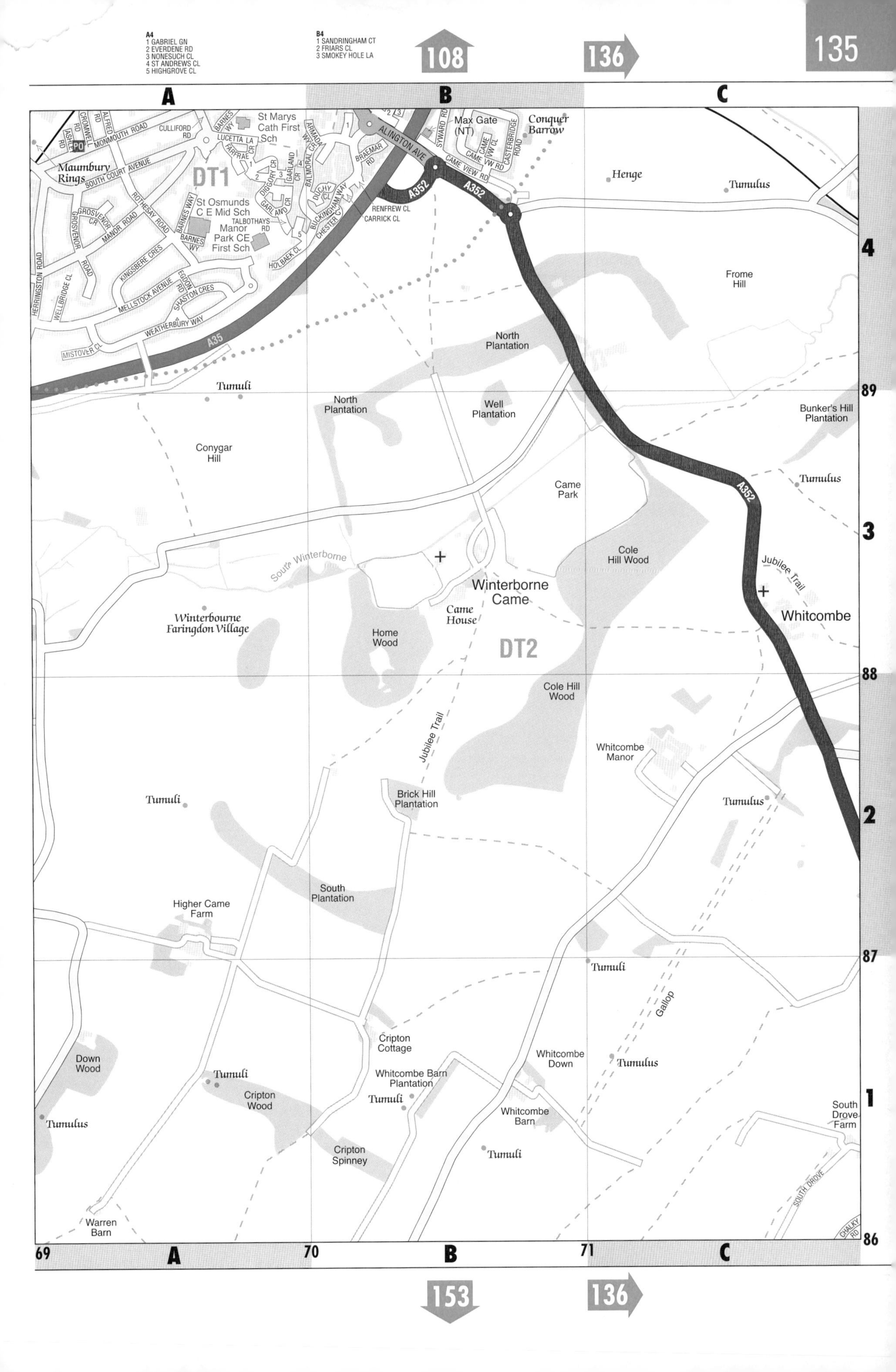

A4
1 GABRIEL GN
2 EVERDENE RD
3 NONESUCH CL
4 ST ANDREWS CL
5 HIGHGROVE CL

B4
1 SANDRINGHAM CT
2 FRIARS CL
3 SMOKEY HOLE LA

108

136

A   **B**   **C**

St Marys
Cath First
Sch

Max Gate
(NT)

Conquer
Barrow

Maumbury
Rings

DT1

St Osmunds
C E Mid Sch

Manor
Park CE
First Sch

Henge

Tumulus

Frome
Hill

4

North
Plantation

Tumuli

North
Plantation

Well
Plantation

89

Bunker's Hill
Plantation

Conygar
Hill

Came Park

Tumulus

3

Cole
Hill Wood

Jubilee Trail

Winterborne
Came

Whitcombe

Winterbourne
Faringdon Village

Home
Wood

Came
House

DT2

88

Cole Hill
Wood

Jubilee Trail

Whitcombe
Manor

Tumuli

Tumulus

2

Brick Hill
Plantation

South
Plantation

Higher Came
Farm

87

Tumuli

Gallop

Down
Wood

Cripton
Cottage

Whitcombe
Down

Tumulus

South
Drove
Farm

1

Tumuli

Whitcombe Barn
Plantation

Cripton
Wood

Tumuli

Whitcombe
Barn

Tumulus

Cripton
Spinney

Tumuli

Warren
Barn

86

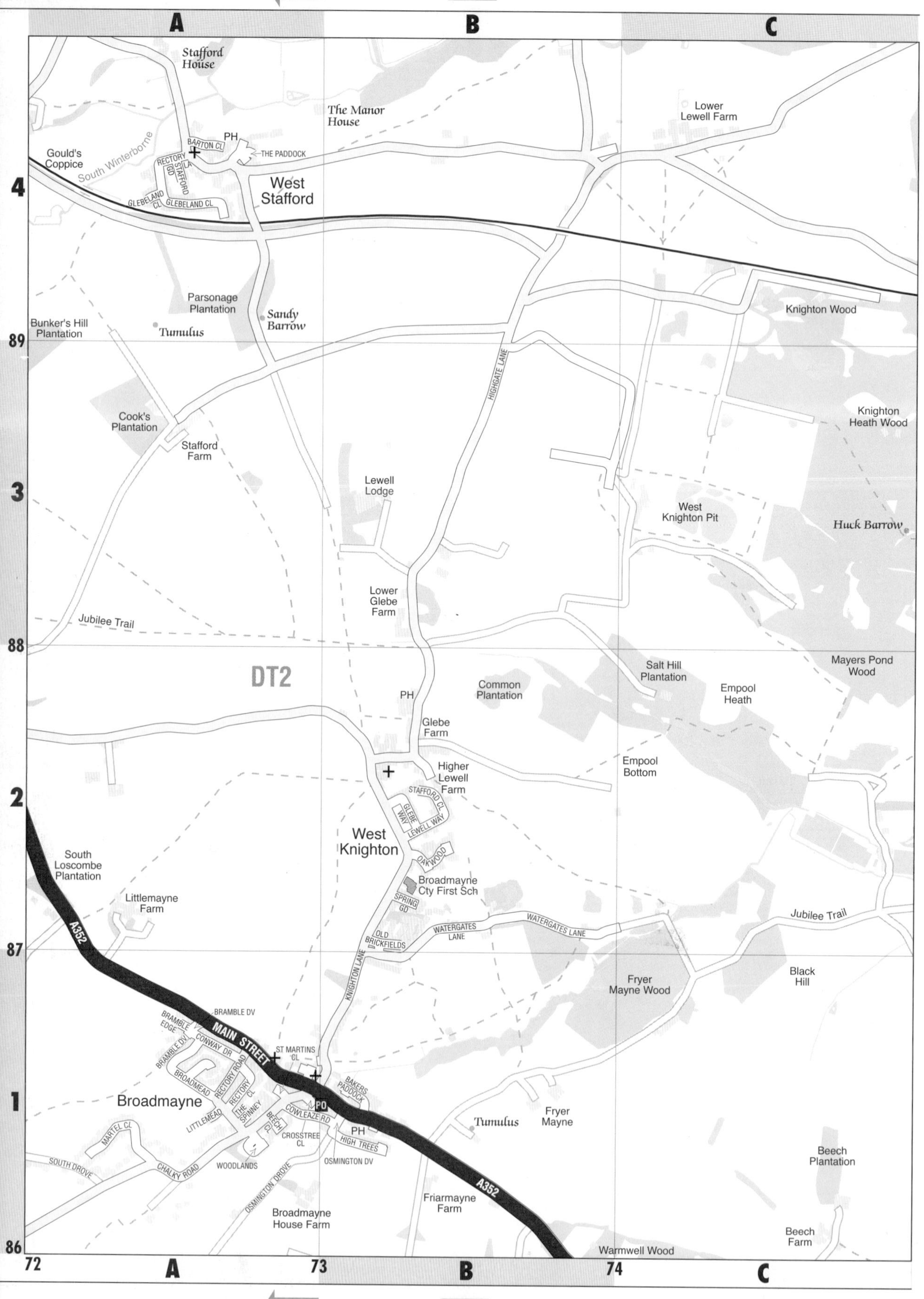

A   B   C

Stafford House

The Manor House

Lower Lewell Farm

PH
BARTON CL
THE PADDOCK
RECTORY STAFFORD RD
Gould's Coppice
South Winterborne
GLEBELAND CL   GLEBELAND CL

West Stafford

4

Knighton Wood

Parsonage Plantation
Sandy Barrow

Bunker's Hill Plantation
Tumulus

89

Cook's Plantation

Knighton Heath Wood

Stafford Farm

Lewell Lodge

3

West Knighton Pit

Huck Barrow

Lower Glebe Farm

Jubilee Trail

88

Salt Hill Plantation

Mayers Pond Wood

DT2

PH
Common Plantation

Empool Heath

Glebe Farm

Empool Bottom

Higher Lewell Farm
STAFFORD CL
GLEBE WAY
LEWELL WAY

2

West Knighton

South Loscombe Plantation

OAKWOOD

Broadmayne Cty First Sch

Jubilee Trail

Littlemayne Farm

SPRING CL

WATERGATES LANE

Fryer Mayne Wood

Black Hill

A352

OLD BRICKFIELDS

WATERGATES LANE

87

KNIGHTON LANE

BRAMBLE DV

MAIN STREET

BRAMBLE EDGE
CONWAY DR
BRAMBLE DV
BROADMEAD

ST MARTINS CL

Tumulus

Fryer Mayne

Beech Plantation

1

Broadmayne

MARTEL CL
LITTLEMEAD
RECTORY ROAD
RECTORY CL
THE SPINNEY
BEECH
PO
BAKERS PADDOCK
COWLEAZE RD
PH
HIGH TREES
CROSSTREE CL

SOUTH DROVE
CHALKY ROAD
Woodlands
OSMINGTON DRIVE
OSMINGTON DV

A352
Friarmayne Farm

Beech Farm

Broadmayne House Farm

Warmwell Wood

86

72   A   73   B   74   C

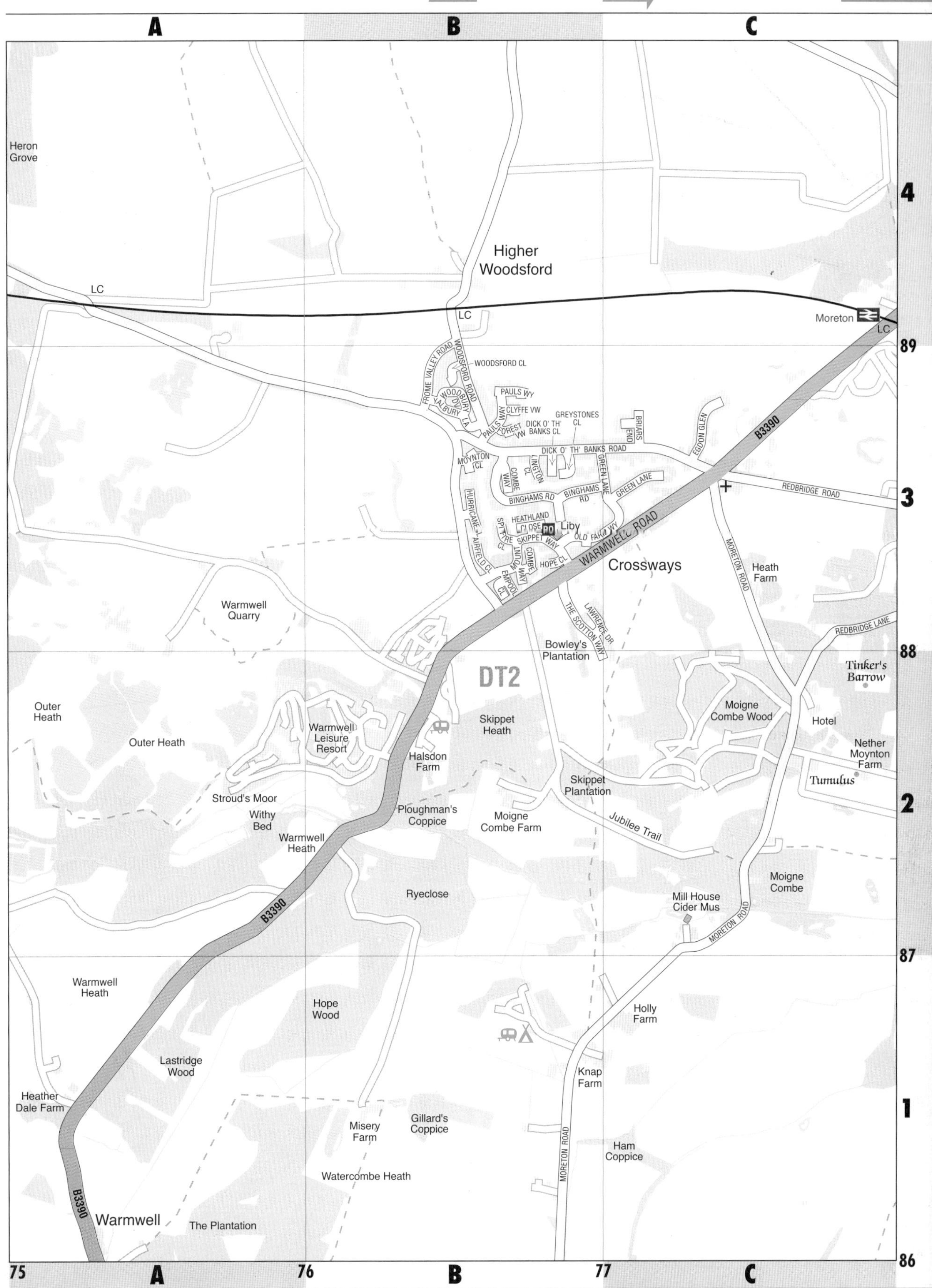

A B C

4

Heron
Grove

Higher
Woodsford

LC

LC

Moreton

89

LC

FROME VALLEY ROAD
WOODSFORD ROAD
WOODBURY
VW
YALBURY
PAULS WAY
FOREST
VW
PAULS WY
CLYFFE VW
WOODSFORD CL
DICK O' TH'
BANKS CL
GREYSTONES
CL
BRIARS
END
GODON GLEN

B3390

MOYNTON
CL
COMBE
WAY
LINGTON
WAY
DICK O' TH' BANKS ROAD
GREEN LANE
GREEN LANE

REDBRIDGE ROAD

3

HURRICANE
BINGHAMS RD
BINGHAMS
RD
HEATHLAND
CLOSE
PO Liby
OLD FARM WY
WARMWELL ROAD

SPITFIRE
AIRFIELD CL
SKIPPET
WAY
COMBI WAY
HOPE CL
Crossways

MORETON ROAD

Heath
Farm

EMMOCK WY
THE SCOTTON WAY
LAWRENCE DR

Warmwell
Quarry

Bowley's
Plantation

REDBRIDGE LANE

88

Tinker's
Barrow

Outer
Heath

DT2

Moigne
Combe Wood

Hotel

Outer Heath

Warmwell
Leisure
Resort

Skippet
Heath

Nether
Moynton
Farm

Tumulus

Stroud's Moor

Halsdon
Farm

Skippet
Plantation

2

Withy
Bed

Ploughman's
Coppice

Moigne
Combe Farm

Jubilee Trail

Moigne
Combe

Warmwell
Heath

Ryeclose

Mill House
Cider Mus

MORETON ROAD

B3390

87

Warmwell
Heath

Hope
Wood

Holly
Farm

Lastridge
Wood

Knap
Farm

1

Heather
Dale Farm

Misery
Farm

Gillard's
Coppice

Ham
Coppice

Watercombe Heath

B3390

Warmwell

The Plantation

75 A 76 B 77 C 86

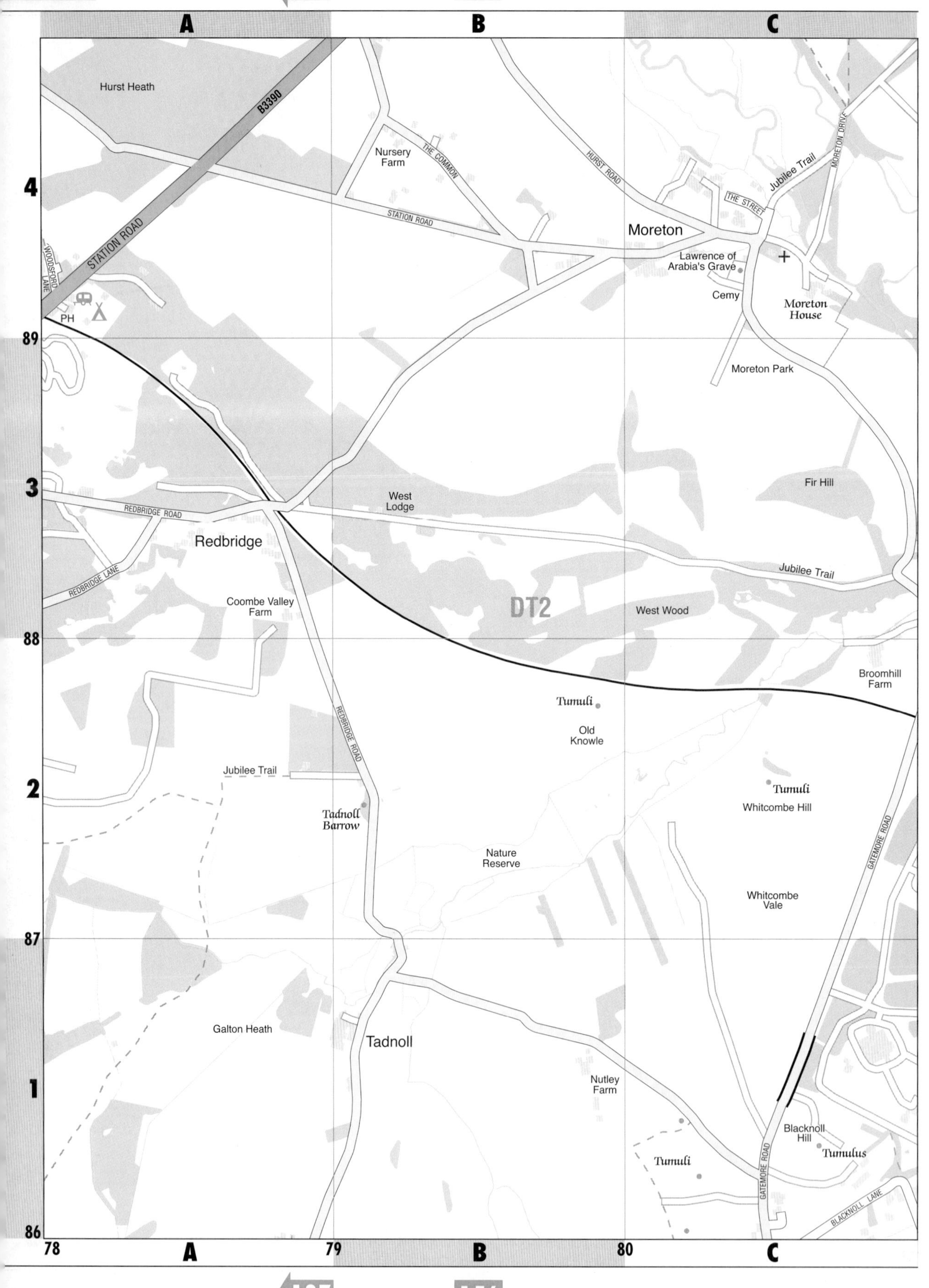

A B C

Hurst Heath

B3390

STATION ROAD

WOODSPORD LANE

Nursery Farm

THE COMMON

STATION ROAD

HURST ROAD

Moreton

THE STREET

Jubilee Trail

MORETON DRIVE

Lawrence of Arabia's Grave

Cemy

Moreton House

PH

4

Moreton Park

89

Fir Hill

3

REDBRIDGE ROAD

West Lodge

Jubilee Trail

Redbridge

REDBRIDGE LANE

Coombe Valley Farm

DT2

West Wood

88

Broomhill Farm

Tumuli

Old Knowle

Tumuli

Whitcombe Hill

Jubilee Trail

REDBRIDGE ROAD

2

Tadnoll Barrow

Nature Reserve

Whitcombe Vale

GATEMORE ROAD

87

Galton Heath

Tadnoll

Nutley Farm

1

Blacknoll Hill

Tumulus

Tumuli

GATEMORE ROAD

BLACKNOLL LANE

86

78 A 79 B 80 C

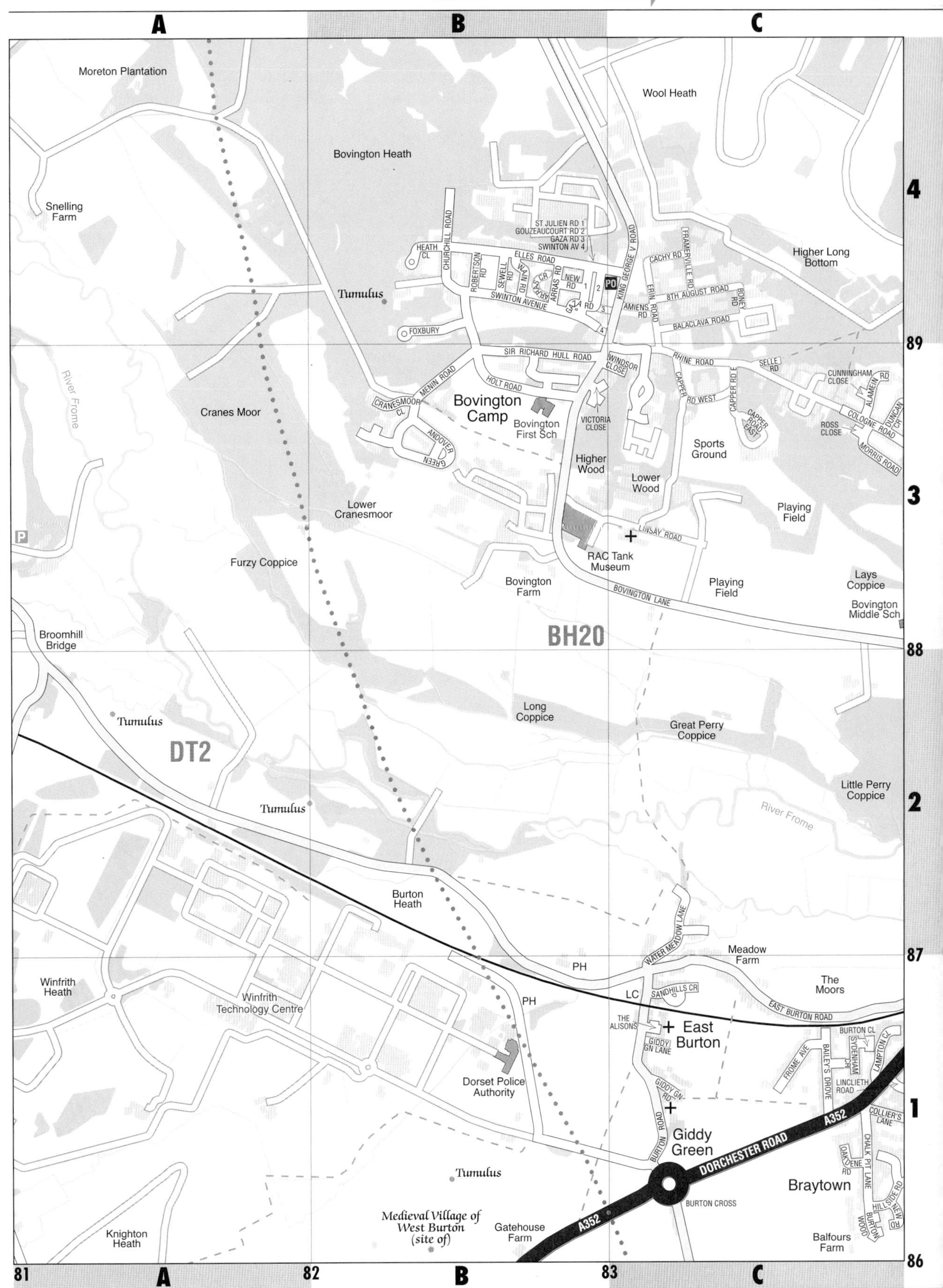

A
B
C

4

Moreton Plantation

Bovington Heath

Wool Heath

Snelling Farm

ST JULIEN RD 1
GOUZEAUCOURT RD 2
GAZA RD 3
SWINTON AV 4

Higher Long Bottom

Tumulus

CHURCHILL ROAD
HEATH CL
ROBERTSON RD
SEWELL RD
WAIN RD
ELLES ROAD
ARRAS RD
NEW RD
CR
PO
KING GEORGE V ROAD
CACHY RD
FRAMEVILLE RD
ERIN ROAD
8TH AUGUST ROAD
BONEY RD
SWINTON AVENUE
AMIENS RD
BALACLAVA ROAD

FOXBURY

89

River Frome

SIR RICHARD HULL ROAD
WINDSOR CLOSE
HOLT ROAD
RHINE ROAD
CAPPER RD WEST
SELLE RD
CUNNINGHAM CLOSE
ALNWICK
DUNCAN CR

Cranes Moor

CRANESMOOR CL
MENIN ROAD

Bovington Camp

Bovington First Sch
VICTORIA CLOSE
CAPPER RD E
ROSS CLOSE
COLOGNE ROAD
MORRIS ROAD

ANDOVER GREEN

Bovington Farm

Higher Wood
Lower Wood

Sports Ground

3

Lower Cranesmoor

Furzy Coppice

P

LINDSAY ROAD
+
RAC Tank Museum
BOVINGTON LANE

Playing Field

Playing Field

Lays Coppice

Bovington Middle Sch

Broomhill Bridge

Bovington Farm

88

BH20

Tumulus

DT2

Long Coppice

Great Perry Coppice

Little Perry Coppice

Tumulus

2

River Frome

Burton Heath

Winfrith Heath

WATER MEADOW LANE
Meadow Farm

PH

The Moors

87

Winfrith Technology Centre

PH
LC
SANDHILLS CR
EAST BURTON ROAD

THE ALISONS
+ East Burton
GIDDY GN LANE
FROME AVE
BAILEY'S DROVE
LINCLIETH ROAD
BURTON CL
SYDENHAM CR
LAMPTON CL
COLLIER'S LANE

Dorset Police Authority

GIDDY GN RD
+
BURTON ROAD
CHALK PIT LANE
OAKLYNE RD

1

Tumulus

Giddy Green

A352
DORCHESTER ROAD
BURTON CROSS
Braytown

HILL SILVER RD
BURTON WOOD

Medieval Village of West Burton (site of)

Gatehouse Farm

A352

Balfours Farm

Knighton Heath

86

139
113

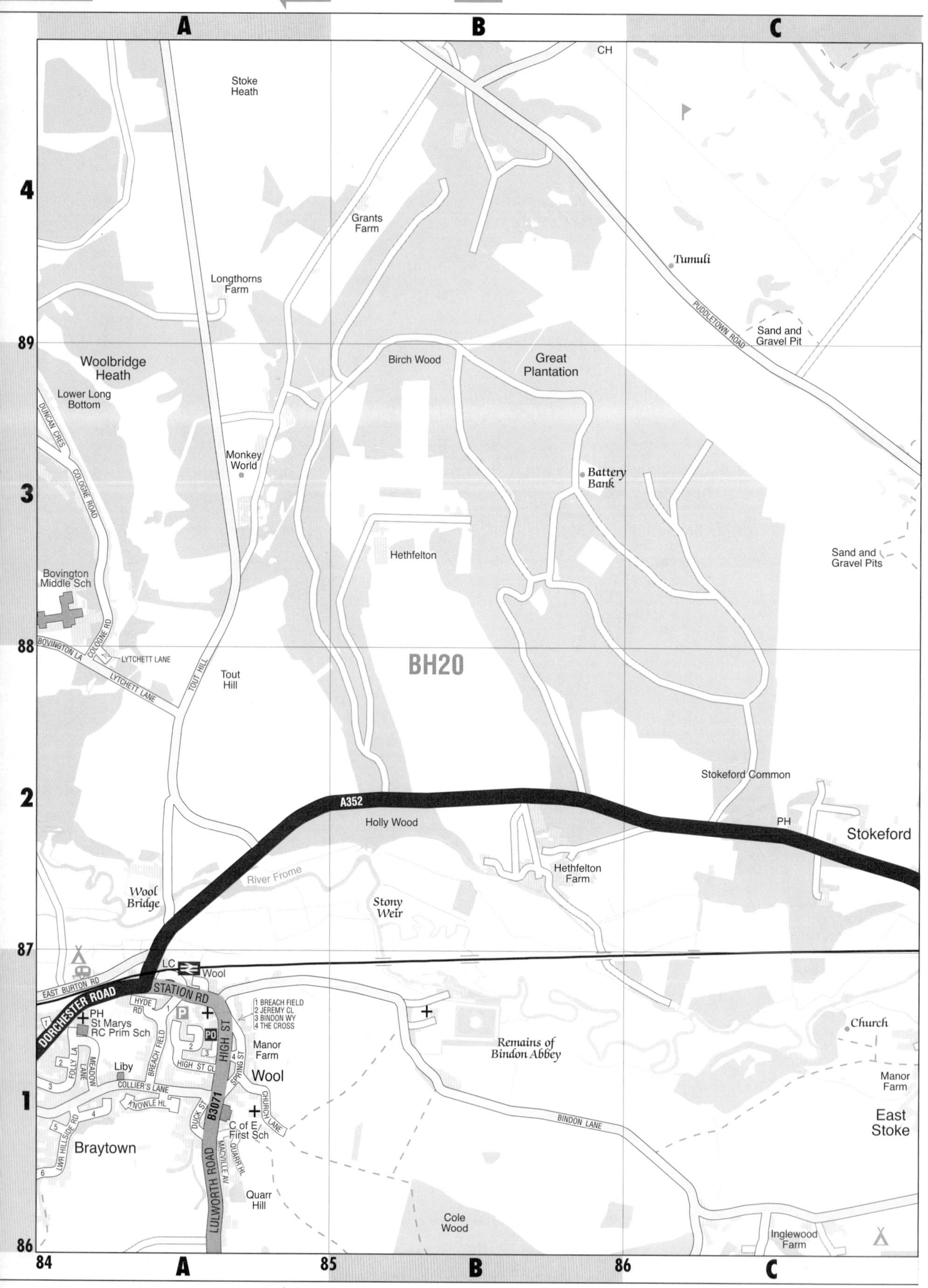
A
B
C
4
3
2
1
89
88
87
86
84
85
86
Stoke Heath
Grants Farm
Longthorns Farm
CH
Tumuli
PUDDLETOWN ROAD
Sand and Gravel Pit
Woolbridge Heath
Lower Long Bottom
Birch Wood
Great Plantation
DUNCAN CRES
COLOGNE ROAD
Monkey World
Battery Bank
Hethfelton
Sand and Gravel Pits
Bovington Middle Sch
COLOGNE RD
BOVINGTON LA
LYTCHETT LANE
LYTCHETT LANE
TOUT HILL
Tout Hill
BH20
Stokeford Common
A352
Holly Wood
PH
Stokeford
River Frome
Hethfelton Farm
Wool Bridge
Stony Weir
LC
Wool
EAST BURTON RD
DORCHESTER ROAD
STATION RD
HYDE RD
1 BREACH FIELD
2 JEREMY CL
3 BINDON WY
4 THE CROSS
PH
St Marys RC Prim Sch
P
PO
HIGH ST
Manor Farm
Remains of Bindon Abbey
Church
Liby
FOLLY LA
MEADOW LANE
BREACH FIELD
HIGH ST CL
SPRING ST
Wool
COLLIER'S LANE
KNOWLE HL
CHURCH LANE
Manor Farm
DUCK ST
B3071
C of E First Sch
BINDON LANE
East Stoke
HILLSIDE RD
LWR HILLSIDE RD
Braytown
LULWORTH ROAD
MACVILLE AV
QUARR HL
Quarr Hill
Cole Wood
Inglewood Farm

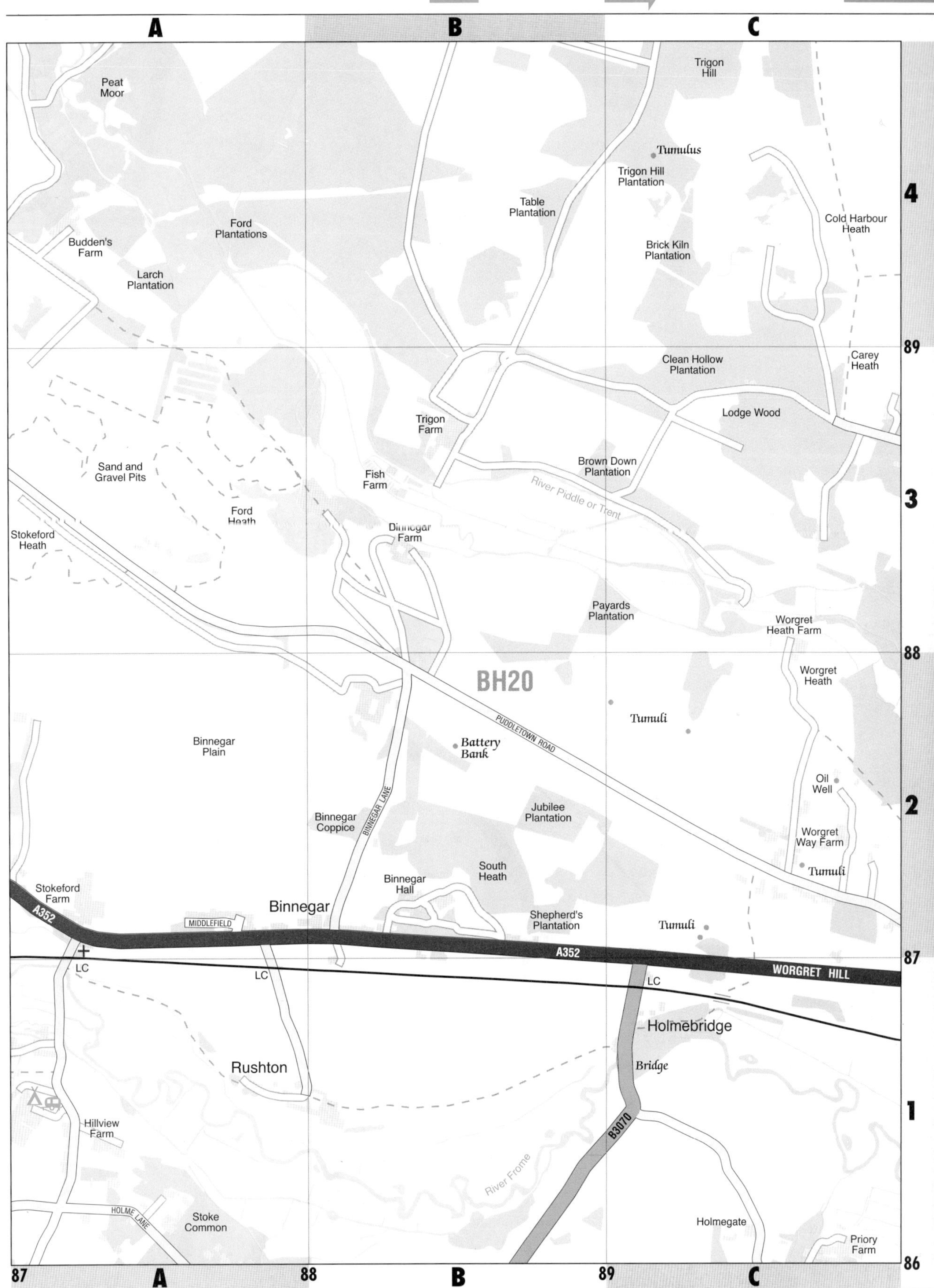

Peat Moor

Ford Plantations

Budden's Farm

Larch Plantation

Trigon Hill

Tumulus

Trigon Hill Plantation

Table Plantation

Brick Kiln Plantation

Cold Harbour Heath

Carey Heath

Clean Hollow Plantation

Lodge Wood

Trigon Farm

Fish Farm

Brown Down Plantation

River Piddle or Trent

Sand and Gravel Pits

Ford Heath

Stokeford Heath

Binnegar Farm

Payards Plantation

Worgret Heath Farm

Worgret Heath

BH20

PUDDLETOWN ROAD

Tumuli

Binnegar Plain

Battery Bank

Binnegar Coppice

BINNEGAR LANE

Jubilee Plantation

Oil Well

Worgret Way Farm

Tumuli

South Heath

Binnegar Hall

Shepherd's Plantation

Tumuli

Stokeford Farm

A352

MIDDLEFIELD

Binnegar

A352

WORGRET HILL

+
LC

LC

LC

Holmebridge

Rushton

Bridge

B3070

Hillview Farm

River Frome

Holmegate

Priory Farm

HOLME LANE

Stoke Common

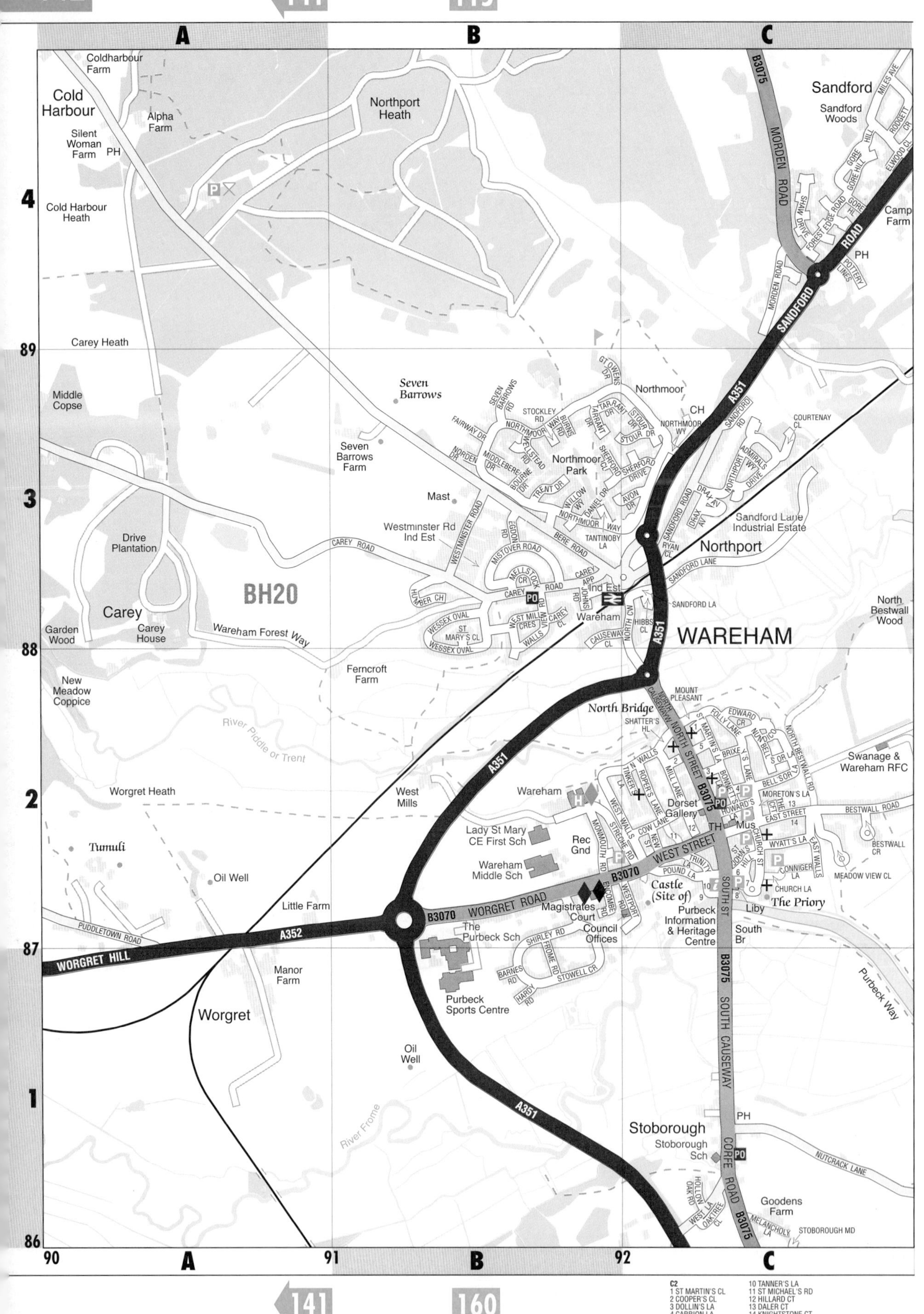

C2
1 ST MARTIN'S CL
2 COOPER'S CL
3 DOLLIN'S LA
4 CARRION LA
5 KENNINGTON SQ
6 HEMSBACH CT
7 CHURCH GN
8 THE QUAY
9 ABBOTS QUAY
10 TANNER'S LA
11 ST MICHAEL'S RD
12 HILLARD CT
13 DALER CT
14 KNIGHTSTONE CT

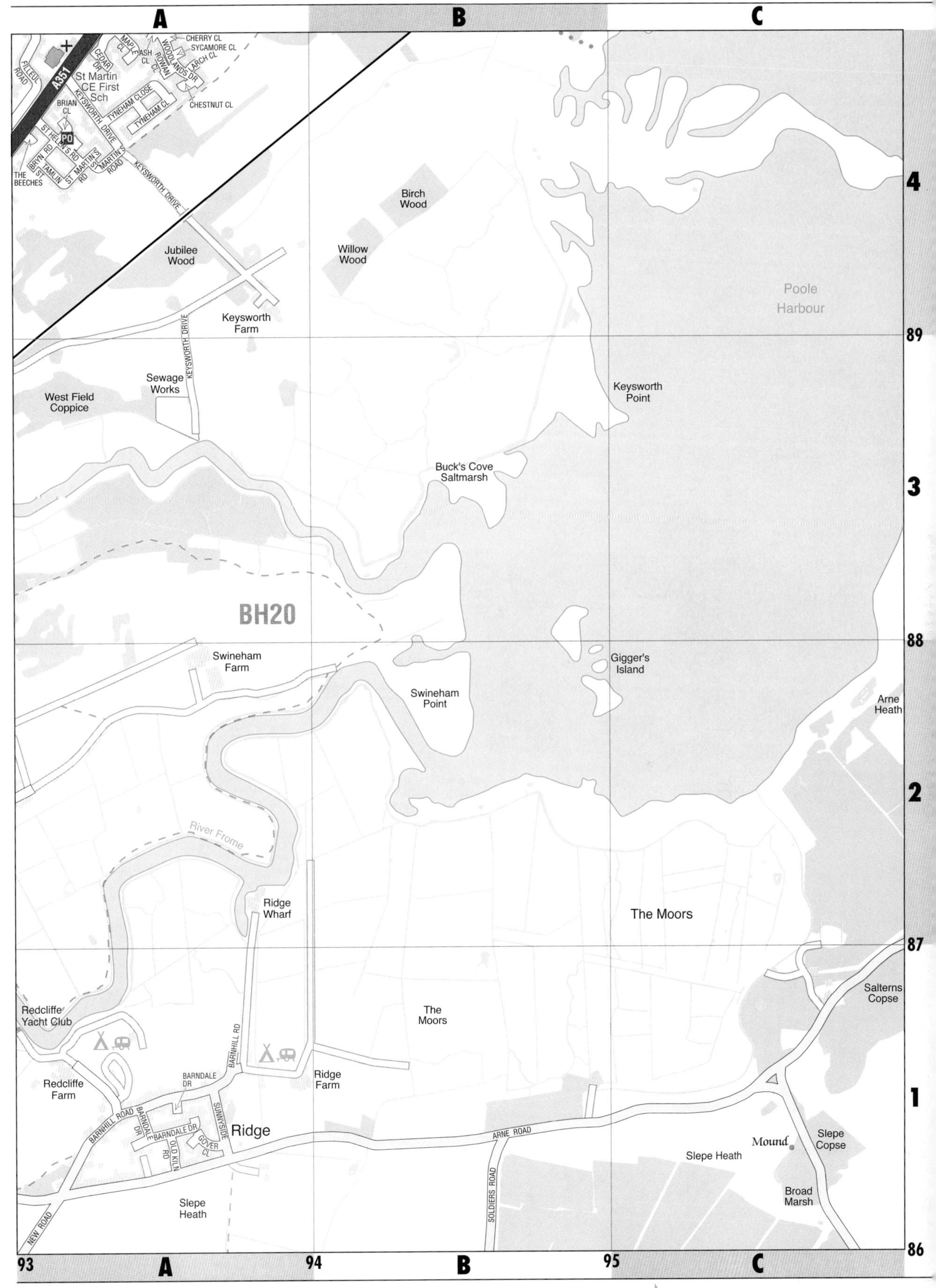

4

Poole
Harbour

89

Birch
Wood

Willow
Wood

St Martin
CE First
Sch

CHERRY CL
SYCAMORE CL

CHESTNUT CL

TYNEHAM CLOSE

TYNEHAM CL

THE
BEECHES

Jubilee
Wood

Keysworth
Farm

Keysworth
Point

West Field
Coppice

Sewage
Works

Buck's Cove
Saltmarsh

3

BH20

88

Swineham
Farm

Gigger's
Island

Arne
Heath

Swineham
Point

2

River Frome

The Moors

Ridge
Wharf

87

Redcliffe
Yacht Club

The
Moors

Salterns
Copse

Redcliffe
Farm

BARNDALE
DR

Ridge
Farm

BARNHILL RD

SUNNYSIDE

1

Ridge

BARNHILL ROAD

BARNDALE DR

GOVER CL

OLD KILN CL

ARNE ROAD

SOLDIERS ROAD

Slepe Heath

Mound

Slepe
Copse

Slepe
Heath

NEW ROAD

Broad
Marsh

86

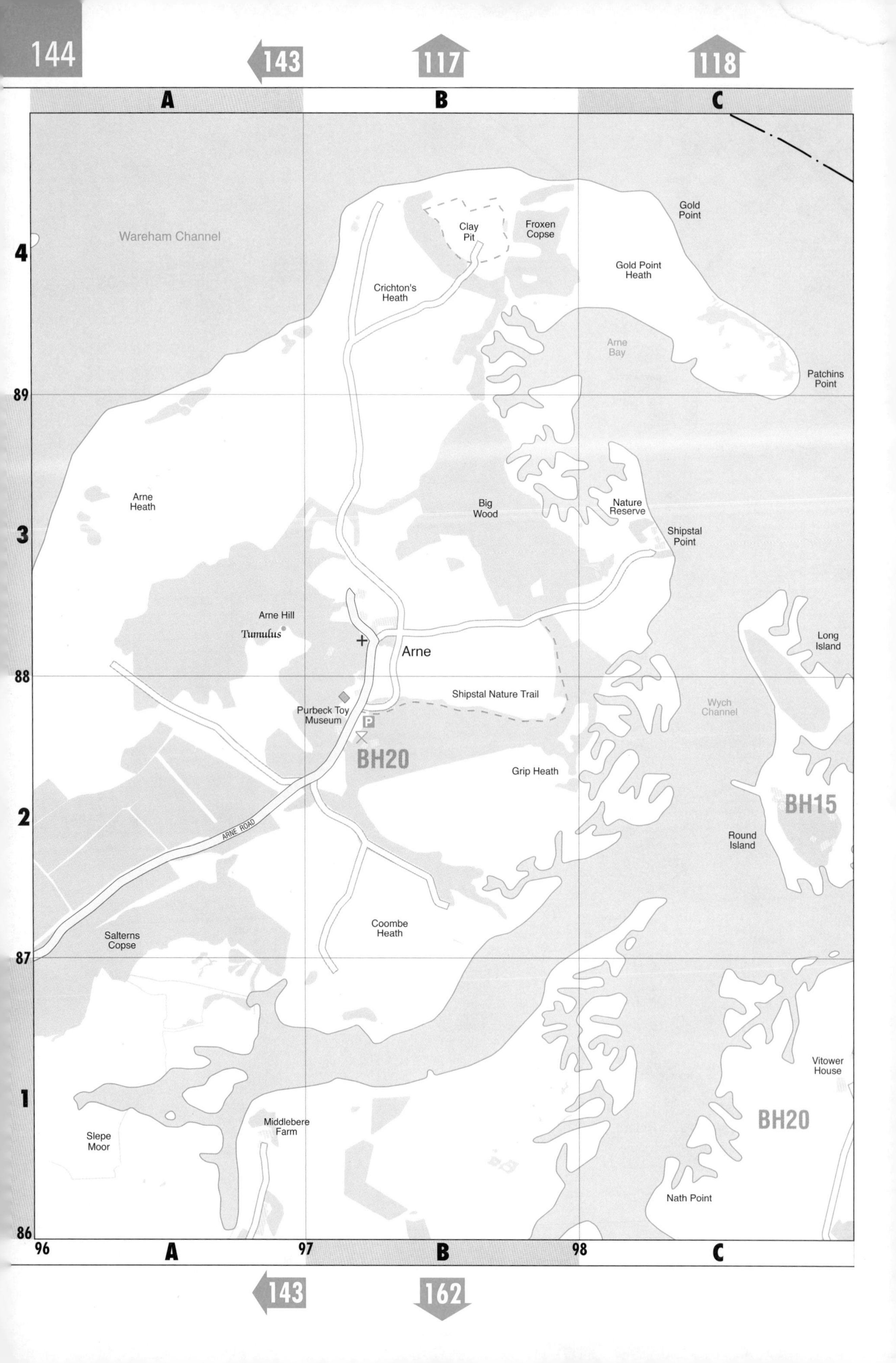

A

B

C

4

Wareham Channel

Clay Pit

Froxen Copse

Gold Point

Crichton's Heath

Gold Point Heath

Arne Bay

89

Arne Heath

Big Wood

Nature Reserve

Patchins Point

3

Shipstal Point

Arne Hill

Tumulus

Arne

Long Island

88

Shipstal Nature Trail

Purbeck Toy Museum

P

Wych Channel

BH20

Grip Heath

BH15

2

ARNE ROAD

Round Island

Salterns Copse

Coombe Heath

87

Vitower House

1

Slepe Moor

Middlebere Farm

BH20

Nath Point

86

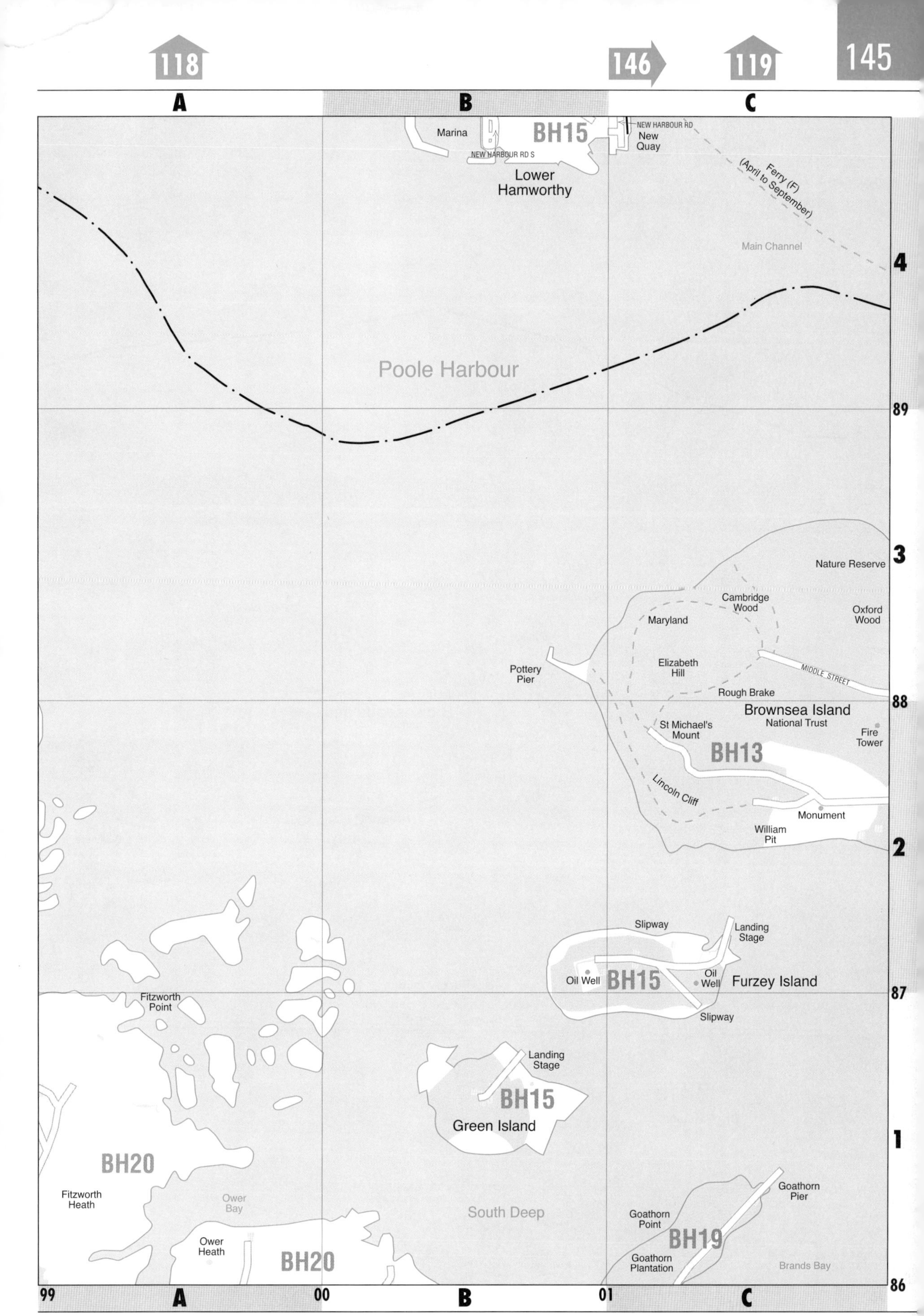

A

B

C

Marina

NEW HARBOUR RD S

BH15

NEW HARBOUR RD

New Quay

Lower
Hamworthy

Ferry (F)
(April to September)

Main Channel

4

Poole Harbour

89

Nature Reserve

3

Cambridge
Wood

Maryland

Oxford
Wood

Pottery
Pier

Elizabeth
Hill

MIDDLE STREET

Rough Brake

88

Brownsea Island
National Trust

St Michael's
Mount

Fire
Tower

BH13

Lincoln Cliff

Monument

William
Pit

2

Slipway

Landing
Stage

Oil Well

BH15

Oil
Well

Furzey Island

87

Slipway

Landing
Stage

BH15

Green Island

1

BH20

Fitzworth
Point

Fitzworth
Heath

Ower
Bay

South Deep

Goathorn
Pier

Goathorn
Point

BH19

Ower
Heath

BH20

Goathorn
Plantation

Brands Bay

86

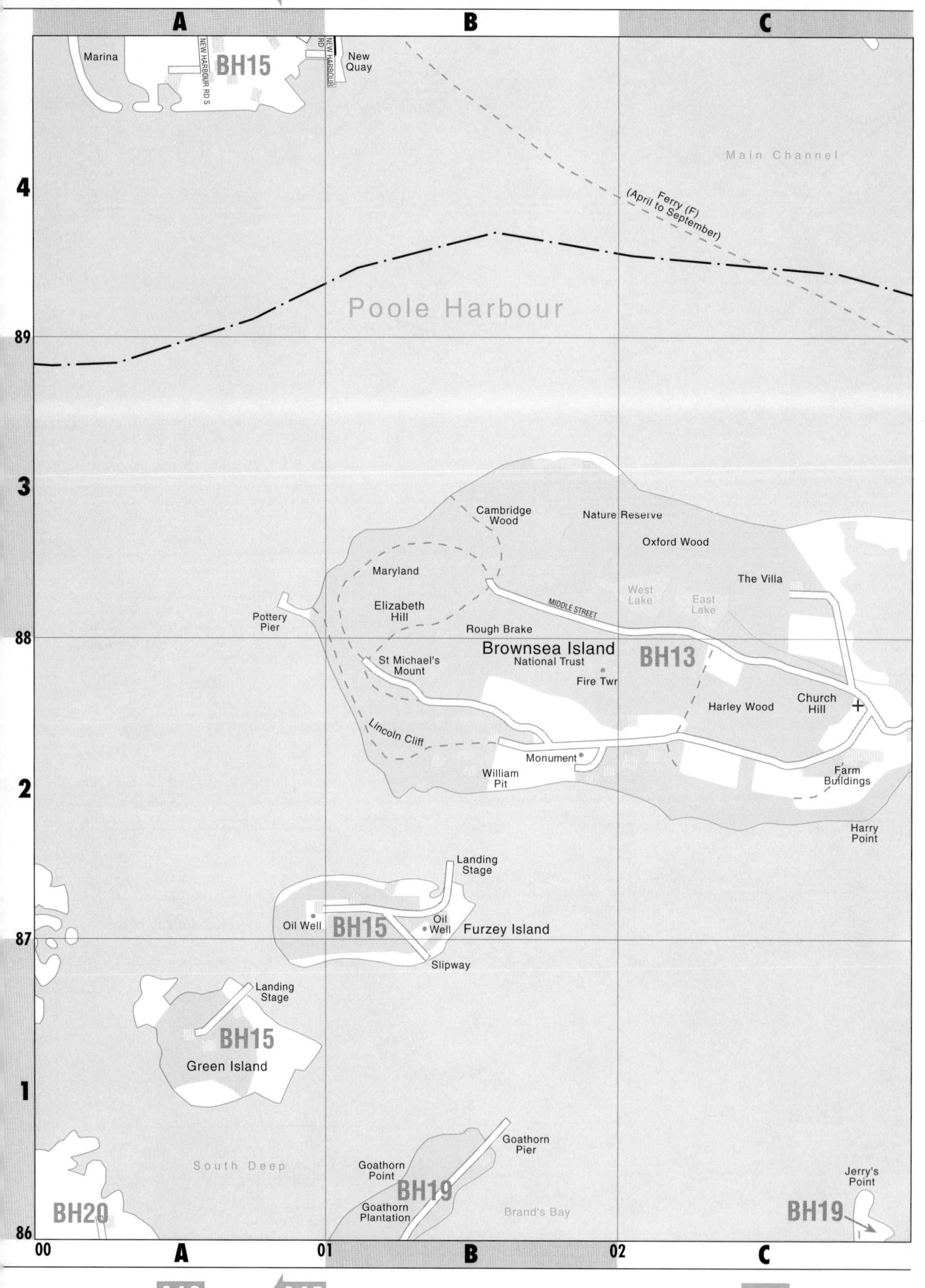

A   B   C

Marina

BH15

NEW HARBOUR RD S

NEW HARBOUR RD

New
Quay

Main Channel

4

Ferry (F)
(April to September)

Poole Harbour

89

3

Cambridge
Wood

Nature Reserve

Oxford Wood

Maryland

The Villa

West
Lake

East
Lake

Pottery
Pier

Elizabeth
Hill

MIDDLE STREET

Rough Brake

88

St Michael's
Mount

Brownsea Island
National Trust

BH13

Fire Twr

Harley Wood

Church
Hill

Lincoln Cliff

Monument

Farm
Buildings

2

William
Pit

Harry
Point

Landing
Stage

Oil Well

BH15

Oil
Well

Furzey Island

87

Slipway

Landing
Stage

BH15

Green Island

1

Goathorn
Pier

Goathorn
Point

South Deep

BH19

Jerry's
Point

BH20

Goathorn
Plantation

Brand's Bay

BH19

86

00   A   01   B   02   C

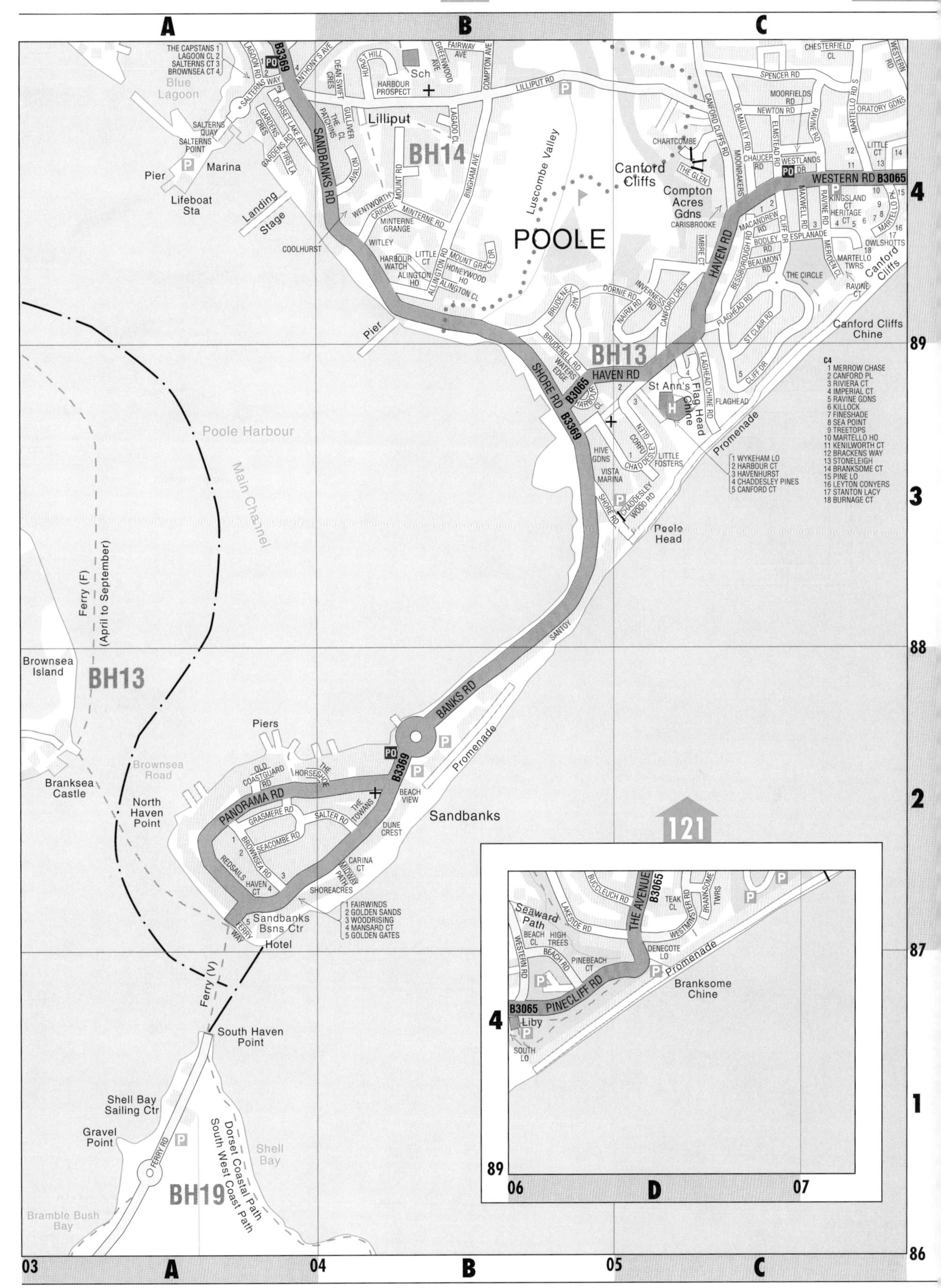

THE CAPSTANS 1
LAGOON CL 2
SALTERNS CT 3
BROWNSEA CT 4

Blue Lagoon

SALTERNS QUAY
SALTERNS POINT

Pier
Marina
Lifeboat Sta
Landing Stage
COOLHURST

Lilliput

BH14

HARBOUR PROSPECT
Sch
FAIRWAY AVE
LILLIPUT RD

Luscombe Valley

Canford Cliffs
Compton Acres Gdns
CARISBROOKE

POOLE

CHARTCOMBE
THE GLEN
WESTERN RD B3065

CHESTERFIELD CL
SPENCER RD
MOORFIELDS RD
NEWTON RD
ORATORY GDNS
LITTLE CT

KINGSLAND CT
HERITAGE

OWLSHOTTS
MARTELLO TWRS
THE CIRCLE
RAVINE CT

Canford Cliffs

89

Poole Harbour

Main Channel

Ferry (F)
(April to September)

BH13

Brownsea Island

Pier

Shore RD B3369
WATERS EDGE
B3065
HAVEN RD

BH13

HAVEN RD
St Ann's Chine
Flag Head Chine
FLAGHEAD

HIVE GDNS
VISTA MARINA
LITTLE FOSTERS

Promenade

Poole Head

C4
1 MERROW CHASE
2 CANFORD PL
3 RIVIERA CT
4 IMPERIAL CT
5 RAVINE GDNS
6 KILLOCK
7 FINESHADE
8 SEA POINT
9 TREETOPS
10 MARTELLO HO
11 KENILWORTH CT
12 BRACKENS WAY
13 STONELEIGH
14 BRANKSOME CT
15 PINE LO
16 LEYTON CONYERS
17 STANTON LACY
18 BURNAGE CT

1 WYKEHAM LO
2 HARBOUR CT
3 HAVENHURST
4 CHADDESLEY PINES
5 CANFORD CT

88

Brownsea Castle
North Haven Point
Brownsea Road

Piers
Old Coastguard RD
PANORAMA RD
GRASMERE RD
SEACOMBE RD
REDSAILS
BROWNSEA RD
HAVEN CT
SHOREACRES
SALTER RD
THE TOWANS
BEACH VIEW
DUNE CREST
CARINA CT
MIDWAY RD

Sandbanks

BANKS RD
PO
B3369
Promenade

Sandbanks Bsns Ctr
Hotel
Ferry (V)

1 FAIRWINDS
2 GOLDEN SANDS
3 WOODRISING
4 MANSARD CT
5 GOLDEN GATES

South Haven Point

121

Seaward Path
BEACH CL
HIGH TREES
WESTERN RD
BEACH RD
PINEBEACH CT

BUCCLEUCH RD
LAKESIDE RD
THE AVENUE B3065
TEAK CL
WESTMINSTER RD
BRANKSOME TWRS

DENECOTE LO
Promenade

Branksome Chine

B3065 PINECLIFF RD
Liby
SOUTH LO

87

Shell Bay Sailing Ctr
Gravel Point
FERRY RD

Dorset Coastal Path
South West Coast Path

Shell Bay

BH19

Bramble Bush Bay

86

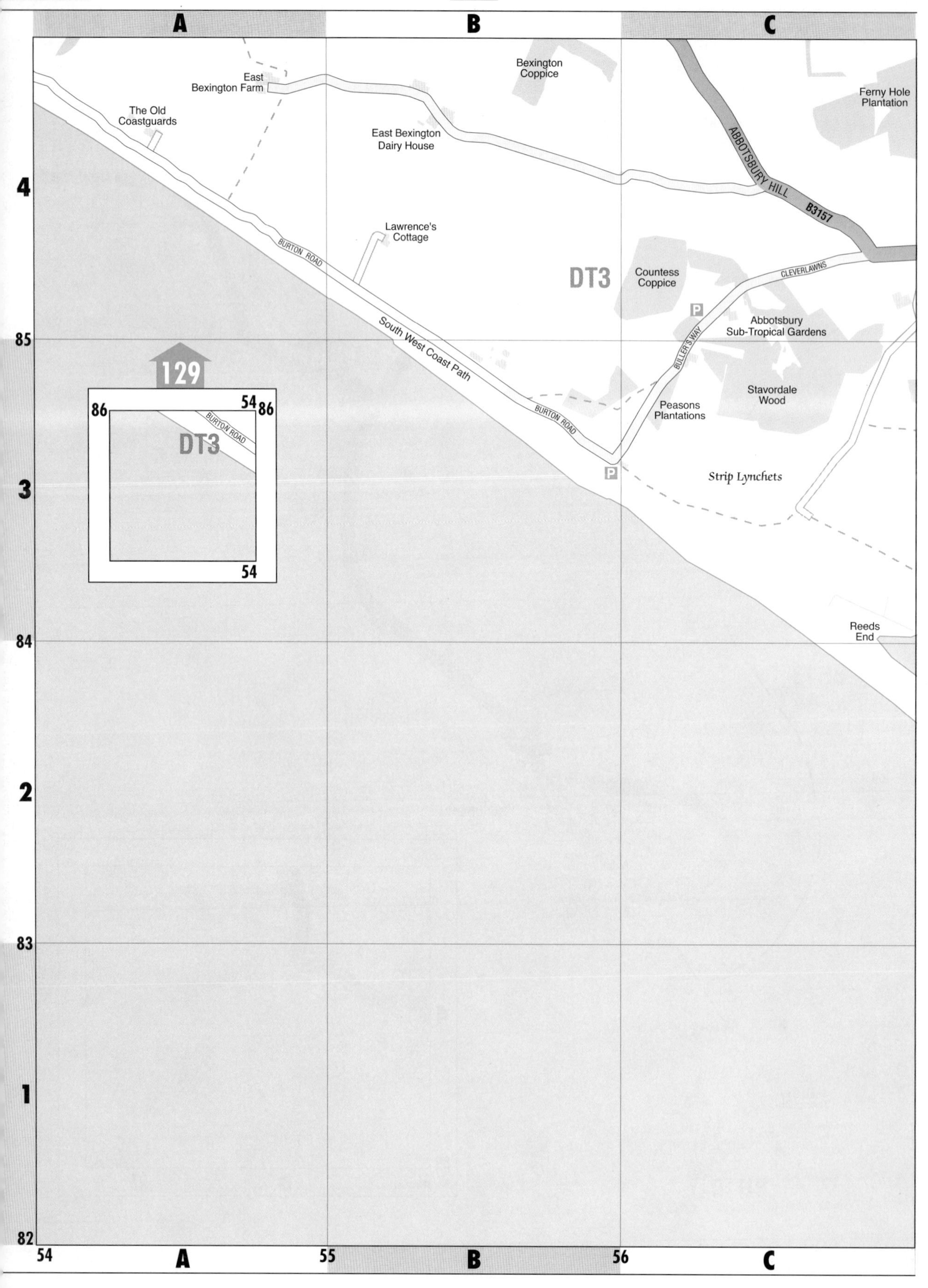

A

B

C

The Old
Coastguards

East
Bexington Farm

Bexington
Coppice

Ferny Hole
Plantation

East Bexington
Dairy House

ABBOTSBURY HILL

B3157

BURTON ROAD

Lawrence's
Cottage

DT3

Countess
Coppice

CLEVERLAWNS

4

South West Coast Path

BULLER'S WAY

P

Abbotsbury
Sub-Tropical Gardens

85

BURTON ROAD

Stavordale
Wood

129

86   54   86

Peasons
Plantations

DT3   BURTON ROAD

P

3

Strip Lynchets

54

84

Reeds
End

2

83

1

82

54   A   55   B   56   C

131
150

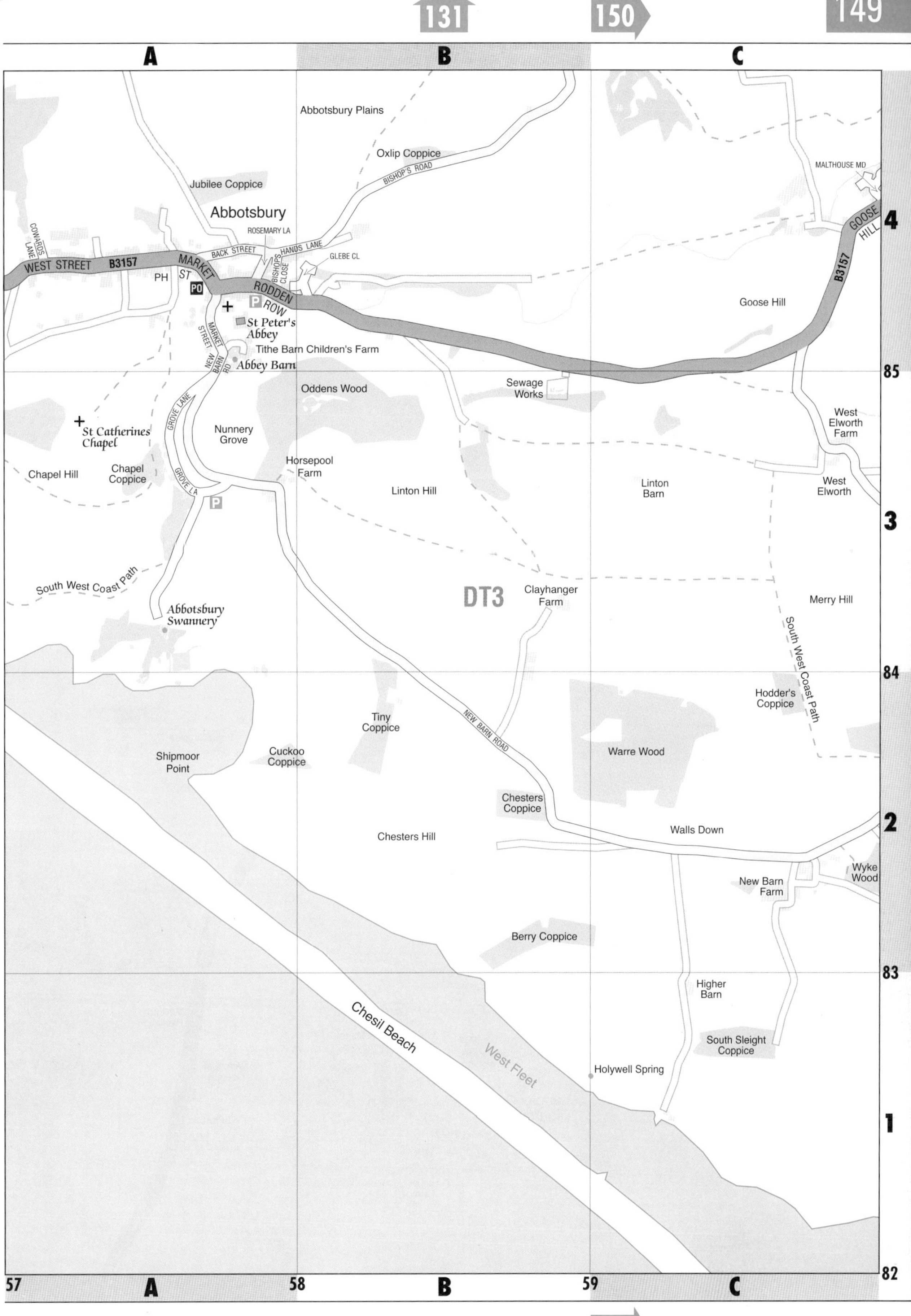
A
B
C
Abbotsbury Plains
Oxlip Coppice
BISHOP'S ROAD
MALTHOUSE MD
Jubilee Coppice
Abbotsbury
ROSEMARY LA
COWARDS LANE
BACK STREET
HANDS LANE
GLEBE CL
WEST STREET
B3157
MARKET ST
BISHOPS CLOSE
GOOSE HILL
PH
PO
RODDEN ROW
P
St Peter's Abbey
Goose Hill
MARKET STREET
NEW BARN RD
Tithe Barn Children's Farm
Abbey Barn
Oddens Wood
Sewage Works
GROVE LANE
St Catherines Chapel
Nunnery Grove
West Elworth Farm
Chapel Hill
Chapel Coppice
Horsepool Farm
GROVE LA
Linton Hill
Linton Barn
West Elworth
South West Coast Path
DT3
Clayhanger Farm
Merry Hill
Abbotsbury Swannery
Hodder's Coppice
Tiny Coppice
NEW BARN ROAD
Shipmoor Point
Cuckoo Coppice
Warre Wood
Chesters Coppice
Walls Down
Chesters Hill
Wyke Wood
New Barn Farm
Berry Coppice
Higher Barn
Chesil Beach
West Fleet
South Sleight Coppice
Holywell Spring
4
85
3
84
2
83
1
82
57
58
59

150

150

A4
1 MANOR CL
2 WESTFIELD
3 WALNUT ORCH
4 MALTHOUSE MDW
5 BRAMDON CL
6 WINTERS CL

◄ 149

▲ 132

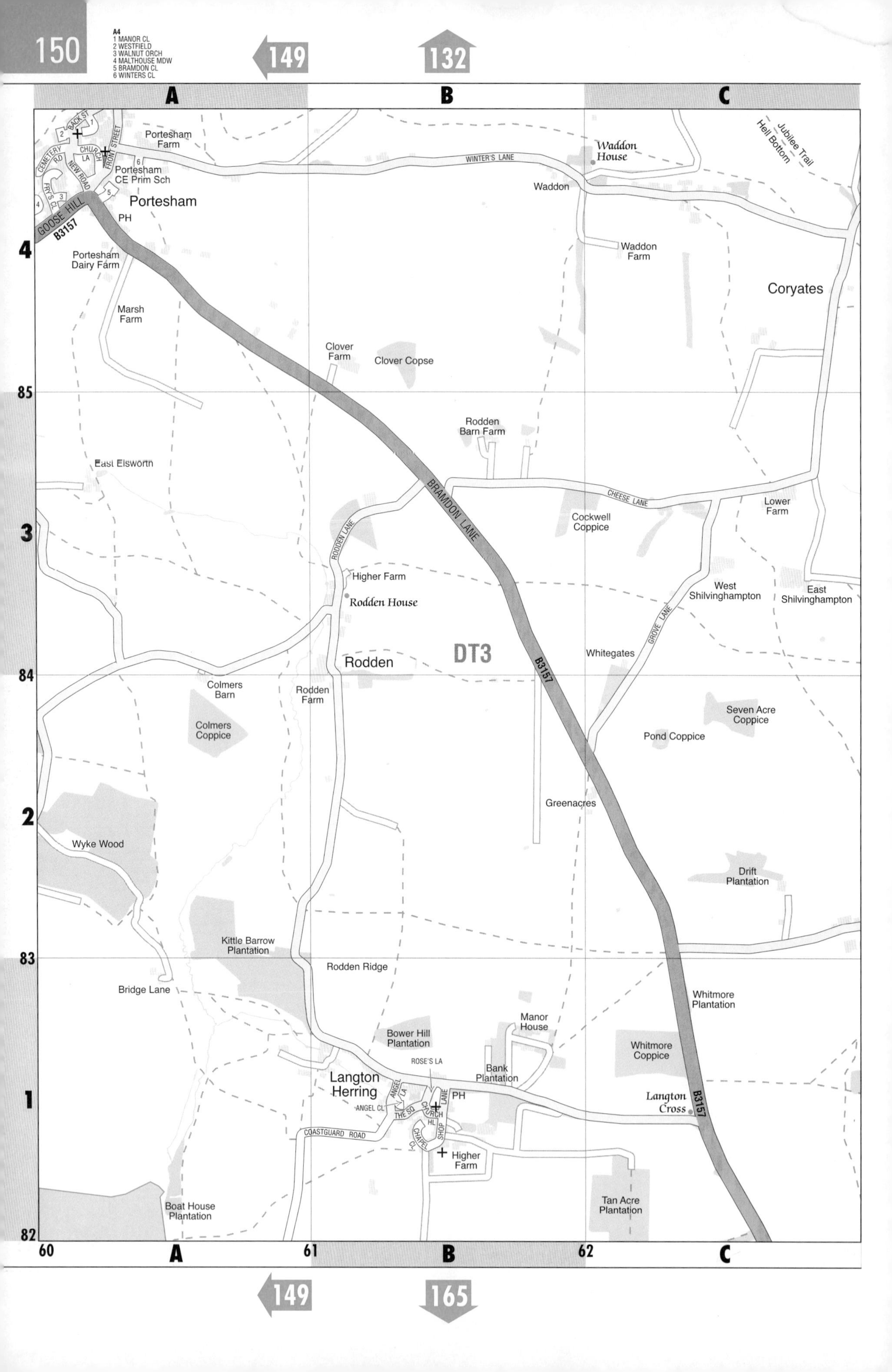

A · B · C

4

85

3

84

2

83

1

82

60 · A · 61 · B · 62 · C

Portesham Farm
BACK ST
CEMETERY RD
CHURCH LA
NEW ROAD
FROM STREET
FRY'S CL
GOOSE HILL
B3157
Portesham CE Prim Sch
Portesham
PH
Portesham Dairy Farm
Marsh Farm
East Elsworth
Clover Farm
Clover Copse
Winter's Lane
Waddon House
Waddon
Waddon Farm
Coryates
Jubilee Trail
Hell Bottom
Rodden Barn Farm
Cheese Lane
Cockwell Coppice
Lower Farm
BRAMDON LANE
RODDEN LANE
Higher Farm
Rodden House
Rodden
West Shilvinghampton
East Shilvinghampton
GROVE LANE
DT3
Whitegates
B3157
Colmers Barn
Rodden Farm
Colmers Coppice
Seven Acre Coppice
Pond Coppice
Wyke Wood
Greenacres
Drift Plantation
Kittle Barrow Plantation
Rodden Ridge
Whitmore Plantation
Bridge Lane
Bower Hill Plantation
ROSE'S LA
Manor House
Bank Plantation
Whitmore Coppice
Langton Herring
ANGEL CL
ANGEL CL
THE SQ
CHURCH LANE
PH
CHAPEL CL
HL
SHOP
COASTGUARD ROAD
Higher Farm
Langton Cross
B3157
Boat House Plantation
Tan Acre Plantation

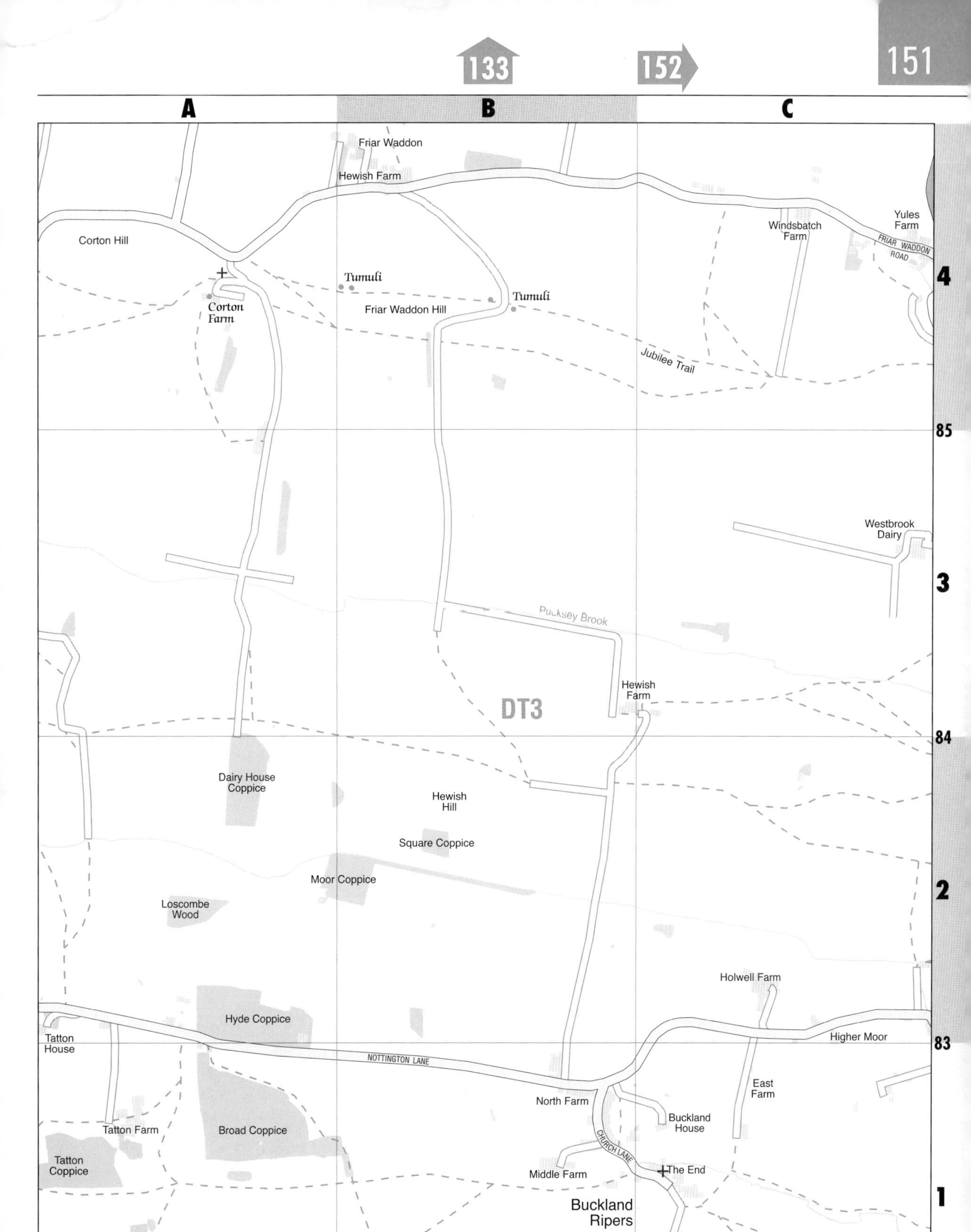

Friar Waddon

Hewish Farm

Corton Hill

Windsbatch Farm

Yules Farm

FRIAR WADDON ROAD

4

Tumuli

Corton Farm

Friar Waddon Hill

Tumuli

Jubilee Trail

85

Westbrook Dairy

3

Pucksey Brook

Hewish Farm

DT3

84

Dairy House Coppice

Hewish Hill

Square Coppice

2

Moor Coppice

Loscombe Wood

Holwell Farm

Hyde Coppice

Higher Moor

83

Tatton House

NOTTINGTON LANE

East Farm

Tatton Farm

Broad Coppice

North Farm

Buckland House

CHURCH LANE

Tatton Coppice

Middle Farm

The End

1

Buckland Ripers

Coverwell Coppice

Higher Barn

82

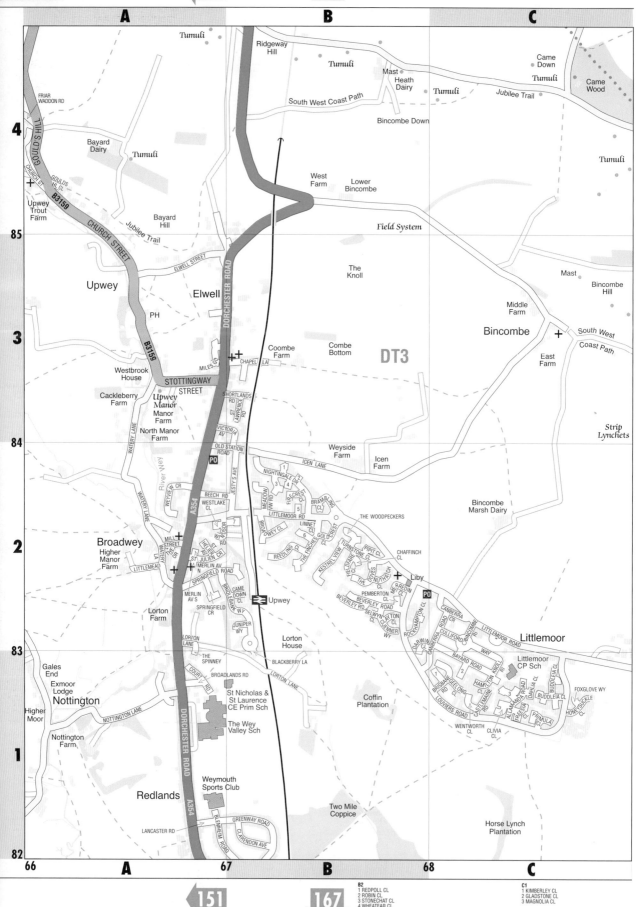

A **B** **C**

Tumuli
Ridgeway Hill
Tumuli
Mast
Heath Dairy
South West Coast Path
Bincombe Down
Came Down
Tumuli
Came Wood
Jubilee Trail

4

FRIAR WADDON RD
Bayard Dairy
Tumuli
West Farm
Lower Bincombe
Tumuli

GOULDS HILL S
CHURCH ST
Upwey Trout Farm
B3159
Bayard Hill
Jubilee Trail
Field System

85

CHURCH STREET
ELWELL STREET
DORCHESTER ROAD
The Knoll
Mast
Bincombe Hill
Upwey
Elwell
Middle Farm
Bincombe

3

B3159
PH
MILES CL
CHAPEL LA
Coombe Farm
Combe Bottom
DT3
East Farm
South West Coast Path

STOTTINGWAY STREET
Westbrook House
Cackleberry Farm
Upwey Manor
Manor Farm
North Manor Farm
SHORTLANDS RD
ST LAWRENCE RD
Strip Lynchets

84

WATERY LANE
VICTORIA AV
OLD STATION ROAD
PO
Weyside Farm
Icen Farm
ICEN LANE
Bincombe Marsh Dairy

River Way
WEYVIEW CR
JESTY'S AVE
BEECH RD
WESTLAKE CL
MEADOW VW RD
Nightingale Dr
FIR CL
CREST
BRAMBLING CL
THE WOODPECKERS

A354
WINDSOR RD
BROADWEY CL
LITTLEMOOR RD
LINNET
GOLDCREST
TURNSTONE CL
PIPIT CL
CHAFFINCH CL

2

Broadwey
Higher Manor Farm
MILL STREET
WATERY
THE DR
ST JULIEN CR
MERLIN AV
SPRINGFIELD ROAD
REEDLING CL
THE FINCHES
KESTREL VIEW
THE DOVES
NUTHATCH
FIELDFARE
Liby
PO

LITTLEMEAD
MERLIN AV S
CAME DOWN CL
SPRINGFIELD CR
JUNIPER WY
Upwey
BEVERLEY CL
BEVERLEY ROAD
SELWYN CL
CLAYTON CL
GLENNER CL
PEMBERTON CL
RD
REDPOLL
ROCKHAMPTON CL
CANBERRA CR
CULLIFORD RD
BINCOMBE
Littlemoor
LITTLEMOOR ROAD

Lorton Farm
LORTON LANE
THE SPINNEY
Lorton House
BLACKBERRY LA
LORTON LANE
DARWIN CL
CANBERRA RD
BAYARD ROAD
WAY
Littlemoor CP Sch
BUDDLEIA CL
FOXGLOVE WY

83

Gales End
Exmoor Lodge
Nottington
BROADLANDS RD
St Nicholas & St Laurence CE Prim Sch
Coffin Plantation
BRISBANE RD
GEELONG
HAMILTON
CASTLEMAINE RD
COUVIERS ROAD
ALLAMANDA ROAD
DAHLIA CL
BUDDLEIA CL
HONEYSUCKLE CL
FRESIA
PRIMULA CL
CLIVIA CL

Higher Moor
NOTTINGTON LANE
The Wey Valley Sch
WENTWORTH CL

1

Nottington Farm
DORCHESTER ROAD
A354
Weymouth Sports Club
Redlands
LANCASTER RD
GREENWAY ROAD
BLENHEIM ROAD
CLARENDON AVE
Two Mile Coppice
Horse Lynch Plantation

82

66 **A** 67 **B** 68 **C**

B2
1 REDPOLL CL
2 ROBIN CL
3 STONECHAT CL
4 WHEATEAR CL
5 JORDAN WY
6 SANDERLING CL
7 REGENCY DR

C1
1 KIMBERLEY CL
2 GLADSTONE CL
3 MAGNOLIA CL

A   B   C

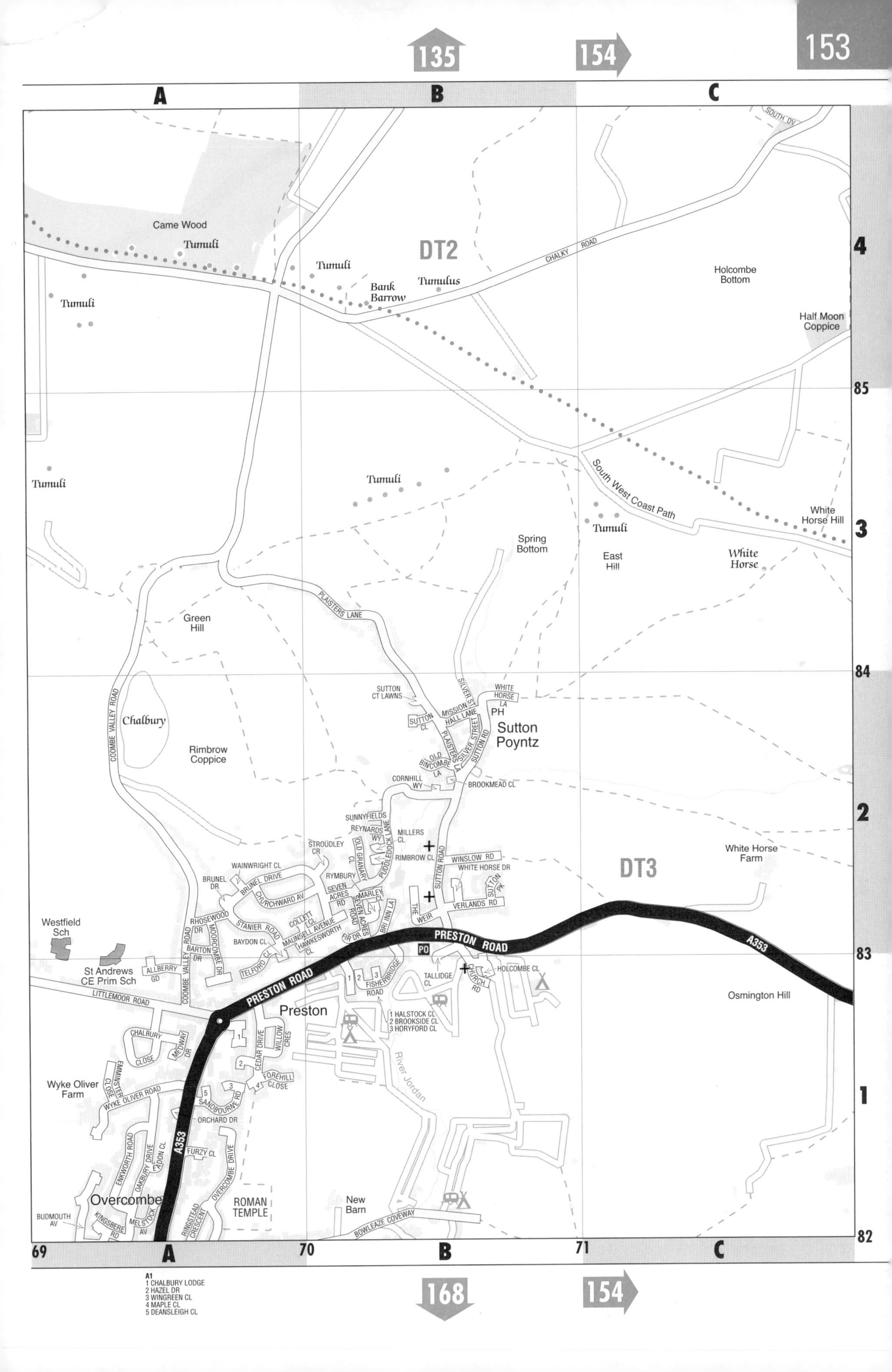

4

Came Wood
Tumuli
Tumuli
Bank Barrow
Tumulus
DT2
CHALKY ROAD
Holcombe Bottom
Half Moon Coppice

Tumuli

85

Tumuli
Tumuli
South West Coast Path
White Horse Hill

3

Spring Bottom
East Hill
Tumuli
White Horse

PLAISTERS LANE

Green Hill

84

SUTTON CT LAWNS
WHITE HORSE PH
Sutton Poyntz

Chalbury
Rimbrow Coppice
SUTTON CL
MISSION ST
HALL LANE
SILVER STREET
SUTTON RD
OLD BINCOMBE LA
PLAISTERS LA
SILVER STREET
CORNHILL WY
BROOKMEAD CL

2

COOMBE VALLEY ROAD
SUNNYFIELDS
REYNARDS WY
MILLERS CL
STROUDLEY CR
OLD GRANARY
PUDDLEDOCK LANE
RIMBROW CL
SUTTON ROAD
WINSLOW RD
WHITE HORSE DR
WHITE HORSE FARM
DT3
WAINWRIGHT CL
RYMBURY
SEVEN ACRES RD
MARLEY RD
SUTTON PK
BRUNEL DR
BRUNEL DRIVE
CHURCHWARD AV
COLLETT
SEVEN ACRES RD
BRI INN LA
THE WEIR
VERLANDS RD
RHOSEWOOD DR
MOORCOMBE DR
STANIER ROAD
BAYDON CL
MAUNSELL AVENUE
HAWKESWORTH CL

Westfield Sch
St Andrews CE Prim Sch
ALLBERRY GD
BARTON DR
TELFORD CL
PO
PRESTON ROAD   A353

83

Osmington Hill

LITTLEMOOR ROAD
PRESTON ROAD
Preston
1 2 3
FISHERBRIDGE ROAD
TALLIDGE CL
HOLCOMBE CL
CLUTCH RD

CHALBURY CLOSE
MIDWAY DR
CEDAR DRIVE
WILLOW CRES
1 HALSTOCK CL
2 BROOKSIDE CL
3 HORYFORD CL

EMMINSTER CLOSE
WYKE OLIVER ROAD
WYKE OLIVER ROAD
SANDBOURNE RD
FOREHILL CLOSE
River Jordan

Wyke Oliver Farm
1

ORCHARD DR

ENKWORTH ROAD
OAKBURY DRIVE
EDON CL
FURZY CL
A353
RINGSTEAD CRESCENT
OVERCOMBE DRIVE
ROMAN TEMPLE
New Barn

BUDMOUTH AV
KINGSBERE RD
MELSTOCK AV
Overcombe
BOWLEAZE COVEWAY

82

69   A   70   B   71   C   82

A1
1 CHALBURY LODGE
2 HAZEL DR
3 WINGREEN CL
4 MAPLE CL
5 DEANSLEIGH CL

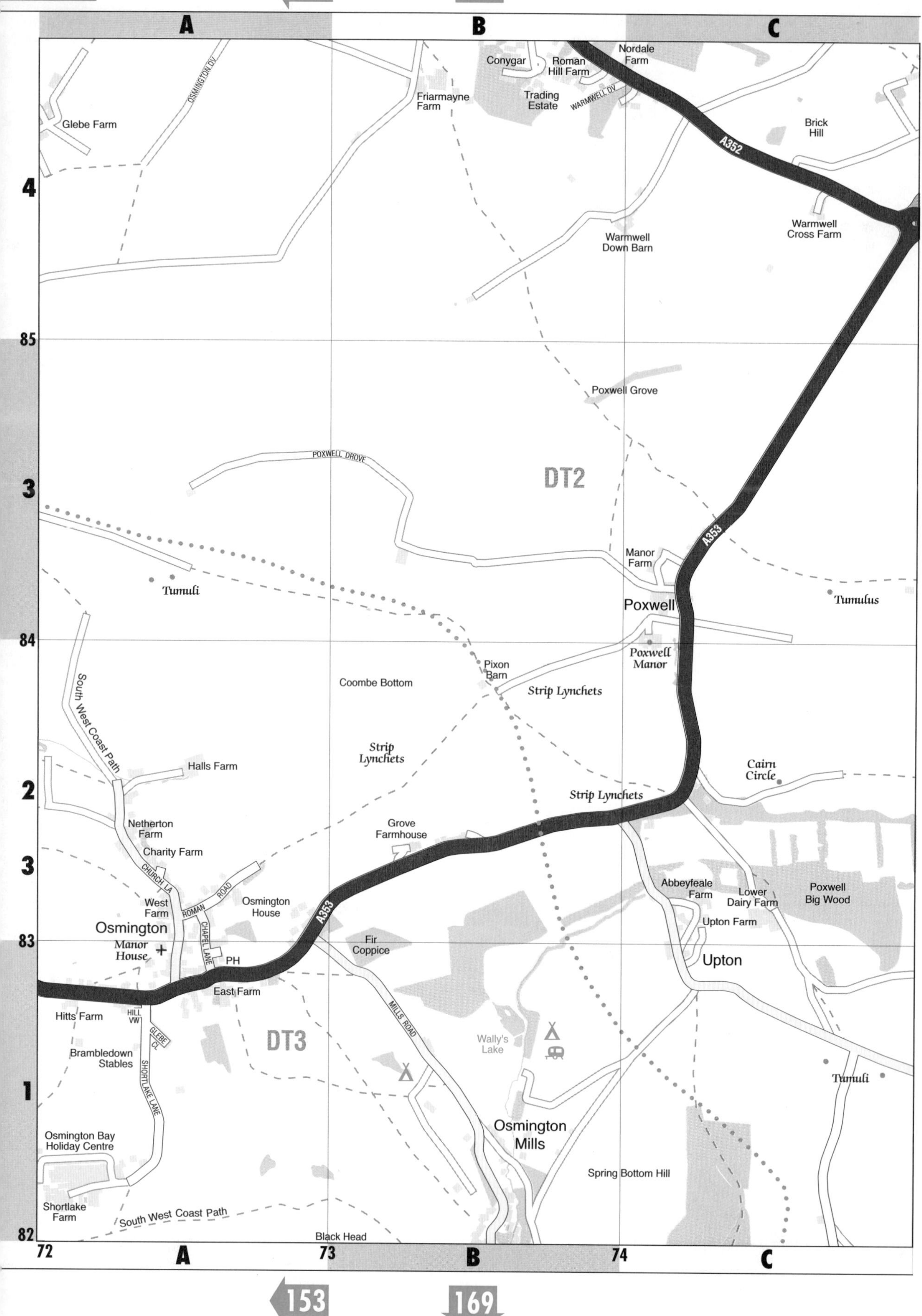

A   B   C

Glebe Farm

Friarmayne
Farm

Conygar   Roman
Hill Farm

Nordale
Farm

Trading
Estate

Brick
Hill

A352

Warmwell
Down Barn

Warmwell
Cross Farm

4

85

Poxwell Grove

DT2

POXWELL DROVE

A353

3

Tumuli

Manor
Farm

Poxwell

Tumulus

84

Coombe Bottom

Pixon
Barn

Strip Lynchets

Poxwell
Manor

South West Coast Path

Strip
Lynchets

Strip Lynchets

Cairn
Circle

2

Halls Farm

Netherton
Farm

Grove
Farmhouse

Strip Lynchets

Abbeyfeale
Farm

Lower
Dairy Farm

Poxwell
Big Wood

Charity Farm

3

CHURCH LA

ROMAN   ROAD

West
Farm

Osmington
House

Upton Farm

Osmington

CHAPEL LANE

Fir
Coppice

83

Manor
House

PH

Upton

East Farm

Hitts Farm

HILL
VW

MILLS ROAD

Wally's
Lake

GLEBE CL

DT3

SHORTLAKE LANE

Brambledown
Stables

Tumuli

1

Osmington
Mills

Osmington Bay
Holiday Centre

Spring Bottom Hill

Shortlake
Farm

South West Coast Path

82

Black Head

72   A   73   B   74   C

Warmwell House
Warmwell
B3390
Ower Wood
CASTLE LA
Moigne Court
Bartlett's Coppice
Moat
MORETON RD
Owermoigne
CE Prim Sch
4
HOLLANDS MD AV
Orchard Coppice
Galton
West Barn
E FARM LA
East Farm
POLLARDS LA
CHURCH LA
GLEBEFORD CL
Manor Farm
Chilbury Plantation
CHILBURY GD
KIT LA
WAREHAM ROAD
WAREHAM ROAD
85
Newgate Farm
A352
Watercombe
Glebe Farm
Watercombe Farm
GALLOWS HILL
East Farm
Hill Dairy
3
Owermoigne Down Barn
DT2
Lord's Barrow
Tumulus
Tumulus
Moigns Down Barn
84
Tumuli
Northground Dairy
Moigns Down
North Holworth Farm
2
South Holworth Farm
Clayland Coppice
Holworth Village
83
West Chaldon
Tumuli
Brimstone Bottom
1
Brimstone Bottom Barn
P
Falcon Barn
South Down Farm
Ringstead Farm
82

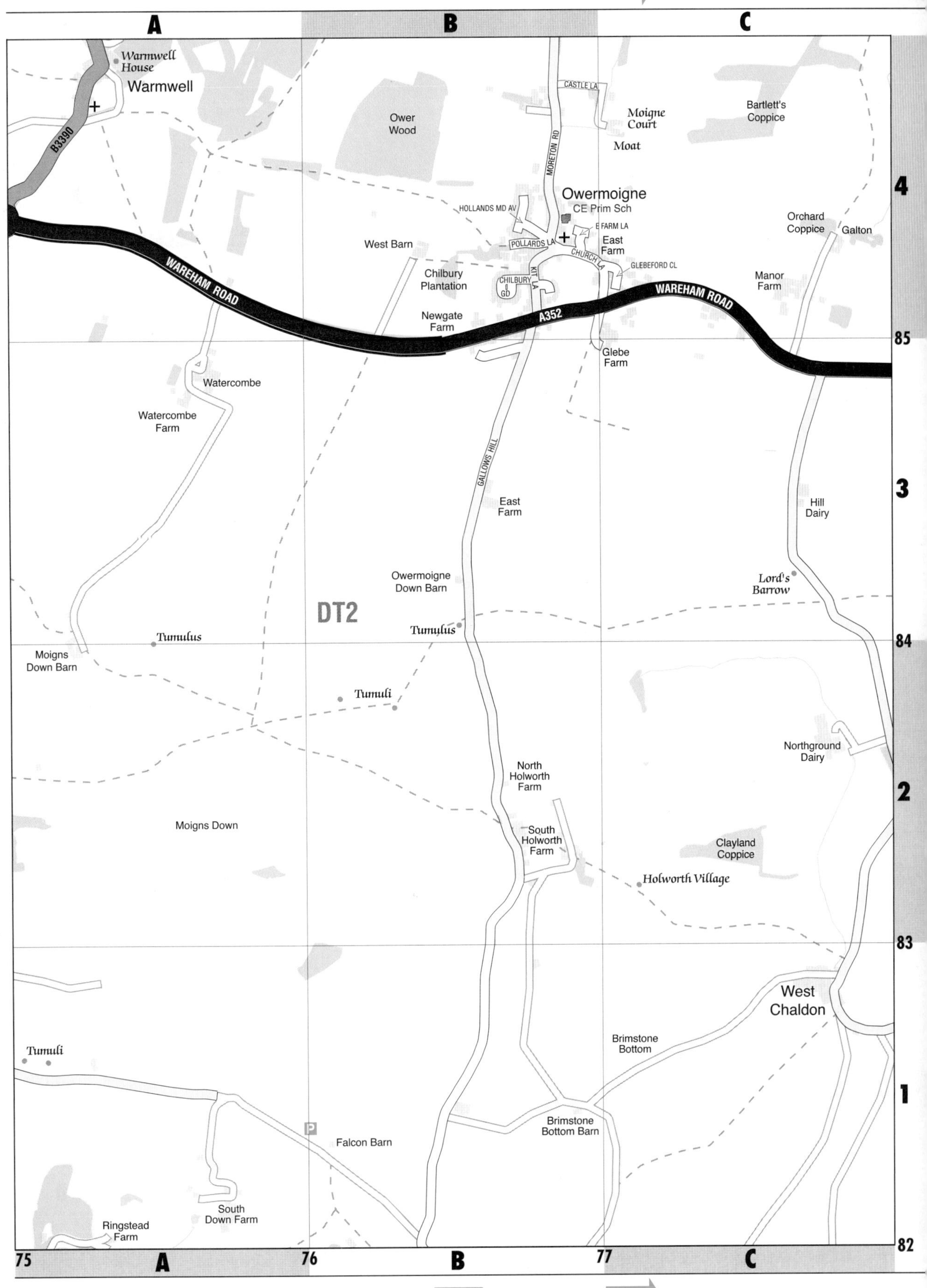

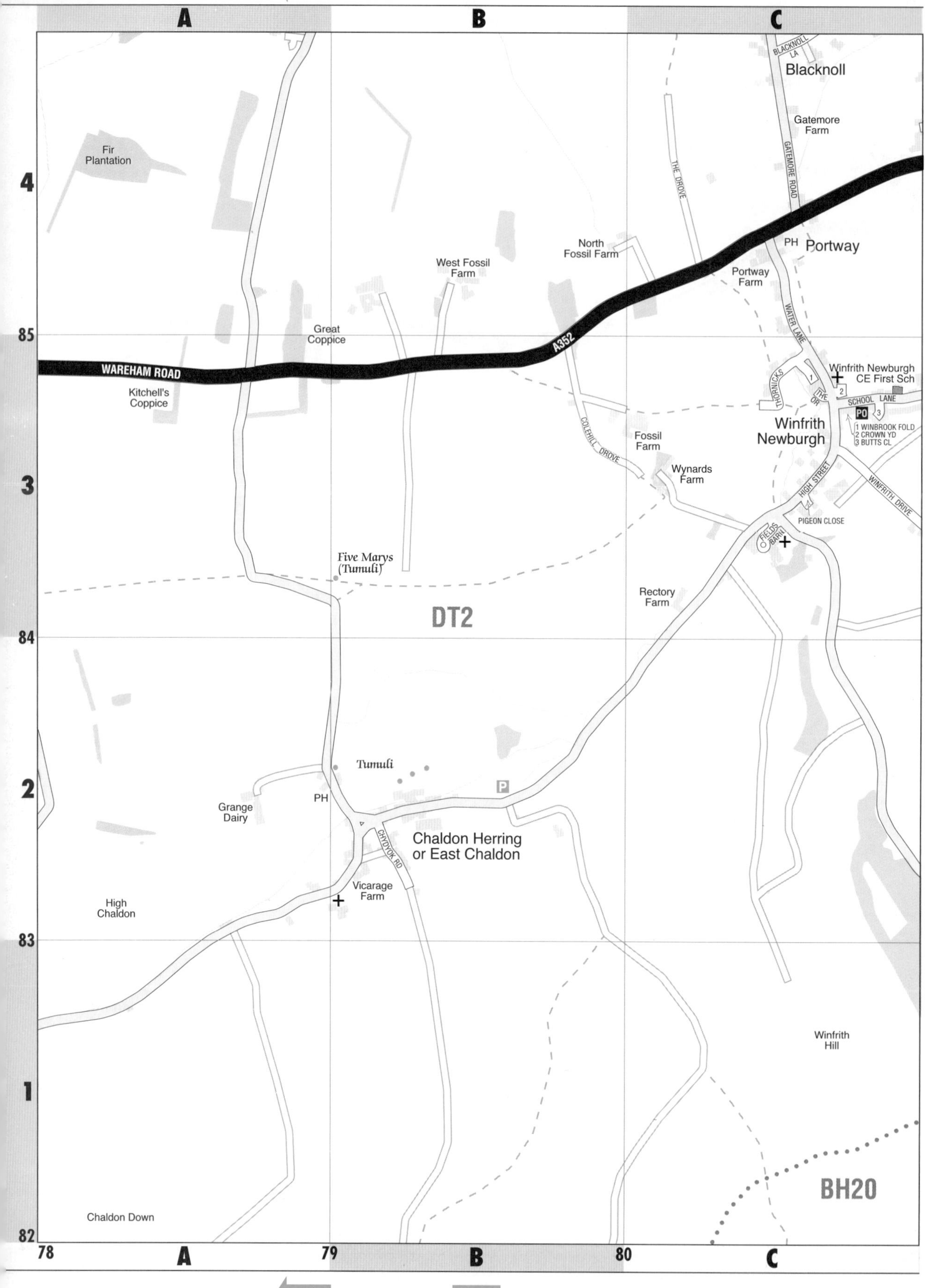

155
138

A   **B**   **C**

4

Blacknoll

BLACKNOLL LA

Gatemore
Farm

THE DROVE

GATEMORE ROAD

PH **Portway**

Fir
Plantation

Portway
Farm

WATER LANE

85

West Fossil
Farm

North
Fossil Farm

Winfrith Newburgh
CE First Sch

THORNICKS

TYE DR

Great
Coppice

A352

1

SCHOOL LANE

WAREHAM ROAD

Kitchell's
Coppice

COLEHILL DROVE

Fossil
Farm

**Winfrith
Newburgh**

PO

2

1 WINBROOK FOLD
2 CROWN YD
3 BUTTS CL

3

Wynards
Farm

HIGH STREET

WINFRITH DRIVE

PIGEON CLOSE

*Five Marys
(Tumuli)*

FIELDS BARN

DT2

Rectory
Farm

84

2

Tumuli

P

High
Chaldon

Grange
Dairy

PH

CHYDOK RD

**Chaldon Herring
or East Chaldon**

Winfrith
Hill

Vicarage
Farm

83

1

BH20

82

Chaldon Down

78   **A**   79   **B**   80   **C**

155
171

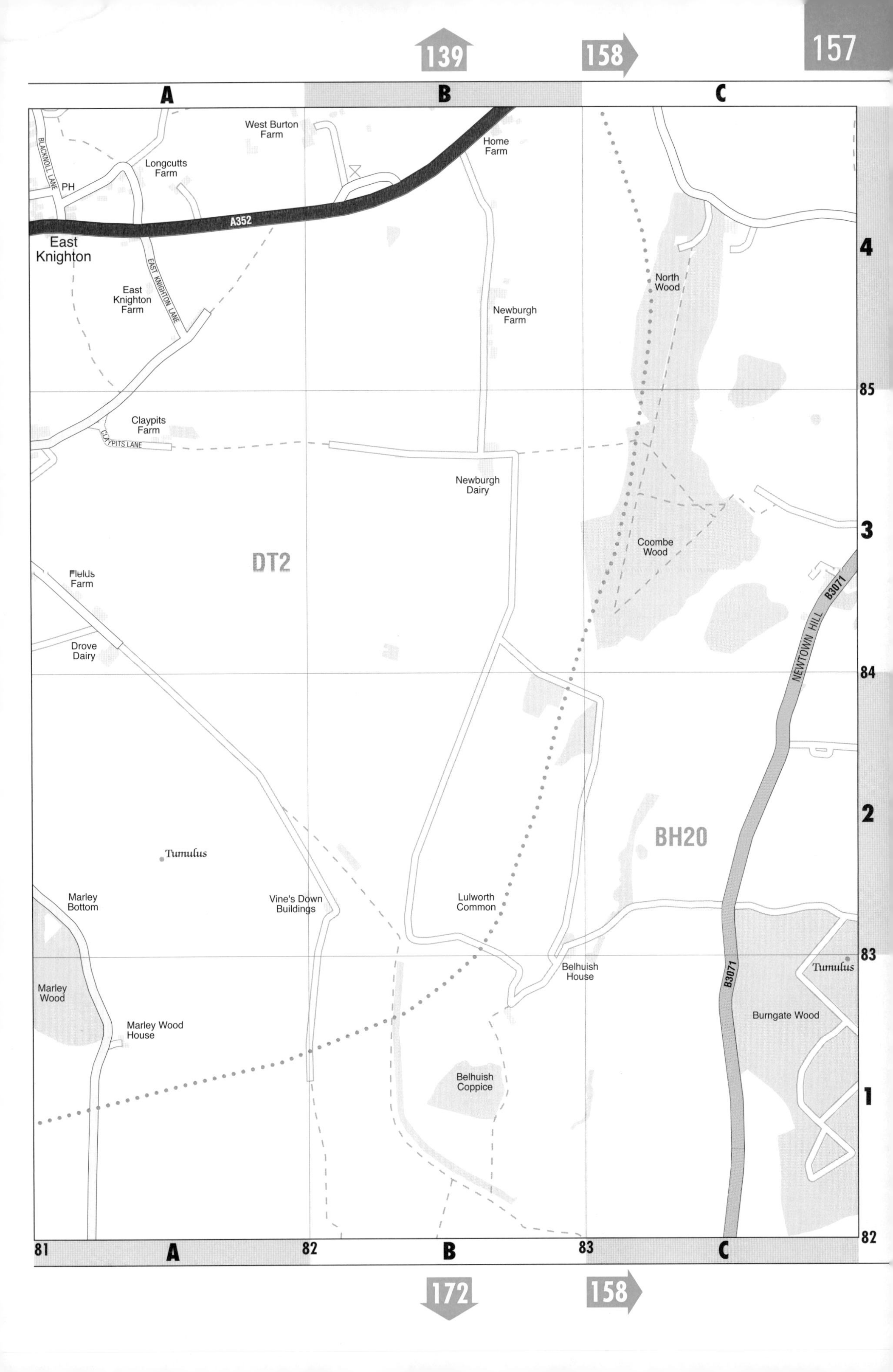

139
158

A   B   C

BLACKNOLL LANE

PH

Longcutts
Farm

West Burton
Farm

Home
Farm

A352

East
Knighton

EAST KNIGHTON LANE

East
Knighton
Farm

Newburgh
Farm

North
Wood

4

85

Claypits
Farm

CLAYPITS LANE

Newburgh
Dairy

DT2

Coombe
Wood

3

Fields
Farm

NEWTOWN HILL

B3071

Drove
Dairy

84

Tumulus

BH20

2

Marley
Bottom

Vine's Down
Buildings

Lulworth
Common

B3071

Tumulus

83

Marley
Wood

Belhuish
House

Burngate
Wood

Marley Wood
House

Belhuish
Coppice

1

81   82   83   **82**

A   B   C

157 140

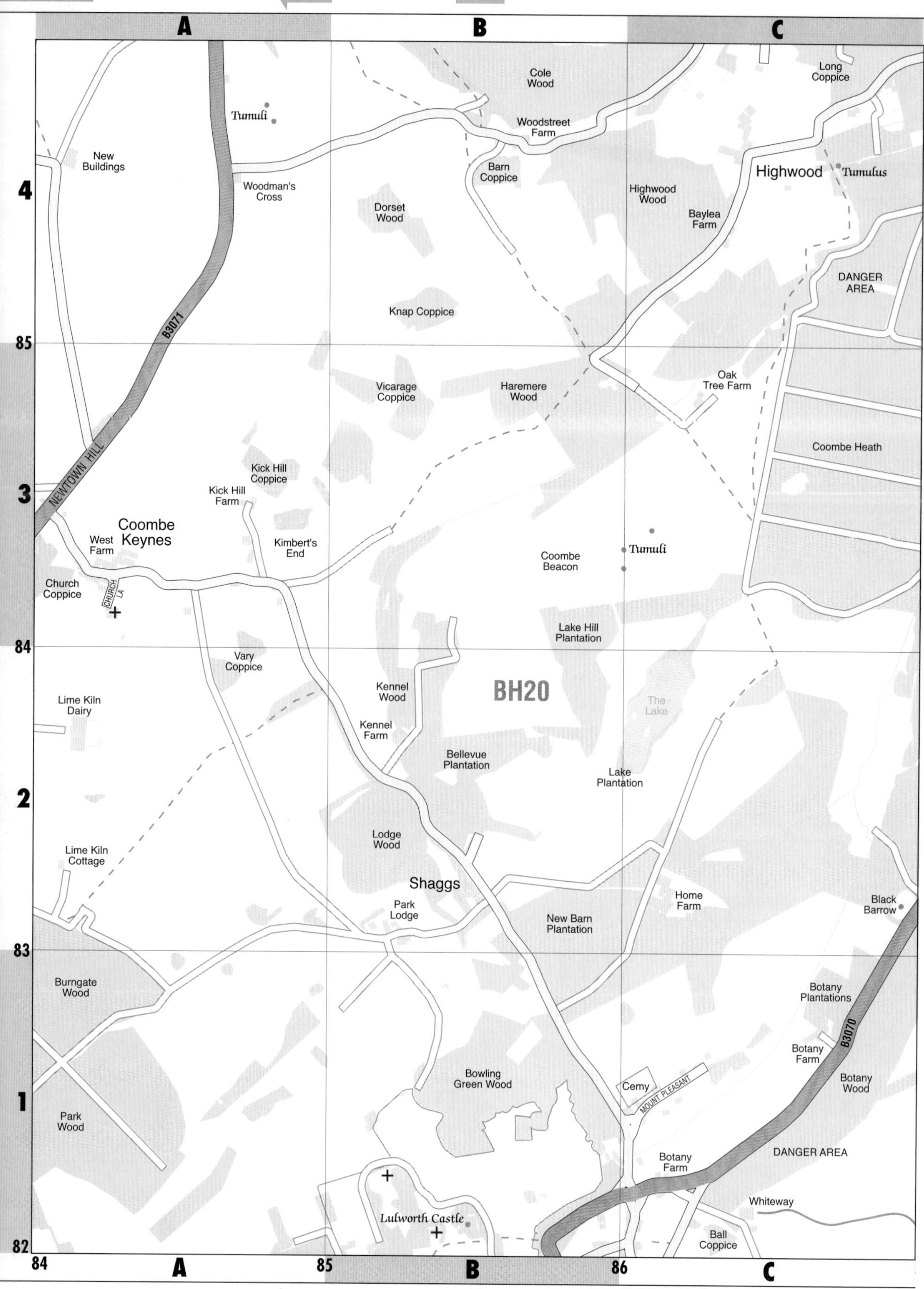

New Buildings

Tumuli

Cole Wood

Woodstreet Farm

Woodman's Cross

Barn Coppice

Highwood Wood

Long Coppice

Highwood

Tumulus

Dorset Wood

Baylea Farm

4

DANGER AREA

Knap Coppice

85

Vicarage Coppice

Haremere Wood

Oak Tree Farm

Coombe Heath

Kick Hill Coppice

Kick Hill Farm

3

Coombe Keynes

Kimbert's End

NEWTOWN HILL B3071

West Farm

Coombe Beacon

Tumuli

Church Coppice

CHURCH LA

Vary Coppice

84

Lake Hill Plantation

Kennel Wood

BH20

The Lake

Lime Kiln Dairy

Kennel Farm

Bellevue Plantation

Lake Plantation

2

Lodge Wood

Lime Kiln Cottage

Shaggs

Home Farm

Black Barrow

Park Lodge

New Barn Plantation

83

Burngate Wood

Botany Plantations

B3070

Botany Farm

Bowling Green Wood

Botany Wood

1

Cemy

MOUNT PLEASANT

Park Wood

DANGER AREA

Botany Farm

Whiteway

Lulworth Castle

Ball Coppice

82

157 173

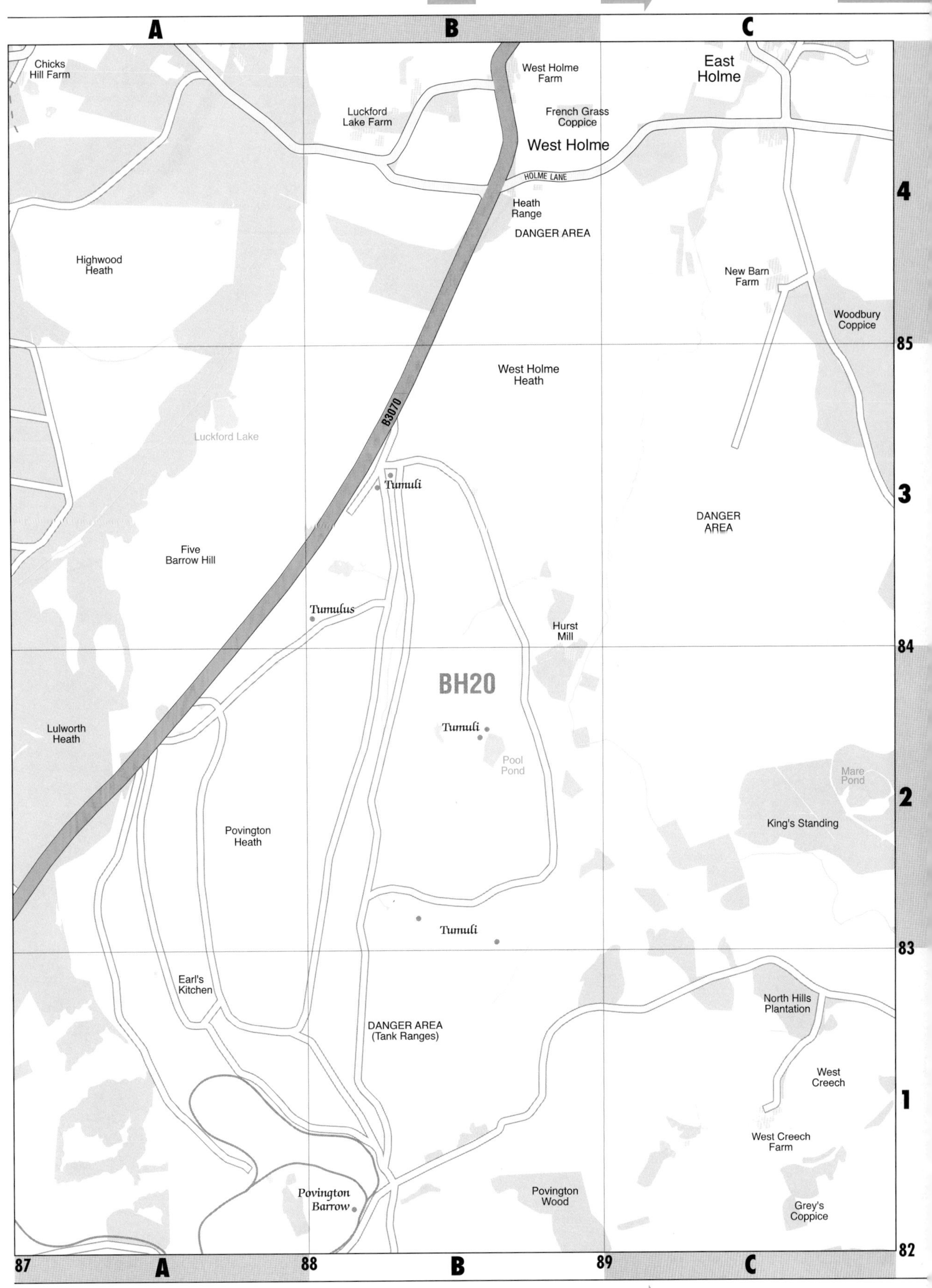

Chicks
Hill Farm

West Holme
Farm

East
Holme

Luckford
Lake Farm

French Grass
Coppice

West Holme

HOLME LANE

4

Heath
Range

Highwood
Heath

New Barn
Farm

DANGER AREA

Woodbury
Coppice

West Holme
Heath

85

Luckford Lake

B3070

Tumuli

3

DANGER
AREA

Five
Barrow Hill

Tumulus

Hurst
Mill

84

BH20

Lulworth
Heath

Tumuli

Pool
Pond

Mare
Pond

2

Povington
Heath

King's Standing

Tumuli

83

Earl's
Kitchen

North Hills
Plantation

DANGER AREA
(Tank Ranges)

West
Creech

1

West Creech
Farm

Povington
Barrow

Povington
Wood

Grey's
Coppice

82

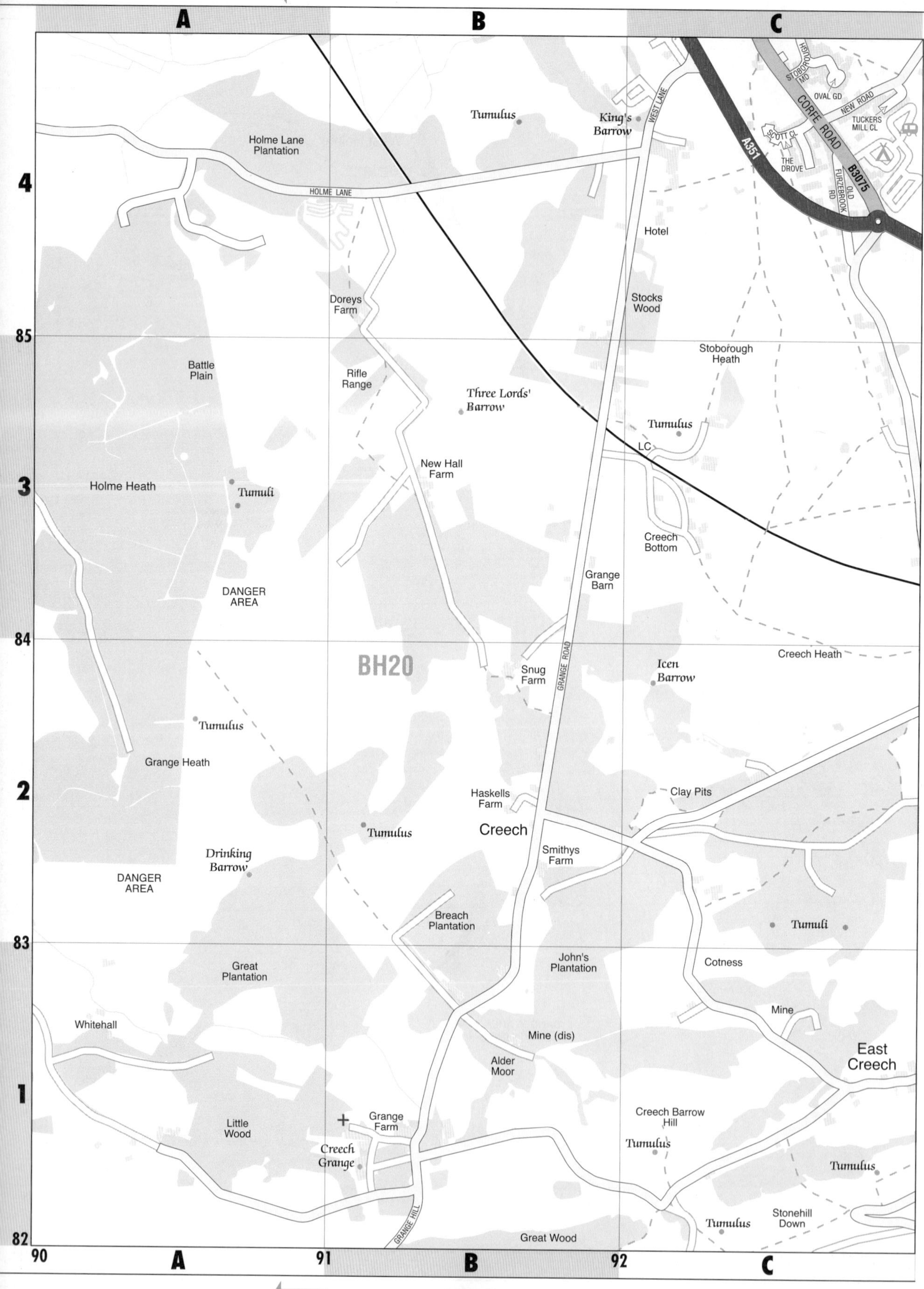

A   B   C

4

Holme Lane
Plantation

Tumulus

King's
Barrow

WEST LANE

A351

CORFE ROAD

OVAL GD

NEW ROAD

SCOTT CL

THE
DROVE

TUCKERS
MILL CL

HORTON RD

STOBOROUGH RD

OLD FURZEBROOK RD

B3075

HOLME LANE

Hotel

Doreys
Farm

Stocks
Wood

85

Battle
Plain

Rifle
Range

Three Lords'
Barrow

Stoborough
Heath

Tumulus

LC

3

Holme Heath

Tumuli

New Hall
Farm

Creech
Bottom

DANGER
AREA

Grange
Barn

84

BH20

Snug
Farm

Icen
Barrow

Creech Heath

Tumulus

Grange Heath

GRANGE ROAD

Tumulus

Haskells
Farm

Clay Pits

2

DANGER
AREA

Drinking
Barrow

Tumulus

Creech

Smithys
Farm

Tumuli

83

Great
Plantation

Breach
Plantation

John's
Plantation

Cotness

Whitehall

Mine

Mine (dis)

East
Creech

Alder
Moor

1

Little
Wood

Grange
Farm

Creech Barrow
Hill

Creech
Grange

Tumulus

Tumulus

GRANGE HILL

Tumulus

Stonehill
Down

82

Great Wood

90   A   **91**   B   **92**   C

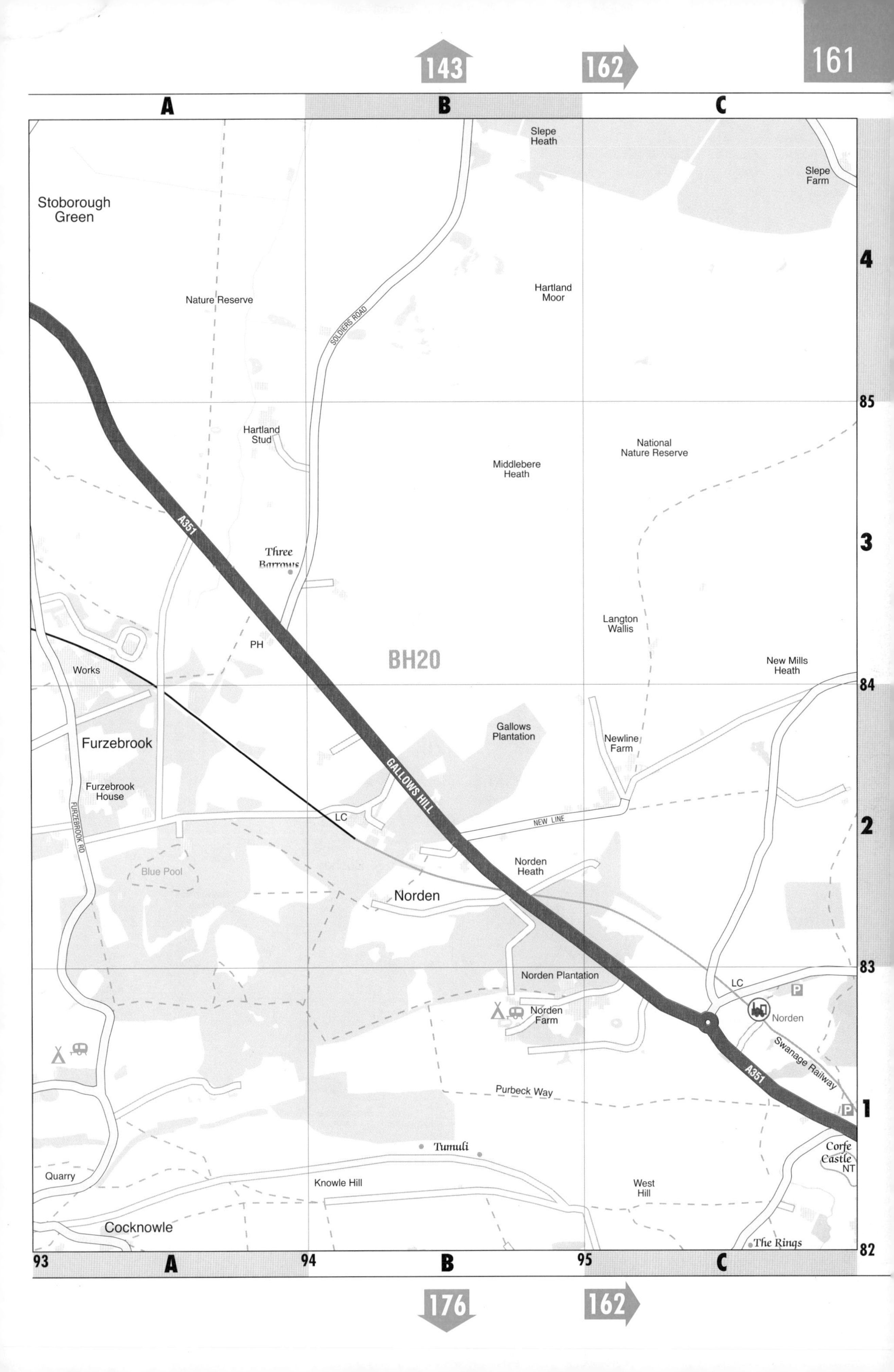

A B C

4

85

3

84

BH20

2

83

1

82

Stoborough
Green

Nature Reserve

Slepe
Heath

Slepe
Farm

Hartland
Moor

Hartland
Stud

SOLDIERS ROAD

National
Nature Reserve

Middlebere
Heath

Three
Barrows

A351

Langton
Wallis

New Mills
Heath

PH

Works

Gallows
Plantation

Newline
Farm

Furzebrook

GALLOWS HILL

Furzebrook
House

FURZEBROOK RD

LC

NEW LINE

Blue Pool

Norden
Heath

Norden

Norden Plantation

LC

Norden

P

Norden
Farm

Swanage Railway

A351

Purbeck Way

P

Tumuli

Quarry

Knowle Hill

West
Hill

Corfe
Castle
NT

Cocknowle

The Rings

93 A 94 B 95 C 82

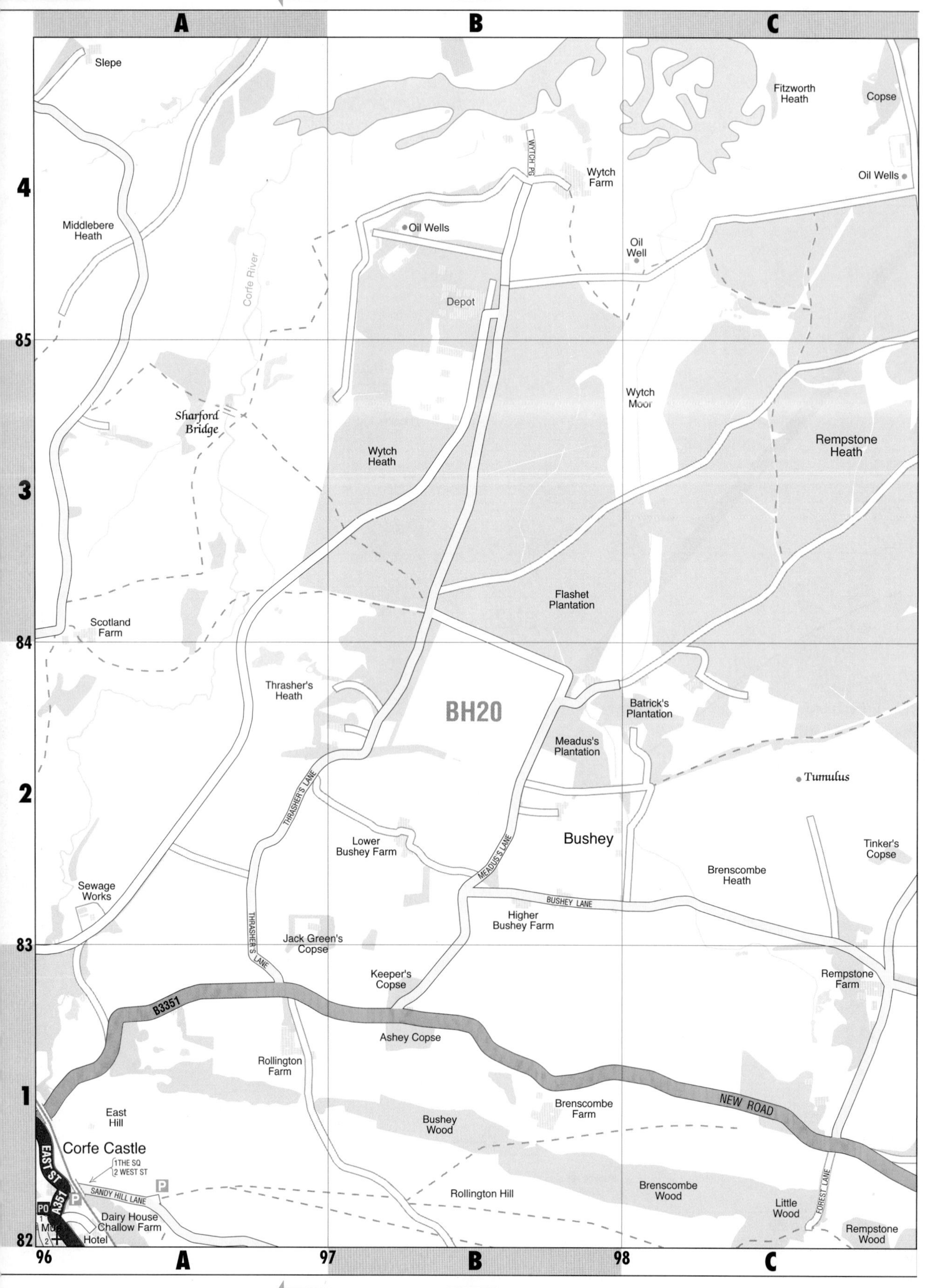
Slepe
Fitzworth Heath
Copse
Wytch Farm
Oil Wells
Middlebere Heath
Oil Wells
Oil Well
Corfe River
Depot
Wytch Moor
Sharford Bridge
Wytch Heath
Rempstone Heath
Flashet Plantation
Scotland Farm
Thrasher's Heath
BH20
Batrick's Plantation
Meadus's Plantation
Tumulus
Lower Bushey Farm
Bushey
Tinker's Copse
Brenscombe Heath
Sewage Works
Higher Bushey Farm
Jack Green's Copse
Keeper's Copse
Rempstone Farm
Ashey Copse
Rollington Farm
East Hill
Brenscombe Farm
Bushey Wood
Corfe Castle
Rollington Hill
Brenscombe Wood
Little Wood
Rempstone Wood
Dairy House
Challow Farm
Hotel
WYTCH PG
THRASHER'S LANE
MEADUS'S LANE
BUSHEY LANE
B3351
NEW ROAD
FOREST LANE
SANDY HILL LANE
EAST ST
A351
1 THE SQ
2 WEST ST
PO
P
4
85
3
84
2
83
1
82
96
97
98

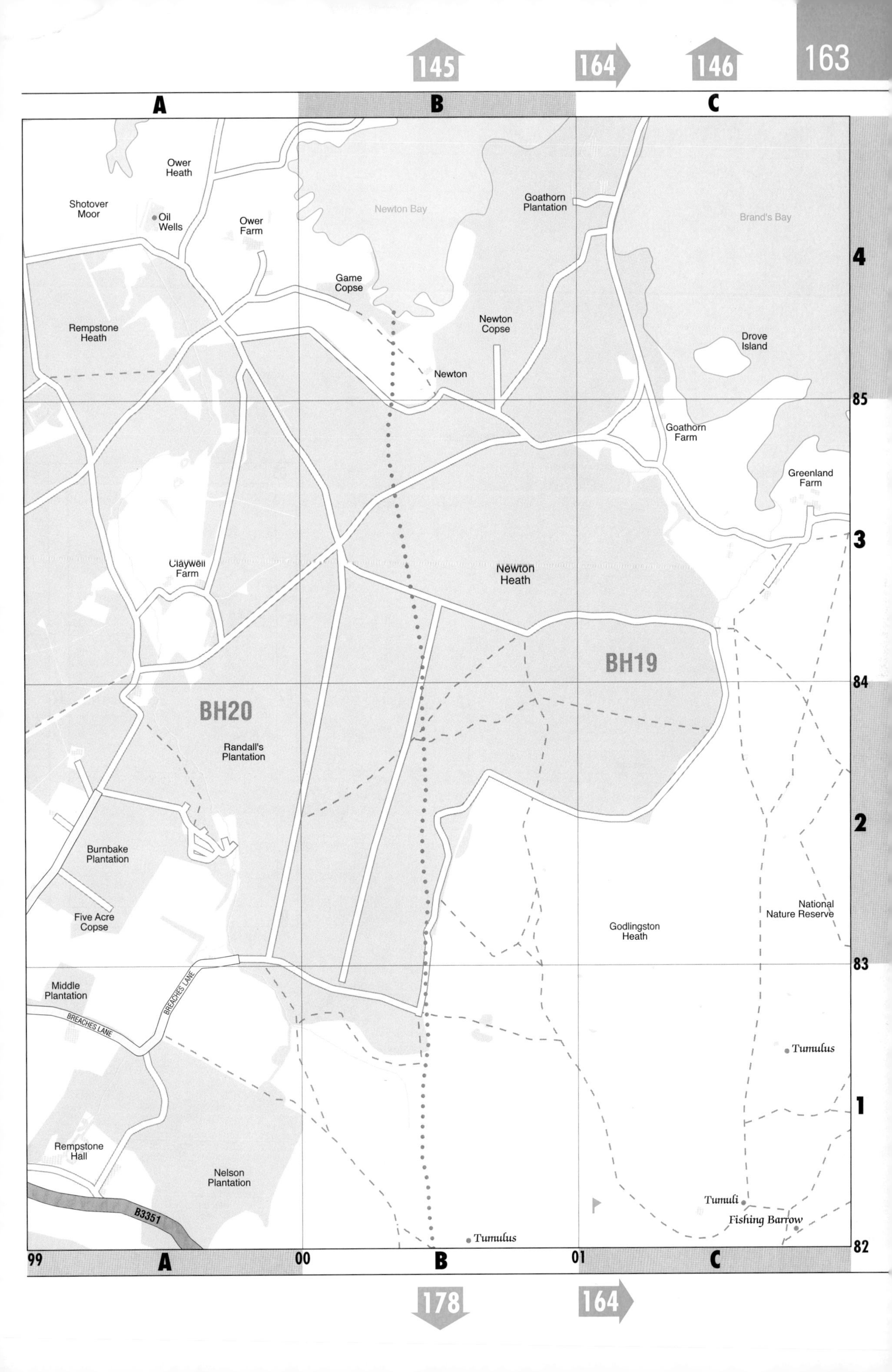

A
B
C

Ower
Heath

Shotover
Moor
● Oil
Wells

Newton Bay

Goathorn
Plantation

Brand's Bay

Ower
Farm

4

Rempstone
Heath

Game
Copse

Newton
Copse

Drove
Island

85

Newton

Goathorn
Farm

Greenland
Farm

Claywell
Farm

3

Newton
Heath

BH19

BH20

84

Randall's
Plantation

2

Burnbake
Plantation

Godlingston
Heath

National
Nature Reserve

Five Acre
Copse

83

Middle
Plantation

BREACHES LANE

BREACHES LANE

● Tumulus

Rempstone
Hall

1

Nelson
Plantation

B3351

● Tumuli

Fishing Barrow

82

● Tumulus

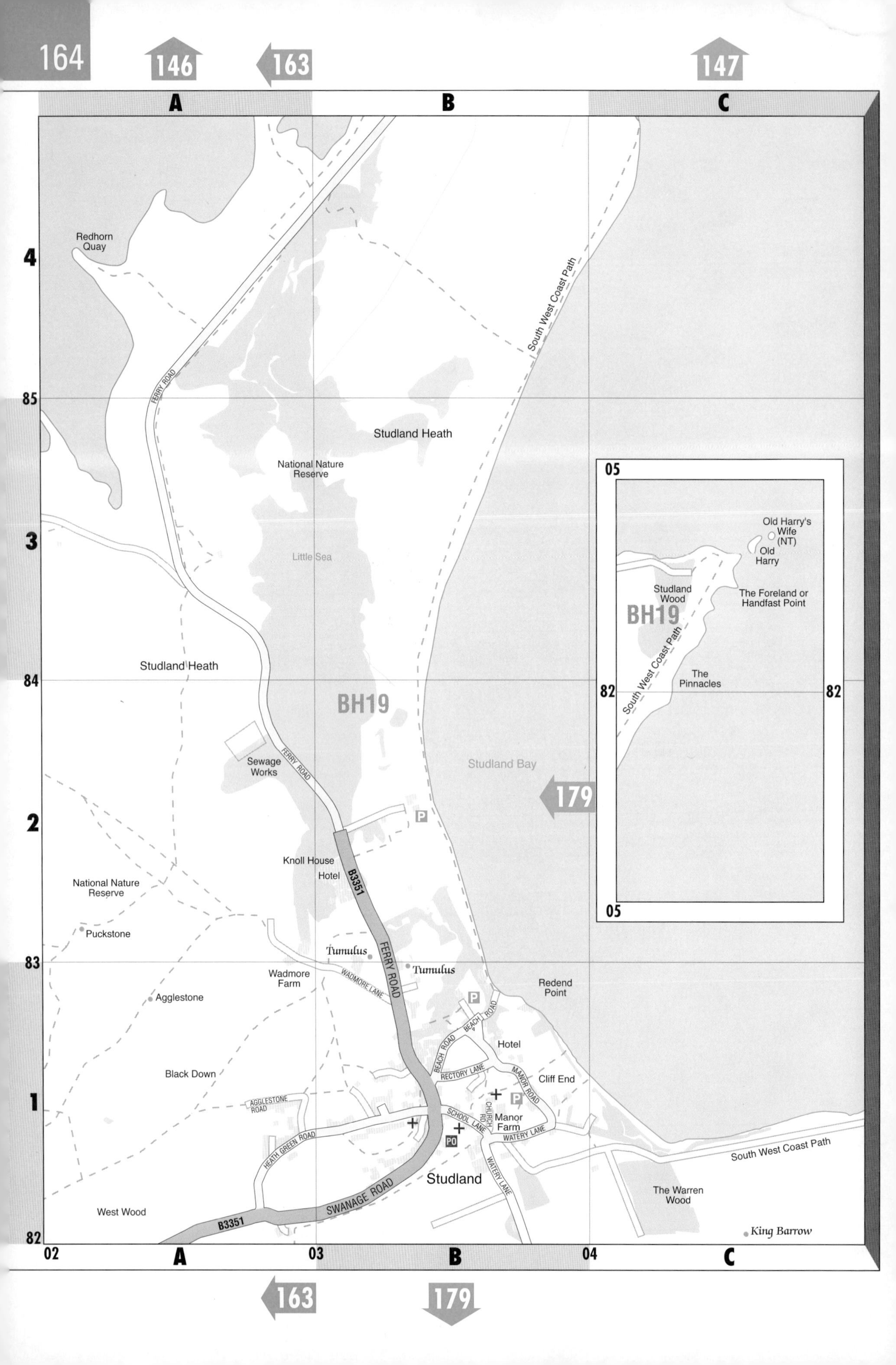
146
163
147
A
B
C
4
85
3
84
2
83
1
82
02
03
04
Redhorn Quay
FERRY ROAD
Studland Heath
National Nature Reserve
South West Coast Path
Little Sea
Studland Heath
BH19
Sewage Works
Studland Bay
179
Knoll House Hotel
B3351
National Nature Reserve
Puckstone
Tumulus
Tumulus
Wadmore Farm
WADMORE LANE
Agglestone
Redend Point
BEACH ROAD
Hotel
RECTORY LANE
MANOR ROAD
Cliff End
Black Down
AGGLESTONE ROAD
SCHOOL LANE
CHURCH RD
Manor Farm
WATERY LANE
HEATH GREEN ROAD
PO
Studland
SWANAGE ROAD
West Wood
The Warren Wood
King Barrow
05
Old Harry's Wife (NT)
Old Harry
Studland Wood
The Foreland or Handfast Point
The Pinnacles
82
82
05

163
179

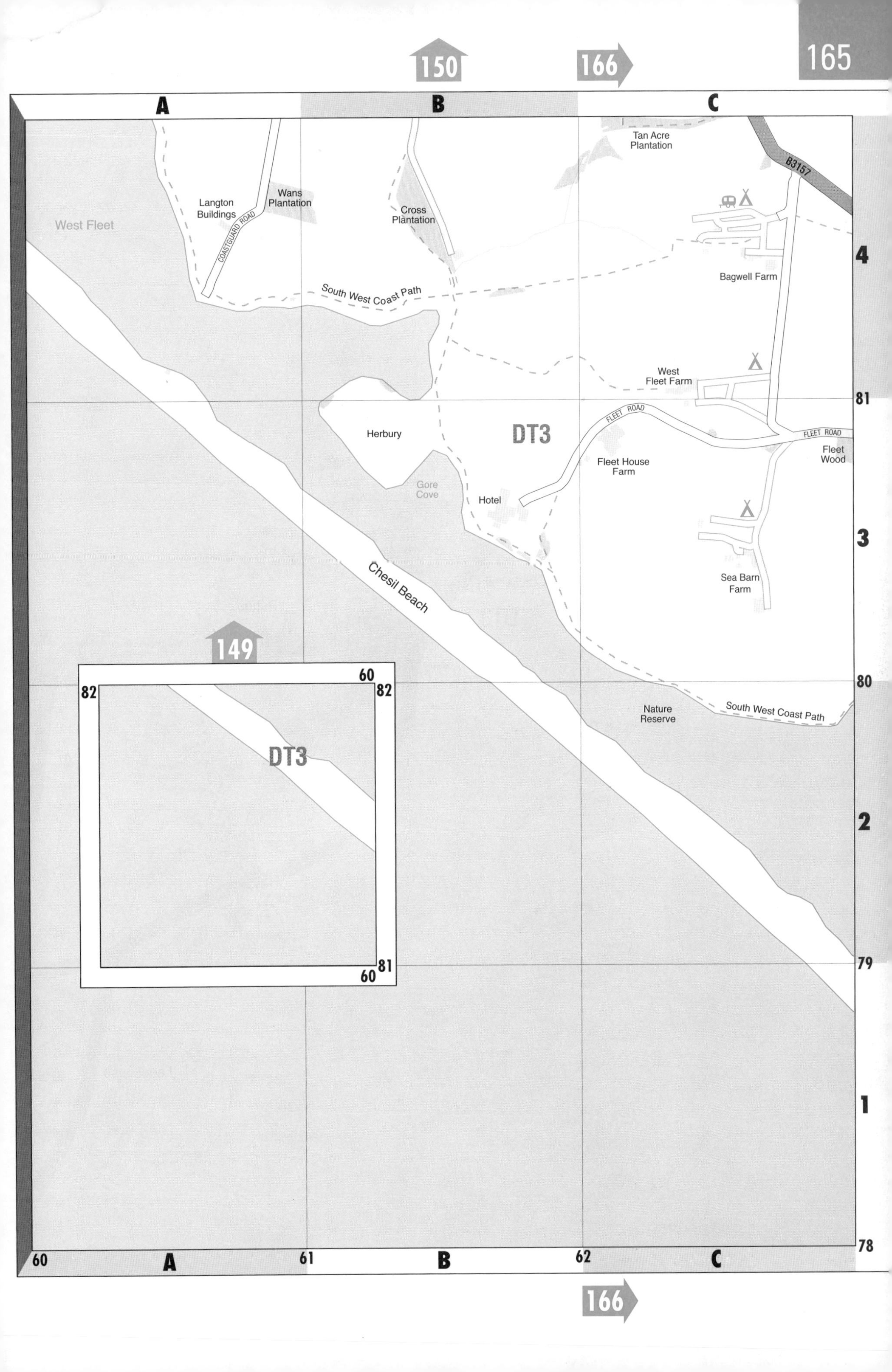
150
166
A
B
C
Tan Acre Plantation
B3157
Langton Buildings
Wans Plantation
Cross Plantation
West Fleet
COASTGUARD ROAD
4
Bagwell Farm
South West Coast Path
West Fleet Farm
81
FLEET ROAD
Herbury
DT3
FLEET ROAD
Fleet Wood
Fleet House Farm
Gore Cove
Hotel
3
Sea Barn Farm
Chesil Beach
149
60
82
82
80
Nature Reserve
South West Coast Path
DT3
2
81
60
79
1
78
60
A
61
B
62
C
166

166

← 165

↑ 151

B3
1 CURLEW CL
2 GREBE CL
3 HERON CL

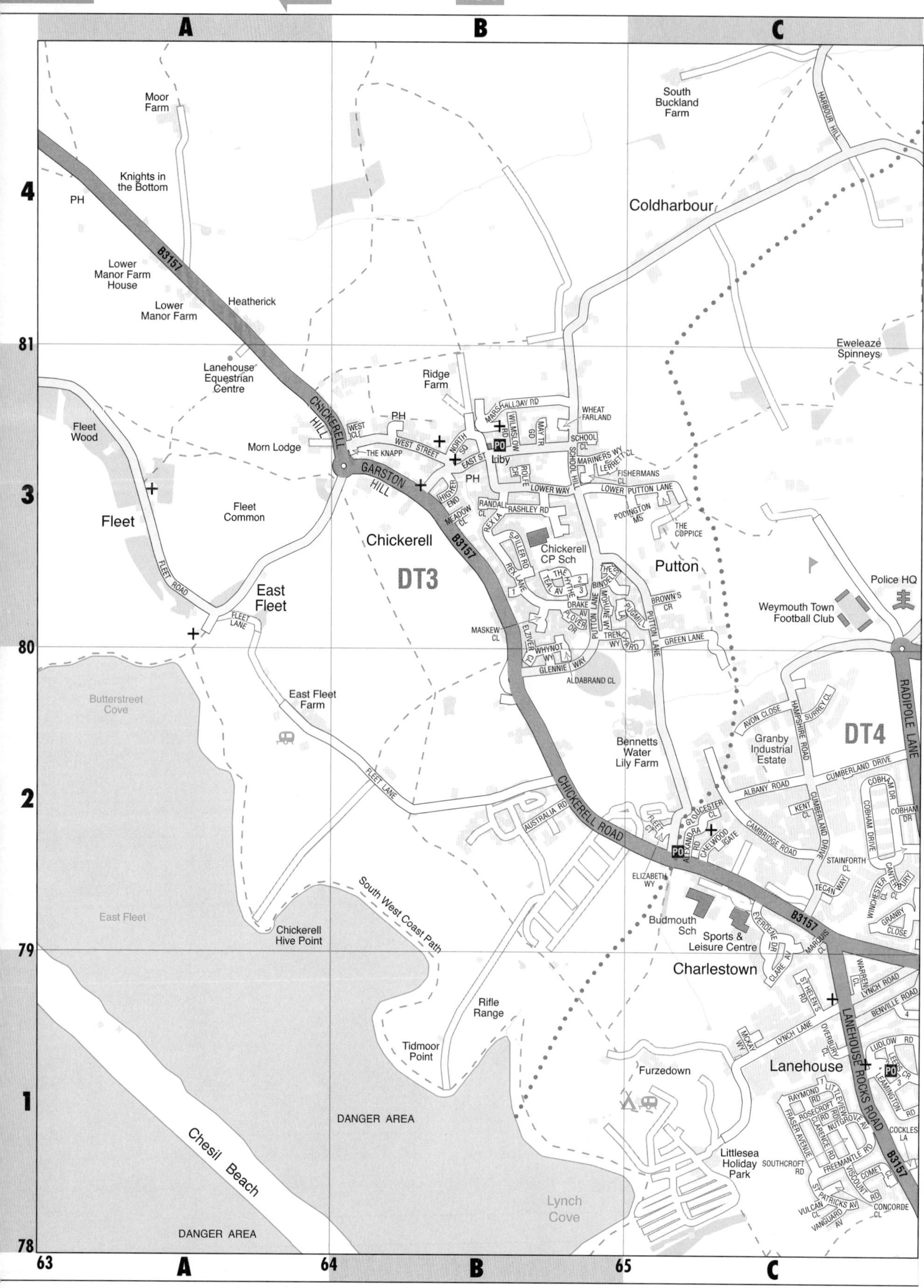

Moor Farm

Knights in the Bottom

PH

B3157

Lower Manor Farm House

Heatherick

Lower Manor Farm

Lanehouse Equestrian Centre

South Buckland Farm

Coldharbour

Eweleaze Spinneys

81

Fleet Wood

Morn Lodge

CHICKERELL HILL

WEST CL

PH

Ridge Farm

WEST STREET

THE KNAPP

NORTH SQ

EAST ST

MARSHALLDAY RD

WILMSLOW

MAY TR

WHEAT FARLAND

SCHOOL CL

GARSTON HILL

PH

ROFE

Liby

SCHOOL HILL

MARINERS WY

LERRETT CL

FISHERMANS CL

Fleet

+

Fleet Common

Chickerell

DT3

3

HIGHER END

MEADOW CL

RANDALL RD

REXLA

RASHLEY RD

LOWER WAY

LOWER PUTTON LANE

POXINGTON MS

THE COPPICE

80

Putton

Police HQ

Weymouth Town Football Club

East Fleet

FLEET ROAD

FLEET LANE

+

S.PILLER RD

Chickerell CP Sch

THE TEA AV

2 3

1

MASKEW CL

ELZIVER CL

WHYNOT

DRAKE AV

PLOVER DR

THE HYTHE

BINDALL

PUTTON LANE

BROWN'S CR

PUTTON LANE

GREEN LANE

AVON CLOSE

HAMPSHIRE ROAD

SURREY CL

DT4

Granby Industrial Estate

CUMBERLAND DRIVE

COBH.

COBHAM DR

East Fleet Farm

GLENNIE WAY

ALDABRAND CL

RADIPOLE LANE

2

Butterstreet Cove

FLEET LANE

Bennetts Water Lily Farm

ALBANY ROAD

KENT CL

CUMBERLAND ROAD

COBHAM DRIVE

STAINFORTH CL

CAREY CL

CARY COURT

South West Coast Path

AUSTRALIA RD

CHICKERELL ROAD

PO

ALEXANDRA RD

CAELWOOD

GLOUCESTER

CAMBRIDGE ROAD

WINSFORD CL

GRANBY CLOSE

TECAV WAY

B3157

79

East Fleet

Chickerell Hive Point

ELIZABETH WY

Budmouth Sch

Sports & Leisure Centre

EVERDENE DR

MARQUIS

WARREN ROAD

CLARE AV

Charlestown

LYNCH ROAD

BENVILLE ROAD

Rifle Range

Tidmoor Point

ST HELEN'S RD

LYNCH LANE

MAY WY

LYNCH

OVERBURY

Furzedown

Lanehouse

LUDLOW RD

LAMINGTON

PO

COCKLES LA

1

RAYMOND RD

ROSECROFT RD

FRASER AVENUE

CLARENCE RD

NUTGROVE AV

FREEMANTLE RD

SOUTHCROFT RD

LANEHOUSE ROCKS ROAD

B3157

DANGER AREA

Littlesea Holiday Park

VULCAN CL

VANGUARD AV

ST PATRICKS AV

VISCOUNT RD

COMET CL

CONCORDE CL

Chesil Beach

DANGER AREA

Lynch Cove

78

63   A   64   B   65   C

← 165

↓ 180

C1
1 GORDON CR
2 LINCOLN RD
3 LIVERPOOL RD
4 TOLLERDOWN RD

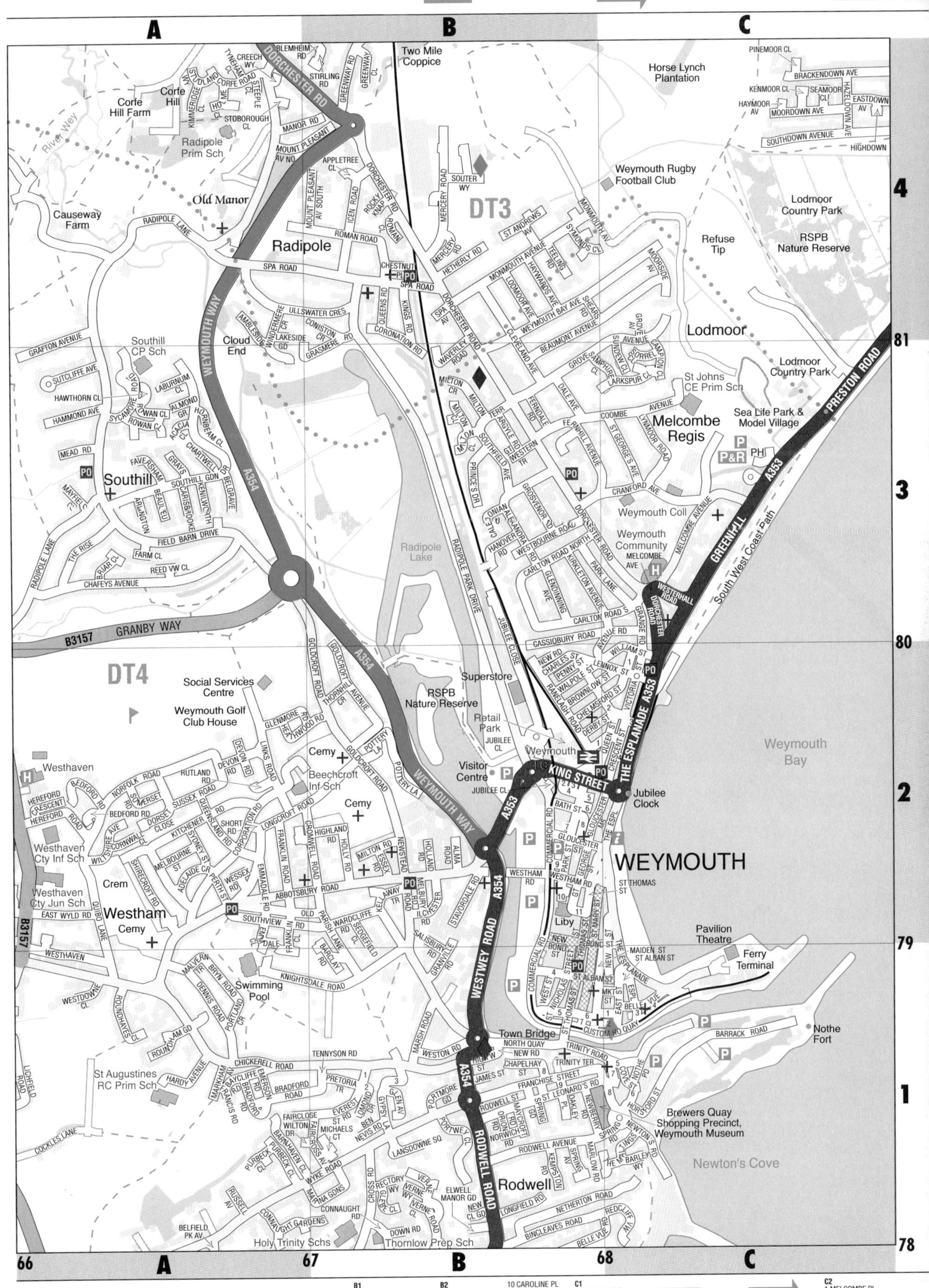

B1
1 ASHTON RD
2 GYPSY LA
3 PRINCE OF WALES RD
4 LWR ST ALBAN ST
5 LWR ST EDMUND ST
6 ST EDMUND ST
7 ST MARY ST
8 DORSET TR
9 PROSPECT PL

B2
1 STANLEY ST
2 UPWAY ST
3 TERMINUS RD
4 EDWARD ST
5 ALBERT ST
6 CLIFTON PL
7 QUEBEC PL
8 TURTON ST
9 WOOPERTON ST

10 CAROLINE PL
11 SCHOOL ST

C1
1 MITCHELL ST
2 HELEN LA
3 SOUTH PD
4 PILGRIMS WY
5 COVE ROW
6 SPRING RD
7 TRINITY ST
8 NEWBERRY GD

C2
1 MELCOMBE PL
2 HARDWICK ST
3 ASTRID WY
4 MUSGRAVE PL

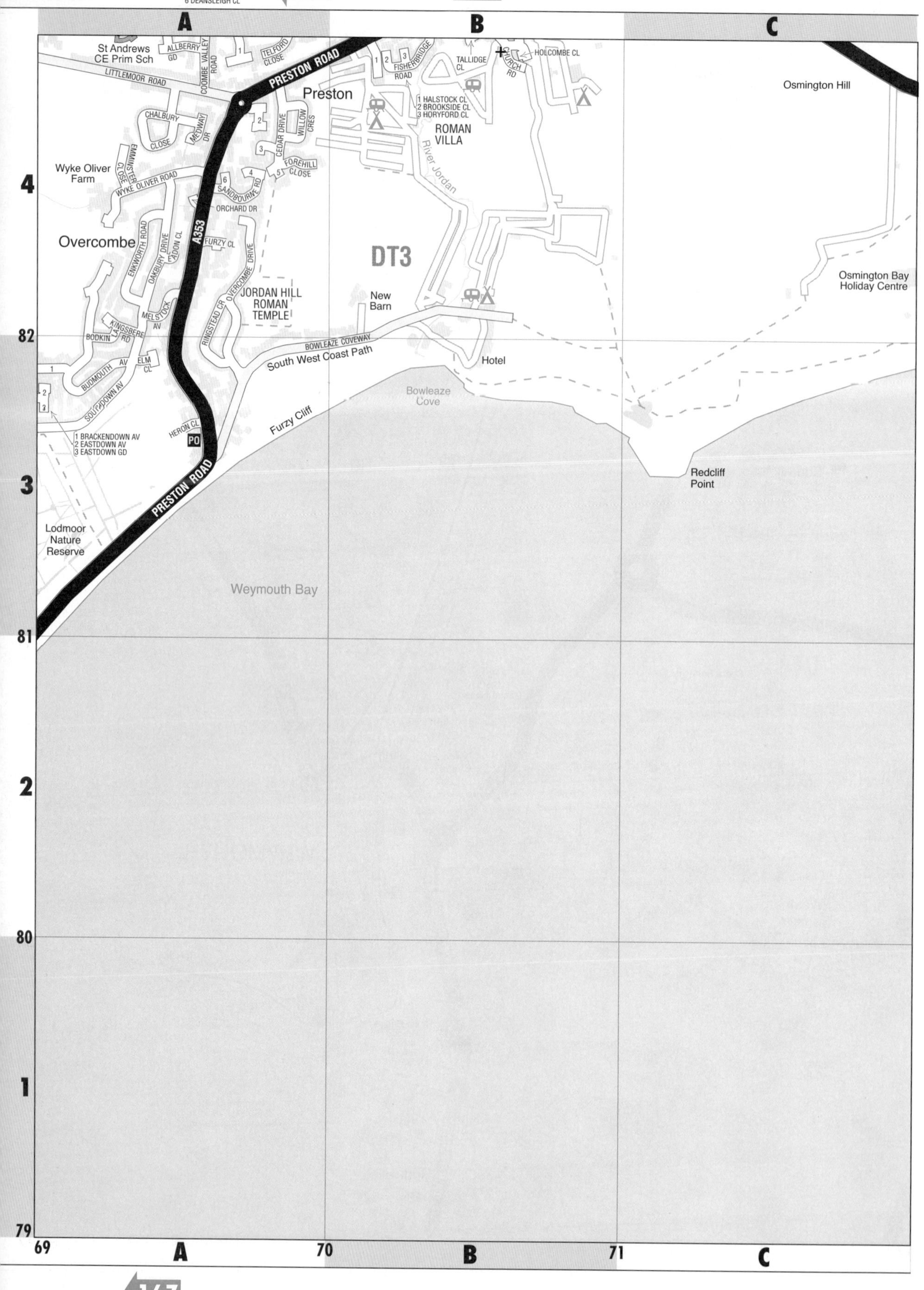

A4
1 MOORCOMBE DR
2 CHALBURY LODGE
3 HAZEL DR
4 WINGREEN CL
5 MAPLE CL
6 DEANSLEIGH CL

167
153

A **B** **C**

St Andrews
CE Prim Sch

ALLBERRY GD

TELFORD CLOSE

LITTLEMOOR ROAD

PRESTON ROAD

Preston

COOMBE VALLEY ROAD

CHALBURY CLOSE

MIDWAY DR

CEDAR DRIVE

WILLOW CRES

FISHERBRIDGE ROAD

TALLIDGE CL

HOLCOMBE CL

CHURCH RD

Osmington Hill

1 HALSTOCK CL
2 BROOKSIDE CL
3 HORYFORD CL

ROMAN VILLA

River Jordan

4

Wyke Oliver Farm

EMMINSTER CLOSE

WYKE OLIVER ROAD

EMKWORTH ROAD

OAKBURY DRIVE

ZION CL

FURZY CL

FOREHILL CLOSE

SANDBOURNE RD

ORCHARD DR

DT3

Osmington Bay
Holiday Centre

Overcombe

A353

RINGSTEAD CR

OVERCOMBE DRIVE

JORDAN HILL
ROMAN
TEMPLE

New
Barn

MELSTOCK AV

KINGSBERE RD

BODKIN

ELM CL

BUDMOUTH AV

SOUTHDOWN AV

82

BOWLEAZE COVEWAY

South West Coast Path

Hotel

1

2

3

HERON CL

PO

1 BRACKENDOWN AV
2 EASTDOWN AV
3 EASTDOWN GD

Furzy Cliff

Bowleaze
Cove

Redcliff
Point

3

PRESTON ROAD

Lodmoor
Nature
Reserve

Weymouth Bay

81

2

80

1

79

69 **A** 70 **B** 71 **C**

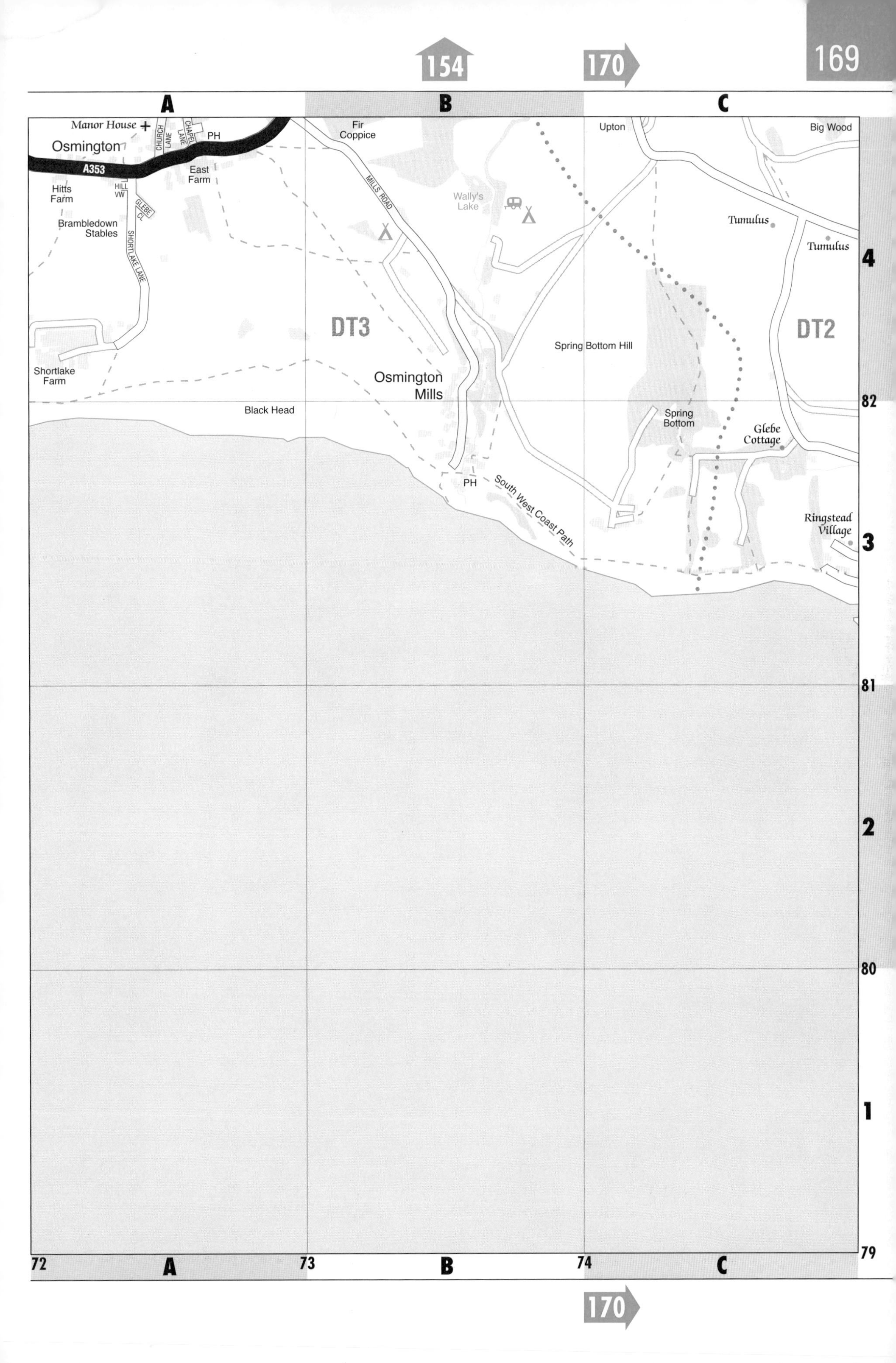
154
170
A
B
C
Manor House
Osmington
CHURCH LANE
CHAPEL LANE
PH
A353
East Farm
Hitts Farm
HILL VW
GLEBE CL
Brambledown Stables
SHORTLAKE LANE
Shortlake Farm
Fir Coppice
MILLS ROAD
Wally's Lake
DT3
Osmington Mills
Black Head
PH
South West Coast Path
Upton
Spring Bottom Hill
Spring Bottom
Big Wood
Tumulus
Tumulus
DT2
Glebe Cottage
Ringstead Village
4
82
3
81
2
80
1
79
72
73
74
170

169
155

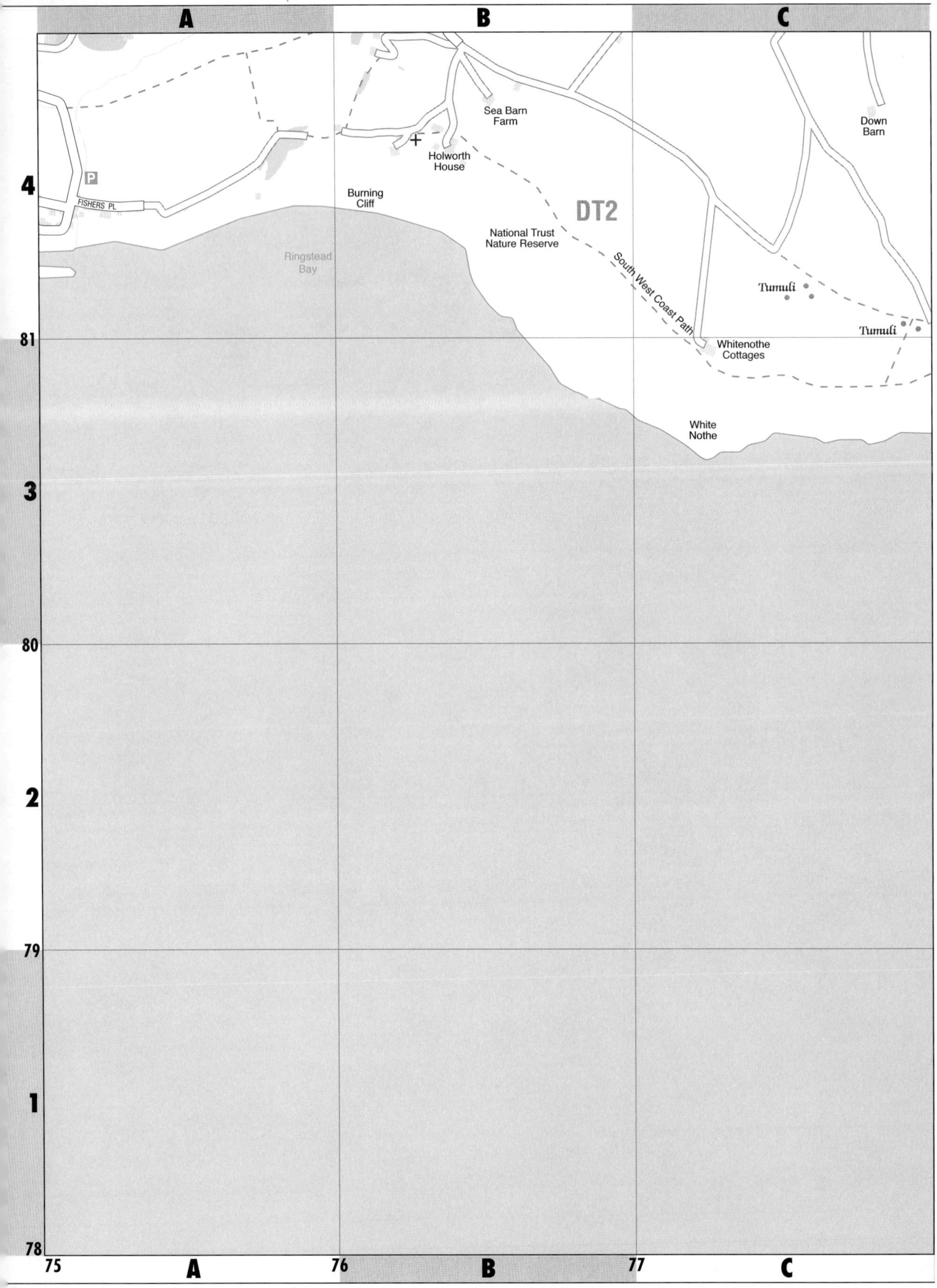

A | B | C

4

P

FISHERS PL

Ringstead
Bay

Burning
Cliff

Sea Barn
Farm

Holworth
House

National Trust
Nature Reserve

DT2

South West Coast Path

Down
Barn

Tumuli

Tumuli

Whitenothe
Cottages

81

White
Nothe

3

80

2

79

1

78

75 | A | 76 | B | 77 | C

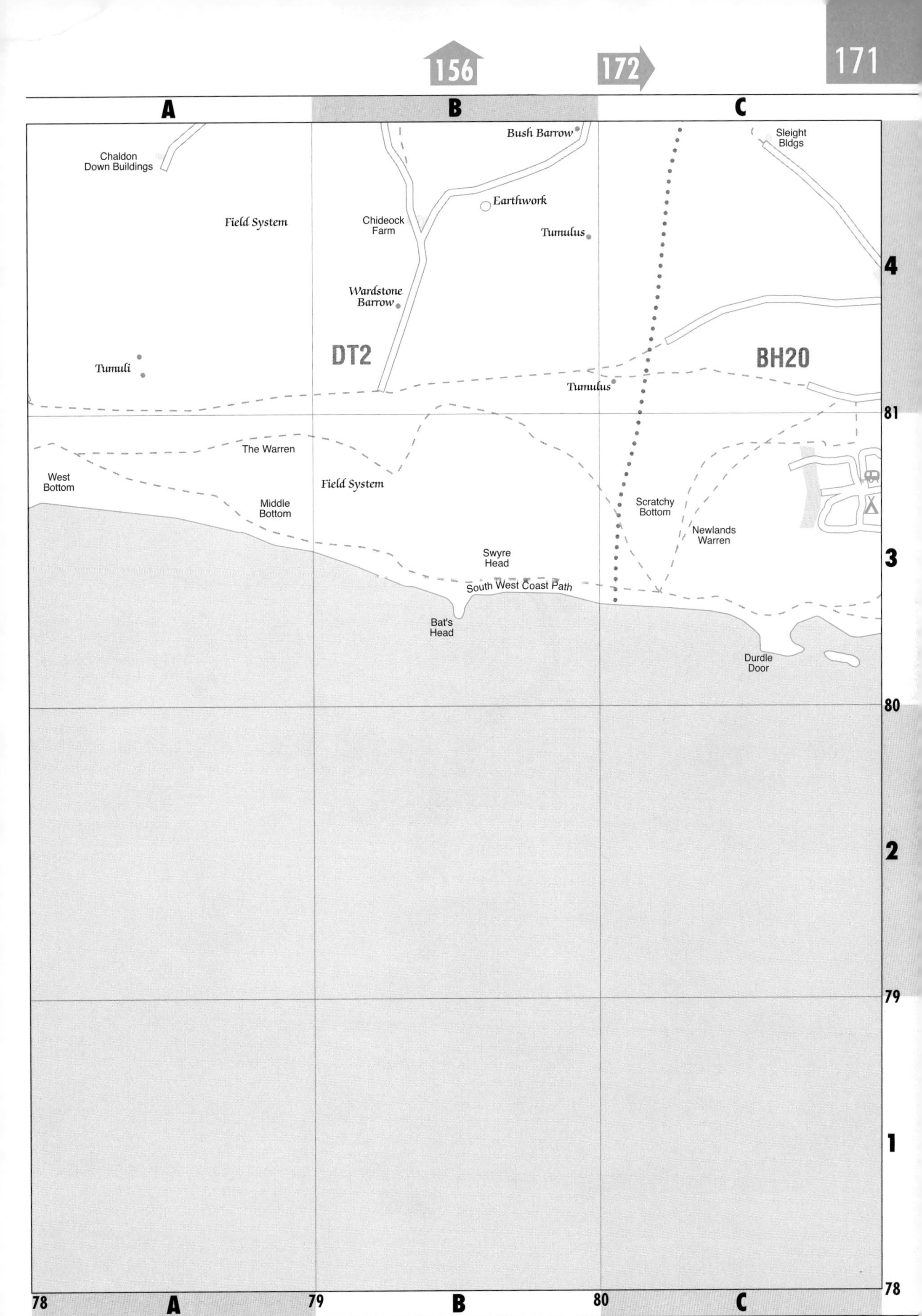

A   B   C

Chaldon
Down Buildings

Bush Barrow

Sleight
Bldgs

Field System

Chideock
Farm

Earthwork

Tumulus

4

Wardstone
Barrow

DT2

BH20

Tumuli

Tumulus

81

The Warren

West
Bottom

Field System

Scratchy
Bottom

Middle
Bottom

Newlands
Warren

3

Swyre
Head

South West Coast Path

Bat's
Head

Durdle
Door

80

2

79

1

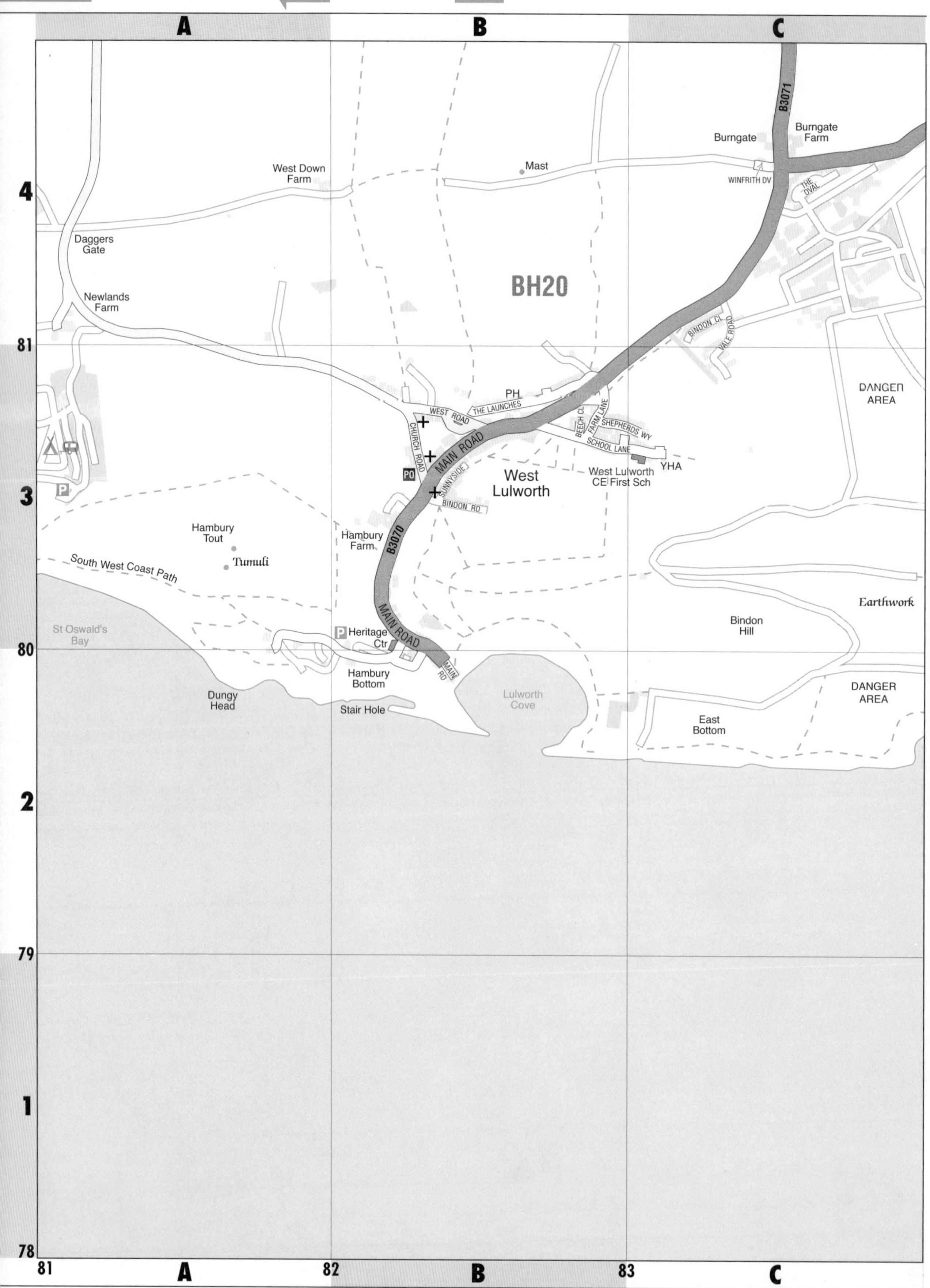

A **B** **C**

West Down Farm

Mast

Burngate

Burngate Farm

B3071

WINFRITH DV

THE OVAL

Daggers Gate

BH20

Newlands Farm

Bindon Cl

Vale Road

4

81

DANGER AREA

PH

THE LAUNCHES

West Road

Church Road

Main Road

Beech Cl

Farm Lane

Shepherds Wy

School Lane

PO

Sunnyside

West Lulworth

West Lulworth CE First Sch

YHA

Bindon Rd

Hambury Tout

Tumuli

Hambury Farm

B3070

3

South West Coast Path

St Oswald's Bay

P

Heritage Ctr

Main Road

Main Rd

Hambury Bottom

Stair Hole

Lulworth Cove

Bindon Hill

Earthwork

DANGER AREA

East Bottom

Dungy Head

80

2

79

1

78

81 **A** **82** **B** **83** **C**

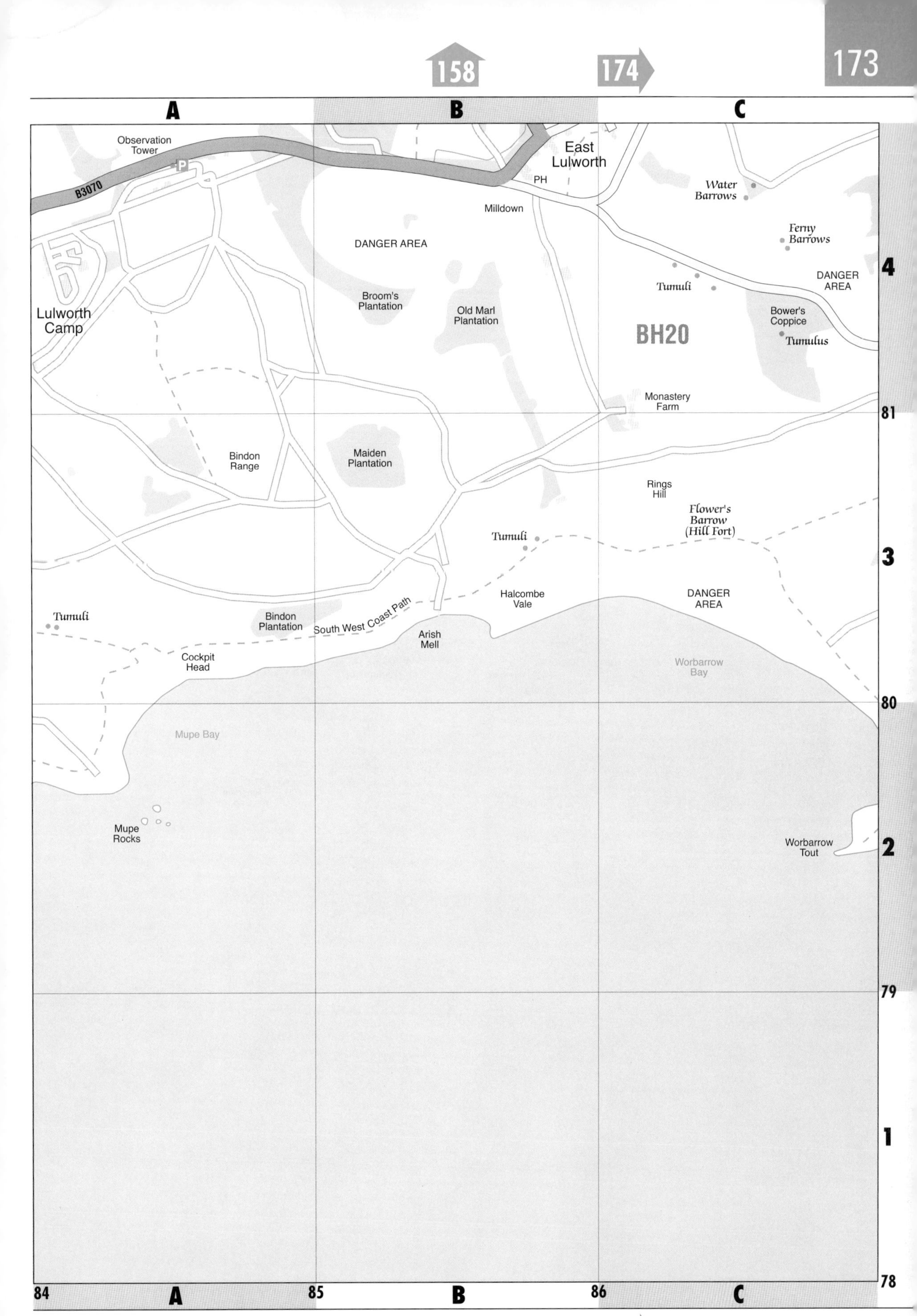

Observation Tower

B3070

Lulworth Camp

East Lulworth

PH

Milldown

DANGER AREA

Broom's Plantation

Old Marl Plantation

Water Barrows

Ferny Barrows

4

Tumuli

DANGER AREA

BH20

Bower's Coppice

Tumulus

Monastery Farm

81

Bindon Range

Maiden Plantation

Rings Hill

Flower's Barrow (Hill Fort)

3

Tumuli

Halcombe Vale

DANGER AREA

Bindon Plantation

South West Coast Path

Arish Mell

Tumuli

Worbarrow Bay

Cockpit Head

80

Mupe Bay

Worbarrow Tout

2

Mupe Rocks

79

1

84 **A** 85 **B** 86 **C** 78

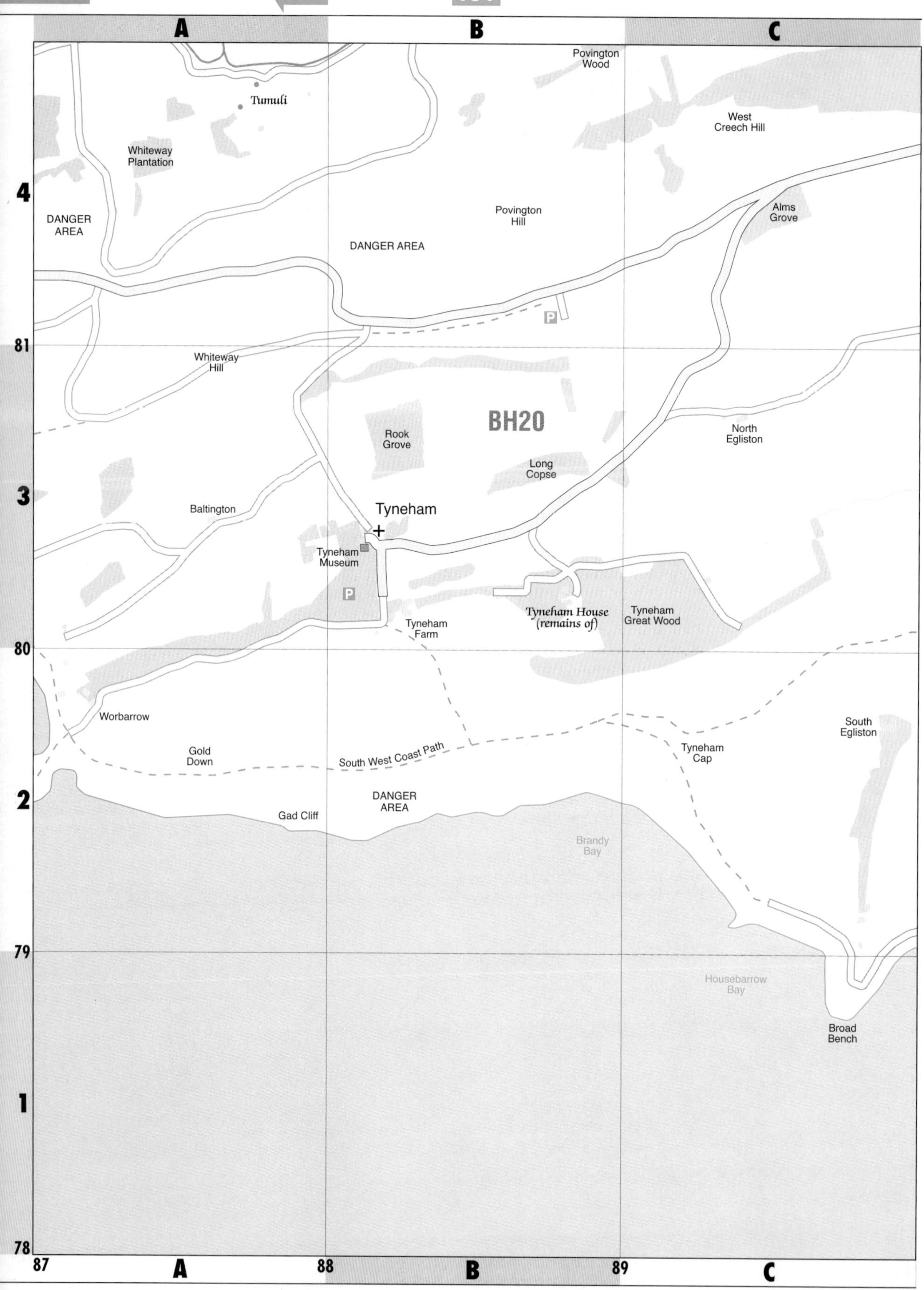

A **B** **C**

Povington
Wood

West
Creech Hill

Tumuli

Whiteway
Plantation

4

DANGER
AREA

Povington
Hill

Alms
Grove

DANGER AREA

81

Whiteway
Hill

P

North
Egliston

BH20

Rook
Grove

Long
Copse

3

Baltington

Tyneham

+

Tyneham
Museum

P

Tyneham House
(remains of)

Tyneham
Great Wood

Tyneham
Farm

80

Worbarrow

South
Egliston

Gold
Down

South West Coast Path

Tyneham
Cap

2

Gad Cliff

DANGER
AREA

Brandy
Bay

79

Housebarrow
Bay

Broad
Bench

1

78

87 **A** 88 **B** 89 **C**

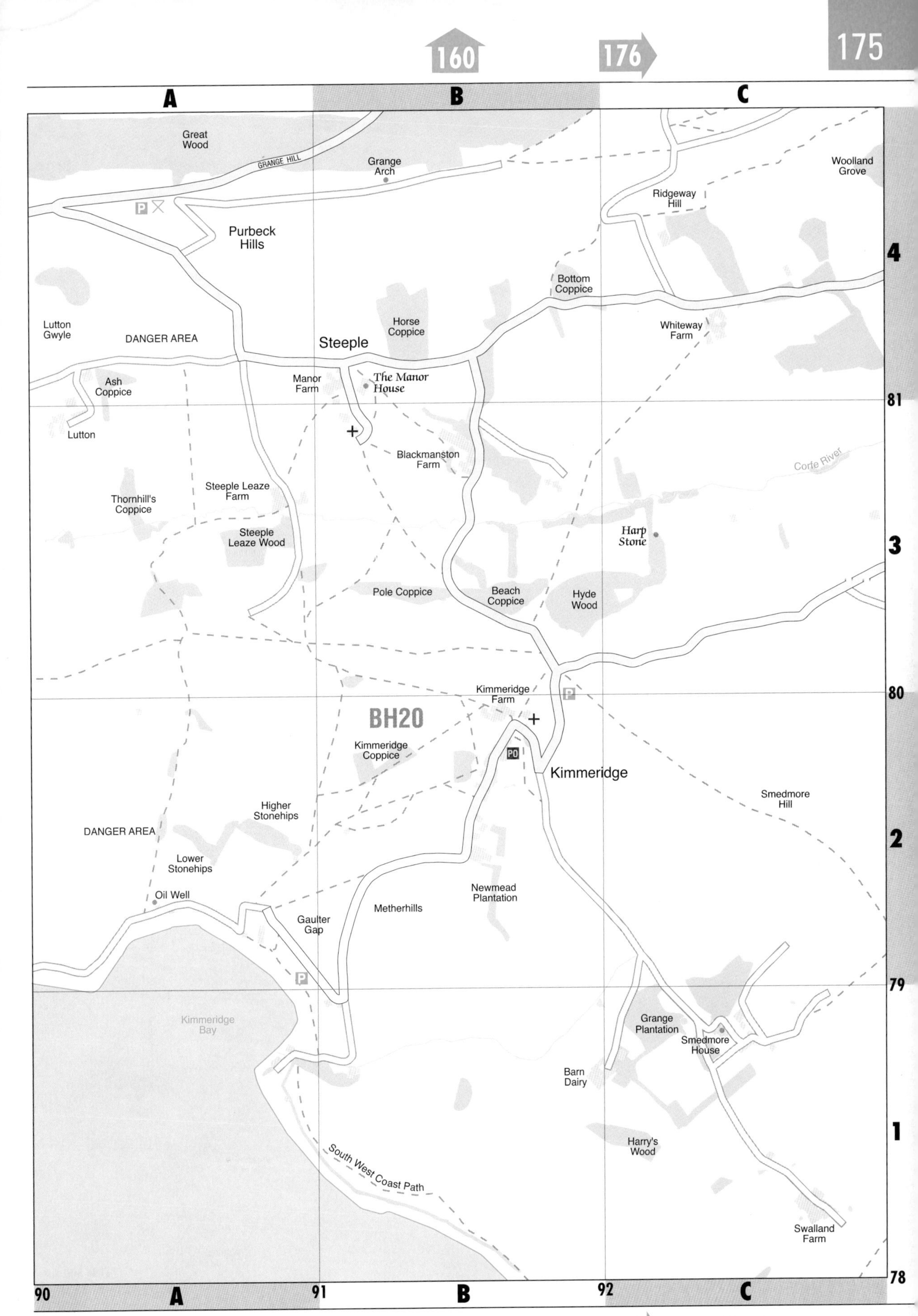

A   B   C

Great
Wood

GRANGE HILL

Grange
Arch

Woolland
Grove

Ridgeway
Hill

P ✕

Purbeck
Hills

Bottom
Coppice

4

Lutton
Gwyle

DANGER AREA

Steeple

Horse
Coppice

Whiteway
Farm

Ash
Coppice

Manor
Farm

The Manor
House

81

Lutton

✚

Blackmanston
Farm

Corfe River

Thornhill's
Coppice

Steeple Leaze
Farm

Harp
Stone

3

Steeple
Leaze Wood

Pole Coppice

Beach
Coppice

Hyde
Wood

Kimmeridge
Farm

P

80

BH20

Kimmeridge
Coppice

✚

PO

Kimmeridge

Smedmore
Hill

Higher
Stonehips

2

DANGER AREA

Lower
Stonehips

Oil Well

Newmead
Plantation

Gaulter
Gap

Metherhills

P

79

Kimmeridge
Bay

Grange
Plantation

Smedmore
House

Barn
Dairy

1

Harry's
Wood

South West Coast Path

Swalland
Farm

78

90   A   91   B   92   C

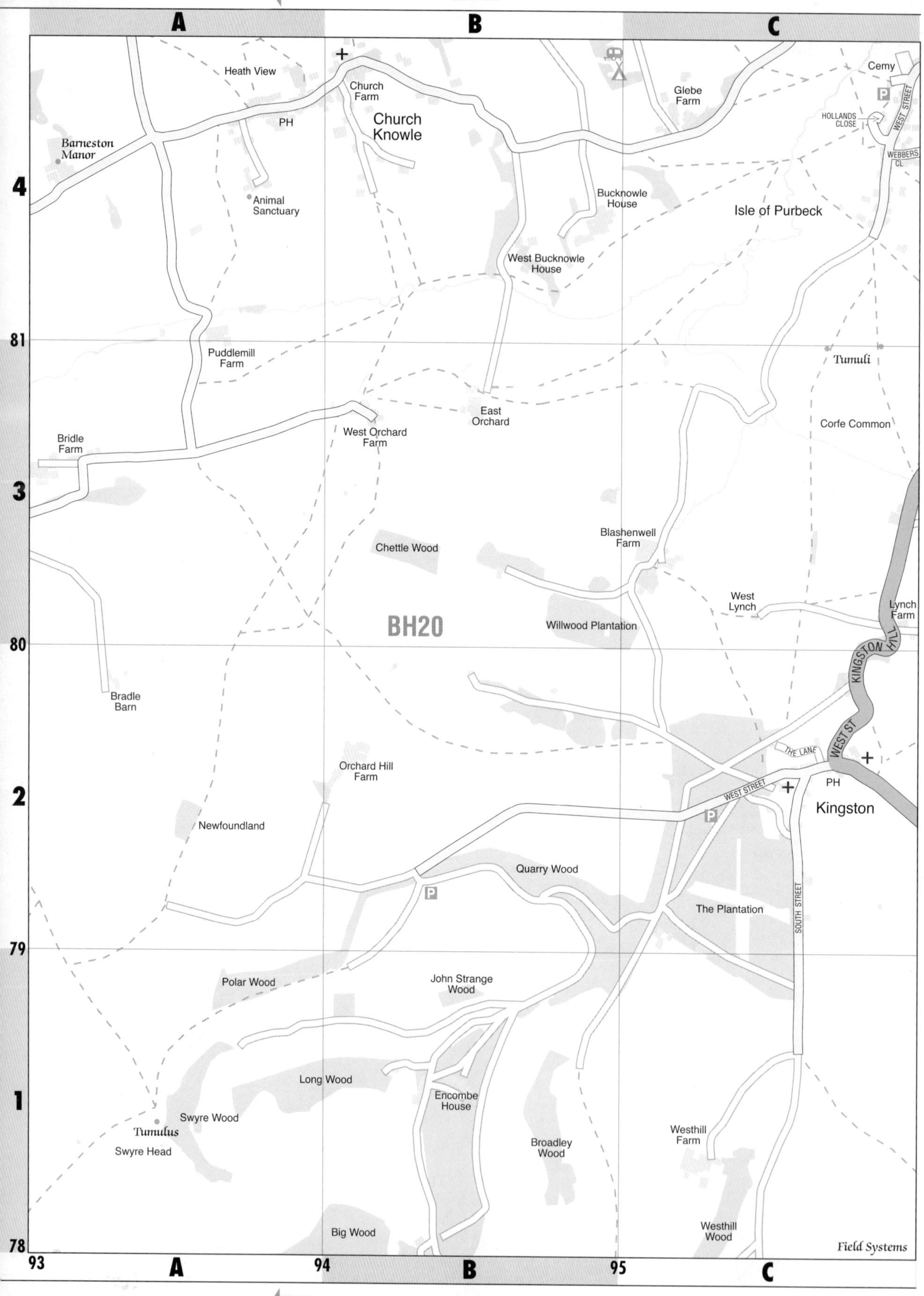

A B C

Heath View

Church Farm

Church Knowle

PH

Barneston Manor

Animal Sanctuary

Glebe Farm

Bucknowle House

Isle of Purbeck

Cemy

HOLLANDS CLOSE

WEBBERS CL

West Bucknowle House

4

81

Puddlemill Farm

Tumuli

Corfe Common

West Orchard Farm

East Orchard

Bridle Farm

Chettle Wood

Blashenwell Farm

3

West Lynch

Lynch Farm

Willwood Plantation

BH20

80

Bradle Barn

Orchard Hill Farm

THE LANE

WEST ST

KINGSTON

Newfoundland

WEST STREET

Kingston

PH

2

Quarry Wood

The Plantation

SOUTH STREET

79

Polar Wood

John Strange Wood

Long Wood

Encombe House

Westhill Farm

1

Swyre Wood

Broadley Wood

Tumulus

Swyre Head

Big Wood

Westhill Wood

Field Systems

78

93 A 94 B 95 C

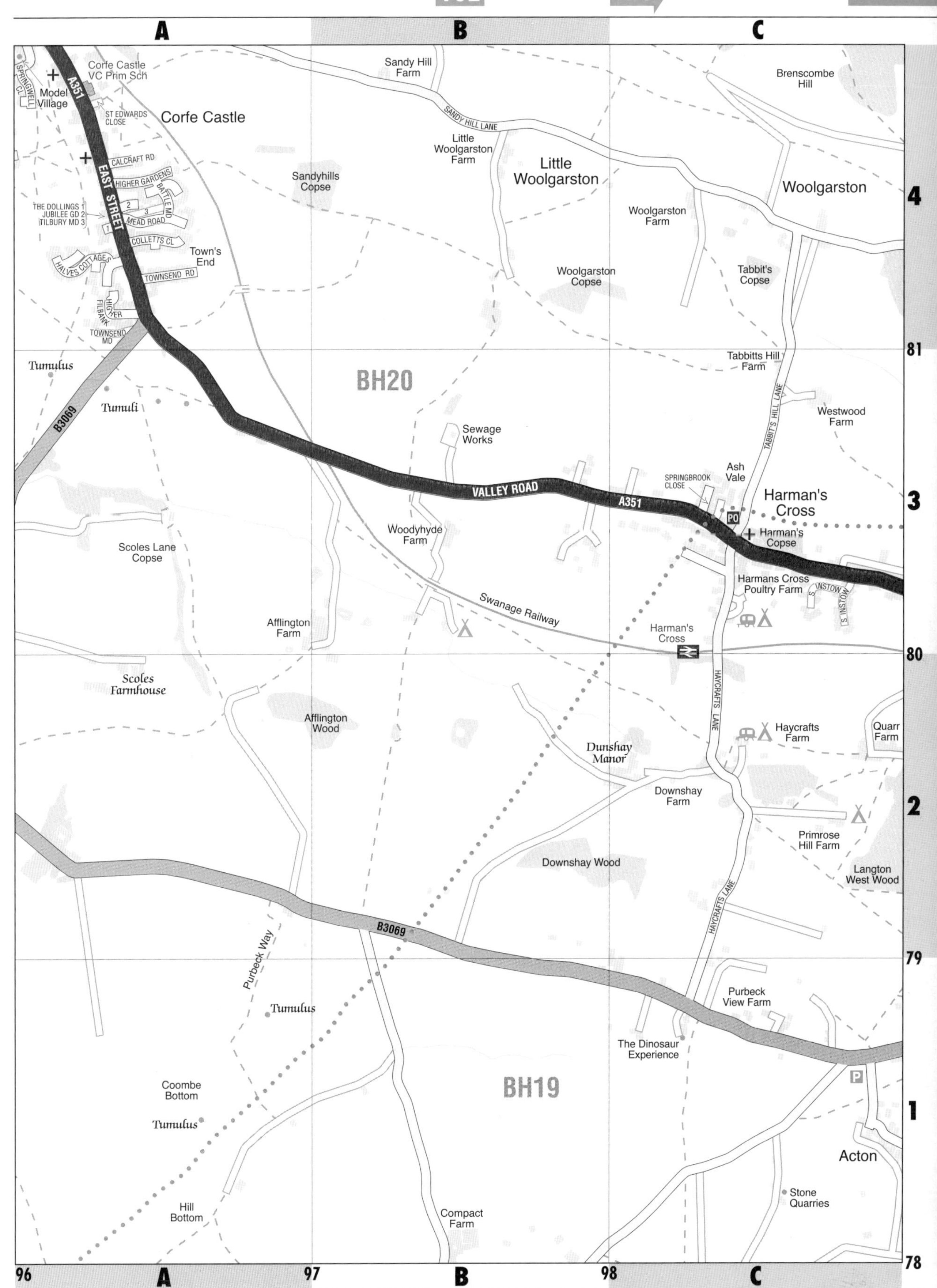

A

B

C

Corfe Castle VC Prim Sch

Model Village

St Edwards Close

Corfe Castle

CALCRAFT RD

HIGHER GARDENS

THE DOLLINGS 1
JUBILEE GD 2
TILBURY MD 3

BAFFTE MD

MEAD ROAD

COLLETTS CL

Town's End

TOWNSEND RD

HALVES COTTAGES

HIGH VER
FILBANK

TOWNSEND MD

A351

EAST STREET

Sandy Hill Farm

SANDY HILL LANE

Little Woolgarston Farm

Little Woolgarston

Sandyhills Copse

Woolgarston Farm

Woolgarston Copse

Brenscombe Hill

Woolgarston

Tabbit's Copse

4

Tumulus

Tumuli

B3069

BH20

Sewage Works

Tabbitts Hill Farm

TABBIT'S HILL LANE

Westwood Farm

81

Ash Vale

SPRINGBROOK CLOSE

VALLEY ROAD

A351

PO

Harman's Cross

Harman's Copse

3

Scoles Lane Copse

Woodyhyde Farm

Swanage Railway

Harmans Cross Poultry Farm

INSTOW

Afflington Farm

Harman's Cross

80

Scoles Farmhouse

Afflington Wood

Dunshay Manor

Downshay Farm

HAYCRAFTS LANE

Haycrafts Farm

Quarr Farm

Primrose Hill Farm

Langton West Wood

2

Downshay Wood

Purbeck Way

B3069

79

Tumulus

HAYCRAFTS LANE

Purbeck View Farm

Coombe Bottom

BH19

The Dinosaur Experience

P

Tumulus

1

Acton

Hill Bottom

Compact Farm

Stone Quarries

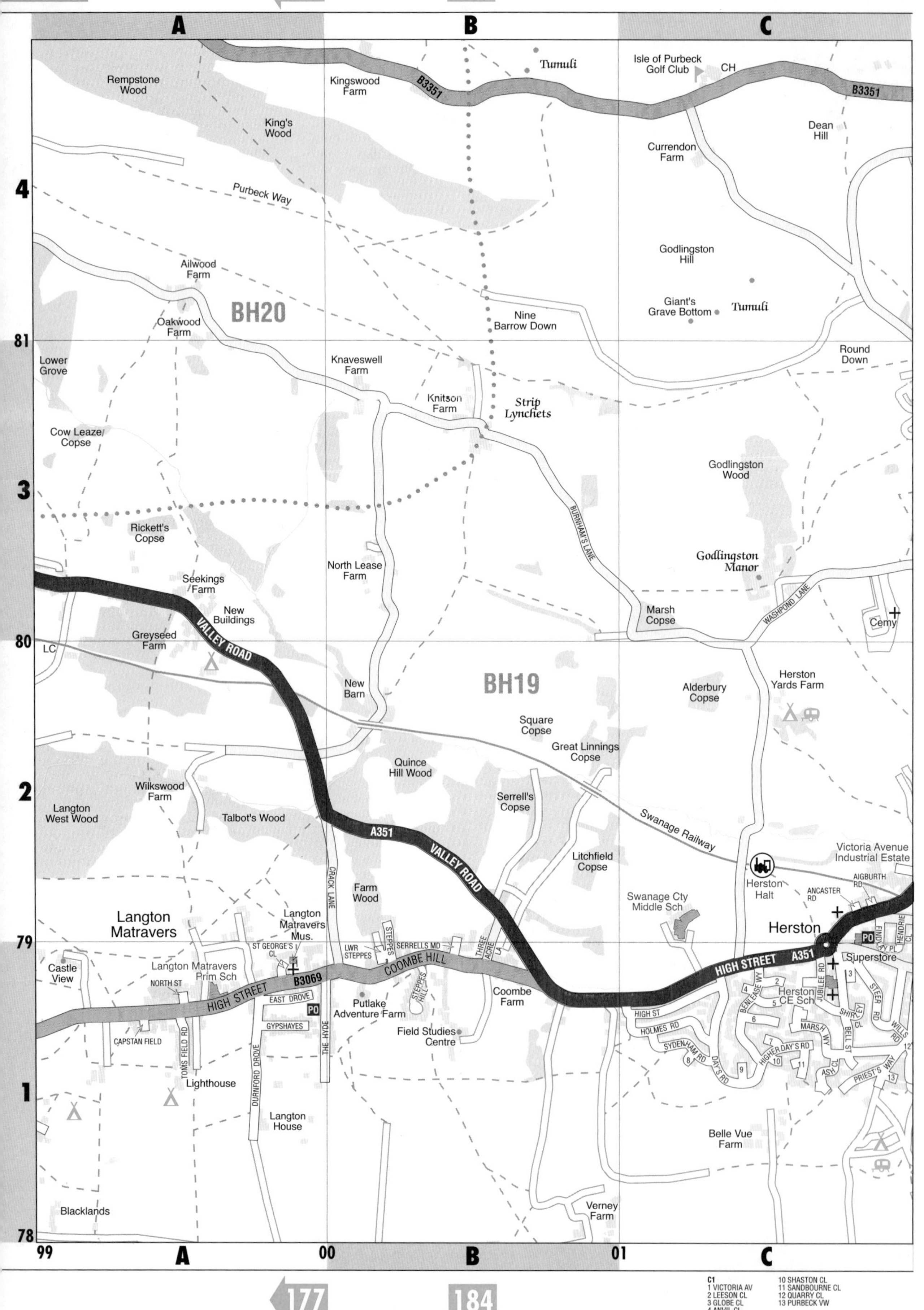

C1
1 VICTORIA AV
2 LEESON CL
3 GLOBE CL
4 ANVIL CL
5 ALDERBURY CL
6 KINGSWOOD CL
7 SHOTTSFORD CL
8 BAY VIEW
9 CASTERBRIDGE CL
10 SHASTON CL
11 SANDBOURNE CL
12 QUARRY CL
13 PURBECK VW

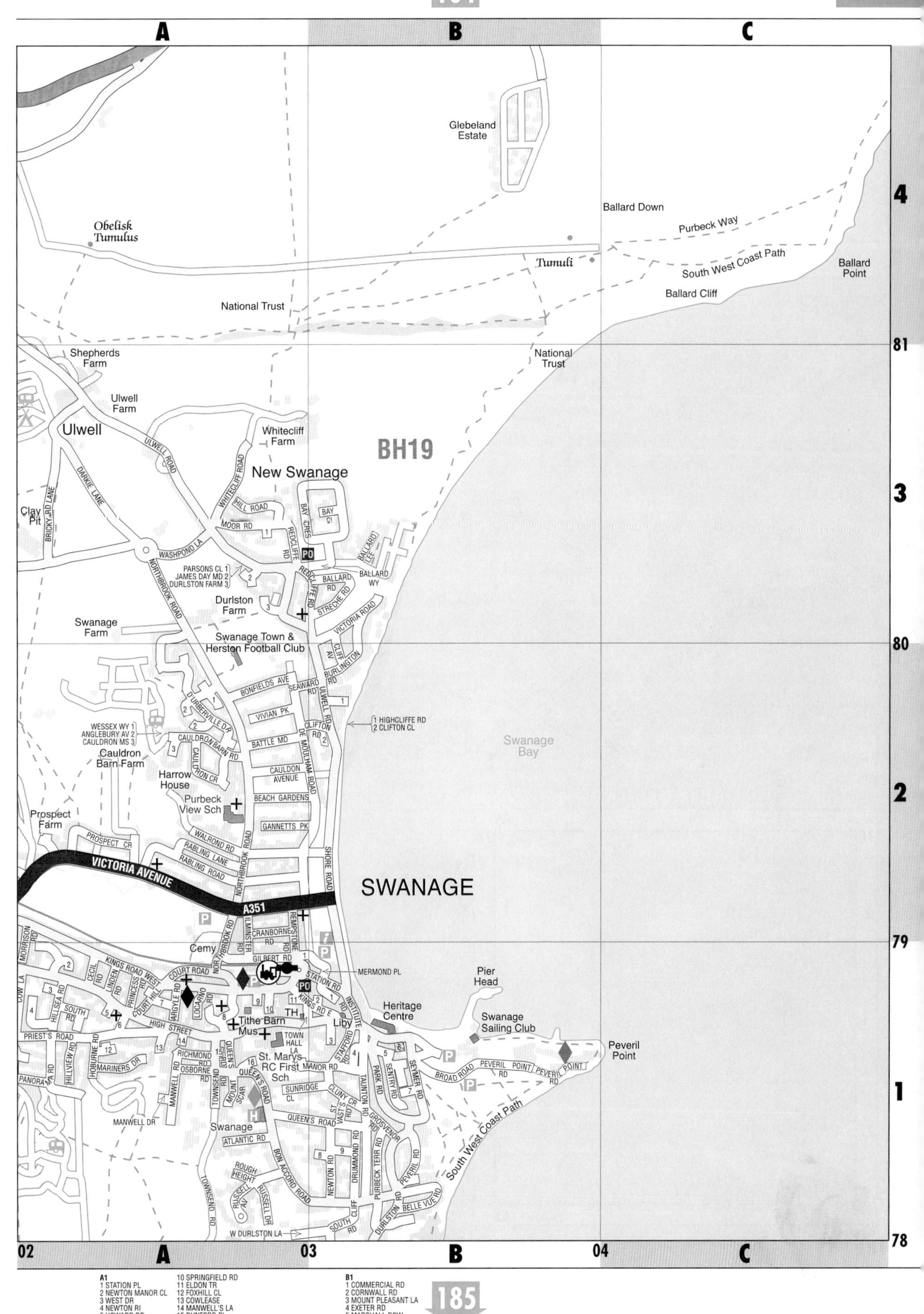

4

81

3

80

2

79

1

78

Glebeland
Estate

Obelisk
Tumulus

Ballard Down

Purbeck Way

Tumuli

South West Coast Path

Ballard Cliff

Ballard
Point

National Trust

National
Trust

Shepherds
Farm

Ulwell
Farm

Whitecliff
Farm

Ulwell

BH19

New Swanage

Clay
Pit

BRICKYARD LANE

DARKIE LANE

ULWELL ROAD

WHITECLIFF ROAD

HILL ROAD

MOOR RD

WASHPOND LA

NORTHBROOK ROAD

BAY
CRES

BAY
CL

REDCLIFFE RD

BALLARD
LEE

PARSONS CL 1
JAMES DAY MD 2
DURLSTON FARM 3

BALLARD
RD

STRECHE RD

BALLARD
WY

Durlston
Farm

VICTORIA ROAD

Swanage
Farm

Swanage Town &
Herston Football Club

CLIFF
AV

BURLINGTON

BONFIELDS AVE

SEAWARD
RD

ULWELL RD

VIVIAN PK

DE MOULHAM ROAD

CLIFTON
RD

1 HIGHCLIFFE RD
2 CLIFTON CL

WESSEX WY 1
ANGLEBURY AV 2
CAULDRON MS 3

DURBERVILLE DR

CAULDRON BARN RD

BATTLE MD

Cauldron
Barn Farm

CAULDRON CR

CAULDON
AVENUE

Swanage
Bay

Harrow
House

BEACH GARDENS

Prospect
Farm

Purbeck
View Sch

WALROND RD

NORTHBROOK ROAD

GANNETTS PK

PROSPECT CR

RABLING LANE

RABLING ROAD

SHORE ROAD

SWANAGE

VICTORIA AVENUE

A351

P

ELMINSTER

CRANBORNE
RD

REMPSTONE
RD

i

P

Cemy

KINGS ROAD WEST

COURT ROAD

GILBERT RD

STATION RD

MERMOND PL

Pier
Head

MORRISON

CECIL

PRINCESS RD

ARGYLE RD

LOCARNO

NORTHBROOK ROAD

KINGS RD E

INSTITUTE RD

PO

Heritage
Centre

Swanage
Sailing Club

Peveril
Point

LOW LA

LINDEN RD

HIGH STREET

STAFFORD RD

BROAD ROAD

PEVERIL POINT
RD

PEVERIL
POINT

HOBORNE RD

HILLSEA
RD

SOUTH
RD

Tithe Barn
Mus

TH

Liby

SEYMER RD

PRIEST'S RD

HILLVIEW RD

MARINERS DR

MANWELL RD

OSBORNE

RICHMOND
RD

TOWNSEND RD

TOWN
HALL

St. Marys
RC First
Sch

MANOR RD

TAUNTON RD

CLUNY CR

VAST'S RD

SENTRY RD

GROSVENOR RD

South West Coast Path

PANORA

MANWELL DR

Swanage

MOUNT
SCAR

H

ATLANTIC RD

QUEEN'S ROAD

SUNRIDGE
CL

NEWTON RD

DRUMMOND RD

PURBECK TERR RD

PEVERIL RD

ROUGH
HEIGHT

BON ACCORD ROAD

RUSSELL
AV

RUSSELL DR

SOUTH
CLIFF

DURLSTON RD

BELLE VUE RD

W DURLSTON LA

A4
1 BEACHVIEW CL
2 JASMINE WY
3 CUNNINGHAM CL
4 FOSSETT WY
5 WESTHILL CL

B4
1 LANEHOUSE ROCKS RD
2 WYKE RD
3 LYMES CL
4 CHURCHILL CL
5 SWAFFIELD GD
6 MARTLEAVES CL

7 BELFIELD PK DR
8 BUXTON CL
9 BELFIELD CL
10 CARRINGTON CL
11 HILLBOURNE RD
12 DOWNCLOSE

C4
1 CROSS RD
2 CONNAUGHT RD

A   B   C

Little Bridge Farm

B3157

Mast

Church Knap

BOULTON CL

Belfield Park Ave

BUXTON ROAD

Southlands

Western Ledges

PORTLAND ROAD

PO

All Saints CE Sch

Liby

Wyke Regis Inf Sch

Wyke Regis

Sandsfoot Castle

Wyke Regis CE Jun Sch

A354

DT4

Wyke Regis Community & Sports Centre

LESSINGHAM AV

South West Coast Path

4

77

Nature Reserve

Chesil Beach Holiday Village

1 KINGFISHER CL
2 AVOCET CL
3 WHITEHEAD DR
4 SMALLMOUTH CL
5 FERRYMANS WY

3

PH

PORTLAND RD

Small Mouth

Ferry Bridge

Boat Yard

76

Chesil Beach

West Bay

Chesil Beach Visitor Centre

P

2

64   65

78   DT3   78

PORTLAND BEACH ROAD

Parasite Academy

DT4

75

A354

1

Works

77   77

DT5

74

64   65

65   A   66   B   67   C

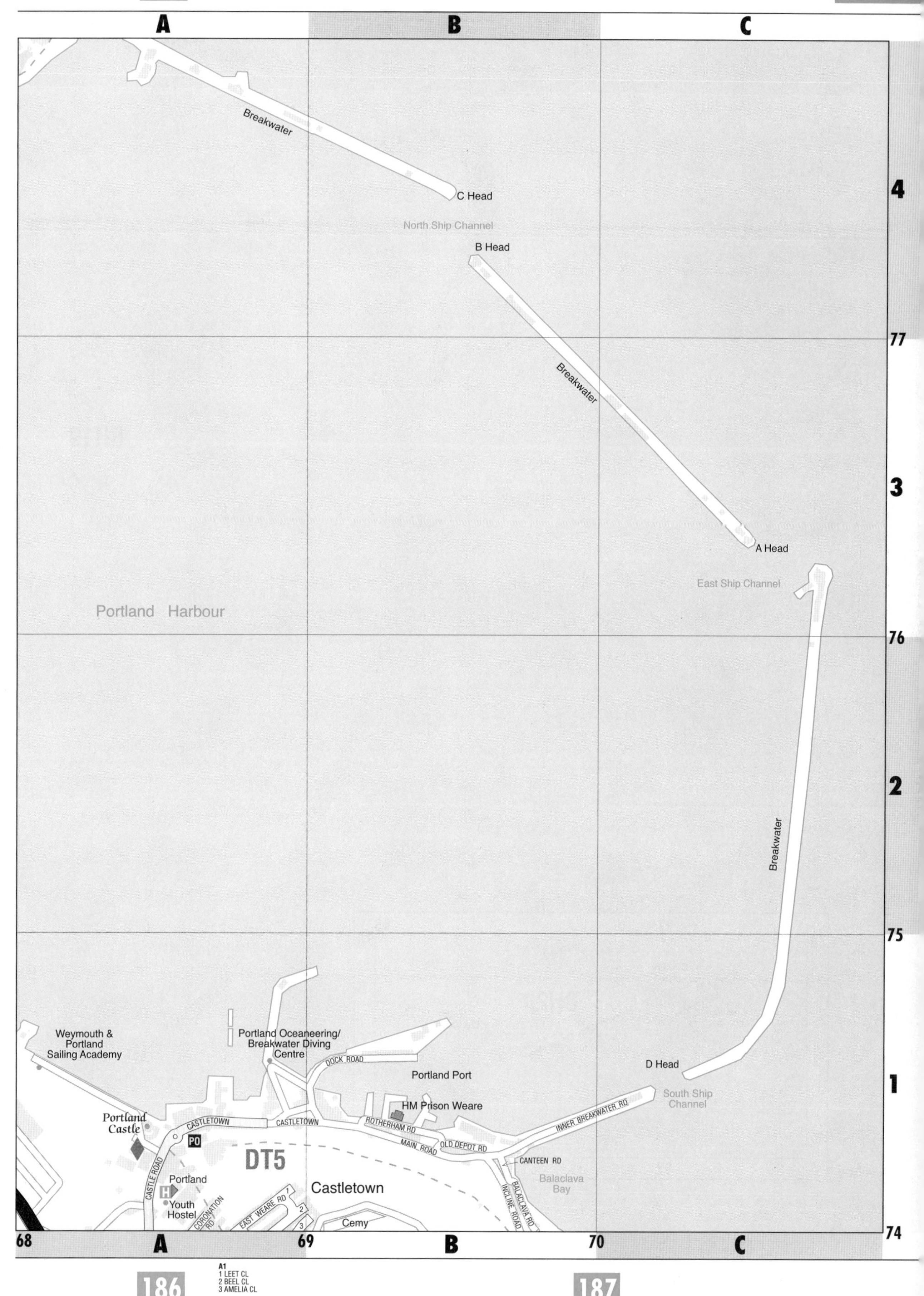

A   B   C

Breakwater

C Head

North Ship Channel

B Head

Breakwater

4

77

3

A Head

East Ship Channel

Portland Harbour

76

Breakwater

2

75

Weymouth & Portland Sailing Academy

Portland Oceaneering/ Breakwater Diving Centre

DOCK ROAD

Portland Port

HM Prison Weare

D Head

South Ship Channel

1

Portland Castle

CASTLETOWN

CASTLETOWN

ROTHERHAM RD

OLD DEPOT RD

INNER BREAKWATER RD

CASTLE ROAD

PO

MAIN ROAD

CANTEEN RD

BALACLAVA RD

INCLINE ROAD

DT5

Castletown

Balaclava Bay

Portland Youth Hostel

CORONATION RD

EAST WEARE RD

2

3

Cemy

74

68   A   69   B   70   C

A1
1 LEET CL
2 BEEL CL
3 AMELIA CL

176

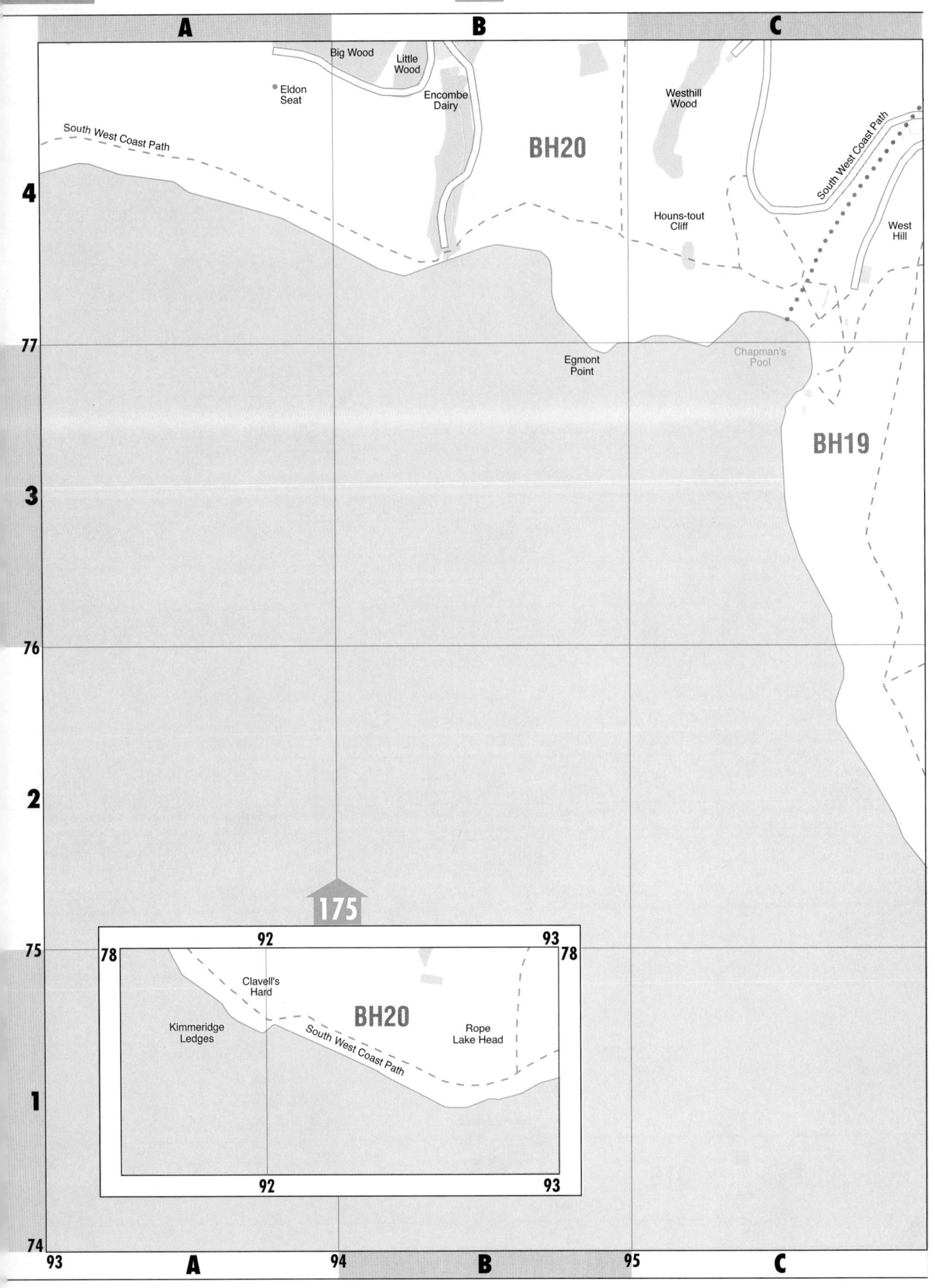

A   B   C

Big Wood

Little Wood

Eldon Seat

Encombe Dairy

BH20

Westhill Wood

South West Coast Path

Houns-tout Cliff

West Hill

South West Coast Path

4

77

Egmont Point

Chapman's Pool

BH19

3

76

2

175

75

92   93

78   78

Clavell's Hard

BH20

Kimmeridge Ledges

Rope Lake Head

South West Coast Path

1

92   93

74

93   A   94   B   95   C

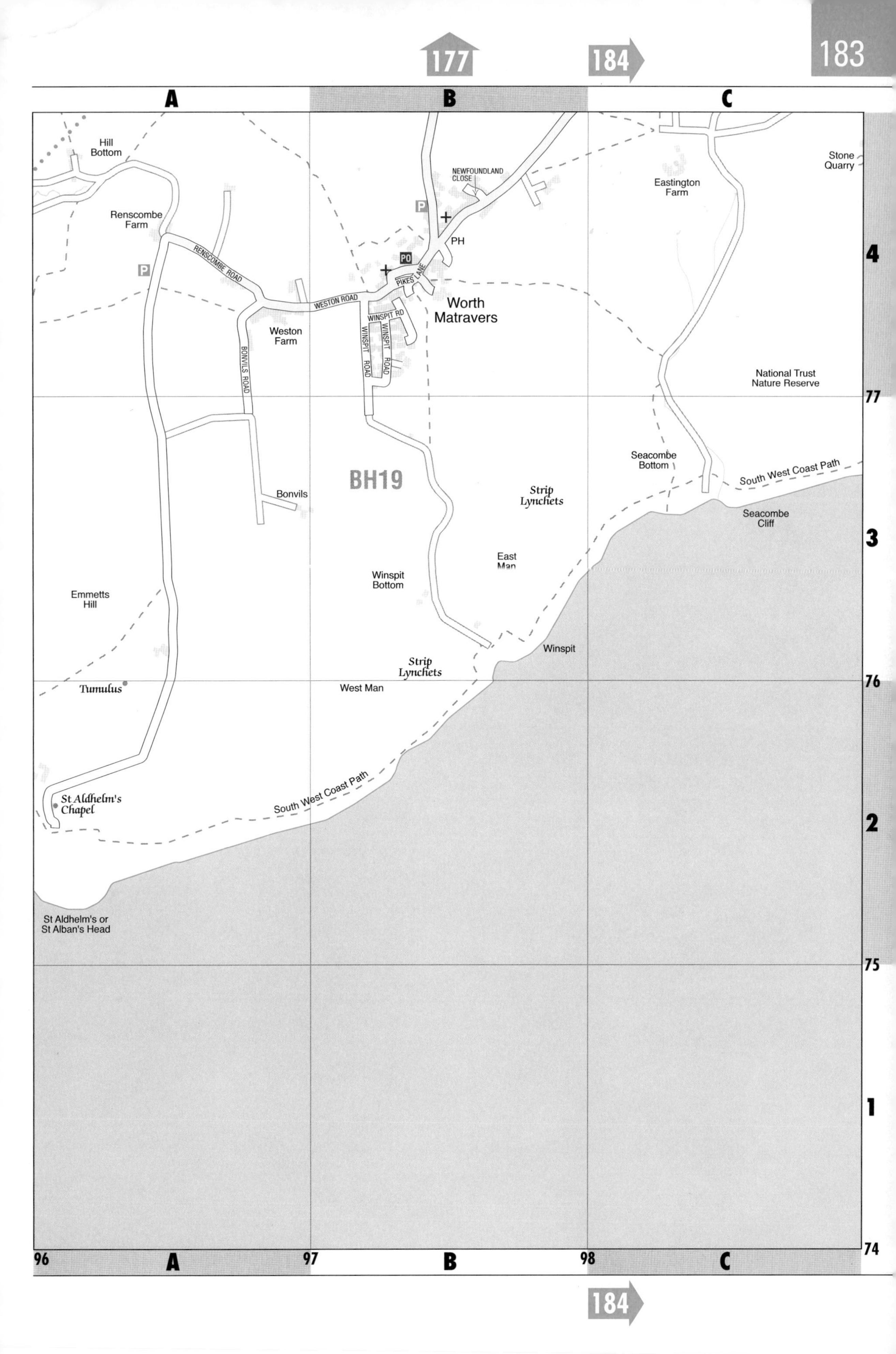

A
B
C

Hill Bottom

Renscombe Farm

NEWFOUNDLAND CLOSE

Eastington Farm

Stone Quarry

P

RENSCOMBE ROAD

P

PO

PH

4

Weston Farm

WESTON ROAD

PIKES LANE

Worth Matravers

WINSPIT RD

BONVILS ROAD

WINSPIT ROAD

WINSPIT ROAD

National Trust Nature Reserve

77

Bonvils

BH19

Seacombe Bottom

South West Coast Path

Strip Lynchets

Seacombe Cliff

3

Emmetts Hill

Winspit Bottom

East Man

Strip Lynchets

Winspit

76

Tumulus

West Man

South West Coast Path

St Aldhelm's Chapel

South West Coast Path

2

St Aldhelm's or St Alban's Head

75

1

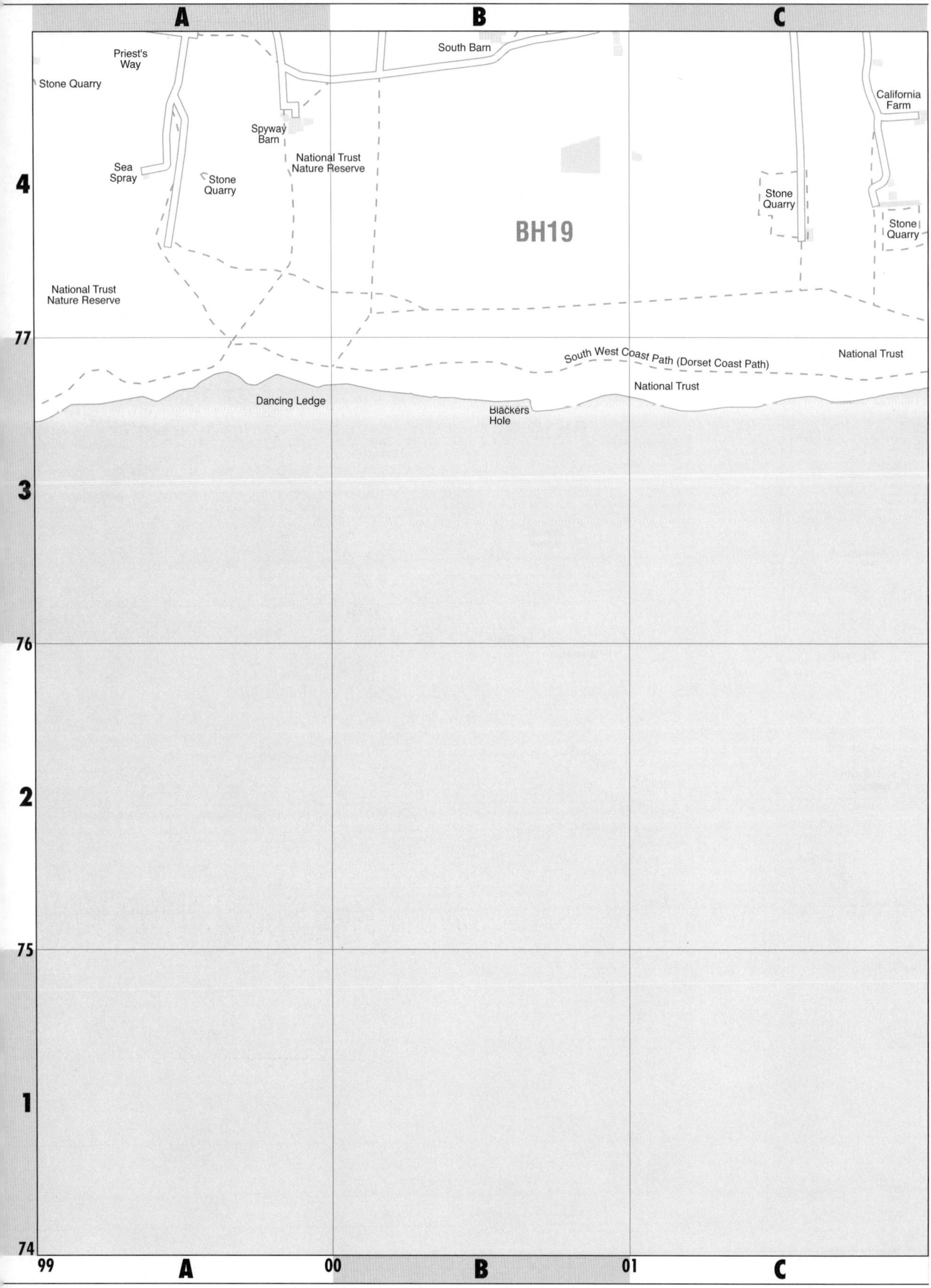

A

B

C

Priest's
Way

Stone Quarry

South Barn

California
Farm

Spyway
Barn

Sea
Spray

Stone
Quarry

National Trust
Nature Reserve

4

Stone
Quarry

BH19

Stone
Quarry

National Trust
Nature Reserve

77

South West Coast Path (Dorset Coast Path)

National Trust

Dancing Ledge

Blackers
Hole

National Trust

3

76

2

75

1

74

99

A

00

B

01

C

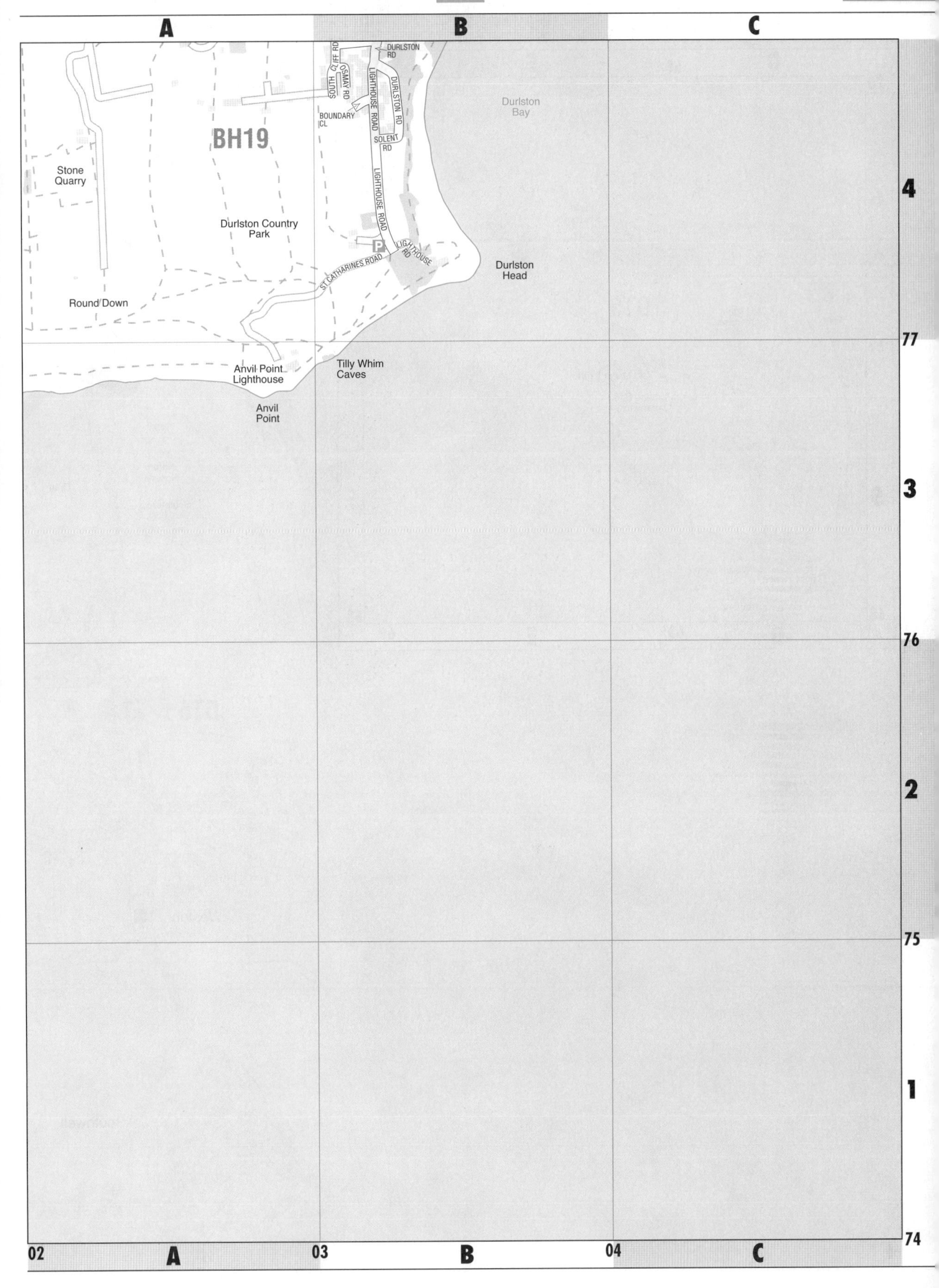

A

B

C

Stone
Quarry

SOUTH CLIFF RD

OSMAY RD

DURLSTON
RD

DURLSTON RD

LIGHTHOUSE ROAD

BOUNDARY
CL

SOLENT
RD

Durlston
Bay

BH19

Durlston Country
Park

LIGHTHOUSE ROAD

LIGHTHOUSE
RD

Round Down

P

LIGHTHOUSE

ST CATHARINES ROAD

Durlston
Head

Anvil Point
Lighthouse

Tilly Whim
Caves

Anvil
Point

4

77

3

76

2

75

1

74

02

A

03

B

04

C

180

181

A   B   C

D   68   E   69

70   70

4   6   6

Parrys Dive Centre & Sch

Chesil

CHISWELL

FORTUNESWELL

HIGH ST   A354   A354

Liby   P

Brackenbury Cty Infs Sch

Chesil Cove

Underhill Junior Sch

Wallsend Cove

Field System

DT5

Old Higher Lighthouse

PORTLAND BILL RD

Cave Hole

FORTUNESWELL

NEW ROAD

Hotel

PRIORY RD

YEATE'S ROAD

73   69   69

Old Lower Light

Portland Bird Observatory

West Weare

West Cliff

Tout Quarry Nature Reserve

Quarry

PH

Sculpture Park

WIDE STREET

3   5   5

Clay Ope

TRADECROFT

P

Pulpit Rock   Trinity House Lighthouse   Visitor Centre

Bill of Portland

Cemy

Royal Manor Sch

REFORNE

GROSVENOR ROAD

CHANNEL VW RD

72   D   68   E   69   68

DT5

WESTON ROAD

BLINDMERE RD

PARK ESTATE

HAMCROFT

POUND

PIECE

GREENWAYS

FURLANDS

St. Georges Cty Inf Sch

2   2

ROAD

CROFT

ROAD

Blacknor

WOOLCOMBE RD

COURTLANDS

COURTLANDS RD

BLACKNOR RD.

WESTCLIFF RD

Mutton Cove

FOUR

ISLE RD

GYPSY LA

Weston   PO

71   71

REAP LANE

AVALANCHE ROAD

1   1

RIP CFF

LONGSTONE

Southwell Prim Sch

W. WOOLS RD

BOWN HILL

WHEATLAN

MD BOWER

Southwell

CHURCH RD

SWEET HILL LANE

UNDERLEDGE

CLIFF WAY   SOUTH WAY   WEST WAY   SWEET HILL RD

70   70

66   A   67   B   68   C

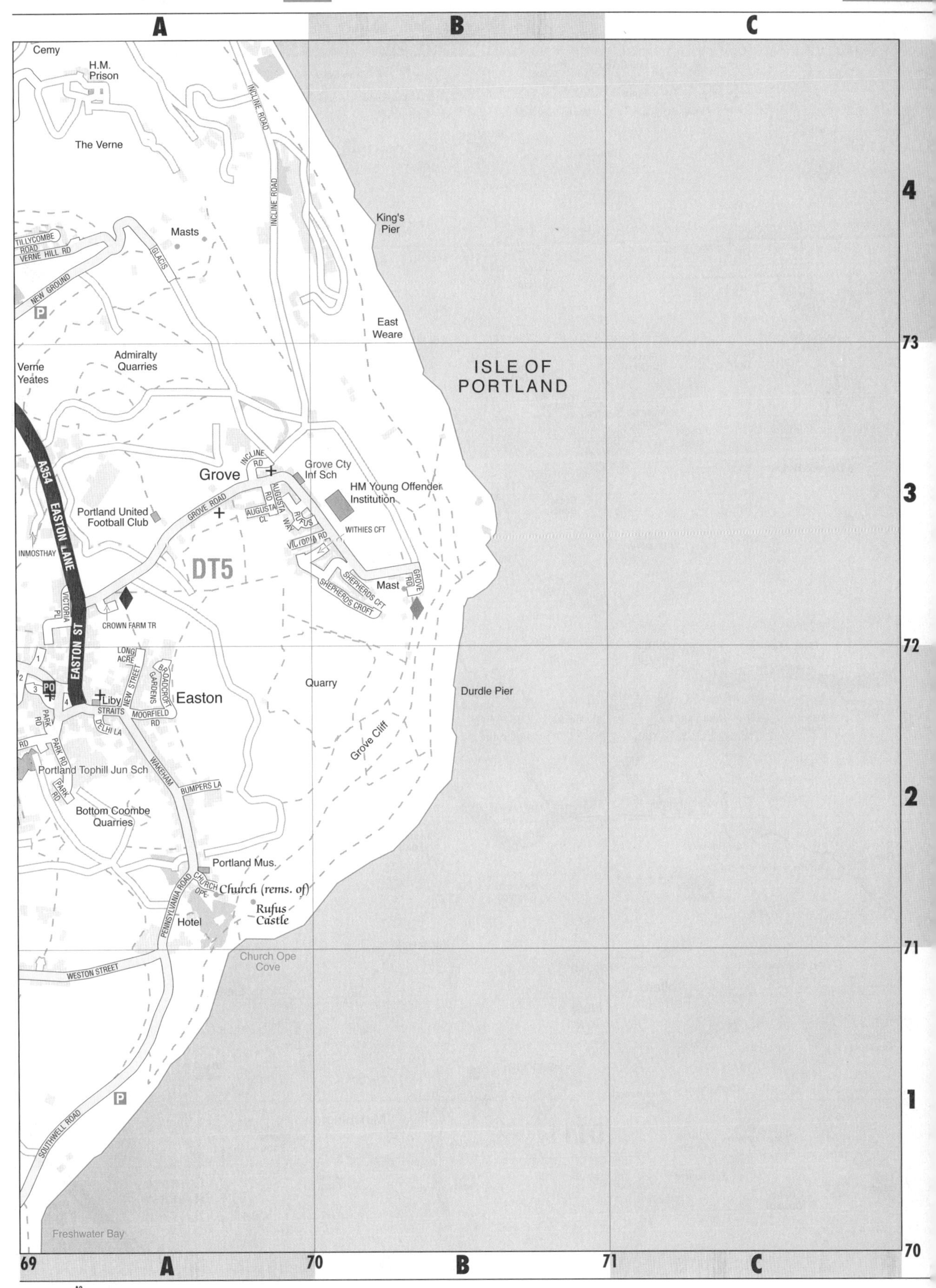

A
B
C

Cemy

H.M. Prison

The Verne

Masts

King's Pier

East Weare

4

73

TILLYCOMBE ROAD
VERNE HILL RD

NEW GROUND

Verne Yeates

Admiralty Quarries

ISLE OF PORTLAND

A354 EASTON LANE

INMOSTHAY

Grove

INCLINE RD

Grove Cty Inf Sch

HM Young Offender Institution

WITHIES CFT

Portland United Football Club

GROVE ROAD

AUGUSTA WAY
AUGUSTA RD
AUGUSTA CL
RUS

VICTORIA RD

GROVE RD

Mast

3

DT5

VICTORIA PL

CROWN FARM TR

SHEPHERDS CFT
SHEPHERDS CROFT

72

EASTON ST

LONG ACRE
NEW STREET
BROADCROFT
GARDENS

PO

Liby

STRAITS
DELHI LA
MOORFIELD RD

Easton

Quarry

Durdle Pier

PARK RD
PARK RD
PARK RD

Portland Tophill Jun Sch

WANGHAM

BUMPERS LA

Grove Cliff

2

Bottom Coombe Quarries

Portland Mus.

CHURCH OPE
PENNSYLVANIA ROAD

Church (rems. of)

Hotel

Rufus Castle

71

WESTON STREET

Church Ope Cove

1

SOUTHWELL ROAD

P

Freshwater Bay

70

69
A
70
B
71
C
70

25

Scale: 1¾ inches to 1 mile

| 0 | ¼ | ½ | mile |
| 0 | 250m | 500m | 750m | 1 km |

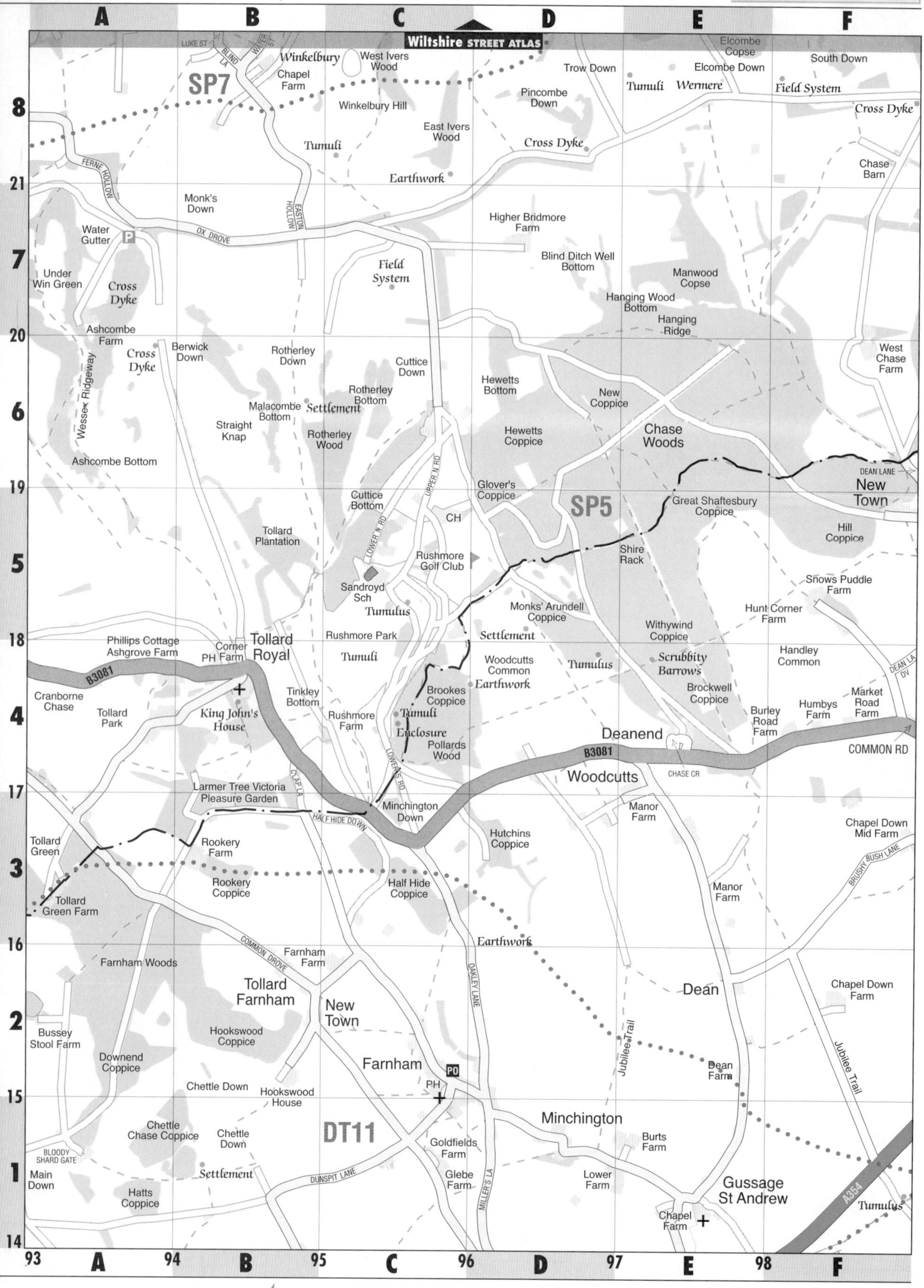

A **B** **C** **D** **E** **F**

Wiltshire STREET ATLAS

8

Luke St
Winkelbury
West Ivers Wood
SP7
Chapel Farm
Trow Down
Elcombe Copse
Elcombe Down
South Down
Tumuli
Wermere
Field System
Winkelbury Hill
East Ivers Wood
Pincombe Down
Cross Dyke

21

Tumuli
FERNE HOLLOW
Earthwork
Cross Dyke
Chase Barn

Monk's Down
OX DROVE
EASTON HOLLOW
Higher Bridmore Farm
Cross Dyke

7

Water Gutter
Field System
Blind Ditch Well Bottom
Manwood Copse
Chase Barn

Under Win Green
Cross Dyke
Hanging Wood Bottom
Hanging Ridge

20

Ashcombe Farm
Berwick Down
Rotherley Down
Cuttice Down
Hewetts Bottom
New Coppice
West Chase Farm

Cross Dyke
Wessex Ridgeway
Malacombe Bottom
Settlement
Rotherley Bottom
Hewetts Coppice
Chase Woods

6

Straight Knap
Rotherley Wood
Hewetts Coppice

Ashcombe Bottom

19

Cuttice Bottom
Glover's Coppice
SP5
Great Shaftesbury Coppice
DEAN LANE
New Town
Hill Coppice

Tollard Plantation
UPPER N RD
CH
Shire Rack

5

LOWER N RD
Rushmore Golf Club
Snows Puddle Farm

Sandroyd Sch
Tumulus
Monks' Arundell Coppice
Withywind Coppice
Hunt Corner Farm
DEAN LA DV

18

Phillips Cottage
Ashgrove Farm
Tollard Royal
Rushmore Park
Settlement
Woodcutts Common
Tumulus
Scrubbity Barrows
Handley Common

Corner PH Farm
Tumuli
Earthwork
Brockwell Coppice
Market Road Farm

4

Cranborne Chase
B3081
King John's House
Tinkley Bottom
Brookes Coppice
Deanend
Burley Road Farm
Humbys Farm

Tollard Park
Rushmore Farm
Tumuli
Enclosure
Pollards Wood
B3081
Woodcutts
CHASE CR
COMMON RD

17

Larmer Tree Victoria Pleasure Garden
CLAP LA
HALF HIDE DOWN
Minchington Down
Manor Farm
Chapel Down Mid Farm

Tollard Green
LOWER S RD
Hutchins Coppice
BRUSH BUSH LANE

3

Rookery Farm
Manor Farm

Tollard Green Farm
Rookery Coppice
Half Hide Coppice
Earthwork
Dean

16

COMMON DROVE
Farnham Farm
OAKLEY LANE
Chapel Down Farm

Farnham Woods
Tollard Farnham
New Town
Dean

2

Bussey Stool Farm
Hookswood Coppice
Farnham
Jubilee Trail
Dean Farm
Jubilee Trail

Downend Coppice
PO

15

Chettle Down
Hookswood House
PH
Minchington
Burts Farm

BLOODY SHARD GATE
DT11
Goldfields Farm
Gussage St Andrew
A354

1

Main Down
Chettle Chase Coppice
Chettle Down
Settlement
DUNSPIT LANE
Glebe Farm
MILLER S LA
Lower Farm
Tumulus

Hatts Coppice
Chapel Farm

14

93 **A** 94 **B** 95 **C** 96 **D** 97 **E** 98 **F**

39

200

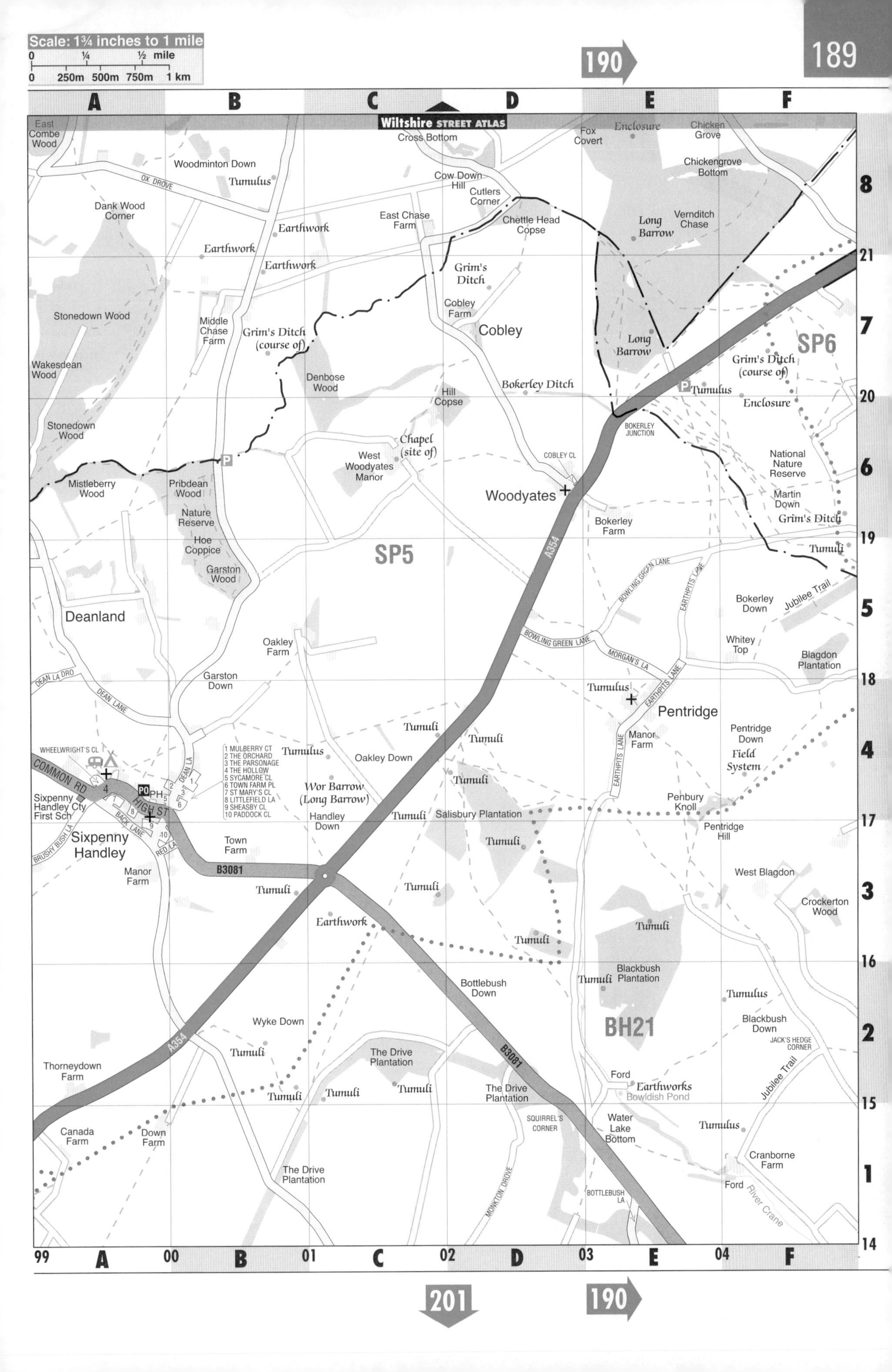
Scale: 1¾ inches to 1 mile
0 ¼ ½ mile
0 250m 500m 750m 1 km
190
Wiltshire STREET ATLAS
East Combe Wood
Cross Bottom
Fox Covert
Enclosure
Chicken Grove
Woodminton Down
OX DROVE
Tumulus
Cow Down Hill
Cutlers Corner
Chickengrove Bottom
Dank Wood Corner
East Chase Farm
Chettle Head Copse
Earthwork
Earthwork
Earthwork
Long Barrow
Vernditch Chase
Grim's Ditch
Cobley Farm
Cobley
Stonedown Wood
Middle Chase Farm
Grim's Ditch (course of)
Long Barrow
SP6
Grim's Ditch (course of)
Wakesdean Wood
Denbose Wood
Bokerley Ditch
Tumulus
Enclosure
Hill Copse
Stonedown Wood
BOKERLEY JUNCTION
Chapel (site of)
West Woodyates Manor
COBLEY CL
National Nature Reserve
Mistleberry Wood
Pribdean Wood
Woodyates
Martin Down
Nature Reserve
Hoe Coppice
Bokerley Farm
Grim's Ditch
SP5
Tumuli
A354
Garston Wood
BOWLING GREEN LANE
EARTHPITS LANE
Bokerley Down
Jubilee Trail
Deanland
Oakley Farm
BOWLING GREEN LANE
Whitey Top
MORGAN'S LA
Blagdon Plantation
DEAN LA DRO
Garston Down
Tumulus
EARTHPITS LANE
DEAN LANE
Pentridge
Tumuli
Tumuli
Pentridge Down
Manor Farm
WHEELWRIGHT'S CL
DEAN LA
1 MULBERRY CT
2 THE ORCHARD
3 THE PARSONAGE
4 THE HOLLOW
5 SYCAMORE CL
6 TOWN FARM PL
7 ST MARY'S CL
8 LITTLEFIELD LA
9 SHEASBY CL
10 PADDOCK CL
Tumulus
Oakley Down
Field System
COMMON RD
Tumuli
Sixpenny Handley Cty First Sch
PO
PH
HIGH ST
Wor Barrow (Long Barrow)
EARTHPITS LANE
Penbury Knoll
BACK LANE
BRUSHY BUSH LA
Handley Down
Tumuli
Salisbury Plantation
Pentridge Hill
Sixpenny Handley
RED LA
Town Farm
Tumuli
Manor Farm
B3081
West Blagdon
Tumuli
Tumuli
Crockerton Wood
Earthwork
Tumuli
Tumuli
Bottlebush Down
Tumuli
Blackbush Plantation
Tumulus
Wyke Down
BH21
Blackbush Down
A354
JACK'S HEDGE CORNER
Tumuli
The Drive Plantation
B3081
Thorneydown Farm
Ford
Earthworks
Jubilee Trail
Tumuli
Tumuli
Tumuli
The Drive Plantation
Bowldish Pond
SQUIRREL'S CORNER
Water Lake Bottom
Tumulus
Canada Farm
Down Farm
Cranborne Farm
The Drive Plantation
MONKTON DROVE
BOTTLEBUSH LA
Ford
River Crane
A B C D E F
8 21 7 20 6 19 5 18 4 17 3 16 2 15 1 14
99 00 01 02 03 04

Scale: 1¾ inches to 1 mile
0 ¼ ½ mile
0 250m 500m 750m 1 km

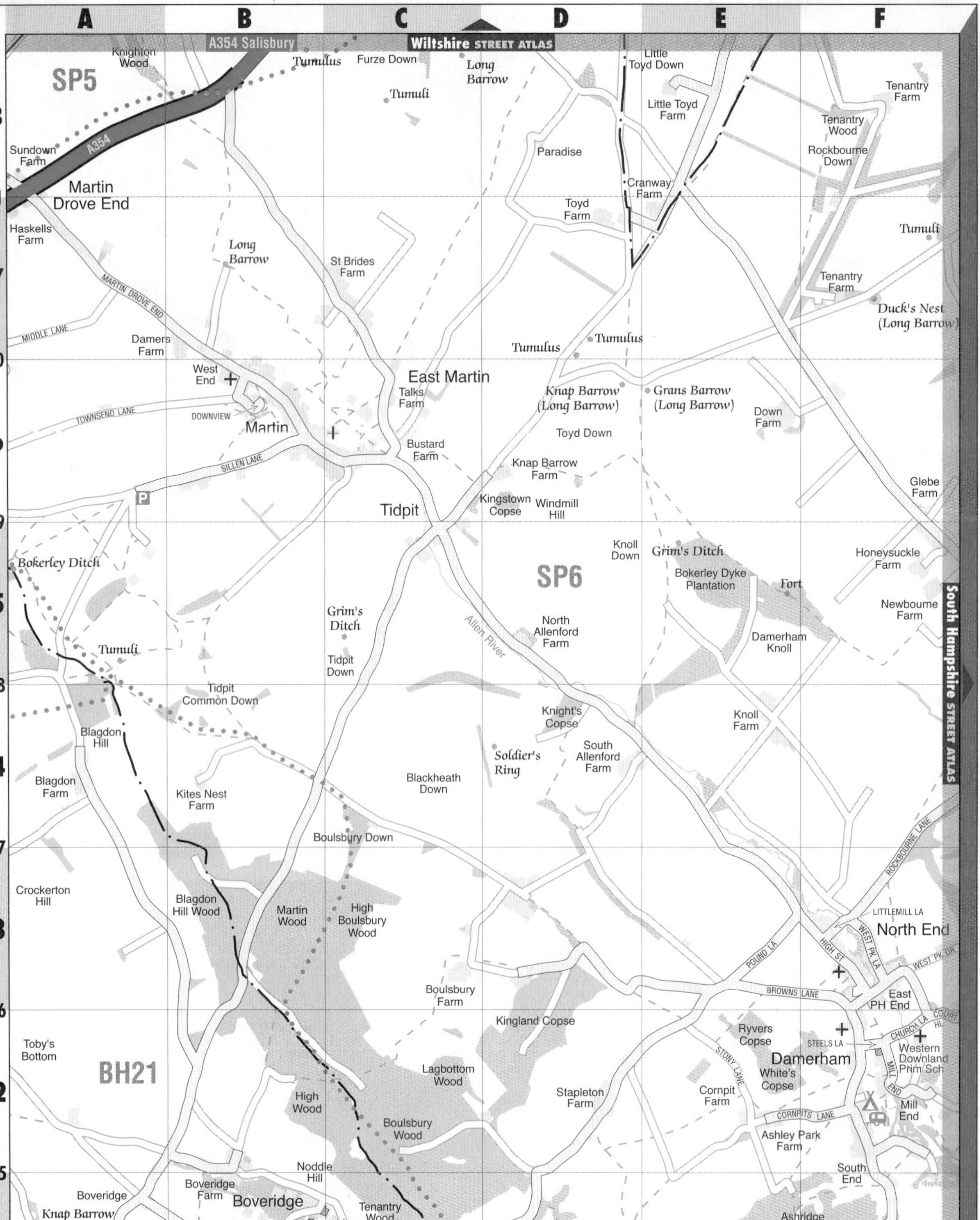

	A	B	C	D	E	F

Wiltshire STREET ATLAS

South Hampshire STREET ATLAS

SP5

A354 Salisbury

Tumulus
Furze Down
Long Barrow
Tumuli
Little Toyd Down
Little Toyd Farm
Tenantry Farm
Tenantry Wood
Rockbourne Down

Sundown Farm
Paradise
Toyd Farm
Cranway Farm

Martin Drove End
A354

Haskells Farm
Long Barrow
St Brides Farm
Tumuli

Tenantry Farm
Duck's Nest (Long Barrow)

MARTIN DROVE END
MIDDLE LANE
Damers Farm
West End
East Martin
Talks Farm
Tumulus
Tumulus
Knap Barrow (Long Barrow)
Grans Barrow (Long Barrow)
Down Farm

TOWNSEND LANE
DOWNVIEW
Martin
Bustard Farm
Toyd Down
Knap Barrow Farm
Glebe Farm

SILLEN LANE
Tidpit
Kingstown Copse
Windmill Hill
Knoll Down
Grim's Ditch
Honeysuckle Farm

P
Bokerley Ditch
Grim's Ditch
SP6
Bokerley Dyke Plantation
Fort
Newbourne Farm

Tumuli
Allen River
North Allenford Farm
Damerham Knoll

Tidpit Down
Tidpit Common Down
Knight's Copse
Knoll Farm

Blagdon Hill
Soldier's Ring
South Allenford Farm

Blagdon Farm
Blackheath Down
Kites Nest Farm
Boulsbury Down

Crockerton Hill
LITTLEMILL LA
North End

Blagdon Hill Wood
Martin Wood
High Boulsbury Wood
POUND LA
HIGH ST
WEST PK LA
WEST PK DR
BROWNS LANE
East PH End

Toby's Bottom
Boulsbury Farm
Kingland Copse
Ryvers Copse
STEELS LA
CHURCH LA COURT HL
Western Downland Prim Sch

BH21
High Wood
Lagbottom Wood
Stapleton Farm
Cornpit Farm
White's Copse
Damerham
Mill End

Boulsbury Wood
CORNPITS LANE
Ashley Park Farm
South End

Noddle Hill
Boveridge Farm
Boveridge
Tenantry Wood
Ashridge Copse

Knap Barrow
Boveridge House Sch
White House Copse

Burwood
Biddlesgate Farm
Hyde Farm
Sinkhole Copse
Pond Copse

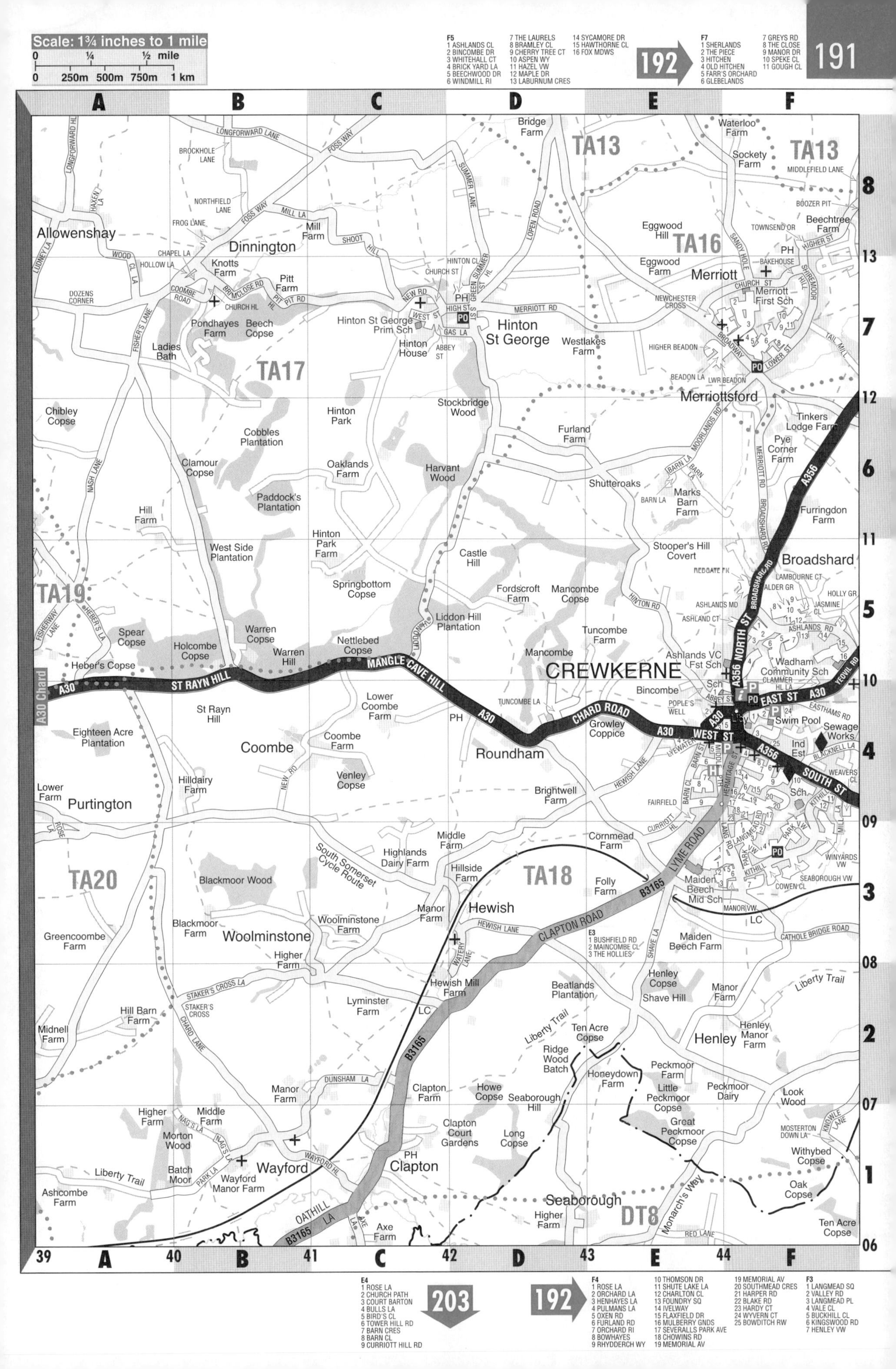

Scale: 1¾ inches to 1 mile
0 ¼ ½ mile
0 250m 500m 750m 1 km

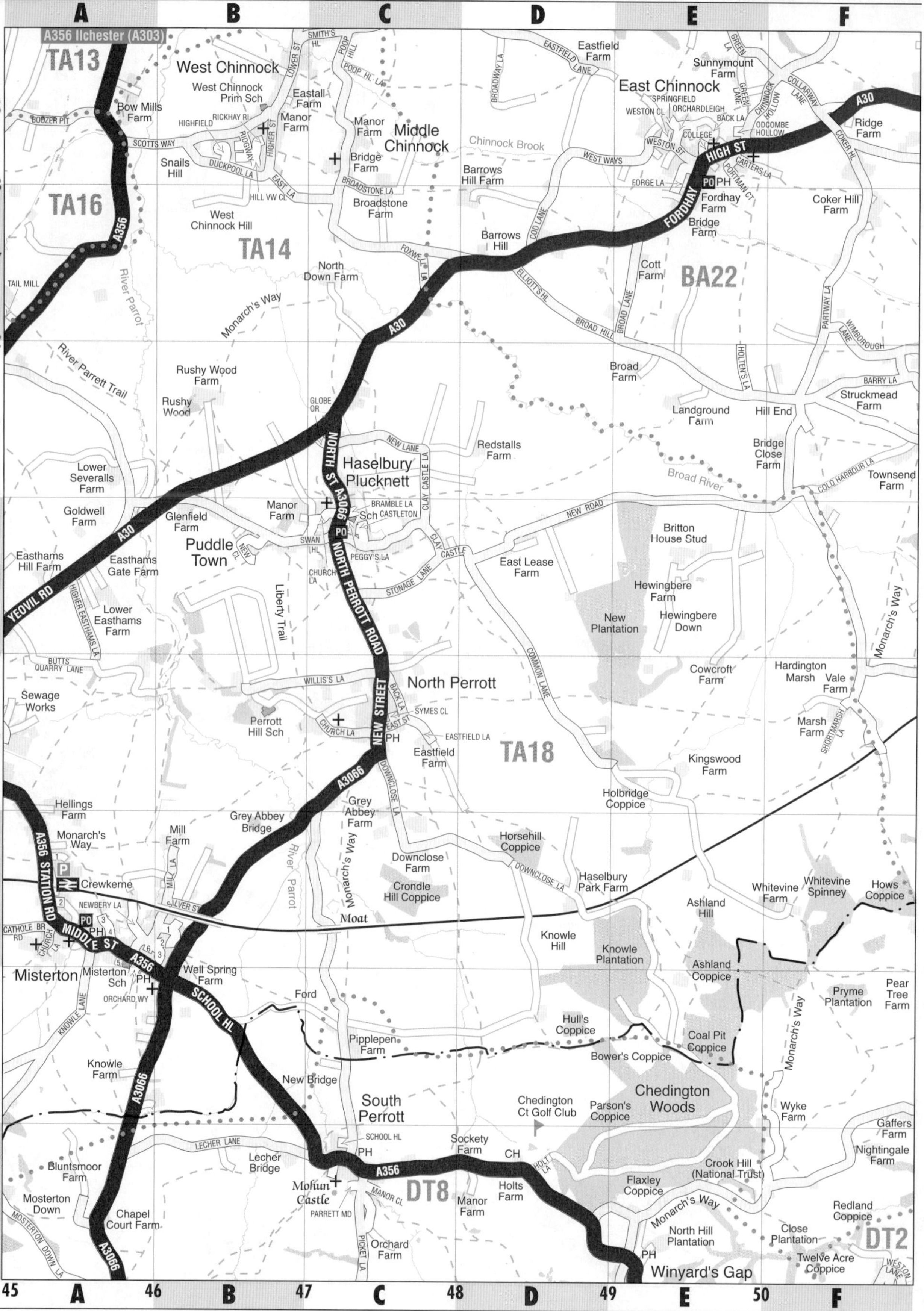

A B C D E F

8
A356 Ilchester (A303)
TA13
West Chinnock
West Chinnock Prim Sch
SMITH'S HL
POOP HILL
POOP HL LA
EASTFIELD LANE
Eastfield Farm
Sunnymount Farm
GREEN LANE
A30
East Chinnock
Springfield
ORCHARDLEIGH
WESTON CL
Back La
COLLARWAY LANE
Bow Mills Farm
BOOZER PIT
SCOTTS WAY
Highfield
RICKHAY RI
Eastall Farm
RICKHAY RI
Manor Farm
Manor Farm
Middle Chinnock
Chinnock Brook
WESTON ST
WEST WAYS
COLLEGE
HIGH ST
ODCOMBE HOLLOW
CHINNOCK HOLLOW
COKER HL
Ridge Farm

13
TA16
Snails Hill
HIGHER ST
DUCKPOOL LA
HILL VW CL
West Chinnock Hill
FOXWE LA
BROADSTONE LA
Broadstone Farm
Barrows Hill Farm
COLD LANE
FORDHAY
PO PH
FORGE LA
Fordhay Farm
Bridge Farm
Coker Hill Farm

7
TA14
North Down Farm
TA14
Barrows Hill
ELLIOTT'S HL
BROAD LANE
BROAD HILL
Cott Farm
BA22
PARTWAY LA
WINDROUGH LA

12
River Parrot
TAIL MILL
River Parrett Trail
Monarch's Way
A30
Broad Farm
Broad River
BARRY LA
Struckmead Farm

6
Lower Severalls Farm
Rushy Wood Farm
Rushy Wood
GLOBE OR
NORTH ST A3066
New Lane
NEW LANE
Redstalls Farm
Landground Farm
Hill End
Bridge Close Farm
HOLTEN'S LA
Townsend Farm
COLD HARBOUR LA

11
Goldwell Farm
A30
Glenfield Farm
Haselbury Plucknett
Manor Farm
BRAMBLE LA
CASTLETON
Sch
CLAY CASTLE LA
NEW ROAD
Britton House Stud

5
Easthams Hill Farm
YEOVIL RD
A30
HIGHER EASTHAMS LA
Easthams Gate Farm
Lower Easthams Farm
Puddle Town
NORTH PERROTT ROAD
SWAN HL
PO
PEGGY'S LA
CHURCH LA
STONAGE LANE
CLAY CASTLE
East Lease Farm
Hewingbere Farm
Hewingbere Down

10
BUTTS QUARRY LANE
Liberty Trail
WILLIS'S LA
New Plantation
Cowcroft Farm
Hardington Marsh
Vale Farm
Monarch's Way

4
Sewage Works
Perrott Hill Sch
CHURCH LA
SYMES CL
PH
North Perrott
BACK LA
EAST ST
EASTFIELD LA
Eastfield Farm
NEW STREET
TA18
COMMON LANE
Kingswood Farm
Holbridge Coppice
Marsh Farm
SHORTMARSH LA

09
Hellings Farm
Monarch's Way
Mill Farm
MILL LA
Grey Abbey Bridge
A3066
Grey Abbey Farm
DOWNCLOSE LA
Horsehill Coppice
Haselbury Park Farm
Whitevine Farm
Whitevine Spinney
Hows Coppice

3
A356 STATION RD
P
Crewkerne
NEWBERY LA
SILVER ST
River Parrot
Downclose Farm
Crondle Hill Coppice
Moat
DOWNCLOSE LA
Knowle Hill
Knowle Plantation
Ashland Hill
Ashland Coppice
Pear Tree Farm

08
CATHOLE BR RD
CHURCH ST
PO
PH
MIDDLE ST
A356
Misterton
Misterton Sch
PH
ORCHARD WY
Well Spring Farm
Ford
Monarch's Way
Pryme Plantation

2
Misterton
Knowle Farm
KNOWLE LANE
SCHOOL HL
A3066
New Bridge
Pipplepen Farm
Hull's Coppice
Bower's Coppice
Coal Pit Coppice
Monarch's Way

07
LECHER LANE
South Perrott
SCHOOL HL
PH
Sockety Farm
CH
Chedington Ct Golf Club
Parson's Coppice
Chedington Woods
Wyke Farm
Gaffers Farm
Nightingale Farm

1
Bluntsmoor Farm
Lecher Bridge
A356
Mohun Castle
PARRETT MD
PICKET LA
MANOR CL
DT8
Manor Farm
HOLT LA
Holts Farm
Flaxley Coppice
Crook Hill (National Trust)
Monarch's Way
North Hill Plantation
Close Plantation
Redland Coppice
DT2

06
Mosterton Down
MOSTERTON DOWN LA
A3066
Chapel Court Farm
Orchard Farm
PH
Winyard's Gap
Twelve Acre Coppice
WESTON LA

45 A 46 B 47 C 48 D 49 E 50 F

A3
1 BRADFORD ROAD
2 BROUGHTONS DRIVE
3 CLARK'S LANE
4 UNITY LANE
5 CLOSE DRIVE
6 THE AVENUE

B3
1 PACKERS' WAY
2 TURNPIKE CLOSE
3 TURNPIKE GREEN

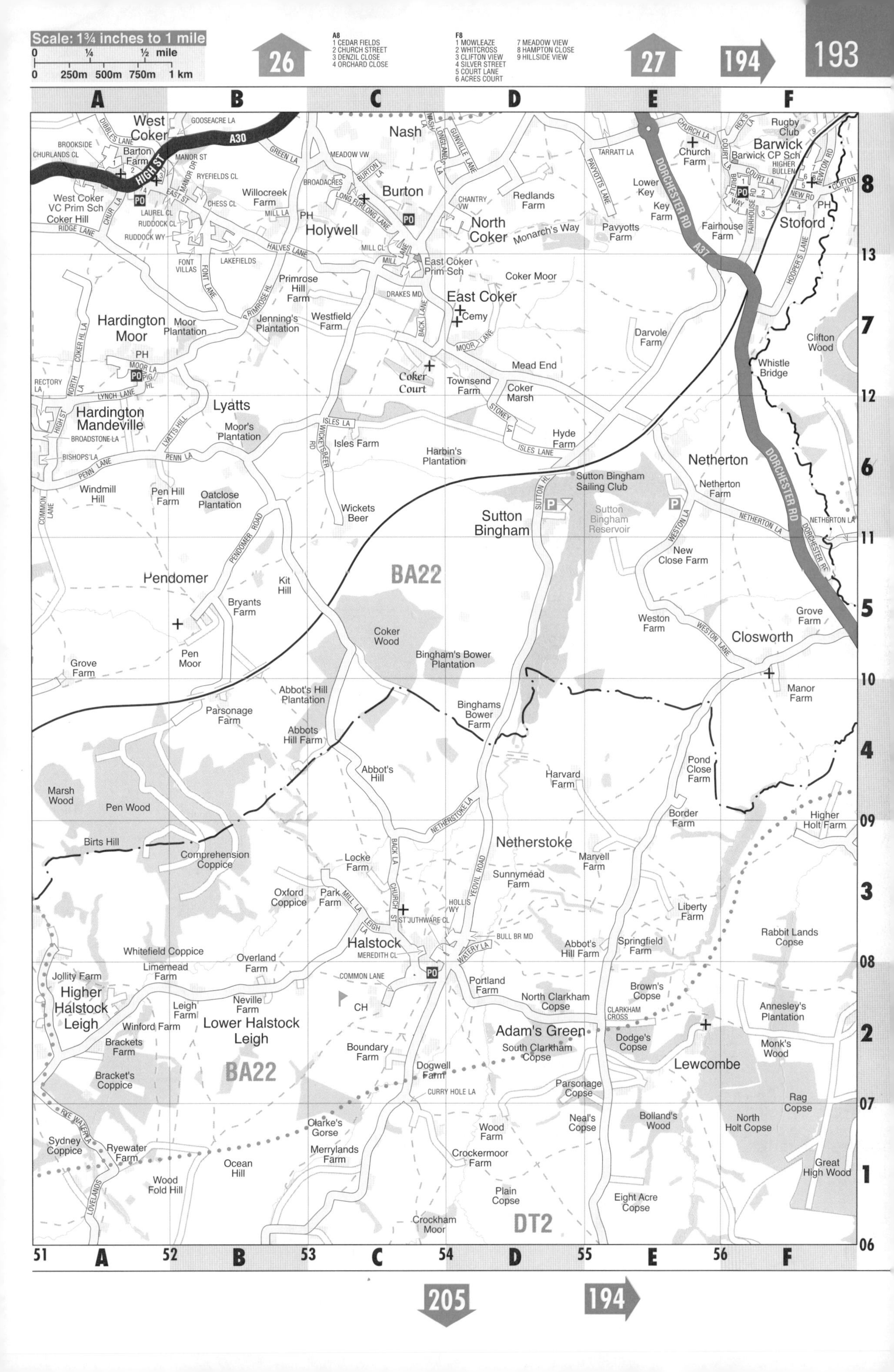

193 28 29

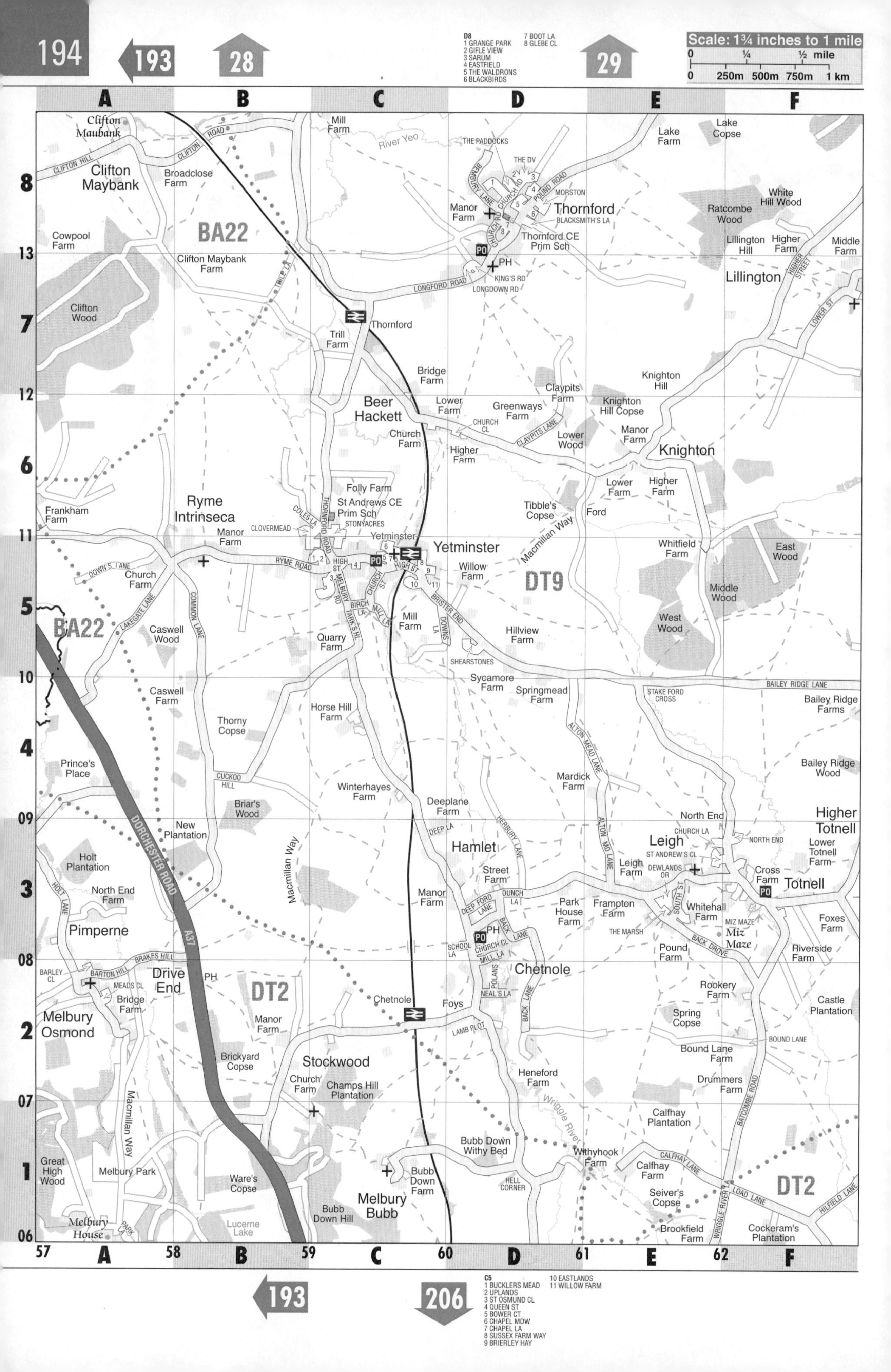
D8
1 GRANGE PARK
2 GIFLE VIEW
3 SARUM
4 EASTFIELD
5 THE WALDRONS
6 BLACKBIRDS
7 BOOT LA
8 GLEBE CL
Scale: 1¾ inches to 1 mile
0 ¼ ½ mile
0 250m 500m 750m 1 km
Clifton Maubank
Clifton Maybank
Broadclose Farm
Cowpool Farm
BA22
Clifton Maybank Farm
Clifton Wood
Mill Farm
River Yeo
THE PADDOCKS
THE DV
MORSTON
Thornford
BLACKSMITH'S LA
Manor Farm
Thornford CE Prim Sch
KING'S RD
LONGDOWN RD
LONGFORD ROAD
Thornford
Trill Farm
Bridge Farm
Lake Farm
Lake Copse
White Hill Wood
Ratcombe Wood
Lillington Hill
Higher Farm
Middle Farm
Lillington
Knighton Hill
Claypits Farm
Knighton Hill Copse
Beer Hackett
Lower Farm
Greenways Farm
Church Farm
Higher Farm
Lower Wood
Manor Farm
Knighton
Folly Farm
St Andrews CE Prim Sch
STONYACRES
CLOVERMEAD
Ryme Intrinseca
Frankham Farm
Manor Farm
Tibble's Copse
Lower Farm
Higher Farm
Ford
Macmillan Way
Yetminster
Willow Farm
DT9
Whitfield Farm
East Wood
Middle Wood
West Wood
Church Farm
Caswell Wood
Quarry Farm
Mill Farm
Hillview Farm
SHEARSTONES
Caswell Farm
Sycamore Farm
Springmead Farm
BAILEY RIDGE LANE
STAKE FORD CROSS
Bailey Ridge Farms
Horse Hill Farm
Thorny Copse
Prince's Place
Winterhayes Farm
Mardick Farm
Bailey Ridge Wood
Briar's Wood
New Plantation
Deeplane Farm
North End
Higher Totnell
Leigh
Lower Totnell Farm
Holt Plantation
Hamlet
Street Farm
Leigh Farm
Cross Farm
Totnell
North End Farm
Manor Farm
Park House Farm
Frampton Farm
Whitehall Farm
Foxes Farm
Pimperne
Miz Maze
THE MARSH
Pound Farm
Riverside Farm
DORCHESTER ROAD
A37
Drive End
Chetnole
Rookery Farm
Castle Plantation
Bridge Farm
DT2
Manor Farm
Chetnole
Foys
Spring Copse
Melbury Osmond
BOUND LANE
Bound Lane Farm
Brickyard Copse
Stockwood
Heneford Farm
Drummers Farm
Church Farm
Champs Hill Plantation
Calfhay Plantation
Wriggle River
Bubb Down Withy Bed
Withyhook Farm
Great High Wood
Melbury Park
Ware's Copse
Bubb Down Farm
HELL CORNER
Calfhay Farm
Seiver's Copse
DT2
Melbury Bubb
Bubb Down Hill
Lucerne Lake
Melbury House
Brookfield Farm
Cockeram's Plantation
C5
1 BUCKLERS MEAD
2 UPLANDS
3 ST OSMUND CL
4 QUEEN ST
5 BOWER CT
6 CHAPEL MDW
7 CHAPEL LA
8 SUSSEX FARM WAY
9 BRIERLEY HAY
10 EASTLANDS
11 WILLOW FARM

193 206

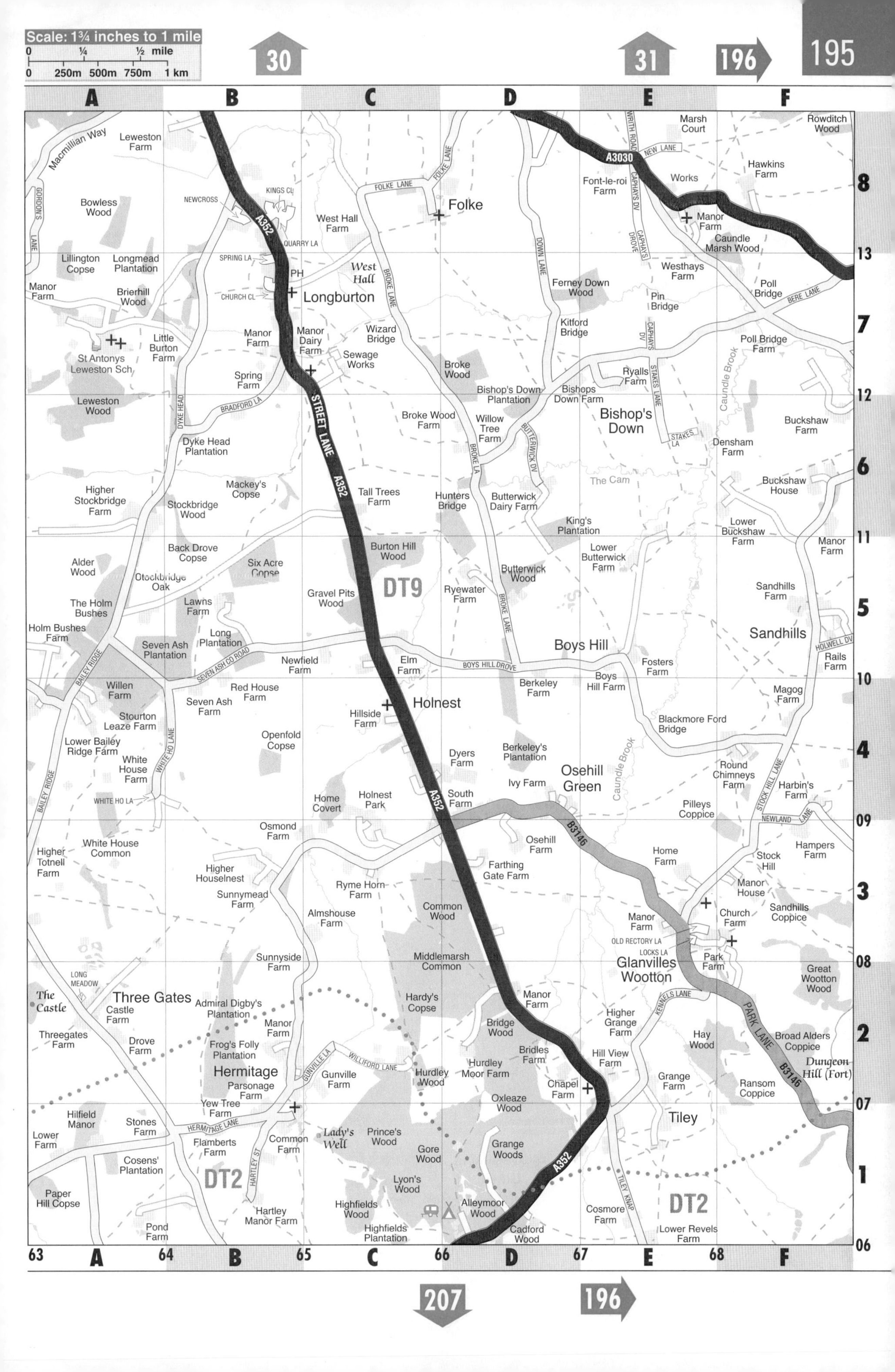
Scale: 1¾ inches to 1 mile
0 ¼ ½ mile
0 250m 500m 750m 1 km
30
31
196
A B C D E F
8 13 7 12 6 11 5 10 4 09 3 08 2 07 1 06
63 64 65 66 67 68
Macmillian Way
Leweston Farm
GORDON'S LANE
Bowless Wood
NEWCROSS
KINGS CL
A352
QUARRY LA
SPRING LA
Lillington Copse
Longmead Plantation
PH
CHURCH CL
Longburton
Manor Farm
Brierhill Wood
St Antonys Leweston Sch
Little Burton Farm
Manor Farm
Manor Dairy Farm
Sewage Works
Wizard Bridge
West Hall
West Hall Farm
FOLKE LANE
Folke
BROKE LANE
Spring Farm
Leweston Wood
DYKE HEAD
BRADFORD LA
Dyke Head Plantation
STREET LANE
Broke Wood
Broke Wood Farm
Willow Tree Farm
Bishop's Down Plantation
Bishops Down Farm
Bishop's Down
Higher Stockbridge Farm
Mackey's Copse
Stockbridge Wood
Tall Trees Farm
Hunters Bridge
BROKE LA
Butterwick Dairy Farm
BUTTERWICK DV
DOWN LANE
Ferney Down Wood
Kitford Bridge
Font-le-roi Farm
WRITH ROAD
A3030
NEW LANE
Marsh Court
Works
CAPHAYS DV
CAPHAYS DROVE
Manor Farm
Caundle Marsh Wood
Westhays Farm
Pin Bridge
Rowditch Wood
Hawkins Farm
Poll Bridge
BERE LANE
Poll Bridge Farm
Ryalls Farm
STAKES LANE
STAKES LA
Caundle Brook
Densham Farm
Buckshaw Farm
Buckshaw House
The Cam
King's Plantation
Lower Buckshaw Farm
Manor Farm
Alder Wood
Back Drove Copse
Six Acre Copse
Stockbridge Oak
Burton Hill Wood
DT9
Gravel Pits Wood
Ryewater Farm
Butterwick Wood
Lower Butterwick Farm
Sandhills Farm
Sandhills
The Holm Bushes
Holm Bushes Farm
Lawns Farm
Long Plantation
Seven Ash Plantation
SEVEN ASH CO ROAD
BAILEY RIDGE
Newfield Farm
Elm Farm
BOYS HILL DROVE
Boys Hill
Boys Hill Farm
Fosters Farm
HOLWELL DV
Rails Farm
Willen Farm
Red House Farm
Seven Ash Farm
Holnest
Hillside Farm
Berkeley Farm
Magog Farm
Stourton Leaze Farm
Lower Bailey Ridge Farm
WHITE HO LANE
Openfold Copse
Blackmore Ford Bridge
White House Farm
Dyers Farm
Berkeley's Plantation
Osehill Green
Ivy Farm
Round Chimneys Farm
STOCK HILL LANE
Harbin's Farm
WHITE HO LA
Home Covert
Holnest Park
South Farm
Pilleys Coppice
NEWLAND LANE
Osmond Farm
B3146
Osehill Farm
Higher Totnell Farm
White House Common
Higher Houselnest
Farthing Gate Farm
Home Farm
Stock Hill
Hampers Farm
Sunnymead Farm
Ryme Horn Farm
Manor House
Common Wood
Almshouse Farm
Manor Farm
Church Farm
Sandhills Coppice
OLD RECTORY LA
LOCKS LA
Sunnyside Farm
Middlemarsh Common
Glanvilles Wootton
Park Farm
Great Wootton Wood
LONG MEADOW
The Castle
Three Gates
Castle Farm
Admiral Digby's Plantation
Hardy's Copse
Manor Farm
KENNELS LANE
PARK LANE
Threegates Farm
Drove Farm
Manor Farm
Frog's Folly Plantation
Bridge Wood
Higher Grange Farm
Hay Wood
Broad Alders Coppice
Bridles Farm
Hurdley Moor Farm
Hill View Farm
Dungeon Hill (Fort)
Hermitage
GUNVILLE LA
WILLIFORD LANE
Hurdley Wood
Gunville Farm
Parsonage Farm
Chapel Farm
Grange Farm
Ransom Coppice
Yew Tree Farm
Oxleaze Wood
Tiley
Hilfield Manor
Stones Farm
HERMITAGE LANE
Lower Farm
Flamberts Farm
Common Farm
Lady's Well
Prince's Wood
Gore Wood
Grange Woods
Cosens' Plantation
DT2
HARTLEY ST
Lyon's Wood
TILEY KNAP
Paper Hill Copse
Hartley Manor Farm
Highfields Wood
Alleymoor Wood
Cosmore Farm
DT2
Pond Farm
Highfields Plantation
Cadford Wood
Lower Revels Farm
207
196

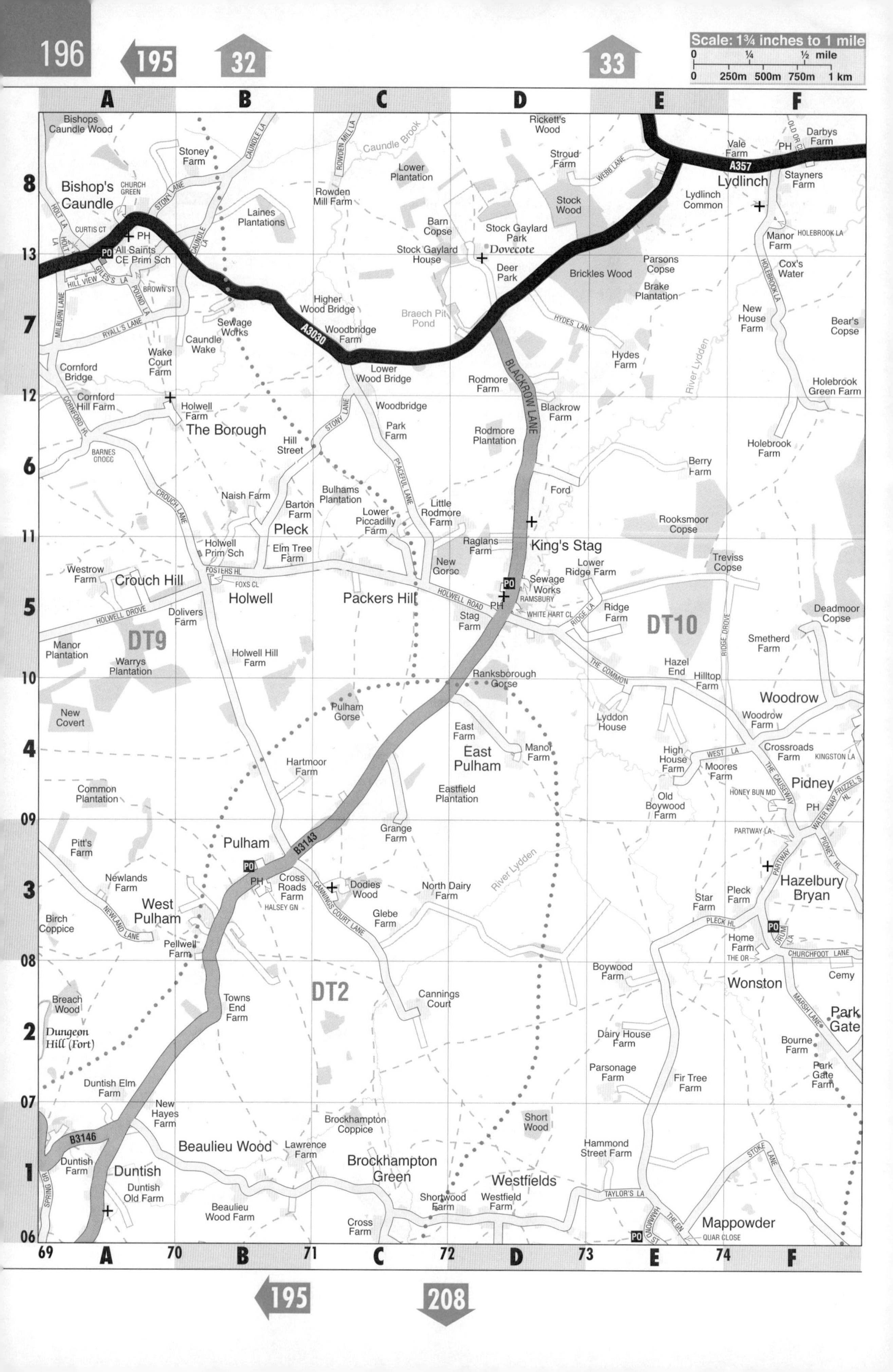
195
32
33
Scale: 1¾ inches to 1 mile
Bishop's Caundle
Lydlinch
The Borough
Pleck
King's Stag
Crouch Hill
Holwell
Packers Hill
DT9
DT10
East Pulham
Woodrow
Pidney
Pulham
West Pulham
Hazelbury Bryan
Wonston
DT2
Dungeon Hill (Fort)
Beaulieu Wood
Duntish
Brockhampton Green
Westfields
Mappowder
Park Gate
A3030
A357
B3143
B3146
BLACKROW LANE
208

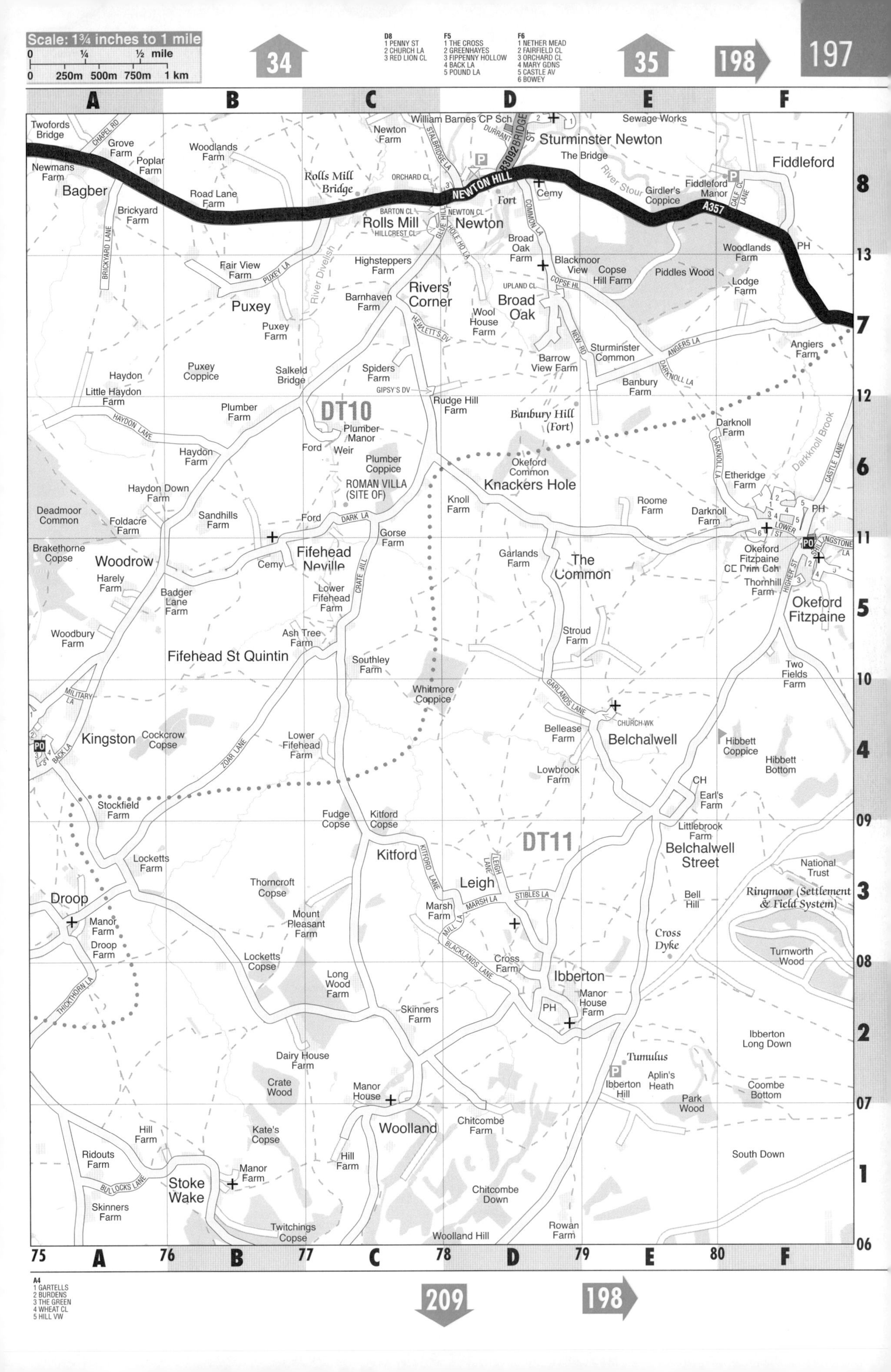
Scale: 1¾ inches to 1 mile
0 ¼ ½ mile
0 250m 500m 750m 1 km
D8
1 PENNY ST
2 CHURCH LA
3 RED LION CL
F5
1 THE CROSS
2 GREENHAYES
3 FIPPENNY HOLLOW
4 BACK LA
5 POUND LA
F6
1 NETHER MEAD
2 FAIRFIELD CL
3 ORCHARD CL
4 MARY GDNS
5 CASTLE AV
6 BOWEY
Twofords Bridge
Grove Farm
Poplar Farm
Woodlands Farm
Newton Farm
William Barnes CP Sch
Sewage Works
Sturminster Newton
The Bridge
Fiddleford
Newmans Farm
Bagber
Road Lane Farm
Rolls Mill Bridge
Newton Hill
River Stour
Girdler's Coppice
Fiddleford Manor
Brickyard Farm
Rolls Mill
Newton
Fort
Cemy
A357
B3092
Broad Oak Farm
Blackmoor View
Copse Hill Farm
Piddles Wood
Woodlands Farm
Lodge Farm
Fair View Farm
Highsteppers Farm
Puxey
Barnhaven Farm
Rivers' Corner
Wool House Farm
Broad Oak
Puxey Farm
River Divelish
Sturminster Common
Angiers Farm
Haydon
Puxey Coppice
Salkeld Bridge
Spiders Farm
Barrow View Farm
Banbury Farm
Little Haydon Farm
Plumber Farm
DT10
Rudge Hill Farm
Banbury Hill (Fort)
Darknoll Farm
Plumber Manor
Ford
Weir
Haydon Farm
Plumber Coppice
Okeford Common
Knackers Hole
Etheridge Farm
Darknoll Brook
Roman Villa (site of)
Haydon Down Farm
Knoll Farm
Roome Farm
Darknoll Farm
Deadmoor Common
Foldacre Farm
Sandhills Farm
Gorse Farm
Brakethorne Copse
Woodrow
Fifehead Neville
Garlands Farm
The Common
Okeford Fitzpaine CE Prim Sch
Harely Farm
Badger Lane Farm
Lower Fifehead Farm
Thornhill Farm
Okeford Fitzpaine
Woodbury Farm
Ash Tree Farm
Stroud Farm
Fifehead St Quintin
Southley Farm
Two Fields Farm
Whitmore Coppice
Belchalwell
Bellease Farm
Hibbett Coppice
Kingston
Cockcrow Copse
Lower Fifehead Farm
Hibbett Bottom
Lowbrook Farm
Earl's Farm
Stockfield Farm
Fudge Copse
Kitford Copse
Littlebrook Farm
DT11
Belchalwell Street
National Trust
Locketts Farm
Kitford
Thorncroft Copse
Leigh
Bell Hill
Ringmoor (Settlement & Field System)
Droop
Marsh Farm
Mount Pleasant Farm
Manor Farm
Droop Farm
Cross Dyke
Turnworth Wood
Locketts Copse
Cross Farm
Long Wood Farm
Ibberton
Manor House Farm
Skinners Farm
Ibberton Long Down
Dairy House Farm
Tumulus
Aplin's Heath
Ibberton Hill
Crate Wood
Manor House
Park Wood
Coombe Bottom
Kate's Copse
Woolland
Chitcombe Farm
Hill Farm
Ridouts Farm
South Down
Stoke Wake
Manor Farm
Hill Farm
Chitcombe Down
Skinners Farm
Twitchings Copse
Woolland Hill
Rowan Farm
A4
1 GARTELLS
2 BURDENS
3 THE GREEN
4 WHEAT CL
5 HILL VW

34 35 198 209 198

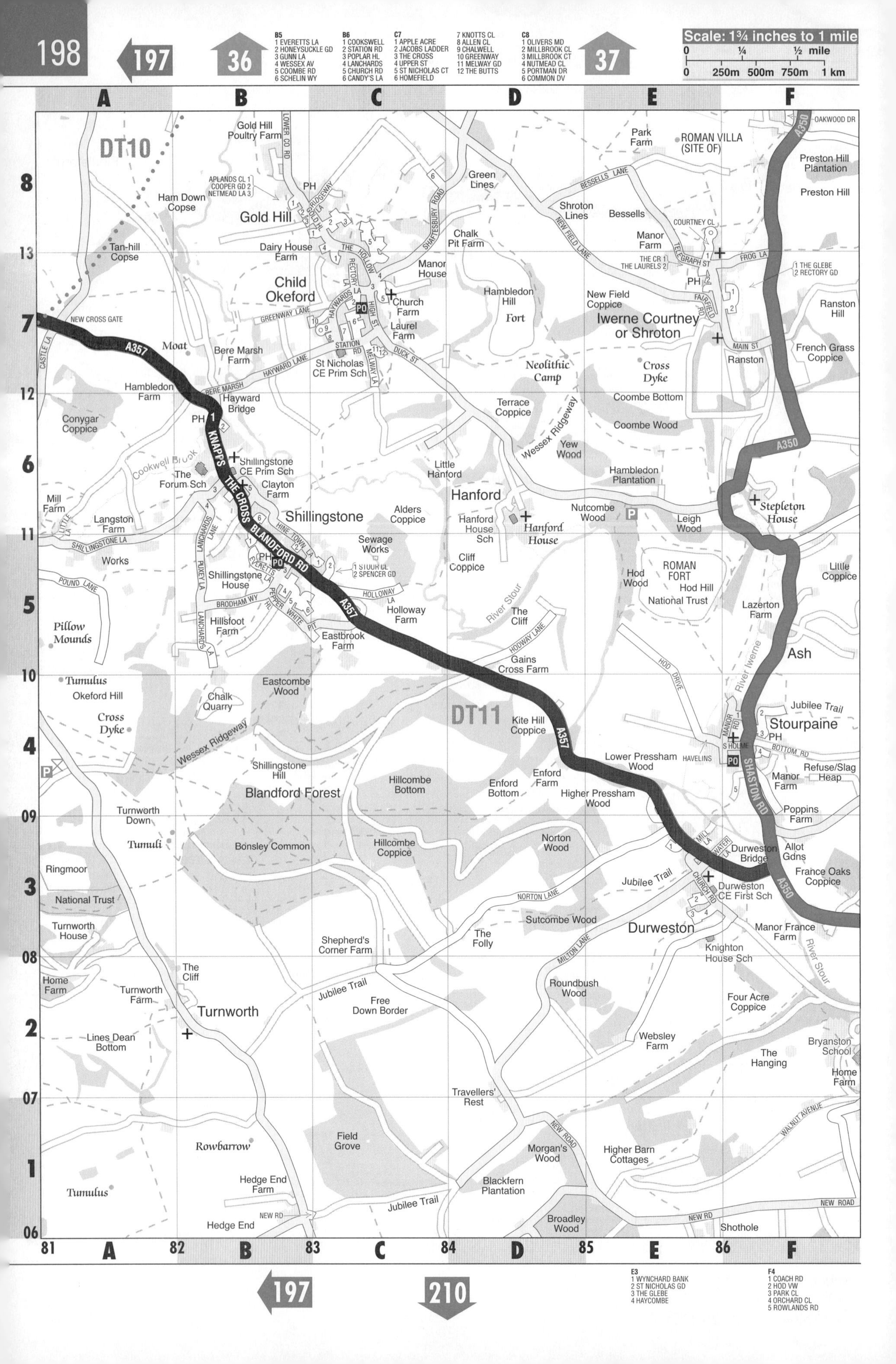
198
197
36
B5
1 EVERETTS LA
2 HONEYSUCKLE GD
3 GUNN LA
4 WESSEX AV
5 COOMBE RD
6 SCHELIN WY
B6
1 COOKSWELL
2 STATION RD
3 POPLAR HL
4 LANCHARDS
5 CHURCH RD
6 CANDY'S LA
C7
1 APPLE ACRE
2 JACOBS LADDER
3 THE CROSS
4 UPPER ST
5 ST NICHOLAS CT
6 HOMEFIELD
7 KNOTTS CL
8 ALLEN CL
9 CHALWELL
10 GREENWAY
11 MELWAY GD
12 THE BUTTS
C8
1 OLIVERS MD
2 MILLBROOK CL
3 MILLBROOK CT
4 NUTMEAD CL
5 PORTMAN DR
6 COMMON DV
37
Scale: 1¾ inches to 1 mile
0 ¼ ½ mile
0 250m 500m 750m 1 km
A
B
C
D
E
F
DT10
Gold Hill Poultry Farm
LOWER CO RD
Park Farm
ROMAN VILLA (SITE OF)
OAKWOOD DR
A350
Preston Hill Plantation
Preston Hill
APLANDS CL 1
COOPER GD 2
NETMEAD LA 3
PH
Ham Down Copse
Green Lines
BESSELLS LANE
Shroton Lines
Bessells
Gold Hill
RIDGEWAY
GOLD HL
SHAFTESBURY ROAD
Chalk Pit Farm
Manor Farm
COURTNEY CL
NEW FIELD LANE
Tan-hill Copse
Dairy House Farm
THE HOLLOW
THE CR 1
THE LAURELS 2
TELEGRAPH ST
FROG LA
1 THE GLEBE
2 RECTORY GD
Child Okeford
RECTORY LA
Manor House
Hambledon Hill
Fort
New Field Coppice
FAIRFIELD RD
Ranston Hill
HAYWARDS LA
HIGH ST
Church Farm
GREENWAY LANE
NEW CROSS GATE
Laurel Farm
Iwerne Courtney or Shroton
A357
Moat
Bere Marsh Farm
STATION RD
DUCK ST
MAIN ST
Ranston
French Grass Coppice
CASTLE LA
HAYWARD LANE
St Nicholas CE Prim Sch
MELWAY LA
Neolithic Camp
Cross Dyke
BERE MARSH
Hambledon Farm
Hayward Bridge
Terrace Coppice
Coombe Bottom
Wessex Ridgeway
Conygar Coppice
KNAPPS
Coombe Wood
Yew Wood
A350
Cookwell Brook
Shillingstone CE Prim Sch
Little Hanford
Hambledon Plantation
The Forum Sch
THE CROSS
Clayton Farm
Hanford
Mill Farm
Stepleton House
Langston Farm
LITTLE LA
Shillingstone
Alders Coppice
Hanford House Sch
Hanford House
Nutcombe Wood
Leigh Wood
SHILLINGSTONE LA
LANCHARDS LANE
HINE TOWN LA
BLANDFORD RD
Sewage Works
Works
Cliff Coppice
ROMAN FORT
Little Coppice
POUND LANE
PUXEY LA
EVERETTS LA
1 STOUR CL
2 SPENCER GD
Shillingstone House
HOLLOWAY LA
Hod Wood
Hod Hill
National Trust
BRODHAM WY
PEPPER HL
Holloway Farm
River Stour
The Cliff
Lazerton Farm
Pillow Mounds
Hillsfoot Farm
WHITE PIT
Eastbrook Farm
HODWAY LANE
Ash
LANCHARDS LA
Gains Cross Farm
HOD DRIVE
River Iwerne
Tumulus
Eastcombe Wood
Okeford Hill
Chalk Quarry
DT11
Jubilee Trail
Cross Dyke
Kite Hill Coppice
Stourpaine
MANOR RD
Wessex Ridgeway
Lower Pressham Wood
HAVELINS
S HOLME
BOTTOM RD
Shillingstone Hill
Enford Farm
Refuse/Slag Heap
Blandford Forest
Hillcombe Bottom
Enford Bottom
Higher Pressham Wood
SHASTON RD
Manor Farm
Turnworth Down
Poppins Farm
Tumuli
Bonsley Common
Hillcombe Coppice
Norton Wood
MILL LA
WATER LA
Durweston Bridge
Allot Gdns
Ringmoor
Jubilee Trail
CHURCH RD
Durweston CE First Sch
France Oaks Coppice
National Trust
NORTON LANE
Turnworth House
Shepherd's Corner Farm
The Folly
Sutcombe Wood
Durweston
Manor France Farm
Knighton House Sch
River Stour
MILTON LANE
The Cliff
Home Farm
Turnworth Farm
Jubilee Trail
Free Down Border
Roundbush Wood
Four Acre Coppice
Turnworth
Lines Dean Bottom
Websley Farm
Bryanston School
The Hanging
Home Farm
Travellers' Rest
WALNUT AVENUE
NEW ROAD
Rowbarrow
Field Grove
Morgan's Wood
Higher Barn Cottages
Hedge End Farm
Blackfern Plantation
Tumulus
Jubilee Trail
NEW ROAD
NEW RD
NEW RD
Broadley Wood
Hedge End
Shothole
8
13
7
12
6
11
5
10
4
09
3
08
2
07
1
06
81
82
83
84
85
86
197
210
E3
1 WYNCHARD BANK
2 ST NICHOLAS GD
3 THE GLEBE
4 HAYCOMBE
F4
1 COACH RD
2 HOD VW
3 PARK CL
4 ORCHARD CL
5 ROWLANDS RD

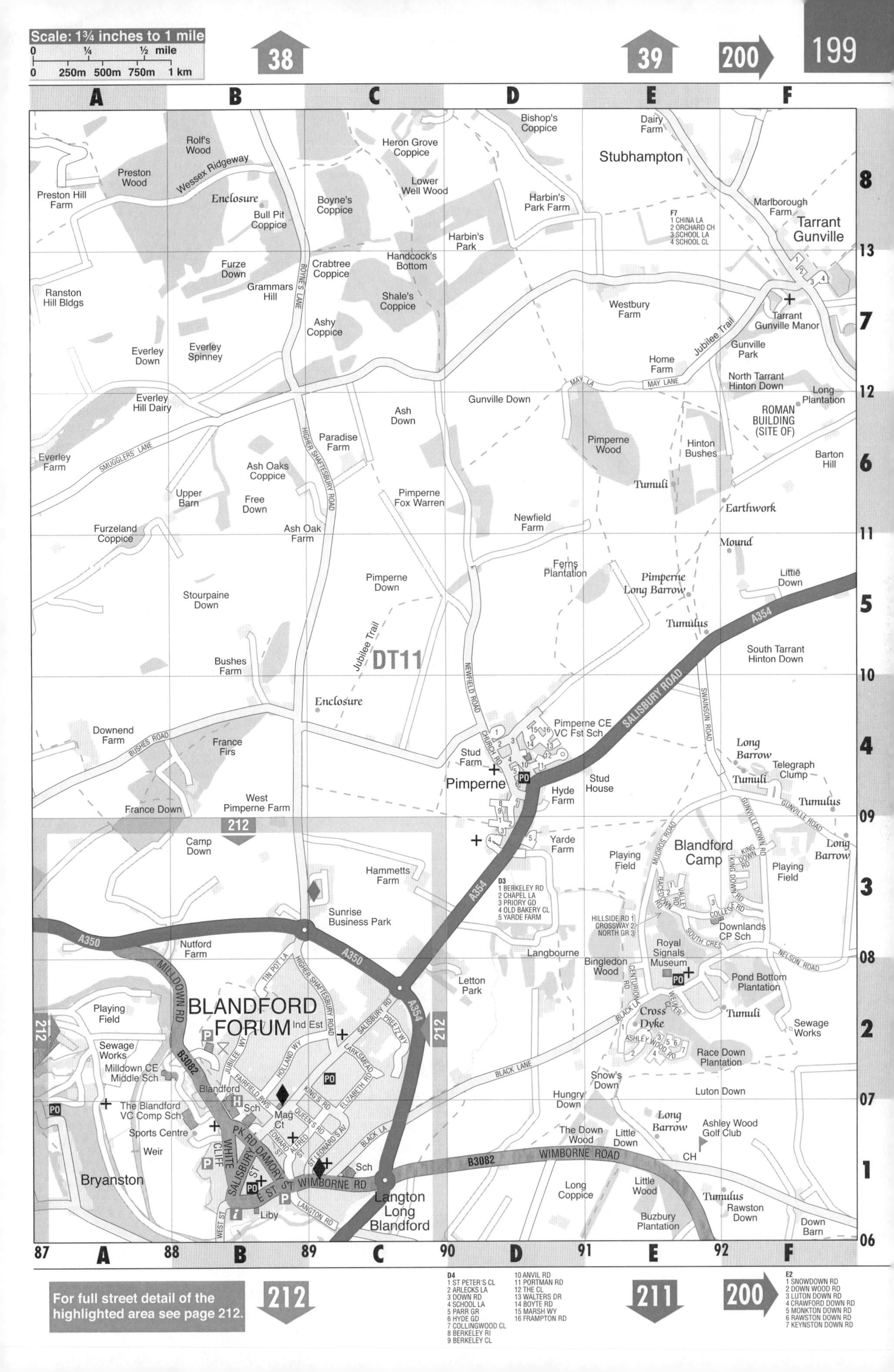

A B C D E F

8

Preston Hill Farm
Preston Wood
Rolf's Wood
Wessex Ridgeway
Enclosure
Bull Pit Coppice
Boyne's Coppice
Heron Grove Coppice
Lower Well Wood
Bishop's Coppice
Harbin's Park Farm
Dairy Farm
Stubhampton
Marlborough Farm
Tarrant Gunville

13

Ranston Hill Bldgs
Furze Down
Grammars Hill
Crabtree Coppice
Handcock's Bottom
Harbin's Park
Shale's Coppice
F7
1 CHINA LA
2 ORCHARD CH
3 SCHOOL LA
4 SCHOOL CL

Tarrant Gunville Manor

7

Everley Down
Everley Spinney
Ashy Coppice
Westbury Farm
Gunville Park
North Tarrant Hinton Down
Long Plantation

12

Everley Hill Dairy
SMUGGLERS' LANE
Paradise Farm
Ash Down
Gunville Down
Home Farm
MAY LANE
Hinton Bushes
ROMAN BUILDING (SITE OF)
Barton Hill

6

Everley Farm
Ash Oaks Coppice
Free Down
Pimperne Fox Warren
Pimperne Wood
Tumuli
Earthwork

Furzeland Coppice
Upper Barn
Ash Oak Farm
Newfield Farm
Mound

11

Stourpaine Down
Bushes Farm
Pimperne Down
Ferns Plantation
Pimperne Long Barrow
Little Down

Jubilee Trail
DT11
Tumulus
A354
South Tarrant Hinton Down

5

BUSHES ROAD
Downend Farm
France Firs
Enclosure
SALISBURY ROAD
SWAINSON ROAD
Long Barrow
Telegraph Clump
Tumuli
Tumulus

10

France Down
West Pimperne Farm
CHURCH RD
NEWFIELD ROAD
Stud Farm
Pimperne
Pimperne CE VC Fst Sch
Hyde Farm
Stud House
Blandford Camp
Long Barrow

4

D3
1 BERKELEY RD
2 CHAPEL LA
3 PRIORY GD
4 OLD BAKERY CL
5 YARDE FARM
Yarde Farm
Playing Field
MADROS RD
KING DOWN RD
COLLEGE RD
GUNVILLE DOWN RD
Playing Field

09

212
Camp Down
Hammetts Farm
Sunrise Business Park
A354
Langbourne
HILLSIDE RD 1
CROSSWAY 2
NORTH GR 3
Downlands CP Sch
SOUTH CRES
Tumuli

3

A350
Nutford Farm
MILLDOWN RD
HIGHER SHAFTESBURY ROAD
A350
Letton Park
Bingledon Wood
BLACK LA
CENTURION RD
Royal Signals Museum
PO
NELSON ROAD
Pond Bottom Plantation

08

212
Playing Field
Sewage Works
Milldown CE Middle Sch
B3082
BLANDFORD FORUM Ind Est
Blandford
SALISBURY RD
PRIEST WY
PO
KING'S RD
ELIZABETH RD
A354
212
BLACK LANE
Cross Dyke
ASHLEY WOOD RD
Snow's Down
Race Down Plantation
Sewage Works

2

The Blandford VC Comp Sch
Sports Centre
Weir
Bryanston
PO
JUBILEE WY
FAIRFIELD RD
HOLLAND WY
Mag Ct
PK RD DAMORY
Sch
QUEEN'S RD
EDWARD ST
ALFRED ST
ST LEONARD'S AV
Sch
WIMBORNE RD
B3082 WIMBORNE ROAD
Hungry Down
The Down Wood
Little Down
Long Barrow
Luton Down
Ashley Wood Golf Club
CH

07

PO
WHITE CLIFF
SALISBURY ST
WEST ST
PO
EYE ST
P
LANGTON RD
i Liby
Langton Long Blandford
Long Coppice
Little Wood
Buzbury Plantation
Tumulus
Rawston Down
Down Barn

06

A B C D E F

87 88 89 90 91 92

For full street detail of the highlighted area see page 212.

D4
1 ST PETER'S CL
2 ARLECKS LA
3 DOWN RD
4 SCHOOL LA
5 PARR GR
6 HYDE GD
7 COLLINGWOOD CL
8 BERKELEY RI
9 BERKELEY CL

10 ANVIL RD
11 PORTMAN RD
12 THE CL
13 WALTERS DR
14 BOYTE RD
15 MARSH WY
16 FRAMPTON RD

E2
1 SNOWDOWN RD
2 DOWN WOOD RD
3 LUTON DOWN RD
4 CRAWFORD DOWN RD
5 MONKTON DOWN RD
6 RAWSTON DOWN RD
7 KEYNSTON DOWN RD

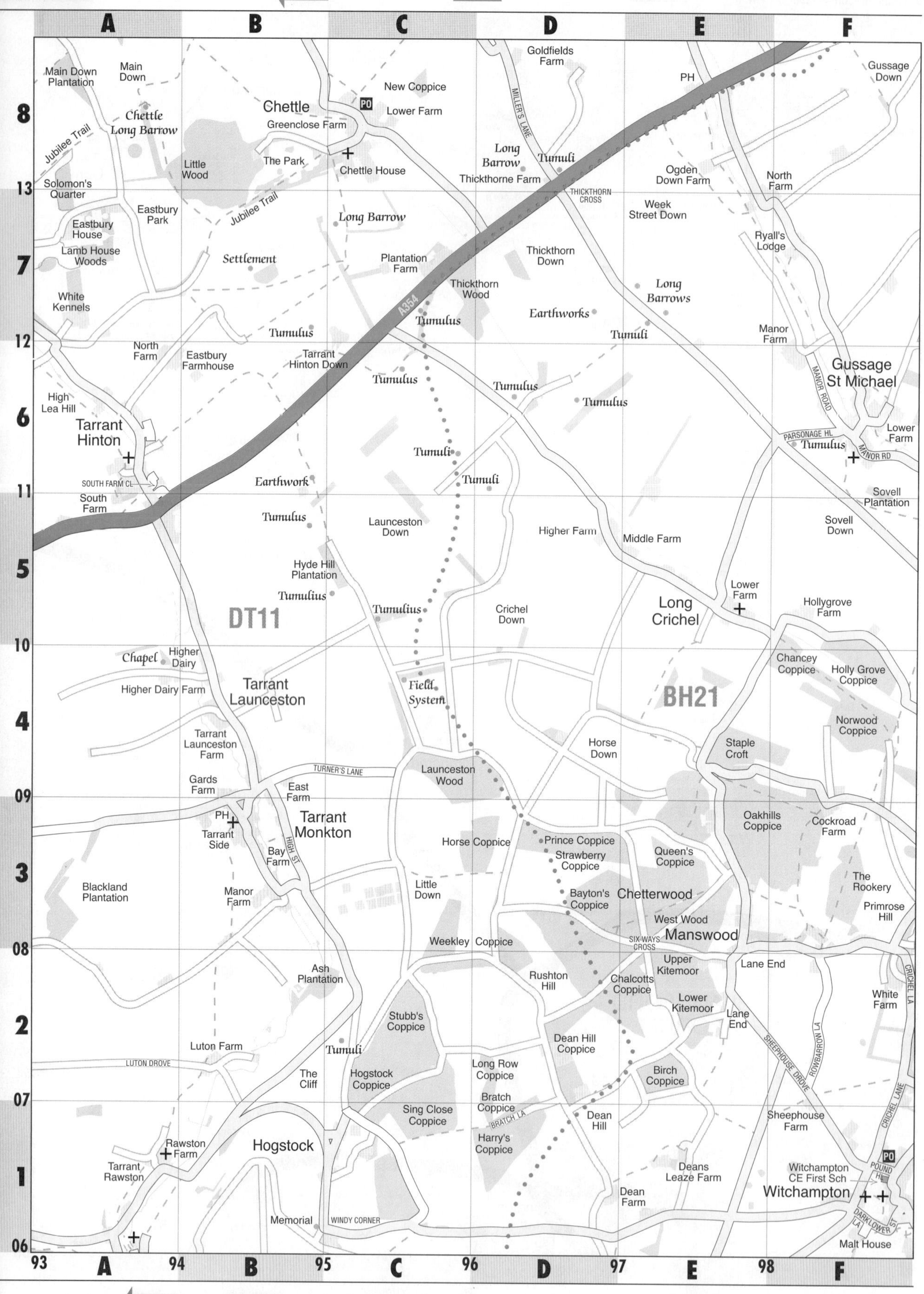
A
B
C
D
E
F
Main Down Plantation
Main Down
Chettle Long Barrow
Chettle
Greenclose Farm
New Coppice
Lower Farm
Goldfields Farm
MILLER'S LANE
PH
Gussage Down
Jubilee Trail
Solomon's Quarter
Little Wood
The Park
Chettle House
Long Barrow
Tumuli
Thickthorne Farm
THICKTHORN CROSS
Ogden Down Farm
North Farm
Eastbury Park
Eastbury House
Lamb House Woods
Long Barrow
Week Street Down
Ryall's Lodge
Settlement
Plantation Farm
Thickthorn Down
White Kennels
Thickthorn Wood
A354
Long Barrows
Earthworks
Tumulus
Tumuli
Manor Farm
North Farm
Eastbury Farmhouse
Tarrant Hinton Down
Gussage St Michael
MANOR ROAD
High Lea Hill
Tarrant Hinton
Tumulus
Tumulus
Tumulus
PARSONAGE HL
Lower Farm
MANOR RD
Tumuli
Tumuli
SOUTH FARM CL
South Farm
Earthwork
Sovell Plantation
Tumulus
Launceston Down
Higher Farm
Middle Farm
Sovell Down
Hyde Hill Plantation
Tumulus
Tumulus
DT11
Crichel Down
Long Crichel
Lower Farm
Hollygrove Farm
Chapel
Higher Dairy
Higher Dairy Farm
Tarrant Launceston
Field System
BH21
Chancey Coppice
Holly Grove Coppice
Norwood Coppice
Tarrant Launceston Farm
Horse Down
Staple Croft
TURNER'S LANE
Launceston Wood
Gards Farm
East Farm
PH
Tarrant Side
Tarrant Monkton
Horse Coppice
Prince Coppice
Strawberry Coppice
Queen's Coppice
Oakhills Coppice
Cockroad Farm
Bay Farm
HIGH ST
Blackland Plantation
Manor Farm
Little Down
Bayton's Coppice
Chetterwood
The Rookery
Primrose Hill
West Wood
Manswood
SIX WAYS CROSS
Weekley Coppice
Upper Kitemoor
Lane End
Ash Plantation
Rushton Hill
Chalcotts Coppice
Lower Kitemoor
White Farm
CRICHEL LA
Stubb's Coppice
Lane End
ROWBARROW LA
SHEEPHOUSE DROVE
Luton Farm
LUTON DROVE
Tumuli
Dean Hill Coppice
Long Row Coppice
Birch Coppice
The Cliff
Hogstock Coppice
Bratch Coppice
Sing Close Coppice
BRATCH LA
Dean Hill
Sheephouse Farm
CRICHEL LANE
Rawston Farm
Hogstock
Harry's Coppice
Tarrant Rawston
Deans Leaze Farm
PO
POUND HL
Witchampton CE First Sch
Witchampton
Dean Farm
Memorial
WINDY CORNER
DARKLOWER LA
LOWER ST
Malt House
8
13
7
12
6
11
5
10
4
09
3
08
2
07
1
06
93
94
95
96
97
98

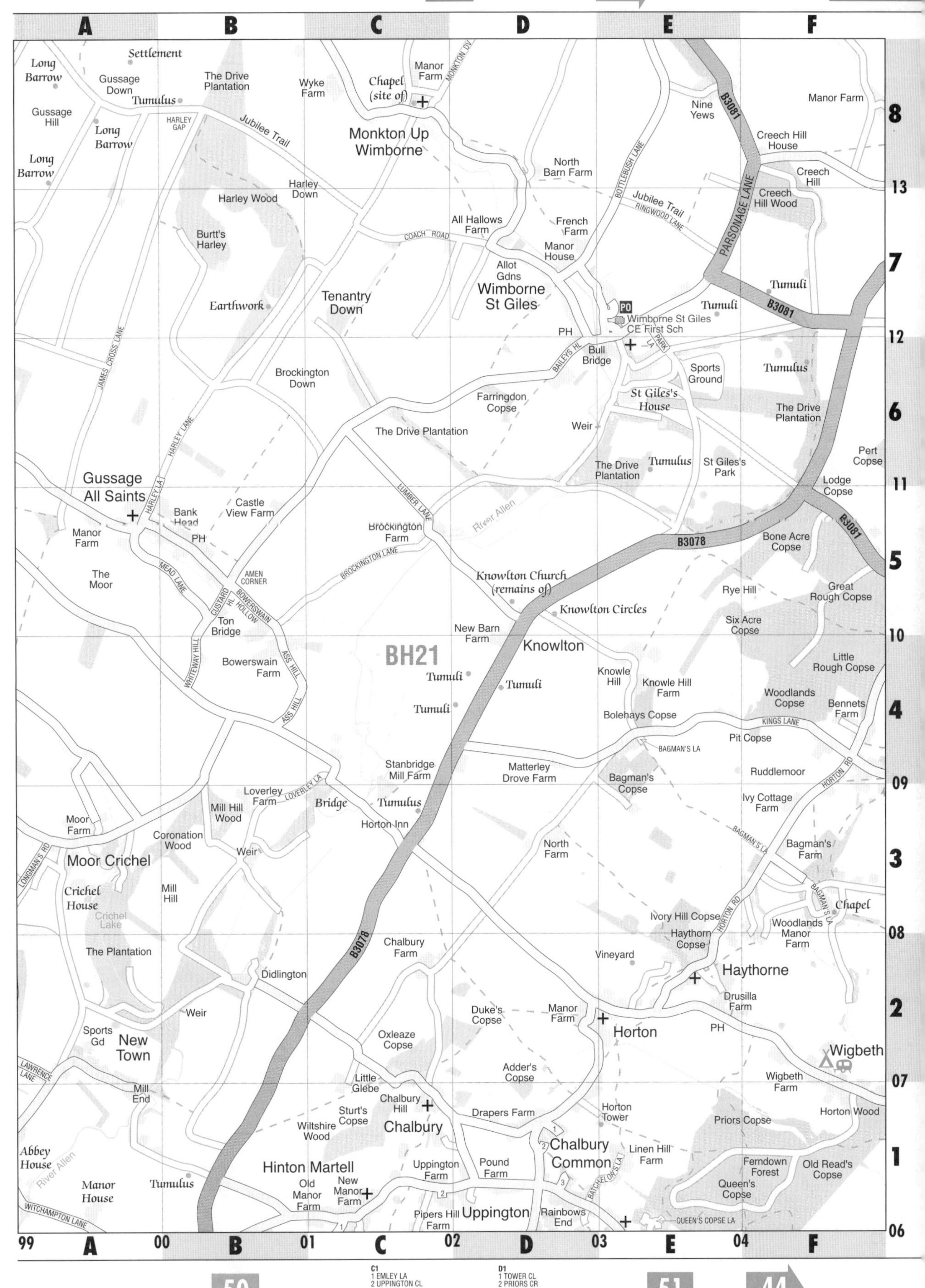

Long Barrow
Settlement
Gussage Down
Tumulus
The Drive Plantation
Wyke Farm
Chapel (site of)
Manor Farm
MONKTON DV
Nine Yews
Manor Farm

Gussage Hill
Long Barrow
HARLEY GAP
Monkton Up Wimborne
Creech Hill House
Creech Hill

Long Barrow
Jubilee Trail
Harley Down
North Barn Farm
French Farm
Jubilee Trail
RINGWOOD LANE
Creech Hill Wood

Harley Wood
COACH ROAD
All Hallows Farm
Manor House
BOTTLEBUSH LANE
PARSONAGE LANE

Burtt's Harley
Earthwork
Tenantry Down
Allot Gdns
Wimborne St Giles
PO
PH
Wimborne St Giles CE First Sch
Tumuli
B3081
Tumuli

Brockington Down
Farringdon Copse
BAILEYS HL
Bull Bridge
St Giles's House
Sports Ground
Tumulus
The Drive Plantation

JAMES CROSS LANE
HARLEY LANE
The Drive Plantation
Weir
The Drive Plantation
Tumulus
St Giles's Park
Pert Copse
Lodge Copse

Gussage All Saints
Bank Head
PH
Castle View Farm
Brockington Farm
LUMBER LANE
River Allen
B3078
Bone Acre Copse
B3081

Manor Farm
HARLEY LA
AMEN CORNER
BROCKINGTON LANE
Knowlton Church (remains of)
Knowlton Circles
Rye Hill
Great Rough Copse

The Moor
MEAD LANE
BOWERSWAIN HOLLOW
New Barn Farm
Knowlton
Knowle Hill
Six Acre Copse

CUSTARD'S HL
BOWERSWAIN HL
Ton Bridge
BH21
Tumuli
Tumuli
Knowle Hill Farm
Woodlands Copse
Little Rough Copse

WHITEWAY HILL
ASS HILL
Bowerswain Farm
Tumuli
Bolehays Copse
KINGS LANE
Bennets Farm

Moor Farm
Loverley Farm
LOVERLEY LA
Bridge
Tumulus
Matterley Drove Farm
BAGMAN'S LA
Bagman's Copse
Pit Copse
Ruddlemoor
HORTON RD
Ivy Cottage Farm

Moor Crichel
Mill Hill Wood
Coronation Wood
Weir
Horton Inn
North Farm
BAGMAN'S LA
Bagman's Farm

LONGMAN'S RD
Crichel House
Crichel Lake
Mill Hill
Ivory Hill Copse
Haythorn Copse
HORTON RD
Chapel
Woodlands Manor Farm

The Plantation
Didlington
B3078
Chalbury Farm
Vineyard
Haythorne
Drusilla Farm

LAWRENCE LANE
Sports Gd
New Town
Weir
Oxleaze Copse
Duke's Copse
Manor Farm
Horton
PH
Wigbeth

WITCHAMPTON LANE
Mill End
Little Glebe
Sturt's Copse
Adder's Copse
Wigbeth Farm

Abbey House
River Allen
Manor House
Tumulus
Wiltshire Wood
Chalbury Hill
Chalbury
Drapers Farm
Horton Tower
Priors Copse
Horton Wood

Hinton Martell
Old Manor Farm
New Manor Farm
Uppington Farm
Pound Farm
Chalbury Common
Linen Hill Farm
Ferndown Forest
Old Read's Copse

Pipers Hill Farm
Uppington
Rainbows End
BATCHELOR'S LA
Queen's Copse
QUEEN'S COPSE LA

C1
1 EMLEY LA
2 UPPINGTON CL

D1
1 TOWER CL
2 PRIORS CR
3 BAKERS LA

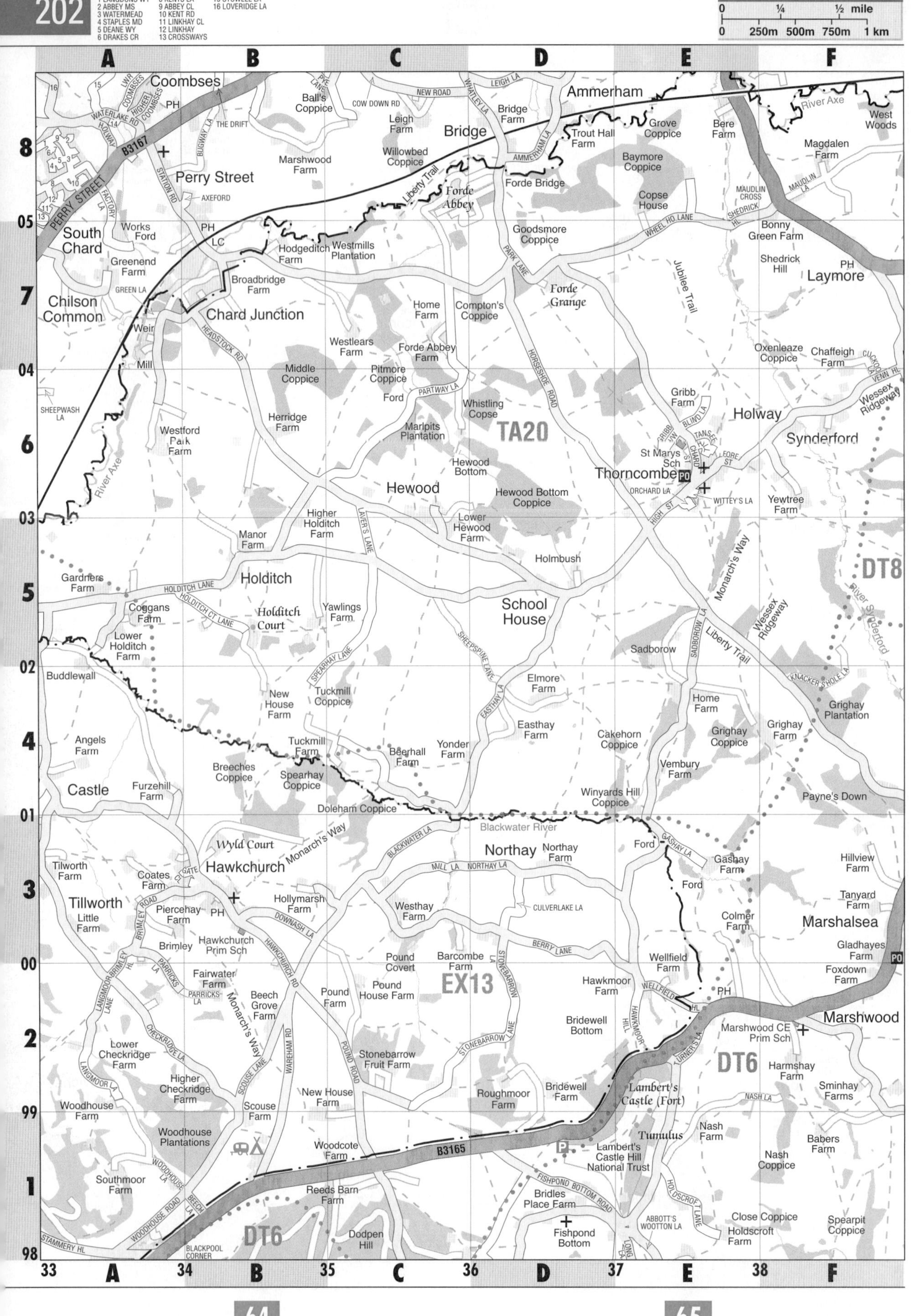

A8
1 LANGDONS WY
2 ABBEY MS
3 WATERMEAD
4 STAPLES MD
5 DEANE WY
6 DRAKES CR
7 GULWAY MD
8 KENTS LA
9 ABBEY CL
10 KENT RD
11 LINKHAY CL
12 LINKHAY
13 CROSSWAYS
14 HOLLEYS CL
15 STOWELL LA
16 LOVERIDGE LA

Coombses
Ball's Coppice
COW DOWN RD
NEW ROAD
Leigh Farm
Ammerham
River Axe
West Woods
Marshwood Farm
Willowbed Coppice
Bridge Farm
Trout Hall Farm
Grove Coppice
Bere Farm
Magdalen Farm
Perry Street
Bridge
Forde Bridge
Baymore Coppice
Copse House
MAUDLIN CROSS
SHEDRICK HL
Axeford
Forde Abbey
Goodsmore Coppice
Bonny Green Farm
Shedrick Hill
PH Laymore
South Chard
Works Ford
Hodgeditch
Westmills Plantation
Forde Grange
Oxenleaze Coppice
Chaffeigh Farm
Greenend Farm
Broadbridge Farm
Home Farm
Compton's Coppice
Holway
Wessex Ridgeway
Chilson Common
Weir
Chard Junction
Westlears Farm
Forde Abbey Farm
Synderford
Mill
Middle Coppice
Pitmore Coppice
PARTWAY LA
Whistling Copse
TA20
Gribb Farm
SHEEPWASH LA
Herridge Farm
Ford
Marlpits Plantation
St Marys Sch
Thorncombe
Westford Park Farm
Hewood Bottom
Hewood
Hewood Bottom Coppice
Yewtree Farm
Higher Holditch Farm
Lower Hewood Farm
Holmbush
DT8
Gardners Farm
HOLDITCH LANE
Manor Farm
Holditch
Holbush
River Synderford
Coggans Farm
Holditch Court
Yawlings Farm
School House
Sadborow
Wessex Ridgeway
Lower Holditch Farm
Buddlewall
New House Farm
Tuckmill Coppice
Elmore Farm
Home Farm
Grighay Plantation
Angels Farm
Tuckmill Farm
Beerhall Farm
Yonder Farm
Easthay Farm
Cakehorn Coppice
Grighay Coppice
Grighay Farm
Castle
Furzehill Farm
Breeches Coppice
Spearhay Coppice
Winyards Hill Coppice
Vembury Farm
Payne's Down
Doleham Coppice
Blackwater River
Liberty Trail
Tilworth Farm
Wyld Court
Monarch's Way
Northay
Northay Farm
Ford
Gashay Farm
Hillview Farm
Tillworth
Coates Farm
Hawkchurch
Hollymarsh Farm
Ford
Tanyard Farm
Little Farm
Piercehay Farm
PH
Westhay Farm
CULVERLAKE LA
Colmer Farm
Marshalsea
Brimley
Hawkchurch Prim Sch
BERRY LANE
Wellfield Farm
Gladhayes Farm
Fairwater Farm
Pound Covert
Barcombe Farm
EX13
Hawkmoor Farm
Foxdown Farm
Lower Checkridge Farm
Beech Grove Farm
Pound Farm
Pound House Farm
Bridewell Bottom
Marshwood CE Prim Sch
Marshwood
Higher Checkridge Farm
Stonebarrow Fruit Farm
Roughmoor Farm
Bridewell Farm
Lambert's Castle (Fort)
Harmshay Farm
DT6
Woodhouse Farm
Scouse Farm
New House Farm
Tumulus
Nash Farm
Sminhay Farms
Southmoor Farm
Woodhouse Plantations
Woodcote Farm
B3165
Lambert's Castle Hill National Trust
Babers Farm
Nash Coppice
Reeds Barn Farm
Bridles Place Farm
ABBOTT'S WOOTTON LA
Close Coppice
Spearpit Coppice
STAMMERY HL
BLACKPOOL CORNER
DT6
Dodpen Hill
Fishpond Bottom
Holdscroft Farm
Holdscroft

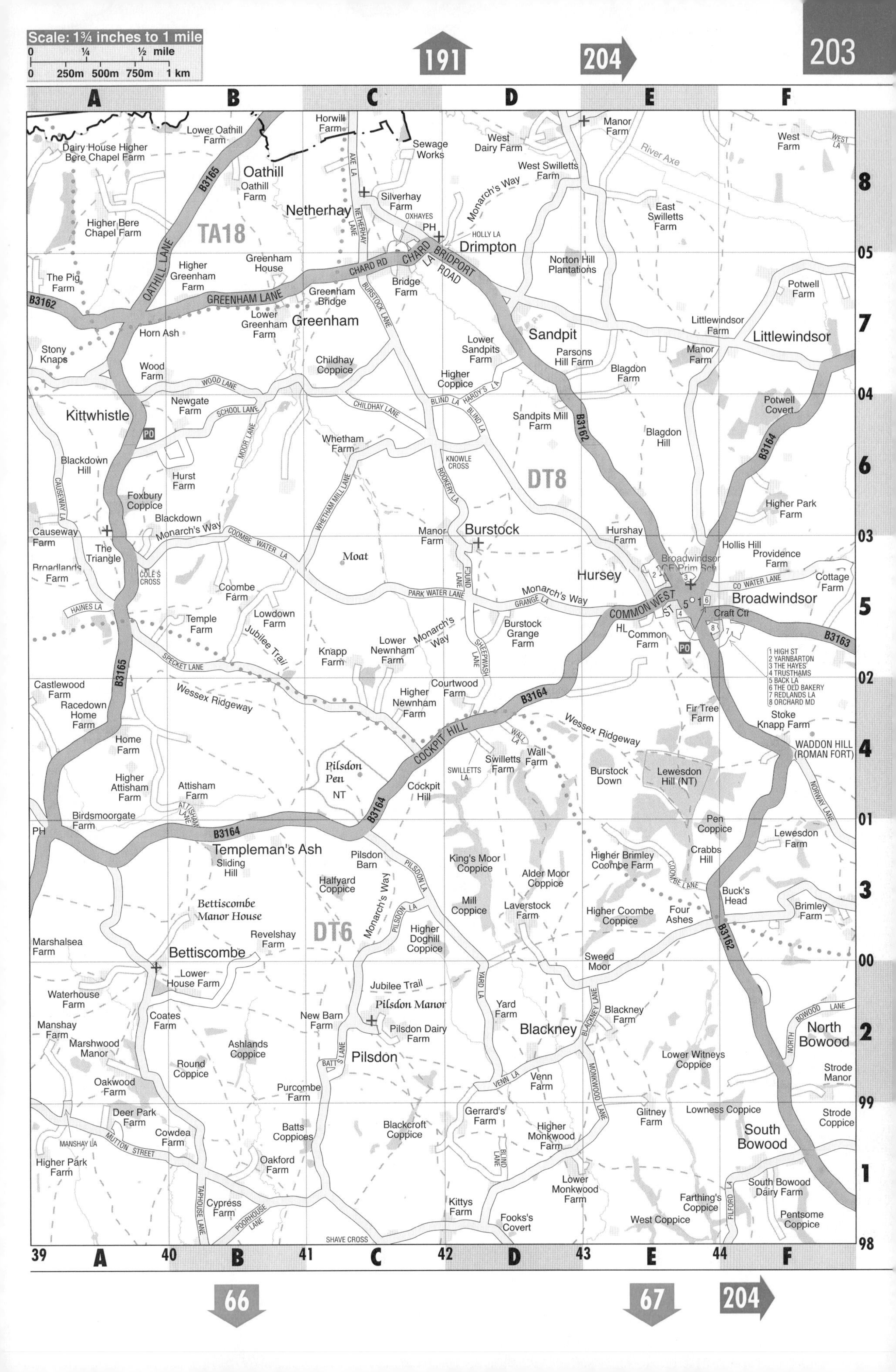
Scale: 1¾ inches to 1 mile
191
204
A B C D E F
Lower Oathill Farm
Dairy House Higher Bere Chapel Farm
Horwill Farm
Sewage Works
West Dairy Farm
Manor Farm
West Farm
River Axe
Oathill
Oathill Farm
Netherhay
Silverhay Farm
West Swilletts Farm
Monarch's Way
East Swilletts Farm
Higher Bere Chapel Farm
TA18
Drimpton
Norton Hill Plantations
The Pig Farm
Higher Greenham Farm
Greenham House
CHARD RD
CHARD LA
BRIDPORT ROAD
Bridge Farm
Potwell Farm
B3162
GREENHAM LANE
Greenham Bridge
Lower Greenham Farm
Greenham
Sandpit
Littlewindsor Farm
Littlewindsor
Horn Ash
Stony Knaps
Wood Farm
Childhay Coppice
Lower Sandpits Farm
Higher Coppice
Parsons Hill Farm
Blagdon Farm
Manor Farm
Kittwhistle
Newgate Farm
SCHOOL LANE
WOOD LANE
CHILDHAY LANE
BLIND LA
HARDY'S LA
Sandpits Mill Farm
Potwell Covert
Blackdown Hill
Whetham Farm
KNOWLE CROSS
DT8
Blagdon Hill
B3164
Hurst Farm
Foxbury Coppice
Blackdown
Burstock
Higher Park Farm
Causeway Farm
The Triangle
Manor Farm
Hurshay Farm
Hollis Hill
Providence Farm
Broadlands Farm
COLE'S CROSS
COOMBE WATER LA
Moat
Hursey
Broadwindsor CE Prim Sch
Cottage Farm
Coombe Farm
PARK WATER LANE
GRANGE LA
COMMON WEST
Broadwindsor
HAINES LA
Temple Farm
Lowdown Farm
Jubilee Trail
Burstock Grange Farm
Common Farm
Craft Ctr
B3163
Knapp Farm
Lower Newnham Farm
SPECKET LANE
SHEEPWASH LANE
1 HIGH ST
2 YARNBARTON
3 THE HAYES
4 TRUSTHAMS
5 BACK LA
6 THE OLD BAKERY
7 REDLANDS LA
8 ORCHARD MD
Castlewood Farm
Racedown Home Farm
Wessex Ridgeway
Courtwood Farm
Higher Newnham Farm
Fir Tree Farm
Stoke Knapp Farm
Home Farm
COCKPIT HILL
Swilletts Farm
Wall Farm
Burstock Down
Lewesdon Hill (NT)
WADDON HILL (ROMAN FORT)
Higher Attisham Farm
Attisham Farm
Pilsdon Pen
NT
Cockpit Hill
SWILLETTS LA
NORWAY LANE
Birdsmoorgate Farm
Pen Coppice
Lewesdon Farm
Templeman's Ash
Pilsdon Barn
King's Moor Coppice
Higher Brimley Coombe Farm
Crabbs Hill
Sliding Hill
Halfyard Coppice
Alder Moor Coppice
COOMBE LANE
Bettiscombe Manor House
Mill Coppice
Laverstock Farm
Higher Coombe Coppice
Four Ashes
Buck's Head
Brimley Farm
Marshalsea Farm
Revelshay Farm
DT6
Higher Doghill Coppice
PILSDON LA
Bettiscombe
Sweed Moor
Lower House Farm
Jubilee Trail
Pilsdon Manor
YARD LA
Yard Farm
Blackney Farm
Waterhouse Farm
Coates Farm
New Barn Farm
Pilsdon Dairy Farm
Blackney
North Bowood
Manshay Farm
Marshwood Manor
Ashlands Coppice
BLACKNEY LANE
Lower Witneys Coppice
Round Coppice
BATT'S LANE
Pilsdon
Strode Manor
Oakwood Farm
Purcombe Farm
VENN LA
Venn Farm
MONKWOOD LANE
Deer Park Farm
Gerrard's Farm
Glitney Farm
Lowness Coppice
Strode Coppice
Cowdea Farm
Batts Coppices
Blackcroft Coppice
Higher Monkwood Farm
South Bowood
MANSHAY LA
MUTTON STREET
Higher Park Farm
Oakford Farm
BLIND LANE
Cypress Farm
Kittys Farm
Lower Monkwood Farm
Farthing's Coppice
South Bowood Dairy Farm
TAPHOUSE LANE
POORHOUSE LANE
SHAVE CROSS
Fooks's Covert
West Coppice
FILFORD LA
Pentsome Coppice
39 40 41 42 43 44
98 99 00 01 02 03 04 05
1 2 3 4 5 6 7 8
66
67
204

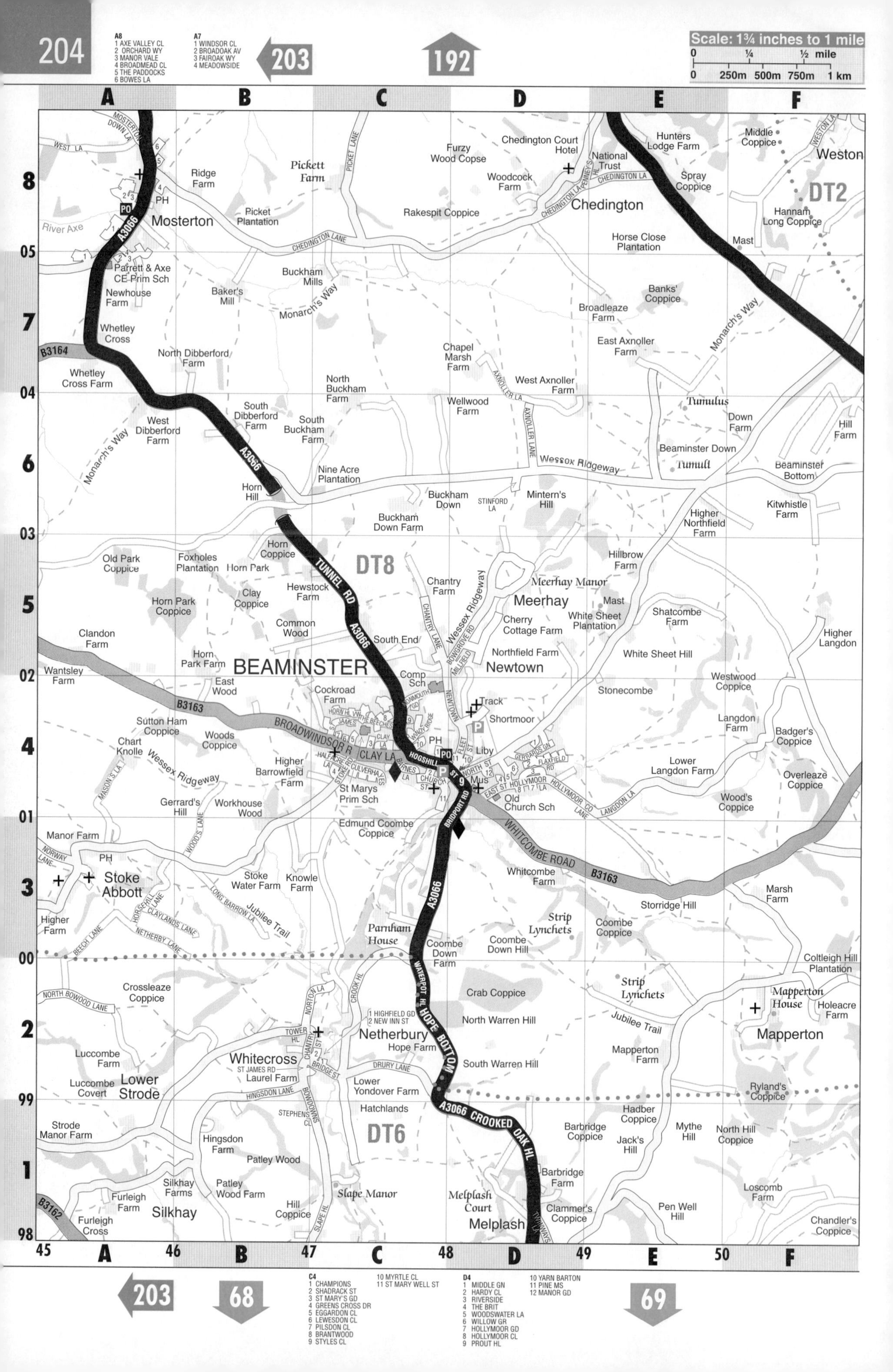
Mosterton
Ridge Farm
Pickett Farm
Furzy Wood Copse
Chedington Court Hotel
National Trust
Hunters Lodge Farm
Middle Coppice
Weston
Woodcock Farm
Spray Coppice
DT2
Chedington
Picket Plantation
Rakespit Coppice
Hannam Long Coppice
River Axe
Horse Close Plantation
Mast
Parrett & Axe CE Prim Sch
Buckham Mills
Baker's Mill
Newhouse Farm
Banks' Coppice
Monarch's Way
Broadleaze Farm
Whetley Cross
East Axnoller Farm
North Dibberford Farm
Chapel Marsh Farm
Whetley Cross Farm
North Buckham Farm
West Axnoller Farm
Wellwood Farm
Tumulus
South Dibberford Farm
West Dibberford Farm
South Buckham Farm
Down Farm
Hill Farm
Beaminster Down
Tumuli
Nine Acre Plantation
Wessex Ridgeway
Beaminster Bottom
Horn Hill
Buckham Down
Mintern's Hill
Kitwhistle Farm
Buckham Down Farm
Higher Northfield Farm
Horn Coppice
Old Park Coppice
Foxholes Plantation
Horn Park
DT8
Hillbrow Farm
Chantry Farm
Meerhay Manor
Hewstock Farm
Clay Coppice
Horn Park Coppice
Meerhay
Mast
Shatcombe Farm
White Sheet Plantation
Cherry Cottage Farm
Common Wood
Higher Langdon
Clandon Farm
South End
Northfield Farm
White Sheet Hill
Horn Park Farm
BEAMINSTER
Newtown
Wantsley Farm
Comp Sch
Westwood Coppice
East Wood
Cockroad Farm
Stonecombe
Track
Sutton Ham Coppice
Shortmoor
Langdon Farm
Badger's Coppice
Chart Knolle
Woods Coppice
Liby
Higher Barrowfield Farm
Lower Langdon Farm
Overleaze Coppice
St Marys Prim Sch
Mus
Old Church Sch
Gerrard's Hill
Workhouse Wood
Wood's Coppice
Edmund Coombe Coppice
Manor Farm
WHITCOMBE ROAD
Stoke Abbott
Stoke Water Farm
Knowle Farm
Whitcombe Farm
B3163
Marsh Farm
Storridge Hill
Higher Farm
Jubilee Trail
Strip Lynchets
Coombe Coppice
Parnham House
Coombe Down Farm
Coombe Down Hill
Coltleigh Hill Plantation
Crossleaze Coppice
Crab Coppice
Strip Lynchets
Mapperton House
Holeacre Farm
North Warren Hill
Netherbury
Hope Farm
Mapperton
Mapperton Farm
Luccombe Farm
Whitecross
Laurel Farm
South Warren Hill
Luccombe Covert
Lower Strode
Lower Yondover Farm
Ryland's Coppice
Hatchlands
Hadber Coppice
Strode Manor Farm
Barbridge Coppice
Jack's Hill
Mythe Hill
North Hill Coppice
DT6
Hingsdon Farm
Patley Wood
Barbridge Farm
Silkhay Farms
Patley Wood Farm
Furleigh Farm
Slape Manor
Melplash Court
Loscomb Farm
Silkhay
Hill Coppice
Clammer's Coppice
Pen Well Hill
Furleigh Cross
Melplash
Chandler's Coppice
A3066
B3164
B3163
B3162
TUNNEL RD
CLAY LA
HOGSHILL
BRIDPORT RD
WATERPOT HL
HOPE BOTTOM
A3066 CROOKED OAK HL
CHEDINGTON LANE
BROADWINDSOR R
1 HIGHFIELD GD
2 NEW INN ST
A B C D E F
8 7 6 5 4 3 2 1
05 04 03 02 01 00 99 98
45 46 47 48 49 50

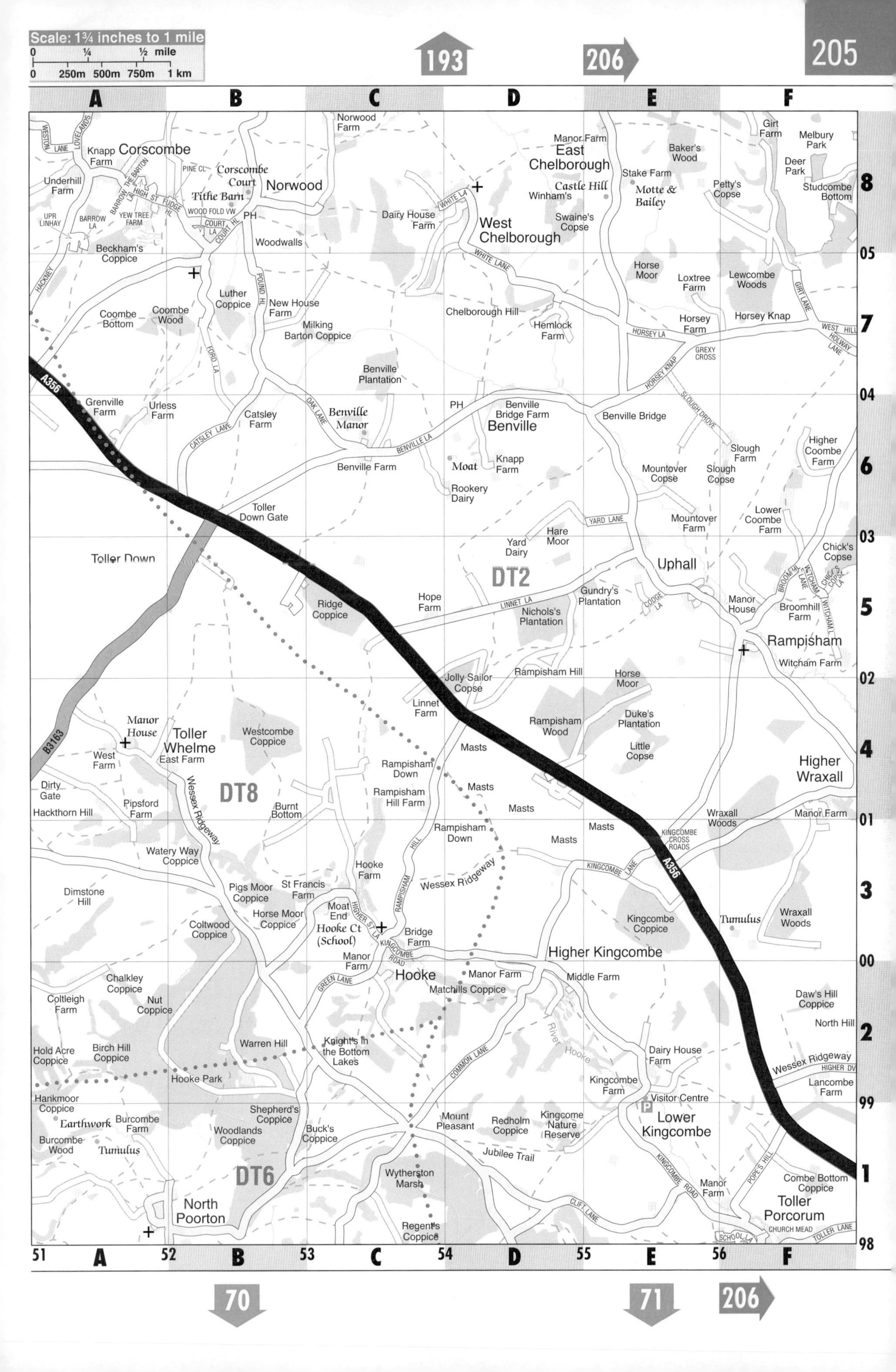
Scale: 1¾ inches to 1 mile
0 ¼ ½ mile
0 250m 500m 750m 1 km
193
206
A B C D E F
Corscombe
Knapp Farm
Underhill Farm
Corscombe Court
Tithe Barn
Norwood
Norwood Farm
Woodwalls
Beckham's Coppice
Luther Coppice
New House Farm
Coombe Bottom
Coombe Wood
Milking Barton Coppice
Dairy House Farm
West Chelborough
Manor Farm
East Chelborough
Castle Hill
Winham's
Swaine's Copse
Stake Farm
Motte & Bailey
Baker's Wood
Petty's Copse
Girt Farm
Melbury Park
Deer Park
Studcombe Bottom
Horse Moor
Loxtree Farm
Lewcombe Woods
Chelborough Hill
Hemlock Farm
Horsey Farm
Horsey Knap
Grexy Cross
Benville Plantation
Grenville Farm
Urless Farm
Catsley Farm
Benville Manor
Benville Bridge Farm
Benville
Benville Bridge
Benville Farm
Moat
Knapp Farm
Rookery Dairy
Mountover Copse
Slough Farm
Slough Copse
Higher Coombe Farm
Toller Down Gate
Toller Down
Mountover Farm
Lower Coombe Farm
Yard Dairy
Hare Moor
Chick's Copse
DT2
Uphall
Ridge Coppice
Hope Farm
Gundry's Plantation
Nichols's Plantation
Manor House
Broomhill Farm
Rampisham
Witcham Farm
Jolly Sailor Copse
Rampisham Hill
Horse Moor
Linnet Farm
Rampisham Wood
Duke's Plantation
Manor House
Toller Whelme
Westcombe Coppice
West Farm
East Farm
Masts
Little Copse
Higher Wraxall
Dirty Gate
DT8
Rampisham Down
Rampisham Hill Farm
Pipsford Farm
Burnt Bottom
Hackthorn Hill
Wraxall Woods
Manor Farm
Watery Way Coppice
Rampisham Down
Wessex Ridgeway
Hooke Farm
Dimstone Hill
Pigs Moor Coppice
St Francis Farm
Moat End
Hooke Ct (School)
Horse Moor Coppice
Bridge Farm
Kingcombe Coppice
Tumulus
Wraxall Woods
Coltwood Coppice
Manor Farm
Higher Kingcombe
Hooke
Manor Farm
Middle Farm
Chalkley Coppice
Matchills Coppice
Coltleigh Farm
Nut Coppice
Daw's Hill Coppice
North Hill
Hold Acre Coppice
Birch Hill Coppice
Warren Hill
Knight's in the Bottom Lakes
River Hooke
Dairy House Farm
Hooke Park
Kingcombe Farm
Visitor Centre
Lancombe Farm
Hankmoor Coppice
Shepherd's Coppice
Earthwork
Burcombe Farm
Mount Pleasant
Redholm Coppice
Kingcome Nature Reserve
Lower Kingcombe
Burcombe Wood
Tumulus
Woodlands Coppice
Buck's Coppice
Jubilee Trail
DT6
Wytherston Marsh
Manor Farm
Combe Bottom Coppice
North Poorton
Toller Porcorum
Regent's Coppice
A356
B3163
51 52 53 54 55 56
98 99 00 01 02 03 04 05
1 2 3 4 5 6 7 8
70
71
206

Scale: 1¾ inches to 1 mile

0	¼	½ mile
0	250m 500m 750m	1 km

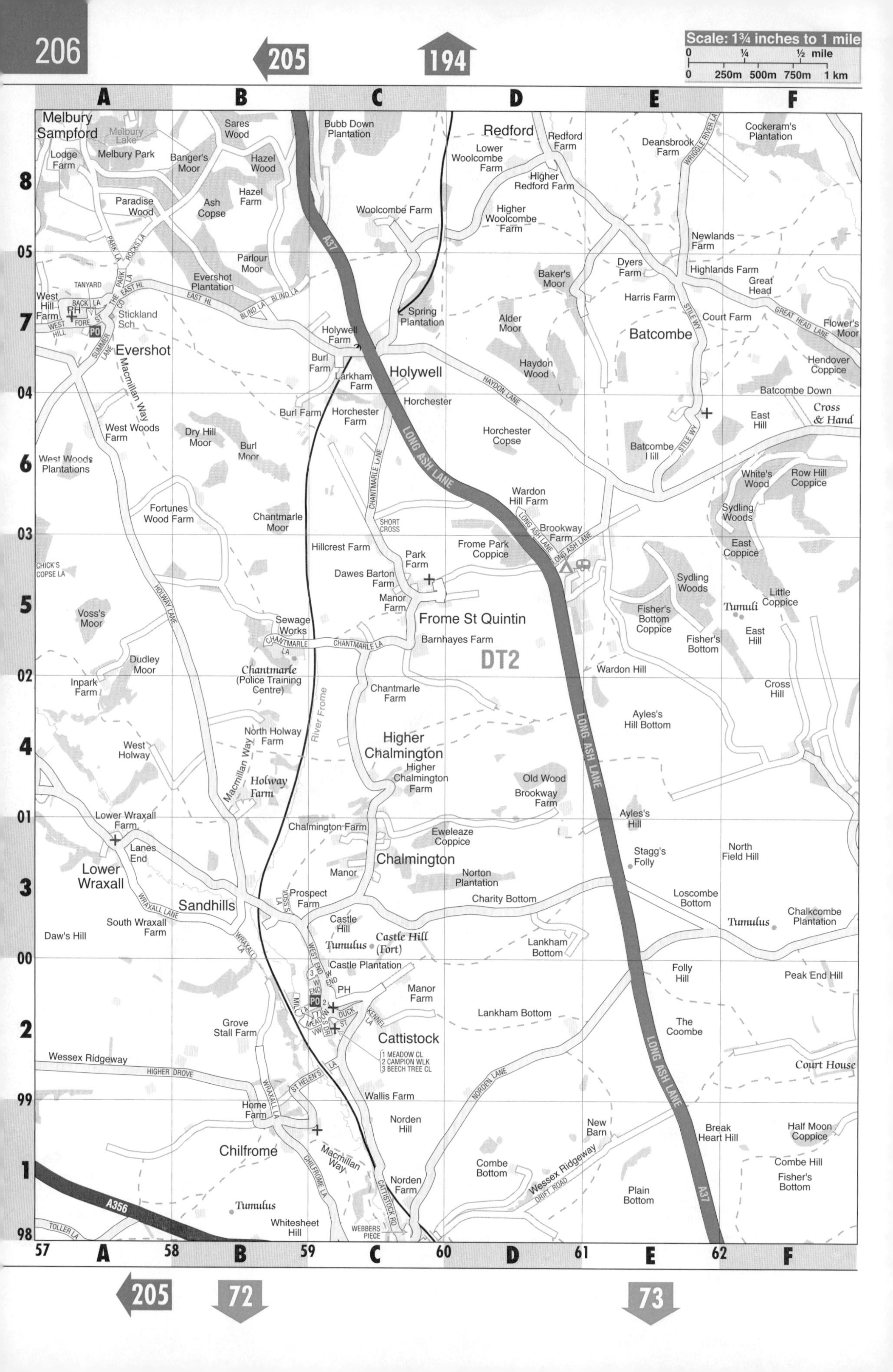

A **B** **C** **D** **E** **F**

Melbury Sampford
Melbury Lake
Lodge Farm
Melbury Park
Banger's Moor
Sares Wood
Hazel Wood
Bubb Down Plantation
Redford
Redford Farm
Deansbrook Farm
Cockeram's Plantation

8

Paradise Wood
Ash Copse
Hazel Farm
Lower Woolcombe Farm
Higher Redford Farm
Newlands Farm
Highlands Farm
Great Head

05

Parlour Moor
Evershot Plantation
Woolcombe Farm
Higher Woolcombe Farm
Baker's Moor
Dyers Farm
Harris Farm
Court Farm
Flower's Moor

7

West Hill Farm
TANYARD
Stickland Sch
BACK LA
FORE ST
PO
WEST HILL
Evershot
East Hl
Blind La
Blind La
Holywell Farm
Burl Farm
Larkham Farm
Holywell
Spring Plantation
Horchester
Alder Moor
Haydon Wood
Batcombe
Stile Way
Hendover Coppice

04

Macmillan Way
West Woods Farm
Dry Hill Moor
Burl Farm
Horchester Farm
Burl Moor
Horchester
Chantmarle Lane
Horchester Copse
Batcombe Hill
Stile W'Y
East Hill
Batcombe Down
Cross & Hand

6

West Woods Plantations
Fortunes Wood Farm
Chantmarle Moor
Short Cross
Wardon Hill Farm
Long Ash Lane
Brookway
Long Ash Lane
White's Wood
Row Hill Coppice
Sydling Woods

03

CHICK'S COPSE LA
Holway Lane
Hillcrest Farm
Dawes Barton Farm
Park Farm
Frome Park Coppice
East Coppice
Sydling Woods

5

Voss's Moor
Sewage Works
Chantmarle La
Chantmarle La
Manor Farm
Frome St Quintin
Barnhayes Farm
DT2
Wardon Hill
Fisher's Bottom Coppice
Tumuli
Little Coppice
Fisher's Bottom
East Hill

02

Inpark Farm
Dudley Moor
Chantmarle (Police Training Centre)
River Frome
Chantmarle Farm
Wardon Hill
Cross Hill

4

West Holway
North Holway Farm
Macmillan Way
Higher Chalmington
Higher Chalmington Farm
Old Wood
Brookway Farm
Ayles's Hill Bottom

01

Lower Wraxall Farm
Lanes End
Holway Farm
Chalmington Farm
Eweleaze Coppice
Ayles's Hill
North Field Hill

3

Lower Wraxall
Wraxall Lane
Sandhills
Prospect Farm
Manor
Chalmington
Norton Plantation
Charity Bottom
Stagg's Folly
Loscombe Bottom
Tumulus
Chalkcombe Plantation

Daw's Hill
South Wraxall Farm
Castle Hill
Tumulus
Castle Hill (Fort)
Lankham Bottom

00

WRAXALL LA
WEST END W
Castle Plantation
PH
Manor Farm
Folly Hill
Peak End Hill

2

MILL LA
PO
DUCK ST
KENNEL LA
Grove Stall Farm
Cattistock
Lankham Bottom
The Coombe
Court House

Wessex Ridgeway
HIGHER DROVE
ST HELEN'S LA
Wallis Farm
1 MEADOW CL
2 CAMPION WLK
3 BEECH TREE CL
Norden Lane

99

WRAXALL LA
Home Farm
Norden Hill
New Barn
Break Heart Hill
Half Moon Coppice

1

Chilfrome
Macmillan Way
CHILFROME LA
Norden Farm
Combe Bottom
Wessex Ridgeway
DRIFT ROAD
Plain Bottom
Combe Hill
Fisher's Bottom

A356
Tumulus
Whitesheet Hill
WEBBERS PIECE
Cattistock Rd
A37

98

TOLLER LA

57 **A** **58** **B** **59** **C** **60** **D** **61** **E** **62** **F**

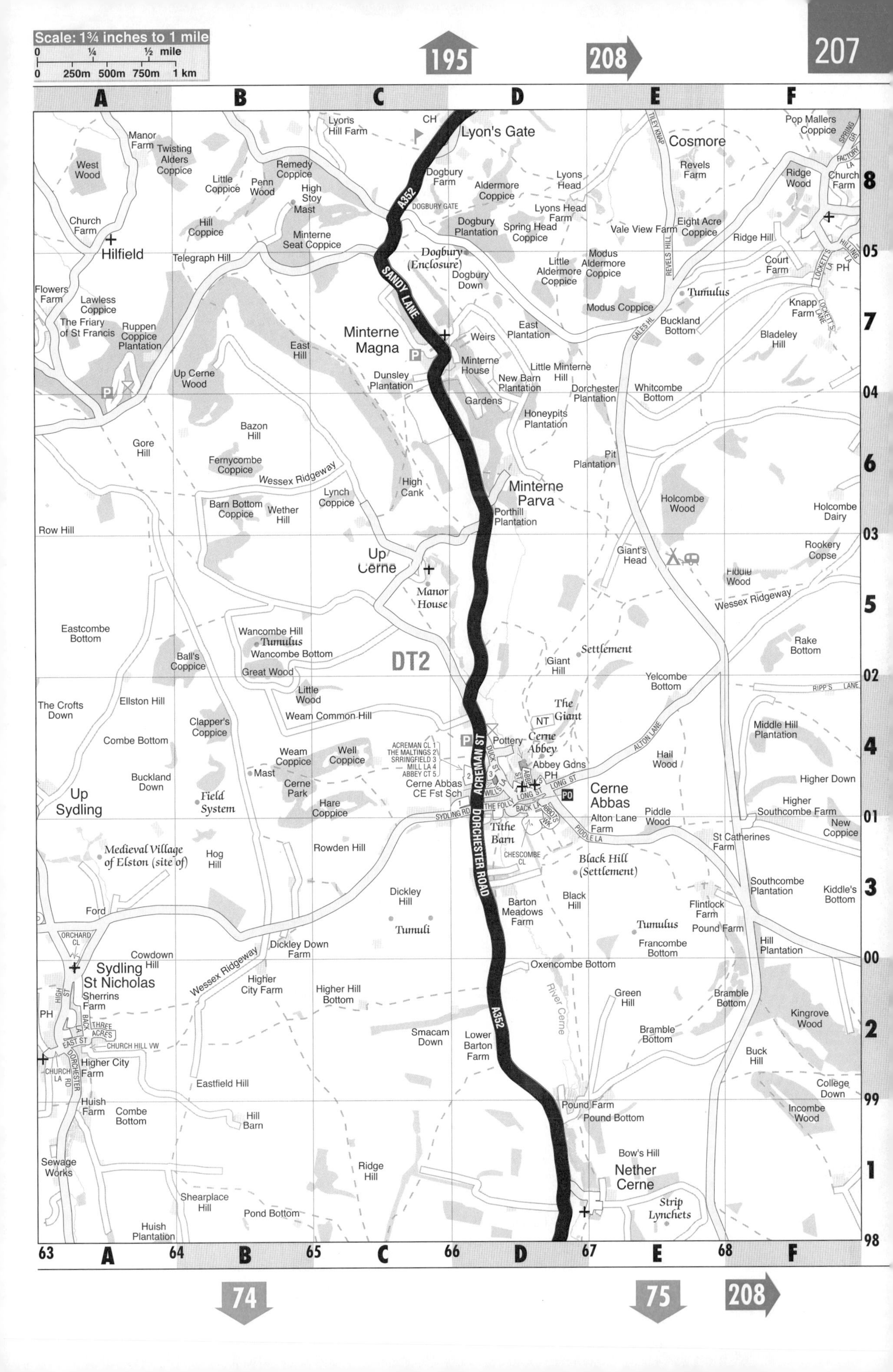
Scale: 1¾ inches to 1 mile
0 ¼ ½ mile
0 250m 500m 750m 1 km
195
208
A B C D E F
Lyons Hill Farm
CH
Lyon's Gate
Cosmore
Pop Mallers Coppice
Manor Farm
Twisting Alders Coppice
West Wood
Little Coppice
Penn Wood
Remedy Coppice
High Stoy Mast
Dogbury Farm
Aldermore Coppice
Lyons Head
Revels Farm
Ridge Wood
Church Farm
A352
DOGBURY GATE
Lyons Head Farm
Church Farm
Hill Coppice
Minterne Seat Coppice
Dogbury Plantation
Spring Head Coppice
Vale View Farm
Eight Acre Coppice
Ridge Hill
Hilfield
Telegraph Hill
Dogbury (Enclosure)
Little Aldermore Coppice
Modus Aldermore Coppice
Court Farm
PH
SANDY LANE
Dogbury Down
REVELS HILL
Tumulus
Flowers Farm
Lawless Coppice
Modus Coppice
Knapp Farm
The Friary of St Francis
Ruppen Coppice Plantation
Minterne Magna
East Hill
East Plantation
Weirs
Buckland Bottom
Bladeley Hill
GALES HL
Up Cerne Wood
Dunsley Plantation
Minterne House
Little Minterne Hill
New Barn Plantation
Dorchester Plantation
Whitcombe Bottom
Gardens
Honeypits Plantation
Bazon Hill
Gore Hill
Fernycombe Coppice
Wessex Ridgeway
Pit Plantation
High Cank
Minterne Parva
Lynch Coppice
Barn Bottom Coppice
Wether Hill
Holcombe Wood
Holcombe Dairy
Porthill Plantation
Row Hill
Up Cerne
Giant's Head
Rookery Copse
Piddle Wood
Manor House
Wessex Ridgeway
Eastcombe Bottom
Wancombe Hill
Tumulus
Wancombe Bottom
Rake Bottom
Ball's Coppice
DT2
Settlement
Giant Hill
Great Wood
Yelcombe Bottom
RIPP'S LANE
The Crofts Down
Ellston Hill
Little Wood
Weam Common Hill
The Giant
NT
Clapper's Coppice
Middle Hill Plantation
Combe Bottom
ALTON LANE
ACREMAN CL 1
THE MALTINGS 2
SRRINGFIELD 3
MILL LA 4
ABBEY CT 5
Pottery
Cerne Abbey
Weam Coppice
Well Coppice
Abbey Gdns
PH
Hail Wood
Higher Down
Mast
ACREMAN ST
DUCK ST
Buckland Down
Cerne Park
Cerne Abbas CE Fst Sch
WILLS LA
LONG ST
Cerne Abbas
Up Sydling
Field System
Hare Coppice
THE FOLLY
BACK LA
ABBOTS WK
PO
Higher Southcombe Farm
SYDLING RD
Alton Lane Farm
Piddle Wood
New Coppice
Tithe Barn
PIDDLE LA
St Catherines Farm
Medieval Village of Elston (site of)
Hog Hill
Rowden Hill
DORCHESTER ROAD
CHESCOMBE CL
Black Hill (Settlement)
Southcombe Plantation
Kiddle's Bottom
Dickley Hill
Black Hill
Barton Meadows Farm
Flintlock Farm
Ford
Tumuli
Tumulus
Pound Farm
ORCHARD CL
Dickley Down Farm
Francombe Bottom
Hill Plantation
Cowdown Hill
Oxencombe Bottom
Sydling St Nicholas
Wessex Ridgeway
Higher City Farm
Higher Hill Bottom
Green Hill
Bramble Bottom
Sherrins Farm
River Cerne
A352
HIGH ST
PH
BACK LA
THREE ACRES
Kingrove Wood
EAST ST
CHURCH HILL VW
Smacam Down
Lower Barton Farm
Bramble Bottom
Buck Hill
Higher City Farm
CHURCH LA
DORCHESTER RD
Eastfield Hill
College Down
Huish Farm
Combe Bottom
Hill Barn
Pound Farm
Pound Bottom
Incombe Wood
Sewage Works
Ridge Hill
Bow's Hill
Nether Cerne
Shearplace Hill
Pond Bottom
Strip Lynchets
Huish Plantation
8 05 7 04 6 03 5 02 4 01 3 00 2 99 1 98
63 64 65 66 67 68
74
75
208

Scale: 1¾ inches to 1 mile
0   ¼   ½   mile
0   250m 500m 750m   1 km

A B C D E F

8

SPRING
GR
FACTORY LA
Woolford's
Water
B3143
Buckland Newton
Prim Sch
LANDSCOMBE
VALE
CRANES MD
PO
Higher Farm

Rew
REW LA
Millers
Farm
CASTLE LA
Rew Head
Farm
Castle
Lane Farm
Ball
Farm
Wreth
Farm

Brockhampton
Farm
CHASTON LA
Chaston
Farm
Sharnhill Green

Lower
Thurnwood
Farm
Thurnwood
Dairy Farm

+
HAMMOND ST
QUAR LA
Mappowder
Court
DT10
Saunders
Farm
Cockroad
Copse

05

HILLING LA
MAJOR'S COMMON
Buckland Newton
FORD DOWN LA

Higher
Henley Farm
Bookham
BOOKHAM LANE

Noake Farm

Monkwood
Hill Farm
Humber
Wood
DT11

7

Old Henley
Farm
Henley
CRONTHORNE LA
Bookham
Cottage Farm
WHITE WAY
Alton Common
Farm
Alton
Common

Little Monkwood
Hill Farm
Park Farm
Melcombe
Park

04

Henley House
Farm
Narn
Farm

Ivest Wood
Church Hill
Hill Wood
Ball Bottom
Copse
Ball
Copse
Armswell
Farm
Woodlands
Farm
Lovelace's
Copse
Springwood
Farm
Hill Wood

6

Barcombe
Farm
HOLCOMBE MD
Field
System
Penny Farthing
Wood
Little Elias
Copse
Watcombe
Wood
Field System
Ball Hill
Kithill Plantation
Folly
Nettlecombe
Tout
Fort
Aldermore
Copse
Dorsetshire
Gap
Cony-gar
Copse
Tumulus
Little Wood
Nordon
Hill

03

Alton
Pancras
Watcombe
Bottom
Fetchum
Wood
Rock Pits
Farm
Folly
Farm
Sheepland
Copse
Cross
Dyke
Round Copse
Rough Copse
Melcombe Horsey
Bowdens
Cross
Well Dykes
Copse
Higher Melcombe
Farm
Higher
Melcombe

5

Austral Farm
+
Manor
House
Tumulus
West
Hill
Settlement
Harveys
Farm
PH
Plush
Higher
Hill
Tumuli
Hanover
Copse
Cross
Dyke
Lyscombe Hill
Lyscombe
Bottom
Settlement
Tumulus
Nettlecombe
Farm
Hog Hill
Summer House
Plantation

02

RIPP'S LANE
Rake
Bottom
Bulland's
Plantation
+
Lower Farm
Firland Wood

4

Rake Hill
Enclosures
Tenant's
Bottom
Plush Hill
DT2
Stickley
Coppice
Thorncombe
Bottom
Cross Dyke
Hog Hill

01

Tenant's Hill
Lower
Down
New
Coppice
Morning Well
Plantation
Ash Bed
Coppice
Lower
Southcombe
Farm
Tumulus
Slovens
Corner Coppice
Lyscombe
Farm
Chapel

3

Kiddles Farm
East
Hill
Redlands
Coppice
New Barn
Farm
Tokenhills
Coppice
Dole's Ash
Farm
Thorncombe
Farm
DRAKE'S LANE
Kiddle's
Bottom
Piddletrenthide
CHURCH LA
SMITH'S LA
Manor
House
Kingcombe

00

Rogers'
Bottom
Hillside Farm
Kingrove
Down
PO
PH
WIGHTMAN'S ORCHARD
NORTHOVER CL
Piddle Valley
First Sch
Whitcombe
Hill
Tumulus

2

Kingrove
Wood
Dutnole
Coppice
South House
Tumulus
Tumuli

99

Coll Down
Kingrove
Bottom
Highlands
SUN LA
Hog Leaze
Cheselbourne
West Down

1

Well Bottom Down
Lackington
Farm
SWAN LA
SOUTH VW
+
PH
White
Lackington
LACKINGTON
DROVE
Tumulus
Dole's Hill
Plantation
Tumulus

98

69   A   70   B   71   C   72   D   73   E   74   F

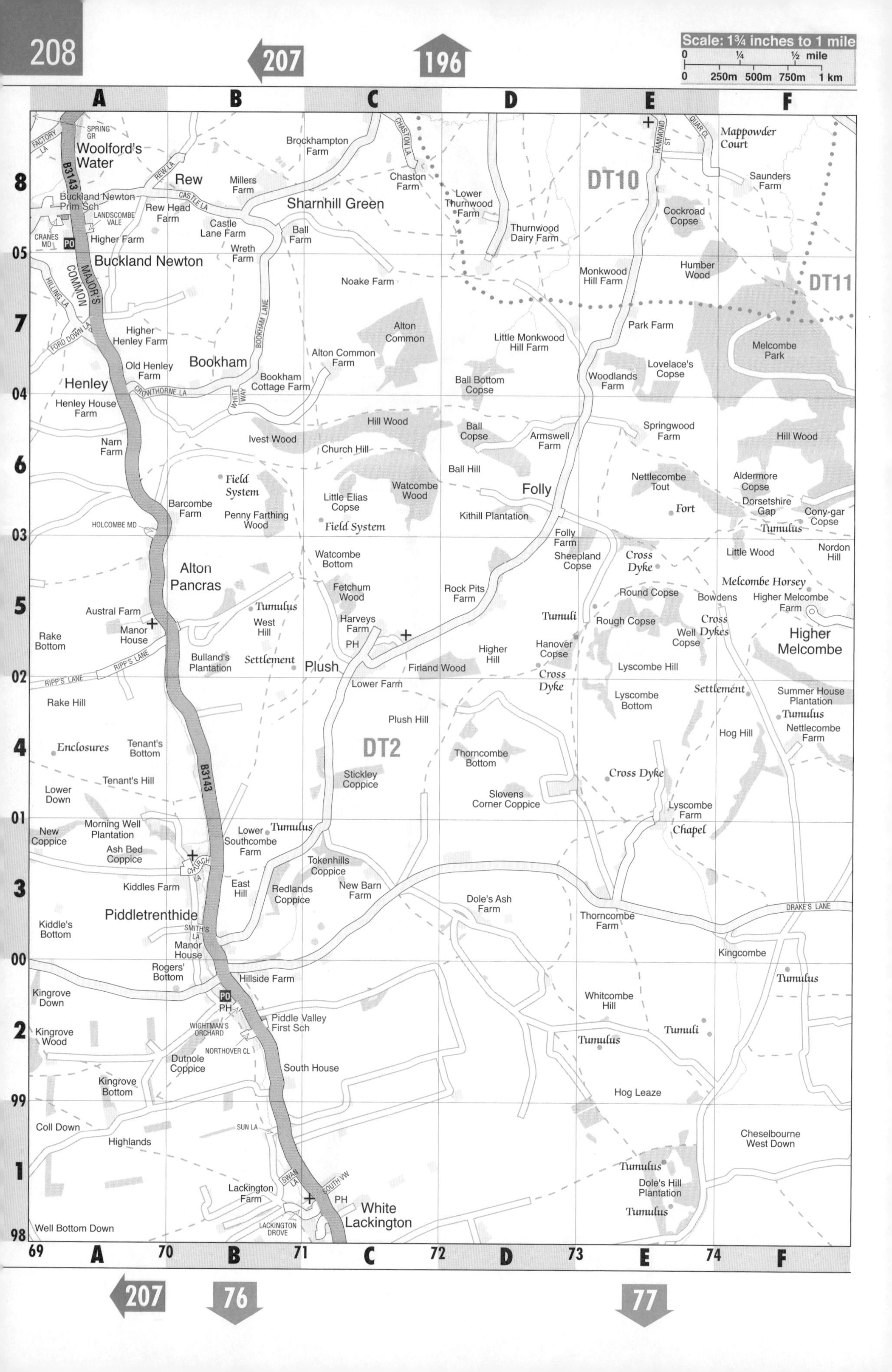

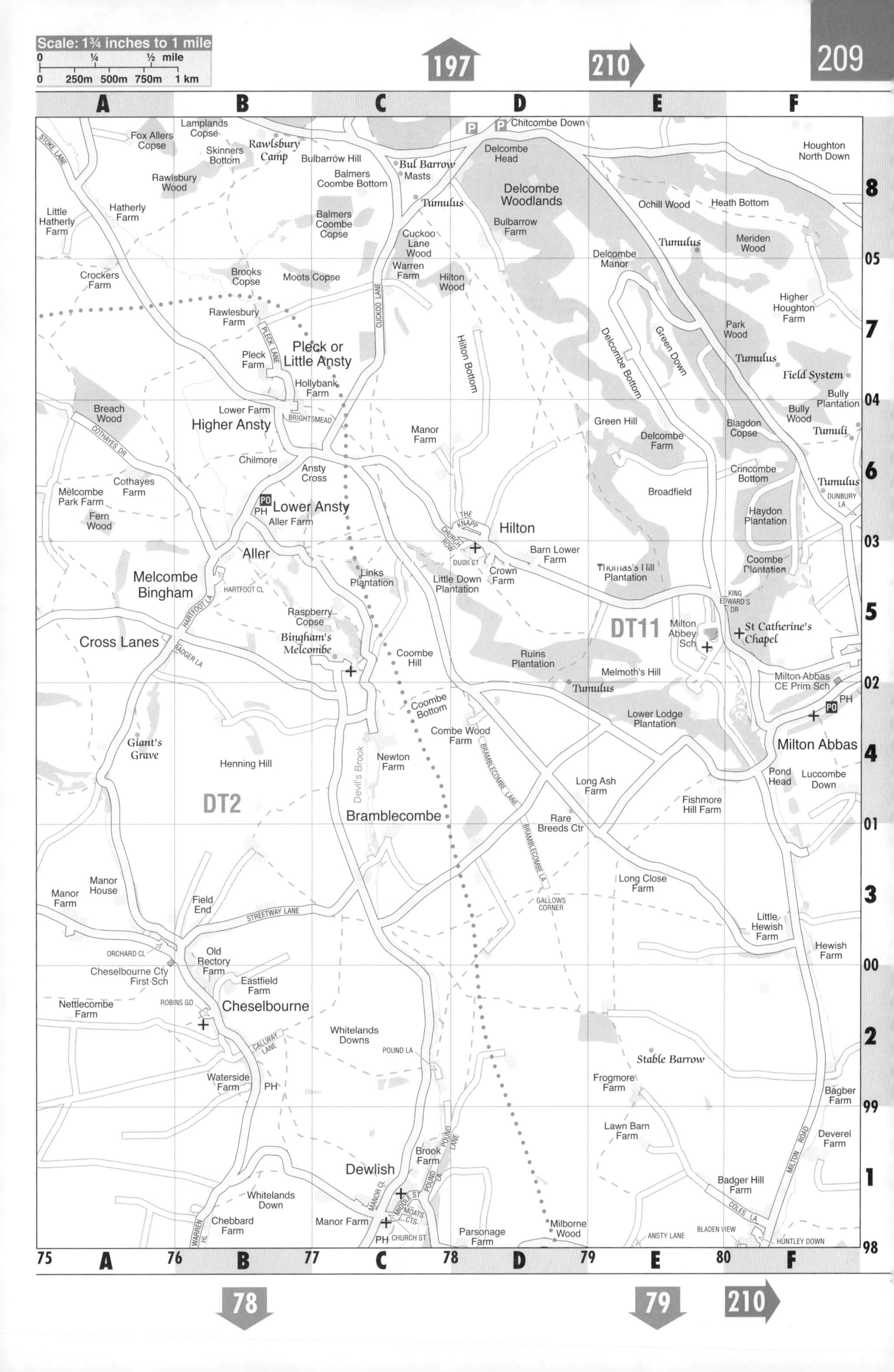
Scale: 1¾ inches to 1 mile
0 ¼ ½ mile
0 250m 500m 750m 1 km
197
210
A B C D E F
Lamplands Copse
Fox Allers Copse
Skinners Bottom
Rawlsbury Camp
Bulbarrow Hill
Bul Barrow Masts
Chitcombe Down
Delcombe Head
Houghton North Down
Rawlsbury Wood
Balmers Coombe Bottom
Delcombe Woodlands
Tumulus
Little Hatherly Farm
Hatherly Farm
Balmers Coombe Copse
Cuckoo Lane Wood
Bulbarrow Farm
Ochill Wood
Heath Bottom
Meriden Wood
Delcombe Manor
Crockers Farm
Brooks Copse
Moots Copse
Warren Farm
Hilton Wood
Higher Houghton Farm
Rawlesbury Farm
Cuckoo Lane
Park Wood
Pleck Lane
Pleck or Little Ansty
Pleck Farm
Hilton Bottom
Delcombe Bottom
Green Down
Field System
Hollybank Farm
Bully Plantation
Breach Wood
Lower Farm
Higher Ansty
Brightsmead
Green Hill
Bully Wood
Manor Farm
Delcombe Farm
Blagdon Copse
Tumuli
Cothayes Dr
Chilmore
Ansty Cross
Crincombe Bottom
Cothayes Farm
Melcombe Park Farm
Broadfield
Dunbury La
PO
PH
Lower Ansty
Aller Farm
Fern Wood
The Knapp
Church Row
Hilton
Haydon Plantation
Aller
Barn Lower Farm
Duck Ct
Coombe Plantation
Melcombe Bingham
Links Plantation
Little Down Plantation
Crown Farm
Thomas's Hill Plantation
Hartfoot Cl
King Edward's Dr
Hartfoot La
Raspberry Copse
DT11
Milton Abbey Sch
St Catherine's Chapel
Cross Lanes
Bingham's Melcombe
Coombe Hill
Ruins Plantation
Badger La
Melmoth's Hill
Milton Abbas CE Prim Sch
Coombe Bottom
Lower Lodge Plantation
Combe Wood Farm
Giant's Grave
Henning Hill
Devil's Brook
Newton Farm
Bramblecombe Lane
Milton Abbas
Pond Head
Luccombe Down
Long Ash Farm
DT2
Bramblecombe
Fishmore Hill Farm
Rare Breeds Ctr
Bramblecombe La
Manor Farm
Manor House
Long Close Farm
Field End
Gallows Corner
Streetway Lane
Little Hewish Farm
Hewish Farm
Orchard Cl
Old Rectory Farm
Cheselbourne Cty First Sch
Eastfield Farm
Nettlecombe Farm
Robins Gd
Cheselbourne
Callway Lane
Whitelands Downs
Pound La
Stable Barrow
Waterside Farm
Frogmore Farm
Bagber Farm
Lawn Barn Farm
Pound Lane
Deverel Farm
Brook Farm
Milton Road
Dewlish
Badger Hill Farm
Whitelands Down
Manor Cl
Middle St
Moats Cts
Coles La
Chebbard Farm
Warren Hl
Manor Farm
Church St
Parsonage Farm
Milborne Wood
Ansty Lane
Bladen View
Huntley Down
8
05
7
04
6
03
5
02
4
01
3
00
2
99
1
98
75 76 77 78 79 80
78
79
210

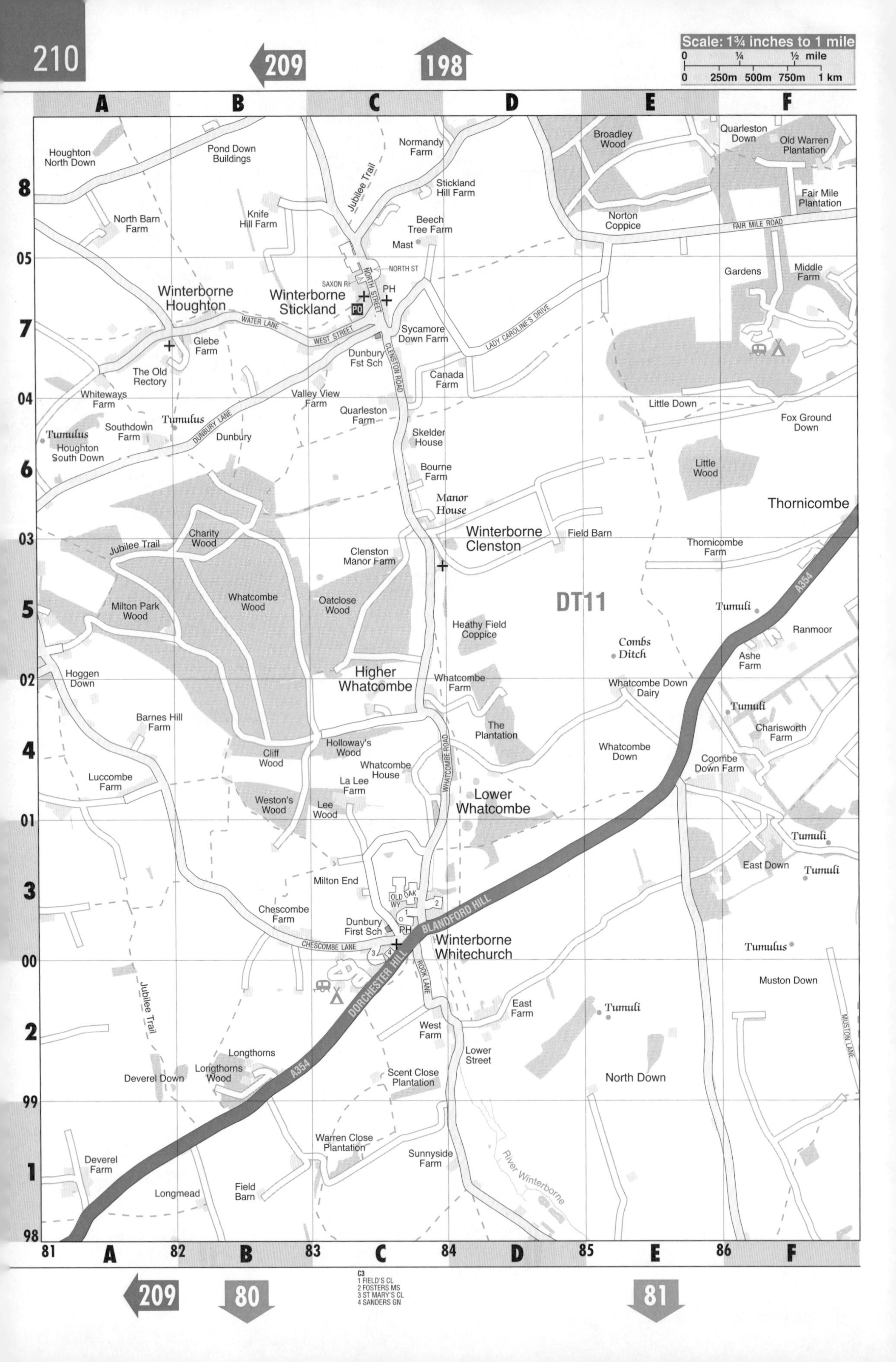

Scale: 1¾ inches to 1 mile

0   ¼   ½   mile
0   250m   500m   750m   1 km

A   **B**   **C**   **D**   **E**   **F**

8

Houghton
North Down

Pond Down
Buildings

Normandy
Farm

Broadley
Wood

Quarleston
Down

Old Warren
Plantation

North Barn
Farm

Knife
Hill Farm

Stickland
Hill Farm

Norton
Coppice

Fair Mile
Plantation

FAIR MILE ROAD

05

Beech
Tree Farm

Mast

Gardens

Middle
Farm

NORTH ST

SAXON RI

PH

7

Winterborne
Houghton

Winterborne
Stickland

PO

Sycamore
Down Farm

LADY CAROLINE'S DRIVE

WATER LANE

Glebe
Farm

WEST STREET

Dunbury Fst Sch

Canada
Farm

The Old
Rectory

CLENSTON ROAD

04

Whiteways
Farm

Valley View
Farm

Quarleston
Farm

Little Down

Fox Ground
Down

Tumulus

DUNBURY LANE

Skelder
House

Southdown
Farm

Dunbury

6

Tumulus
Houghton
South Down

Bourne
Farm

Little
Wood

Manor
House

Thornicombe

03

Jubilee Trail

Charity
Wood

Clenston
Manor Farm

Winterborne
Clenston

Field Barn

Thornicombe
Farm

Milton Park
Wood

Whatcombe
Wood

Oatclose
Wood

DT11

Tumuli

5

Heathy Field
Coppice

Ranmoor

Combs
Ditch

Ashe
Farm

02

Hoggen
Down

Higher
Whatcombe

Whatcombe
Farm

Whatcombe Down
Dairy

Tumuli

Barnes Hill
Farm

The
Plantation

Charisworth
Farm

4

Cliff
Wood

Holloway's
Wood

Whatcombe
House

Whatcombe
Down

Coombe
Down Farm

Luccombe
Farm

La Lee
Farm

Lower
Whatcombe

01

Weston's
Wood

Lee
Wood

Tumuli

East Down

Tumuli

3

Milton End

Chescombe
Farm

OLD OAK WY

2

Dunbury
First Sch

RH

Winterborne
Whitechurch

BLANDFORD HILL

Tumulus

CHESCOMBE LANE

1

3

00

DORCHESTER HILL

ROOK LANE

Muston Down

MUSTON LANE

Jubilee Trail

West
Farm

East
Farm

Tumuli

2

Longthorns

A354

Longthorns
Wood

North Down

Deverel Down

Scent Close
Plantation

Lower
Street

99

Deverel
Farm

Warren Close
Plantation

Sunnyside
Farm

River Winterborne

1

Longmead

Field
Barn

98

81   **A**   **82**   **B**   **83**   **C**   **84**   **D**   **85**   **E**   **86**   **F**

C3
1 FIELD'S CL
2 FOSTERS MS
3 ST MARY'S CL
4 SANDERS GN

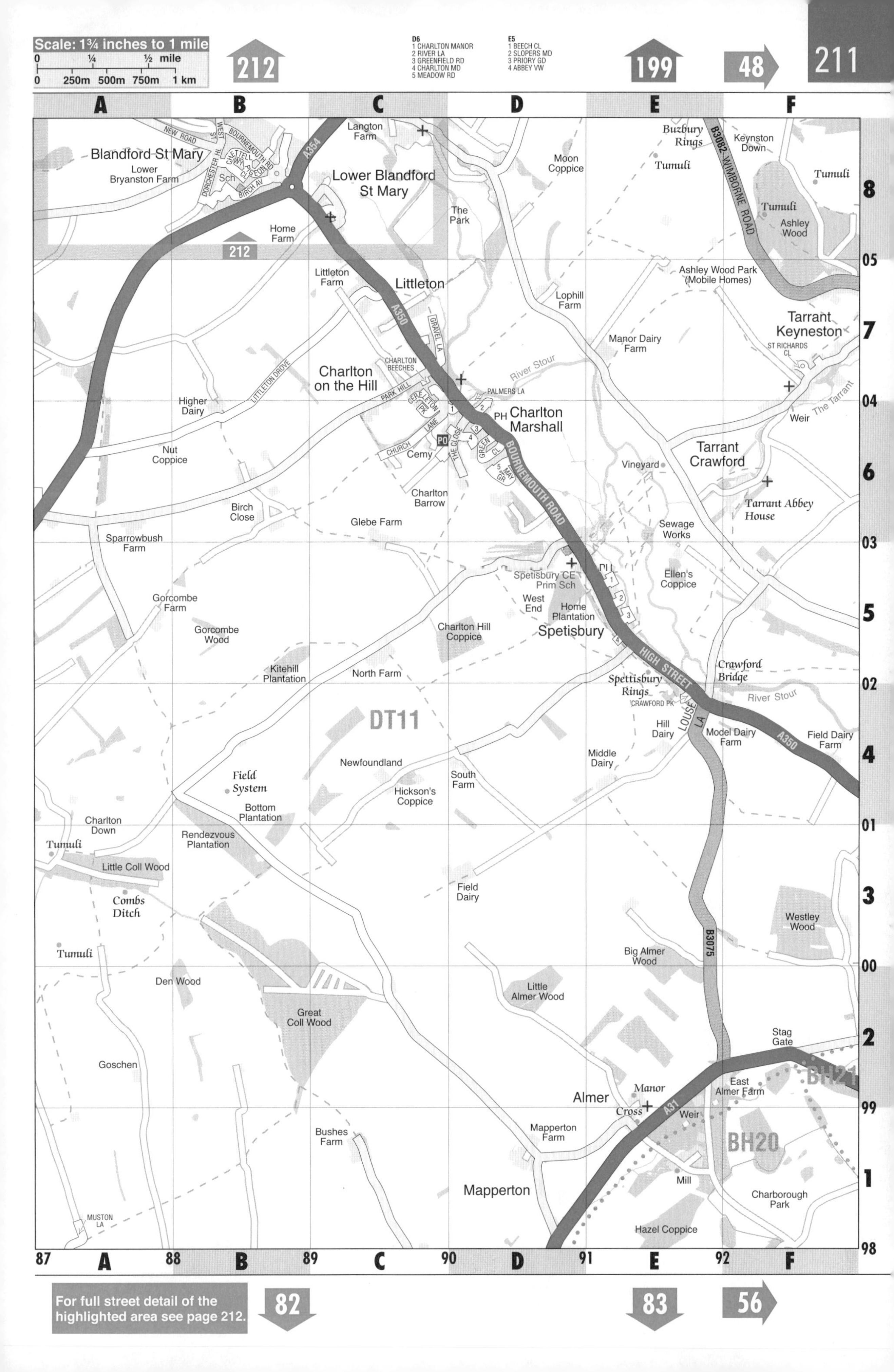
Scale: 1¾ inches to 1 mile
0 ¼ ½ mile
0 250m 500m 750m 1 km
212
D6
1 CHARLTON MANOR
2 RIVER LA
3 GREENFIELD RD
4 CHARLTON MD
5 MEADOW RD
E5
1 BEECH CL
2 SLOPERS MD
3 PRIORY GD
4 ABBEY VW
199
48
A B C D E F
Blandford St Mary
Lower Bryanston Farm
NEW ROAD
WEST ST
BOURNEMOUTH RD
DORCHESTER HL
Sch
BIRCH AV
A354
Langton Farm
Lower Blandford St Mary
Home Farm
212
The Park
Moon Coppice
Buzbury Rings
Tumuli
B3082 WIMBORNE ROAD
Keynston Down
Tumuli
Tumuli
Ashley Wood
8
05
Littleton Farm
Littleton
A350
GRAVEL LA
Lophill Farm
Ashley Wood Park (Mobile Homes)
Tarrant Keyneston
7
ST RICHARDS CL
Manor Dairy Farm
LITTLETON DROVE
Charlton on the Hill
CHARLTON BEECHES
River Stour
PARK HILL
PALMERS LA
Higher Dairy
PH
Charlton Marshall
04
Weir
The Tarrant
Nut Coppice
CHURCH
Cemy
PO
THE CLOSE
GREEN CL
MAY GR
BOURNEMOUTH ROAD
Tarrant Crawford
Vineyard
6
Tarrant Abbey House
Charlton Barrow
Birch Close
Glebe Farm
Sewage Works
Sparrowbush Farm
03
Spetisbury CE Prim Sch
Ellen's Coppice
Gorcombe Farm
West End
Home Plantation
5
Gorcombe Wood
Charlton Hill Coppice
Spetisbury
HIGH STREET
Crawford Bridge
Kitehill Plantation
North Farm
Spettisbury Rings
02
CRAWFORD PK
River Stour
DT11
Hill Dairy
LOUSE LA
Model Dairy Farm
A350
Field Dairy Farm
Middle Dairy
4
Newfoundland
Field System
South Farm
Hickson's Coppice
Bottom Plantation
Charlton Down
Rendezvous Plantation
01
Tumuli
Little Coll Wood
Combs Ditch
Field Dairy
3
Westley Wood
B3075
Tumuli
Big Almer Wood
00
Den Wood
Little Almer Wood
Great Coll Wood
Stag Gate
2
Goschen
East Almer Farm
BH21
Manor
Almer
Cross
A31
Weir
99
Bushes Farm
Mapperton Farm
BH20
1
Mill
Mapperton
Charborough Park
MUSTON LA
Hazel Coppice
98
87 A 88 B 89 C 90 D 91 E 92 F
For full street detail of the highlighted area see page 212.
82
83
56

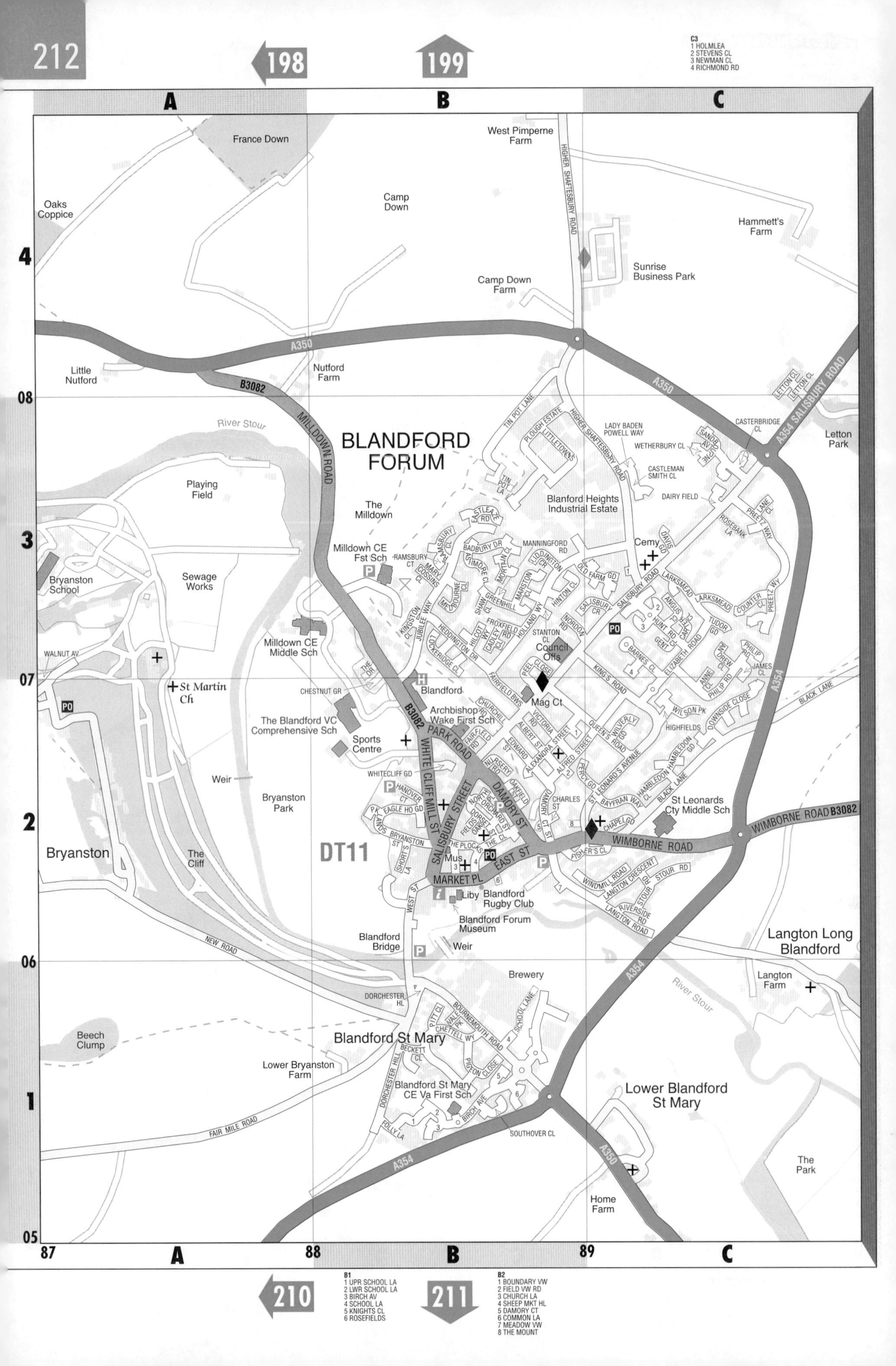

198
199

C3
1 HOLMLEA
2 STEVENS CL
3 NEWMAN CL
4 RICHMOND RD

A   B   C

France Down

West Pimperne
Farm

Camp
Down

Oaks
Coppice

4

Camp Down
Farm

Hammett's
Farm

Sunrise
Business Park

A350

Little
Nutford

B3082

Nutford
Farm

LETTON CL
LETTON CL

CASTERBRIDGE
CL

A354 SALISBURY ROAD

08

River Stour

MILLDOWN ROAD

**BLANDFORD
FORUM**

A350

TIN POT LANE

PLOUGH ESTATE
LITTLETOWNS

HIGHER SHAFTESBURY ROAD

LADY BADEN
POWELL WAY

WETHERBURY CL

SANDR
AV

Letton
Park

Playing
Field

The
Milldown

Blanford Heights
Industrial Estate

CASTLEMAN
SMITH CL

DAIRY FIELD

ROSEBANK
LA

PREETZ WAY

PREETZ LANE

3

Milldown CE
Fst Sch

Bryanston
School

Sewage
Works

RAMSBURY
CT

ST LEA
RD

BADBURY DR

MANNINGFORD RD

OLD FARM GD

Cemy

DAVIS

LARKSMEAD

LARKSMEAD

COUNTER WY

ANGUS

Walnut AV

Milldown CE
Middle Sch

CHESTNUT GR

St Martin
Ch

PO

Blandford

H

The Blandford VC
Comprehensive Sch

Sports
Centre

Weir

Bryanston
Park

PARK ROAD

B3082

WHITE CLIFF

Archbishop
Wake First Sch

Council
Offs

Mag Ct

PO

HUNT RD

GERT

TUDOR GD

PHILIP RD

JAMES CL

PHILIP RD

BLACK LANE

A354

QUEEN'S ROAD

KING'S ROAD

WILSON PK

HIGHFIELDS

DOWNSIDE CLOSE

St Leonards
Cty Middle Sch

07

WALNUT AV

WHITECLIFF GD

HANOVER
CT

SALISBURY STREET

DAMORY ST

ALEXANDRA STREET

LEONARD'S AVENUE

HAMBLEDON RD

HAMBLEDON

BLACK LANE

2

DT11

Bryanston

The
Cliff

EAGLE HO GD

BRYANSTON

LANDS

SHORTS LA

WEST ST

THE PLOCKS

MARKET PL

EAST ST

i

Liby

Mus

PO

P

Blandford
Rugby Club

CHARLES
ST

CHAPEL GD

FISHER'S CL

WINDMILL ROAD

LANGTON CRESCENT

RIVERSIDE
RD

STOUR RD

STOUR RD

WIMBORNE ROAD

B3082

Langton Long
Blandford

NEW ROAD

Blandford
Bridge

P

Weir

Blandford
Forum Museum

LANGTON ROAD

A354

River Stour

Langton
Farm

06

Beech
Clump

DORCHESTER
HL

Blandford
Bridge

Brewery

SCHOOL LANE

BOURNEMOUTH ROAD

Blandford St Mary

PITT CL

WALK

CHETTELL WY

BECKETT CL

PIGEON CLOSE

Lower
Blandford
St Mary

Langton
Farm

Lower Bryanston
Farm

DORCHESTER HILL

Blandford St Mary
CE Va First Sch

BIRCH AVE

SOUTHOVER CL

A350

The
Park

1

FAIR MILE ROAD

FOLLY LA

A354

Home
Farm

05

87   A   88   B   89   C

210
211

B1
1 UPR SCHOOL LA
2 LWR SCHOOL LA
3 BIRCH AV
4 SCHOOL LA
5 KNIGHTS CL
6 ROSEFIELDS

B2
1 BOUNDARY VW
2 FIELD VW RD
3 CHURCH LA
4 SHEEP MKT HL
5 DAMORY CT
6 COMMON LA
7 MEADOW VW
8 THE MOUNT

A3
1 CHANCERY CL
2 HIGHBURY CL
3 KENSINGTON RD
4 RICHMOND RD
5 JUBILEE CT
6 HAWTHORN CL
7 CHARLES ST
8 MEADOW RD
9 GEORGE ST (STH)
10 MEADOW RD (STH)
11 WINDSOR ST
12 WINDSOR RD
13 STATION TERR
14 SANDOWN PL
15 SOUTH ST

B3
1 THE VENTRY
2 VENTRY CLOSE
3 SWAYNES CL
4 BELLE VUE RD
5 CHAPEL PL
6 SUMMERLOCK APP
7 GRIFFINS CT
8 MALTHOUSE LA
9 PRIORY SQ
10 CHEESE MARKET
11 MINSTER ST
12 ROLLESTONE ST
13 ST EDMUNDS CHURCH ST
14 BROWN ST

A B C

Salisbury Rugby Club
Playing Field
Bishopdown
Wyndham Park Sch
St Marks CE Junior Sch
SP1
Salisbury Crem
Cemy
Cowslip Farm
Victoria Park
South Wilts Grammar Sch For Girls
Exeter House Specl Sch
Sports Ground
Salisbury Leisure Centre
Allot Gdns
Laverstock & Ford Sports Club
Sarum St Pauls CE Sch
La Retraite Sch
Superstore
Chafyn Grove Sch
Highbury First Sch
Fisherton Manor Middle Sch
Swimming Baths
Council Offices
Old Manor
Ashfield Trad Est
SP2
Arts Ctr
Barton Heritage Collection
Mag Ct
Mus, Liby & Art Gall
Laverstock Mill Bridge
Salisbury
Churchfields Ind Est
Milford
Godolphin Sch Douglas Ho
Godolphin Sch
YHA
Rainbows End
Mompesson House
Sarum Coll
Sch Of English
Milford Ind Est
Regimental Museum
Bishop Wordsworths Sch
St Martins CE (aided) Junior Sch
Milford Farm
Medieval Hall
Salisbury Cathedral
St Martins CE Inf Sch
Salisbury & South Wiltshire Museum
King's House
Cath Sch
Bishop's Palace
Dolphin Industrial Estate
Recreation Ground
Old Mill
Coll Of Tech
Salisbury Cathedral Sch
Salisbury Business Park
Leaden Hall Sch
St Osmonds Sch
Retail Park
Manor Farm
Churchill Gardens
Hatches Bridge
Harnham Bridge
SALISBURY
Harnham CE Jun & Inf Sch
Sewage Works
Harnham
East Harnham Dairy Farm
Harnham Hill
Drove End
SP5
Long Barn Bridge Farm
Britford Prim Sch
River Avon
River Nadder
River Bourne
Avon Valley Path

4 3 2 1
31 30 29 28

13 A 14 B 15 C

A1
1 GRASMERE CL
2 HARVARD CL
3 CHRISTOPHER CL

A2
1 STEPHENS CL
2 TURNER CL
3 MUNKS CL

B1
1 BRITFORD LA WEST
2 SWALLOWMEAD
3 MARTINS CL
4 MAPLECROFT
5 HAWKSRIDGE
6 SWIFTDOWN
7 LINNETSDENE
8 RAVENSCROFT
9 WRENSCROFT
10 OWLSWOOD
11 LONGHILL DR

B2
1 ROSEMARY LA
2 CULVER ST
3 HILL VIEW RD
4 BARNARD ST
5 PAYNE'S HILL
6 ST MARTIN'S CHURCH ST
7 GREEN'S CT
8 FRIAR'S ORCHARD
9 WHITEFRIARS RD

C2
1 METHUEN DR
2 ST MARGARET'S CL
3 COURTWOOD CL
4 BYWAYS CL
5 THE BEECHES
6 MILFORD HOLLOW
7 POLDEN RD
8 BOURNE CL
9 ST JOHN'S CL

Index

Church Rd 6 Beckenham BR2..........53 C6

- **Place name** May be abbreviated on the map
- **Location number** Present when a number indicates the place's position in a crowded area of mapping
- **Locality, town or village** Shown when more than one place has the same name
- **Postcode district** District for the indexed place
- **Page and grid square** Page number and grid reference for the standard mapping

Public and commercial buildings are highlighted in **magenta** **Places of interest** are highlighted in **blue** with a star★

Abbreviations used in the index

Acad	**Academy**	Comm	**Common**	Gd	**Ground**	L	**Leisure**	Prom	**Promenade**
App	**Approach**	Cott	**Cottage**	Gdn	**Garden**	La	**Lane**	Rd	**Road**
Arc	**Arcade**	Cres	**Crescent**	Gn	**Green**	Liby	**Library**	Recn	**Recreation**
Ave	**Avenue**	Cswy	**Causeway**	Gr	**Grove**	Mdw	**Meadow**	Ret	**Retail**
Bglw	**Bungalow**	Ct	**Court**	H	**Hall**	Meml	**Memorial**	Sh	**Shopping**
Bldg	**Building**	Ctr	**Centre**	Ho	**House**	Mkt	**Market**	Sq	**Square**
Bsns, Bus	**Business**	Ctry	**Country**	Hospl	**Hospital**	Mus	**Museum**	St	**Street**
Bvd	**Boulevard**	Cty	**County**	HQ	**Headquarters**	Orch	**Orchard**	Sta	**Station**
Cath	**Cathedral**	Dr	**Drive**	Hts	**Heights**	Pal	**Palace**	Terr	**Terrace**
Cir	**Circus**	Dro	**Drove**	Ind	**Industrial**	Par	**Parade**	TH	**Town Hall**
Cl	**Close**	Ed	**Education**	Inst	**Institute**	Pas	**Passage**	Univ	**University**
Cnr	**Corner**	Emb	**Embankment**	Int	**International**	Pk	**Park**	Wk, Wlk	**Walk**
Coll	**College**	Est	**Estate**	Intc	**Interchange**	Pl	**Place**	Wr	**Water**
Com	**Community**	Ex	**Exhibition**	Junc	**Junction**	Prec	**Precinct**	Yd	**Yard**

Index of localities, towns and villages

A

Abbotsbury 149 A4
Acton 177 C1
Adam's Green 193 D2
Adber 14 C3
Affpuddle 111 C4
Alcester 12 B1
Alderholt 42 A3
Alderney 88 B1
Aller 209 B5
Allington 100 A4
Allowenshay 191 A8
Almer 211 E2
Alton Pancras 208 B5
Alvington 26 B2
Alweston 31 A1
Ameysford 52 C1
Ammerham 202 D8
Anderson 82 A4
Arne 144 B3
Ash 68 B3
Ash 198 F5
Ashington 59 A1
Ashley 54 C3
Ashley 95 B2
Ashley Heath 53 C3
Ashmore 39 B4
Askerswell 102 B3
Athelhampton 78 C1
Atrim 68 A2
Avon 63 C1

B

Bagber 197 A8
Barrow Hill 84 C2
Barrow Street 3 C1
Barton on Sea 126 A4
Barwick 193 F8
Bashley 95 A4
Batcombe 206 E7
Bay 6 A1
Beaminster 204 B5
Bear Cross 88 C3
Bearwood 88 C3
Beaulieu Wood 196 B1
Beckley 94 B3
Bedchester 37 B4
Beer Hackett 194 C6
Belchalwell 197 E4
Belchalwell Street 197 E3
Benville 205 D6
Bere Regis 81 A1
Bettiscombe 203 B3
Bickton 43 A3
Bincombe 152 C3
Binnegar 141 A2
Bishop's Caundle 196 A8
Bishop's Down 195 E6
Bishopdown 213 C4
Bisterne 63 C3
Bittles Green 12 B4
Blackney 203 D2
Blacknoll 156 C4
Blackwater 91 B2
Blandford Camp 199 E3
Blandford Forum 212 B3
Blandford St Mary 212 B1
Blashford 47 B1
Bleak Hill 42 C2
Bloxworth 82 A1
Bluntshay 66 C4
Bookham 208 B7
Boscombe 122 C2
Bothenhampton 100 C2
Bournemouth 123 A2
Bourton 1 C1
Boveridge 209 B1
Bovington Camp 139 B3
Bowden 9 C2
Bowridge Hill 6 A2
Boys Hill 195 E5
Bradford Abbas 28 B1
Bradford Peverell 106 C3
Bradpole 69 A1
Bramblecombe 209 C4
Branksome 120 C3
Branksome Park 120 C1
Bransgore 93 A2
Braytown 139 C1
Briantspuddle 112 A4
Bridge 202 D8
Bridport 100 A3
Broad Oak 197 D7
Broadmayne 136 A1
Broadoak 67 B3
Broadshard 191 F5
Broadstone 87 A1
Broadwey 152 A2
Broadwindsor 203 F5
Brockhampton Green 196 C1
Broom Hill 51 B1
Bryanston 212 B2
Brympton D'Evercy 26 A2
Buckhorn Weston 9 A3
Buckland Newton 208 A7
Buckland Ripers 151 B1
Bugley 10 A3
Burleston 78 C1
Burstock 203 D6
Burton 3 B3
Burton 92 B1
Burton 107 C2
Burton 193 C8
Burton Bradstock 101 A1
Bushey 162 B2

C

Camel Green 42 B3
Camesworth 68 C4
Canford Cliffs 147 C4
Canford Heath 87 C1
Canford Magna 60 A1
Cann 24 A4
Cann Common 24 B4
Carey 142 A3
Castle 202 A4
Castle Park 134 B4
Castletown 181 B1
Catherston Leweston 65 B1
Cattistock 206 C2
Cerne Abbas 207 E4
Chalbury 201 C1
Chalbury Common 201 D1
Chaldon Herring 156 B2
Chalmington 206 C3
Chard Junction 202 B7
Charing Cross 42 A3
Charlestown 166 C1
Charlton Down 75 B2
Charlton Marshall 211 D6
Charlton on the Hill 211 C7
Charminster 107 C3
Charminster 90 B1
Charmouth 97 A4
Charnage 3 C2
Chedington 204 E8
Cheselbourne 209 B2
Chesil 186 C4
Chetnole 194 D2
Chettle 200 B8
Chickerell 166 B3
Chideock 99 A3
Chilbridge 58 C4
Chilcombe 102 B2
Child Okeford 198 B7
Chilfrome 206 B1
Chilson Common 202 A7
Chilton Cantelo 14 A4
Christchurch 124 A3
Church Knowle 176 B4
Clapgate 50 C1
Clapton 191 C1
Clifton Maybank 194 A8
Closworth 193 F5
Cobb 96 A2
Cobley 189 D7
Cocknowle 161 A1
Cold Harbour 142 A4
Coldharbour 166 C4
Colehill 59 C4
Colesbook 5 C2
Combe Almer 84 B4
Compton Abbas 24 A1
Compton Valence 104 C4
Coneygar 100 B4
Coombe 13 C1
Coombe 65 A4
Coombe 191 B4
Coombe Keynes 158 A3
Coombses 202 B8
Corfe Castle 162 A1
Corfe Mullen 86 A1
Corscombe 205 A8
Coryates 150 C4
Cosmore 207 E8
Court Orchard 100 B4
Crab Orchard 45 A1
Cranborne 40 A4
Creech 160 B2
Crendell 41 A4
Crewkerne 191 E5
Cripplestyle 41 A3
Crooked Withies 52 A4
Cross Lanes 209 A5

Crossways 137 C3
Crouch Hill 196 A5
Crow 55 C2
Cruxton 73 A3
Cucklington 4 A2

D

Daggons 41 C3
Damerham 209 F2
Dean 188 E2
Deanend 188 E4
Deanland 189 A5
Dewlands Common 44 C3
Dewlish 209 C1
Dinnington 191 B8
Dorchester 107 B1
Dottery 68 A2
Downton 127 C4
Drimpton 203 D8
Drive End Farm 194 A2
Droop 197 A3
Dudsbury 61 B1
Duntish 196 A1
Durweston 198 E3

E

East Bloxworth 82 C1
East Brook 59 B3
East Burton 139 C1
East Chaldon 156 B2
East Chelborough 205 D8
East Chinnock 192 E8
East Coker 193 D7
East Compton 24 A1
East Creech 160 C1
East End 58 C1
East Fleet 166 A3
East Holme 159 C4
East Holton 117 A2
East Howe 89 B2
East Knighton 157 A4
East Lulworth 173 B4
East Martin 209 C6
East Melbury 24 B3
East Morden 83 B2
East Orchard 36 C4
East Parley 90 A4
East Pulham 196 D4
East Stoke 140 C1
East Stour 10 C2
East Stour Common 11 A2
Easton 187 A2
Ebblake 45 C2
Eccliffe 10 B1
Edmondsham 40 B2
Ellingham 47 A3
Elm Hill 7 A1
Elwell 152 A3
Enbury 89 C3
Enmore Green 12 B2
Ensbury Park 89 B1
Evershot 206 A7

F

Fairmile 91 C1
Farnham 188 C2
Farrington 37 A2
Ferndown 61 B3
Fiddleford 197 F8
Fifehead Magdalen 20 C4
Fifehead Neville 197 C5
Fifehead St Quintin 197 A8
Filford 67 C4
Fleet 166 A3
Folke 195 D8
Folly 208 D6
Fontmell Magna 37 C4
Fontmell Parva 36 B1
Fordingbridge 43 A4
Forston 75 A2
Fortuneswell 186 C4
Foxholes 120 A3
Frampton 73 C2
Friars Cliff 125 B4
Frogham 43 C4
Frome St Quintin 206 D5
Furzebrook 161 A2
Furzehill 50 C1

G

Gannetts 21 B2
Gasper 1 B4
Gaunt's Common 51 A4
Giddy Green 139 C1
Gillingham 5 C1
Glanvilles Wootton 195 E2

Goathill 31 B4
God's Blessing Green 51 B2
Godmanstone 75 A4
Godwinscroft 93 A3
Gold Hill 198 B8
Gore 14 C2
Gotham 41 A2
Grange 50 C1
Grange Estate 62 C4
Greenham 203 C7
Grimstone 74 A1
Grove 187 A3
Gussage All Saints 201 A5
Gussage St Andrew 188 E1
Gussage St Michael 200 F6
Guy's Marsh 23 A3

H

Hains 20 C2
Hale 4 A2
Halstock 193 C3
Ham Common 6 A1
Hamlet 194 D3
Hammoon 36 A4
Hampreston 60 C1
Hamworthy 118 B2
Hanford 198 D6
Harbridge 43 A1
Harbridge Green 43 A1
Harcombe Bottom 64 A2
Hardington Mandeville 193 A6
Hardington Moor 193 A7
Harman's Cross 177 C3
Harnham 213 A1
Hartgrove 22 C1
Haselbury Plucknett 192 C6
Hawkchurch 202 B3
Haydon 31 B2
Haythorne 201 F2
Hazelbury Bryan 196 F3
Hemsworth 49 A4
Henbury 56 C1
Henley 191 E2
Henley 208 A7
Henstridge 19 A2
Henstridge Ash 19 A3
Henstridge Bowden 18 A3
Henstridge Marsh 19 C3
Hermitage 195 B2
Herston 178 C2
Hewish 191 D3
Hewood 202 C6
Highcliffe 125 C4
Higher Ansty 209 B6
Higher Bockhampton 109 A3
Higher Chalmington 206 C4
Higher Eype 99 C3
Higher Halstock Leigh 193 A2
Higher Kingcombe 205 E3
Higher Melcombe 208 F5
Higher Nyland 8 C1
Higher Row 51 C3
Higher Sandford 15 C3
Higher Totnell 194 F4
Higher Whatcombe 210 C5
Higher Woodsford 137 B4
Higher Wraxall 205 F4
Highlands 100 A2
Hightown 55 C3
Highwood 158 C4
Hilfield 207 A7
Hillbourne 87 A1
Hillbutts 58 C3
Hilton 209 D6
Hincknowle 69 A4
Hinton 14 A3
Hinton 94 A2
Hinton Martell 201 B1
Hinton Parva 50 A3
Hinton St George 191 D7
Hinton St Mary 35 A2
Hogstock 200 B1
Holdenhurst 91 A2
Holditch 202 B5
Hollands 27 B4
Hollow Oak 113 A4
Holmebridge 141 C1
Holnest 195 C4
Holt 51 B2
Holt Heath 52 B3
Holt Wood 51 B4
Holton Heath 116 A2
Holway 16 A3
Holway 202 E6
Holwell 3 A3
Holwell 196 B5
Holwell 193 C8
Holywell 206 C7
Hooke 205 C2
Hordle 95 C2
Horton 201 E2
Horton Common 44 C1
Horton Heath 44 B1
Hound Hill 58 C4
Houndstone 26 B3

Hummer 14 B2
Hungerford 43 C3
Huntingford 5 C4
Hurn 91 A3
Hursey 203 E5
Hurst 111 B1
Hyde 43 C3
Hyde 100 C3

I

Ibberton 197 D2
Ibsley 47 B4
Iford 123 B4
Ivy Cross 13 A2
Iwerne Courtney 198 E7
Iwerne Minster 37 C1

K

Kimmeridge 175 B2
King's Stag 196 D5
Kingsbury Regis 17 B2
Kingsland 68 A4
Kingston 55 A1
Kingston 63 C4
Kingston 176 C2
Kingston 197 A4
Kingston Maurward 108 C1
Kingston Russell 104 B2
Kington Magna 9 B2
Kinson 89 A3
Kit Hill 23 A2
Kitford 197 C3
Kittwhistle 203 A6
Knackers Hole 197 D6
Knapp Hill 7 B1
Knighton 194 E6
Knob's Crook 44 A2
Knowlton 201 D4

L

Lake 117 C1
Lambrook 68 C3
Lambs' Green 58 C1
Lane End 113 B3
Lanehouse 166 C1
Langham 9 C4
Langton Herring 150 B1
Langton Long Blandford 212 C2
Langton Matravers 178 A2
Laymore 202 F7
Leigh 194 E3
Leigh 197 D3
Leigh 59 C2
Leigh Park 59 C2
Lewcombe 193 E2
Lillington 194 F7
Lilliput 147 B4
Limpers Hill 3 B2
Little Canford 60 B2
Little Pamphill 58 C3
Little Woolgarston 177 B4
Littlebredy 131 b4
Littledown 123 A4
Littlemoor 152 C2
Littleton 211 C7
Littlewindsor 203 F7
Litton Cheney 103 B1
Loders 69 B1
Lodmoor 167 C4
Long Bredy 103 C1
Long Crichel 200 E5
Long Cross 2 B3
Longburton 195 C7
Longfleet 119 B2
Longham 61 A1
Loscombe 69 C4
Lower Ansty 209 B6
Lower Blandford St Mary 212 C1
Lower Bockhampton 109 A1
Lower Daggons 41 B4
Lower Eype 99 C2
Lower Halstock Leigh 193 B2
Lower Hamworthy 119 A1
Lower Holwell 40 C3
Lower Kingcombe 205 E1
Lower Mannington 52 B4
Lower Nyland 19 C4
Lower Odcombe 26 A3
Lower Parkstone 120 A2
Lower Row 51 C4
Lower Strode 204 A2
Lower Turmer 46 C4
Lower Whatcombe 210 D4
Lower Wraxall 206 A3
Lower Zeals 2 B3
Lufton 26 A3
Lulworth Camp 173 A4

Lyatts 193 B6
Lydlinch 196 F8
Lyme Regis 96 B3
Lyon's Gate 207 D8
Lytchett Matravers 84 B2
Lytchett Minster 116 C4

M

Madjeston 10 C4
Maiden Newton 73 A4
Mangerton 69 A2
Mannington 52 B4
Manston 36 A2
Manswood 200 E3
Mapperton 204 F2
Mapperton 211 D1
Mappowder 196 F1
Margaret Marsh 22 B1
Marnhull 20 C1
Marshalsea 202 F3
Marshwood 202 F2
Martin 209 B6
Martin Drove End 209 A8
Martinstown or Winterbourne St Martin 133 B3
Meerhay 204 D5
Melbury Abbas 24 C3
Melbury Bubb 194 C1
Melbury Osmond 194 A2
Melbury Sampford 206 A8
Melcombe Bingham 209 A5
Melcombe Regis 167 C3
Melplash 204 D1
Mere 3 A3
Merley 59 B1
Merriott 70 A2
Merriott 191 E7
Merriottsford 191 E7
Merritown 90 C4
Middle Bockhampton 92 C3
Middle Chinnock 192 C8
Milborne Port 17 B1
Milborne St Andrew 79 C4
Milborne Wick 17 A3
Miles Cross 99 C4
Milford 213 C3
Milton Abbas 209 F4
Milton on Stour 5 B3
Minchington 188 D1
Minterne Magna 207 C7
Minterne Parva 207 D6
Misterton 192 A2
Mockbeggar 47 C4
Monkton Up Wimborne 201 C8
Monkton Wyld 64 A3
Moor Crichel 201 A3
Moorbath 67 B2
Moordown 90 A1
Moorside 21 B2
Moortown 55 B3
Morcombelake 98 B4
Moreton 138 C4
Mosterton 204 A8
Motcombe 12 A4
Mount Pleasant 86 C4
Mounters 20 C1
Muckleford 106 A4
Mudeford 125 A3
Mudford 14 A2
Muscliffe 90 B2

N

Nash 193 C8
Neacroft 93 A3
Nether Cerne 207 E1
Nether Compton 28 C4
Netherbury 204 C2
Netherhay 203 C8
Netherstoke 193 D3
Netherton 193 E6
Nettlecombe 70 A2
New Milton 94 C1
New Swanage 179 A3
New Town 9 B1
New Town 17 A1
New Town 27 C3
New Town 188 C2
New Town 188 F6
New Town 201 A2
New Town 120 A4
Newport 82 B1
Newton 197 D8
Newton Peveril 56 C4
Newtown 204 D5
Norden 161 B2
North Bockhampton 92 C4
North Bowood 203 F2
North Chideock 99 A4
North Coker 193 D6
North End 7 A2
North Gorley 43 B2
North Kingston 55 C1

North Perrott 192 C4
North Poorton 205 B1
North Poulner 47 C1
North Wootton 30 C1
Northay 202 D3
Northbourne 89 C2
Northbrook 78 A1
Northport 142 C3
Norwood 205 B8
Nottington 152 A1
Notton 73 A2

O

Oakdale 119 B3
Oakley 59 C1
Oathill 203 B8
Oborne 16 C1
Okeford Fitzpaine 197 F5
Old Milton 94 C1
Organford 116 A3
Osehill Green 195 E4
Osmington 169 A4
Osmington Mills 169 B4
Over Compton 28 C4
Overcombe 168 A4
Owermoigne 155 B4
Oxbridge 68 C4

P

Packers Hill 196 C5
Pallington 111 B2
Pamphill 58 A3
Park Gate 196 F2
Parkstone 120 A2
Parkway 14 C4
Parley Green 90 B4
Peacemarsh 5 C2
Pear Ash 1 B2
Pen Mill 28 A3
Pendomer 193 B5
Penn 64 B2
Penselwood 1 A2
Pentridge 189 E4
Perry Street 202 B8
Piddlehinton 76 C4
Piddletrenthide 208 A3
Pidney 196 F4
Pig Oak 51 A2
Pilford 60 A4
Pillwell 21 A2
Pilsdon 203 C2
Pimperne 194 A3
Pimperne 199 D4
Pleck 34 C4
Pleck 196 B6
Pleck or Little Ansty 209 C7
Plush 208 C5
Pokesdown 123 A2
Poole 119 A1
Poolestown 33 C3
Portesham 132 A1
Portway 156 C4
Post Green 116 C4
Poulner 47 C1
Powerstock 70 A3
Poxwell 154 C3
Poyntington 16 C2
Preston 168 A4
Preston Plucknett 26 C2
Puddle Town 192 B5
Puddletown 78 A1
Pulham 196 B3
Puncknowle 129 C3
Purewell 124 B4
Purse Caundle 32 A4
Purtington 191 A4
Putton 166 C3
Puxey 197 B7
Pymore 68 B1

Q

Queen Oak 2 A2

R

Radipole 167 A4
Rampisham 205 F5
Red Hill 89 C3
Redbridge 138 A3
Redford 206 D8
Redlands 152 A1
Rew 208 B8
Ridge 143 A1
Rimpton 15 A4
Ringwood 47 B1
Rivers' Corner 197 C7
Rixon 35 B1

Rockford 47 C2
Rodden 150 B3
Rodgrove 8 C3
Rodwell 167 B1
Rolls Mill 197 C8
Romford 44 C4
Rook Street 3 A4
Rossmore 120 C4
Roundham 191 D4
Rowlands 59 B3
Rushton 141 A1
Ryall 66 B1
Ryme Intrinseca 194 B6

S

St Andrew's Well 100 C4
St Ives 54 B3
St James 12 C1
St Johns 59 B2
St Leonards 54 A1
Salisbury 213 B1
Salwayash 68 A3
Sandbanks 147 B2
Sandford 142 C4
Sandford Orcas 15 C3
Sandhills 195 F5
Sandhills 206 B3
Sandpit 203 D7
School House 202 D5
Seaborough 191 D1
Seatown 99 A2
Sedgehill 7 C3
Shaftesbury 12 C2
Shaggs 158 B2
Shapwick 56 B4
Sharnhill Green 208 C8
Sherborne 30 A4
Sherford 115 B4
Shillingstone 198 C6
Shipton Gorge 101 B2
Shroton 198 E7
Silkhay 204 A1
Silton 5 A4
Sitterton 80 C2
Sixpenny Handley 189 A3
Skilling 100 A3
Slepe 115 C4
Somerford 124 C4
Sopley 92 A3
South Bockhampton . .92 C2
South Bowood 203 F1
South Chard 202 A7
South Gorley 43 C1
South Perrott 192 C2
South Poorton 70 B4
Southbourne 123 C2
Southbrook 3 A5
Southill 167 A3
Southlands 180 C4
Southover 73 B1

Southover 128 A4
Southwell 186 C1
Spetisbury 211 D5
Springbourne 122 B3
Spyway 102 B4
Stafford's Green 16 A4
Stalbridge 33 C4
Stalbridge Weston 33 A3
Stallen 29 A3
Stanbridge 50 B2
Stanley Green 119 B3
Stanpit 124 C3
Stapehill 60 C3
Steeple 175 B4
Sterte 119 A2
Stinsford 108 C2
Stoborough 142 C1
Stoborough Green 161 A4
Stockwood 194 C2
Stoford 193 F8
Stoke Abbott 204 A3
Stoke Wake 197 B1
Stokeford 140 C2
Stone 101 A4
Stone 59 A3
Stour Provost 21 B4
Stour Row 22 B4
Stourpaine 198 F4
Stourton Caundle 32 C2
Stratton 106 C4
Strouden 90 C1
Stubhampton 199 E8
Stuckton 43 C4
Studland 164 B1
Sturminster Marshall . . .56 C2
Sturminster Newton . . .35 A1
Summerlands 27 A3
Sutton Bingham 193 D6
Sutton Holms 44 A4
Sutton Poyntz 153 B2
Sutton Waldron 37 C3
Swanage 179 B2
Swyre 129 B3
Sydling St Nicholas 207 A2
Symondsbury 99 C4
Synderford 202 F6

T

Tadnoll 138 B1
Talbot Village 89 B1
Tarrant Crawford 211 E6
Tarrant Gunville 199 F8
Tarrant Hinton 200 A6
Tarrant Keyneston 48 A3
Tarrant Launceston . . .200 B4
Tarrant Monkton 200 B3
Tarrant Rushton 48 A4
Templeman's Ash 203 B3
The Borough 196 B6
The Causeway 3 B2

The Common 197 D5
The Mount 69 A3
Thorncombe 202 E6
Thorne Coffin 26 B4
Thornford 194 D8
Thornicombe 210 F6
Three Gates 195 A2
Three Legged Cross 45 A1
Throop 112 B4
Throop 90 C2
Tidpit 209 C6
Tiley 195 E1
Tillworth 202 A3
Tincleton 110 B2
Tiptoe 95 B4
Todber 21 B2
Tollard Farnham 188 B2
Tollard Royal 188 B4
Toller Fratrum 72 B4
Toller Porcorum 71 C4
Toller Whelme 205 B4
Tollerford 72 C4
Tolpuddle 79 B1
Totnell 194 F3
Town's End 81 B2
Trent 14 C1
Trickett's Cross 61 C4
Tuckton 123 C3
Turlin Moor 117 B2
Turmer 46 C4
Turners Puddle 112 B4
Turnworth 198 B2
Twyford 23 B1
Tyneham 174 B3

U

Ulwell 179 A3
Up Cerne 207 C5
Up Mudford 14 C1
Up Sydling 207 A4
Uphall 205 E5
Uploders 101 C4
Upper Parkstone 120 A3
Uppington 201 D1
Upton 118 B4
Upwey 152 A3

V

Verwood 45 A3

W

Walditch 101 A3
Walkford 94 B1
Wallisdown 89 A1

Walton Elm 34 C4
Wareham 142 C3
Warmwell 137 A1
Warren 113 B2
Waterditch 93 A3
Waterloo 87 A1
Watton 100 A2
Wayford 191 B1
Waytown 68 C4
Well Bottom 39 B3
West Bay 100 B1
West Bexington 129 C1
West Bourton 4 B4
West Chaldon 155 C1
West Chelborough 205 D8
West Chinnock 192 B8
West Cliff 121 B1
West Coker 193 A8
West Compton 71 C1
West End 29 C3
West Holme 159 B4
West Howe 88 C2
West Hurn 90 C3
West Knighton 136 B2
West Lulworth 172 B3
West Melbury 24 A3
West Milton 69 C3
West Moors 53 A1
West Morden 83 A2
West Orchard 36 B3
West Parley 89 F4
West Pulham 196 A3
West Southbourne 123 B3
West Stafford 136 A4
West Stour 10 A1
Westbourne 121 B2
Westfields 196 D1
Westham 167 A2
Weston 186 C2
Weston 204 F8
Weymouth 167 C2
Whitchurch 19 A3
Whitchurch
  Canonicorum 66 A2
Whitcombe 135 C3
White Cross 1 C3
White Hill 3 B1
White Lackington 208 C1
Whitecross 204 B2
Whitefield 83 A1
Whitmore 44 A3
Wick 124 A2
Wigbeth 201 F2
Wimborne Minster 59 A1
Wimborne St Giles 201 D7
Winfrith Newburgh 156 C3
Winkton 92 B1
Winterborne Came 135 B3
Winterborne Clenston .210 D6
Winterborne
  Herringston 134 C3
Winterborne Houghton .210 B7
Winterborne Kingston . .81 B4

Winterborne Monkton .134 B2
Winterborne Muston . . .82 A4
Winterborne Stickland .210 C7
Winterborne Tomson . . .82 B4
Winterborne
  Whitechurch 210 D3
Winterborne Zelston . . .82 C4
Winterbourne Abbas . . .105 B1
Winterbourne
  Steepleton 132 C4
Winton 121 C4
Winyard's Gap 192 E1
Witchampton 200 F1
Wolverton 2 A2
Wonston 196 F2
Woodbridge 23 B1
Woodcutts 188 D4
Woodlands 44 A3
Woodlands Common . . .44 B3
Woodrow 196 F4
Woodsford 110 B1
Woodville 21 C4
Woodyates 189 D6
Wool 140 A1
Woolbridge Heath 140 A3
Woolford's Water 208 A8
Woolgarston 177 C4
Woolland 197 C1
Woolminstone 191 B3
Woolsbridge 53 B4
Wooth 68 C2
Wooton 95 A4
Wootton Fitzpaine 65 A2
Worgret 142 A1
Worth Matravers 183 D4
Wych 100 C1
Wyke 5 B1
Wyke Regis 180 B4
Wynford Eagle 72 B2

Y

Yenston 18 C4
Yeovil 27 A2
Yetminster 194 D5
Yondover 101 B4

Z

Zeals 1 C2

8

8th August Rd BH20 . . .139 C4

A

Aaron Cl BH17 . . . . .119 C4
Abbey Barn★ DT3 . . . . .149 A4
Abbey CE VC Prim Sch The
DT9 . . . . .29 C2
Abbey CE Voluntary Aided
Fst Sch The SP7 . . . . . . .12 B1
Abbey Cl 9 TA20 . . . . . .202 A8
Abbey Ct DT2 . . . . .207 D4
Abbey Gdns★
Cerne Abbas DT2 . . . . . . .207 D4
Ferndown BH21 . . . . .60 B3
Abbey House★ BH21 . . .201 A1
Abbey Mews 2 TA20 . . .202 A8
Abbey Mus★ SP7 . . . . . . .12 C1
Abbey Rd Sherborne DT9 . .30 A3
West Moors BH22 . . . . .62 A4
Yeovil BA21 . . . . .26 C3
Abbey St
Cerne Abbas DT2 . . . . . . .207 D4
Crewkerne TA18 . . . . .191 E4
Hinton St George TA17 . . .191 C7
Abbey View 4 DT11 . . . .211 E5
Abbey Wlk SP7 . . . . .12 C1
Abbot Rd SP1 . . . . .213 C4
Abbots Cl BH23 . . . . .125 C4
Abbots Meade BA21 . . . . .26 C3
Abbots Quay 9 BH20 . . .142 C2
Abbots Way
Sherborne DT9 . . . . .29 C3
Yeovil BA21 . . . . .26 C4
Abbots Wlk DT2 . . . . . . .207 D4
Abbotsbury Castle (Fort)★
DT3 . . . . .130 B1
Abbotsbury Hill DT3 . . .130 B1
Abbotsbury La DT2 . . . .130 C4
Abbotsbury Rd
Broadstone BH18 . . . . .86 C3
Weymouth DT4 . . . . .167 A2
Abbotsbury Swannery★
DT3 . . . . .149 A3
Abbott Cl BH9 . . . . .122 A4
Abbott Rd BH9 . . . . .122 A4
Abbott St BH21 . . . . .58 B3
Abbott's Way SP8 . . . . .5 C2
Abbott's Wootton La
Marshwood DT6 . . . . .202 E1
Whitechurch Canonicorum
DT6 . . . . .65 B4
Abbotts Mdw BH16 . . . . . .84 B2
Abbotts Way BH22 . . . . . .62 A4
Abder Cross DT9 . . . . .14 C2
Abels La DT9 . . . . .14 C1
Aberdare Rd BH10 . . . . . . .89 C1
Abingdon Dr BH23 . . . . .126 B4
Abingdon Rd BH17 . . . . .119 B4
Abinger Rd BH7 . . . . . . .123 A3
Abney Rd BH10 . . . . .89 B2
Acacia Ave BH31 . . . . .45 C2
Acacia Cl DT4 . . . . .167 A3
Acacia Rd SO41 . . . . .95 C2
Acer Ave 2 Bridport DT6 .68 C1
Bridport DT6 . . . . .100 C4
Acer Dr BA21 . . . . .26 C4
Ackerman Rd DT1 . . . . .108 B1
Acland Rd
Bournemouth BH9 . . . . . .122 A4
7 Dorchester DT1 . . . . . .108 A1
Acorn Bsns Pk BH12 . . .120 A4
Acorn Cl
Christchurch BH23 . . . . . .123 C4
New Milton BH25 . . . . .95 B2
St.Leonards BH24 . . . . .54 A2
Acorn Way BH31 . . . . .45 B3
Acorns The BH21 . . . . .60 A2
Acreman Cl DT2 . . . . . . .207 D4
Acreman Pl DT9 . . . . .30 A3
Acreman St
Cerne Abbas DT2 . . . . . . .207 D4
Sherborne DT9 . . . . .30 A3
Acres Ct 6 BA22 . . . . . . .193 F8
Acres Rd BH11 . . . . .89 A1
Acton Rd BH10 . . . . .89 A1
Ad Astro Fst Sch BH17 . . .87 C1
Adamsfield Gdns BH10 . . .89 B1
Adastral Rd BH17 . . . . . .119 C4
Adastral Sq BH17 . . . . . .119 C4
Adber Cl BA21 . . . . .28 A4
Addington Pl BH23 . . . . .124 B3
Addiscombe Rd BH23 . . .124 A4
Addison Cl SP8 . . . . .6 A1
Addison Sq BH24 . . . . . . .55 B4
Addlewell La BA20 . . . . . .27 B2
Adelaide Cl BH23 . . . . . .123 C4
Adelaide Cres DT4 . . . . .167 A2
Adelaide La 40 BH1 . . . .121 C2
Adeline Rd BH5 . . . . . . .122 C2
Admirals Cl DT9 . . . . .30 B4
Admirals Way BH20 . . . .142 C3
Admirals Wlk BH2 . . . . .121 B1
Admiralty Rd BH6 . . . . . .123 C2
Aggis Farm Rd BH31 . . . .45 A3
Agglestone Rd BH19 . . .164 A1
Aigburth Rd BH19 . . . . .178 C2
Airetons Cl BH18 . . . . . . .87 B2
Airfield Cl DT2 . . . . .137 B3
Airfield Ind Est BH23 . . .124 C3
Airfield Rd BH23 . . . . . .124 C3
Airfield Way BH23 . . . . .124 C4
Airspeed Rd BH23 . . . . .125 A4
Akeshill Cl BH25 . . . . .95 A3
Alamein Rd BH20 . . . . . .139 C3
Alan Ct 16 BH23 . . . . . . .126 A4
Alastair Cl BA21 . . . . .27 A4
Alastair Dr BA21 . . . . .27 A4
Albany BH1 . . . . .122 B2
Albany Cl
Barton on Sea BH25 . . . . . .94 C1
Sherborne DT9 . . . . .30 B4
Albany Dr Horton BH21 . . .52 C4
Three Legged Cross BH21 . .45 A1
Albany Gdns BH15 . . . . .118 C1
Albany Pk BH17 . . . . . . .119 A4
Albany Rd
Salisbury SP1 . . . . .213 B3
Weymouth DT4 . . . . .166 C2
Albemarle Rd BH3 . . . . .121 C4
Albert Cl BA21 . . . . .27 A4
Albert Rd
Bournemouth BH1 . . . . . .121 C2
Corfe Mullen BH21 . . . . . . .86 B3
Dorchester DT1 . . . . .107 C1
Ferndown BH22 . . . . .61 B3
New Milton BH25 . . . . .94 C1
Poole BH12 . . . . .120 B3
Albert St
Blandford Forum DT11 . . .212 B1
5 Radipole DT4 . . . . .167 B2
Albert Terr 5 DT5 . . . . .186 C4
Albion Cl BH12 . . . . .120 A4
Albion Rd BH23 . . . . .91 C1
Albion Way BH31 . . . . . . .44 C3
Alby Rd BH12 . . . . .120 C3
Alcester Rd BH12 . . . . . .120 B3
Aldabrand Cl DT3 . . . . . .166 B2
Aldbury Ct BH25 . . . . . .127 A4
Alder Cl Burton BH23 . . . . .92 B1
3 Sandford BH20 . . . . . .116 A1
Sturminster Newton DT10 . .35 B1
Alder Cres BH12 . . . . . . .120 C4
Alder Dr SP6 . . . . .42 A3
Alder Gr
Crewkerne TA18 . . . . .191 F5
Yeovil BA20 . . . . .27 A1
Alder Hills BH12 . . . . . . .121 A4
Alder Hills Ind Est BH12 121 A4
Alder Rd Poole BH12 . . . .120 C3
Sturminster Newton DT10 . .35 B1
Alderbury Cl 5 BH19 . . .178 C1
Alderbury Ct 6 BH23 . . .124 C3
Alderholt Pk★ SP6 . . . . . .42 A4
Alderley Rd BH10 . . . . . . .89 C2
Alderney Mid Sch BH12 . .88 B1
Alderney Ave BH12 . . . . . .88 B1
Alderney Hospl BH12 . . . .88 B1
Aldis Gdns BH15 . . . . . . .118 C1
Aldondale Gdns BA20 . . . .27 B2
Aldridge Rd
Bournemouth BH10 . . . . . . .89 B3
Ferndown BH22 . . . . .61 C2
Aldridge Way BH22 . . . . . .61 C2
Alexander Cl BH23 . . . . .124 C3
Alexandra Ct DT6 . . . . . .100 B3
Alexandra Lodge 6
BH1 . . . . .122 A2
Alexandra Rd
Bournemouth BH6 . . . . . . .123 B3
Bridport DT6 . . . . .100 B3
Dorchester DT1 . . . . .107 C1
Poole BH14 . . . . .120 C2
Radipole DT4 . . . . .167 B3
Weymouth DT4 . . . . .166 C2
Yeovil BA21 . . . . .27 C3
Alexandra St DT11 . . . . .212 B1
Alexandria Ct BH22 . . . . .61 C2
Alford Rd BH3 . . . . .121 B4
Alfred Pl DT1 . . . . .108 A1
Alfred Rd DT1 . . . . .108 A1
Alfred St DT11 . . . . .212 B1
Alice in Wonderland Family
Pk★ BH23 . . . . .90 C4
Alice Rd DT1 . . . . .107 C1
Alington 18 BH4 . . . . . . .121 B2
Alington Ave DT1 . . . . . .135 B4
Alington Cl BH14 . . . . . .147 B4
Alington House BH14 . . .147 B4
Alington Rd
Bournemouth BH3 . . . . . .122 A3
Dorchester DT1 . . . . .108 A1
Alington St 4 DT1 . . . . .108 A1
Alipore Cl BH14 . . . . . . .120 B2
Alipore Hts BH14 . . . . . .120 B2
Alisons The BH20 . . . . . .139 C1
All Saints CE Prim Sch
DT9 . . . . .196 A8
All Saints CE Sch DT4 . .180 B4
All Saints' Rd
Dorchester DT1 . . . . .108 A1
Weymouth DT4 . . . . .180 B4
Allamanda Rd DT3 . . . . .152 C1
Allberry Gdns DT3 . . . . .168 A4
Allen Cl 8 DT11 . . . . . . .198 C7
Allen Ct BH21 . . . . .59 B3
Allen Rd BH21 . . . . .59 B2
Allenbourn Mid Sch
BH21 . . . . .59 B3
Allenby Cl BH17 . . . . .87 A1
Allenby Rd BH17 . . . . .87 A1
Allens La BH16 . . . . .118 B3
Allens Rd BH16 . . . . .118 B3
Allenview Rd BH21 . . . . . .59 B3
Allingham Rd BA21 . . . . . .27 C4
Allington Gdns 3 DT6 . .100 A4
Allington Mead 3 DT6 . .100 B4
Allington Pk DT6 . . . . . .100 A4
Allington Rd BH14 . . . . .147 B4
Alma Rd
Bournemouth BH9 . . . . . .122 A4
Weymouth DT4 . . . . .167 B2
Almer Rd BH15 . . . . .118 C2
Almond Gr Poole BH12 . .120 B4
Radipole DT4 . . . . .167 A3
Almshouses BH10 . . . . . . .89 B1
Alpha Ctr The BH17 . . . .119 A4
Alpine Rd BH24 . . . . .54 C1
Alton La DT2 . . . . .207 E4
Alton Mead La DT9 . . . .194 E4
Alton Rd
Bournemouth BH10 . . . . . . .89 A1
Poole BH14 . . . . .120 B2
Alton Rd E BH14 . . . . . . .120 B1
Alum Chine Rd BH4 . . . .121 A2
Alumdale Rd BH4 . . . . . .121 A1
Alumhurst Rd BH4 . . . . .121 A1
Alvandi Gdns 12 BH25 . . .95 A2
Alverton Ave BH15 . . . . .119 C2
Alverton Hall BH4 . . . . . .121 B1
Alvington La BA22 . . . . . .26 B2
Alyth Rd BH3 . . . . .121 B3
Ambassador Cl BH23 . . .125 A3
Ambassador Ind Est
BH23 . . . . .125 A3
Amber Rd BH21 . . . . .86 B2
Amberley Cl BH23 . . . . .125 C4
Amberley Ct 8 BH1 . . . .122 A2
Amberwood BH22 . . . . . . .61 C3
Amberwood Dr BH23 . . . .93 C1
Amberwood Gdns BH23 .94 A1
Amberwood House BH23 94 A1
Ambleside
Christchurch BH23 . . . . . . .91 C2
Radipole DT4 . . . . .167 A4
Ambrose Cl DT9 . . . . .28 B1
Ambury La BH23 . . . . . . .124 C4
Amelia Cl 3 DT5 . . . . . . .181 A1
Amen Cnr BH21 . . . . .201 B5
Amesbury Rd BH6 . . . . . .123 B3
Amethyst Rd BH23 . . . . .124 C4
Ameys La BH22 . . . . .61 C4
Ameysford Rd BH22 . . . . .52 B1
Amiens Rd BH20 . . . . . . .139 C4
Amira Ct 9 BH2 . . . . . . .121 C2
Ammerham La TA20 . . . .202 D8
Ampfield Rd BH8 . . . . .90 B2
Amsterdam Sq BH23 . . . .124 B3
Ancaster Rd BH19 . . . . . .178 C2
Anchor Cl
Bournemouth BH11 . . . . . . .88 C3
Christchurch BH23 . . . . . .125 A3
Anchor Rd BH11 . . . . .88 C3
Ancrum Lodge BH4 . . . . .121 A2
Andbourne Ct BH6 . . . . .123 C2
Anderson Manor★
DT11 . . . . .82 B4
Anderson Rd SP1 . . . . . .213 C4
Andover Cl BH23 . . . . . .125 A4
Andover Gn BH20 . . . . . .139 B3
Andree Ct BH23 . . . . . . .126 A4
Andrew Cl DT11 . . . . . . .212 C2
Andrew La BH25 . . . . .95 B1
Andrews Cl BH11 . . . . . . .89 A2
Andrews Way SP2 . . . . .213 A1
Angel Cl DT3 . . . . .150 B1
Angel La
Barton on Sea BH25 . . . . .127 B4
Ferndown BH22 . . . . .61 A2
Langton Herring DT3 . . . .150 B1
Mere BA12 . . . . .3 A3
Shaftesbury SP7 . . . . .12 C2
Stour Provost SP8 . . . . . . .10 C1
Angeline Cl BH23 . . . . . .125 C4
Angers La DT10 . . . . .197 E7
Anglebury Ave BH19 . . .179 A2
Anglewood Mans 9
BH4 . . . . .121 B2
Anglo-European Coll of
Chiropractic BH5 . . . . .123 A2
Angus Cl DT11 . . . . .212 C2
Anjou Cl BH11 . . . . .88 B3
Annandale Ct BH6 . . . . . .123 B2
Anncott Cl BH16 . . . . .84 B2
Anne Cl
Blandford Forum DT11 . . .212 C1
Christchurch BH23 . . . . . . .92 A1
Annerley Rd BH1 . . . . . . .122 B2
Annet Cl BH15 . . . . .118 C1
Anning Rd DT7 . . . . .96 B3
Annings La DT6 . . . . . . .101 C1
Anson Cl
Christchurch BH23 . . . . . .124 C3
Ringwood BH24 . . . . .55 C4
Anstey Cl BH11 . . . . .89 A3
Anstey Rd BH11 . . . . .89 A3
Ansty La DT11 . . . . .79 B4
Antell's Way SP6 . . . . . . .42 B3
Antelope Wlk DT1 . . . . .108 A1
Anthony's Ave BH14 . . . .120 B1
Antler Dr BH25 . . . . .94 C2
Anvil Cl 4 BH19 . . . . . . .178 C1
Anvil Cres BH18 . . . . .86 C3
Anvil Rd 10 DT11 . . . . . .199 D4
Aplands Cl DT11 . . . . . . .198 B8
Apollo Cl
Dorchester DT1 . . . . .134 C4
Poole BH12 . . . . .120 B4
Apple Acre 1 DT11 . . . . .198 C7
Apple Cl BH12 . . . . .121 A2
Apple Gr BH23 . . . . .91 C1
Apple Tree Gr BH22 . . . . .61 C3
Apple Tree Rd SP6 . . . . . .42 A3
Apple Trees La DT6 . . . . .99 A3
Appleslade Way BH25 . . .95 A3
Appletree Cl
Bournemouth BH6 . . . . . .123 B3
New Milton BH25 . . . . .95 A1
Radipole DT3 . . . . .167 B4
Approach Rd BH14 . . . . .120 A2
April Cl BH11 . . . . .89 A2
Apsley Cres BH17 . . . . . . .87 B1
Apsley Ct 2 BH8 . . . . . .122 A3
Aragon Cl DT4 . . . . .180 C4
Aragon Way BH9 . . . . . . .90 A2
Arbutus Cl DT1 . . . . . . .108 A1
Arcade BH4 . . . . .121 A2
Arcade The 37 BH1 . . . .121 C2
Arcadia Ave BH8 . . . . . . .122 A4
Arcadia Rd BH23 . . . . . . .91 C1
Archbishop Wake Fst Sch
DT11 . . . . .212 B1
Archdale Cl BH10 . . . . . . .89 B1
Archway Rd BH14 . . . . . .120 C2
Arden Rd BH9 . . . . .89 C2
Arden Wlk BH25 . . . . .95 A1
Ardmore Rd BH14 . . . . . .120 A2
Argyle Rd
Christchurch BH23 . . . . . .124 C3
Radipole DT4 . . . . .167 B3
Swanage BH19 . . . . .179 A1
Argyll Mans 11 BH5 . . . .122 C2
Argyll Rd
Bournemouth BH5 . . . . . .122 C2
Poole BH12 . . . . .120 B3
Ariel Cl BH6 . . . . .124 A2
Ariel Dr BH6 . . . . .124 A2
Ark Dr BH22 . . . . .61 C2
Arlecks La 2 DT11 . . . . .199 D4
Arley Rd BH14 . . . . .120 A1
Arlington DT4 . . . . .167 A3
Arlington Cl BA21 . . . . . . .26 C4
Arlington Ct BH25 . . . . . .127 A4
Armada Way DT1 . . . . . .135 B4
Armoury Rd BA22 . . . . . . .26 B3
Armoury Yd SP7 . . . . .12 C2
Armstrong Rd DT6 . . . . .100 B4
Arne Ave BH12 . . . . .120 C4
Arne Cres BH12 . . . . . . .120 C4
Arne Rd BH20 . . . . .143 B1
Arnewood Ct BH2 . . . . . .121 C1
Arnewood Gdns BA20 . . . .27 A1
Arnewood Rd BH6 . . . . . .123 B3
Arnewood Sch The BH25 94 C1
Arnold Cl BH22 . . . . .53 A2
Arnold Rd BH22 . . . . .53 A2
Arnolds Cl BH25 . . . . . . .126 C4
Arran Way BH23 . . . . .94 A1
Arras Cres BH20 . . . . . . .139 B4
Arras Rd BH20 . . . . .139 B4
Arrow Field DT6 . . . . . . .100 B3
Arrowfield DT6 . . . . .100 B3
Arrowsmith Ct BH18 . . . .87 A2
Arrowsmith La BH21 . . . .87 C4
Arrowsmith Rd BH21 . . . .87 C4
Arthur Cl BH2 . . . . .121 C3
Arthur La 3 BH23 . . . . . .124 A4
Arthur Rd BH23 . . . . .124 A4
Artillery Rd BA22 . . . . . . .26 B3
Artist Row DT5 . . . . .186 C4
Arts Inst of Bournemouth The
BH12 . . . . .121 B4
Arun Cl 2 SP8 . . . . .5 C2
Arundel Cl BH25 . . . . .94 C2
Arundel Rd BA21 . . . . .28 A3
Arundel Way BH23 . . . . .125 C4
Ascham Rd BH8 . . . . . . .122 A3
Ascot Rd BH18 . . . . .87 A2
Ash Ave BH20 . . . . .116 A2
Ash Cl Alderholt SP6 . . . . . .42 B3
Sandford BH20 . . . . .143 A4
Shaftesbury SP7 . . . . .13 A2
Swanage BH19 . . . . .178 C1
Upton BH16 . . . . .118 A4
Ash End BA8 . . . . .19 A3
Ash Gr BH24 . . . . .55 C4
Ash Hill DT2 . . . . .106 C4
Ash La DT6 . . . . .68 B3
Ash Tree Cl 2 DT2 . . . . . .78 A1
Ash Tree La SP7 . . . . .24 B3
Ash Wlk BA8 . . . . .19 A3
Ashbourne Ct 1 BH1 . . .122 A2
Ashbourne Rd BH5 . . . .123 A3
Ashbrook Wlk BH16 . . . .117 A3
Ashburn Garth 5 BH24 . .55 C3
Ashburton Gdns BH10 . . .89 B1
Ashcombe La DT9 . . . . . .31 B2
Ashdene Cl BH21 . . . . . . .59 B3
Ashdown BH2 . . . . .121 B1
Ashdown Cl BH17 . . . . . . .87 C1
Ashdown Sch BH17 . . . . . .87 C1
Ashdown Wlk BH25 . . . . .95 B1
Ashfield Rd SP2 . . . . . . .213 A3
Ashfield Trad Est SP2 . .213 A3
Ashford Gr BA21 . . . . .27 B4
Ashford Rd
Bournemouth BH6 . . . . . . .123 B4
Fordingbridge SP6 . . . . . . .42 C4
Ashgrove BA12 . . . . .3 A2
Ashington Gdns BH21 . . .86 C4
Ashington La BH21 . . . . . .59 A1
Ashington Pk BH25 . . . . .95 A1
Ashington St 3 DT1 . . . .107 B1
Ashland Ct TA18 . . . . . . .191 E5
Ashlands Cl 1 TA18 . . . .191 F5
Ashlands Mdw TA18 . . . .191 F5
Ashlands Rd TA18 . . . . . .191 F5
Ashlands VC Fst Sch
TA18 . . . . .191 E5
Ashleigh Ave DT2 . . . . . . .72 C4
Ashleigh Rise BH10 . . . . .89 B1
Ashlett Gdns BH25 . . . . . .95 B2
Ashley Arnewood Ct 9
BH25 . . . . .95 A1
Ashley Cl
Bournemouth BH1 . . . . . .122 C3
Ringwood BH24 . . . . .55 C3
Ashley Comm Rd BH25 . .95 B2
Ashley Ct BH22 . . . . .62 A4
Ashley Dr BH24 . . . . .46 C1
Ashley Dr N BH24 . . . . . . .54 A3
Ashley Dr S BH24 . . . . . . .54 A3
Ashley Dr W BH24 . . . . . .54 A3
Ashley Inf Sch BH25 . . . . .95 B2
Ashley Jun Sch BH25 . . . .95 B2
Ashley La SO41 . . . . .95 C2
Ashley Meads BH25 . . . . .95 B2
Ashley Pk BH24 . . . . .54 B3
Ashley Rd
Bournemouth BH1 . . . . . .122 C3
Dorchester DT1 . . . . .135 A4
Marnhull DT10 . . . . .21 A1
New Milton BH25 . . . . .95 B2
Poole BH14 . . . . .120 B3
Salisbury SP2 . . . . .213 A3
Ashley Wood Golf Club
DT11 . . . . .199 E1
Ashley Wood Pk DT11 . . .211 E7
Ashley Wood Rd DT11 . .199 E2
Ashling Cl BH8 . . . . . . .122 B4
Ashling Cres BH8 . . . . . .122 A4
Ashmead BA20 . . . . .26 C1
Ashmeads Cl BH21 . . . . . .60 A3
Ashmeads Way BH21 . . . .60 A3
Ashmede BH4 . . . . .121 B1
Ashmore BH21 . . . . .59 B2
Ashmore Ave
Barton on Sea BH25 . . . . .127 A4
Hamworthy BH15 . . . . . . .118 C1
Ashmore Bottom DT11 . . .39 B1
Ashmore Cl DT11 . . . . . .212 B2
Ashmore Cres BH15 . . . .118 C1
Ashmore Gr BH23 . . . . . . .93 C1
Ashridge Ave 1 BH10 . . .89 B3
Ashridge Gdns BH10 . . . .89 B3
Ashridge Par 2 BH10 . . .89 B3
Ashton Ct
13 New Milton BH25 . . . . . .95 A2
Poole BH13 . . . . .121 A1
Ashton Rd
Bournemouth BH9 . . . . .89 C1
1 Weymouth DT4 . . . . . . .167 B1
Ashtree Cl BH25 . . . . .95 B1
Ashurst Rd
Bournemouth BH8 . . . . .90 B2
Ferndown BH22 . . . . .53 A2
Ashwell Ct BH23 . . . . .91 C1
Ashwood Dr
Broadstone BH18 . . . . .87 B2
Yeovil Without BA21 . . . . .28 A4
Asker Gdns DT6 . . . . . . .100 B3
Askwith Cl DT9 . . . . .29 C3
Aspen Dr BH31 . . . . .45 B3
Aspen Gdns BH12 . . . . . .120 C4
Aspen Pl BH25 . . . . .95 A1
Aspen Rd BH12 . . . . .120 C4
Aspen Way
10 Crewkerne TA18 . . . . .191 F5
Poole BH12 . . . . .120 C4
Asquith Cl BH23 . . . . . . .124 B3
Ass Hill BH21 . . . . .201 B4
Assisi Rd SP1 . . . . .213 B4
Astbury Ave BH12 . . . . . . .89 A1
Aston Mead
Christchurch BH23 . . . . . . .91 C2
Salisbury SP1 . . . . .213 C4
Astrid Way 3 DT4 . . . . .167 C2
Athelhampton House★
DT2 . . . . .78 C1
Athelhampton Rd DT2 . . .78 C1
Athelney Ct 18 BH1 . . . .122 A2
Athelney Way BA21 . . . . .26 C3
Athelstan Rd
Bournemouth BH6 . . . . . .123 C3
15 Dorchester DT1 . . . . . .108 A1
Atlantic Rd BH19 . . . . . .179 A1
Attisham La DT6 . . . . . . .203 B4
Attwood Cl SP6 . . . . .42 A3
Attwood Rd SP1 . . . . . . .213 B4
Auckland Rd BH23 . . . . .125 B4
Audemer Ct BH24 . . . . . . .55 C4
Audrayton Ct 9 BH6 . . .123 C2
Augusta Cl DT5 . . . . . . .187 A3
Augusta Rd DT5 . . . . . . .187 A3
Augustan Cl 1 DT1 . . . .134 C4
Austen Ave BH10 . . . . .89 C3
Auster Cl BH23 . . . . .125 A4
Austin Ave BH14 . . . . . . .120 A1
Austin Cl BH1 . . . . .122 B3
Australia Rd DT3 . . . . . .166 B2
Autumn Cl BH22 . . . . .61 A4
Autumn Copse BH25 . . . . .95 B1
Autumn Rd BH11 . . . . .88 B2
Avalanche Rd DT5 . . . . .186 C1
Avalon BH14 . . . . .147 B4
Avebury Ave BH10 . . . . . .89 C3
Avenue Ct BH13 . . . . . . .121 A2
Avenue La 20 BH2 . . . . .121 C2
Avenue Rd
Bournemouth BH2 . . . . . .121 C2
Christchurch BH23 . . . . . . .94 B1
Lyme Regis DT7 . . . . .96 A3
New Milton BH25 . . . . .95 A2
Radipole DT4 . . . . .167 B2
Wimborne Minster BH21 . . .59 B2
Avenue Shopping Ctr The 21
BH2 . . . . .121 C2
Avenue The
Bournemouth BH9 . . . . .89 C2
6 Crewkerne TA18 . . . . . .192 A3
Ferndown BH22 . . . . .53 A2
Poole BH13 . . . . .121 A1
Salisbury SP1 . . . . .213 C3

Avenue The *continued*
Sherborne DT9 30 B4
Yeovil BA21 27 B3
Avocet Cl DT4 180 B3
Avon Approach SP2 213 B3
Avon Ave BH24 54 C2
Avon Bldgs BH23 124 A4
Avon Castle★ BH24 54 C2
Avon Castle Dr BH24 54 C2
Avon Cl
Bournemouth BH8 122 B3
Weymouth DT4 166 C2
Yeovil BA21 27 C3
Avon Cotts BH23 92 B3
Avon Cswy BH23 91 B4
Avon Ct BH23 124 B3
Avon Dr BH20 142 C3
Avon Farm Cotts BH23 63 C2
Avon Heath Ctry Pk★ BH24 54 B2
Avon Heath Ctry Pk (South Pk)★ BH24 63 A4
Avon House BH2 121 C1
Avon Mews BH8 122 B3
Avon Pk BH24 54 C3
Avon Rd
Bournemouth BH8 122 B3
Ferndown BH22 53 A1
Avon Rd E BH23 124 A4
Avon Rd W BH23 123 C4
Avon Run Cl BH23 125 A3
Avon Run Rd BH23 125 A3
Avon Terr SP2 213 A3
Avon View Par BH23 92 B2
Avon View Rd BH23 92 B2
Avon Wharf BH23 124 B3
Avonbourne Girls Sch BH7 123 A4
Avoncliffe Rd BH6 123 C2
Avondale Gdns SP8 5 C2
Avonlea Prep Sch BH24 55 B4
Award Rd BH21 60 C3
Axe La
Broadwindsor DT8 203 C8
West Crewkerne TA18 191 C1
Axe Valley Cl 1 DT8 204 A8
Axeford TA20 202 B8
Axford Cl BH8 90 B2
Axminster Rd DT6 96 C4
Axnoller La DT8 204 D6
Aylesbury Rd BH1 122 C2
Ayleswade Rd SP2 213 B1
Aysha Cl BH25 95 A1
Azalea Cl BH24 54 B3
Azura Cl BH21 53 B3

B

Babwell Rd BA9 4 A2
Babylon Hill DT9 28 B3
Babylon View BA21 28 A4
Back Dro DT9 194 E3
Back La Bere Regis BH20 81 A2
Bradford Abbas DT9 28 B1
Broadwindsor DT8 203 E5
Cerne Abbas DT2 207 D4
Chetnole DT9 194 D3
East Chinnock BA22 192 E8
East Coker BA22 193 C7
Evershot DT2 206 A7
Frome Vauchurch DT2 72 C4
Gillingham SP8 5 B3
Halstock BA22 193 C3
Hazelbury Bryan DT10 197 A4
Kington Magna SP8 9 B2
North Perrott TA18 192 C4
4 Okeford Fitzpaine DT11 197 F5
Rimpton BA22 15 A4
Sherborne DT9 30 A3
Sixpenny Handley SP5 189 A4
Sturminster Marshall BH21 56 B3
Swyre DT2 129 B3
Sydling St Nicholas DT2 207 A2
Back St Abbotsbury DT3 149 A4
East Stour SP8 10 C2
Portesham DT3 132 A1
Badbury Cl BH18 87 B2
Badbury Ct 8 BH23 124 C3
Badbury Dr DT11 212 B2
Badbury Rings (Hill Fort)★ DT11 49 A2
Badbury View BH21 59 B3
Badbury View Rd BH21 86 B4
Baden Cl BH25 95 A1
Baden Powell & St Peter's Mid Sch BH14 120 A2
Bader Rd BH17 119 C4
Badger Hts BA22 26 B3
Badger La DT2 209 A5
Badger Way BH31 45 A3
Badgers Cl BH24 54 A3
Badgers Copse BH25 95 B3
Badgers Way DT10 35 A1
Badgers Wlk BH22 61 C4
Baglake DT2 103 B1
Bagman's La BH21 201 E3
Bagwood Rd 8 DT11 81 C4
Bailey Cl BH25 95 B2
Bailey Cres BH15 119 B4
Bailey Dr BH23 123 C4
Bailey Gate Ind Est BH21 56 C2
Bailey Hall BH23 123 C4
Bailey Ridge DT9 195 A4
Bailey Ridge La DT9 194 F4
Bailey's Dro BH20 139 C1
Baileys Hill BH21 201 D6
Baiter Gdns BH15 119 B1
Bakehouse TA16 191 F7
Bakehouse La 1 DT9 28 B1
Baker Rd BH11 89 A3
Baker's Cross DT6 65 B2
Bakers Farm Rd BH31 45 A4
Bakers La 3 BH21 201 D1
Bakers Paddock DT2 136 B1
Balaclava Rd
Bovington Camp BH20 139 C4
Fortuneswell DT5 181 B1
Balcombe Rd BH13 121 A2
Baldwin Cl BH23 124 B3
Balena Cl BH17 119 A4
Balfour Cl BH23 125 B4
Balfour Rd BH9 89 C1
Ball La 17 BH15 119 B1
Ball's Hill BA22 26 A4
Ball's La BH21 56 B3
Ballam Cl BH16 118 B4
Ballands Castle★ BA9 1 A1
Ballard Cl
Lytchett Matravers BH16 84 B2
New Milton BH25 95 A2
Poole BH15 119 B1
Ballard Coll BH25 95 A2
Ballard Lee BH19 179 B3
Ballard Rd Poole BH15 119 B1
Swanage BH19 179 B3
Ballard Sch BH25 95 A2
Ballard Way BH19 179 B3
Balmoor Cl BA12 3 A2
Balmoral Ave BH8 90 C1
Balmoral Cres DT1 135 B4
Balmoral Ct 7 BH23 126 A4
Balmoral House BH2 121 B2
Balmoral Rd Poole BH14 120 B2
Salisbury SP1 213 B4
Yeovil BA21 28 A3
Balmoral Wlk BH25 94 C2
Balston Rd BH14 120 A3
Balston Terr BH15 119 A1
Banbury Hill (Fort)★ DT10 197 D6
Banbury Rd BH17 119 B4
Bank Chambers BH14 120 C2
Bank Cl BH23 124 A3
Banks Rd BH13 147 B2
Bankside Rd BH9 90 A2
Banocroft Ct 1 BH15 119 C2
Banstead Rd BH18 87 A3
Banton Shard DT6 68 C1
Barberry Way BH31 45 C3
Barbers Gate 15 BH15 119 A1
Barbers Piles 8 BH15 119 A1
Barbers Wharf 16 BH15 119 A1
Barclay Mans BH2 121 C3
Barclay Rd DT4 167 B2
Bardolfeston Village★ DT2 78 B1
Bargates BH23 124 A4
Barges Cl DT2 103 B1
Baring Rd BH6 124 A2
Barlake Ct 5 DT1 107 B1
Barlands Cl BH23 92 B1
Barley Cl DT2 194 A2
Barley Way DT4 167 C1
Barleycroft Rd 3 DT5 186 C2
Barleyfields 10 SP8 5 C2
Barlynch Ct 6 BA21 26 C3
Barn Cl
8 Crewkerne TA18 191 E4
Upton BH16 118 A4
Barn Cres 7 TA18 191 E4
Barn La TA18 191 E6
Barn Rd BH18 87 A2
Barn St TA18 191 E4
Barnaby Mead SP8 5 C1
Barnard St 4 SP1 213 B2
Barndale Dr BH20 143 A1
Barnes Cl
Blandford Forum DT11 212 C2
Bournemouth BH10 89 B2
Marnhull DT10 21 A1
Sturminster Newton DT10 35 A1
Barnes Cres
Bournemouth BH10 89 B2
Wimborne Minster BH21 59 C2
Barnes Cross DT9 196 A6
Barnes La DT8 204 C4
Barnes Pl BA12 3 A3
Barnes Rd
Bournemouth BH10 89 B2
Wareham Town BH20 142 B1
Barnes Way 18 DT1 108 A1
Barneston Manor★ BH20 176 A4
Barnet Cl BA21 27 A4
Barney's Cl DT6 97 A4
Barnfield BH23 125 B4
Barnhaven Cl DT4 167 A1
Barnhill Rd BH20 143 A1
Barns Rd BH22 62 A3
Barnsfield Rd BH24 54 B1
Barnsley Dro BH21 50 A2
Barons Ct 3 BH12 121 A2
Barons Rd BH11 88 B3
Barr La DT6 101 B2
Barr's La DT6 97 A4
Barrack La BH24 55 C2
Barrack Rd
Christchurch BH23 123 C4
Ferndown BH22 62 A1
Weymouth DT4 167 C1
Barrack St DT6 100 B4
Barrie Rd BH9 89 C2
Barrington Rd SP1 213 C4
Barrow Cl DT1 134 C4
Barrow Dr BH8 90 C1
Barrow Hill
Bere Regis BH20 81 A2
Stalbridge DT10 33 B4
Stourton Caundle DT10 32 C1
Barrow La DT2 205 A8
Barrow Rd BH8 90 C1
Barrow Rise DT4 180 A4
Barrow St La BA12 3 C2
Barrow View BH22 61 A3
Barrow Way BH8 90 C1
Barrowfield Cl DT6 128 A4
Barrowgate Rd BH8 90 B2
Barrowgate Way BH8 90 B2
Barrowland La DT2 71 A3
Barrs Ave BH25 95 A2
Barrs Wood Dr BH25 95 A2
Barrs Wood Rd BH25 95 A2
Barry Gdns BH18 86 C3
Barry La BA22 192 F6
Barters La
Broadstone BH18 86 C2
Donhead St Mary SP7 25 A4
Bartlets Cl DT2 133 B3
Bartlett Dr BH7 123 A4
Bartlett Rd SP1 213 B4
Bartletts The BA12 3 A2
Bartley Ct 6 BH21 59 A3
Bartom's La BH16 84 A1
Barton Cl
Sturminster Newton DT10 197 C8
Toller Porcorum DT2 71 B4
West Stafford DT2 136 A4
Barton Comm La BH25 127 A4
Barton Comm Rd BH25 127 A4
Barton Croft BH25 127 A4
Barton Ct BH25 127 A3
Barton Ct Ave BH25 127 A4
Barton Ct Rd BH25 95 A1
Barton Dr
Barton on Sea BH25 126 C4
Overcombe/Preston DT3 153 A2
Barton Gdns DT9 29 C3
Barton Gn BH25 127 A3
Barton Heritage Collection★ SP2 213 A3
Barton Hill
Kington Magna SP8 9 B2
Melbury Osmond DT2 194 A2
Shaftesbury SP7 12 C2
Barton Hill House Sch SP7 12 C2
Barton House BH25 126 C4
Barton La
Barton on Sea BH25 126 C4
Mere BA12 3 A3
Barton Lodge BH12 120 A3
Barton The DT2 205 A8
Barton Way BH25 126 C4
Barton Wood Rd BH25 126 C4
Bartonside Rd BH25 126 B4
Barwick CP Sch BA22 193 F8
Bascott Cl BH11 89 A1
Bascott Rd BH11 89 A1
Bashley Comm Rd BH25 95 A4
Bashley Cross Rd BH25 94 C3
Bashley Dr BH25 95 A3
Bashley Rd BH25 95 A3
Bassett Rd BH12 120 A3
Bastone Way BH22 61 A3
Bat Alley DT10 20 C1
Batchelor Cres BH11 88 C2
Batchelor Rd BH11 88 C2
Batchelor's La BH21 201 D1
Batchpool La BA8 8 A4
Batcombe Cl BH11 88 C2
Batcombe Rd DT9 194 F1
Bath Hill Ct 9 BH1 122 A2
Bath Orch 6 DT6 68 C1
Bath Rd
Bournemouth BH1 122 A2
Sturminster Newton DT10 35 A1
Bath St DT4 167 B2
Bathwell La DT9 17 B1
Bats La DT2 106 C1
Batten Cl BH23 124 B4
Batterley Dro BH21 41 A2
Battle Mead
Corfe Castle BH20 177 A4
Swanage BH19 179 A2
Batts La DT6 203 C2
Baunton's Orch DT9 17 B1
Bauntons Cl 10 DT9 17 B1
Baverstock Rd BH12 121 A4
Bay Cl Swanage BH19 179 B3
Three Legged Cross BH21 53 A4
Upton BH16 118 A3
Bay Cres BH19 179 A3
Bay Hog La BH15 119 A1
Bay La SP8 6 A1
Bay Rd SP8 5 C1
Bay Tree Way BH23 93 B1
Bay View 8 BH19 178 C1
Bayard Rd DT3 152 C1
Baycliffe Rd DT4 167 A1
Baydon Cl DT3 153 A2
Bayfran Way DT11 212 C1
Baynard's Rd DT1 107 B1
Bayview Rd DT7 96 A3
Beach Ave BH25 126 C4
Beach Cl BH13 147 D4
Beach Gdns BH19 179 A2
Beach Rd
Burton Bradstock DT6 128 B4
Poole BH13 147 D4
Studland BH19 164 B1
Upton BH16 118 A3
Beach View BH13 147 B2
Beachcroft BH13 121 A2
Beachview Cl 1 DT4 180 A4
Beacon Ct BH23 125 C4
Beacon Dr BH23 125 C4
Beacon Gdns BH18 86 C2
Beacon Hill La BH21 86 A2
Beacon Pk Cres BH16 118 A4
Beacon Pk Rd BH16 118 A4
Beacon Rd
Bournemouth BH2 121 C1
Broadstone BH18 86 C2
Upton BH16 118 A4
Beacon Way BH18 86 C2
Beaconfield Rd BA20 27 A1
Beaconsfield Rd
Christchurch BH23 124 A4
Poole BH12 120 B3
Beadon La TA16 191 E7
Beaminster Mus★ DT8 204 D4
Beaminster Rd DT6 68 C1
Beaminster VC Comp Sch DT8 204 C4
Beamish Rd BH17 119 C4
Bear Cross Ave BH11 88 C3
Bearwood Prim Sch BH11 88 B3
Beatrice Rd SP1 213 B4
Beatty Cl BH24 55 C4
Beatty Rd BH9 90 A1
Beau Ct
31 Bournemouth BH4 121 B2
9 New Milton BH25 95 A2
Beauchamps Gdns BH7 123 A4
Beaucroft La BH21 59 C3
Beaucroft Rd BH21 59 C3
Beaucroft Sch BH21 59 C3
Beaufort Cl BH23 125 A4
Beaufort Dr BH21 59 B3
Beaufort Mews BH21 59 A2
Beaufort Rd BH6 123 B3
Beaufoy Cl SP7 13 A2
Beaufoys Ave BH22 61 B4
Beaufoys Cl BH22 61 B4
Beaufoys Ct BH22 61 B3
Beaulieu DT4 167 A3
Beaulieu Ave BH23 123 C4
Beaulieu Cl BH25 94 C4
Beaulieu Dr BA21 26 C3
Beaulieu Rd
Bournemouth BH4 121 A1
Christchurch BH23 123 C4
Beaumont Ave
Bridport DT6 100 B4
Radipole DT4 167 B3
Beaumont Rd BH13 147 C4
Beaver Ind Est BH23 125 A3
Beccles Cl BH15 118 C1
Becher Rd BH14 120 C2
Becket Way SP1 213 C3
Beckett Cl DT11 211 B1
Beckhampton Rd BH15 118 C2
Becklands La DT6 65 C2
Beckley Copse BH23 94 A1
Becton La BH25 127 A4
Becton Mead BH25 95 A1
Bedale Way BH15 119 C3
Bedford Cres BH7 123 B4
Bedford Pl DT6 100 B4
Bedford Rd
Salisbury SP2 213 A3
Weymouth DT4 167 A2
Yeovil BA21 27 C4
Bedford Rd N BH12 88 B1
Bedford Rd S BH12 88 B1
Bedford Terr DT6 100 B4
Bedwin St SP1 213 B3
Beech Ave
Bournemouth BH6 123 B2
Holton Heath BH20 116 A2
Beech Cl Alderholt SP6 42 B3
Broadmayne DT2 136 A1
Broadstone BH18 86 C2
1 Spetisbury DT11 211 E5
Verwood BH31 45 A3
West Lulworth BH20 172 B3
Beech Ct BH21 59 C2
Beech La
Hawkchurch EX13 202 B1
Netherbury DT8 204 A3
St.Leonards BH24 54 A1
Beech Rd
Puddletown DT2 78 A1
Radipole DT3 152 A2
Beech Tree Cl DT2 206 C2
Beech Wood Cl BH18 87 A2
Beechbank Ave BH17 86 C1
Beechcroft BH1 122 A3
Beechcroft Inf Sch DT4 167 B2
Beechcroft La 1 BH24 55 B4
Beechcroft Mews 2 BH24 55 B4
Beechcroft Rd SP1 213 C3
Beeches The
Beaminster DT8 204 C4
Bournemouth BH7 123 A4
5 Salisbury SP1 213 C2
1 Shaftesbury SP7 12 C2
Wareham St Martin BH20 143 A4
Beechey Ct 6 BH8 122 A3
Beechey Rd BH8 122 A3
Beechfield 30 BH4 121 B2
Beechwood BA20 27 A1
Beechwood Ave
Bournemouth BH5 122 C2
New Milton BH25 94 C2
Beechwood Ct BH2 121 C1
Beechwood Dr 5 TA18 191 F5
Beechwood Gdns BH5 123 A2
Beechwood Rd BH22 53 A1
Beel Cl 2 DT5 181 A1
Beer St BA20 27 A2
Belben Cl BH12 88 B1
Belben Rd BH12 88 B1
Belfield Pk Ave DT4 167 A1
Belfield Rd BH6 124 A2
Belgrave DT4 167 A3
Belgrave Ct BH1 122 B2
Belgrave Pl 3 DT5 186 C4
Belgrave Rd BH13 121 A1
Bell Heather Cl BH16 118 A4
Bell La 18 BH15 119 A1
Bell St Shaftesbury SP7 12 C2
Swanage BH19 178 C1
Bell's Orch La BH20 142 C2
Bellamy La SP1 213 B3
Bellbury Cl 1 DT2 78 A1
Belle Vue DT4 167 C1
Belle Vue Cl BH6 123 B2
Belle Vue Cres BH6 123 C2
Belle Vue Gdns 2 BH6 123 C2
Belle Vue Gr BH22 53 A1
Belle Vue Mans 7 BH6 123 C2
Belle Vue Rd
Bournemouth BH6 123 C2
Poole BH14 120 B2
4 Salisbury SP1 213 B3
Swanage BH19 179 B1
Weymouth DT4 167 B1
Belle Vue Terr 15 DT5 186 C4
Belle Vue Wlk BH22 61 C1
Bellflower Cl BH23 125 A4
Bellman's Cross BA8 19 B3
Bellows Cross BH21 40 B4
Bells House BH21 59 B3
Bells La BA12 1 C4
Belmont Ave BH8 90 B1
Belmont Cl
Shaftesbury SP7 12 C1
Verwood BH31 45 B3
Belmont Rd
New Milton BH25 95 B2
Poole BH14 120 B3
Belmour Lodge 26 BH4 121 B2
Belvedere Rd
Bournemouth BH3 122 A3
Christchurch BH23 124 A4
7 Swanage BH19 179 B1
Yeovil BA21 28 A3
Bembury La DT9 194 D8
Bemister Rd BH9 122 A4
Ben Nevis Rd DT4 167 B1
Benbow Cres BH12 88 C1
Benbridge Ave BH11 88 C3
Bendigo Rd BH23 123 C4
Benellen Ave BH4 121 B2
Benellen Gdns BH4 121 B2
Benellen Rd BH4 121 B3
Benellen Twrs BH4 121 B2
Bengal Rd BH9 121 C4
Benjamin Ct BH23 123 C4
Benjamin Rd BH15 118 C1
Benlease Way BH19 178 C1
Benmoor Rd BH17 119 A4
Benmore Cl BH25 95 B1
Benmore Rd BH9 90 A1
Bennett House 11 BH4 121 B2
Bennett Rd BH8 122 B3
Bennett's Alley 22 BH15 119 A1
Bennetts Hill La DT6 101 B1
Bennion Rd BH10 89 B2
Benridge Cl BH18 87 A2
Benson Rd BH17 119 B4
Bentley Rd BH9 89 C2
Benville La DT2 205 C6
Benville Manor★ DT2 205 C6
Benville Rd DT4 166 C1
Bere Cl BH17 87 B1
Bere Down La BH20 80 C3
Bere La DT9 195 F7
Bere Marsh DT11 198 B7
Bere Rd
Northport BH20 142 B3
Winterborne Kingston DT11 81 C4
Bere Regis Cty Fst Sch BH20 81 A1
Bere Regis Sports Club BH20 81 B2
Beresford Cl BH12 120 B3
Beresford Gdns BH23 124 C3
Beresford Rd
Bournemouth BH6 123 A2
Poole BH12 120 B3
Berkeley Ave BH12 120 B4
Berkeley Cl
9 Pimperne DT11 199 D4
Verwood BH31 45 A4
Berkeley Ct DT6 100 B3
Berkeley Rd
Bournemouth BH3 121 C4
1 Pimperne DT11 199 D3
16 Yeovil BA20 27 B2
Berkeley Rise 8 DT11 199 D4
Berkley Ave BH22 61 B1
Berkshire Rd SP2 213 A2
Bermuda Ct 9 BH23 126 A4
Bernards Cl BH23 123 C4

Berne Ct 11 BH1 122 A2
Beron Ct BH15 119 C2
Berrans Ave BH11 89 A3
Berrans Ct BH11 89 A3
Berry La EX13 202 D3
Bertram Rd BH25 95 B2
Berwick La DT6 129 B3
Berwick Rd BH3 121 C3
Berwyn Ct BH18 87 A2
Bessborough Rd BH13 147 C4
Bessells La DT11 198 D8
Bessemer Cl BH31 45 C2
Bestwall Cres BH20 142 C2
Bestwall Rd BH20 142 C2
Beswick Ave BH10 89 B1
Bethany Ct BH12 121 A4
Bethany House BH1 122 B3
Bethany Jun CE Sch BH1 122 B3
Bethia Cl BH8 122 B3
Bethia Rd BH8 122 B3
Bettiscombe Cl BH17 87 C1
Bettiscombe Manor House* DT6 203 B3
Beverley Gdns BH10 89 B2
Beverley Grange 29 BH4 121 B2
Beverley Rd DT3 152 B2
Bexington Cl BH11 88 C2
Bickerley Gdns BH24 55 A3
Bickerley Rd BH24 55 A3
Bicknell Boys Sch BH7 123 A4
Bicknell Ct 10 BH4 121 B2
Bicknell Gdns BA21 27 B4
Bicton Rd BH10 89 A2
Biddlecome Orch 5 DT6 100 B4
Big Ope DT5 186 C4
Bilshay La DT6 68 A2
Bimport SP7 12 B1
Bincleaves Rd DT4 167 B1
Bincombe Dr 2 TA18 191 F5
Bincombe Rise DT3 152 C2
Bindbarrow Rd DT6 128 B3
Bindells The DT3 166 B3
Bindon Abbey (rems of)* BH20 140 B1
Bindon Cl Poole BH12 120 C4
West Lulworth BH20 172 C4
Bindon La BH20 140 B1
Bindon Rd BH20 172 B3
Bindon Way BH20 140 A1
Bingham Ave BH14 147 B4
Bingham Cl
Christchurch BH23 124 C4
Verwood BH31 45 B2
Bingham Dr BH31 45 B2
Bingham Rd
Bournemouth BH9 122 A4
Christchurch BH23 124 C4
Salisbury SP1 213 C4
Verwood BH31 45 B2
Binghams Rd DT2 137 B3
Binnegar La BH20 141 B2
Binnie Rd BH12 120 C3
Birch Ave
3 Blandford St Mary DT11 222 B1
Burton BH23 92 B2
Ferndown BH22 61 C1
Holton Heath BH20 116 A2
New Milton BH25 94 B3
Birch Cl Corfe Mullen BH21 86 B3
Poole BH14 120 C2
St.Leonards BH24 53 C2
Birch Dr BH8 91 A1
Birch Gr Ferndown BH22 52 C1
New Milton BH25 95 A1
Birch La Puddletown DT2 77 C2
Yetminster DT9 194 C5
Birch Rd BH24 54 B2
Birch Wlk BH22 61 C2
Birchdale 6 BA20 26 C1
Birchdale Rd BH21 59 B3
Birchfield Prim Sch BA21 27 C4
Birchfield Rd BA21 27 C4
Birchwood Cl BH23 125 A4
Birchwood Dr SP6 42 B3
Birchwood Mews BH14 120 B2
Birchwood Rd
Poole BH14 120 B2
Upton BH16 118 A3
Bird's Cl 5 TA18 191 E4
Bird's Hill Rd BH15 119 C2
Birds Hill Gdns 5 BH15 119 C2
Birkdale Ct BH18 87 A3
Birkdale Rd BH18 87 A3
Bishop Cl BH12 121 B4
Bishop Ct BH24 55 B4
Bishop Rd BH9 122 A4
Bishop Wordsworths Sch SP1 213 B2
Bishop's La DT9 28 B1
Bishop's Palace* SP1 213 B2
Bishop's Rd
Abbotsbury DT3 149 B4
Portesham DT3 131 B1
Bishop's Wlk SP1 213 B2
Bishopdown Rd SP1 213 B4
Bishops Cl
Abbotsbury DT3 149 A4
Bournemouth BH7 122 C4
Mere BA12 3 A3
Bishops Dr SP2 213 A1
Bishops La BA22 193 A6
Bitchams Mead BH20 81 A1
Bitterne Way BH31 45 B3
Black Hill BH31 45 B3
Black La DT11 212 C1
Black Lawn SP8 5 C2
Black Mere BA22 26 B3
Black Moor Rd BH31 45 C2
Blackberry La
Christchurch BH23 124 C3
Radipole DT3 152 B1
Sherborne DT9 30 A4
Blackbird Cl BH17 118 C4
Blackbird Way BH23 93 B4
Blackbirds 6 DT9 194 D8
Blackburn Rd BH12 120 A3
Blackers Hole (Cave)* BH19 184 B3
Blackfield La BH22 53 A2
Blackfield Rd BH8 90 B2
Blackfriars Way SP1 213 B2
Blackhill Rd BH16 116 B2
Blackhill Rd W BH16 116 B1
Blacklands La DT11 197 D3
Blackmoor BA8 19 A3
Blackmoor La BA8 19 A2
Blackmore Rd
Shaftesbury SP7 13 A2
Stalbridge DT10 33 B4
Blacknell La TA18 191 F4
Blackney La DT6 203 E2
Blacknoll La DT2 138 C1
Blacknor Rd DT5 186 C2
Blackpool Cnr DT6 202 B1
Blackrow La DT10 196 D7
Blacksmith Cl BH21 86 B3
Blacksmith's La DT9 194 D8
Blacksmith's Piece DT2 105 B1
Blackthorn Way
New Milton BH25 95 B2
Verwood BH31 45 B3
Blackwater Dr BH21 87 B4
Blackwater Gr SP6 42 A3
Blackwater La EX13 202 C3
Bladen View DT11 79 C4
Blagdon Cl DT2 133 B3
Blagdon Rd DT1 107 B1
Blair Ave BH14 120 B2
Blair Cl BH25 94 C2
Blake Dene Rd BH14 120 A1
Blake Hill Ave BH14 120 B1
Blake Hill Cres BH14 120 B1
Blake Rd 22 TA18 191 F4
Blakey Rd SP1 213 C2
Blandford Cl BH15 118 C1
Blandford Hill
Milborne St Andrew DT11 79 C4
Winterborne Whitechurch DT11 210 C3
Blandford Hospl DT11 212 B1
Blandford Rd
Corfe Mullen BH21 86 B4
Hamworthy BH15 118 B2
Iwerne Minster DT11 37 C1
Pamphill BH21 58 B4
Shapwick DT11 48 C1
Shillingstone DT11 198 B6
Sturminster Marshall BH21 56 B2
Blandford Rd N
Lytchett Minster & Upton BH16 85 A1
Upton BH16 118 A4
Blandford Sports Ctr DT11 212 B1
Blandford St Mary CE VA Fst Sch DT11 211 B1
Blandford VC Comp Sch The DT11 212 B1
Blaney Way BH21 86 B3
Blanford Hts Ind Est DT11 212 B2
Blashford Lakes Study Ctr* BH24 47 B2
Bleak St BA9 1 B2
Bleax Cl SP7 22 C1
Bleet La SP8 10 B3
Bleke St SP7 12 C2
Blemheim Rd DT3 152 A1
Blenheim Cres SO41 95 C2
Blenheim Ct
25 Bournemouth BH4 121 B2
Christchurch BH23 124 A4
Blenheim Dr BH23 125 A3
Blenheim Rd BA21 27 C4
Blind La
Berwick St John SP7 188 B8
Burstock DT8 203 C6
Ellingham Harbridge & Ibsley SP6 43 C1
Evershot DT2 206 B7
Marshwood DT6 203 D1
Thorncombe TA20 202 E6
Wimborne Minster BH21 59 A3
Blind La Cl DT6 68 C1
Blind St BH20 81 A1
Blindmere Rd DT5 186 C2
Blissford Hill SP6 43 C3
Bloody Shard Gate DT11 188 A1
Bloomfield Ave BH9 89 C1
Bloomfield Pl BH9 89 C1
Bloxworth Rd BH12 120 C4
Blue Boar Row SP1 213 B3
Bluebell Cl BH23 125 A4
Bluebell La BH17 86 C1
Bluebell Rd BA22 26 B3
Bluntshay La DT6 66 C4
Blyth Cl BH23 91 B2
Blyth Way SP1 213 C4
Blythe Rd BH21 86 B3
Blythswood Ct BH25 126 C4
Boar St BA12 3 A3
Bob Hann Cl BH12 120 B3
Bockhampton Cross DT2 109 A2
Bockhampton La DT2 109 A2
Bockhampton Rd BH23 92 C3
Bodkin La DT3 168 A3
Bodley Rd BH13 147 C4
Bodorgan Rd BH2 121 C2
Bodowen Cl BH23 92 B1
Bodowen Rd BH23 92 B1
Bodsmarsh La DT10 21 C1
Bognor Rd BH18 86 C2
Bohay's Dr DT4 180 B4
Bokerley Ditch* SP6 190 A5
Boldre Cl
Barton on Sea BH25 126 B4
Poole BH12 120 B4
Boleyn Cl BH9 90 A2
Boleyn Cres DT4 180 C4
Bolton Cl BH6 123 C2
Bolton Cres BH22 62 A3
Bolton Ct 4 BH6 123 C2
Bolton Rd BH6 123 C2
Bon Accord Rd BH19 179 A1
Bond Ave BH22 52 C2
Bond Rd BH15 119 C3
Bond St Radipole DT4 167 B2
4 Yeovil BA20 27 B2
Boney Rd BH20 139 C4
Bonfields Ave BH19 179 A2
Bonham La BA12 1 C4
Bonham Rd BH3 121 C4
Bonhole La DT6 101 C2
Bonington Cl BH23 124 C4
Bonnett's La BH20 142 C2
Bonscombe La DT6 101 B3
Bonvils Rd BH19 183 A4
Bookham La DT2 208 B7
Boot La 7 DT9 194 D8
Boozer Pit TA16 191 F8
Border Dr BH16 118 B3
Border Lodge BH23 94 B1
Border Rd BH16 118 B3
Boreham Rd BH6 123 B3
Borley Rd BH17 119 A4
Borthwick Rd BH1 122 C3
Boscombe Cliff Rd BH5 122 C2
Boscombe Gr Rd BH1 122 B3
Boscombe Overcliff Dr BH5 123 A2
Boscombe Spa Rd BH5 122 B2
Bosley Cl BH23 91 C1
Bosley Way BH23 91 C1
Boston Lodge 22 BH4 121 B2
Boswell's Cl BH20 81 A2
Bosworth Mews BH9 90 A2
Bothen Dr DT6 100 C3
Bottlebush La BH21 189 E1
Bottom Rd DT11 198 F4
Bouchers Way SP2 213 B1
Boulnois Ave BH14 120 C2
Boulton Cl DT4 180 B4
Bound La DT9 194 F2
Boundary Ave BA22 26 B4
Boundary Cl
Swanage BH19 185 B4
Yeovil BA21 27 A4
Boundary Dr BH21 59 B3
Boundary La BH24 53 C1
Boundary Rd
Bournemouth BH10 89 C1
Yeovil BA22 26 B3
Boundary View 1 DT11 212 B1
Bountys La BH12 120 C3
Bourne Ave
Bournemouth BH2 121 C2
Salisbury SP1 213 C3
Bourne Cl
Bournemouth BH4 121 B2
8 Salisbury SP1 213 C2
Bourne Ct
24 Bournemouth BH2 121 C2
Wimborne Minster BH21 59 B3
Bourne Dr BH20 142 B3
Bourne Dro DT2 76 C3
Bourne Hill SP1 213 B3
Bourne Pines 3 BH1 121 C2
Bourne Valley Rd BH12 121 A3
Bourne Way
Gillingham SP8 5 C2
Salisbury SP1 213 C2
Bournemouth & Poole Coll of F Ed BH14 119 C2
Bournemouth & Poole Coll The BH1 122 A2
Bournemouth Aquarium* BH2 121 C1
Bournemouth Aviation Mus* BH23 91 A4
Bournemouth Central Bsns Pk BH1 122 B3
Bournemouth Crown & Cty Cts* BH7 91 B1
Bournemouth Gram Sch (Boys) BH8 90 B1
Bournemouth Gram Sch (Girls) BH8 90 B1
Bournemouth Int Airport BH23 90 C4
Bournemouth Int Ctr* BH2 121 C1
Bournemouth Meml Homes BH8 90 C1
Bournemouth Nuffield Hospl BH8 122 A3
Bournemouth Rd
Charlton Marshall DT11 211 D6
Poole BH14 120 B2
Bournemouth Sta BH1 122 A2
Bournemouth Univ BH12 121 B4
Bournewood Dr BH4 121 B2
Bourton Gdns BH7 123 A4
Bourton Prim Sch SP8 1 C1
Bouverie Ave SP2 213 B1
Bouverie Ave S SP2 213 A1
Bouverie Cl
23 Barton on Sea BH25 95 A1
Salisbury SP2 213 A1
Boveridge Gdns BH9 90 A2
Boveridge House Sch BH21 190 B1
Bovington Cl BH17 87 C1
Bovington Fst Sch BH20 139 B3
Bovington La BH20 139 C3
Bovington Mid Sch BH20 139 C3
Bow The 3 DT1 108 A1
Bowden La BA8 18 B3
Bowden Rd
Abbas & Templecombe BA8 18 A4
Poole BH12 88 B1
Bowditch Row 25 TA18 191 F4
Bowdowns DT6 204 B2
Bower Ct 5 DT9 194 C5
Bower Gdns SP1 213 C2
Bower Hill Rd SP1 213 C3
Bower Rd BH8 122 B4
Bowers Rd 6 DT5 186 C2
Bowerswain Hollow BH21 201 B5
Bowerwood Rd SP6 42 C4
Bowes La 6 DT8 204 A8
Bowey 6 DT11 197 F6
Bowgrove Rd DT8 204 D5
Bowhayes Bridport DT6 100 C3
8 Crewkerne TA18 191 F4
Bowland Rise BH25 95 B1
Bowleaze BA21 26 C3
Bowleaze Coveway DT3 168 A3
Bowling Gn La SP5 189 D5
Bown Hill DT5 186 C1
Box Cl BH17 119 A4
Boyd Rd BH12 120 C3
Boyle Cl DT10 33 B4
Boyne's La
Iwerne Minster DT11 38 B1
Iwerne Stepleton DT11 199 B7
Boys Hill Dro DT9 195 D5
Boyte Rd 14 DT11 199 D4
Bozley Hill SP7 24 A4
Brabazon Dr BH23 125 A4
Brabazon Rd BH21 59 C1
Brabourne Ave BH22 61 B2
Bracken Cl BH24 53 C2
Bracken Glen BH15 119 C3
Bracken Lodge 3 BH6 123 C2
Bracken Rd
Bournemouth BH6 123 B2
Ferndown BH22 61 A4
Bracken Way BH23 94 A1
Brackenbury Cty Infs Sch DT5 186 C4
Brackendale Ct BH21 52 C4
Brackendale Rd BH8 122 B4
Brackendown Ave DT3 167 C4
Brackenhill BH13 121 A1
Brackenhill Rd BH21 60 A4
Brackens Way 12 BH13 147 C4
Brackley Cl BH23 91 A4
Bradbourne Rd BH2 121 C2
Bradford Abbas Prim Sch DT9 28 B1
Bradford La DT9 195 B6
Bradford Rd
Bournemouth BH9 90 B2
1 Crewkerne TA18 192 A3
Sherborne DT9 29 C3
Weymouth DT4 167 A1
Bradpole Rd BH8 90 C1
Bradstock Cl BH12 120 C4
Braemar Ave BH6 124 A2
Braemar Cl BH6 124 A2
Braemar Dr BH23 93 C1
Braemar Rd DT1 135 B4
Braemar Rise SP1 213 B4
Braeside Rd
Ferndown BH22 53 A2
St.Leonards BH24 54 A2
Braidley Rd BH2 121 C2
Brailswood Rd BH15 119 C2
Braishfield Gdns BH8 90 B1
Brakes Hill DT2 194 A2
Bramar Ct BH4 121 B1
Bramble Cl SP6 42 B3
Bramble Ct BH22 53 A1
Bramble Dr DT6 100 B1
Bramble Dro DT2 136 A1
Bramble Edge DT2 136 A1
Bramble La
Christchurch BH23 94 A1
Haselbury Plucknett TA18 192 C5
Bramblecombe La DT11 209 D4
Brambles The SP1 213 C3
Brambling Cl DT3 152 B2
Bramdon Cl 5 DT3 150 A4
Bramdon La DT3 150 B3
Bramley Cl 8 TA18 191 F5
Bramley Ct BH22 61 B3
Bramley Hill
Bridport DT6 100 C4
Mere BA12 2 C3
Bramley Rd
Bournemouth BH10 89 B3
Ferndown BH22 61 B3
Brampton Rd BH15 119 B3
Bramshaw Gdns BH8 90 B2
Bramshaw Way BH25 126 B4
Branders Cl BH6 124 A2
Branders La BH6 124 A3
Brandwood Ct 4 BH14 120 A2
Brandy La 9 DT5 186 C4
Brandy Row 8 DT5 186 C4
Branksea Ave BH15 118 C1
Branksea Cl BH15 118 C1
Branksome Cl BH25 95 A1
Branksome Ct 14 BH13 147 C4
Branksome Dene Rd BH4 121 A1
Branksome Heath Mid Sch BH12 120 B3
Branksome Hill Rd BH4 121 A3
Branksome Sta BH12 120 C2
Branksome Twrs BH13 147 D4
Branksome Wood Gdns BH2 121 B2
Branksome Wood Rd BH2 121 B2
Branscombe Cl 1 DT5 186 C1
Bransgore CE Prim Sch BH23 93 B4
Brantwood 8 DT8 204 C4
Branwell Cl BH23 92 A1
Brassey Cl BH9 90 A1
Brassey Rd BH9 90 A1
Brassey Terr BH9 89 C1
Bratch La DT11 200 D1
Breach Cl SP8 1 C1
Breach Field BH20 140 A1
Breach La
Kington Magna SP8 9 B2
Shaftesbury SP7 12 B1
Breaches La BH20 163 A1
Breamore Cl BH25 94 C2
Brearley Ct BH23 126 A4
Brecon Cl
Bournemouth BH10 89 C3
New Milton BH25 95 B1
Bredy Cl BH17 87 B1
Bredy La DT6 101 C1
Bredy Rd DT6 128 B4
Bremble Cl BH12 88 B1
Brendon Cl BH8 90 C1
Breston Cl 5 DT5 186 C1
Brian Cl BH20 143 A4
Briar Cl
Christchurch BH23 124 C3
Gillingham SP8 5 C1
Mudford BA21 28 A4
Poole BH15 119 C3
Radipole DT4 167 A3
Briar Way BH21 60 A3
Briarfield 28 BH4 121 B2
Briars End DT2 137 C3
Briars The 3 BA20 26 C1
Briarswood Rd BH16 118 B4
Brick Yd La 4 TA18 191 F5
Brickyard La Bourton SP8 1 C1
Broadstone BH21 58 A1
Ferndown BH21 61 A3
1 Gillingham SP8 6 A1
Gillingham SP8 10 C4
Silton SP8 4 C4
Sturminster Newton DT10 197 A7
Swanage BH19 179 A3
Bridewell La SP7 7 A2
Bridge App BH15 119 A1
Bridge Cl SP8 6 A1
Bridge Inn La DT3 153 B2
Bridge Pl BH10 89 B4
Bridge Rd DT6 97 A4
Bridge St Bourton SP8 1 C1
Christchurch BH23 124 B3
6 Lyme Regis DT7 96 B3
Netherbury DT6 204 C2
Salisbury SP2 213 B2
Sturminster Marshall BH21 56 B2
Sturminster Newton DT10 197 D8
Bridges Cl BH22 53 A2
Bridges The BH24 55 A4
Bridgewater Rd BH12 120 B3
Bridle Cl BH16 118 B4
Bridle Cres BH7 123 B4
Bridle Way
Stofold BA22 193 F8
Wimborne Minster BH21 60 B3
Bridlebank Way DT3 152 A2
Bridleways BH31 45 A3
Bridport & W Dorset Golf Club DT6 100 B1
Bridport Com Hospl DT6 100 A4
Bridport CP Sch DT6 100 C4
Bridport Leisure Ctr DT6 100 B3
Bridport Rd
Beaminster DT8 204 D3
Broadwindsor DT8 203 C8
Dorchester DT1 107 B1

Bridport Rd *continued*
Poole BH12 120 C4
Verwood BH31 45 A3
Brierley Ave BH22 61 C1
Brierley Cl BH10 89 C3
Brierley Hay 9 DT9 194 C5
Brierley Rd BH10 89 C2
Brigadier Cl 1 BA22 26 B3
Bright Rd BH15 119 B3
Brighthay La DT6 67 A1
Brightlands Ave BH6 123 C3
Brightsmead DT2 209 B6
Brimclose Rd TA17 191 B7
Brimley Hill EX13 202 A2
Brimley Rd EX13 202 A3
Brinscombe La 3 SP7 13 A1
Brinsley Cl DT10 35 A1
Brinsons Cl BH23 92 B2
Brionne Way SP7 13 A2
Brisbane Rd
Christchurch BH23 91 C1
Radipole DT3 152 C1
Brister End DT9 194 C5
Bristol Rd DT9 30 A4
Brit The 4 DT8 204 D4
Brit View Rd DT6 100 A1
Britannia Ct BH12 120 A4
Britannia Rd BH14 120 A2
Britannia Way
Christchurch BH23 125 A4
Dorchester DT1 134 C4
Britford La SP2 213 B1
Britford La W 1 SP2 213 B1
Britford Prim Sch
SP5 213 C1
Britmore La SP7 13 C4
Brixey Cl BH12 120 B4
Brixey Rd BH12 120 B4
Brixey's La BH20 142 C2
Broad Ave BH8 122 B4
Broad Cl DT11 81 C4
Broad Hill BA22 192 D7
Broad La Bridport DT6 100 A3
East Chinnock BA22 192 E7
Broad Mead Rd BH21 45 A1
Broad Rd BH19 179 B1
Broad Robin SP8 5 C1
Broad St DT7 96 B3
Broad Stone The★
DT2 104 C1
Broadacres
East Coker BA22 193 C8
Gillingham SP8 5 C2
Broadcroft Gdns DT5 187 A2
Broadhill La SP6 43 C4
Broadhurst Ave BH10 89 C2
Broadlands Ave BH6 123 C2
Broadlands Cl
Bournemouth BH8 90 B2
Christchurch BH23 94 A1
Salisbury SP1 213 B4
Broadlands Rd DT3 152 A1
Broadleaze BA21 26 C3
Broadmayne Cty Fst Sch
DT2 136 B2
Broadmayne Rd BH12 121 A4
Broadmead DT2 136 A1
Broadmead Ave DT6 100 B4
Broadmead Cl 4 DT8 204 A8
Broadmeadow Rd
DT4 180 B4
Broadmoor Rd BH21 86 B4
Broadoak Ave 2 DT8 204 A7
Broadoak Rd DT6 67 C1
Broads The BH21 58 C3
Broadshard La BH24 47 B1
Broadshard Rd TA18 191 F5
Broadstone Fst Sch
BH18 87 A2
Broadstone La
Hardington Mandeville
BA22 193 A6
West Chinnock TA18 192 C8
Broadstone Mid Sch
BH18 87 B3
Broadstone Way BH18 86 C1
Broadwater Ave BH14 120 B1
Broadway
Bournemouth BH6 124 A2
Merriott TA16 191 E7
Broadway Ct BH12 121 A3
Broadway Gables BH14 120 C2
Broadway Gdns 6 BH21 59 B2
Broadway La
Bournemouth BH8 90 B2
West Chinnock BA22 192 D8
Broadway Mews BH14 119 C2
Broadway Pk 4 BH21 59 B2
Broadway The BH10 89 B3
Broadwey Cl DT3 152 B2
Broadwindsor CE Prim Sch
DT8 203 E5
Broadwindsor Craft & Design
Ctr★ DT8 203 E5
Broadwindsor Rd DT8 204 B4
Brockenhurst Rd BH9 90 A1
Brockhills La BH25 95 B3
Brockhole La TA17 191 B8
Brockington La BH21 201 C5
Brockley Rd BH10 89 C2
Brocks Pine BH24 54 A2
Brodham Way DT11 198 B5
Brog St BH21 58 B1
Broke La DT9 195 D6
Brombys The 7 BH15 119 B1
Bromley House BH12 121 A3
Bronte Ave BH23 92 A1
Brook Ave BH25 95 A2
Brook Ave N BH25 95 A2
Brook Cl BH10 89 B2
Brook Dr BH31 45 B2
Brook La Bransgore BH23 93 A4
Corfe Mullen BH21 86 B3
Henstridge BA8 19 A2
Woodlands BH21 44 A4
Brook Rd
Bournemouth BH10 89 B2
Poole BH12 120 B3
Wimborne Minster BH21 59 C2
Brook St
Milborne Port DT9 17 B1
Shipton Gorge DT6 101 B2
Brook Terr SP6 43 A4
Brook Way BH23 125 B4
Brookdale Cl BH18 87 A2
Brookdale Farm BH18 87 A2
Brookhouse St 8 DT1 107 B1
Brookland Way 4 BA8 19 A2
Brooklands BH4 121 A2
Brooklyn Ct BH25 94 C2
Brookmead Cl DT3 153 B2
Brooks Cl BH24 55 B3
Brookside
Ellingham Harbridge & Ibsley
SP6 43 C1
8 Gillingham SP8 5 C2
Milborne Port DT9 17 B1
West Coker BA22 193 A8
Brookside Cl DT3 168 B4
Brookside Pk Homes
BH21 86 A2
Brookside Rd
Bransgore BH23 93 A4
Wimborne Minster BH21 59 C2
Brookside Way BH23 93 C1
Broom Hill DT2 205 F5
Broom Rd BH12 88 B1
Broomfield Ct BH22 61 C3
Broomfield Dr SP6 42 B3
Broughton Ave BH10 89 C2
Broughton Cl BH10 89 C2
Broughton Cres DT4 180 B4
Broughtons Dr 2 TA18 192 A3
Brown St
Bishop's Caundle DT9 196 A7
14 Salisbury SP1 213 B3
Brown's Cres DT3 166 C3
Brown's La SP8 10 C2
Brownen Rd BH9 122 A4
Brownes Pl DT2 73 C2
Browning Ave BH5 123 A2
Browning Rd BH12 120 B3
Brownlow Ct 23 BH4 121 B2
Brownlow St DT4 167 B2
Browns La SP6 190 E3
Brownsea Ave BH21 86 B3
Brownsea Cl BH25 94 C2
Brownsea Ct BH14 147 A4
Brownsea Island (NT)★
BH15 146 B2
Brownsea Rd BH13 147 A2
Brownsea View Ave
BH14 120 B1
Brownsea View Cl BH14 120 B1
Brudenell Ave BH13 147 B4
Brudenell Rd BH13 147 B3
Brune Way BH22 61 B2
Brunel Cl BH31 45 C2
Brunel Dr DT3 153 A2
Brunsell's Knap DT10 33 A1
Brunstead Pl BH12 121 A2
Brunstead Rd BH12 121 A2
Brunswick St BA20 27 B2
Brushy Bush La SP5 188 F3
Brutus Cl DT1 134 C4
Bryanston Pk★ DT11 212 A1
Bryanston Sch DT11 212 A2
Bryanston St DT11 212 B1
Bryanstone Rd BH3 121 C4
Bryant Rd BH12 121 A4
Bryants La DT4 180 A4
Brymer Rd
4 Puddletown DT2 78 A1
Puddletown DT2 110 A4
Brymers Ave 14 DT5 186 C4
Brympton Ave BA22 26 A2
Brympton Way BA20 26 C2
Bryn Rd Sandford BH20 143 A4
Weymouth DT4 167 A1
Bryony Cl BH18 86 C2
Bryony Gdns SP8 5 B1
Bub La BH23 124 C3
Buccaneers Cl BH23 124 C3
Buccleuch Rd BH13 121 A1
Bucehayes Cl BH23 126 A4
Buchanan Ave BH7 122 C3
Buckhill Cl 5 TA18 191 F3
Buckhorn Cl DT6 69 A4
Buckingham Ct
2 Christchurch BH23 126 A4
Poole BH15 119 B2
Buckingham Mans 5
BH1 122 A2
Buckingham Rd
Gillingham SP8 5 C1
Poole BH12 120 B4
Buckingham Way DT1 135 B4
Buckingham Wlk BH25 94 C2
Buckland Gr BH23 93 C1
Buckland Newton Prim Sch
DT2 208 A8
Buckland Rd Poole BH12 120 B3
Yeovil BA21 28 A3
Buckland Terr BH12 120 B3
Buckle Pl BA22 26 B3
Bucklers Mead 1 DT9 194 C5
Bucklers Mead Rd
BA21 27 C4
Bucklers Mead Sch
BA21 27 C4
Bucklers Way BH8 90 B2
Buckthorn Cl BH17 86 C1
Buddens La SP7 23 C2
Buddle Hill SP6 43 C2
Buddleia Cl DT3 152 C1
Budmouth Ave DT3 168 A3
Budmouth Sch DT4 166 C2
Buffalo Mews BH15 119 A1
Buffetts Rd DT10 35 A1
Bugdens La BH31 45 B3
Bugway La TA20 202 B8
Bulbury Woods Golf Club
BH16 115 C4
Bull Bridge Mead
BA22 193 D3
Bull Cl DT2 106 C4
Bull Gd La DT10 35 B1
Bull La
Maiden Newton DT2 72 C4
16 Poole BH15 119 B1
Puncknowle DT2 129 B3
Buller Ave BA22 26 B3
Buller's Way DT3 148 C3
Bullfinch Cl BH17 86 C1
Bullocks La DT11 197 A1
Bulls La 4 TA18 191 E4
Bumpers La DT5 187 A2
Bunford La BA20 26 C2
Bunting Rd BH22 61 A4
Burbidge Cl BH16 84 B1
Burbitt La DT6 101 B2
Burbridge Cl BH17 119 C4
Burcombe Rd BH10 89 B3
Burdens 2 DT10 197 A4
Burdock Cl BH23 93 A1
Bure Cl BH23 125 A3
Bure Haven Dr BH23 125 A3
Bure Homage Gdns
BH23 125 A3
Bure Homage La BH23 125 A3
Bure La BH23 125 A3
Bure Pk BH23 125 A3
Bure Rd BH23 125 A3
Burford Ave SP2 213 B1
Burford Cl BH23 91 C1
Burford Ct 15 BH1 122 A2
Burford Rd SP2 213 B1
Burges Cl DT10 20 C2
Burgess Cl BH11 88 C2
Burgess Field BH21 44 B3
Burgess Gn SP1 213 C4
Burleigh Rd BH6 123 B3
Burleston Dro DT2 78 C1
Burley Cl
Barton on Sea BH25 126 B4
Verwood BH31 45 A3
Burley Rd Bransgore BH23 93 A4
Burton BH23 92 B3
Poole BH12 120 B3
Burling Terr 1 BH12 121 A2
Burlington Arc 34 BH1 121 C2
Burlington Rd BH19 179 B2
Burn Cl BH31 45 B2
Burn View DT2 107 C3
Burnaby Ct BH4 121 B1
Burnaby Rd BH4 121 B1
Burnage Ct 18 BH13 147 C4
Burnbake Rd BH31 45 A3
Burnbrae Rd BH22 61 B1
Burnet Way SP1 213 C4
Burnett Ave BH23 123 C4
Burnett Rd BH23 123 C4
Burngate Rd BH15 118 C1
Burnham Dr BH8 122 B4
Burnham Rd BH23 92 B1
Burnham's La BH19 178 B3
Burnleigh Gdns BH25 95 B2
Burns Rd
Bournemouth BH6 123 B4
Northport BH20 142 B3
Burnside
Christchurch BH23 125 B4
Winterborne St Martin
DT2 133 B3
Burraton Sq 6 DT1 107 B1
Burroughes Ave BA21 27 A3
Burrows La BH31 41 A1
Burrywells DT2 102 B3
Burstock La DT8 203 C7
Burt's La Holt BH21 52 B4
Horton BH21 44 B1
Burt's Pl 6 BH19 179 B1
Burtley Rd BH6 123 C2
Burton Bradstock VC Prim
Sch DT6 128 A4
Burton CE Prim Sch
BH23 92 B2
Burton Cl Burton BH23 92 B1
Shaftesbury SP7 13 A2
St.Leonards BH24 53 C3
Wool BH20 139 C1
Burton Cross BH20 139 C1
Burton Hall BH23 92 B2
Burton Hall Pl BH23 92 B2
Burton La BA22 193 C8
Burton Rd
Abbotsbury DT3 148 A4
Bothenhampton DT6 100 C1
Burton Bradstock DT6 128 A4
Christchurch BH23 124 C4
Poole BH13 121 A2
Burton Rd *continued*
Puncknowle DT2 129 C1
Wool BH20 139 C1
Burton St DT10 20 C2
Burton Wood BH20 139 C1
Burtoncroft BH23 92 B2
Burts Hill BH21 59 B3
Bury Rd BH13 120 C1
Bush Pk DT11 81 C4
Bushell Rd BH15 119 B4
Bushells Farm SP6 43 A4
Bushes Hill SP8 5 A4
Bushes Rd DT11 199 A4
Bushey La BH20 162 B2
Bushey Rd BH8 90 B1
Bushfield Rd 1 TA18 191 E3
Bushmead Dr BH24 54 A3
Bute Dr BH23 126 A4
Butler Cl SP2 213 B1
Butlers La BH24 47 C1
Butt Cl DT2 78 A1
Butt Farm Cl DT2 105 B1
Butt La Bere Regis BH20 81 A2
Chideock DT6 66 C1
Butt La Hollow BH20 81 A2
Buttercup Cl 2 SP8 5 B1
Buttercup Dr BH23 93 A1
Buttercup Way DT6 100 B1
Butterwick Dro DT9 195 D6
Buttery The BH23 124 B4
Button's La 18 BH15 119 B1
Butts Cl Marnhull DT10 20 C1
Winfrith Newburgh DT2 156 C3
Butts La SP8 21 B4
Butts Mead 1 SP7 13 A1
Butts Quarry La TA18 192 A4
Butts Rd SP1 213 B3
Butts Terr SP2 213 B3
Butts The
10 Child Okeford DT11 198 C7
Shaftesbury SP7 12 B2
Buxton Cl 8 DT4 180 B4
Buxton Rd DT4 180 B4
Buzbury Rings★ DT11 211 E8
Byron Ct BH22 61 B3
Byron House 16 BH25 95 A1
Byron Rd
Barton on Sea BH25 126 C4
Bournemouth BH5 122 C2
Wimborne Minster BH21 59 B3
Byways Cl 4 SP1 213 C2

C

Cabot Bsns Village
BH17 119 A4
Cabot La BH17 119 A4
Cabot Way BH25 94 C2
Cachy Rd BH20 139 C4
Caddy La BA12 2 C3
Cadhay Cl BH25 94 C2
Cadley Cl DT11 212 B2
Cadnam Way BH8 90 B2
Cadogan Rd BH24 55 B4
Caesar's Way BH18 86 C2
Caird Ave BH25 95 B1
Cairns Cl BH23 123 C4
Caister Cl BH22 61 B3
Calcraft Rd BH20 177 A4
Calder Rd BH17 119 C4
Caledon Rd BH14 120 C2
Caledonian Cl
Christchurch BH23 125 A4
Radipole DT4 167 B3
Caley Way DT6 69 A1
Calf Cl La DT10 197 F8
Calfhay La DT9 194 E1
Calkin Cl BH23 92 A1
Calluna Rd BH12 120 A4
Callway La DT2 209 B2
Calmore Cl BH8 90 B2
Calves La SP7 12 A2
Calvin Rd BH9 121 C4
Camborne Pl BA21 28 A3
Camborne St BA21 28 A3
Cambridge Cl BA20 26 C3
Cambridge Gdns BH23 91 C1
Cambridge Rd
Bournemouth BH2 121 B2
Dorchester DT1 107 B1
Salisbury SP1 213 B4
Weymouth DT4 166 C2
Cambridge Wlk 1 DT1 107 B1
Camden Cl BH9 90 A1
Camden Way DT1 134 C4
Came Down Cl DT3 152 B2
Came Down Golf Club
DT2 134 C1
Came House★ DT2 135 B3
Came View Cl DT1 135 B4
Came View Rd DT1 135 B4
Camel Gn Rd SP6 42 B3
Camellia Cl BH21 45 A1
Camellia Gdns BH25 95 A1
Camelot Way SP8 5 B1
Cameron Rd BH23 124 B4
Camesworth La DT6 69 A4
Cammel Rd BH22 61 B1
Camp Rd
Chickerell DT4 180 A4
West Coker BA22 26 B1
Campbell Rd
Bournemouth BH1 122 C3
Burton BH23 92 B2
Salisbury SP1 213 B3
Campion Cl
5 Gillingham SP8 5 B1
Campion Cl *continued*
Radipole DT4 167 C4
Campion Dr BA22 26 B3
Campion Gr BH23 124 C3
Canberra Cres DT3 152 C2
Canberra Rd
Christchurch BH23 91 C1
Radipole DT3 152 C1
Candy's La 6 DT11 198 B6
Candys Cl BH21 58 C1
Candys La BH21 58 C1
Canford Ave BH11 89 A1
Canford Bottom BH21 60 B3
Canford Cliffs Ave
BH14 120 C1
Canford Cliffs Rd BH13 120 C1
Canford Cres BH13 147 C4
Canford Ct BH13 147 C3
Canford Gdns BH11 89 A1
Canford Heath Fst & Mid
Schs BH17 119 B4
Canford Heath Nature
Reserve★ BH11 88 A2
Canford Heath Rd BH17 87 C1
Canford Magna BH21 60 A1
Canford Pl 2 BH13 147 C4
Canford Rd
Bournemouth BH11 89 A1
Poole BH15 119 B2
Canford Sch BH21 60 A1
Canford View Dr BH21 60 A3
Canford Way BH12 88 B1
Cann Hill SP7 24 A3
Cannings Ct La DT2 196 C3
Cannington Coll BA20 26 C3
Cannon Cl BH18 87 A1
Cannon Ct Mews 8 DT9 17 B1
Cannon Hill Gdns BH21 60 A4
Cannon Hill Rd BH21 60 A4
Canteen Rd DT5 181 B1
Canterbury Cl
Ferndown BH22 53 A1
Weymouth DT4 166 C2
Capella Ct BH2 121 C1
Capesthorne BH23 125 A3
Caphays Dro DT9 195 E7
Capitol Cl DT1 134 C4
Capper Rd E BH20 139 C3
Capper Rd W BH20 139 C3
Capstan Field BH19 178 A1
Capstans The BH14 147 A4
Capstone Pl BH8 122 B3
Capstone Rd BH8 122 A3
Capulet Rd SP1 213 A4
Carbery Ave BH6 123 B3
Carbery Gdns BH6 123 C3
Carbery La 3 BH6 123 B2
Carbery Row 2 BH6 123 B2
Cardigan Rd
Bournemouth BH9 121 C4
Poole BH12 120 C2
Cards Mill La DT6 66 A4
Carent Cl DT10 21 A1
Carey App BH20 142 B3
Carey Cl BH20 142 B3
Carey Rd
Bournemouth BH9 89 C2
Northport BH20 142 B3
Careys Rd BH8 90 B2
Carina Ct BH13 147 B2
Carisbrook Cres BH15 118 B2
Carisbrooke Poole BH13 147 C4
Radipole DT4 167 A3
Carisbrooke Ct
4 Christchurch BH23 126 A4
New Milton BH25 94 C2
Carisbrooke Gdns
BA20 27 A3
Carisbrooke Way BH23 93 C1
Carlinford 29 BH5 122 C2
Carlton Ave BH25 126 C4
Carlton Gr BH12 120 B3
Carlton Rd BH1 122 B2
Carlton Rd N DT4 167 B3
Carlton Rd S DT4 167 B3
Carlyle Rd BH6 123 B3
Carmel Cl BH15 118 B1
Carmelite Way SP1 213 B2
Carnarvon Rd 4 BH1 122 C2
Carnegie Cl BH14 120 B3
Caroline Ave BH23 124 C3
Caroline Pl 10 DT4 167 B2
Caroline Rd BH11 89 A2
Carpenters Cl DT2 106 C4
Carradale BH23 125 A4
Carraway La DT10 20 C1
Carrbridge Cl BH3 121 B4
Carrbridge Gdns BH3 121 B4
Carrbridge Rd BH3 121 B4
Carrick Cl DT1 135 B4
Carrick Way BH25 95 B1
Carrington Cl 10 DT4 180 B4
Carrion La 4 BH20 142 C2
Carroll Ave BH22 61 C3
Carroll Cl BH12 121 A3
Carsworth Way BH17 88 A1
Carter Cl DT11 212 C2
Carter Com Sch BH15 118 C1
Carter's La Chideock DT6 98 C4
9 Poole BH15 119 B1
Carters Ave BH15 118 B2
Carters La BA22 192 E8
Cartref Cl BH31 45 A3
Cartwright Cl BH10 89 B2
Carvers La BH24 55 B4
Carysfort Rd BH1 122 B2
Caseberry Ct 7 DT1 107 B1
Cashmoor Cl BH12 120 C4

Caslake Cl BH25 ....94 C1
Cassel Ave BH13 ....121 A1
Casselles Ct 33 BH25 ....95 A1
Cassiobury Rd DT4 ......167 B2
Casterbridge Cl
  Pimperne DT11 ....212 C2
  9 Swanage BH19 .....178 C1
Casterbridge Rd
  Dorchester DT1 ......135 B4
  Ferndown BH22 ....61 B2
Castle Ave
  Christchurch BH23 ....125 C4
  5 Okeford Fitzpaine DT11 197 F6
Castle Cl
  Cranborne BH21 ......40 A4
  Dorchester DT1 ......107 B1
Castle Ct 3 BH21 .....126 A4
Castle Ct Sch BH21 .....86 A1
Castle Farm Rd BH16 ....84 B2
Castle Gate Cl BH8 .....90 B1
Castle Hill BH14 ......120 A2
Castle Hill Cl SP7 ......12 B2
Castle Hill Cres BA12 ....3 A3
Castle Hill La
  Cranborne BH21 ......40 A3
  Mere BA12 ....3 A3
Castle Hill Rd DT4 .....180 A4
Castle Keep SP1 ......213 A4
Castle La
  Buckland Newton DT2 .208 B8
  Okeford Fitzpaine DT11 197 F6
  Owermoigne DT2 .....155 B4
Castle La E DT7 ......123 B4
Castle La W BH8 ....90 B1
Castle Par BH7 ....123 B4
Castle Rd
  Bournemouth BH9 ......90 A1
  Fortuneswell DT5 .....181 A1
  Salisbury SP1 ....213 B4
  Sherborne DT9 ....30 B4
Castle Sq DT6 ....100 B3
Castle St
  Christchurch BH23 ....124 B3
  Cranborne BH21 ......40 A4
  Mere BA12 ....2 C3
  Poole BH15 ....119 B1
  Salisbury SP2 ....213 B3
Castle Town Way DT9 ....16 C1
Castle View Dr BH16 ....84 B1
Castledene Cres BH14 ..120 A1
Castlemain Ave BH6 ....123 B4
Castlemaine Rd DT3 ....152 C1
Castleman Smith Cl
  DT11 ....212 C2
Castleman Way BH24 ....55 B2
Castlemews BH24 ......54 C3
Castleton TA18 ....192 C5
Castleton Ave BH10 ....89 B3
Castleton Rd DT9 ......30 B3
Castletown DT5 ....181 A1
Castlewood BH24 ......54 C3
Cat La DT10 ....33 A1
Catalina Cl BH23 .....125 A3
Catalina Dr BH15 .....119 C1
Caters Pl DT1 ....108 A1
Cathedral Sch SP1 ....213 B2
Catherine St SP1 .....213 B2
Catherine Wheel Gdns
  BH23 ....91 C2
Cathole Bridge Rd
  TA18 ....191 F3
Caton Cl BH12 ....121 A4
Catsley La DT2 ....205 B6
Cattistock Rd
  Bournemouth BH8 ......90 C1
  Maiden Newton DT2 ....72 C4
Cauldon Ave BH19 .....179 A2
Cauldron Barn Rd
  BH19 ....179 A2
Cauldron Cres BH19 ...179 A2
Cauldron Mdws BH19 ...179 A2
Caundle La
  Stalbridge DT10 ......33 A3
  Stourton Caundle DT10 .32 C1
Causeway Cl BH20 .....142 B3
Causeway La DT8 .....203 A6
Causeway The
  Hazelbury Bryan DT10 .196 F4
  Milborne St Andrew DT11 .79 C4
Cavalier Cl BA21 ......27 C4
Cavalier Way BA21 .....27 C4
Cavan Cres BH17 ......87 A1
Cavendish Hall BH1 ...122 A4
Cavendish Pl BH1 .....122 A3
Cavendish Rd BH1 ....122 A3
Caversham Cl BH15 ...118 C2
Cawdor Rd BH3 ......121 B4
Caxton Cl BH23 ......125 A4
Cecil Ave
  Bournemouth BH8 ....122 B4
  Salisbury SP2 ....213 B1
Cecil Cl BH21 ....86 C3
Cecil Ct BH8 ....122 A4
Cecil Hill BH8 ....122 A4
Cecil Rd
  Bournemouth BH5 ....122 C4
  Poole BH12 ....120 B3
  Swanage BH19 ......179 A1
Cecil St BA20 ....27 B3
Cedar Ave
  Bournemouth BH10 ....89 B3
  Christchurch BH23 ...123 B4
  3 St.Leonards BH24 ...53 C2
Cedar Cl Upton BH16 ..118 A4
  1 Wool BH20 ....140 A1
Cedar Ct BH4 ....121 A1
Cedar Dr
  11 Easton/Weston DT5 .186 C1

Cedar Dr continued
  Overcombe/Preston
  DT3 ....168 A4
  Sandford BH20 ......116 A1
  Wimborne Minster BH21 .60 A3
Cedar Fields 1 BA22 ..193 A8
Cedar Gdns BH25 ......94 C1
Cedar Gr BA21 ....27 A3
Cedar Manor BH4 ....121 B2
Cedar Rd DT1 ....107 C1
Cedar Trad Pk BH21 ....60 C3
Cedar Way BH22 ......61 B4
Cedars The BH4 ......121 B2
Celandine Cl BH23 ....125 A4
Celandine Rd 3 BA22 ...26 B3
Cellars Farm Rd BH6 ..124 A2
Celtic Cres DT1 ......134 C4
Cemetery Ave BH15 ...119 C3
Cemetery Rd
  10 Gillingham SP8 ......5 C1
  Portesham DT3 ......150 A4
  Wimborne Minster BH21 .59 A3
Centenary Gdns BA8 ....19 A2
Centenary House 6
  BH23 ....124 A4
Centenary Way BH1 ...122 C3
Central Acre 13 BA20 ...27 B2
Central Ave
  Corfe Mullen BH21 ....86 B4
  Poole BH12 ....120 C3
Central Dr BH2 ......121 C3
Central Rd 2 BA20 ....27 C2
Centre Pl BH24 ....55 A4
Centurion Rd DT11 ...199 E2
Cereleton Pk DT11 ...211 C6
Cerne Abbas DT2 ....207 D4
Cerne Abbas CE Fst Sch
  DT2 ....207 D4
Cerne Abbas Giant* ...207 D4
Cerne Abbey* DT2 ...207 D4
Cerne Cl BH9 ....90 A2
Chaddesley Glen BH13 147 C3
Chaddesley Pines BH13 147 C3
Chaddesley Wood Rd
  BH13 ....147 C3
Chafeys Ave DT4 ....167 A3
Chaffey Cl BH24 ......55 C4
Chaffeymoor Hill SP8 ....1 A1
Chaffinch Cl
  Bincombe DT3 ......152 B2
  Broadstone BH17 .....86 C1
  New Milton BH25 .....94 C1
Chafyn Gr Sch SP1 ...213 C4
Chalbury (Hill Fort)*
  DT3 ....153 A2
Chalbury Cl
  Overcombe/Preston
  DT3 ....168 A4
  Poole BH17 ....88 A1
Chalbury Ct
  7 Christchurch BH23 ..124 C3
  11 Poole BH14 ....120 A2
Chalbury Lodge 1 DT3 .168 A4
Chaldecott Gdns BH10 ..89 B2
Chaldon Rd BH17 ......87 C1
Chalfont Ave BH23 .....91 B2
Chalice Cl BH4 ......120 A2
Chalk Pit Cl BH20 .....81 A1
Chalk Pit La
  Litton Cheney DT2 ...103 A1
  Wool BH20 ....139 C1
Chalk The 2 DT11 .....37 C1
Chalky Rd DT2 ......135 C1
Chalwell 9 DT11 .....198 C7
Chalwyn Ind Est BH12 .120 A4
Chamberlaine Rd DT4 ..180 B4
Champernhayes La
  DT6 ....64 C3
Champions 1 DT8 ....204 C4
Chancery Cl 1 SP2 ...213 A3
Chancery La DT6 .....100 B3
Chander Cl BH22 ......61 C2
Chandlers DT9 ....30 B4
Chandlers Ct 3 BH7 ..123 A4
Chandos Ave BH12 ...121 A4
Channel Cl
  Barton on Sea BH25 ..126 C4
  Bournemouth BH6 ....123 B2
Channel View Rd DT5 ..186 C4
Chant Cl BH23 ....124 B4
Chantmarle La DT2 ...206 B5
Chantry Cl BH23 ......93 C1
Chantry La DT8 .....204 C5
Chantry St DT6 .....204 C5
Chantry The* BA12 .....3 A3
Chantry View BA22 ...193 D8
Chapel Cl
  Corfe Mullen BH21 ....86 B3
  Langton Herring DT3 ..150 B1
Chapel Gate BH23 .....90 B4
Chapel Gdns DT11 ...212 C1
Chapel Hill SP8 ....9 B1
Chapel La Bransgore BH23 93 A4
  Corfe Mullen BH21 ....86 B3
  Dinnington TA17 ....191 B8
  Henstridge BA8 ....18 B3
  Hurn BH23 ....90 B4
  Maiden Newton DT2 ...72 C4
  7 Milborne Port DT9 ...17 B1
  Osmington DT3 .....154 A2
  Pen Selwood BA9 ......1 B2
  2 Pimperne DT11 ....199 D3
  Poole BH15 ....119 B1
  Radipole DT3 ....152 B2
  Wimborne Minster BH21 .59 A3
  Woodlands BH21 .....44 A4

Chapel La continued
  7 Yetminster DT9 ....194 C5
  Zennor BA12 ....1 C3
Chapel Mdw 6 DT9 ...194 C5
Chapel Pl 5 SP2 .....213 B3
Chapel Rd Poole BH14 .120 A2
  Sturminster Newton
  DT10 ....197 A8
Chapel Rise BH24 .....54 C1
Chapel St
  Milborne St Andrew DT11 .79 C4
  Shipton Gorge DT6 ...101 B2
Chapel View 6 DT2 .....78 A1
Chapelhay St DT4 ....167 B1
Charberry Rise DT6 ....96 C4
Charborough Cl BH16 ...84 B2
Charborough House*
  BH20 ....83 C4
Charborough Pk*
  BH20 ....211 F1
Charborough Rd BH18 ..87 A2
Charborough Way 1
  BH21 ....56 B2
Chard La
  Broadwindsor DT8 ...203 C7
  Wayford TA18 ....191 B2
Chard Rd
  Broadwindsor DT8 ...203 C7
  Crewkerne TA18 ....191 D4
Chard St TA20 ....202 E6
Chards Mead Rd DT6 ..100 B4
Charing Cl 2 BH24 ....55 B3
Charing Cross SP6 .....42 A3
Charles Cres BH25 .....95 A3
Charles Garrett Cl 7
  SP7 ....12 C2
Charles Gdns BH10 ....89 B1
Charles Keightley Ct
  BH21 ....59 B2
Charles Rd
  Burton Bradstock DT6 .128 A4
  Christchurch BH23 ...124 C4
  Poole BH15 ....119 B2
  Yeovil BA21 ....27 C3
Charles St
  Blandford Forum DT11 .212 B1
  Dorchester DT1 .....108 A1
  Radipole DT4 ....167 B2
  7 Salisbury SP2 .....213 A3
Charles's La DT01 .....55 C1
Charlotte Cl
  Charminster DT2 ....107 C3
  Christchurch BH23 ...125 A3
  3 New Milton BH25 ...95 A1
  Poole BH12 ....121 B4
Charlton Beeches
  DT11 ....211 C7
Charlton Cl
  Bournemouth BH9 .....90 B2
  12 Crewkerne TA18 ..191 F4
  Hordle SO41 ....95 C2
Charlton La SP7 ....13 C1
Charlton Manor 1
  DT11 ....211 D6
Charlton Mead 4 DT11 211 D6
Charltons The DT11 ...121 C3
Charminster Ave BH9 ...90 A1
Charminster Cl 5 BH8 ..90 A1
Charminster Pl BH8 ....90 B1
Charminster Rd BH8 ..122 A4
Charminster St Marys Fst Sch
  DT2 ....107 B3
Charmouth Cl DT7 .....96 B3
Charmouth CP Sch
  DT6 ....97 A4
Charmouth Gr BH14 ..120 A2
Charmouth Heritage Coast
  Ctr* DT6 ....97 A4
Charmouth Rd DT7 ....96 B3
Charnock Cl SO41 .....95 C2
Charnwood Ave 8 BH9 ..90 A2
Charnwood Cl BH22 ....53 A1
Charnwood Rd SP2 ...213 A3
Chartcombe BH13 ....147 C4
Charter Rd BH11 ......88 B3
Chartwell DT4 ....167 A3
Chase Cres SP5 .....188 E4
Chase The
  St.Leonards BH24 .....54 C3
  Verwood BH31 ....45 C3
Chaseborough Sq 4
  DT1 ....107 B1
Chaseside BH7 ......123 A4
Chaston La DT2 .....208 C8
Chatham Cl SP1 .....213 A4
Chatsworth Rd
  Bournemouth BH8 ...122 B4
  Poole BH14 ....120 A3
  Yeovil BA21 ....27 C4
Chatsworth Way BH25 ..94 C2
Chaucer Cl BH21 ......59 B3
Chaucer Rd BH13 ....147 C4
Chaucombe Pl BH25 ...94 C1
Cheam Rd BH18 ......86 C2
Cheap St DT9 ....30 A3
Checkridge La EX13 ..202 A2
Cheddington Rd BH9 ...90 A2
Chedington Cl BH17 ...87 C1
Chedington Ct Golf Club
  DT8 ....192 D2
Chedington La DT8 ...204 D8
Cheese La DT3 ......150 C3
Cheese Mkt 10 SP1 ...213 B3
Chelmsford Rd BH16 ..118 A4
Chelmsford St DT4 ...167 B2
Chelston Ave BA21 ....27 C4
Cheltenham Rd BH12 .120 B3
Chelwood Gate DT4 ..166 C4

Chene Rd BH21 ....59 B2
Cherford Rd BH11 .....89 A1
Cherita Ct BH15 .....119 C3
Cheriton Ave BH7 ....123 B4
Cheriton Way BH21 ....59 B2
Cherrett Cl BH11 ......88 C2
Cherries Dr BH9 ......89 C1
Cherry Cl Poole BH14 .120 A2
  Sandford BH20 .....143 A4
Cherry Ct BH14 ......120 A3
Cherry Gr BH22 ....61 B3
Cherry Hill Gdns BH16 .118 A3
Cherry Hill Gr BH16 ..118 A3
Cherry Orch La
  Cann SP7 ....11 C1
  Gillingham SP8 ....5 B1
Cherry Tree DT6 .....100 A4
Cherry Tree Cl BH24 ...53 C2
Cherry Tree Ct
  9 Crewkerne TA18 ...191 F5
  31 New Milton BH25 ...95 A1
Cherry Tree Dr BA20 ...26 C1
Cherryfields SP8 ......5 C2
Chescombe Cl DT2 ...207 D3
Chescombe La DT11 ..210 B3
Cheselbourne Cty Fst Sch
  DT2 ....209 A3
Chesil Beach Visitor Ctr*
  ....180 B2
Chesil View DT4 .....180 A4
Chesildene Ave BH8 ...90 B2
Chesildene Dr BH8 ....90 B2
Chessel Ave BH5 ....122 C4
Chessels Cl BA22 ....193 B8
Chester Cl DT1 ......135 B4
Chester Rd BH13 ....121 A4
Chesterfield Cl BH13 .147 C4
Chesterfield Ct BH1 ..122 B2
Chestnut Ave
  Barton on Sea BH25 ..127 A4
  Bournemouth BH6 ...123 B2
  Ellingham Harbridge & Ibsley
  BH24 ....46 B3
  Wareham St Martin
  BH20 ....116 A2
Chestnut Cl BH20 ....143 A4
Chestnut Dr BA20 .....27 A2
Chestnut Gr
  Blandford Forum DT11 .212 A1
  Ferndown BH21 ......60 C3
Chestnut Pl DT3 .....167 B4
Chestnut Rd DT6 ....100 B2
Chestnut Way
  Burton BH23 ....92 B2
  Dorchester DT1 .....107 B1
  Gillingham SP8 ....5 B1
Chetcombe Rd BA12 ....3 A3
Chetnole Cl BH11 .....88 A1
Chetnole Sta DT9 ....194 C2
Chettell Way DT11 ...212 B1
Chetwode Way BH17 ...87 A1
Cheverell Ave SP1 ...213 C4
Cheviot Ct Flats BH23 .124 C4
Cheviot Way BH31 .....45 A3
Cheviots The BH14 ...120 B2
Chewton Comm Rd
  BH23 ....126 A4
Chewton Farm Rd BH23 .94 B3
Chewton Lodge BH23 .126 A4
Chewton Way BH23 ....94 A3
Cheyne Cl 4 DT5 .....186 C1
Cheyne Gdns BH4 ....121 B1
Chichester Cl SP2 ....213 B1
Chichester Rd 1 BH24 ..47 C1
Chichester Way BH23 .125 A3
Chichester Wlk BH21 ..59 C1
Chick's Copse La
  Cattistock DT2 ......206 A5
  Rampisham DT2 ....205 F5
Chickerell Cl BH9 .....90 A2
Chickerell CP Sch
  DT3 ....166 B3
Chickerell Hill DT3 ...166 B3
Chickerell Rd DT3 ...166 B2
Chideock Cl BH12 ....120 C3
Chideock Ct BH12 ....120 C3
Chideock Hill DT6 .....98 C4
Chigwell Rd BH8 ......90 A1
Chilbury Gdns DT2 ...155 B4
Chilcombe Hill (Fort)*
  DT2 ....102 C2
Chilcombe La
  Chilcombe DT6 ......102 B2
  Shipton Gorge DT6 ..102 B3
Chilcombe Rd BH16 ..123 A3
Childhay La DT8 .....203 C6
Chilfrome Cl BH17 .....87 B1
Chilfrome La
  Chilfrome DT2 ......206 B1
  Maiden Newton DT2 ...72 C4
Chiltern Cl
  Barton on Sea BH25 ...94 C1
  Poole BH12 ....121 A3
Chiltern Ct 5 BH23 ..124 C4
Chiltern Dr
  Barton on Sea BH25 ..126 C4
  Verwood BH31 ....45 A3
Chilton Gr BA21 ....27 B4
Chimes The BH4 .....121 A2
China La 1 DT11 ....199 F7
Chine Cres BH2 ......121 B1
Chine Cres Rd BH2 ..121 B1
Chine Wlk BH22 ......61 C1
Chinnock Hollow
  BA22 ....192 E8
Chippel La DT10 ......20 C1
Chipper La SP1 .....213 B3

Chiselbury Gr SP2 ...213 B1
Chisels La BH23 ......93 A3
Chiswell DT5 ....186 C4
Chiswell Rd BH17 .....87 B1
Chitten Hill BH20 ....115 B4
Choristers Sq SP1 ...213 B3
Chorley Cl BH15 .....119 B3
Chowins Rd 18 TA18 ..191 F4
Chris Cres BH15 .....118 B4
Christ the King RC Prim Sch
  BH11 ....89 A3
Christchurch Bay Rd
  BH25 ....126 C4
Christchurch By-pass
  BH23 ....124 B4
Christchurch Castle*
  BH23 ....124 B3
Christchurch Cty Jun Sch
  BH23 ....124 A4
Christchurch Cty Prim Sch
  BH23 ....124 A4
Christchurch Hospl
  BH23 ....123 C4
Christchurch Priory*
  BH23 ....124 B3
Christchurch Rd
  Barton on Sea BH25 ..126 B4
  Bournemouth BH1 ...122 B2
  Ferndown BH22 ......61 B1
  Hurn BH23 ....91 B3
  Ringwood BH24 ......55 A4
Christchurch Ski Ctr*
  BH23 ....63 A2
Christchurch Sta BH23 124 A4
Christie Miller Rd
  SP2 ....213 A3
Christopher Cl
  3 Salisbury SP2 ....213 A1
  Yeovil BA20 ....27 A3
Christopher Cres BH15 119 B3
Christophers BH21 ....59 B1
Christy's La SP7 ......12 C2
Chur La BA22 ....193 A8
Church Acre 22 DT1 ..108 A1
Church La
  Beer Hackett DT9 ...194 D6
  Bourton SP8 ....1 B1
  Bridport DT6 ....69 A1
  Chetnole DT9 ....194 D3
  6 Dorchester DT1 ..108 A1
  Fontmell Magna SP7 ..37 C4
  Longburton DT9 ....195 B7
  Stour Provost SP7 ....22 B4
  9 Swanage BH19 ...179 A1
  Todber DT10 ....21 B2
Church Farm SP6 ......43 A4
Church Gn
  Bishop's Caundle DT9 .196 A8
  7 Wareham BH20 ...142 C2
Church Hill
  Buckhorn Weston SP8 ..9 A3
  Dinnington TA17 ....191 B7
  Iwerne Minster DT11 ..37 C1
  Kington Magna SP8 ....9 B2
  Langton Herring DT3 .150 B1
  Marnhull DT10 ....21 A2
  Milborne St Andrew DT11 .79 C4
  Piddlehinton DT2 .....76 C4
  Shaftesbury SP7 .....12 B2
  Stalbridge DT10 ......19 B1
  8 Swanage BH19 ...179 A1
  Verwood BH31 ....45 A3
  West Stour SP8 ......10 A2
  Woodlands BH21 .....44 A4
Church Hill La DT2 ...104 B4
Church Hill View DT2 .207 A2
Church Knap DT4 ....180 B4
Church Knowle Animal
  Sanctuary & Rehoming Ctr*
  BH20 ....176 A4
Church La
  Barwick BA22 ....193 E8
  Bere Regis BH20 .....81 A1
  3 Blandford Forum DT11 212 B1
  Charlton Marshall DT11 211 C6
  Chickerell DT3 ......151 B1
  Christchurch BH23 ...124 A3
  Coombe Keynes BH20 .158 A3
  Crewkerne TA18 ....192 A3
  Damerham SP6 .....190 F2
  East Orchard SP7 .....36 C4
  Easton/Weston DT5 ..186 C1
  Ferndown BH22 ......89 C4
  Frampton DT2 ....73 C2
  Godmanstone DT2 ....75 A4
  Haselbury Plucknett
  TA18 ....192 C5
  Leigh DT9 ....194 E3
  Margaret Marsh SP7 ..22 B3
  New Milton BH25 .....94 C1
  Osmington DT3 .....154 A2
  Owermoigne DT2 ...155 B4
  Piddletrenthide DT2 .208 B3
  Portesham DT3 .....150 A4
  Rimpton BA22 ....15 A4
  Shaftesbury SP7 .....12 C1
  Stinsford DT2 ......108 C2
  Stour Provost SP8 ....21 B4
  2 Sturminster Newton
  DT10 ....197 D8
  Sutton Waldron DT11 ..37 C2
  Sydling St Nicholas DT2 207 A2
  Wareham BH20 .....142 C2
  Wool BH20 ....140 A1
Church Mead DT2 ...205 F1

Church Ope DT5 ......**187** A2
Church Path
　2 Crewkerne TA18 ...**191** E4
　Litton Cheney DT2 ......**103** B1
　Yeovil BA22 ....**27** B3
Church Rd
　Bournemouth BH6 ......**123** C2
　Bradford Abbas DT9 ....**28** B1
　Durweston DT11 ......**198** E3
　Ferndown BH22 ....**61** B3
　Iwerne Minster DT11 ....**37** C1
　Maiden Newton DT2 ....**72** C4
　Overcombe/Preston
　　DT3 ....**168** B4
　Pimperne DT11 ......**199** D4
　Poole BH14 ....**120** A2
　5 Shillingstone DT11 ..**198** B6
　Silton SP8 ....**2** A1
　Studland BH19 ......**164** B1
　Thornford DT9 ......**194** D8
　Three Legged Cross BH21 .**45** A1
　West Lulworth BH20 ...**172** B3
Church Row DT11 ...**209** C6
Church St
　Beaminster DT8 ......**204** C4
　Bridport DT6 ....**100** B3
　Burton Bradstock DT6 ..**128** A4
　Christchurch BH23 ....**124** A3
　Cranborne BH21 ......**40** A4
　Dewlish DT2 ....**209** C1
　5 Dorchester DT1 ....**108** A1
　Fontmell Magna SP7 ...**37** C1
　Fordingbridge SP6 .....**43** A4
　Halstock BA22 ......**193** C3
　Henstridge BA8 ......**19** A2
　Hinton St George TA17 ..**191** C7
　Kington Magna SP8 ....**9** B2
　Lyme Regis DT7 ....**96** B3
　Mere BA12 ....**3** B1
　Merriott TA16 ......**191** F7
　Milborne Port DT9 .....**17** B1
　Poole BH15 ....**119** A1
　Puncknowle DT2 ......**129** C3
　Radipole DT3 ......**152** A4
　Shapwick DT11 ......**56** A4
　Sturminster Newton DT10 .**35** A1
　Wareham BH20 ......**142** C2
　2 West Coker BA22 ...**193** A8
　West Stour SP8 ....**10** A1
　10 Wimborne Minster BH21 **59** A3
　Winterborne Kingston
　　DT11 ....**81** C4
　Yeovil BA20 ....**27** B3
　Yetminster DT9 ......**194** C5
Church Track SP8 ......**1** B1
Church View SP8 ....**5** C1
Church Wlk
　Littlebredy DT2 ......**131** B4
　Motcombe SP7 ....**12** A4
　Okeford Fitzpaine DT11 ..**197** E4
Churchfield BH31 ......**45** A3
Churchfield Cres BH15 .**119** C2
Churchfield Ct BH15 ...**119** C2
Churchfield La BH24 ....**43** A1
Churchfield Rd BH15 ..**119** C2
Churchfields Ind Est
　SP2 ....**213** A3
Churchfields Rd SP2 ...**213** A3
Churchfoot La DT10 ...**196** F3
Churchill Cl
　Alderholt SP6 ....**42** A1
　Sturminster Marshall
　　BH21 ....**56** B2
　4 Weymouth DT4 ....**180** B4
Churchill Cres BH12 ...**120** B3
Churchill Ct BH25 .....**94** C1
Churchill Dro BH21 ....**40** C4
Churchill Gdns BH12 ..**120** B3
Churchill Rd
　Blandford Forum DT11 ..**212** B1
　Bournemouth BH1 .....**122** B3
　Bovington Camp BH20 ..**139** B4
　Poole BH12 ....**120** B3
　Wimborne Minster BH21 ..**59** C2
Churchill Way E SP1 ...**213** B3
Churchill Way N SP1 ..**213** B3
Churchill Way S SP1 ..**213** B3
Churchill Way W SP2 ..**213** B3
Churchmoor Rd BH21 ...**60** A3
Churchward Ave DT3 ...**153** A2
Churchwell St DT9 .....**28** B1
Churlands Cl BA22 ....**193** A8
Chydyok Rd DT2 ......**156** B2
Cinnamon La **10** BH15 .**119** A1
Circle The
　3 Bournemouth BH9 ....**90** A2
　Poole BH13 ....**147** C4
Claire Ct BH23 ......**126** A4
Clammer Hill La TA18 ..**191** F4
Clanfield DT9 ....**29** C2
Clap La SP5 ....**188** B4
Clappentail La DT7 ....**96** A3
Clappentail Pk DT7 ....**96** A3
Clapton Ct Gdns★
　TA18 ....**191** D1
Clapton Rd TA18 ....**191** D3
Clare Ave DT4 ......**166** C1
Claremont Ave
　Bournemouth BH9 ......**90** A1
　Gillingham SP8 ....**5** C1
Claremont Gdns DT6 ..**100** B4
Claremont Rd
　Bournemouth BH9 ......**90** A1
　Bridport DT6 ....**100** B4
Clarence Cl **2** DT5 ..**186** C2

Clarence Pk Rd BH7 ...**123** A3
Clarence Rd
　Dorchester DT1 ......**134** C4
　Easton/Weston DT5 ...**186** C2
　3 Poole BH14 ......**120** A2
　Weymouth DT4 ......**166** C1
Clarence St BA20 ......**27** B2
Clarendon Ave DT3 ...**152** B1
Clarendon Cl
　Broadstone BH18 ......**87** A2
　Gillingham SP8 ....**5** B1
Clarendon Ct BH2 ....**121** B1
Clarendon Rd
　Bournemouth BH4 ....**121** B2
　Broadstone BH18 ......**86** C2
　Christchurch BH23 ....**124** A4
　Salisbury SP1 ......**213** C3
Clark's Cl BH24 ....**55** B4
Clark's La **3** TA18 ..**192** A3
Clarkham Cross BA22 ..**193** A7
Clarks BA22 ....**26** B3
Clatcombe La DT9 .....**15** C2
Claudius Cl DT1 ......**134** C4
Clay Castle TA18 ....**192** C5
Clay Castle La TA18 ..**192** C5
Clay La Beaminster DT8 **204** C4
　Puncknowle DT2 ......**129** C2
Claydon Prep Sch
　DT11 ....**37** C1
Clayesmore Sch DT11 ..**37** C1
Clayford Ave BH22 .....**61** A4
Clayford Cl BH17 ......**87** B1
Claylake Dr BH31 ......**45** B3
Claylands La DT8 ....**204** A3
Claypits La
　Beer Hackett DT9 ....**194** D6
　Winfrith Newburgh DT2 .**157** A3
Clayton Cl
　Radipole DT3 ......**152** B2
　Yeovil BA22 ....**26** B3
Clearmount Rd DT4 ...**180** C4
Cleasby Grange **26** BH5 .**122** C2
Cleeves Cl BH12 ....**88** B1
Clematis Cl BH23 ....**125** B4
Clement Mews BH4 ...**121** A2
Clement's La BA12 ......**3** A2
Clements La DT5 ....**186** C4
Clenston Rd DT11 ....**210** C2
Cleve The BA21 ......**26** C3
Cleveland Ave DT4 ...**167** B4
Cleveland Cl BH25 ...**126** B4
Cleveland Ct BH2 ....**121** B1
Cleveland Gdns BH1 ..**122** B3
Cleveland Rd BH1 ....**122** B3
Cleverlawns DT3 ....**148** C4
Cleves Cl DT4 ......**180** C4
Cliff Ave BH19 ......**179** B2
Cliff Cres BH25 ......**126** C4
Cliff Dr
　Christchurch BH23 ....**125** B3
　Poole BH13 ....**147** C3
Cliff House **10** BH6 ...**123** C2
Cliff Rd DT6 ....**128** A4
Cliff Terr BH25 ......**126** C3
Cliff Way DT5 ......**186** B1
Cliffe Rd BH25 ......**126** C4
Clifford Rd BH9 ......**90** A1
Clift La DT2 ....**205** D1
Clifton Cl
　Swanage BH19 ......**179** B2
　Yeovil BA21 ....**28** A3
Clifton Ct
　18 Bournemouth BH5 ..**122** C2
　19 New Milton BH25 ...**95** A1
Clifton Gdns BH22 .....**61** B2
Clifton Hill BA22 ....**193** F8
Clifton Pl **6** DT4 ....**167** B2
Clifton Rd
　Bournemouth BH6 ....**123** B2
　Clifton Maybank BA22 .**194** B8
　Poole BH14 ....**120** C1
　Salisbury SP2 ......**213** A3
　Swanage BH19 ......**179** A2
Clifton View **3** BA22 .**193** F8
Clingan Rd BH6 ......**123** B4
Clinton Cl BH23 ......**94** A1
Clive Ct **19** BH4 ....**121** A2
Clive Rd Bournemouth BH9 **89** C1
　Christchurch BH23 .....**93** C1
Cliveden Cl BH22 ......**61** B4
Clivia Cl DT3 ......**152** C1
Cloisters The
　Christchurch BH23 ....**124** A3
　2 Ringwood BH24 ....**55** C3
Close Dr **5** TA18 ...**192** A3
Close The
　Barton on Sea BH25 ..**127** A4
　Blandford Forum DT11 .**212** B1
　Broadstone BH18 ......**86** C2
　Charlton Marshall DT11 .**211** D6
　8 Merriott TA16 ....**191** F7
　12 Pimperne DT11 ...**199** D4
　Ringwood BH24 ......**55** A4
　St.Leonards BH24 ....**54** B2
Clough's Rd BH24 .....**55** B4
Clovens Rd DT5 ....**186** C4
Clover Cl BH23 ......**125** A4
Clover Ct BH25 ....**95** B2
Clover Dr BH17 ......**86** C1
Cloverfields SP8 ....**5** C2
Clovermead DT9 ....**194** B6
Clovers The BH12 ....**121** A4
Clowes Ave BH6 ....**124** A4
Clump Hill BH21 ......**44** B1
Cluny Cres BH19 ....**179** B1
Clyde Rd BH17 ....**87** A1
Clyffe View DT2 ....**137** B3

Clyppetts **2** DT11 .....**81** C4
Coach House Pl BH1 ...**122** A3
Coach Rd
　1 Stourpaine DT11 ..**198** F4
　Wimborne St Giles
　　BH21 ....**201** C7
Coach Rd The DT7 .....**64** A1
Coastguard Rd
　6 Fortuneswell DT5 ..**186** C4
　Langton Herring DT3 ..**150** A1
Coastguard Way BH23 .**124** C3
Cobb Rd DT7 ....**96** A2
Cobb's Rd BH21 ....**59** C3
Cobbs La BH15 ......**119** C3
Cobham Dr DT4 ......**166** C1
Cobham Rd
　Bournemouth BH9 ......**90** A2
　Ferndown BH21 ....**61** A4
　Ferndown Town BH22 ..**52** B1
Cobham Way BH21 .....**59** C1
Cobley Cl SP5 ......**189** D6
Coburg Rd DT1 ......**107** C1
Cockerell Cl BH21 .....**59** C1
Cocklands DT2 ......**107** C3
Cockles La Fleet DT4 ..**166** C1
Cockpit Hill DT6 ....**203** C4
Cod La BA22 ....**192** D7
Codge La DT2 ......**205** E5
Codogan Ct **14** BH1 ...**122** A2
Cogdean Cl BH21 ......**86** C4
Cogdean Way BH21 ....**86** C4
Cogdean Wlk BH21 ....**86** C4
Cogdeane Rd BH17 .....**87** B1
Coker Ct★ BA22 ....**193** C7
Coker Hill BA22 ....**192** F8
Coker Hill La BA22 ..**193** A7
Colber Medieval Village of★
　DT10 ....**34** C1
Colborne Ave BH21 ....**59** C3
Colbourne Cl
　Bransgore BH23 ....**93** A4
　Poole BH15 ....**119** B1
Cold Harbour
　Milborne Port DT9 .....**17** B1
　Sherborne DT9 ....**30** B4
Cold Harbour La BA22 .**192** F6
Coldharbour SP8 ....**5** C1
Coldharbour La SP2 ..**213** A3
Cole St La SP8 ....**11** A3
Cole's Cross DT8 ....**203** A5
Cole's La SP7 ....**12** A1
Colehill Cres BH9 .....**90** A2
Colehill Dro DT2 ....**156** B3
Colehill Fst Sch BH21 ..**60** A4
Colehill La Holt BH21 ..**51** B1
　Wimborne Minster BH21 .**59** C4
Colehill Rd BH20 ......**83** C3
Coleman Rd BH11 ......**89** A2
Colemore Rd BH7 ....**123** B4
Coleridge Gn BH23 ...**124** C4
Coles Ave BH15 ......**118** C1
Coles Cl DT10 ....**35** B1
Coles Gdns BH15 ....**118** C1
Coles La
　Milborne St Andrew
　　DT11 ....**209** F1
　Yetminster DT9 ......**194** B6
Colin Cl BH21 ....**86** B3
Coll of Air Traffic Control
　BH23 ....**90** C4
Collarway La BA22 ...**192** F8
College Cl BA22 ......**192** E8
College Arms Cl SP7 ...**22** A4
College Gn BA21 ......**27** B3
College Rd
　Blandford Camp DT11 ..**199** E3
　Bournemouth BH5 ....**123** A2
　Ringwood BH24 ......**55** B4
College St SP1 ......**213** B3
Collett Cl DT3 ......**153** A2
Colletts Cl BH20 ....**177** A4
Collier's La BH20 ....**139** C1
Collingbourne Ave BH6 .**123** B4
Collingwood Cl **7** DT11 **199** D4
Collingwood Rd BH21 ..**53** A3
Collins La
　Ringwood BH24 ......**55** B4
　Weymouth DT4 ......**180** B4
Colliton St DT1 ......**108** A1
Collwood Cl BH15 ....**119** B4
Collyer's Rise SP7 .....**37** C3
Colman Ct BH1 ......**122** B2
Colmer Rd BA21 ......**27** B3
Cologne Rd
　Bovington Camp BH20 .**140** A3
　Wool BH20 ....**139** C3
Colombine Cl BH23 ....**93** A1
Colonnade Rd **5** BH5 .**123** A4
Colonnade Rd W **4**
　BH5 ....**123** A3
Colt Cl BH21 ....**60** C3
Columbia Rd BH10 .....**89** B1
Columbia Trees La BH10 .**89** B1
Columbian Way BH10 ...**89** B1
Colville Cl BH5 ......**123** A3
Colville Rd **6** BH5 ...**123** A3
Colway Cl DT7 ....**96** A4
Colway La DT7 ....**96** A3
Combe Hill
　Milborne Port DT9 .....**17** A2
　Templecombe BA8 .....**18** C4
Combe Pk BA21 ....**27** A4
Combe Way DT2 ....**137** B3
Comber Rd **5** BH9 ....**90** A2
Comet Cl DT4 ......**166** C1
Comet Way BH23 ....**125** A3
Comley Rd BH9 ....**89** C1

Commercial Rd
　Bournemouth BH2 ....**121** C2
　Poole BH14 ....**120** A2
　Radipole DT4 ......**167** B1
Common Dro
　6 Child Okeford DT11 .**198** C8
　Farnham DT11 ......**188** B3
Common Hill DT8 ....**203** E5
Common La
　6 Blandford Forum DT11 **212** B1
　Burton Bradstock DT6 .**128** B4
　East Stour SP8 ....**11** A2
　Halstock BA22 ......**193** C2
　Haselbury Plucknett
　　TA18 ....**192** D5
　Henstridge BA8 ....**18** C4
　Kington Magna SP8 .....**9** B1
　Marnhull DT10 ....**34** B4
　Ryme Intrinseca DT9 ..**194** B5
　Sturminster Newton
　　DT10 ....**197** D8
　Toller Porcorum DT2 ..**205** D2
Common Mead Ave SP8 ..**5** C1
Common Mead La SP8 ...**5** B1
Common Rd SP5 ......**188** F4
Common The
　Evershot DT2 ....**206** A7
　Hazelbury Bryan DT10 .**196** E5
　Moreton DT2 ....**138** B4
Common Wr La DT8 ..**203** F5
Compton Abbas Airfield
　SP5 ....**24** C1
Compton Acres Gdns★
　BH13 ....**147** C4
Compton Ave BH14 ...**120** B1
Compton Beeches
　BH24 ....**54** B3
Compton Cl
　Verwood DT31 ....**45** A3
　Yeovil BA21 ....**28** A4
Compton Cres BH22 ....**53** B1
Compton Ct BH14 ....**120** B2
Compton Dr BH14 ...**120** B1
Compton Gdns BH14 ..**120** B1
Compton Rd
　New Milton BH25 ......**95** A1
　Over Compton DT9 .....**28** B3
Concorde Cl DT4 ....**166** C1
Condor Cl BH21 ....**53** B3
Coney's Castle (Fort)★
　DT6 ....**65** B4
Coneygar Cl DT6 ....**100** B4
Coneygar La DT6 ....**100** B4
Coneyggar Rd DT6 ...**100** B4
Conifer Ave BH14 ...**120** A1
Conifer Cl
　Christchurch BH23 ....**91** B2
　Ferndown BH22 ....**61** C1
　St.Leonards BH24 .....**53** C2
Coniston Ave BH11 ....**88** C3
Coniston Cl BH31 ......**45** A3
Coniston Cres DT3 ...**167** B4
Coniston Gdns BA21 ...**27** A4
Coniston Rd BH24 ......**55** B3
Connaught Cl BH25 ....**94** C1
Connaught Cres BH12 .**120** C3
Connaught Gdns DT4 .**167** A1
Connaught Rd
　Bournemouth BH5 ....**123** A3
　2 Weymouth BH14 ..**180** C4
Connell Rd BH15 ....**119** B3
Conniger La BH20 ...**142** C2
Consort Cl BH12 ....**120** B3
Constable Cl BA21 .....**28** A4
Constable Way SP2 ...**213** A2
Constitution Hill Gdns
　BH14 ....**120** A3
Constitution Hill Rd
　BH14 ....**120** A3
Conway Cl BH25 ....**95** A2
Conway Ct **20** BH25 ...**95** A2
Conway Dr DT2 ......**136** A1
Conways Dr BH14 ....**120** A2
Cook Cl BH24 ....**55** C4
Cook Row BH21 ....**59** A2
Cook's La DT10 ....**33** B2
Cooke Gdns BH12 ....**120** C3
Cooke Rd BH12 ......**120** C3
Cooks La DT9 ....**30** A3
Cookswell **1** DT11 ..**198** B3
Coolhurst BH14 ......**147** B4
Coombe DT9 ....**30** A4
Coombe Ave
　Bournemouth BH10 ....**89** C2
　Radipole DT4 ......**167** C3
Coombe Cl BA21 ....**27** B4
Coombe Gdns BH10 ....**89** C1
Coombe Hill BH19 ...**178** B1
Coombe La
　Castleton DT9 ....**15** B1
　Stoke Abbott DT8 ....**203** B3
Coombe Rd
　Dinnington TA17 ....**191** B7
　Puddletown DT2 ....**78** A1
　Salisbury SP2 ......**213** A1
　5 Shillingstone DT11 .**198** B5
　Winterbourne Steepleton
　　DT2 ....**105** A2
Coombe St
　Lyme Regis DT7 ....**96** B3
　Pen Selwood BA9 ......**1** B2
Coombe St La BA21 ....**27** A4
Coombe Valley Rd
　Bincombe DT3 ......**153** A2
　Overcombe/Preston
　　DT3 ....**168** A4
Coombe Wr La DT8 ..**203** B6

Coombes Cl DT2 ....**103** B1
Cooper Dean Dr BH8 ...**90** C1
Cooper Gdns DT11 ...**198** B8
Cooper's Cl **2** BH20 .**142** C2
Coopers Dr DT6 ......**100** B2
Coopers La BH31 ......**45** A4
Copeland Dr BH14 ...**120** A1
Copper Beech Cl BH12 .**121** A2
Copper Beech Gdns
　BH10 ....**89** B1
Coppercourt Leaze **5**
　BH21 ....**59** B2
Coppern Way DT10 ....**33** B4
Coppers Cl SP6 ....**42** B3
Coppice Ave BH22 .....**61** A4
Coppice Cl
　New Milton BH25 ......**95** B2
　St.Leonards BH24 ......**54** A2
Coppice St SP7 ....**12** C1
Coppice The
　Chickerell DT3 ......**166** C3
　Christchurch BH23 ...**125** A3
Coppice View BH10 ....**89** C2
Copse Ave BH25 ....**95** A1
Copse Cl BH14 ......**119** C2
Copse Hill DT10 ....**197** D7
Copse Rd
　Brympton BA22 ....**26** B4
　New Milton BH25 ......**95** A1
　Verwood BH31 ....**45** A4
Copse Way BH23 ....**125** C4
Copsewood Ave BH8 ...**90** C1
Copythorne Cl BH8 ....**90** B1
Coral Ct **2** BH12 ...**121** A2
Coram Ave DT7 ....**96** A2
Corbar Rd BH23 ....**123** C4
Corbiere Ave BH12 .....**88** B1
Corbin Ave BH22 ......**62** A3
Corbin Way DT6 ......**68** C1
Cordery Gdns SP8 ......**5** C2
Cordova Gdns DT6 ...**100** B4
Corfe Castle★ BH20 .**161** C3
Corfe Castle Model Village★
　BH20 ....**177** A4
Corfe Castle Mus★
　BH20 ....**162** A1
Corfe Castle VC Prim Sch
　BH20 ....**177** A4
Corfe Halt Cl BH21 ....**58** C1
Corfe Hills Sch BH18 ...**86** C3
Corfe Lodge Rd BH18 ..**86** B2
Corfe Mews BH15 ....**119** B2
Corfe Rd Arne BH20 ..**160** C4
　Radipole DT3 ......**167** A4
Corfe View Rd
　Corfe Mullen BH21 .....**86** B3
　Poole BH14 ....**120** B2
Corfe Way BH18 ....**86** C2
Corfu BH13 ....**147** C3
Corhampton Rd BH6 ..**123** B3
Cornelia Cres BH12 ...**121** A3
Corner Cl DT10 ....**21** A2
Corner La SP7 ....**7** B1
Corner The DT11 ....**198** E7
Cornerways Ct **7** BH25 .**95** A1
Cornflower Dr BH23 ..**125** B4
Cornford Hill DT9 ...**196** A6
Cornford Way BH23 ..**125** B4
Cornhill Way DT3 ...**153** B2
Cornish Gdns BH10 ....**89** B1
Cornpits La SP6 ......**190** E2
Cornwall Cl DT4 ....**167** A2
Cornwall Rd
　10 Dorchester DT1 ...**107** C1
　Salisbury SP1 ......**213** B4
　2 Swanage BH19 ...**179** B1
Coronation Ave
　Bournemouth BH9 .....**89** C1
　Upton BH16 ....**118** A4
　Yeovil BA21 ....**27** A4
Coronation Cl BH31 ....**45** A4
Coronation Rd
　Bridport DT6 ....**100** B3
　1 Fortuneswell DT5 ..**186** C4
　Gillingham SP8 ....**5** C1
　Radipole DT3 ......**167** B4
　Verwood BH31 ....**45** A4
Corporation Rd
　Bournemouth BH1 ....**122** B3
　Weymouth DT4 ......**167** A2
Corpus Christi RC Prim Sch
　BH5 ....**123** A3
Corscombe Cl BH17 ....**87** C1
Corscombe Ct★ DT2 .**205** B8
Corton Cl BA21 ....**28** A4
Cortry Cl BH12 ......**121** A4
Cossins La **1** TA18 ..**191** F4
Cotes Ave BH14 ....**120** A3
Cotes Ct BH14 ......**120** A3
Cothayes Dro DT2 ...**209** A6
Cotlands Rd BH1 ....**122** A2
Cotswold Cl BH31 .....**45** A3
Cotswold Ct **6** BH23 .**124** C4
Cottage Cl **2** BH20 ..**140** A1
Cottage Gdns BH12 ..**120** B3
Cottage Mews BH24 ...**55** A4
Cotton Cl BH18 ....**86** C3
Counter Cl DT11 ....**212** C2
Countess Cl BH21 .....**87** C4
Countess Gdns BH7 ..**122** C4
County Mus★ DT1 ...**108** A1
Court Ash BA20 ....**27** B3
Court Barton
　3 Crewkerne TA18 ..**191** E4
　Easton/Weston DT5 ..**186** C2
Court Cl Bridport DT6 ..**68** C3
　12 Christchurch BH23 .**124** C4
Court Gdns BA21 .....**27** A4

Court Hill
Corscombe DT2 205 B8
Damerham SP6 190 F2
Swanage BH19 179 A1
Court La
Corscombe DT2 205 B8
Milborne Port DT9 17 B2
5 Stofold BA22 193 F8
Court Orch Rd DT6 100 B4
Court Rd
Bournemouth BH9 90 A1
Radipole DT3 152 A1
Swanage BH19 179 A1
Courtauld Dr DT4 180 B4
Courtenay Cl BH20 142 C3
Courtenay Dr BH21 59 B3
Courtenay Rd BH14 120 A2
Courthill Fst Sch BH14 120 B2
Courthill Rd BH14 120 B2
Courtlands Rd DT5 186 C2
Courtleigh Manor 6 BH5 122 B2
Courtney Cl DT11 198 E8
Courtney Pl BH21 86 B3
Courtwood Cl 3 SP1 213 C2
Courtyard Craft Ctr* BH16 117 A4
Courtyard The
Christchurch BH23 124 B3
Poole BH12 88 B1
Cove Rd BH10 89 B1
Cove Row 5 DT4 167 C1
Cove St DT4 167 C1
Covena Rd BH6 123 C3
Coventry Cl BH21 86 B2
Coventry Cres BH17 87 A1
Cow Down Rd TA20 202 C8
Cow Dro BH20 81 B1
Cow La Laverstock SP1 213 C3
Long Bredy DT2 103 B1
Salisbury SP1 213 C3
Swanage BH19 179 A1
Wareham BH20 142 C2
Cowards La DT3 149 A4
Cowdrey Gdns BH8 90 C1
Cowdrys Field 2 BH21 59 A3
Cowell Dr BH7 123 A4
Cowen Cl TA18 191 F3
Cowgrove Rd BH21 58 C3
Cowlease 13 BH19 179 A1
Cowleaze DT2 133 B3
Cowleaze Rd DT2 136 A1
Cowley Cl 7 DT1 107 C1
Cowley Rd BH17 119 B4
Cowleys Rd BH23 92 B1
Cowper Ave BH25 95 A1
Cowper Rd BH9 89 C1
Cowpitts La BH24 47 C1
Cowslip Rd BH18 86 C1
Cox Ave BH9 90 A2
Cox Cl BH9 90 A2
Cox Hill DT10 34 B4
Cox's La DT2 130 B4
Coxstone La BH24 55 A3
Coy Pond Rd BH12 121 A3
Crab La BA12 2 A4
Crab Orch Way BH21 45 A1
Crabbswood La SO41 95 C4
Crabton Cl Rd BH5 122 C2
Crabtree Cl BH23 92 B1
Crack La BH19 178 B2
Crackmore DT9 17 B1
Craigmoor Ave BH8 90 C1
Craigmoor Cl BH8 90 C1
Craigmoor Way BH8 90 C1
Craigside Rd BH24 53 C2
Craigwood Dr BH22 61 C2
Cranborne CE Fst Sch BH21 40 A4
Cranborne Cres BH12 120 C4
Cranborne Ct
14 Bournemouth BH4 121 B2
Bournemouth BH9 122 A4
Cranborne Cty Mid Sch BH21 40 A4
Cranborne Dr 9 SP7 12 C2
Cranborne Lodge* BH21 40 A4
Cranborne Pl BH25 94 C2
Cranborne Rd
Alderholt SP6 41 B3
Bournemouth BH2 121 C1
Hinton Parva BH21 50 B3
Swanage BH19 179 A2
Wimborne Minster BH21 59 B4
Cranbourne Ct BH17 88 A1
Cranbrook Mews BH12 120 A3
Cranbrook Rd BH12 120 A3
Crane Cl BH31 45 A4
Crane Dr BH31 45 A3
Crane St BH21 40 A4
Crane Valley Golf Club BH21 44 B3
Crane Way BH21 53 B3
Cranebridge Rd SP2 213 B2
Cranemoor Ave BH23 93 C1
Cranemoor Cl BH23 93 C1
Cranemoor Gdns BH23 93 C1
Cranes Mdw DT2 208 A8
Cranes Mews BH15 119 B2
Cranesmoor Cl BH20 139 B3
Cranfield Ave BH21 59 B3
Cranford Ave DT4 167 C3
Cranleigh Cl BH6 123 C3
Cranleigh Ct BH6 123 C3
Cranleigh Gdns BH6 123 C3
Cranleigh Rd BH6 123 C3
Cranmer Rd BH9 121 C4
Cransley Ct BH4 121 B1
Crantock Gr BH8 90 C1
Cranwell Cl BH11 88 C2
Crate Hill DT10 197 C5
Crate La SP7 7 C3
Crawford Bridge* DT11 211 E5
Crawford Down Rd 4 DT11 199 E2
Crawford Pk DT11 211 E4
Crawshaw Rd BH14 120 A1
Creasey Rd BH11 89 A3
Creech Grange* BH20 160 B1
Creech Rd BH12 120 B3
Creech Way DT3 167 A4
Creekmoor La BH17 119 A4
Crescent Ct BH25 126 C4
Crescent Dr BH25 126 C4
Crescent Rd
Bournemouth BH2 121 C2
Poole BH14 120 C2
Verwood BH31 45 B3
Wimborne Minster BH21 59 B2
Crescent St DT4 167 C2
Crescent The
Barton on Sea BH25 126 B4
3 Bournemouth BH7 122 C2
14 Yeovil BA20 27 B2
Crescent Wlk BH22 61 C1
Crest Rd BH12 120 B3
Cresta Gdns BH22 61 C1
Crewkerne Sta TA18 192 A3
Cribb Cl BH17 119 C4
Crichel House* BH21 201 A3
Crichel La BH21 200 F1
Crichel Mount Rd BH14 147 B4
Crichel Rd BH9 122 A4
Cricket Cl BH23 124 C3
Crimea Rd BH9 121 C4
Cringle Ave BH6 124 A2
Crispen Cl BH23 125 C4
Criterion Arc 39 BH1 121 C2
Crock La DT6 100 C3
Crockford Cl BH25 95 A3
Croft Cl BH21 86 B4
Croft Rd Bournemouth BH9 89 C1
Bransgore BH23 93 A3
Christchurch BH23 124 C4
Easton/Weston DT5 186 C2
Poole BH12 120 A3
Ringwood BH24 47 C1
Croft The
Wareham BH20 142 C2
10 Yeovil BA20 26 C1
Crofton Ave BA21 27 B3
Crofton Cl BH23 91 C1
Crofton Pk BA21 27 B3
Crofton Rd BA21 27 B3
Cromer Gdns BH12 120 C3
Cromer Rd
Bournemouth BH8 122 B4
Poole BH12 120 C3
Cromwell Pl 9 BH5 123 A3
Cromwell Rd
Bournemouth BH5 123 A3
13 Dorchester DT1 108 A1
Poole BH12 120 B3
Weymouth DT4 167 A2
16 Wimborne Minster BH21 59 B2
Yeovil BA21 27 C3
Crook Hill (National Trust)* DT8 192 E1
Crook Hill DT6 204 C2
Crooked La BA9 4 B2
Crooked Oak Hill DT6 204 D1
Crookhays SP7 12 C2
Cropmead Ind Est TA18 191 F4
Crosby Rd BH4 121 B1
Cross La SP8 5 C4
Cross Rd
Bradford Abbas DT9 28 B1
1 Weymouth DT4 180 C4
Cross The
2 Bradford Abbas DT9 28 B1
3 Child Okeford DT11 198 C7
5 Henstridge BA8 19 A2
1 Okeford Fitzpaine DT11 197 F5
Shillingstone DT11 198 B6
Wool BH20 140 A1
Cross Way
Bradford Abbas DT9 28 B1
Christchurch BH23 91 B1
Crossfields DT9 28 C4
Crossmead Ave BH25 95 A1
Crosstree Cl DT2 136 A1
Crossway DT11 199 E3
Crossways 18 TA20 202 A8
Crossways The BH16 118 B4
Crouch La DT9 196 A6
Crow Arch La 5 BH24 55 B3
Crow La BH24 55 C3
Crowe Hill Ct 2 BH15 119 C2
Crown Cl BH12 120 B3
Crown Ct
Milborne St Andrew DT11 79 C4
8 Wimborne Minster BH21 59 A3
Crown Farm Terr DT5 187 A3
Crown Mead BH21 59 B2
Crown Rd DT10 21 A1
Crown Wlk 9 BH7 122 C2
Crown Yd DT2 156 C3
Crowthorne La DT2 208 A7
Crumpets Dr BH16 84 C3
Crumplers Cl BH16 84 A2
Crusader Rd BH11 88 B2
Cruxton Farm Ctyd BH21 59 B1
Cruxton La DT2 73 A3
Cucklington Gdns BH9 90 A2
Cuckoo Hill DT9 194 B4
Cuckoo La
Broadwindsor TA20 202 F7
Hilton DT11 209 C7
Stinsford DT2 109 A3
Cuckoo Rd BH12 120 A4
Cudnell Ave BH11 89 A3
Cuffnells Cl BH24 47 B4
Cul-de-sac BH25 126 B4
Culford Cl BH8 90 C1
Culford Ct 1 BH8 122 A3
Cull Cl BH12 121 B4
Cull La BH25 95 A3
Cull Peppers Dish (Sink Hole)* DT2 112 A3
Culliford Cres BH17 87 C1
Culliford Rd DT1 135 A4
Culliford Rd N 19 DT1 108 A1
Culliford Way DT3 152 C2
Cullwood La BH25 95 B3
Culver Rd BH25 94 C1
Culver St 2 SP1 213 B2
Culverhayes DT8 204 C4
Culverhayes Pl BH21 59 A3
Culverhayes Rd BH21 59 A3
Culverlake La EX13 202 D3
Culvers Cl DT9 30 A3
Culvers La SP8 5 B1
Cumberland Dr DT4 166 C2
Cumnor Rd BH1 122 A2
Cunnage La BA12 3 C1
Cunningham Cl
Bournemouth BH11 89 A2
Bovington Camp BH20 139 C3
Christchurch BH23 125 A3
4 Ringwood BH24 55 C4
3 Weymouth DT4 180 A4
Cunningham Cres BH11 89 A2
Cunningham Ct BH25 94 C2
Cunningham Pl BH11 89 A2
Cunnington Cl DT1 134 C4
Curlew Cl
1 Chickerell DT3 166 B3
Ferndown BH22 61 A4
Curlew Rd
Bournemouth BH8 90 B1
Christchurch BH23 125 A2
Curlews The BH31 45 B3
Curlieu Rd BH15 119 B3
Curriott Hill TA18 191 E3
Curriott Hill Rd 9 TA18 191 E4
Curry Hole La DT2 193 D2
Curtis Ct DT9 196 A8
Curtis Rd BH12 120 B3
Curzon Ct 32 BH4 121 B2
Curzon Rd
Bournemouth BH1 122 B3
Poole BH14 120 A2
Curzon Way BH23 125 B4
Custard Hill BH21 201 B5
Custom House Quay DT4 167 B1
Cuthburga Rd BH21 59 B2
Cuthbury Cl BH21 59 A2
Cuthbury Gdns BH21 59 A3
Cutler Cl New Milton BH25 95 B2
Poole BH12 121 B4
Cutlers Pl BH21 60 A3
Cutt Mill La DT10 34 C3
Cynthia Cl BH12 120 A4
Cynthia House BH12 120 A4
Cynthia Rd BH12 120 A4
Cypress Dr BA20 27 A1
Cypress Way 9 SP8 5 C1
Cyril Rd BH8 122 B3

D

D'Urberville Cl 4 DT1 134 C4
D'Urberville Dr BH19 179 A2
Dacombe Cl BH16 118 B4
Dacombe Dr BH16 118 B4
Daggons Rd SP6 41 C3
Dagmar Rd DT1 107 C1
Dahlia Cl DT3 152 C1
Dairy Cl
Christchurch BH23 124 B4
Corfe Mullen BH21 86 A2
Dairy Field DT11 212 C2
Dairy Mdw La SP1 213 C2
Dakota Cl BH23 125 A4
Dale Ave DT4 167 B3
Dale Cl BH15 119 C3
Dale Rd BH15 119 C3
Dale Valley Rd BH15 119 C4
Daler Ct 18 BH20 142 C2
Dales Cl BH21 60 B3
Dales Dr BH21 60 A3
Dales La BH23 90 C4
Dalewood Ave BH11 88 C3
Dalkeith Rd
Corfe Mullen BH21 86 B2
Poole BH13 121 A1
Dalling Rd BH12 121 A3
Dalmeny Rd BH6 124 A2
Dalwoods DT9 30 A3
Damer's Rd DT1 107 B1
Damerham Rd BH8 90 B2
Damers Cty Fst Sch DT1 107 C1
Damory Ct 5 DT11 212 B1
Damory Ct St DT11 212 B1
Damory St DT11 212 B1
Dampier Pl 2 BA21 27 C3
Dampier St 3 BA21 27 C3
Dane Ct BH14 120 A2
Dane Dr BH22 61 C2
Danecourt Cl BH14 119 C2
Danecourt Rd BH14 119 C2
Danecrest Rd SO41 95 C2
Danehurst New Rd SO41 95 B4
Danes Cl BH25 127 A4
Danesbury Ave BH6 123 C2
Danesbury Mdws BH25 95 B3
Daneswood Rd BH25 95 B2
Daniel Dr BH20 142 B3
Daniel Gdns 18 BH15 119 B1
Danielsfield Rd BA20 27 A1
Dansie Cl BH14 120 A2
Darby La 6 DT6 128 A4
Darby's Cl BH15 119 B3
Darby's Cnr BH17 87 B1
Darby's La BH15 119 B3
Darby's La N BH17 119 B4
Dark La Bransgore BH23 94 A2
Fifehead Neville DT10 197 C6
Mere BA12 3 A3
Sandford Orcas DT9 15 B3
Tincleton DT2 110 B3
Witchampton BH21 200 F1
Darkie La BH19 179 A3
Darknoll La DT11 197 E6
Darley Rd BH22 61 B2
Darracott Rd BH5 123 A3
Darrian Ct BH16 118 A4
Darwin Ave BH23 91 C1
Darwin Cl DT3 152 B2
Darwin Ct 4 BH12 121 A2
Dashwood Cl DT10 35 B1
Davenant Cl 5 SP8 5 C1
Davenport Cl BH16 118 B4
David Way BH15 118 C1
David's La BH24 54 C3
David's Wlk DT1 134 C4
Davis Ct BH12 120 C3
Davis Field BH25 94 C1
Davis Gdns DT11 212 C2
Davis Rd BH12 120 C3
Dawkins Bsns Ctr BH15 118 B2
Dawkins Rd BH15 118 B2
Dawkins Way BH25 95 A1
Dawlish Cres DT4 180 B4
Dawn Chorus BH14 120 A2
Dawn Cl BH10 89 B1
Daws Ave BH11 89 A1
Day's Ct BH21 59 B2
Day's Rd BH19 178 C1
Daylesford Cl BH14 120 A1
De Courtenai Cl BH11 88 C3
De Haviland Cl BH21 59 C1
De Havilland Ho BH23 125 A3
De Havilland Way BH23 125 A3
De Lisle Rd BH3 121 C4
De Mauley Rd BH13 147 C4
De Montfort Rd BH21 59 B1
De Moulham Rd BH19 179 A2
De Redvers Rd BH14 120 B1
De Vaux Pl SP1 213 B2
Deacon Gdns BH11 89 A3
Deacon Rd BH11 89 A3
Dean Cl BH15 118 C2
Dean La SP5 188 F6
Dean La Dro SP5 188 F4
Dean Pk Cres BH1 121 C2
Dean Pk Rd BH1 121 C2
Dean Swift Cres BH14 147 B4
Dean's Rd 18 BH5 123 A3
Deane Ave SP8 5 C1
Deane Way 5 TA20 202 A8
Deans Ct La BH21 59 B2
Deans Dro BH16 84 B1
Deans Gr BH21 59 B4
Deans The BH1 121 C2
Deanscroft Rd BH10 89 C2
Deansleigh Cl 5 DT3 168 A4
Deansleigh Rd BH7 91 A1
Dear Hay La BH15 119 B1
Decies Rd BH14 120 A3
Dee Way BH15 119 A1
Deep Ford La DT9 194 D3
Deep La DT9 194 C3
Deepdene La BH11 88 C3
Deer Pk Cl BH25 94 C2
Deerleap Way BH25 95 A3
Delamere Gdns BH10 89 C2
Delft Mews BH23 124 B3
Delhi Cl BH14 120 B2
Delhi La DT5 187 A2
Delhi Rd BH9 89 C1
Delilah Rd BH15 118 B1
Delkeith Ct BH22 61 B2
Dell Cl BH18 86 C2
Dell The BH25 126 B4
Delph Rd BH21 87 B4
Delph Woods Woodland Trail* BH21 87 B4
Delta Cl BH23 125 A4
Denby Rd BH15 119 C2
Dene Cl BH24 47 C1
Dene Wlk BH22 61 C1
Denecote Lodge BH13 147 D4
Denes Ave BA12 3 A3
Deneve Ave BH17 87 B1
Denewood Copse BH22 52 C2
Denewood Rd BH22 52 C2
Denhall Cl DT10 35 A1
Denham Cl BH17 87 C2
Denham Dr Cann SP7 23 A3
Christchurch BH23 93 C1
Denhay La DT6 67 B3
Denholm Cl BH24 47 C1
Denison Rd BH17 87 B1
Denison Rise SP1 213 C4
Denmark La BH15 119 B2
Denmark Rd
Bournemouth BH9 89 C1
Poole BH15 119 B2
Denmark Terr BH1 122 C3
Denmead BH25 95 B2
Denmead Rd BH6 123 B4
Dennetts La 19 BH15 119 A1
Dennis Rd
Corfe Mullen BH21 86 B3
Weymouth DT4 167 A1
Dennistoun Ave BH23 124 C4
Denwood Rd BH4 121 A2
Denzil Cl 3 BA22 193 A8
Derby Rd BH1 122 B2
Derby St DT4 167 B2
Dereham Way BH12 120 C3
Derritt La BH23 92 B4
Derrybrian Gdns BH25 95 A1
Derwent Cl
Bournemouth BH9 90 A1
Ferndown BH22 62 A3
Derwent Gdns BA21 27 C3
Derwent Rd
New Milton BH25 95 A3
Weymouth DT4 180 B3
Derwent Way 3 BA21 26 C3
Derwentwater Rd BH21 59 B1
Deverel Cl BH23 124 A4
Devizes Rd SP2 213 A3
Devon Rd
Christchurch BH23 123 C4
Poole BH15 119 C3
Weymouth DT4 167 A2
Devonshire Rd SP1 213 B4
Dew's Rd SP2 213 A3
Dewey's Way SP8 5 C1
Dewlands Orch DT9 194 E3
Dewlands Rd BH31 44 C3
Dewlands Way BH31 45 A3
Dewlish Cl BH17 88 A1
Dewlish House* DT2 78 C4
Diamond Cl SP6 43 A4
Diana Cl DT1 134 C4
Diana Ct BH23 126 A4
Diana Way BH21 86 C4
Dibbles La BA22 193 A8
Dibden Cl BH8 90 B2
Dick o' Th' Banks Cl DT2 137 B3
Dick o' Th' Banks Rd DT2 137 B3
Dickens Rd BH6 123 B4
Didcot Rd BH17 119 B4
Digby Rd DT9 30 A3
Diggory Cres DT1 135 A4
Dillons Gdns BH16 84 B1
Dilly La BH25 127 A4
Diments Gdns 2 DT6 100 B4
Dinah's Hollow SP7 24 B3
Dingle Rd BH5 123 A2
Dingley Rd BH15 119 B3
Dinham Ct BH25 95 B2
Dinham Rd BH25 95 B2
Dinhay DT10 20 C2
Dinosaur Experience The* BH19 177 C1
Dinosaur Mus* DT1 108 A1
Diprose Rd BH21 86 C4
Discover Salisbury (Medieval Hall)* SP1 213 B2
Disraeli Rd BH23 124 B3
Dock Rd DT5 181 B1
Dodhams Farm Cl DT6 68 C1
Doe Copse Way BH25 94 C2
Dogbury Gate DT2 207 C8
Dogdean BH21 59 B4
Dogwood Rd BH18 86 C1
Dolbery Rd N BH12 88 B1
Dolbery Rd S BH12 88 B1
Dollin's La 3 BH20 142 C2
Dollings The BH20 177 A4
Dolmans Hill BH16 84 A2
Dolphin Ave BH10 89 C3
Dolphin Cl 2 DT7 96 B3
Dolphin Ctr BH15 119 B1
Dolphin Ind Est SP1 213 C2
Dolphin La SP8 5 C2
Dolphin Pl BH25 127 A4
Dolphin St SP1 213 B2
Dominion Ctr* BH11 88 C2
Dominion Rd BH11 88 C2
Donaldson Rd SP1 213 B3
Doncaster Rd DT4 180 B3
Donhead Hollow SP7 25 B4
Donkey La
Bere Regis BH20 113 A3
Bridport DT6 100 B4
5 Burton Bradstock DT6 128 A4
Donnelly Rd BH6 123 C3
Donnington Dr BH23 125 A4
Donoughmore Rd 1 BH1 122 C2
Dorchester Cty Mid Sch DT1 134 C4
Dorchester Gdns BH15 119 C3
Dorchester Hill
Blandford St Mary DT11 212 B1
Milborne St Andrew DT11 79 C4
Winterborne Whitechurch DT11 210 C2
Dorchester Mans BH1 122 B2
Dorchester Mus* DT1 108 A1

Dorchester Prep Sch DT1 108 A1
Dorchester Rd
Affpuddle DT2 79 C1
Askerswell DT2 103 A2
Bincombe DT3 134 B1
Cerne Abbas DT2 207 D4
Closworth BA22 193 F6
Frampton DT2 74 A1
Loders DT6 101 B3
Lytchett Minster & Upton BH16 117 A4
Maiden Newton DT2 73 A4
Melbury Osmond BA22 194 A4
Poole BH15 119 C3
Radipole DT3 152 A1
Stratton DT2 106 B4
Sydling St Nicholas DT2 207 A2
Tolpuddle DT2 79 A1
Upton BH16 118 A4
Wool BH20 139 C1
Yeovil BA20 27 B1
Dorchester S Sta DT1 108 A1
Dorchester W Sta DT1 107 C1
Dormers The BH25 94 C1
Dornie Rd BH13 147 C4
Dorset Ave BH22 61 B2
Dorset Cl DT4 167 A2
Dorset Cty Hospl DT1 107 C1
Dorset Gall* BH20 142 C2
Dorset Grange BH23 123 C4
Dorset House BH13 121 A1
Dorset Lake Ave BH14 147 A4
Dorset Lake Manor BH14 120 A1
Dorset Leisure Ctr DT6 97 A4
Dorset Rare Breeds Ctr* SP8 11 B4
Dorset Rd
Bournemouth BH4 121 B3
Christchurch BH23 124 C4
Salisbury SP1 213 B4
Dorset St DT11 212 B1
Dorset Terr 8 DT4 167 B1
Dottery Rd DT6 68 A1
Double Comm DT6 97 A4
Douglas Ave BH23 124 A3
Douglas Cl BH16 118 B4
Douglas Gdns BH12 120 C3
Douglas Haig Rd SP1 213 B3
Douglas Mews
Bournemouth BH6 123 B3
Upton BH16 118 B4
Douglas Rd
Bournemouth BH6 123 C2
Poole BH12 120 C3
Weymouth DT4 180 B3
Doulton Gdns BH14 120 A1
Doussie Cl BH16 118 A4
Dover Cl BH13 121 A2
Dover Rd Poole BH13 121 A2
Weymouth DT4 180 B3
Dover St SP7 21 C3
Doves The DT3 152 B2
Doveshill Cres BH10 89 B2
Doveshill Gdns BH10 89 B2
Doveshill Mobile Home Pk BH10 89 B2
Dowlands Cl BH10 89 B2
Dowlands Rd BH10 89 B2
Dowman Pl DT4 180 B3
Down End DT2 107 C3
Down House La DT6 99 C2
Down La Folke DT9 195 D8
Trent DT9 14 C1
Down Lodge Cl SP6 42 B3
Down Rd
3 Pimperne DT11 199 D4
Weymouth DT4 167 B1
Down Wood Rd 2 DT11 199 E2
Down's La DT9 194 A5
Downash La EX13 202 B3
Downclose 12 DT4 180 B4
Downclose La TA18 192 C4
Downes St DT6 100 B3
Downey Cl BH11 88 C1
Downlands CP Sch DT11 199 E3
Downlands Pl BH17 119 C4
Downleaze 1 BA20 26 C1
Downs La DT9 194 C5
Downside Cl
Blandford Forum DT11 212 C1
Charmouth DT6 97 A4
Mere BA12 3 A3
Downsview Dr SP8 5 C2
Downsway SP1 213 B4
Downton Cl BH8 90 B2
Downton La SO41 127 C4
Downton Rd SP2 213 B1
Downview Rd SP6 190 B6
Doyne Rd BH14 120 C2
Dozens Cnr TA17 191 A7
Dragons Hill DT7 96 B4
Dragoon Way BH23 123 C4
Drake Ave DT3 166 B3
Drake Cl
Christchurch BH23 124 C3
New Milton BH25 94 C2
Ringwood BH24 47 C1
Drake Ct 22 BH15 119 B1
Drake Rd BH15 119 B1
Drake's La DT2 208 F3
Drakes Cres 6 TA20 202 A8
Drakes Mdw BA22 193 C7
Drakes Rd BH22 61 C2
Draper Rd
Bournemouth BH11 89 A2
Christchurch BH23 124 C4
Drax Ave BH20 142 C3
Draycott Rd BH10 89 B1
Dreswick Cl BH23 91 B2
Drew Cl Bridport DT6 68 C1
Poole BH12 121 B4
Drew's La DT10 19 B1
Drewitt Ind Est BH11 88 C2
Drift Rd DT2 72 C4
Drift The TA20 202 B8
Drive The BH12 120 B3
Drones La SP7 23 B1
Drove La SP7 36 C3
Drove Rd DT10 32 C2
Drove The Arne BH20 160 C4
Shapwick DT11 56 C4
Thornford DT9 194 D8
Winfrith Newburgh DT2 156 C4
Droveway La BA21 14 A3
Droxford Rd BH6 123 A3
Druce La DT2 77 C2
Druids Cl BH22 61 B1
Druitt Rd BH23 124 C4
Drum La DT10 196 F3
Drummond Rd
Bournemouth BH1 122 B2
Swanage BH19 179 B1
Drury La DT6 204 C2
Drury Rd BH4 121 A1
Dry La SP8 5 B1
Dryden Cl
Salisbury SP2 213 B1
St.Leonards BH24 54 A3
Duart Ct BH25 95 B2
Duchy Cl DT1 135 B4
Duchy Manor Mid Sch BA12 3 A3
Duck Island La BH24 55 A3
Duck La
Bournemouth BH11 88 C2
Salisbury SP1 213 C3
Stalbridge DT10 19 B1
Duck St Bridport DT6 100 C2
Cattistock DT2 206 C2
Cerne Abbas DT2 207 D4
Chideock DT6 99 A3
Child Okeford DT11 198 C7
Hilton DT11 209 D5
Symondsbury DT6 99 C4
Winterborne Kingston DT11 81 C4
Wool BH20 140 A1
Duck's Nest (Long Barrow)* SP6 190 F7
Ducking Stool La BH23 124 A3
Duckpool La TA18 192 B8
Dudley Ave SO41 95 C2
Dudley Gdns BH10 89 B3
Dudley Pl 29 BH25 95 A1
Dudley Rd BH10 89 B3
Dudmoor Farm Rd BH23 91 C2
Dudmoor La BH23 91 C2
Dudsbury Ave BH22 61 B2
Dudsbury Cres BH22 61 C2
Dudsbury Ct 9 BH23 124 C3
Dudsbury Gdns BH22 89 C4
Dudsbury Rd BH22 61 B1
Dudsway Ct BH22 61 B2
Dugberry Hill DT6 70 A3
Dugdell Cl BH22 61 C3
Duke's Ave DT1 108 A1
Dukes Dr BH11 88 C3
Dukesfield BH23 91 B1
Dullar La BH21 56 B1
Dulsie Rd BH3 121 B4
Dumbarton Rd DT4 180 B3
Dumpton Sch BH21 59 B4
Dunbar Cres BH23 93 C1
Dunbar Rd BH3 121 C3
Dunbury Fst Sch
Winterborne Kingston DT11 81 C4
Winterborne Stickland DT11 210 C7
Winterborne Whitechurch DT11 210 C3
Dunbury La DT11 209 F6
Duncan Cres BH20 139 C3
Duncan Rd BH25 95 B2
Dunch La DT9 194 D3
Duncliff Rd BH6 124 A2
Duncliffe Cl DT10 33 C4
Duncombe Dr BH24 46 C2
Dundas Rd BH17 119 C4
Dundee Rd DT4 180 B3
Dune Crest BH13 147 B2
Dunedin Cl BH22 61 A2
Dunedin Dr BH22 61 A2
Dunedin Gdns BH22 61 A2
Dunedin Gr BH23 125 B4
Dunford Cl
Barton on Sea BH25 126 C4
New Milton BH25 94 C1
Dunford Pl 15 BH19 179 A1
Dunford Rd BH12 120 B3
Dungeon Hill (Fort)* DT9 195 F2
Dunkeld Rd BH3 121 C3
Dunlin Cl BH23 125 A3
Dunn's La
Iwerne Minster DT11 37 C1
Silton SP8 2 A1
Dunnock Cl BH22 61 A4
Dunsham La TA18 191 C2
Dunshay Manor* BH19 177 B2
Dunspit La DT11 188 B1
Dunstans La BH15 120 A3
Dunyeats Rd BH18 87 A2
Durdells Ave BH11 89 A3
Durdells Gdns BH11 89 A3
Durland Cl BH25 95 A1
Durley Chine Ct BH2 121 B1
Durley Chine Rd BH2 121 B1
Durley Chine Rd S BH2 121 B1
Durley Gdns BH2 121 B1
Durley Rd BH2 121 C1
Durley Rd S BH2 121 B1
Durlston Cres BH23 91 B2
Durlston Ct Sch BH25 127 A4
Durlston Ctry Pk* BH19 185 A4
Durlston Farm BH19 179 A3
Durlston Rd Poole BH14 120 B1
Swanage BH19 179 B1
Durnford Dro BH19 178 A1
Durngate St DT1 108 A1
Durnover Ct DT1 108 A1
Durrant DT10 197 D8
Durrant Cl DT9 30 A3
Durrant Rd
7 Bournemouth BH2 121 C2
Poole BH14 120 B2
Durrington Pl BH7 123 A3
Durrington Rd BH7 123 A4
Durweston CE Fst Sch DT11 198 E3
Durweston Cl BH9 90 A2
Dyke Head DT9 195 B6
Dymewood Rd BH21 53 A4

E

Eadon Cl DT3 168 A4
Eagle House Gdns DT11 212 B1
Eagle House Sch BH14 120 A2
Eagle Rd BH12 121 A2
Eaglehurst 5 BH12 121 A2
Earl Cl 14 DT1 108 A1
Earle Rd BH4 121 B1
Earle St BA20 27 C2
Earlham Dr BH14 120 B2
Earls Cl DT9 30 B4
Earlsdon Way BH23 125 C4
Earlswood Dr SP6 42 A3
Earlswood Pk BH25 95 B2
Earthpits La SP5 189 E4
East Ave
Barton on Sea BH25 126 B4
Bournemouth BH3 121 B3
East Borough BH21 59 A3
East Burton Rd BH20 139 C1
East Cl BH25 126 B4
East Cliff DT7 96 B3
East Cliff Way BH23 125 B4
East Coker Prim Sch BA22 193 C7
East Coker Rd BA20 27 A1
East Dro BH19 178 A1
East Farm La DT2 155 B4
East Hill
Charminster DT2 107 B3
Evershot DT2 206 A7
East Howe La BH10 89 B2
East Knighton La DT2 157 A4
East La TA18 192 B8
East Mill La DT9 30 B3
East Morden Dro BH20 83 B3
East Overcliff Dr BH1 122 B2
East Quay BH15 119 B1
East Quay Rd BH15 119 B1
East Rd DT6 100 C3
East St Beaminster DT8 204 D4
Blandford Forum DT11 212 B1
Bourton SP8 1 C1
Bridport DT6 100 B3
Chickerell DT3 166 B3
Corfe Castle BH20 162 A1
Crewkerne TA18 191 F4
Fortuneswell DT5 186 C4
Milborne Port DT9 17 B1
North Perrott TA18 192 C4
Poole BH15 119 B1
Radipole DT4 167 C1
Salisbury SP2 213 A3
Sydling St Nicholas DT2 207 A2
Wareham BH20 142 C2
West Coker BA22 193 A8
Wimborne Minster BH21 59 B2
9 Winterborne Kingston DT11 81 C4
East View Rd BH24 55 B4
East Walls BH20 142 C2
East Way
Bournemouth BH8 90 B1
Corfe Mullen BH21 86 B3
East Weare Rd DT5 181 A1
East Wyld Rd DT4 167 A2
Eastbrook Row BH21 59 B2
Eastbury Ct BH23 124 C2
Eastcott Cl BH7 123 A4
Eastdown Ave DT3 167 C4
Eastdown Gdns DT3 168 A3
Easter Rd BH9 90 A1
Eastfield 4 DT9 194 D8
Eastfield Cl BH24 55 C4
Eastfield La
North Perrott TA18 192 C4
Ringwood BH24 55 C4
West Chinnock BA22 192 D8
Easthams Rd TA18 191 F4
Easthay La TA20 202 D4
Eastlake Ave BH12 120 B3
Eastland Rd BA21 27 C3
Eastlands
New Milton BH25 95 A1
10 Yetminster DT9 194 C5
Eastleaze Rd DT11 212 B2
Easton Hollow SP5 188 B7
Easton La DT5 187 A3
Easton Sq 4 DT5 187 A2
Easton St DT5 187 A2
Eastop La DT10 33 A3
Eastville BA21 27 C3
Eastwell La DT10 35 A4
Eastwood Ave BH22 61 C3
Eastworth Rd BH31 45 A4
Eaton Rd BH13 121 A1
Ebor Cl BH22 61 C1
Ebor Rd Poole BH12 120 B3
Weymouth DT4 180 B4
Eccles Rd BH15 119 A1
Eddison Ave DT1 108 B1
Eddy Green Rd BH16 84 A1
Eden Ct 20 BH1 122 A2
Eden Gr BH21 59 B2
Edgarton Rd BH17 87 B2
Edgehill Rd
Bournemouth BH9 89 C1
Bridport DT6 100 A3
Edgemoor Rd BH22 53 B1
Edifred Rd BH9 90 A2
Edison Rd SP2 213 A2
Edith Ct 2 SP8 5 C1
Edmondsham House* BH21 40 B2
Edmondsham Rd BH31 45 A4
Edmonsham House 23 BH2 121 C2
Edmunds Cl BH25 95 A1
Edward Cl BA22 26 B3
Edward Cres BH20 142 C2
Edward Rd
Bournemouth BH11 89 A2
Christchurch BH23 124 C4
Dorchester DT1 107 C1
Poole BH14 120 B3
Edward St
Blandford Forum DT11 212 B1
4 Radipole DT4 167 B2
Edward Way Ct BH11 89 A2
Edwina Cl BH24 47 C1
Edwina Dr BH17 87 A1
Egdon Cl
Bere Regis BH20 81 A1
Ferndown BH22 61 A2
Egdon Ct BH16 118 A4
Egdon Dr BH21 87 C4
Egdon Glen DT2 137 C3
Egdon Rd
Dorchester DT1 135 A4
Northport BH20 142 B3
Egerton Gdns BH8 122 B3
Egerton Rd BH8 122 B3
Eggardon Cl 5 DT8 204 C4
Eggardon Hill (Fort)* DT6 71 A1
Egmont Cl BH24 54 C1
Egmont Dr BH24 54 C1
Egmont Gdns BH24 54 C1
Egmont Rd BH16 118 A2
Elbury View SP7 37 C4
Elder Rd BH20 81 A1
Elderberry La BH23 124 C3
Eldon Ave BH25 126 C4
Eldon Cl BH25 126 C4
Eldon Ct 9 BH14 120 A2
Eldon Pl BH4 121 A2
Eldon Rd BH9 89 C1
Eldon Terr 11 BH19 179 A1
Eldons Dro BH16 84 B2
Eldridge Cl 3 DT1 134 C4
Eleanor Dr BH11 88 B3
Eleanor Gdns BH23 123 C4
Elfin Dr BH22 61 B4
Elgar Rd BH10 89 B2
Elgin Rd
Bournemouth BH3 121 B3
Poole BH14 120 B1
Elijah Cl BH15 118 C1
Eliot House 14 BH25 95 A1
Eliotts Dr BA21 27 A4
Elise Cl BH7 123 A4
Elizabeth Ave
Bridport DT6 100 B3
Christchurch BH23 123 C4
Elizabeth Cl 1 DT7 96 B3
Elizabeth Ct
12 Bournemouth BH1 122 A2
11 New Milton BH25 95 A1
Elizabeth Gdns BH23 125 B4
Elizabeth Pl DT1 107 B1
Elizabeth Rd
Blandford Forum DT11 212 C2
Poole BH15 119 B2
Upton BH16 118 B4
Wimborne Minster BH21 59 B3
Elizabeth Way DT3 166 C2
Ellerslie Cl DT2 107 C3
Elles Rd BH20 139 B4
Ellesdon DT6 97 A4
Ellesfield Dr BH22 61 B1
Ellingham Dr BH24 46 C2
Ellingham Dro BH24 47 C3
Ellingham Rd BH25 126 B4
Elliot Rd BH11 88 C2
Elliott's Hill BA22 192 D7
Elm Ave Christchurch BH23 91 C1
Elm Ave *continued*
Holton Heath BH20 116 A2
New Milton BH25 95 A1
Elm Cl Motcombe SP7 7 A1
Overcombe/Preston DT3 168 A3
Salisbury SP1 213 C4
Sturminster Newton DT10 35 B1
Elm Ct 4 BH25 95 A1
Elm Gdns BH4 121 B3
Elm Gr SP1 213 C3
Elm Gr Rd SP1 213 B3
Elm Tree Wlk BH22 89 C4
Elmes Rd BH9 89 C1
Elmgate Dr BH7 123 A4
Elmhurst Ave BA21 27 B4
Elmhurst Rd
Bournemouth BH11 89 A3
Ferndown BH22 53 A1
Elmhurst Way BH22 53 A1
Elmore Dr BH24 54 A3
Elmrise Prim Sch BH11 89 A2
Elms Ave BH14 120 A1
Elms Cl BH14 120 A1
Elms Way BH6 123 C2
Elmstead Rd BH13 147 C4
Elmwood Way BH23 126 A4
Elphinstone Rd BH23 94 A1
Elsdon's La DT6 64 A2
Elston Medieval Village of* DT2 207 A3
Eltham Cl BH7 123 A4
Elvin Cl SO41 95 C2
Elwell DT6 100 C3
Elwell Manor Gdns DT4 167 B1
Elwell St DT3 152 A3
Elwood Cl BH20 142 C4
Elwyn Rd BH1 122 B3
Elysium Ct BH22 61 C2
Elziver Cl DT3 166 B3
Embankment Way BH24 55 B3
Emberley Cl BH22 62 A3
Emerald Cl BH24 54 A3
Emerson Cl BH15 119 B1
Emerson Rd Poole BH15 119 B1
Weymouth DT4 167 A1
Emily Cl BH23 92 A1
Emily Ct BH14 120 C3
Emley La 1 BH21 201 C1
Emmadale Rd DT4 167 A2
Emmanuel CE Mid Sch BH31 45 A3
Emmdale Cl DT4 167 A2
Emminster Cl DT3 168 A4
Empool Cl DT2 137 B3
Encombe Cl BH12 120 C4
Encombe Rd BH20 142 B2
Endfield Cl BH23 91 C1
Endfield Rd
Bournemouth BH9 90 A1
Christchurch BH23 91 C1
Endless St SP1 213 B3
Enfield Cres BH15 119 C3
Enfield Rd BH15 119 C3
Englands Way BH11 88 B2
Enkworth Rd DT3 168 A4
Ensbury Ave BH10 89 B1
Ensbury Cl BH10 89 B1
Ensbury Ct BH10 89 C1
Ensbury Pk Rd BH9 89 C1
Enterprise Way BH23 90 B4
Epiphany CE Prim Sch BH9 90 A2
Erica Dr BH21 86 B3
Ericksen Rd BH11 89 B2
Erin Rd BH20 139 C4
Erinbank Mans BH1 122 B2
Erpingham Rd BH12 121 A3
Esmonde Way BH17 119 C4
Esplanade
Bridport DT6 100 A1
Poole BH13 147 C4
Portland DT5 186 C4
Radipole DT4 167 C2
Essex Ave BH23 91 C1
Essex Rd DT4 167 B2
Essex Sq SP2 213 A1
Estcourt Rd SP1 213 B3
Ethelbert Rd BH21 59 B2
Eton Gdns BH4 121 B2
Ettrick Rd BH13 121 A1
Eucalyptus Ave BH24 54 B1
Euston Gr BH24 55 B3
Evans Cl
Bournemouth BH11 88 C1
St.Leonards BH24 54 A3
Evelyn Mews 1 BH9 89 C1
Evelyn Rd BH9 90 A1
Evening Glade BH22 61 C2
Eventide Homes BH8 90 C1
Everdene Cl BH22 61 B1
Everdene Dr DT4 166 C2
Everdene Rd 2 DT1 135 A4
Everest Rd
Christchurch BH23 124 C4
Weymouth DT4 167 B1
Everetts La 1 DT11 198 B5
Everglades Cl BH22 61 B4
Evergreen Cl BH21 53 A4
Evergreens BH24 54 A3
Evering Ave BH12 88 B1
Evering Gdns BH12 88 B1
Everon Gdns BH25 95 A1
Evershot Rd BH8 90 C1
Eversleigh BH2 121 B1
Everton Rd 15 BA20 27 B2

Evesham Ave BA21 26 C3
Evesham Cl BH7 123 A4
Evesham Ct BH13 121 A1
Exbourne Manor BH1 122 B2
Exbury Dr BH11 88 C3
Excelsior Rd BH14 120 B2
Exeter Cres BH2 121 C2
Exeter Ct 10 BH23 126 A4
Exeter House Specl Sch
SP1 213 B4
Exeter La BH2 121 C1
Exeter Pk Mans BH2 121 C1
Exeter Pk Rd BH2 121 C1
Exeter Rd
Bournemouth BH2 121 C2
4 Swanage BH19 179 B1
Exeter St SP1 213 B2
Exton Rd BH6 123 B4
Eynon Mews BH24 55 A3
Eype Down Rd DT6 99 C3
Eyres Way SP1 213 B2

F

Factory Hill SP8 1 C2
Factory La
Buckland Newton DT2 207 F8
Tatworth & Forton
TA20 202 A8
Factory Rd BH16 118 B3
Fair Lea BH2 121 C1
Fair Mile Rd DT11 210 F8
Fairclose DT4 167 A1
Faircourt 18 BH25 95 A2
Faircross Ave DT4 167 B1
Fairey Cl SP8 5 C2
Fairfax DT6 99 A3
Fairfield
Christchurch BH23 124 A4
Crewkerne TA18 191 E4
Sherborne DT9 30 A4
Fairfield Bglws DT11 212 B2
Fairfield Cl
Christchurch BH23 124 A4
2 Okeford Fitzpaine DT11 197 F6
Wimborne Minster BH21 59 C3
Fairfield Pk DT7 96 B3
Fairfield Rd
Barton on Sea BH25 126 C4
Blandford Forum DT11 212 B1
11 Dorchester DT1 108 A1
Iwerne Courtney or Shroton
DT11 198 E7
Salisbury SP1 213 B4
Wimborne Minster BH21 59 B2
Fairhavon Ct 12 BH5 122 C2
Fairhouse Rd BA22 193 F8
Fairies Dr BH22 61 C2
Fairlane SP7 13 A1
Fairlie BH24 47 C1
Fairlie Pk BH24 47 B1
Fairlight La SO41 95 B4
Fairmead Rd BA21 27 C4
Fairmead Sch BA21 27 C4
Fairmile Par BH23 91 C1
Fairmile Rd BH23 91 C1
Fairoak Way 3 DT8 204 A7
Fairthorn Ct 2 BH2 121 C2
Fairview Cres BH18 87 A3
Fairview Dr BH18 87 A3
Fairview Pk BH14 120 B2
Fairview Rd
Broadstone BH18 87 A3
Salisbury SP1 213 C3
Weymouth DT4 180 B4
Fairway Ave BH14 147 B4
Fairway Dr
Christchurch BH23 123 C3
Wareham Town BH20 142 B3
Fairway The BH25 127 A4
Fairway View BA21 27 C3
Fairways BH22 61 C3
Fairwinds BH13 147 A2
Fairwood Rd BH31 45 A4
Fairy Bridge Wlk 1 SP8 5 C2
Fairy Cres SP8 5 C2
Falcon Dr BH23 125 A3
Falconer Dr BH15 118 C2
Falconsway SP2 213 B1
Falkland Sq 2 BH15 119 B1
Fallows The BH25 95 A3
Fancy Rd BH12 120 A4
Fancy's Row BH20 116 A2
Fantley La SP8 2 A1
Far Ends 18 BH14 120 A2
Faraday Rd SP2 213 A3
Farcroft Rd BH12 120 A3
Farfrae Cres DT1 135 A4
Farley Rd SP1 213 C2
Farm Cl Radipole DT4 167 A3
Ringwood BH24 55 B4
Farm La
Christchurch BH23 125 A3
Salisbury SP2 213 A3
West Lulworth BH20 172 B3
Farm La N BH25 127 A4
Farm La S BH25 127 A4
Farm Rd
Bradford Abbas DT9 28 B1
Ferndown BH22 52 C1
Farmdene Cl BH23 125 B4
Farmer Palmers Farm Pk*
BH16 116 A3
Farmers Wlk 1 BH21 59 A3
Farnham Rd BH12 121 A4
Farr's Orch 5 TA16 191 F7
Farriers Cl BH21 60 A3
Farringdon Cl 2 DT1 134 C4
Farrington BH4 121 B1
Farwell Cl BH23 92 B2
Farwell Rd BH12 88 B1
Faversham
Bournemouth BH2 121 B1
Radipole DT4 167 A3
Fawcett Rd BH25 94 C1
Fawley Gn BH8 90 B2
Fawn Gdns BH25 94 C2
Fellowsmead DT10 20 C1
Felton Cres BH23 125 C4
Felton Ct BH14 119 C3
Felton Rd BH14 119 C3
Fenleigh Cl BH25 95 A1
Fennel Rd BA12 3 A3
Fennel Way BA22 26 B3
Fenton Rd BH6 123 B3
Fenway Cl DT1 108 B1
Fenwick Ct BH8 122 A3
Fern Bank
28 Bournemouth BH2 121 C2
Three Legged Cross BH21 53 A4
Fern Barrow BH12 121 A4
Fern Cl Alderholt SP6 42 B3
Burton BH23 92 B1
Fern Hill SP8 11 A2
Ferncroft Gdns BH10 89 B3
Ferncroft Rd BH10 89 B3
Ferndale Gdns BA21 27 A3
Ferndale Rd
New Milton BH25 95 A3
Radipole DT4 167 B3
Ferndown Forest Golf Club
BH22 52 C1
Ferndown Fst Sch BH22 61 B3
Ferndown Ind Est BH21 60 C4
Ferndown Mid Sch BH22 61 B3
Ferndown Rd DT7 96 B3
Ferndown Upper Sch
BH22 61 A3
Ferne Hollow SP5 188 A8
Fernery Rd BA21 27 C3
Fernglade BH25 95 A2
Fernheath Cl BH11 89 A2
Fernheath Rd BH11 89 A2
Fernhill Ave DT4 167 B3
Fernhill Cl BH17 88 A1
Fernhill Flats 29 BH2 121 C2
Fernhill Gate BH25 95 A2
Fernhill La BH25 95 A2
Fernhill Rd BH25 95 A2
Fernlea Ave BH22 61 B2
Fernlea Cl Ferndown BH22 61 B2
St.Leonards BH24 54 A2
Fernlea Gdns BH22 61 B2
Fernside Ave BH14 119 C2
Fernside Ct BH15 119 C2
Fernside Rd
Bournemouth BH9 121 C4
Ferndown BH22 53 A1
Poole BH15 119 C2
Fernway Cl BH21 60 A2
Fernwood Cl BH24 54 B3
Ferris Ave BH8 90 B1
Ferris Cl BH8 90 B1
Ferris Pl BH8 90 B1
Ferry Rd
Bournemouth BH6 123 C2
Hamworthy BH15 119 A1
Poole BH19 147 A1
Studland BH19 164 A2
Ferry Way BH13 147 A2
Ferrymans Way DT4 180 B3
Feversham Ave BH8 90 C1
Feversham Rd SP1 213 B4
Fiddleford Manor*
DT10 197 F8
Field Barn Dr DT4 167 A3
Field La Gillingham SP8 5 A2
Kington Magna SP8 9 B1
Pen Selwood BA9 1 A2
Field Pl
Barton on Sea BH25 126 B4
Verwood BH31 45 A4
Field View Rd 2 DT11 212 B1
Field Way
Christchurch BH23 93 B1
Corfe Mullen BH21 86 C4
Field's Cl 1 DT11 210 C3
Fieldfare Cl DT3 152 B2
Fielding Rd BA21 27 C3
Fieldings The SP8 10 B2
Fields Barn DT2 156 C3
Fields Mead DT6 100 A4
Fields Oak DT11 212 B1
Fields The BA12 3 A3
Fieldway BH24 55 B4
Fifehead Hill SP8 20 C4
Filbridge Rise DT10 35 B1
Filford La DT6 67 C4
Filleul Rd BH20 115 C1
Finches The DT3 152 B2
Finchfield Ave BH11 88 C3
Finchley Rd SP2 213 A3
Findlay Pl BH19 178 C2
Fineshade 7 BH13 147 C4
Fippenny Hollow 3
DT11 197 F5
Fir Ave
Holton Heath BH20 116 A2
New Milton BH25 95 A1
Fir Cl BH22 53 A2
Fir Dr DT3 153 B2
Fir Tree Cl
Dorchester DT1 107 B1
Netherbury DT6 68 A3
St.Leonards BH24 53 C1
Fir Tree Hill SP6 42 B3
Fir Tree La BH23 93 B1
Fir Vale Rd BH1 121 C2
Firbank Rd BH9 122 A4
Firch La DT6 101 A3
Firecrest Cl DT3 152 B2
Firmain Rd BH12 88 B1
Firs Glen Rd
Bournemouth BH9 121 C4
Ferndown BH22 53 A1
Verwood BH31 45 A3
Firs La BH14 147 A4
Firs The BH1 122 A2
Firshill BH23 125 C4
Firside Rd BH21 86 B2
First Cliff Wlk 1 DT6 100 A1
First Marine Ave BH25 126 C4
Firsway BH16 118 B4
Firtree Cres SO41 95 C2
Fisher's Cl DT11 212 B1
Fisher's La TA17 191 A7
Fisherbridge Rd DT3 168 B4
Fisherman's Ave BH5 123 A2
Fisherman's Wlk BH5 123 A2
Fishermans Cl DT3 166 B3
Fishermans Rd BH15 119 B1
Fishers Cl DT9 14 C1
Fishers Pl DT2 170 A4
Fisherton Island SP2 213 A3
Fisherton Manor Mid Sch
SP2 213 A3
Fisherton St SP2 213 A3
Fisherway La TA19 191 A5
Fishey La SP7 36 C3
Fishpond Bottom Rd
DT6 202 D1
Fishweir Fields 1 DT6 68 C1
Fishweir La DT6 68 C1
Fitzharris Ave BH9 122 A4
Fitzmaurice Rd BH23 123 C4
Fitzpain Cl BH22 61 B1
Fitzpain Rd BH22 61 B1
Fitzwilliam Cl BH11 88 C3
Fitzworth Ave BH16 118 B2
Five Acres DT6 97 A4
Five Marys (Tumuli)*
DT2 156 B3
Fiveways Specl Sch
BA21 27 C3
Flaghead BH13 147 C3
Flaghead Chine Rd
BH13 147 C3
Flaghead Rd BH13 147 C4
Flambard Ave BH23 92 A1
Flambard Rd BH14 120 B2
Flanders Cl DT10 21 A1
Flax La DT9 28 C4
Flax Way BA21 26 C3
Flaxfield Dr 15 TA18 191 F4
Flaxfield Rd DT8 204 D4
Flazen Cl BH11 88 B2
Fleet Ct DT3 166 C2
Fleet La DT3 166 A3
Fleet Rd DT3 165 C3
Fleet St DT8 204 D4
Fleet View DT4 180 B4
Fleet's Cnr BH17 119 A4
Fleetpoint Bsns Ctr
BH15 119 A3
Fleets Est BH15 119 A3
Fleets La BH15 119 B3
Fleetsbridge Bsns Ctr
BH17 119 A4
Fleetwood Ct BH15 119 B4
Fletcher Cl BH10 89 B2
Fletcher Rd BH10 89 B2
Flood La DT6 100 B2
Floral Farm BH21 60 A1
Florence Rd
Bournemouth BH5 122 C2
Dorchester DT1 134 C4
Poole BH14 120 B2
Florin Mall 7 BH7 122 C2
Floriston Gdns BH25 95 B2
Flower Ct 10 BH21 59 B2
Flowers Dro BH16 84 B2
Flushing Mdw BA21 28 A3
Folke La DT9 31 A1
Folkstone Rd SP2 213 A1
Folly Cl SP2 213 A1
Folly Farm La BH24 54 C3
Folly Fields BA21 27 B4
Folly La
Blandford St Mary DT11 211 B1
Gillingham SP8 10 B3
Kington Magna SP8 9 C2
Nether Compton DT9 28 C4
Wareham BH20 142 C2
Wool BH20 140 A1
Folly Mill Gdns DT6 100 B3
Folly Mill La DT6 100 B3
Folly The DT2 207 D4
Font La BA22 193 B7
Font Villas BA22 193 B7
Fontmell Magna St Andrews
CE Sch SP7 37 C3
Fontmell Rd BH18 87 B2
Foot's Hill SP7 24 A4
Footners La BH23 92 B1
Ford Cl BH22 61 C4
Ford Down La DT2 208 A7
Ford La Corscombe DT2 205 B7
Ferndown BH22 62 A4
Forde Abbey* TA20 202 D8
Forde Pk BA21 26 C4
Fordhay BA22 192 E7
Fordingbridge Rd SP6 42 B4
Fordington Gdns 16
DT1 108 A1
Fore St Evershot DT2 206 A7
Thorncombe TA20 202 E6
Forehill Cl DT3 168 A4
Foreland Cl BH23 91 B2
Foreland Rd BH16 118 B2
Forest Cl
Christchurch BH23 93 B1
Verwood BH24 45 C2
Forest Ct BH25 95 A1
Forest Ct Hills 6 BH24 55 C3
Forest Edge Dr BH24 53 C3
Forest Edge Rd BH20 142 C4
Forest Hill BA20 27 A1
Forest La
Corfe Castle BH20 162 C1
Verwood BH31 45 A4
Forest Links Rd BH21 52 B1
Forest Oak Dr BH25 95 A3
Forest Pines BH25 95 A2
Forest Rd
Ferndown BH22 53 A2
Poole BH13 121 A1
Forest Rise BH23 93 B1
Forest View
Crossways DT2 137 B3
New Milton BH25 94 B3
Forest View Cl BH9 90 A1
Forest View Dr BH21 61 A3
Forest View Rd BH9 90 A1
Forest Way
Christchurch BH23 93 B1
Ferndown BH21 61 A3
Forestlake Ave BH24 55 C3
Forestside Gdns BH24 47 C1
Forestside The BH31 45 C3
Forge End SP8 10 B1
Forge La
East Chinnock BA22 192 E8
Zennor BA12 1 C2
Forsters La DT6 69 A1
Forsyth Gdns BH10 89 B1
Fort Cumberland Pl
BH15 118 B1
Fortescue Rd
Bournemouth BH3 122 A3
Poole BH12 120 B3
Fortuneswell DT5 186 C4
Forty Foot Way DT6 100 A1
Forum Sch The DT11 198 B6
Foss Way TA17 191 C8
Fosse Cl BA21 26 C4
Fosse Way BA21 26 C4
Fossett Way 4 DT4 180 A4
Fosters DT9 30 B3
Fosters Hill DT9 196 B5
Fosters Mdws 2 DT11 210 C3
Fosters Spring BH16 84 B1
Fotherby Cres SP1 213 C4
Foundry Cl DT6 100 A4
Foundry Knapp DT6 100 A4
Foundry La DT6 100 B3
Foundry Sq 13 TA18 191 F4
Fountain Mead 11 SP7 12 C2
Fountain Way BH23 124 A3
Four Acres DT5 186 C2
Four Wells Rd BH21 60 A4
Fouracre Cl DT6 100 B4
Fourgates Rd 6 DT1 107 C1
Fourth Cliff Wlk DT6 100 A1
Fowler's Hill SP1 213 C2
Fowler's Rd SP1 213 B2
Fox Cl DT6 69 A1
Fox La BH21 60 B3
Fox La Terr DT10 35 A1
Fox Mdws 16 TA18 191 F5
Foxbury BH20 139 B4
Foxbury Rd
St Leonards BH24 62 C4
St.Leonards BH24 54 A1
Foxcote 8 BA20 26 C1
Foxcote Gdns BH25 94 C2
Foxcroft Dr BH21 60 A3
Foxes Cl BH31 45 A3
Foxglove Cl
Christchurch BH23 125 B4
Gillingham SP8 5 C1
Foxglove Pl BH25 95 B2
Foxglove Way
Radipole DT3 152 C1
Yeovil BA22 26 B3
Foxgloves BH16 118 A4
Foxhill Cl 12 BH19 179 A1
Foxhills BH31 45 B3
Foxhills Cres BH16 84 B2
Foxhills Dr BH16 84 B2
Foxhills La BH16 84 B1
Foxhills Rd BH16 84 B2
Foxholes 1 BH6 123 C2
Foxholes Rd
Bournemouth BH6 123 C2
Poole BH15 119 C3
Foxs Cl DT9 196 B5
Foxwell La TA18 192 C7
Foxwood Ave BH23 124 C3
Foyle Hill SP7 12 B1
Framerville Rd BH20 139 C4
Frampton Cl BH25 95 B3
Frampton Pl BH24 55 B4
Frampton Rd
Bournemouth BH9 122 A4
16 Pimperne DT11 199 D4
Frances Ct 13 BH23 126 A4
Frances Rd BH1 122 B2
Francesca Ct 14 BH23 124 C4
Francesca Grange 13
BH23 124 C4
Francesca Lodge 1
BH23 124 C3
Franchise St DT4 167 B1
Francis Ave BH11 88 B2
Francis Ave Ind Est BH11 88 B2
Francis Rd Poole BH12 120 C3
Weymouth DT4 167 A1
Francis Way SP2 213 B1
Frank Wareham Cottage
Homes The BH9 90 A2
Frankland Cres BH14 120 C2
Franklin Cl DT4 167 A1
Franklin Rd
Bournemouth BH9 90 A2
New Milton BH25 95 B2
Weymouth DT4 167 A2
Franklyn Cl BH16 118 A4
Franks Way BH12 120 A4
Frankston Rd BH6 123 B2
Fraser Ave DT4 166 C1
Fraser Ct BH25 94 C2
Fraser Rd BH12 120 C4
Freame Way SP8 5 B1
Freda Rd BH23 123 C3
Frederica Rd BH9 121 C4
Freedom Ave BA21 27 A3
Freemans Cl BH21 60 A3
Freemans La BH21 60 A3
Freemantle Rd DT4 166 C1
Freesia Cl DT3 152 C1
Fremington Ct 16 BH25 95 A2
French Mill La
Cann SP7 23 C4
Shaftesbury SP7 12 C1
French Mill Rise SP7 12 C1
French Rd BH17 87 A1
French's Farm Rd
BH16 117 A4
Frensham Cl BH10 89 C2
Freshwater Cl 8 DT5 186 C1
Freshwater Dr BH15 118 B2
Freshwater Rd BH23 125 B3
Friar Waddon Rd
Chickerell DT3 151 C4
Radipole DT3 152 A4
Friar's Orch 9 SP1 213 B2
Friars Ave BA21 26 C3
Friars Cl 2 DT1 135 B4
Friars Gate BH23 125 B3
Friars Moor DT10 35 B1
Friars Rd BH23 125 A3
Friars Wlk BH25 127 A4
Friary Hill DT1 108 A1
Friary La
Dorchester DT1 108 A1
Salisbury SP1 213 B2
Friary The SP1 213 B2
Friday's Heron BH21 40 A4
Frinton Ct 6 BH14 120 A2
Fritham Gdns BH8 90 B2
Frizzel's Hill DT10 196 F4
Frobisher Ave BH12 88 C1
Frobisher Cl
Christchurch BH23 124 C3
3 Ringwood BH24 47 C1
Frog La
Dinnington TA17 191 B8
Fordingbridge SP6 43 A4
Iwerne Courtney or Shroton
DT11 198 F7
Motcombe SP7 12 B4
Frogham Hill SP6 43 C3
Frogmore La DT2 71 C4
Frome Ave BH20 139 C1
Frome Bridge* DT2 110 B1
Frome La DT2 72 C4
Frome Rd BH20 142 B2
Frome Terr DT1 108 A1
Frome Valley Rd DT2 137 B3
Frome View
Bradford Peverell DT2 107 A3
Maiden Newton DT2 73 A4
Front La BH21 56 B3
Front St East Stour SP8 10 C2
Portesham DT3 132 A1
Froom's La BH20 81 B1
Frost Rd BH11 88 C2
Froud Way BH21 86 B2
Froxfield Rd DT11 212 B2
Fry's Cl DT3 150 A4
Fry's La DT2 75 A4
Fryer Cl BH11 89 A3
Fryers Copse BH21 60 B3
Fryers Rd BH21 52 C4
Frys Cl BH16 84 B2
Fudge Hill DT2 205 A8
Fulbrooks Cl DT6 100 B4
Fulbrooks La DT6 100 B4
Fulmar Rd BH23 125 A3
Fulwood Ave BH11 88 C3
Furge Gr BA8 19 A2
Furge La BA8 19 A2
Furland Rd 6 TA18 191 F4
Furlands DT5 186 C2
Furlong La DT9 17 A2
Furlong The BH24 55 A4
Furlongs The DT9 30 A4
Furnell Rd BH15 119 B1
Furze Croft BH25 95 A1
Furze Hill Dr BH14 120 B1
Furze The 9 BA20 26 C1
Furzebrook Cl BH17 87 C2
Furzebrook Rd BH20 161 A2
Furzehill BH21 50 C1

Furzelands Rd
Verwood BH21 45 A1
Verwood BH21 53 A4
Furzey Rd BH16 118 A3
Furzy Cl DT3 168 A4

G

Gabriel Gn 1 DT1 135 A4
Gainsborough DT9 17 B1
Gainsborough Ave BH25 95 A3
Gainsborough Ct 11 BH5 123 A3
Gainsborough Dr DT9 29 C3
Gainsborough Hill DT9 30 B2
Gainsborough Rd
Bournemouth BH7 122 C4
St.Leonards BH24 54 A3
Gainsborough Way BA21 28 A4
Gale Cres DT6 100 B3
Gales Hill DT2 207 E7
Gallop Way BH12 121 B4
Gallop's La BH20 83 B1
Galloway Rd BH15 118 B2
Gallows Cnr
Iwerne Courtney or Shroton DT11 36 C1
Milton Abbas DT11 209 D3
Gallows Dr BH22 61 C1
Gallows Hill Arne BH20 161 B2
Owermoigne DT2 155 B3
Gallwey Rd DT4 180 B4
Galton Ave BH23 123 C3
Gannetts Pk BH19 179 A2
Garden Cl Bridport DT6 100 B4
Litton Cheney DT2 103 A1
New Milton BH25 95 A1
Garden Ct BH1 122 B3
Garden House 17 BH1 122 A2
Garden Wlk BH22 61 C4
Garden-Lane BH24 54 A2
Gardens Cres BH14 147 A4
Gardens Ct 7 BH15 119 C2
Gardens Rd BH14 147 A4
Gardenside 1 DT6 97 A4
Gardner Ct BH23 123 C4
Gardner Rd
Christchurch BH23 123 C4
Ringwood BH24 55 B3
Garfield Ave
Bournemouth BH1 122 B3
Dorchester DT1 134 C4
Garland Cres DT1 135 A4
Garland Rd BH15 119 B2
Garlands La DT11 197 D4
Garrett Rd BA20 26 C2
Garsdale Cl BH11 89 A3
Garston Hill DT3 166 B3
Gartells 1 DT10 197 A4
Garth Cl BH24 53 C2
Garth Rd BH9 90 A1
Gas La
Hinton St George TA17 191 C7
Salisbury SP2 213 A3
Gascoigne's La SP7 12 C1
Gascoyne La DT2 107 A3
Gashay La EX13 202 E3
Gasper St BA12 1 B3
Gassons La DT6 66 A2
Gate Cl EX13 202 A3
Gatemore Rd DT2 138 C1
Gateway The BH13 120 C2
Gawthorne Dr SP2 213 A1
Gaydon Rise BH11 88 C2
Gaza Rd BH20 139 B4
Gazelle Rd BA20 26 C2
Geelong Cl DT3 152 C1
Geneva Ave BH6 123 B3
Gent Cl DT11 212 C2
George St Bridport DT6 100 B1
Salisbury SP2 213 A3
Sherborne DT9 30 A3
George St (South) 9 SP2 213 A3
Georges Cl DT6 97 A4
Georges Mews BH21 86 B4
Georgian Cl BH24 55 B4
Georgian Way BH10 89 C2
Georgina Cl BH12 121 B4
Georgina Talbot House BH12 121 A4
Gerald Rd BH3 122 A3
Germaine Cl BH23 125 C4
Gerrards Gn DT8 204 D4
Gervis Cres BH14 120 A2
Gervis Pl BH2 121 C2
Gervis Rd BH1 122 A2
Giant's Grave* DT2 209 A4
Gibbs Gn BH16 84 B1
Gibbs La DT6 66 B1
Gibbs Marsh Trading Est DT10 20 A2
Gibson Rd BH17 119 C4
Giddy Gn La BH20 139 C1
Giddy Gn Rd BH20 139 C1
Giddylake BH21 59 B3
Gifle View 2 DT9 194 D8
Gigant St SP1 213 B2
Gigg La SP8 8 C2
Gilbert Cl SP6 42 B3
Gilbert Ct 5 BH23 124 A4
Gilbert Rd
Bournemouth BH1 122 B3
Gilbert Rd *continued*
Swanage BH19 179 A1
Gilbert Way SP1 213 C4
Giles Cl DT2 107 A3
Giles's La
Bishop's Caundle DT9 196 A7
Morden BH20 83 B2
Gillam Rd BH10 89 B3
Gillett Rd BH12 121 B4
Gillingham Cl BH9 90 B2
Gillingham CP Sch SP8 5 C1
Gillingham Milton Prim Sch SP8 5 C3
Gillingham Mus* SP8 5 C1
Gillingham Sch SP8 6 A1
Gillingham Sta SP8 5 C1
Gillion Ct 2 BH23 124 C3
Gipsy La DT6 68 C1
Gipsy's Dro DT10 197 C7
Girt La DT2 205 F7
Glacis DT5 187 A4
Gladdis Rd BH11 88 C2
Glade The BH24 54 A3
Gladelands Cl BH18 86 C2
Gladelands Mobile Home Pk BH22 61 C4
Gladelands Way BH18 86 C2
Gladstone Cl
Bridport DT6 100 C4
Christchurch BH23 124 B3
2 Radipole DT3 152 C1
Gladstone Rd
Bournemouth BH7 122 C3
Poole BH12 120 B3
Gladstone Rd E BH7 122 C3
Gladstone Rd W BH1 122 C3
Glamis Ave BH10 89 C3
Glastonbury Ct BA21 26 C3
Gleadowe Ave BH23 123 C3
Glebe Cl
Abbotsbury DT3 149 B4
Bridport DT6 100 B3
Maiden Newton DT2 72 C4
Osmington DT3 169 A4
8 Thornford DT9 194 D8
Weymouth DT4 167 B1
Glebe Cottage* DT2 169 C3
Glebe Ct 4 DT11 37 C1
Glebe Gdns SP7 12 A4
Glebe Rd BH16 84 B1
Glebe The
3 Durweston DT11 198 E3
3 Iwerne Minster DT11 37 C1
Glebe Way DT2 136 B2
Glebefields DT2 106 C4
Glebeford Cl DT2 155 C4
Glebeland Cl DT2 136 A4
Glebeland La DT6 65 C4
Glebelands 6 TA16 191 F7
Glen Ave DT4 167 B1
Glen Cl BH25 126 B4
Glen Fern Rd BH1 122 A2
Glen Rd
Bournemouth BH5 122 C2
Poole BH14 120 A2
Glen Spey BH25 95 B1
Glen The BH12 120 B3
Glenair Ave BH14 120 A2
Glenair Cres BH14 120 A2
Glenair Rd BH14 120 A2
Glenavon BH25 95 B1
Glenavon Rd BH23 93 C1
Glencoe Rd
Bournemouth BH7 122 C4
Poole BH12 120 B3
Glendale Ave BH22 61 C3
Glendale Cl
Christchurch BH23 91 B2
Wimborne Minster BH21 59 B3
Glendale Cres SP1 213 C2
Glendale Ct BH23 91 B2
Glendale Rd BH6 124 A2
Glendinning Ave DT4 167 B3
Glendon Ave BH10 89 B3
Glendrive BH25 126 B4
Gleneagles BH23 123 C3
Gleneagles Ave BH14 120 B1
Gleneagles Cl BH22 61 C3
Glenferness Ave BH3 121 B3
Glengariff Rd BH14 120 B2
Glengarry BH25 95 B1
Glengarry Way BH23 125 B3
Glenives Cl BH24 54 A2
Glenmeadows Dr BH10 89 A3
Glenmoor (Girls) Sch BH10 89 B1
Glenmoor Cl BH10 89 B1
Glenmoor Rd
Bournemouth BH9 121 C4
Ferndown BH22 61 B2
Glenmore Rd
Salisbury SP1 213 C4
Weymouth DT4 167 A2
Glenmount Dr BH14 120 A2
Glennie Way DT3 166 B2
Glenroyd Gdns BH6 123 C2
Glenside BH25 126 A4
Glenthorne Ave BA21 27 B4
Glenville Cl BH23 94 A1
Glenville Gdns BH10 89 B1
Glenville Rd
Bournemouth BH10 89 B1
Christchurch BH23 94 A1
Yeovil BA21 27 C3
Glenwood Cl BH22 53 A1
Glenwood La BH22 53 A1
Glenwood Rd
Ferndown BH22 53 A1
Glenwood Rd *continued*
Verwood BH31 45 A3
Glenwood Way BH22 53 A1
Glissons BH22 61 A1
Globe Cl 3 BH19 178 C1
Globe La BH15 119 B1
Globe Orch TA18 192 C6
Gloucester Cl DT3 166 C2
Gloucester Mews DT4 167 B2
Gloucester Rd
Bournemouth BH7 122 C3
8 Dorchester DT1 107 C1
Poole BH12 120 C3
Gloucester St DT4 167 B2
Glovers Cl 2 DT9 17 B1
Glue Hill DT10 197 C8
Glyde Path Rd DT1 108 A1
Glyn Pl SP7 24 B3
Glynville Cl BH21 60 A4
Glynville Ct BH21 60 A4
Glynville Rd BH21 60 A4
Goathill Rd DT9 17 B1
Goathorn Cl BH16 118 B2
God's Blessing La BH21 51 A2
Godley Rd SP2 213 B1
Godlingston Manor* BH19 178 C3
Godmanston Cl BH17 88 A1
Godolphin Sch SP1 213 C2
Godolphin Sch Douglas House SP1 213 C3
Godshill Cl BH8 90 B2
Gold Hill
Child Okeford DT11 198 B8
Shaftesbury SP7 12 C1
Gold St DT10 33 B4
Goldcrest Cl DT3 152 B2
Goldcroft BA21 27 B3
Goldcroft Ave DT4 167 B3
Goldcroft Rd DT4 167 B2
Golden Gates BH13 147 A2
Golden Hill DT10 32 C1
Golden Sands BH13 147 A2
Goldenleas Ct BH11 88 B2
Goldenleas Dr BH11 88 B2
Goldenstones Pool & Leisure Ctr BA20 27 B2
Goldfinch Cl BH25 94 C1
Goldfinch Rd BH17 118 C4
Golding's La DT9 17 B1
Golf Links Rd
Broadstone BH18 87 A3
Ferndown BH22 61 C2
Goliath Rd BH15 118 B1
Good Rd BH12 120 B4
Goodwin's La BH20 83 B1
Goose Hill DT3 149 C4
Gooseacre La BA22 26 B1
Gordon Cres 1 DT4 166 C1
Gordon Ct BH4 121 B2
Gordon Mount BH23 126 A4
Gordon Rd
Bournemouth BH1 122 B2
Christchurch BH23 126 A4
Poole BH12 121 A3
6 Swanage BH19 179 A1
Wimborne Minster BH21 59 C2
Yeovil BA21 27 C3
Gordon Rd S BH12 121 A3
Gordon Way BH23 92 B1
Gordon's La DT9 195 A8
Gore Cross DT6 68 C1
Gore Cross Way 5 DT6 68 C1
Gore Grange BH25 94 C1
Gore Hill BH20 142 C4
Gore La DT6 68 C1
Gore Rd BH25 94 C1
Gore Rd Ind Est BH25 94 C1
Gorey Ave BH12 88 B1
Gorleston Rd BH12 120 C3
Gorley Lynch SP6 43 C2
Gorley Rd BH24 47 C1
Gorse Cl New Milton BH25 95 B2
St.Leonards BH24 53 C2
Gorse Hill Cl BH15 119 C3
Gorse Hill Cres BH15 119 C3
Gorse Hill Rd BH15 119 C3
Gorse La BH16 118 B4
Gorse Rd BH21 86 B3
Gorsecliff Ct 7 BH5 122 B2
Gorsecliff Rd BH10 89 B1
Gorsefield Rd BH25 95 A2
Gorseland Ct BH22 61 C2
Gort Rd
Bournemouth BH11 89 A2
Poole BH17 87 A1
Gosling Cl BH17 119 C4
Gough Cl 11 TA16 191 F7
Gough Cres BH17 87 A1
Goughs Cl DT10 35 A1
Gould's Hill
Radipole DT3 152 A4
Winterborne St Martin DT2 133 C2
Goulds Hill Cl DT3 152 A4
Gover Cl BH20 143 A1
Gower Rd SP7 13 A1
Grafton Ave DT4 167 A3
Grafton Cl
Bournemouth BH3 122 A4
Christchurch BH23 124 B3
Grafton Rd BH3 122 A3
Grammar Sch La BH21 59 A2
Granby Cl DT4 166 C2
Granby Ind Est DT4 166 C2
Granby Rd BH9 90 A2
Granby Way DT4 167 A3
Grand Ave BH6 123 B2
Grand Par 20 BH15 119 A1
Grange BH21 50 C1
Grange Arch* BH20 175 B4
Grange Ct 16 BH1 122 A2
Grange Gdns
Poole BH12 120 C4
Salisbury SP1 213 C3
Grange Hill BH20 160 B1
Grange La DT8 203 D5
Grange Pk 1 DT9 194 D8
Grange Rd
Bournemouth BH6 123 B2
Broadstone BH18 87 A2
Christchurch BH23 125 A4
Church Knowle BH20 160 B2
Radipole DT4 167 C3
St.Leonards BH24 53 C1
Grange Rd Bsns Ctr BH23 125 A4
Grange Sch The BH23 124 C4
Grangecroft Rd 5 DT5 186 C2
Grangewood Hall BH21 59 B3
Grans Barrow (Long Barrow)* SP6 190 E6
Grant's Ave BH1 122 B3
Grantham Rd BH1 122 C3
Grantley Rd 16 BH5 122 C2
Grants Cl BH1 122 C3
Granville Gdns 6 SP7 12 C2
Granville Pl 32 BH1 121 C2
Granville Rd
Bournemouth BH5 123 A3
Poole BH12 120 A3
Weymouth DT4 167 B1
Granville Way DT9 30 B4
Grasmere Cl
Christchurch BH23 91 B2
1 Salisbury SP2 213 A1
Grasmere Gdns BH25 95 A3
Grasmere Rd
Bournemouth BH5 123 A2
Poole BH13 147 A2
Radipole DT3 167 B3
Grass Royal BA21 27 C3
Grass Royal Jun Sch BA21 27 C3
Gravel Hill BH18 87 B3
Gravel La
Charlton Marshall DT11 211 C7
Ringwood BH24 55 A4
Gray Cl BH17 119 C4
Gray's Yd 23 BH15 119 B1
Graycot Cl BH10 89 B3
Grays DT4 167 A3
Grays Cl SP7 12 A4
Grayson Ct BH22 61 C2
Great Cnr BA21 26 C3
Great Down La DT10 21 A2
Great George St DT4 167 B2
Great Head La DT2 206 F7
Great Hill BA9 1 A2
Great La SP7 12 C1
Great Owens Dr BH20 142 B3
Great Pit La BA22 15 A3
Great Western Rd 11 DT1 107 C1
Great Western Terr
Radipole DT4 167 B3
Yeovil BA21 27 C3
Greaves Cl BH10 89 B2
Grebe Cl
Broadstone BH17 118 C4
2 Chickerell DT3 166 B3
Christchurch BH23 125 A3
Green Acres BH23 124 C4
Green Acres Cl BH24 54 C3
Green Bottom BH21 60 A4
Green Cl
Bere Regis BH20 81 A1
Bradpole DT6 100 C4
Charlton Marshall DT11 211 D6
Poole BH15 119 B1
Sturminster Newton DT10 35 B1
Green Dr SP6 42 B3
Green Gdns BH15 119 B1
Green La Ashmore SP5 39 B4
Barton on Sea BH25 127 A4
Bournemouth BH10 89 B2
Bridport DT6 100 C3
Chickerell DT3 166 C3
Crossways DT2 137 B3
East Chinnock BA22 192 E8
Ferndown BH22 61 A1
Hooke DT8 205 C2
Kington Magna SP8 9 B2
New Milton BH25 94 C4
Ringwood BH24 55 B2
Stour Provost SP7 22 B2
Sturminster Marshall DT11 56 A3
Tatworth & Forton TA20 202 A7
West Coker BA22 193 B8
Weymouth DT4 180 C4
Green Loaning 5 BH23 124 C3
Green Mead BA21 26 C3
Green Pit Knapp DT6 65 A1
Green Pk BH1 122 B2
Green Rd
Bournemouth BH9 122 A4
Poole BH15 119 B1
Green St TA17 191 D7
Green The
3 Hazelbury Bryan DT10 197 A4
Mappowder DT10 196 E1
Puddletown DT2 78 A1
Salisbury SP1 213 C3
Sherborne DT9 30 A3
Green's Ct 7 SP1 213 B2
Greenacre
Barton on Sea BH25 127 A4
Charminster DT2 107 C3
Greenacre Cl BH16 118 B3
Greenacres BH13 121 A2
Greenacres Cl BH10 89 C3
Greenclose La BH21 59 B2
Greencroft St SP1 213 B3
Greenfield Gdns BH25 127 A4
Greenfield Rd
3 Charlton Marshall DT11 211 D6
Poole BH15 119 C4
Greenfields BH12 120 C4
Greenfinch Cl BH17 86 C1
Greenfinch Wlk BH24 55 C3
Greenford CE Prim Sch DT2 72 C4
Greenford La
Compton Valence DT2 104 B4
Frome Vauchurch DT2 72 C4
Greenham La TA18 203 B7
Greenhayes
Broadstone BH18 87 B1
Charmouth DT6 96 C4
2 Okeford Fitzpaine DT11 197 F5
Greenhays Rise BH21 59 B3
Greenhill
Blandford Forum DT11 212 B2
Radipole DT4 167 C3
Sherborne DT9 30 A3
Greenhill Cl BH21 59 B3
Greenhill La BH21 59 B3
Greenhill Rd
Wimborne Minster BH21 59 B3
Yeovil BA21 27 C4
Greenhill Terr 4 DT5 186 C4
Greenings Ct DT1 108 A1
Greens Cross Dr 4 DT8 204 C4
Greenside Ct BH25 127 A3
Greensleeves Ave BH18 87 A3
Greensome Dr BH22 61 C3
Greenway
10 Child Okeford DT11 198 C7
Lyme Regis DT7 96 A3
Greenway Cl DT3 167 B4
Greenway Cres BH16 118 A4
Greenway La DT11 198 B7
Greenway Rd DT3 152 B1
Greenways
Christchurch BH23 125 C4
Easton/Weston DT5 186 C2
Greenways Ave BH8 90 B2
Greenways Ct BH22 61 C2
Greenwood Ave
Ferndown BH22 61 C3
Poole BH14 147 B4
Salisbury SP1 213 C3
Greenwood Copse BH24 54 A2
Greenwood Rd
Bournemouth BH9 121 C4
Yeovil BA21 26 C4
Greenwood Way BH24 54 A2
Greenwoods 32 BH25 95 A1
Grenfell Rd BH9 89 C2
Grenville Cl BH24 47 C1
Grenville Ct
6 Bournemouth BH4 121 B2
11 Poole BH15 119 B1
Grenville Rd BH21 59 B2
Gresham Rd BH9 90 A1
Grexy Cross DT2 205 E7
Grey Mare & Her Colts (Long Barrow) The* DT3 131 B2
Greyfriars Cl SP1 213 B2
Greys Bridge* DT1 108 B1
Greys Rd 7 TA16 191 F7
Greystoke Ave BH11 88 C3
Greystones Cl DT2 137 B3
Gribb View TA20 202 E6
Griffin Ct 12 BH21 59 B2
Griffins Ct 7 SP2 213 B3
Griffiths Gdns BH10 89 A3
Grimsey La SP8 4 C4
Grosvener Ct 19 BH1 122 A2
Grosvenor Cl BH24 53 C3
Grosvenor Cres DT1 135 A4
Grosvenor Ct
2 Bournemouth BH1 122 B2
Christchurch BH23 126 A4
Grosvenor Gdns BH1 122 C2
Grosvenor Rd
Bournemouth BH4 121 B2
Dorchester DT1 135 A4
Easton/Weston DT5 186 C2
Radipole DT4 167 B3
Shaftesbury SP7 12 C2
Stalbridge DT10 33 B4
Swanage BH19 179 B1
Grove Ave
Radipole DT4 167 B3
Yeovil BA20 27 A3
Grove Cty Inf Sch DT5 187 A3
Grove La
Abbotsbury DT3 149 A3
Bothenhampton DT6 101 A3
Portesham DT3 150 C3
Stalbridge DT10 33 B4
Grove La Cl DT10 33 B4
Grove Mans 21 BH1 122 A2
Grove Orch 3 DT6 128 A4
Grove Rd
Barton on Sea BH25 127 A4
Bournemouth BH1 122 A2
Burton Bradstock DT6 128 A4
Easton/Weston DT5 187 A3

Grove Rd *continued*
Poole BH12 120 A3
Wimborne Minster BH21 59 B2
Grove Rd E BH23 124 A4
Grove Rd W BH23 123 C4
Grove The
Bournemouth BH9 89 C2
Christchurch BH23 91 C1
Dorchester DT1 107 C1
Ferndown BH22 61 B2
Verwood BH31 45 B3
Groveley Bsns Ctr BH23 124 C3
Groveley Rd
Bournemouth BH4 121 A1
Christchurch BH23 124 C3
Grovely Ave BH5 122 C2
Grower Gdns BH11 89 A2
Grugs La BH21 40 A4
Gryphon Leisure Ctr DT9 30 A4
Gryphon Sch The DT9 30 B4
Guard Ave BA22 26 B3
Guernsey Rd BH12 88 B1
Guernsey St 11 DT5 186 C4
Guest Ave BH12 121 A3
Guest Cl BH12 121 A3
Guest Rd BH16 118 A4
Guilder La SP1 213 B3
Guildford Ct BH4 121 B2
Guildhall Ct 4 BH15 119 A1
Guildhall Mus★ BH15 119 A1
Guildhill Rd BH6 123 C2
Guinevere Cl BA21 26 C4
Gulliver Cl BH14 147 B4
Gulliver Ct 1 BH21 59 B3
Gullivers Orch DT6 101 B2
Gulway Mead 7 TA20 202 A8
Gundry La DT6 100 B3
Gundry Rd DT6 100 C4
Gunn La 3 DT11 198 B5
Gunners La BA22 26 B3
Gunville Cres BH9 90 A2
Gunville Down Rd DT11 199 F4
Gunville La
East Coker BA22 193 D8
Hermitage DT2 195 C2
Gunville Rd DT11 199 F4
Gurjun Cl BH16 118 A4
Gurney Rd BH21 86 C3
Gussage Rd BH12 120 C4
Gwenlyn Rd BH16 118 B3
Gwynne Rd BH12 120 C3
Gyllas Way SP8 5 C2
Gypshayes BH19 178 A1
Gypsy La
Easton/Weston DT5 186 C2
Ringwood BH24 55 B4
2 Weymouth DT4 167 B1

H

Haarlem Mews BH23 124 B4
Hackney DT2 205 A7
Hadden Rd BH8 122 B4
Haddon La DT10 19 C1
Haddons Dr BH21 52 C3
Hadley Way BH18 86 C2
Hadow Rd BH10 89 B2
Hadrian Cl BH22 61 B1
Hadrian Way BH21 86 C4
Hahnemann Rd BH2 121 C1
Haig Ave BH13 120 C1
Haimes La SP7 12 C2
Hainault Dr BH31 45 B3
Haines La DT8 203 A5
Hains La DT10 20 C3
Haking Rd BH23 124 B4
Halcyon Ct BH15 119 B3
Hale Ave BH25 95 A1
Hale Gdns BH25 95 A1
Hales Mdw BA21 14 A2
Halewood Way BH23 123 C4
Half Acre La DT8 204 C4
Half Acres DT9 30 A3
Half Hide Down SP5 188 B3
Half Moon St DT9 30 A3
Halfpenny La SP5 39 B4
Halifax Way BH23 125 A4
Hall Rd BH11 88 C2
Hallet Ct DT7 96 A3
Hallet Gdns BA20 27 B2
Halls Rd BH16 84 A1
Hallum Cl SP1 213 C4
Halsey Gn DT2 196 B3
Halstock Cl DT3 168 B4
Halstock Cres BH17 87 B1
Halter Path BH15 118 C2
Halter Rise BH21 60 B3
Halton Cl BH23 93 A4
Halves Cotts BH20 177 A4
Halves La BA22 193 B8
Ham La Ferndown BH21 60 C2
5 Gillingham SP8 6 A1
Marnhull DT10 20 B2
Trent DT9 15 A1
Ham Mdw DT10 20 B2
Hamble Rd BH15 120 A3
Hambledon Cl
Blandford Forum DT11 212 C1
Todber DT10 21 B2
Hambledon Gdns
Blandford Forum DT11 212 C1
Bournemouth BH6 123 B3
Hambledon Hill (Hill Fort)★ DT11 198 D7
Hambledon View DT10 35 B1
Hambleton Rd BH7 123 A4
Hambro Rd DT5 186 C4
Hamcroft DT5 186 C2
Hamilton Cl
Bournemouth BH1 122 B3
Christchurch BH23 124 C2
Hamworthy BH15 118 C1
Radipole DT3 152 C1
Hamilton Cres BH15 118 C1
Hamilton Ct
10 Bournemouth BH8 122 A3
5 Wimborne Minster BH21 59 A3
Hamilton Rd
Bournemouth BH1 122 B2
Corfe Mullen BH21 86 C3
Hamworthy BH15 118 C1
Salisbury SP1 213 B3
Hamilton Way BH25 94 C1
Hamlands DT2 105 C1
Hamlon Cl BH11 89 A2
Hammett Cl DT2 79 B1
Hammond Ave DT4 167 A3
Hammond St DT10 196 E1
Hammonds Mead DT6 97 A4
Hampden La BH6 123 A3
Hampreston CE Fst Sch BH21 60 C2
Hampshire Cl BH23 91 C1
Hampshire Ct 26 BH2 121 C2
Hampshire Ctr The BH8 90 C1
Hampshire Hatches La BH24 55 A2
Hampshire House 25 BH2 121 C2
Hampshire Rd DT4 166 C2
Hampton DT3 132 A1
Hampton Cl 8 BA22 193 F8
Hampton Dr BH24 47 B1
Hampton Stone Circle★ DT3 131 C1
Hamworthy Fst Sch BH15 118 C1
Hamworthy Mid Sch BH15 118 C1
Hamworthy Park★ BH15 118 C1
Hamworthy Sta BH16 118 B2
Hanbury Rd 7 BH19 179 A1
Handley Ct BH24 55 A4
Handley Lodge BH12 120 C4
Hands La DT3 149 A4
Hanford House★ DT11 198 D6
Hanford House Sch DT11 198 D6
Hanham Ct BH12 121 A4
Hanham Rd
Corfe Mullen BH21 86 B3
Wimborne Minster BH21 59 B3
Hankinson Rd BH9 122 A4
Hannam's Cl BH16 84 B2
Hannington Pl BH7 123 A3
Hannington Rd BH7 123 A3
Hanover Cl DT10 35 A1
Hanover Ct DT11 212 B1
Hanover Gn BH17 119 C4
Hanover House BH15 119 B2
Hanover La SP8 5 B1
Hanover Rd DT4 167 B3
Happy Island Way DT6 100 C4
Harbeck Rd BH8 90 B2
Harbin's Pk★ DT11 199 D8
Harbour BA21 26 C3
Harbour Cl BH13 147 B3
Harbour Cres BH23 124 C3
Harbour Ct
Barton on Sea BH25 126 C4
Christchurch BH23 124 C3
Poole BH13 147 C3
Harbour Hill DT3 166 C4
Harbour Hill Cres BH15 119 C3
Harbour Hill Rd BH15 119 C3
Harbour Hospl The BH15 119 B2
Harbour Lights BH15 119 C2
Harbour Prospect BH14 147 B4
Harbour Rd
Bournemouth BH6 124 A2
Sherborne DT9 30 B4
Harbour View Cl BH14 120 A3
Harbour View Ct BH23 124 A3
Harbour View Rd
Fortuneswell DT5 186 C4
Poole BH14 120 A2
Harbour Watch BH14 147 B4
Harbour Way DT9 30 A4
Harbridge Dro BH24 42 C2
Harbridge Sch BH24 46 C4
Harcombe Cl BH17 87 C2
Harcombe Rd DT7 64 A2
Harcourt Mews 7 BH5 123 A3
Harcourt Rd BH5 123 A3
Harcourt Terr SP2 213 A2
Harding's La SP8 6 A1
Hardwick St 2 DT4 167 C2
Hardy Ave DT4 167 A1
Hardy Cl
2 Beaminster DT8 204 D4
Ferndown BH22 53 A1
Marnhull DT10 21 A2
Martinstown DT2 133 B3
New Milton BH25 94 C2
Hardy Cres
Stalbridge DT10 33 B4
Wimborne Minster BH21 59 B2
Hardy Ct 23 TA18 191 F4
Hardy Mon (National Trust)★ DT2 132 B2
Hardy Rd Bridport DT6 100 C4
Ferndown BH22 53 A1
Poole BH14 120 B2
Wareham BH20 142 B1
Hardy's Birthplace (National Trust)★ DT2 109 A3
Hardy's La DT8 203 D6
Hare La Cranborne BH21 40 C3
Hordle SO41 95 C2
Hare La Pottery★ BH21 41 A3
Hares Gn BH7 123 A4
Harewood Ave BH7 123 A3
Harewood Cres BH7 122 C4
Harewood Gdns BH7 122 C4
Harewood Pl BH7 123 A3
Harford Rd BH12 120 B4
Hargrove La DT10 33 C2
Harkwood Dr BH15 118 C2
Harland Rd BH6 124 A2
Harleston Villas 17 BH21 59 B2
Harley Gap BH21 201 B8
Harley La BH21 201 A5
Harman's Cross Sta BH19 177 C3
Harness Cl BH21 60 A3
Harnham CE Jun & Inf Sch SP2 213 A1
Harnham Rd SP2 213 A2
Harnwood Rd SP2 213 A1
Harp Stone★ BH20 175 C3
Harper Rd
21 Crewkerne TA18 191 F4
Salisbury SP2 213 A4
Harpitts La
Kington Magna SP8 9 C2
West Stour SP8 10 A2
Harpway La BH23 92 B3
Harrier Dr BH21 59 B1
Harriers Cl BH23 125 B4
Harrington Ct BH23 125 C4
Harris Way BH25 95 A3
Harrison Ave BH1 122 B3
Harrison Cl BH23 92 B2
Harrison Way BH22 53 A2
Harrow Cl BH23 93 A4
Harrow Rd BH23 93 A3
Harry Barrow Cl 1 BH24 55 B3
Harry Lodge's La SP8 5 A1
Hart Cl BH25 94 C2
Hart's La Holt BH21 51 B2
Nether Compton DT9 29 A3
Hartfoot Cl DT2 209 B5
Hartfoot La DT2 209 B5
Harting Rd BH6 123 B4
Hartington Rd SP2 213 A3
Hartley St DT2 195 B1
Hartmoor Hill SP8 9 B3
Hartnell Ct BH21 86 B3
Hartsbourne Dr BH7 123 A4
Harvard Cl 2 SP2 213 A1
Harvey Rd
Bournemouth BH5 123 A3
Oakley BH21 87 C4
Harveys Cl DT2 73 A4
Harwell Rd BH17 119 B4
Harwood Ct BH25 94 C2
Haselbury Plucknett VC Fst Sch TA18 192 C5
Haskells Rd BH12 120 A4
Haslemere Ave BH23 126 A4
Haslemere Pl BH23 126 A4
Hasler Rd BH17 87 B1
Haslop Rd BH21 60 A4
Hastings Rd
Bournemouth BH8 90 C1
Poole BH17 87 A1
Hatch Pond Rd BH17 119 B4
Hatches La SP1 213 C2
Hatfield Ct BH25 94 C2
Hatfield Gdns BH7 123 A4
Hathaway Cl SP1 213 A4
Hathaway Rd BH6 123 B2
Hatherden Ave BH14 119 C3
Hathermead Gdns BA21 27 C4
Havelins DT11 198 E4
Havelock Rd BH12 121 A3
Havelock Way BH23 93 B1
Haven Ct BH13 147 A2
Haven Gdns BH25 95 A1
Haven Rd
Corfe Mullen BH21 86 B3
Poole BH13 147 C4
Havenhurst BH13 147 C3
Haverstock Rd BH9 90 A2
Haviland Mews BH7 122 C3
Haviland Rd
Bournemouth BH1 122 C3
Ferndown BH21 61 A4
Haviland Rd E BH7 122 C3
Haviland Rd W 5 BH7 122 C3
Hawden Rd BH11 89 A1
Hawk Cl BH21 60 A4
Hawkchurch Gdns BH17 87 C1
Hawkchurch Prim Sch EX13 202 B3
Hawkchurch Rd EX13 202 B3
Hawkcombe La SP7 23 C1
Hawker Cl BH21 59 C1
Hawker's La SP7 22 A4
Hawkesdene SP7 12 C1
Hawkesdene La SP7 12 C1
Hawkesworth Cl DT3 153 A2
Hawkins Cl 2 BH24 47 C1
Hawkins Rd BH12 88 C1
Hawkins Way BA21 26 C3
Hawkmoor Hill EX13 202 E2
Hawksridge 5 SP2 213 B1
Hawkwood Rd BH5 122 C2
Haworth Cl BH23 92 A1
Hawthorn Ave SP8 5 C1
Hawthorn Cl
5 Dorchester DT1 107 C1
New Milton BH25 95 B2
Radipole DT4 167 A3
6 Salisbury SP2 213 A3
1 Shaftesbury SP7 13 A2
Hawthorn Dr BH17 86 C1
Hawthorn Rd
Bournemouth BH9 121 C4
Burton BH23 92 C2
Yeovil BA21 27 C4
Hawthorne Cl 15 TA18 191 F5
Hawthorne Rd DT1 107 C1
Hawthorns The
Christchurch BH23 124 C3
Stalbridge DT10 33 C4
Haxen La TA17 191 A8
Haycock Way 2 BH21 56 B2
Haycombe 4 DT11 198 E3
Haycrafts La BH19 177 C2
Haydon Hollow DT9 31 B3
Haydon La
Frome St Quintin DT2 206 D7
Lydlinch DT10 197 A6
Haydon Rd BH13 121 A1
Haye Cl DT7 96 A3
Haye La DT7 96 A3
Hayes Ave BH7 122 C3
Hayes Cl BH21 60 A2
Hayes La BH21 60 A3
Hayes The DT8 203 E5
Hayeswood Fst Sch BH21 60 A3
Hayeswood Rd BH21 60 A3
Haylands DT5 186 C2
Haymoor Ave DT3 167 C4
Haymoor Mid Sch BH17 87 C1
Haymoor Rd BH15 120 A4
Haynes Ave BH15 119 B2
Haysoms Cl BH25 95 A1
Hayters Way SP6 42 B3
Hayward Cres BH31 45 A3
Hayward La DT11 198 B7
Hayward Way BH31 44 C3
Haywards Ave DT3 167 B4
Haywards Farm Cl BH31 45 A3
Haywards La
Child Okeford DT11 198 C7
Corfe Mullen BH21 86 B4
Hazel Cl Alderholt SP6 42 B3
Christchurch BH23 93 B1
Hazel Ct Bournemouth BH9 90 B2
27 New Milton BH25 95 A1
Hazel Dr Ferndown BH22 61 B4
2 Overcombe/Preston DT3 168 A4
Hazel La DT2 129 C4
Hazel View 11 TA18 191 F5
Hazeldene BH18 87 A2
Hazeldown Ave DT3 167 C4
Hazell Ave BH10 89 A1
Hazelton Cl BH7 123 A4
Hazelwood Ave BH25 94 C2
Hazelwood Dr BH31 45 B2
Hazlebury Rd BH17 119 A4
Hazlemere Dr BH24 54 A2
Hazzard's Hill BA12 3 A3
Head La SP8 10 B2
Head's La BH10 89 C3
Headland Cl 6 DT5 186 C1
Headlands Bsns Pk BH24 47 B1
Headless Cross BH10 89 B3
Heads Farm Cl BH10 89 C3
Headstock Rd TA20 202 B7
Headswell Ave BH10 89 C2
Headswell Cres BH10 89 C2
Headswell Gdns BH10 89 C2
Heanor Cl BH10 89 B1
Heath Ave BH15 119 B3
Heath Cl
Bovington Camp BH20 139 B4
Wimborne Minster BH21 60 A4
Heath Farm Cl BH22 61 B2
Heath Farm Rd BH22 61 B2
Heath Farm Way BH22 61 B2
Heath Gn Rd BH19 164 A1
Heath Rd
Christchurch BH23 94 A1
Hordle SO41 95 C2
St.Leonards BH24 53 C2
Heathcote Rd BH5 122 C2
Heather Cl
Bournemouth BH8 90 B2
Christchurch BH23 94 A1
Corfe Mullen BH21 86 C3
St.Leonards BH24 54 A2
Heather Dell BH16 118 A3
Heather Dr BH22 61 A2
Heather Fields 14 SP8 5 C2
Heather Lodge 2 BH25 95 A2
Heather Rd
Bournemouth BH10 89 B2
Yeovil BA21 27 C4
Heather View Rd BH12 120 C4
Heather Way
Ferndown BH22 61 B4
Yeovil BA22 26 B3
Heatherbank Rd BH4 121 B2
Heatherbrae La BH16 118 A3
Heatherdown Rd BH22 53 B1
Heatherdown Way BH22 53 B1
Heatherlands Fst Sch BH12 120 C3
Heatherlands Rise BH12 120 B3
Heatherlea Rd BH6 123 B2
Heathfield Ave BH12 121 A4
Heathfield Rd BH22 53 B1
Heathfield Way BH22 53 A1
Heathfields Way SP7 12 C2
Heathland Cl DT2 137 B3
Heathlands Ave BH22 61 B1
Heathlands Cl
Burton BH23 92 B2
Verwood BH31 45 B3
Heathlands Prim Sch BH11 89 A2
Heathwood Ave BH25 126 C4
Heathwood Rd
Bournemouth BH9 121 C4
Weymouth DT4 167 A2
Heathy Cl BH25 126 C4
Heaton Rd BH10 89 A1
Heavy Horse Ctr★ BH21 40 C1
Heavytree Rd BH14 120 A2
Heber's La TA17 191 A5
Heckford La BH15 119 B2
Heckford Rd
Corfe Mullen BH21 86 B3
Poole BH15 119 B2
Heddington Dr DT11 212 B2
Hedgerley BH25 127 A4
Heights App BH16 118 B4
Heights Rd BH16 118 B4
Helen La 2 DT4 167 C1
Helena Rd BA20 26 C1
Helena Terr SP1 213 B3
Helic Ho 2 BH21 59 B3
Hell Cnr DT2 194 D1
Hell La DT6 99 A4
Helston Cl DT3 132 A1
Helyar Rd BH8 90 C1
Hembury Rd DT2 102 B4
Hemlet's Cl DT6 68 C1
Hemsbach Ct 6 BH20 142 C2
Henbest Cl BH21 60 B3
Henbury Cl
Corfe Mullen BH21 86 B3
Poole BH17 88 A1
Henbury Hall (English Heritage)★ BH21 56 C1
Henbury Rise BH21 86 B3
Henbury View Fst Sch BH21 86 B3
Henbury View Rd BH21 86 B3
Henchard Cl BH22 61 B1
Hendford 6 BA20 27 B2
Hendford Gdns BH10 89 B1
Hendford Gr BA20 27 B2
Hendford Hill BA20 27 A2
Hendford Rd BH10 89 B1
Hendrie Cl BH19 178 C1
Hengist Rd BH1 122 B2
Hengistbury Head Nature Reserve★ BH6 124 C1
Hengistbury Head Nature Trail★ BH6 124 B2
Hengistbury Rd
Barton on Sea BH25 126 C4
Bournemouth BH6 124 A2
Henhayes La 3 TA18 191 F4
Henley Gdns BH7 123 A4
Henley View 7 TA18 191 F3
Henning Way DT9 17 B2
Henning's Pk Rd BH15 119 C3
Henry Cl DT4 180 C4
Henry's Way DT7 96 B3
Henstridge CE VC Prim Sch BA8 19 A3
Henstridge Trad Est BA8 20 A3
Henville Rd 6 BH8 122 B3
Herbert Ave BH12 120 B4
Herbert Ct BH12 120 B4
Herbert Hospl BH4 121 A1
Herbert Rd
Bournemouth BH4 121 A1
New Milton BH25 95 A2
Poole BH13 121 A1
Herberton Rd BH6 123 B3
Herblay Cl BA21 28 A3
Herbury La DT9 194 D4
Hercules Rd BH15 118 B2
Hereford Cres DT4 167 A2
Hereford Rd DT4 167 A2
Heritage Ct BH13 147 C4
Herm Rd BH12 88 B1
Hermitage La DT2 195 B1
Hermitage Rd BH14 120 A3
Hermitage St TA18 191 F4
Hermitage The BH14 120 A3
Hern La SP6 43 B3
Heron Cl
3 Chickerell DT3 166 B3
Overcombe/Preston DT3 168 A3
Heron Ct Rd BH3 122 A4
Heron Dr BH21 60 A4
Heronswood SP2 213 B1
Herrington Rd DT1 135 A4
Herrison Rd DT2 75 C1
Herston CE Sch BH19 178 C1

Herston Halt Sta
BH19 178 C2
Herstone Cl BH17 87 C1
Hertford Ct 12 BH23 126 A4
Hertford Rd BA21 28 A4
Hesketh Cl BH24 54 B3
Hestan Cl BH23 91 B2
Heston Way BH22 52 C2
Hetherly Rd DT3 167 B4
Hewish La TA18 191 E4
Hewitt Rd BH15 118 C2
Hewlett's Dro DT10 197 C7
Heysham Rd BH18 87 A2
Heytesbury Rd BH6 123 B3
Hibberd Way BH10 89 B1
Hibberds Field BH21 40 A4
Hibbs Cl
Northport BH20 142 C3
Upton BH16 118 B4
Hickes Cl BH11 88 C2
Hickory Cl BH16 118 A4
High Brow BH22 61 B3
High Cl BH21 56 B2
High E St DT1 108 A1
High Howe Cl BH11 88 C2
High Howe Gdns BH11 88 C2
High Howe La BH11 88 C2
High Lea BA21 27 B4
High Lea Sch BH21 50 B4
High Marryats BH25 127 A4
High Mead BH22 61 A1
High Mead La BH22 61 A1
High Oaks Gdns BH11 88 C2
High Pines BH23 125 B4
High Pk Rd BH18 86 C2
High Ridge Cres BH25 95 B1
High St Ashmore SP5 39 B4
Broadwindsor DT8 203 E5
Burton Bradstock DT6 128 A4
Child Okeford DT11 198 C7
Christchurch BH23 124 A3
Corscombe DT2 205 A8
Cranborne BH21 40 A4
Damerham SP6 190 F3
East Chinnock BA22 192 E8
13 Easton/Weston DT5 186 C1
Fortuneswell DT5 186 C4
Gillingham SP8 5 C1
Hardington Mandeville
BA22 193 A6
Henstridge BA8 19 A2
Hinton St George TA17 191 C7
Lytchett Matravers BH16 84 A2
Milborne Port DT9 17 B1
Piddlehinton DT2 76 C4
Poole BH15 119 B1
Puddletown DT2 78 A1
Rimpton BA22 15 A4
Ringwood BH24 55 A4
Salisbury SP1 213 B2
Shaftesbury SP7 12 C1
Shapwick DT11 48 B1
Sixpenny Handley SP5 189 A4
Spetisbury DT11 211 E5
St.Leonards BH24 54 A3
Stalbridge DT10 33 B4
Sturminster Marshall
BH21 56 B2
Swanage BH19 178 A1
Sydling St Nicholas DT2 207 A2
Tarrant Monkton DT11 200 B3
Thorncombe TA20 202 E5
Toller Porcorum DT2 71 B4
Weymouth DT4 180 B4
Wimborne Minster BH21 59 A2
Winfrith Newburgh DT2 156 C3
Wool BH20 140 A1
Yeovil BA20 27 B2
Yetminster DT9 194 C5
Zeale SP8 1 C2
High St Cl BH20 140 A1
High St Fordington
DT1 108 A1
High St N BH15 119 B2
High Trees
Broadmayne DT2 136 B1
Poole BH13 147 D4
High Trees Wlk BH22 61 B4
High W St
Dorchester DT1 107 C1
Weymouth DT4 167 B1
High Way BH18 86 C2
Highacres DT6 69 B1
Highbridge Rd BH14 120 B2
Highbury Ave SP2 213 A3
Highbury Cl
New Milton BH25 95 A1
2 Salisbury SP2 213 A3
Highbury Fst Sch SP2 213 A3
Highcliff Rd DT7 96 A3
Highcliffe Castle*
BH23 125 C4
Highcliffe Cnr BH23 126 A4
Highcliffe Jun Sch BH23 93 C1
Highcliffe Rd
Christchurch BH23 125 B4
Swanage BH19 179 B2
Highcliffe Sch BH23 93 B1
Highdown DT3 167 C4
Higher Barn Cl SP7 24 B3
Higher Beadon TA16 191 E7
Higher Blandford Rd
Corfe Mullen BH18 86 C3
Shaftesbury SP7 13 A1
Higher Bullen BA22 193 F8
Higher Cheap St DT9 30 A3
Higher Coombses
TA20 202 A8
Higher Day's Rd BH19 178 C1
Higher Dro DT2 205 F2
Higher Easthams La
TA18 192 A5
Higher End DT3 166 B3
Higher Eype Rd DT6 99 C3
Higher Filbank BH20 177 A4
Higher Gdns BH20 177 A4
Higher Gunville 5 DT9 17 B1
Higher Kingsbury DT9 17 B2
Higher Kingsbury Cl
DT9 17 B2
Higher Kingston BA21 27 B3
Higher Mere Pk* BA12 7 A4
Higher Merley La BH21 86 C4
Higher Ream BA21 26 C3
Higher Sea La DT6 97 A4
Higher Shaftesbury Rd
DT11 212 B3
Higher St Bridport DT6 69 A1
Iwerne Minster DT11 37 C1
Lillington DT9 194 F7
Merriott TA16 191 F8
Morden BH20 83 B2
Okeford Fitzpaine DT11 197 F5
West Chinnock TA18 192 B8
Higher St La DT8 205 C3
Higher Westbury DT9 28 B1
Highfield TA18 192 B8
Highfield Ave BH24 55 B4
Highfield Cl
Charminster DT2 107 B4
Corfe Mullen BH21 86 C3
Highfield Dr BH24 47 B1
Highfield Gdns DT6 204 C2
Highfield House 12
BH14 120 A2
Highfield Rd
Bournemouth BH9 89 C1
Corfe Mullen BH21 86 C3
Ferndown BH22 53 A2
Ringwood BH24 55 B4
Salisbury SP2 213 A3
Yeovil BA21 27 C3
Highfields DT11 212 C1
Highgate La DT2 136 B3
Highgrove SP8 5 C2
Highgrove Cl 5 DT1 135 A4
Highland Ave BH23 94 A1
Highland Rd Poole BH14 120 A3
Weymouth DT4 167 B2
Wimborne Minster BH21 59 B3
Highland View Cl BH21 59 B3
Highlands Cres BH10 89 B2
Highlands Rd
Barton on Sea BH25 127 A4
Salisbury SP2 213 B1
Highmoor Cl
Corfe Mullen BH21 86 B3
Poole BH14 120 A2
Highmoor Rd
Bournemouth BH11 89 A1
Corfe Mullen BH21 86 B3
Poole BH14 120 B2
Hightown Gdns BH24 55 B3
Hightown Rd BH24 55 B3
Hightrees Ave BH8 90 C1
Highview Cl BH23 91 C2
Highview Gdns BH12 120 B4
Highwood Cl SP6 41 C3
Highwood La BH24 47 C1
Highwood Rd BH14 120 C2
Hilary Rd BH17 87 B1
Hilcot Way DT11 212 B2
Hilda Rd BH12 120 C4
Hiley Rd BH15 119 B3
Hilfield La DT2 194 F1
Hill Brow DT9 29 C2
Hill Cl Bransgore BH23 93 A4
5 Bridport DT6 100 A1
Hill Crest Rd BA21 27 C3
Hill House Cl DT9 30 B4
Hill La Bransgore BH23 93 A4
Burton BH23 92 C1
Hill Rd Lyme Regis DT7 96 A3
Swanage BH19 179 A3
Hill Rise DT6 100 A1
Hill Rise Rd DT7 96 A3
Hill St BH15 119 B1
Hill View
Bishop's Caundle DT9 196 A7
Charminster DT2 107 B3
5 Hazelbury Bryan DT10 197 A4
Maiden Newton DT2 73 A4
Osmington DT3 169 A4
Yeovil BA20 27 C3
Hill View Cl TA18 192 B7
Hill View Prim Sch BH10 89 C2
Hill View Rd
Ferndown BH22 61 B4
3 Salisbury SP1 213 B2
Hill Way BH24 54 A3
Hillard Ct 12 BH20 142 C2
Hillary Rd BH23 124 C4
Hillborne Gdns 4 BA21 26 C3
Hillbourne Fst & Mid Schs
BH17 87 A1
Hillbourne Rd Poole BH17 87 A1
11 Weymouth DT4 180 B4
Hillbrow Rd BH6 123 A3
Hillbury Rd SP6 42 B3
Hillcrest Ave BH22 61 B4
Hillcrest Cl
Bournemouth BH9 90 A2
Hillcrest Cl *continued*
Sturminster Newton
DT10 197 C8
Hillcrest Hospl BH10 89 B1
Hillcrest Rd
Bournemouth BH9 90 A2
Corfe Mullen BH21 86 B3
Weymouth DT4 180 C4
Hillfort Cl DT1 134 C4
Hillgrove Ave BA20 27 A1
Hilling La DT2 207 F8
Hillingdon DT6 100 C4
Hillingdon Ct BA21 26 C3
Hillman Rd BH14 120 B3
Hillmeadow BH31 45 B2
Hillsea Rd BH19 179 A1
Hillside Cl BA12 2 C3
Hillside Cty Fst Sch
BH31 45 B4
Hillside Dr BH23 91 B2
Hillside Gdns BH21 86 B2
Hillside Mews BH21 86 B2
Hillside Rd
Blandford Camp DT11 199 E3
Corfe Mullen BH21 86 B3
Poole BH12 88 C1
Verwood BH31 45 B4
Woodlands BH21 44 B3
6 Wool BH20 140 A1
Hillside Terr 4 BA20 27 C2
Hillside View 9 BA22 193 F8
Hilltop Cl BH22 61 A4
Hilltop Rd
Corfe Mullen BH21 86 C3
Ferndown BH22 61 A4
Hillview DT6 68 C1
Hillview Est 1 DT6 100 B4
Hillview Rd
Bournemouth BH10 89 B2
Swanage BH19 179 A1
Hilmar Dr SP8 5 C1
Hiltom Rd BH24 55 B4
Hilton Cl BH15 120 A3
Hilton Rd BH25 95 A2
Hilton Rd Cl DT11 79 C4
Hinchcliffe Cl BH15 118 C1
Hinchcliffe Rd BH15 118 C1
Hine Town La DT11 198 B6
Hine's Mead La DT2 103 B1
Hingsdon La DT6 204 B2
Hintock St DT1 107 B1
Hinton Admiral Mews
BH23 93 C1
Hinton Admiral Sta BH23 93 C1
Hinton Cl
Blandford Forum DT11 212 B2
Hinton St George TA17 191 D7
Hinton Cross BA22 14 A3
Hinton La DT10 35 B4
Hinton Rd
Bournemouth BH1 121 C2
West Crewkerne TA18 191 E5
Hinton St George Prim Sch
TA17 191 C7
Hinton St Mary Roman Villa
(site of)* DT10 35 A2
Hinton View DT10 35 A1
Hinton Wood BH1 122 A1
Hinton Wood Ave BH23 93 C1
Hintonwood La BH23 93 C1
Hitchen 3 TA16 191 F7
Hive Cl DT6 128 B4
Hive Gdns BH13 147 B3
Hoadley Gn SP1 213 C4
Hobart Rd BH25 94 C1
Hobbs Pk BH24 54 A2
Hobbs Rd BH12 120 B4
Hobgoblin DT11 37 C1
Hoburne Ct BH23 93 B1
Hoburne Gdns BH23 93 B1
Hoburne La BH23 125 B4
Hoburne Rd BH19 179 A1
Hod Dr DT11 198 E5
Hod Hill (Roman Fort)*
DT11 198 E5
Hod View 2 DT11 198 F4
Hodder's La DT7 64 A1
Hodges Cl BH17 119 C4
Hodway La DT11 198 D5
Hogarth Way BH8 91 A1
Hogshill St DT8 204 C4
Hogue Ave BH10 89 B3
Holbaek Cl DT1 135 A4
Holbury Cl BH8 90 C2
Holcombe Cl DT3 168 B4
Holcombe Mead DT2 208 A6
Holcombe Rd BH16 118 A3
Holdenhurst Ave BH7 123 B4
Holdenhurst Rd BH8 91 A2
Holditch Ct* TA20 202 B5
Holditch Ct La TA20 202 A5
Holditch La TA20 202 A5
Holdscroft La DT6 202 E1
Hole House La DT10 197 D8
Holebrook La DT10 196 F7
Holes Bay Rd BH15 119 A2
Holes Cl SO41 95 C2
Holland Rd DT4 167 B2
Holland Way
Blandford Forum DT11 212 B2
Corfe Mullen BH18 86 C3
Hollands Cl BH20 176 C4
Hollands Mead Ave
DT2 155 B4
Hollands Wood Dr BH25 95 A3
Holleys Cl 14 TA20 202 A8
Hollies The
3 Crewkerne TA18 191 E3
Hollies The *continued*
Yeovil BA21 27 C4
Hollis Way BA22 193 D3
Hollow Hill DT2 108 C2
Hollow La TA17 191 B7
Hollow Oak BH20 113 A4
Hollow Oak Rd BH20 142 C1
Hollow The
Affpuddle DT2 112 A3
Child Okeford DT11 198 C8
Sixpenny Handley SP5 189 A4
Hollow Way DT6 100 B2
Holloway Ave BH11 88 C3
Holloway La DT11 198 C5
Holloway Rd DT1 108 A1
Hollows Cl SP2 213 A1
Holly Cl
3 Dorchester DT1 107 C1
2 Sandford BH20 116 A1
1 St.Leonards BH24 53 C2
Upton BH16 118 A4
Holly Ct BH15 119 B2
Holly Gdns BH23 92 B1
Holly Gn Rise BH11 88 C2
Holly Gr Merriott TA18 191 F5
Verwood BH31 45 A3
Holly Hedge La BH17 119 B4
Holly La
Broadwindsor DT8 203 D8
Christchurch BH23 94 B1
New Milton BH25 95 B2
Holly Lodge 13 BH12 121 A2
Holly Rd DT4 167 B2
Hollymoor Cl 8 DT8 204 D4
Hollymoor Comm La
DT8 204 D4
Hollymoor Gdns 7 DT8 204 D4
Hollymoor La DT8 204 D4
Holm Cl BH24 47 C1
Holm Hill La BH23 94 A4
Holm Oak Cl BH31 45 A4
Holme Cl DT3 167 A4
Holme La
East Holme BH20 160 A4
East Stoke BH20 141 A1
Holme Rd BH23 126 A4
Holmead Wlk DT1 107 B1
Holmes Rd BH19 178 C1
Holmfield Ave BH7 123 B4
Holmhurst Ave BH23 93 C1
Holmlea DT11 212 C2
Holmwood Garth 4
BH24 55 C3
Holnest Pk* DT9 195 C4
Holnest Rd BH17 87 B1
Holt Heath National Nature
Reserve* BH21 52 B3
Holt Hill DT9 31 C1
Holt La
Bishop's Caundle DT9 196 A8
Holt BH21 51 A2
Melbury Osmond DT2 194 A3
South Perrott DT8 192 D1
Stourton Caundle DT10 32 A1
Holt Rd Holt BH21 51 B3
Horton BH21 52 C4
Poole BH12 120 C3
Wool BH20 139 B3
Holten's La BA22 192 E6
Holton Heath Sta
BH16 116 B1
Holton Heath Trading Pk
BH16 116 B1
Holton Rd BH16 116 B1
Holway TA20 202 A8
Holway La
Cattistock DT2 206 A5
Evershot DT2 205 F7
Holwell Dro DT9 195 F5
Holwell Prim Sch DT9 196 B5
Holwell Rd DT10 196 C5
Holworth Cl BH11 88 C2
Holy Trinity Jun & Inf Sch
DT4 167 B1
Holy Trintiy CE VA Prim Sch
BA20 27 A2
Holyrood Cl BH17 119 A4
Holywell Cl BH17 87 B2
Home Dr BA21 27 A3
Home Farm Cl DT6 101 C4
Home Farm La BA22 15 A4
Home Farm Way BH31 45 A3
Home Rd BH11 89 A3
Homedale House BH2 121 C3
Homedene House BH15 119 B2
Homefield
6 Child Okeford DT11 198 C7
Mere BA12 2 C3
Milborne St Andrew DT11 79 C4
Shaftesbury SP7 12 C2
Homefield House 13
BH25 95 A1
Homefield Ind Prep Sch
BH6 123 C3
Homefield Ind Senior Sch
BH23 92 B3
Homelake House BH14 120 A2
Homelands Est BH23 123 C3
Homelands House BH22 61 B3
Homeleigh House 5
BH8 122 A3
Homemill House 5
BH25 95 A2
Homeoaks House BH2 121 C3
Homeside Rd BH9 90 A1
Homestour House 1
BH23 124 A3
Homeview House BH15 119 B2
Homewood Cl BH25 95 B2
Honey Bun Mdw DT10 196 F4
Honeybourne Cres BH6 124 A2
Honeycombe Rise DT9 29 C2
Honeyfields 15 SP8 5 C2
Honeymead La DT10 35 A1
Honeysuckle Cl DT3 152 C1
Honeysuckle Gdns 2
DT11 198 B5
Honeysuckle La BH17 86 C1
Honeysuckle Way BH23 125 A4
Honeywood House
BH14 147 B4
Hood Cl BH10 89 A1
Hood Cres BH10 89 A1
Hooke Cl BH17 88 A1
Hooke Ct (School)*
DT8 205 C3
Hooper's La
Barwick BA22 193 F7
Puncknowle DT2 129 C3
Hop Cl BH16 117 A4
Hope Bottom DT6 204 C2
Hope Cl DT2 137 B3
Hope Cross SP8 9 A3
Hopkins Cl BH8 91 A1
Hopmans Cl BH16 84 A2
Hopsfield DT11 79 C4
Horace Rd 10 BH5 122 C2
Hordle House Sch SO41 127 C3
Horn Hill View DT8 204 C4
Horn Pk* DT8 204 B5
Hornbeam Cl DT4 167 A3
Hornbeam Way BH21 59 C3
Horncastles La 1 DT9 30 A3
Horning Rd BH12 120 C3
Horsa Cl BH6 123 C2
Horsa Ct BH6 123 C2
Horsa Rd BH6 123 C2
Horsecastles DT9 30 A3
Horsecastles La DT9 29 C3
Horsefields SP8 5 C2
Horsehill La DT8 204 A3
Horseponds SP7 12 B2
Horseshoe Cl BH21 60 A3
Horseshoe Ct 4 BH1 121 C2
Horseshoe Rd TA20 202 D7
Horseshoe The BH13 147 B2
Horsey Knap DT2 205 E7
Horsey La
East Chelborough DT2 205 E7
Yeovil BA20 27 B2
Horsford St DT4 167 C1
Horsham Ave BH10 89 B3
Horton Cl
Bournemouth BH9 90 B2
Yeovil BA21 26 C3
Horton Rd Horton BH21 44 B1
St Leonards & St Ives
BH24 53 C3
St.Leonards BH24 54 B3
Wimborne St Giles BH21 40 A1
Woodlands BH21 201 F3
Horton Twr* BH21 201 E1
Horton Way BH31 44 C3
Horyford Cl DT3 168 B4
Hosier's La 23 BH15 119 A1
Hosker Rd BH5 123 A3
Hospital La
Allington DT6 100 A4
Sherborne DT9 30 A3
Hotton Heath Nature
Reserve* BH16 116 C2
Houlton Rd BH15 119 C2
Hound St DT9 30 A3
Hounds Way BH21 60 A3
Houndstone Cl BA21 26 C3
Houndstone Ct 2 BA22 26 B3
Hounslow Cl BH15 118 C1
Howard Cl
Bothenhampton DT6 101 A4
Christchurch BH23 124 C3
Weymouth DT4 180 C4
Howard Rd
Bournemouth BH8 122 B4
Bridport DT6 100 C3
5 Swanage BH19 179 A1
Verwood BH31 45 A3
Yeovil BA21 28 A3
Howard's La BH20 142 C2
Howarth Cl 1 DT6 128 A4
Howe Cl
Christchurch BH23 124 C3
New Milton BH25 94 C2
Howe La BH31 45 A2
Howe's Eype La DT6 99 C3
Howell House BH21 59 C4
Howeth Cl BH10 89 B2
Howeth Rd BH10 89 B2
Howton Cl BH10 89 B3
Howton Rd BH10 89 B3
Hoxley Rd BH10 89 B2
Hoyal Rd BH15 118 B2
Hudson Cl Poole BH12 88 B1
Ringwood BH24 55 C4
Hudson Rd SP1 213 A4
Hughes Bsns Ctr BH23 125 A4
Huish BA20 27 B2
Huish CP Sch BA20 27 B3
Hull Cres BH11 88 C2
Hull Rd BH11 88 C2
Hull Way BH11 88 C2
Hulse Rd SP1 213 B3
Humber Chase BH20 142 B3
Humber Rd BH22 62 A3
Humpy La DT9 31 A1
Hundred Stone* BA21 27 B4
Hundredstone Cl BA21 27 B4

Hunger Hill BH15 ....119 B1
Hungerford Hill SP6 ....43 C3
Hungerford Rd BH8 ....90 B2
Hunt Rd
Blandford Forum DT11 ....212 C2
Christchurch BH23 ....124 C4
Poole BH15 ....119 C2
Hunt's Hill DT10 ....21 C3
Hunter Cl
Christchurch BH23 ....125 A4
Wimborne Minster BH21 ....60 B3
Hunters Cl BH31 ....45 C3
Hunters Mead SP7 ....7 A1
Huntfield Rd BH9 ....90 A1
Huntick Rd
Lytchett Matravers BH16 ....84 C2
Lytchett Minster & Upton BH16 ....85 A1
Huntingdon Dr BH21 ....59 C1
Huntingdon Gdns BH23 ....92 A1
Huntley Down DT11 ....209 F1
Huntly Rd BH3 ....121 B4
Hunts Mead DT9 ....29 C2
Huntvale Rd BH9 ....90 A2
Hurdles The BH23 ....123 C4
Hurn Cl BH24 ....54 C3
Hurn Ct BH8 ....91 A2
Hurn Ct La BH23 ....90 C3
Hurn La BH24 ....54 C3
Hurn Rd Christchurch BH23 ....91 B2
St Leonards & St Ives BH24 ....54 C2
Hurn Way BH23 ....91 B1
Hurricane Cl DT2 ....137 B3
Hursley Cl BH7 ....123 B4
Hurst Bridges* DT2 ....111 B1
Hurst Cl
Barton on Sea BH25 ....126 B4
Christchurch BH23 ....94 B1
Hurst Ct 6 BH23 ....126 A4
Hurst Hill BH14 ....147 B4
Hurst Rd Moreton DT2 ....111 B1
Ringwood BH24 ....47 B1
Hurstbourne Ave BH23 ....93 C1
Hurstdene Rd BH8 ....90 B1
Hussar Cl BH23 ....123 C4
Hussey's DT10 ....20 C1
Hutchins Cl DT1 ....134 C4
Hyacinth Cl BH17 ....86 C1
Hyde CE Prim Sch SP6 ....43 C3
Hyde Ct BA21 ....26 C3
Hyde Gdns 6 DT11 ....199 D4
Hyde La SP6 ....43 C3
Hyde Rd
Bournemouth BH10 ....89 B3
Gillingham SP8 ....5 C2
Wool BH20 ....140 A1
Hyde The New Milton BH25 ....94 C2
Swanage BH19 ....178 B1
Hydes La DT10 ....196 D7
Hynesbury Rd BH23 ....125 B4
Hythe Rd BH15 ....120 A4
Hythe The DT3 ....166 B3

I

Ibbertson Cl BH8 ....90 C1
Ibbertson Rd BH8 ....90 C1
Ibbertson Way BH8 ....90 C1
Ibbett Rd BH10 ....89 B2
Ibsley Cl BH8 ....122 B3
Ibsley Dro BH24 ....43 B1
Icen La Bincombe DT3 ....152 B2
Shipton Gorge DT6 ....101 C2
Icen Rd DT3 ....167 B4
Icen Way DT1 ....108 A1
Iddesleigh Rd BH3 ....122 A3
Iford Bridge Home Pk BH6 ....123 B4
Iford Cl BH6 ....123 C3
Iford Gdns BH7 ....123 B4
Iford La BH6 ....123 C3
Ilchester Rd
Weymouth DT4 ....167 B2
Yeovil BA21 ....27 A4
Ilminster Rd BH19 ....179 A1
Ilsington House* DT2 ....78 B1
Ilsington Rd DT2 ....109 C2
Imber Dr BH23 ....125 C4
Imber Rd SP7 ....13 A2
Imbre Ct BH13 ....147 C4
Imperial Ct 4 BH13 ....147 C4
Incline Rd
Fortuneswell DT5 ....181 B1
Portland DT5 ....187 A3
India Ave SP2 ....213 A3
Ingarth 8 BH6 ....123 C2
Inglegreen Cl BH25 ....94 C1
Inglesham Way BH15 ....118 C2
Inglewood Ave BH8 ....90 C1
Inglewood Dr BH25 ....95 A1
Ingram Wlk 13 BH21 ....59 B2
Ingworth Rd BH12 ....121 A3
Inmosthay DT5 ....187 A3
Inner Breakwater Rd DT5 ....181 B1
Insley Cres BH18 ....86 C3
Institute Rd BH19 ....179 B1
Inveravon BH23 ....124 C2
Inverclyde House BH14 ....120 A2
Inverclyde Rd BH14 ....120 B2
Inverleigh Rd BH6 ....123 B3
Inverness Rd BH13 ....147 C4
Ipswich Rd BH4 ....121 A2
Iris Gdns 6 SP8 ....5 C1
Iris Rd BH9 ....89 C1
Irvine Way BH23 ....124 C4
Irving Rd BH6 ....123 B3
Isaacs Cl BH12 ....121 A4
Island View Ave BH23 ....125 A3
Island View Rd BH25 ....126 B4
Isle of Purbeck Golf Club BH19 ....178 C4
Isle Rd DT5 ....186 C2
Isles La BA22 ....193 D6
Ivamy Pl BH11 ....88 C1
Ivel Ct BA20 ....27 C2
Ivelway 14 TA18 ....191 F4
Ivers Coll DT10 ....20 C2
Ivor Rd Corfe Mullen BH21 ....86 B2
Poole BH15 ....119 A1
Ivy Cl 4 Gillingham SP8 ....5 B1
St.Leonards BH24 ....53 C2
Ivy La BH24 ....47 B2
Ivy Mead BA12 ....3 A3
Ivy Rd BH21 ....87 B4
Ivy St SP1 ....213 B2
Iwerne Cl BH9 ....90 A2

J

Jack Paul Cl BA12 ....3 A3
Jack the Treacle Eater (Folly)* BA22 ....27 C1
Jack's Hedge Cnr BH21 ....189 F2
Jacklin Ct BH18 ....87 A3
Jackson Gdns BH12 ....120 B3
Jackson Rd BH12 ....120 B3
Jacmar Ct 8 BH25 ....95 A1
Jacobean Cl BH23 ....94 A1
Jacobs Ladder 2 DT11 ....198 C7
Jacobs Rd BH15 ....118 C1
Jacqueline Rd BH12 ....120 B4
James Cl DT11 ....212 C2
James Cross La BH21 ....201 A6
James Day Mead BH19 ....179 A3
James Rd
Dorchester DT1 ....134 C4
Poole BH12 ....121 A3
James St Salisbury SP2 ....213 A3
Weymouth DT4 ....167 B1
Jameson Rd BH9 ....89 C1
Janred Ct BH25 ....126 C4
Jarvis Cl DT10 ....33 B4
Jarvis Way DT10 ....33 B4
Jasmine Cl
Crewkerne TA18 ....191 F5
Yeovil BA22 ....26 B3
Jasmine Way 2 DT4 ....180 A4
Jaundrells Cl BH25 ....95 B2
Jay's Ct BH23 ....126 A4
Jeanneau Cl 8 SP7 ....12 C2
Jefferson Ave BH1 ....122 B3
Jellicoe Cl BH14 ....119 C3
Jellicoe Dr BH23 ....124 C3
Jenner Way DT3 ....152 B2
Jennings Rd BH14 ....120 B1
Jennys La BH16 ....84 A2
Jephcote Rd BH11 ....88 C2
Jeremy Cl BH20 ....140 A1
Jersey Cl BH12 ....88 B1
Jersey Rd BH12 ....88 B1
Jesmond Ave BH23 ....125 C4
Jesop Cl 1 SP8 ....5 C1
Jessica Ave BH31 ....44 C4
Jessop Cl BH10 ....89 C2
Jessop Rd BH21 ....60 A3
Jessopp Ave DT6 ....100 C4
Jessopp House 6 BH21 ....59 B3
Jesty's Ave DT3 ....152 B2
Jewell Cl SP1 ....213 C4
Jewell Rd BH8 ....91 A1
Jimmy Brown Ave BH21 ....53 A3
Johns Rd BH20 ....142 B3
Johnson Rd BH21 ....61 A4
Johnston Rd BH15 ....119 B4
Johnstone Rd BH23 ....124 C3
Jolliffe Ave BH15 ....119 B2
Jolliffe Rd BH15 ....119 B2
Jopps Cnr BH23 ....92 B2
Jordan Hill Roman Temple* DT3 ....168 A4
Jordan Way 5 DT3 ....152 B2
Joshua Cl BH15 ....118 C1
Journeys End DT6 ....100 A3
Jowitt Dr BH25 ....94 C1
Joyce Dickson Cl 6 BH24 ....55 B3
Joys Rd BH21 ....53 A4
Juan's La SP8 ....9 B1
Jubilee Cl
Corfe Mullen BH21 ....86 C4
Radipole DT4 ....167 B2
Ringwood BH24 ....55 C4
Jubilee Cres BH12 ....120 B3
Jubilee Cross BH16 ....85 A2
Jubilee Ct 5 SP2 ....213 A3
Jubilee Gdns
Bournemouth BH10 ....89 B1
Corfe Castle BH20 ....177 A4
Jubilee Rd
Corfe Mullen BH21 ....86 C4
Poole BH12 ....120 B3
Swanage BH19 ....178 C1
Jubilee Way DT11 ....212 B2
Julia Cl BH23 ....125 C4
Julian's Rd BH21 ....59 A2
Julyan Ave BH12 ....121 A4
Jumpers Ave BH23 ....123 C4
Jumpers Rd BH23 ....123 C4
Junction Rd
Bournemouth BH9 ....121 C4
Hamworthy BH16 ....118 B2
Juniper Cl Ferndown BH22 ....61 B4
Three Legged Cross BH21 ....53 A4
Yeovil BA20 ....27 A2
Juniper Flats BH23 ....123 C4
Juniper Gdns 7 SP8 ....5 C1
Juniper Way DT3 ....152 B2
Jupiter Way BH21 ....86 C4
Justin Gdns BH10 ....89 C2

K

Kamptee Copse BH25 ....95 A3
Kangaw Pl BH15 ....118 B1
Katherine Chance Cl BH23 ....92 B2
Katterns Cl BH23 ....91 C1
Kay Cl BH23 ....124 C3
Kayes Cl DT4 ....180 B4
Keats House 17 BH25 ....95 A1
Keeble Cl BH10 ....89 B3
Keeble Cres BH10 ....89 B3
Keeble Rd BH10 ....89 B3
Keepers La BH21 ....60 C2
Keighley Ave BH18 ....86 C1
Keith Rd BH3 ....121 B4
Kellaway Rd BH17 ....119 C4
Kellaway Terr DT4 ....167 B2
Kelly Cl BH17 ....119 C4
Kelsall Gdns BH25 ....95 A2
Kelsey Rd SP1 ....213 B3
Kemp Rd BH9 ....121 C4
Kemp Welch Ct BH12 ....121 A4
Kempston Rd DT4 ....167 B1
Ken Rd BH6 ....123 C2
Kendalls La SP8 ....5 C3
Kenilworth DT4 ....167 A3
Kenilworth Cl BH25 ....95 A2
Kenilworth Ct
2 Christchurch BH23 ....124 A4
11 Poole BH13 ....147 C4
Kenmoor Cl DT3 ....167 C4
Kenmore Dr BA21 ....27 B3
Kennard Ct BH25 ....94 C2
Kennard Rd BH25 ....94 C2
Kennart Rd BH17 ....119 A4
Kennel La DT2 ....206 C2
Kennels La DT9 ....195 E2
Kenneth Ct 15 BH23 ....126 A4
Kennington Rd BH17 ....119 B4
Kennington Sq 5 BH20 ....142 C2
Kensington Dr BH2 ....121 B2
Kensington Rd 3 SP2 ....213 A3
Kent Cl DT4 ....166 C2
Kent House 20 BH4 ....121 B2
Kent La BH24 ....43 A1
Kent Rd Poole BH12 ....120 C3
Salisbury SP2 ....213 A1
10 Tatworth TA20 ....202 A8
Kentisworth Rd DT10 ....20 C1
Kents La 8 TA20 ....202 A8
Kenwyn Rd DT6 ....100 C4
Kenyon Cl BH15 ....119 C4
Kenyon Rd BH15 ....119 C4
Keppel Cl BH24 ....55 B4
Kerley Rd BH2 ....121 C1
Kestrel Cl Ferndown BH22 ....61 A4
Upton BH16 ....118 A4
Kestrel Ct BH24 ....55 B4
Kestrel Dr BH23 ....125 A3
Kestrel View DT3 ....152 B2
Kestrel Way SP6 ....42 B3
Keswick Ct BH25 ....95 A3
Keswick Rd
Bournemouth BH5 ....123 A2
New Milton BH25 ....95 A3
Keswick Way BH31 ....45 A3
Keverstone Ct BH1 ....122 B2
Key La 21 BH15 ....119 A1
Keyes Cl
Christchurch BH23 ....124 C3
Poole BH12 ....88 C1
Keynston Down Rd 7 DT11 ....199 E2
Keysworth Ave BH25 ....126 C4
Keysworth Dr BH20 ....143 A4
Keysworth Rd BH16 ....118 B2
Khartoum Rd DT4 ....180 C4
Khyber Rd BH12 ....120 B3
Kiddles BA21 ....27 C3
Kidmore Cl 2 DT6 ....97 A4
Kilbride 11 BH12 ....121 A2
Killicks Hill DT5 ....186 C4
Killock 6 BH13 ....147 C4
Kilmarnock Rd BH9 ....89 C1
Kilmington Way BH23 ....125 C4
Kiln Cl BH21 ....86 B2
Kimber Rd BH11 ....88 C2
Kimberley Cl
Christchurch BH23 ....123 C4
1 Radipole DT3 ....152 C1
Kimberley Rd
Bournemouth BH6 ....123 B3
Poole BH14 ....120 A2
Kimmeridge Ave BH12 ....120 B4
Kimmeridge Cl DT3 ....167 A4
Kine Bush La SP8 ....10 A4
King Alfred's Mid Sch SP7 ....13 A2
King Arthur Dr BA21 ....26 C4
King Barrow (Tumulus)*
Alderholt SP6 ....41 B3
Studland BH19 ....164 C1
King Charles Way DT6 ....100 C4
King Cl BH24 ....54 A2
King Down Dro BH21 ....49 B2
King Down Rd DT11 ....199 F3
King Edmund Ct SP8 ....5 C1
King Edward Ave BH9 ....90 A1
King Edward Ct BH9 ....89 C1
King Edward's Dr DT11 ....209 F5
King Fisher Way BH23 ....125 A3
King George Ave BH9 ....89 C1
King George Mobile Home Pk BH25 ....94 C1
King George St 7 BA20 ....27 B2
King George V Rd BH20 ....139 C4
King John Ave BH11 ....88 B3
King John Cl BH11 ....88 B3
King John's House* SP5 ....188 B4
King Richard Dr BH11 ....88 B3
King St Bridport DT6 ....100 B3
Fortuneswell DT5 ....186 C4
Radipole DT4 ....167 B2
Wimborne Minster BH21 ....59 A2
Yeovil BA21 ....27 B3
King's Ave BH23 ....123 C3
King's Barrow* BH20 ....160 C4
King's Cres BH14 ....120 C1
King's Ct Pal* SP8 ....6 A1
King's House* SP2 ....213 A2
King's La DT6 ....70 B3
King's Mill Rd DT10 ....34 A3
King's Pk Athletic Ctr BH7 ....122 C3
King's Pk Dr BH7 ....122 C3
King's Pk Rd BH7 ....122 C3
King's Pk Sch BH1 ....122 C3
King's Rd
Blandford Forum DT11 ....212 C2
Bournemouth BH3 ....122 A4
Salisbury SP1 ....213 B3
Thornford DT9 ....194 D7
King's St BH21 ....56 B3
Kingcombe Cross Roads DT2 ....205 E3
Kingcombe La DT2 ....205 E3
Kingcombe Rd DT8 ....205 C3
Kingcome Nature Reserve* DT2 ....205 D1
Kingcup Cl BH18 ....86 C1
Kingfisher Cl
Bournemouth BH6 ....123 C3
Ferndown BH22 ....53 A1
Salisbury SP2 ....213 B1
Weymouth DT4 ....180 B3
Kingfisher Pk Homes 3 BH10 ....89 C2
Kingfisher Way BH24 ....47 B1
Kingfishers 9 BH23 ....124 A3
Kingfishers The BH31 ....45 B3
Kinghton Heath Ind Est BH11 ....88 C2
Kingland Cres BH15 ....119 B1
Kingland Rd BH15 ....119 B1
Kings Arms La BH24 ....55 A4
Kings Arms Row BH24 ....55 A4
Kings Ave BH14 ....120 B1
Kings Cl Ferndown BH22 ....53 A1
Longburton DT9 ....195 B8
Kings Cres DT9 ....30 A4
Kings Hill 2 SP7 ....12 C2
Kings La BH21 ....201 F4
Kings Mead DT2 ....78 A1
Kings Pk Com Hospl BH7 ....122 C3
Kings Rd
Dorchester DT1 ....108 A1
New Milton BH25 ....95 B2
Radipole DT3 ....167 B4
Sherborne DT9 ....30 A4
Kings Rd E BH19 ....179 A1
Kings Rd W BH19 ....179 A1
Kingsbere Ave BH10 ....89 A1
Kingsbere Cres DT1 ....135 A4
Kingsbere Gdns BH23 ....126 A4
Kingsbere La SP7 ....13 A2
Kingsbere Rd
Overcombe/Preston DT3 ....168 A4
Poole BH15 ....119 C3
Kingsbridge Rd BH14 ....120 B2
Kingsbury's La BH24 ....55 A4
Kingscourt Cl 6 SP8 ....6 A1
Kingscourt Rd SP8 ....6 A1
Kingsfield BH24 ....55 B4
Kingsland Ct BH13 ....147 C4
Kingsland Rd SP2 ....213 A3
Kingsleigh Fst Sch BH10 ....89 B2
Kingsleigh Jun Sch BH10 ....89 B2
Kingsleigh Sec Sch BH10 ....89 B2
Kingsley Ave BH6 ....124 A2
Kingsley Cl BH6 ....124 A2
Kingsman La SP7 ....12 C1
Kingsmead Ct 9 BH21 ....59 A3
Kingsmill Rd BH17 ....119 C4
Kingsnorth Cl DT6 ....100 C4
Kingston BA20 ....27 B3
Kingston Cl DT11 ....212 B2
Kingston Hill BH20 ....176 C2
Kingston La DT10 ....196 F4
Kingston Lacy House (NT)* BH21 ....58 A4
Kingston Maurward Agricultural Coll DT2 ....108 C2
Kingston Maurward Gdns & Animal Pk* DT2 ....108 C2
Kingston Rd BH15 ....119 B2
Kingston Russell House* DT2 ....131 A4
Kingston Russell Stone Circle* DT3 ....131 A2
Kingston View BA21 ....27 B3
Kingsway Ferndown BH22 ....61 A4
Lyme Regis DT7 ....96 B3
Kingsway Cl BH23 ....91 C1
Kingswell Cl BH10 ....89 B1
Kingswell Gdns BH10 ....89 A1
Kingswell Gr BH10 ....89 A1
Kingswell Rd BH10 ....89 B1
Kingswood BH4 ....121 B1
Kingswood Cl 6 BH19 ....178 C1
Kingswood Rd 6 TA18 ....191 F3
Kinross Rd BH3 ....121 C3
Kinsbourne Ave BH10 ....89 B1
Kinson Ave BH15 ....120 A4
Kinson Gr BH10 ....89 B3
Kinson Pk Rd BH10 ....89 B3
Kinson Pottery Ind Est BH14 ....120 A3
Kinson Prim Sch BH11 ....89 A3
Kinson Rd BH10 ....89 B2
Kiosks The 20 BH15 ....119 B1
Kipling Rd BH14 ....120 A3
Kirby Cl BH15 ....119 C3
Kirby Way BH6 ....123 B2
Kirkham Ave BH23 ....92 B2
Kirkleton Ave DT4 ....167 B3
Kirkway BH18 ....87 A2
Kit La DT2 ....155 B4
Kitchener Cres BH17 ....87 A1
Kitchener Rd DT4 ....167 A2
Kite's Nest La SP8 ....1 C1
Kitford La DT11 ....197 C3
Kithill TA18 ....191 F3
Kitscroft Rd BH10 ....89 B3
Kitt Hill DT9 ....30 A3
Kittiwake Cl BH6 ....123 C3
Kivel Ct SP2 ....213 B3
Kiwi Cl BH15 ....119 C2
Knacker's Hole La TA20 ....202 F4
Knap Barrow (Long Barrow)* SP6 ....190 D6
Knapp Cl BH23 ....124 A4
Knapp Mill Ave BH23 ....124 A4
Knapp The
Chickerell DT3 ....166 B3
Fontmell Magna SP7 ....37 C3
Hilton DT11 ....209 D6
Shaftesbury SP7 ....12 B2
Knapps DT11 ....198 B6
Knighton Heath Cl BH11 ....88 C2
Knighton Heath Rd BH11 ....88 C2
Knighton House Sch DT11 ....198 E3
Knighton La
Broadmayne DT2 ....136 B1
Oakley BH21 ....88 B4
Knighton Pk BH25 ....126 C4
Knights Cl 5 DT11 ....211 B1
Knights Rd BH11 ....88 B3
Knightsbridge Ct BH2 ....121 C1
Knightsdale Rd DT4 ....167 A1
Knightsdale Rd Swimming Pool DT4 ....167 A1
Knightstone Ct 14 BH20 ....142 C2
Knightstone Rise DT6 ....68 C1
Knightwood Cl BH23 ....125 B4
Knobcrook Rd 3 BH21 ....59 A3
Knole Ct 5 BH1 ....122 B2
Knole Gdns BH1 ....122 B2
Knole Rd BH1 ....122 B2
Knoll Gdns*
Ferndown BH21 ....60 C2
St.Leonards BH24 ....54 A2
Knoll La BH21 ....86 A4
Knoll Manor BH2 ....121 C3
Knoll Pl SP8 ....5 C2
Knoll Rise DT3 ....152 C1
Knollsea Cl 8 BH19 ....179 B1
Knotts Cl 7 DT11 ....198 C7
Knotts Paddock DT9 ....30 B3
Knowl La DT6 ....101 B4
Knowle Cross DT8 ....203 D6
Knowle Hill BH20 ....140 A1
Knowle La TA18 ....191 F1
Knowle Wood Knap 4 BH20 ....140 A1
Knowles Cl BH23 ....124 C4
Knowlton Church (remains of)* BH21 ....201 D5
Knowlton Circles* BH21 ....201 D5
Knowlton Gdns BH9 ....90 A2
Knowlton Rd BH17 ....87 C1
Knyveton House BH1 ....122 A2
Knyveton Rd BH1 ....122 B2
Kyrchil La BH21 ....59 C3
Kyrchil Way BH21 ....59 C4

L

La Retraite Sch SP1 ....213 B3
Labrador Dr BH15 ....119 B1
Laburnam Way SP8 ....5 B1
Laburnum Cl
Ferndown BH22 ....61 A3
Radipole DT4 ....167 A3
1 Sandford BH20 ....116 A1
Verwood BH31 ....45 C3
Laburnum Cres 13 TA18 ....191 F5

Laburnum House [8]
BH10 .89 C2
Laburnum Way BA20 .26 C1
Lacey Cres BH15 .120 A3
Lackington Dro DT2 .208 B1
Lacy Cl BH21 .59 B3
Lacy Dr BH21 .59 B3
Lady Baden Powell Way
DT11 .212 C2
Lady Caroline's Dr
DT11 .210 D7
Lady Mead Cl [3] DT5 .187 A2
Lady's Well★ DT2 .195 C1
Ladysmith Rd BH23 .124 C4
Lagado Cl BH14 .147 B4
Lagland Ct [12] BH15 .119 B1
Lagland St BH15 .119 B1
Lagoon Cl BH14 .147 A4
Lagoon Rd BH14 .147 A4
Laidlaw Cl BH12 .121 A4
Lake Ave BH15 .118 B1
Lake Cres BH15 .118 C2
Lake Dr BH15 .118 B1
Lake Gr Rd BH25 .95 A2
Lake La DT6 .100 B2
Lake Rd
Bournemouth BH11 .89 A3
Hamworthy BH15 .118 C1
Verwood BH31 .45 B2
Lake View Manor BH25 .95 A2
Lakefields BA22 .193 B7
Lakegate La DT9 .194 A5
Lakeside BH24 .55 C3
Lakeside Gdns DT3 .167 A4
Lakeside Pines BH25 .95 A2
Lakeside Rd BH13 .121 A1
Lakeview Dr BH24 .55 C3
Lakewood Rd BH23 .93 C1
Lamb Plot DT9 .194 D2
Lambert Cl [13] DT9 .17 B1
Lambert's Castle (Fort)★
DT6 .202 E2
Lambourne Ct TA18 .191 F5
Lambs Cl BH17 .87 B1
Lambs La BH21 .56 B2
Lambsfield DT9 .30 B4
Lambsgreen La BH21 .58 C1
Lammas Cl SP8 .5 C2
Lampton Cl BH20 .139 C1
Lampton Gdns BH9 .89 C1
Lancaster Cl
Christchurch BH23 .125 B4
Corfe Mullen BH18 .86 C3
Lancaster Dr
Corfe Mullen BH18 .86 C3
Verwood BH31 .45 A3
Lancaster Rd
Dorchester DT1 .108 A1
Ferndown BH21 .61 A4
Radipole DT3 .152 A1
Lancer Cl BH23 .123 C4
Lanchards [4] DT11 .198 B6
Lanchards La DT11 .198 B5
Lander Cl BH15 .119 B1
Landers Reach BH16 .84 B1
Landford Gdns BH8 .90 B1
Landford Way BH8 .90 B1
Landscombe Vale
DT2 .208 A8
Landseer Rd [13] BH4 .121 B2
Landshire La
Fifehead Magdalen SP8 .20 B3
Henstridge DT10 .18 C1
Stalbridge BA8 .19 B2
Lane Cl DT11 .212 C2
Lane End DT11 .79 C4
Lane The
[4] Bournemouth BH8 .122 B3
Corfe Castle BH20 .176 C2
Lane-side SP7 .12 C2
Lanehouse Rocks Rd [1]
DT4 .180 B4
Lanes The BH25 .95 A3
Lang Rd TA18 .191 E3
Langdon Ct BH14 .120 B2
Langdon La
Beaminster DT8 .204 E4
Chideock DT6 .98 C4
Langdon Rd BH14 .120 B2
Langdons DT9 .30 B4
Langdons Way [1] TA20 .202 A8
Langfords La SP7 .12 B1
Langham Ct BH23 .91 C1
Langham La SP8 .4 C1
Langley Chase BH24 .54 A3
Langley Rd
Christchurch BH23 .93 C1
Poole BH14 .120 C2
Langmead Pl [3] TA18 .191 F3
Langmead Rd TA18 .191 F3
Langmead Sq [1] TA18 .191 F3
Langmoor La EX13 .202 A2
Langside Ave BH12 .121 A4
Langside Sch BH12 .121 A4
Langton Ave DT4 .180 B3
Langton Cl BH25 .127 A4
Langton Cres DT11 .212 C1
Langton Cross★ DT3 .150 C1
Langton Dene [27] BH4 .121 B2
Langton Matravers Mus★
BH19 .178 A2
Langton Matravers Prim Sch
BH19 .178 A1
Langton Rd
Blandford Forum DT11 .212 C1
Langton Rd *continued*
Bournemouth BH7 .122 C3
Lansdell Ct [6] BH15 .119 C2
Lansdowne Cres BH1 .122 A2
Lansdowne Gdns BH1 .122 A2
Lansdowne House [13]
BH1 .122 A2
Lansdowne Rd
Bournemouth BH1 .122 A3
Bridport DT6 .100 B2
Lansdowne Sq DT4 .167 B1
Lansdowne The BH1 .122 A2
Lapwing Rd BH21 .60 A4
Lara Cl BH8 .90 B2
Larch Cl Broadstone BH17 .86 C1
Hordle SO41 .95 C2
Sandford BH20 .143 A4
St.Leonards BH24 .54 B2
Larch Way BH22 .61 B4
Larcombe La DT6 .69 B3
Lark Rd BH23 .125 A3
Larkhill Rd Yeovil BA21 .27 A3
Yeovil Without BA21 .26 C4
Larks Cl BH22 .61 A4
Larks Rise BH22 .61 A4
Larksfield Ave BH9 .90 B2
Larkshill Cl BH25 .95 A2
Larksmead DT11 .212 C2
Larkspur Cl DT4 .167 C3
Larkspur Cres BA21 .26 C4
Larmer Tree Victorian
Pleasure Gdn★ SP5 .188 B3
Lascelles Ct [1] BH7 .123 A3
Lascelles Rd BH7 .123 A3
Latch Farm Ave BH23 .124 A4
Latimer Rd BH9 .121 C4
Latimers Cl BH23 .93 C1
Launches The BH20 .172 B3
Laundry La SP7 .12 B1
Laurel Ave BH20 .116 A1
Laurel Cl [1] Bridport DT6 100 A4
Christchurch BH23 .93 B1
Corfe Mullen BH21 .86 B3
Hordle SO41 .95 C2
St.Leonards BH24 .54 A2
West Coker BA22 .193 B8
Laurel Dr BH18 .87 B2
Laurel Gdns BH18 .87 B2
Laurel La BH24 .54 A2
Laurels The
[7] Crewkerne TA18 .191 F5
Ferndown BH22 .61 B4
[8] Gillingham SP8 .5 C1
Iwerne Courtney or Shroton
DT11 .198 E7
Lavender Cl BH31 .45 C3
Lavender Rd
Bournemouth BH8 .90 B2
Hordle SO41 .95 C2
Lavender Villas [1]
BH23 .126 A4
Lavender Way BH18 .86 B2
Laver's La TA20 .202 C6
Laverstock [27] BH5 .122 C2
Laverstock Pk SP1 .213 C3
Laverstock Pk W SP1 .213 C3
Laverstock Rd SP1 .213 C3
Lavinia Rd BH12 .120 B4
Lawford Rd BH9 .90 A2
Lawn View BH25 .94 B3
Lawns Cl BH21 .60 B3
Lawns Rd BH21 .60 A3
Lawns The Charmouth DT6 97 A4
Christchurch BH23 .126 A4
Lawrence Ct BH8 .122 B3
Lawrence Dr
Crossways DT2 .137 B3
Poole BH13 .120 C1
Lawrence La Hyde SP6 .43 B2
Witchampton BH21 .201 A2
Lawrence of Arabia's
Cottage★ BH20 .112 B1
Lawrence of Arabia's Grave★
DT2 .138 C4
Lawrence Rd BH24 .47 C1
Lawson Rd BH12 .120 A3
Layard Dr BH21 .59 B1
Laymoor La BH21 .60 B3
Layton Ct BH12 .120 B3
Layton La SP7 .12 C1
Layton Rd BH12 .120 B3
Le Neubourg Way SP8 .5 C1
Le Patourel Cl BH23 .124 B4
Lea Cl BA21 .27 B4
Lea Rd DT4 .180 A4
Lea The BH31 .45 B3
Lea Way BH11 .88 C3
Leaden Hall Sch SP2 .213 B2
Leamington Rd
Bournemouth BH9 .122 A4
Weymouth DT4 .166 C1
Leaphill Rd BH7 .123 A3
Learoyd Rd BH17 .119 C4
Leaze La BA21 .28 A2
Lecher La DT8 .192 B1
Lechlade Gdns BH7 .123 A4
Ledbury Rd BH23 .124 C3
Ledgard Cl BH14 .120 A2
Lee Ct BH22 .61 B2
Lee La DT6 .101 A4
Leedam Rd BH10 .89 B2
Leeds Cres DT4 .166 C1
Lees Cl BH23 .91 B2
Leeson Cl [2] BH19 .178 C1
Leeson Dr BH22 .61 A4
Leeson House Field Studies
Ctr★ BH19 .178 B1
Leeson Rd BH7 .122 C4
Leet Cl [1] DT5 .181 A1
Leet Ct DT9 .29 C2
Legg La BH21 .59 B2
Legion Cl
Dorchester DT1 .134 C4
Hamworthy BH15 .118 C1
Legion Rd
Hamworthy BH15 .118 C1
Yeovil BA21 .27 A3
Leicester Rd BH13 .120 C2
Leigh Comm BH21 .59 C3
Leigh Gdns BH21 .59 B2
Leigh La Halstock BA22 .193 C3
Ibberton DT11 .197 D3
Wimborne Minster BH21 .59 C3
Winsham TA20 .202 D8
Leigh Rd New Milton BH25 95 A2
Wimborne Minster BH21 .59 C2
Leigham Vale Rd BH6 .123 B2
Lennox St DT4 .167 B2
Lentham Cl BH17 .87 B1
Lenthay Cl DT9 .29 C2
Lenthay Rd DT9 .29 C2
Lerrett Cl DT3 .166 B3
Leslie Rd
Bournemouth BH9 .121 C4
Poole BH14 .120 A2
Lessingham Ave DT4 .180 B3
Letton Cl DT11 .212 C2
Letton Pk★ DT11 .212 C2
Leven Ave BH4 .121 B3
Leven Cl BH4 .121 B2
Levet's La [5] BH15 .119 A1
Lewell Way DT2 .136 B2
Lewens Cl BH21 .59 B2
Lewens La BH21 .59 B2
Lewesdon Cl [6] DT8 .204 C4
Lewesdon Dr BH18 .86 C2
Lewesdon Hill (National
Trust)★ DT8 .203 E4
Leybourne Ave BH10 .89 B2
Leybourne Cl BH10 .89 B3
Leydene Ave BH8 .90 C1
Leydene Cl BH8 .90 C1
Leyland Rd BH12 .88 C1
Leyside BH23 .124 C3
Leyton Conyers [16]
BH13 .147 C4
Liberty Cl BH21 .53 B3
Liberty Ct BH23 .123 C4
Library Mews BH12 .120 B3
Library Rd
Bournemouth BH9 .89 C1
Ferndown BH22 .61 B3
Poole BH12 .120 C3
Lichfield Rd DT4 .167 A1
Liddington Cres DT11 .212 B2
Liddon Hill TA18 .191 C5
Lighthouse Rd BH19 .185 B4
Lilac Cl BH24 .55 B4
Lilliput CE Fst Sch
BH14 .147 B4
Lilliput Ct BH14 .120 A2
Lilliput Rd BH14 .147 B4
Limber Rd BA22 .26 B3
Lime Cl Dorchester DT1 .134 C4
Poole BH15 .119 C3
Lime Hill DT6 .70 A4
Lime Kiln BA21 .26 C3
Lime Kiln La BA8 .19 A2
Lime Kiln Rd BH16 .84 B2
Lime Kiln Way SP2 .213 B1
Lime Tree Ave BA20 .27 A1
Lime Tree Cl SP6 .42 A3
Limekiln Cl [2] DT5 .186 C1
Limerick Cl [3] DT9 .17 B1
Limes The SP7 .12 A4
Limited Rd BH9 .90 A1
Lin Brook Dr BH24 .47 C1
Linclieth Rd [3] BH20 .140 A1
Lincoln Ave
Bournemouth BH1 .122 B3
Christchurch BH23 .91 C1
Lincoln Rd Poole BH12 .120 B4
[2] Weymouth DT4 .166 C1
Lindbergh Rd BH21 .61 A4
Linden Ave DT1 .108 A1
Linden Cl Ferndown BH22 .61 B1
Salisbury SP1 .213 C3
Linden Gdns [1] BH24 .55 A4
Linden Pk SP7 .13 A1
Linden Rd
Bournemouth BH9 .90 A2
Ferndown BH22 .61 B1
Poole BH12 .120 B3
Swanage BH19 .179 A1
Yeovil BA20 .27 A3
Lindens The BH23 .92 B2
Lindford Rd BH24 .47 C1
Lindlar Cl SP7 .12 C2
Lindsay Manor [10] BH12 121 A2
Lindsay Pk [15] BH13 .121 A2
Lindsay Rd BH13 .121 A2
Lindum Ct [3] BH12 .121 A2
Lineside BH23 .124 B4
Linford Cl BH25 .95 A2
Linford Rd BH24 .47 C1
Ling Rd BH12 .88 A1
Lingdale Rd BH6 .123 B3
Lingfield Ave BA21 .27 C4
Lingfield Grange BH4 .121 A2
Lington Cl DT2 .137 B3
Lingwood Ave BH23 .124 C3
Linhorns La BH25 .95 A3
Link Rd BH24 .47 C1
Link Rise BH21 .86 C3
Link Way SP1 .213 C4
Linkhay [12] TA20 .202 A8
Linkhay Cl [11] TA20 .202 A8
Links Dr BH23 .91 B1
Links Rd Poole BH14 .120 B1
Weymouth DT4 .167 A2
Links View Ave BH14 .120 C1
Linkside Ave BH8 .122 C4
Linmead Dr BH11 .89 A3
Linnet Cl Radipole DT3 .152 B2
Ringwood BH24 .55 C3
Linnet Ct BH25 .94 C2
Linnet La DT2 .205 D5
Linnet Rd BH17 .118 C4
Linnetsdene [7] SP2 .213 B1
Linsay Rd BH20 .139 C3
Lintern La SP8 .11 A3
Linthorpe Rd BH15 .119 C2
Linwood Mix Sch BH9 .122 A4
Linwood Rd BH9 .122 A4
Lionheart Cl BH11 .88 B3
Lions Hill Way BH24 .53 C2
Lions La BH24 .53 C2
Lions Wood BH24 .54 A2
Liscombe Cl DT1 .107 B1
Litchford Rd BH25 .95 B2
Little Barrs Dr BH25 .95 A2
Little Britain DT1 .108 B1
Little Content La SP7 .12 C2
Little Croft Rd BH12 .120 A3
Little Ct BH14 .147 B4
Little Dewlands BH31 .44 C3
Little England DT11 .79 C4
Little Forest Mans [10]
BH1 .122 A2
Little Forest Rd BH4 .121 C3
Little Fosters BH13 .147 C3
Little La DT11 .198 A6
Little Lonnen BH21 .59 C4
Littlecroft Ave BH9 .90 A2
Littledown SP7 .12 C3
Littledown Ave BH7 .122 C4
Littledown Dr BH7 .122 C4
Littlefield DT9 .29 C2
Littlefield La SP5 .189 A4
Littlemead
Broadmayne DT2 .136 A1
Radipole DT3 .152 A2
Littlemead Cl BH17 .119 A4
Littlemill La SP6 .190 F3
Littlemoor Ave BH11 .88 B2
Littlemoor CP Sch
DT3 .152 C1
Littlemoor Rd
Overcombe/Preston
DT3 .168 A4
Radipole DT3 .152 B2
Littleton Dro DT11 .211 B6
Littletowns DT11 .212 B2
Littleview Rd DT4 .166 C1
Litton Hill DT2 .103 A1
Litton La
Askerswell DT2 .102 C3
Litton Cheney DT2 .103 A1
Puncknowle DT2 .129 C4
Liverpool Rd [3] DT4 .166 C1
Livingston Rd BH12 .120 B3
Livingstone Rd
Bournemouth BH5 .123 A3
Christchurch BH23 .124 B4
Wimborne Minster BH21 .59 C2
Llewellin Cl BH16 .118 B4
Llewellin Ct BH16 .118 B4
Load La DT2 .194 F1
Loaders Cl BH9 .122 A4
Locarno Rd BH19 .179 A1
Loch Rd BH14 .120 C3
Lockeridge Cl DT11 .212 B2
Lockett's La DT2 .207 F7
Locks La
Glanvilles Wootton DT9 .195 E3
Loders DT6 .101 C3
Stratton DT2 .106 C4
Locksley Dr BH22 .61 B2
Lockwood Terr SP8 .11 A4
Lockyer's Mid Sch BH21 .86 B4
Lockyer's Rd BH21 .86 C4
Lockyer's Way BH16 .84 B2
Lockyers Dr BH22 .61 C3
Lodbourne Gdns [6] SP8 .5 C2
Lodbourne Gn [7] SP8 .5 C2
Lodbourne Terr [5] SP8 .5 C2
Lodden View SP8 .11 A4
Loders CE Prim Sch
DT6 .69 B1
Loders Cl BH17 .87 B2
Loders La DT6 .101 C2
Lodge Cl BH14 .120 C2
Lodge Ct BH14 .120 C2
Lodge Rd
Christchurch BH23 .123 C4
Holt BH21 .51 A3
Lodge The BH2 .121 C2
Lodge Way DT4 .180 B4
Lodmoor Ave DT3 .167 B4
Lodmoor Ctry Pk★
DT3 .167 C3
Loewy Cres BH12 .88 B1
Lombard Ave BH6 .123 B3
Lombardy Cl BH31 .45 B3
Lomer La SP6 .42 C2
Lomond Dr DT4 .167 B1
London Cl
[20] Dorchester DT1 .108 A1
Piddlehinton DT2 .76 C4
London La BH23 .63 C1
London Rd
Dorchester DT1 .108 A1
Milborne Port DT9 .17 C1
London Rd *continued*
Salisbury SP1 .213 C4
London Row DT2 .76 C4
Lone Pine Dr BH22 .61 C2
Lone Pine Way BH22 .61 C1
Long Acre DT5 .187 A2
Long Ash La
Cattistock DT2 .206 E2
Frampton DT2 .74 A2
Frome St Quintin DT2 .206 D6
Maiden Newton DT2 .73 C3
Long Barrow La DT8 .204 B3
Long Bredy Hut La
DT2 .103 C1
Long Cl BA21 .26 C3
Long Cross SP7 .12 C2
Long Entry DT7 .96 B3
Long Furlong La BA22 .193 C8
Long Hill BA12 .2 C3
Long La
Bothenhampton DT6 .100 C2
Bourton SP8 .1 A1
Cann SP7 .24 A4
Colehill BH21 .51 A1
Cucklington BA9 .4 A1
Puddletown DT2 .78 A1
Ringwood BH24 .55 B2
Whitechurch Canonicorum
DT6 .65 B4
Wimborne Minster BH21 .59 C4
Long Mdw DT9 .195 A2
Long Mead BA21 .26 C3
Long Rd BH10 .89 B3
Long St
Cerne Abbas DT2 .207 D4
Sherborne DT9 .30 B3
Long's La DT6 .100 C4
Longacre Dr BH22 .61 B2
Longbarrow Cl BH8 .91 A1
Longbury Hill La SP8 .5 A2
Longcroft Rd
Weymouth DT4 .167 A2
Yeovil BA21 .27 B3
Longdown Rd DT9 .194 D7
Longespee Rd BH21 .87 C4
Longfield Dr
Bournemouth BH11 .89 A3
Ferndown BH22 .89 C4
Longfield Rd DT4 .167 B1
Longfleet CE Comb Sch
BH15 .119 B2
Longfleet Rd BH15 .119 C2
Longford Rd DT9 .194 C7
Longforward Hill
TA17 .191 A8
Longforward La TA17 .191 B8
Longhayes Ave DT6 .100 A4
Longhill Dr [11] SP2 .213 B1
Longland SP2 .213 A3
Longland's La
Littlebredy DT2 .131 C4
Winterbourne Abbas
DT2 .105 A1
Longlands La BA22 .193 C8
Longleat Gdns BH25 .94 C2
Longman's Rd BH21 .201 A3
Longmead SP7 .12 C2
Longmeadow La BH17 .118 C4
Longspee Sch BH17 .119 B4
Longstone Cl DT5 .186 C1
Lonnen Rd BH21 .51 B1
Lonnen Wood Cl BH21 .60 A4
Lonsdale Rd BH3 .121 C3
Looke La DT2 .129 C3
Lopen Rd TA17 .191 D8
Loraine Ave BH23 .126 B4
Lord Cl BH17 .119 C4
Lordsmead Rd BA12 .3 A2
Lorne Pk Rd BH1 .122 A2
Lorne Rd DT1 .107 C1
Lorton La DT3 .152 A2
Loscombe's Well Rd
DT6 .66 B1
Lotmoor Hill SP8 .10 B1
Louise Rd DT1 .107 C1
Louse La DT11 .211 E4
Louviers Rd DT3 .152 C1
Love La Marnhull DT10 .21 A2
Salisbury SP1 .213 B2
Shaftesbury SP7 .12 B1
Love's La DT6 .66 B1
Lovelands DT2 .193 A1
Lovells Mead DT10 .20 C2
Loveridge La [16] TA20 .202 A8
Loverley La BH21 .201 B3
Lovett Gn SP1 .213 C4
Low's Hill La DT9 .29 B3
Lower Acreman St DT9 .30 A3
Lower Ashley Rd BH25 .95 B1
Lower Beadon TA16 .191 F7
Lower Blandford Rd
Broadstone BH18 .87 A2
Cann SP7 .24 A4
[1] Shaftesbury SP7 .12 C1
[2] Shaftesbury SP7 .13 A1
Lower Boyston La DT9 .16 C2
Lower Catherston Rd
DT6 .65 A1
Lower Comm La BH21 .53 B4
Lower Comm Rd DT11 .36 B1
Lower Coombses
TA20 .202 A8
Lower E Coker Rd
BA20 .27 A1
Lower Fairmead Rd
BA21 .27 C4
Lower Golf Links Rd
BH18 .87 A3

Lower Gunville 4 DT9 17 B1
Lower Hillside Rd
BH20 140 A1
Lower Kingsbury DT9 17 B2
Lower N Rd SP5 188 C5
Lower Odcombe BA22 26 A2
Lower Putton La DT3 166 B3
Lower Rd Britford SP5 213 C1
Stalbridge DT10 33 C4
Toller Porcorum DT2 71 C4
Lower Ream BA21 26 C3
Lower S Rd SP5 188 C4
Lower Sch La 2 DT11 211 B1
Lower Sea La DT6 97 A4
Lower St Lillington DT9 194 F7
Merriott TA16 191 F7
Morden BH20 83 B1
Okeford Fitzpaine DT11 197 F6
Salisbury SP2 213 A2
West Chinnock TA18 192 B8
Witchampton BH21 200 F1
Lower St Alban St 4
DT4 167 B1
Lower St Edmund St 5
DT4 167 B1
Lower Steppes BH19 178 B1
Lower Townsend DT6 128 A4
Lower Turners Barn La
BA20 27 A1
Lower Walditch La
DT6 100 C3
Lower Way DT3 166 B3
Lower Wraxhill Rd
BA20 27 A1
Lowesmore Ct BH14 120 B2
Lowther Gdns 3 BH8 122 B3
Lowther Rd
Bournemouth BH8 122 A3
Yeovil BA21 28 A4
Lox La SP7 11 C2
Lubbecke Way DT1 108 B1
Lucas Rd BH15 119 A1
Lucerne Ave BH6 123 B3
Lucetta La DT1 135 A4
Luckham Cl BH9 90 A1
Luckham Gdns BH9 90 B1
Luckham Pl BH9 90 A1
Luckham Rd BH9 90 A1
Luckham Rd E BH9 90 A1
Ludbourne Rd DT9 30 B3
Ludlow Rd DT4 166 C1
Ludney La TA17 191 A7
Lufton Manor Coll
BA22 26 A4
Lufton Trad Est BA22 26 B4
Lufton Way BA22 26 B3
Lulworth Ave BH15 118 C1
Lulworth Castle★
BH20 158 B1
Lulworth Cl BH15 118 C1
Lulworth Cove Heritage Ctr★
BH20 172 B3
Lulworth Cres BH15 118 C1
Lulworth Rd BH20 140 A1
Lumber La BH21 201 C5
Lumby Dr BH24 55 B4
Lumby Dr Pk BH24 55 B4
Lurmer St SP7 37 C3
Luscombe Rd BH14 120 B1
Luther Rd BH9 121 C4
Luton Down Rd 3 DT11 199 E2
Luton Dro DT11 200 A2
Lyatts Hill BA22 193 A6
Lych Gate Ct BH24 55 C3
Lyde La BA21 28 A3
Lyde Rd BA21 27 C3
Lydford Gdns BH11 89 A1
Lydford Rd BH11 89 A1
Lydfords La SP8 5 B1
Lydlinch Cl BH22 61 B1
Lydwell Cl
Bournemouth BH11 88 C3
Weymouth DT4 180 C4
Lyell Rd BH12 120 B3
Lyewater TA18 191 E4
Lym Cl DT7 96 B3
Lyme Cres BH23 125 C4
Lyme Rd
Crewkerne TA18 191 E3
Lyme Regis DT7 96 A4
Lyme Regis Golf Club
DT7 96 B4
Lyme Regis Leisure Ctr
DT7 96 A3
Lyme Regis Marine
Aquarium★ DT7 96 A2
Lyme Regis Philpot Mus★
DT7 96 B3
Lymes Cl 3 DT4 180 B4
Lymington Rd
Barton on Sea BH25 95 B1
Christchurch BH23 125 C4
Lynch Cl Mere BA12 3 A3
Milborne St Andrew DT11 79 B4
Lynch La
Hardington Mandeville
BA22 193 A6
Weymouth DT4 166 C1
Lynch Rd DT4 166 C1
Lyndale Rd DT4 180 B3
Lyndhurst Rd BH23 93 B3
Lyndon Ct BH23 91 C1
Lynes La BH24 55 A4
Lynmoor Rd DT4 167 C3
Lynn Rd BH17 87 C1
Lynric Cl BH25 127 A4
Lynton Cres BH23 91 B2
Lynwood Cl BH22 61 B4
Lynwood Dr BH21 87 C4
Lynx Trad Est BA20 26 C2
Lynx W Trading Est
BA20 26 C2
Lyon Ave BH25 95 A2
Lyon Rd BH12 88 C1
Lysander Cl BH23 125 B4
Lysander Rd BA20 26 C2
Lystra Rd BH9 90 A2
Lytchett Dr BH18 87 A2
Lytchett La BH20 140 A2
Lytchett Matravers CP Sch
BH16 84 B1
Lytchett Minst Upper Sch
BH16 117 A4
Lytchett Way BH16 118 A3
Lytham Rd BH18 87 A2
Lytton Rd BH1 122 B3

M

Mabey Ave BH10 89 B1
Macandrew Rd BH13 147 C4
Macaulay Rd BH18 87 A2
Macklin Rd SP2 213 A3
Maclaren Rd BH9 89 C2
Maclean Rd BH11 88 C2
Macmillan Way DT2 131 A3
Macville Ave BH20 140 A1
Madeira Rd
Bournemouth BH1 122 A2
Poole BH14 120 B3
Madeline Cl BH12 120 A4
Madeline Cres BH12 120 A4
Madison Ave BH1 122 B3
Mag's Barrow BH22 61 C1
Magdalen La
Bridport DT6 100 A3
Christchurch BH23 124 A3
Magna Cl
Bournemouth BH11 88 C3
Yeovil BA21 27 C4
Magna Gdns BH11 88 C3
Magna Rd BH11 88 B4
Magnolia Cl
Bournemouth BH6 124 A3
3 Radipole DT3 152 C1
Verwood BH31 45 C2
Magnolia House 6 BH10 89 C2
Magpie Cl BH8 90 B2
Magpie Gr BH25 94 C1
Maiden Beech Mid Sch
TA18 191 E3
Maiden Castle★ DT2 134 A3
Maiden Castle Rd DT2 134 B4
Maiden Newton Sta
DT2 73 A4
Maiden St DT4 167 C1
Maidment Cl BH11 88 C2
Main Rd
Fortuneswell DT5 181 B1
Tolpuddle DT2 79 B1
West Lulworth BH20 172 B2
Main St Bridport DT6 100 C2
Broadmayne DT2 136 A1
Chideock DT6 99 A3
Iwerne Courtney or Shroton
DT11 198 F7
Maincombe Cl 2 TA18 191 E3
Maitlands The BH2 121 B1
Major's Comm DT2 208 A7
Majorca Mans 11 BH2 121 C2
Malan Cl BH17 119 C4
Malcomb Cl BH6 124 A2
Mallams DT5 186 C4
Mallard Bldgs 6 BH25 95 A2
Mallard Cl
Bournemouth BH8 90 B1
Christchurch BH23 125 A3
Salisbury SP2 213 A2
Mallard Rd
Bournemouth BH8 90 B1
Wimborne Minster BH21 60 A4
Mallory Cl BH23 124 C4
Mallow Cl
Broadstone BH18 86 C2
Christchurch BH23 125 B4
Mallows The BH25 95 B2
Malmesbury Ct BH8 122 B3
Malmesbury Pk Pl 7
BH8 122 B3
Malmesbury Pk Prim Sch
BH8 122 A3
Malmesbury Pk Rd BH8 122 A3
Malmesbury Rd BH24 54 A2
Malmesbury Way BA21 26 C3
Maloren Way BH22 53 B1
Malta Cl 2 DT1 107 C1
Malthouse BH15 119 B1
Malthouse La
8 Salisbury SP2 213 B3
Trent DT9 14 C1
Malthouse Mdw 4 DT3 150 A4
Maltings The
Bournemouth BH11 88 C3
Cerne Abbas DT2 207 D4
Poole BH15 119 C2
Salisbury SP2 213 B3
Weymouth DT4 167 B1
Malvern Cl BH9 90 A2
Malvern Ct
4 Bournemouth BH9 90 A1
2 Christchurch BH23 124 C4
7 Yeovil BA21 26 C3
Malvern Rd BH9 90 A1
Malvern Terr DT4 167 A1
Mampitts La SP7 13 A1
Mampitts Rd SP7 13 A1
Mandalay Cl BH31 45 A3
Mandale Cl BH11 89 A2
Mandale Rd BH11 88 C2
Mandeville Cl DT4 180 A4
Mandeville Rd DT4 180 A4
Mandeville Stoke La
DT6 66 A4
Mangerton La DT6 69 A2
Mangerton Water Mill★
DT6 69 B2
Mangle Cave Hill
TA18 191 C5
Manning Ave BH23 93 B1
Manning's Heath Rd
BH12 88 A1
Manningford Rd DT11 212 B2
Mannings Heath Works
BH12 88 A1
Mannington Pl 19 BH2 121 C2
Mannington Way BH22 52 C1
Manor Ave
Lyme Regis DT7 96 A3
Poole BH12 88 B1
Manor Cl
Bradford Abbas DT9 28 B1
Dewlish DT2 209 C1
Ferndown BH22 61 C3
1 Portesham DT3 150 A4
South Perrott DT8 192 C1
Stratton DT2 106 C4
Templecombe BA8 18 B4
Manor Ct
Ringwood BH24 55 B4
Verwood BH31 45 A3
Manor Dr
9 Merriott TA16 191 F7
West Coker BA22 193 B8
Manor Farm Cl
Litton Cheney DT2 103 B1
New Milton BH25 94 C1
Manor Farm Ct DT2 133 C3
Manor Farm Rd
Bere Regis BH20 81 A1
Bournemouth BH10 89 B4
Salisbury SP1 213 C3
Manor Farmyard BH8 91 A2
Manor Fields DT6 100 C3
Manor Gdns
12 Beaminster DT8 204 D4
2 Ringwood BH24 55 A4
Verwood BH31 45 A3
Manor Gr DT2 133 B3
Manor La
Bradford Peverell DT2 106 C3
Verwood BH31 45 A3
Manor Pk BH15 119 A3
Manor Pk CE Fst Sch
DT1 135 A4
Manor Rd
Bournemouth BH1 122 B2
Christchurch BH23 124 A3
Dorchester DT1 135 A4
Gussage St Michael
BH21 200 F6
Mere BA12 2 C4
Milborne Port DT9 17 B2
New Milton BH25 95 A2
Radipole DT3 167 A4
Ringwood BH24 55 B4
Salisbury SP1 213 C3
Stourpaine DT11 198 F4
Studland BH19 164 B1
Swanage BH19 179 A1
Verwood BH31 45 A3
Yeovil BA20 27 B2
Manor St BA22 193 B8
Manor Vale 3 DT8 204 A8
Manor View TA18 191 F3
Manor Way BH31 45 A4
Mansard Ct BH13 147 A2
Manscombe Abbey★
DT6 66 A1
Mansel Cl BH12 121 B4
Mansfield Ave BH14 120 B2
Mansfield Cl
Ferndown BH22 61 B1
Poole BH14 120 B2
Mansfield Rd
Bournemouth BH9 89 C1
Poole BH14 120 B2
Ringwood BH24 55 A4
Manshay La DT6 203 A1
Manston Rd DT10 35 B1
Manton Cl BH15 118 C2
Manton Rd BH15 118 C2
Manwell Dr BH19 179 A1
Manwell Rd BH19 179 A1
Manwell's La 14 BH19 179 A1
Maple Cl
Barton on Sea BH25 127 A4
Christchurch BH23 125 C4
4 Overcombe/Preston
DT3 168 A4
Sandford BH20 143 A4
Shaftesbury SP7 12 C2
Maple Dr
12 Crewkerne TA18 191 F5
Ferndown BH22 61 B4
Yeovil BA20 27 A2
Maple Gdns DT6 100 B3
Maple Lodge BH16 118 B4
Maple Rd
Bournemouth BH9 121 C4
Poole BH15 119 B2
Maple Way SP8 5 B1
Maplecroft 4 SP2 213 B1
Mapperton Cl BH17 87 C1
Mapperton Hill SP8 2 C1
Mapperton House★
DT8 204 F2
Mapperton La DT6 69 A4
Mappowder Ct★ DT10 208 F8
Marabout Cl BH23 124 B4
Marchwood Rd BH10 89 B2
Margards La BH31 45 A3
Margaret Pl DT1 107 C1
Marian Cl BH21 86 B2
Marian Rd BH21 86 B2
Marianne Rd Poole BH12 121 B4
Wimborne Minster BH21 60 A4
Marie Cl BH12 120 B4
Marie Rd DT1 107 C1
Marina Ct
21 Bournemouth BH5 122 C2
Christchurch BH23 126 A4
Marina Dr BH14 120 A1
Marina Gdns DT4 167 A1
Marina Rd SP1 213 C2
Marina The BH5 122 C2
Marina Twrs 24 BH5 122 C2
Marina View 6 BH23 124 A3
Marine Ct BH25 126 B4
Marine Dr BH25 126 C4
Marine Dr E BH25 127 A3
Marine Dr W BH25 126 C4
Marine Par DT7 96 A2
Marine Rd BH6 123 B2
Mariners Ct BH23 125 A3
Mariners Dr BH19 179 A1
Mariners Way DT3 166 B3
Marion Ct BH23 124 A4
Mark's La BH25 95 A3
Market Cl BH15 119 B1
Market Pl
Blandford Forum DT11 212 B1
Ringwood BH24 55 A4
Sturminster Newton DT10 35 A1
Market St
Abbotsbury DT3 149 A4
Poole BH15 119 A1
Radipole DT4 167 B1
Yeovil BA20 27 B3
Market Way BH21 59 B2
Markets La DT6 101 C2
Markham Ave
Bournemouth BH10 89 B4
Weymouth DT4 167 A1
Markham Cl BH10 89 B3
Markham Rd BH9 122 A4
Marks Rd BH9 89 C2
Marl Cl BA21 27 A4
Marl La DT9 28 B3
Marlborough Ave DT4 180 B4
Marlborough Ct
21 Bournemouth BH4 121 B2
7 Poole BH12 121 A2
3 Wimborne Minster BH21 59 B3
Marlborough Mans 2
BH7 123 A3
Marlborough Pl BH21 59 B3
Marlborough Rd
Bournemouth BH4 121 B2
Poole BH14 120 B2
Salisbury SP1 213 B3
Yeovil BA21 28 A3
Marler House BH4 121 A2
Marley Ave BH25 94 C2
Marley Cl
New Milton BH25 94 C2
Overcombe/Preston
DT3 153 B2
Marline Rd BH12 120 B3
Marlott Rd Gillingham SP8 5 C2
Poole BH15 119 B3
Marlow Dr BH23 91 C2
Marlow Rd DT4 167 B1
Marlpit Dr BH23 94 A1
Marlpit La BH25 95 A4
Marmion Gn BH23 124 C4
Marnhull Rd
Hinton St Mary DT10 35 A3
Poole BH15 119 B2
Marpet Cl BH11 88 C3
Marquis Cl DT4 166 C1
Marquis Way BH11 88 B3
Marriage La DT10 35 A3
Marrowbone La DT6 100 C2
Marryat Ct
Christchurch BH23 126 A4
New Milton BH25 94 C2
Marryat Rd BH25 94 C2
Marsh Gate DT6 100 B2
Marsh La
Christchurch BH23 91 C1
Hazelbury Bryan DT10 196 F2
Henstridge BA8 19 B3
Ibberton DT11 197 D3
Pen Selwood BA9 1 A2
Salisbury SP2 213 A3
Upton BH16 118 A4
Wincanton BA9 8 C4
Winterborne Kingston
DT11 81 C4
Yeovil BA21 27 A4
Marsh Rd DT4 167 B1
Marsh The DT9 194 E3
Marsh Way
15 Pimperne DT11 199 D4
Swanage BH19 178 C1
Marshal Rd BH17 87 A1
Marshall Row 5 BH19 179 B1
Marshallsay Rd DT3 166 B3
Marshfield BH21 59 C4
Marshlands Cl BH23 124 B3
Marshwood Ave BH17 87 C2
Marshwood CE Prim Sch
DT6 202 F2
Marston Cl
Blandford Forum DT11 212 B2
New Milton BH25 95 A3
Marston Gr BH23 93 C1
Marston Rd
Castleton DT9 29 C4
New Milton BH25 95 A3
2 Poole BH15 119 A1
Sherborne DT9 30 A4
Martel Cl DT2 136 A1
Martello House 10
BH13 147 C4
Martello Pk BH13 147 C4
Martello Rd BH13 120 C1
Martello Rd S BH13 147 C4
Martello Twrs BH13 147 C4
Martells The BH25 127 A4
Martin Cl BH17 118 C4
Martin Dro End SP6 190 A7
Martin Kemp-Welch Sch The
BH12 120 B4
Martin's La SP8 5 B4
Martin's St SP7 12 C1
Martindale Ave BH21 60 A3
Martingale Cl BH16 118 B4
Martins Cl Ferndown BH22 61 C4
3 Salisbury SP2 213 B1
Martins Dr BH22 61 C4
Martins Hill Cl BH23 92 B1
Martins Hill La BH23 92 B1
Martins Way BH22 61 C4
Martinscroft Rd 4 DT5 186 C2
Martleaves Cl 6 DT4 180 B4
Martyr Cl DT1 134 C4
Marwell Cl BH7 123 A4
Mary Cossins Cl DT11 212 B2
Mary Gdns 4 DT11 197 F6
Mary La BH22 52 C1
Mary St BA21 27 B3
Maryland Rd BH16 118 B2
Maskew Cl DT3 166 B3
Mason's La DT8 204 A4
Masters Ct BH4 121 B2
Masterson Cl BH23 124 B4
Matchams Cl BH24 63 A4
Matchams La BH23 63 A2
Matlock Rd BH22 61 B2
Matthews Rd BA21 27 C3
Maud Rd DT1 107 C1
Maudlin Cross TA20 202 E8
Maudlin La TA20 202 F8
Maumbury Rd DT1 107 C1
Maumbury Rings★
DT1 135 A4
Maundeville Cres BH23 123 B4
Maundville Rd BH23 123 C4
Maunsell Ave DT3 153 A2
Maureen Cl BH12 120 A4
Maurice Rd BH8 122 B4
Mavis Rd BH9 90 A1
Max Gate (NT)★ DT1 135 B4
Maxwell Rd
Bournemouth BH9 122 A4
Broadstone BH18 86 C2
Poole BH13 147 C4
May Gdns
Bournemouth BH11 88 C2
Christchurch BH23 94 A1
May Gr DT11 211 D6
May La DT11 199 D7
May Terr Gdns DT3 166 B3
Maycroft Rd DT4 167 B1
Mayfair BH4 121 B1
Mayfair Gdns BH11 89 A2
Mayfair Rd SP1 213 C3
Mayfield Ave BH14 120 C2
Mayfield Cl
Ferndown BH22 61 B3
Radipole DT4 167 A3
Mayfield Dr BH22 61 B3
Mayfield Rd
Bournemouth BH9 90 A1
Yeovil BA21 27 C3
Mayfield Way BH22 61 B3
Mayford Rd BH12 121 A3
Maylyn Rd BH16 85 A1
Mc Creery Rd DT9 30 A4
Mcintyre Rd BH23 91 A4
Mckay Way DT4 166 C1
Mckinley Rd BH4 121 B1
Mcwilliam Cl BH12 121 B4
Mcwilliam Rd 2 BH9 90 A1
Mead Ave BA22 26 B3
Mead Bower DT5 186 C1
Mead Cl BH18 87 A1
Mead La Allington DT6 100 A4
Gussage All Saints BH21 201 A5
Mead Rd
Corfe Castle BH20 177 A4
Radipole DT4 167 A3
Meadow Cl
Bransgore BH23 93 A4
Cattistock DT2 206 C2
Chickerell DT3 166 B3
Ferndown BH22 61 B1
Henstridge BA8 19 A3
Ringwood BH24 55 B4
Sopley BH23 92 A4
Stalbridge DT10 33 B4
Meadow Ct
6 Bournemouth BH9 90 A2
15 Wimborne Minster BH21 59 B2
Meadow Ct Cl BH9 90 A2

Meadow Farm La BH21 86 B4
Meadow Gr BH31 45 B3
Meadow La Burton BH23 92 B1
Wool BH20 140 A1
Meadow Rd
5 Charlton Marshall DT11 211 D6
New Milton BH25 95 A2
Ringwood BH24 55 B4
8 Salisbury SP2 213 A3
Yeovil BA21 27 C4
Meadow Rd (South) 10 SP2 213 A3
Meadow Rise BH18 86 C3
Meadow View
7 Blandford Forum DT11 212 B1
Bradford Peverell DT2 107 A3
Cattistock DT2 206 B2
Charminster DT2 107 B3
7 Stofold BA22 193 F8
Meadow View Cl BH20 142 C2
Meadow View Rd
Bournemouth BH11 88 C2
Radipole DT3 152 B2
Meadow Way
Barton on Sea BH25 127 A4
Charmouth DT6 97 A4
Ringwood BH24 55 B4
Verwood BH31 45 B2
Meadowbank BH16 118 B4
Meadowcroft SP8 11 A4
Meadowland BH23 124 C3
Meadowlands DT6 100 B1
Meadows Cl BH16 118 B4
Meadows Dr BH16 118 B4
Meadows The
Gillingham SP8 11 A4
Salisbury SP1 213 C2
Meadowside 4 DT8 204 A7
Meadowsweet Rd BH17 118 C4
Meads Cl DT2 194 A2
Meads The DT9 17 B1
Meadus's La BH20 162 B2
Meadway 4 DT6 100 A1
Meadway The BH23 93 B1
Medbourne Cl DT11 212 B2
Medina Way BH23 125 B3
Medlar Cl BH23 92 B1
Medway Dr DT3 168 A4
Medway Rd BH22 62 A3
Meech Cl DT6 100 B2
Meech Way DT2 75 C1
Meerhay La DT6 65 A2
Meerhay Manor* DT8 204 D5
Meeting House La BH24 55 A4
Melancholy La BH20 142 C1
Melbourne Rd BH23 91 C1
Melbourne Rd BH8 122 B3
Melbourne St DT4 167 A2
Melbury Abbas Mill* SP7 24 A3
Melbury Ave BH12 120 C4
Melbury Cl BH22 61 B2
Melbury Down* SP5 24 C2
Melbury House* DT2 194 A1
Melbury Pk* DT2 194 A1
Melbury Rd
Weymouth DT4 167 B2
Yetminster DT9 194 C5
Melbury St SP7 24 B2
Melbury Way SP7 13 A2
Melchester Cl 11 SP8 5 C2
Melcombe Ave DT4 167 C3
Melcombe Pl 1 DT4 167 C2
Melford Ct BH1 122 A2
Mellstock Ave DT1 135 A4
Mellstock Cres BH20 142 B3
Mellstock Rd BH15 119 B3
Melplash Ct* DT6 204 D1
Melrose Ct SO40 95 B2
Melrose Rd BA21 27 B3
Melstock Ave DT3 168 A4
Melton Ct BH13 120 C2
Melverley Gdns BH21 59 B3
Melville Rd BH9 121 C4
Melvin Cl SP1 213 C3
Melway Gdns 11 DT11 198 C7
Melway La DT11 198 C7
Memorial Ave 19 TA18 191 F4
Memorial Rd BA22 26 B3
Mendip Cl
New Milton BH25 95 B1
Verwood BH31 45 A3
Mendip Ct 4 BH23 124 C4
Mendip Rd BH31 45 A3
Menin Rd BH20 139 B3
Mentone Rd 2 BH14 120 A2
Meon Rd BH7 123 A4
Mercery Rd DT3 167 B4
Mere Castle* BA12 2 C3
Mere Fst Sch BA12 3 A3
Meredith Cl
Christchurch BH23 124 B4
Halstock BA22 193 C3
Meriden Cl BH13 147 C4
Meridians The BH23 123 C3
Merino Way BH22 53 A1
Merlewood Cl BH2 121 C2
Merlewood Ct 19 BH25 95 A2
Merley Dr BH23 126 A4
Merley Fst Sch BH21 59 B1
Merley Gdns BH21 59 C1
Merley House BH21 59 A1
Merley House La BH21 59 B1
Merley House Mus* BH21 59 A1
Merley La BH21 59 C1
Merley Pk Rd
Corfe Mullen BH21 86 C4
Wimborne Minster BH21 59 B1
Merley Rd DT4 180 B3
Merley Ways BH21 59 B1
Merlin Ave N DT3 152 A2
Merlin Ave S DT3 152 A2
Merlin Cl BH24 55 C3
Merlin Way BH23 125 A3
Mermaid Ct 22 BH5 122 C2
Mermond Pl BH19 179 B1
Merredin Cl DT3 152 B2
Merriefield Ave BH18 87 A3
Merriefield Cl BH18 87 A3
Merriefield Dr BH18 87 A3
Merrifield BH21 59 C4
Merriott Fst Sch TA16 191 F7
Merriott Rd
Hinton St George TA17 191 D7
Merriott TA18 191 F6
Merritown La BH23 90 B4
Merrivale Ave BH6 123 C3
Merrow Ave BH12 121 A4
Merrow Chase 1 BH13 147 C4
Merryfield Cl
Bransgore BH23 93 A4
Verwood BH31 45 A4
Merryfield Ct BH10 89 B2
Merryfield La BH10 89 B2
Merton Ct
8 Christchurch BH23 126 A4
3 Poole BH15 119 C2
Merville Gdns BH9 121 C4
Methuen Cl 2 BH8 122 B3
Methuen Dr 1 SP1 213 C2
Methuen Rd
Bournemouth BH8 122 A3
Poole BH17 87 A1
Mews The 1 BH2 121 B2
Meyrick Ave SP2 213 B1
Meyrick Cl BH23 93 A4
Meyrick Pk Cres BH3 121 C3
Meyrick Pk Mans 5 BH2 121 C2
Meyrick Rd BH1 122 A2
Michelgrove Rd BH5 122 C2
Michelmersh Gn BH8 90 B1
Mickleham Cl BH12 121 A4
Middle Brook BH11 89 A3
Middle Field La DT9 15 B3
Middle Gn 1 DT8 204 D4
Middle La Martin SP6 190 A7
Ringwood BH24 55 B4
Middle Path TA18 191 E4
Middle Rd
Bournemouth BH10 89 B3
Lytchett Matravers BH16 84 A1
New Milton SO41 95 C4
Poole BH15 119 C3
Sturminster Marshall BH21 56 C2
Sway SO41 95 C4
Middle St Bridport DT6 69 A1
Burton Bradstock DT6 128 A4
Crewkerne TA18 192 A3
Dewlish DT2 209 C1
Rimpton BA22 15 A4
Salisbury SP2 213 A2
3 Yeovil BA20 27 C2
Middlebere Cres BH16 118 B2
Middlebere Dr BH20 142 B3
Middlefield BH20 141 A2
Middlefield La TA13 191 F8
Middlehill Dr BH21 60 A3
Middlehill Rd BH21 60 A3
Middlemarsh St DT1 107 B1
Middleton Rd
Bournemouth BH9 89 C1
Ringwood BH24 55 B4
Salisbury SP2 213 A3
Midland Rd BH9 89 C1
Midleaze DT9 29 C3
Midney La SP8 4 A4
Midway Path BH13 147 B2
Midwood Ave BH8 90 C1
Milborne Cres BH12 120 C4
Milborne Port CP Sch DT9 17 B1
Milborne St Andrew C Fst Sch DT11 79 C4
Milbourne Rd BH22 61 B3
Milburn Cl 12 BH4 121 B2
Milburn La DT9 196 A7
Milburn Rd BH4 121 A2
Miles Ave BH20 142 C4
Miles Gdns DT3 152 A3
Milestone Rd BH15 119 B3
Milestone Way SP8 5 B1
Milford Cl BH22 53 A1
Milford Ct SP8 5 B1
Milford Cty Jun Sch BA21 27 B4
Milford Dr BH11 88 C3
Milford Hill SP1 213 B2
Milford Hollow 6 SP1 213 C2
Milford Ind Est SP1 213 C2
Milford Manor Gdns SP1 213 C2
Milford Mill Rd SP1 213 C2
Milford Pk SP1 213 C2
Milford Rd
Barton on Sea BH25 127 A4
Dorchester DT1 107 C1
Milford Rd *continued*
Yeovil BA21 27 B3
Milford St SP1 213 B2
Military La DT10 197 A4
Mill Cl BA22 193 C8
Mill End SP6 190 F2
Mill Gn DT7 96 B3
Mill Hill Cl BH14 120 A2
Mill Hollow La SP7 24 A3
Mill House Cider Mus* DT2 137 C2
Mill La Bourton SP8 1 C1
Bradford Abbas DT9 28 B1
Cann SP7 24 A3
Cattistock DT2 206 B2
Cerne Abbas DT2 207 D4
Charminster DT2 107 B4
Chetnole DT9 194 D2
Chideock DT6 99 A2
Christchurch BH23 126 A4
Cranborne BH21 40 B3
Crewkerne TA18 191 F3
Durweston DT11 198 E3
East Coker BA22 193 C7
Edmondsham BH21 40 C2
Halstock BA22 193 C3
Hawkchurch EX13 202 C3
Hurn BH23 91 A3
Ibberton DT11 197 D3
Kingstone TA17 191 B8
Lyme Regis DT7 96 B3
Lyme Regis DT7 96 A4
Marnhull DT10 20 C2
Mere BA12 3 A3
Misterton TA18 192 B3
Poole BH14 120 A2
Shapwick DT11 56 C3
Stour Provost SP8 21 B4
Stratton DT2 106 C4
Symondsbury DT6 99 C4
Trent DT9 14 C1
Wareham BH20 142 C2
West Coker BA22 193 B8
Wimborne Minster BH21 59 A3
Winterbourne Abbas DT2 132 C4
Wootton Fitzpaine DT6 64 B2
Yeovil BA20 27 B2
Yetminster DT9 194 C5
Zeale SP8 1 C1
Mill Rd
Christchurch BH23 124 A4
Salisbury SP2 213 A2
Mill Rd N BH8 90 B2
Mill Rd S BH8 90 B1
Mill Rise SP8 1 C1
Mill St
Blandford Forum DT11 212 B1
Broadstone BH21 58 A1
Burton Bradstock DT6 128 A4
Corfe Mullen BH21 57 A1
Dorchester DT1 108 A1
Fontmell Magna SP7 37 C3
Puddletown DT2 78 A1
Radipole DT3 152 A2
Rimpton BA22 15 A4
Mill Stream App SP2 213 B3
Millbank House 5 BH21 59 B3
Millbrook
Salisbury SP1 213 C3
17 Yeovil BA20 27 B2
Millbrook Cl 2 DT11 198 C8
Millbrook Ct 3 DT11 198 C8
Milldown CE Fst Sch DT11 212 B2
Milldown CE Mid Sch DT11 212 B2
Milldown Rd DT11 212 A2
Millennium Way SP2 213 B1
Miller Cl BH25 95 B2
Miller Rd BH23 124 B4
Miller's Cl DT1 107 C2
Miller's Hill DT9 17 A3
Miller's La
Farnham DT11 200 D8
Sixpenny Handley DT11 188 D1
Millers Cl DT3 153 B2
Millfield
Beaminster DT8 204 D5
Broadstone BH17 119 A4
New Milton BH25 94 C2
Millhams Cl BH10 89 A3
Millhams Dr BH10 89 A3
Millhams Rd BH10 89 A3
Millhams St BH23 124 A3
Millhams St N BH23 124 A3
Mills Rd DT3 169 B4
Mills The BH12 120 C4
Millstream Cl
Broadstone BH17 119 A4
Wimborne Minster BH21 59 B2
Millyford Cl BH25 126 B4
Milne Rd BH17 87 A1
Milner Rd BH4 121 B1
Milom La
Athelhampton DT2 110 B4
Puddletown DT2 78 B1
Milton Abbas CE Prim Sch DT11 209 F5
Milton Abbey Sch DT11 209 E5
Milton Cl Poole BH14 120 B2
Radipole DT4 167 B3
Yeovil BA21 26 C3
Milton Cres DT3 167 B3
Milton Ct BH22 61 B3
Milton Gr BH25 95 A1
Milton La DT11 198 D2
Milton Mead BH25 94 C1
Milton Rd
Bournemouth BH8 122 A3
Milborne St Andrew DT11 79 C4
Poole BH14 120 B2
Salisbury SP2 213 B1
Weymouth DT4 167 B2
Wimborne Minster BH21 59 B3
Milton Terr DT4 167 B3
Milton Villas BH8 122 A3
Milvers La DT6 101 A2
Milverton Cl BH23 93 C1
Mimosa Ave BH21 87 C4
Minerva Cl DT1 134 C4
Minstead Rd BH10 89 B2
Minster St 11 SP1 213 B3
Minster View BH21 59 B3
Minster Way BH16 118 A4
Minterne Gdns* DT2 207 D6
Minterne Grange BH14 147 B4
Minterne Rd
3 Bournemouth BH9 90 A1
Christchurch BH23 124 C3
Poole BH14 147 B4
Minton Mews BH2 121 C3
Mission Hall La DT3 153 B2
Mission Rd BH18 87 A1
Misterton Sch TA18 192 A2
Mistover Cl DT1 135 A4
Mistover Rd BH20 142 B3
Mitchell Cl BH25 127 A4
Mitchell Rd
Ferndown BH21 61 A4
Poole BH17 119 C4
Mitchell St 1 DT4 167 C1
Mitchelmore Rd BA21 27 B3
Mithras Cl DT1 134 C4
Miz Maze* DT9 194 F3
Moat Ct BH4 121 B3
Moat La BH25 126 C4
Moats Cotts DT2 209 C1
Moberly Rd SP1 213 B4
Mockbeggar La BH24 47 B4
Modbury Village* DT6 129 A4
Moffat Rd BH23 124 B4
Mohun Castle* DT8 192 C1
Mohune Way DT3 166 B3
Mohuns Pk* BA8 19 B4
Moigne Ct* DT2 155 C4
Molyneux Rd BH25 95 B2
Mompesson House* SP1 213 B2
Monaco Ct BH9 122 A4
Moneyfly Rd BH31 45 B3
Monkey World* BH20 140 A3
Monks Cl BH22 62 A4
Monks Dale BA21 26 C4
Monks Way BH11 88 B3
Monkshood Cl BH23 93 A1
Monkswell Gn BH23 124 B3
Monkton Cl BH22 61 B3
Monkton Cres BH12 120 C4
Monkton Down Rd 5 DT11 199 E2
Monkton Dro BH21 189 D1
Monkton Hill DT2 134 C3
Monkton Wyld Cross DT6 64 A4
Monkton Wyld La DT6 64 B3
Monkwood La DT6 203 E2
Monkworthy Dr BH24 54 A3
Monmouth Ave DT3 167 B4
Monmouth Cl BH31 45 B2
Monmouth Dr BH31 45 B2
Monmouth Gdns DT8 204 C4
Monmouth Rd
Dorchester DT1 108 A1
Wareham BH20 142 B2
Yeovil BA21 27 C4
Monmouth St 5 DT7 96 B3
Monsal Ave BH22 61 B2
Montacute Sch BH17 87 B1
Montacute Way BH21 87 C4
Montagu Pk BH23 126 A4
Montagu Rd BH23 126 A4
Montague Rd BH5 123 A2
Monterey Dr SO41 95 C2
Montgomery Ave BH11 89 A2
Montgomery Gdns SP2 213 A3
Montrose Cl
1 Easton/Weston DT5 186 C2
Verwood BH31 45 A3
Montrose Dr BH10 89 A1
Montrose Rd BA21 28 A4
Moonrakers BH13 147 C4
Moonrakers Way BH23 93 C1
Moor La
Broadwindsor DT8 203 B6
Buckhorn Weston SP8 4 B1
East Coker BA22 193 D7
Gillingham SP8 9 B4
Hardington Mandeville BA22 193 A7
Sturminster Marshall BH21 56 B2
Moor Rd Broadstone BH18 87 A3
Swanage BH19 179 A3
Moor The DT2 78 A1
Moor View Rd BH15 119 C4
Moorcombe Dr DT3 153 A2
Moorcroft Ave BH23 92 B1
Moordown Ave DT3 167 C4
Moordown Cl BH9 90 A2
Moordown St John's CE Prim Sch BH9 89 C1
Moore Ave BH11 89 A2
Moore Cl BH25 94 C1
Moorfield Gr BH9 89 C1
Moorfield Rd DT5 187 A2
Moorfields Rd BH13 147 C4
Moorhaven BH22 61 B3
Moorhills 14 BH21 59 B2
Moorings Cl BH15 118 C1
Moorings The 7 BH23 124 A3
Moorland Ave BH25 126 C4
Moorland Cres BH16 118 A4
Moorland Gate BH24 55 B3
Moorland Par BH16 118 A4
Moorland Rd BH1 122 B2
Moorland Way BH16 118 A4
Moorlands Coll BH23 92 A3
Moorlands Rd
Ferndown BH22 53 A2
Merriott TA18 191 E6
Verwood BH31 45 A4
Moorlands Rise BH22 53 A2
Moorlea 11 BH8 122 A3
Moors Cl BH23 91 A4
Moors Valley Ctry Pk* BH24 46 A1
Moorside Ave DT4 167 C4
Moorside Cl BH11 89 A2
Moorside Rd
Bournemouth BH11 89 A2
Corfe Mullen BH21 86 B3
Ferndown BH22 53 A1
Moortown Dr BH21 88 A4
Moortown House BH24 55 B3
Moortown La BH24 55 B2
Moorvale Rd BH9 90 A1
Moorway La DT9 15 C2
Morant Ct 14 BH25 95 A2
Morant Rd BH24 47 B1
Moray Ct 14 BH21 59 A3
Morden Ave BH22 61 B2
Morden La BH20 82 B2
Morden Rd
Bournemouth BH9 89 C1
Sandford BH20 142 C4
Wareham St Martin BH20 115 C2
Moreton Dr
Moreton DT2 138 C4
Turners Puddle DT2 112 A1
Moreton House* DT2 138 C4
Moreton Pk* DT2 138 C3
Moreton Rd
Bournemouth BH9 90 A2
Crossways DT2 137 C3
Moreton Sta DT2 137 C4
Moreton's La BH20 142 C2
Morgan's La SP5 189 E5
Moriconium Quay BH15 118 B1
Morington Ct 8 BH8 122 A3
Morley Cl
Bournemouth BH5 123 A3
Burton BH23 92 B2
Morley Rd BH5 123 A3
Morley Way BH22 61 C2
Mornish Rd BH13 120 C1
Morris Rd Poole BH17 119 B4
Wool BH20 139 C3
Morrison Ave BH12 120 C3
Morrison Rd BH19 179 A1
Morston DT9 194 D8
Mortain Cl DT11 212 B2
Mortimer Cl BH23 125 A3
Mortimer Rd BH8 90 A1
Mossley Ave BH12 89 A1
Mosterton Down La
Misterton TA18 191 F1
Mosterton DT8 192 A1
Motcombe CE Sch SP7 12 A4
Motcombe Grange Prep Sch SP7 7 A1
Motcombe Rd
Poole BH13 121 A1
Shaftesbury SP7 12 C2
Mount Ave BH25 95 A1
Mount Cl BH25 95 A1
Mount Grace Dr BH14 147 B4
Mount Heatherbank 30 BH1 121 C2
Mount Joy DT6 100 B2
Mount La DT6 99 C2
Mount Pleasant
Bridport DT6 100 B4
Christchurch BH23 125 A3
East Lulworth BH20 158 C1
Ringwood BH24 55 B4
Wareham Town BH20 142 C2
Yeovil BA21 27 C3
Mount Pleasant Ave N DT3 167 A4
Mount Pleasant Ave S DT3 167 B4
Mount Pleasant Dr BH8 90 C1
Mount Pleasant La 3 BH19 179 B1
Mount Pleasant Rd BH15 119 B2
Mount Rd
Bournemouth BH11 89 A2
Poole BH14 120 A3
Mount Scar BH19 179 A1
Mount Skippet Way DT2 137 B3
Mount The
8 Blandford Forum DT11 212 B1
Ringwood BH24 55 C4
Mountain Ash Rd 4 DT1 107 C1

Mountbatten Cl
Christchurch BH23 ......125 A3
Weymouth DT4 ....180 A4
Mountbatten Ct BH25 ...94 C2
Mountbatten Dr BH22 ...61 B3
Mountbatten Gdns BH8 ..91 C1
Mountbatten Rd BH13 ..121 A1
Mounters Cl DT10 ....20 C1
Mountjoy Cl BH21 ....59 C1
Mountjoy Sch DT6 .....100 B2
Mower La DT11 ....37 A3
Mowes La DT10 ....34 C4
Mowleaze 1 BA22 .....193 F8
Moyles Ct Sch BH24 .....47 C3
Moynton Cl DT2 ....137 B3
Muchelney Way BA21 ...26 C4
Muddox Barrow La
BH20 ....81 A3
Muddyford La DT6 ......98 B4
Mude Gdns BH23 ......125 A3
Mudeford BH23 ....125 A3
Mudeford Cty Inf Sch
BH23 ....124 C3
Mudeford Cty Jun Sch
BH23 ....124 C3
Mudeford Gn Cl BH23 ..124 C3
Mudeford La BH23 .....124 C3
Mudford Rd BA21 ....27 B4
Mudros Rd DT11 ....199 E3
Mulberry Ct
4 Christchurch BH23 ....124 A4
Sixpenny Handley SP5 ....189 B4
Mulberry Gdns
16 Crewkerne TA18 ......191 F4
Fordingbridge SP6 ....43 A4
Mullins Cl BH12 ....121 B4
Munden's La DT9 ....31 A1
Munks Cl 3 SP2 ....213 A2
Munster Rd BH14 ......120 B2
Murley Rd BH9 ....122 A4
Murray-Smith Dr BA22 ..26 B3
Musbury Cl DT10 ....20 C2
Musbury La DT10 ....20 C2
Muscliff Prim Sch BH9 ..90 B2
Muscliffe La BH9 ....90 A3
Muscliffe Rd BH9 ....89 C1
Museum of Childhood*
BH8 ....122 C3
Museum of Electricity*
BH23 ....124 A4
Museum of S Somerset*
BA20 ....27 B2
Musgrave Pl 4 DT4 ....167 C2
Muston La DT11 ....82 A4
Mustons La 4 SP7 ......12 C2
Mutton St DT6 ....203 A1
Myrtle Cl
10 Beaminster DT8 ......204 C4
Hordle SO41 ....95 C2
Myrtle Rd BH8 ....122 B3

N

Nada Rd BH23 ....93 B1
Nag's La TA18 ....191 B1
Nairn Ct BH3 ....121 C4
Nairn Rd
Bournemouth BH3 ......121 C3
Poole BH13 ....147 C4
Naish Holiday Village*
BH25 ....126 B4
Naish Rd BH25 ....126 C4
Nallers La DT2 ....102 C3
Namu Rd BH9 ....89 C1
Nansen Ave BH15 ......119 B3
Napier Cres SP1 ....213 C3
Napier Rd BH15 ....118 B2
Napiers Way DT11 ......37 C2
Narrow La BH24 ....47 C1
Naseby Rd BH9 ....90 A1
Nash Ct* DT10 ....21 A2
Nash La
Chillington TA17 ....191 A6
East Coker BA20 ....193 C8
Marnhull DT10 ....21 A2
Marshwood DT6 ....202 E2
Yeovil BA20 ....26 C1
Nathan Cl BA20 ....26 C1
Nathen Gdns BH15 .....118 B2
Nations Rd SP8 ....10 A3
Navarac Ct BH14 ......120 B2
Nea Cl BH23 ....125 B4
Nea Dr BH24 ....46 C2
Nea Rd BH23 ....125 C4
Neacroft Cl BH25 ......126 B4
Neal's La DT9 ....194 D2
Neathem Rd BA21 ....27 C4
Neighbourhood Ctr BH17 87 C1
Nelson Cl BH25 ....94 C2
Nelson Ct 10 BH15 .....119 B1
Nelson Dr BH23 ....124 C3
Nelson Rd
Bournemouth BH4 ......121 A2
Salisbury SP2 ....213 B3
Tarrant Monkton DT11 ...199 F3
Nether Abber Village (site of)* BA22 ....14 B4
Nether Mead 1 DT11 ...197 F6
Netheravon Rd SP1 ....213 B3
Netherby La DT8 ......204 A3
Nethercoombe La DT9 ..30 A4
Netherhall Gdns BH4 ..121 B2
Netherhay La DT8 .....203 C8
Netherstoke La BA22 ..193 C3
Netherton La BA22 .....193 F6
Netherton Rd
Weymouth DT4 ....167 B1
Netherton Rd *continued*
Yeovil BA21 ....27 C4
Netherwood Pl BH21 ....59 A3
Netley 8 BA21 ....26 C3
Netley Cl BH15 ....120 A4
Netmead La DT11 ......198 B8
Nettlebed Nursery SP7 ..12 C2
Nettlecombe SP7 ....13 A2
Nettleton Cl BH17 .....119 C4
Neville Cl SP1 ....213 C4
New Barn Rd DT3 ......149 A4
New Bond St DT4 ......167 B2
New Borough Rd BH21 ..59 B2
New Bridge Rd SP1 ...213 B2
New Canal SP1 ....213 B2
New Cl Bourton SP8 ....1 C1
Haselbury Plucknett
TA18 ....192 B5
New Cl Gdns DT4 ......167 B1
New Cotts BH21 ....60 C1
New Cross Gate DT11 ..198 A7
New Cut BA12 ....3 A3
New Field La DT11 .....198 D8
New Fields Bsns Pk
BH17 ....119 B4
New Gd DT5 ....187 A4
New Harbour Rd BH15 .119 A1
New Harbour Rd S
BH15 ....146 A4
New Harbour Rd W
BH15 ....119 A1
New Harnham Rd SP2 ..213 B1
New Inn St DT6 ....204 C2
New La Cann SP7 ....13 A1
Caundle Marsh DT9 .....195 E8
Haselbury Plucknett
TA18 ....192 C6
Morden BH20 ....83 B2
Motcombe SP7 ....12 A4
New Milton BH25 ....94 C3
Stour Provost SP8 ....11 A1
New Line BH20 ....161 B2
New Merrifield BH21 ....59 C4
New Milton Inf Sch BH25 95 A1
New Milton Jun Sch
BH25 ....95 A1
New Milton Sta BH25 ...95 A2
New Orch DT15 ....119 A1
New Par BH10 ....89 C2
New Pk Rd BH6 ....123 B2
New Quay Rd BH15 ....119 A1
New Rd Arne BH20 .....143 A1
Bournemouth BH10 ....89 C3
Bovington Camp BH20 ...139 B4
Bryanston DT11 ....212 B1
Brympton BA22 ....26 B3
Castleton DT9 ....30 A2
Corfe Castle BH20 ......162 C1
Ellingham Harbridge & Ibsley
BH24 ....47 B4
Ferndown BH22 ....61 C2
Gillingham SP8 ....6 A1
Haselbury Plucknett
TA18 ....192 D5
Hinton St George TA17 ..191 C7
Loders DT6 ....101 C4
Lytchett Minster & Upton
BH16 ....116 C4
Odcombe BA22 ....26 A3
Poole BH12 ....120 B3
Portesham DT3 ....150 A4
Portland DT5 ....186 C3
Radipole DT4 ....167 B2
Shaftesbury SP7 ....12 B2
Shapwick DT11 ....48 B1
Stalbridge DT10 ....33 B4
Stoborough Green BH20 ..160 C4
Stofold BA22 ....193 F8
Sturminster Newton
DT10 ....197 D7
West Crewkerne TA18 ....191 B4
Weymouth DT4 ....167 B1
Winsham TA20 ....202 C8
Winterborne Stickland
DT11 ....198 B1
Woodlands BH21 ....44 B4
Wool BH20 ....139 C1
Zeale SP8 ....2 A2
New St
9 Dorchester DT1 ......108 A1
Easton/Weston DT5 .....187 A2
Marnhull DT10 ....20 C1
North Perrott TA18 ......192 C4
9 Poole BH15 ....119 A1
Puddletown DT2 ....78 A1
Radipole DT4 ....167 C1
Ringwood BH24 ....55 B3
Salisbury SP1 ....213 B2
Wareham BH20 ....142 C2
New St La Loders DT6 ...69 B1
Symondsbury DT6 ....99 C3
Newberry Gdns 8 DT4 .167 C1
Newberry Rd DT4 ......167 B1
Newbery La TA18 ......192 A3
Newbury SP8 ....6 A1
Newbury Dr BH10 ......89 B1
Newchester Cross
TA16 ....191 E7
Newcombe La DT2 .....108 C2
Newcombe Rd
Bournemouth BH6 ......123 C3
Ferndown BH22 ....53 A2
Newcroft Gdns BH23 ..124 A2
Newcross DT9 ....195 B8
Newell DT9 ....30 A3
Newell House Sch DT9 ..30 A3
Newfield Rd DT11 .....199 D5
Newfoundland Cl
BH19 ....183 B4
Newfoundland Dr BH15 119 B1
Newhaven DT2 ....105 C1
Newland DT9 ....30 B3
Newland La DT9 ......195 F3
Newlands Rd
Bournemouth BH7 ......123 A3
Christchurch BH23 ......124 C4
New Milton BH25 ....95 A1
Newlands Way BH18 ....86 B2
Newlyn Way BH12 ....120 C4
Newman Cl DT11 ......212 C2
Newman's La BH22 .....52 C3
Newmans Cl BH22 ......53 A3
Newmorton Rd BH9 .....90 A2
Newport La BH20 ....82 B1
Newstead Rd
Bournemouth BH6 ....123 B2
Weymouth DT4 ....167 B2
Newton Cl Gillingham SP8 ..5 C1
Sturminster Newton
DT10 ....197 D8
Newton Hill DT10 .....197 D8
Newton Manor Cl 2
BH19 ....179 A1
Newton Morrell BH14 ..120 B2
Newton Rd
Barton on Sea BH25 .....127 A4
Barwick BA20 ....27 C2
Maiden Newton DT2 ......73 A4
Poole BH13 ....147 C4
Stofold BA22 ....193 F8
Sturminster Marshall
BH21 ....56 B2
Swanage BH19 ....179 B1
1 Yeovil BA20 ....27 C2
Newton Rise 4 BH19 ..179 A1
Newton Surmaville*
BA20 ....27 C2
Newton's Rd DT4 ......167 C1
Newtown DT8 ....204 C4
Newtown Bsns Ctr
BH12 ....120 A4
Newtown Hill BH20 ....157 C2
Newtown La
Corfe Mullen BH21 ....86 B4
Ellingham Harbridge & Ibsley
BH24 ....43 C1
Verwood BH31 ....45 B3
Newtown Rd BH31 ......45 B2
Nicholas Cl BH23 ......94 A1
Nicholas Gdns BH10 ...89 B1
Nichole Ct BH12 ......120 A4
Nicholson Cl BH17 ....119 C4
Nightingale Cl BH31 ...45 B3
Nightingale Dr DT3 ...152 B2
Nightingale La 4 BH15 .119 B1
Nightjar Cl BH17 ......118 C4
Nimrod Way BH21 ......60 C3
Nine Stones (Stone Circle)*
DT2 ....105 B1
Noade St SP5 ....25 B1
Noah Henville Cnr 4
DT11 ....81 C4
Noake Rd DT9 ....29 C3
Noble Cl BH11 ....88 C1
Noel Rd BH10 ....89 A1
Noel The BH25 ....95 B2
Nonesuch Cl 3 DT1 ...135 A4
Noon Gdns BH31 ....45 B3
Noon Hill Dr BH31 .....45 B3
Noon Hill Rd BH31 .....45 B3
Norburton DT6 ....128 A4
Norcliffe Cl BH10 ......89 A2
Norden Dr BH20 ......142 B3
Norden La DT2 ....72 C4
Norden Sta BH20 ......161 C1
Nordon Rd DT11 ......212 B2
Nordons DT6 ....100 C3
Norfolk Ave BH23 ....91 C1
Norfolk Rd
Salisbury SP2 ....213 A2
Weymouth DT4 ....167 A2
Norleywood BH23 .....125 C4
Norman Ave BH12 .....121 A3
Norman Cl DT6 ....100 C4
Norman Gdns BH12 ...121 A3
Normandy Dr BH23 ....124 B4
Normandy Way
Dorchester DT1 ....107 C1
Hamworthy BH15 ....118 B1
Normanhurst Ave BH8 ...90 C1
Normanton Cl BH23 .....91 C1
Norris Cl BH24 ....54 A2
Norris Gdns BH25 ....95 A1
Norrish Rd BH12 ......120 B3
North Allington DT6 ...100 B4
North Ave
Bournemouth BH10 ....89 B3
Lyme Regis DT7 ....96 A3
North Bestwall Rd
BH20 ....142 C2
North Bowood La DT6 ..203 F2
North Bridge* BH20 ...142 B2
North Cres DT9 ....17 B2
North Cswy BH20 .....142 C3
North Dorset Leisure Ctr
SP8 ....6 A1
North End DT9 ....194 F3
North End La SP6 ....42 C2
North Gr DT11 ....199 E3
North Hill Cl DT6 .....128 A4
North Hill Way DT6 ....100 B2
North La
Hardington Mandeville
BA22 ....193 A7
Yeovil BA20 ....27 B3
North Lodge Rd BH14 ..120 C2
North Mills Rd DT6 ....100 B4
North Perrott Rd
TA18 ....192 C5
North Pk DT2 ....73 C2
North Pl DT11 ....212 B1
North Poulner Rd BH24 ..47 B1
North Quay DT4 ....167 B1
North Rd Ashmore SP5 ...25 B1
Bournemouth BH7 ......122 C3
Chideock DT6 ....99 A4
Mere BA12 ....3 A3
Poole BH14 ....120 A2
Sherborne DT9 ....30 B4
Weymouth DT4 ....180 A4
North Rew La DT2 .....106 A1
North Sq Chickerell DT3 .166 B3
2 Dorchester DT1 ......108 A1
North St
Beaminster DT8 ....204 D4
Bere Regis BH20 ....81 A1
Bradford Abbas DT9 ......28 B1
Bridport DT6 ....100 B4
Charminster DT2 ....75 B1
Crewkerne TA18 ....191 F5
Fontmell Magna SP7 ......37 C4
Haselbury Plucknett
TA18 ....192 C6
Langton Matravers
BH19 ....178 A1
Mere BA12 ....3 A3
Milborne Port DT9 ....17 B1
Poole BH15 ....119 B1
Salisbury SP2 ....213 A3
Wareham BH20 ....142 C2
Winterborne Kingston
DT11 ....81 C4
Winterborne Stickland
DT11 ....210 C7
North Terr BA21 ....27 C3
North Walls BH20 .....142 C2
North Wlk SP1 ....213 B2
Northay La EX13 ......202 C3
Northbourne Ave BH10 ..89 B3
Northbourne Gdns BH10 .89 C3
Northbourne Pl 3 BH10 .89 B3
Northbrook Rd
Broadstone BH18 ....87 A1
Swanage BH19 ....179 A1
Yeovil BA21 ....27 C4
Northcote Rd BH1 ....122 A2
Northernhay 1 DT1 ...108 A1
Northey Rd BH6 ....123 C3
Northfield La TA17 ....191 B8
Northfield Rd BH24 .....47 B1
Northleigh La BH21 .....59 C3
Northmead Dr BH17 ...118 C4
Northmere Dr BH12 ...120 C4
Northmere Rd BH12 ...120 C4
Northmoor Way BH20 ..142 B3
Northover BH3 ....121 C3
Northover Cl
Burton Bradstock DT6 ....128 B4
Piddletrenthide DT2 .....208 B2
Northover La SO41 .....95 C4
Northport Dr BH20 ....142 C3
Nortoft Rd BH8 ....122 A3
Norton Cl BH23 ....124 B4
Norton La
Durweston DT11 ....198 D3
Netherbury DT6 ....204 C2
Norton Rd BH9 ....121 C4
Norway Cl 3 BH9 ......89 C1
Norway La DT8 ....203 F4
Norwich Ave BH2 .....121 B2
Norwich Ave W BH2 ...121 B2
Norwich Ct 12 BH2 ....121 C2
Norwich Mans 4 BH2 ..121 B2
Norwich Rd
Bournemouth BH2 ......121 C2
Weymouth DT4 ....167 B1
Norwood Pl BH5 ......123 A3
Nothe Fort* DT4 ......167 C1
Nothe Par DT4 ....167 C1
Nottington La
Chickerell DT3 ....151 B1
Radipole DT3 ....152 A1
Nouale La BH24 ....55 C4
Noyce Gdns BH8 ....91 A1
Nuffield Hospl BH5 ...122 C2
Nuffield Ind Est BH17 ..119 B4
Nuffield Rd BH17 .....119 B4
Nugent Rd BH6 ....124 A2
Nundico BH20 ....142 C2
Nursery Gdns
Bridport DT6 ....100 C4
Mere BA12 ....3 A3
Nursery Rd
Blandford Forum DT11 ...212 B1
Bournemouth BH9 ....90 A2
Ringwood BH24 ....55 B3
Salisbury SP2 ....213 A3
Yeovil BA20 ....27 B2
Nursling Gn BH8 ....90 B1
Nutcombe Cl DT6 ....97 A4
Nutcrack La BH20 .....142 C1
Nutgrove Ave DT4 .....166 C1
Nuthatch Cl
Broadstone BH17 ....118 C4
Ferndown BH22 ....61 A4
Radipole DT3 ....152 B2
Nutley Cl BH11 ....88 C2
Nutley Way BH11 ....88 C2
Nutmead Cl 4 DT11 ...198 C8
Nyland La SP8 ....8 B1

O

Oak Ave
Christchurch BH23 ......123 B4
Holton Heath BH20 ......116 A2
Oak Cl Corfe Mullen BH21 .86 B3
Ferndown BH22 ....61 C1
Oak La Corscombe DT2 ..205 C6
Ringwood BH24 ....55 B4
Oak Mews BH12 ....120 B3
Oak Rd Alderholt SP6 .....42 A3
Bournemouth BH8 ....122 B3
New Milton BH25 ....95 B2
Upton BH16 ....118 B3
Oak Vale La BA8 ....19 A2
Oakbury Dr DT3 ....168 A4
Oakdale Rd BH15 ......119 C3
Oakdale S Rd Mid Sch
BH15 ....119 B3
Oakdene Cl BH21 ....59 B3
Oakdene Rd BH20 .....139 C1
Oakfield Rd BH15 .....119 B3
Oakfield St DT11 ......212 B1
Oakford Ct BH8 ....90 B2
Oakham Grange BH22 ...61 C3
Oakhurst Cl BH22 ......53 A1
Oakhurst La BH22 ......53 A1
Oakhurst Rd BH22 ......53 A1
Oakland Wlk BH22 ......61 C1
Oaklands Cl BH31 ......45 A3
Oaklands Rd BA21 ......27 C4
Oakleigh 4 BA20 ....26 C1
Oakleigh Way BH23 ...125 C4
Oakley Gdns BH16 .....118 A4
Oakley Hill BH21 ....59 B1
Oakley La
Farnham DT11 ....188 D2
Oakley BH21 ....59 C1
Oakley Pl DT4 ....167 B1
Oakley Rd BH21 ....59 B1
Oakley Straight BH21 ...59 C1
Oakmead Coll of Tech
BH11 ....88 C2
Oakmead Gdns DT11 ....88 C2
Oakmead Rd BH17 .....118 C4
Oaks Dr BH24 ....53 C2
Oaks Mead BH31 ....45 A3
Oaks The Gillingham SP8 ...5 C1
Verwood BH31 ....45 A4
Oaktree Cl BH20 ......142 C1
Oakwood
Bournemouth BH3 ......121 C4
West Knighton DT2 .....136 B2
Oakwood Ave BH25 .....95 B2
Oakwood Cl BH9 ....90 A1
Oakwood Ct BH25 ....95 A2
Oakwood Dr 5 DT11 ....37 C1
Oakwood Rd
Bournemouth BH9 ....90 A1
Christchurch BH23 ....93 C1
Oasis Mews BH16 .....118 A4
Oasis The 12 BH12 ....121 A2
Oates Rd BH9 ....89 C1
Oathill La
Broadwindsor TA18 ......203 A7
West Crewkerne TA18 ....191 B1
Oban Rd BH3 ....121 C4
Oborne Rd DT9 ....30 B4
Ocean Hts 28 BH5 .....122 C2
Octagon Theatre*
BA20 ....27 B2
Odcombe Hollow
BA22 ....192 E8
Odstock Rd SP2 ......213 B1
OK Mobile Home Pk
BH23 ....125 A4
Okeford Fitzpaine CE Prim
Sch DT11 ....197 F5
Okeford Rd BH18 ....87 B2
Old Bakery Cl 4 DT11 ..199 D3
Old Bakery The DT8 ....203 E5
Old Barn Cl
Christchurch BH23 ....91 B1
Ringwood BH24 ....55 B4
Old Barn Farm Rd
BH21 ....53 B3
Old Barn Rd
Bere Regis BH20 ....81 A1
Christchurch BH23 ....91 B1
Old Barn Way BA20 .....27 A1
Old Bincombe La DT3 ..153 B2
Old Blandford Rd SP2 ..213 A1
Old Bound Rd BH16 ...118 B3
Old Boundary Rd SP7 ...12 C1
Old Bowden Way DT9 ...17 B2
Old Brickfields DT2 ...136 B2
Old Bridge Rd BH6 ....123 B4
Old Cann Sch SP7 ....13 A1
Old Castle Rd DT4 ....180 C4
Old Chalk Pit BH20 ......81 A1
Old Chapel Dr BH16 .....84 B2
Old Christchurch La 35
BH1 ....121 C2
Old Christchurch Rd
BH1 ....121 C2
Old Church Rd DT6 ....100 C2
Old Church Sch DT8 ...204 D4
Old Coastguard Rd
BH13 ....147 A2
Old Ct Mews BH14 .....120 A2
Old Depot Rd DT5 .....181 B1
Old Farm Cl BH24 ......47 C1
Old Farm Gdns DT11 ..212 B2

Old Farm Rd BH15 119 C3
Old Farm Way DT2 137 B3
Old Forge Cl BH16 116 C3
Old Forge Rd BH21 60 C3
Old Furzebrook Rd
BH20 160 C4
Old Generator House The
BH12 121 A3
Old Granary Cl DT3 153 B2
Old Ham La BH21 60 B2
Old Highway Mews BH21 59 B2
Old Hitchen 4 TA16 191 F7
Old Hollow BA12 3 A3
Old Kiln Rd
Ridge BH20 143 A1
Upton BH16 118 B3
Old Lifeboat House (Mus)★
BH15 119 B1
Old Lyme Hill DT6 96 C4
Old Lyme Rd DT6 96 C4
Old Manor Cl BH21 59 B2
Old Manor Hospl SP2 213 A3
Old Mdws Wlk SP2 213 A2
Old Mill La DT10 21 A2
Old Mills DT2 71 C4
Old Milton Gn BH25 94 C1
Old Milton Rd BH25 95 A1
Old Mkt Rd BH21 85 A4
Old Mulberry Cl BH10 89 A1
Old Oak Way DT11 210 C3
Old Orch BH15 119 B1
Old Orch Cl DT10 196 F8
Old Parish La DT4 167 A2
Old Pines Cl BH22 61 C2
Old Pound Cl BH16 84 B2
Old Pound Ct SP8 1 D1
Old Priory Rd BH6 123 C2
Old Rd Odcombe BA22 26 A2
Wimborne Minster BH21 59 A3
Old Rd The DT9 18 A1
Old Rectory Cl
4 Charmouth DT6 97 A4
Corfe Mullen BH21 86 B4
Old Rectory La DT9 195 E3
Old Rope Wlk The BH15 118 C1
Old Ropewalk BH15 119 A1
Old Sandpit La BH16 86 A1
Old Sawmill Cl BH31 45 A4
Old Sch Cl Ferndown BH22 61 B3
Folke DT9 31 A1
Poole BH14 120 A2
Old Sch La
Hinton St Mary DT10 35 A3
Iwerne Minster DT11 37 C1
Old Sch The DT2 72 C4
Old St Salisbury SP2 213 B1
Sturminster Marshall
BH21 56 C2
Old St John's Mews BH9 89 C2
Old Sta Gdns BA8 19 A3
Old Sta Rd
Radipole DT3 152 A2
4 Yeovil BA20 27 C2
Old Stacks Gdns 1 BH24 55 C3
Old Town Mews 5
BH15 119 B1
Old Vicarage Cl BH10 89 C3
Old Vicarage Gdn DT7 96 A3
Old Wareham Rd
Corfe Mullen BH21 86 A2
Poole BH12 120 A4
Olga Rd DT1 107 C1
Olivers Mead 1 DT11 198 C8
Olivers Rd BH21 60 A3
Olivers Way BH21 60 A3
Onslow Gdns BH21 59 B3
Onslow House BH21 59 B3
Ophir Gdns 1 BH8 122 B3
Ophir Rd BH8 122 A3
Oratory Gdns BH13 147 C4
Orchard Ave
Bridport DT6 100 B4
Poole BH14 119 C1
Orchard Chase 2 DT11 199 F7
Orchard Cl
3 Charmouth DT6 97 A4
Cheselbourne DT2 209 A3
Christchurch BH23 124 A3
Corfe Mullen BH21 86 B4
Ferndown BH22 61 C3
Fontmell Magna SP7 37 C3
Lytchett Minster & Upton
BH16 116 C3
3 Okeford Fitzpaine DT11 197 F6
Ringwood BH24 55 B4
4 Stourpaine DT11 198 F4
Sturminster Newton
DT10 197 C8
Sydling St Nicholas DT2 207 A3
4 West Coker BA22 193 A8
Orchard Cres DT6 100 B4
Orchard Ct
10 New Milton BH25 95 A2
Verwood BH31 45 B3
Orchard Dr DT3 168 A4
Orchard Gr BH25 95 A1
Orchard La
Corfe Mullen BH21 86 B4
2 Crewkerne TA18 191 F4
Thorncombe TA20 202 E6
7 Winterborne Kingston
DT11 81 C4
Orchard Leigh 6 BH25 95 A1
Orchard Mead DT8 203 E5
Orchard Mews
2 Christchurch BH23 124 A3
7 Gillingham SP8 5 B1
Orchard Rd
Gillingham SP8 5 C1
Milborne Port DT9 17 B1
Orchard Rise
7 Crewkerne TA18 191 F4
Milborne St Andrew DT11 79 C4
Orchard St
Blandford Forum DT11 212 B1
Bournemouth BH2 121 C2
Dorchester DT1 108 A1
Yeovil BA20 27 A2
Orchard The
Blandford Forum DT11 212 B2
Bournemouth BH11 88 B3
Bransgore BH23 93 B4
Hazelbury Bryan DT10 196 F3
Radipole DT3 152 A2
Sixpenny Handley SP5 189 B4
Winfrith Newburgh DT2 156 C3
Orchard Way
Misterton TA18 192 A2
2 Mosterton DT8 204 A8
Orchard Wlk
22 Bournemouth BH2 121 C2
Milborne Port DT9 17 B1
Orchardleigh BA22 192 E8
Orcheston Rd BH8 122 B3
Orchid Way BH23 124 B4
Orestes Gate BH23 125 A3
Orford Cl BH23 91 B2
Orford St DT2 78 A1
Organford Rd BH16 116 B2
Orion Rd DT4 167 B1
Ormonde Rd BH13 121 A1
Osborne Rd
Bournemouth BH9 121 C4
New Milton BH25 95 A2
Poole BH14 120 A2
Swanage BH19 179 A1
Wimborne Minster BH21 59 B2
Yeovil BA20 27 B3
Osbourne House 4
BH25 95 A2
Osbourne Rd DT6 100 B4
Osmay Rd BH19 185 B4
Osmington Dro DT2 136 A1
Osmington White Horse★
DT3 153 C2
Osprey Cl BH23 125 A3
Osprey Rd DT4 180 B3
Ossemsley Manor House
BH23 94 B3
Ossemsley S Dr BH25 94 C4
Oswald Cl BH9 89 C1
Oswald Rd BH9 89 C1
Otter Cl Upton BH16 118 A3
Verwood BH31 45 B3
Otter Rd BH15 119 C3
Otters Wlk BH25 95 B3
Ottery La DT9 30 A3
Oval Gdn BH20 160 C4
Oval The BH20 172 C4
Over Links Dr BH14 120 B1
Overbury Cl DT4 166 C1
Overbury Rd BH14 120 B2
Overcliffe Mans BH1 122 B2
Overcombe BA8 18 B4
Overcombe Cl BH17 87 C1
Overcombe Dr DT3 168 A4
Overlands Rd DT4 180 A4
Overton Cl DT7 96 B4
Ovington Ave BH7 123 B4
Ovington Gdns BH7 123 B4
Owermoigne CE Prim Sch
DT2 155 B4
Owl Sanctuary★ BH24 55 C3
Owls Rd
Bournemouth BH5 122 C2
Verwood BH31 45 B3
Owlshotts BH13 147 C4
Owlswood 10 SP2 213 B1
Ox Dro
Berwick St John SP5 188 B7
Bower Chalke SP5 189 A8
Oxen Rd 5 TA18 191 F4
Oxencroft 12 SP7 12 C2
Oxey Cl BH25 95 A1
Oxford Ave BH6 123 A3
Oxford La BH11 89 A3
Oxford Rd
Bournemouth BH1 122 A2
Yeovil BA21 28 A4
Oxhayes DT8 203 C8
Ozone Terr DT7 96 A2

P

Paceycombe Way DT1 107 B1
Packers' Way 1 TA18 192 B3
Paddington Cl BH11 88 B2
Paddington Gr BH11 88 B2
Paddock Cl
Ferndown BH21 61 A3
Lytchett Matravers BH16 84 B2
Shaftesbury SP7 13 A1
Sixpenny Handley SP5 189 A3
St.Leonards BH24 54 A2
Paddock Gr BH31 45 B3
Paddock The DT2 136 A4
Paddock Wlk DT9 17 B1
Paddock's Cross DT6 67 A4
Paddock's La DT6 67 A4
Paddocks Cl BH12 120 A4
Paddocks The
Bournemouth BH10 89 B2
1 Iwerne Minster DT11 37 C1
5 Mosterton DT8 204 A8
Thornford DT9 194 D8
Padfield Cl BH6 123 C3
Padget Rd BH24 47 C1
Padstow Pl SP6 43 A4
Page Dr 10 DT5 186 C1
Pageant Dr DT9 30 A3
Pageants Cl DT6 68 C1
Paget Cl BH21 60 A4
Paget Rd BH11 89 A2
Paisley Rd BH6 123 B3
Palfrey Rd BH10 89 B3
Palma Ct BH23 126 A4
Palmer Pl BH25 95 A2
Palmer Rd Poole BH15 119 B3
Salisbury SP2 213 A3
Palmers La DT11 211 D7
Palmers Orch BH16 84 B2
Palmerston Ave BH23 124 B3
Palmerston Cl BH16 118 B4
Palmerston Rd
Bournemouth BH1 122 C3
Poole BH14 120 B2
Upton BH16 118 B4
Pamphill CE Fst Sch
BH21 58 C3
Panorama Rd
Poole BH13 147 A2
Swanage BH19 179 A1
Pans Cnr BH22 61 C2
Parade The
Barton on Sea BH25 94 C1
5 Bournemouth BH6 123 C2
New Milton BH25 95 B2
Poole BH17 87 A1
Paradise La BH20 83 B2
Paradise Rd BH21 51 C4
Paradise St 17 BH15 119 A1
Parcroft Gdns BA20 27 A3
Parcroft Jun Sch BA20 27 A3
Pardys Hill BH21 86 B4
Parfields BA20 27 A3
Parham Cl BH25 94 C2
Parham Rd BH10 89 B1
Parish Rd BH15 119 C2
Park Ave BH10 89 B3
Park Cl Burton BH23 92 B2
New Milton BH25 95 B3
Salisbury SP1 213 B4
3 Stourpaine DT11 198 F4
Park Cnr BH20 115 B4
Park Dr
Holton Heath BH20 116 A2
Verwood BH31 45 A4
Park Est Rd DT5 186 C2
Park Gate Mews 14
BH2 121 C2
Park Gdns
Christchurch BH23 124 C4
Yeovil BA20 27 B3
Park Gr DT10 33 B4
Park Hill DT11 211 C6
Park Homer Dr BH21 60 A3
Park Homer Rd BH21 59 C3
Park La Alderholt SP6 42 A3
Bournemouth BH10 89 C2
Evershot DT2 206 A7
Glanvilles Wootton DT9 195 F2
Henstridge BA8 19 A4
Melbury Sampford DT2 194 A1
Radipole DT4 167 B3
Salisbury SP1 213 B4
Shapwick DT11 48 B1
Thorncombe TA20 202 D7
Wayford TA18 191 B1
Wimborne Minster BH21 59 B2
Wimborne St Giles BH21 201 E7
Woodlands BH21 44 A3
Park La Rd BH15 119 C1
Park Lands DT11 212 B1
Park Mead Rd DT4 180 B4
Park Pl BH14 119 C2
Park Rd
Barton on Sea BH25 94 C1
Blandford Forum DT11 212 B1
Bournemouth BH8 122 A3
Bridport DT6 100 B4
Easton/Weston DT5 187 A2
Henstridge BA8 19 A2
New Milton BH25 95 B3
Poole BH14 119 C2
Stalbridge DT10 33 B4
Swanage BH19 179 B1
Yeovil BA20 27 B3
Park St Radipole DT4 167 B2
Salisbury SP1 213 B3
Yeovil BA20 27 B2
Park The
Barton on Sea BH25 126 B4
Yeovil BA20 27 B3
Park View
Crewkerne TA18 191 F3
New Milton BH25 95 A1
9 Poole BH15 119 C2
Park View Mews BH25 95 A1
Park Way BH22 53 A1
Park Wr La DT8 203 C5
Park's La DT2 130 B4
Parkelea 3 BH21 56 B2
Parker Rd BH9 121 C4
Parkers Cl BH24 47 C1
Parkland Cl BH24 45 C2
Parkland Dr BH25 126 C4
Parkland Pl BH25 95 A1
Parkside
Christchurch BH23 93 B1
Ringwood BH24 55 A3
Parkside Gdns BH10 89 C1
Parkside Rd BH14 120 B2
Parkstone Ave BH14 120 B2
Parkstone Gram Sch
BH17 87 A1
Parkstone Hts BH14 119 C3
Parkstone Rd BH15 119 C2
Parkstone Sta BH14 120 A2
Parkview BH2 121 C2
Parkway DT6 97 A4
Parkway Dr BH8 122 C4
Parkwood La 14 BH5 123 A3
Parkwood Rd
Bournemouth BH5 123 A2
Wimborne Minster BH21 59 B2
Parley Cl BH22 61 C1
Parley Cross BH22 89 C4
Parley Fst Sch BH22 61 B2
Parley La BH23 90 B4
Parley Rd BH9 90 A1
Parmiter Dr BH21 59 C2
Parmiter Rd BH21 59 C2
Parmiter Way BH21 59 C2
Parnham House★
DT8 204 C3
Parr Gr 5 DT11 199 D4
Parr House 5 BH14 120 A2
Parr St BH14 120 A2
Parrett & Axe CE Prim Sch
DT8 204 A7
Parrett Mead DT8 192 C1
Parricks La EX13 202 A3
Parsonage Barn La
BH24 55 B4
Parsonage Ct 9 BH8 122 A3
Parsonage Gn SP2 213 A1
Parsonage Hill BH21 200 F6
Parsonage La BH21 201 E7
Parsonage Rd
Bournemouth BH1 122 A2
Bridport DT6 100 B4
Parsonage St SP7 37 C3
Parsonage The SP5 189 B4
Parsons Cl BH19 179 A3
Parsons La DT2 102 C3
Parsons Pool 3 SP7 12 C2
Partridge Cl BH23 125 A3
Partridge Dr BH14 120 B1
Partridge Gr BH25 95 A3
Partridge Wlk BH14 120 A1
Partway DT10 196 F3
Partway La
Hardington Mandeville
BA22 192 F7
Hazelbury Bryan DT10 196 F3
Thorncombe TA20 202 C6
Pascoe Cl BH14 120 A2
Pasture Way DT6 100 B3
Patchins Rd BH16 118 A2
Patchins The BH14 147 B4
Patson Hill La DT9 15 B1
Pattinson Cl BA21 27 C3
Paul's Mead DT5 186 C4
Pauls Way DT2 137 B3
Pauncefote Rd BH5 123 A3
Pauntley Rd BH23 124 C3
Pavan Gdns BH10 89 B1
Pavilion Theatre★
DT4 167 C2
Pavyotts La BA22 193 E8
Payne Cl BH21 53 A3
Payne's Hill 5 SP1 213 B2
Paynes Cl DT2 76 C4
Peace Cl BH23 93 A4
Peaceful La DT10 196 C6
Peacemarsh Farm Cl 12
SP8 5 C2
Pear Ash La BA9 1 B2
Pear Cl BH12 121 A2
Pear Tree Cl
Alderholt SP6 42 A3
Bransgore BH23 93 A4
Pearce Ave BH14 120 A1
Pearce Gdns BH14 120 A1
Pearce Rd BH16 118 A3
Pearce-Smith Ct BH25 126 C4
Pearl Gdns BH10 89 B2
Pearl Rd BH10 89 B2
Pearson Ave BH14 120 A3
Pearson Gdns BH10 89 B3
Peatons La BH16 84 A2
Peckham Ave BH25 95 A1
Peeks Mews BH6 123 C3
Peel Cl
Blandford Forum DT11 212 B2
Poole BH12 120 B3
Pegasus Ct
Bournemouth BH1 122 A3
8 New Milton BH25 95 A2
Pegasus Lodge BH22 61 B3
Peggy's La TA18 192 C5
Pelham Cl BH23 124 B3
Pelican Mead BH24 55 C3
Pemberton Cl DT3 152 B2
Pembroke Cl BA21 28 A4
Pembroke Ct 11 BH23 126 A4
Pembroke Rd
Bournemouth BH4 121 A1
Poole BH12 120 B4
Pen Mill Cty Inf Sch
BA21 27 C3
Pen Mill Hill BA9 1 C2
Pen Mill Trading Est
BA21 28 A3
Pencraig BH13 121 A2
Pendomer Rd BA22 193 B5
Penelope Ct 18 BH23 126 A4
Pengelly Ave BH10 89 C3
Penmore Rd DT9 15 B3
Penn Cl BH25 94 C1
Penn Cross DT6 64 B1
Penn Hill BA20 27 B2
Penn Hill Ave BH14 120 B2
Penn Hill Pk BA20 27 B2
Penn House Day Hospl
BA20 27 B2
Penn La BA22 193 A6
Pennant Way BH23 124 C4
Penney's Hill DT8 204 D8
Pennine Ct 8 BH23 124 C4
Pennine Way BH31 45 A3
Pennington Cl BH22 52 C1
Pennington Cres BH22 52 C1
Pennington Rd BH22 52 C1
Pennsylvania Rd DT5 187 A2
Penny Hedge BH25 127 A4
Penny La 6 BH7 122 C2
Penny Plot DT7 96 A3
Penny St Radipole DT4 167 B2
1 Sturminster Newton
DT10 197 D8
Penny Way BH23 125 B3
Penny's Cnr SO41 95 C2
Penny's Ct BH22 61 B3
Penny's La BH21 40 A4
Penny's Mead BH21 40 A4
Penny's Wlk BH22 61 B3
Pennyfarthing St SP1 213 B3
Pennywell Gdns BH25 95 B2
Penrith Cl BH31 45 A3
Penrith Rd BH5 123 A2
Penrose Cl BH16 84 B1
Penrose Rd BH22 61 B3
Pentons Hill SP6 43 C3
Pentridge La DT10 34 B2
Pepper Hill DT11 198 B5
Percy Gdns DT11 212 B1
Percy Rd
Bournemouth BH5 122 C2
Yeovil BA21 27 C3
Peregrine Rd BH23 125 A3
Pergin Cres BH17 119 A4
Pergin Way BH17 119 A4
Perrott Hill Sch TA18 192 B4
Perry Gdns BH15 119 B1
Perry St TA20 202 A7
Perryfield Gdns BH7 123 A4
Persley Rd BH10 89 C2
Perth Cl BH23 91 C1
Perth St DT4 167 A2
Peter Grant Way BH22 61 B3
Peter St 3 BA20 27 B2
Peters Cl BH16 118 B3
Peters Rd BH22 61 C2
Petersfield Pl BH7 123 A4
Petersfield Rd BH7 123 A4
Petersham La BH21 51 A2
Petersham Rd BH17 119 A4
Petit Rd BH9 90 A2
Petter's Way BA20 27 B2
Pettitts Cl DT9 28 B1
Pettridge La BA12 3 A3
Pettycrate La DT6 98 C3
Petwyn Cl BH22 62 A3
Peverell Ave E DT1 107 B1
Peverell Rd BH16 118 A2
Peveril Cl BH24 54 A3
Peveril Point Rd BH19 179 B1
Peveril Rd BH19 179 B1
Phelipps Rd BH21 86 C3
Philip Rd DT11 212 C1
Phillips Rd DT10 21 A1
Phyldon Cl BH12 120 A3
Phyldon Rd BH12 120 A3
Piccadilly La DT11 56 B4
Pickard Rd BH22 61 C4
Pickering Cl BH18 87 A1
Picket La DT8 192 C1
Pickett La BA21 27 B4
Picketts Cross DT2 74 A2
Pickford Rd BH9 89 C1
Piddle La DT2 207 D3
Piddle Valley Fst Sch
DT2 208 B2
Pidney Hill DT10 196 F3
Piece Rd DT9 17 B2
Piece The 2 TA16 191 F7
Pierston Fields SP8 5 B3
Pig Hill BA22 193 A7
Pig Shoot La BH23 90 C3
Pigeon Cl
Blandford Forum DT11 212 B1
Winfrith Newburgh DT2 156 C3
Pikes La BH19 183 B4
Pile La DT10 32 C3
Pilford Heath Rd BH21 60 A4
Pilford La BH21 51 B1
Pilgrim Pk BH24 55 C4
Pilgrim's Cl BH25 95 B2
Pilgrims Way
Broadstone BH17 119 A4
4 Radipole DT4 167 C1
Pill Mdw SP8 9 B2
Pilot Hight Rd BH11 89 A2
Pilsdon Cl 7 DT8 204 C4
Pilsdon Dr BH17 87 C2
Pilsdon La DT6 203 C3
Pilsdon Manor★ DT6 203 C2
Pilsdon Pen (Hill Fort)★
DT6 203 C4
Pilwell DT10 21 A2
Pimperleaze Rd BA12 3 C1
Pimpern Cl BH17 87 C1

Pimperne CE VC Fst Sch
DT11 ....199 D4
Pimpernel Ct **6** SP8 ......5 B1
Pine Ave
 Bournemouth BH6 ....123 B2
 Poole BH12 ....120 C3
Pine Cl
 Barton on Sea BH25 ......126 C4
 Corscombe DT2 ....205 B8
 Ferndown BH22 ....61 B4
Pine Cres
 Christchurch BH23 ....125 C4
 Holton Heath BH16 ......116 A2
Pine Dr Poole BH13 ....120 C2
 St.Leonards BH24 ....54 A2
Pine Glen Ave BH22 ......61 B4
Pine Grange **4** BH1 .....122 A2
Pine House BH5 ....95 A2
Pine Lodge **15** BH13 .....147 C4
Pine Manor Rd BH24 ......53 C3
Pine Mans **3** BH1 ....122 B2
Pine Pk Mans BH13 ......121 A2
Pine Rd Alderholt SP6 .....42 A1
 Bournemouth BH9 ....122 A4
 Broadstone BH18 ....58 C1
Pine Ridge DT7 ....96 B4
Pine Tree Ave BH20 ....27 A2
Pine Tree Cl BH21 ....59 B3
Pine Tree Glen BH4 ......121 B2
Pine Vale Cres BH10 ......89 C2
Pine View DT6 ....100 A3
Pine View Cl Upton BH16 118 B3
 Verwood BH31 ....44 C4
Pine View Rd BH31 ....44 C4
Pine Wlk
 Lyme Regis DT7 ....96 A2
 Verwood BH9 ....45 B3
Pineapple La DT6 ....68 B3
Pinebeach Ct BH13 ....147 D4
Pinecliffe Ave BH6 ....123 B2
Pinecliffe Rd BH25 ....126 B4
Pineholt Cl BH24 ....54 B3
Pinehurst Ave BH23 ......124 C3
Pinehurst Rd BH22 ....53 C1
Pinemoor Cl DT3 ....167 C4
Pines Mews **11** DT8 ...204 D4
Pines The BH13 ....121 A1
Pineside BH9
122 A4
Pinesprings Dr BH18 ......86 C1
Pinetree Wlk BH17 ......118 C4
Pinewood Ave BH10 ......89 B3
Pinewood Cl
 Bournemouth BH10 ....89 B3
 Christchurch BH23 ....94 A1
 Upton BH16 ....118 A4
Pinewood Gdns BH22 .....61 B4
Pinewood Rd
 Christchurch BH23 ....93 C1
 Ferndown BH22 ....61 B4
 Hordle SO41 ....95 C2
 Poole BH13 ....121 A1
 St.Leonards BH24 ....54 A2
 Upton BH16 ....118 A4
Pinford La DT9 ....30 C3
Pink End BH22 ....61 C2
Pink Knoll Hollow DT9 ....15 C4
Pipers Ash **2** BH24 ......55 C4
Pipers Dr BH23 ....125 A4
Pipit Cl DT3 ....152 B2
Pippin Cl BH21 ....91 C1
Pirates La DT4 ....180 A4
Pit Hill TA17 ....191 B7
Pit Rd TA17 ....191 B7
Pitcher Cl **3** DT11 ....81 C4
Pitchers DT6 ....68 A3
Pitfield Cnr BA22 ....15 A3
Pitman's La DT6 ....66 A1
Pitt Cl DT11 ....211 B1
Pitt La DT6 ....65 C2
Pitt's Dro BH21 ....49 C1
Pittmore Rd BH23 ....92 B1
Pitts La
 Melbury Abbas SP7 ....23 C3
 Sedgehill And Semley SP7 ..7 B3
Pitts Orch DT10 ....35 A1
Pitts Pl BH25 ....95 B1
Pitwines Cl BH15 ....119 B1
Pix Mead Gdns SP7 ....13 C1
Place Mill ★ BH23 ....124 A3
Placket La BA20 ....27 A1
Plain The DT2 ....109 A3
Plaisters La DT3 ....153 B2
Plant Pk Rd BH24 ....54 C1
Plantaganet Chase
 BA20 ....27 A1
Plantagenet Cres BH11 ...88 B3
Plantagenet Pk BA20 .....27 A2
Plantagenet Way **8** SP8 ..5 B1
Plantation Ct BH17 ....87 B1
Plantation Dr BH23 ....94 A1
Plantation Rd BH17 ....87 B1
Plassey Cl DT1 ....107 C1
Plassey Cres BH10 ....89 B3
Playfield Cl **2** BA8 ......19 A2
Playfields Dr BH12 ......120 C3
Pleasance Way BH25 ......94 C2
Pleck Hill DT10 ....196 E3
Pleck La DT2 ....209 B7
Plecy Cl BH22 ....61 B1
Plemont Cl DT2 ....88 C1
Plocks The DT11 ....212 B1
Plot La DT9 ....14 C1
Plott La BA8 ....19 B3
Plough Est DT11 ....212 B2
Plover Cl **11** DT9 ....17 B1
Plover Ct BA21 ....26 C3
Plover Dr DT3 ....166 B3

Plover Rd DT9 ....17 B1
Plowman Cl DT10 ....21 A2
Plum Orch DT9 ....28 C4
Plumbley Mdws **6** DT11 .81 C4
Plumer Rd DT6 ....87 A1
Podington Mdws DT3 ...166 B3
Pokesdown Com Prim Sch
 BH5 ....123 A3
Pokesdown Sta BH7 .....123 A3
Polans DT9 ....194 D2
Polden Rd **7** SP1 ....213 C2
Policemans La BH16 .....117 A4
Pollards La DT2 ....155 B4
Pomona Cl BH22 ....61 B3
Pompey's Cnr BH21 ....61 A2
Pompey's La BH21 ....61 A1
Pond Cl Henstridge BA8 ...19 A2
 New Milton BH25 ....95 A2
Pond Head BH21 ....51 B3
Pond Wlk DT10 ....33 B4
Ponsonby Rd BH14 ......120 B2
Pony Dr BH16 ....118 B4
Poole Aquarium &
 Serpentarium ★ BH15 .119 B1
Poole Commerce Ctr
 BH12 ....120 C3
Poole Gram Sch BH17 ....87 B1
Poole High Sch BH15 ....119 B2
Poole Hill BH2 ....121 C2
Poole Hospl BH15 ....119 B2
Poole La BH11 ....89 A3
Poole Rd
 Bournemouth BH2 ....121 B2
 Lytchett Matravers BH16 ..84 C3
 Poole BH12 ....121 A2
Sturminster Marshall
 BH21 ....56 B1
 Upton BH16 ....118 B4
 Wimborne Minster BH21 ..59 B2
Poole Sta BH15 ....119 B2
Poole's Ct **4** DT7 ....96 B3
Poop Hill TA18 ....192 C8
Poop Hill La TA18 ....192 C8
Poorhouse La DT6 ....66 B4
Pope's Hill DT2 ....205 F1
Pope's La DT9 ....17 B1
Popes Rd BH15 ....119 B3
Poplar Cl Bransgore BH23 .93 B4
 Christchurch BH23 ....126 A4
 6 Poole BH15 ....119 A1
 Wimborne Minster BH21 ..59 B3
Poplar Cres BH24 ....55 B4
Poplar Hill **3** DT11 ....198 B6
Poplar La BH23 ....93 A4
Poplar Rd BH25 ....95 B2
Poplar Way BH24 ....55 B4
Pople's Well TA18 ......191 E4
Poppy Cl
 Christchurch BH23 ....125 B4
 Upton BH16 ....117 A4
 Yeovil BA22 ....26 B3
Poppyfields SP8 ....5 C2
Porchester Ct **12** BH1 ...122 A4
Porchester Pl BH8 ......122 A3
Porchester Rd BH8 ......122 A4
Port La DT6 ....101 B2
Port Regis Sch SP7 ....12 A3
Portarlington Cl BH2 ....121 B1
Portarlington Rd BH4 ....121 B1
Portchester Boys Sch
 BH7 ....123 A4
Portelet Cl BH12 ....88 B1
Porter Rd BH17 ....119 A4
Porters La BH21 ....60 B3
Portesham CE Prim Sch
 DT3 ....150 A4
Portesham Gdns BH9 .....90 A2
Portesham Hill DT3 .....132 A1
Portesham Way BH17 .....87 C2
Portfield Cl BH23 ....124 A4
Portfield Rd BH23 ....124 A4
Portfield Sch BH23 ......124 A3
Portiere House BH11 .....89 A2
Portland Ave BH23 ......213 A1
Portland Beach Rd
 DT4 ....180 C2
Portland Castle ★ DT5 ..181 A1
Portland Cres DT4 ......167 A4
Portland Ct DT7 ....96 A3
Portland Hospl DT5 .....181 A1
Portland Mus ★ DT5 ....187 A2
Portland Pl BH2 ....121 C2
Portland Port DT5 ......181 B4
Portland Rd
 Bournemouth BH9 ....122 A4
 Weymouth DT4 ....180 B4
Portland Tophill Jun Sch
 DT5 ....187 A2
Portman Cres BH5 ......123 A4
Portman Ct BA22 ....192 E8
Portman Dr **5** DT11 ....198 C8
Portman Rd
 Bournemouth BH7 ....122 C3
 11 Pimperne DT11 ....199 D4
Portman Terr BH5 ....123 A4
Portmore Cl BH18 ....87 B3
Portmore Gdns DT4 .....167 B3
Portnell's La BA12 ....1 C1
Portreeve Dr BA21 ....27 B3
Portswood Dr **2** BH9 ...90 A2
Portway DT2 ....102 B3
Portwey Cl DT4 ....167 A4
Possessions Cnr SP5 .....26 A2
Post Gn Rd BH16 ....116 C4
Post Office Bldgs BH9 ..121 C4
Post Office La
 6 Poole BH15 ....119 B1
 St.Leonards BH24 ....54 B1

Post Office Rd
 41 Bournemouth BH1 ..121 C2
 Gillingham SP8 ....5 B3
Potterne Way BH21 ....45 B2
Potters Way Poole BH14 .120 B1
 Salisbury SP1 ....213 C2
Pottery La DT4 ....167 B2
Pottery Lines BH20 .....142 C4
Pottery Rd BH14 ....120 A1
Poulner Hill BH24 ....55 C4
Poulner Jun & Inf Sch
 BH24 ....47 C1
Poulner Pk BH24 ....47 C1
Pound Cl
 Charminster DT2 ....107 B3
 Poole BH15 ....119 C3
 Ringwood BH24 ....55 B4
 Stalbridge DT10 ....33 B4
 Yeovil BA21 ....26 C3
Pound Cottage Visitor Ctr ★
 DT2 ....205 E2
Pound Hill
 Corscombe DT2 ....205 B7
 Witchampton BH21 ......200 F1
Pound La
 Bishop's Caundle DT9 ...196 A4
 Burstock DT8 ....203 D5
 3 Christchurch BH23 ..124 A3
 Damerham SP6 ....190 E3
 Dewlish DT2 ....209 C1
 21 Dorchester DT1 .....108 A1
 Gillingham SP8 ....5 B3
 5 Okeford Fitzpaine DT11 197 F5
 Poole BH15 ....119 C3
 Shaftesbury SP7 ....13 A2
 Wareham BH20 ....142 C2
 Wootton Fitzpaine DT6 ....64 A3
Pound Piece
 Easton/Weston DT5 ......186 C2
 Maiden Newton DT2 ......72 C4
Pound Rd
 Hawkchurch EX13 ....202 A3
 Lyme Regis DT7 ....96 A3
 Thornford DT9 ....194 D8
Pound St DT7 ....96 A3
Poundbury Cres DT1 .....107 C1
Poundbury Rd DT1 ......107 C2
Poundbury W Ind Est
 DT1 ....107 C1
Povington Barrow ★
 BH20 ....159 B1
Powell Rd BH14 ....120 A4
Powerscourt Rd BH25 ...126 C4
Powis Cl BH25 ....95 A2
Powys Cl DT1 ....134 C4
Poxwell Dro DT2 ....154 A3
Poxwell Manor ★ DT2 ..154 C2
Prankerds Rd **12** DT9 ...17 B1
Preetz Way DT11 ....212 C2
Preston Cl BH23 ....118 B4
Preston Cty Comp Sch
 BA21 ....26 C3
Preston Gr BA20 ....27 A3
Preston La BH23 ....92 B1
Preston Rd
 Overcombe/Preston
 DT3 ....153 B2
 Poole BH15 ....119 B3
 Radipole DT3 ....167 C3
 Yeovil BA22 ....26 B3
Preston VC Prim Sch
 BA21 ....27 A3
Preston Way BH23 ......125 B4
Prestwood Cl BH25 ......94 C1
Pretoria Terr DT4 ....167 B1
Priest La BH23 ....92 A4
Priest's House Mus & Gdns ★
 BH21 ....59 A2
Priest's Rd BH19 ....179 A1
Priest's Way BH19 ......178 C1
Priestlands DT9 ....30 A4
Priestlands La DT9 ....30 A4
Priestley Rd BH10 ....89 A1
Prime La DT6 ....65 C4
Primrose Cl **3** SP8 ......5 B1
Primrose Gdns BH17 ......86 C1
Primrose Hill BA22 .....193 B7
Primrose La BA21 ....14 A1
Primrose Way
 Christchurch BH23 ....125 B4
 Corfe Mullen BH21 ....86 C4
Primula Cl DT3 ....152 C1
Prince of Wales Rd
 Bournemouth BH4 ....121 B2
 Dorchester DT1 ....108 A1
 3 Weymouth DT4 .....167 B1
Prince of Wales Sch The
 DT1 ....134 B4
Prince's Dr DT4 ....167 B3
Prince's Pl BH25 ....95 B2
Prince's St DT1 ....108 A1
Princes Cl BH22 ....61 B3
Princes Ct **6** BH12 ....121 A2
Princes St BA20 ....27 B2
Princess Ave BH23 ......124 A4
Princess Rd
 Bournemouth BH4 ....121 A2
 Bridport DT6 ....100 B3
 Poole BH12 ....121 A2
 Swanage BH19 ....179 A1
Pringles Cl BH22 ....61 C3
Pringles Dr BH22 ....61 C3
Priors Cl BH23 ....125 B4
Priors Cnr **2** BH21 ....201 D1
Priors Rd BH17 ....119 A4
Priors Wlk **7** BH21 .....59 A1
Priory CE Prim Sch The
 BH23 ....124 A3

Priory Cl BA20 ....26 C1
Priory Gdns
 3 Pimperne DT11 .....199 D3
 3 Spetisbury DT11 ....211 E5
 West Moors BH22 ....62 A4
Priory Glade BA21 ....26 C3
Priory House BH23 ......124 B3
Priory Ind Pk BH23 .....125 A4
Priory La DT6 ....100 B3
Priory Quay BH23 ......124 B3
Priory Rd
 Bournemouth BH2 ....121 C1
 Portland DT5 ....186 C3
 West Moors BH22 ....62 A4
Priory Sq **9** SP2 ......213 B3
Priory View Ct **5** BH23 .124 A3
Priory View Pl **7** BH9 ..90 A2
Priory View Rd
 Bournemouth BH9 ....90 A2
 Burton BH23 ....92 B1
Privet Rd BH9 ....121 C1
Promenade BH23 ....125 A3
Prospect Cl **2** SP8 ....6 A1
Prospect Cres BH19 ....179 A2
Prospect Pl Mere BA12 ....2 C3
 9 Weymouth DT4 ....167 B1
Prospect Rd
 Dorchester DT1 ....107 C1
 Lytchett Matravers BH16 ..84 B2
Prosperous St **14** BH15 .119 B1
Prout Hill **9** DT8 ......204 D4
Prunus Cl BH22 ....61 A4
Prunus Dr BH22 ....61 A4
Pryors Wlk BH21 ....84 B1
Pud Brook **9** DT9 ....17 B1
Puddledock La **13** BA22 .153 B2
Puddletown CE Fst Sch
 DT2 ....78 A1
Puddletown Cres BH17 ...87 C1
Puddletown Rd
 Arne BH20 ....142 A2
 Bere Regis BH20 ....140 C4
 East Stoke BH20 ....113 A1
Pugmill La DT3 ....166 B3
Pullman Ct BH22 ....52 C1
Pullman Way BH24 ....55 B3
Pulmans La **4** TA18 ...191 F4
Purbeck Ave BH15 ......118 C1
Purbeck Cl Loders DT6 ...101 C4
 Lytchett Matravers BH16 ..84 B2
 Upton BH16 ....118 A4
 Weymouth DT4 ....167 A1
Purbeck Ct
 Bournemouth BH5 ......123 A2
 3 Christchurch BH23 ..124 C4
Purbeck Dr BH31 ....45 A3
Purbeck Gdns BH14 .....119 C3
Purbeck Hts BH14 ......120 A3
Purbeck Information &
 Heritage Ctr ★ BH20 ..142 C2
Purbeck Rd
 Barton on Sea BH25 .....126 B4
 Bournemouth BH2 ....121 C1
 Lytchett Matravers BH16 ..84 B2
Purbeck Sch The
 BH20 ....142 B2
Purbeck Sports Ctr
 BH20 ....142 B1
Purbeck Terr Rd
 BH19 ....179 B1
Purbeck Toy Mus ★
 BH20 ....144 B2
Purbeck View **13** BH19 .178 C1
Purbeck View Sch
 BH19 ....179 A2
Purchase Rd BH12 ....121 B4
Purewell BH23 ....124 B3
Purewell Cl BH23 ....124 C3
Purewell Cross BH23 ...124 C3
Purewell Cross Rd
 BH23 ....124 B4
Purewell Ct **11** BH23 ..124 C4
Purns Mill La SP8 ....5 C3
Pussex La BH23 ....91 A4
Putt's La BH21 ....16 A4
Putton La DT3 ....166 B3
Puxey La
 Shillingstone DT11 ......198 B5
 Sturminster Newton
 DT10 ....197 B2
Pye Cl BH21 ....86 C4
Pye Cnr BH21 ....59 A2
Pye La Cranborne BH21 ..41 A3
 Tatworth & Forton
 TA20 ....202 B8
 Wimborne Minster BH21 ..59 A2
Pymore La DT6 ....68 B2
Pymore Rd
 Bradpole DT6 ....68 C2
 Bridport DT6 ....100 B4

Q

Quantock Ct **7** BH23 ..124 C4
Quar Cl DT10 ....196 E1
Quarr Dr DT9 ....30 A4
Quarr Hill Morden BH20 ..83 B1
 Wool BH20 ....140 A1
Quarr La Sherborne DT9 ...30 A4
 Symondsbury DT6 ....99 B3
Quarry Chase **7** BH4 ..121 B2
Quarry Cl
 Shipton Gorge DT6 ......101 B2
 Stour Provost SP8 ....21 B4
 Sturminster Newton DT10 .35 A1

Pim – Ram 235

Quarry Dr BH21 ....60 A4
Quarry Fields Ind Est
 BA12 ....2 C3
Quarry La
 Bothenhampton DT6 .....100 C2
 Bradford Abbas DT9 ......28 B3
 Longburton DT9 ....195 B8
 Melbury Abbas SP7 ....24 A3
Quarry Rd BH21 ....60 A4
Quarterjack Mews **1**
 ....59 B2
Quay Point **19** BH15 ...119 B1
Quay Rd BH23 ....124 A3
Quay The Poole BH15 ...119 B1
 8 Wareham Town BH20 .142 C2
Quayle Dr BH21 ....88 C3
Quayside DT6 ....100 B1
Quebec Pl **7** DT4 .....167 B2
Queen Anne Dr BH21 ....87 C4
Queen Elizabeth Ct BH21 59 A2
Queen Elizabeth's Sch
 BH21 ....58 C3
Queen Manor Rd SP1 ...213 C2
Queen Mary Ave BH9 ....89 C1
Queen St Gillingham SP8 ...5 C1
 Radipole DT4 ....167 C2
 Salisbury SP1 ....213 B3
 4 Yetminster DT9 .....194 C5
Queen's Ave
 Christchurch BH23 ....124 A3
 Dorchester DT1 ....134 C4
Queen's Copse La BH21 ..51 B4
Queen's Pk Ave BH8 ....122 B4
Queen's Pk Gdns BH8 ...122 B4
Queen's Pk Rd BH8 .....122 B4
Queen's Pk S Dr BH8 ...122 B4
Queen's Pk W Dr BH8 ..122 B4
Queen's Rd
 Blandford Forum DT11 ..212 C1
 Bournemouth BH4 ....121 B2
 Christchurch BH23 ......124 C3
 Corfe Mullen BH21 ....86 B3
 Poole BH14 ....120 B2
 Swanage BH19 ....179 A1
Queen's Cl BH22 ....52 C1
Queens Ct
 5 Bournemouth BH4 ..121 B2
 New Milton BH25 ....95 B2
Queens Gdns BH2 ......121 B2
Queens Gr
 New Milton BH25 ....95 B2
 Pen Selwood BA9 ....3 A3
Queens Mead **16** BH19 .179 A1
Queens Rd
 Bradford Abbas DT9 ......28 B1
 Bridport DT6 ....100 B3
 Ferndown BH22 ....61 B4
 Fortuneswell DT5 ....186 C4
 Mere BA12 ....3 A3
 Radipole DT3 ....167 B4
 Salisbury SP1 ....213 B3
Queens Wlk DT7 ....96 A3
Queensbury Rd SP1 .....213 B4
Queensbury Mans **7**
 BH1 ....122 A2
Queensland Rd
 Bournemouth BH5 ......123 A3
 Weymouth DT4 ....167 A2
Queensmead **4** BH21 ...59 B3
Queensway
 New Milton BH25 ....94 C2
 Ringwood BH24 ....55 B4
 Yeovil BA20 ....27 B3
Queensway Pl BA20 ......27 B2
Queenswood Ave BH8 ....90 C1
Queenswood Dr BH22 ....61 B4
Queenwell DT4 ....68 C1
Quibo La DT4 ....167 A2
Quince La BH21 ....59 C3
Quinton Cl BH23 ....125 C4
Quomp The BH24 ....55 B4

R

R L Stevenson Ave BH4 121 A2
Rabin Hill DT10 ....35 A1
Rabling La BH19 ....179 A1
Rabling Rd BH19 ....179 A2
Racedown Rd DT11 .....199 E3
Rachel Cl BH12 ....120 B4
Radcliffe Rd SP2 ....213 B1
Radipole La
 Chickerell DT4 ....166 C2
 Radipole DT4 ....167 A3
Radipole Lake Nature
 Reserve ★ DT4 ....167 B2
Radipole Pk Dr DT4 ....167 B3
Radipole Prim Sch
 DT3 ....167 A4
Radipole Rd BH17 ....88 A1
Radnor Rd SP1 ....213 B4
Raglan Gdns BH11 ....89 A1
Raglan Terr BA21 ....27 A4
Railway Dr DT1 ....56 B2
Railway Terr **4** SP8 .....6 A1
Raleigh Cl
 Christchurch BH23 ......124 C3
 New Milton BH25 ....94 C2
 3 Ringwood BH24 .....55 C4
Raleigh Rd Poole BH12 ...88 C4
 Stalbridge DT10 ....33 C4
Ralph Rd BH21 ....86 C4
Ram La DT11 ....48 B1
Ram's Hill DT10 ....21 C1

Rampant Wlk DT1 134 C4
Rampart Rd SP1 213 B3
Rampisham Hill DT8 205 C3
Ramsbury DT10 196 D5
Ramsbury Cl DT11 212 B2
Ramsbury Ct DT11 212 B2
Ramsey Ct BH25 94 C2
Randall Cl DT3 166 B3
Randalls Hill BH16 85 A1
Randolph Rd
2 Bournemouth BH1 122 C2
Poole BH14 120 B3
Ranelagh Ct BH23 125 C4
Ranelagh Rd
Christchurch BH23 125 C4
Radipole DT4 167 B2
Rashley Rd DT3 166 B3
Raspberry La SP7 12 B1
Ratcliff's Gdn SP7 12 B1
Ratleigh La DT9 29 A3
Ravana Ct 4 BH8 122 A3
Raven Way BH23 125 A3
Ravenscourt Rd BH6 123 B3
Ravenscroft 8 SP2 213 B1
Ravensdale Cl BH12 120 B3
Ravenshall BH2 121 B1
Ravine Ct BH13 147 C4
Ravine Gdns 5 BH13 147 C4
Ravine Rd
Bournemouth BH5 123 A2
Poole BH13 147 C4
Rawles Way DT6 100 B4
Rawlsbury Camp* DT11 209 B8
Rawston Down Rd 6 DT11 199 E2
Rax La DT6 100 B4
Raymond Cl BH31 45 B3
Raymond Rd DT4 166 C1
Rayners Dr BH12 120 B3
Reap La DT5 186 C1
Rebbeck Rd BH7 123 A3
Reckleford BA20 27 B3
Reckleford Cty Inf Sch BA21 27 C3
Recreation Rd BH12 120 C3
Rectory Ave BH21 58 B1
Rectory Cl DT2 136 A1
Rectory Gdns DT11 198 F7
Rectory La
Child Okeford DT11 198 C7
Hardington Mandeville BA22 193 A7
Puncknowle DT2 129 C3
Studland BH19 164 B1
West Stafford DT2 136 A4
Rectory Rd
Broadmayne DT2 136 A1
Piddlehinton DT2 76 C4
Poole BH15 119 B3
Salisbury SP2 213 A2
Rectory Way DT4 167 B1
Red Horn Cl BH16 118 B2
Red House Mus & Gdns* BH23 124 A3
Red La Corfe Mullen BH21 86 A4
Seaborough DT8 191 E1
Sixpenny Handley SP5 189 A3
Todber DT10 21 B2
Red Lion Cl 3 DT10 197 D8
Red Oaks Cl BH22 61 A4
Red Post Bloxworth DT11 82 B4
Poyntington DT9 16 B2
Red Roofs BH22 61 C2
Red Wing Rd DT9 17 B1
Redan Cl BH23 125 C4
Redbreast Rd BH9 90 A2
Redbreast Rd N BH9 90 A2
Redbridge La DT2 137 C3
Redbridge Rd DT2 137 C3
Redcliff View DT4 167 C1
Redcliffe Cl BH23 92 B2
Redcliffe Rd BH19 179 A3
Redcotts La BH21 59 A3
Redcotts Rd BH21 59 A3
Redford Cl SP1 213 C4
Redgate Pk TA18 191 E5
Redhill Ave BH9 89 C2
Redhill Cl BH10 89 C2
Redhill Cres BH9 89 C2
Redhill Ct BH10 89 C2
Redhill Dr BH10 89 C2
Redhill Pk Homes 1 BH10 89 C2
Redhoave Rd BH17 87 C1
Redhole La
Castleton DT9 16 A1
Sherborne DT9 30 A4
Redlands
Christchurch BH23 125 A4
Poole BH12 120 C3
Redlands La DT8 203 F5
Redmans La SP7 24 A3
Redmans View BH31 45 A3
Redpoll Cl 1 DT3 152 B2
Redsails BH13 147 A2
Redshank Cl BH17 86 C1
Redvers Rd BH23 124 C4
Redwood Cl BH24 55 B4
Redwood Dr BH22 61 B4
Redwood Rd Upton BH16 118 A4
Yeovil BA21 28 A4
Reed View Cl DT4 167 A3
Reedling Cl DT3 152 B2
Reeves Orch BH21 56 B3
Reforne DT5 186 C2
Reforne Cl 1 DT5 187 A2
Regency Cres BH23 123 C4
Regency Dr 7 DT3 152 B2
Regent Dr BH7 122 C4
Regent Way BH23 124 A3
Regents The 2 BA21 26 C3
Regimental Mus* SP1 213 B2
Reid St BH23 124 A4
Rempstone Rd
Oakley BH21 87 B4
Swanage BH19 179 A2
Remus Cl DT1 134 C4
Renault Dr BH18 87 A1
Renfrew Cl DT1 135 B4
Renscombe Rd BH19 183 A4
Restharrow BH1 122 A2
Retreat Rd BH21 59 B2
Revels Hill DT2 207 E7
Rew La DT2 208 A8
Rex La DT3 166 B3
Rex's La BA22 27 C1
Reynard Ct BH15 119 C2
Reynards Way DT3 153 B2
Rhine Rd BH20 139 C3
Rhode La DT7 64 A1
Rhosewood Dr DT3 153 A2
Rhydderch Way 9 TA18 191 F4
Ribble Cl BH18 87 A1
Ribbonwood Hts BH14 120 A2
Ricardo Cres BH23 125 A3
Rice Gdns BH16 118 B2
Rice Terr BH16 118 B2
Richard Cl BH16 118 A4
Richards Way SP2 213 A2
Richmond Cl DT9 30 A3
Richmond Ct
15 Bournemouth BH5 122 C2
7 New Milton BH25 95 A2
Richmond Gdns BH1 121 C2
Richmond Gn DT9 30 A3
Richmond Hill BH1 121 C2
Richmond Hill Dr BH2 121 C2
Richmond Pk Ave BH8 122 B4
Richmond Pk Cl BH8 122 B3
Richmond Pk Cres BH8 122 B4
Richmond Pk Rd BH8 122 B4
Richmond Rd
Blandford Forum DT11 212 C2
Poole BH14 120 B2
4 Salisbury SP2 213 A3
Sherborne DT9 30 A3
Swanage BH19 179 A1
Wimborne Minster BH21 59 B2
Yeovil BA20 27 B2
Richmond Rise BH8 122 B3
Richmond Way BA21 26 C3
Richmond Wood Rd BH8 122 B4
Ricketts La DT10 35 A1
Rickhay Rise TA18 192 B8
Ridge Dro DT10 196 F5
Ridge La
Hazelbury Bryan DT10 196 D5
West Coker BA22 193 A8
Ridge The DT9 16 C3
Ridge Way
Puddletown DT2 76 C1
Shaftesbury SP7 12 C2
Ridgeback La DT6 69 C4
Ridgefield Gdns BH23 125 B4
Ridgemead 5 BA20 26 C1
Ridgemount Gdns BH15 118 C2
Ridgeway Bradpole DT6 68 C1
Broadstone BH18 87 A2
Corfe Mullen BH21 86 B4
Ferndown BH22 89 C4
3 Sherborne DT9 30 A3
Ridgeway La
Child Okeford DT11 198 C8
Hinton St Mary DT10 35 A2
Ridgeway Rd SP1 213 B3
Ridgway TA18 192 B8
Ridley Rd BH9 121 C4
Ridout Cl BH10 89 A1
Ridwood DT6 99 A3
Rigg La DT9 14 C1
Riggs Gdns BH11 88 C1
Rigler Rd BH15 119 A1
Rimbrow Cl DT3 153 B2
Rimbury Way BH23 124 A4
Ring St DT10 33 B4
Ringmoor (Settlement & Field System)* DT11 197 F3
Rings The DT11 79 C4
Ringstead Cres DT3 168 A3
Ringwood CE Inf Sch BH24 55 B4
Ringwood Cty Jun Sch BH24 55 B3
Ringwood La BH21 201 E7
Ringwood Rd
Alderholt SP6 42 B3
Bournemouth BH11 88 C2
Bransgore BH23 93 B3
Christchurch BH23 94 A1
Ferndown BH22 61 B2
Fordingbridge SP6 43 B3
Hyde SP6 43 C2
Poole BH12 120 A4
Sopley BH23 92 A4
St.Leonards BH24 53 C1
Three Legged Cross BH21 52 C4
Verwood BH31 45 B3
Ringwood Recn Ctr BH24 55 B4
Ringwood Ret Pk BH11 88 C2
Ringwood Sch BH24 55 B4
Rip Croft DT5 186 C1
Ripon Rd BH9 90 A1
Ripp's La DT2 207 F4
Rise The DT4 167 A3
Ritchie Pl BH22 52 C2
Ritchie Rd
Bournemouth BH11 89 A2
Yeovil BA22 26 B3
River Cl BH21 59 B3
River La 2 DT11 211 D6
River Pk BH6 123 C3
River View SP8 5 C1
River Way
Charmouth DT6 97 A4
Christchurch BH23 91 B1
Riverbourne Rd SP1 213 C2
Riverdale La BH23 124 A3
Riverlea Rd BH23 124 A3
Rivermead Gdns BH23 91 C1
Rivers Mead DT10 35 B1
Rivers Rd BA21 27 C4
Riversdale 8 BH21 59 B2
Riversdale Rd BH6 124 A2
Riversdene DT11 48 A3
Riverside
3 Beaminster DT8 204 D4
4 Bournemouth BH10 89 C2
Ringwood BH24 55 A3
Riverside Ave BH7 91 B1
Riverside Cl SP1 213 C3
Riverside La BH6 123 C3
Riverside Pk BH23 124 A3
Riverside Pk Ind Est BH21 59 B2
Riverside Rd
Blandford Forum DT11 212 C1
Bournemouth BH6 123 C3
Ferndown BH22 52 C1
Salisbury SP1 213 C3
Riverslea Mews BH23 124 B3
Riversmeet Ct BH23 124 B3
Rivervale DT6 100 B4
Riviera Ct
3 Bournemouth BH2 121 B2
3 Poole BH13 147 C4
Rivirea 22 BH1 122 A2
Rixon Cl DT10 35 B1
Rixon Hill DT10 35 B1
Roberts La BH17 119 A4
Roberts Pl DT1 107 C1
Roberts Rd
Bournemouth BH7 123 A3
Poole BH17 87 A1
Robertson Rd BH20 139 B4
Robin Cl 2 DT3 152 B2
Robin Cres BH25 94 B3
Robin Gr BH25 94 C1
Robins Ct 7 BH21 59 B2
Robins Garth DT1 108 A1
Robins Gdn DT2 209 A2
Robins Way BH23 125 A3
Robinson Hts DT10 33 B4
Robinswood Dr BH22 61 B4
Robsall Cl BH12 120 C4
Robville Ct BH6 123 A3
Rochester Rd BH11 89 A2
Rockbourne Gdns BH25 126 B4
Rockbourne La SP6 190 F3
Rockford Cl BH6 123 C2
Rockhampton Cl DT3 152 B2
Rockley Rd BH15 118 C1
Rocks La DT2 206 A7
Rockway DT6 101 B2
Rocky Knap DT3 167 B4
Rod Hill La DT2 78 A1
Rodden Cl DT4 180 B4
Rodden House* DT3 150 B3
Rodden La DT3 150 B3
Rodden Row DT3 149 A4
Rodgett Cres BH20 142 C4
Rodney Cl BH12 121 A4
Rodney Ct
Christchurch BH23 125 A3
Poole BH15 119 B1
Rodney Dr BH23 124 C3
Rodway BH21 59 B2
Rodwell Ave DT4 167 B1
Rodwell Cl BH10 89 B3
Rodwell Rd DT4 167 B1
Rodwell St DT4 167 B1
Roe Ave BA22 26 B3
Roe La BA22 15 A4
Roebuck Cl BH25 95 A2
Roeshot Cres BH23 93 C1
Roeshot Hill BH23 93 B1
Roke Rd BH20 80 C2
Rolfe Cres DT3 166 B3
Rollestone St 12 SP1 213 B3
Rolls Bridge La SP8 5 C1
Rolls Bridge Way SP8 5 B1
Rolls Dr BH6 124 A2
Rolls Mill Bridge* DT10 197 C8
Roman Cl DT3 167 B4
Roman Hts BH21 86 C4
Roman Rd
Corfe Mullen BH18 86 C3
Dorchester DT1 134 C4
Osmington DT3 154 A2
Radipole DT3 167 B4
Roman Way BH21 58 B3
Romer Rd SP2 213 B1
Romney Cl BH10 89 C2
Romney Rd BH10 89 C2
Romsey Rd BA21 28 A4
Romulus Cl DT1 134 C4
Rook Hill Rd BH23 125 B3
Rook La DT11 210 C2
Rook St BA12 3 A2
Rookery Cl
7 Gillingham SP8 6 A1
Gillingham SP8 11 A4
Rookery La
Burstock DT8 203 C6
Uplyme DT7 64 A1
Rookery The DT2 130 C4
Roosevelt Cres BH11 89 A3
Rope Walks DT6 100 B3
Roper's La BH20 142 C2
Ropers La BH16 118 B4
Roping Rd BA21 27 B3
Ropley Rd BH7 123 B4
Rosamond Ave DT6 101 B2
Rosamund Ave BH21 59 C2
Roscrea Cl BH6 124 A2
Roscrea Dr BH6 124 A2
Rose Cres BH15 119 C3
Rose Ct 3 Gillingham SP8 6 A1
Poole BH15 119 C2
Rose Gdn The BH23 91 B1
Rose Gdns BH9 90 A2
Rose La 1 TA18 191 E4
Rose's La DT3 150 B1
Rosebank La DT11 212 C2
Roseberry Gdns 3 SP8 5 C2
Rosebery Ave BA21 27 C3
Rosebery Cl BH31 45 C3
Rosebery Rd BH5 123 A3
Rosebud Ave 1 BH9 90 A1
Rosecrae Cl BH25 94 C2
Rosecroft Rd DT4 166 C1
Rosedale Cl 3 BH23 124 C3
Rosefields 6 DT11 211 B1
Roselyn Cres DT9 31 A1
Rosemary Cl SP1 213 C3
Rosemary Ct 14 BH23 126 A4
Rosemary Gdns BH12 120 A4
Rosemary La
Abbotsbury DT3 149 A4
1 Salisbury SP1 213 B2
Rosemary Rd BH12 120 B4
Rosemary St DT9 17 B1
Rosemount Rd BH4 121 A1
Rosewood Gdns BH25 94 C2
Roslin Gdns BH3 121 B4
Roslin Rd BH3 121 C4
Roslin Rd S BH3 121 C4
Ross Cl BH20 139 C3
Ross Gdns BH11 88 B3
Ross Glades BH3 121 C3
Ross Rd BH24 47 C1
Rossiters Quay BH23 124 B3
Rossley Cl BH23 93 C1
Rossmore Par BH12 120 A4
Rossmore Rd BH12 120 B4
Rotary Cl BH21 59 C4
Rothbury Pk BH25 95 A1
Rotherfield Rd
Bournemouth BH5 123 A2
Christchurch BH23 94 A1
Rotherham Rd DT5 181 B1
Rothesay Dr BH23 125 C4
Rothesay Rd
Bournemouth BH4 121 B3
Dorchester DT1 135 A4
Rotterdam Dr BH23 124 B4
Rougemont Cl SP1 213 B3
Rough Down La DT6 65 A1
Rough Height BH19 179 A1
Roumelia La BH5 122 C2
Roundham Gdns
Bridport DT6 100 B2
Weymouth DT4 167 A1
Roundhaye Rd BH11 88 C3
Roundhayes Cl DT4 167 A1
Roundways* BH11 88 C2
Row The DT10 35 A1
Rowan Cl
Christchurch BH23 125 B4
Radipole DT4 167 A3
St Leonards & St Ives BH24 53 C2
Sandford BH20 143 A4
Rowan Dr
Broadstone BH17 86 C1
Christchurch BH23 125 B4
Verwood BH31 45 B2
Rowan Way BA20 27 A2
Rowbarrow Cl Poole BH17 87 C1
Salisbury SP2 213 B1
Rowbarrow Hill DT9 14 C2
Rowbarrow La BH21 200 F2
Rowden Mill La DT10 32 C1
Rowena Rd BH6 123 C3
Rowland Ave BH15 119 C3
Rowlands Hill BH21 59 B3
Rowlands Rd 5 DT11 198 F4
Rowls La BA9 4 A2
Rownhams Rd BH8 90 B2
Royal Arc 5 BH7 122 C2
Royal Armoured Corps Tank Mus* BH20 139 C3
Royal Bournemouth Gen Hospl The BH7 91 A1
Royal Manor Sch DT5 186 C2
Royal Oak Rd BH10 89 B3
Royal Signals Mus* DT11 199 E3
Royal Victoria Hospl BH4 121 B2
Royster Cl BH17 87 B1
Royston Dr BH21 59 B3
Royston Pl BH25 127 A4
Rozel Manor BH13 121 A1
Rozelle Rd BH14 120 B2
Ruben Dr BH15 118 B1
Rubens Cl BH25 95 A2
Ruddock Cl BA22 193 B8
Ruddock Way BA22 193 A8
Rue La DT9 31 C2
Rufford Gdns BH6 123 C3
Rufus Castle* DT5 187 A2
Rufus Way DT5 187 A3
Rugby Rd BH17 87 A1
Ruins La DT6 99 A3
Runnymede Ave BH11 88 C3
Runnymede Rd BA21 27 C4
Runton Rd BH12 120 C3
Runway The BH23 125 A4
Rural La DT2 73 C2
Ruscombe La DT6 69 C3
Rushall La BH21 86 A3
Rushcombe Fst Sch BH21 86 B3
Rushcombe Way BH21 86 C3
Rushetts Cl 7 DT5 186 C1
Rushford Warren BH23 124 C2
Rushmere Rd BH6 123 B4
Rushmore Golf Club SP5 188 C5
Rushmore Pk* SP5 188 C5
Rushton Cres BH3 121 C3
Ruskin Ave BH9 90 A2
Russel Rd BH10 89 B3
Russell Ave
Swanage BH19 179 A1
Weymouth DT4 167 A1
Russell Cotes Art Gall & Mus* BH1 122 A1
Russell Cotes Rd BH1 122 A1
Russell Ct 3 BH25 95 A2
Russell Dr
Christchurch BH23 124 B3
Swanage BH19 179 A1
Russell Gdns
Hamworthy BH16 118 B2
St.Leonards BH24 54 B3
Russell Rd SP2 213 A3
Russet Cl BH22 61 B3
Russet Way BA20 26 C1
Rutland Manor 9 BH12 121 A2
Rutland Rd
Bournemouth BH9 122 A4
Christchurch BH23 91 C1
Weymouth DT4 167 A2
Ryall Rd Poole BH17 87 B1
Whitechurch Canonicorum DT6 66 B1
Ryall's La DT9 196 A7
Ryan Cl Ferndown BH22 61 B4
Northport BH20 142 C3
Ryan Gdns
Bournemouth BH11 89 A3
Ferndown BH22 61 B4
Rydal Cl BH23 91 B2
Rydal Mews BH21 59 B3
Rye Gdns BA20 26 C1
Rye Hill BH20 81 A1
Rye Hill Cl BH20 81 A1
Rye Wr La TA18 193 A1
Ryecroft Ave BH11 88 C3
Ryefields Cl BA22 193 B8
Ryemead La DT4 180 B3
Ryland's La DT4 180 B4
Rymbury DT3 153 B2
Ryme Rd DT9 194 B5

S

Sackmore Gn DT10 20 C2
Sackmore La DT10 20 C2
Sackville St DT11 81 C4
Sadborow La TA20 202 E5
Saddle Cl BH21 60 B3
Saffron Ct BH11 88 B2
Saffron Dr BH23 125 A4
Saffron Way BH11 88 B2
St Adlem's CE Comb Sch BH12 121 A3
St Alban St DT4 167 B1
St Alban's Ave BH8 122 B4
St Alban's Cres BH8 122 A4
St Alban's Rd BH8 122 A4
St Aldhelm's BH14 120 C2
St Aldhelm's Chapel* BH19 183 A2
St Aldhelm's Cl BH13 120 C2
St Aldhelm's Rd
Poole BH13 120 C2
Sherborne DT9 30 A4
St Andrew's Cl DT9 194 E3
St Andrew's Rd DT6 68 C1
St Andrews BH23 124 A3
St Andrews Ave DT3 167 B4
St Andrews CE Prim Sch
Overcombe/Preston DT3 168 A4
Yetminster DT9 194 C6
St Andrews Cl 4 DT1 135 A4
St Andrews Dr DT6 97 A4
St Andrews Ind Est DT6 100 C4
St Andrews Mdw DT7 96 A3
St Andrews Rd
Broadstone BH18 87 A3
Yeovil BA20 27 A3
St Andrews View SP7 37 C4
St Ann Pl SP1 213 B2
St Ann St SP1 213 B2
St Ann's Ct 1 BH1 122 C3
St Ann's Hospl BH13 147 C3

St Anne's Ave BH6 .....123 C3
St Anne's Gdns BA21 ....27 A3
St Anne's Rd Upton BH16 118 A4
Weymouth DT4 ....180 C4
St Annes Cl SP7 ....23 A3
St Anthony's Rd BH2 ...121 C3
St Antonys Leweston Sch
DT9 ....195 A7
St Aubyns Ct 3 BH15 ..119 A1
St Augustin's Rd BH2 ..121 C3
St Augustines RC Prim Sch
DT4 ....167 A1
St Bartholomews CE VC Fst
Sch TA18 ....191 F4
St Brelades BH14 ......120 B1
St Brelades Ave BH12 ...88 B1
St Catharines Rd
BH19 ....185 B4
St Catherine's Chapel★
DT11 ....209 F5
St Catherine's Cres 2
DT9 ....30 A3
St Catherine's Par BH23 .91 C1
St Catherine's RC Prim Sch
BH21 ....60 A3
St Catherine's Rd BH6 .123 C2
St Catherine's Way BH23 91 B2
St Catherines BH21 .....59 B2
St Catherines Chapel★
DT3 ....149 A3
St Catherines RC Sch
DT6 ....100 B4
St Clair Rd Poole BH13 ..147 C4
Salisbury SP2 ....213 B1
St Cleeves Way BH22 ....61 B2
St Clement & St John CE Inf
Sch BH8 ....122 B3
St Clement's Gdns BH1 .122 B3
St Clement's Rd BH8 ...122 B3
St Clements La BH15 ...119 A1
St Clements Rd BH15 ..120 A4
St David's Cres BA21 ....27 B4
St David's Ct 3 BH1 ...122 C3
St David's Rd
Upton BH16 ....118 A4
Weymouth DT4 ....180 B4
St Denys 28 BH25 ....95 A1
St Edmund St 6 DT4 ...167 B1
St Edmund's Church St 13
SP1 ....213 B3
St Edward's Sch BH15 ..119 C4
St Edwards 5 SP7 ....12 C2
St Edwards Cl BH20 ....177 A4
St Francis Rd SP1 .....213 B4
St Gabriel's Cl DT6 .....98 B4
St George's Almshos 11
BH15 ....119 A1
St George's Ave
Bournemouth BH8 ....122 B4
Poole BH12 ....120 A4
Radipole DT4 ....167 C3
Yeovil BA21 ....27 B4
St George's Cl
Bournemouth BH8 ....122 B4
Christchurch BH23 ......125 B4
Langton Matravers
BH19 ....178 A1
St George's Ct 2 BH1 ..122 C3
St George's Dr BH22 ....61 B2
St George's Rd
Portland DT5 ....186 C2
Shaftesbury SP7 ....12 C1
St Georges Cl
Bransgore BH23 ....93 A4
Dorchester DT1 ....108 B1
St Georges Cty Inf Sch
DT5 ....186 C2
St Georges Est Rd
DT5 ....186 C2
St Georges Hill DT7 .....96 A3
St Georges Mans 18
BH5 ....122 C2
St Georges Rd DT1 .....108 B1
St Gildas Sch BA21 ......27 B3
St Giles Cl DT6 ....99 A4
St Giles's House★
BH21 ....201 E6
St Gregorys CE Prim Sch
DT10 ....20 C1
St Helen's La DT2 ......206 B2
St Helen's Rd
Dorchester DT1 ....107 C1
Sandford BH20 ....143 A4
Weymouth DT4 ....166 C1
St Helier Ave DT3 ......152 A2
St Helier Rd BH12 ....88 B1
St Ives CP Sch BH24 ....54 B3
St Ives End La BH24 .....54 B2
St Ives Gdns BH2 ......121 C3
St Ives Pk BH24 ....54 B3
St Ives Wood BH24 ......54 B3
St James DT8 ....204 C4
St James CE Fst Sch
SP6 ....42 B3
St James CE Prim Sch
BH7 ....123 A3
St James Cl 7 BH15 ...119 A1
St James Fst Sch BH21 ..51 A3
St James Pk DT6 ....69 A1
St James Rd BH22 ....61 A3
St James St SP7 ....12 C1
St James's 20 BH5 .....122 C2
St James's Cl BA21 ......26 C3
St James's Pk BA21 ......26 C3
St James's Sq BH5 .....123 A3
St John's Cl
9 Salisbury SP1 ....213 C2
Wimborne Minster BH21 ...59 B2
St John's Ct 4 BH1 ....122 C3
St John's Gdns 3 BH9 ...89 C1
St John's Hill
Shaftesbury SP7 ....12 B1
Wareham BH20 ....142 C2
Wimborne Minster BH21 ...59 B3
St John's Rd
Bournemouth BH5 ......122 C2
Christchurch BH23 ......124 A3
Poole BH15 ....119 B2
Yeovil BA21 ....27 C4
St John's St SP1 ....213 B2
St Johns CE Fst Sch
BH21 ....59 B2
St Johns CE Prim Sch
DT4 ....167 C3
St Johns Rd BH25 ....95 A4
St Joseph's RC Comb Sch
BH12 ....120 C4
St Joseph's RC Prim Sch
BH23 ....125 A4
St Judes Cl SP1 ....213 C4
St Julien Cres DT3 .....152 A2
St Julien Rd BH20 .....139 B4
St Just Cl BH22 ....61 B2
St Juthware Cl BA22 ...193 C3
St Katharine's CE Prim Sch
BH6 ....124 A2
St Katherine's Ave
DT6 ....100 C4
St Katherine's CE Prim Sch
BH6 ....123 A2
St Katherine's Dr DT6 ..100 C4
St Lawrence 4 DT6 ....128 A4
St Lawrence Cres SP7 ...12 C2
St Lawrence Rd DT3 ...152 B3
St Ledger's Pl BH1 .....122 B3
St Ledger's Rd BH8 ....122 B3
St Leonard's Ave
DT11 ....212 C1
St Leonard's Rd
Bournemouth BH8 ......122 A3
Weymouth DT4 ....167 B1
St Leonards Cty Mid Sch
DT11 ....212 C1
St Leonards Hospl
BH24 ....53 C1
St Leonards Way BH24 ...53 C3
St Luke's CE Prim Sch
BH9 ....121 C4
St Luke's Ct 2 DT6 ....100 A4
St Luke's Rd BH3 ......121 C4
St Margaret's Almshouses
BH21 ....59 A3
St Margaret's Ave BH23 124 A3
St Margaret's Cl 2 SP1 213 C2
St Margaret's Rd
Bournemouth BH10 ....89 B1
Poole BH15 ....119 B2
St Margarets BH2 ......121 C3
St Margarets Cl BH21 ....59 A3
St Margarets Hill BH21 ..59 A3
St Mark's Ave SP1 .....213 B4
St Mark's CE Prim Sch
BH10 ....89 B1
St Mark's Rd
Bournemouth BH11 ....89 A2
Salisbury SP1 ....213 B3
St Marks CE Jun Sch
SP1 ....213 B2
St Martin's 6 SP1 .....213 B2
St Martin's Cl 1 BH20 .142 C2
St Martin's La BH20 ....142 C2
St Martin's Rd
12 Fortuneswell DT5 ....186 C4
Sandford BH20 ....143 A4
Weymouth DT4 ....180 C4
St Martin's Sq SP8 ....5 C1
St Martins CE Inf Sch
SP1 ....213 B2
St Martins CE Jun Sch
SP1 ....213 C2
St Martins Ch★ DT11 ...212 A1
St Martins Cl DT2 ......136 A1
St Martins Field DT2 ...133 B4
St Martins Rd BH16 ....118 A4
St Martins Sch TA18 ...191 E4
St Mary St 7 DT4 ......167 B1
St Mary Well St 11 DT8 .204 C4
St Mary's Church (remains
of)★ SP7 ....24 A1
St Mary's Cl
Northport BH20 ....142 B3
Sixpenny Handley SP5 ...189 A4
3 Winterborne Whitechurch
DT11 ....210 C3
St Mary's Cres BA21 ....27 C4
St Mary's Ct BH6 ......123 C2
St Mary's Gdns 3 DT8 .204 C4
St Mary's Maternity Hospl
BH15 ....119 B2
St Mary's Mews BH22 ...61 B2
St Mary's Rd
Bournemouth BH1 ....122 B3
Ferndown BH22 ....61 B3
Poole BH15 ....119 C2
Salisbury SP2 ....213 A2
Sherborne DT9 ....29 C3
St Marys Cath Fst Sch
DT1 ....135 A4
St Marys CE Mid Sch
DT2 ....78 A1
St Marys CE Prim Sch
DT6 ....100 B3
St Marys Cl BH23 ....93 B4
St Marys Fst Sch BH22 ..52 C2
St Marys Prim Sch
DT8 ....204 C4
St Marys RC Fst Sch
BH19 ....179 A1
St Marys RC Prim Sch
BH20 ....140 A1
St Marys RC Sch DT10 ...21 A3
St Marys Sch
Donhead St Mary SP7 .....13 B1
Thorncombe TA20 ....202 E6
St Merrin's Cl BH10 .....89 B2
St Michael's 2 BH2 ....121 B2
St Michael's Ave BA21 ...27 C4
St Michael's CE Mid Sch
BH21 ....59 C4
St Michael's CE Prim Sch
BH2 ....121 B2
St Michael's La DT6 ...100 B3
St Michael's Mews 16
BH2 ....121 C2
St Michael's Pl 18 BH2 .121 C2
St Michael's Rd
Bournemouth BH2 ......121 C1
11 Wareham BH20 ......142 C2
Yeovil BA21 ....27 C3
St Michael's Trading Est
DT6 ....100 B3
St Michaels DT7 ....96 B3
St Michaels Cl
Hamworthy BH15 ....118 C1
Over Compton DT9 ....28 C4
Verwood BH31 ....45 A3
St Michaels Ct
1 Bournemouth BH6 ....123 B2
Weymouth DT4 ....167 B1
St Michaels Rd BH31 ....45 A2
St Michaels VC Inf Sch
DT7 ....96 B3
St Nicholas & St Laurence CE
Prim Sch DT3 ....152 B1
St Nicholas CE Prim Sch
DT11 ....198 C7
St Nicholas Cl
3 Henstridge BA8 ....19 A2
11 Yeovil BA20 ....27 B2
St Nicholas Ct 5 DT11 .198 C7
St Nicholas Gdns 2
DT11 ....198 E3
St Nicholas St DT4 .....167 B1
St Nicholas' Rd SP1 ....213 B2
St Osmonds Sch SP1 ...213 B2
St Osmund Cl 3 DT9 ...194 C5
St Osmund's Rd BH14 ..120 B2
St Osmunds CE Mid Sch
DT1 ....135 A4
St Patrick's Rd BA21 ....26 C4
St Patricks Ave DT4 ....166 C1
St Paul's Cl DT9 ....30 B4
St Paul's Gn DT9 ....30 B4
St Paul's La BH1 ....122 A2
St Paul's Pl BH1 ....122 A2
St Paul's Rd
Bournemouth BH1 ......122 A2
13 Fortuneswell DT5 ....186 C4
Salisbury SP2 ....213 A3
St Peter's Abbey★
DT3 ....149 A4
St Peter's Cl 1 DT11 ...199 D4
St Peter's Cres 36 BH1 .121 C2
St Peter's Ct 7 BH14 ..120 A2
St Peter's RC Comp Sch
BH6 ....123 C2
St Peter's RC Sch BH7 .123 A4
St Peter's Rd
Bournemouth BH1 ......122 A2
Poole BH14 ....120 A2
St Peter's Wlk 38 BH1 ..121 C2
St Peters Ct BH1 ....122 A2
St Rayn Hill TA18 ......191 A4
St Richards Cl DT11 ....211 F7
St Rumbold's Rd SP7 ....12 C1
St Saviors Cl BH7 ......123 B4
St Stephen's Ct 6 BH2 .121 C2
St Stephen's Rd BH2 ...121 C2
St Stephen's Way 27
BH2 ....121 C2
St Stephens La BH31 ....45 B3
St Swithin's Rd DT9 .....30 B3
St Swithins Ave DT6 ...100 B4
St Swithins Cl DT9 ......30 B3
St Swithins Rd DT6 ....100 B4
St Swithun's Rd BH1 ...122 A2
St Swithun's Rd S BH1 .122 A2
St Thomas Cross 1
BA21 ....27 C3
St Thomas Garnet's RC Sch
BH5 ....123 A3
St Thomas Rd DT1 .....107 C1
St Thomas St DT4 ......167 B1
St Thomas's Cl BH10 ....89 C1
St Valerie Rd BH2 ......121 C3
St Vast's Rd BH19 ......179 B1
St Walburga's RC Prim Sch
BH9 ....90 A1
St Winifred's Rd BH2 ..121 C3
Salerno Pl BH15 ....118 B1
Salisbury & S Wiltshire Mus★
SP2 ....213 A2
Salisbury Arts Ctr★
SP1 ....213 B3
Salisbury Bsns Pk
SP1 ....213 C2
Salisbury Cath★ SP1 ...213 B2
Salisbury Cath Sch
SP1 ....213 B2
Salisbury Coll of Tech
SP1 ....213 B2
Salisbury Cres DT11 ...212 B2
Salisbury Leisure Ctr
SP1 ....213 A4
Salisbury Rd
Blandford Forum DT11 ...212 C2
Bournemouth BH1 ......122 C2
Burton BH23 ....92 B2
Donhead St Mary SP7 .....13 B1
Ellingham Harbridge & Ibsley
SP6 ....43 B1
Pimperne DT11 ....199 E4
Poole BH14 ....120 B3
Shaftesbury SP7 ....12 C1
Sopley BH23 ....92 A3
9 Swanage BH19 ....179 B1
Weymouth DT4 ....167 B2
Salisbury Sch of English
SP1 ....213 B2
Salisbury St
Blandford Forum DT11 ...212 B1
Cranborne BH21 ....40 A4
Dorchester DT1 ....108 A1
Marnhull DT10 ....21 A1
Mere BA12 ....3 A3
Shaftesbury SP7 ....12 C1
Salisbury Sta SP2 ......213 A3
Salisbury Swimming Baths
SP1 ....213 B3
Sally Kings La SP7 ......12 B2
Sally Lovell's La BA8 ....18 C4
Salt La SP1 ....213 B3
Salter Rd BH13 ....147 B2
Salterns Ct BH14 ......147 A4
Salterns Point BH14 ...147 A4
Salterns Quay BH14 ...147 A4
Salterns Rd BH14 ......120 A2
Salterns Way BH14 ....147 A4
Salthouse La BA20 ......27 B2
Saltings Rd BH16 ......118 A3
Salway Dr DT6 ....68 A3
Salwayash Prim Sch
DT6 ....68 A4
Sammy Miller's Motorcycle
Mus★ BH25 ....94 C3
Samphire Cl DT4 ......167 B3
Samples Way BH17 ....119 C4
Samson Rd BH15 ......118 B1
Samways Cl BA22 ....26 B3
San Remo Twrs 23 BH5 .122 C2
Sancreed Rd BH12 .....120 C4
Sancroft BH21 ....60 A1
Sandbanks Bsns Ctr
BH13 ....147 A2
Sandbanks Rd BH14 ...120 A1
Sandbourne Ave DT11 ..212 C2
Sandbourne Cl 11 BH19 178 C1
Sandbourne Rd
Bournemouth BH4 ......121 B1
Overcombe/Preston
DT3 ....168 A4
Poole BH15 ....119 B2
Sandecotes Rd BH14 ...120 B2
Sanderling Cl 6 DT3 ...152 B2
Sanderlings 3 BH24 .....55 C3
Sanders Gn 4 DT11 ...210 C3
Sandford Cl BH9 ....90 B2
Sandford Dr BH20 ......116 A1
Sandford La BH20 .....142 C3
Sandford La Ind Est
BH20 ....142 C3
Sandford Mid Sch
BH20 ....116 A1
Sandford Orcas Rd
Castleton DT9 ....15 C2
Sandford Orcas DT9 ......15 C2
Sandford Rd
Northport BH20 ....142 C3
Wareham St Martin
BH20 ....116 A1
Sandford St Martin CE Fst
Sch BH20 ....143 A4
Sandford Way BH18 .....86 C1
Sandhills Cl BH17 ....87 B1
Sandhills Cres BH20 ...139 C1
Sandhurst Dr BH21 ......53 B4
Sandhurst Rd BA20 ......27 A1
Sandilands Cl SP8 ....10 C2
Sandleheath Rd SP6 .....42 A4
Sandlewood Cl BA21 .....28 A4
Sandmartin Cl BH25 ...126 C4
Sandown Cl BA20 ....27 B3
Sandown Pl 14 SP2 ....213 A3
Sandown Rd BH23 .....124 C3
Sandpiper Cl BH17 ......86 C1
Sandpiper Way DT4 ...180 B3
Sandpit La BH15 ....119 B2
Sandringham Cl BH9 ....90 A2
Sandringham Ct
Bournemouth BH8 ......122 B3
1 Dorchester DT1 ......135 B4
Sandringham Gdns BH9 .90 A2
Sandringham Rd
Poole BH14 ....120 B2
Yeovil BA21 ....28 A3
Sandringham Sports Ctr
DT1 ....108 A1
Sandroyd Sch SP5 .....188 C5
Sandsfoot Castle★
DT4 ....180 C4
Sandy Cl BH21 ....60 A4
Sandy Hill La BH20 ....162 A1
Sandy Hole TA16 ......191 F8
Sandy La
Bournemouth BH6 ......123 A3
Christchurch BH23 ....91 C1
Lytchett Matravers BH16 ..84 C3
Minterne Magna DT2 ....207 C7
Pamphill BH21 ....58 A3
St.Leonards BH24 ....54 B3
Upton BH16 ....118 A3
Verwood BH21 ....45 A1
Sandy La *continued*
Whitechurch Canonicorum
DT6 ....65 A4
Wimborne Minster BH21 ...60 A4
Sandy Mead Rd BH8 ....90 C1
Sandy Plot BH23 ....124 B4
Sandy Way BH10 ....89 C2
Sandyhurst Cl BH17 .....87 B1
Sansome's Hill 6 DT9 ...17 B1
Santoy BH13 ....147 B3
Sarah Cl BH7 ....123 A4
Sarah Sands Cl BH23 ..124 B4
Sark Rd BH12 ....120 B4
Sarum 3 DT9 ....194 D8
Sarum Ave BH22 ....53 A2
Sarum Cl SP2 ....213 A4
Sarum Coll SP1 ....213 B2
Sarum Ct BH14 ....120 B2
Sarum St 14 BH15 .....119 A1
Sarum St Pauls CE Sch
SP2 ....213 A3
Saulfland Dr BH23 .....125 B4
Saulfland House BH23 ..125 B4
Saulfland Pl BH23 .....125 B4
Saville Ct 9 BH21 ....59 B2
Sawyers La DT2 ....106 C4
Saxon Hts BH6 ....123 C3
Saxon King Gdns BH6 ..124 A2
Saxon Mead Cl SP8 ....5 C2
Saxon Rd SP2 ....213 A1
Saxon Rise DT11 ......210 C7
Saxon Spur SP7 ....12 C2
Saxon Sq Sh Ctr 4
BH23 ....124 A3
Saxon Way SP6 ....42 B3
Saxonbury Rd BH6 .....123 C3
Saxonford Rd BH23 ....125 B4
Saxonhurst Cl BH10 .....89 C3
Saxonhurst Gdns BH10 ..89 C2
Saxonhurst Rd BH10 ....89 C2
Scadden's Cnr DT6 .....66 A4
Scamell's Rd SP2 ......213 B3
Scaplen's Ct Mus★
BH15 ....119 A1
Scarf Rd BH17 ....119 C4
Schelin Way 0 DT11 ...198 B5
School Cl
Chickerell DT3 ....166 B3
4 Tarrant Gunville DT11 .199 F7
Verwood BH31 ....45 B4
School Hill
Chickerell DT3 ....166 B3
Cucklington BA9 ....4 A2
Powerstock DT6 ....70 A3
South Perrott DT8 ......192 C1
School House La DT2 ..103 A1
School La
Askerswell DT2 ....102 B4
4 Blandford Forum DT11 .211 B1
Bournemouth BH11 ....89 A3
Broadwindsor DT8 ......203 B6
Chetnole DT9 ....194 D3
9 Dorchester DT1 ......107 C1
Gillingham SP8 ....6 A1
4 Pimperne DT11 ......199 D4
Poole BH15 ....119 B3
Ringwood BH24 ....55 B4
St.Leonards BH24 ....54 B3
Studland BH19 ....164 B1
3 Tarrant Gunville DT11 .199 F7
Toller Porcorum DT2 .....71 C4
Verwood BH21 ....53 A4
West Lulworth BH20 ....172 B3
Wimborne Minster BH21 ...59 A3
Winfrith Newburgh DT2 ..156 C3
Woodsford DT2 ....110 B1
School Rd SP8 ....5 C1
School St 11 DT4 ......167 B2
Schoolhouse La DT10 ...21 A1
Scotchey Hill SP8 ....10 B1
Scotchey La SP8 ....10 C1
Scots La SP1 ....213 B3
Scott Cl Poole BH12 .....88 C1
Stoborough Green BH20 ..160 C4
Scott Rd BH12 ....88 C1
Scott's Gn BH23 ....124 C4
Scott's La DT6 ....64 A3
Scotter Rd BH7 ....123 A3
Scotton Way The DT2 ..137 B3
Scotts Hill La BH23 ....124 B4
Scotts Way TA18 ....192 A8
Scouse La EX13 ....202 B2
Scrubbity Barrows★
SP5 ....188 E4
Scutts Cl BH16 ....84 B2
Sea Hill La DT6 ....99 A3
Sea King Rd BA20 ....26 C2
Sea Life Pk & Model
Village★ DT4 ....167 C3
Sea Point 8 BH13 .....147 C4
Sea Rd
Barton on Sea BH25 .....126 C4
Bournemouth BH5 ......122 C2
Sea Rd N DT6 ....100 C4
Sea Rd S DT6 ....100 B3
Sea View 7 DT5 ....186 C4
Sea View Rd Poole BH12 .120 A3
Upton BH16 ....118 A4
Sea Vixen Ind Est BH23 .125 A4
Seabank Cl BH16 ......118 A4
Seaborough View
TA18 ....191 F3
Seabourne Pl 12 BH5 ..123 A3
Seabourne Rd BH5 ....123 A3
Seacombe Rd BH13 ....147 A2

Seacroft Ave BH25 ... 126 C4
Seafield Cl BH25 ... 126 C4
Seafield Dr BH6 ... 123 C3
Seafield Rd
Barton on Sea BH25 ... 126 C4
Bournemouth BH6 ... 123 B2
Christchurch BH23 ... 125 B4
Seagull Rd BH8 ... 90 B1
Seamoor Cl DT3 ... 167 C4
Seamoor La BH4 ... 121 A2
Seamoor Rd BH4 ... 121 A2
Seaton Cl BH23 ... 126 A4
Seaton Rd
Christchurch BH23 ... 126 A4
Yeovil BA20 ... 27 A2
Seatown Cl BH17 ... 88 A1
Seaview Rd
Barton on Sea BH25 ... 126 B4
Christchurch BH23 ... 94 B1
Seaward Ave BH25 ... 126 C4
Seaward Gdns DT6 ... 100 B1
Seaward Rd BH19 ... 179 A2
Seaway BH25 ... 127 A4
Seaway Ave BH23 ... 125 B4
Second Cliff Wlk 2 DT6 ... 100 A1
Second Marine Ave BH25 ... 127 A3
Sedgefield Cl DT4 ... 167 B2
Sedgemoor Cl BA21 ... 27 C3
Sedgley Rd BH9 ... 121 C4
Seed Warehouse The 15 BH15 ... 119 B1
Selby Cl BH18 ... 87 A2
Seldown BH15 ... 119 B2
Seldown Bridge BH15 ... 119 B1
Seldown La BH15 ... 119 B2
Seldown Rd BH15 ... 119 B2
Self Rd BH15 ... 119 A1
Selfridge Ave BH6 ... 124 A2
Selfridge Cl BH6 ... 124 A2
Seliot Cl BH15 ... 119 B3
Selkirk Cl BH21 ... 59 C1
Selle Rd BH20 ... 139 C3
Sellwood Way BH25 ... 126 B4
Selwood Cl DT10 ... 35 B1
Selwood Pk BH10 ... 89 B4
Selworthy Cl BH14 ... 120 A1
Selwyn Cl DT3 ... 152 B2
Senior Dr SP2 ... 213 B1
Sentinal Ct BH15 ... 119 C2
Sentry Rd BH19 ... 179 B1
Serpentine Rd BH15 ... 119 B2
Serrells Mead BH19 ... 178 B1
Seth Ward Dr SP1 ... 213 C4
Setley Gdns BH8 ... 90 C2
Seven Acres 9 DT5 ... 186 C1
Seven Acres Rd DT3 ... 153 B2
Seven Ash Comm Rd DT9 ... 195 B4
Seven Barrows Rd BH20 ... 142 B3
Sevenoaks Dr BH7 ... 123 A4
Severalls Pk Ave 17 TA18 ... 191 F4
Severn Rd BH22 ... 62 A3
Seward Ave BH6 ... 123 B2
Sewell Rd BH20 ... 139 B4
Seymer Rd BH19 ... 179 B1
Seymour Rd BH24 ... 47 B1
Shadrack DT6 ... 128 A4
Shadrack St 2 DT8 ... 204 C4
Shady Bower SP1 ... 213 C2
Shaftesbury Cl BH22 ... 53 A1
Shaftesbury Fst Sch SP7 ... 13 A1
Shaftesbury Mus★ SP7 ... 12 C1
Shaftesbury Rd
Child Okeford DT11 ... 198 C8
Ferndown BH22 ... 53 A1
Gillingham SP8 ... 6 A1
Henstridge BA8 ... 19 B3
Kington Magna SP8 ... 20 A4
Mere BA12 ... 3 A2
Poole BH15 ... 119 B2
Shaftesbury Upper Sch SP7 ... 12 C1
Shaftsbury Rd BH8 ... 122 B3
Shakespeare Rd
Bournemouth BH6 ... 123 B4
Salisbury SP1 ... 213 A4
Wimborne Minster BH21 ... 59 B3
Shamrock Ct 2 BH21 ... 59 B2
Shapland Ave BH11 ... 88 C3
Shapwick Rd BH15 ... 119 A1
Shard Cl BH31 ... 45 B3
Sharford Bridge★ BH20 ... 162 A3
Sharlands Cl BH18 ... 87 A2
Sharp Rd BH12 ... 121 A4
Shaston Cl 10 BH19 ... 178 C1
Shaston Cres DT1 ... 135 A4
Shaston Rd DT11 ... 198 F4
Shatcombe La DT2 ... 71 B2
Shatter's Hill BH20 ... 142 C2
Shave Cross DT6 ... 203 C1
Shave Hill SP8 ... 9 A4
Shave La Todber DT10 ... 21 B3
West Crewkerne TA18 ... 191 E3
Shaves La BH25 ... 95 A3
Shaw Cl DT11 ... 212 B2
Shaw Dr BH20 ... 142 C4
Shaw Rd BH24 ... 47 C1
Shawford Gdns BH8 ... 90 B1
Shawford Rd BH8 ... 90 B2
Shear Plot DT6 ... 99 C4
Shears Rd DT4 ... 167 B4
Shearstones DT9 ... 194 D5
Sheasby Cl SP5 ... 189 A3
Shedbush La DT6 ... 98 B4
Shedrick Hill TA20 ... 202 E8
Sheep Mkt Hill 4 DT11 ... 212 B1
Sheepcroft La BH21 ... 51 B2
Sheephouse Dro BH21 ... 200 E2
Sheeplands La DT9 ... 29 C3
Sheeplands The DT9 ... 29 C4
Sheepspine La TA20 ... 202 C5
Sheepwash La
Burstock DT8 ... 203 D5
Tatworth & Forton TA20 ... 202 A6
Shelbourne Cl BH8 ... 122 B3
Shelbourne Rd BH8 ... 122 A3
Sheldrake Rd BH23 ... 125 A3
Shell Bay Sailing Ctr★ BH19 ... 147 A1
Shelley Cl
Bournemouth BH1 ... 122 C3
Christchurch BH23 ... 125 B4
St.Leonards BH24 ... 53 C3
Yeovil BA21 ... 26 C3
Shelley Ct BH22 ... 61 B3
Shelley Dr SP1 ... 213 A4
Shelley Gdns BH1 ... 122 C3
Shelley Hamlets BH23 ... 125 B4
Shelley Hill BH23 ... 125 B4
Shelley House 15 BH25 ... 95 A1
Shelley Pk (Bournemouth & Poole Coll) BH5 ... 122 C2
Shelley Rd
Bournemouth BH1 ... 122 C3
Poole BH12 ... 120 B3
Shelley Rd E BH7 ... 122 C3
Shelton Rd BH6 ... 123 B3
Shenstone Ct 18 BH25 ... 95 A1
Shepherd Cl BH23 ... 93 C1
Shepherd's Hill SP8 ... 9 B4
Shepherds Croft DT5 ... 187 B3
Shepherds Hill BH24 ... 46 C3
Shepherds La BH24 ... 46 B3
Shepherds Way
Bournemouth BH7 ... 123 A4
West Lulworth BH20 ... 172 B3
Sheppards Field 4 BH21 ... 59 A3
Sherborn Cres BH17 ... 88 A1
Sherborne Abbey DT9 ... 30 A3
Sherborne Castle★ DT9 ... 30 B3
Sherborne CP Sch DT9 ... 30 B4
Sherborne Cswy SP7 ... 11 C2
Sherborne Dr BH22 ... 61 B2
Sherborne Golf Club DT9 ... 16 A2
Sherborne Hill DT9 ... 30 B2
Sherborne Mus★ DT9 ... 30 B3
Sherborne Rd
Henstridge BA8 ... 18 C2
Milborne Port DT9 ... 17 B1
Purse Caundle DT10 ... 18 B1
Yeovil BA21 ... 27 C3
Sherborne Sch DT9 ... 30 A3
Sherborne Sta DT9 ... 30 A3
Sherbourne La 3 DT7 ... 96 B3
Sherbourne Old Castle★ DT9 ... 30 B3
Sherfield Cl BH8 ... 90 B1
Sherford Cl BH20 ... 142 B3
Sherford Dr BH20 ... 142 C3
Sheridan Cl DT2 ... 73 C2
Sheriden Way 5 BH21 ... 56 B2
Sheringham Rd BH12 ... 120 C3
Sherlands 1 TA16 ... 191 F7
Sherren Ave DT2 ... 75 C1
Sherrin Cl BH15 ... 119 B3
Sherwood Ave
Ferndown BH22 ... 61 B2
Poole BH14 ... 120 A2
Sherwood Dr BH31 ... 45 B3
Shetland View BH31 ... 45 B3
Shiller's La DT9 ... 15 C3
Shillingstone CE Prim Sch DT11 ... 198 B6
Shillingstone Dr BH9 ... 90 A2
Shillingstone Gdns BH12 ... 120 C4
Shillingstone La DT11 ... 197 F5
Shillito Rd BH12 ... 120 C3
Ship Knapp DT6 ... 66 A1
Shipney La DT10 ... 19 C1
Shipstal Cl BH16 ... 118 B2
Shipstal Nature Trail★ BH20 ... 144 B2
Shipton La
Burton Bradstock DT6 ... 101 B1
Loders DT6 ... 101 C3
Shipton Rd DT6 ... 101 B2
Shirecroft Rd DT4 ... 167 A2
Shiremoor Hill TA16 ... 191 F7
Shires Cl BH24 ... 55 B2
Shires Copse BH6 ... 123 C2
Shires Mead BH31 ... 45 B3
Shirley Cl
Ferndown BH22 ... 53 A1
Swanage BH19 ... 178 C1
Shirley Rd
Bournemouth BH9 ... 90 A1
Poole BH12 ... 120 A3
Upton BH16 ... 118 B4
Wareham BH20 ... 142 B2
Shoe La DT6 ... 100 C4
Shoot Hill TA17 ... 191 C8
Shop La DT3 ... 150 B1
Shore Ave BH16 ... 118 B3
Shore Cl BH16 ... 118 B3
Shore Gdns BH16 ... 118 A3
Shore La BH16 ... 118 B3
Shore Rd Poole BH13 ... 147 B3
Swanage BH19 ... 179 B2
Shoreacres BH13 ... 147 B2
Shoredown La DT9 ... 17 B3
Short Cl BH12 ... 121 A4
Short Cross DT2 ... 206 C6
Short Rd DT4 ... 167 A2
Short's La DT11 ... 212 B1
Shortedge DT10 ... 35 B1
Shortlake La DT3 ... 169 A4
Shortlands DT5 ... 186 C2
Shortlands Rd DT3 ... 152 A3
Shortmarsh La TA18 ... 192 F4
Shorts Cl BH23 ... 92 B1
Shorts Gn La SP7 ... 12 A4
Shottsford Cl 7 BH19 ... 178 C1
Shottsford Rd BH15 ... 119 B3
Shreen Cl 9 SP8 ... 5 C2
Shreen Way SP8 ... 5 C2
Shrubbery La DT4 ... 180 B4
Shute La DT11 ... 37 C1
Shute Lake La 11 TA18 ... 191 F4
Shute's La SP8 ... 9 B4
Sidmouth Rd DT7 ... 96 A3
Sidney Gdns 11 BH9 ... 90 A2
Sidney Smith Ct BH17 ... 87 C1
Sidney St SP2 ... 213 A3
Silchester Cl BH2 ... 121 C3
Silk House Barton DT10 ... 33 B4
Sillen La SP6 ... 190 B6
Silton Rd SP8 ... 1 C1
Silver Birch Cl BH12 ... 121 A2
Silver Bsns Pk BH23 ... 124 C4
Silver St
Christchurch BH23 ... 124 A3
Crewkerne TA18 ... 192 B3
Lyme Regis DT7 ... 96 A3
Overcombe/Preston DT3 ... 153 B2
Salisbury SP1 ... 213 B2
4 Stofold BA22 ... 193 F8
Yeovil BA20 ... 27 B3
Silver Way BH23 ... 125 C4
Silverdale BH25 ... 127 A4
Silverdale Cl BH18 ... 86 C2
Silverdale Cres SP6 ... 42 B3
Silverwood Cl BH21 ... 59 B1
Simmonds Cl BH15 ... 119 B3
Simons Rd DT9 ... 30 A4
Sinclair Ct 8 BH14 ... 120 A2
Singleton Dr BH10 ... 89 B1
Sir John Colfox Sch DT6 ... 68 C1
Sir Richard Hull Rd BH20 ... 139 B3
Siskin Cl BH22 ... 61 A4
Sitterton Cl BH20 ... 81 A2
Six Ways Cross BH21 ... 200 E3
Sixpenny Cl BH12 ... 120 C4
Sixpenny Handley Cty Fst Sch SP5 ... 189 A4
Skilling Hill Rd DT6 ... 100 B3
Skilling La DT6 ... 100 A3
Skinner St BH15 ... 119 B1
Skipton Cl BH18 ... 87 A1
Slade La BA22 ... 15 A3
Slade's La BH10 ... 121 B4
Slades Farm Rd BH10 ... 89 B1
Slades Farm Specl Sch BH10 ... 89 B1
Slades Gn DT6 ... 100 C3
Slape Hill DT6 ... 68 B4
Slape Manor★ DT6 ... 204 C1
Sleepbrook Cl BH31 ... 45 A3
Sleight Cl BA21 ... 26 C3
Sleight La BH21 ... 86 B4
Slepe Cres BH12 ... 120 C4
Slinn Rd BH23 ... 124 C4
Slip Way BH15 ... 119 A1
Slodbrook La SP8 ... 2 B1
Slopers Mead 2 DT11 ... 211 E5
Slough Dro DT2 ... 205 E7
Slough La Horton BH21 ... 44 A1
Lytchett Minster & Upton BH16 ... 117 A3
Upton BH16 ... 118 A3
Woodlands BH21 ... 44 A2
Slyer's La
Puddletown DT2 ... 76 C1
Stinsford DT2 ... 108 B3
Smacombe La DT6 ... 101 B2
Smallmouth Cl DT4 ... 180 B3
Smeaton Rd SP2 ... 213 A3
Smedmore House★ BH20 ... 175 C1
Smishops La DT6 ... 69 B1
Smith's Hill TA18 ... 192 B8
Smith's La DT2 ... 208 B3
Smith's Terr BA21 ... 27 C3
Smithfield Pl BH9 ... 89 C1
Smithson Cl BH12 ... 121 B4
Smithy La BH25 ... 94 C3
Smokey Hole La 3 DT1 ... 135 B4
Smugglers La BH21 ... 59 C4
Smugglers La N BH23 ... 93 C1
Smugglers La S BH23 ... 125 C4
Smugglers Reach BH23 ... 125 A3
Smugglers Wood Rd BH23 ... 93 B1
Smugglers' La
Colehill BH21 ... 50 C1
Stourpaine DT11 ... 199 A6
Snag La DT11 ... 79 C3
Snail's La BH24 ... 47 B2
Snails La BH24 ... 47 A1
Snow Down Rd 1 DT11 ... 199 E2
Snow Hill BH20 ... 81 A1
Snow Hill La BH20 ... 81 A1
Snowdon Rd BH4 ... 121 B2
Snowdrop Gdns BH23 ... 93 A1
Soberton Rd BH8 ... 122 B3
Sodern La DT2 ... 107 B4
Sodom La DT10 ... 21 A2
Solar Ct BH13 ... 121 A1
Soldiers Rd BH20 ... 143 B1
Solent Dr BH25 ... 127 A4
Solent Lodge 21 BH25 ... 95 A1
Solent Rd
Barton on Sea BH25 ... 126 B4
Bournemouth BH6 ... 124 A2
Christchurch BH23 ... 94 A1
Swanage BH19 ... 185 B4
Solent View BH6 ... 124 A2
Solly Cl BH12 ... 120 C4
Solomon Way BH15 ... 118 B1
Somerby Rd BH15 ... 119 B3
Somerfields DT7 ... 96 A3
Somerford Ave BH23 ... 125 A4
Somerford Bsns Pk BH23 ... 125 A4
Somerford Ct BH23 ... 125 C4
Somerford Cty Inf Sch BH23 ... 124 C4
Somerford Cty Jun Sch BH23 ... 124 C4
Somerford Rd BH23 ... 124 C4
Somerford Way BH23 ... 124 C3
Somerley Pk★ BH24 ... 46 C3
Somerley Rd BH9 ... 122 A4
Somerley View BH24 ... 55 A4
Somers Rd DT7 ... 96 A3
Somerset Cl SP8 ... 5 C2
Somerset Rd
Bournemouth BH7 ... 123 A3
Salisbury SP1 ... 213 B4
Weymouth DT4 ... 167 A2
Somerton Cl BH25 ... 95 B2
Somerville Ct BH25 ... 94 C2
Somerville Rd
Bournemouth BH2 ... 121 B2
Ringwood BH24 ... 55 C4
Sonning Way BH8 ... 90 A1
Soper's La BH23 ... 124 A3
Sopers La BH17 ... 87 A1
Sopley Cl BH25 ... 126 B4
Sopley Farm Bldgs BH23 ... 92 A3
Sopwith Cl BH23 ... 125 A3
Sopwith Cres BH21 ... 59 C1
Sorrel Cl DT4 ... 167 C3
Sorrel Gdns BH18 ... 86 C1
Sorrel Way SP8 ... 5 B1
Sorrell Ct BH23 ... 125 A4
Sorrell Way BH23 ... 125 A4
Souter Way DT3 ... 167 B4
South Annings 2 DT6 ... 128 A4
South Ave
Lyme Regis DT7 ... 96 A3
New Milton BH25 ... 95 A1
Sherborne DT9 ... 29 C2
South Bridge★ BH20 ... 142 C2
South Cliff Rd
Bournemouth BH2 ... 121 C1
Swanage BH19 ... 179 B1
South Cres DT11 ... 199 E3
South Cswy BH20 ... 142 C1
South Ct DT9 ... 29 C2
South Ct Ave DT1 ... 135 A4
South Dr DT2 ... 206 C2
South Dro DT2 ... 135 C1
South Farm Cl DT11 ... 200 A6
South Haven Cl BH16 ... 118 A2
South Hill SP6 ... 42 B3
South Holme DT11 ... 198 F4
South Instow BH19 ... 177 C3
South Kinson Dr BH11 ... 89 A2
South Lawns DT6 ... 100 B3
South Mead BH20 ... 81 A1
South Mill La DT6 ... 100 B3
South Par 3 DT4 ... 167 C1
South Pk Rd BH12 ... 121 A4
South Rd
Bournemouth BH1 ... 122 C3
Corfe Mullen BH21 ... 86 C3
Poole BH15 ... 119 B1
Swanage BH19 ... 179 A1
Weymouth DT4 ... 180 B3
South Rd Comb Sch BH15 ... 119 B1
South St Arne BH20 ... 142 C2
Bridport DT6 ... 100 B3
Corfe Castle BH20 ... 176 C2
Crewkerne TA18 ... 191 F4
Dorchester DT1 ... 108 A1
11 Gillingham SP8 ... 5 C1
Hinton St George TA17 ... 191 D7
Kington Magna SP8 ... 9 B1
Leigh DT9 ... 194 E3
Milborne Port DT9 ... 17 B1
15 Salisbury SP2 ... 213 A3
Sherborne DT9 ... 30 A3
Yeovil BA20 ... 27 B2
South View
Bournemouth BH2 ... 121 C3
Bradford Abbas DT9 ... 28 B1
Piddletrenthide DT2 ... 208 C1
South View Pl 17 BH2 ... 121 C2
South View Rd
Christchurch BH23 ... 124 A3
Milborne Port DT9 ... 17 B1
South Walks Rd DT1 ... 108 A1
South Way DT5 ... 186 B1
South Western Cres BH14 ... 120 A1
South Western Rd SP2 ... 213 A3
South Wilts Gram Sch For Girls SP1 ... 213 B4
South Wlk DT6 ... 100 B3
Southampton Rd
Ringwood BH24 ... 55 A4
Salisbury SP1 ... 213 C2
Southbourne Coast Rd BH6 ... 123 C2
Southbourne Cross Roads 6 BH6 ... 123 C2
Southbourne Gr BH6 ... 123 B2
Southbourne Overcliff Dr BH6 ... 123 B2
Southbourne Rd BH5 ... 123 B2
Southbourne Sands BH6 ... 123 B2
Southbrook
Bere Regis BH20 ... 81 A1
Mere BA12 ... 3 B2
Southbrook Cl BH17 ... 88 A1
Southbrook Gdns BA12 ... 3 A2
Southcliffe Rd
Barton on Sea BH25 ... 126 B4
Christchurch BH23 ... 125 B3
Southcote Rd BH1 ... 122 B2
Southcroft Rd DT4 ... 166 C1
Southdown Ave DT3 ... 167 C4
Southdown Ct 1 BH23 ... 124 C4
Southdown Rd DT4 ... 180 C4
Southdown Way BH22 ... 53 A1
Southern Ave BH22 ... 53 B1
Southern La BH25 ... 126 C4
Southern Oaks BH25 ... 94 C1
Southern Rd BH6 ... 123 B2
Southernhay Rd BH31 ... 45 B3
Southey Rd BH23 ... 124 C4
Southfield Ave DT4 ... 167 B3
Southfield Mews 4 BH24 ... 55 B3
Southill Ave BH12 ... 120 B3
Southill CP Sch DT4 ... 167 A4
Southill Gdn Dr DT4 ... 167 A3
Southill Gdns BH9 ... 90 A1
Southill Rd
Bournemouth BH9 ... 90 A1
Poole BH12 ... 120 B4
Southlands Ave
Bournemouth BH6 ... 123 C2
Corfe Mullen BH21 ... 86 C3
Southlands Cl BH21 ... 86 B3
Southlands Ct BH18 ... 87 A2
Southlands Rd DT4 ... 180 C4
Southlawns Wlk BH25 ... 94 C1
Southlea Ave BH6 ... 123 C2
Southmead Cres 20 TA18 ... 191 F4
Southmead La BA8 ... 19 A2
Southover DT6 ... 128 A4
Southover Cl DT11 ... 211 B1
Southover La DT2 ... 79 B1
Southview Rd DT4 ... 167 A2
Southville BA21 ... 27 C3
Southville Rd BH5 ... 123 A3
Southway Cl BA21 ... 27 A4
Southway Cres BA21 ... 27 A3
Southway Dr BA21 ... 27 A4
Southwell Prim Sch DT5 ... 186 C1
Southwell Rd
12 Easton/Weston DT5 ... 186 C1
Portland DT5 ... 187 A1
Southwick Pl BH6 ... 123 B4
Southwick Rd BH6 ... 123 B3
Southwood Ave
Bournemouth BH6 ... 123 B2
Christchurch BH23 ... 94 A1
Southwood Cl
Christchurch BH23 ... 94 A1
Ferndown BH22 ... 61 B3
Southwood Ct BH23 ... 94 A1
Southwoods BA20 ... 27 B2
Sovereign Bsns Ctr BH15 ... 119 A3
Sovereign Cl BH7 ... 122 C4
Sovereign Ctr BH1 ... 122 C3
Sovereign Sq 8 BH7 ... 122 C2
Spa Ave DT3 ... 167 B4
Spa Rd DT3 ... 167 A4
Sparacre Gdns DT6 ... 100 B4
Sparkford Cl BH7 ... 123 A4
Sparrow Rd BA21 ... 27 B3
Spearhay La TA20 ... 202 B4
Specket La DT6 ... 203 A5
Speedwell Dr BH23 ... 125 A4
Speke Cl 10 TA16 ... 191 F7
Spence La DT6 ... 64 C3
Spencer Ct 5 BH25 ... 95 A1
Spencer Gdns DT11 ... 198 C5
Spencer Rd
Bournemouth BH1 ... 122 B2
New Milton BH25 ... 95 A1
Poole BH13 ... 147 C4
Spetisbury CE Prim Sch DT11 ... 211 D5
Spetisbury Cl BH9 ... 90 A2
Spettisbury Rings★ DT11 ... 211 E5
Spicer La BH11 ... 88 C3
Spiller Rd DT3 ... 166 B3
Spinacre BH25 ... 127 A4
Spindle Cl BH18 ... 86 C1
Spindlewood Cl 26 BH25 ... 95 A1
Spingfield Rd BA12 ... 3 A3
Spinners Cl BH22 ... 53 A1

Spinners Way BA12 ......3 A3
Spinners' La DT6 ......101 A3
Spinney Cl 2 BH24 ......53 C2
Spinney The
Broadmayne DT2 ......136 A1
Lytchett Matravers BH16 ..84 B1
Radipole DT3 ......152 A1
St.Leonards BH24 ......54 A3
7 Yeovil BA20 ......26 C1
Spinney Way BH25 ......95 A3
Spinneys La BH22 ......61 B3
Spitfire Cl DT2 ......137 B3
Spittlefields BH24 ......55 B4
Spittles La DT7 ......96 B3
Spread Eagle Hill SP7 ......8 B2
Spring Ave DT4 ......167 B1
Spring Cl 4 Bridport DT6 ..68 C1
Verwood BH31 ......45 A3
Spring Ct BH12 ......120 B3
Spring Gdns
10 Fortuneswell DT5 ......186 C4
Poole BH12 ......120 B3
West Knighton DT2 ......136 B2
Weymouth DT4 ......167 B1
Spring Gr DT2 ......196 A1
Spring La
Longburton DT9 ......195 B7
New Milton BH25 ......95 A4
Sandford Orcas DT9 ......15 C3
Spring Rd
Bournemouth BH1 ......122 B3
6 Weymouth DT4 ......167 C1
Spring St BH20 ......140 A1
Springbank Rd BH12 ......122 C4
Springbourne Ct BH1 ......122 B3
Springbourne Mews
BH1 ......122 B3
Springbrook Cl BH20 ......177 C3
Springdale Ave BH18 ......86 C2
Springdale Fst Sch BH18 ..86 C2
Springdale Gr BH21 ......86 C2
Springdale Rd BH18 ......86 C2
Springfield
East Chinnock BA22 ......192 E8
Puncknowle DT2 ......129 C3
Springfield Ave
Bournemouth BH6 ......124 A1
Christchurch BH23 ......91 B1
Springfield Cl
2 Shaftesbury SP7 ......13 A2
Verwood BH31 ......45 A3
Springfield Cres
Poole BH14 ......120 A2
Radipole DT3 ......152 A2
5 Sherborne DT9 ......30 A3
Springfield Gdns BH25 ..95 B1
Springfield Pl BA21 ......27 A4
Springfield Rd
Milborne Port DT9 ......17 B2
Poole BH14 ......120 A2
Radipole DT3 ......152 A2
10 Swanage BH19 ......179 A1
Verwood BH31 ......45 A3
Yeovil BA21 ......27 A4
Springfields Holt BH21 ......51 A2
Stalbridge DT10 ......33 C4
Springhill Gdns DT7 ......96 A3
Springvale Ave BH7 ......123 A4
Springwater Cl BH11 ......89 A2
Springwater Ct BH23 ......124 B3
Springwater Dr BH23 ......124 B3
Springwater Rd BH11 ......89 A2
Springwell Cl BH20 ......177 A4
Spruce Cl BH17 ......86 C1
Spur Cl BH21 ......60 B3
Spur Hill Ave BH14 ......120 B2
Spur Rd BH14 ......120 B2
Spurgeon Rd BH7 ......123 A4
Spy Cl BH16 ......84 B2
Spyway Rd DT2 ......102 B4
Square The
Bournemouth BH2 ......121 C2
Cattistock DT2 ......206 C2
Corfe Castle BH20 ......162 A1
Cranborne BH21 ......40 A4
12 Gillingham SP8 ......5 C1
Langton Herring DT3 ......150 B1
Mere BA12 ......3 A3
Milborne St Andrew DT11 ..79 C4
Powerstock DT6 ......70 A2
Puddletown DT2 ......78 A1
Wimborne Minster BH21 ..59 A3
Squirrel's Cl BH23 ......91 B1
Squirrel's Cnr BH21 ......189 D1
Srringfield DT7 ......207 D4
Stables The BH23 ......123 C4
Stacey Cl BH12 ......120 B4
Stacey Gdns BH8 ......90 C1
Stafford Cl DT2 ......136 B2
Stafford Gdns DT2 ......136 A4
Stafford House★ DT2 ..136 A4
Stafford Rd
Bournemouth BH1 ......122 A2
Swanage BH19 ......179 B1
Stag Cl BH25 ......94 C2
Stag Gate★ DT11 ......211 F2
Stagg's Folly★ DT2 ......206 E3
Stagswood BH31 ......44 C3
Stainers Mead SP7 ......7 A1
Stainforth Cl DT4 ......166 C4
Stake Ford Cross DT9 ..194 E4
Staker's Cross TA18 ......191 B2
Staker's Cross La
TA18 ......191 B2
Stakes La DT9 ......195 E6
Stalbridge CE Prim Sch
DT10 ......19 B1
Stalbridge Cl DT10 ......33 B4

Stalbridge Dr BH22 ......61 B2
Stalbridge La DT10 ......34 B2
Stalbridge Pk★ DT10 ......19 A1
Stalbridge Rd
Broadstone BH17 ......119 A4
Henstridge BA8 ......19 A2
Stalbridge DT10 ......32 C2
Stalham Rd BH12 ......120 C3
Stallards La BH24 ......55 A4
Stamford Rd BH6 ......123 B3
Stammery Hill EX13 ......202 A1
Stanbarrow Cl BH20 ......81 A1
Standpitts La SP8 ......10 C3
Stanfield Cl BH12 ......120 B4
Stanfield Rd
Bournemouth BH9 ......121 C4
Ferndown BH22 ......61 B3
Poole BH12 ......120 B4
Stanier Rd DT3 ......153 A2
Staniforth Ct BH23 ......124 B3
Stanley Cl BH31 ......45 B3
Stanley Ct
Bournemouth BH1 ......122 B3
Poole BH15 ......119 B3
Stanley Gn Cres BH15 ..119 B3
Stanley Gn Fst Sch
BH15 ......119 B3
Stanley Gn Ind Est
BH15 ......119 B3
Stanley Gn Rd BH15 ......119 B3
Stanley Pearce House
BH17 ......87 B1
Stanley Rd
Bournemouth BH1 ......122 B3
Christchurch BH23 ......126 A4
Poole BH15 ......119 B1
Stanley St 1 DT4 ......167 B2
Stannington Cl BH25 ......95 A1
Stanpit BH23 ......124 C3
Stanpit Marsh Nature
Reserve★ BH23 ......124 B3
Stanstead Rd DT2 ......73 A4
Stanton Cl DT11 ......212 B2
Stanton Lacy 17 BH13 ..147 C4
Stanton Rd BH10 ......89 B1
Stapehill Cres BH21 ......60 B3
Stapehill Mus & Gdns★
BH21 ......60 B3
Stapehill Rd BH21 ......60 C2
Staple Cl La BH15 ......119 B3
Staple Cross BH23 ......124 C4
Staplecross La BH23 ......124 B4
Stapleford Ave BH22 ......61 C3
Staples Mdw 4 TA20 ..202 A8
Staples Terr DT7 ......96 B3
Star Cottage Gdn★ BH31 58 B3
Star La DT6 ......98 B4
Starlight Farm Cl BH31 ..45 B4
Stars La BA20 ......27 B2
Station App
Broadstone BH18 ......87 A2
Dorchester DT1 ......108 A1
Station Pl 1 BH19 ......179 A1
Station Rd Alderholt SP6 ..42 A3
Child Okeford DT11 ......198 C7
Christchurch BH23 ......93 C1
2 Easton/Weston DT5 ..187 A2
Edmondsham BH31 ......44 C4
Ferndown BH22 ......52 C1
Gillingham SP8 ......5 C1
Hamworthy BH15 ......119 A1
Henstridge BA8 ......19 A3
Holton Heath BH20 ......116 B2
Maiden Newton DT2 ......72 C4
Misterton TA18 ......192 A3
Moreton DT2 ......138 A4
New Milton BH25 ......95 A1
Poole BH14 ......120 A2
Sherborne DT9 ......30 A3
2 Shillingstone DT11 ..198 B6
Stalbridge DT10 ......19 B1
Sturminster Marshall
BH21 ......56 B2
Sturminster Newton DT10 ..35 A1
Swanage BH19 ......179 A1
Tatworth & Forton
TA20 ......202 A8
Verwood BH31 ......45 A4
Wareham St Martin
BH16 ......116 B1
Wimborne Minster BH21 ..59 B2
Wool BH20 ......140 A1
Station Terr
13 Salisbury SP2 ......213 A3
Wimborne Minster BH21 ..59 B2
Station Yd SP6 ......42 A3
Staunton BH2 ......121 C1
Stavordale Rd DT4 ......167 B2
Stearts La DT10 ......35 A3
Stedman Rd BH5 ......123 A3
Steel Well La BA8 ......19 A2
Steel's La BA9 ......1 A2
Steels La SP6 ......190 F2
Steep St BA12 ......3 A3
Steepdene BH14 ......120 A2
Steeple Cl Poole BH17 ......87 B2
Radipole DT3 ......167 A4
Steepleton Rd BH18 ......87 B2
Steer Rd BH19 ......178 C1
Stella Ct 19 BH23 ......126 A4
Stem La DT6 ......94 C2
Stenhurst Rd BH15 ......119 C3
Stephen Langton Dr
BH11 ......88 B3
Stephen's Castle (Tumulus)★
BH31 ......45 B4

Stephens Cl
Netherbury DT6 ......204 B1
1 Salisbury SP2 ......213 A2
Stephenson Rd SP2 ......213 A2
Stepleton House★
DT11 ......198 F6
Stepnell Reach BH16 ......118 B3
Steppes BH19 ......178 A2
Steppes Hill BH19 ......178 B1
Sterte Ave BH15 ......119 A2
Sterte Ave W BH15 ......119 A2
Sterte Cl BH15 ......119 B2
Sterte Ct BH15 ......119 B2
Sterte Espl BH15 ......119 B2
Sterte Ind Est BH15 ......119 A2
Sterte Rd BH15 ......119 B2
Stevens Cl DT11 ......212 C2
Stevenson Cres BH14 ..120 C2
Stevenson Rd BH6 ......124 A2
Stevensons Cl 3 BH21 ..59 B2
Steward's La BH6 ......56 A4
Stewart Cl 5 BH8 ......122 B3
Stewart Rd BH8 ......122 A3
Stewarts Way BH22 ......61 C4
Stibles La DT11 ......197 D3
Stiby Rd BA21 ......27 A4
Stickland Sch DT2 ......206 A7
Stile La DT7 ......96 A2
Stile Way DT2 ......206 E6
Stileham Bank DT11 ......79 C4
Stillmore Rd BH11 ......88 B2
Stinford Cl DT8 ......204 D6
Stinsford Cl BH9 ......90 A2
Stinsford Hill DT2 ......108 B2
Stinsford La BH17 ......119 B4
Stinsford Rd BH17 ......87 B1
Stinsford View DT1 ......108 B1
Stirling Cl BH25 ......95 A2
Stirling Ct
Bournemouth BH4 ......121 B1
21 New Milton BH25 ......95 A2
Stirling Rd
Bournemouth BH3 ......121 C4
Radipole DT3 ......167 B4
Stirling Way BH23 ......125 A3
Stirrup Cl Upton BH16 ..118 B4
Wimborne Minster BH21 ..60 B3
Stoborough Cl DT3 ......167 A4
Stoborough Dr BH18 ......87 A1
Stoborough Mdw
BH20 ......142 C1
Stoborough Sch BH20 ..142 C1
Stock Hill La DT9 ......195 F4
Stock La SP8 ......5 A1
Stockbridge Cl BH17 ......88 A1
Stockley Rd BH20 ......142 B3
Stockwood Cl SP1 ......213 C4
Stoke La
Mappowder DT10 ......196 F1
Stoke Wake DT11 ......209 A8
Stoke Mill La DT6 ......67 A3
Stoke Rd
Beaminster DT8 ......204 C4
Weymouth DT4 ......180 B4
Stoke Wood Rd BH3 ......121 C3
Stokehouse St DT1 ......107 B1
Stokes Ave BH15 ......119 B2
Stokes La DT10 ......32 C2
Stonage La TA18 ......192 C5
Stone Gdns BH8 ......91 A1
Stone La
Wimborne Minster BH21 ..59 A3
Yeovil BA21 ......27 B4
Stone La Ind Est BH21 ..59 A3
Stonebarrow La
Charmouth DT6 ......97 B4
Hawkchurch EX13 ......202 C2
Stanton St Gabriel DT6 ..97 C4
Stonechat Cl
Ferndown BH22 ......61 A4
3 Radipole DT3 ......152 B2
Stonechat Ct BH23 ......124 C4
Stonecrop Cl BH18 ......86 C1
Stonedene DT9 ......30 A4
Stoneleigh 18 BH13 ......147 C4
Stoneleigh Ave SO41 ......95 C2
Stoney La BA22 ......193 D6
Stoney Lawn DT11 ......81 B4
Stoneylawn DT10 ......21 A1
Stony Down La DT6 ......65 A2
Stony La
Bishop's Caundle DT9 ..196 A8
Burton BH23 ......190 A8
Damerham SP6 ......190 E2
Holwell DT10 ......196 C6
Stony La S BH23 ......124 B3
Stony Weir★ BH20 ......140 B2
Stonyacres DT9 ......194 C6
Stopples La SO41 ......95 C2
Story La BH18 ......87 A2
Stottingway St DT3 ......152 A3
Stour Cl East Stour SP8 ..10 B1
Ferndown BH21 ......60 B2
Shillingstone DT11 ......198 C5
Stour Dr BH20 ......142 B3
Stour Gdns SP8 ......9 C1
Stour Hill SP8 ......9 C1
Stour Hill Pk SP8 ......9 C1
Stour La SP8 ......9 C1
Stour Mdws SP8 ......5 C1
Stour Pk BH10 ......89 C3
Stour Rd
Blandford Forum DT11 ..212 C4
Bournemouth BH8 ......122 B3
Christchurch BH23 ......124 A3
Stour View Cl DT10 ......35 A1
Stour View Gdns BH21 ..58 C1
Stour Way BH23 ......91 B1

Stour Wlk
Bournemouth BH8 ......90 B2
11 Wimborne Minster BH21 59 B2
Stourbank Rd BH23 ......124 A3
Stourcliffe Ave BH6 ......123 B2
Stourcroft Dr BH23 ......91 C1
Stourfield Fst & Jun Schs
BH6 ......123 B3
Stourfield Rd BH5 ......123 B3
Stourpaine Rd BH17 ......87 B1
Stourton Cl 17 BH4 ......121 B2
Stourton Way BA21 ......26 C4
Stourvale Ave BH23 ......123 B4
Stourvale Pl 10 BH5 ......123 A3
Stourvale Rd BH5 ......123 B3
Stourwood Ave BH6 ......123 B2
Stourwood Mans 4
BH6 ......123 B2
Stourwood Rd BH6 ......123 B2
Stowcastle St 9 DT1 ..107 B1
Stowell Cres BH20 ......142 B3
Stowell La 15 TA20 ......202 A8
Stower Provost CP Sch
SP8 ......21 C4
Stowey St DT1 ......107 B1
Straits DT5 ......187 A2
Strand St BH15 ......119 B1
Stratfield Pl BH25 ......94 C2
Stratford Rd
Salisbury SP1 ......213 B4
Yeovil BA21 ......26 C3
Strathmore Dr BH31 ......45 B3
Strathmore Rd BH9 ......90 A2
Stratton Rd BH9 ......90 B2
Straw Barrow★ DT11 ..48 B2
Streche Rd
Swanage BH19 ......179 B3
Wareham BH20 ......142 B2
Street La
Longburton DT9 ......195 C6
Sedgehill and Semley SP7 ..7 C2
Street The
Charmouth DT6 ......97 A4
Moreton DT2 ......138 C4
Motcombe SP7 ......7 A1
Sutton Waldron DT11 ......37 B3
Winterborne Zelston
DT11 ......82 C4
Streets La BH24 ......55 C2
Streetway La DT2 ......209 B3
Strete Mount 10 BH23 ..124 C4
Stretton Ct BH14 ......120 A2
Strides La BH24 ......55 A4
Strode Gdns BH24 ......54 B3
Strodes La DT1 ......75 B1
Strongate La DT6 ......68 A4
Stroud Cl BH21 ......60 A3
Stroud Gdns 4 BH23 ..124 C3
Stroud La BH23 ......124 C3
Stroud Pk Ave BH23 ......124 C3
Strouden Ave BH8 ......122 B4
Strouden Rd BH9 ......90 A1
Stroudley Cres DT3 ......153 B2
Struan Ct BH24 ......54 B3
Struan Dr BH24 ......54 A4
Struan Gdns BH24 ......54 A3
Stuart Cl BH16 ......118 A4
Stuart La SP8 ......5 B1
Stuart Rd BH23 ......126 A4
Stuart Way DT6 ......100 C4
Stubhampton Bottom
DT11 ......38 C3
Stuckton Rd SP6 ......43 B4
Student Village DT12 ..121 B4
Studland Heath (National
Nature Reserve)★
BH19 ......164 A3
Studland Rd BH4 ......121 B1
Studland Way DT3 ......167 A4
Studley Cl BH23 ......126 B4
Studley Ct BH5 ......126 B4
Sturminster Marshall Fst Sch
BH21 ......56 C2
Sturminster Newton High
Sch DT10 ......35 A1
Sturminster Newton Leisure
Ctr DT10 ......35 A2
Sturminster Newton Mill &
Mus★ DT10 ......35 A1
Sturminster Rd 10 BH9 ..90 A2
Sturt La BH20 ......81 B2
Styles Cl 9 DT8 ......204 C4
Styles La DT8 ......78 A1
Sudan Rd DT4 ......180 C4
Suffolk Ave BH23 ......91 C1
Suffolk Cl BH21 ......60 B3
Suffolk Rd
Bournemouth BH2 ......121 C2
Salisbury SP2 ......213 A1
Suffolk Rd S BH2 ......121 B2
Sugar Hill
Bere Regis BH20 ......113 C4
Bloxworth BH20 ......114 A3
Summer Field Cl BH21 ..60 A2
Summer Fields BH31 ......45 A3
Summer Hill TA17 ......191 D7
Summer House Terr
BA20 ......27 B2
Summer La
Evershot DT2 ......206 A7
Hinton St George TA17 ..191 D8
Summerbee Comp Sch
BH8 ......90 C1
Summerbee Fst Sch BH8 90 B1
Summerbee Jun Sch
BH8 ......90 B1
Summercroft Way
BH22 ......53 A2

Summerfield Cl BH23 ......92 B1
Summerfields
Bournemouth BH7 ......122 C4
Henstridge BA8 ......19 A3
Summerhill Rd DT7 ......96 B3
Summerhouse View
BA21 ......27 C3
Summerlands
Ferndown BH22 ......61 B3
Yeovil BA21 ......27 A3
Summerlands Hospl
BA21 ......27 A3
Summerleaze Pk BA20 ..27 A3
Summerlock App 6
SP2 ......213 B3
Summers Ave BH11 ......89 A3
Summers La BH23 ......92 B1
Summertrees Ct BH25 ..95 B2
Sun La
Piddletrenthide DT2 ......208 B1
Whitchurch Canonicorum
DT6 ......98 B4
Sunbury Cl BH11 ......89 A3
Sunbury Ct 8 BH2 ......121 C2
Sunderland Dr BH23 ......125 A4
Sundew Cl
Christchurch BH23 ......93 B1
New Milton BH25 ......95 A4
Radipole DT4 ......167 C4
Sundew Rd BH18 ......86 C1
Sunningdale
Christchurch BH23 ......123 C3
8 Poole BH15 ......119 C2
Sunningdale Cres BH10 ..89 B2
Sunningdale Gdns BH18 ..87 A3
Sunningdale Rd BA21 ......27 C3
Sunny Hill Ct BH12 ......120 B3
Sunny Hill Rd BH12 ......120 B3
Sunnybank Dr BH21 ......60 A3
Sunnybank Rd BH21 ......60 A3
Sunnybank Way BH21 ..60 A3
Sunnyfield Rd BH25 ......127 A4
Sunnyfields DT3 ......153 B2
Sunnyhill Rd
Bournemouth BH6 ......123 B3
Salisbury SP1 ......213 B4
Sunnylands Ave BH6 ......123 C2
Sunnymoor Rd BH11 ......89 A1
Sunnyside Ridge BH20 ..143 A1
West Lulworth BH20 ......172 B3
Sunnyside Rd
Poole BH12 ......120 B3
Weymouth DT4 ......180 B4
Sunridge Cl Poole BH12 ..121 A3
Swanage BH19 ......179 A1
Sunrise Bsns Pk DT11 ..212 C3
Sunrise Ct BH22 ......61 B3
Sunset Lodge BH13 ......121 A1
Surrey Cl
Christchurch BH23 ......91 C1
Weymouth DT4 ......166 C2
Surrey Gdns BH4 ......121 B2
Surrey Rd BH2 ......121 A2
Surrey Rd S BH4 ......121 B2
Sussex Farm Way 8
DT9 ......194 C5
Sussex Rd
Salisbury SP2 ......213 A1
Weymouth DT4 ......167 A2
Sutcliffe Ave DT4 ......167 A3
Sutherland Ave BH18 ......86 C3
Sutton Cl 4 Gillingham SP8 ..5 C1
Overcombe/Preston
DT3 ......153 B2
Poole BH17 ......88 A1
Sutton Ct Lawns DT3 ..153 A2
Sutton Grange BA21 ......26 C3
Sutton Hill BA22 ......193 D6
Sutton Pk DT3 ......153 B2
Sutton Rd
Bournemouth BH9 ......90 A1
Overcombe/Preston
DT3 ......153 B2
Swaffield Gdns 5 DT4 ..180 B4
Swainson Rd DT11 ......199 E4
Swallow Cl BH17 ......118 C4
Swallow Way BH21 ......60 A4
Swallowcliffe Gdns
BA20 ......27 B3
Swallowfields 13 SP8 ......5 C1
Swallowmead 2 SP2 ..213 B1
Swan Cl SP2 ......213 B1
Swan Gn 8 BH23 ......124 A3
Swan Hill TA18 ......192 B5
Swan La DT2 ......208 B1
Swan Mead BH24 ......55 C3
Swan St BH21 ......40 A4
Swanage Cty Mid Sch
BH19 ......178 C2
Swanage Her Ctr★
BH19 ......179 B1
Swanage Hospl BH19 ..179 A1
Swanage Rd BH19 ......164 B1
Swanage Rly★ BH20 ..177 B3
Swanmore Cl DT11 ......123 A4
Swanmore Rd BH7 ......123 A4
Swansbury Dr BH8 ......91 A1
Sway Gdns BH8 ......90 B1
Sway Rd BH25 ......95 B3
Swaynes Cl 3 SP1 ......213 B3
Sweep The DT4 ......55 B4
Sweet Hill La DT5 ......186 C1
Sweet Hill Rd DT5 ......186 C1
Sweetmans Rd SP7 ......12 C2

Swift Cl BH17 ....118 C4
Swiftdown 6 SP2 .....213 B1
Swilletts La DT6 ....203 D4
Swinton Ave BH20 .....139 B4
Swordfish Dr BH23 .....125 A4
Swyre Rd DT2 ....129 C1
Sycamore Ave BH20 ....116 A2
Sycamore Cl
Broadstone BH17 ....86 C1
Christchurch BH23 ......123 B4
Sandford BH20 ....143 A4
Sixpenny Handley SP5 ...189 A4
Sycamore Dr
14 Crewkerne TA18 ......191 F5
Yeovil BA20 ....27 A1
Sycamore Pl BH21 ......60 B3
Sycamore Rd Hordle SO41 95 C2
Radipole DT4 ....167 A3
Sycamore Way SP8 ....5 B1
Sydenham Cres BH20 ..139 C1
Sydenham Rd BH19 ....178 C1
Sydenham Way 17 DT1 .108 A1
Sydling Cl BH17 ....88 A1
Sydling Rd
Cerne Abbas DT2 ....207 C3
Yeovil BA21 ....27 C3
Sydney Pl 3 SP8 ....5 C1
Sydney Rd
Broadstone BH18 ....87 A2
Christchurch BH23 ....91 C1
Sydney St DT4 ....167 A2
Sylmor Gdns BH9 ....90 A1
Sylvan Cl 4 Gillingham SP8 .5 C2
St.Leonards BH24 ....53 C2
Sylvan Fst Sch BH12 ...120 A3
Sylvan Rd BH12 ....120 A3
Sylvan Way SP8 ....5 C2
Symes Cl TA18 ....192 C4
Symes Rd BH15 ....118 C2
Symonds Cl DT3 ....167 B4
Symondsbury Prim Sch
DT6 ....99 C4
Syward Cl DT1 ....108 B1
Syward Rd DT1 ....108 B1

T

Tabbit's Hill La BH20 ...177 C3
Tabernacle La 8 BA20 ...27 B2
Tadden Cotts BH21 ......58 B4
Tadden Wlk BH18 ....86 C1
Tadnoll Barrow★ DT2 ..138 B2
Tail Mill TA16 ....191 F7
Tait Cl BH17 ....119 C4
Talbot Ave BH3 ....121 C4
Talbot Cl SP1 ....213 C4
Talbot Comb Sch BH12 .121 A4
Talbot Ct BH9 ....89 C1
Talbot Dr
Christchurch BH23 ....93 C1
Poole BH12 ....121 A4
Talbot Heath Sch BH4 ..121 B3
Talbot Hill Rd BH9 .....121 B4
Talbot House Prep Sch
BH9 ....121 C4
Talbot Manor BH3 ......121 B4
Talbot Mdws BH12 .....121 A4
Talbot Mews BH10 ......89 A1
Talbot Rd
Bournemouth BH9 ......121 C4
Lyme Regis DT7 ....96 A4
Talbot Rise BH10 ....89 B1
Talbothays Rd DT1 ....135 A4
Tall Trees BH14 ....120 A3
Tallidge Cl DT3 ....168 B4
Tamar Cl BH22 ....62 A3
Tamlin St BH20 ....143 A4
Tamworth Rd BH7 ......122 C3
Tan Howse Cl BH7 .....123 A4
Tan La SP8 ....2 A1
Tanglewood Ct 11 BH25 .95 A2
Tanglewood Lodge
BH17 ....118 C4
Tangmere Cl BH23 .....125 A3
Tangmere Pl BH17 .....119 C4
Tanner's La 10 BH20 ...142 C2
Tannery Rd DT6 ....100 B3
Tansee Hill TA20 ....202 E6
Tantinoby La BH20 .....142 B3
Tanyard DT2 ....206 A7
Tanyard La SP7 ....12 B1
Tanzey La DT10 ....21 A2
Taphouse La DT6 ....66 B4
Tapper Ct BH21 ....59 C2
Tark's Hill DT9 ....194 C5
Tarn Dr BH17 ....118 C4
Tarrant Abbey House★
DT11 ....211 F6
Tarrant Cl BH17 ....87 C1
Tarrant Dr BH20 ....142 B3
Tarrant Rd BH9 ....90 A2
Tarratt La BA20 ....27 A1
Tarratt Rd BA20 ....27 A1
Tasman Cl BH23 ....123 C4
Tatnam Rd BH15 ....119 B2
Tattershall Gdns 4 BH21 56 B2
Tatum Cres BH15 ......119 B2
Taunton Rd BH19 ......179 B1
Taverner Cl BH15 ......119 B1
Taylor Dr BH8 ....90 B2
Taylor Way BH31 ....45 A3
Taylor's Bldgs 21 BH15 .119 B1
Taylor's La
Mappowder DT10 ....196 E1
Taylor's La *continued*
Whitechurch Canonicorum
DT6 ....66 A1
Teal Ave DT3 ....166 B3
Teasel Way BH22 ....53 A1
Tecan Way DT4 ....166 C2
Technology Rd BH17 ...119 A4
Tedder Cl BH11 ....89 A2
Tedder Gdns BH11 ....89 A2
Tedder Rd BH11 ....89 A2
Teeling Rd DT3 ....167 B4
Telegraph St DT11 .....198 E8
Telford Cl DT3 ....168 A4
Telford Rd Ferndown BH21 61 A4
Salisbury SP2 ....213 A2
Temple Cl DT1 ....134 C4
Temple La BA8 ....8 A1
Temple Mews BH1 ......122 B3
Templecombe La SP8 ....8 C3
Templer Cl BH11 ....88 C1
Ten Acres SP7 ....12 C2
Tennyson Rd
Bournemouth BH9 ....89 C1
1 Poole BH14 ....120 A2
Weymouth DT4 ....167 B1
Wimborne Minster BH21 ...59 B3
Tensing Rd BH23 ......124 C4
Terence Ave BH17 ....87 B1
Terence Rd BH21 ....86 B3
Termare Cl BA22 ....26 B3
Terminus St 3 DT4 ....167 B2
Tern Ct BH6 ....123 B3
Terrace Rd BH2 ....121 C2
Terrington Ave BH23 ....93 C1
Tewkesbury 9 BA21 .....26 C3
Thames Alley 13 BH15 ..119 A1
Thames Cl BH22 ....62 A3
Thames Mews 12 BH15 .119 A1
Thames St BH15 ....119 A1
Thatcham Ct BA21 ....27 A4
Thatcham Pk BA21 ......27 A4
Thatcham Pk Cl BA21 ...27 A4
Theobold Rd BH23 ....91 A4
Thessaly Ct 17 BH5 ....122 C2
Thetchers Cl BH25 ......95 A3
Thetford Rd BH12 ......120 C3
Thickthorn Cross
BH21 ....200 D7
Thickthorn La DT10 ....197 A2
Third Cliff Wlk 3 DT6 ..100 A1
Thistlebarrow Rd
Bournemouth BH7 ......122 C3
Salisbury SP1 ....213 B4
Thomas Hardy Cl DT10 ..35 A1
Thomas Hardy Dr SP7 ...13 A2
Thomas Hardye Leisure Ctr
DT1 ....134 B4
Thomas Hardye Sch
DT1 ....134 C4
Thomas's London Day Schs
BH24 ....55 A4
Thompson Cl
Britford SP2 ....213 A1
Puddletown DT2 ....78 A1
Thomson Dr 10 TA18 ...191 F4
Thoresby Ct BH25 ....94 C2
Thorn Rd BH17 ....87 B2
Thornbury 15 BH4 .....121 B2
Thornbury Rd BH6 .....124 A2
Thorncombe Beacon★
DT6 ....99 B2
Thorncombe Cl
Bournemouth BH9 ....90 A2
Poole BH17 ....87 C1
Thorne Cl BH31 ....45 A4
Thorne Gdns BA21 ....26 C4
Thorne La
Brympton BA21 ....26 C4
Yeovil BA21 ....27 A4
Thorners CE Prim Sch
DT2 ....103 B1
Thornfield Dr BH23 ......93 C1
Thornford CE Prim Sch
DT9 ....194 D8
Thornford Rd DT9 .....194 C6
Thornford Sta DT9 .....194 C7
Thornham Rd BH25 .....95 B2
Thornhill Cl DT1 ....134 C4
Thornhill Cres DT4 .....167 B2
Thornhill Rd DT10 ....33 B4
Thornicks DT2 ....156 C3
Thornley Rd BH10 ....89 B2
Thornlow Prep Sch
DT4 ....167 B1
Thornton Cl BH21 ....86 B3
Thornton Rd BA21 ....26 C4
Thorny La BA22 ....14 B4
Thorogood Ct 4 BH15 ..119 C2
Thrasher's La BH20 ....162 A2
Three Acre Dr BH25 ....126 C4
Three Acre La BH19 ....178 B1
Three Acres DT2 ....207 A2
Three Barrows★
BH20 ....161 A3
Three Cnr Mead 5 BA21 26 C3
Three Cross Rd BH21 ....53 A3
Three Legged Cross Fst Sch
BH21 ....45 A1
Three Lions Cl 12 BH21 ..59 A3
Three Lords' Barrow★
BH20 ....160 B3
Three Yards Cl DT5 ....186 C4
Thrift Cl DT10 ....33 C4
Throop Cl BH8 ....91 A1
Throop Hollow DT2 ....112 B3
Throop Rd
Abbas & Templecombe
BA8 ....8 A2
Throop Rd *continued*
Bournemouth BH8 ....90 C2
Throopside Ave BH9 ....90 B2
Thrush Rd BH12 ....88 B1
Thursby Rd BH23 ....93 C1
Thwaite Rd BH12 ......121 A3
Tidemill Cl BH23 ....124 A4
Tiffany Cl SO41 ....95 C2
Tilburg Rd BH23 ....124 B4
Tilbury Mead BH20 ....177 A4
Tiley Knap DT2 ....207 E8
Tilly Whim Caves★
BH19 ....185 B3
Tilly Whim La DT2 .....106 C2
Tillycombe Rd DT5 ....187 A4
Timber Hill DT7 ....96 B4
Timothy Cl BH10 ....89 B3
Tin Pot La DT11 ....212 B2
Tincleton Cross DT2 ...110 B3
Tincleton Gdns BH9 .....90 A2
Tinker's Barrow★
DT2 ....137 C2
Tinker's La
Cucklington BA9 ....4 A3
Wareham Town BH20 ....142 C2
Tinneys La DT9 ....30 B3
Tintagel Rd BA21 ....26 C4
Tintern BA21 ....26 C3
Tintinhull Rd
Yeovil BA21 ....27 A4
Yeovil Without BA21 .....26 C4
Tiptoe Prim Sch SO41 ...95 B4
Tithe Barn Children's Farm★
DT3 ....149 B4
Tithe Barn Mus★
BH19 ....179 A1
Tiverton Ct 24 BH4 ....121 B2
Tizard's Knap DT6 ......66 A1
Toby's Cl DT5 ....186 C2
Tobys Ct SP7 ....12 C2
Todber Cl BH11 ....88 C2
Tollard Cl BH12 ....120 C4
Toller La DT2 ....72 A4
Tollerdown Rd 4 DT4 ..166 C1
Tollerford Rd BH17 .....87 B1
Tollgate Pk SP7 ....12 C3
Tollgate Rd SP1 ....213 B2
Tolpuddle Gdns BH9 ....90 A2
Tolstoi Rd BH14 ....120 A3
Tomlins La SP8 ....5 C1
Toms Field Rd BH19 ...178 A1
Tonge Rd BH11 ....89 A3
Toose The BA21 ....26 C3
Top La Ringwood BH24 ....55 B4
Stourton with Gasper BA12 ..1 B4
Torbay Rd BH14 ....120 B2
Torre The BA21 ....26 C3
Totmel Rd BH17 ....88 A1
Tourney Rd BH11 ....88 C3
Tout Hill
East Stoke BH20 ....140 A2
Shaftesbury SP7 ....12 B2
Tout Hill La DT2 ....104 C3
Tout Quarry Nature
Reserve★ DT5 ....186 C3
Tout Quarry Sculpture Pk★
DT5 ....186 C3
Towans The BH13 ......147 B2
Tower Cl 1 BH21 ....201 D1
Tower Ct BH2 ....121 C1
Tower Hill
Bere Regis BH20 ....81 A1
Iwerne Minster DT11 .....37 C1
Netherbury DT6 ....204 B2
Tower Hill Rd 6 TA18 ..191 E4
Tower La BH21 ....59 B3
Tower Mews SP1 ....213 B3
Tower Rd
Bournemouth BH1 ......122 C3
Poole BH13 ....121 A1
Yeovil BA21 ....27 B4
Tower Rd W BH13 ......121 A1
Towers Farm BH21 ......86 B4
Towers Way BH21 ....86 B4
Town Farm Pl SP5 .....189 B4
Town Hall La BH19 .....179 A1
Town Path SP2 ....213 A2
Towngate Bridge BH15 .119 B2
Towngate Sh Ctr 1
BH15 ....119 B1
Townsend BH21 ....56 B2
Townsend Cl
Bournemouth BH11 ....89 A3
Mere BA12 ....2 C3
Townsend Gn BA8 ....19 A2
Townsend La SP6 ......190 A6
Townsend Mead
BH20 ....177 A4
Townsend Orch TA16 ...191 F8
Townsend Prim & Com Sch
BH8 ....91 A1
Townsend Rd
Corfe Castle BH20 ......177 A4
Swanage BH19 ....179 A1
Townsend Way DT6 .....68 C1
Townsville Rd BH9 ......90 A1
Tozer Cl BH11 ....88 C1
Tracey Ct BH23 ....126 A4
Tradecroft DT5 ....186 C3
Trafalgar Ct BH23 .....124 C3
Trafalgar Rd BH9 ......121 C4
Tree Hamlets BH16 ....118 B3
Treebys Cl BH23 ....92 B1
Treeside BH23 ....93 B1
Treetops 9 BH13 ....147 C4
Trefoil Way BH23 ......125 B4
Tregonwell Rd BH2 ....121 C1
Trellech Ct 1 BA22 .....26 C3
Treloen Ct 3 BH8 ......122 A3
Trenchard Mdw BH16 ....84 B2
Trenchard Way DT3 ....166 B3
Trendle St DT9 ....30 A3
Trent Cl Tolpuddle DT2 ...79 B1
Yeovil BA21 ....28 A4
Trent Dr BH20 ....142 B3
Trent Path La DT9 ......29 C3
Trent Way BH22 ....62 A3
Trent Youngs CE Prim Sch
DT9 ....14 C1
Trentham Ave BH7 .....123 A4
Trentham Cl BH7 ......123 A4
Tresco Spinney BA21 ....26 C3
Tresillian Cl BH23 ....94 A1
Tresillian Way BH23 .....94 A1
Treves Rd DT1 ....134 C4
Trevone 15 BH25 ....95 A2
Triangle The
Bournemouth BH2 ......121 C2
Upton BH16 ....118 A4
Tricketts La BH22 ....61 C3
Trigon Rd BH15 ....119 B4
Trill La DT9 ....194 B7
Trinidad Cres BH12 ....120 B4
Trinidad Fst Sch BH12 ..120 B4
Trinidad House BH12 ..120 B4
Trinity 2 BH1 ....122 A2
Trinity Ind Est BH21 ....59 C2
Trinity La BH20 ....142 C2
Trinity Rd
Bournemouth BH1 ......122 A2
Weymouth DT4 ....167 B1
Trinity St
Dorchester DT1 ....108 A1
Salisbury SP1 ....213 B2
7 Weymouth DT4 ......167 C1
Trinity Terr DT4 ....167 B1
Trinity Way DT6 ....68 C1
Troak Cl BH23 ....124 C4
Troon Rd BH18 ....87 A3
Trotters La BH21 ....60 A3
Truman Rd BH10 ....89 A3
Truscott Ave BH9 ......122 A4
Trusthams DT8 ....203 E5
Trustin Cl 6 DT6 ....100 B4
Trystworthy 10 BH2 ....121 C2
Tuckers La BH15 ....118 C1
Tuckers Mill Cl BH20 ...160 C4
Tucks Cl BH23 ....93 A4
Tuckton Cl BH6 ....123 B2
Tuckton Rd BH6 ....123 C2
Tudor Cl SP6 ....42 B3
Tudor Ct
Bournemouth BH1 ......122 A3
Poole BH15 ....119 C3
Tudor Gdns DT11 ......212 C2
Tudor Rd BH18 ....87 A2
Tulse Hill Zeale BA12 .....2 A2
Zennor BA12 ....1 C2
Tuncombe La TA18 ....191 D4
Tunnel Rd DT8 ....204 C5
Turbary Ct
Bournemouth BH12 ......89 A1
Ferndown BH22 ....61 C3
Upton BH16 ....118 B4
Turbary Hts BH11 ....88 C1
Turbary Pk Ave BH11 ....89 A1
Turbary Rd BH22 ....61 C3
Turbary Ret Pk BH11 ....88 C2
Turberville Rd BH20 .....81 A1
Turbetts Cl BH16 ....84 B2
Turbury Cl BH12 ....120 B4
Turbury Rd BH12 ....120 B4
Turf Croft Ct BH23 ......94 A1
Turk's La BH14 ....120 A1
Turlin Moor Fst Sch
BH16 ....118 B2
Turlin Moor Mid Sch
BH16 ....118 B2
Turlin Rd BH16 ....118 B2
Turnberry Cl BH23 .....123 C3
Turner Cl 2 SP2 ....213 A2
Turner's Barn La BA20 ..27 A1
Turner's La
Marshwood DT6 ....202 E2
Tarrant Monkton DT11 ...200 B4
Turners La SP8 ....5 C1
Turnpike Cl 2 TA18 ....192 B3
Turnpike Gn 3 TA18 ...192 B3
Turnstone Cl DT3 ......152 B2
Turnworth Cl BH18 .....87 B2
Turton St 8 DT4 ......167 B2
Tut Hill DT9 ....31 C1
Tweedale Rd BH9 ....90 B2
Twemlow Ave BH14 ....119 C2
Twin Oaks Cl BH18 ......87 A2
Twinways La DT6 ....69 A4
Two Droves DT2 ....109 C4
Two Elms BA22 ....14 B4
Two Riversmeet Leisure Ctr
BH23 ....124 B3
Two Twr La BA20 ....27 B1
Twyford Cl BH8 ....90 B1
Twyford Way BH17 ......88 A1
Twynham Ave BH23 ....124 A4
Twynham Rd BH6 ......123 C2
Twynham Sch BH23 ....124 A3
Tynedale Cl BH9 ....90 A2
Tyneham Ave BH12 .....120 B4
Tyneham Cl
Radipole DT3 ....167 A4
Sandford BH20 ....143 A4
Tyneham House (remains
of)★ BH20 ....174 B3
Tyneham Mus★ BH20 ...174 B3
Tyrrell Gdns BH8 ....91 A1
Tytherley Gn BH8 ....90 B1

U

Ubsdell Cl BH25 ....95 A2
Uddens Dr
Ferndown Town BH21 ....51 C1
Wimborne Minster BH21 ..60 B4
Uddens Trad Est BH21 ...60 C3
Ullswater Cres DT3 ....167 A4
Ullswater Rd BH21 ......59 B3
Ulwell Rd BH19 ....179 A3
Umbers Hill SP7 ....12 B1
Undercliff Dr BH1 .....122 B1
Undercliff Rd BH5 .....122 C2
Underdown Hollow
DT9 ....28 B2
Underhedge Gdns
DT5 ....186 C1
Underhill Mere BA12 ......2 C3
Pen Selwood BA9 ....1 A1
Underhill Jun Sch
DT5 ....186 C4
Underwood Cl BH17 .....87 A1
Union St 2 BA20 ....27 B2
Unity La 4 TA18 ....192 A3
Upland Cl DT10 ....197 D7
Uplands
Bothenhampton DT6 .....101 A3
2 Yetminster DT9 ....194 C5
Uplands Ave BH25 .....127 A4
Uplands Cl BH22 ....62 A4
Uplands Rd
Bournemouth BH8 ....90 B1
Ferndown BH22 ....53 A1
Uplands Sch BH14 .....120 B2
Uplyme Cl BH17 ....88 A1
Uplyme Rd DT7 ....96 A3
Upper Fairfield Rd
13 Dorchester DT1 ......107 C1
12 Dorchester DT1 ......108 A1
Upper Golf Links Rd
BH18 ....87 A3
Upper Gordon Rd BH23 ..94 A1
Upper Hinton Rd BH1 ..121 C2
Upper Linhay DT2 .....205 A8
Upper N Rd SP5 ....188 C5
Upper Norwich Rd 13
BH2 ....121 C2
Upper Rd BH12 ....120 B3
Upper Sch La 1 DT11 ..211 B1
Upper St 4 DT11 ......198 C7
Upper Terr Rd BH2 .....121 C2
Upper Westhill Rd DT7 ..96 A3
Upper Wr St BA12 ....3 A3
Uppington Cl 2 BH21 ..201 C1
Uppleby Rd BH12 ......120 B3
Upton Cl BH16 ....118 A4
Upton Cross Mobile Home Pk
BH16 ....118 B4
Upton Ct BH16 ....118 B4
Upton Ctry Pk★ BH17 ..118 C3
Upton Heath Est BH16 ..118 B4
Upton Ind Est BH16 ....116 B3
Upton Inf Sch BH16 ....118 A4
Upton Jun Sch BH16 ...118 A4
Upton Rd
Broadstone BH17 ....119 A4
Poole BH17 ....118 C4
Upton Way BH18 ....86 C2
Upway St 2 DT4 ....167 B2
Upwey Ave BH15 ....118 C2
Upwey Sta DT3 ....152 B2
Utrecht Ct BH23 ....124 B4

V

Vaggs La SO41 ....95 C3
Vale Cl
4 Crewkerne TA18 ......191 F3
Poole BH14 ....120 C2
Vale Lodge BH1 ....122 B3
Vale Mans 4 BH1 ......122 B2
Vale Pk DT11 ....211 B1
Vale Rd
Bournemouth BH1 ......122 B2
Poole BH14 ....120 C2
Stalbridge DT10 ....33 B4
West Lulworth BH20 .....172 C3
Yeovil BA21 ....28 A3
Vale St BA8 ....19 A2
Vale View Pk SO41 ......95 C4
Valencia Cl BH23 ....91 B2
Valette Rd BH9 ....90 A2
Valiant Way BH23 ......125 A4
Valley Bladen DT2 .....112 A4
Valley Cl
Christchurch BH23 ....91 C2
Yeovil BA21 ....27 B3
Valley Rd
Blandford Camp DT11 ...199 E3
Bournemouth BH8 ....90 C2
Bridport DT6 ....100 B2
2 Crewkerne TA18 ......191 F3
Langton Matravers
BH19 ....178 A3
Worth Matravers BH20 ...177 B3
Valley View BH12 ......121 A4
Vallis Cl BH15 ....119 B1
Vanessa Ave SP1 ......213 C3
Vanguard Ave DT4 .....166 C1
Vanguard Rd
Bournemouth BH8 ....90 C1
Poole BH15 ....119 B1
Veals La DT10 ....35 A3
Vearse Cl DT6 ....100 A3
Vecta Cl BH23 ....125 B3
Vectis Rd BH25 ....126 B4

Velvet Lawn Rd BH25 ...94 C2
Venator Pl BH21 ...59 B3
Venn Hill TA20 ...202 F6
Venn La Chideock DT6 ...66 C1
  Stoke Abbott DT6 ...203 D2
Venn The SP7 ...12 C2
Venning Ave BH11 ...88 C3
Ventnor Rd DT5 ...186 C4
Ventry Cl Poole BH13 ...120 C2
  2 Salisbury SP1 ...213 B3
Ventry The 1 SP1 ...213 B3
Ventura Ctr The BH16 ...118 B3
Ventura Pl BH16 ...118 B3
Verity Cres BH17 ...88 A1
Verlands Rd DT3 ...153 B2
Vermin La BH20 ...83 A4
Vernalls Cl BH10 ...89 B3
Vernalls Ct BH25 ...95 B3
Vernalls Gdns BH10 ...89 B3
Vernalls Rd DT9 ...30 A4
Verne Cl DT4 ...167 B1
Verne Comm Rd DT5 ...186 C4
Verne Hill Rd DT5 ...187 A4
Verne Rd Verwood BH31 ...45 B3
  Weymouth DT4 ...167 B1
Verne Way DT4 ...167 B1
Verney Cl BH11 ...89 A2
Verney Rd BH11 ...89 A2
Verno La BH23 ...93 B1
Verona Ave BH6 ...123 B3
Verona Gr SP1 ...213 A4
Verriott's La DT6 ...66 B1
Verulam Pl 31 BH1 ...121 C2
Verulam Rd BH14 ...119 C2
Verwood CE Fst Sch
  BH31 ...45 A3
Verwood Cres BH6 ...124 C2
Verwood Ind Est BH31 ...45 B3
Verwood Leisure Ctr
  BH31 ...45 A3
Verwood Rd
  Ellingham Harbridge & Ibsley
  BH24 ...46 B1
  St Leonards & St Ives
  BH24 ...54 C4
  Three Legged Cross BH21 ...45 A4
  Verwood BH31 ...53 A4
  Woodlands BH21 ...44 B4
Verwood Sports Ctr
  BH31 ...45 B3
Vespasian Way DT1 ...134 C4
Vetch Cl BH23 ...125 B4
Vian Ct BH25 ...94 C2
Vicarage Cl 5 BH20 ...140 A1
Vicarage Cotts BH8 ...90 C2
Vicarage Ct 4 DT6 ...100 B4
Vicarage La DT2 ...107 C3
Vicarage Rd
  Bournemouth BH9 ...89 C1
  Poole BH15 ...119 B3
  Verwood BH31 ...45 A3
Vicarage St 9 BA20 ...27 B2
Vicarage Way BH23 ...92 B1
Vickers Cl BH8 ...91 A1
Vickery Way BH23 ...124 B4
Victoria Ave
  Bournemouth BH9 ...89 C1
  Radipole DT3 ...152 A3
  1 Swanage BH19 ...178 C1
Victoria Ave Ind Est
  BH19 ...178 C2
Victoria Cl
  Corfe Mullen BH21 ...86 B3
  Wool BH20 ...139 B3
  Yeovil BA21 ...27 C3
Victoria Cres BH12 ...120 B3
Victoria Ct SP1 ...213 B4
Victoria Gdns
  Ferndown BH22 ...61 B3
  Ringwood BH24 ...55 B3
Victoria Gr DT6 ...100 B4
Victoria Hospl BH21 ...59 A3
Victoria Pk Rd BH9 ...89 C1
Victoria Pl
  Bournemouth BH1 ...122 B3
  Easton/Weston DT5 ...187 A3
  Wimborne Minster BH21 ...59 A3
Victoria Rd
  Blandford Forum DT11 ...212 B1
  Bournemouth BH1 ...122 B3
  Christchurch BH23 ...124 C3
  Dorchester DT1 ...107 C1
  Easton/Weston DT5 ...187 A3
  Ferndown BH22 ...61 B3
  Gillingham SP8 ...6 A1
  Poole BH12 ...120 B2
  Salisbury SP1 ...213 B3
  Swanage BH19 ...179 B3
  Weymouth DT4 ...180 B4
  Wimborne Minster BH21 ...59 A3
  Yeovil BA21 ...27 C3
Victoria Sq DT5 ...186 C4
Victoria St
  Radipole DT4 ...167 C2
  Shaftesbury SP7 ...12 C1
Victory Cl BH21 ...53 B3
Victory Rd DT5 ...186 C4
View Rd DT7 ...96 A3
Viewside Cl BH21 ...86 B3
Viking Cl BH6 ...124 A2
Viking Way
  Bournemouth BH6 ...124 A3
  Christchurch BH23 ...125 A3
  Salisbury SP2 ...213 B1
Village Rd DT6 ...68 C1
Villette Cl BH23 ...92 A1
Vince Cl BH11 ...89 A3
Vincent Cl 2 BH25 ...95 A1

Vincent Pl BA20 ...27 B3
Vincent Rd 1 BH25 ...95 A1
Vincents Cl DT9 ...31 A1
Vine Cl BH7 ...123 A4
Vine Farm Cl BH12 ...121 B4
Vine Farm Rd BH12 ...121 A4
Vine Hill DT6 ...58 C3
Vineries Cl BH21 ...59 C3
Vineries The BH21 ...59 C3
Vinery The BH25 ...95 A1
Vineyard St 6 AH16 ...84 B2
Vinney Cross DT6 ...102 A3
Vinneys Cl BH23 ...92 B1
Violet Farm Cl BH21 ...86 B3
Violet La BH25 ...95 A2
Virginia Cl
  1 Henstridge BA8 ...19 A2
  Poole BH12 ...120 B4
Viscount Ct BH11 ...88 B3
Viscount Dr BH23 ...125 A3
Viscount Rd DT4 ...166 C1
Viscount Wlk BH11 ...88 B3
Vista Marina BH13 ...147 B3
Vivian Pk BH19 ...179 A2
Vixen Wlk BH25 ...95 A3
Voss's La DT2 ...206 B3
Vulcan Cl DT4 ...166 C1
Vulcan Way BH23 ...125 A4

W

W Burton Medieval Village
  of* DT2 ...139 B1
Waddock Dro DT2 ...111 C2
Waddon Hill (Roman Fort)*
  DT8 ...203 F4
Waddon House* DT3 ...150 C4
Waddon Way DT6 ...69 B1
Wadham Com Sch
  TA18 ...191 F5
Wadmore La BH19 ...164 B1
Wagtail Dr BH25 ...94 C1
Wain Rd BH20 ...139 B4
Wain-a-long Rd SP1 ...213 C3
Wainwright Cl DT3 ...153 A2
Wakefield Ave BH10 ...89 C3
Wakeham DT5 ...187 A2
Wakely Gdns BH11 ...89 A3
Wakely Rd BH11 ...89 A3
Walcheren Pl BH15 ...118 B2
Walcott Ave BH23 ...91 C1
Walditch Gdns BH17 ...87 C1
Walditch Rd DT6 ...100 C3
Waldren Cl BH15 ...119 C1
Waldrons The 5 DT9 ...194 B8
Walford Cl BH21 ...59 B3
Walford Gdns BH21 ...59 A3
Walford Mill Craft Ctr*
  BH21 ...59 A3
Walker Cres DT4 ...180 B3
Walkford La BH25 ...94 B2
Walkford Rd BH23 ...94 B1
Walkford Way BH23 ...94 A1
Walkingfield La BH15 ...119 B1
Walkwood Ave BH7 ...123 A4
Wall La DT6 ...203 D4
Wallace Rd BH18 ...87 A2
Wallis Rd BH10 ...89 A1
Walliscott Rd BH11 ...89 A1
Wallisdown Rd BH10 ...121 B4
Wallsend Cl 3 DT5 ...186 C1
Walnut Ave DT11 ...212 A2
Walnut Cl BH25 ...94 C2
Walnut Orch 3 DT5 ...150 A4
Walpole Rd BH1 ...122 C3
Walpole St DT4 ...167 B2
Walrond Rd BH19 ...179 A2
Walsford Rd BH4 ...121 B3
Walsingham Dene BH7 ...122 C4
Walters Dr 16 DT11 ...199 D4
Waltham Rd BH7 ...123 A3
Walton Elm Hill DT10 ...35 A4
Walton Rd
  Bournemouth BH10 ...89 B1
  Poole BH15 ...120 A3
Wanchard La DT2 ...107 B4
Wanderwell DT6 ...100 B2
Wanderwell Farm La
  DT6 ...100 B2
Wanstead Dr BH24 ...47 B1
Warbler Cl BH16 ...118 A4
Warburton Rd BH17 ...119 C4
Wardcliffe Rd DT4 ...167 B2
Wardstone Barrow*
  DT2 ...171 B4
Ware La DT7 ...96 A2
Wareham Ct BH7 ...123 A3
Wareham Golf Club
  BH20 ...142 C3
Wareham Hospl BH20 ...142 B2
Wareham Lady St Mary CE
  Fst Sch BH20 ...142 B2
Wareham Mid Sch
  BH20 ...142 B2
Wareham Mus* BH20 ...142 C2
Wareham Rd
  Corfe Mullen BH21 ...86 B3
  Hawkchurch EX13 ...202 B2
  Lytchett Matravers BH16 ...84 B1
  Lytchett Minster & Upton
  BH16 ...116 A3
  Owermoigne DT2 ...155 C4
  Wareham St Martin
  BH16 ...116 B2
  Warmwell DT2 ...155 A4
Wareham Sta BH20 ...142 B3

Wares Cl 5 DT11 ...81 C4
Warland Way BH21 ...86 C4
Warmwell Cl
  9 Bournemouth BH9 ...90 A2
  Poole BH17 ...87 C1
Warmwell Dro DT2 ...154 B4
Warmwell House*
  DT2 ...155 A4
Warmwell Rd DT2 ...137 B3
Warne Hill DT6 ...100 C4
Warnford Rd BH6 ...123 B4
Warren Ave BH23 ...124 C3
Warren Cl
  St.Leonards BH24 ...54 C3
  Weymouth DT4 ...166 C1
Warren Dr BH24 ...54 C3
Warren Edge Cl BH6 ...123 C2
Warren Edge Ct BH6 ...123 C2
Warren Edge Rd BH6 ...123 C2
Warren Hill DT2 ...78 B4
Warren La BH24 ...54 C3
Warren Rd
  Bere Regis BH20 ...113 B2
  Bournemouth BH4 ...121 A1
  Poole BH14 ...120 B2
  Puddletown DT2 ...78 A3
Warren Way BH16 ...116 B1
Warren Wlk BH22 ...61 A4
Warwick Ave BH25 ...95 A2
Warwick Cl SP1 ...213 A4
Warwick Ct 14 BH5 ...122 C2
Warwick Pl 3 BH7 ...123 A3
Warwick Rd
  Bournemouth BH7 ...123 A3
  Poole BH14 ...120 B2
Washington Ave BH8 ...122 B3
Washpond La BH19 ...178 C3
Watcombe Rd BH6 ...123 B3
Water Barrows*
  BH20 ...173 C4
Water Knap DT10 ...196 F3
Water La
  Bournemouth BH6 ...123 B4
  Durweston DT11 ...198 E3
  Swyre DT6 ...129 B4
  Winfrith Newburgh DT2 ...156 C4
  Winterborne Stickland
  DT11 ...210 D7
Water La Farm BH10 ...89 C3
Water Mdw La BH20 ...139 C1
Water St
  Cranborne BH21 ...40 A4
  Mere BA12 ...3 A3
Water Twr Rd BH18 ...87 B2
Watercombe Hts BA20 ...26 C1
Watercombe La BA20 ...26 C1
Watercombe Pk BA20 ...26 C2
Waterditch Rd BH23 ...93 A2
Waterford Cl BH14 ...120 A1
Waterford Gdns BH23 ...126 A4
Waterford Lodge BH23 ...125 A3
Waterford Pl BH23 ...126 A4
Waterford Rd
  Christchurch BH23 ...126 A4
  New Milton BH25 ...95 B2
Waterfront Mus* BH15 ...119 A1
Watergates La DT2 ...136 B2
Waterlake Rd TA20 ...202 A8
Waterloo House BH17 ...87 A1
Waterloo La Silton SP8 ...5 A4
  Stourton Caundle DT10 ...33 A1
Waterloo Rd
  Bournemouth BH9 ...121 C4
  Broadstone BH17 ...119 B4
  Corfe Mullen BH21 ...86 A3
  Salisbury SP1 ...213 C2
Waterloo Way 3 BH24 ...55 B3
Watermead
  Christchurch GU21 ...124 A3
  3 Tatworth TA20 ...202 A8
Watermill Rd BH23 ...124 A4
Waterpot Hill DT6 ...204 C2
Waters Edge BH13 ...147 B3
Waters Rd SP1 ...213 B4
Watership Dr BH24 ...55 C3
Waterside BH23 ...124 C2
Waterside Cl BH24 ...47 B1
Watersmeet Rd SP2 ...213 B3
Waterston Cl BH17 ...87 C1
Waterston La DT2 ...77 B2
Waterston Manor*
  DT2 ...77 B2
Watery La
  Christchurch BH23 ...125 A4
  Donhead St Mary SP7 ...24 C4
  Halstock BA22 ...193 D2
  Iwerne Minster DT11 ...37 C1
  Lytchett Minster & Upton
  BH16 ...117 A3
  Radipole DT3 ...152 A2
  Shaftesbury SP7 ...12 C1
  Studland BH19 ...164 B1
  Tincleton DT2 ...110 B2
  Upton BH16 ...118 A4
  West Crewkerne TA18 ...191 D2
Watford La DT6 ...68 C1
Watkin Rd 19 BH5 ...122 C2
Watton Cl BH8 ...91 A1
Watton Cross BH20 ...100 A3
Watton Gdns DT6 ...100 C4
Watton La DT6 ...100 A3
Watton Pk DT6 ...100 B3
Wavell Ave BH17 ...87 A4
Wavell Rd
  Bournemouth BH11 ...89 A2
  Salisbury SP2 ...213 A1
Wavendon Ave BH25 ...126 C4
Wavering La SP8 ...5 A2

Waverley Cres BH15 ...119 B3
Waverley House 12 BH25 ...95 A1
Waverley Rd
  New Milton BH25 ...95 A1
  Radipole DT3 ...167 B3
Wayclose La
  Buckhorn Weston SP8 ...9 A4
  Cucklington SP8 ...4 A1
Wayford Hill TA18 ...191 B1
Wayground Rd BH21 ...58 C1
Wayman Rd BH21 ...86 C3
Wayne Rd BH12 ...120 A3
Wayside Rd
  Bournemouth BH6 ...123 C4
  St Leonards BH24 ...62 C4
  St.Leonards BH24 ...53 C1
Waytown Cl BH17 ...87 B1
Weare Cl DT5 ...186 C4
Weatherbury Way
  DT1 ...135 A4
Weatherby Castle (Fort)*
  BH20 ...79 C3
Weavers Cl
  Crewkerne TA18 ...191 F4
  Ferndown BH22 ...53 A1
Webb La DT10 ...196 E8
Webb's Way BH11 ...88 C1
Webbers Cl BH20 ...176 C4
Webbers Piece DT2 ...206 C1
Webbs Cl BH23 ...53 C1
Webster Rd BH9 ...90 A2
Wedgwood Dr BH14 ...120 A1
Weiner Cl DT11 ...199 E2
Weir The DT3 ...153 B2
Weir View DT2 ...107 B3
Welbeck Rd BA21 ...28 A4
Weldon Ave BH11 ...88 C3
Well Cl
  Bradford Abbas DT9 ...28 B1
  New Milton BH25 ...94 C1
Well La Poole BH15 ...119 B2
  Powerstock DT6 ...70 C2
  Shaftesbury SP7 ...12 B2
Well Plot DT6 ...101 B4
Welland Rd
  Wimborne Minster BH21 ...59 B2
  Yeovil BA21 ...27 C4
Wellbridge Cl DT1 ...135 A4
Wellesley Ave BH23 ...125 B4
Wellfield Hill EX13 ...202 E2
Wellfields Dr DT6 ...100 C4
Wellington Ave BH23 ...125 B4
Wellington Ct
  7 Bournemouth BH8 ...122 A3
  New Milton BH25 ...95 A2
Wellington Rd
  Bournemouth BH1 ...122 A3
  Poole BH14 ...120 B2
Wellstead Rd BH20 ...142 B3
Wendover Cl BH25 ...94 C1
Wendy Cres BH22 ...61 C2
Wenlock Ct 9 BH21 ...124 C4
Wentwood Gdns BH25 ...95 B1
Wentworth BH14 ...147 B4
Wentworth Ave BH5 ...123 A2
Wentworth Cl
  Bournemouth BH5 ...123 A2
  Radipole BH20 ...152 C1
Wentworth Coll BH5 ...123 A2
Wentworth Dr
  Broadstone BH18 ...87 A3
  Christchurch BH23 ...123 C3
Wentworth Rd BA21 ...28 A4
Wescott Way BH11 ...88 C2
Wesley Cl
  8 Bournemouth BH8 ...122 B3
  Charmouth DT6 ...97 A4
Wesley Grange 33 BH21 ...59 C3
Wesley Rd Poole BH12 ...120 B3
  Wimborne Minster BH21 ...59 C3
Wessex Ave
  New Milton BH25 ...95 A1
  4 Shillingstone DT11 ...198 B5
Wessex Cl BH23 ...125 B4
Wessex Dr DT9 ...28 B1
Wessex Est BH24 ...55 B4
Wessex Gate Ret Pk
  BH17 ...119 A3
Wessex Oval BH20 ...142 B3
Wessex Rd
  Dorchester DT1 ...107 B1
  Poole BH20 ...120 A2
  Ringwood BH24 ...55 B4
  Salisbury SP1 ...213 C3
  Stalbridge DT10 ...33 B4
  Weymouth DT4 ...167 A4
  Yeovil BA21 ...26 C4
Wessex Trad Ctr BH12 ...120 A4
Wessex Way
  Bournemouth BH8 ...122 B3
  Dorchester DT1 ...107 B1
  Gillingham SP8 ...5 C2
  Swanage BH19 ...179 A2
West Allington DT6 ...100 A4
West Ave BH21 ...53 A4
West Bay Cres DT4 ...180 B4
West Bay Rd DT6 ...100 B1
West Borough BH21 ...59 A3
West Bourton Rd SP8 ...1 B1
West Brook BA21 ...26 C3
West Butts St 1 BH15 ...119 A1
West Chinnock Prim Sch
  TA18 ...192 B8
West Cl Chickerell DT3 ...166 B3
  Verwood BH31 ...44 C3
West Cl Ct BH6 ...124 A2
West Cl House BH6 ...124 A2
West Cliff Cotts BH2 ...121 C1

West Cliff Gdns BH2 ...121 C1
West Cliff Mews BH2 ...121 C1
West Cliff Rd
  Bournemouth BH2 ...121 B1
  Bridport DT6 ...100 A1
West Coker Rd
  East Coker BA20 ...26 C1
  Yeovil BA20 ...27 A1
West Coker VC Prim Sch
  BA22 ...193 A8
West Dr 3 BH19 ...179 A1
West Durlston La
  BH19 ...179 A1
West End DT2 ...206 B3
West Gables Cl DT6 ...100 A4
West Hall* DT9 ...195 C7
West Hendford BA20 ...27 A2
West Hill
  Charminster DT2 ...107 B3
  Evershot DT2 ...205 F7
  Milborne Port DT9 ...17 B1
West Hill Pl 16 BH2 ...121 C2
West Hill Rd
  Bournemouth BH2 ...121 C1
  Lyme Regis DT7 ...96 A3
West Howe Cl BH11 ...89 A2
West Howe Ind Est BH11 ...88 C2
West La Arne BH20 ...142 C1
  Hazelbury Bryan DT10 ...196 E4
  Melbury Abbas SP7 ...24 C1
  Mosterton DT8 ...203 F8
  North Wootton DT9 ...30 C1
West Lulworth CE Fst Sch
  BH20 ...172 C3
West Mans 8 BH4 ...121 B2
West Mead DT6 ...100 A4
West Mill Cres BH20 ...142 B3
West Mill La
  Castleton DT9 ...30 A2
  Stalbridge DT10 ...20 A2
West Mills Rd DT1 ...107 C2
West Moors Mid Sch
  BH22 ...53 A1
West Moors Rd
  Ferndown BH22 ...61 B4
  Three Legged Cross BH21 ...53 A4
  West Moors BH22 ...52 C2
West Overcliff Dr BH4 ...121 B1
West Pk BA20 ...27 A3
West Pk Dr SP6 ...190 F3
West Pk La SP6 ...190 F3
West Quay Rd BH15 ...119 A1
West Rd
  Bournemouth BH5 ...123 A2
  Bransgore BH23 ...93 A4
  Symondsbury DT6 ...99 B3
  West Lulworth BH20 ...172 B3
West Row BH21 ...59 A2
West Row Mews BH21 ...59 A2
West St
  Abbotsbury DT3 ...149 A4
  Bere Regis BH20 ...81 A2
  Blandford Forum DT11 ...212 B2
  Bridport DT6 ...100 B3
  Broadwindsor DT8 ...203 E5
  Chickerell DT3 ...166 B3
  Corfe Castle BH20 ...162 A1
  Crewkerne TA18 ...191 E4
  Fontmell Magna SP7 ...37 C3
  Hinton St George TA17 ...191 C7
  Kington Magna SP8 ...9 B1
  Poole BH15 ...119 A1
  Radipole DT4 ...167 B1
  Ringwood BH24 ...55 A4
  Salisbury SP2 ...213 A3
  Shapwick DT11 ...56 A4
  Templecombe BA8 ...18 B4
  Wareham BH20 ...142 C2
  Wimborne Minster BH21 ...59 A3
  Winterborne Kingston
  DT11 ...81 B4
  Winterbourne Stickland
  DT11 ...210 C7
  Yeovil BA20 ...27 A2
West St Ct 11 BH21 ...59 A3
West Sta Terr BH4 ...121 B2
West View SP7 ...37 C4
West View Rd
  Christchurch BH23 ...124 C3
  Poole BH15 ...119 B2
West Walks Rd 8 DT1 ...108 A1
West Walls BH20 ...142 B2
West Way
  Bournemouth BH9 ...90 A1
  Broadstone BH18 ...87 A1
  Easton/Weston DT5 ...186 C1
  Winterbourne Abbas
  DT2 ...105 B1
West Way Cl BH9 ...90 A1
West Ways BA22 ...192 D8
West Wlk Bridport DT6 ...100 A1
  Salisbury SP1 ...213 B2
West Wools DT5 ...186 C1
Westbourne Cl
  Bournemouth BH4 ...121 B2
  Salisbury SP1 ...213 C2
  Yeovil BA20 ...27 A3
Westbourne Gr BA20 ...27 A3
Westbourne Pk Rd BH4 ...121 A1
Westbridge Pk DT9 ...29 C2
Westbrook Cl BH10 ...89 B1
Westbrook Rd SP8 ...5 A1
Westbury
  Bradford Abbas DT9 ...28 B1

Westbury continued
Sherborne DT9 ....30 A2
Westbury Cl
Barton on Sea BH25 ....127 A4
Bransgore BH23 ....93 A4
Westbury Ct 10 BH14 ...120 A2
Westbury Rd BH24 ......55 B4
Westby Rd BH5 ....122 C2
Westcliff Rd
Charmouth DT6 ....96 C4
Easton/Weston DT5 ....186 C2
Westcroft Par 10 BH25 ..95 A1
Westcroft Pk BH18 .....87 B2
Westdown Rd BH11 .....89 A3
Westdowne Cl DT4 .....167 A1
Westerhall Rd DT4 ....167 C3
Westerham Rd BH4 ....121 A2
Westerleigh BH4 ......121 B1
Western Ave
Barton on Sea BH25 ...126 B4
Bournemouth BH10 .....89 C2
Poole BH13 ....120 C1
Yeovil BA22 ....26 A4
Western Cl BH10 ....89 B3
Western Downland Prim Sch
SP6 ....190 F2
Western Rd BH13 ......121 A1
Western St DT9 ....28 B4
Westerngate BH13 .....121 A2
Westfield
2 Portesham DT3 ......150 A4
Sherborne DT9 ....29 C2
13 Wimborne Minster BH21 59 A3
Westfield Ave BA21 ....27 A3
Westfield Cl BH21 ......59 A3
Westfield Com Sch
BA21 ....27 A3
Westfield Cres BA21 ...27 A3
Westfield Est BA12 ......1 C1
Westfield Gdns BH23 ...93 A1
Westfield Gr BA21 ......27 A4
Westfield Inf Sch BA21 ..27 A4
Westfield Pl BA21 ......27 A4
Westfield Rd
Bournemouth BH6 .....123 C2
Yeovil BA21 ....27 A4
Westfield Sch DT3 ....153 A2
Westgate Pk BH4 ......121 A2
Westham Cl BH17 ....87 C2
Westham Rd DT4 ......167 B2
Westhaven DT4 ....167 A1
Westhaven Cty Inf Sch
DT4 ....167 A2
Westhaven Cty Jun Sch
DT4 ....167 A2
Westheath Rd BH18 ....87 A2
Westhill Cl 5 DT4 .....180 A4
Westhill Rd DT4 ......180 B4
Westlake Cl DT3 ......152 A2
Westland Rd BA20 .....27 A2
Westlands Cl BH23 .....93 A4
Westlands Dr BH13 ....147 C4
Westleaze DT2 ....107 C3
Westleaze Cl DT2 .....107 C3
Westminster BA22 .....26 B3
Westminster Cl 10 SP7 ..12 C2
Westminster Ct BH25 ...126 C4
Westminster Meml Hospl
SP7 ....12 C1
Westminster Rd
Northport BH20 ....142 B3
Poole BH13 ....121 A1
Salisbury SP2 ....213 A1
Westminster Rd E BH13 121 A1
Westminster Rd Ind Est
BH20 ....142 B3
Westminster St 10 BA20 .27 B2
Westmoreland Ct SO41 ..95 C2
Weston Cl BA22 ....192 E8
Weston Dr BH1 ....122 A2
Weston Hill SP8 ....9 A3
Weston La
Closworth BA22 ......193 E5
Corscombe DT2 ....192 F1
Weston Rd
Easton/Weston DT5 ....186 C2
Weymouth DT4 ....167 B1
Wimborne Minster BH21 ..59 C4
Worth Matravers BH19 ..183 B4
Weston St
East Chinnock BA22 ...192 E8
Easton/Weston DT5 ...187 A1
Westons La 8 BH15 ...119 B1
Westover Hill DT6 ......64 C1
Westover La BH24 .....54 C3
Westover Rd
Bournemouth BH1 .....121 C2
14 Dorchester DT1 ....107 C1
Westport Rd BH20 ....142 B2
Westray Hall BH4 .....121 B1
Westridge 6 DT9 ......30 A3
Westville DT4 ....27 C3
Westwey Rd DT4 ......167 B1
Westwood Ave BH22 ...61 B3
Westwoods & Glendene Pk
BH25 ....94 B3
Wet La BA12 ....3 B1
Wetherbury Cl DT11 ...212 C2
Wetherby Cl
Broadstone BH18 ......87 A1
Milborne St Andrew DT11 .79 C4
Wey Valley Sch The
DT3 ....152 B1
Weyman's Ave BH10 ...89 B3

Weymans Dr BH10 ......89 B3
Weymouth & Portland Sailing
Acad★ DT5 ....181 A1
Weymouth Ave
10 Dorchester DT1 .....108 A1
Dorchester DT1 ....134 C4
Weymouth Bay Ave
DT4 ....167 B4
Weymouth Coll
Dorchester DT1 ....107 B1
Radipole DT4 ....167 C3
Weymouth Com Hospl
DT4 ....167 C3
Weymouth Golf Club
DT4 ....167 A2
Weymouth Mus★ DT4 .167 C1
Weymouth Rd
Dorchester DT1 ....134 C4
Poole BH14 ....120 B3
Winterborne Monkton
DT2 ....134 C3
Weymouth Rugby Football
Club DT3 ....167 C4
Weymouth Sports Club
DT3 ....152 A1
Weymouth Sta DT4 ....167 B3
Weymouth Way DT4 ...167 A3
Weyview Cres DT3 ....152 A2
Wharf Cl BH12 ....120 C3
Wharfdale Rd
Bournemouth BH4 ....121 B2
Poole BH12 ....120 C3
Wharncliffe Ct BH23 ..125 C4
Wharncliffe Gdns BH23 126 A4
Wharncliffe Rd
Bournemouth BH5 ....122 C4
Christchurch BH23 ....126 A4
Whatcombe Rd DT11 ..210 D4
Whatleigh Cl BH15 ....119 B1
Whatley La TA20 .....202 C8
Wheat Cl 4 DT10 .....197 A4
Wheat Farland DT3 ...166 B3
Wheatear Cl 4 DT3 ...152 B2
Wheathill Cl 1 DT9 ....17 B1
Wheathill La DT9 ......17 C2
Wheathill Way DT9 ....17 B1
Wheatlands DT5 ......186 C1
Wheaton Grange BH4 .121 B2
Wheaton Rd BH7 .....123 A3
Wheatplot Pk Homes 2
BH10 ....89 C2
Wheel House La TA20 .202 E7
Wheelers La BH11 .....89 A4
Wheelwright's Cl SP5 .189 A4
Whetham Mill La DT8 .203 C6
Whetland's La DT6 .....69 B1
Whimbrel Ct BH23 ....125 A3
Whincroft Cl BH22 .....61 C4
Whincroft Dr BH22 .....61 C3
Whitby Ave BH18 ......87 A1
Whitby Cl BH23 ....91 B2
Whitby Cres BH18 .....87 A1
Whitchurch Ave BH18 ..87 B2
Whitchurch La BA8 .....19 A3
Whitcombe Rd DT8 ...204 D3
Whitcross 2 BA22 ....193 F8
White Cl 3 Bridport DT6 .68 C1
Poole BH15 ....120 A4
White Cliff DT11 ......212 B1
White Farm Cl BH21 ..121 B4
White Hart Cl DT10 ...196 D5
White Hart La SP7 .....12 C1
White Hill
5 Puddletown DT2 ....78 A1
Tolpuddle DT2 ....79 B1
White Hill La DT2 ......79 B1
White Horse Dr
Overcombe/Preston
DT3 ....153 B2
Poole BH15 ....119 B3
White Horse La
Hinton St Mary DT10 ...35 A3
Overcombe/Preston
DT3 ....153 B2
White Horse Mews
DT2 ....72 C4
White Horses BH25 ...126 C4
White House La DT9 ..195 A4
White Knights BH25 ..126 C4
White La DT2 ....205 C8
White La Cl DT10 ......35 A1
White Lodge BH15 ...119 C2
White Lovington BH20 ..81 A1
White Mead BA21 ......26 C3
White Mill Bridge★
BH21 ....56 C3
White Pit DT11 ....198 B5
White Pit La SP7 ....24 B2
White Rd BA12 ....3 A3
White Way
Buckland Newton DT2 .208 B6
Litton Cheney DT2 ....103 B2
White Way La DT10 ....21 C1
Whitebeam Way BH31 ..45 B3
Whitebridge Rd SP1 ..213 B1
Whitecliff Cres BH14 ..120 A1
Whitecliff Gdns DT11 ..212 B1
Whitecliff Rd
Poole BH14 ....119 C1
Swanage BH19 ......179 A3
Whitecross DT4 ....87 C2
Whitecross Dr DT4 ...180 C4
Whitefield Dr SP8 ......10 B1
Whitefield Lodge 1
BH25 ....95 A2
Whitefield Rd
New Milton BH25 ......95 A1
Poole BH14 ....120 A1

Whitefriars Rd 9 SP1 ..213 B2
Whitehall BH23 ....124 A3
Whitehall Ct 3 TA18 ..191 F5
Whitehart Fields 1
BH24 ....55 C4
Whitehayes Cl BH23 ...92 B1
Whitehayes Rd BH23 ...92 B1
Whitehead Dr DT4 ....180 B3
Whitehouse Rd BH21 ...59 B1
Whitelegg Way BH10 ...89 C3
Whitemarsh BA12 ......3 A2
Whites Cl DT2 ....76 C4
Whiteway Hill DT2 ....201 B4
Whiteways BH21 ....59 C3
Whitfield Pk BH24 .....54 B3
Whitfield Rd DT1 .....107 B1
Whithay La DT6 ....68 A4
Whitingham St 8 BH5 .123 A3
Whitley Way BH25 .....95 A3
Whitmore La BH21 .....44 A4
Whitsbury Cl BH8 ......90 B1
Whittle Rd BH21 ....60 C1
Whittles Way BH15 ...119 A1
Whynot Way DT3 .....166 B2
Wick 1 Ind Est BH25 ...94 C1
Wick 2 Ind Est BH25 ...94 C1
Wick Cl BH25 ....94 C1
Wick Dr BH25 ....94 C1
Wick Farm BH6 ......124 A3
Wick Hill DT9 ....17 A3
Wick La BH6 ....124 A3
Wick Rd DT9 ....17 B2
Wicket Rd BH10 ....89 B3
Wicketsbeer Rd BA22 193 C6
Wickfield Ave BH23 ...124 A3
Wickfield Cl BH23 ....124 A3
Wickford House BH23 .124 A3
Wickham Cl BH22 ......61 C3
Wickham Dr BH21 ......86 B2
Wickham Rd BH7 ....123 A3
Wicklea Rd BH6 ......124 A2
Wickmeads Rd BH6 ...124 A3
Widdicombe Ave BH14 .120 C1
Wide St DT5 ....186 C3
Widget Cl BH11 ....89 A1
Widworthy Dr BH18 ...86 C3
Wight Wlk BH22 ....61 C1
Wightman's Orch DT2 .208 B2
Wilderness The DT9 ....30 B2
Wilderton Rd BH13 ...120 C2
Wilderton Rd W BH13 .121 A2
Wildfell Cl DT3 ....92 A1
Wildown Gdns BH6 ...124 A2
Wildown Rd BH6 .....124 A2
Wilfred Rd BH5 ......122 C2
Wilkins Way BH15 ....119 A1
Wilkinson Dr BH8 ......91 A1
Willett Rd BH21 ....59 A1
William Barnes CP Sch
DT10 ....197 D8
William Cl
Christchurch BH23 .....94 A1
Laverstock SP1 ......213 C3
William Ct 17 BH23 ...126 A4
William Rd BH7 ......122 C4
William St DT4 ....167 C2
William's Ind Pk BH25 .94 C1
Williams Ave DT1 ....107 C1
Williams' Ave DT4 ....180 B4
Williford La DT2 .....195 C2
Willis Way BH15 .....119 A3
Willis's La TA18 .....192 B4
Willoughby Cl 3 DT2 ..78 A1
Willow Cl
Bournemouth BH4 ....121 B1
Salisbury SP1 ....213 C3
St.Leonards BH24 .....53 C2
Upton BH16 ....118 B3
Willow Cres
Holton Heath BH20 ...116 A1
Overcombe/Preston
DT3 ....168 A4
Willow Ct BH7 ....123 B3
Willow Dr
Christchurch BH23 ....124 A3
Ringwood BH24 ....55 B3
Wimborne Minster BH21 .60 B3
Willow Farm 11 DT9 ..194 C5
Willow Gr 6 DT8 .....204 D4
Willow Lodge 1 BH1 ..122 B2
Willow Lodge Montessori
Sch BH16 ....117 A4
Willow Mead BH8 .....90 B2
Willow Pk BH14 ......120 A2
Willow Pl BH23 ......124 B3
Willow Rd BA21 ....27 A3
Willow Tree Rise BH11 ..89 A2
Willow View BH16 .....118 B2
Willow Way
Bridport DT6 ....100 C4
Christchurch BH23 ....124 A3
Ferndown BH22 ....61 B4
Motcombe SP7 ....12 A4
Northport BH20 ......142 B3
Willow Wlk BH25 .....127 A4
Willowdene Cl BH25 ...95 B2
Willows The BH25 ....127 A4
Wills Cl BH21 ....86 B2
Wills La DT2 ....207 D4
Wills Rd Poole BH12 ..120 C2
Swanage BH19 ......178 C1
Willwood Cl BH17 .....87 C2
Wilman Way SP2 .....213 A1
Wilmslow Rd DT3 ....166 B3
Wilmur Cres BH15 ...119 C3
Wilson Pk DT1 ....212 C1
Wilson Rd
Bournemouth BH1 ....122 C3

Wilson Rd continued
Dorchester DT1 ....108 B1
Poole BH14 ....120 B2
Wilton Cl BH23 ....91 B1
Wilton Dr DT4 ....167 A1
Wilton Gdns BH25 .....94 C2
Wilton Rd
Bournemouth BH7 ....122 C3
Salisbury SP2 ....213 A3
Yeovil BA21 ....28 A4
Wiltshire Ave DT4 ...167 A2
Wiltshire Cl SP8 ....5 C3
Wiltshire Gdns BH23 ..92 C4
Wiltshire Rd
Bransgore BH23 ......92 C3
Salisbury SP2 ....213 A1
Wilverley Ave BH8 .....90 C1
Wilverley Rd BH23 ...125 A4
Wilverly Gdns DT11 ..212 C1
Wimberne Fst Sch BH21 .59 A3
Wimborne Minst Model Town
& Gdns★ BH21 ....59 A2
Wimborne Rd
Blandford Forum DT11 .212 C1
Bournemouth BH10 ....89 B3
Broadstone BH21 ......58 C1
Lytchett Matravers BH16 .84 C2
Poole BH15 ....119 B3
Tarrant Keyneston DT11 211 E8
Tarrant Rushton DT11 ..48 A3
Wimborne Minster BH21 .59 A3
Wimborne Rd E BH22 ..61 B3
Wimborne Rd W BH21 ..60 B3
Wimborne St BH21 ....40 A4
Wimborne St Giles CE Fst
Sch BH21 ....201 F7
Wimborough La BA22 .192 F7
Win Gn View SP7 ......13 A3
Winbrook Fold DT2 ...156 C3
Winchelsea Sch BH12 ..88 B1
Winchester Cl DT4 ...166 C2
Winchester Gdns BA21 .27 C4
Winchester Pl 3 BH15 119 B1
Winchester Rd BH25 ...95 B2
Winchester St SP1 ...213 B1
Wincombe Bsns Pk
SP7 ....13 A3
Wincombe Cl BH22 ....61 B2
Wincombe Dr BH22 ....61 B2
Wincombe La SP7 .....12 C2
Wincombe Pk★ SP7 ...13 B3
Wind Whistle Farm 1
DT11 ....81 C4
Windermere Cl BA20 ...27 A1
Windermere Cres
DT3 ....167 A3
Windermere Rd BH3 ..122 A4
Windgreen Est BH21 ...86 C4
Windham Mews BH1 ..122 B3
Windham Rd BH1 .....122 B3
Windlesham Rd SP1 ..213 B4
Windmill Barrow★
BH21 ....84 A4
Windmill Cl
Shaftesbury SP7 ......12 C2
St.Leonards BH24 .....54 C2
Windmill La
St Leonards & St Ives
BH24 ....55 A2
St.Leonards BH24 .....54 C2
Windmill Rd DT11 ....212 B1
Windmill Rise 6 TA18 .191 F5
Windsor Cl
Bovington Camp BH20 .139 C3
Hordle SO41 ....95 C2
1 Mosterton DT8 .....204 A7
St.Leonards BH24 .....54 A3
Windsor Ct
5 Christchurch BH23 .126 A4
Poole BH14 ....120 A2
Windsor La SP8 ....5 B1
Windsor Rd
Bournemouth BH5 ....122 C2
Christchurch BH23 ....123 C4
Dorchester DT1 ....107 C1
Radipole DT3 ....152 A2
12 Salisbury SP2 .....213 A1
Windsor St 11 SP2 ...213 A1
Windsor Way SO41 ....42 B3
Windwhistle Cnr SP7 ..13 C2
Windy Cnr DT11 .....200 C1
Windy Ridge DT8 ....204 C4
Wine St 1 BA20 ....27 B2
Winfrith Cres BH12 ..120 C4
Winfrith Dro
West Lulworth BH20 ..172 C4
Winfrith Newburgh DT2 156 C3
Winfrith Newburgh CE Fst
Sch DT2 ....156 C3
Winfrith Tech Ctr DT2 .139 A1
Wingate Ave BA21 ....27 C4
Wingfield Ave
Christchurch BH23 .....93 B1
Poole BH15 ....119 B3
Wingfield Cl BH1 .....122 B2
Wingfield Rd DT9 ......30 A3
Wingreen Cl 3 DT3 ..168 A4
Winifred Rd BH15 ....119 C3
Winkelbury Hill (Hill Fort)★
SP7 ....188 C8
Winkton Cl BH23 ......92 B1
Winkton House BH23 ..92 B1
Winnards Cl BH22 .....61 C1
Winniford Cl DT6 ......99 A4
Winsford Cl BH23 ......93 B1
Winsley Ave BH6 ....123 B3
Winslow Rd DT3 .....153 B2

Winspit Cl BH15 ......118 C2
Winspit Rd BH19 .....183 B4
Winston Ave BH12 ....121 A3
Winston Ct
1 Christchurch BH23 .124 A4
20 New Milton BH25 ...95 A1
Winston Dr BA21 ......27 A4
Winston Gdns BH12 ..121 A3
Winston Par 22 BH25 ..95 A1
Winston Pk BH12 ....121 A3
Winston Rd BH9 ....90 A2
Winston Way BH24 ....55 B4
Winter La DT9 ....15 C3
Winter's La DT3 .....150 B4
Winterborne La BH20 ..82 C3
Winterbourne Cl BH15 119 B2
Winterbourne Copse
DT4 ....180 B4
Winterbourne Faringdon
Village★ DT2 ....135 A3
Winterbourne Hospl
DT1 ....134 C4
Winterbourne Rd BH15 119 B3
Winterbourne Valley CE Fst
Sch DT2 ....105 B3
Winterhayes Cl BH17 ..87 C2
Winters Cl 6 DT3 ....150 A4
Winton (Boys) Sch BH10 .89 B1
Winton Prim Sch BH9 ..89 C1
Winton Way
Bournemouth BH10 ....89 B1
New Milton BH25 ......95 A3
Winyards View TA18 ..191 F3
Wisbech Way SO41 ....95 C2
Wishart Gdns BH9 .....90 A3
Wishay St 8 DT1 .....107/ B1
Wistaria Ho 7 BH4 ...89 C2
Wisteria Dr BA22 ......26 B3
Wisteria Dr BH31 ......45 C2
Witch Cl SP8 ....10 B2
Witch La SP8 ....10 B2
Witcham La DT2 .....205 F5
Witchampton CE Fst Sch
BH21 ....200 F1
Witchampton La
Hinton Martell BH21 ...50 A4
Witchampton BH21 ...201 A1
Withermoor Rd BH9 ..121 C4
Withies Croft DT5 ....187 B3
Withingham Rd BH13 .120 C2
Withybed La BA9 ....4 B2
Witley BH14 ....147 B4
Witney Rd BH17 ....87 B1
Wittey's La TA20 ....202 E6
Woburn Rd BA21 ......28 A4
Woking Rd BH14 .....120 B2
Wolfe Cl BH23 ....124 B4
Wolfeton House★
DT2 ....107 B3
Wollaston Rd
Bournemouth BH6 ....123 C2
Dorchester DT1 ....108 A1
Wollaton Cres BH22 ...61 B2
Wollaton Rd BH22 ....61 B2
Wollstonecraft Rd 25
BH5 ....122 C2
Wolseley Rd BH12 ...120 B3
Wolterton Rd BH12 ..121 B2
Wolverley Ct 16 BH4 .121 B2
Wolverton Rd BH7 ...122 C3
Wonderholm Par BH11 .89 A1
Wood Cl La TA17 ....191 A8
Wood Fold View DT2 .205 B8
Wood La
Bournemouth BH11 ....88 C3
Broadwindsor DT8 ...203 B7
Hinton St Mary DT10 ..35 A2
Stalbridge DT10 ....33 B4
Symondsbury DT6 .....67 B3
Wood Lawn Cl BH25 .126 C4
Wood Row BH9 ....90 C2
Wood View BH21 ......60 A4
Wood's La DT8 ......204 B3
Woodacre Gdns BH22 ..61 C2
Woodbury BH1 ....122 A1
Woodbury Ave BH8 ...90 C1
Woodbury Cl BH23 ....91 C2
Woodbury Dro DT2 ..137 B3
Woodbury Gdns SP2 .213 B1
Woodbury Hill (Fort)★
BH20 ....81 B1
Woodcocks Cres BH7 .123 A4
Woodcote 2 BA20 ....26 C1
Woodcote Dr BH16 ..118 A3
Woodcutts La BH21 ...50 B4
Woodend Rd BH9 ....121 C4
Woodfield Gdns BH23 ..93 B1
Woodfield Rd BH11 ...89 A3
Woodford Cl BH24 ....55 B4
Woodford Rd BH1 ...122 B2
Woodgreen Dr BH11 ...88 B2
Woodhayes BA8 ......19 A2
Woodhayes Ave BH23 ..93 C1
Woodhenge BA22 .....26 B3
Woodhouse Cross SP8 ..4 C2
Woodhouse La EX13 ..202 A1
Woodhouse Rd EX13 .202 A1
Woodlake Cl BH17 .....87 B1
Woodland Ave BH5 ..123 A2
Woodland Cl BH31 ....45 A4
Woodland Dr BH7 ....122 C3
Woodland Gr 12 BA20 ..27 B2
Woodland Mans BH14 .120 A4
Woodland Way BH23 .125 B4
Woodland Wlk
Bournemouth BH5 ....123 A2
Ferndown BH22 ....61 C4

Woodlands DT2 . . . . .136 A1
Woodlands Ave BH15 . .118 C2
Woodlands Cl BH23 . . . . .93 A4
Woodlands Cres BH15 . .118 C2
Woodlands Dr BH20 . . . .116 A1
Woodlands Manor★
  BA12 . . . . .3 A2
Woodlands Mead DT10 . .20 C2
Woodlands Rd
  Barton on Sea BH25 . . . . .126 C4
  Mere BA12 . . . . .3 A1
Woodlands Way
  New Milton BH25 . . . . .95 A3
  St.Leonards BH24 . . . . .54 A2
Woodleaze Cl BH18 . . . .87 A3
Woodlinken Cl BH31 . . .45 B2
Woodlinken Dr BH31 . . .45 B2
Woodlinken Way BH31 . .45 C2
Woodmead Rd DT7 . . .96 A3
Woodpecker Cl BH15 . . .45 A3
Woodpecker Dr BH17 . .118 C4
Woodpeckers The
  DT3 . . . . .152 B2
Woodrising BH13 . . . . .147 A2
Woodrisings The BH2 . .121 B2
Woodroffe Sch DT7 . . .96 A3
Woodruff Cl BH23 . . . . .125 B4
Woods View Rd BH9 . . .121 B4
Woodsage Dr SP8 . . . . . . .5 B1
Woodsford Castle★
  DT2 . . . . .110 A1
Woodsford Cl DT2 . . . .137 B3
Woodsford House Sch
  DT2 . . . . .110 B1
Woodsford La DT2 . . . .138 A4
Woodsford Rd DT2 . . . .137 B4
Woodside Cl BH22 . . . . .61 C3
Woodside Rd
  Bournemouth BH5 . . . . . .123 A2
  Ferndown BH22 . . . . .52 C2
  Poole BH14 . . . . .120 B2
Woodstock Cl BH14 . . .120 A1
Woodstock Ct BH22 . . . .61 C2
Woodstock La BH24 . . . .55 B4
Woodstock Rd
  Burton BH23 . , , , , , , , ,92 B1
  Poole BH14 . . . . .120 A1
  Salisbury SP1 . . . . .213 B3
  Yeovil BA21 . . . . .27 C4
Woodswater La 5 DT8 .204 D4
Woodvale Gdns BH25 . . .95 B2
Woodvill Rd SP1 . . . . . .213 C4

Wool Bridge★ BH20 . . .140 A2
Wool CE Fst Sch
  BH20 . . . . .140 A1
Wool Rd BH12 . . . . . . .120 A4
Wool Sta BH20 . . . . . . .140 A1
Wooland Gdns DT4 . . . .180 B4
Woolands La SP7 . . . . . . .12 B2
Woolcombe Rd DT5 . . . .186 C2
Woolcott La SP8 . . . . .1 B1
Woolmer La BH24 . . . . . .47 B1
Woolsbarrow (Fort)★
  BH20 . . . . .114 C3
Woolsbridge Ind Est
  BH21 . . . . .53 B3
Woolsbridge Rd BH24 . . .54 A2
Woolslope Cl BH22 . . . .53 A1
Woolslope Gdns BH22 . .53 A1
Woolslope Rd BH22 . . . .53 A1
Woolven Cl BH14 . . . . . .120 A1
Wooperton St 9 DT4 . .167 B2
Wootton Cross DT6 . . . .65 B2
Wootton Gdns BH1 . . . .122 A2
Wootton Gr DT9 . . . . . . .30 A4
Wootton La DT6 . . . . . . .65 A2
Wootton Mount BH1 . . .122 A2
Wootton Rd BH25 . . . . . .95 B4
Wootton Rough BH25 . . .95 A4
Worbarrow Gdns BH12 .120 B4
Wordsworth Ave BH8 . . .90 C1
Wordsworth Rd SP1 . . . .213 B3
Worgret Hill BH20 . . . . .141 C1
Worgret Rd Poole BH15 . .119 B4
  Wareham BH20 . . . . .142 B2
Worrell Dr BH12 . . . . . .120 B4
Worthington Cres BH14 .120 A2
Worthy Rd BH25 . . . . . . .95 A1
Wortley Rd BH23 . . . . . .126 A4
Wrackle Cl DT2 . . . . . . .106 C4
Wraxall Cl BH17 . . . . . . .87 B1
Wraxall La DT2 . . . . . . .206 B2
Wraxhill Rd BA20 . . . . . .27 A1
Wren Cl
  Christchurch BH23 . . . . . .125 A3
  New Milton BH25 . . . . . . .94 C1
Wren Cres BH12 . . . . . . .121 A3
Wren Gdns SP6 . . . . .42 B3
Wrenscroft 9 SP2 . . . . .213 B1
Wriggle River La DT2 . .194 E1
Writh Rd DT9 . . . . .31 B1

Wroxham Rd BH12 . . . . .120 C3
Wyatt's La BH20 . . . . . .142 C2
Wyatts Cl BH21 . . . . .86 B3
Wyatts La BH21 . . . . .86 B3
Wych Hill DT6 . . . . .100 B2
Wych Ridge DT6 . . . . . .100 B2
Wychwood Cl BH2 . . . . .121 C2
Wychwood Dr BH2 . . . . .121 C2
Wychwood Grange 1
  BH2 . . . . .121 C2
Wycliffe Rd BH9 . . . . . .121 C4
Wydford Cl DT9 . . . . . . .29 C3
Wyelands Ave BH21 . . . .60 B3
Wyke CP Sch SP8 . . . . . . .5 B1
Wyke Oliver Rd DT3 . . .168 A4
Wyke Rd Gillingham SP8 . . . .5 C1
  Weymouth DT4 . . . . .167 A1
Wyke Regis CE Jun Sch
  DT4 . . . . .180 B4
Wyke Regis Com & Sports Ctr
  DT4 . . . . .180 B3
Wyke Regis Inf Sch
  DT4 . . . . .180 B4
Wykeham Cl BH17 . . . . .119 C4
Wykeham Lodge BH13 .147 C3
Wynchard Bank 1
  DT11 . . . . .198 E3
Wyncombe Rd BH5 . . . .123 A3
Wyndham Cl BH23 . . . . .94 A1
Wyndham Pk Sch SP1 . .213 B4
Wyndham Rd
  Christchurch BH23 . . . . . .94 A1
  Poole BH14 . . . . .120 A2
  Salisbury SP1 . . . . .213 B3
Wyndham St 5 BA20 . . .27 C3
Wyndham Terr SP1 . . . .213 B3
Wyndham View BA21 . . .27 C3
Wynford Rd
  Bournemouth BH9 . . . . . . .90 A2
  Poole BH14 . . . . .120 B2
Wynne Cl BH18 . . . . .86 C2
Wynnes Cl 4 DT9 . . . . . .30 A3
Wynnes Rise DT9 . . . . . .30 A3
Wynter Cl BH7 . . . . .122 C4
Wytch Pas BH20 . . . . . .162 B4
Wyvern Cl
  Fast Coker BA20 . . . . .26 C1
  Poole BH12 . . . . .120 B4
Wyvern Ct 24 TA18 . . . .191 F4
Wyvern Rd 1 DT1 . . . . .107 C1

Y

Yalbury La DT2 . . . . . . .137 B3
Yard La
  Marshwood DT6 . . . . . . .203 D2
  Rampisham DT2 . . . . . . .205 E6
Yarde Farm 5 DT11 . . . .199 D3
Yarmouth Cl BH12 . . . . .121 A3
Yarmouth Rd BH12 . . . .120 C3
Yarn Barton
  10 Beaminster DT8 . . . . .204 D4
  18 Yeovil BA20 . . . . .27 B2
Yarnbarton DT8 . . . . . . .203 E5
Yarrells Cl BH16 . . . . . .118 B3
Yarrells Dr BH16 . . . . . .118 A4
Yarrells La BH16 . . . . . .118 B3
Yarrells Sch BH16 . . . . .118 A4
Yarrow Cl BH23 . . . . . . .125 A4
Yarrow Ct 1 SP8 . . . . . . .5 B1
Yarrow Rd BH12 . . . . . .120 A4
Yearlings' Dro BH20 . . .113 A4
Yeates Rd DT5 . . . . .186 C3
Yeatman Hospl The
  DT9 . . . . .30 A3
Yeatmans Cl SP7 . . . . . .12 B2
Yeatmans La SP7 . . . . . .12 B2
Yeatminster Rd BH17 . . .87 C1
Yellow La DT6 . . . . .69 B1
Yellowham Hill DT2 . . . .109 B4
Yelverton Rd 33 BH1 . . .121 C2
Yenston Hill BA8 . . . . . . .18 C4
Yeolands Rd 7 DT5 . . . .186 C2
Yeomans Ind Pk BH8 . . .90 C1
Yeomans Rd BH8 . . . . . .90 C2
Yeomans Way BH8 . . . . .90 C1
Yeovil Coll BA22 . . . . . . .26 B4
Yeovil Coll iT Ctr BA20 . .27 C2
Yeovil Golf Club BA21 . .28 A2
Yeovil Junc Sta BA22 . . .28 A1
Yeovil Pen Mill Sta
  BA21 . . . . .28 A3
Yeovil Rd
  Crewkerne TA18 . . . . . . .191 F4
  Halstock BA22 . . . . .193 D3
  Sherborne DT9 . . . . .29 C3
  Yeovil BA20 . . . . .27 A1
Yeovil Ski Activity Ctr
  BA20 . . . . .27 C2
Yeovil Sports Club
  BA21 . . . . .27 A4
Yerville Gdns SO41 . . . . .95 C2

Yetminster Sta DT9 . . . .194 C5
Yew La BH25 . . . . .95 B2
Yew Tree Cl
  Wimborne Minster BH21 . .59 B3
  Yeovil BA20 . . . . .27 A1
Yew Tree Ct 30 BH25 . . .95 A1
Yew Tree Farm DT2 . . . .205 A8
Yew Tree La DT2 . . . . . .106 C3
Yews The BA12 . . . . .3 A3
Yewstock Sch DT10 . . . .35 A1
York Ave BH25 . . . . .95 A2
York Cl Broadstone BH18 . .87 A1
  Charminster DT2 . . . . . . .107 C3
  Christchurch BH23 . . . . . .123 C4
York Pl Bournemouth BH7 123 A3
  17 New Milton BH25 . . . . .95 A2
  Yeovil BA20 . . . . .27 B3
York Rd
  Bournemouth BH1 . . . . . .122 A2
  Broadstone BH18 . . . . . . .87 A1
  Dorchester DT1 . . . . .108 A1
  Salisbury SP2 . . . . .213 A3
Youngs Rd BH11 . . . . . . .89 A3

Z

Zamek Cl BH11 . . . . .89 A3
Zeals Fst Sch BA12 . . . . . .2 A3
Zeals Gn Dr BA12 . . . . . . .2 A2
Zeals Rise BA12 . . . . .1 C2
Zetland Ct BH4 . . . . .121 A1
Zig Zag Hill SP7 . . . . . . .24 C3
Zinnia Cl BH10 . . . . .89 C1
Zoar La DT10 . . . . .197 B4

Notes

NG NH NJ NK
NM NN NO NP
NR NS NT NU
NX NY NZ
SC SD SE TA
SH SJ SK TF TG
SM SN SO SP TL TM
SR SS ST SU TQ TR
SW SX SY SZ TV

Any feature in this atlas can be given a unique reference to help you find the same feature on other Ordnance Survey maps of the area, or to help someone else locate you if they do not have a Street Atlas.

The grid squares in this atlas match the Ordnance Survey National Grid and are at 1 kilometre intervals. The small figures at the bottom and sides of every other grid line are the National Grid kilometre values (**00** to **99** km) and are repeated across the country every 100 km (see left).

To give a unique National Grid reference you need to locate where in the country you are. The country is divided into 100 km squares with each square given a unique two-letter reference. Use the administrative map to determine in which 100 km square a particular page of this atlas falls.

The bold letters and numbers between each grid line (**A** to **C**, **1** to **4**) are for use within a specific Street Atlas only, and when used with the page number, are a convenient way of referencing these grid squares.

Example   The railway bridge over DARLEY GREEN RD in grid square A1

Step 1: Identify the two-letter reference, in this example the page is in **SP**

Step 2: Identify the 1 km square in which the railway bridge falls. Use the figures in the southwest corner of this square: Eastings **17**, Northings **74**. This gives a unique reference: **SP 17 74**, accurate to 1 km.

Step 3: To give a more precise reference accurate to 100 m you need to estimate how many tenths along and how many tenths up this 1 km square the feature is. This makes the bridge about **8** tenths along and about **1** tenth up from the southwest corner.

This gives a unique reference: **SP 178 741**, accurate to 100 m.

Eastings (read from left to right along the bottom) come before Northings (read from bottom to top). If you have trouble remembering say to yourself "Along the hall, THEN up the stairs"!

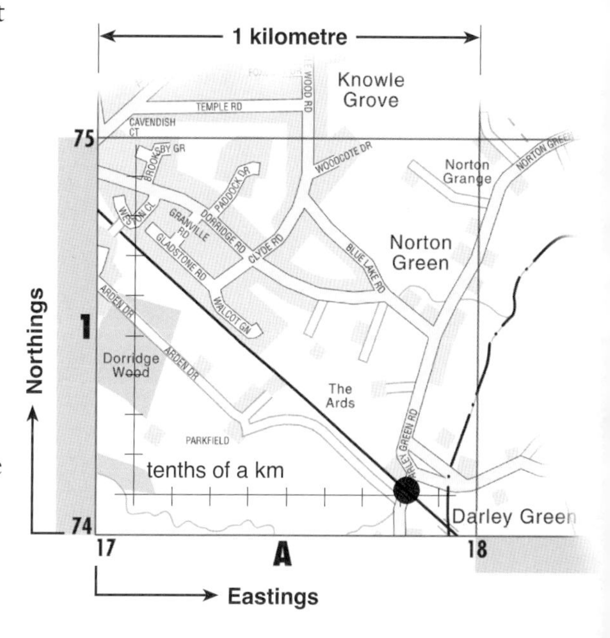

Addresses

Name and Address	Telephone	Page	Grid reference

Name and Address	Telephone	Page	Grid reference

Street Atlases from Philip's

Philip's publish an extensive range of regional and local street atlases which are ideal for motoring, business and leisure use. They are widely used by the emergency services and local authorities throughout Britain.

Key features include:

◆ Superb county-wide mapping at an extra-large scale of 3½ inches to 1 mile, or 2½ inches to 1 mile in pocket editions

◆ Complete urban and rural coverage, detailing every named street in town and country

◆ Each atlas available in three handy formats – hardback, spiral, pocket paperback

'The mapping is very clear... great in scope and value'
★★★★ BEST BUY   AUTO EXPRESS

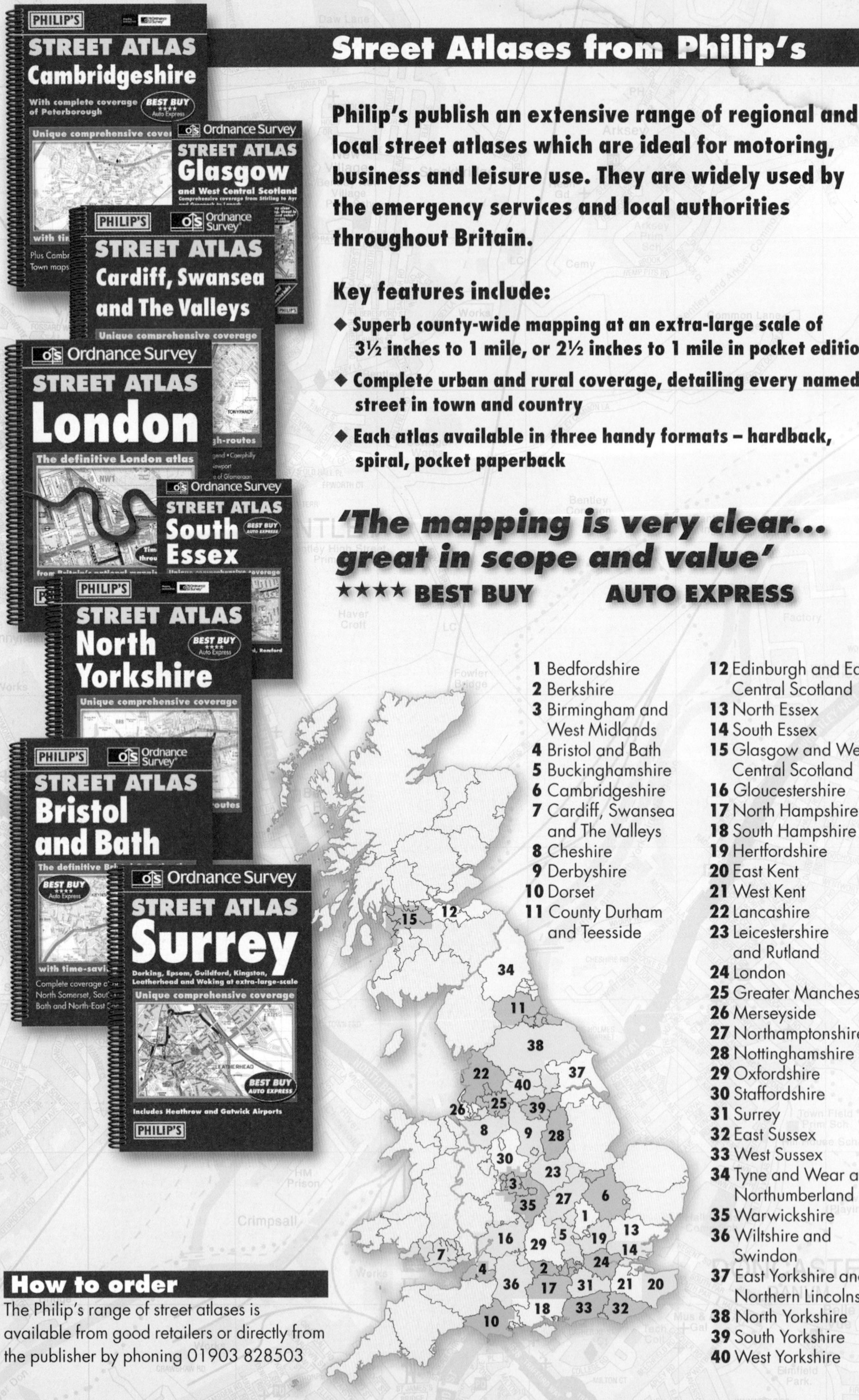

PHILIP'S
STREET ATLAS
Cambridgeshire
With complete coverage of Peterborough
BEST BUY ★★★★ Auto Express
OS Ordnance Survey

STREET ATLAS
Glasgow
and West Central Scotland

PHILIP'S   OS Ordnance Survey
STREET ATLAS
Cardiff, Swansea and The Valleys
Unique comprehensive coverage

OS Ordnance Survey
STREET ATLAS
London
The definitive London atlas

OS Ordnance Survey
STREET ATLAS
South Essex
BEST BUY AUTO EXPRESS

PHILIP'S
STREET ATLAS
North Yorkshire
BEST BUY Auto Express
Unique comprehensive coverage

PHILIP'S   OS Ordnance Survey
STREET ATLAS
Bristol and Bath
The definitive Bristol
BEST BUY ★★★★ Auto Express

OS Ordnance Survey
STREET ATLAS
Surrey
Dorking, Epsom, Guildford, Kingston, Leatherhead and Woking at extra-large-scale
Unique comprehensive coverage
BEST BUY AUTO EXPRESS
Includes Heathrow and Gatwick Airports
PHILIP'S

1 Bedfordshire	**12** Edinburgh and East Central Scotland
2 Berkshire	**13** North Essex
3 Birmingham and West Midlands	**14** South Essex
4 Bristol and Bath	**15** Glasgow and West Central Scotland
5 Buckinghamshire	**16** Gloucestershire
6 Cambridgeshire	**17** North Hampshire
7 Cardiff, Swansea and The Valleys	**18** South Hampshire
8 Cheshire	**19** Hertfordshire
9 Derbyshire	**20** East Kent
10 Dorset	**21** West Kent
11 County Durham and Teesside	**22** Lancashire
	23 Leicestershire and Rutland
	24 London
	25 Greater Manchester
	26 Merseyside
	27 Northamptonshire
	28 Nottinghamshire
	29 Oxfordshire
	30 Staffordshire
	31 Surrey
	32 East Sussex
	33 West Sussex
	34 Tyne and Wear and Northumberland
	35 Warwickshire
	36 Wiltshire and Swindon
	37 East Yorkshire and Northern Lincolnshire
	38 North Yorkshire
	39 South Yorkshire
	40 West Yorkshire

How to order
The Philip's range of street atlases is available from good retailers or directly from the publisher by phoning 01903 828503